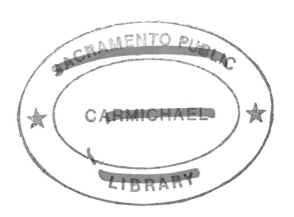

Handbook of Mortgage Mathematics & Financial Tables

Paul R. Goebel
Assistant Professor of Finance
Texas Tech University

Norman G. Miller
Associate Professor of Real Estate
University of Cincinnati

Prentice-Hall, Inc., Englewood Cliffs, New Jersey 07632

Library of Congress Cataloging in Publication Data

Goebel, Paul R.
Handbook of mortgage mathematics and financial tables.

1. Real estate business—Tables. 2. Interest and usury—Tables. 3. Business mathematics—Real estate business. I. Miller, Norman G. II. Title.
HF5716.R4G63 332.8'0212 81-5880
ISBN 0-13-380410-0 AACR2
ISBN 0-13-380402-X (pbk.)

Printed in the United States of America

10 9 8 7 6 5 4 3 2

Prentice-Hall International, Inc., *London*
Prentice-Hall of Australia Pty. Limited, *Sydney*
Prentice-Hall of Canada, Ltd., *Toronto*
Prentice-Hall of India Private Limited, *New Delhi*
Prentice-Hall of Japan, Inc., *Tokyo*
Prentice-Hall of Southeast Asia Pte. Ltd., *Singapore*
Whitehall Books Limited, *Wellington, New Zealand*

Contents

Preface

Handbook of Mortgage Mathematics and Financial Tables is a useful and up-to-date handbook designed for the mortgage lender, real estate practitioner, and student of real estate finance. The condensed treatment of mortgage finance provides the mathematical foundation necessary for the complete understanding of financial tables by the novice as well as mathematical extensions for the experienced user. With fixed rate mortgages giving way to a multitude of new mortgage instruments, such an understanding of real estate finance becomes increasingly necessary.

Chapter 1 illustrates the essential concepts of mortgage mathematics. Building upon the concepts of present value analysis, the mathematics necessary for the myriad of mortgage types now available are developed and illustrated with examples. Included are fixed rate mortgages, variable rate mortgages, renegotiated rate mortgages, as well as discussion on other types of instruments now offered by real estate lenders. The mathematics of discount point calculations and their effect on yields are discussed in detail for various types of prepayment assumptions. In addition, calculation of the annual percentage rate required for disclosure under federal Regulation Z is discussed and illustrated.

Chapter 2 illustrates the use of tables in solving the types of problems developed in Chapter 1. Numerous examples are given to demonstrate the adaptability of the tables to various types of financial problems and needs.

Chapter 3 includes the financial tables required for the most common needs of a mortgage lender. The tables are intended to provide all of the essential information needed by primary and secondary mortgage market participants. Included are present and future value factors for both single sums and annuities, mortgage constant factors for fixed rate mortgages, mortgage balance remaining percentage factors, discount point tables, and annual percentage rate tables. The range of interest rates and terms covered is far beyond those available in most other financial tables. The accuracy of the financial tables in *Handbook of Mortgage Mathematics and Financial Tables* is far superior to most tables currently available because the factors are taken to 5 decimal places.

Creation and inclusion of discount point tables, unlike any available elsewhere, was prompted by the inaccuracy of "rule of thumb" methods of finding discount points. Rules of thumb such as "eight points will raise the yield on a mortgage by one percent" hold only under very limited conditions, primarily when contract rates are between 7% and 9%, with only a small change in the effective yield desired. Yet this rule is being used in interest rate ranges much different from those for which it holds. Under other conditions, rules of thumb provide erroneous conclusions, by either under- or overstating the yield actually realized. For this reason, a table of accurate discount point charges is developed to bring any given contract interest rate up to a given effective yield for a variety of mortgage terms and prepayment assumptions. With this unique table, lenders may instantly and accurately determine necessary point charges for desired effective yields. The point charges are given in both positive and negative form so that they may also be used to determine the premium or discount from par value to pay for a mortgage in the secondary market. The use of the table is discussed fully in Chapter 2.

The last table, which provides the annual percentage rate resulting from origination fees and discount point charges that raise the effective yield above the contract rate, is necessary to provide information that must be disclosed to borrowers. The table may be used as a follow-up to the discount point table, where the lender determines the accurate point charges necessary for a desired yield, then rounds off the point charges to the nearest quarter of a percent, and may then determine the annual percentage rate for disclosure purposes in the Annual Percentage Rate table.

The authors wish to acknowledge the capable computer assistance of Robert Plante of Purdue University. Computer software programs currently being developed with Dr. Plante include the information in these tables as well as extension and other needs of real estate lenders. Any errors or omissions in this text are, of course, the sole responsibility of the authors.

chapter 1

The Mathematics of Real Estate Finance

PRESENT VALUE FORMULATIONS

"Yield," "interest rate," and "discount rate" are all terms applied to return *on* investments. The yields required for any given type of investment depend on the risk of the investment and the type of market returns available for that given risk level. Risk is measured by the variance of returns, but it is a function of economic and financial factors. The market keeps risk-return relationships in equilibrium through adjustments in price each time that an asset is traded.

Given that we know the risk and market-required yield on an investment, the present or future value of an investment in terms of price can be derived.

Future Value of a Single Sum

The future value of a single sum compounded per period at a given yield is:

$$\$FV = (1 + i)^n(\$PV),$$

where

$$PV = \text{initial sum invested at } n = 0,$$
$$i = \text{yield per period, and}$$
$$n = \text{number of periods.}$$

Example:

What is the future value of a \$1 investment that yields a 9% annual rate of return, compounded monthly for 30 years?

Solution:

$$\begin{aligned} FV &= (1 + .09/12)^{12 \times 30}(\$1), \\ &= (1 + .0075)^{360}(\$1), \\ &= \$14.73. \end{aligned}$$

Because the problem calls for monthly compounding, the 30-year term must be multiplied by 12 and the 9% interest divided by 12 to change the yearly factors to monthly ones. If \$1 is invested at a 9% annual rate, it will grow to \$14.73 in 30 years, with monthly compounding.

Present Value of a Single Sum

If \$1 invested for 360 months at 9% annually or .75% monthly becomes \$14.73, then \$1 in 30 years at this same yield is worth only 1/14.73 today. This is the fraction of each dollar that will become a full dollar in 30 years. Thus, the present value of a single sum is the reciprocal of the future value. The present value of a single sum discounted at a given yield per period is:

$$\$PV = \left[\frac{1}{(1+i)^n}\right] (\$FV).$$

Example:

What is the present value of \$15 dollars at an annual rate of 12%, discounted monthly for 5 years?

Solution:

$$\$PV = \left[\frac{1}{(1+.12/12)^{5\times 12}}\right] (\$15),$$

$$= \left[\frac{1}{(1+.01)^{60}}\right] (\$15),$$

$$= (.55045)(\$15),$$

$$= \$8.257.$$

If $15 can be received in 5 years, it is worth $8.26 today, assuming an annual rate of 12% compounded monthly.

Future Value of an Annuity

The mathematics of compounding or discounting an annuity must be used in order to develop a simplified procedure for obtaining the future or present value of an annuity over a large number of periods. This is because each yield per period is further compounded in the case of future value or further discounted in the case of present value.

If we add together the future value of single sums each period:

$$FV_A = (\$)(1+i)^1 + (\$)(1+i)^2 + \cdots + (\$)(1+i)^{n.}$$

we get a geometric progression of n terms with a periodic yield of i. Each dollar compounded per period is related by the relationship, shown as follows:

$$\begin{array}{lcccc} & \textit{Period 1} \rightarrow & \textit{Period 2} \rightarrow & \textit{Period 3} \rightarrow \ldots \rightarrow & \textit{Period n} \\ FV = & (\$)(1+i) \rightarrow & (\$)_1(1+i) \rightarrow & (\$)_2(1+i) \rightarrow \ldots \rightarrow & (\$)_{n-1}(1+i). \end{array}$$

Example:

At 10% for 4 years the value progresses as:

$$\begin{array}{llll} \textit{Period 1} \rightarrow & \textit{Period 2} \rightarrow & \textit{Period 3} \rightarrow & \textit{Period 4} \\ (\$1)(1.10) \rightarrow & (\$)(1.10)(1.10) \rightarrow & (\$)(1.21)(1.10) \rightarrow & (\$)(1.331)(1.10) = \$1.46. \end{array}$$

In general this relationship is:

$$\$_n = \$_1 r^n,$$

where r is the common ratio or relationship between any two periods, such as 1.10 in the previous example: $r = (1+i)$.

The sum of the n terms of a geometric progression is:

$$S_n = \$_1 + \$_1 r + \$_1 r^2 + \$_1 r^3 + \cdots + \$_1 r^{n-1} \tag{I-1}$$

Then multiplying both sides by r yields:

$$rS_n = \$_1 r + \$_1 r^2 + \cdots + \$_1 r^n, \tag{I-2}$$

and, subtracting the members of (I-1) from (I-2), all terms on the right except the first and last cancel out, and we obtain:

$$rS_n - S_n = \$_1 r^n - \$_1 \tag{I-3}$$

or

$$S_n(r-1) = \$_1(r^n - 1).$$

Therefore we can separate the sum S_n out, as:

$$S_n = \frac{\$_1(r^n - 1)}{r-1}. \tag{I-4}$$

Substituting $(1+i)$ for r we get:

$$S_{FV} = (\$)\left[\frac{(1+i)^n - 1}{(1+i) - 1}\right] \tag{I-5}$$

or

$$FV_A = (\$)\left[\frac{(1+i)^n - 1}{i}\right], \tag{I-6}$$

where (I-6) is the formula used to calculate the future value of \$1 per period, commonly referred to as the future value of an annuity.

Example:

Find the future value of \$1 per month for 5 years, with an annual yield of 12%, compounded monthly.

Solutions:

$$FV_A = \left[\frac{(1 + 12/12)^{5\times12} - 1}{.12/12}\right] (\$1),$$

$$= \left[\frac{(1+.01)^{60}-1}{.01}\right](\$1),$$

$$= \left[\frac{1.8167-1}{.01}\right](\$1),$$

$$= (81.669)(\$1),$$

$$= \$81.67.$$

One dollar deposited at the end of each month for 5 years will be worth \$81.67, if compounded monthly at a 12% annual yield.

Present Value of an Annuity

The present value of a stream or annuity of identical or level dollar flows at a given yield per period is the sum of all of the present value of single sums from 1 to *n*, the term of the investment.

$$PV_{Annuity} = (\$)\left[\frac{1}{(1+i)^1}\right] + (\$)\left[\frac{1}{(1+i)^2}\right] + \cdots + (\$)\left[\frac{1}{(1+i)^n}\right]. \quad \text{(I-7)}$$

Example:

What is the present value of \$1 paid in each year at the end of the year for 3 years, with a discount rate of 10%?

Solution:

$$PV_{Annuity} = (\$1)\left[\frac{1}{(1+.10)^1}\right] + (\$1)\left[\frac{1}{(1+.10)^2}\right] + (\$1)\left[\frac{1}{(1+.10)^3}\right],$$

$$= (\$1)(.909091) + (\$1)(.82645) + (\$1)(.75131),$$

$$= (\$1)(2.48685),$$

$$= \$2.486.$$

Note that the answer must be under \$3.00, the sum of the annuity, unless the discount rate is zero, in which case the sum would be \$3.00. The geometric progression rules also apply for the present value of an annuity, except that we are discounting so that:

$$PV_A = (\$)\left[\frac{1}{(1+i)^1}\right] + (\$)\left[\frac{1}{(1+i)^2}\right] + \cdots + (\$)\left[\frac{1}{(1+i)^n}\right] \quad \text{(I-8)}$$

or

$$PV_A = (\$)(1+i)^{-1} + (\$)(1+i)^{-2} + \cdots + (\$)(1+i)^{-n}, \qquad \text{(I-9)}$$

which reduces to:

$$PV_A = \left[\frac{1-(1+i)^{-n}}{i}\right] \qquad \text{(I-10)}$$

or

$$PV_A = \left[\frac{1-1/(1+i)^{n}}{i}\right] \qquad \text{(I-11)}$$

where (I-11) is the most commonly used form because of the ease of putting the present value of a single sum for $1/(1+i)^n$.

Example:

Find the present value of a yearly annuity for \$50 for 10 years with an annual discount rate of 15%.

Solution:

$$PV_A = \left[\frac{1-1/(1+.15)^{10}}{.15}\right](\$50) = \left[\frac{1-.24718}{.15}\right](\$50),$$

$$= (5.018769)(\$50),$$

$$= \$250.94.$$

Tables have been developed that provide the calculations, at various yields and periods for all the future and present value concepts discussed. These tables and their use are discussed in Chapter II.

MORTGAGE MATHEMATICS

Mortgage Payments

When we consider the fact that a mortgage loan is merely the present value of an annuity, where the annuity is the mortgage payments, we develop a new relationship:

$$\$PV = PV_A(\text{annuity})$$

or

$$\text{Mortgage} = PV_A(\text{mortgage payments}).$$

Thus, Mortgage payments = Mortgage / PV_A, or the mortgage payment per period will be $1/PV_A$ times the original mortgage. We call $1/PV_A$ the loan or mortgage constant, MC.

Example:

Find the monthly mortgage payments, $\$MP$, for a mortgage of \$50,000 with an annual rate of interest of 9% and a 30-year term.

Solution:

$$MC = \frac{1}{PV_A} = \frac{1}{\left[\dfrac{1-1/(1+i)^n}{i}\right]}$$

or

$$MC = \frac{1}{\left[\dfrac{1-1/(1+.0075)^{360}}{.0075}\right]},$$

$$= \frac{1}{124.28186},$$

$$= .008046226.$$

The resulting mortgage constant is then multiplied by the initial mortgage amount to find the monthly mortgage payment:

$$\$MP = MC(\$50{,}000),$$

$$= .008046226(\$50{,}000),$$

$$= \$402.31 \text{ to be paid monthly 360 times.}$$

Note that the mortgage constant includes both principal repayment (\$50,000 in the previous case) and the yield desired on the loan.

Mortgage Balance Remaining

The yield or interest portion of each mortgage payment is always based on the outstanding mortgage balance:

$$\text{Interest per period} = i \text{ (mortgage balance)},$$

where i is the periodic interest rate (.09/12 in the previous example, or .0075).

Example:

What is the first month's interest on a monthly paid $50,000 loan at a 9% annual interest rate and a 30-year term?

Solution:

$$\$ \text{ Interest} = .09/12(\$50{,}000),$$

$$= .0075(\$50{,}000),$$

$$= \$375.00.$$

Because the payment is $402.31, the difference between the monthly payment and the interest, $402.31 − $375.00 = $27.31, must go toward principal repayment, reducing the remaining loan balance. The interest in the second month is computed as:

$$\$ \text{ Interest} = .09/12(\$50{,}000.00 - \$27.31),$$

$$= .0075(\$49{,}972.69),$$

$$= \$374.79,$$

and the loan is reduced further by $27.51. Note that the loan constant is the percentage of the mortgage that includes both principal repayment and interest, paid on a level basis. However, the interest decreases as a proportion of the level mortgage payment each period and the principal repayment proportion increases. Rather than repeat monthly calculations to determine the principal repaid over long terms, another procedure is available. Recall that the mortgage is merely the present value of an annuity for a lender. Then, if a borrower pays a mortgage over only part of the term, the present value of the remaining payments divided by the present value of the full-term mortgage is the remaining mortgage proportion to be paid off. This equation, where n is the full term of the mortgage and j is the number of periods actually paid, is:

$$MB_j = \frac{PV_a^{n-j}}{PV_a^n} = \frac{\left[\dfrac{1-1/(1+i)^{n-j}}{i}\right]}{\left[\dfrac{1-1/(1+i)^{n}}{i}\right]}, \qquad (1) \qquad \text{(I-12)}$$

which reduces to a shorter version:

$$MB_j = \frac{1-1/(1+i)^{n-j}}{\left[1-1/(1+i)^{n}\right]}, \qquad \text{(I-13)}$$

where MB_j is the percentage of the mortgage balance remaining in period j.

Note that the remaining mortgage balance in dollars is simply the present value of the remaining mortgage payments discounted at the contract mortgage rate of interest.

Example:

What is the mortgage balance remaining on a \$50,000 mortgage at 11%, with monthly payments, paid for 12 years of an original 30-year term?

Solution:

$$MB_{144} = \frac{[1-1/(1+.009167)^{360-144}]}{[1-1/(1+.009167)^{360}]} = \frac{1-1/7.177708}{1-1/26.708098}$$

$$= \frac{.860679}{.967558},$$

$$= .8941587.$$

After paying on the mortgage for 12 years, 89.41587% of the original loan still remains to be paid. Therefore:

$$(.8941587)(\$50{,}000) = \$44{,}707.94,$$

which is the remaining balance. Note that in the preceding example only $5,292.06 of an original $50,000 mortgage, or 10.58% of the balance, has been paid off even though 12 of 30 years, or 40% of the term, of the mortgage has expired. While this may seem inequitable, it is interesting to look at the result if a borrower insisted on using a stright principal amortization mortgage, paying off an equal amount of the mortgage principal, plus interest, each period.

As an example, assume a $50,000 mortgage at 12% for 25 years, payable monthly. With level payment amortization, the monthly mortgage payment is $526.61, of which (.01) ($50,000), or $500, is interest in the first month. If a borrower decided to pay off the principal on a level basis, that would mean $50,000 ÷ 300 months, or $166.67 per period. In the first month the payment would be $500 + $166.67, or $666.67, declining each month thereafter as the interest portion declines. The conclusion is that the traditional fully amortized level payment plan makes a mortgage of a given size more affordable and feasible when the borrower may not otherwise be able to "afford" the loan.

APPLICATIONS AND VARIATIONS

Discount Points

A discount point is a finance charge that raises the yield on a mortgage loan. A point is 1% or .01 of the initial mortgage. The effect of "points" is to reduce the lender's net cash outflow or present value of the mortgage loan. Because loan payments are based on the contract rate and full mortgage, the yield to the lender on the net cash mortgage loan increases with the payment of points.

Example:

What is the overall effective lender yield on a $50,000 mortgage at 10%, monthly payments for 30 years, with 4 points charged at closing?

Solutions:

Four points equals (.04) $50,000 = $2,000. Thus, the mortgage lender lends out $50,000 − $2,000, or $48,000, but receives payments based on a $50,000 mortgage. The payments represent an annuity, which when discounted to $48,000 will give an effective yield of *r*, for which we must solve:

$$\$48{,}000 = PV_{A_r}(\$438.78),$$

where \$438.78 is the monthly mortgage payment, based on the contract rate, *i*. Solving for the relationship:

$$PV_{A_{r?}} = \frac{\$48{,}000.00}{\$438.78} = 109.394.$$

We can then solve for the present value of an annuity, which equals 109.394, by solving for *i*:

$$109.394 = \frac{1 - 1/(1+i)^{360}}{i}.$$

The *i* that equates the two sides of the equation is the effective yield, in this case .87431522 monthly for an annual yield of 10.4918%.

The effective yield resulting from charging discount points and other fees that must be included according to federal Regulation Z is called the annual percentage rate, *APR*. The Annual Percentage Rate is calculated with no prepayment assumption and must be disclosed to the borrower within the nearest quarter of a percentage point. The use of the Chapter III Annual Percentage Rate table is discussed in Chapter II.

Let's approach points from another perspective. Suppose we wish to raise the contract or stated rate of interest on a mortgage loan, *i*, up to some desired yield, *r*, by charging points. The question then is how many points do we charge?

Assuming the full term required to pay off a mortgage loan, *PV*, we have the following relationship:

$$PV - \text{points} = PV_{a_r}(MP_i) \qquad \text{(I-14)}$$

or

$$\text{Points} = PV - PV_{a_r}(MP_i). \qquad \text{(I-15)}$$

More explicitly, for each dollar of mortgage loan, we can use \$1 for the *PV* and determine the percentage of each dollar we need of the loan as points:

$$\text{Percentage points} = 1 - \left[\frac{1 - 1/(1+r)^n}{r}\right]\left[\frac{1 - 1/(1+i)^n}{i}\right]^{-1}, \qquad \text{(I-16)}$$

where

PV = the initial mortgage amount,

PV_{a_r} = the present value of an annuity at r, the desired effective yield; and

MP_i = the mortgage payment at the contract rate of interest i.

Example:

How many points are needed to bring the yield up to 12.5% from 11.0% on a 360-month (30-year) loan, assuming no early prepayment?

Solution:

$$\text{Points} = 1 - \left[\frac{1 - 1/(1 + .125/12)^{360}}{.125/12}\right] \left[\frac{1 - 1/(1 + .11/12)^{360}}{.11/12}\right]^{-1},$$

$$= 1 - \left[\frac{1 - 1/(1 + .01041667)^{360}}{.01041667}\right] \left[\frac{1 - 1/(1 + .00916667)^{360}}{.00916667}\right]^{-1},$$

$$= 1 - (93.698077)(.00952323),$$

$$= 1 - .8923087,$$

$$= .1076912,$$

which means that 10.76912% of every dollar must be charged as points at the closing on the loan to bring the yield up to 12.5% from the contract rate of 11.0%.

Proof:

Assume that a loan of \$50,000 is made at 11.0% for 30 years, payable monthly, and that the lender charges (.1076912)(\$50,000), or \$5,384.56, in "points." What is the effective yield? As can be seen, \$50,000 – \$5,384.56 equals the net loan (\$44,615.44) and \$476.162 is the monthly payment:

$$\$44{,}615.44 = PV_A(\$476.162)$$

and

$$PV_A = 93.698,$$

which is the present value of a monthly annuity factor for 12.5% for 30 years.

What happens if the loan is not paid over the full term but is paid off early? Then our effective yield will differ from that in the previous case. Let us say that we want to assume a 12-year prepayment and desire to charge the amount of points that will bring an 11.0% yield up to 12.5% based on a 30-year monthly amortization schedule.

The monthly payment is still the same $476.162 based on a $50,000 loan, but now the present value of the annuity is only over 12 years or 144 months, and we also must consider the present value of a single sum, the mortgage balance remaining in year 12. The solution as to how many points per dollar of mortgage loan will bring the yield to 12.5% is:

$$\text{Points} = 1 - PV_{a_r}(MC_i) - PV_{s_r}(\%MB_i), \qquad \text{(I-17)}$$

where we must discount both the mortgage payment, which for $1 is the same as the mortgage constant, MC_i, as an annuity at r, the desired yield, and the percentage mortgage balance remaining, $\%MB_i$, at a single sum at the desired yield. More explicitly, for each dollar of mortgage loan:

$$\text{Points} = 1 - \left[\frac{1 - 1/(1+i)^j}{r}\right]\left[\frac{1 - 1/(1+i)^n}{i}\right]^{-1} - \frac{1}{(1+r)^j}\left[\frac{1 - 1/(1+i)^{n-j}}{1 - 1/(1+i)^n}\right], \qquad \text{(I-18)}$$

where

j = the number of months actually paid,

n = the full term in months of the mortgage,

i = the contract rate, and

r = the desired yield.

Example:

How many points should be charged to bring a $50,000 mortgage at an 11.0% contract rate up to 12.5% based on a 30-year term (monthly payments) and an assumed prepayment in 12 years.

Solution:

$$\text{Points} = 1 - PV_{a_r}(MC_i) - PV_{s_r}(MB_i),$$

$$= 1 - PV_{a_{.125/12}}(MC_{.110/12}) - PV_{s_{.125/12}}(MB_{.110/12}),$$

$$= 1 - \left[\frac{1-1/(1+.125/12)^{144}}{.125/12}\right]\left[\frac{1-1/(1+.11/12)^{360}}{.11/12}\right]^{-1}$$

$$- \frac{1}{(1+.125/12)^{144}}\left[\frac{1-1/(1+.11/12)^{216}}{1-1/(1+.11/12)^{360}}\right],$$

$$= 1 - (74.412).00952323 - (.22486808).894158693,$$

$$= 1 - .7086492 - .2010677,$$

$$= .09028304,$$

or 9.028 points should be charged to raise the contract rate of 11.0% up to the desired yield of 12.5%, with a 12-year assumed prepayment. The dollar value of the points is .09028304 ($50,000) = $4,514.15. Note the significant effect of reducing the assumed prepayment period. The points in dollars required to change the yield 1½% is $5,384.56 for the full-term example and $4,514.15 for the assumed 12-year prepayment example.

Wraparound Mortgages

In some cases, it may not be desirable to pay off an existing mortgage. This may be because of high prepayment penalties or low existing interest cost. However, new funds may be desired by the borrower for a variety of reasons, such as the current value of a property and the borrower's credit justifying additional funds. The new funds may be provided by a lender who will then collect payments on both the new and old money and pass through or service the old loan payments. This is called a wraparound mortgage, where a new second mortgage encompasses, or "wraps around," the existing first mortgage, keeping the first mortgage intact. In this way a new lender has better control over the lien position.

Example:

A borrower arranges a $125,000 mortgage at 7%, for 30 years monthly). The sum of the monthly payments for 1 year is $9,979.54. Five years later, the mortgage balance is $117,664.48, with current first mortgage rates up to 9.00% and 10.25% for second mortgages. Because the existing mortgage rate is below the current first mortgage rates, the borrower does not want to refinance. Instead, the borrower arranges for an addditional (second) wraparound mortgage of $50,000. The wraparound note is based upon $167,664, which is the sum of $117,664 and $50,000. The term is 25 years at 8%, so that the payments are $1,294.06 monthly or $15,528.74 yearly. What is the effective yield on the additional $50,000?

Solution:

$15,528.74	collected each year
9,979.54	passed through to old mortgage lender
$ 5,549.20	the net debt service ($462.43 per month) to the new lender

$$\frac{\$462.43}{\$50{,}000.00} = .0092486,$$

which is the loan constant for a 25-year monthly loan.

Now we can solve for the effective interest rate for a 25-year monthly mortgage loan constant that matches .0092486, or we can divide $50,000.00 by $462.43 to get the present value of annuity factor and solve for the effective yield to the wraparound lender:

$$PV_{a_r} = \frac{\$50{,}000.00}{\$462.43},$$

$$PV_{a_r} = 108.1245,$$

$$\left[\frac{1 - 1/(1+r)^n}{r}\right] = 108.1245,$$

and

$$r = 10.228\%.$$

As a further variation on wraparound mortgages, how do we solve for a wraparound yield when the term on the wraparound is longer than the remaining term on the old money?

Example:

A lender agrees to advance $100,000 on a wraparound mortgage of $250,000 for 25 years, with a remaining balance on the existing first mortgage of \$150,000. The first mortgage has a remaining term of 10 years and requires monthly payments of \$2,152.06. The wraparound note of \$250,000 has a contract rate of 12.5%, requiring monthly payments of \$2,725.89. What is the effective yield on the wraparound note?

Solution:

$$\text{New money} = (\$2{,}725.89 - \$2{,}152.06)PV_{A_{120\ mo,r}} + PV_{s_{120\ mo,r}} PV_{A_{300-120,r}}(\$2{,}725.89),$$

$$\$100{,}000 = (\$573.83)PV_{A_{120,r}} + PV_{s_{120,r}} PV_{A_{180,r}}(\$2{,}725.89),$$

where $PV_{s_{120}}$ is the present value of a single sum that discounts the final 15 years of wraparound income to the present. Through an interative approach, we may try various yields until we solve for the effective yield r. At 14%, we get:

$$\$100{,}000 = \$573.83\left[\frac{1-1/(1+.011667)^{120}}{.011667}\right] + \left[\frac{1}{(1+.011667)^{120}}\right] \times \left[\frac{1-1/(1+.011667)^{180}}{.011667}\right](\$2{,}725.89),$$

$$= \$573.83(64.40542) + .2486034(\$204{,}686.14),$$

$$= \$87{,}843.44.$$

Because this answer is too low, we must try a lower yield, such as 13%. At 13%, the sum of the discounted flows is \$97,559.24; therefore, we must go even lower, but we know that the yield has to be above 12.50%. So let us try 12.75%. At 12.75% the result is \$100,218.51; therefore our solution is approximately 12.77% as the effective yield.

Graduated Payment Mortgages

To facilitate younger borrowers who aspire to homeownership but cannot afford fixed rate mortgage payments, yet expect increasing income, a beneficial variation on mortgage payments is possible. A graduated payment mortgage, *GPM*, begins with some base mortgage payment that increases over time. The initial payments may be lower than the interest due, thus increasing the principal in the early years. In other words, the mortgage balance may actually increase in the early years as a result of unpaid interest.

If the initial payment is set at interest only, the mortgage balance does not increase, but this will have a smaller impact on easing the monthly payment burden on borrowers. Once the initial payment is set, then the following payments in each period will be:

$$MP_t = \frac{[(1+i)/(1+g)-1](PV)\,[(1+g)^t]}{1-[(1+g)/(1+i)]^n},$$

where:

MP_t = the mortgage payment in period t, where the maximum t is the length of the graduation period,
i = the interest rate (contract rate) on the mortgage per period,
g = the growth rate in the monthly payments,
PV = the original mortgage balance, and
n = the full term of the mortgage.

Example:

Assume a \$50,000 mortgage with an interest rate of 12% per year, paid monthly, with a 300-month or 25-year term. The fixed level payments per month are \$526.21, of which \$500 is interest the first month. If we set up a graduated payment mortgage with a 3% annual growth rate (.25% monthly) over the full term, but graduate payments for the first 10 years only, with fixed level payments thereafter, what is the first payment?

Solution:

$$MP_1 = \frac{[(1+.01)/(1+.0025)-1]\ (\$50{,}000)\ (1+.0025)^1}{1-[(1+.0025)/(1+.01)]^{300}}.$$

$$= \frac{(.0074813)(\$50{,}000)(1.0025)}{.89311857},$$

$$= \$419.87.$$

Because the interest in the first month is \$500, the mortgage balance in the first month increases by \$500 − \$419.87 = \$80.13, or a new principal balance of \$50,080.13.

In the second month the payment is:

$$MP_2 = \frac{[(1+.01)/(1+.0025)-1](\$50{,}000)(1+.0025)^2}{1-[(1+.0025)/(1+.01)]^{300}},$$

$$= \$420.93.$$

Following up on this example, how is the payment in year 11 and in subsequent years calculated? The solution is found by treating the mortgage principal balance at the end of 10 years as a new mortgage with a term of 15 years at 12% per year and solving for the fixed mortgage constant to determine the new mortgage payment.

Further variation on the graduated payment mortgage is possible in a number of ways. Suppose that a lending institution did not wish to allow the original mortgage balance to increase but wished to keep the initial payments as low as possible. In this case, the borrower could make interest only payments for a number of years and then pay the mortgage off over some remaining term on a graduated basis.

Example:

Take the same $50,000 mortgage at 12% as before, but assume that the borrower will pay interest only for 5 years of the 25-year term (or $500 per month). What is the graduated payment schedule over the remaining 20 years? The solution is found by treating the 20 years as a full-term graduated payment mortgage, but constraining the result so that the first payment starts at $500 or more, so as not to increase the loan balance. One approach is to use trial and error in testing out various growth rates and solve for *MP* in period one.

Try a growth rate of .6% per year or .0005 in decimal form per month for the remaining 20 years. Solving for MP_1 over 20 years:

$$MP_1 = \frac{[(1+.01)/(1+.0005)-1)](\$50{,}000)(1+.0005)^1}{1-[(1+.0005)/(1+.01)]^{240}},$$

$$= \frac{(.00949525)(\$50{,}000)(1.0005)}{.89649231},$$

$$= \frac{\$475}{.89649231} = \$529.84,$$

which is the first payment in year 6.

Because the result is $29.84 above the interest-only payment in the first month, the assumed growth rate is satisfactory as a solution. We could, if desired, increase the growth rate just slightly and reduce further the first principal and interest mortgage payment of $529.84.

Another variation on the graduated payment mortgage that many borrowers and lenders might prefer is to graduate the payments each year but to hold the monthly payments constant during each year. To solve for such payments requires a two-stage approach. First, we need to solve for graduated mortgage payments on an annual payment basis. Then, to derive the monthly payments, we need to solve for the constant monthly annuity, which sums to the annual payment when compounded at the appropriate yield. This is done by dividing the annual graduated mortgage payments by a 12-month future value of annuity factor.

Example:

Find the monthly graduated payments on a $50,000 mortgage, at a 12% annual interest rate, with a 25-year term and a 3% annual growth rate, holding payments constant during each year.

Solution:

Step 1. Find the annual sum due at the end of 1 year of annual payments.

$$MP_{1yr} = \frac{[(1+.12)/(1+.03)-1](\$50{,}000)(1+.03)^{1}}{1-[(1+.03)/(1+.12)]^{25}},$$

$$MP_{1yr} = \frac{\$4{,}500.00}{.87684} = \$5{,}132.08$$

Step 2. Find the monthly annuity that if compounded at 12% annually (.01 monthly) sums to $5,132.08 for 12 periods.

$$FV_A\,(\text{monthly mortgage payments}_1) = \$5{,}132.08$$

or

$$\text{Monthly mortgage payments}_1 = \frac{\$5{,}132.08}{FV_A},$$

$$= \frac{\$5{,}132.08}{[(1+.01)^{12}-1]/.01},$$

$$= \$404.66.$$

The constant monthly payments in the first year are \$404.66. In year 2, MP_{2yr} = \$5,286.03 and the monthly payments are:

$$\text{Monthly mortgage payments}_2 = \frac{\$5,286.03}{12.8625},$$
$$= \$410.96.$$

The monthly payment for any year can be calculated in this manner using any combination of increase in graduation rate or graduation term.

For federally regulated real estate lenders, several general graduated payment mortgage plans are allowed with various rates of annual increases in payment size over 5- or 10-year periods, with payments fixed after the graduated term is over. The mathematics are identical to that just shown, where the payments graduate per annum by some percentage for 5 or 10 years but are held constant during each year. After the graduated period is over, the payments are fixed as with the traditional fixed rate mortgage instrument for the remaining term.

FHA Graduated Payment Mortgage Plans

Plan I	5 years of increasing payments at 2½% each year
Plan II	5 years of increasing payments at 5% each year
Plan III	5 years of increasing payments at 7½% each year
Plan IV	10 years of increasing payments at 2% each year
Plan V	10 years of increasing payments at 3% each year

The maximum loan balances for a plan I mortgage at 12% or 13% will be at the end of year 4 and about 2% more than the original loan balance. With plan II at the end of year 5 the mortgage will be at its maximum balance some 5% above the original loan. Plan II will also reach its maximum level at the end of year 5 some 8% to 9% above the original loan in the 12% to 13% interest range. Plan IV will reach its maximum level some 4% to 5% above the original loan in 84 months. Plan V will reach its maximum level some 8% to 9½% above the original loan in 96 months.

Variations of Graduated Payment Mortgages Using Escrow Accounts

Several forms of graduated payment mortgages have been devised by financial institutions, some called "flips" for flexible payment plans, others called "equalizer" loans. However, the basis upon which most privately developed plans reduce mortgage payments in the early years is through the use of escrow accounts, not through increasing loan balances. Typically, part of the "down payment" on a home purchase is placed in an escrow account administered by the lending institution. The funds in the escrow account earn rather conservative yields, such as those paid on passbook savings accounts. For a period of 2 to 5 years, the funds in the escrow account are used to reduce the monthly mortgage payments. As with FHA-approved plans, the monthly mortgage payments stay constant, increasing annually to a new level. A major advantage for a lender using this technique is that the mortgage balance need not increase in the early years. From the borrower's point of view, the burden of the cash outflow each month is easier to carry, even though one is subsidizing one's self through the escrow account funds. This plan seems especially appropriate for homebuyers on their second or third homes who have substantial market equities, increasing income, and higher aspirations.

Most escrow account graduated payment mortgages carry interest yields ¼% to ⅜% above conventional fixed rate plans. In addition, the lender is able to produce an even greater overall yield through the use of lower-cost stable funds from the escrow account deposits.

Example:

Start with a fixed rate mortgage at an interest rate of 13% for a 30-year term. For a $100,000 mortgage the payments are $1,106.70 monthly. Suppose that the borrower has $50,000 of cash that could be put toward a home purchase and that the borrower puts a contract on a home for $143,000. The lender estimates closing costs of $3,000, so the borrower will need $46,000 of cash to close. However, the borrower prefers a lower monthly cash payment, at least in the early years, and the lender does not mind bringing the loan to value ratio up to 80%. So the borrower decides to take $10,000 and place it in an escrow account at 5½% monthly to be used to subsidize the monthly payments for 3 years. Simultaneously the borrower increases the loan to $110,000 requiring new monthly payments of $1,216.82 on a fixed rate basis. How much can the monthly payments be reduced using the $10,000 in the escrow account, if the payments are to be held constant for 3 years and then are at $1,216.82 from year 4 on?

Solution:

The $10,000 is the present value of an annuity that will be used to reduce the monthly required interest payments. A 36-month mortgage constant at 5.5% interest annually or .00458333 monthly will give us the monthly percentage to allocate, in this case .030196. Therefore:

$$.030196(\$10{,}000) = \$301.96 \text{ escrow monthly subsidy,}$$

and for 3 years the payments will be:

$$\$1{,}216.82 - \$301.96 = \$914.86 \text{ net monthly payment,}$$

which is $191.34 less than the monthly payment if constant payments are used and the escrowed funds are put toward the purchase.

Note that, even though $914.86 is the monthly required cash payment for 3 years, the borrower may deduct the actual interest portion of the $1,216.82 cash received monthly by the lender. In month 1 this will be $1,191.67. As a result of the tax deduction of interest, the annual net cash outlay for the escrow account subsidized mortgage is reduced even further.

Note also that there is no reason why an escrow subsidy account cannot be used to reduce the payments on a variable rate or negotiated rate mortgage. In fact, in an uncertain inflationary economy, that could be an optimal combination for both lender and borrower. Further, mortgage payments may be graduated for 3, 5 or even 10 years on an escrow account subsidized mortgage.

Variable Rate Mortgages

Variable rate mortgages, *VRM,* are mortgages with yields that vary according to some index to which the interest rate is tied. Typically, variable rate mortgages are restricted in movement to only a limited amount, such as .25% semiannually, thus limiting extreme variations in the interest rate over short time periods. Also, variable rate mortgages are typically constrained to a maximum and minimum amount, such as ± 2% or 5%. As a result of interest rate changes, consumers generally have the right to either increase (decrease) their mortgage payments or increase (decrease) the term of the mortgage. The index is typically some long-term index of a federal institution, such as the Federal Home Loan Bank Board.

Today, lenders have no regulatory minimum or maximum constraints on the interest rate changes which may occur. The intervals between adjustments also have been liberalized. Indexes as well may be one of several which relate to the cost of the lender's funds.

Example:

Assume that an individual borrows on a variable rate mortgage of $80,000 at 10% for 25 years (300 months) with monthly payments initially of $726.96. Also assume initially that the FHLBB index is at 8.0%, but 1 year later moves to 8.5%. The new interest rate on the variable rate mortgage is:

$$\text{New variable rate} = \frac{\text{Index (end of period)}}{\text{Index base (beginning of period)}}\text{(beg. per. var. rate)},$$

$$= \frac{8.5\%}{8.0\%}(10.0) = 10.625\% \text{ beginning in period 2.}$$

Now the borrower can either increase the size of the monthly payment or increase the term to keep the payment the same. Suppose on the mortgage that the borrower decides to increase the mortgage payment. To solve for the new payment, we develop the new mortgage payment based on a 24-year term at 10.625% interest, the present value being the loan balance at the end of year 1.

Solution:

Step 1. Derive the mortgage balance:

$$MB_1 = \frac{[1 - 1/(1 + .0083333)^{288}]}{[1 - 1/(1 + .008333)^{300}]}(\$80{,}000) = \frac{.90837537}{.91706025}, (\$80{,}000)$$

$$= (.99052965)(\$80{,}000),$$

$$= \$79{,}242.37.$$

Step 2. Solve for the mortgage payments based on the $79,242.37 balance, 24 years at 10.625%. The solution is:

$$MP = \$79{,}242.37(1/PV_{a_{10.625}}),$$

$$= \$761.78 \text{ per month.}$$

Next assume that the borrower decides to hold the monthly mortgage payment constant at $726.96 per month and extend the term. How far must we extend the term to hold the mortgage payment constant? The solution is found by:

$$\$726.96 = \$79{,}242.37 \text{ (mortgage constant)}$$

or

$$\frac{\$726.96}{\$79{,}242.37} = .00917388.$$

Now, because we know the yield desired is 10.625%, we examine various mortgage constants at that yield extending the term until we reach .00917381. To do this, we merely plug longer terms into *n* until the *MC* solution matches .00917388.

Try 30 years or 360 months, and we get a mortgage constant of .00924098 or $732.28 per month in payments, which is too high.

Try 32 years or 384 months, and we get a mortgage constant of .00916463 or $726.23 per month, which is very close.

Try 31 years 9 months or 381 months, and we get a mortgage constant of .00917325 or $726.92, which is about as close as we will ever need. Now we merely adjust the new payments to $726.92 down by $0.04 and increase the term to 31 years 9 months.

The problem with this solution is obvious; by regulation one may not be able to fully extend the term of the mortgage to that which holds payments constant.

If by regulation we cannot go longer than, say, 30 years, the increased mortgage payment with the term fully extended will be solved as follows:

$$MP = \frac{1}{\left[\dfrac{1 - 1/(1 + .10625/12)^{360}}{.10625/12}\right]} (\$79{,}242.37) = \$732.28,$$

which is our new payment.

Renegotiated Rate Mortgages

With a renegotiated rate mortgage, *RRM*, sometimes called "roll-overs," the unpaid balance is refinanced every few years, such as 3 or 5 years. At that time the interest rate is adjusted upward or downward depending on prevailing market conditions. These renegotiated rate mortgages are limited to no more than a 5% increase or decrease over the life of the loan for Federal Home Loan Bank Board members. Also, rates cannot fluctuate by more than half a percentage point a year, or 1.5% for 3 years, 2.5% for 5 years, and so on. Fluctuation in the rates will be tied to changes in mortgage market rates as measured by the bank board's national index. The index is an average of new mortgages throughout the United States issued during the previous month on existing homes.

The mathematical mechanics of renegotiated rate mortgages are similar to those for variable rate mortgages, the primary difference being that for the former adjustment periods between interest rate changes are longer.

Variable Balance Mortgages

Variable balance mortgages are similar to variable rate mortgages except that, instead of varying the payment or term in response to an interest rate change, the payments and term can be held stable and the balance owed varied. The result is a much more stable position for the borrower. Over the average life of a mortgage, often assumed to be 12 years, the principal balance may increase and decrease several times, yet the borrower need not react to these changes instantaneously. Over the typical term of 12 years the principal balance changes may average out to only a small difference in what would have resulted with a traditional level amortization fixed rate mortgage.

Example:

Assume a \$100,000 mortgage at 12.0%, 30-year term, with payments set at \$1,028.61 monthly. Now suppose that the index increases, requiring a new interest rate of 12.5% at the end of one year. What is the effect on the mortgage balance remaining?

Solution:

The mortgage balance is \$99,637.12 at the end of 1 year. If the interest rate is still 12.0%, then in the first month of the second year a payment of \$1,028.61 is made of which initially .120/12 (\$99,637.12), or \$996.37, is interest, leaving \$32.23 to go toward the mortgage balance. But, with the interest rate at 12.5%, .125/12 (\$99,637.12), or \$1,037.89, is now needed to cover interest. Because the payment is only \$1,028.61, an additional \$9.28 is due and will be added to the mortgage balance at the end of month 13. So, for month 14, the new balance is \$99,637.12 + \$9.28 = \$99,646.39. In month 14, we continue this same process with interest owed in period t equal to:

$$\$I_t = \frac{i}{12}(MB_{t-1}),$$

where i is the current annual interest rate and MB_{t-1} is the mortgage balance from the last period. Over time, as i moves up or down, the MB will move up or down. Allowing the term or payments to vary slightly in addition will result in constraining the movement of the mortgage balance.

Reverse Annuity Mortgages

The reverse annuity mortgage, *RAM*, has great appeal for older owners of homes who live on fixed incomes and have accumulated substantial equity in their homes. The reverse annuity mortgage reverses the flow of payments, from borrower to lender to lender to borrower. With a reverse annuity mortgage, a homeowner can use the equity built up in the home to acquire a stream of income from a lender, while still living in the house until death or some other predetermined date. The debt obligation accruing while the annuity is received is paid off at death or other predetermined date.

Reverse annuity mortgages can be based on fixed term and interest rate contracts or on variable rate contracts. Maximum balances or loan-to-value ratios can be built into the reverse annuity mortgage contracts to protect lenders. The annuity amount will be determined as if it was a mortgage, taking any of the forms already discussed. Upon full payment or death, the lender then owns the equity and may sell it to liquidate the capital investment.

PROBLEM SETS

Present Value and Annuity Problems

1. What is the present value of $1,217 to be received 5 years from now if you expect a 4% annual yield on your money?
2. You lend someone $1,000 today in return for a promise to repay $1,311 4 years from now. What annual rate of interest are you charging?
3. Someone offers to buy your car for $7,000 or to rent the car for $1,000 a year for 5 years and then buy it for $5,000. If you expect a 10% annual return on this deal, which is the better offer?
4. A bond pays $50 a year for 15 years and then $1,000 at maturity at the end of the 15 years. What is the bond worth to you if you expect a 6% annual return?
5. You borrow $2,000 today to be paid off annually over 4 years at 10%. What are the annual payments?

6. To what amount will $100 dollars grow in 50 years if yielding 18% per year?

7. To what amount will $100 dollars *per year*, deposited at the end of the year, grow in 50 years if yielding 18% per year?

8. A person buys a house, makes a down payment of $3,000, and agrees to pay $40 at the end of each month for 16½ years. If the yield expected by the seller is 4.5% annually, what is the equivalent cash price of the house? (assume monthly compounding)

Present Value and Annuity Solutions

1. $x = \$1{,}217\ (PV_{s_{4\%}}) = \$1{,}217\left[\frac{1}{(1+.04)^5}\right],$

$= \$1{,}217\ (.821927) = \$1{,}000.28.$

That is, the right to receive $1,217 in 5 years is worth $1,000.28 today, given a 4% annual yield.

2. You know that the present value is $1,000 and that the future value is $1,311 4 years from now. Therefore, the relationship is:

$$\$1{,}000 = \$1{,}311\ (PV_{s_{\%?}}),$$
$$PV_{s_{\%?}} = \frac{\$1{,}000}{\$1{,}311} = .76277651,$$
$$.76277651 = \frac{1}{(1+\%?)^4},$$

or

$$1.311 = (1+\%?)^4.$$

By iterative method, we see that 7% approximately equates the two sides of the equation, meaning in this example that an annual yield of 7% is charged.

3. You have a choice between $7,000 now or an annuity of $1,000 per year plus a single sum ($5,000) in 5 years. Discounting this second alternative at 10% results in:

$$\$1{,}000\left[\frac{1-1/(1+.10)^5}{.10}\right] + \$5{,}000\left[\frac{1}{(1+.10)^5}\right]$$
$$= \$1{,}000\ (3.7980) + \$5{,}000\ (.62092) = \$6{,}895.40.$$

Because $6,895.40 is less than $7,000, the $7,000 is the best alternative.

4. $$\$50\left[\frac{1-1/(1+.06)^{15}}{.06}\right]+\$1{,}000\left[\frac{1}{(1+.06)^{15}}\right]=\$902.88.$$

To earn a 6% annual return, you should pay $902.88 for the bond.

5. $$PV=PV_{A_{10\%}}(x),$$

$$\$2{,}000=\left[\frac{1-1/(1+.10)^{4}}{.10}\right](x),$$

$$\$2{,}000=3.1698654(x),$$

$$\frac{\$2{,}000}{3.16987}=\$630.94.$$

Or you could have solved for $1/PV_{A_{10\%}}$, the loan constant, $1/3.16987=.31547035$, so $\$2{,}000\ (.31547035)=\$630.94$, which is the yearly payment to amortize $2,000 over 4 years.

6. $\$100(FV_{s_{18\%}})=\$100(1.18)^{50}=\$392{,}735.68.$

7. $$\$100(FV_{A_{18\%}})=\$100\left[\frac{(1+.18)^{50}-1}{.18}\right],$$

$$=\$100(\$21{,}813.093),$$

$$=\$2{,}181{,}309.30.$$

8 $$PV_A=(40)\left[\frac{1-1/(1+.00375)^{198}}{.00375}\right],$$

$$=\$5{,}583.10.$$

Add the down payment of $3,000 for a total cash price of $8,583.10.

Problems on the Mathematics of Mortgages

1. What is the monthly loan constant on a 10%, 25-year term loan?
2. Given the monthly loan constant as in Problem 1, what are the monthly and sum of monthly payments for one year on a $75,000 mortgage?
3. What are the first month's interest and principal on the mortgage payment?

4. What is the total interest cost if the mortgage is paid over the 25-year term?

5. What are the monthly and annual payments on a 30-year, 10%, monthly payment loan for $75,000?

6. What is the mortgage balance in dollars after 5 years of payments on the $75,000, 10% monthly, 30-year term mortgage?

7. If a lender makes a $20,000 loan with the monthly payments at $170.41 for 20 years, what annual interest rate is being charged?

8. A lender makes a 9.0%, $30,000 loan for 31 years, with monthly payments of $239.89. The lender wants to bring the yield up to 9.5%. How much in points must be charged to produce this yield, assuming no prepayments?

9. A borrower arranges a wraparound mortgage with the terms based on $192,814 at 10.5%, payable monthly for 10 years. The old mortgage was originally for $200,000 at 10.0% for 30 years, but it has been paid down to $132,814 with 10 years to go. What is the effective yield on the new money?

Solutions to Problems on the Mathematics of Mortgages

1. $$MC = \frac{1}{\left[\dfrac{1 - 1/(1 + .10/12)^{300}}{.10/12}\right]} = .009087007.$$

2. .00909($75,000) = $681.52 monthly or $8,178.31 yearly.

3. .10/12($75,000) = $625 in interest:

$681.52 − $625.00 = $56.52 in principal reduction.

4. $8,178.31 × 25 = $204,457.75
204,457.75 − 75,000.00 (principal) = $129,457.75 (interest)

5. $$\frac{1}{\left[\dfrac{1 - 1/(1 + .10/12)^{360}}{.10/12}\right]}(\$75{,}000) = .0087757(\$75{,}000)$$

$$= \$658.18.$$

Note that, by increasing the term from 25 to 30 years, the monthly payment decreases from \$681.52 to \$658.18. The annual payment is $\$658.18 \times 12 = \$7,898.16$.

6. $$MB_{5yr} = \frac{[1 - 1/(1 + .008333)^{360-60}]}{[1 - 1/(1 + .008333)^{360}]} (\$75,000)$$

$$= .96574321, (\$75,000)$$

$$= .9654321(\$75,000) = \$72,430.74,$$

or \$72,430.74 remains to be paid after 5 years of the 30-year loan.

7. $\$170.41 / \$20,000.00 = \text{loan constant} = .0085205$. Solving, $.0085205 = 1/PV_{A_{\%?}}$ or take the inverse of $.0085205 = 117.364$ and solve for the $PV_{A\%?}$ directly:

$$PV_A = \frac{1 - 1/(1 + \%?)^{240}}{\%?} = 117.364$$

The interest rate being charged is approximately .006865 monthly or 8.25% annually.

8. There are several ways of solving for "points." The standard approach is:

$$\text{Points} = PV - PV_{a_r}(MP_i),$$

$$= \$30,000 - \frac{1 - 1/(1 + .095/12)^{372}}{.095/12} (\$240.00),$$

$$= \$30,000 - (119.59382)(\$240.00),$$

$$= \$1,297.48,$$

which divided by \$30,000 is .04325 or approximately 4.325 "points." The lender must charge 4.325 points, or \$1,297.48, to raise the yield from 9.0% to 9.5%.

9. The monthly payment on the full note is \$2,601.74, with \$1,755.14 needed for the first mortgage, leaving a net of \$846.59 on the new money. The loan constant for 10 years is therefore:

$$\frac{\$846.59}{\$60,000} = .01410987,$$

and the PV_A is 70.872338. Solving for these results:

$$70.872338 = PV_{A_{?\%}},$$

$$= \frac{1 - 1/(1+?\%)^{120}}{?\%},$$

$$?\% = 11.5878.$$

The effective yield on the new money is slightly over 11.5%.

chapter 2

Time Value, Yield, and Point Table Illustration

PRESENT VALUE TABLES

As demonstrated in Chapter I, formulas can be used to solve virtually all problems concerning the time value of money. The repetitious use of some of these formulas becomes tedious. As a result, tables have been developed to assist the user in solving the more common time value problems. This chapter will show how the tables are developed and will illustrate their use in place of, or in conjunction with, formulas in carrying out various time value and mortgage mathematic calculations.

Future Value of a Single Sum

The future value was developed in Chapter I as:

$$FV = (1 + i)^n(\$PV),$$
$$= \text{Future value factor} \times PV.$$

In solving this equation for the future value, the user simply plugs in the interest rate, i, and the number of compounding periods, n, solves for the future value factor, and then multiplies the factor by the beginning dollar amount PV. The future value tables in Chapter III have been developed by calculating this factor for $1 at various interest rates and terms. The tables are based on an annual yield, with monthly compounding. The user now, instead of calculating the factor, can go to the tables and get the future value factor and then multiply it by the initial present value to solve any future value of a single-sum problem.

Example:

What is the future value of a $1 investment that yields a 9% annual rate of return, compounded monthly for 30 years?

Solution:

$FV = \$1 \times$ table factor FV of $1, 9%, 30 years. From the Future Value of One Dollar table, under the 9%, 30-year period column, the factor is 14.73058:

$$FV = \$1(14.73058),$$
$$= \$14.73.$$

If $1 is invested at a 9% annual rate, compounded monthly, it will grow to $14.73 in 30 years.

Example:

You have a chance to sell your vacant lot to a local broker for $5,000. Your brother-in-law, who is in the service and will not return for 6 years, has offered to pay $10,000 for the lot upon his return. If you can invest the $5,000 now at a 10% annual return, compounded monthly, should you sell to the broker or wait for your brother-in-law?

Solution:

You need to determine the future value of your $5,000 investment to solve this problem. $FV = \$5{,}000 \times$ table factor FV of $1, 10%, 6 years. Going to the Future Value of One Dollar table, under the 10%, 6-year column, a factor of 1.81759 is obtained. Multiplying this by the initial investment yields:

$$FV = \$5{,}000(1.81759),$$
$$= \$9{,}087.95.$$

If the property is sold to the broker and the proceeds are invested at 10% for 6 years, it will be worth $9,087.95. Because this is less than the $10,000 your brother-in-law will pay in 6 years, you should not sell to the broker.

Present Value of a Single Sum

It was shown in Chapter I that the present value of a single sum is simply the reciprocal of the future value factor:

$$\$PV = \frac{1}{(1+i)^n}(\$FV),$$
$$= \text{Present value factor} \times FV.$$

The user can solve for the present value factor by plugging in the interest, i, and term, n, values. The Present Value of One Dollar tables have been developed by doing this calculation for a variety of interest rates and terms. As such, the user now needs only to get the proper table factor and then multiply that factor by the future value amount to get the present value, $\$PV$.

Example:

What is the present value of \$1 at an annual rate of 12%, discounted monthly for 5 years?

Solution:

$$PV = \$1 \times \text{table factor } PV \text{ of } \$1,\ 12\%,\ 5 \text{ years},$$
$$= \$1(.55045),$$
$$= \$.55045.$$

From the Present Value of One Dollar table column 12%, 5 years, the factor of .55045 is obtained; when multiplied by \$1, we find that \$1 to be received in 5 years is worth \$.55 in the present.

Example:

Your grandfather's will provides you with \$1,000,000 when you reach age 21, which is in 3 years. If the current annual yield on safe investments is 13%, compounded monthly, what is the present value of your inheritance?

Solution:

The following relationship will solve this problem:

$$PV = \$1{,}000{,}000 \times \text{table factor } PV \text{ of } \$1,\ 13\%,\ 3 \text{ years},$$
$$= \$1{,}000{,}000(.67848),$$
$$= \$678{,}480.00$$

By going to the 13%, 3-year column of the Present Value of One Dollar Table, a factor of .67848 is obtained. Multiplying this by the amount to be received in 3 years gives the value of the amount in the present. The $1,000,000 inheritance then is found to be worth a mere $678,480.00 today.

Future Value of an Annuity

We saw in Chapter I that the formula for calculating the future value of an annuity factor was:

$$FV_a = \frac{(1+i)^n - 1}{i}(\$).$$

Chapter III includes future value of annuity factors for a number of different interest rates and terms. These were developed using the formula just given, based on an annual yield with monthly compounding and assuming that payment is made at the end of the period.

Example:

Find the future value of a $1 monthly deposit for 5 years, with an annual yield of 12%, compounded monthly.

Solution:

$$FV_a = \$1 \times \text{table factor } FV \text{ of annuity, } 12\%\text{, 5 years,}$$
$$= \$1(81.66967),$$
$$= \$81.67.$$

By going to the Future Value of One Dollar Per Period table for 12%, 5 years, a factor of 81.6697 is obtained. Multiplying this factor by the $1 monthly payment gives a future value of $81.67, meaning that, if $1 is deposited at the end of each month for 5 years, it will accumulate to $81.67 if compounded at 12% annually. Note that payments are made at the end of each period, making this an ordinary annuity. If payments were made at the beginning of the period, this would then become an annuity due. In a situation that dictates that payments be made at the beginning of the compounding period, a simple adjustment can be made to convert the ordinary annuity to an annuity due. We must move each installment forward one period. In other words, each installment will be subject to one more period of compounding than each installment in the ordinary annuity. This conversion is accomplished by multiplying the ordinary annuity factor by its base. The base is simply one plus the periodic interest factor.

Example:

Find the future value of a \$1 monthly deposit, deposited at the beginning of the period for 5 years. Assume an annual yield of 12%, compounded monthly.

Solution:

$$
\begin{aligned}
FV_a &= \$1 \times \text{table factor } FV \text{ of annuity, } 12\%, 5 \text{ years} \times \text{base},\\
&= \$1(81.66967)\left(1+\frac{.12}{12}\right),\\
&= \$1(81.66967)(1.01),\\
&= \$82.4863.
\end{aligned}
$$

After finding the compound amount of \$1 per period factor, an adjustment is made for the deposit's being at the beginning of the period. The base is calculated by dividing the annual yield by the compounding period, in this case 12 to represent monthly compounding. The table factor is then multiplied by the base to get the annuity due factor. If \$1 is deposited at the beginning of the month each month for 5 years, it will grow to \$82.49, compounded monthly at a 12% annual rate. Note that the annuity due result of \$82.49 is greater than the ordinary annuity example of \$81.67. The difference is due to the interest on one additional period earned by depositing payments at the beginning of the period.

Present Value of an Annuity

Just as we have used the formulas in developing tables for the other factors, so too can we develop tables for the present value of an annuity. As given in Chapter I, the present value of a stream of payments was:

$$PV_a = \frac{1 - 1/(1+i)^n}{i}.$$

By using a range of interest rates and payment periods in this formula, the tables in Chapter III have been generated. These tables, as the others do, assume an annual nominal yield with monthly compounding for a \$1 value. Payment is also assumed to be made at the end of the compounding period. In using the tables, simply find the table factor and then multiply it by the value of an annuity to get the present value of the income stream.

Example:

What is the present value of \$1 paid at the end of each month for 8 years, with an annual discount rate of 14.25%, compounded monthly?

Solution:

$$PV_a = \$1 \times \text{table factor } PV \text{ of annuity, 14.25\%, 8 years,}$$
$$= \$1(57.09692),$$
$$= \$57.09.$$

To solve this problem, we need to get the Present Value of One Dollar Per Period table factor under the 14.25%, 8-year column. That factor is 57.09692, which, when multiplied by the annuity amount of \$1, yields a present value of \$57.09.

Example:

You have an opportunity to buy a rental property that will provide net returns of \$800 per month during your 15-year expected holding period. If you desire a 15% monthly compounded annual return on your investment, how much should you pay for the property?

Solution:

$$PV = \$800 \times \text{table factor } PV \text{ of annuity, 15\%, 15 years,}$$
$$= \$800(71.44964),$$
$$= \$57{,}159.71.$$

By looking at the Present Amount of One Per Period table under the 15%, 15-year column, we get a factor of 71.44964. Multiplying this by the net monthly income of \$800, we find that the property value is \$57,159.71.

Table Use in Mortgage Mathematics

We have seen that in determining a mortgage payment we need simply to find the mortgage constant by taking the reciprocal of the present worth of one per period factor. This is due to the fact that a mortgage loan is the present value of an annuity, where the annuity is the mortgage payment:

$$\text{Mortgage} = PV_a(\text{mortgage payments})$$

or

$$\text{Mortgage payments} = \text{Mortgage}\left(\frac{1}{PV_a}\right).$$

Instead of substituting the interest rate and compounding period in the present value of an annuity formula, we can go directly to the Present Value of One Per Period tables to get this factor. The reciprocal of this factor is then multiplied by the initial mortgage amount to get the periodic payment necessary to amortize the mortgage amount over the loan period.

Example:

Find the monthly mortgage payments necessary to amortize a $50,000 loan with an annual rate of interest of 9% and a 30-year term.

Solution:

$$\$MP = \$50{,}000(MC),$$

where

$MC = 1/PV_a$ and $MC = 1/$(Table factor PV of annuity, 9%, 30 years).

Therefore:

$$\$MP = \$50{,}000\left(\frac{1}{124.28187}\right),$$

$$= \$50{,}000(.00804623),$$

$$= \$402.31.$$

By going to the Present Value of One Per Period table under 9% and 30 years, the factor of 124.28187 is obtained. Taking the reciprocal of this factor gives us the mortgage constant of .00804623, which, when multiplied by the loan amount of $50,000, yields the monthly mortgage payment of $402.31.

Mortgage Constant

Although this procedure can be applied for virtually any interest rate or compounding period in finding the mortgage constant, it is still rather tedious, as several steps are involved. Consequently, tables have been developed by taking the reciprocal of the present value of annuity factors for many common interest rates and loan terms. The resulting factors, the mortgage constants, are included in the Chapter III tables. The Mortgage Constant tables assume an annual nominal yield with monthly compounding and payment made at the end of the period.

Example:

In the previous example, a 9%, 30-year term, \$50,000 mortgage was obtained. Find the monthly mortgage payment required to amortize this mortgage, using the Mortgage Constant tables.

Solution:

$$
\begin{aligned}
\$MP &= \$50{,}000(MC),\\
&= \$50{,}000(.00805),\\
&= \$402.50.
\end{aligned}
$$

By going to the Mortgage Constant table under 9% and 30 years, a factor of .00805 is obtained. Multiplying this by the initial mortgage amount of \$50,000 gives a monthly payment for principal and interest of \$402.50. Note that this amount is slightly larger than the \$402.31 payment calculated in the preceding example. The difference is due to rounding error in that the Mortgage Constant tables truncate the present value of an annuity reciprocal to 5 places.

Example:

You borrow \$65,000 on a fully amortized mortgage loan at 15.5% annual interest. The monthly payment is \$825.50. What is the term of the mortgage?

Solution:

$$\$MP = \$65{,}000(MC)$$

or

$$\frac{\$\mathrm{MP}}{\$65{,}000} = MC,$$

and

$$\frac{\$825.50}{\$65{,}000} = MC,$$

$$.01270 = \text{Table factor } MC,\ 15.5\%,\ ?\ \text{years}.$$

In the Mortgage Constant table under 15.5%, we need to find the year that has a factor of .01270. This factor corresponds to the 28-year period, indicating that the mortgage loan carries a 28-year amortization term.

Mortgage Balance Remaining

The Present Value of One Dollar Per Period tables can also be used to calculate the percentage of mortgage balance remaining. We developed in Chapter I the relationship:

$$MB_j = \frac{PV_a^{n-j}}{PV_a^n} = \frac{\left[\dfrac{1-1/(1+i)^{n-j}}{i}\right]}{\left[\dfrac{1-1/(1+i)^n}{i}\right]}.$$

Instead of carrying out the calculations by plugging in the interest rate and compounding period and then churning out the numbers, we can now go directly to the Present Value of One Per Period tables to get the appropriate factors.

Example:

You have a 30-year, 11.5% mortgage with a $61,000 initial loan balance. After 5 years, you decide to sell and pay off your remaining balance. How much will you have to pay off?

Solution:

$$\begin{aligned} MB_{60} &= \frac{PV_a^{360-60}}{PV_a^{360}} (\$61{,}000), \\ &= \frac{98.37979}{100.98037}(\$61{,}000), \\ &= .9742467(\$61{,}000), \\ &= \$59{,}429.04. \end{aligned}$$

To solve this problem, we need first to calculate the present value of an annuity factor for the remaining term, 300 months, and the present value of an annuity factor for the original terrn, 360 months. Getting these factors from Chapter III, under the 11.5% Present Value of One Per

Period table, we then divide the 300-month factor, 98.37979, by the 360-month factor, 100.98037. This yields .97425, which is the percentage of the mortgage still left to be paid. Multiplying this by the initial loan amount of $61,000 gives a $59,429.04 mortgage loan left to be paid at the end of 5 years.

Once again, using the present value of an annuity factors in deriving the mortgage balance remaining is unnecessarily tedious. By carrying out the calculations for a variety of interest rates, loan term to maturity, and number of years paid, the Mortgage Balance Remaining tables have been generated. To use the tables, we simply need to find the contract rate and go down the original loan term column until we locate the age of the loan. The corresponding factor represents the percentage of the initial mortgage balance still remaining to be paid.

Example:

After paying monthly for 12 years on an original $45,000 mortgage at 9.5%, for a 30-year original loan term, you decide to sell the property and pay off the remaining balance. How much of the original loan is still outstanding?

Solution:

$$\begin{aligned} \$MB_{144} &= \$45{,}000 \times MBR_{144},\ 9.5\%,\ 30\text{-year term}, \\ &= \$45{,}000(.8687305), \\ &= \$39{,}092.87. \end{aligned}$$

Going to the Mortgage Balance Remaining 9.5% contract rate table under a 30-year original loan term, the factor corresponding to the 12-year payment period is .8687305. Multiplying this percentage of mortgage remaining by the original loan amount, $45,000, gives the dollar amount of mortgage remaining to be paid, $39,092.87.

Discount Point Applications

The Present Value of an Annuity tables can also be used in solving discount point problems. The relationship concerning discount points was developed in Chapter 1 as:

$$\text{Percentage (discount) points} = 1 - \left[\frac{1 - 1/(1+r)^n}{r}\right]\left[\frac{1 - 1/(1+i)^n}{i}\right]^{-1},$$

where

$r =$ the desired yield,

$i =$ the contract or stated interest rate, and

$n =$ the loan compounding period as before.

This reduces to:

$$\text{Percentage (discount) points} = 1 - \frac{PV_{a_r}}{PV_{a_i}},$$

where PV_{a_r} is the present value of an annuity at the desired yield and PV_{a_i} is the present value of an annuity at the contract rate.

Example:

How many discount points, DP, are required to be charged to raise the lender's desired yield on a 13.00% contract rate, 30-year, \$70,000 mortgage to 15.25%, assuming no prepayment?

Solution:

$$DP = 1 - \frac{PV_{a_{15.25\%}}}{PV_{a_{13.00\%}}},$$

$$= 1 - \frac{77.85382}{90.39961},$$

$$= 1 - .8612185,$$

$$= .13878, \text{ or } 13.878 \text{ points.}$$

By going to the Present Value of One Per Period tables, the factor for 15.25% and 30 years is found to be 77.85382, and the 30-year 13.00% factor is 90.39961. Dividing the desired yield factor by the contract rate factor gives .861218, which when subtracted from 1 provides the percentage points necessary to raise the lender's yield. The dollar value of the points the lender should charge is calculated as:

$$\$DP = \$70{,}000(.13878),$$

$$= \$9{,}714.60.$$

By multiplying the initial mortgage amount by the percentage discount points (recall that 1 discount point equals 1% of the initial mortgage), we get the dollar value of points. In this example, the lender must charge \$9,714.60 in points to raise the yield from 13.00% to 15.25% on a \$70,000, 30-year mortgage.

Proof:

Assume that the lender in the example charges \$9,714.60 in points at the loan closing. What is the effective yield?

$$\begin{aligned}\text{Amount actually lent} &= \$70{,}000.00 - \$9{,}714.60,\\ &= \$60{,}285.40.\\ \text{Monthly loan payment} &= \$70{,}000 \times MC\ 13\%,\ 30\ \text{years},\\ &= \$70{,}000(.01106),\\ &= \$774.20.\end{aligned}$$

Because the amount actually lent equals $PV_{a_r} \times$ monthly payment, solving for the effective yield *r* results in:

$$\begin{aligned}PV_{a_{r?}} &= \frac{\$60{,}285.40}{\$774.20},\\ &= 77.86799.\end{aligned}$$

By looking under the 30-year row in the Present Value of One Per Period tables, the factor of 77.86799 is found to correspond approximately to the 15.25% column. This indicates that the effective yield is approximately equal to the desired 15.25%, the slight difference being due to rounding.

To this point, our discussion of discount points has assumed that the loan will be held to maturity, that is, paid over its full term. This is unrealistic in most cases, as loans are often paid off prior to their maturity dates. If lenders have records or experience that indicate the typical prepayment period in their portfolio, this can be incorporated in the discount point calculations. When prepayment occurs, the lender's effective yield as a result of point charges will increase. By assuming a most probable prepayment period, the lender can more accurately estimate the discount points necessary to achieve a desired yield. It was shown in Chapter I that the adjustment necessary to incorporate a prepayment was:

$$\text{Percentage points} = 1 - PV_{a_r}(MC_i) - PV_{s_r}(\%MB_j),$$

where the contract rate mortgage constant, MC_i, is discounted by the present value of an annuity for the expected payment period at the desired rate, PV_{a_r}, and the percentage mortgage balance remaining, $\%MB_j$, in the year of prepayment is discounted by the present value of one at the desired rate, PV_{s_r}, at the expected prepayment period.

The discount points can be calculated, incorporating prepayment assumptions, by simply going to the appropriate tables and obtaining the needed factors.

Example:

How many discount points, *DP*, should be charged to raise the yield from 11.50% on a $48,000, 25-year term mortgage to 12.25%, assuming that the loan will be paid off after 9 years?

Solution:

$$DP = 1 - PV_{a_{12.25\%}}(MC_{11.50\%}) - PV_{s_{12.25\%}}(MB_{11.50\%}),$$
$$= 1 - 65.25051(.01016) - .33390(.890729),$$
$$= 1 - .662945 - .2974144,$$
$$= .03964, \text{ or } 3.964 \text{ points.}$$

This problem is solved by going to the Present Value of One Per Period table under 12.25% and 9 years to get a factor of 65.25051. This factor is then multiplied by the mortgage constant .01016, which is obtained under the 11.50%, 25-year column of the Mortgage Constant table. The present value of one factor for 12.25% and 9 years, .33390, is obtained from Chapter III and is multiplied by the mortgage balance remaining after 9 years. The mortgage balance remaining is obtained from the Mortgage Balance Remaining table under the 11.50% contract rate, 25-year original term, and 9-year prepayment period. The result of all these calculations is 3.964 points, which must be charged by the lender to raise the yield from 11.50% to 12.25%, with a prepayment expected after 9 years. The dollar value of the points is calculated as:

$$DP = \$48{,}000(.03964),$$
$$= \$1{,}902.74.$$

The lender needs to charge $1,902.74 at closing to raise the yield from 11.50% to 12.25%.

Discount Point Table Derivation

It is readily apparent that calculating discount points, especially when prepayment is assumed, can become very cumbersome. Several factors coming from different tables are necessary. To simplify the discount point calculation process, the factor derivation and calculations have been done for some of the most common interest rates, loan term, and prepayment assumptions. The resulting Discount Percentage Point table is in Chapter III. This table has been calculated for desired (effective) yields ranging from 7.00% to 20.75%, with corresponding contract rates. The initial original terms of the loans are from 15 to 35 years, in 5-year increments, with prepayment assumptions for 5, 7, 9, 12, 15, and full-term years for each original term table. Contract and desired rates are again specified in yearly nominal interest rates, with monthly compounding at the end of the month.

In using the table, one now has only to go to the correct beginning loan term, with the appropriate prepayment assumption, and find the specified contract rate and desired (effective) yield. The corresponding factor is interpreted as the percentage (discount) points that must be charged to raise the contract rate to the desired yield. If the desired yield is greater than the contract rate, the percentage points to be charged will be positive. If the desired (effective) yield is less than the contract rate, the percentage points will be negative. When multiplied by the loan amount, this will provide the amount of discount or premium to be charged or paid off for the loan to give the desired yield.

Example:

How many points are needed to raise the yield on an $80,000, 30-year loan from a contract rate of 15.00% to a desired yield of 16.25%, assuming no prepayment?

Solution:

$DP = DP$ 360-month term, 360-month prepayment,
15% contract, 16.25% desired,

= .07362 or 7.362 points.

By going to the 30-year Discount Point table with no prepayment assumed, under the 15.00% contract rate row and 16.25% effective rate column, we find 7.362 points need to be charged.

As before, it is realistic to expect some loans to be paid off before maturing. In this case, the assumed prepayment period must be incorporated in the calculation. The table provides this incorporation, so the user needs only to find the correct table given any original term and prepayment assumption.

Example:

A potential borrower is negotiating a loan with a local lender for \$54,000 and a period of 30 years. The contract interest rate will be 12.50%; however, the lender wants to charge points to make the effective yield 12.75%. What should the points be if it is assumed that the loan will be paid off after 5 years?

Solution:

$$\$DP = \$54{,}000 \times DP \text{ 360-month term, 60-month prepayment, 12.50\% contract, 12.75\% desired,}$$

$$= \$54{,}000(.00913),$$

$$= \$493.02.$$

The percentage points needed to be charged to raise the lender's yield by .25% is found under the 360-month contract, 60-month prepayment Discount Point table. By looking under the 12.50% column and the 12.75% row, the percentage point factor of .00913 is obtained. Because .913 points need to be charged, multiplying the percentage points by the loan amount gives the dollar value of the points, \$493.02.

Annual Percentage Rate Table Derivation

Another application of the Discount Point table is to use it in determining effective annual yields for federal disclosure purposes. Because the annual percentage rate, *APR*, that a lender actually charges is a function of the contract rate and the total points charged at closing, the Discount Point table can be used in deriving the annual percentage rate once the total points charged have been estimated. To simplify the process, the Annual Percentage Rate table has been developed in Chapter III, allowing the user to find the annual percentage rate directly by looking under the appropriate contract rate, term to maturity, and total points charged at closing columns. No prepayment is assumed in this table. In using the Annual Percentage Rate table, all the charges that the federal regulators require to be used in the annual percentage rate calculation must be summed and converted to a percentage of the mortgage loan. These are the "points" that must be used in selecting the annual percentage rate for federal Regulation Z disclosure purposes.

Example:

On a 20-year (240-month) mortgage at a contract rate of 15.50%, with no prepayment assumed, a lender is charging a 1-point origination fee, 4 discount points, and half a percentage point of prepaid interest for a total of 5.50% of the mortgage in points. What is the effective yield?

Solution:

In the Discount Point table we must first find the 20-year mortgages. Then in the 15.50% contract rate we go across the columns to find .055 corresponding to the points charged. Then the effective yield that corresponds to .055 column will be the actual effective yield (or annual percentage rate), which in this case is 16.55%.

Secondary Market Application

The Discount Point table can also be used in pricing mortgages in the secondary market. The table allows determination of how much to pay for a mortgage at given contract rates to yield a desired (effective) rate. To solve this problem, we need to find the amount of points necessary to bring a contract rate yield up or down to some effective yield and use that as the discount or premium necessary to achieve the desired yield.

Example:

A life insurance company wants to buy a pool of $9.50%, 30-year term government-insured mortgages with a face amount of $1,000,000. The life insurance company believes that the common assumption of a 12-year prepayment will hold. If it desires the current market rate of 10.25% as its yield, what should the company pay for the mortgage pool?

Solution:

$$\begin{aligned}\$\text{ Purchase price} &= \$1{,}000{,}000 \times (1 - DP,\ \text{30-year, 9.50\% contract,}\\ &\qquad \text{10.25\% desired, 12-year prepayment}),\\ &= \$1{,}000{,}000(1 - .04958),\\ &= \$1{,}000{,}000(.95042),\\ &= \$950{,}420.\end{aligned}$$

The discount point factor under the 360-month loan term, 144-month prepayment Discount Point table is .04958. This factor corresponds to the 9.50% contract rate and 10.25% desired yield. Subtracting this factor from 1 (for 100%) gives the amount that should be paid for each dollar of original loan to increase the yield to the desired level. Multiplying by the $1,000,000 pool amount gives the solution: The life insurance company should pay $950,420 for the mortgages to earn a 10.25% effective yield, with the contract rate of 9.50% based on the $1,000,000 for the mortgage payment calculation. When mortgage market yields decline so that some mortgage contract rates are above the current market-required yields, a premium must be paid for these mortgages.

Example:

A mortgage company wants to buy a pool of mortgages with a face (par) value of $2,000,000 and a contract rate of 12.0% with 25 years to maturity and a prepayment assumption of 7 years. Current market yields for such mortgages are 11.5%. What price should the mortgage company pay for the package?

Solution:

$ Purchase price = (Face value of package) (1 − *DP*, 300-month term, 12.0% contract, 11.5% desired effective yield, 84-month prepayment assumption),

= $2,000,000[1 − (−.02336)],

= $2,000,000(1 + .02336),

= $2,046,720.

As in the previous example, find the market price of the mortgages by multiplying the face value of the mortgages (which is equal to the principal balance remaining based on the contract rate of interest) by 1 − *DP*, the percentage by which the face value of the mortgage package must be multiplied to derive the market price. Whenever contract rates exceed market rates, *DP* will appear as a negative in the table so that 1 − (− *DP*) becomes 1 + *DP*, where the negative *DP* in the table is actually a premium percentage to be added onto the mortgage principal value.

In the solution the *DP* factor is found under the 300-month loan term, 84-month prepayment Discount Point table, with a contract rate of 12.0% and an effective yield of 11.5% desired. The factor of − .02336 is then the premium to be added to 1 to derive the multiple of the mortgage principal to derive market price.

Interpolation in the Tables

Often the terms or periods used, or factors derived, will not match the given table values. In that case, one has to either use formulas to solve the problem or make adjustments in the table used. The table adjustments can be made relatively easily through interpolation. Useful approximations of the interest and term factors can be obtained through simple arithmetic manipulation.

Example:

Approximately how long will it take for money to double itself at 10%, compounded monthly?

Solution:

For money to double, the compound amount of $1 must grow to $2. That means that we need to look under the 10% column in the Chapter III Future Value of One Dollar table until we find the 2.000 factor. At 72 months, the factor is 1.81759. At 84 months, the factor is 2.00792. Our answer lies between and is derived as follows:

at $n=72$	$i=1.81759$	.18241	.19033
at $n=?$	$i=2.00000$		
at $n=84$	$i=2.00792$		

$$2.00792-1.81759=.19033$$

$$2.00000-1.81759=.18241$$

Interpolating,

$$?-72/84-72=(2.0000-1.81759)/(2.00792-1.81759),$$

$$?-72=(.18241/.19033)(12),$$

$$?=.958388(12)+72,$$

$$=83.50065.$$

In carrying out the interpolation, a ratio is set up and solved between the known compounding periods and their factors and the unknown period and its given factor. The result of the ratio between the difference in the known factors and their compounding periods is 83.5 periods, or 83.5 months for any money invested at 10% annual yield, with monthly compounding, to double.

Example:

A purchaser agrees to pay $35,000 for a house, putting up $5,000 of cash and paying the balance monthly over 20 years. If the payments are $345 per month, what is the approximate rate of interest, compounded monthly, being paid on the debt?

Solution:

Because \$345 per month will amortize the \$30,000 debt over the 240-month period, the mortgage constant is calculated to be:

$$MC = \frac{\$345}{\$30{,}000},$$
$$= .01150.$$

To solve the problem, we need to find this factor in the Mortgage Constant table at the 240-month term and corresponding interest rate. Going to the table yields:

at $i = .1250$	$MC = .01136$	.00014	.00018
at $i = ?$	$MC = .01150$		
at $i = .1275$	$MC = .01154$		

Taking the ratio and interpolating provides:

$$(? - .1250)/(.1275 - .1250) = (0.1150 - .01136)/(.01154 - .01136),$$
$$? - .1250 = .00014/.00018(.0025),$$
$$? = .77777(.0025) + .1250,$$
$$= .001944 + .1250,$$
$$= .126944.$$

At the given terms, the borrower is paying a 12.694% annual nominal interest rate on the loan.

Example:

Assume that a full-term loan of \$65,000 is made at 11.5% for 30 years, payable monthly. If the lender charges 4 points at closing, what is the annual yield earned by the lender?

Solution:

Using the Discount Point tables will help to solve this problem. Looking at the 360-month full-term table under the 11.5% contract rate column gives desired yield factors of:

at $r = .1200$	$DP = .03726$	.00274	.01771
at $r = ?$	$DP = .04000$		
at $r = .1255$	$DP = .05497$		

and the relationship is interpolated as:

$$(? - .1200) / (.1225 - .1200) = (.04 - .03726) / (.05497 - .03726),$$

$$? - .1200 = .15471485(.1225 - .1200),$$

$$? = .000386787 + .1200,$$

$$= .1203867.$$

If the lender charges 4 points at closing, the annual yield on the 11.5% contract rate mortgage, amortized over 30 years, will be 12.039%.

It must be noted that interpolation in a linear table will provide useful approximations only. If a more accurate calculation is required, a formula using at least 8 significant digits should be used.

PROBLEM SETS

Time Value of Money Problem Set

1. You have an opportunity to invest in a speculative oil company at $30 per share. If you buy 100 shares, at what price will you have to sell your shares 3 years hence to realize a 20% annual rate of return, assuming monthly compounding and no dividends?

2. An investor makes a $200-per-month investment in a real estate venture that guarantees an annual yield of 13.5% interest, compounded monthly. After 4 years, how much should this investment be worth?

3. An investment opportunity promises to pay $425 per month for 8 years. You believe that a return of 18% per year should be earned to adequately compensate for the risk being taken. How much should be paid for this investment today?

4. You have an opportunity to invest in a property with an asking price of $90,000. You believe that the property could be held and sold for $110,000 in 2 years. What rate of return would you earn on this investment if you paid the asking price?

5. What should you pay for the property in Problem 4 if you require a 12% annual return, compounded monthly?

6. A developer comes to you with the following deal: You will receive $500 per month for the first year of operation, $1,000 a month for the second year, and $2,000 a month for the third year, at which time your interest will cease. At a promised 15% return, how much is the developer asking in this deal?

7. A rental property can be purchased for $58,000 that will provide income of $350 per month. If this property is sold after 6 years for $70,000, what is the internal rate of return of the investment?

8. A lender makes a $25,000 improvement loan with monthly payments of $393. A balloon payment of $5,000 in principal is due at the end of the loan term. If a yield of 14.5% is desired, what will the term of the loan be?

Solutions to Time Value Problem Set

1. Selling price = $3,000 × table factor *FV* of $1 per period, 3 years, 20%,

   = $3,000(1.81313),

   = $5,439.39.

   You need to sell for $5,439.39 to realize a 20% annual return on your investment.

2. *FV* = $200 × table factor *FV* of $1 per period, 4 years, 13.5%,

   = $200(63.18587),

   = $12,637.17.

   At the end of 4 years, the $200-per-month investment will have grown to $12,637.17, at a 13.5% yield.

3. *PV* = $425 × table factor *PV* of $1 per period, 8 years, 18%,

   = $425(50.70168),

   = $21,548.21.

   $21,548.21 should be paid for the right to receive $425 per month, for an 18% annual yield.

4. $90,000 = $110,000 × table factor *PV* of $1 per period, 2 years ?%,

   $$\frac{\$90,000}{\$110,000} = 8.181818.$$

   at $i = .1000$ $PV = .81941$

   at $i = ?$ $PV = .81818$

   at $i = .1025$ $PV = .81536$

Interpolating,

$$i = .100759.$$

If the asking price is paid, a 10.07% annual return will be earned.

5. $PV = \$110{,}000 \times$ table factor PV of \$1 per period, 2 years, 12%,

$= \$110{,}000(.78757)$,

$= \$86{,}632.70$.

To earn a 12% annual yield over the 2-year holding period, \$86,632.70 should be paid for the property.

6. $PV = \$500$(table factor PV of \$1 per period, 1 year, 15%) + \$1,000(PV of \$1 per period, 2 years, 15% − PV of \$1 per period, 1 year, 15%) + \$2,000(PV of \$1 per period, 3 years, 15% − PV of \$1 per period, 2 years, 15%),

$= \$500(11.07931) + \$1{,}000(20.62423 - 11.07931) + \$2{,}000(28.84727 - 20.62423)$,

$= \$5{,}539.65 + \$9{,}544.92 + \$16{,}446.08$,

$= \$31{,}530.65$.

The developer should be trying to get \$31,530.65 from you if he or she plans to return a 15% annual yield.

7. \$58,000 − \$350(table factor PV of \$1 per period, 6 years, ?%) + \$70,000(table factor PV of \$1 per period, 6 years, ?%).

At 10.00%,

$$\$58{,}000 \stackrel{?}{=} \$350(53.97867) + \$70{,}000(.55018),$$
$$\$58{,}000 \neq \$57{,}405.13.$$

At 9.00%

$$\$58{,}000 \stackrel{?}{=} \$350(55.47685) + \$70{,}000(.58392),$$
$$\$58{,}000 \neq \$60{,}291.30.$$

At 9.75%

$$\$58{,}000 \stackrel{?}{=} \$350(54.34778) + \$70{,}000(.55842),$$
$$\$58{,}000 \cong \$58{,}111.12.$$

The property would return approximately 9.75% annual return over the 6-year holding period.

8. \$25,000 = \$393(table factor PV of \$1 per period, ? years, 14.5%) + \$5,000(table factor PV of \$1, ? years, 14.5%).

At 10 years,

$$\$25{,}000 \stackrel{?}{=} \$393(63.17647) + \$5{,}000(.23662),$$
$$\$25{,}000 \neq \$26{,}011.45.$$

At 8 years,

$$\$25{,}000 \stackrel{?}{=} \$393(56.63394) + \$5{,}000(.31567),$$
$$\$25{,}000 \neq \$23{,}835.49.$$

At 9 years,

$$\$25{,}000 \stackrel{?}{=} \$393(60.14054) + \$5{,}000(.27330),$$
$$\$25{,}000 \cong \$25{,}001.73.$$

To provide the lender with a 14.5% annual return, the term of the loan and balloon payment should be 9 years.

Mortgage Mathematic Problem Set

1. A fully amortized mortgage loan is contracted for $70,000 at 15%, with monthly payments over 30 years. What will the payments be?

2. In Problem 1, if the lender charges "points" to the buyer of $2,100, what is the effective interest cost to the buyer?

3. If the lender assumes that the loan will be paid off in 9 years, what does the yield become in the previous example?

4. A lender is considering making a $55,000, 12%, 30-year FHA-insured loan. The current market interest is 15%. If the lender desires the market rate as a yield, how many points should be charged the seller?

5. A borrower takes out a partially amortized loan for $200,000 to be paid over a 20-year period. Monthly payments are to be based on a 30-year amortization schedule, with a 13% contract rate. What will the monthly payments and balloon payment be?

6. In Problem 5, if the lender charges points of $2,000, what will the effective interest rate on the loan be? What will the effective interest rate be if the buyer decides to prepay the loan after 9 years?

7. A variable interest rate loan is made for $65,000 at a beginning rate of 14.0%, with monthly payments of $761.15 for 40 years. Six months later, the index to which the mortgage is tied decreases and the new interest rate is to be 13.5%. What will the new payments beginning in month 7 be?

8. A mortgage loan is applied for with the following amounts: \$61,000 loan amount, 30-year term fully amortized, 11.5% contract rate, 5 discount points charged at closing, 1-point origination fee, and \$300 in prepaid interest. What is the annual percentage rate on this loan, assuming no prepayment?

Solutions to Mortgage Mathematic Problem Set

1. $\$MP = \$70,000 \times$ table factor MC, 30 years, 15%,

$= \$70,000(.01264),$

$= \$884.80.$

A monthly payment of \$884.80 will amortize this loan over the 30 year period.

2. $DP =$ Table factor DP, \$2,100/\$70,000, 30 years, 15% contract, ?% desired,

$= .03.$

at $r = .1525$	$DP = .01558$
at $r = ?$	$DP = .03000$
at $r = .1550$	$DP = .03072$

Through interpolation,

$$r = .15488.$$

The effective interest cost to the buyer is 15.49%.

3. $DP =$ Table factor DP, \$2,000/\$70,000, 30 years, 9-year prepayment, 15% contract, ?% desired,

$= .03.$

at $r = .1550$	$DP = .02397$
at $r = ?$	$DP = .03$
at $r = .1575$	$DP = .03564$

Through interpolation,

$$r = .15629.$$

With a 9-year prepayment and 3 points, the yield to the lender is raised from the contract rate of 15.00% to 15.63%.

4. DP = Table factor DP, 30 years, 12% contract, 15% desired,

= .18651.

The lender should charge 18.65 points to increase the yield to 15%. The dollar value of the points will be:

$\$DP = \$55{,}000(.18651),$

$= \$10{,}258.05.$

5. $\$MP = \$200{,}000 \times$ table factor MC, 30 years, 13%,

$= \$200{,}000(.01106),$

$= \$2{,}212.$

The monthly payment, based on a 30-year amortization schedule, is \$2,212. Because the loan is to be paid over a 20-year period, a balloon payment is required at the end of year 20.

$\$MBR_{240} = \$200{,}000 \times$ table factor MBR, 30 years, 13%, payment in year 20,

$= \$200{,}000(.7408),$

$= \$148{,}160.$

The balloon payment in year 20 is \$148,160.

6. DP = (Table factor DP, \$2,000/\$200,000, 30 years, 13% contract, ?% desired),

= .01.

at $i = .1300$	$r = .00000$
at $i = ?$	$r = .01000$
at $i = .1325$	$r = .01739$

Through interpolation,

$i = .131437.$

If the lender charges \$2,000, or 1 point, the yield will be 13.14%. If a 9-year prepayment is assumed, the yield becomes:

DP = Table factor DP, \$2,000/\$200,000, 30 years, 9-year prepayment, 13% contract, ?% desired,

= .01.

$$\text{at } i = .1300 \qquad r = .00000$$

$$\text{at } i = ? \qquad r = .01000$$

$$\text{at } i = .1325 \qquad r = .01292$$

Through interpolation,

$$r = .1319.$$

If the loan is prepaid in year 10, the yield to the lender will rise to 13.19%.

7. *Step 1*

$$MBR_{6mo} = \$65{,}000 \times \text{table factor } MBR, \text{ 6 months, } 14\%,$$

$$= \$65{,}000(.99972),$$

$$= \$64{,}981.80.$$

After 6 months, $64,981.80 remains to be paid on the original mortgage.

Step 2

$$\$MP = \$64{,}981.80 \times \text{table factor } MC, \text{ 474 months, } 13.5\%,$$

$$= \$64{,}981.80(?).$$

$$\text{at } n = 468 \qquad MC = .01131$$

$$\text{at } n = 474 \qquad MC = ?$$

$$\text{at } n = 480 \qquad MC = .01130$$

Through interpolation,

$$MC = .011305.$$

$$\$MP = \$64{,}981.80(.011305),$$

$$= \$734.62.$$

The new mortgage payment will fall from $761.15 to $734.62.

8. $APR = \text{Table factor } APR, \text{ 11.5\% contract rate, 360-month term, 6.5 points,}$

$$= 12.3952\%.$$

The total points charged in this problem amount to approximately 6.5, and finding the corresponding Annual Percentage Rate table factor for 11.5% contract rate yields an annual percentage rate of 12.395%.

chapter 3

Financial Tables

All the financial tables developed in the previous chapters are presented in this chapter. Preceding each table is a brief description and illustration of its use. Extreme care has been taken to ensure accuracy in these tables. Although these tables are accurate to the fifth decimal place, slight rounding differences will still exist from a factor taken to 6 or more decimal places. For calculations requiring greater accuracy, use of the formulas provided is recommended.

Summary of Algebraic Formulas in Tables

Future Value of One Dollar:

$$FV_s = (1+i)^n.$$

Present Value of One Dollar:

$$PV_s = \frac{1}{(1+i)^n}.$$

Future Value of One Per Period:

$$FV_a = \frac{(1+i)^n - 1}{i}.$$

Present Value of One Per Period:

$$PV_a = \frac{1 - 1/(1+i)^n}{i}.$$

Mortgage Constant:

$$MC = \frac{1}{PV_a} = \frac{1}{\left[\dfrac{1 - 1/(1+i)^n}{i}\right]}.$$

Mortgage Balance Remaining:

$$MB_j = \frac{PV_a^{n-j}}{PV_a^n} = \frac{1 - 1/(1+i)^{n-j}}{1 - 1(1+i)^n},$$

where n is the full term and j is the term of prepayment.

Discount Points:

$$\text{Percentage points} = 1 - \left[\frac{1 - 1/(1+r)^j}{r}\right] \left[\frac{1 - 1/(1+i)^n}{i}\right]^{-1} - \frac{1}{(1+r)^j} \left[\frac{1 - 1/(1+i)^{n-j}}{1 - 1/(1+i)^n}\right],$$

where:

n = full term,

j = term of prepayment,

i = contract rate, and

r = effective yield.

Annual Percentage Rate:

$APR = r$ when the equality following is solved,

$$= \frac{1 - 1/(1+r)^n}{r} = \frac{1 - \text{points}}{\text{Mortgage constant}}.$$

Note that the correct amount of points to use in the annual percentage rate calculation is the percentage of the mortgage that includes all the charges that federal regulations require to be included under Regulation Z.

FUTURE VALUE OF ONE DOLLAR TABLE

Description:

The Future Value of One Dollar table may be used to determine what a given sum will grow to over a given period. To use the table, find the factor under the appropriate interest rate and term; then multiply the factor by the initial amount to obtain the future value of the investment.

Table Calculation Formula:

$$FV_s = (1 + i)^n.$$

Table Range:

Annual interest rate, with monthly compounding, from 7.00% to 24.75%, in .25% increments. Term from 1 to 12 months in 1-month increments, 1 to 40 years in 1-year increments.

Example:

What is the future value of a $1,000 investment that yields a 10% annual rate of return, with monthly compounding, over a 10-year period?

Solution:

Finding the factor under 10% and 10 years yields:

$$FV_s = \$1{,}000 \times \text{table factor } FV_s\text{, } 10\%\text{, } 10 \text{ years,}$$

$$= \$1{,}000(2.70704),$$

$$= \$2{,}707.04.$$

The $1,000 investment, earning a 10% annual yield, will be worth $2,707.04 in 10 years.

FUTURE VALUE OF ONE DOLLAR

ANNUAL INTEREST RATE

PERIOD YR	MOS	.07000	.07250	.07500	.07750	.08000	.08250	.08500	.08750	.09000
	1	1.00583	1.00604	1.00625	1.00646	1.00667	1.00688	1.00708	1.00729	1.00750
	2	1.01170	1.01212	1.01254	1.01296	1.01338	1.01380	1.01422	1.01464	1.01506
	3	1.01760	1.01823	1.01887	1.01950	1.02013	1.02077	1.02140	1.02203	1.02267
	4	1.02354	1.02439	1.02524	1.02608	1.02693	1.02778	1.02864	1.02949	1.03034
	5	1.02951	1.03058	1.03164	1.03271	1.03378	1.03485	1.03592	1.03699	1.03807
	6	1.03551	1.03680	1.03809	1.03938	1.04067	1.04197	1.04326	1.04456	1.04585
	7	1.04155	1.04307	1.04458	1.04609	1.04761	1.04913	1.05065	1.05217	1.05370
	8	1.04763	1.04937	1.05111	1.05285	1.05459	1.05634	1.05809	1.05984	1.06160
	9	1.05374	1.05571	1.05768	1.05965	1.06163	1.06360	1.06559	1.06757	1.06956
	10	1.05989	1.06209	1.06429	1.06649	1.06870	1.07092	1.07313	1.07536	1.07758
	11	1.06607	1.06850	1.07094	1.07338	1.07583	1.07828	1.08074	1.08320	1.08566
1	12	1.07229	1.07496	1.07763	1.08031	1.08300	1.08569	1.08839	1.09110	1.09381
2	24	1.14981	1.15554	1.16129	1.16708	1.17289	1.17873	1.18459	1.19049	1.19641
3	36	1.23293	1.24215	1.25145	1.26081	1.27024	1.27974	1.28930	1.29894	1.30865
4	48	1.32205	1.33526	1.34860	1.36207	1.37567	1.38940	1.40326	1.41727	1.43141
5	60	1.41763	1.43535	1.45329	1.47146	1.48985	1.50846	1.52730	1.54637	1.56568
6	72	1.52011	1.54294	1.56612	1.58964	1.61350	1.63772	1.66230	1.68724	1.71255
7	84	1.62999	1.65860	1.68770	1.71730	1.74742	1.77806	1.80923	1.84094	1.87320
8	96	1.74783	1.78292	1.81872	1.85523	1.89246	1.93043	1.96915	2.00864	2.04892
9	108	1.87418	1.91657	1.95991	2.00422	2.04953	2.09585	2.14321	2.19162	2.24112
10	120	2.00966	2.06023	2.11206	2.16519	2.21964	2.27545	2.33265	2.39127	2.45136
11	132	2.15494	2.21466	2.27603	2.33908	2.40387	2.47044	2.53883	2.60911	2.68131
12	144	2.31072	2.38067	2.45272	2.52694	2.60339	2.68213	2.76324	2.84679	2.93284
13	156	2.47776	2.55912	2.64314	2.72989	2.81947	2.91197	3.00749	3.10612	3.20796
14	168	2.65688	2.75095	2.84833	2.94913	3.05348	3.16150	3.27332	3.38907	3.50889
15	180	2.84895	2.95716	3.06945	3.18599	3.30692	3.43242	3.56265	3.69780	3.83804
16	192	3.05490	3.17882	3.30774	3.44186	3.58139	3.72655	3.87756	4.03465	4.19808
17	204	3.27574	3.41710	3.56453	3.71829	3.87865	4.04589	4.22030	4.40219	4.59189
18	216	3.51254	3.67324	3.84125	4.01692	4.20057	4.39259	4.59334	4.80322	5.02264
19	228	3.76646	3.94858	4.13946	4.33953	4.54922	4.76900	4.99935	5.24077	5.49380
20	240	4.03874	4.24456	4.46082	4.68805	4.92680	5.17766	5.44124	5.71818	6.00915
21	252	4.33070	4.56272	4.80712	5.06456	5.33572	5.62135	5.92220	6.23908	6.57285
22	264	4.64377	4.90474	5.18031	5.47131	5.77859	6.10305	6.44567	6.80744	7.18943
23	276	4.97946	5.27239	5.58247	5.91073	6.25821	6.62604	7.01541	7.42757	7.86385
24	288	5.33943	5.66759	6.01585	6.38543	6.77764	7.19384	7.63550	8.10419	8.60153
25	300	5.72542	6.09243	6.48288	6.89827	7.34018	7.81029	8.31041	8.84244	9.40841
26	312	6.13931	6.54911	6.98616	7.45229	7.94941	8.47957	9.04498	9.64795	10.29099
27	324	6.58312	7.04002	7.52852	8.05080	8.60920	9.20621	9.84447	10.52684	11.25635
28	336	7.05901	7.56772	8.11298	8.69739	9.32376	9.99511	10.71463	11.48579	12.31228
29	348	7.56931	8.13499	8.74281	9.39590	10.09763	10.85161	11.66171	12.53210	13.46725
30	360	8.11650	8.74477	9.42153	10.15051	10.93573	11.78151	12.69250	13.67372	14.73058
31	372	8.70324	9.40027	10.15295	10.96573	11.84339	12.79109	13.81440	14.91934	16.11241
32	384	9.33240	10.10489	10.94115	11.84642	12.82639	13.88718	15.03547	16.27843	17.62386
33	396	10.00704	10.86234	11.79054	12.79784	13.89097	15.07721	16.36447	17.76133	19.27710
34	408	10.73045	11.67656	12.70587	13.82568	15.04391	16.36920	17.81094	19.37931	21.08543
35	420	11.50615	12.55182	13.69226	14.93606	16.29255	17.77192	19.38526	21.14469	23.06338
36	432	12.33793	13.49268	14.75523	16.13562	17.64482	19.29483	21.09874	23.07088	25.22689
37	444	13.22984	14.50407	15.90072	17.43152	19.10934	20.94825	22.96368	25.17254	27.59334
38	456	14.18623	15.59127	17.13513	18.83150	20.69540	22.74335	24.99346	27.46565	30.18179
39	468	15.21175	16.75996	18.46537	20.34391	22.41311	24.69227	27.20265	29.96766	33.01305
40	480	16.31141	18.01626	19.89889	21.97779	24.27339	26.80820	29.60712	32.69759	36.10990

FUTURE VALUE OF ONE DOLLAR

ANNUAL INTEREST RATE

PERIOD YR	MOS	.09250	.09500	.09750	.10000	.10250	.10500	.10750	.11000	.11250
	1	1.00771	1.00792	1.00813	1.00833	1.00854	1.00875	1.00896	1.00917	1.00938
	2	1.01548	1.01590	1.01632	1.01674	1.01716	1.01758	1.01800	1.01842	1.01884
	3	1.02330	1.02394	1.02457	1.02521	1.02584	1.02648	1.02712	1.02775	1.02839
	4	1.03119	1.03204	1.03290	1.03375	1.03461	1.03546	1.03632	1.03717	1.03803
	5	1.03914	1.04022	1.04129	1.04237	1.04344	1.04452	1.04560	1.04668	1.04776
	6	1.04715	1.04845	1.04975	1.05105	1.05236	1.05366	1.05497	1.05628	1.05758
	7	1.05522	1.05675	1.05828	1.05981	1.06135	1.06288	1.06442	1.06596	1.06750
	8	1.06336	1.06512	1.06688	1.06864	1.07041	1.07218	1.07395	1.07573	1.07751
	9	1.07155	1.07355	1.07555	1.07755	1.07955	1.08156	1.08358	1.08559	1.08761
	10	1.07981	1.08205	1.08429	1.08653	1.08878	1.09103	1.09328	1.09554	1.09781
	11	1.08814	1.09061	1.09310	1.09558	1.09808	1.10057	1.10308	1.10558	1.10810
1	12	1.09652	1.09925	1.10198	1.10471	1.10746	1.11020	1.11296	1.11572	1.11849
2	24	1.20237	1.20835	1.21435	1.22039	1.22646	1.23255	1.23868	1.24483	1.25101
3	36	1.31842	1.32827	1.33819	1.34818	1.35825	1.36838	1.37859	1.38888	1.39924
4	48	1.44568	1.46010	1.47466	1.48935	1.50420	1.51918	1.53432	1.54960	1.56503
5	60	1.58523	1.60501	1.62504	1.64531	1.66583	1.68660	1.70763	1.72892	1.75046
6	72	1.73824	1.76430	1.79075	1.81759	1.84483	1.87247	1.90052	1.92898	1.95787
7	84	1.90602	1.93941	1.97337	2.00792	2.04307	2.07883	2.11520	2.15220	2.18985
8	96	2.09000	2.13189	2.17461	2.21818	2.26261	2.30792	2.35413	2.40125	2.44931
9	108	2.29173	2.34347	2.39637	2.45045	2.50574	2.56226	2.62005	2.67912	2.73952
10	120	2.51294	2.57606	2.64074	2.70704	2.77499	2.84463	2.91600	2.98915	3.06412
11	132	2.75550	2.83172	2.91004	2.99050	3.07318	3.15812	3.24539	3.33505	3.42717
12	144	3.02147	3.11276	3.20680	3.30365	3.40341	3.50615	3.61198	3.72098	3.83324
13	156	3.31312	3.42170	3.53382	3.64958	3.76912	3.89254	4.01998	4.15157	4.28743
14	168	3.63291	3.76129	3.89419	4.03174	4.17413	4.32151	4.47407	4.63198	4.79543
15	180	3.98358	4.13459	4.29130	4.45392	4.62266	4.79776	4.97945	5.16799	5.36362
16	192	4.36809	4.54494	4.72892	4.92030	5.11939	5.32649	5.54192	5.76602	5.99913
17	204	4.78971	4.99602	5.21116	5.43552	5.66950	5.91349	6.16793	6.43326	6.70995
18	216	5.25203	5.49186	5.74258	6.00469	6.27871	6.56518	6.86464	7.17771	7.50498
19	228	5.75898	6.03691	6.32819	6.63346	6.95339	7.28868	7.64006	8.00830	8.39421
20	240	6.31486	6.63606	6.97352	7.32807	7.70057	8.09192	8.50307	8.93502	9.38881
21	252	6.92440	7.29467	7.68467	8.09542	8.52804	8.98367	9.46356	9.96896	10.50125
22	264	7.59277	8.01865	8.46833	8.94311	9.44442	9.97371	10.53254	11.12256	11.74550
23	276	8.32566	8.81449	9.33190	9.87958	10.45927	11.07284	11.72228	12.40965	13.13718
24	288	9.12929	9.68930	10.28354	10.91410	11.58317	12.29311	13.04640	13.84568	14.69375
25	300	10.01048	10.65094	11.33223	12.05695	12.82784	13.64785	14.52010	15.44789	16.43475
26	312	10.97674	11.70802	12.48786	13.31946	14.20626	15.15189	16.16026	17.23550	18.38204
27	324	12.03626	12.87001	13.76134	14.71419	15.73279	16.82168	17.98569	19.22997	20.56005
28	336	13.19804	14.14733	15.16468	16.25495	17.42336	18.67549	20.01732	21.45524	22.99613
29	348	14.47198	15.55142	16.71113	17.95706	19.29559	20.73359	22.27843	23.93802	25.72085
30	360	15.86887	17.09486	18.41529	19.83740	21.36900	23.01851	24.79496	26.70810	28.76841
31	372	17.40060	18.79149	20.29323	21.91463	23.66521	25.55523	27.59575	29.79873	32.17706
32	384	19.08018	20.65650	22.36267	24.20938	26.20816	28.37150	30.71291	33.24700	35.98959
33	396	20.92188	22.70660	24.64316	26.74442	29.02436	31.49814	34.18218	37.09431	40.25385
34	408	22.94134	24.96018	27.15620	29.54491	32.14318	34.96934	38.04333	41.38682	45.02337
35	420	25.15573	27.43742	29.92551	32.63865	35.59713	38.82309	42.34063	46.17605	50.35800
36	432	27.58387	30.16051	32.97723	36.05634	39.42223	43.10152	47.12334	51.51949	56.32472
37	444	30.24638	33.15387	36.34016	39.83191	43.65835	47.85146	52.44630	57.48126	62.99840
38	456	33.16589	36.44431	40.04603	44.00284	48.34966	53.12486	58.37053	64.13293	70.46283
39	468	36.36720	40.06132	44.12981	48.61051	53.54508	58.97940	64.96395	71.55432	78.81168
40	480	39.87751	44.03731	48.63005	53.70066	59.29878	65.47913	72.30215	79.83450	88.14976

FUTURE VALUE OF ONE DOLLAR

ANNUAL INTEREST RATE

PERIOD YR	MOS	.11500	.11750	.12000	.12250	.12500	.12750	.13000	.13250	.13500
	1	1.00958	1.00979	1.01000	1.01021	1.01042	1.01063	1.01083	1.01104	1.01125
	2	1.01926	1.01968	1.02010	1.02052	1.02094	1.02136	1.02178	1.02221	1.02263
	3	1.02903	1.02966	1.03030	1.03094	1.03158	1.03221	1.03285	1.03349	1.03413
	4	1.03889	1.03975	1.04060	1.04146	1.04232	1.04318	1.04404	1.04490	1.04577
	5	1.04884	1.04993	1.05101	1.05209	1.05318	1.05427	1.05535	1.05644	1.05753
	6	1.05890	1.06021	1.06152	1.06283	1.06415	1.06547	1.06679	1.06811	1.06943
	7	1.06904	1.07059	1.07214	1.07368	1.07524	1.07679	1.07834	1.07990	1.08146
	8	1.07929	1.08107	1.08286	1.08464	1.08644	1.08823	1.09002	1.09182	1.09362
	9	1.08963	1.09166	1.09369	1.09572	1.09775	1.09979	1.10183	1.10388	1.10593
	10	1.10007	1.10235	1.10462	1.10690	1.10919	1.11148	1.11377	1.11607	1.11837
	11	1.11062	1.11314	1.11567	1.11820	1.12074	1.12329	1.12584	1.12839	1.13095
1	12	1.12126	1.12404	1.12683	1.12962	1.13242	1.13522	1.13803	1.14085	1.14367
2	24	1.25722	1.26346	1.26973	1.27604	1.28237	1.28873	1.29512	1.30154	1.30799
3	36	1.40967	1.42018	1.43077	1.44143	1.45217	1.46299	1.47389	1.48486	1.49592
4	48	1.58061	1.59634	1.61223	1.62827	1.64446	1.66082	1.67733	1.69400	1.71084
5	60	1.77227	1.79435	1.81670	1.83932	1.86222	1.88539	1.90886	1.93261	1.95665
6	72	1.98718	2.01692	2.04710	2.07773	2.10880	2.14034	2.17234	2.20481	2.23777
7	84	2.22814	2.26709	2.30672	2.34703	2.38804	2.42976	2.47219	2.51536	2.55927
8	96	2.49832	2.54830	2.59927	2.65125	2.70426	2.75831	2.81344	2.86965	2.92698
9	108	2.80127	2.86439	2.92893	2.99490	3.06235	3.13130	3.20178	3.27384	3.34751
10	120	3.14095	3.21969	3.30039	3.38309	3.46785	3.55471	3.64373	3.73496	3.82846
11	132	3.52182	3.61906	3.71896	3.82160	3.92705	4.03538	4.14669	4.26104	4.37851
12	144	3.94887	4.06796	4.19062	4.31694	4.44705	4.58105	4.71906	4.86120	5.00759
13	156	4.42771	4.57255	4.72209	4.87649	5.03591	5.20051	5.37045	5.54590	5.72706
14	168	4.96461	5.13972	5.32097	5.50857	5.70275	5.90373	6.11174	6.32705	6.54989
15	180	5.56661	5.77725	5.99580	6.22258	6.45788	6.70204	6.95536	7.21821	7.49094
16	192	6.24162	6.49385	6.75622	7.02913	7.31301	7.63829	7.91543	8.23490	8.56719
17	204	6.99847	7.29934	7.61308	7.94023	8.28137	8.63709	9.00802	9.39479	9.79808
18	216	7.84710	8.20474	8.57861	8.96942	9.37796	9.80501	10.25142	10.71805	11.20582
19	228	8.79864	9.22245	9.66659	10.13202	10.61975	11.13085	11.66644	12.22769	12.81581
20	240	9.86555	10.36640	10.89255	11.44530	12.02597	12.63598	13.27679	13.94996	14.65711
21	252	11.06184	11.65223	12.27400	12.92881	13.61841	14.34463	15.10942	15.91481	16.76296
22	264	12.40319	13.09756	13.83065	14.60461	15.42170	16.28433	17.19501	18.15642	19.17137
23	276	13.90720	14.72217	15.58473	16.49762	17.46378	18.48631	19.56848	20.71376	21.92581
24	288	15.59357	16.54830	17.56126	18.63600	19.77627	20.98605	22.26957	23.63130	25.07598
25	300	17.48444	18.60093	19.78847	21.05155	22.39496	23.82381	25.34349	26.95977	28.67876
26	312	19.60459	20.90817	22.29814	23.78019	25.36042	27.04529	28.84172	30.75706	32.79917
27	324	21.98183	23.50160	25.12610	26.86252	28.71854	30.70238	32.82281	35.08920	37.51157
28	336	24.64733	26.41672	28.31272	30.34437	32.52134	34.85399	37.35342	40.03152	42.90102
29	348	27.63605	29.69342	31.90348	34.27753	36.82769	39.56699	42.50941	45.66997	49.06480
30	360	30.98718	33.37657	35.94964	38.72049	41.70426	44.91728	48.37709	52.10260	56.11416
31	372	34.74467	37.51656	40.50896	43.73934	47.22658	50.99104	55.05470	59.44127	64.17633
32	384	38.95778	42.17008	45.64651	49.40871	53.48013	57.88610	62.65404	67.81359	73.39683
33	396	43.68178	47.40082	51.43562	55.81294	60.56176	65.71352	71.30233	77.36515	83.94208
34	408	48.97860	53.28037	57.95895	63.04727	68.58111	74.59938	81.14437	88.26205	96.00241
35	420	54.91771	59.88921	65.30959	71.21929	77.66235	84.68678	92.34492	100.69378	109.79550
36	432	61.57699	67.31781	73.59249	80.45055	87.94609	96.13822	105.09152	114.87653	125.57031
37	444	69.04378	75.66784	82.92586	90.87833	99.59156	109.13814	119.59757	131.05692	143.61155
38	456	77.41598	85.05361	93.44293	102.65774	112.77908	123.89591	136.10591	149.51632	164.24486
39	468	86.80339	95.60358	105.29383	115.96397	127.71284	140.64925	154.89295	170.57573	187.84265
40	480	97.32911	107.46215	118.64773	130.99491	144.62407	159.66800	176.27321	194.60137	214.83084

FUTURE VALUE OF ONE DOLLAR

ANNUAL INTEREST RATE

PERIOD YR	MOS	.13750	.14000	.14250	.14500	.14750	.15000	.15250	.15500	.15750
	1	1.01146	1.01167	1.01188	1.01208	1.01229	1.01250	1.01271	1.01292	1.01313
	2	1.02305	1.02347	1.02389	1.02431	1.02473	1.02516	1.02558	1.02600	1.02642
	3	1.03477	1.03541	1.03605	1.03669	1.03733	1.03797	1.03861	1.03925	1.03989
	4	1.04663	1.04749	1.04835	1.04922	1.05008	1.05095	1.05181	1.05268	1.05354
	5	1.05862	1.05971	1.06080	1.06189	1.06299	1.06408	1.06518	1.06627	1.06737
	6	1.07075	1.07207	1.07340	1.07473	1.07605	1.07738	1.07871	1.08005	1.08138
	7	1.08302	1.08458	1.08615	1.08771	1.08928	1.09085	1.09242	1.09400	1.09557
	8	1.09543	1.09723	1.09904	1.10086	1.10267	1.10449	1.10631	1.10813	1.10995
	9	1.10798	1.11004	1.11209	1.11416	1.11622	1.11829	1.12036	1.12244	1.12452
	10	1.12068	1.12299	1.12530	1.12762	1.12994	1.13227	1.13460	1.13694	1.13928
	11	1.13352	1.13609	1.13866	1.14125	1.14383	1.14642	1.14902	1.15162	1.15423
1	12	1.14651	1.14934	1.15219	1.15504	1.15789	1.16075	1.16362	1.16650	1.16938
2	24	1.31447	1.32099	1.32753	1.33411	1.34071	1.34735	1.35402	1.36072	1.36745
3	36	1.50705	1.51827	1.52956	1.54094	1.55240	1.56394	1.57557	1.58728	1.59908
4	48	1.72784	1.74501	1.76234	1.77984	1.79751	1.81535	1.83337	1.85156	1.86993
5	60	1.98098	2.00561	2.03054	2.05578	2.08132	2.10718	2.13335	2.15985	2.18666
6	72	2.27120	2.30513	2.33956	2.37450	2.40995	2.44592	2.48242	2.51946	2.55704
7	84	2.60394	2.64938	2.69561	2.74263	2.79046	2.83911	2.88861	2.93895	2.99016
8	96	2.98544	3.04505	3.10584	3.16783	3.23105	3.29551	3.36125	3.42828	3.49664
9	108	3.42282	3.49980	3.57850	3.65896	3.74120	3.82528	3.91123	3.99909	4.08891
10	120	3.92428	4.02247	4.12310	4.22623	4.33191	4.44021	4.55120	4.66494	4.78150
11	132	4.49920	4.62319	4.75058	4.88144	5.01588	5.15400	5.29589	5.44165	5.59140
12	144	5.15836	5.31363	5.47355	5.63824	5.80785	5.98253	6.16242	6.34768	6.53848
13	156	5.91408	6.10718	6.30654	6.51236	6.72486	6.94424	7.17074	7.40457	7.64598
14	168	6.78053	7.01924	7.26630	7.52201	7.78666	8.06056	8.34404	8.63743	8.94107
15	180	7.77391	8.06751	8.37213	8.68819	9.01611	9.35633	9.70933	10.07556	10.45552
16	192	8.91283	9.27232	9.64625	10.03516	10.43968	10.86041	11.29800	11.75313	12.22650
17	204	10.21860	10.65707	11.11426	11.59097	12.08801	12.60627	13.14662	13.71003	14.29745
18	216	11.71568	12.24862	12.80569	13.38798	13.99661	14.63278	15.29773	15.99274	16.71918
19	228	13.43208	14.07785	14.75453	15.46359	16.20656	16.98507	17.80080	18.65553	19.55111
20	240	15.39995	16.18027	16.99996	17.86099	18.76544	19.71549	20.71343	21.76166	22.86271
21	252	17.65612	18.59666	19.58711	20.63008	21.72835	22.88485	24.10264	25.38497	26.73524
22	264	20.24283	21.37393	22.56798	23.82847	25.15908	26.56369	28.04641	29.61156	31.26371
23	276	23.20850	24.56595	26.00250	27.52272	29.13149	30.83392	32.63547	34.54188	36.55922
24	288	26.60867	28.23468	29.95970	31.78972	33.73110	35.79062	37.97541	40.29309	42.75169
25	300	30.50697	32.45131	34.51913	36.71825	39.05697	41.54412	44.18910	47.00187	49.99305
26	312	34.97639	37.29765	39.77244	42.41087	45.22374	48.22253	51.41948	54.82766	58.46097
27	324	40.10061	42.86776	45.82523	48.98606	52.36419	55.97451	59.83294	63.95645	68.36321
28	336	45.97555	49.26972	52.79916	56.58063	60.63206	64.97267	69.62303	74.60518	79.94270
29	348	52.71120	56.62776	60.83442	65.35263	70.20536	75.41732	81.01502	87.02691	93.48355
30	360	60.43366	65.08466	70.09254	75.48459	81.29020	87.54100	94.27100	101.51686	109.31798
31	372	69.28749	74.80454	80.75961	87.18737	94.12525	101.61361	109.69599	118.41938	127.83447
32	384	79.43846	85.97600	93.05004	100.70450	108.98685	117.94845	127.64486	138.13616	149.48732
33	396	91.07659	98.81583	107.21091	116.31726	126.19497	136.90920	148.53060	161.13578	174.80778
34	408	104.41977	113.57318	123.52685	134.35054	146.12010	158.91797	172.83375	187.96483	204.41706
35	420	119.71779	130.53443	142.32584	155.17963	169.19125	184.46475	201.11347	219.26090	239.04162
36	432	137.25705	150.02871	163.98577	179.23795	195.90515	214.11829	234.02042	255.76776	279.53095
37	444	157.36589	172.43430	188.94202	207.02617	226.83694	248.53878	272.31174	298.35300	326.87845
38	456	180.42079	198.18599	217.69625	239.12255	262.65262	288.49251	316.86843	348.02866	382.24576
39	468	206.85334	227.78349	250.82645	276.19500	304.12328	334.86898	368.71565	405.97531	446.99130
40	480	237.15839	261.80114	288.99859	319.01499	352.14182	388.70068	429.04631	473.57004	522.70355

FUTURE VALUE OF ONE DOLLAR

PERIOD YR	MOS	.16000	.16250	.16500	.16750	.17000	.17250	.17500	.17750	.18000
		ANNUAL INTEREST RATE								
	1	1.01333	1.01354	1.01375	1.01396	1.01417	1.01438	1.01458	1.01479	1.01500
	2	1.02684	1.02727	1.02769	1.02811	1.02853	1.02896	1.02938	1.02980	1.03023
	3	1.04054	1.04118	1.04182	1.04246	1.04310	1.04375	1.04439	1.04503	1.04568
	4	1.05441	1.05528	1.05614	1.05701	1.05788	1.05875	1.05962	1.06049	1.06136
	5	1.06847	1.06957	1.07067	1.07177	1.07287	1.07397	1.07507	1.07618	1.07728
	6	1.08271	1.08405	1.08539	1.08673	1.08807	1.08941	1.09075	1.09210	1.09344
	7	1.09715	1.09873	1.10031	1.10190	1.10348	1.10507	1.10666	1.10825	1.10984
	8	1.11178	1.11361	1.11544	1.11728	1.11911	1.12096	1.12280	1.12464	1.12649
	9	1.12660	1.12869	1.13078	1.13287	1.13497	1.13707	1.13917	1.14128	1.14339
	10	1.14162	1.14397	1.14633	1.14869	1.15105	1.15341	1.15579	1.15816	1.16054
	11	1.15685	1.15947	1.16209	1.16472	1.16735	1.16999	1.17264	1.17529	1.17795
1	12	1.17227	1.17517	1.17807	1.18098	1.18389	1.18681	1.18974	1.19268	1.19562
2	24	1.37422	1.38102	1.38784	1.39471	1.40160	1.40853	1.41549	1.42248	1.42950
3	36	1.61096	1.62292	1.63498	1.64711	1.65934	1.67166	1.68406	1.69656	1.70914
4	48	1.88848	1.90720	1.92611	1.94520	1.96448	1.98395	2.00360	2.02344	2.04348
5	60	2.21381	2.24128	2.26909	2.29724	2.32573	2.35457	2.38376	2.41331	2.44322
6	72	2.59518	2.63388	2.67314	2.71299	2.75342	2.79444	2.83606	2.87830	2.92116
7	84	3.04226	3.09524	3.14915	3.20398	3.25975	3.31648	3.37418	3.43288	3.49259
8	96	3.56635	3.63743	3.70991	3.78382	3.85919	3.93604	4.01441	4.09432	4.17580
9	108	4.18072	4.27458	4.37053	4.46860	4.56886	4.67135	4.77611	4.88320	4.99267
10	120	4.90094	5.02334	5.14878	5.27732	5.40904	5.54402	5.68234	5.82408	5.96932
11	132	5.74523	5.90326	6.06561	6.23239	6.40371	6.57971	6.76051	6.94624	7.13703
12	144	6.73497	6.93732	7.14570	7.36033	7.58130	7.80889	8.04326	8.28462	8.53316
13	156	7.89520	8.15250	8.41812	8.69235	8.97544	9.26770	9.56940	9.88087	10.20241
14	168	9.25532	9.58054	9.91712	10.26546	10.62595	10.99903	11.38512	11.78468	12.19818
15	180	10.84974	11.25873	11.68305	12.12326	12.57998	13.05379	13.54535	14.05532	14.58437
16	192	12.71883	13.23088	13.76342	14.31729	14.89333	15.49242	16.11547	16.76345	17.43734
17	204	14.90991	15.54848	16.21425	16.90839	17.63209	18.38661	19.17325	19.99337	20.84839
18	216	17.47845	18.27205	19.10149	19.96841	20.87448	21.82147	22.81121	23.84563	24.92672
19	228	20.48948	21.47269	22.50286	23.58223	24.71313	25.89801	27.13945	28.44012	29.80284
20	240	24.01922	25.23398	26.50990	27.85006	29.25767	30.73611	32.28894	33.91987	35.63282
21	252	28.15703	29.65412	31.23047	32.89027	34.63791	36.47803	38.41549	40.45543	42.60324
22	264	33.00767	34.84852	36.79162	38.84264	41.00754	43.29261	45.70451	48.25025	50.93721
23	276	38.69392	40.95280	43.34304	45.87225	48.54849	51.38026	54.37657	57.54694	60.90145
24	288	45.35976	48.12635	51.06105	54.17406	57.47615	60.97878	64.69407	68.63489	72.81488
25	300	53.17392	56.55645	60.15340	63.97829	68.04554	72.37043	76.96923	81.85923	87.05880
26	312	62.33423	66.46323	70.86480	75.55687	80.55855	85.89020	91.57351	97.63159	104.08908
27	324	73.07260	78.10534	83.48356	89.23090	95.37260	101.93564	108.94882	116.44292	124.45080
28	336	85.66088	91.78676	98.34933	105.37961	112.91083	120.97858	129.62095	138.87874	148.79564
29	348	100.41774	107.86469	115.86221	124.45086	133.67420	143.57900	154.21545	165.63743	177.90277
30	360	117.71679	126.75894	136.49357	146.97355	158.25578	170.40149	183.47656	197.55189	212.70378
31	372	137.99595	148.96282	160.79873	173.57233	187.35771	202.23477	218.28971	235.61552	254.31251
32	384	161.76862	175.05607	189.43186	204.98487	221.81124	240.01494	259.70837	281.01312	304.06065
33	396	189.63663	205.71997	223.16363	242.08234	262.60050	284.85295	308.98588	335.15778	363.54044
34	408	222.30549	241.75516	262.90196	285.89359	310.89056	338.06730	367.61339	399.73485	434.65556
35	420	260.60223	284.10249	309.71642	337.63365	368.06076	401.22281	437.36499	476.75441	519.68208
36	432	305.49639	333.86764	364.86704	398.73745	435.74409	476.17661	520.35137	568.61384	621.34134
37	444	358.12449	392.34996	429.83824	470.89962	515.87382	565.13279	619.08372	678.17244	742.88700
38	456	419.81889	461.07640	506.37873	556.12145	610.73875	670.70717	736.54972	808.84041	888.20920
39	468	492.14142	541.84140	596.54864	656.76644	723.04855	796.00427	876.30392	964.68505	1061.95906
40	480	576.92302	636.75369	702.77494	775.62582	856.01120	944.70854	1042.57533	1150.55731	1269.69754

FUTURE VALUE OF ONE DOLLAR

ANNUAL INTEREST RATE

PERIOD YR	MOS	.18250	.18500	.18750	.19000	.19250	.19500	.19750	.20000	.20250
	1	1.01521	1.01542	1.01563	1.01583	1.01604	1.01625	1.01646	1.01667	1.01688
	2	1.03065	1.03107	1.03149	1.03192	1.03234	1.03276	1.03319	1.03361	1.03403
	3	1.04632	1.04697	1.04761	1.04826	1.04890	1.04955	1.05019	1.05084	1.05148
	4	1.06224	1.06311	1.06398	1.06485	1.06573	1.06660	1.06748	1.06835	1.06923
	5	1.07839	1.07950	1.08060	1.08171	1.08282	1.08393	1.08505	1.08616	1.08727
	6	1.09479	1.09614	1.09749	1.09884	1.10019	1.10155	1.10290	1.10426	1.10562
	7	1.11144	1.11304	1.11464	1.11624	1.11784	1.11945	1.12106	1.12266	1.12428
	8	1.12834	1.13020	1.13205	1.13391	1.13577	1.13764	1.13951	1.14138	1.14325
	9	1.14550	1.14762	1.14974	1.15187	1.15399	1.15613	1.15826	1.16040	1.16254
	10	1.16293	1.16531	1.16771	1.17010	1.17251	1.17491	1.17732	1.17974	1.18216
	11	1.18061	1.18328	1.18595	1.18863	1.19132	1.19400	1.19670	1.19940	1.20211
1	12	1.19857	1.20152	1.20448	1.20745	1.21043	1.21341	1.21640	1.21939	1.22239
2	24	1.43656	1.44365	1.45078	1.45794	1.46513	1.47236	1.47962	1.48691	1.49424
3	36	1.72181	1.73458	1.74744	1.76039	1.77343	1.78657	1.79980	1.81313	1.82655
4	48	2.06371	2.08413	2.10476	2.12558	2.14661	2.16784	2.18927	2.21092	2.23277
5	60	2.47349	2.50413	2.53515	2.56654	2.59831	2.63047	2.66302	2.69597	2.72932
6	72	2.96464	3.00877	3.05354	3.09697	3.14506	3.19183	3.23929	3.28744	3.33630
7	84	3.55332	3.61510	3.67794	3.74185	3.80687	3.87299	3.94026	4.00868	4.07827
8	96	4.25889	4.34362	4.43001	4.51810	4.60793	4.69952	4.79292	4.88815	4.98525
9	108	5.10457	5.21895	5.33587	5.45539	5.57756	5.70243	5.83008	5.96056	6.09393
10	120	6.11816	6.27068	6.42696	6.58711	6.75122	6.91938	7.09169	7.26825	7.44918
11	132	7.33302	7.53435	7.74117	7.95362	8.17185	8.39603	8.62630	8.86285	9.10582
12	144	8.78911	9.05268	9.32410	9.60360	9.89142	10.18780	10.49300	10.80727	11.13090
13	156	10.53434	10.87699	11.23072	11.59588	11.97283	12.36195	12.76364	13.17829	13.60633
14	168	12.62610	13.06894	13.52721	14.00146	14.49222	15.00009	15.52564	16.06949	16.63228
15	180	15.13322	15.70261	16.29329	16.90607	17.54176	18.20122	18.88533	19.59500	20.33118
16	192	18.13817	18.86702	19.62499	20.41325	21.23301	22.08550	22.97204	23.89397	24.85270
17	204	21.73980	22.66912	23.63796	24.64800	25.70098	26.79871	27.94309	29.13609	30.37976
18	216	26.05659	27.23743	28.47152	29.76126	31.10913	32.51776	33.98986	35.52829	37.13600
19	228	31.23055	32.72635	34.29346	35.93526	37.65530	39.45730	41.34513	43.32288	45.39479
20	240	37.43189	39.32140	41.30588	43.39006	45.57896	47.87779	50.29205	52.82753	55.49027
21	252	44.86461	47.24550	49.75222	52.39138	55.16995	58.09527	61.17505	64.41742	67.83092
22	264	53.77321	56.76647	59.92569	63.26002	66.77914	70.49324	74.41309	78.55003	82.91604
23	276	64.45076	68.20612	72.17946	76.38337	80.83120	85.53703	90.51578	95.78320	101.35598
24	288	77.24851	81.95110	86.93891	92.22918	97.84018	103.79128	110.10303	116.79718	123.89684
25	300	92.58747	98.46599	104.71642	111.36222	118.42829	125.94113	133.92888	142.42145	151.45063
26	312	110.97222	118.30897	126.12913	134.46442	143.34868	152.81792	162.91054	173.66744	185.13219
27	324	133.00758	142.15075	151.92036	162.35920	173.51295	185.43042	198.16373	211.76853	226.30428
28	336	159.41841	170.79714	182.98546	196.04078	210.02458	225.00268	241.04556	258.22866	276.63276
29	348	191.07354	205.21639	220.40283	236.70963	254.21919	273.01996	293.20684	314.88172	338.15394
30	360	229.01432	246.57185	265.47141	285.81528	307.71351	331.28448	356.65561	383.96396	413.35700
31	372	274.48886	296.26131	319.75574	345.10795	372.46441	401.98310	433.83445	468.20223	505.28470
32	384	328.99312	355.96426	385.14028	416.70094	450.84057	487.76935	527.71447	570.92163	617.65646
33	396	394.32009	427.69861	463.89483	503.14596	545.70912	591.86302	641.90975	696.17675	755.01891
34	408	472.61880	513.88896	558.75333	607.52409	660.54047	718.17108	780.81643	848.91172	922.92981
35	420	566.46500	617.44850	673.00876	733.55557	799.53531	871.43423	949.78194	1035.15538	1128.18291
36	432	678.94590	741.87748	810.62745	885.73241	967.77828	1057.40489	1155.31092	1262.25924	1379.08286
37	444	813.76172	891.38154	976.38680	1069.47848	1171.42392	1283.06311	1405.31553	1539.18767	1685.78119
38	456	975.34744	1071.01385	1176.04108	1291.34286	1417.92189	1556.87850	1709.42014	1876.87172	2060.68708
39	468	1169.01864	1286.84588	1416.52122	1559.23322	1716.28942	1889.12818	2079.33175	2288.64064	2518.96940
40	480	1401.14642	1546.17265	1706.17540	1882.69771	2077.44122	2292.28245	2529.29074	2790.74799	3079.17048

FUTURE VALUE OF ONE DOLLAR

ANNUAL INTEREST RATE

PERIOD YR	MOS	.20500	.20750	.21000	.21250	.21500	.21750	.22000	.22250	.22500
	1	1.01708	1.01729	1.01750	1.01771	1.01792	1.01813	1.01833	1.01854	1.01875
	2	1.03446	1.03488	1.03531	1.03573	1.03615	1.03658	1.03700	1.03743	1.03785
	3	1.05213	1.05278	1.05342	1.05407	1.05472	1.05537	1.05601	1.05666	1.05731
	4	1.07010	1.07098	1.07186	1.07274	1.07362	1.07450	1.07537	1.07626	1.07714
	5	1.08839	1.08950	1.09062	1.09173	1.09285	1.09397	1.09509	1.09621	1.09733
	6	1.10698	1.10834	1.10970	1.11107	1.11243	1.11380	1.11517	1.11654	1.11791
	7	1.12589	1.12750	1.12912	1.13074	1.13236	1.13399	1.13561	1.13724	1.13887
	8	1.14512	1.14700	1.14888	1.15077	1.15265	1.15454	1.15643	1.15832	1.16022
	9	1.16469	1.16683	1.16899	1.17114	1.17330	1.17547	1.17763	1.17980	1.18198
	10	1.18458	1.18701	1.18944	1.19188	1.19432	1.19677	1.19922	1.20168	1.20414
	11	1.20482	1.20754	1.21026	1.21299	1.21572	1.21846	1.22121	1.22396	1.22672
1	12	1.22540	1.22842	1.23144	1.23447	1.23750	1.24055	1.24360	1.24665	1.24972
2	24	1.50161	1.50901	1.51644	1.52391	1.53142	1.53896	1.54653	1.55414	1.56179
3	36	1.84007	1.85369	1.86741	1.88122	1.89513	1.90915	1.92326	1.93748	1.95180
4	48	2.25483	2.27711	2.29960	2.32231	2.34524	2.36839	2.39176	2.41536	2.43919
5	60	2.76307	2.79724	2.83182	2.86682	2.90224	2.93810	2.97439	3.01112	3.04830
6	72	3.38587	3.43617	3.48721	3.53899	3.59154	3.64485	3.69894	3.75382	3.80951
7	84	4.14905	4.22105	4.29429	4.36878	4.44454	4.52160	4.59999	4.67971	4.76080
8	96	5.08426	5.18521	5.28815	5.39312	5.50014	5.60926	5.72053	5.83398	5.94965
9	108	6.23026	6.36961	6.51204	6.65763	6.80644	6.95855	7.11403	7.27295	7.43538
10	120	7.63457	7.82453	8.01918	8.21863	8.42300	8.63241	8.84698	9.06684	9.29212
11	132	9.35541	9.61179	9.87514	10.14564	10.42350	10.70891	11.00208	11.30320	11.61251
12	144	11.46414	11.80729	12.16063	12.52448	12.89913	13.28491	13.68215	14.09117	14.51234
13	156	14.04817	14.50427	14.97508	15.46107	15.96273	16.48056	17.01507	17.56681	18.13631
14	168	17.21466	17.81730	18.44090	19.08620	19.75395	20.44490	21.15988	21.89971	22.66525
15	180	21.09487	21.88707	22.70885	23.56131	24.44559	25.36286	26.31436	27.30134	28.32513
16	192	25.84968	26.88645	27.96458	29.08570	30.25152	31.46382	32.72445	34.03530	35.39838
17	204	31.67624	33.02778	34.43668	35.90537	37.43639	39.03235	40.69601	42.43021	44.23793
18	216	38.81612	40.57188	42.40668	44.32405	46.32769	48.42147	50.60942	52.89575	55.28487
19	228	47.56534	49.83919	52.22125	54.71664	57.33072	60.06911	62.93770	65.94265	69.09041
20	240	58.28664	61.22332	64.30730	67.54596	70.94700	74.51855	78.26910	82.20760	86.34341
21	252	71.42455	75.20777	79.19054	83.38335	87.79722	92.44376	97.33519	102.48435	107.90478
22	264	87.52376	92.38651	97.51835	102.93411	108.64943	114.68083	121.04571	127.76243	134.85037
23	276	107.25175	113.48916	120.08792	127.06890	134.45414	142.26696	150.53203	159.27542	168.52472
24	288	131.42647	139.41202	147.88099	156.86254	166.38757	176.48885	187.20112	198.56119	210.60810
25	300	161.05022	171.25611	182.10647	193.64184	205.90533	218.94271	232.80267	247.53691	263.20039
26	312	197.35120	210.37393	224.25306	239.04473	254.80872	271.60872	289.51260	308.59264	328.92583
27	324	241.83448	258.42692	276.15404	295.09316	315.32687	336.94339	360.03688	384.70795	411.06400
28	336	296.34436	317.45604	340.06694	364.28317	390.21835	417.99410	447.74064	479.59734	513.71342
29	348	363.14086	389.96842	418.77180	449.69605	482.39687	518.54133	556.80872	597.89148	641.99607
30	360	444.99340	479.04387	515.69206	555.13556	597.58694	643.27488	692.44542	745.36322	802.31300
31	372	545.29564	588.46567	635.04347	685.29729	739.51638	798.01272	861.12276	929.20932	1002.66370
32	384	668.20617	722.88127	782.01750	845.97783	915.15467	989.97228	1070.88932	1158.40162	1253.04524
33	396	818.82092	887.99969	963.00710	1044.33287	1132.50780	1228.10713	1331.75429	1444.12490	1565.95116
34	408	1003.38449	1090.83398	1185.88480	1289.19590	1401.48323	1523.52461	1656.16508	1800.32269	1956.99481
35	420	1229.54899	1339.99908	1460.34516	1591.47157	1734.34148	1890.00387	2059.60122	2244.37774	2445.68846
36	432	1506.69133	1646.07775	1798.32645	1964.62132	2146.25497	2344.63862	2561.31303	2797.96032	3056.41692
37	444	1846.30200	2022.07001	2214.52989	2425.26289	2655.99967	2908.63438	3185.24012	3488.08573	3819.65428
38	456	2262.46148	2483.94531	2727.05917	2993.91034	3286.31091	3608.29763	3961.15371	4348.43266	4773.48450
39	468	2772.42398	3051.32083	3358.20788	3695.88763	4067.44250	4476.26277	4926.07720	5420.98677	5965.50176
40	480	3397.33285	3748.29459	4135.42921	4562.45639	5033.47743	5553.01432	6126.05275	6758.08961	7455.18524

FUTURE VALUE OF ONE DOLLAR

ANNUAL INTEREST RATE

PERIOD YR	MOS	.22750	.23000	.23250	.23500	.23750	.24000	.24250	.24500	.24750
	1	1.01896	1.01917	1.01938	1.01958	1.01979	1.02000	1.02021	1.02042	1.02063
	2	1.03828	1.03870	1.03913	1.03955	1.03998	1.04040	1.04083	1.04125	1.04168
	3	1.05796	1.05861	1.05926	1.05991	1.06056	1.06121	1.06186	1.06251	1.06316
	4	1.07802	1.07890	1.07978	1.08066	1.08155	1.08243	1.08332	1.08420	1.08509
	5	1.09845	1.09958	1.10070	1.10183	1.10295	1.10408	1.10521	1.10634	1.10747
	6	1.11928	1.12065	1.12203	1.12341	1.12478	1.12616	1.12754	1.12893	1.13031
	7	1.14050	1.14213	1.14377	1.14541	1.14704	1.14869	1.15033	1.15197	1.15362
	8	1.16212	1.16402	1.16593	1.16784	1.16975	1.17166	1.17358	1.17549	1.17742
	9	1.18415	1.18633	1.18852	1.19071	1.19290	1.19509	1.19729	1.19949	1.20170
	10	1.20660	1.20907	1.21155	1.21402	1.21651	1.21899	1.22149	1.22398	1.22648
	11	1.22948	1.23225	1.23502	1.23780	1.24058	1.24337	1.24617	1.24897	1.25178
1	12	1.25279	1.25586	1.25895	1.26204	1.26514	1.26824	1.27135	1.27447	1.27760
2	24	1.56947	1.57719	1.58495	1.59274	1.60057	1.60844	1.61634	1.62428	1.63226
3	36	1.96622	1.98074	1.99537	2.01010	2.02494	2.03989	2.05494	2.07010	2.08537
4	48	2.46325	2.48754	2.51207	2.53683	2.56183	2.58707	2.61256	2.63829	2.66427
5	60	3.08593	3.12401	3.16256	3.20157	3.24106	3.28103	3.32148	3.36242	3.40386
6	72	3.86601	3.92333	3.98150	4.04051	4.10039	4.16114	4.22278	4.28532	4.34877
7	84	4.84328	4.92717	5.01250	5.09928	5.18755	5.27733	5.36865	5.46152	5.55598
8	96	6.06760	6.18786	6.31047	6.43549	6.56296	6.69293	6.82545	6.96056	7.09832
9	108	7.60141	7.77111	7.94456	8.12184	8.30305	8.48826	8.67756	8.87104	9.06880
10	120	9.52294	9.75945	10.00178	10.25008	10.50449	10.76516	11.03225	11.30590	11.58629
11	132	11.93021	12.25654	12.59172	12.93600	13.28962	13.65283	14.02589	14.40906	14.80262
12	144	14.94601	15.39254	15.85232	16.32574	16.81319	17.31509	17.83187	18.36396	18.91181
13	156	18.72416	19.33094	19.95725	20.60371	21.27098	21.95972	22.67061	23.40436	24.16170
14	168	23.45738	24.27702	25.12513	26.00269	26.91070	27.85023	28.82236	29.82822	30.86896
15	180	29.38709	30.48863	31.63123	32.81640	34.04572	35.32083	36.64342	38.01525	39.43814
16	192	36.81575	38.28957	39.82207	41.41558	43.07250	44.79535	46.58675	48.44939	50.38611
17	204	46.12228	48.08649	50.13391	52.26807	54.49261	56.81134	59.22824	61.74743	64.37322
18	216	57.78138	60.39008	63.11598	65.96433	68.94061	72.05052	75.30004	78.69541	82.24313
19	228	72.38774	75.84171	79.45973	83.24955	87.21930	91.37748	95.73298	100.29514	105.07371
20	240	90.68639	95.24685	100.03565	105.06417	110.34435	115.88874	121.71049	127.82342	134.24203
21	252	113.61069	119.61707	125.93967	132.59507	139.60070	146.97494	154.73708	162.90745	171.50742
22	264	142.32996	150.22275	158.55148	167.34013	176.61399	186.39976	196.72556	207.62109	219.11764
23	276	178.30907	188.65931	199.60804	211.18975	223.44087	236.39996	250.10778	264.60740	279.94439
24	288	223.38321	236.93039	251.29612	266.52967	282.68328	299.81231	317.97545	337.23489	357.65656
25	300	279.85150	297.55229	316.36870	336.37080	357.63304	380.23451	404.25927	429.79665	456.94152
26	312	350.59421	373.68514	398.29170	424.51303	452.45473	482.22929	513.95653	547.76407	583.78785
27	324	439.21973	469.29763	501.42848	535.75194	572.41715	611.58335	653.42056	698.11033	745.84653
28	336	550.24860	589.37389	631.27231	676.13978	724.18603	775.63556	830.72866	889.72253	952.89248
29	348	689.34409	740.17332	794.73891	853.31468	916.19444	983.69344	1056.14997	1133.92703	1217.41409
30	360	863.60105	929.55685	1000.53485	1076.91630	1159.11134	1247.56113	1342.74020	1445.15899	1555.36653
31	372	1081.90783	1167.39677	1259.62119	1359.11023	1466.43447	1582.20916	1707.09775	1841.81561	1987.13409
32	384	1355.39966	1466.09131	1585.79739	1715.24994	1855.24028	2006.62379	2170.32509	2347.34363	2538.75972
33	396	1698.02655	1841.21096	1996.43622	2164.71210	2347.13284	2544.88416	2759.25088	2991.62526	3243.51585
34	408	2127.26494	2312.31014	2513.40909	2731.95082	2969.44425	3227.52845	3507.98389	3812.74458	4143.91128
35	420	2665.00904	2903.94653	3164.25097	3447.82813	3756.75334	4093.28647	4459.88838	4859.23870	5294.25523
36	432	3338.68766	3646.96124	3983.62695	4351.29313	4752.80708	5191.27698	5670.09571	6192.96684	6763.93303
37	444	4182.66322	4580.08649	5015.17859	5491.50107	6012.95136	6583.79443	7208.69730	7892.76687	8641.59132
38	456	5239.98451	5751.96468	6313.84830	6930.48781	7607.20634	8349.84327	9164.80416	10059.11554	11040.48492
39	468	6564.58247	7223.68405	7948.80575	8746.54501	9624.15705	10589.62021	11651.70790	12820.06766	14105.30800
40	480	8224.02106	9071.96309	10007.13191	11038.47980	12175.87572	13430.19894	14813.44224	16338.82564	18020.92166

PRESENT VALUE OF ONE DOLLAR TABLE

Description:

The Present Value of One Dollar table may be used to find what a sum to be received in the future is worth today. To use the table, find the factor that corresponds to the appropriate annual interest rate and term; then multiply by the future sum to derive the present value.

Table Calculation Formula:

$$PV_s = \frac{1}{(1-i)^n}.$$

Table Range:

Annual interest rate, with monthly compounding, from 7.00% to 24.75%, in .25% increments. Term from 1 to 12 months in 1-month increments, 1 to 40 years, in 1-year increments.

Example:

If $3,000 is to be received in 3 years, what is the present value of this sum, assuming an annual yield of 15%, with monthly compounding?

Solution:

Finding the table factor corresponding to 15% interest and 3 years provides:

$$PV_s = \$3{,}000 \times \text{table factor}, PV_s, 15\%, 3 \text{ years},$$
$$= \$3{,}000(.63941),$$
$$= \$1{,}918.23.$$

The $3,000 to be received in 3 years is worth $1,918.23 in the present, with a 15% annual discount rate and monthly compounding.

PRESENT VALUE OF ONE DOLLAR

PERIOD YR	MOS	ANNUAL INTEREST RATE .07000	.07250	.07500	.07750	.08000	.08250	.08500	.08750	.09000
	1	.99420	.99399	.99379	.99358	.99338	.99317	.99297	.99276	.99256
	2	.98843	.98803	.98762	.98721	.98680	.98639	.98598	.98557	.98517
	3	.98270	.98209	.98148	.98087	.98026	.97966	.97905	.97844	.97783
	4	.97700	.97619	.97539	.97458	.97377	.97297	.97216	.97136	.97055
	5	.97134	.97033	.96933	.96832	.96732	.96632	.96532	.96433	.96333
	6	.96570	.96450	.96331	.96211	.96092	.95972	.95853	.95735	.95616
	7	.96010	.95871	.95732	.95594	.95455	.95317	.95179	.95042	.94904
	8	.95453	.95295	.95138	.94980	.94823	.94666	.94510	.94354	.94198
	9	.94900	.94723	.94547	.94371	.94195	.94020	.93845	.93670	.93496
	10	.94350	.94154	.93960	.93765	.93571	.93378	.93185	.92992	.92800
	11	.93802	.93589	.93376	.93164	.92952	.92740	.92530	.92319	.92109
1	12	.93258	.93027	.92796	.92566	.92336	.92107	.91879	.91651	.91424
2	24	.86971	.86540	.86111	.85684	.85260	.84837	.84417	.83999	.83583
3	36	.81108	.80505	.79908	.79314	.78725	.78141	.77561	.76986	.76415
4	48	.75640	.74892	.74151	.73418	.72692	.71974	.71262	.70558	.69861
5	60	.70541	.69669	.68809	.67960	.67121	.66293	.65475	.64667	.63870
6	72	.65785	.64811	.63852	.62907	.61977	.61060	.60158	.59268	.58392
7	84	.61350	.60292	.59252	.58231	.57227	.56241	.55272	.54320	.53385
8	96	.57214	.56088	.54984	.53902	.52841	.51802	.50783	.49785	.48806
9	108	.53357	.52177	.51023	.49895	.48792	.47713	.46659	.45628	.44620
10	120	.49760	.48538	.47347	.46185	.45052	.43947	.42870	.41819	.40794
11	132	.46405	.45154	.43936	.42752	.41600	.40479	.39388	.38327	.37295
12	144	.43277	.42005	.40771	.39574	.38411	.37284	.36189	.35127	.34097
13	156	.40359	.39076	.37834	.36632	.35468	.34341	.33250	.32195	.31172
14	168	.37638	.36351	.35108	.33908	.32749	.31631	.30550	.29507	.28499
15	180	.35101	.33816	.32579	.31387	.30240	.29134	.28069	.27043	.26055
16	192	.32734	.31458	.30232	.29054	.27922	.26834	.25789	.24785	.23820
17	204	.30527	.29265	.28054	.26894	.25782	.24716	.23695	.22716	.21778
18	216	.28469	.27224	.26033	.24895	.23806	.22766	.21771	.20819	.19910
19	228	.26550	.25326	.24158	.23044	.21982	.20969	.20003	.19081	.18202
20	240	.24760	.23560	.22417	.21331	.20297	.19314	.18378	.17488	.16641
21	252	.23091	.21917	.20802	.19745	.18742	.17789	.16886	.16028	.15214
22	264	.21534	.20388	.19304	.18277	.17305	.16385	.15514	.14690	.13909
23	276	.20082	.18967	.17913	.16918	.15979	.15092	.14254	.13463	.12716
24	288	.18729	.17644	.16623	.15661	.14754	.13901	.13097	.12339	.11626
25	300	.17466	.16414	.15425	.14496	.13624	.12804	.12033	.11309	.10629
26	312	.16288	.15269	.14314	.13419	.12580	.11793	.11056	.10365	.09717
27	324	.15190	.14205	.13283	.12421	.11615	.10862	.10158	.09500	.08884
28	336	.14166	.13214	.12326	.11498	.10725	.10005	.09333	.08706	.08122
29	348	.13211	.12293	.11438	.10643	.09903	.09215	.08575	.07980	.07425
30	360	.12321	.11435	.10614	.09852	.09144	.08488	.07879	.07313	.06789
31	372	.11490	.10638	.09849	.09119	.08444	.07818	.07239	.06703	.06206
32	384	.10715	.09896	.09140	.08441	.07796	.07201	.06651	.06143	.05674
33	396	.09993	.09206	.08481	.07814	.07199	.06633	.06111	.05630	.05188
34	408	.09319	.08564	.07870	.07233	.06647	.06109	.05615	.05160	.04743
35	420	.08691	.07967	.07303	.06695	.06138	.05627	.05159	.04729	.04336
36	432	.08105	.07411	.06777	.06197	.05667	.05183	.04740	.04334	.03964
37	444	.07559	.06895	.06289	.05737	.05233	.04774	.04355	.03973	.03624
38	456	.07049	.06414	.05836	.05310	.04832	.04397	.04001	.03641	.03313
39	468	.06574	.05967	.05416	.04915	.04462	.04050	.03676	.03337	.03029
40	480	.06131	.05551	.05025	.04550	.04120	.03730	.03378	.03058	.02769

PRESENT VALUE OF ONE DOLLAR

ANNUAL INTEREST RATE

PERIOD YR	MOS	.09250	.09500	.09750	.10000	.10250	.10500	.10750	.11000	.11250
	1	.99235	.99215	.99194	.99174	.99153	.99133	.99112	.99092	.99071
	2	.98476	.98435	.98395	.98354	.98313	.98273	.98232	.98192	.98151
	3	.97723	.97662	.97602	.97541	.97481	.97420	.97360	.97300	.97239
	4	.96975	.96895	.96815	.96735	.96655	.96575	.96496	.96416	.96336
	5	.96233	.96134	.96035	.95936	.95836	.95738	.95639	.95540	.95442
	6	.95497	.95379	.95261	.95143	.95025	.94907	.94790	.94672	.94555
	7	.94767	.94630	.94493	.94356	.94220	.94084	.93948	.93812	.93677
	8	.94042	.93886	.93731	.93577	.93422	.93268	.93114	.92960	.92807
	9	.93322	.93149	.92976	.92803	.92631	.92459	.92287	.92116	.91945
	10	.92609	.92417	.92227	.92036	.91846	.91657	.91468	.91279	.91091
	11	.91900	.91692	.91483	.91276	.91068	.90862	.90656	.90450	.90245
1	12	.91197	.90971	.90746	.90521	.90297	.90074	.89851	.89628	.89407
2	24	.83169	.82758	.82348	.81941	.81536	.81132	.80731	.80332	.79935
3	36	.75848	.75286	.74728	.74174	.73624	.73079	.72538	.72001	.71467
4	48	.69172	.68489	.67812	.67143	.66481	.65825	.65176	.64533	.63897
5	60	.63083	.62305	.61537	.60779	.60030	.59291	.58561	.57840	.57128
6	72	.57530	.56680	.55842	.55018	.54205	.53405	.52617	.51841	.51076
7	84	.52465	.51562	.50675	.49803	.48946	.48104	.47277	.46464	.45665
8	96	.47847	.46907	.45985	.45082	.44197	.43329	.42479	.41645	.40828
9	108	.43635	.42672	.41730	.40809	.39908	.39028	.38167	.37326	.36503
10	120	.39794	.38819	.37868	.36941	.36036	.35154	.34294	.33454	.32636
11	132	.36291	.35314	.34364	.33439	.32540	.31664	.30813	.29985	.29179
12	144	.33096	.32126	.31184	.30270	.29382	.28521	.27686	.26875	.26088
13	156	.30183	.29225	.28298	.27400	.26531	.25690	.24876	.24087	.23324
14	168	.27526	.26587	.25679	.24803	.23957	.23140	.22351	.21589	.20853
15	180	.25103	.24186	.23303	.22452	.21633	.20843	.20083	.19350	.18644
16	192	.22893	.22002	.21146	.20324	.19534	.18774	.18044	.17343	.16669
17	204	.20878	.20016	.19190	.18397	.17638	.16910	.16213	.15544	.14903
18	216	.19040	.18209	.17414	.16654	.15927	.15232	.14567	.13932	.13324
19	228	.17364	.16565	.15802	.15075	.14381	.13720	.13089	.12487	.11913
20	240	.15836	.15069	.14340	.13646	.12986	.12358	.11760	.11192	.10651
21	252	.14442	.13709	.13013	.12353	.11726	.11131	.10567	.10031	.09523
22	264	.13170	.12471	.11809	.11182	.10588	.10026	.09494	.08991	.08514
23	276	.12011	.11345	.10716	.10122	.09561	.09031	.08531	.08058	.07612
24	288	.10954	.10321	.09724	.09162	.08633	.08135	.07665	.07222	.06806
25	300	.09990	.09389	.08824	.08294	.07796	.07327	.06887	.06473	.06085
26	312	.09110	.08541	.08008	.07508	.07039	.06600	.06188	.05802	.05440
27	324	.08308	.07770	.07267	.06796	.06356	.05945	.05560	.05200	.04864
28	336	.07577	.07068	.06594	.06152	.05739	.05355	.04996	.04661	.04349
29	348	.06910	.06430	.05984	.05569	.05183	.04823	.04489	.04177	.03888
30	360	.06302	.05850	.05430	.05041	.04680	.04344	.04033	.03744	.03476
31	372	.05747	.05322	.04928	.04563	.04226	.03913	.03624	.03356	.03108
32	384	.05241	.04841	.04472	.04131	.03816	.03525	.03256	.03008	.02779
33	396	.04780	.04404	.04058	.03739	.03445	.03175	.02926	.02696	.02484
34	408	.04359	.04006	.03682	.03385	.03111	.02860	.02629	.02416	.02221
35	420	.03975	.03645	.03342	.03064	.02809	.02576	.02362	.02166	.01986
36	432	.03625	.03316	.03032	.02773	.02537	.02320	.02122	.01941	.01775
37	444	.03306	.03016	.02752	.02511	.02291	.02090	.01907	.01740	.01587
38	456	.03015	.02744	.02497	.02273	.02068	.01882	.01713	.01559	.01419
39	468	.02750	.02496	.02266	.02057	.01868	.01696	.01539	.01398	.01269
40	480	.02508	.02271	.02056	.01862	.01686	.01527	.01383	.01253	.01134

PRESENT VALUE OF ONE DOLLAR

PERIOD YR	MOS	.11500	.11750	.12000	.12250	.12500	.12750	.13000	.13250	.13500
		ANNUAL INTEREST RATE								
	1	.99051	.99030	.99010	.98989	.98969	.98949	.98928	.98908	.98888
	2	.98111	.98070	.98030	.97989	.97949	.97908	.97868	.97828	.97787
	3	.97179	.97119	.97059	.96999	.96939	.96879	.96819	.96759	.96700
	4	.96257	.96177	.96098	.96019	.95940	.95861	.95782	.95703	.95624
	5	.95343	.95245	.95147	.95048	.94951	.94853	.94755	.94657	.94560
	6	.94438	.94321	.94205	.94088	.93972	.93856	.93740	.93624	.93508
	7	.93542	.93407	.93272	.93137	.93003	.92869	.92735	.92601	.92468
	8	.92654	.92501	.92348	.92196	.92044	.91892	.91741	.91590	.91439
	9	.91774	.91604	.91434	.91264	.91095	.90926	.90758	.90590	.90422
	10	.90903	.90716	.90529	.90342	.90156	.89970	.89785	.89600	.89416
	11	.90040	.89836	.89632	.89429	.89227	.89025	.88823	.88622	.88421
1	12	.89185	.88965	.88745	.88526	.88307	.88089	.87871	.87654	.87437
2	24	.79540	.79148	.78757	.78368	.77981	.77596	.77213	.76832	.76453
3	36	.70938	.70413	.69892	.69375	.68862	.68353	.67848	.67346	.66849
4	48	.63267	.62643	.62026	.61415	.60810	.60211	.59619	.59032	.58451
5	60	.56425	.55731	.55045	.54368	.53699	.53039	.52387	.51744	.51108
6	72	.50323	.49581	.48850	.48130	.47420	.46722	.46033	.45355	.44687
7	84	.44880	.44109	.43352	.42607	.41875	.41156	.40450	.39756	.39074
8	96	.40027	.39242	.38472	.37718	.36979	.36254	.35544	.34847	.34165
9	108	.35698	.34911	.34142	.33390	.32655	.31936	.31233	.30545	.29873
10	120	.31838	.31059	.30299	.29559	.28836	.28132	.27444	.26774	.26120
11	132	.28394	.27632	.26889	.26167	.25464	.24781	.24116	.23468	.22839
12	144	.25324	.24582	.23863	.23165	.22487	.21829	.21191	.20571	.19970
13	156	.22585	.21870	.21177	.20507	.19857	.19229	.18620	.18031	.17461
14	168	.20143	.19456	.18794	.18154	.17535	.16938	.16362	.15805	.15267
15	180	.17964	.17309	.16678	.16071	.15485	.14921	.14377	.13854	.13349
16	192	.16021	.15399	.14801	.14227	.13674	.13144	.12634	.12143	.11672
17	204	.14289	.13700	.13135	.12594	.12075	.11578	.11101	.10644	.10206
18	216	.12744	.12188	.11657	.11149	.10663	.10199	.09755	.09330	.08924
19	228	.11365	.10843	.10345	.09870	.09416	.08984	.08572	.08178	.07803
20	240	.10136	.09647	.09181	.08737	.08315	.07914	.07532	.07168	.06823
21	252	.09040	.08582	.08147	.07735	.07343	.06971	.06618	.06283	.05966
22	264	.08062	.07635	.07230	.06847	.06484	.06141	.05816	.05508	.05216
23	276	.07191	.06792	.06417	.06061	.05726	.05409	.05110	.04828	.04561
24	288	.06413	.06043	.05694	.05366	.05057	.04765	.04490	.04232	.03988
25	300	.05719	.05376	.05053	.04750	.04465	.04197	.03946	.03709	.03487
26	312	.05101	.04783	.04485	.04205	.03943	.03698	.03467	.03251	.03049
27	324	.04549	.04255	.03980	.03723	.03482	.03257	.03047	.02850	.02666
28	336	.04057	.03785	.03532	.03296	.03075	.02869	.02677	.02498	.02331
29	348	.03618	.03368	.03134	.02917	.02715	.02527	.02352	.02190	.02038
30	360	.03227	.02996	.02782	.02583	.02398	.02226	.02067	.01919	.01782
31	372	.02878	.02665	.02469	.02286	.02117	.01961	.01816	.01682	.01558
32	384	.02567	.02371	.02191	.02024	.01870	.01728	.01596	.01475	.01362
33	396	.02289	.02110	.01944	.01792	.01651	.01522	.01402	.01293	.01191
34	408	.02042	.01877	.01725	.01586	.01458	.01340	.01232	.01133	.01042
35	420	.01821	.01670	.01531	.01404	.01288	.01181	.01083	.00993	.00911
36	432	.01624	.01485	.01359	.01243	.01137	.01040	.00952	.00870	.00796
37	444	.01448	.01322	.01206	.01100	.01004	.00916	.00836	.00763	.00696
38	456	.01292	.01176	.01070	.00974	.00887	.00807	.00735	.00669	.00609
39	468	.01152	.01046	.00950	.00862	.00783	.00711	.00646	.00586	.00532
40	480	.01027	.00931	.00843	.00763	.00691	.00626	.00567	.00514	.00465

PRESENT VALUE OF ONE DOLLAR

ANNUAL INTEREST RATE

PERIOD YR	MOS	.13750	.14000	.14250	.14500	.14750	.15000	.15250	.15500	.15750
	1	.98867	.98847	.98826	.98806	.98786	.98765	.98745	.98725	.98705
	2	.97747	.97707	.97667	.97626	.97586	.97546	.97506	.97466	.97426
	3	.96640	.96580	.96520	.96461	.96401	.96342	.96282	.96223	.96164
	4	.95545	.95466	.95388	.95309	.95231	.95152	.95074	.94996	.94918
	5	.94463	.94365	.94268	.94171	.94074	.93978	.93881	.93785	.93688
	6	.93393	.93277	.93162	.93047	.92932	.92817	.92703	.92589	.92474
	7	.92335	.92201	.92069	.91936	.91804	.91672	.91540	.91408	.91276
	8	.91288	.91138	.90988	.90838	.90689	.90540	.90391	.90242	.90094
	9	.90254	.90087	.89920	.89754	.89588	.89422	.89257	.89092	.88927
	10	.89232	.89048	.88865	.88682	.88500	.88318	.88137	.87955	.87775
	11	.88221	.88021	.87822	.87624	.87425	.87228	.87031	.86834	.86638
1	12	.87222	.87006	.86792	.86577	.86364	.86151	.85938	.85727	.85515
2	24	.76076	.75701	.75328	.74957	.74587	.74220	.73854	.73490	.73129
3	36	.66355	.65865	.65378	.64895	.64416	.63941	.63469	.63001	.62536
4	48	.57876	.57306	.56743	.56185	.55632	.55086	.54544	.54008	.53478
5	60	.50480	.49860	.49248	.48643	.48046	.47457	.46875	.46300	.45732
6	72	.44030	.43381	.42743	.42114	.41495	.40884	.40283	.39691	.39108
7	84	.38403	.37745	.37097	.36461	.35836	.35222	.34619	.34026	.33443
8	96	.33496	.32840	.32197	.31567	.30950	.30344	.29751	.29169	.28599
9	108	.29216	.28573	.27945	.27330	.26729	.26142	.25567	.25006	.24456
10	120	.25482	.24860	.24254	.23662	.23085	.22521	.21972	.21437	.20914
11	132	.22226	.21630	.21050	.20486	.19937	.19402	.18883	.18377	.17885
12	144	.19386	.18820	.18270	.17736	.17218	.16715	.16227	.15754	.15294
13	156	.16909	.16374	.15857	.15355	.14870	.14400	.13946	.13505	.13079
14	168	.14748	.14247	.13762	.13294	.12842	.12406	.11985	.11578	.11184
15	180	.12864	.12395	.11944	.11510	.11091	.10688	.10299	.09925	.09564
16	192	.11220	.10785	.10367	.09965	.09579	.09208	.08851	.08508	.08179
17	204	.09786	.09383	.08997	.08627	.08273	.07933	.07607	.07294	.06994
18	216	.08536	.08164	.07809	.07469	.07145	.06834	.06537	.06253	.05981
19	228	.07445	.07103	.06778	.06467	.06170	.05888	.05618	.05360	.05115
20	240	.06494	.06180	.05882	.05599	.05329	.05072	.04828	.04595	.04374
21	252	.05664	.05377	.05105	.04847	.04602	.04370	.04149	.03939	.03740
22	264	.04940	.04679	.04431	.04197	.03975	.03765	.03566	.03377	.03199
23	276	.04309	.04071	.03846	.03633	.03433	.03243	.03064	.02895	.02735
24	288	.03758	.03542	.03338	.03146	.02965	.02794	.02633	.02482	.02339
25	300	.03278	.03082	.02897	.02723	.02560	.02407	.02263	.02128	.02000
26	312	.02859	.02681	.02514	.02358	.02211	.02074	.01945	.01824	.01711
27	324	.02494	.02333	.02182	.02041	.01910	.01787	.01671	.01564	.01463
28	336	.02175	.02030	.01894	.01767	.01649	.01539	.01436	.01340	.01251
29	348	.01897	.01766	.01644	.01530	.01424	.01326	.01234	.01149	.01070
30	360	.01655	.01536	.01427	.01325	.01230	.01142	.01061	.00985	.00915
31	372	.01443	.01337	.01238	.01147	.01062	.00984	.00912	.00844	.00782
32	384	.01259	.01163	.01075	.00993	.00918	.00848	.00783	.00724	.00669
33	396	.01098	.01012	.00933	.00860	.00792	.00730	.00673	.00621	.00572
34	408	.00958	.00880	.00810	.00744	.00684	.00629	.00579	.00532	.00489
35	420	.00835	.00766	.00703	.00644	.00591	.00542	.00497	.00456	.00418
36	432	.00729	.00667	.00610	.00558	.00510	.00467	.00427	.00391	.00358
37	444	.00635	.00580	.00529	.00483	.00441	.00402	.00367	.00335	.00306
38	456	.00554	.00505	.00459	.00418	.00381	.00347	.00316	.00287	.00262
39	468	.00483	.00439	.00399	.00362	.00329	.00299	.00271	.00246	.00224
40	480	.00422	.00382	.00346	.00313	.00284	.00257	.00233	.00211	.00191

PRESENT VALUE OF ONE DOLLAR

ANNUAL INTEREST RATE

PERIOD YR	MOS	.16000	.16250	.16500	.16750	.17000	.17250	.17500	.17750	.18000
	1	.98684	.98664	.98644	.98623	.98603	.98583	.98563	.98542	.98522
	2	.97386	.97346	.97306	.97266	.97226	.97186	.97146	.97106	.97066
	3	.96104	.96045	.95986	.95927	.95868	.95809	.95750	.95691	.95632
	4	.94840	.94762	.94684	.94606	.94528	.94451	.94373	.94296	.94219
	5	.93592	.93496	.93400	.93304	.93208	.93112	.93017	.92921	.92826
	6	.92360	.92247	.92133	.92019	.91906	.91793	.91680	.91567	.91454
	7	.91145	.91014	.90883	.90753	.90622	.90492	.90362	.90232	.90103
	8	.89946	.89798	.89651	.89503	.89356	.89210	.89063	.88917	.88771
	9	.88762	.88598	.88435	.88271	.88108	.87945	.87783	.87621	.87459
	10	.87594	.87415	.87235	.87056	.86877	.86699	.86521	.86344	.86167
	11	.86442	.86247	.86052	.85858	.85664	.85470	.85278	.85085	.84893
1	12	.85305	.85094	.84885	.84676	.84467	.84259	.84052	.83845	.83639
2	24	.72769	.72410	.72054	.71700	.71347	.70996	.70647	.70300	.69954
3	36	.62075	.61617	.61163	.60712	.60265	.59821	.59380	.58943	.58509
4	48	.52953	.52433	.51918	.51408	.50904	.50405	.49910	.49421	.48936
5	60	.45171	.44617	.44070	.43530	.42997	.42471	.41950	.41437	.40930
6	72	.38533	.37967	.37409	.36860	.36319	.35785	.35260	.34743	.34233
7	84	.32870	.32308	.31755	.31211	.30677	.30152	.29637	.29130	.28632
8	96	.28040	.27492	.26955	.26428	.25912	.25406	.24910	.24424	.23947
9	108	.23919	.23394	.22881	.22378	.21887	.21407	.20938	.20478	.20029
10	120	.20404	.19907	.19422	.18949	.18488	.18037	.17598	.17170	.16752
11	132	.17406	.16940	.16486	.16045	.15616	.15198	.14792	.14396	.14011
12	144	.14848	.14415	.13994	.13586	.13190	.12806	.12433	.12071	.11719
13	156	.12666	.12266	.11879	.11504	.11142	.10790	.10450	.10121	.09802
14	168	.10805	.10438	.10084	.09741	.09411	.09092	.08783	.08486	.08198
15	180	.09217	.08882	.08559	.08249	.07949	.07661	.07383	.07115	.06857
16	192	.07862	.07558	.07266	.06985	.06714	.06455	.06205	.05965	.05735
17	204	.06707	.06431	.06167	.05914	.05671	.05439	.05216	.05002	.04797
18	216	.05721	.05473	.05235	.05008	.04791	.04583	.04384	.04194	.04012
19	228	.04881	.04657	.04444	.04240	.04046	.03861	.03685	.03516	.03355
20	240	.04163	.03963	.03772	.03591	.03418	.03254	.03097	.02948	.02806
21	252	.03552	.03372	.03202	.03040	.02887	.02741	.02603	.02472	.02347
22	264	.03030	.02870	.02718	.02574	.02439	.02310	.02188	.02073	.01963
23	276	.02584	.02442	.02307	.02180	.02060	.01946	.01839	.01738	.01642
24	288	.02205	.02078	.01958	.01846	.01740	.01640	.01546	.01457	.01373
25	300	.01881	.01768	.01662	.01563	.01470	.01382	.01299	.01222	.01149
26	312	.01604	.01505	.01411	.01324	.01241	.01164	.01092	.01024	.00961
27	324	.01369	.01280	.01198	.01121	.01049	.00981	.00918	.00859	.00804
28	336	.01167	.01089	.01017	.00949	.00886	.00827	.00771	.00720	.00672
29	348	.00996	.00927	.00863	.00804	.00748	.00696	.00648	.00604	.00562
30	360	.00849	.00789	.00733	.00680	.00632	.00587	.00545	.00506	.00470
31	372	.00725	.00671	.00622	.00576	.00534	.00494	.00458	.00424	.00393
32	384	.00618	.00571	.00528	.00488	.00451	.00417	.00385	.00356	.00329
33	396	.00527	.00486	.00448	.00413	.00381	.00351	.00324	.00298	.00275
34	408	.00450	.00414	.00380	.00350	.00322	.00296	.00272	.00250	.00230
35	420	.00384	.00352	.00323	.00296	.00272	.00249	.00229	.00210	.00192
36	432	.00327	.00300	.00274	.00251	.00229	.00210	.00192	.00176	.00161
37	444	.00279	.00255	.00233	.00212	.00194	.00177	.00162	.00147	.00135
38	456	.00238	.00217	.00197	.00180	.00164	.00149	.00136	.00124	.00113
39	468	.00203	.00185	.00168	.00152	.00138	.00126	.00114	.00104	.00094
40	480	.00173	.00157	.00142	.00129	.00117	.00106	.00096	.00087	.00079

PRESENT VALUE OF ONE DOLLAR

ANNUAL INTEREST RATE

PERIOD YR	MOS	.18250	.18500	.18750	.19000	.19250	.19500	.19750	.20000	.20250
	1	.98502	.98482	.98462	.98441	.98421	.98401	.98381	.98361	.98341
	2	.97026	.96987	.96947	.96907	.96867	.96828	.96788	.96748	.96709
	3	.95573	.95514	.95455	.95397	.95338	.95279	.95221	.95162	.95104
	4	.94141	.94064	.93987	.93910	.93833	.93756	.93679	.93602	.93525
	5	.92731	.92636	.92541	.92446	.92351	.92257	.92162	.92068	.91973
	6	.91342	.91229	.91117	.91005	.90893	.90781	.90670	.90558	.90447
	7	.89973	.89844	.89715	.89587	.89458	.89330	.89202	.89074	.88946
	8	.88625	.88480	.88335	.88190	.88046	.87901	.87757	.87614	.87470
	9	.87298	.87137	.86976	.86816	.86656	.86496	.86336	.86177	.86019
	10	.85990	.85814	.85638	.85462	.85287	.85113	.84938	.84765	.84591
	11	.84702	.84511	.84320	.84130	.83941	.83752	.83563	.83375	.83187
1	12	.83433	.83228	.83023	.82819	.82616	.82413	.82210	.82008	.81807
2	24	.69611	.69269	.68928	.68590	.68253	.67918	.67585	.67253	.66923
3	36	.58078	.57651	.57227	.56806	.56388	.55973	.55562	.55153	.54748
4	48	.48456	.47982	.47511	.47046	.46585	.46129	.45677	.45230	.44787
5	60	.40429	.39934	.39445	.38963	.38487	.38016	.37551	.37092	.36639
6	72	.33731	.33236	.32749	.32269	.31796	.31330	.30871	.30419	.29973
7	84	.28143	.27662	.27189	.26725	.26268	.25820	.25379	.24946	.24520
8	96	.23480	.23022	.22573	.22133	.21702	.21279	.20864	.20458	.20059
9	108	.19590	.19161	.18741	.18331	.17929	.17536	.17152	.16777	.16410
10	120	.16345	.15947	.15559	.15181	.14812	.14452	.14101	.13758	.13424
11	132	.13637	.13273	.12918	.12573	.12237	.11910	.11592	.11283	.10982
12	144	.11378	.11046	.10725	.10413	.10110	.09816	.09530	.09253	.08984
13	156	.09493	.09194	.08904	.08624	.08352	.08089	.07835	.07588	.07350
14	168	.07920	.07652	.07393	.07142	.06900	.06667	.06441	.06223	.06012
15	180	.06608	.06368	.06137	.05915	.05701	.05494	.05295	.05103	.04919
16	192	.05513	.05300	.05096	.04899	.04710	.04528	.04353	.04185	.04024
17	204	.04600	.04411	.04230	.04057	.03891	.03732	.03579	.03432	.03292
18	216	.03838	.03671	.03512	.03360	.03214	.03075	.02942	.02815	.02693
19	228	.03202	.03056	.02916	.02783	.02656	.02534	.02419	.02308	.02203
20	240	.02672	.02543	.02421	.02305	.02194	.02089	.01988	.01893	.01802
21	252	.02229	.02117	.02010	.01909	.01813	.01721	.01635	.01552	.01474
22	264	.01860	.01762	.01669	.01581	.01497	.01419	.01344	.01273	.01206
23	276	.01552	.01466	.01385	.01309	.01237	.01169	.01105	.01044	.00987
24	288	.01295	.01220	.01150	.01084	.01022	.00963	.00908	.00856	.00807
25	300	.01080	.01016	.00955	.00898	.00844	.00794	.00747	.00702	.00660
26	312	.00901	.00845	.00793	.00744	.00698	.00654	.00614	.00576	.00540
27	324	.00752	.00703	.00658	.00616	.00576	.00539	.00505	.00472	.00442
28	336	.00627	.00585	.00546	.00510	.00476	.00444	.00415	.00387	.00361
29	348	.00523	.00487	.00454	.00422	.00393	.00366	.00341	.00318	.00296
30	360	.00437	.00406	.00377	.00350	.00325	.00302	.00280	.00260	.00242
31	372	.00364	.00338	.00313	.00290	.00268	.00249	.00231	.00214	.00198
32	384	.00304	.00281	.00260	.00240	.00222	.00205	.00189	.00175	.00162
33	396	.00254	.00234	.00216	.00199	.00183	.00169	.00156	.00144	.00132
34	408	.00212	.00195	.00179	.00165	.00151	.00139	.00128	.00118	.00108
35	420	.00177	.00162	.00149	.00136	.00125	.00115	.00105	.00097	.00089
36	432	.00147	.00135	.00123	.00113	.00103	.00095	.00087	.00079	.00073
37	444	.00123	.00112	.00102	.00094	.00085	.00078	.00071	.00065	.00059
38	456	.00103	.00093	.00085	.00077	.00071	.00064	.00058	.00053	.00049
39	468	.00086	.00078	.00071	.00064	.00058	.00053	.00048	.00044	.00040
40	480	.00071	.00065	.00059	.00053	.00048	.00044	.00040	.00036	.00032

PRESENT VALUE OF ONE DOLLAR

PERIOD YR	MOS	.20500	.20750	.21000	.21250	.21500	.21750	.22000	.22250	.22500
		ANNUAL INTEREST RATE								
	1	.98320	.98300	.98280	.98260	.98240	.98220	.98200	.98180	.98160
	2	.96669	.96629	.96590	.96550	.96511	.96471	.96432	.96392	.96353
	3	.95045	.94987	.94929	.94870	.94812	.94754	.94696	.94638	.94580
	4	.93449	.93372	.93296	.93219	.93143	.93067	.92991	.92915	.92839
	5	.91879	.91785	.91691	.91597	.91504	.91410	.91317	.91223	.91130
	6	.90336	.90225	.90114	.90004	.89893	.89783	.89673	.89563	.89453
	7	.88819	.88691	.88564	.88438	.88311	.88185	.88058	.87932	.87806
	8	.87327	.87184	.87041	.86899	.86757	.86615	.86473	.86332	.86190
	9	.85860	.85702	.85544	.85387	.85230	.85073	.84916	.84760	.84604
	10	.84418	.84245	.84073	.83901	.83729	.83558	.83387	.83217	.83047
	11	.83000	.82813	.82627	.82441	.82256	.82071	.81886	.81702	.81518
1	12	.81606	.81406	.81206	.81007	.80808	.80610	.80412	.80215	.80018
2	24	.66595	.66269	.65944	.65621	.65299	.64979	.64661	.64344	.64029
3	36	.54346	.53946	.53550	.53157	.52767	.52379	.51995	.51613	.51235
4	48	.44349	.43915	.43486	.43061	.42640	.42223	.41810	.41402	.40997
5	60	.36192	.35750	.35313	.34882	.34456	.34036	.33620	.33210	.32805
6	72	.29534	.29102	.28676	.28257	.27843	.27436	.27035	.26640	.26250
7	84	.24102	.23691	.23287	.22890	.22500	.22116	.21739	.21369	.21005
8	96	.19669	.19286	.18910	.18542	.18181	.17828	.17481	.17141	.16808
9	108	.16051	.15700	.15356	.15020	.14692	.14371	.14057	.13750	.13449
10	120	.13098	.12780	.12470	.12167	.11872	.11584	.11303	.11029	.10762
11	132	.10689	.10404	.10126	.09856	.09594	.09338	.09089	.08847	.08611
12	144	.08723	.08469	.08223	.07984	.07752	.07527	.07309	.07097	.06891
13	156	.07118	.06895	.06678	.06468	.06265	.06068	.05877	.05693	.05514
14	168	.05809	.05613	.05423	.05239	.05062	.04891	.04726	.04566	.04412
15	180	.04740	.04569	.04404	.04244	.04091	.03943	.03800	.03663	.03530
16	192	.03869	.03719	.03576	.03438	.03306	.03178	.03056	.02938	.02825
17	204	.03157	.03028	.02904	.02785	.02671	.02562	.02457	.02357	.02261
18	216	.02576	.02465	.02358	.02256	.02159	.02065	.01976	.01891	.01809
19	228	.02102	.02006	.01915	.01828	.01744	.01665	.01589	.01516	.01447
20	240	.01716	.01633	.01555	.01480	.01410	.01342	.01278	.01216	.01158
21	252	.01400	.01330	.01263	.01199	.01139	.01082	.01027	.00976	.00927
22	264	.01143	.01082	.01025	.00971	.00920	.00872	.00826	.00783	.00742
23	276	.00932	.00881	.00833	.00787	.00744	.00703	.00664	.00628	.00593
24	288	.00761	.00717	.00676	.00638	.00601	.00567	.00534	.00504	.00475
25	300	.00621	.00584	.00549	.00516	.00486	.00457	.00430	.00404	.00380
26	312	.00507	.00475	.00446	.00418	.00392	.00368	.00345	.00324	.00304
27	324	.00414	.00387	.00362	.00339	.00317	.00297	.00278	.00260	.00243
28	336	.00337	.00315	.00294	.00275	.00256	.00239	.00223	.00209	.00195
29	348	.00275	.00256	.00239	.00222	.00207	.00193	.00180	.00167	.00156
30	360	.00225	.00209	.00194	.00180	.00167	.00155	.00144	.00134	.00125
31	372	.00183	.00170	.00157	.00146	.00135	.00125	.00116	.00108	.00100
32	384	.00150	.00138	.00128	.00118	.00109	.00101	.00093	.00086	.00080
33	396	.00122	.00113	.00104	.00096	.00088	.00081	.00075	.00069	.00064
34	408	.00100	.00092	.00084	.00078	.00071	.00066	.00060	.00056	.00051
35	420	.00081	.00075	.00068	.00063	.00058	.00053	.00049	.00045	.00041
36	432	.00066	.00061	.00056	.00051	.00047	.00043	.00039	.00036	.00033
37	444	.00054	.00049	.00045	.00041	.00038	.00034	.00031	.00029	.00026
38	456	.00044	.00040	.00037	.00033	.00030	.00028	.00025	.00023	.00021
39	468	.00036	.00033	.00030	.00027	.00025	.00022	.00020	.00018	.00017
40	480	.00029	.00027	.00024	.00022	.00020	.00018	.00016	.00015	.00013

PRESENT VALUE OF ONE DOLLAR

ANNUAL INTEREST RATE

PERIOD YR	MOS	.22750	.23000	.23250	.23500	.23750	.24000	.24250	.24500	.24750
	1	.98139	.98119	.98099	.98079	.98059	.98039	.98019	.97999	.97979
	2	.96313	.96274	.96235	.96195	.96156	.96117	.96078	.96038	.95999
	3	.94522	.94464	.94406	.94348	.94290	.94232	.94175	.94117	.94059
	4	.92763	.92687	.92611	.92536	.92460	.92385	.92309	.92234	.92158
	5	.91037	.90944	.90851	.90758	.90666	.90573	.90481	.90388	.90296
	6	.89343	.89234	.89124	.89015	.88906	.88797	.88688	.88580	.88471
	7	.87681	.87556	.87430	.87305	.87181	.87056	.86932	.86807	.86684
	8	.86050	.85909	.85769	.85628	.85489	.85349	.85210	.85071	.84932
	9	.84449	.84293	.84138	.83984	.83829	.83676	.83522	.83369	.83215
	10	.82877	.82708	.82539	.82371	.82203	.82035	.81867	.81700	.81534
	11	.81335	.81153	.80970	.80789	.80607	.80426	.80246	.80066	.79886
1	12	.79822	.79626	.79431	.79237	.79043	.78849	.78656	.78464	.78272
2	24	.63716	.63404	.63093	.62785	.62478	.62172	.61868	.61566	.61265
3	36	.50859	.50486	.50116	.49749	.49384	.49022	.48663	.48307	.47953
4	48	.40597	.40200	.39808	.39419	.39035	.38654	.38277	.37903	.37534
5	60	.32405	.32010	.31620	.31235	.30854	.30478	.30107	.29740	.29378
6	72	.25866	.25489	.25116	.24749	.24388	.24032	.23681	.23335	.22995
7	84	.20647	.20296	.19950	.19611	.19277	.18949	.18627	.18310	.17999
8	96	.16481	.16161	.15847	.15539	.15237	.14941	.14651	.14367	.14088
9	108	.13155	.12868	.12587	.12312	.12044	.11781	.11524	.11273	.11027
10	120	.10501	.10246	.09998	.09756	.09520	.09289	.09064	.08845	.08631
11	132	.08382	.08159	.07942	.07730	.07525	.07324	.07130	.06940	.06756
12	144	.06691	.06497	.06308	.06125	.05948	.05775	.05608	.05445	.05288
13	156	.05341	.05173	.05011	.04853	.04701	.04554	.04411	.04273	.04139
14	168	.04263	.04119	.03980	.03846	.03716	.03591	.03470	.03353	.03240
15	180	.03403	.03280	.03161	.03047	.02937	.02831	.02729	.02631	.02536
16	192	.02716	.02612	.02511	.02415	.02322	.02232	.02147	.02064	.01985
17	204	.02168	.02080	.01995	.01913	.01835	.01760	.01688	.01620	.01553
18	216	.01731	.01656	.01584	.01516	.01451	.01388	.01328	.01271	.01216
19	228	.01381	.01319	.01258	.01201	.01147	.01094	.01045	.00997	.00952
20	240	.01103	.01050	.01000	.00952	.00906	.00863	.00822	.00782	.00745
21	252	.00880	.00836	.00794	.00754	.00716	.00680	.00646	.00614	.00583
22	264	.00703	.00666	.00631	.00598	.00566	.00536	.00508	.00482	.00456
23	276	.00561	.00530	.00501	.00474	.00448	.00423	.00400	.00378	.00357
24	288	.00448	.00422	.00398	.00375	.00354	.00334	.00314	.00297	.00280
25	300	.00357	.00336	.00316	.00297	.00280	.00263	.00247	.00233	.00219
26	312	.00285	.00268	.00251	.00236	.00221	.00207	.00195	.00183	.00171
27	324	.00228	.00213	.00199	.00187	.00175	.00164	.00153	.00143	.00134
28	336	.00182	.00170	.00158	.00148	.00138	.00129	.00120	.00112	.00105
29	348	.00145	.00135	.00126	.00117	.00109	.00102	.00095	.00088	.00082
30	360	.00116	.00108	.00100	.00093	.00086	.00080	.00074	.00069	.00064
31	372	.00092	.00086	.00079	.00074	.00068	.00063	.00059	.00054	.00050
32	384	.00074	.00068	.00063	.00058	.00054	.00050	.00046	.00043	.00039
33	396	.00059	.00054	.00050	.00046	.00043	.00039	.00036	.00033	.00031
34	408	.00047	.00043	.00040	.00037	.00034	.00031	.00029	.00026	.00024
35	420	.00038	.00034	.00032	.00029	.00027	.00024	.00022	.00021	.00019
36	432	.00030	.00027	.00025	.00023	.00021	.00019	.00018	.00016	.00015
37	444	.00024	.00022	.00020	.00018	.00017	.00015	.00014	.00013	.00012
38	456	.00019	.00017	.00016	.00014	.00013	.00012	.00011	.00010	.00009
39	468	.00015	.00014	.00013	.00011	.00010	.00009	.00009	.00008	.00007
40	480	.00012	.00011	.00010	.00009	.00008	.00007	.00007	.00006	.00006

FUTURE VALUE OF ONE PER PERIOD TABLE

Description:

The Future Value of One Per Period table, also known as future value of an annuity, may be used to find what a series of equal dollar flows will be worth in the future, with a given interest rate and term. To use the table, find the factor corresponding to the appropriate interest rate and term; then multiply the factor by the amount of the period flow.

Table Calculation Formula:

$$FV_a = \frac{(1+i)^n - 1}{i}.$$

Table Range:

Annual interest rate, with monthly compounding, from 7.00% to 24.75% in .25% increments. Term from 1 to 12 months in 1-month increments, 1 to 40 years in 1-year increments. Flows assumed made at the end of the compounding period.

Example:

What is the future value of a stream of $50 per month for 4 years, with an annual yield of 12.75%, monthly compounding, payments made at the end of the month?

Solution:

Finding the table factor corresponding to 12.75% interest and 4 years provides:

$$FV_a = \$50 \times \text{table factor } FV_a,\ 12.75\%,\ 4 \text{ years},$$

$$= \$50(62.19454),$$

$$= \$3{,}109.73.$$

If monthly deposits of $50 are made, after 4 years the value will grow to $3,109.73, assuming a 12.75% annual yield, with monthly compounding.

FUTURE VALUE OF ONE DOLLAR PER PERIOD

ANNUAL INTEREST RATE

PERIOD YR	MOS	.07000	.07250	.07500	.07750	.08000	.08250	.08500	.08750	.09000
	1	1.00000	1.00000	1.00000	1.00000	1.00000	1.00000	1.00000	1.00000	1.00000
	2	2.00583	2.00604	2.00625	2.00646	2.00667	2.00687	2.00708	2.00729	2.00750
	3	3.01753	3.01816	3.01879	3.01942	3.02004	3.02067	3.02130	3.02193	3.02256
	4	4.03514	4.03640	4.03766	4.03892	4.04018	4.04144	4.04270	4.04396	4.04523
	5	5.05867	5.06078	5.06289	5.06500	5.06711	5.06922	5.07134	5.07345	5.07556
	6	6.08818	6.09136	6.09453	6.09771	6.10089	6.10408	6.10726	6.11044	6.11363
	7	7.12370	7.12816	7.13263	7.13709	7.14157	7.14604	7.15052	7.15500	7.15948
	8	8.16525	8.17123	8.17720	8.18319	8.18918	8.19517	8.20117	8.20717	8.21318
	9	9.21288	9.22059	9.22831	9.23604	9.24377	9.25151	9.25926	9.26702	9.27478
	10	10.26663	10.27630	10.28599	10.29569	10.30540	10.31512	10.32485	10.33459	10.34434
	11	11.32651	11.33839	11.35028	11.36218	11.37410	11.38603	11.39798	11.40994	11.42192
1	12	12.39259	12.40689	12.42122	12.43556	12.44993	12.46431	12.47872	12.49314	12.50759
2	24	25.68103	25.74378	25.80672	25.86986	25.93319	25.99672	26.06044	26.12436	26.18847
3	36	39.93010	40.08038	40.23138	40.38311	40.53556	40.68874	40.84266	40.99732	41.15272
4	48	55.20924	55.49163	55.77586	56.06196	56.34992	56.63976	56.93149	57.22514	57.52071
5	60	71.59290	72.05808	72.52711	73.00002	73.47686	73.95765	74.44244	74.93125	75.42414
6	72	89.16094	89.86632	90.57879	91.29843	92.02533	92.75955	93.50119	94.25032	95.00703
7	84	107.99898	109.00944	110.03187	111.06644	112.11331	113.17263	114.24456	115.32927	116.42693
8	96	128.19882	129.58749	130.99515	132.42208	133.86858	135.33494	136.82145	138.32843	139.85616
9	108	149.85891	151.70804	153.58586	155.49286	157.42954	159.39639	161.39394	163.42271	165.48322
10	120	173.08481	175.48670	177.93034	180.41652	182.94604	185.51972	188.13842	190.80298	193.51428
11	132	197.98971	201.04778	204.16475	207.34187	210.58039	213.88161	217.24686	220.67747	224.17484
12	144	224.69498	228.52487	232.43581	236.42968	240.50839	244.67390	248.92822	253.27341	257.71157
13	156	253.33079	258.06159	262.90162	267.85361	272.92039	278.10484	283.40993	288.83870	294.39428
14	168	284.03668	289.81234	295.73257	301.80130	308.02257	314.40055	320.93950	327.64384	334.51808
15	180	316.96230	323.94307	331.11228	338.47543	346.03822	353.80652	361.78635	369.98396	378.40577
16	192	352.26811	360.63218	369.23860	378.09497	387.20915	396.58926	406.24369	416.18110	426.41043
17	204	390.12619	400.07145	410.32477	420.89647	431.79724	443.03816	454.63066	466.58660	478.91825
18	216	430.72103	442.46701	454.60056	467.13549	480.08613	493.46735	507.29459	521.58383	536.35167
19	228	474.25047	488.04048	502.31360	517.08810	532.38297	548.21794	564.61353	581.59108	599.17275
20	240	520.92666	537.03005	553.73073	571.05255	589.02042	607.66022	626.99895	647.06474	667.88687
21	252	570.97708	589.69180	609.13950	629.35106	650.35875	672.19623	694.89867	718.50277	743.04685
22	264	624.64564	646.30099	668.84979	692.33169	716.78813	742.26248	768.80011	796.44851	825.25736
23	276	682.19391	707.15350	733.19556	760.37048	788.73111	818.33285	849.23377	881.49479	915.17978
24	288	743.90235	772.56741	802.53665	833.87368	866.64533	900.92185	936.77702	974.28842	1013.53754
25	300	810.07169	842.88464	877.26087	913.28013	951.02639	990.58808	1032.05831	1075.53516	1121.12194
26	312	881.02443	918.47273	957.78613	999.06396	1042.41104	1087.93800	1135.76159	1186.00506	1238.79849
27	324	957.10634	999.72677	1044.56277	1091.73734	1141.38057	1193.63005	1248.63131	1306.53831	1367.51392
28	336	1038.68822	1087.07148	1138.07611	1191.85360	1248.56452	1308.37907	1371.47768	1438.05163	1508.30375
29	348	1126.16766	1180.96339	1238.84913	1300.01050	1364.64469	1432.96118	1505.18255	1581.54527	1562.30063
30	360	1219.97100	1281.89329	1347.44542	1416.85380	1490.35945	1568.21900	1650.70571	1738.11057	1830.74348
31	372	1320.55538	1390.38872	1464.47233	1543.08114	1626.50847	1715.06735	1809.09180	1908.93833	2014.98744
32	384	1428.41102	1507.01678	1590.58434	1679.44617	1773.95780	1874.49945	1981.47778	2095.32777	2216.51474
33	396	1544.06356	1632.38708	1726.48675	1826.76309	1933.64535	2047.59363	2169.10111	2298.69652	2436.94670
34	408	1668.07662	1767.15493	1872.93962	1985.91147	2106.58689	2235.52062	2373.30864	2520.59130	2678.05670
35	420	1801.05460	1912.02475	2030.76201	2157.84153	2293.88248	2439.55147	2595.56626	2762.69978	2941.78447
36	432	1943.64557	2067.75376	2200.83655	2343.57982	2496.72353	2661.06616	2837.46943	3026.86333	3230.25173
37	444	2096.54445	2235.15595	2384.11443	2544.23530	2716.40027	2901.56293	3100.75463	3315.09107	3545.77922
38	456	2260.49640	2415.10632	2581.62065	2761.00602	2954.31008	3162.66837	3387.31186	3629.57516	3890.90535
39	468	2436.30046	2608.54547	2794.45978	2995.18625	3211.96629	3446.14850	3699.19814	3972.70743	4268.40670
40	480	2624.81340	2816.48449	3023.82217	3248.17420	3491.00783	3753.92064	4038.65233	4347.09761	4681.32027

FUTURE VALUE OF ONE DOLLAR PER PERIOD

ANNUAL INTEREST RATE

PERIOD YR	MOS	.09250	.09500	.09750	.10000	.10250	.10500	.10750	.11000	.11250
	1	1.00000	1.00000	1.00000	1.00000	1.00000	1.00000	1.00000	1.00000	1.00000
	2	2.00771	2.00792	2.00813	2.00833	2.00854	2.00875	2.00896	2.00917	2.00937
	3	3.02318	3.02381	3.02444	3.02507	3.02570	3.02633	3.02696	3.02758	3.02821
	4	4.04649	4.04775	4.04901	4.05028	4.05154	4.05281	4.05407	4.05534	4.05660
	5	5.07768	5.07980	5.08191	5.08403	5.08615	5.08827	5.09039	5.09251	5.09463
	6	6.11682	6.12001	6.12320	6.12640	6.12959	6.13279	6.13599	6.13919	6.14240
	7	7.16397	7.16846	7.17295	7.17745	7.18195	7.18645	7.19096	7.19547	7.19998
	8	8.21919	8.22521	8.23123	8.23726	8.24330	8.24933	8.25538	8.26143	8.26748
	9	9.28255	9.29033	9.29811	9.30591	9.31371	9.32152	9.32933	9.33716	9.34499
	10	10.35410	10.36388	10.37366	10.38346	10.39326	10.40308	10.41291	10.42275	10.43260
	11	11.43392	11.44592	11.45795	11.46998	11.48204	11.49411	11.50619	11.51829	11.53040
1	12	12.52205	12.53654	12.55104	12.56557	12.58011	12.59468	12.60927	12.62387	12.63850
2	24	26.25278	26.31729	26.38201	26.44692	26.51203	26.57734	26.64285	26.70857	26.77448
3	36	41.30886	41.46576	41.62341	41.78182	41.94099	42.10093	42.26164	42.42312	42.58538
4	48	57.81822	58.11767	58.41909	58.72249	59.02788	59.33528	59.64470	59.95615	60.26965
5	60	75.92112	76.42225	76.92755	77.43707	77.95085	78.46891	78.99131	79.51808	80.04926
6	72	95.77140	96.54351	97.32345	98.11131	98.90718	99.71114	100.52328	101.34369	102.17247
7	84	117.53770	118.66176	119.79927	120.95042	122.11538	123.29433	124.48745	125.69494	126.91697
8	96	141.40498	142.97519	144.56711	146.18108	147.81742	149.47647	151.15858	152.86408	154.59335
9	108	167.57602	169.70166	171.86070	174.05371	176.28127	178.54397	180.84241	183.17721	185.54899
10	120	196.27321	199.08068	201.93762	204.84498	207.80371	210.81481	213.87928	216.99814	220.17243
11	132	227.74036	231.37550	235.08170	238.86049	242.71341	246.64201	250.64792	254.73278	258.89827
12	144	262.24486	266.87549	271.60572	276.43788	281.37432	286.41749	291.56988	296.83404	302.21257
13	156	300.07987	305.89878	311.85436	317.95010	324.18955	330.57637	337.11430	343.80720	350.65901
14	168	341.56688	348.79503	356.20745	363.80920	371.60550	379.60171	387.80333	396.21604	404.84568
15	180	387.05838	395.94863	405.08353	414.47035	424.11654	434.02981	444.21809	454.68957	465.45270
16	192	436.94092	447.78211	458.94387	470.43638	482.27015	494.45607	507.00535	519.92960	533.24079
17	204	491.63832	504.75994	518.29673	532.26278	546.67267	561.54151	576.88493	592.71912	609.06083
18	216	551.61534	567.39268	583.70223	600.56322	617.99558	636.02000	654.65797	673.93176	693.86447
19	228	617.38159	636.24157	655.77761	676.01560	696.98249	718.70628	741.21610	764.54223	788.71616
20	240	689.49587	711.92355	735.20303	759.36884	784.45696	810.50488	837.55166	865.63804	894.80643
21	252	768.57093	795.11677	822.72803	851.45024	881.33100	912.41999	944.76910	978.43254	1013.46691
22	264	855.27863	886.56673	919.17859	953.17378	988.61466	1025.56650	1064.09761	1104.27949	1146.18698
23	276	950.35572	987.09287	1025.46491	1065.54910	1107.42650	1151.18215	1196.90522	1244.68929	1294.63252
24	288	1054.61005	1097.59599	1142.59001	1189.69158	1239.00529	1290.64107	1344.71452	1401.34716	1460.66677
25	300	1168.92744	1219.06628	1271.65920	1326.83340	1384.72289	1445.46885	1509.22007	1576.13330	1646.37374
26	312	1294.27922	1352.59220	1413.89052	1478.33577	1546.09859	1617.35919	1692.30783	1771.14548	1854.08438
27	324	1431.73046	1499.37025	1570.62618	1645.70241	1724.81495	1808.19243	1896.07683	1988.72425	2086.40580
28	336	1582.44908	1660.71566	1743.34532	1830.59452	1922.73529	2020.05616	2122.86316	2231.48098	2346.25405
29	348	1747.71568	1838.07421	1933.67787	2034.84726	2141.92320	2255.26800	2375.26683	2502.32924	2636.89066
30	360	1928.93450	2033.03517	2143.42000	2260.48792	2384.66397	2516.40099	2656.18151	2804.51974	2961.96362
31	372	2127.64531	2247.34554	2374.55106	2509.75612	2653.48849	2806.31174	2968.82776	3141.67937	3325.55316
32	384	2345.53651	2482.92569	2629.25221	2785.12595	2951.19958	3128.17166	3316.78991	3517.85472	3732.22294
33	396	2584.45947	2741.88661	2909.92709	3089.33060	3280.90125	3485.50165	3704.05717	3937.56065	4187.07738
34	408	2846.44427	3026.54877	3219.22440	3425.38945	3646.03107	3882.21064	4135.06937	4405.83446	4695.82567
35	420	3133.71693	3339.46295	3560.06300	3796.63805	4050.39596	4322.63833	4614.76785	4928.29637	5264.85347
36	432	3448.71834	3683.43312	3935.65937	4206.76124	4498.21194	4811.60266	5148.65211	5511.21696	5901.30307
37	444	3794.12499	4061.54150	4349.55801	4659.82968	4994.14805	5354.45256	5742.84289	6161.59245	6613.16300
38	456	4172.87172	4477.17622	4805.66489	5160.34030	5543.37505	5957.12639	6404.15227	6887.22863	7409.36831
39	468	4588.17666	4934.06168	5308.28428	5713.26094	6151.61930	6626.21695	7140.16184	7696.83458	8299.91276
40	480	5043.56855	5436.29191	5862.15939	6324.07958	6825.22253	7369.04360	7959.30959	8600.12720	9295.97421

FUTURE VALUE OF ONE DOLLAR PER PERIOD

ANNUAL INTEREST RATE

PERIOD YR	MOS	.11500	.11750	.12000	.12250	.12500	.12750	.13000	.13250	.13500
	1	1.00000	1.00000	1.00000	1.00000	1.00000	1.00000	1.00000	1.00000	1.00000
	2	2.00958	2.00979	2.01000	2.01021	2.01042	2.01062	2.01083	2.01104	2.01125
	3	3.02884	3.02947	3.03010	3.03073	3.03136	3.03199	3.03262	3.03325	3.03388
	4	4.05787	4.05913	4.06040	4.06167	4.06294	4.06420	4.06547	4.06674	4.06801
	5	5.09676	5.09888	5.10101	5.10313	5.10526	5.10738	5.10951	5.11164	5.11377
	6	6.14560	6.14881	6.15202	6.15523	6.15844	6.16165	6.16487	6.16808	6.17130
	7	7.20450	7.20901	7.21354	7.21806	7.22259	7.22712	7.23165	7.23619	7.24073
	8	8.27354	8.27960	8.28567	8.29174	8.29782	8.30391	8.31000	8.31609	8.32219
	9	9.35283	9.36067	9.36853	9.37639	9.38426	9.39214	9.40002	9.40791	9.41581
	10	10.44246	10.45233	10.46221	10.47211	10.48201	10.49193	10.50185	10.51179	10.52174
	11	11.54253	11.55468	11.56683	11.57901	11.59120	11.60340	11.61562	11.62786	11.64011
1	12	12.65315	12.66781	12.68250	12.69721	12.71194	12.72669	12.74146	12.75625	12.77106
2	24	26.84061	26.90693	26.97346	27.04020	27.10715	27.17430	27.24166	27.30922	27.37700
3	36	42.74843	42.91226	43.07688	43.24229	43.40851	43.57552	43.74335	43.91198	44.08143
4	48	60.58522	60.90287	61.22261	61.54446	61.86843	62.19454	62.52281	62.85325	63.18587
5	60	80.58489	81.12501	81.66967	82.21890	82.77274	83.33125	83.89445	84.46240	85.03513
6	72	103.00971	103.85550	104.70993	105.57311	106.44512	107.32608	108.21607	109.11520	110.02356
7	84	128.15374	129.40545	130.67227	131.95443	133.25211	134.56552	135.89486	137.24035	138.60220
8	96	156.34673	158.12459	159.92729	161.75522	163.60876	165.48830	167.39423	169.32694	171.28685
9	108	187.95837	190.40602	192.89258	195.41872	197.98513	200.59250	203.24153	205.93294	208.66746
10	120	223.40323	226.69161	230.03869	233.44559	236.91348	240.44352	244.03692	247.69489	251.41870
11	132	263.14610	267.47803	271.89586	276.40141	280.99657	285.68324	290.46340	295.33904	300.31220
12	144	307.70817	313.32356	319.06156	324.92504	330.91696	337.04033	343.29824	349.69387	356.23045
13	156	357.67380	364.85572	372.20905	379.73818	387.44762	395.34198	403.42601	411.70459	420.18272
14	168	413.69823	422.77988	432.09698	441.65606	451.46384	461.52724	471.85336	482.44954	493.32330
15	180	476.51615	487.88890	499.58020	511.59957	523.95684	536.66214	549.72591	563.15894	576.97231
16	192	546.95132	561.07398	575.62197	590.60897	606.04907	621.95686	638.34741	655.23627	672.63955
17	204	625.92742	643.33686	661.30775	679.85936	699.01163	718.78523	739.20154	760.28272	782.05172
18	216	714.48011	735.80355	757.86063	780.67815	804.28393	828.73683	853.97683	880.12500	907.18362
19	228	813.77063	839.73972	866.65883	894.56481	923.49597	953.49216	984.59483	1016.84709	1050.29378
20	240	925.10106	956.56802	989.25537	1023.21316	1058.49359	1095.15109	1133.24235	1172.82652	1213.96522
21	252	1049.93134	1087.88760	1127.40021	1168.53656	1211.36707	1255.96529	1302.40807	1350.77569	1401.15205
22	264	1189.89846	1235.49593	1283.06528	1332.69641	1384.48345	1438.52496	1494.92414	1553.78906	1615.23285
23	276	1346.83789	1401.41345	1458.47257	1518.13422	1580.52322	1645.77055	1714.01369	1785.39690	1860.07159
24	288	1522.80770	1587.91122	1656.12591	1727.60799	1802.52179	1881.04011	1963.34472	2049.62678	2140.08740
25	300	1720.11548	1797.54199	1878.84663	1964.23320	2053.91654	2148.12308	2247.09152	2351.07350	2460.33432
26	312	1941.34868	2033.17515	2129.81391	2231.52915	2338.59999	2451.32129	2570.00460	2694.97908	2826.59254
27	324	2189.40846	2298.03602	2412.61013	2533.47130	2660.98009	2795.51829	2937.49017	3087.32384	3245.47270
28	336	2467.54781	2595.74998	2731.27198	2874.55039	3026.04850	3186.25799	3355.70069	3534.93047	3724.53524
29	348	2779.41414	2930.39208	3090.34813	3259.83926	3439.45782	3629.83392	3831.63784	4045.58261	4272.42682
30	360	3129.09718	3306.54286	3494.96413	3695.06825	3907.60916	4133.39068	4373.26978	4628.16024	4899.03641
31	372	3521.18255	3729.35101	3950.89557	4186.71048	4437.75126	4705.03892	4989.66452	5292.79409	5615.67379
32	384	3960.81193	4204.60388	4464.65052	4742.07808	5038.09268	5353.98605	5691.14176	6051.04178	6435.27364
33	396	4453.75047	4738.80664	5043.56246	5369.43097	5717.92893	6090.68452	6489.44564	6916.08887	7372.62905
34	408	5006.46240	5339.27140	5695.89492	6078.09969	6487.78642	6927.00015	7397.94139	7902.97806	8444.65846
35	420	5626.19582	6014.21721	6430.95947	6878.62418	7359.58538	7876.40328	8431.83906	9028.87086	9670.71111
36	432	6321.07769	6772.88264	7259.24860	7782.91055	8346.82452	8954.18573	9608.44818	10313.34595	11072.91618
37	444	7100.22047	7625.65219	8192.58553	8804.40814	9464.78997	10177.70709	10947.46759	11778.73970	12676.58228
38	456	7973.84158	8584.19845	9244.29294	9958.30956	10730.79198	11566.67432	12471.31517	13450.53455	14510.65421
39	468	8953.39740	9661.64183	10429.38317	11261.77664	12164.43296	13143.45921	14205.50321	15357.80215	16608.23540
40	480	10051.73351	10872.73025	11764.77251	12734.19569	13787.91103	14933.45865	16179.06553	17533.70889	19007.18539

FUTURE VALUE OF ONE DOLLAR PER PERIOD

ANNUAL INTEREST RATE

PERIOD YR	MOS	.13750	.14000	.14250	.14500	.14750	.15000	.15250	.15500	.15750
	1	1.00000	1.00000	1.00000	1.00000	1.00000	1.00000	1.00000	1.00000	1.00000
	2	2.01146	2.01167	2.01187	2.01208	2.01229	2.01250	2.01271	2.01292	2.01312
	3	3.03451	3.03514	3.03577	3.03640	3.03703	3.03766	3.03829	3.03892	3.03955
	4	4.06928	4.07055	4.07182	4.07309	4.07436	4.07563	4.07690	4.07817	4.07944
	5	5.11590	5.11804	5.12017	5.12230	5.12444	5.12657	5.12871	5.13085	5.13298
	6	6.17452	6.17775	6.18097	6.18420	6.18742	6.19065	6.19389	6.19712	6.20035
	7	7.24527	7.24982	7.25437	7.25892	7.26348	7.26804	7.27260	7.27717	7.28173
	8	8.32829	8.33440	8.34052	8.34663	8.35276	8.35889	8.36502	8.37116	8.37731
	9	9.42372	9.43164	9.43956	9.44749	9.45543	9.46337	9.47133	9.47929	9.48726
	10	10.53170	10.54167	10.55165	10.56165	10.57165	10.58167	10.59169	10.60173	10.61178
	11	11.65238	11.66466	11.67695	11.68927	11.70159	11.71394	11.72630	11.73867	11.75106
1	12	12.78589	12.80075	12.81562	12.83051	12.84543	12.86036	12.87532	12.89029	12.90529
2	24	27.44498	27.51318	27.58159	27.65021	27.71904	27.78808	27.85734	27.92682	27.99651
3	36	44.25170	44.42280	44.59472	44.76748	44.94107	45.11551	45.29079	45.46692	45.64390
4	48	63.52069	63.85774	64.19701	64.53853	64.88232	65.22839	65.57675	65.92743	66.28045
5	60	85.61269	86.19513	86.78248	87.37480	87.97213	88.57451	89.18199	89.79462	90.41245
6	72	110.94127	111.86843	112.80513	113.75149	114.70762	115.67362	116.64961	117.63569	118.63198
7	84	139.98062	141.37583	142.78805	144.21751	145.66443	147.12904	148.61158	150.11228	151.63138
8	96	173.27437	175.28993	177.33393	179.40683	181.50906	183.64106	185.80329	187.99621	190.22029
9	108	211.44583	214.26883	217.13720	220.05175	223.01326	226.02255	229.08045	232.18781	235.34547
10	120	255.20960	259.06891	262.99795	266.99806	271.07063	275.21706	279.43879	283.73728	288.11404
11	132	305.38499	310.55953	315.83803	321.22271	326.71585	332.31981	338.03695	343.86973	349.82065
12	144	362.91132	369.73987	376.71961	383.85409	391.14700	398.60208	406.22317	414.01421	421.97924
13	156	428.86554	437.75832	446.86647	456.19556	465.75129	475.53952	485.56627	495.83772	506.36020
14	168	504.48239	515.93478	527.68867	539.75251	552.13498	564.84501	577.89180	591.28481	605.03377
15	180	591.17749	605.78627	620.81084	636.26375	652.15794	668.50676	685.32398	702.62380	720.42086
16	192	690.57385	709.05637	728.10485	747.73763	767.97369	788.83260	810.33463	832.50070	855.35244
17	204	804.53229	827.74903	851.72744	876.49391	902.07578	928.50137	955.80000	984.00205	1013.13900
18	216	935.18620	964.16750	994.16360	1025.21197	1057.35149	1090.62252	1125.06697	1160.72833	1197.65175
19	228	1084.98157	1120.95897	1158.27647	1196.98658	1237.14394	1278.80538	1322.03004	1366.87946	1413.41763
20	240	1256.72272	1301.16601	1347.36493	1395.39233	1445.32412	1497.23948	1551.22097	1607.35468	1665.73036
21	252	1453.62480	1508.28552	1565.22991	1624.55798	1686.37422	1750.78785	1817.91300	1887.86893	1960.78031
22	264	1679.37403	1746.33669	1816.25078	1889.25241	1965.48414	2045.09527	2128.24219	2215.08870	2305.80640
23	276	1938.19666	2019.93890	2105.47337	2194.98384	2288.66320	2386.71394	2489.34863	2596.79045	2709.27367
24	288	2234.93810	2334.40142	2438.71144	2548.11444	2662.86954	2783.24935	2909.54069	3042.04539	3181.08102
25	300	2575.15366	2695.82641	2822.66350	2955.99278	3096.15996	3243.52962	3398.48618	3561.43512	3732.80403
26	312	2965.21250	3111.22734	3265.04748	3427.10667	3597.86335	3777.80202	3967.43481	4167.30304	4377.97894
27	324	3412.41692	3588.66509	3774.75587	3971.25988	4178.78153	4397.95112	4629.47698	4874.04775	5132.43485
28	336	3925.13904	4137.40436	4362.03448	4599.77607	4851.42187	5117.81360	5399.84502	5698.46520	6014.68197
29	348	4512.97753	4768.09347	5038.68836	5325.73448	5630.26653	5953.38562	6296.26363	6660.14784	7046.36583
30	360	5186.93731	5492.97097	5818.31912	6164.24212	6532.08430	6923.27961	7339.35768	7781.95029	8252.79831
31	372	5959.63558	6326.10314	6716.59835	7132.74808	7576.29161	8049.08845	8553.12676	9090.53244	9663.57868
32	384	6845.53803	7283.65697	7751.58263	8251.40671	8785.37059	9355.87614	9965.49739	10616.99302	11313.31978
33	396	7861.22964	8384.21383	8944.07647	9543.49697	10185.35310	10872.73586	11608.96550	12397.60873	13242.49724
34	408	9025.72517	9649.13008	10318.05055	11035.90691	11806.38123	12633.43763	13521.34414	14474.69630	15498.44255
35	420	10360.82516	11102.95149	11901.12351	12759.69314	13683.35624	14677.18016	15746.63349	16897.61818	18136.50428
36	432	11891.52399	12773.88954	13725.11718	14750.72718	15856.69002	17049.46354	18336.03320	19723.95566	21221.40604
37	444	13646.47790	14694.36887	15826.69617	17050.44188	18373.17517	19803.10219	21349.12038	23020.87728	24828.83449
38	456	15658.54138	16901.65648	18248.10494	19706.69367	21286.99243	22999.40070	24855.22042	26866.73514	29047.29620
39	468	17965.38226	19438.58490	21038.01694	22774.75839	24660.87724	26709.51863	28935.00194	31352.92690	33980.28919
40	480	20610.18693	22354.38336	24252.51300	26318.48160	28567.47046	31016.05477	33682.33293	36586.06794	39748.84216

FUTURE VALUE OF ONE DOLLAR PER PERIOD

ANNUAL INTEREST RATE

PERIOD YR	MOS	.16000	.16250	.16500	.16750	.17000	.17250	.17500	.17750	.18000
	1	1.00000	1.00000	1.00000	1.00000	1.00000	1.00000	1.00000	1.00000	1.00000
	2	2.01333	2.01354	2.01375	2.01396	2.01417	2.01437	2.01458	2.01479	2.01500
	3	3.04018	3.04081	3.04144	3.04207	3.04270	3.04333	3.04396	3.04459	3.04522
	4	4.08071	4.08199	4.08326	4.08453	4.08581	4.08708	4.08835	4.08963	4.09090
	5	5.13512	5.13726	5.13940	5.14155	5.14369	5.14583	5.14798	5.15012	5.15227
	6	6.20359	6.20683	6.21007	6.21331	6.21656	6.21980	6.22305	6.22630	6.22955
	7	7.28631	7.29088	7.29546	7.30004	7.30462	7.30921	7.31380	7.31840	7.32299
	8	8.38346	8.38961	8.39577	8.40194	8.40811	8.41428	8.42046	8.42665	8.43284
	9	9.49524	9.50322	9.51121	9.51921	9.52722	9.53524	9.54326	9.55129	9.55933
	10	10.62184	10.63191	10.64199	10.65209	10.66219	10.67231	10.68243	10.69257	10.70272
	11	11.76346	11.77588	11.78832	11.80077	11.81324	11.82572	11.83822	11.85073	11.86326
1	12	12.92031	12.93535	12.95041	12.96549	12.98059	12.99572	13.01086	13.02603	13.04121
2	24	28.06641	28.13653	28.20687	28.27743	28.34821	28.41921	28.49042	28.56186	28.63352
3	36	45.82174	46.00045	46.18003	46.36048	46.54180	46.72401	46.90710	47.09109	47.27597
4	48	66.63580	66.99353	67.35363	67.71613	68.08105	68.44840	68.81820	69.19047	69.56522
5	60	91.03552	91.66388	92.29757	92.93666	93.58118	94.23119	94.88674	95.54788	96.21465
6	72	119.63859	120.65564	121.68324	122.72151	123.77058	124.83056	125.90157	126.98374	128.07720
7	84	153.16913	154.72577	156.30155	157.89673	159.51156	161.14630	162.80121	164.47657	166.17264
8	96	192.47601	194.76384	197.08429	199.43784	201.82501	204.24630	206.70225	209.19338	211.72023
9	108	238.55432	241.81523	245.12913	248.49692	251.91955	255.39797	258.93315	262.52608	266.17777
10	120	292.57057	297.10844	301.72922	306.43455	311.22606	316.10545	321.07442	326.13474	331.28819
11	132	355.89224	362.08714	368.40799	374.85753	381.43855	388.15390	395.00649	401.99931	409.13539
12	144	430.12239	438.44791	446.96012	455.66348	464.56254	473.66197	482.96656	492.48120	502.21092
13	156	517.14023	528.18450	539.49988	551.09341	562.97234	575.14410	587.61632	600.39684	613.49372
14	168	619.14870	633.63992	648.51802	663.79394	679.47889	695.58445	712.12250	729.10530	746.54545
15	180	738.73025	757.56756	776.94883	796.89062	817.41003	838.52467	860.25270	882.61287	905.62451
16	192	878.91222	903.20313	928.24906	954.07470	980.70557	1008.16804	1036.48937	1065.69776	1095.82234
17	204	1043.24343	1074.34912	1106.49104	1139.70542	1174.02980	1209.50306	1246.16550	1284.05883	1323.22631
18	216	1235.88412	1275.47411	1316.47224	1358.93097	1402.90476	1448.45018	1495.62592	1544.49297	1595.11463
19	228	1461.71118	1511.82939	1563.84439	1617.83121	1673.86794	1732.03581	1792.41940	1855.10669	1920.18925
20	240	1726.44164	1789.58613	1855.26565	1923.58636	1994.65900	2068.59905	2145.52697	2225.56840	2308.85437
21	252	2036.77743	2115.99646	2198.57974	2284.67604	2374.44088	2468.03682	2565.63378	2667.40943	2773.54945
22	264	2400.57501	2499.58284	2603.02712	2711.11452	2824.06151	2942.09491	3065.45238	3194.38289	3329.14734
23	276	2827.04429	2950.36058	3079.49370	3214.72840	3356.36365	3504.71342	3660.10740	3822.89181	3993.43026
24	288	3326.98178	3480.09934	3640.80379	3809.48462	3986.55176	4172.43661	4367.59328	4572.49972	4787.65900
25	300	3913.04390	4102.63042	4302.06531	4511.87783	4732.62624	4964.89946	5209.31875	5466.53954	5737.25331
26	312	4600.06740	4834.20789	5081.07644	5341.38780	5615.89765	5905.40499	6210.75464	6532.83993	6872.60552
27	324	5405.44500	5693.93300	5998.80462	6321.01970	6661.59537	7021.60956	7402.20468	7804.59148	8230.05326
28	336	6349.56563	6704.25287	7079.95094	7477.94208	7899.58825	8346.33613	8819.72249	9321.37983	9853.04244
29	348	7456.33068	7891.54663	8353.61497	8844.24039	9365.23777	9918.53938	10506.20254	11130.41782	11793.51780
30	360	8753.75903	9286.81411	9854.07796	10457.80677	11100.40813	11784.45130	12512.67820	13288.01515	14113.58539
31	372	10274.69640	10926.48527	11621.72558	12363.39096	13154.66195	13998.94058	14899.86597	15861.33104	16887.50037
32	384	12057.64686	12853.37137	13704.13491	14613.84138	15586.67607	16627.12617	17740.00283	18930.46474	20204.04353
33	396	14147.74761	15117.78276	16157.35497	17271.57075	18465.91746	19746.29208	21119.03210	22590.94875	24169.36279
34	408	16597.91170	17778.84246	19047.41534	20410.28704	21874.62753	23448.16002	25139.20415	26956.72245	28910.37055
35	420	19470.16751	20906.02984	22452.10335	24117.03766	25910.17118	27841.58655	29922.17050	32163.67868	34578.80559
36	432	22837.22912	24580.99470	26463.05777	28494.62353	30687.81793	33055.76408	35612.66505	38373.89364	41356.08952
37	444	26784.33712	28899.68915	31188.23535	33664.45018	36344.03440	39244.01991	42382.88375	45780.67183	49459.13334
38	456	31411.41656	33974.87283	36754.81645	39769.89468	43040.38228	46588.32493	50437.69530	54614.56303	59147.27978
39	468	36835.60668	39939.05708	43312.62823	46980.28199	50968.13316	55304.64465	60020.84054	65150.53853	70730.60371
40	480	43194.22635	46947.96474	51038.17727	55495.58096	60353.73184	65649.28980	71422.30810	77716.55020	84579.83629

FUTURE VALUE OF ONE DOLLAR PER PERIOD

PERIOD YR	PERIOD MOS	ANNUAL INTEREST RATE .18250	.18500	.18750	.19000	.19250	.19500	.19750	.20000	.20250
	1	1.00000	1.00000	1.00000	1.00000	1.00000	1.00000	1.00000	1.00000	1.00000
	2	2.01521	2.01542	2.01562	2.01583	2.01604	2.01625	2.01646	2.01667	2.01687
	3	3.04586	3.04649	3.04712	3.04775	3.04838	3.04901	3.04965	3.05028	3.05091
	4	4.09218	4.09345	4.09473	4.09601	4.09728	4.09856	4.09984	4.10112	4.10239
	5	5.15441	5.15656	5.15871	5.16086	5.16301	5.16516	5.16731	5.16947	5.17162
	6	6.23280	6.23606	6.23932	6.24257	6.24583	6.24910	6.25236	6.25563	6.25889
	7	7.32759	7.33220	7.33680	7.34141	7.34603	7.35064	7.35526	7.35989	7.36451
	8	8.43904	8.44524	8.45144	8.45765	8.46387	8.47009	8.47632	8.48255	8.48879
	9	9.56738	9.57543	9.58350	9.59157	9.59964	9.60773	9.61582	9.62393	9.63204
	10	10.71288	10.72305	10.73324	10.74343	10.75364	10.76386	10.77409	10.78433	10.79458
	11	11.87581	11.88837	11.90095	11.91354	11.92615	11.93877	11.95141	11.96406	11.97674
1	12	13.05642	13.07165	13.08690	13.10217	13.11746	13.13277	13.14811	13.16347	13.17884
2	24	28.70540	28.77751	28.84984	28.92239	28.99517	29.06818	29.14142	29.21488	29.28857
3	36	47.46175	47.64844	47.83603	48.02454	48.21397	48.40433	48.59561	48.78783	48.98098
4	48	69.94248	70.32226	70.70457	71.08945	71.47690	71.86695	72.25961	72.65490	73.05285
5	60	96.88712	97.56533	98.24934	98.93920	99.63496	100.33668	101.04441	101.75821	102.47813
6	72	129.18206	130.29846	131.42653	132.56640	133.71820	134.88206	136.05812	137.24652	138.44739
7	84	167.88969	169.62802	171.38789	173.16960	174.97343	176.79968	178.64865	180.52064	182.41596
8	96	214.28336	216.88331	219.52066	222.19597	224.90984	227.66285	230.45561	233.28873	236.16283
9	108	269.88925	273.66155	277.49575	281.39292	285.35416	289.38060	293.47338	297.63366	301.86263
10	120	336.53659	341.88181	347.32575	352.87033	358.51754	364.26939	370.12795	376.09530	382.17359
11	132	416.41786	423.84990	431.43477	439.17580	447.07639	455.14001	463.37025	471.77072	480.34516
12	144	512.16087	522.33631	532.74265	543.38542	554.27031	565.40312	576.78980	588.43648	600.34939
13	156	626.91521	640.66981	654.76624	669.21344	684.02062	699.19720	714.75290	730.69766	747.04171
14	168	764.45591	782.85003	801.74155	821.14461	841.07375	861.54396	882.57064	904.16967	926.35738
15	180	929.30756	953.68258	978.77078	1004.59404	1031.17494	1058.53674	1086.70347	1115.69991	1145.55159
16	192	1126.89321	1158.94151	1191.99944	1226.10025	1261.27834	1297.56928	1335.00982	1373.63798	1413.49305
17	204	1363.71272	1405.56448	1448.82968	1493.55814	1539.80147	1587.61317	1637.04867	1688.16538	1741.02281
18	216	1647.55663	1701.88722	1758.17728	1816.50043	1876.93309	1939.55463	2004.44749	2071.69727	2141.39288
19	228	1987.76238	2057.92527	2130.78114	2206.43743	2285.00594	2366.60306	2451.34994	2539.37265	2630.80245
20	240	2395.52157	2485.71256	2579.57607	2677.26724	2778.94790	2884.78687	2994.96027	3109.65184	3229.05326
21	252	2884.24801	2999.70806	3120.14183	3245.77117	3376.82805	3513.55502	3656.20568	3805.04519	3960.35085
22	264	3470.01908	3617.28458	3771.24397	3932.21181	4100.51770	4276.50707	4460.54192	4653.00165	4854.28387
23	276	4172.10460	4359.31587	4555.48528	4761.05524	4976.49041	5202.27886	5438.93328	5686.99220	5947.02132
24	288	5013.60068	5250.88222	5500.09043	5761.84307	6036.79049	6325.61737	6629.04457	6947.83105	7282.77589
25	300	6022.18959	6322.11813	6637.85106	6970.24533	7320.20520	7688.68483	8076.69114	8485.28671	8915.59289
26	312	7231.05034	7609.23081	8008.26412	8429.33185	8873.68364	9342.64122	9837.60258	10360.04643	10911.53691
27	324	8679.95019	9155.72402	9658.90305	10191.10733	10754.05424	11349.56444	11979.56814	12646.11172	13351.36484
28	336	10416.55281	11013.86846	11647.06921	12318.36488	13030.10356	13784.78029	14585.04639	15433.71935	16333.79336
29	348	12497.98631	13246.46845	14041.78108	14886.92414	15785.09268	16739.68965	17754.33960	18832.90325	19979.49301
30	360	14992.72251	15928.98474	16926.17027	17988.33358	19119.80294	20325.19906	21609.45506	22977.83779	24435.97063
31	372	17982.82943	19152.08502	20400.36735	21733.13350	23156.22271	24675.88336	26298.80193	28032.13402	29883.53754
32	384	21566.67102	23024.70844	24584.97788	26254.79591	28042.00987	29955.03666	32002.90452	34195.29778	36542.60503
33	396	25862.14302	27677.74771	29625.26916	31714.48169	33955.89333	36360.80128	38941.35185	41710.60473	44682.60231
34	408	31010.55132	33268.47318	35696.21316	38306.78475	41114.21121	44133.60463	47381.25115	50874.70301	54632.87775
35	420	37181.26036	39985.84854	43008.56061	46266.66764	49778.82479	53565.18312	57647.51056	62049.32277	66796.02450
36	432	44577.26470	48056.91765	51816.15712	55877.83620	60266.69775	65009.53194	70135.34703	75675.55447	81664.16958
37	444	53441.86678	57754.47856	62424.75536	67482.85126	72961.49112	78896.19153	85325.50084	92291.25993	99838.88558
38	456	64066.68072	69406.30393	75202.62916	81495.33827	88327.59818	95746.36953	103802.74257	112552.30304	122055.53064
39	468	76801.22540	83406.21943	90593.35800	98414.72971	106927.13262	116192.50322	126278.38474	137258.43838	149213.00137
40	480	92064.42240	100227.41519	109131.22570	118844.06579	129440.49138	141001.99680	153617.66507	167384.87955	182410.10265

FUTURE VALUE OF ONE DOLLAR PER PERIOD

ANNUAL INTEREST RATE

PERIOD YR	MOS	.20500	.20750	.21000	.21250	.21500	.21750	.22000	.22250	.22500
	1	1.00000	1.00000	1.00000	1.00000	1.00000	1.00000	1.00000	1.00000	1.00000
	2	2.01708	2.01729	2.01750	2.01771	2.01792	2.01813	2.01833	2.01854	2.01875
	3	3.05154	3.05217	3.05281	3.05344	3.05407	3.05470	3.05534	3.05597	3.05660
	4	4.10367	4.10495	4.10623	4.10751	4.10879	4.11007	4.11135	4.11263	4.11391
	5	5.17378	5.17593	5.17809	5.18025	5.18241	5.18457	5.18673	5.18889	5.19105
	6	6.26216	6.26543	6.26871	6.27198	6.27526	6.27854	6.28182	6.28510	6.28838
	7	7.36914	7.37377	7.37841	7.38305	7.38769	7.39233	7.39698	7.40163	7.40629
	8	8.49503	8.50128	8.50753	8.51379	8.52005	8.52632	8.53259	8.53887	8.54516
	9	9.64015	9.64828	9.65641	9.66455	9.67270	9.68086	9.68902	9.69720	9.70538
	10	10.80484	10.81511	10.82540	10.83570	10.84600	10.85632	10.86666	10.87700	10.88735
	11	11.98942	12.00213	12.01484	12.02758	12.04033	12.05310	12.06588	12.07868	12.09149
1	12	13.19424	13.20966	13.22510	13.24057	13.25605	13.27156	13.28709	13.30264	13.31821
2	24	29.36249	29.43664	29.51102	29.58563	29.66047	29.73555	29.81086	29.88641	29.96219
3	36	49.17508	49.37013	49.56613	49.76309	49.96101	50.15990	50.35977	50.56062	50.76244
4	48	73.45347	73.85677	74.26278	74.67153	75.08302	75.49728	75.91432	76.33418	76.75686
5	60	103.20424	103.93658	104.67522	105.42021	106.17161	106.92948	107.69388	108.46487	109.24252
6	72	139.66088	140.88713	142.12628	143.37848	144.64387	145.92260	147.21483	148.52070	149.84037
7	84	184.33491	186.27782	188.24499	190.23676	192.25345	194.29540	196.36294	198.45641	200.57617
8	96	239.07854	242.03651	245.03739	248.08183	251.17052	254.30413	257.48337	260.70893	263.98153
9	108	306.16148	310.53145	314.97378	319.48974	324.08064	328.74779	333.49252	338.31621	343.22025
10	120	388.36501	394.67179	401.09620	407.64055	414.30723	421.09864	428.01724	435.06557	442.24617
11	132	489.09736	498.03123	507.15073	516.45994	525.96301	535.66420	545.56787	555.67845	566.00049
12	144	612.53494	624.99972	637.75045	650.79403	664.13752	677.78817	691.75342	706.04086	720.65829
13	156	763.79556	780.96999	798.57608	816.62521	835.12906	854.09964	873.54927	893.49061	913.93667
14	168	949.15056	972.56653	996.62309	1021.33856	1046.73182	1072.82229	1099.62997	1127.17542	1155.47983
15	180	1176.28488	1207.92699	1240.50595	1274.05072	1308.59114	1344.15803	1380.78315	1418.49929	1457.34028
16	192	1454.61565	1497.04779	1540.83290	1586.01589	1632.64317	1680.76276	1730.42429	1781.67908	1834.58022
17	204	1795.68263	1852.20873	1910.66732	1971.12702	2033.65893	2098.33674	2165.23681	2234.43827	2306.02315
18	216	2213.62665	2288.49448	2366.09596	2446.53453	2529.91765	2616.35689	2705.96817	2798.87189	2895.19310
19	228	2725.77594	2824.43535	2926.92869	3033.41008	3144.03992	3258.98522	3378.41984	3502.52477	3631.48844
20	240	3353.36452	3482.79426	3617.56017	3757.88937	3904.01885	4056.19587	4214.67844	4379.73577	4551.64878
21	252	4122.41258	4291.53358	4468.03092	4652.23615	4844.49601	5045.17314	5254.64677	5473.31352	5701.58823
22	264	5064.80532	5285.00277	5515.33403	5756.27896	6008.34051	6272.04592	6547.94783	6836.62555	7138.68638
23	276	6219.61492	6505.39728	6805.02427	7119.18489	7448.60304	7794.03926	8156.29260	8536.20263	8934.65149
24	288	7634.72048	8004.55073	8393.19953	8801.64917	9230.93406	9682.14351	10156.42465	10654.98555	11179.09849
25	300	9368.79313	9846.13643	10348.94098	10878.59810	11436.57629	12024.42556	12643.78202	13296.37271	13984.02067
26	312	11493.72859	12108.37173	12757.31789	13442.52588	14166.06794	14930.13651	15737.05114	16589.26603	17489.37785
27	324	14097.62795	14887.34019	15723.08791	16607.61363	17543.82550	18534.80749	19583.83003	20694.36148	21870.08012
28	336	17288.45046	18301.07248	19375.25371	20514.81436	21723.81487	23006.57122	24367.67110	25811.99118	27344.71549
29	348	21198.48955	22494.55950	23872.67426	25338.13009	26896.56953	28554.00427	30316.83948	32191.89978	34186.45697
30	360	25989.85782	27645.91055	29410.97474	31292.36081	33297.87546	35435.85565	37715.20491	40145.43219	42736.69334
31	372	31861.20829	33973.91811	36231.05569	38642.67034	41219.51884	43973.11568	46915.78685	50060.72752	53422.06376
32	384	39055.97070	41747.35062	44629.57150	47716.39499	51022.58627	54563.98791	58357.59907	62421.66053	66775.74616
33	396	47872.44426	51296.36781	54971.83406	58917.62110	63153.92399	67702.46261	72586.59758	77831.45519	83464.06175
34	408	58676.16531	63026.54353	67707.70278	72745.18048	78166.50612	84001.35786	90281.73144	97042.12246	104319.72303
35	420	71915.06265	77436.09162	83391.15224	89814.86523	96744.64047	104220.90333	112287.33936	120991.15912	130383.38448
36	432	88138.02899	95137.02648	102704.36848	110886.85120	119735.16091	129304.19963	139653.43806	150847.29836	162955.56904
37	444	108017.67833	116881.15702	126487.42227	136899.55146	148186.02793	160421.20739	173685.82475	188067.54495	203661.56150
38	456	132378.23297	143592.01816	155774.80974	169011.40725	183394.09710	199023.31775	216008.38439	234468.27834	254532.50690
39	468	162229.69624	176404.09596	191840.45009	208652.47766	226964.23274	246911.04962	268640.57472	292313.89343	318106.76047
40	480	198809.72789	216711.01243	236253.09754	257588.12538	280882.46127	306318.03132	334093.78650	364427.30505	397556.54628

FUTURE VALUE OF ONE DOLLAR PER PERIOD

PERIOD YR	MOS	ANNUAL INTEREST RATE .22750	.23000	.23250	.23500	.23750	.24000	.24250	.24500	.24750
	1	1.00000	1.00000	1.00000	1.00000	1.00000	1.00000	1.00000	1.00000	1.00000
	2	2.01896	2.01917	2.01938	2.01958	2.01979	2.02000	2.02021	2.02042	2.02062
	3	3.05723	3.05787	3.05850	3.05913	3.05977	3.06040	3.06103	3.06167	3.06230
	4	4.11519	4.11648	4.11776	4.11904	4.12032	4.12161	4.12289	4.12418	4.12546
	5	5.19321	5.19538	5.19754	5.19971	5.20187	5.20404	5.20621	5.20838	5.21055
	6	6.29167	6.29495	6.29824	6.30153	6.30483	6.30812	6.31142	6.31472	6.31802
	7	7.41095	7.41561	7.42027	7.42494	7.42961	7.43428	7.43896	7.44364	7.44832
	8	8.55145	8.55774	8.56404	8.57034	8.57665	8.58297	8.58929	8.59562	8.60195
	9	9.71357	9.72176	9.72997	9.73818	9.74640	9.75463	9.76286	9.77111	9.77936
	10	10.89772	10.90810	10.91849	10.92889	10.93930	10.94972	10.96016	10.97060	10.98106
	11	12.10432	12.11717	12.13003	12.14291	12.15580	12.16872	12.18164	12.19459	12.20755
1	12	13.33380	13.34941	13.36505	13.38071	13.39639	13.41209	13.42781	13.44356	13.45933
2	24	30.03821	30.11446	30.19095	30.26768	30.34465	30.42186	30.49931	30.57701	30.65494
3	36	50.96526	51.16907	51.37388	51.57970	51.78653	51.99437	52.20323	52.41312	52.62404
4	48	77.18240	77.61080	78.04209	78.47629	78.91343	79.35352	79.79658	80.24264	80.69172
5	60	110.02687	110.81800	111.61597	112.42084	113.23268	114.05154	114.87750	115.71061	116.55095
6	72	151.17399	152.52173	153.88374	155.26018	156.65122	158.05702	159.47775	160.91357	162.36466
7	84	202.72256	204.89593	207.09665	209.32509	211.58162	213.86661	216.18044	218.52350	220.89619
8	96	267.30190	270.67079	274.08894	277.55711	281.07609	284.64666	288.26962	291.94579	295.67598
9	108	348.20605	353.27505	358.42873	363.66857	368.99611	374.41288	379.92047	385.52048	391.21455
10	120	449.56168	457.01475	464.60813	472.34459	480.22696	488.25815	496.44111	504.77886	513.27448
11	132	576.53865	587.29769	598.28246	609.49794	620.94921	632.64148	644.58007	656.77042	669.21808
12	144	735.61371	750.91530	766.57146	782.59080	798.98212	815.75446	832.91709	850.47949	868.45140
13	156	934.90081	956.39673	978.43854	1001.04071	1024.21810	1047.98599	1072.36006	1097.35642	1122.99161
14	168	1184.56502	1214.45342	1245.16815	1276.73300	1309.17245	1342.51172	1376.77677	1411.99430	1448.19183
15	180	1497.34100	1538.53747	1580.96682	1624.66738	1669.67870	1716.04157	1763.79808	1812.99168	1863.66717
16	192	1889.18257	1945.54288	2003.71983	2063.77410	2125.76844	2189.76773	2255.83908	2324.05187	2394.47789
17	204	2380.07644	2456.68623	2535.94382	2617.94384	2702.78437	2790.56704	2881.39722	2975.38412	3072.64091
18	216	2995.06171	3098.61264	3205.98607	3317.32760	3432.78848	3552.52584	3676.70291	3805.48925	3939.06102
19	228	3765.50702	3904.78477	4049.53433	4199.97709	4356.34359	4518.87384	4687.81775	4863.43553	5045.99815
20	240	4730.71060	4917.22714	5111.51758	5313.91506	5524.76719	5744.43676	5973.30237	6211.75914	6460.21946
21	252	5939.90473	6188.71682	6448.49912	6719.74807	7002.98294	7298.74687	7607.60803	7930.16071	8267.02663
22	264	7454.76695	7785.53466	8131.68916	8493.96399	8873.12815	9269.98792	9685.38861	10120.21652	10575.40091
23	276	9352.56607	9790.92032	10250.73764	10733.09343	11239.11777	11769.99821	12326.98270	12911.38275	13524.57666
24	288	11730.10341	12309.41152	12918.50917	13558.96183	14232.41843	14940.61574	15685.38318	16468.64779	17292.43944
25	300	14708.65037	15472.29339	16277.09440	17125.31760	18019.35338	18961.72540	19955.09814	21002.28479	22106.25563
26	312	18440.13413	19444.44211	20505.37805	21626.19721	22810.34433	24061.46474	25383.41616	26780.28117	28256.38042
27	324	23114.88706	24432.91979	25828.56667	27306.48224	28871.60353	30529.16732	32284.72850	34144.17955	36113.77120
28	336	28971.35496	30697.76818	32530.18353	34475.22274	36539.92588	38731.77803	41058.73764	43529.26664	46152.36262
29	348	36308.25957	38565.56429	40967.16968	43522.45192	46241.40305	49134.67177	52213.60683	55490.30349	58977.65288
30	360	45499.83547	48446.44439	51588.89525	54940.40682	58515.09931	62328.05639	66395.39134	70734.31785	75363.22569
31	372	57014.91876	60855.48371	64961.09383	69350.30973	74043.00471	79060.45817	84425.45589	90162.39727	96297.41046
32	384	71440.86099	76439.54663	81795.99449	87536.16736	93687.93000	100281.18944	107348.04561	114922.95319	123042.89547
33	396	89513.48835	96011.00663	102990.25647	110487.42659	118541.44888	127194.20775	136490.76543	146479.60458	157212.88950
34	408	112154.63405	120590.09418	129672.72705	139452.80789	149984.55142	161326.42238	173541.47082	186697.69379	200868.42580
35	420	140519.15837	151458.07974	163264.56601	176008.24503	189764.37907	204614.32353	220646.02312	237954.54863	256642.67758
36	432	176053.85483	190224.06446	205554.93947	222142.62767	240091.30484	259513.84895	280532.57113	303280.00839	327899.78320
37	444	220571.24700	238908.86018	258796.31423	280366.01188	303761.75311	329139.72160	356669.55699	386535.52039	418937.76110
38	456	276342.04014	300050.33129	325824.42852	353846.18599	384313.58336	417442.16327	453466.59756	492642.39363	535247.75361
39	468	346210.94339	376835.68972	410209.32893	446581.02202	486222.67201	529431.01036	576529.87561	627872.70184	683845.23644
40	480	433741.77034	473267.63944	516445.51790	563615.98985	615151.61524	671459.94677	732986.83253	800220.03148	873693.17147

PRESENT VALUE OF ONE PER PERIOD TABLE

Description:

The Present Value of One Per Period table, also known as present value of an annuity, may be used to find the current worth of a series of equal dollar flows to be received in the future, at a given interest rate and term. To use the table, find the factor corresponding to the given annual interest rate and term of dollar receipt; then multiply by the amount of receipt per period.

Table Calculation Formula:

$$PV_a = \frac{1 - 1/(1+i)^n}{i}.$$

Table Range:

Annual interest rate, with monthly compounding, from 7.00% to 24.75% in .25% increments. Term from 1 to 12 months in 1-month increments, 1 to 40 years in 1-year increments. Flows assumed made at the end of the compounding period.

Example:

What is the present value of a series of \$300 monthly rent payments to be received for 15 years, if an annual yield of 12% is desired, with monthly compounding and rent received at the end of each month?

Solution:

Finding the table factor corresponding to 12% annual interest and 15-year term provides:

$$\begin{aligned} PV_a &= \$300 \times \text{table factor } PV_a,\ 12\%,\ 15 \text{ years}, \\ &= \$300(83.32166), \\ &= \$24{,}996.50. \end{aligned}$$

If monthly rental payments of \$300 are received for 15 years, the value of the stream is \$24,996.50, given a 12% annual yield and monthly compounding.

PRESENT VALUE OF ONE DOLLAR PER PERIOD

ANNUAL INTEREST RATE

PERIOD YR	MOS	.07000	.07250	.07500	.07750	.08000	.08250	.08500	.08750	.09000
	1	.99420	.99399	.99379	.99358	.99338	.99317	.99297	.99276	.99256
	2	1.98264	1.98202	1.98141	1.98079	1.98018	1.97956	1.97895	1.97834	1.97772
	3	2.96534	2.96411	2.96289	2.96166	2.96044	2.95922	2.95800	2.95678	2.95556
	4	3.94234	3.94031	3.93827	3.93624	3.93421	3.93218	3.93016	3.92813	3.92611
	5	4.91368	4.91064	4.90760	4.90457	4.90154	4.89851	4.89548	4.89246	4.88944
	6	5.87938	5.87514	5.87091	5.86668	5.86245	5.85823	5.85402	5.84980	5.84560
	7	6.83948	6.83385	6.82823	6.82261	6.81701	6.81140	6.80581	6.80022	6.79464
	8	7.79402	7.78681	7.77961	7.77242	7.76524	7.75807	7.75091	7.74375	7.73661
	9	8.74302	8.73404	8.72508	8.71613	8.70719	8.69827	8.68936	8.68046	8.67158
	10	9.68651	9.67558	9.66467	9.65378	9.64290	9.63205	9.62121	9.61038	9.59958
	11	10.62454	10.61147	10.59843	10.58541	10.57242	10.55945	10.54650	10.53358	10.52067
1	12	11.55712	11.54174	11.52639	11.51107	11.49578	11.48052	11.46529	11.45009	11.43491
2	24	22.33510	22.27866	22.22242	22.16638	22.11054	22.05490	21.99945	21.94420	21.88915
3	36	32.38646	32.26688	32.14791	32.02956	31.91181	31.79466	31.67811	31.56216	31.44681
4	48	41.76020	41.55861	41.35837	41.15948	40.96191	40.76567	40.57074	40.37712	40.18478
5	60	50.50199	50.20241	49.90531	49.61066	49.31843	49.02862	48.74118	48.45611	48.17337
6	72	58.65444	58.24347	57.83652	57.43356	57.03452	56.63938	56.24808	55.86058	55.47685
7	84	66.25729	65.72382	65.19638	64.67488	64.15926	63.64943	63.14532	62.64686	62.15396
8	96	73.34757	72.68255	72.02602	71.37787	70.73797	70.10619	69.48243	68.86655	68.25844
9	108	79.95985	79.15604	78.36367	77.58255	76.81250	76.05333	75.30488	74.56695	73.83938
10	120	86.12635	85.17812	84.24474	83.32595	82.42149	81.53107	80.65447	79.79142	78.94169
11	132	91.87713	90.78028	89.70215	88.64238	87.60060	86.57646	85.56961	84.57971	83.60642
12	144	97.24022	95.99179	94.76640	93.56357	92.38280	91.22362	90.08558	88.96822	87.87109
13	156	102.24174	100.83989	99.46583	98.11891	96.79850	95.50399	94.23480	92.99033	91.77002
14	168	106.90607	105.34993	103.82671	102.33559	100.87578	99.44652	98.04705	96.67663	95.33456
15	180	111.25596	109.54548	107.87343	106.23879	104.64059	103.07787	101.54969	100.05517	98.59341
16	192	115.31259	113.44846	111.62862	109.85182	108.11687	106.42260	104.76788	103.15162	101.57277
17	204	119.09573	117.07929	115.11329	113.19626	111.32673	109.50334	107.72471	105.98956	104.29661
18	216	122.62383	120.45693	118.34693	116.29205	114.29060	112.34091	110.44141	108.59056	106.78686
19	228	125.91408	123.59905	121.34762	119.15770	117.02731	114.95453	112.93748	110.97439	109.06353
20	240	128.98251	126.52206	124.13213	121.81031	119.55429	117.36185	115.23084	113.15920	111.14495
21	252	131.84407	129.24125	126.71605	124.26572	121.88761	119.57917	117.33795	115.16160	113.04787
22	264	134.51272	131.77082	129.11382	126.53859	124.04210	121.62147	119.27393	116.99682	114.78759
23	276	137.00146	134.12401	131.33886	128.64248	126.03148	123.50258	121.05269	118.67882	116.37811
24	288	139.32242	136.31310	133.40361	130.58997	127.86839	125.23522	122.68699	120.22039	117.83222
25	300	141.48690	138.34954	135.31961	132.39268	129.56452	126.83110	124.18857	121.63325	119.16162
26	312	143.50547	140.24398	137.09759	134.06137	131.13067	128.30102	125.56820	122.92815	120.37701
27	324	145.38795	142.00632	138.74748	135.60601	132.57679	129.65493	126.83579	124.11494	121.48817
28	336	147.14351	143.64577	140.27851	137.03581	133.91208	130.90197	128.00043	125.20264	122.50403
29	348	148.78073	145.17090	141.69924	138.35932	135.14503	132.05058	129.07049	126.19953	123.43278
30	360	150.30757	146.58968	143.01763	139.58444	136.28349	133.10854	130.05364	127.11319	124.28187
31	372	151.73147	147.90952	144.24104	140.71848	137.33471	134.08299	130.95696	127.95057	125.05814
32	384	153.05938	149.13733	145.37631	141.76821	138.30536	134.98053	131.78691	128.71804	125.76783
33	396	154.29777	150.27952	146.42980	142.73990	139.20162	135.80723	132.54946	129.42143	126.41666
34	408	155.45267	151.34207	147.40740	143.63935	140.02919	136.56868	133.25008	130.06609	127.00985
35	420	156.52971	152.33052	148.31457	144.47194	140.79334	137.27003	133.89380	130.65693	127.55216
36	432	157.53414	153.25005	149.15639	145.24263	141.49892	137.91602	134.48524	131.19844	128.04797
37	444	158.47085	154.10546	149.93756	145.95602	142.15043	138.51103	135.02865	131.69474	128.50125
38	456	159.34442	154.90122	150.66246	146.61638	142.75201	139.05907	135.52793	132.14961	128.91566
39	468	160.15909	155.64149	151.33513	147.22765	143.30749	139.56385	135.98667	132.56649	129.29453
40	480	160.91884	156.33014	151.95935	147.79347	143.82039	140.02880	136.40814	132.94858	129.64090

PRESENT VALUE OF ONE DOLLAR PER PERIOD

ANNUAL INTEREST RATE

PERIOD YR	MOS	.09250	.09500	.09750	.10000	.10250	.10500	.10750	.11000	.11250
	1	.99235	.99215	.99194	.99174	.99153	.99133	.99112	.99092	.99071
	2	1.97711	1.97650	1.97589	1.97527	1.97466	1.97405	1.97344	1.97283	1.97222
	3	2.95434	2.95312	2.95190	2.95069	2.94947	2.94826	2.94704	2.94583	2.94462
	4	3.92409	3.92207	3.92005	3.91804	3.91602	3.91401	3.91200	3.90999	3.90798
	5	4.88642	4.88341	4.88040	4.87739	4.87439	4.87138	4.86838	4.86539	4.86239
	6	5.84140	5.83720	5.83301	5.82682	5.82463	5.82045	5.81628	5.81211	5.80794
	7	6.78906	6.78350	6.77793	6.77238	6.76683	6.76129	6.75576	6.75023	6.74471
	8	7.72948	7.72236	7.71525	7.70615	7.70105	7.69397	7.68690	7.67983	7.67278
	9	8.66271	8.65385	8.64501	8.63618	8.62736	8.61856	8.60977	8.60099	8.59223
	10	9.58879	9.57802	9.56727	9.55654	9.54582	9.53513	9.52445	9.51378	9.50314
	11	10.50780	10.49494	10.48211	10.46930	10.45651	10.44374	10.43100	10.41828	10.40558
1	12	11.41977	11.40465	11.38957	11.37451	11.35948	11.34448	11.32951	11.31456	11.29965
2	24	21.83428	21.77962	21.72514	21.67085	21.61676	21.56286	21.50914	21.45562	21.40228
3	36	31.33204	31.21786	31.10426	30.99124	30.87879	30.76692	30.65561	30.54487	30.43470
4	48	39.99373	39.80395	39.61543	39.42816	39.24214	39.05734	38.87378	38.69142	38.51027
5	60	47.89295	47.61483	47.33897	47.06537	46.79399	46.52483	46.25785	45.99303	45.73037
6	72	55.09683	54.72049	54.34778	53.97867	53.61310	53.25106	52.89248	52.53735	52.18561
7	84	61.66657	61.18460	60.70799	60.23667	59.77056	59.30961	58.85375	58.40290	57.95701
8	96	67.65799	67.06509	66.47963	65.90149	65.33057	64.76677	64.20998	63.66010	63.11703
9	108	73.12200	72.41465	71.71715	71.02935	70.35110	69.68223	69.02259	68.37204	67.73043
10	120	78.10503	77.28121	76.47000	75.67116	74.88449	74.10976	73.34676	72.59528	71.85511
11	132	82.64942	81.70839	80.78301	79.87299	78.97801	78.09779	77.23204	76.38049	75.54285
12	144	86.79378	85.73585	84.69690	83.67653	82.67434	81.68996	80.72300	79.77311	78.83992
13	156	90.57332	89.39968	88.24860	87.11954	86.01202	84.92555	83.85965	82.81386	81.78773
14	168	94.02015	92.73272	91.47162	90.23620	89.02585	87.83996	86.67795	85.53923	84.42326
15	180	97.16357	95.76483	94.39638	93.05744	91.74725	90.46508	89.21021	87.98194	86.77960
16	192	100.03029	98.52318	97.05048	95.61126	94.20460	92.82961	91.48546	90.17129	88.88632
17	204	102.64465	101.03249	99.45898	97.92301	96.42351	94.95944	93.52978	92.13358	90.76987
18	216	105.02888	103.31524	101.64459	100.01563	98.42712	96.87784	95.36663	93.89234	92.45388
19	228	107.20323	105.39188	103.62794	101.90990	100.23633	98.60582	97.01704	95.46868	93.95950
20	240	109.18618	107.28104	105.42775	103.62462	101.86999	100.16227	98.49995	96.88154	95.30562
21	252	110.99457	108.99962	107.06101	105.17680	103.34514	101.56423	99.83235	98.14786	96.50915
22	264	112.64378	110.56365	108.54313	106.58186	104.67715	102.82701	101.02952	99.28284	97.58518
23	276	114.14781	111.98531	109.88809	107.85373	105.87992	103.96445	102.10519	100.30010	98.54722
24	288	115.51945	113.27916	111.10859	109.00504	106.96599	104.98898	103.07168	101.21185	99.40734
25	300	116.77034	114.45623	112.21614	110.04723	107.94668	105.91182	103.94009	102.02904	100.17636
26	312	117.91112	115.52697	113.22120	110.99063	108.83221	106.74305	104.72035	102.76148	100.86390
27	324	118.95148	116.50105	114.13325	111.84461	109.63182	107.49176	105.42142	103.41795	101.47861
28	336	119.90026	117.38720	114.96090	112.61764	110.35385	108.16616	106.05134	104.00633	102.02821
29	348	120.76553	118.19333	115.71196	113.31739	111.00582	108.77361	106.61733	104.53369	102.51958
30	360	121.55462	118.92668	116.39351	113.95082	111.59453	109.32077	107.12587	105.00635	102.95890
31	372	122.27425	119.59382	117.01200	114.52421	112.12611	109.81361	107.58279	105.42998	103.35168
32	384	122.93054	120.20073	117.57325	115.04324	112.60612	110.25753	107.99335	105.80968	103.70285
33	396	123.52906	120.75284	118.08256	115.51308	113.03955	110.65738	108.36223	106.15000	104.01682
34	408	124.07488	121.25510	118.54474	115.93839	113.43093	111.01755	108.69368	106.45502	104.29753
35	420	124.57267	121.71201	118.96415	116.32338	113.78433	111.34196	108.99148	106.72841	104.54850
36	432	125.02663	122.12767	119.34474	116.67188	114.10345	111.63417	109.25906	106.97344	104.77289
37	444	125.44063	122.50580	119.69012	116.98734	114.39159	111.89737	109.49948	107.19306	104.97350
38	456	125.81819	122.84979	120.00354	117.27290	114.65179	112.13445	109.71551	107.38990	105.15287
39	468	126.16251	123.16273	120.28795	117.53140	114.88673	112.34799	109.90960	107.56632	105.31323
40	480	126.47652	123.44741	120.54604	117.76539	115.09888	112.54034	110.08400	107.72445	105.45660

PRESENT VALUE OF ONE DOLLAR PER PERIOD

ANNUAL INTEREST RATE

PERIOD YR	MOS	.11500	.11750	.12000	.12250	.12500	.12750	.13000	.13250	.13500
	1	.99051	.99030	.99010	.98989	.98969	.98949	.98928	.98908	.98888
	2	1.97161	1.97100	1.97040	1.96979	1.96918	1.96857	1.96796	1.96736	1.96675
	3	2.94341	2.94219	2.94099	2.93978	2.93857	2.93736	2.93615	2.93495	2.93374
	4	3.90597	3.90397	3.90197	3.89996	3.89796	3.89597	3.89397	3.89198	3.88998
	5	4.85940	4.85642	4.85343	4.85045	4.84747	4.84449	4.84152	4.83855	4.83558
	6	5.80378	5.79963	5.79548	5.79133	5.78719	5.78305	5.77892	5.77479	5.77066
	7	6.73920	6.73369	6.72819	6.72270	6.71722	6.71174	6.70626	6.70080	6.69534
	8	7.66574	7.65870	7.65168	7.64466	7.63766	7.63066	7.62367	7.61670	7.60973
	9	8.58348	8.57474	8.56602	8.55731	8.54861	8.53992	8.53125	8.52259	8.51395
	10	9.49251	9.48190	9.47130	9.46073	9.45017	9.43963	9.42910	9.41860	9.40811
	11	10.39291	10.38026	10.36763	10.35502	10.34244	10.32987	10.31733	10.30481	10.29232
1	12	11.28476	11.26991	11.25508	11.24028	11.22550	11.21076	11.19604	11.18135	11.16669
2	24	21.34913	21.29617	21.24339	21.19079	21.13838	21.08616	21.03411	20.98225	20.93057
3	36	30.32508	30.21602	30.10751	29.99954	29.89213	29.78525	29.67892	29.57312	29.46785
4	48	38.33032	38.15155	37.97396	37.79754	37.62227	37.44816	37.27519	37.10335	36.93264
5	60	45.46982	45.21139	44.95504	44.70075	44.44852	44.19831	43.95011	43.70390	43.45966
6	72	51.83722	51.49217	51.15039	50.81187	50.47655	50.14442	49.81542	49.48953	49.16672
7	84	57.51602	57.07985	56.64845	56.22176	55.79972	55.38226	54.96933	54.56087	54.15683
8	96	62.58068	62.05093	61.52770	61.01090	60.50043	59.99620	59.49812	59.00610	58.52005
9	108	67.09761	66.47344	65.85779	65.25051	64.65148	64.06055	63.47760	62.90251	62.33515
10	120	71.12606	70.40793	69.70052	69.00365	68.31713	67.64078	66.97442	66.31787	65.67097
11	132	74.71885	73.90824	73.11075	72.32614	71.55415	70.79455	70.04710	69.31157	68.58773
12	144	77.92310	77.02228	76.13716	75.26739	74.41266	73.57267	72.74710	71.93566	71.13807
13	156	80.78081	79.79269	78.82294	77.87115	76.93692	76.01987	75.11961	74.23578	73.36802
14	168	83.32948	82.25738	81.20643	80.17614	79.16601	78.17557	77.20436	76.25193	75.31783
15	180	85.60253	84.45009	83.32166	82.21665	81.13445	80.07450	79.03625	78.01916	77.02270
16	192	87.62975	86.40083	85.19882	84.02302	82.87271	81.74724	80.64595	79.56821	78.51339
17	204	89.43774	88.13630	86.86471	85.62211	84.40772	83.22073	82.06041	80.92601	79.81682
18	216	91.05020	89.68027	88.34309	87.03772	85.76323	84.51871	83.30331	82.11617	80.95650
19	228	92.48828	91.05385	89.65509	88.29090	86.96024	85.66208	84.39545	83.15940	81.95301
20	240	93.77084	92.27586	90.81942	89.40028	88.01728	86.66926	85.35513	84.07383	82.82433
21	252	94.91469	93.36302	91.85270	90.38237	88.95072	87.55647	86.19841	84.87536	83.58619
22	264	95.93485	94.33021	92.76968	91.25177	89.77501	88.33800	86.93941	85.57794	84.25235
23	276	96.84467	95.19066	93.58346	92.02141	90.50291	89.02644	87.59053	86.19377	84.83481
24	288	97.65611	95.95617	94.30565	92.70273	91.14570	89.63288	88.16268	86.73358	85.34411
25	300	98.37979	96.63720	94.94655	93.30588	91.71332	90.16708	88.66543	87.20673	85.78942
26	312	99.02520	97.24308	95.51532	93.83962	92.21457	90.63765	89.10720	87.62148	86.17879
27	324	99.60082	97.78210	96.02007	94.31250	92.65721	91.05216	89.49539	87.98501	86.51925
28	336	100.11419	98.26164	96.46802	94.73093	93.04809	91.41731	89.83649	88.30367	86.81694
29	348	100.57204	98.68826	96.86555	95.10136	93.39327	91.73896	90.13623	88.58298	87.07723
30	360	100.98037	99.06780	97.21833	95.42928	93.69808	92.02229	90.39961	88.82781	87.30482
31	372	101.34455	99.40546	97.53141	95.71957	93.96725	92.27188	90.63104	89.04242	87.50382
32	384	101.66934	99.70586	97.80925	95.97655	94.20494	92.49174	90.83440	89.23052	87.67782
33	396	101.95901	99.97310	98.05582	96.20405	94.41484	92.68541	91.01310	89.39541	87.82996
34	408	102.21735	100.21086	98.27464	96.40544	94.60020	92.85601	91.17012	89.53993	87.96299
35	420	102.44775	100.42238	98.46883	96.58373	94.76388	93.00629	91.30810	89.66662	88.07930
36	432	102.65324	100.61056	98.64117	96.74155	94.90842	93.13866	91.42934	89.77766	88.18101
37	444	102.83650	100.77798	98.79410	96.88127	95.03606	93.25528	91.53587	89.87499	88.26994
38	456	102.99994	100.92692	98.92983	97.00495	95.14878	93.35800	91.62949	89.96031	88.34769
39	468	103.14571	101.05942	99.05028	97.11445	95.24831	93.44848	91.71175	90.03509	88.41568
40	480	103.27571	101.17730	99.15717	97.21137	95.33621	93.52819	91.78403	90.10065	88.47513

PRESENT VALUE OF ONE DOLLAR PER PERIOD

PERIOD YR	MOS	ANNUAL INTEREST RATE .13750	.14000	.14250	.14500	.14750	.15000	.15250	.15500	.15750
	1	.98867	.98847	.98826	.98806	.98786	.98765	.98745	.98725	.98705
	2	1.96614	1.96554	1.96493	1.96433	1.96372	1.96312	1.96251	1.96191	1.96130
	3	2.93254	2.93134	2.93014	2.92893	2.92773	2.92653	2.92533	2.92414	2.92294
	4	3.88799	3.88600	3.88401	3.88203	3.88004	3.87806	3.87608	3.87410	3.87212
	5	4.83262	4.82966	4.82670	4.82374	4.82079	4.81784	4.81489	4.81194	4.80900
	6	5.76654	5.76243	5.75832	5.75421	5.75011	5.74601	5.74192	5.73783	5.73374
	7	6.68989	6.68444	6.67900	6.67357	6.66814	6.66273	6.65731	6.65191	6.64651
	8	7.60277	7.59582	7.58888	7.58196	7.57503	7.56812	7.56122	7.55433	7.54745
	9	8.50532	8.49670	8.48809	8.47949	8.47091	8.46234	8.45379	8.44525	8.43672
	10	9.39763	9.38718	9.37674	9.36632	9.35591	9.34553	9.33516	9.32480	9.31446
	11	10.27984	10.26739	10.25496	10.24255	10.23017	10.21780	10.20546	10.19314	10.18084
1	12	11.15206	11.13746	11.12288	11.10833	11.09381	11.07931	11.06485	11.05041	11.03599
2	24	20.87907	20.82774	20.77660	20.72563	20.67485	20.62423	20.57380	20.52354	20.47345
3	36	29.36311	29.25890	29.15522	29.05205	28.94940	28.84727	28.74564	28.64453	28.54392
4	48	36.76304	36.59455	36.42715	36.26085	36.09563	35.93148	35.76840	35.60637	35.44540
5	60	43.21737	42.97702	42.73858	42.50204	42.26739	42.03459	41.80364	41.57453	41.34722
6	72	48.84694	48.53017	48.21637	47.90551	47.59755	47.29247	46.99024	46.69082	46.39417
7	84	53.75714	53.36176	52.97063	52.58369	52.20089	51.82219	51.44752	51.07684	50.71009
8	96	58.03990	57.56555	57.09692	56.63394	56.17651	55.72457	55.27803	54.83682	54.40086
9	108	61.77539	61.22311	60.67820	60.14054	59.61001	59.08651	58.56992	58.06012	57.55703
10	120	65.03354	64.40542	63.78645	63.17647	62.57532	61.98285	61.39891	60.82335	60.25604
11	132	67.87535	67.17423	66.48415	65.80489	65.13627	64.47807	63.83010	63.19217	62.56410
12	144	70.35403	69.58327	68.82552	68.08052	67.34800	66.62772	65.91943	65.22288	64.53784
13	156	72.51597	71.67928	70.85764	70.05070	69.25814	68.47967	67.71496	66.96374	66.22570
14	168	74.40164	73.50295	72.62134	71.75643	70.90781	70.07513	69.25802	68.45611	67.66907
15	180	76.04636	75.08965	74.15209	73.23320	72.33253	71.44964	70.58410	69.73548	68.90337
16	192	77.48091	76.47019	75.48065	74.51176	73.56298	72.63379	71.72371	70.83223	69.95889
17	204	78.73215	77.67134	76.63373	75.61870	74.62564	73.65395	72.70307	71.77244	70.86152
18	216	79.82350	78.71641	77.63450	76.57706	75.54339	74.53282	73.54472	72.57845	71.63341
19	228	80.77539	79.62570	78.50309	77.40678	76.33599	75.28998	74.26802	73.26941	72.29349
20	240	81.60565	80.41683	79.25695	78.12514	77.02052	75.94228	74.88961	73.86175	72.85795
21	252	82.32981	81.10516	79.91124	78.74707	77.61170	76.50424	75.42380	74.36954	73.34066
22	264	82.96144	81.70406	80.47911	79.28552	78.12227	76.98837	75.88287	74.80486	73.75345
23	276	83.51235	82.22514	80.97197	79.75170	78.56322	77.40546	76.27739	75.17804	74.10645
24	288	83.99287	82.67851	81.39973	80.15531	78.94404	77.76478	76.61643	75.49795	74.40831
25	300	84.41198	83.07297	81.77099	80.50474	79.27293	78.07434	76.90780	75.77220	74.66645
26	312	84.77754	83.41617	82.09322	80.80727	79.55697	78.34102	77.15820	76.00731	74.88721
27	324	85.09638	83.71478	82.37288	81.06919	79.80228	78.57078	77.37339	76.20885	75.07598
28	336	85.37449	83.97459	82.61560	81.29595	80.01413	78.76871	77.55832	76.38163	75.23741
29	348	85.61705	84.20064	82.82627	81.49228	80.19710	78.93924	77.71724	76.52975	75.37546
30	360	85.82862	84.39732	83.00911	81.66226	80.35512	79.08614	77.85382	76.65673	75.49351
31	372	86.01315	84.56844	83.16780	81.80942	80.49160	79.21270	77.97119	76.76558	75.59447
32	384	86.17411	84.71733	83.30552	81.93682	80.60946	79.32174	78.07206	76.85890	75.68080
33	396	86.31449	84.84687	83.42506	82.04713	80.71125	79.41567	78.15874	76.93889	75.75462
34	408	86.43694	84.95958	83.52881	82.14263	80.79916	79.49660	78.23324	77.00747	75.81776
35	420	86.54374	85.05764	83.61885	82.22531	80.87508	79.56631	78.29726	77.06626	75.87174
36	432	86.63689	85.14297	83.69700	82.29690	80.94065	79.62637	78.35228	77.11666	75.91791
37	444	86.71814	85.21720	83.76483	82.35887	80.99728	79.67812	78.39956	77.15987	75.95739
38	456	86.78901	85.28179	83.82370	82.41253	81.04618	79.72270	78.44019	77.19690	75.99115
39	468	86.85082	85.33799	83.87479	82.45898	81.08842	79.76110	78.47511	77.22866	76.02002
40	480	86.90473	85.38688	83.91914	82.49920	81.12490	79.79419	78.50512	77.25587	76.04471

PRESENT VALUE OF ONE DOLLAR PER PERIOD

ANNUAL INTEREST RATE

PERIOD YR	MOS	.16000	.16250	.16500	.16750	.17000	.17250	.17500	.17750	.18000
	1	.98684	.98664	.98644	.98623	.98603	.98583	.98563	.98542	.98522
	2	1.96070	1.96010	1.95949	1.95889	1.95829	1.95769	1.95709	1.95648	1.95588
	3	2.92174	2.92055	2.91935	2.91816	2.91697	2.91577	2.91458	2.91339	2.91220
	4	3.87014	3.86817	3.86619	3.86422	3.86225	3.86028	3.85831	3.85635	3.85438
	5	4.80606	4.80312	4.80019	4.79726	4.79433	4.79140	4.78848	4.78556	4.78264
	6	5.72966	5.72559	5.72152	5.71745	5.71339	5.70933	5.70528	5.70123	5.69719
	7	6.64112	6.63573	6.63035	6.62498	6.61961	6.61425	6.60890	6.60355	6.59821
	8	7.54058	7.53371	7.52686	7.52001	7.51318	7.50635	7.49953	7.49272	7.48593
	9	8.42820	8.41969	8.41120	8.40272	8.39426	8.38580	8.37736	8.36893	8.36052
	10	9.30414	9.29384	9.28355	9.27328	9.26303	9.25279	9.24257	9.23237	9.22218
	11	10.16856	10.15631	10.14407	10.13186	10.11967	10.10750	10.09535	10.08322	10.07112
1	12	11.02161	11.00725	10.99292	10.97862	10.96434	10.95009	10.93587	10.92167	10.90751
2	24	20.42354	20.37380	20.32423	20.27484	20.22561	20.17656	20.12767	20.07895	20.03041
3	36	28.44381	28.34420	28.24509	28.14647	28.04834	27.95071	27.85355	27.75688	27.66068
4	48	35.28547	35.12657	34.96869	34.81183	34.65599	34.50114	34.34730	34.19443	34.04255
5	60	41.12171	40.89797	40.67600	40.45577	40.23728	40.02049	39.80541	39.59201	39.38027
6	72	46.10028	45.80911	45.52064	45.23482	44.95164	44.67106	44.39306	44.11760	43.84467
7	84	50.34723	49.98822	49.63299	49.28151	48.93372	48.58959	48.24906	47.91209	47.57863
8	96	53.97008	53.54440	53.12375	52.70807	52.29728	51.89131	51.49010	51.09357	50.70168
9	108	57.06052	56.57051	56.08688	55.60953	55.13838	54.67332	54.21425	53.76109	53.31375
10	120	59.69682	59.14556	58.60212	58.06637	57.53818	57.01741	56.50396	55.99768	55.49845
11	132	61.94569	61.33678	60.73717	60.14671	59.56522	58.99253	58.42849	57.87294	57.32571
12	144	63.86409	63.20138	62.54951	61.90825	61.27740	60.65675	60.04610	59.44525	58.85401
13	156	65.50056	64.78805	64.08790	63.39985	62.72364	62.05901	61.40573	60.76356	60.13226
14	168	66.89655	66.13822	65.39377	64.66287	63.94523	63.24055	62.54853	61.86890	61.20137
15	180	68.08739	67.28714	66.50225	65.73234	64.97708	64.23610	63.50907	62.79566	62.09556
16	192	69.10323	68.26480	67.44318	66.63793	65.84865	65.07494	64.31642	63.57271	62.84345
17	204	69.96979	69.09674	68.24188	67.40473	66.58484	65.78175	64.99502	64.22423	63.46898
18	216	70.70900	69.80467	68.91986	68.05403	67.20668	66.37729	65.56539	64.77050	63.99216
19	228	71.33959	70.40708	69.49536	68.60383	67.73193	66.87910	66.04480	65.22851	64.42974
20	240	71.87750	70.91970	69.98387	69.06938	68.17559	67.30191	66.44775	65.61254	64.79573
21	252	72.33637	71.35590	70.39854	69.46358	68.55035	67.65817	66.78643	65.93452	65.10184
22	264	72.72780	71.72709	70.75054	69.79738	68.86689	67.95836	67.07111	66.20449	65.35787
23	276	73.06171	72.04295	71.04933	70.08002	69.13426	68.21129	67.31038	66.43084	65.57200
24	288	73.34655	72.31173	71.30295	70.31935	69.36010	68.42441	67.51149	66.62063	65.75110
25	300	73.58953	72.54045	71.51824	70.52201	69.55087	68.60398	67.68053	66.77976	65.90090
26	312	73.79681	72.73507	71.70099	70.69361	69.71200	68.75529	67.82262	66.91318	66.02619
27	324	73.97362	72.90069	71.85612	70.83891	69.84810	68.88277	67.94204	67.02504	66.13098
28	336	74.12445	73.04161	71.98779	70.96195	69.96307	68.99020	68.04241	67.11884	66.21862
29	348	74.25312	73.16154	72.09957	71.06613	70.06017	69.08071	68.12678	67.19748	66.29193
30	360	74.36288	73.26358	72.19445	71.15434	70.14220	69.15697	68.19769	67.26342	66.35324
31	372	74.45651	73.35042	72.27499	71.22904	70.21148	69.22123	68.25730	67.31870	66.40452
32	384	74.53637	73.42431	72.34335	71.29229	70.27000	69.27538	68.30740	67.36506	66.44741
33	396	74.60451	73.48719	72.40138	71.34585	70.31943	69.32100	68.34950	67.40392	66.48328
34	408	74.66263	73.54070	72.45064	71.39120	70.36118	69.35944	68.38490	67.43651	66.51329
35	420	74.71221	73.58623	72.49245	71.42960	70.39645	69.39183	68.41465	67.46383	66.53838
36	432	74.75450	73.62497	72.52795	71.46212	70.42624	69.41913	68.43965	67.48674	66.55937
37	444	74.79058	73.65794	72.55808	71.48965	70.45140	69.44212	68.46067	67.50595	66.57693
38	456	74.82135	73.68599	72.58365	71.51297	70.47266	69.46150	68.47833	67.52205	66.59161
39	468	74.84760	73.70987	72.60536	71.53271	70.49061	69.47782	68.49318	67.53555	66.60389
40	480	74.87000	73.73018	72.62379	71.54942	70.50577	69.49158	68.50566	67.54687	66.61416

PRESENT VALUE OF ONE DOLLAR PER PERIOD

ANNUAL INTEREST RATE

PERIOD YR	MOS	.18250	.18500	.18750	.19000	.19250	.19500	.19750	.20000	.20250
	1	.98502	.98482	.98462	.98441	.98421	.98401	.98381	.98361	.98341
	2	1.95528	1.95468	1.95408	1.95348	1.95288	1.95229	1.95169	1.95109	1.95049
	3	2.91101	2.90982	2.90864	2.90745	2.90626	2.90508	2.90389	2.90271	2.90153
	4	3.85242	3.85046	3.84850	3.84655	3.84459	3.84263	3.84068	3.83873	3.83678
	5	4.77973	4.77682	4.77391	4.77100	4.76810	4.76520	4.76230	4.75941	4.75652
	6	5.69315	5.68911	5.68508	5.68105	5.67703	5.67301	5.66900	5.66499	5.66099
	7	6.59288	6.58755	6.58223	6.57692	6.57161	6.56631	6.56102	6.55573	6.55045
	8	7.47914	7.47235	7.46558	7.45882	7.45207	7.44532	7.43859	7.43186	7.42515
	9	8.35211	8.34372	8.33534	8.32698	8.31862	8.31028	8.30195	8.29364	8.28533
	10	9.21201	9.20186	9.19172	9.18160	9.17150	9.16141	9.15134	9.14128	9.13124
	11	10.05903	10.04697	10.03493	10.02291	10.01091	9.99893	9.98697	9.97503	9.96312
1	12	10.89336	10.87925	10.86516	10.85110	10.83706	10.82305	10.80907	10.79511	10.78118
2	24	19.98202	19.93381	19.88576	19.83788	19.79016	19.74261	19.69521	19.64799	19.60092
3	36	27.56497	27.46972	27.37495	27.28065	27.18681	27.09343	27.00052	26.90806	26.81606
4	48	33.89165	33.74170	33.59272	33.44468	33.29759	33.15144	33.00622	32.86192	32.71853
5	60	39.17018	38.96173	38.75490	38.54968	38.34605	38.14400	37.94350	37.74456	37.54715
6	72	43.57423	43.30625	43.04072	42.77760	42.51686	42.25849	42.00245	41.74873	41.49729
7	84	47.24865	46.92210	46.59893	46.27912	45.96260	45.64935	45.33932	45.03247	44.72877
8	96	50.31434	49.93149	49.55308	49.17904	48.80931	48.44384	48.08255	47.72541	47.37234
9	108	52.87213	52.43614	52.00571	51.58074	51.16114	50.74685	50.33777	49.93383	49.53495
10	120	55.00617	54.52071	54.04196	53.56980	53.10412	52.64482	52.19179	51.74492	51.30412
11	132	56.78667	56.25565	55.73251	55.21712	54.70932	54.20899	53.71598	53.23017	52.75142
12	144	58.27219	57.69960	57.13607	56.58142	56.03547	55.49805	54.96901	54.44818	53.93541
13	156	59.51160	58.90137	58.30135	57.71131	57.13107	56.56041	55.99914	55.44706	54.90399
14	168	60.54569	59.90158	59.26880	58.64709	58.03621	57.43592	56.84600	56.26622	55.69635
15	180	61.40845	60.73403	60.07200	59.42208	58.78399	58.15745	57.54221	56.93799	56.34456
16	192	62.12828	61.42686	60.73885	60.06393	59.40178	58.75209	58.11456	57.48891	56.87484
17	204	62.72886	62.00349	61.29249	60.59550	59.91217	59.24214	58.58509	57.94070	57.30864
18	216	63.22994	62.48340	61.75214	61.03574	60.33382	59.64600	58.97192	58.31120	57.66352
19	228	63.64800	62.88283	62.13375	61.40035	60.68218	59.97884	59.28993	58.61505	57.95384
20	240	63.99681	63.21526	62.45058	61.70231	60.96998	60.25314	59.55136	58.86423	58.19134
21	252	64.28783	63.49193	62.71363	61.95239	61.20774	60.47919	59.76629	59.06857	58.38563
22	264	64.53063	63.72220	62.93201	62.15951	61.40417	60.66549	59.94298	59.23616	58.54457
23	276	64.73321	63.91385	63.11332	62.33104	61.56645	60.81903	60.08824	59.37359	58.67459
24	288	64.90223	64.07336	63.26385	62.47310	61.70052	60.94556	60.20765	59.48629	58.78096
25	300	65.04325	64.20611	63.38883	62.59076	61.81129	61.04983	60.30582	59.57872	58.86798
26	312	65.16090	64.31660	63.49258	62.68820	61.90279	61.13577	60.38653	59.65451	58.93917
27	324	65.25907	64.40855	63.57873	62.76889	61.97839	61.20659	60.45288	59.71667	58.99740
28	336	65.34097	64.48509	63.65025	62.83573	62.04085	61.26496	60.50743	59.76765	59.04504
29	348	65.40930	64.54878	63.70962	62.89108	62.09245	61.31306	60.55227	59.80945	59.08402
30	360	65.46631	64.60180	63.75892	62.93692	62.13503	61.35270	60.58913	59.84374	59.11590
31	372	65.51388	64.64592	63.79985	62.97489	62.17030	61.38537	60.61944	59.87185	59.14198
32	384	65.55356	64.68264	63.83383	63.00633	62.19939	61.41230	60.64436	59.89491	59.16332
33	396	65.58667	64.71320	63.86204	63.03237	62.22343	61.43449	60.66484	59.91381	59.18077
34	408	65.61430	64.73864	63.88546	63.05394	62.24329	61.45277	60.68168	59.92932	59.19505
35	420	65.63735	64.75981	63.90490	63.07180	62.25969	61.46784	60.69552	59.94204	59.20673
36	432	65.65658	64.77743	63.92105	63.08659	62.27325	61.48026	60.70690	59.95247	59.21629
37	444	65.67262	64.79210	63.93445	63.09884	62.28445	61.49050	60.71626	59.96102	59.22411
38	456	65.68601	64.80430	63.94558	63.10899	62.29370	61.49893	60.72395	59.96803	59.23050
39	468	65.69718	64.81446	63.95482	63.11739	62.30134	61.50589	60.73027	59.97378	59.23573
40	480	65.70650	64.82291	63.96249	63.12435	62.30766	61.51162	60.73547	59.97850	59.24001

PRESENT VALUE OF ONE DOLLAR PER PERIOD

ANNUAL INTEREST RATE

PERIOD YR	MOS	.20500	.20750	.21000	.21250	.21500	.21750	.22000	.22250	.22500
	1	.98320	.98300	.98280	.93260	.98240	.98220	.98200	.98180	.98160
	2	1.94989	1.94930	1.94870	1.94810	1.94751	1.94691	1.94631	1.94572	1.94512
	3	2.90035	2.89916	2.89798	2.89680	2.89563	2.89445	2.89327	2.89209	2.89092
	4	3.83483	3.83289	3.83094	3.82900	3.82706	3.82512	3.82318	3.82124	3.81931
	5	4.75363	4.75074	4.74786	4.74497	4.74210	4.73922	4.73635	4.73348	4.73061
	6	5.65699	5.65299	5.64900	5.64501	5.64103	5.63705	5.63307	5.62910	5.62514
	7	6.54517	6.53990	6.53464	6.52939	6.52414	6.51889	6.51366	6.50843	6.50320
	8	7.41844	7.41174	7.40505	7.39837	7.39170	7.38504	7.37839	7.37174	7.36511
	9	8.27704	8.26876	8.26049	8.25224	8.24400	8.23577	8.22755	8.21934	8.21115
	10	9.12122	9.11121	9.10122	9.09125	9.08129	9.07135	9.06142	9.05151	9.04162
	11	9.95122	9.93935	9.92749	9.91566	9.90385	9.89205	9.88028	9.86853	9.85680
1	12	10.76728	10.75340	10.73955	10.72572	10.71192	10.69815	10.68440	10.67068	10.65698
2	24	19.55401	19.50727	19.46069	19.41426	19.36799	19.32189	19.27594	19.23014	19.18451
3	36	26.72451	26.63341	26.54275	26.45254	26.36278	26.27345	26.18455	26.09610	26.00807
4	48	32.57605	32.43448	32.29380	32.15401	32.01510	31.87707	31.73991	31.60361	31.46816
5	60	37.35126	37.15688	36.96399	36.77257	36.58263	36.39413	36.20707	36.02144	35.83723
6	72	41.24811	41.00117	40.75645	40.51391	40.27354	40.03531	39.79921	39.56520	39.33327
7	84	44.42817	44.13064	43.83614	43.54464	43.25609	42.97046	42.68771	42.40782	42.13074
8	96	47.02329	46.67820	46.33703	45.99972	45.66622	45.33647	45.01042	44.68802	44.36923
9	108	49.14105	48.75206	48.36790	47.98850	47.61379	47.24370	46.87815	46.51708	46.16042
10	120	50.86928	50.44030	50.01709	49.59955	49.18758	48.78111	48.38002	47.98425	47.59370
11	132	52.27961	51.81462	51.35632	50.90460	50.45933	50.02041	49.58771	49.16114	48.74058
12	144	53.43052	52.93339	52.44385	51.96177	51.48700	51.01940	50.55884	50.10518	49.65830
13	156	54.36974	53.84413	53.32699	52.81815	52.31744	51.82469	51.33974	50.86244	50.39264
14	168	55.13619	54.58553	54.04416	53.51188	52.98849	52.47382	51.96768	51.46988	50.98024
15	180	55.76166	55.18907	54.62653	54.07384	53.53076	52.99709	52.47261	51.95713	51.45044
16	192	56.27209	55.68036	55.09946	54.52906	53.96896	53.41889	52.87864	52.34798	51.82667
17	204	56.68862	56.08033	55.48350	54.89783	54.32305	53.75891	53.20514	52.66149	52.12773
18	216	57.02854	56.40592	55.79536	55.19655	54.60919	54.03299	53.46768	52.91298	52.36863
19	228	57.30593	56.67097	56.04861	55.43853	54.84041	54.25393	53.67880	53.11471	52.56140
20	240	57.53230	56.88673	56.25427	55.63456	55.02725	54.43203	53.84856	53.27653	52.71564
21	252	57.71703	57.06237	56.42127	55.79335	55.17824	54.57559	53.98507	53.40633	52.83907
22	264	57.86778	57.20535	56.55689	55.92198	55.30025	54.69132	54.09484	53.51045	52.93783
23	276	57.99080	57.32175	56.66702	56.02618	55.39884	54.78460	54.18310	53.59397	53.01686
24	288	58.09119	57.41650	56.75645	56.11059	55.47851	54.85980	54.25408	53.66097	53.08010
25	300	58.17312	57.49364	56.82907	56.17896	55.54289	54.92042	54.31116	53.71471	53.13070
26	312	58.23997	57.55643	56.88804	56.23435	55.59491	54.96928	54.35705	53.75781	53.17119
27	324	58.29453	57.60754	56.93593	56.27922	55.63695	55.00867	54.39395	53.79239	53.20359
28	336	58.33906	57.64915	56.97482	56.31557	55.67092	55.04042	54.42363	53.82013	53.22951
29	348	58.37539	57.68303	57.00640	56.34501	55.69837	55.06601	54.44749	53.84238	53.25026
30	360	58.40504	57.71060	57.03205	56.36886	55.72055	55.08665	54.46668	53.86023	53.26686
31	372	58.42924	57.73305	57.05287	56.38819	55.73848	55.10328	54.48211	53.87454	53.28014
32	384	58.44898	57.75132	57.06979	56.40384	55.75296	55.11668	54.49452	53.88603	53.29077
33	396	58.46510	57.76620	57.08352	56.41651	55.76467	55.12749	54.50450	53.89524	53.29928
34	408	58.47825	57.77831	57.09467	56.42679	55.77413	55.13620	54.51252	53.90263	53.30608
35	420	58.48898	57.78817	57.10373	56.43510	55.78177	55.14322	54.51897	53.90855	53.31153
36	432	58.49773	57.79619	57.11108	56.44184	55.78795	55.14888	54.52416	53.91331	53.31588
37	444	58.50488	57.80273	57.11705	56.44730	55.79294	55.15345	54.52833	53.91712	53.31937
38	456	58.51071	57.80804	57.12190	56.45173	55.79697	55.15712	54.53168	53.92018	53.32216
39	468	58.51547	57.81237	57.12584	56.45531	55.80023	55.16009	54.53438	53.92264	53.32439
40	480	58.51936	57.81590	57.12904	56.45821	55.80286	55.16248	54.53655	53.92460	53.32618

PRESENT VALUE OF ONE DOLLAR PER PERIOD

ANNUAL INTEREST RATE

PERIOD YR	MOS	.22750	.23000	.23250	.23500	.23750	.24000	.24250	.24500	.24750
	1	.98139	.98119	.98099	.98079	.98059	.98039	.98019	.97999	.97979
	2	1.94453	1.94394	1.94334	1.94275	1.94215	1.94156	1.94097	1.94038	1.93978
	3	2.88974	2.88857	2.88740	2.88623	2.88505	2.88388	2.88271	2.88154	2.88038
	4	3.81737	3.81544	3.81351	3.81158	3.80965	3.80773	3.80580	3.80388	3.80196
	5	4.72774	4.72488	4.72202	4.71916	4.71631	4.71346	4.71061	4.70776	4.70492
	6	5.62118	5.61722	5.61326	5.60932	5.60537	5.60143	5.59749	5.59356	5.58964
	7	6.49798	6.49277	6.48757	6.48237	6.47718	6.47199	6.46681	6.46164	6.45647
	8	7.35848	7.35186	7.34525	7.33865	7.33206	7.32548	7.31891	7.31234	7.30579
	9	8.20297	8.19480	8.18664	8.17849	8.17036	8.16224	8.15413	8.14603	8.13794
	10	9.03174	9.02188	9.01203	9.00220	8.99238	8.98259	8.97280	8.96303	8.95328
	11	9.84509	9.83340	9.82173	9.81008	9.79846	9.78685	9.77526	9.76369	9.75214
1	12	10.64331	10.62967	10.61605	10.60245	10.58888	10.57534	10.56182	10.54833	10.53486
2	24	19.13902	19.09370	19.04852	19.00350	18.95864	18.91393	18.86936	18.82495	18.78069
3	36	25.92047	25.83330	25.74656	25.66023	25.57433	25.48884	25.40377	25.31911	25.23486
4	48	31.33357	31.19982	31.06690	30.93482	30.80356	30.67312	30.54349	30.41467	30.28665
5	60	35.65441	35.47298	35.29292	35.11423	34.93669	34.76089	34.58621	34.41285	34.24078
6	72	39.10339	38.87555	38.64971	38.42587	38.20399	37.98406	37.76606	37.54997	37.33576
7	84	41.85644	41.58490	41.31606	41.04991	40.78640	40.52552	40.26722	40.01147	39.75825
8	96	44.05399	43.74225	43.43398	43.12911	42.82761	42.52943	42.23453	41.94286	41.65438
9	108	45.80811	45.46008	45.11627	44.77661	44.44104	44.10951	43.78195	43.45830	43.13851
10	120	47.20829	46.82792	46.45253	46.08203	45.71634	45.35539	44.99909	44.64738	44.30017
11	132	48.32594	47.91709	47.51395	47.11641	46.72438	46.33776	45.95645	45.58037	45.20943
12	144	49.21807	48.78436	48.35705	47.93602	47.52116	47.11235	46.70947	46.31243	45.92111
13	156	49.93018	49.47493	49.02673	48.58545	48.15095	47.72310	47.30177	46.88684	46.47817
14	168	50.49861	50.02481	49.55867	49.10004	48.64876	48.20468	47.76766	47.33754	46.91418
15	180	50.95234	50.46266	49.98120	49.50778	49.04224	48.58440	48.13410	47.69117	47.25546
16	192	51.31452	50.81130	50.31682	49.83087	49.35326	48.88381	48.42233	47.96865	47.52258
17	204	51.60361	51.08891	50.58340	50.08687	49.59910	49.11989	48.64905	48.18637	47.73166
18	216	51.83438	51.30996	50.79516	50.28972	49.79342	49.30604	48.82737	48.35720	47.89532
19	228	52.01858	51.48596	50.96336	50.45045	49.94701	49.45282	48.96763	48.49124	48.02341
20	240	52.16561	51.62614	51.09696	50.57780	50.06842	49.56855	49.07796	48.59641	48.12367
21	252	52.28297	51.73774	51.20308	50.67872	50.16438	49.65981	49.16474	48.67893	48.20215
22	264	52.37665	51.82660	51.28738	50.75868	50.24023	49.73176	49.23300	48.74368	48.26358
23	276	52.45143	51.89736	51.35433	50.82204	50.30019	49.78849	49.28668	48.79449	48.31165
24	288	52.51112	51.95371	51.40752	50.87224	50.34758	49.83323	49.32891	48.83435	48.34929
25	300	52.55877	51.99857	51.44976	50.91202	50.38504	49.86850	49.36213	48.86563	48.37874
26	312	52.59680	52.03429	51.48332	50.94354	50.41464	49.89631	49.38825	48.89017	48.40180
27	324	52.62716	52.06274	51.50997	50.96852	50.43805	49.91824	49.40880	48.90943	48.41984
28	336	52.65139	52.08539	51.53114	50.98831	50.45655	49.93554	49.42497	48.92454	48.43397
29	348	52.67073	52.10342	51.54796	51.00399	50.47117	49.94917	49.43768	48.93640	48.44502
30	360	52.68617	52.11779	51.56132	51.01641	50.48273	49.95992	49.44768	48.94570	48.45368
31	372	52.69850	52.12922	51.57193	51.02626	50.49186	49.96840	49.45555	48.95300	48.46045
32	384	52.70834	52.13833	51.58036	51.03406	50.49908	49.97508	49.46174	48.95873	48.46575
33	396	52.71619	52.14558	51.58705	51.04024	50.50479	49.98035	49.46660	48.96322	48.46990
34	408	52.72246	52.15135	51.59237	51.04514	50.50930	49.98451	49.47043	48.96675	48.47315
35	420	52.72746	52.15595	51.59659	51.04902	50.51287	49.98778	49.47344	48.96951	48.47569
36	432	52.73145	52.15961	51.59995	51.05209	50.51568	49.99037	49.47581	48.97168	48.47768
37	444	52.73464	52.16252	51.60261	51.05453	50.51791	49.99241	49.47767	48.97339	48.47924
38	456	52.73719	52.16484	51.60473	51.05646	50.51967	49.99401	49.47914	48.97472	48.48046
39	468	52.73922	52.16669	51.60641	51.05799	50.52107	49.99528	49.48029	48.97577	48.48141
40	480	52.74084	52.16816	51.60775	51.05920	50.52217	49.99628	49.48120	48.97659	48.48216

MORTGAGE CONSTANT TABLE

Description:

The Mortgage Constant table can be used to compute the monthly payments required to amortize a loan of any size. To use the table, find the factor that corresponds to the contract interest rate and loan term to maturity; then multiply by the initial loan amount to arrive at the monthly loan payments.

Table Calculation Formula:

$$MC = \frac{1}{\left[\frac{1 - 1/(1+i)^n}{i}\right]}$$

Table Range:

Annual interest rate, with monthly compounding, from 7.00% to 24.75% in .25% increments. Loan terms from 1 to 12 months in 1-month increments, 1 to 40 years in 1 year increments.

Example:

What would the monthly payments be to completely amortize a 9%, $40,000, 25-year term loan?

Solution:

Finding the monthly mortgage constant corresponding to 9% and 25 years provides:

$$\begin{aligned} \text{Monthly payment} &= \$40{,}000 \times \text{table factor } MC,\ 9\%,\ 25 \text{ years}, \\ &= \$40{,}000(.00839), \\ &= \$335.60. \end{aligned}$$

A monthly payment of $335.60 for 25 years will completely amortize the $40,000, 9% contract interest rate loan.

MORTGAGE CONSTANT

PERIOD YR	MOS	.07000	.07250	.07500	.07750	.08000	.08250	.08500	.08750	.09000
		ANNUAL INTEREST RATE								
	1	1.00583	1.00604	1.00625	1.00646	1.00667	1.00688	1.00708	1.00729	1.00750
	2	.50438	.50454	.50469	.50485	.50501	.50516	.50532	.50548	.50563
	3	.33723	.33737	.33751	.33765	.33779	.33793	.33807	.33821	.33835
	4	.25366	.25379	.25392	.25405	.25418	.25431	.25444	.25457	.25471
	5	.20351	.20364	.20377	.20389	.20402	.20414	.20427	.20440	.20452
	6	.17009	.17021	.17033	.17045	.17058	.17070	.17082	.17095	.17107
	7	.14621	.14633	.14645	.14657	.14669	.14681	.14693	.14705	.14717
	8	.12830	.12842	.12854	.12866	.12878	.12890	.12902	.12914	.12926
	9	.11438	.11449	.11461	.11473	.11485	.11497	.11508	.11520	.11532
	10	.10324	.10335	.10347	.10359	.10370	.10382	.10394	.10405	.10417
	11	.09412	.09424	.09435	.09447	.09459	.09470	.09482	.09493	.09505
1	12	.08653	.08664	.08676	.08687	.08699	.08710	.08722	.08734	.08745
2	24	.04477	.04489	.04500	.04511	.04523	.04534	.04546	.04557	.04568
3	36	.03088	.03099	.03111	.03122	.03134	.03145	.03157	.03168	.03180
4	48	.02395	.02406	.02418	.02430	.02441	.02453	.02465	.02477	.02489
5	60	.01980	.01992	.02004	.02016	.02028	.02040	.02052	.02064	.02076
6	72	.01705	.01717	.01729	.01741	.01753	.01766	.01778	.01790	.01803
7	84	.01509	.01522	.01534	.01546	.01559	.01571	.01584	.01596	.01609
8	96	.01363	.01376	.01388	.01401	.01414	.01426	.01439	.01452	.01465
9	108	.01251	.01263	.01276	.01289	.01302	.01315	.01328	.01341	.01354
10	120	.01161	.01174	.01187	.01200	.01213	.01227	.01240	.01253	.01267
11	132	.01088	.01102	.01115	.01128	.01142	.01155	.01169	.01182	.01196
12	144	.01028	.01042	.01055	.01069	.01082	.01096	.01110	.01124	.01138
13	156	.00978	.00992	.01005	.01019	.01033	.01047	.01061	.01075	.01090
14	168	.00935	.00949	.00963	.00977	.00991	.01006	.01020	.01034	.01049
15	180	.00899	.00913	.00927	.00941	.00956	.00970	.00985	.00999	.01014
16	192	.00867	.00881	.00896	.00910	.00925	.00940	.00954	.00969	.00985
17	204	.00840	.00854	.00869	.00883	.00898	.00913	.00928	.00943	.00959
18	216	.00816	.00830	.00845	.00860	.00875	.00890	.00905	.00921	.00936
19	228	.00794	.00809	.00824	.00839	.00855	.00870	.00885	.00901	.00917
20	240	.00775	.00790	.00806	.00821	.00836	.00852	.00868	.00884	.00900
21	252	.00758	.00774	.00789	.00805	.00820	.00836	.00852	.00868	.00885
22	264	.00743	.00759	.00775	.00790	.00806	.00822	.00838	.00855	.00871
23	276	.00730	.00746	.00761	.00777	.00793	.00810	.00826	.00843	.00859
24	288	.00718	.00734	.00750	.00766	.00782	.00798	.00815	.00832	.00849
25	300	.00707	.00723	.00739	.00755	.00772	.00788	.00805	.00822	.00839
26	312	.00697	.00713	.00729	.00746	.00763	.00779	.00796	.00813	.00831
27	324	.00688	.00704	.00721	.00737	.00754	.00771	.00788	.00806	.00823
28	336	.00680	.00696	.00713	.00730	.00747	.00764	.00781	.00799	.00816
29	348	.00672	.00689	.00706	.00723	.00740	.00757	.00775	.00792	.00810
30	360	.00665	.00682	.00699	.00716	.00734	.00751	.00769	.00787	.00805
31	372	.00659	.00676	.00693	.00711	.00728	.00746	.00764	.00782	.00800
32	384	.00653	.00671	.00688	.00705	.00723	.00741	.00759	.00777	.00795
33	396	.00648	.00665	.00683	.00701	.00718	.00736	.00754	.00773	.00791
34	408	.00643	.00661	.00678	.00696	.00714	.00732	.00750	.00769	.00787
35	420	.00639	.00656	.00674	.00692	.00710	.00728	.00747	.00765	.00784
36	432	.00635	.00653	.00670	.00689	.00707	.00725	.00744	.00762	.00781
37	444	.00631	.00649	.00667	.00685	.00703	.00722	.00741	.00759	.00778
38	456	.00628	.00646	.00664	.00682	.00701	.00719	.00738	.00757	.00776
39	468	.00624	.00643	.00661	.00679	.00698	.00717	.00735	.00754	.00773
40	480	.00621	.00640	.00658	.00677	.00695	.00714	.00733	.00752	.00771

MORTGAGE CONSTANT

PERIOD YR	MOS	.09250	.09500	.09750	.10000	.10250	.10500	.10750	.11000	.11250
		ANNUAL INTEREST RATE								
	1	1.00771	1.00792	1.00813	1.00833	1.00854	1.00875	1.00896	1.00917	1.00938
	2	.50579	.50595	.50610	.50626	.50642	.50657	.50673	.50689	.50704
	3	.33849	.33862	.33876	.33890	.33904	.33918	.33932	.33946	.33960
	4	.25484	.25497	.25510	.25523	.25536	.25549	.25562	.25576	.25589
	5	.20465	.20477	.20490	.20503	.20515	.20528	.20541	.20553	.20566
	6	.17119	.17132	.17144	.17156	.17168	.17181	.17193	.17205	.17218
	7	.14730	.14742	.14754	.14766	.14778	.14790	.14802	.14814	.14826
	8	.12937	.12949	.12961	.12973	.12985	.12997	.13009	.13021	.13033
	9	.11544	.11556	.11567	.11579	.11591	.11603	.11615	.11627	.11638
	10	.10429	.10441	.10452	.10464	.10476	.10488	.10499	.10511	.10523
	11	.09517	.09528	.09540	.09552	.09563	.09575	.09587	.09599	.09610
1	12	.08757	.08768	.08780	.08792	.08803	.08815	.08827	.08838	.08850
2	24	.04580	.04591	.04603	.04614	.04626	.04638	.04649	.04661	.04672
3	36	.03192	.03203	.03215	.03227	.03238	.03250	.03262	.03274	.03286
4	48	.02500	.02512	.02524	.02536	.02548	.02560	.02572	.02585	.02597
5	60	.02088	.02100	.02112	.02125	.02137	.02149	.02162	.02174	.02187
6	72	.01815	.01827	.01840	.01853	.01865	.01878	.01891	.01903	.01916
7	84	.01622	.01634	.01647	.01660	.01673	.01686	.01699	.01712	.01725
8	96	.01478	.01491	.01504	.01517	.01531	.01544	.01557	.01571	.01584
9	108	.01368	.01381	.01394	.01408	.01421	.01435	.01449	.01463	.01476
10	120	.01280	.01294	.01308	.01322	.01335	.01349	.01363	.01378	.01392
11	132	.01210	.01224	.01238	.01252	.01266	.01280	.01295	.01309	.01324
12	144	.01152	.01166	.01181	.01195	.01210	.01224	.01239	.01254	.01268
13	156	.01104	.01119	.01133	.01148	.01163	.01178	.01192	.01208	.01223
14	168	.01064	.01078	.01093	.01108	.01123	.01138	.01154	.01169	.01185
15	180	.01029	.01044	.01059	.01075	.01090	.01105	.01121	.01137	.01152
16	192	.01000	.01015	.01030	.01046	.01062	.01077	.01093	.01109	.01125
17	204	.00974	.00990	.01005	.01021	.01037	.01053	.01069	.01085	.01102
18	216	.00952	.00968	.00984	.01000	.01016	.01032	.01049	.01065	.01082
19	228	.00933	.00949	.00965	.00981	.00998	.01014	.01031	.01047	.01064
20	240	.00916	.00932	.00949	.00965	.00982	.00998	.01015	.01032	.01049
21	252	.00901	.00917	.00934	.00951	.00968	.00985	.01002	.01019	.01036
22	264	.00888	.00904	.00921	.00938	.00955	.00973	.00990	.01007	.01025
23	276	.00876	.00893	.00910	.00927	.00944	.00962	.00979	.00997	.01015
24	288	.00866	.00883	.00900	.00917	.00935	.00952	.00970	.00988	.01006
25	300	.00856	.00874	.00891	.00909	.00926	.00944	.00962	.00980	.00998
26	312	.00848	.00866	.00883	.00901	.00919	.00937	.00955	.00973	.00991
27	324	.00841	.00858	.00876	.00894	.00912	.00930	.00949	.00967	.00985
28	336	.00834	.00852	.00870	.00888	.00906	.00925	.00943	.00961	.00980
29	348	.00828	.00846	.00864	.00882	.00901	.00919	.00938	.00957	.00975
30	360	.00823	.00841	.00859	.00878	.00896	.00915	.00933	.00952	.00971
31	372	.00818	.00836	.00855	.00873	.00892	.00911	.00930	.00948	.00968
32	384	.00813	.00832	.00851	.00869	.00888	.00907	.00926	.00945	.00964
33	396	.00810	.00828	.00847	.00866	.00885	.00904	.00923	.00942	.00961
34	408	.00806	.00825	.00844	.00863	.00882	.00901	.00920	.00939	.00959
35	420	.00803	.00822	.00841	.00860	.00879	.00898	.00918	.00937	.00956
36	432	.00800	.00819	.00838	.00857	.00876	.00896	.00915	.00935	.00954
37	444	.00797	.00816	.00835	.00855	.00874	.00894	.00913	.00933	.00953
38	456	.00795	.00814	.00833	.00853	.00872	.00892	.00911	.00931	.00951
39	468	.00793	.00812	.00831	.00851	.00870	.00890	.00910	.00930	.00950
40	480	.00791	.00810	.00830	.00849	.00869	.00889	.00908	.00928	.00948

MORTGAGE CONSTANT

ANNUAL INTEREST RATE

PERIOD YR	MOS	.11500	.11750	.12000	.12250	.12500	.12750	.13000	.13250	.13500
	1	1.00958	1.00979	1.01000	1.01021	1.01042	1.01063	1.01083	1.01104	1.01125
	2	.50720	.50736	.50751	.50767	.50783	.50798	.50814	.50830	.50845
	3	.33974	.33988	.34002	.34016	.34030	.34044	.34058	.34072	.34086
	4	.25602	.25615	.25628	.25641	.25654	.25668	.25681	.25694	.25707
	5	.20579	.20591	.20604	.20617	.20629	.20642	.20655	.20667	.20680
	6	.17230	.17242	.17255	.17267	.17280	.17292	.17304	.17317	.17329
	7	.14839	.14851	.14863	.14875	.14887	.14899	.14911	.14924	.14936
	8	.13045	.13057	.13069	.13081	.13093	.13105	.13117	.13129	.13141
	9	.11650	.11662	.11674	.11686	.11698	.11710	.11722	.11734	.11745
	10	.10535	.10546	.10558	.10570	.10582	.10594	.10605	.10617	.10629
	11	.09622	.09634	.09645	.09657	.09669	.09681	.09692	.09704	.09716
1	12	.08862	.08873	.08885	.08897	.08908	.08920	.08932	.08943	.08955
2	24	.04684	.04696	.04707	.04719	.04731	.04742	.04754	.04766	.04778
3	36	.03298	.03310	.03321	.03333	.03345	.03357	.03369	.03381	.03394
4	48	.02609	.02621	.02633	.02646	.02658	.02670	.02683	.02695	.02708
5	60	.02199	.02212	.02224	.02237	.02250	.02263	.02275	.02288	.02301
6	72	.01929	.01942	.01955	.01968	.01981	.01994	.02007	.02021	.02034
7	84	.01739	.01752	.01765	.01779	.01792	.01806	.01819	.01833	.01846
8	96	.01598	.01612	.01625	.01639	.01653	.01667	.01681	.01695	.01709
9	108	.01490	.01504	.01518	.01533	.01547	.01561	.01575	.01590	.01604
10	120	.01406	.01420	.01435	.01449	.01464	.01478	.01493	.01508	.01523
11	132	.01338	.01353	.01368	.01383	.01398	.01413	.01428	.01443	.01458
12	144	.01283	.01298	.01313	.01329	.01344	.01359	.01375	.01390	.01406
13	156	.01238	.01253	.01269	.01284	.01300	.01315	.01331	.01347	.01363
14	168	.01200	.01216	.01231	.01247	.01263	.01279	.01295	.01311	.01328
15	180	.01168	.01184	.01200	.01216	.01233	.01249	.01265	.01282	.01298
16	192	.01141	.01157	.01174	.01190	.01207	.01223	.01240	.01257	.01274
17	204	.01118	.01135	.01151	.01168	.01185	.01202	.01219	.01236	.01253
18	216	.01098	.01115	.01132	.01149	.01166	.01183	.01200	.01218	.01235
19	228	.01081	.01098	.01115	.01133	.01150	.01167	.01185	.01203	.01220
20	240	.01066	.01084	.01101	.01119	.01136	.01154	.01172	.01189	.01207
21	252	.01054	.01071	.01089	.01106	.01124	.01142	.01160	.01178	.01196
22	264	.01042	.01060	.01078	.01096	.01114	.01132	.01150	.01169	.01187
23	276	.01033	.01051	.01069	.01087	.01105	.01123	.01142	.01160	.01179
24	288	.01024	.01042	.01060	.01079	.01097	.01116	.01134	.01153	.01172
25	300	.01016	.01035	.01053	.01072	.01090	.01109	.01128	.01147	.01166
26	312	.01010	.01028	.01047	.01066	.01084	.01103	.01122	.01141	.01160
27	324	.01004	.01023	.01041	.01060	.01079	.01098	.01117	.01137	.01156
28	336	.00999	.01018	.01037	.01056	.01075	.01094	.01113	.01132	.01152
29	348	.00994	.01013	.01032	.01052	.01071	.01090	.01109	.01129	.01148
30	360	.00990	.01009	.01029	.01048	.01067	.01087	.01106	.01126	.01145
31	372	.00987	.01006	.01025	.01045	.01064	.01084	.01103	.01123	.01143
32	384	.00984	.01003	.01022	.01042	.01062	.01081	.01101	.01121	.01141
33	396	.00981	.01000	.01020	.01039	.01059	.01079	.01099	.01119	.01139
34	408	.00978	.00998	.01018	.01037	.01057	.01077	.01097	.01117	.01137
35	420	.00976	.00996	.01016	.01035	.01055	.01075	.01095	.01115	.01135
36	432	.00974	.00994	.01014	.01034	.01054	.01074	.01094	.01114	.01134
37	444	.00972	.00992	.01012	.01032	.01052	.01072	.01092	.01113	.01133
38	456	.00971	.00991	.01011	.01031	.01051	.01071	.01091	.01112	.01132
39	468	.00970	.00990	.01010	.01030	.01050	.01070	.01090	.01111	.01131
40	480	.00968	.00988	.01008	.01029	.01049	.01069	.01090	.01110	.01130

MORTGAGE CONSTANT

PERIOD YR	MOS	.13750	.14000	.14250	.14500	.14750	.15000	.15250	.15500	.15750
		ANNUAL INTEREST RATE								
	1	1.01146	1.01167	1.01188	1.01208	1.01229	1.01250	1.01271	1.01292	1.01313
	2	.50861	.50877	.50892	.50908	.50924	.50939	.50955	.50971	.50987
	3	.34100	.34114	.34128	.34142	.34156	.34170	.34184	.34198	.34212
	4	.25720	.25733	.25747	.25760	.25773	.25786	.25799	.25812	.25826
	5	.20693	.20705	.20718	.20731	.20744	.20756	.20769	.20782	.20794
	6	.17341	.17354	.17366	.17379	.17391	.17403	.17416	.17428	.17441
	7	.14948	.14960	.14972	.14984	.14997	.15009	.15021	.15033	.15045
	8	.13153	.13165	.13177	.13189	.13201	.13213	.13225	.13237	.13250
	9	.11757	.11769	.11781	.11793	.11805	.11817	.11829	.11841	.11853
	10	.10641	.10653	.10665	.10677	.10688	.10700	.10712	.10724	.10736
	11	.09728	.09740	.09751	.09763	.09775	.09787	.09799	.09811	.09822
1	12	.08967	.08979	.08990	.09002	.09014	.09026	.09038	.09049	.09061
2	24	.04789	.04801	.04813	.04825	.04837	.04849	.04861	.04872	.04884
3	36	.03406	.03418	.03430	.03442	.03454	.03467	.03479	.03491	.03503
4	48	.02720	.02733	.02745	.02758	.02770	.02783	.02796	.02808	.02821
5	60	.02314	.02327	.02340	.02353	.02366	.02379	.02392	.02405	.02419
6	72	.02047	.02061	.02074	.02087	.02101	.02115	.02128	.02142	.02155
7	84	.01860	.01874	.01888	.01902	.01916	.01930	.01944	.01958	.01972
8	96	.01723	.01737	.01751	.01766	.01780	.01795	.01809	.01824	.01838
9	108	.01619	.01633	.01648	.01663	.01678	.01692	.01707	.01722	.01737
10	120	.01538	.01553	.01568	.01583	.01598	.01613	.01629	.01644	.01660
11	132	.01473	.01489	.01504	.01520	.01535	.01551	.01567	.01582	.01598
12	144	.01421	.01437	.01453	.01469	.01485	.01501	.01517	.01533	.01549
13	156	.01379	.01395	.01411	.01428	.01444	.01460	.01477	.01493	.01510
14	168	.01344	.01360	.01377	.01394	.01410	.01427	.01444	.01461	.01478
15	180	.01315	.01332	.01349	.01366	.01383	.01400	.01417	.01434	.01451
16	192	.01291	.01308	.01325	.01342	.01359	.01377	.01394	.01412	.01429
17	204	.01270	.01287	.01305	.01322	.01340	.01358	.01375	.01393	.01411
18	216	.01253	.01270	.01288	.01306	.01324	.01342	.01360	.01378	.01396
19	228	.01238	.01256	.01274	.01292	.01310	.01328	.01346	.01365	.01383
20	240	.01225	.01244	.01262	.01280	.01298	.01317	.01335	.01354	.01373
21	252	.01215	.01233	.01251	.01270	.01288	.01307	.01326	.01345	.01364
22	264	.01205	.01224	.01243	.01261	.01280	.01299	.01318	.01337	.01356
23	276	.01197	.01216	.01235	.01254	.01273	.01292	.01311	.01330	.01349
24	288	.01191	.01210	.01229	.01248	.01267	.01286	.01305	.01325	.01344
25	300	.01185	.01204	.01223	.01242	.01261	.01281	.01300	.01320	.01339
26	312	.01180	.01199	.01218	.01238	.01257	.01276	.01296	.01316	.01335
27	324	.01175	.01195	.01214	.01234	.01253	.01273	.01292	.01312	.01332
28	336	.01171	.01191	.01210	.01230	.01250	.01270	.01289	.01309	.01329
29	348	.01168	.01188	.01207	.01227	.01247	.01267	.01287	.01307	.01327
30	360	.01165	.01185	.01205	.01225	.01244	.01264	.01284	.01305	.01325
31	372	.01163	.01182	.01202	.01222	.01242	.01262	.01283	.01303	.01323
32	384	.01160	.01180	.01200	.01220	.01241	.01261	.01281	.01301	.01321
33	396	.01159	.01179	.01199	.01219	.01239	.01259	.01279	.01300	.01320
34	408	.01157	.01177	.01197	.01217	.01238	.01258	.01278	.01299	.01319
35	420	.01155	.01176	.01196	.01216	.01236	.01257	.01277	.01298	.01318
36	432	.01154	.01174	.01195	.01215	.01235	.01256	.01276	.01297	.01317
37	444	.01153	.01173	.01194	.01214	.01235	.01255	.01276	.01296	.01317
38	456	.01152	.01173	.01193	.01213	.01234	.01254	.01275	.01295	.01316
39	468	.01151	.01172	.01192	.01213	.01233	.01254	.01274	.01295	.01315
40	480	.01151	.01171	.01192	.01212	.01233	.01253	.01274	.01294	.01315

MORTGAGE CONSTANT

ANNUAL INTEREST RATE

PERIOD YR	MOS	.16000	.16250	.16500	.16750	.17000	.17250	.17500	.17750	.18000
	1	1.01333	1.01354	1.01375	1.01396	1.01417	1.01438	1.01458	1.01479	1.01500
	2	.51002	.51018	.51034	.51049	.51065	.51081	.51096	.51112	.51128
	3	.34226	.34240	.34254	.34268	.34282	.34296	.34310	.34324	.34338
	4	.25839	.25852	.25865	.25878	.25892	.25905	.25918	.25931	.25944
	5	.20807	.20820	.20833	.20845	.20858	.20871	.20883	.20896	.20909
	6	.17453	.17465	.17478	.17490	.17503	.17515	.17528	.17540	.17553
	7	.15058	.15070	.15082	.15094	.15107	.15119	.15131	.15143	.15156
	8	.13262	.13274	.13286	.13298	.13310	.13322	.13334	.13346	.13358
	9	.11865	.11877	.11889	.11901	.11913	.11925	.11937	.11949	.11961
	10	.10748	.10760	.10772	.10784	.10796	.10808	.10819	.10831	.10843
	11	.09834	.09846	.09858	.09870	.09882	.09894	.09906	.09917	.09929
1	12	.09073	.09085	.09097	.09109	.09120	.09132	.09144	.09156	.09168
2	24	.04896	.04908	.04920	.04932	.04944	.04956	.04968	.04980	.04992
3	36	.03516	.03528	.03540	.03553	.03565	.03578	.03590	.03603	.03615
4	48	.02834	.02847	.02860	.02873	.02886	.02898	.02911	.02924	.02937
5	60	.02432	.02445	.02458	.02472	.02485	.02499	.02512	.02526	.02539
6	72	.02169	.02183	.02197	.02211	.02225	.02239	.02253	.02267	.02281
7	84	.01986	.02000	.02015	.02029	.02044	.02058	.02073	.02087	.02102
8	96	.01853	.01868	.01882	.01897	.01912	.01927	.01942	.01957	.01972
9	108	.01753	.01768	.01783	.01798	.01814	.01829	.01845	.01860	.01876
10	120	.01675	.01691	.01706	.01722	.01738	.01754	.01770	.01786	.01802
11	132	.01614	.01630	.01646	.01663	.01679	.01695	.01711	.01728	.01744
12	144	.01566	.01582	.01599	.01615	.01632	.01649	.01665	.01682	.01699
13	156	.01527	.01543	.01560	.01577	.01594	.01611	.01629	.01646	.01663
14	168	.01495	.01512	.01529	.01546	.01564	.01581	.01599	.01616	.01634
15	180	.01469	.01486	.01504	.01521	.01539	.01557	.01575	.01592	.01610
16	192	.01447	.01465	.01483	.01501	.01519	.01537	.01555	.01573	.01591
17	204	.01429	.01447	.01465	.01484	.01502	.01520	.01539	.01557	.01576
18	216	.01414	.01433	.01451	.01469	.01488	.01507	.01525	.01544	.01563
19	228	.01402	.01420	.01439	.01458	.01476	.01495	.01514	.01533	.01552
20	240	.01391	.01410	.01429	.01448	.01467	.01486	.01505	.01524	.01543
21	252	.01382	.01401	.01420	.01440	.01459	.01478	.01497	.01517	.01536
22	264	.01375	.01394	.01413	.01433	.01452	.01471	.01491	.01510	.01530
23	276	.01369	.01388	.01407	.01427	.01446	.01466	.01486	.01505	.01525
24	288	.01363	.01383	.01402	.01422	.01442	.01461	.01481	.01501	.01521
25	300	.01359	.01379	.01398	.01418	.01438	.01458	.01478	.01497	.01517
26	312	.01355	.01375	.01395	.01415	.01434	.01454	.01474	.01494	.01515
27	324	.01352	.01372	.01392	.01412	.01432	.01452	.01472	.01492	.01512
28	336	.01349	.01369	.01389	.01409	.01429	.01449	.01470	.01490	.01510
29	348	.01347	.01367	.01387	.01407	.01427	.01448	.01468	.01488	.01508
30	360	.01345	.01365	.01385	.01405	.01426	.01446	.01466	.01487	.01507
31	372	.01343	.01363	.01384	.01404	.01424	.01445	.01465	.01485	.01506
32	384	.01342	.01362	.01382	.01403	.01423	.01444	.01464	.01484	.01505
33	396	.01340	.01361	.01381	.01402	.01422	.01443	.01463	.01484	.01504
34	408	.01339	.01360	.01380	.01401	.01421	.01442	.01462	.01483	.01503
35	420	.01338	.01359	.01379	.01400	.01421	.01441	.01462	.01482	.01503
36	432	.01338	.01358	.01379	.01399	.01420	.01441	.01461	.01482	.01502
37	444	.01337	.01358	.01378	.01399	.01419	.01440	.01461	.01481	.01502
38	456	.01337	.01357	.01378	.01398	.01419	.01440	.01460	.01481	.01502
39	468	.01336	.01357	.01377	.01398	.01419	.01439	.01460	.01481	.01501
40	480	.01336	.01356	.01377	.01398	.01418	.01439	.01460	.01480	.01501

MORTGAGE CONSTANT

ANNUAL INTEREST RATE

PERIOD YR	MOS	.18250	.18500	.18750	.19000	.19250	.19500	.19750	.20000	.20250
	1	1.01521	1.01542	1.01563	1.01583	1.01604	1.01625	1.01646	1.01667	1.01688
	2	.51143	.51159	.51175	.51191	.51206	.51222	.51238	.51253	.51269
	3	.34352	.34366	.34380	.34394	.34408	.34422	.34437	.34451	.34465
	4	.25958	.25971	.25984	.25997	.26011	.26024	.26037	.26050	.26064
	5	.20922	.20934	.20947	.20960	.20973	.20985	.20998	.21011	.21024
	6	.17565	.17577	.17590	.17602	.17615	.17627	.17640	.17652	.17665
	7	.15168	.15180	.15192	.15205	.15217	.15229	.15242	.15254	.15266
	8	.13371	.13383	.13395	.13407	.13419	.13431	.13443	.13456	.13468
	9	.11973	.11985	.11997	.12009	.12021	.12033	.12045	.12057	.12070
	10	.10855	.10867	.10879	.10891	.10903	.10915	.10927	.10939	.10951
	11	.09941	.09953	.09965	.09977	.09989	.10001	.10013	.10025	.10037
1	12	.09180	.09192	.09204	.09216	.09228	.09240	.09251	.09263	.09275
2	24	.05004	.05017	.05029	.05041	.05053	.05065	.05077	.05090	.05102
3	36	.03628	.03640	.03653	.03666	.03678	.03691	.03704	.03716	.03729
4	48	.02951	.02964	.02977	.02990	.03003	.03016	.03030	.03043	.03056
5	60	.02553	.02567	.02580	.02594	.02608	.02622	.02635	.02649	.02663
6	72	.02295	.02309	.02323	.02338	.02352	.02366	.02381	.02395	.02410
7	84	.02116	.02131	.02146	.02161	.02176	.02191	.02206	.02221	.02236
8	96	.01988	.02003	.02018	.02033	.02049	.02064	.02080	.02095	.02111
9	108	.01891	.01907	.01923	.01939	.01955	.01971	.01987	.02003	.02019
10	120	.01818	.01834	.01850	.01867	.01883	.01900	.01916	.01933	.01949
11	132	.01761	.01778	.01794	.01811	.01828	.01845	.01862	.01879	.01896
12	144	.01716	.01733	.01750	.01767	.01785	.01802	.01819	.01837	.01854
13	156	.01680	.01698	.01715	.01733	.01750	.01768	.01786	.01804	.01821
14	168	.01652	.01669	.01687	.01705	.01723	.01741	.01759	.01777	.01795
15	180	.01628	.01647	.01665	.01683	.01701	.01719	.01738	.01756	.01775
16	192	.01610	.01628	.01646	.01665	.01683	.01702	.01721	.01739	.01758
17	204	.01594	.01613	.01632	.01650	.01669	.01688	.01707	.01726	.01745
18	216	.01582	.01600	.01619	.01638	.01657	.01677	.01696	.01715	.01734
19	228	.01571	.01590	.01609	.01629	.01648	.01667	.01687	.01706	.01726
20	240	.01563	.01582	.01601	.01621	.01640	.01660	.01679	.01699	.01718
21	252	.01556	.01575	.01595	.01614	.01634	.01653	.01673	.01693	.01713
22	264	.01550	.01569	.01589	.01609	.01629	.01648	.01668	.01688	.01708
23	276	.01545	.01565	.01584	.01604	.01624	.01644	.01664	.01684	.01704
24	288	.01541	.01561	.01581	.01601	.01621	.01641	.01661	.01681	.01701
25	300	.01537	.01557	.01578	.01598	.01618	.01638	.01658	.01678	.01699
26	312	.01535	.01555	.01575	.01595	.01615	.01636	.01656	.01676	.01697
27	324	.01532	.01553	.01573	.01593	.01613	.01634	.01654	.01675	.01695
28	336	.01530	.01551	.01571	.01591	.01612	.01632	.01653	.01673	.01694
29	348	.01529	.01549	.01570	.01590	.01611	.01631	.01651	.01672	.01693
30	360	.01528	.01548	.01568	.01589	.01609	.01630	.01650	.01671	.01692
31	372	.01526	.01547	.01567	.01588	.01608	.01629	.01650	.01670	.01691
32	384	.01525	.01546	.01567	.01587	.01608	.01628	.01649	.01670	.01690
33	396	.01525	.01545	.01566	.01586	.01607	.01628	.01648	.01669	.01690
34	408	.01524	.01545	.01565	.01586	.01607	.01627	.01648	.01669	.01689
35	420	.01524	.01544	.01565	.01585	.01606	.01627	.01648	.01668	.01689
36	432	.01523	.01544	.01564	.01585	.01606	.01627	.01647	.01668	.01689
37	444	.01523	.01543	.01564	.01585	.01606	.01626	.01647	.01668	.01689
38	456	.01522	.01543	.01564	.01585	.01605	.01626	.01647	.01668	.01688
39	468	.01522	.01543	.01564	.01584	.01605	.01626	.01647	.01667	.01688
40	480	.01522	.01543	.01563	.01584	.01605	.01626	.01646	.01667	.01688

MORTGAGE CONSTANT

ANNUAL INTEREST RATE

PERIOD YR	MOS	.20500	.20750	.21000	.21250	.21500	.21750	.22000	.22250	.22500
	1	1.01708	1.01729	1.01750	1.01771	1.01792	1.01813	1.01833	1.01854	1.01875
	2	.51285	.51301	.51316	.51332	.51348	.51363	.51379	.51395	.51411
	3	.34479	.34493	.34507	.34521	.34535	.34549	.34563	.34577	.34591
	4	.26077	.26090	.26103	.26116	.26130	.26143	.26156	.26169	.26183
	5	.21037	.21049	.21062	.21075	.21088	.21101	.21113	.21126	.21139
	6	.17677	.17690	.17702	.17715	.17727	.17740	.17752	.17765	.17777
	7	.15278	.15291	.15303	.15315	.15328	.15340	.15352	.15365	.15377
	8	.13480	.13492	.13504	.13516	.13529	.13541	.13553	.13565	.13578
	9	.12082	.12094	.12106	.12118	.12130	.12142	.12154	.12166	.12179
	10	.10963	.10975	.10988	.11000	.11012	.11024	.11036	.11048	.11060
	11	.10049	.10061	.10073	.10085	.10097	.10109	.10121	.10133	.10145
1	12	.09287	.09299	.09311	.09323	.09335	.09347	.09359	.09371	.09384
2	24	.05114	.05126	.05139	.05151	.05163	.05175	.05188	.05200	.05213
3	36	.03742	.03755	.03768	.03780	.03793	.03806	.03819	.03832	.03845
4	48	.03070	.03083	.03097	.03110	.03124	.03137	.03151	.03164	.03178
5	60	.02677	.02691	.02705	.02719	.02734	.02748	.02762	.02776	.02790
6	72	.02424	.02439	.02454	.02468	.02483	.02498	.02513	.02527	.02542
7	84	.02251	.02266	.02281	.02296	.02312	.02327	.02343	.02358	.02374
8	96	.02127	.02142	.02158	.02174	.02190	.02206	.02222	.02238	.02254
9	108	.02035	.02051	.02067	.02084	.02100	.02117	.02133	.02150	.02166
10	120	.01966	.01983	.01999	.02016	.02033	.02050	.02067	.02084	.02101
11	132	.01913	.01930	.01947	.01964	.01982	.01999	.02017	.02034	.02052
12	144	.01872	.01889	.01907	.01924	.01942	.01960	.01978	.01996	.02014
13	156	.01839	.01857	.01875	.01893	.01911	.01930	.01948	.01966	.01984
14	168	.01814	.01832	.01850	.01869	.01887	.01906	.01924	.01943	.01962
15	180	.01793	.01812	.01831	.01849	.01868	.01887	.01906	.01925	.01944
16	192	.01777	.01796	.01815	.01834	.01853	.01872	.01891	.01910	.01930
17	204	.01764	.01783	.01802	.01822	.01841	.01860	.01880	.01899	.01918
18	216	.01754	.01773	.01792	.01812	.01831	.01851	.01870	.01890	.01910
19	228	.01745	.01765	.01784	.01804	.01823	.01843	.01863	.01883	.01903
20	240	.01738	.01758	.01778	.01797	.01817	.01837	.01857	.01877	.01897
21	252	.01733	.01752	.01772	.01792	.01812	.01832	.01852	.01872	.01893
22	264	.01728	.01748	.01768	.01788	.01808	.01828	.01849	.01869	.01889
23	276	.01724	.01745	.01765	.01785	.01805	.01825	.01846	.01866	.01886
24	288	.01721	.01742	.01762	.01782	.01802	.01823	.01843	.01864	.01884
25	300	.01719	.01739	.01760	.01780	.01800	.01821	.01841	.01862	.01882
26	312	.01717	.01737	.01758	.01778	.01799	.01819	.01840	.01860	.01881
27	324	.01715	.01736	.01756	.01777	.01797	.01818	.01838	.01859	.01880
28	336	.01714	.01735	.01755	.01776	.01796	.01817	.01837	.01858	.01879
29	348	.01713	.01734	.01754	.01775	.01795	.01816	.01837	.01857	.01878
30	360	.01712	.01733	.01753	.01774	.01795	.01815	.01836	.01857	.01877
31	372	.01711	.01732	.01753	.01773	.01794	.01815	.01835	.01856	.01877
32	384	.01711	.01732	.01752	.01773	.01794	.01814	.01835	.01856	.01876
33	396	.01710	.01731	.01752	.01773	.01793	.01814	.01835	.01855	.01876
34	408	.01710	.01731	.01751	.01772	.01793	.01814	.01834	.01855	.01876
35	420	.01710	.01730	.01751	.01772	.01793	.01813	.01834	.01855	.01876
36	432	.01709	.01730	.01751	.01772	.01793	.01813	.01834	.01855	.01876
37	444	.01709	.01730	.01751	.01772	.01792	.01813	.01834	.01855	.01875
38	456	.01709	.01730	.01751	.01771	.01792	.01813	.01834	.01855	.01875
39	468	.01709	.01730	.01751	.01771	.01792	.01813	.01834	.01855	.01875
40	480	.01709	.01730	.01750	.01771	.01792	.01813	.01834	.01854	.01875

MORTGAGE CONSTANT

PERIOD YR	MOS	.22750	.23000	.23250	.23500	.23750	.24000	.24250	.24500	.24750
		ANNUAL INTEREST RATE								
	1	1.01896	1.01917	1.01938	1.01958	1.01979	1.02000	1.02021	1.02042	1.02063
	2	.51426	.51442	.51458	.51473	.51489	.51505	.51521	.51536	.51552
	3	.34605	.34619	.34633	.34647	.34661	.34675	.34690	.34704	.34718
	4	.26196	.26209	.26223	.26236	.26249	.26262	.26276	.26289	.26302
	5	.21152	.21165	.21177	.21190	.21203	.21216	.21229	.21242	.21254
	6	.17790	.17802	.17815	.17827	.17840	.17853	.17865	.17878	.17890
	7	.15389	.15402	.15414	.15426	.15439	.15451	.15464	.15476	.15488
	8	.13590	.13602	.13614	.13626	.13639	.13651	.13663	.13676	.13688
	9	.12191	.12203	.12215	.12227	.12239	.12252	.12264	.12276	.12288
	10	.11072	.11084	.11096	.11108	.11121	.11133	.11145	.11157	.11169
	11	.10157	.10169	.10182	.10194	.10206	.10218	.10230	.10242	.10254
1	12	.09396	.09408	.09420	.09432	.09444	.09456	.09468	.09480	.09492
2	24	.05225	.05237	.05250	.05262	.05275	.05287	.05300	.05312	.05325
3	36	.03858	.03871	.03884	.03897	.03910	.03923	.03936	.03950	.03963
4	48	.03191	.03205	.03219	.03233	.03246	.03260	.03274	.03288	.03302
5	60	.02805	.02819	.02833	.02848	.02862	.02877	.02891	.02906	.02920
6	72	.02557	.02572	.02587	.02602	.02618	.02633	.02648	.02663	.02678
7	84	.02389	.02405	.02420	.02436	.02452	.02468	.02483	.02499	.02515
8	96	.02270	.02286	.02302	.02319	.02335	.02351	.02368	.02384	.02401
9	108	.02183	.02200	.02216	.02233	.02250	.02267	.02284	.02301	.02318
10	120	.02118	.02135	.02153	.02170	.02187	.02205	.02222	.02240	.02257
11	132	.02069	.02087	.02105	.02122	.02140	.02158	.02176	.02194	.02212
12	144	.02032	.02050	.02068	.02086	.02104	.02123	.02141	.02159	.02178
13	156	.02003	.02021	.02040	.02058	.02077	.02095	.02114	.02133	.02152
14	168	.01980	.01999	.02018	.02037	.02056	.02074	.02093	.02112	.02132
15	180	.01963	.01982	.02001	.02020	.02039	.02058	.02078	.02097	.02116
16	192	.01949	.01968	.01987	.02007	.02026	.02046	.02065	.02085	.02104
17	204	.01938	.01957	.01977	.01997	.02016	.02036	.02056	.02075	.02095
18	216	.01929	.01949	.01969	.01988	.02008	.02028	.02048	.02068	.02088
19	228	.01922	.01942	.01962	.01982	.02002	.02022	.02042	.02062	.02082
20	240	.01917	.01937	.01957	.01977	.01997	.02017	.02038	.02058	.02078
21	252	.01913	.01933	.01953	.01973	.01993	.02014	.02034	.02054	.02075
22	264	.01909	.01930	.01950	.01970	.01990	.02011	.02031	.02052	.02072
23	276	.01907	.01927	.01947	.01968	.01988	.02008	.02029	.02049	.02070
24	288	.01904	.01925	.01945	.01966	.01986	.02007	.02027	.02048	.02068
25	300	.01903	.01923	.01944	.01964	.01985	.02005	.02026	.02046	.02067
26	312	.01901	.01922	.01942	.01963	.01984	.02004	.02025	.02045	.02066
27	324	.01900	.01921	.01941	.01962	.01983	.02003	.02024	.02045	.02065
28	336	.01899	.01920	.01941	.01961	.01982	.02003	.02023	.02044	.02065
29	348	.01899	.01919	.01940	.01961	.01981	.02002	.02023	.02043	.02064
30	360	.01898	.01919	.01939	.01960	.01981	.02002	.02022	.02043	.02064
31	372	.01898	.01918	.01939	.01960	.01981	.02001	.02022	.02043	.02064
32	384	.01897	.01918	.01939	.01959	.01980	.02001	.02022	.02043	.02063
33	396	.01897	.01918	.01938	.01959	.01980	.02001	.02022	.02042	.02063
34	408	.01897	.01917	.01938	.01959	.01980	.02001	.02021	.02042	.02063
35	420	.01897	.01917	.01938	.01959	.01980	.02000	.02021	.02042	.02063
36	432	.01896	.01917	.01938	.01959	.01980	.02000	.02021	.02042	.02063
37	444	.01896	.01917	.01938	.01959	.01979	.02000	.02021	.02042	.02063
38	456	.01896	.01917	.01938	.01959	.01979	.02000	.02021	.02042	.02063
39	468	.01896	.01917	.01938	.01959	.01979	.02000	.02021	.02042	.02063
40	480	.01896	.01917	.01938	.01959	.01979	.02000	.02021	.02042	.02063

MORTGAGE BALANCE REMAINING TABLE

Description:

The Mortgage Balance Remaining table can be used to determine the remaining unpaid principal balance of a loan at any point during the life of the loan. To use the table, find the factor corresponding to the contract rate and original loan term; then multiply this percentage of loan remaining by the initial loan amount to get the dollar amount of principal remaining to be paid.

Table Calculation Formula:

$$MB_j = \frac{1 - 1/(1+i)^{n-j}}{1 - 1/(1+i)^n}$$

where n is the full term and j is the year of prepayment.

Table Range:

Annual interest rate, with monthly compounding, of 7.00% to 19.50%, in .25% increments. Original loan term from 1 to 15 years in 1-year increments, 15 to 40 years in 5-year increments.

Example:

What is the remaining principal balance of a $61,000, 30-year original term 11.5% interest loan at the end of year 7?

Solution:

Finding the mortgage balance remaining table factor corresponding to 11.5% and 30-year original loan term provides:

MB_j = $61,000 × table factor *MBR,* 11.5%, 30-year term, 7-year prepayment,

= $61,000(.95904),

= $58,501.44.

After making monthly payments on the loan for 7 years, $58,501.44 of the initial $61,000 principal still remains to be paid.

REMAINING MORTGAGE BALANCE TABLE FOR 7.000 PERCENT

ORIGINAL LOAN TERM

AGE OF LOAN	1	2	3	4	5	6	7	8	9	10
1	0.00000	.51744	.68964	.77553	.82690	.86101	.88525	.90333	.91730	.92840
2	0.00000	0.00000	.35685	.53484	.64129	.71197	.76221	.79968	.82863	.85163
3	0.00000	0.00000	0.00000	.27675	.44226	.55216	.63027	.68853	.73355	.76930
4	0.00000	0.00000	0.00000	0.00000	.22884	.38079	.48880	.56935	.63159	.68103
5	0.00000	0.00000	0.00000	0.00000	0.00000	.19704	.33710	.44155	.52226	.58637
6	0.00000	0.00000	0.00000	0.00000	0.00000	0.00000	.17443	.30451	.40503	.48487
7	0.00000	0.00000	0.00000	0.00000	0.00000	0.00000	0.00000	.15757	.27933	.37603
8	0.00000	0.00000	0.00000	0.00000	0.00000	0.00000	0.00000	0.00000	.14454	.25933
9	0.00000	0.00000	0.00000	0.00000	0.00000	0.00000	0.00000	0.00000	0.00000	.13419

AGE OF LOAN	11	12	13	14	15	20	25	30	35	40
1	.93741	.94485	.95108	.95637	.96090	.97621	.98470	.98984	.99312	.99528
2	.87029	.88571	.89863	.90959	.91898	.95070	.96830	.97895	.98574	.99022
3	.79832	.82229	.84238	.85942	.87402	.92335	.95071	.96727	.97783	.98479
4	.72115	.75429	.78207	.80563	.82582	.89402	.93185	.95475	.96935	.97897
5	.63840	.68138	.71739	.74794	.77413	.86257	.91162	.94132	.96025	.97272
6	.54967	.60319	.64805	.68609	.71870	.82884	.88993	.92692	.95050	.96603
7	.45452	.51935	.57368	.61977	.65927	.79268	.86668	.91147	.94004	.95885
8	.35250	.42945	.49395	.54865	.59554	.75390	.84174	.89492	.92882	.95116
9	.24310	.33306	.40845	.47240	.52720	.71232	.81501	.87716	.91679	.94291
10	.12579	.22969	.31676	.39063	.45393	.66774	.78633	.85812	.90390	.93406
11	0.00000	.11885	.21845	.30294	.37535	.61993	.75559	.83771	.89007	.92457
12	0.00000	0.00000	.11304	.20892	.29110	.56866	.72262	.81582	.87524	.91440
13	0.00000	0.00000	0.00000	.10811	.20075	.51369	.68727	.79235	.85934	.90349
14	0.00000	0.00000	0.00000	0.00000	.10388	.45475	.64937	.76718	.84229	.89179
15	0.00000	0.00000	0.00000	0.00000	0.00000	.39154	.60872	.74019	.82401	.87924
16	0.00000	0.00000	0.00000	0.00000	0.00000	.32377	.56514	.71125	.80441	.86579
17	0.00000	0.00000	0.00000	0.00000	0.00000	.25109	.51841	.68022	.78339	.85137
18	0.00000	0.00000	0.00000	0.00000	0.00000	.17316	.46829	.64694	.76085	.83590
19	0.00000	0.00000	0.00000	0.00000	0.00000	.08960	.41456	.61126	.73668	.81932
20	0.00000	0.00000	0.00000	0.00000	0.00000	0.00000	.35694	.57300	.71077	.80154
21	0.00000	0.00000	0.00000	0.00000	0.00000	0.00000	.29515	.53197	.68298	.78247
22	0.00000	0.00000	0.00000	0.00000	0.00000	0.00000	.22890	.48798	.65318	.76202
23	0.00000	0.00000	0.00000	0.00000	0.00000	0.00000	.15786	.44081	.62123	.74010
24	0.00000	0.00000	0.00000	0.00000	0.00000	0.00000	.08168	.39023	.58696	.71659
25	0.00000	0.00000	0.00000	0.00000	0.00000	0.00000	0.00000	.33599	.55022	.69138
26	0.00000	0.00000	0.00000	0.00000	0.00000	0.00000	0.00000	.27783	.51083	.66435
27	0.00000	0.00000	0.00000	0.00000	0.00000	0.00000	0.00000	.21547	.46859	.63536
28	0.00000	0.00000	0.00000	0.00000	0.00000	0.00000	0.00000	.14860	.42329	.60428
29	0.00000	0.00000	0.00000	0.00000	0.00000	0.00000	0.00000	.07689	.37472	.57095
30	0.00000	0.00000	0.00000	0.00000	0.00000	0.00000	0.00000	0.00000	.32264	.53522
31	0.00000	0.00000	0.00000	0.00000	0.00000	0.00000	0.00000	0.00000	.26679	.49690
32	0.00000	0.00000	0.00000	0.00000	0.00000	0.00000	0.00000	0.00000	.20690	.45580
33	0.00000	0.00000	0.00000	0.00000	0.00000	0.00000	0.00000	0.00000	.14269	.41174
34	0.00000	0.00000	0.00000	0.00000	0.00000	0.00000	0.00000	0.00000	.07383	.36450
35	0.00000	0.00000	0.00000	0.00000	0.00000	0.00000	0.00000	0.00000	0.00000	.31384
36	0.00000	0.00000	0.00000	0.00000	0.00000	0.00000	0.00000	0.00000	0.00000	.25951
37	0.00000	0.00000	0.00000	0.00000	0.00000	0.00000	0.00000	0.00000	0.00000	.20126
38	0.00000	0.00000	0.00000	0.00000	0.00000	0.00000	0.00000	0.00000	0.00000	.13880
39	0.00000	0.00000	0.00000	0.00000	0.00000	0.00000	0.00000	0.00000	0.00000	.07182

REMAINING MORTGAGE BALANCE TABLE FOR 7.250 PERCENT

ORIGINAL LOAN TERM

AGE OF LOAN	1	2	3	4	5	6	7	8	9	10
1	0.00000	.51806	.69045	.77642	.82782	.86194	.88619	.90426	.91822	.92930
2	0.00000	0.00000	.35770	.53608	.64274	.71353	.76384	.80134	.83031	.85330
3	0.00000	0.00000	0.00000	.27772	.44378	.55400	.63232	.69071	.73581	.77160
4	0.00000	0.00000	0.00000	0.00000	.22990	.38251	.49095	.57178	.63422	.68378
5	0.00000	0.00000	0.00000	0.00000	0.00000	.19816	.33897	.44394	.52502	.58938
6	0.00000	0.00000	0.00000	0.00000	0.00000	0.00000	.17561	.30652	.40764	.48790
7	0.00000	0.00000	0.00000	0.00000	0.00000	0.00000	0.00000	.15880	.28145	.37882
8	0.00000	0.00000	0.00000	0.00000	0.00000	0.00000	0.00000	0.00000	.14581	.26155
9	0.00000	0.00000	0.00000	0.00000	0.00000	0.00000	0.00000	0.00000	0.00000	.13550

AGE OF LOAN	11	12	13	14	15	20	25	30	35	40
1	.93829	.94571	.95192	.95719	.96170	.97690	.98528	.99032	.99351	.99559
2	.87195	.88735	.90024	.91117	.92053	.95206	.96946	.97992	.98654	.99086
3	.80064	.82461	.84469	.86170	.87627	.92537	.95245	.96873	.97904	.98577
4	.72399	.75717	.78497	.80853	.82870	.89667	.93416	.95671	.97098	.98030
5	.64159	.68468	.72077	.75136	.77756	.86582	.91451	.94379	.96231	.97442
6	.55301	.60675	.65176	.68992	.72259	.83266	.89338	.92990	.95300	.96809
7	.45779	.52299	.57758	.62386	.66349	.79731	.87067	.91496	.94299	.96130
8	.35544	.43294	.49784	.55286	.59997	.75870	.84626	.89891	.93222	.95399
9	.24541	.33614	.41212	.47653	.53168	.71751	.82001	.88165	.92066	.94614
10	.12714	.23209	.31998	.39448	.45828	.67323	.79180	.86310	.90822	.93769
11	0.00000	.12024	.22093	.30628	.37937	.62563	.76148	.84316	.89485	.92862
12	0.00000	0.00000	.11446	.21147	.29455	.57447	.72888	.82173	.88048	.91886
13	0.00000	0.00000	0.00000	.10956	.20337	.51947	.69384	.79869	.86503	.90837
14	0.00000	0.00000	0.00000	0.00000	.10536	.46034	.65617	.77392	.84843	.89710
15	0.00000	0.00000	0.00000	0.00000	0.00000	.39679	.61567	.74729	.83058	.88498
16	0.00000	0.00000	0.00000	0.00000	0.00000	.32847	.57215	.71867	.81139	.87196
17	0.00000	0.00000	0.00000	0.00000	0.00000	.25503	.52535	.68791	.79076	.85795
18	0.00000	0.00000	0.00000	0.00000	0.00000	.17609	.47506	.65483	.76859	.84290
19	0.00000	0.00000	0.00000	0.00000	0.00000	.09122	.42099	.61928	.74475	.82672
20	0.00000	0.00000	0.00000	0.00000	0.00000	0.00000	.36287	.58106	.71913	.80933
21	0.00000	0.00000	0.00000	0.00000	0.00000	0.00000	.30039	.53998	.69159	.79063
22	0.00000	0.00000	0.00000	0.00000	0.00000	0.00000	.23323	.49582	.66198	.77053
23	0.00000	0.00000	0.00000	0.00000	0.00000	0.00000	.16103	.44835	.63015	.74892
24	0.00000	0.00000	0.00000	0.00000	0.00000	0.00000	.08342	.39732	.59594	.72570
25	0.00000	0.00000	0.00000	0.00000	0.00000	0.00000	0.00000	.34247	.55917	.70073
26	0.00000	0.00000	0.00000	0.00000	0.00000	0.00000	0.00000	.28350	.51963	.67389
27	0.00000	0.00000	0.00000	0.00000	0.00000	0.00000	0.00000	.22012	.47714	.64504
28	0.00000	0.00000	0.00000	0.00000	0.00000	0.00000	0.00000	.15198	.43146	.61403
29	0.00000	0.00000	0.00000	0.00000	0.00000	0.00000	0.00000	.07874	.38235	.58070
30	0.00000	0.00000	0.00000	0.00000	0.00000	0.00000	0.00000	0.00000	.32956	.54486
31	0.00000	0.00000	0.00000	0.00000	0.00000	0.00000	0.00000	0.00000	.27282	.50634
32	0.00000	0.00000	0.00000	0.00000	0.00000	0.00000	0.00000	0.00000	.21182	.46493
33	0.00000	0.00000	0.00000	0.00000	0.00000	0.00000	0.00000	0.00000	.14625	.42042
34	0.00000	0.00000	0.00000	0.00000	0.00000	0.00000	0.00000	0.00000	.07577	.37257
35	0.00000	0.00000	0.00000	0.00000	0.00000	0.00000	0.00000	0.00000	0.00000	.32113
36	0.00000	0.00000	0.00000	0.00000	0.00000	0.00000	0.00000	0.00000	0.00000	.26584
37	0.00000	0.00000	0.00000	0.00000	0.00000	0.00000	0.00000	0.00000	0.00000	.20640
38	0.00000	0.00000	0.00000	0.00000	0.00000	0.00000	0.00000	0.00000	0.00000	.14251
39	0.00000	0.00000	0.00000	0.00000	0.00000	0.00000	0.00000	0.00000	0.00000	.07383

REMAINING MORTGAGE BALANCE TABLE FOR 7.500 PERCENT

ORIGINAL LOAN TERM

AGE OF LOAN	1	2	3	4	5	6	7	8	9	10
1	0.00000	.51868	.69126	.77730	.82874	.86287	.88711	.90518	.91913	.93019
2	0.00000	0.00000	.35854	.53731	.64418	.71509	.76546	.80299	.83197	.85496
3	0.00000	0.00000	0.00000	.27870	.44529	.55584	.63437	.69288	.73805	.77389
4	0.00000	0.00000	0.00000	0.00000	.23097	.38423	.49309	.57421	.63684	.68653
5	0.00000	0.00000	0.00000	0.00000	0.00000	.19929	.34085	.44634	.52777	.59238
6	0.00000	0.00000	0.00000	0.00000	0.00000	0.00000	.17679	.30853	.41024	.49093
7	0.00000	0.00000	0.00000	0.00000	0.00000	0.00000	0.00000	.16003	.28358	.38160
8	0.00000	0.00000	0.00000	0.00000	0.00000	0.00000	0.00000	0.00000	.14709	.26378
9	0.00000	0.00000	0.00000	0.00000	0.00000	0.00000	0.00000	0.00000	0.00000	.13682

AGE OF LOAN	11	12	13	14	15	20	25	30	35	40
1	.93916	.94656	.95275	.95800	.96249	.97757	.98584	.99078	.99388	.99589
2	.87360	.88897	.90184	.91274	.92206	.95339	.97058	.98085	.98729	.99147
3	.80295	.82691	.84697	.86396	.87350	.92734	.95414	.97014	.98019	.98670
4	.72681	.76004	.78785	.81140	.83155	.89927	.93642	.95861	.97253	.98155
5	.64476	.68797	.72413	.75475	.78096	.86902	.91733	.94617	.96429	.97601
6	.55634	.61031	.65547	.69371	.72644	.83642	.89675	.93278	.95540	.97004
7	.46106	.52661	.58147	.62793	.66769	.80129	.87457	.91834	.94582	.96361
8	.35839	.43642	.50173	.55705	.60438	.76343	.85068	.90278	.93549	.95668
9	.24774	.33923	.41580	.48066	.53615	.72263	.82493	.88602	.92437	.94921
10	.12850	.23450	.32321	.39834	.46263	.67867	.79718	.86795	.91238	.94116
11	0.00000	.12163	.22342	.30963	.38340	.63129	.76727	.84848	.89946	.93248
12	0.00000	0.00000	.11588	.21403	.29802	.58024	.73504	.82750	.88554	.92313
13	0.00000	0.00000	0.00000	.11102	.20600	.52522	.70032	.80489	.87054	.91306
14	0.00000	0.00000	0.00000	0.00000	.10685	.46593	.66289	.78052	.85437	.90220
15	0.00000	0.00000	0.00000	0.00000	0.00000	.40203	.62256	.75427	.83695	.89050
16	0.00000	0.00000	0.00000	0.00000	0.00000	.33318	.57910	.72597	.81818	.87739
17	0.00000	0.00000	0.00000	0.00000	0.00000	.25898	.53227	.69548	.79795	.86430
18	0.00000	0.00000	0.00000	0.00000	0.00000	.17902	.48180	.66262	.77614	.84966
19	0.00000	0.00000	0.00000	0.00000	0.00000	.09286	.42741	.62721	.75265	.83388
20	0.00000	0.00000	0.00000	0.00000	0.00000	0.00000	.36880	.58905	.72733	.81688
21	0.00000	0.00000	0.00000	0.00000	0.00000	0.00000	.30563	.54793	.70004	.79855
22	0.00000	0.00000	0.00000	0.00000	0.00000	0.00000	.23757	.50362	.67064	.77881
23	0.00000	0.00000	0.00000	0.00000	0.00000	0.00000	.16422	.45586	.63896	.75753
24	0.00000	0.00000	0.00000	0.00000	0.00000	0.00000	.08518	.40440	.60481	.73460
25	0.00000	0.00000	0.00000	0.00000	0.00000	0.00000	0.00000	.34895	.56801	.70988
26	0.00000	0.00000	0.00000	0.00000	0.00000	0.00000	0.00000	.28918	.52836	.68325
27	0.00000	0.00000	0.00000	0.00000	0.00000	0.00000	0.00000	.22478	.48563	.65456
28	0.00000	0.00000	0.00000	0.00000	0.00000	0.00000	0.00000	.15538	.43958	.62363
29	0.00000	0.00000	0.00000	0.00000	0.00000	0.00000	0.00000	.08059	.38996	.59030
30	0.00000	0.00000	0.00000	0.00000	0.00000	0.00000	0.00000	0.00000	.33648	.55439
31	0.00000	0.00000	0.00000	0.00000	0.00000	0.00000	0.00000	0.00000	.27886	.51569
32	0.00000	0.00000	0.00000	0.00000	0.00000	0.00000	0.00000	0.00000	.21675	.47398
33	0.00000	0.00000	0.00000	0.00000	0.00000	0.00000	0.00000	0.00000	.14983	.42934
34	0.00000	0.00000	0.00000	0.00000	0.00000	0.00000	0.00000	0.00000	.07772	.38061
35	0.00000	0.00000	0.00000	0.00000	0.00000	0.00000	0.00000	0.00000	0.00000	.32841
36	0.00000	0.00000	0.00000	0.00000	0.00000	0.00000	0.00000	0.00000	0.00000	.27217
37	0.00000	0.00000	0.00000	0.00000	0.00000	0.00000	0.00000	0.00000	0.00000	.21156
38	0.00000	0.00000	0.00000	0.00000	0.00000	0.00000	0.00000	0.00000	0.00000	.14624
39	0.00000	0.00000	0.00000	0.00000	0.00000	0.00000	0.00000	0.00000	0.00000	.07585

REMAINING MORTGAGE BALANCE TABLE FOR 7.750 PERCENT

ORIGINAL LOAN TERM

AGE OF LOAN	1	2	3	4	5	6	7	8	9	10
1	0.00000	.51930	.69206	.77818	.82965	.86379	.88803	.90609	.92002	.93107
2	0.00000	0.00000	.35939	.53855	.64562	.71665	.76708	.80464	.83363	.85661
3	0.00000	0.00000	0.00000	.27967	.44681	.55768	.63641	.69504	.74029	.77617
4	0.00000	0.00000	0.00000	0.00000	.23203	.38595	.49524	.57664	.63946	.68926
5	0.00000	0.00000	0.00000	0.00000	0.00000	.20042	.34274	.44873	.53052	.59538
6	0.00000	0.00000	0.00000	0.00000	0.00000	0.00000	.17798	.31055	.41284	.49396
7	0.00000	0.00000	0.00000	0.00000	0.00000	0.00000	0.00000	.16127	.28571	.38439
8	0.00000	0.00000	0.00000	0.00000	0.00000	0.00000	0.00000	0.00000	.14837	.26602
9	0.00000	0.00000	0.00000	0.00000	0.00000	0.00000	0.00000	0.00000	0.00000	.13815

AGE OF LOAN	11	12	13	14	15	20	25	30	35	40
1	.94002	.94740	.95357	.95880	.96326	.97822	.98638	.99122	.99424	.99617
2	.87523	.89058	.90342	.91428	.92357	.95470	.97167	.98174	.98801	.99204
3	.80523	.82920	.84923	.86619	.88069	.92928	.95578	.97150	.98129	.98757
4	.72962	.76288	.79070	.81424	.83437	.90183	.93861	.96043	.97402	.98274
5	.64792	.69124	.72746	.75812	.78433	.87217	.92007	.94848	.96617	.97753
6	.55967	.61385	.65915	.69749	.73027	.84012	.90003	.93556	.95769	.97189
7	.46433	.53023	.58535	.63159	.67186	.80551	.87839	.92161	.94853	.96581
8	.36133	.43991	.50562	.56123	.60877	.76811	.85500	.90654	.93863	.95923
9	.25007	.34233	.41949	.48478	.54061	.72771	.82974	.89025	.92794	.95213
10	.12986	.23691	.32644	.40220	.46697	.68406	.80245	.87266	.91639	.94446
11	0.00000	.12303	.22591	.31299	.38742	.63691	.77297	.85366	.90391	.93617
12	0.00000	0.00000	.11732	.21660	.30149	.58598	.74112	.83313	.89043	.92721
13	0.00000	0.00000	0.00000	.11248	.20865	.53095	.70671	.81095	.87587	.91754
14	0.00000	0.00000	0.00000	0.00000	.10835	.47150	.66954	.78699	.86014	.90709
15	0.00000	0.00000	0.00000	0.00000	0.00000	.40728	.62938	.76111	.84314	.89580
16	0.00000	0.00000	0.00000	0.00000	0.00000	.33790	.58600	.73314	.82478	.88360
17	0.00000	0.00000	0.00000	0.00000	0.00000	.26295	.53914	.70294	.80495	.87042
18	0.00000	0.00000	0.00000	0.00000	0.00000	.18197	.48851	.67030	.78352	.85619
19	0.00000	0.00000	0.00000	0.00000	0.00000	.09450	.43381	.63504	.76037	.84081
20	0.00000	0.00000	0.00000	0.00000	0.00000	0.00000	.37472	.59696	.73536	.82419
21	0.00000	0.00000	0.00000	0.00000	0.00000	0.00000	.31089	.55581	.70834	.80624
22	0.00000	0.00000	0.00000	0.00000	0.00000	0.00000	.24193	.51136	.67916	.78686
23	0.00000	0.00000	0.00000	0.00000	0.00000	0.00000	.16743	.46334	.64762	.76591
24	0.00000	0.00000	0.00000	0.00000	0.00000	0.00000	.08695	.41146	.61356	.74328
25	0.00000	0.00000	0.00000	0.00000	0.00000	0.00000	0.00000	.35542	.57676	.71883
26	0.00000	0.00000	0.00000	0.00000	0.00000	0.00000	0.00000	.29487	.53701	.69242
27	0.00000	0.00000	0.00000	0.00000	0.00000	0.00000	0.00000	.22946	.49406	.66389
28	0.00000	0.00000	0.00000	0.00000	0.00000	0.00000	0.00000	.15880	.44766	.63307
29	0.00000	0.00000	0.00000	0.00000	0.00000	0.00000	0.00000	.08247	.39754	.59977
30	0.00000	0.00000	0.00000	0.00000	0.00000	0.00000	0.00000	0.00000	.34339	.56380
31	0.00000	0.00000	0.00000	0.00000	0.00000	0.00000	0.00000	0.00000	.28490	.52494
32	0.00000	0.00000	0.00000	0.00000	0.00000	0.00000	0.00000	0.00000	.22170	.48296
33	0.00000	0.00000	0.00000	0.00000	0.00000	0.00000	0.00000	0.00000	.15343	.43760
34	0.00000	0.00000	0.00000	0.00000	0.00000	0.00000	0.00000	0.00000	.07968	.38861
35	0.00000	0.00000	0.00000	0.00000	0.00000	0.00000	0.00000	0.00000	0.00000	.33568
36	0.00000	0.00000	0.00000	0.00000	0.00000	0.00000	0.00000	0.00000	0.00000	.27849
37	0.00000	0.00000	0.00000	0.00000	0.00000	0.00000	0.00000	0.00000	0.00000	.21672
38	0.00000	0.00000	0.00000	0.00000	0.00000	0.00000	0.00000	0.00000	0.00000	.14998
39	0.00000	0.00000	0.00000	0.00000	0.00000	0.00000	0.00000	0.00000	0.00000	.07789

REMAINING MORTGAGE BALANCE TABLE FOR 8.000 PERCENT

ORIGINAL LOAN TERM

AGE OF LOAN	1	2	3	4	5	6	7	8	9	10
1	0.00000	.51992	.69286	.77906	.83056	.86471	.88895	.90700	.92092	.93195
2	0.00000	0.00000	.36024	.53978	.64706	.71820	.76869	.80628	.83527	.85825
3	0.00000	0.00000	0.00000	.28065	.44832	.55952	.63844	.69720	.74252	.77843
4	0.00000	0.00000	0.00000	0.00000	.23309	.38767	.49738	.57907	.64206	.69199
5	0.00000	0.00000	0.00000	0.00000	0.00000	.20156	.34462	.45113	.53327	.59837
6	0.00000	0.00000	0.00000	0.00000	0.00000	0.00000	.17918	.31257	.41545	.49698
7	0.00000	0.00000	0.00000	0.00000	0.00000	0.00000	0.00000	.16251	.28785	.38718
8	0.00000	0.00000	0.00000	0.00000	0.00000	0.00000	0.00000	0.00000	.14966	.26826
9	0.00000	0.00000	0.00000	0.00000	0.00000	0.00000	0.00000	0.00000	0.00000	.13948

AGE OF LOAN	11	12	13	14	15	20	25	30	35	40
1	.94088	.94823	.95438	.95958	.96402	.97886	.98691	.99165	.99457	.99643
2	.87685	.89217	.90498	.91581	.92506	.95597	.97273	.98260	.98869	.99257
3	.80751	.83146	.85147	.86840	.88286	.93118	.95738	.97280	.98233	.98839
4	.73241	.76570	.79353	.81706	.83716	.90433	.94075	.96219	.97543	.98386
5	.65107	.69449	.73078	.76146	.78766	.87526	.92274	.95070	.96797	.97895
6	.56299	.61737	.66281	.70124	.73406	.84377	.90324	.93825	.95988	.97364
7	.46760	.53385	.58921	.63602	.67601	.80966	.88211	.92477	.95113	.96789
8	.36429	.44339	.50950	.56539	.61314	.77273	.85924	.91018	.94164	.96165
9	.25240	.34543	.42317	.48890	.54505	.73273	.83446	.89437	.93137	.95490
10	.13123	.23934	.32967	.40606	.47131	.68941	.80763	.87725	.92025	.94760
11	0.00000	.12444	.22842	.31635	.39145	.64249	.77858	.85870	.90820	.93968
12	0.00000	0.00000	.11876	.21919	.30497	.59168	.74711	.83862	.89515	.93111
13	0.00000	0.00000	0.00000	.11396	.21130	.53665	.71303	.81688	.88102	.92182
14	0.00000	0.00000	0.00000	0.00000	.10986	.47706	.67612	.79332	.86572	.91177
15	0.00000	0.00000	0.00000	0.00000	0.00000	.41252	.63614	.76782	.84915	.90088
16	0.00000	0.00000	0.00000	0.00000	0.00000	.34262	.59285	.74019	.83120	.88908
17	0.00000	0.00000	0.00000	0.00000	0.00000	.26692	.54597	.71027	.81176	.87631
18	0.00000	0.00000	0.00000	0.00000	0.00000	.18494	.49519	.67787	.79071	.86248
19	0.00000	0.00000	0.00000	0.00000	0.00000	.09616	.44020	.64278	.76791	.84750
20	0.00000	0.00000	0.00000	0.00000	0.00000	0.00000	.38065	.60478	.74322	.83127
21	0.00000	0.00000	0.00000	0.00000	0.00000	0.00000	.31615	.56362	.71648	.81370
22	0.00000	0.00000	0.00000	0.00000	0.00000	0.00000	.24630	.51905	.68752	.79468
23	0.00000	0.00000	0.00000	0.00000	0.00000	0.00000	.17065	.47078	.65616	.77407
24	0.00000	0.00000	0.00000	0.00000	0.00000	0.00000	.08873	.41850	.62219	.75175
25	0.00000	0.00000	0.00000	0.00000	0.00000	0.00000	0.00000	.36188	.58541	.72758
26	0.00000	0.00000	0.00000	0.00000	0.00000	0.00000	0.00000	.30056	.54557	.70140
27	0.00000	0.00000	0.00000	0.00000	0.00000	0.00000	0.00000	.23416	.50242	.67305
28	0.00000	0.00000	0.00000	0.00000	0.00000	0.00000	0.00000	.16224	.45570	.64235
29	0.00000	0.00000	0.00000	0.00000	0.00000	0.00000	0.00000	.08435	.40509	.60910
30	0.00000	0.00000	0.00000	0.00000	0.00000	0.00000	0.00000	0.00000	.35029	.57309
31	0.00000	0.00000	0.00000	0.00000	0.00000	0.00000	0.00000	0.00000	.29094	.53409
32	0.00000	0.00000	0.00000	0.00000	0.00000	0.00000	0.00000	0.00000	.22666	.49185
33	0.00000	0.00000	0.00000	0.00000	0.00000	0.00000	0.00000	0.00000	.15704	.44611
34	0.00000	0.00000	0.00000	0.00000	0.00000	0.00000	0.00000	0.00000	.08165	.39657
35	0.00000	0.00000	0.00000	0.00000	0.00000	0.00000	0.00000	0.00000	0.00000	.34292
36	0.00000	0.00000	0.00000	0.00000	0.00000	0.00000	0.00000	0.00000	0.00000	.28481
37	0.00000	0.00000	0.00000	0.00000	0.00000	0.00000	0.00000	0.00000	0.00000	.22189
38	0.00000	0.00000	0.00000	0.00000	0.00000	0.00000	0.00000	0.00000	0.00000	.15374
39	0.00000	0.00000	0.00000	0.00000	0.00000	0.00000	0.00000	0.00000	0.00000	.07993

REMAINING MORTGAGE BALANCE TABLE FOR 8.250 PERCENT

ORIGINAL LOAN TERM

AGE OF LOAN	1	2	3	4	5	6	7	8	9	10
1	0.00000	.52054	.69367	.77994	.83147	.86563	.88986	.90790	.92180	.93281
2	0.00000	0.00000	.36108	.54102	.64849	.71974	.77029	.80791	.83691	.85987
3	0.00000	0.00000	0.00000	.28162	.44984	.56135	.64047	.69935	.74473	.78068
4	0.00000	0.00000	0.00000	0.00000	.23416	.38939	.49953	.58148	.64466	.69470
5	0.00000	0.00000	0.00000	0.00000	0.00000	.20270	.34651	.45352	.53601	.60135
6	0.00000	0.00000	0.00000	0.00000	0.00000	0.00000	.18037	.31459	.41806	.50000
7	0.00000	0.00000	0.00000	0.00000	0.00000	0.00000	0.00000	.16376	.28999	.38997
8	0.00000	0.00000	0.00000	0.00000	0.00000	0.00000	0.00000	0.00000	.15095	.27051
9	0.00000	0.00000	0.00000	0.00000	0.00000	0.00000	0.00000	0.00000	0.00000	.14081

AGE OF LOAN	11	12	13	14	15	20	25	30	35	40
1	.94172	.94906	.95518	.96036	.96477	.97949	.98742	.99205	.99489	.99668
2	.87845	.89375	.90652	.91731	.92652	.95722	.97376	.98342	.98934	.99307
3	.80976	.83370	.85369	.87058	.88500	.93304	.95892	.97405	.98332	.98916
4	.73518	.76851	.79634	.81985	.83991	.90679	.94282	.96388	.97678	.98491
5	.65421	.69773	.73407	.76477	.79097	.87829	.92534	.95284	.96968	.98030
6	.56630	.62088	.66646	.70496	.73782	.84735	.90636	.94085	.96198	.97529
7	.47086	.53746	.59306	.64004	.68013	.81376	.88575	.92783	.95361	.96985
8	.36724	.44688	.51337	.56955	.61749	.77729	.86338	.91370	.94452	.96395
9	.25474	.34854	.42685	.49301	.54948	.73769	.83909	.89836	.93466	.95754
10	.13261	.24177	.33291	.40993	.47565	.69470	.81272	.88170	.92395	.95058
11	0.00000	.12585	.23093	.31972	.39548	.64802	.78409	.86361	.91233	.94302
12	0.00000	0.00000	.12021	.22178	.30845	.59735	.75300	.84398	.89971	.93482
13	0.00000	0.00000	0.00000	.11544	.21396	.54233	.71925	.82266	.88600	.92592
14	0.00000	0.00000	0.00000	0.00000	.11138	.48260	.68261	.79952	.87112	.91625
15	0.00000	0.00000	0.00000	0.00000	0.00000	.41776	.64283	.77439	.85497	.90575
16	0.00000	0.00000	0.00000	0.00000	0.00000	.34735	.59964	.74711	.83743	.89435
17	0.00000	0.00000	0.00000	0.00000	0.00000	.27091	.55275	.71749	.81839	.88198
18	0.00000	0.00000	0.00000	0.00000	0.00000	.18792	.50184	.68533	.79772	.86855
19	0.00000	0.00000	0.00000	0.00000	0.00000	.09782	.44657	.65042	.77528	.85396
20	0.00000	0.00000	0.00000	0.00000	0.00000	0.00000	.38657	.61252	.75091	.83813
21	0.00000	0.00000	0.00000	0.00000	0.00000	0.00000	.32142	.57136	.72446	.82093
22	0.00000	0.00000	0.00000	0.00000	0.00000	0.00000	.25069	.52668	.69574	.80227
23	0.00000	0.00000	0.00000	0.00000	0.00000	0.00000	.17389	.47818	.66456	.78201
24	0.00000	0.00000	0.00000	0.00000	0.00000	0.00000	.09052	.42551	.63070	.76001
25	0.00000	0.00000	0.00000	0.00000	0.00000	0.00000	0.00000	.36834	.59395	.73612
26	0.00000	0.00000	0.00000	0.00000	0.00000	0.00000	0.00000	.30626	.55404	.71019
27	0.00000	0.00000	0.00000	0.00000	0.00000	0.00000	0.00000	.23886	.51072	.68203
28	0.00000	0.00000	0.00000	0.00000	0.00000	0.00000	0.00000	.16569	.46368	.65146
29	0.00000	0.00000	0.00000	0.00000	0.00000	0.00000	0.00000	.08625	.41261	.61828
30	0.00000	0.00000	0.00000	0.00000	0.00000	0.00000	0.00000	0.00000	.35717	.58225
31	0.00000	0.00000	0.00000	0.00000	0.00000	0.00000	0.00000	0.00000	.29697	.54313
32	0.00000	0.00000	0.00000	0.00000	0.00000	0.00000	0.00000	0.00000	.23162	.50066
33	0.00000	0.00000	0.00000	0.00000	0.00000	0.00000	0.00000	0.00000	.16067	.45455
34	0.00000	0.00000	0.00000	0.00000	0.00000	0.00000	0.00000	0.00000	.08363	.40448
35	0.00000	0.00000	0.00000	0.00000	0.00000	0.00000	0.00000	0.00000	0.00000	.35013
36	0.00000	0.00000	0.00000	0.00000	0.00000	0.00000	0.00000	0.00000	0.00000	.29112
37	0.00000	0.00000	0.00000	0.00000	0.00000	0.00000	0.00000	0.00000	0.00000	.22706
38	0.00000	0.00000	0.00000	0.00000	0.00000	0.00000	0.00000	0.00000	0.00000	.15750
39	0.00000	0.00000	0.00000	0.00000	0.00000	0.00000	0.00000	0.00000	0.00000	.08199

REMAINING MORTGAGE BALANCE TABLE FOR 8.500 PERCENT

ORIGINAL LOAN TERM

AGE OF LOAN	1	2	3	4	5	6	7	8	9	10
1	0.00000	.52116	.69447	.78081	.83237	.86654	.89077	.90880	.92268	.93367
2	0.00000	0.00000	.36193	.54225	.64992	.72128	.77189	.80953	.83853	.86148
3	0.00000	0.00000	0.00000	.28260	.45135	.56319	.64250	.70149	.74694	.78291
4	0.00000	0.00000	0.00000	0.00000	.23523	.39111	.50167	.58390	.64725	.69740
5	0.00000	0.00000	0.00000	0.00000	0.00000	.20383	.34839	.45592	.53875	.60432
6	0.00000	0.00000	0.00000	0.00000	0.00000	0.00000	.18157	.31662	.42066	.50302
7	0.00000	0.00000	0.00000	0.00000	0.00000	0.00000	0.00000	.16501	.29214	.39276
8	0.00000	0.00000	0.00000	0.00000	0.00000	0.00000	0.00000	0.00000	.15225	.27276
9	0.00000	0.00000	0.00000	0.00000	0.00000	0.00000	0.00000	0.00000	0.00000	.14215

AGE OF LOAN	11	12	13	14	15	20	25	30	35	40
1	.94256	.94987	.95597	.96112	.96551	.98010	.98791	.99244	.99519	.99691
2	.88004	.89531	.90805	.91880	.92797	.95844	.97475	.98421	.98996	.99355
3	.81200	.83593	.85589	.87274	.88711	.93486	.96043	.97526	.98426	.98989
4	.73794	.77129	.79912	.82261	.84264	.90920	.94484	.96551	.97807	.98590
5	.65734	.70095	.73733	.76805	.79424	.88127	.92787	.95490	.97132	.98157
6	.56961	.62438	.67008	.70866	.74156	.85088	.90940	.94336	.96398	.97685
7	.47413	.54105	.59689	.64403	.68422	.81779	.88930	.93079	.95598	.97171
8	.37020	.45036	.51723	.57368	.62182	.78178	.86743	.91711	.94729	.96612
9	.25709	.35164	.43053	.49712	.55390	.74259	.84362	.90223	.93782	.96004
10	.13399	.24421	.33616	.41379	.47997	.69994	.81771	.88603	.92752	.95342
11	0.00000	.12727	.23345	.32309	.39952	.65351	.78950	.86839	.91630	.94621
12	0.00000	0.00000	.12167	.22438	.31195	.60298	.75880	.84920	.90409	.93836
13	0.00000	0.00000	0.00000	.11654	.21664	.54799	.72539	.82831	.89081	.92983
14	0.00000	0.00000	0.00000	0.00000	.11290	.48813	.68903	.80557	.87635	.92053
15	0.00000	0.00000	0.00000	0.00000	0.00000	.42299	.64945	.78083	.86061	.91042
16	0.00000	0.00000	0.00000	0.00000	0.00000	.35208	.60638	.75390	.84349	.89941
17	0.00000	0.00000	0.00000	0.00000	0.00000	.27491	.55949	.72458	.82484	.88743
18	0.00000	0.00000	0.00000	0.00000	0.00000	.19092	.50846	.69268	.80455	.87439
19	0.00000	0.00000	0.00000	0.00000	0.00000	.09950	.45292	.65796	.78247	.86020
20	0.00000	0.00000	0.00000	0.00000	0.00000	0.00000	.39248	.62016	.75843	.84475
21	0.00000	0.00000	0.00000	0.00000	0.00000	0.00000	.32669	.57903	.73227	.82794
22	0.00000	0.00000	0.00000	0.00000	0.00000	0.00000	.25508	.53426	.70380	.80964
23	0.00000	0.00000	0.00000	0.00000	0.00000	0.00000	.17715	.48553	.67281	.78972
24	0.00000	0.00000	0.00000	0.00000	0.00000	0.00000	.09232	.43250	.63909	.76805
25	0.00000	0.00000	0.00000	0.00000	0.00000	0.00000	0.00000	.37478	.60238	.74445
26	0.00000	0.00000	0.00000	0.00000	0.00000	0.00000	0.00000	.31195	.56242	.71878
27	0.00000	0.00000	0.00000	0.00000	0.00000	0.00000	0.00000	.24358	.51894	.69083
28	0.00000	0.00000	0.00000	0.00000	0.00000	0.00000	0.00000	.16916	.47161	.66041
29	0.00000	0.00000	0.00000	0.00000	0.00000	0.00000	0.00000	.08816	.42009	.62731
30	0.00000	0.00000	0.00000	0.00000	0.00000	0.00000	0.00000	0.00000	.36403	.59127
31	0.00000	0.00000	0.00000	0.00000	0.00000	0.00000	0.00000	0.00000	.30301	.55206
32	0.00000	0.00000	0.00000	0.00000	0.00000	0.00000	0.00000	0.00000	.23659	.50937
33	0.00000	0.00000	0.00000	0.00000	0.00000	0.00000	0.00000	0.00000	.16431	.46291
34	0.00000	0.00000	0.00000	0.00000	0.00000	0.00000	0.00000	0.00000	.08563	.41235
35	0.00000	0.00000	0.00000	0.00000	0.00000	0.00000	0.00000	0.00000	0.00000	.35732
36	0.00000	0.00000	0.00000	0.00000	0.00000	0.00000	0.00000	0.00000	0.00000	.29742
37	0.00000	0.00000	0.00000	0.00000	0.00000	0.00000	0.00000	0.00000	0.00000	.23223
38	0.00000	0.00000	0.00000	0.00000	0.00000	0.00000	0.00000	0.00000	0.00000	.16128
39	0.00000	0.00000	0.00000	0.00000	0.00000	0.00000	0.00000	0.00000	0.00000	.08405

REMAINING MORTGAGE BALANCE TABLE FOR 8.750 PERCENT

ORIGINAL LOAN TERM

AGE OF LOAN	1	2	3	4	5	6	7	8	9	10
1	0.00000	.52178	.69527	.78168	.83327	.86745	.89167	.90968	.92355	.93452
2	0.00000	0.00000	.36278	.54348	.65136	.72282	.77348	.81114	.84014	.86308
3	0.00000	0.00000	0.00000	.28358	.45287	.56502	.64452	.70362	.74913	.78513
4	0.00000	0.00000	0.00000	0.00000	.23630	.39284	.50381	.58631	.64983	.70008
5	0.00000	0.00000	0.00000	0.00000	0.00000	.20498	.35028	.45831	.54149	.60728
6	0.00000	0.00000	0.00000	0.00000	0.00000	0.00000	.18277	.31865	.42327	.50603
7	0.00000	0.00000	0.00000	0.00000	0.00000	0.00000	0.00000	.16626	.29429	.39556
8	0.00000	0.00000	0.00000	0.00000	0.00000	0.00000	0.00000	0.00000	.15355	.27502
9	0.00000	0.00000	0.00000	0.00000	0.00000	0.00000	0.00000	0.00000	0.00000	.14350

AGE OF LOAN	11	12	13	14	15	20	25	30	35	40
1	.94339	.95067	.95675	.96187	.96623	.98069	.98838	.99281	.99548	.99713
2	.88162	.89685	.90955	.92027	.92939	.95963	.97571	.98497	.99054	.99399
3	.81422	.83813	.85806	.87487	.88919	.93664	.96188	.97641	.98516	.99057
4	.74068	.77406	.80188	.82534	.84533	.91156	.94679	.96708	.97929	.98684
5	.66045	.70415	.74058	.77130	.79747	.88420	.93033	.95689	.97288	.98276
6	.57290	.62787	.67369	.71234	.74526	.85434	.91237	.94577	.96588	.97832
7	.47739	.54465	.60071	.64800	.68829	.82177	.89277	.93365	.95825	.97347
8	.37316	.45384	.52109	.57781	.62612	.78622	.87139	.92041	.94993	.96818
9	.25945	.35476	.43421	.50122	.55830	.74744	.84805	.90598	.94085	.96241
10	.13538	.24665	.33941	.41765	.48429	.70513	.82260	.89022	.93094	.95611
11	0.00000	.12870	.23598	.32647	.40355	.65896	.79482	.87304	.92012	.94924
12	0.00000	0.00000	.12313	.22659	.31545	.60858	.76451	.85428	.90832	.94174
13	0.00000	0.00000	0.00000	.11844	.21932	.55362	.73145	.83382	.89545	.93356
14	0.00000	0.00000	0.00000	0.00000	.11444	.49365	.69537	.81149	.88140	.92463
15	0.00000	0.00000	0.00000	0.00000	0.00000	.42821	.65600	.78713	.86608	.91489
16	0.00000	0.00000	0.00000	0.00000	0.00000	.35682	.61305	.76056	.84936	.90426
17	0.00000	0.00000	0.00000	0.00000	0.00000	.27892	.56618	.73156	.83111	.89267
18	0.00000	0.00000	0.00000	0.00000	0.00000	.19392	.51505	.69991	.81121	.88002
19	0.00000	0.00000	0.00000	0.00000	0.00000	.10119	.45925	.66539	.78948	.86621
20	0.00000	0.00000	0.00000	0.00000	0.00000	0.00000	.39838	.62772	.76579	.85115
21	0.00000	0.00000	0.00000	0.00000	0.00000	0.00000	.33196	.58662	.73993	.83472
22	0.00000	0.00000	0.00000	0.00000	0.00000	0.00000	.25949	.54177	.71171	.81679
23	0.00000	0.00000	0.00000	0.00000	0.00000	0.00000	.18041	.49284	.68093	.79722
24	0.00000	0.00000	0.00000	0.00000	0.00000	0.00000	.09414	.43946	.64734	.77588
25	0.00000	0.00000	0.00000	0.00000	0.00000	0.00000	0.00000	.38120	.61069	.75259
26	0.00000	0.00000	0.00000	0.00000	0.00000	0.00000	0.00000	.31765	.57071	.72717
27	0.00000	0.00000	0.00000	0.00000	0.00000	0.00000	0.00000	.24830	.52708	.69945
28	0.00000	0.00000	0.00000	0.00000	0.00000	0.00000	0.00000	.17264	.47948	.66919
29	0.00000	0.00000	0.00000	0.00000	0.00000	0.00000	0.00000	.09008	.42754	.63618
30	0.00000	0.00000	0.00000	0.00000	0.00000	0.00000	0.00000	0.00000	.37087	.60017
31	0.00000	0.00000	0.00000	0.00000	0.00000	0.00000	0.00000	0.00000	.30903	.56087
32	0.00000	0.00000	0.00000	0.00000	0.00000	0.00000	0.00000	0.00000	.24157	.51799
33	0.00000	0.00000	0.00000	0.00000	0.00000	0.00000	0.00000	0.00000	.16795	.47121
34	0.00000	0.00000	0.00000	0.00000	0.00000	0.00000	0.00000	0.00000	.08763	.42017
35	0.00000	0.00000	0.00000	0.00000	0.00000	0.00000	0.00000	0.00000	0.00000	.36447
36	0.00000	0.00000	0.00000	0.00000	0.00000	0.00000	0.00000	0.00000	0.00000	.30370
37	0.00000	0.00000	0.00000	0.00000	0.00000	0.00000	0.00000	0.00000	0.00000	.23740
38	0.00000	0.00000	0.00000	0.00000	0.00000	0.00000	0.00000	0.00000	0.00000	.16506
39	0.00000	0.00000	0.00000	0.00000	0.00000	0.00000	0.00000	0.00000	0.00000	.08612

REMAINING MORTGAGE BALANCE TABLE FOR 9.000 PERCENT

ORIGINAL LOAN TERM

AGE OF LOAN	1	2	3	4	5	6	7	8	9	10
1	0.00000	.52240	.69607	.78256	.83417	.86835	.89257	.91057	.92442	.93537
2	0.00000	0.00000	.36363	.54471	.65278	.72435	.77507	.81275	.84175	.86467
3	0.00000	0.00000	0.00000	.28456	.45438	.56685	.64654	.70575	.75132	.78734
4	0.00000	0.00000	0.00000	0.00000	.23737	.39456	.50595	.58872	.65241	.70276
5	0.00000	0.00000	0.00000	0.00000	0.00000	.20612	.35218	.46070	.54422	.61024
6	0.00000	0.00000	0.00000	0.00000	0.00000	0.00000	.18398	.32068	.42588	.50904
7	0.00000	0.00000	0.00000	0.00000	0.00000	0.00000	0.00000	.16752	.29644	.39835
8	0.00000	0.00000	0.00000	0.00000	0.00000	0.00000	0.00000	0.00000	.15486	.27728
9	0.00000	0.00000	0.00000	0.00000	0.00000	0.00000	0.00000	0.00000	0.00000	.14485

AGE OF LOAN	11	12	13	14	15	20	25	30	35	40
1	.94421	.95147	.95751	.96261	.96695	.98127	.98884	.99317	.99575	.99733
2	.88318	.89838	.91104	.92171	.93079	.96079	.97664	.98570	.99110	.99441
3	.81643	.84031	.86021	.87698	.89125	.93838	.96329	.97752	.98601	.99121
4	.74341	.77680	.80461	.82805	.84799	.91388	.94869	.96858	.98045	.98771
5	.66355	.70733	.74380	.77453	.80068	.88707	.93272	.95880	.97436	.98389
6	.57619	.63134	.67728	.71559	.74893	.85775	.91526	.94810	.96770	.97971
7	.48064	.54823	.60452	.65156	.69232	.82568	.89615	.93640	.96042	.97513
8	.37613	.45732	.52494	.58192	.63041	.79060	.87525	.92361	.95246	.97012
9	.26181	.35787	.43789	.50531	.56268	.75223	.85239	.90961	.94375	.96465
10	.13677	.24911	.34267	.42151	.48861	.71026	.82739	.89430	.93422	.95866
11	0.00000	.13013	.23852	.32986	.40758	.66435	.80004	.87755	.92380	.95211
12	0.00000	0.00000	.12460	.22960	.31895	.61414	.77013	.85923	.91240	.94495
13	0.00000	0.00000	0.00000	.11995	.22201	.55922	.73741	.83919	.89993	.93711
14	0.00000	0.00000	0.00000	0.00000	.11598	.49914	.70162	.81728	.88629	.92854
15	0.00000	0.00000	0.00000	0.00000	0.00000	.43343	.66248	.79330	.87137	.91917
16	0.00000	0.00000	0.00000	0.00000	0.00000	.36155	.61966	.76708	.85505	.90891
17	0.00000	0.00000	0.00000	0.00000	0.00000	.28294	.57282	.73840	.83720	.89770
18	0.00000	0.00000	0.00000	0.00000	0.00000	.19694	.52159	.70703	.81768	.88543
19	0.00000	0.00000	0.00000	0.00000	0.00000	.10288	.46556	.67272	.79632	.87201
20	0.00000	0.00000	0.00000	0.00000	0.00000	0.00000	.40427	.63518	.77297	.85733
21	0.00000	0.00000	0.00000	0.00000	0.00000	0.00000	.33723	.59413	.74742	.84127
22	0.00000	0.00000	0.00000	0.00000	0.00000	0.00000	.26390	.54922	.71947	.82371
23	0.00000	0.00000	0.00000	0.00000	0.00000	0.00000	.18369	.50010	.68890	.80450
24	0.00000	0.00000	0.00000	0.00000	0.00000	0.00000	.09596	.44638	.65547	.78349
25	0.00000	0.00000	0.00000	0.00000	0.00000	0.00000	0.00000	.38761	.61890	.76051
26	0.00000	0.00000	0.00000	0.00000	0.00000	0.00000	0.00000	.32334	.57890	.73537
27	0.00000	0.00000	0.00000	0.00000	0.00000	0.00000	0.00000	.25303	.53514	.70788
28	0.00000	0.00000	0.00000	0.00000	0.00000	0.00000	0.00000	.17613	.48728	.67780
29	0.00000	0.00000	0.00000	0.00000	0.00000	0.00000	0.00000	.09201	.43493	.64491
30	0.00000	0.00000	0.00000	0.00000	0.00000	0.00000	0.00000	0.00000	.37768	.60893
31	0.00000	0.00000	0.00000	0.00000	0.00000	0.00000	0.00000	0.00000	.31505	.56957
32	0.00000	0.00000	0.00000	0.00000	0.00000	0.00000	0.00000	0.00000	.24654	.52652
33	0.00000	0.00000	0.00000	0.00000	0.00000	0.00000	0.00000	0.00000	.17161	.47943
34	0.00000	0.00000	0.00000	0.00000	0.00000	0.00000	0.00000	0.00000	.08965	.42793
35	0.00000	0.00000	0.00000	0.00000	0.00000	0.00000	0.00000	0.00000	0.00000	.37159
36	0.00000	0.00000	0.00000	0.00000	0.00000	0.00000	0.00000	0.00000	0.00000	.30997
37	0.00000	0.00000	0.00000	0.00000	0.00000	0.00000	0.00000	0.00000	0.00000	.24257
38	0.00000	0.00000	0.00000	0.00000	0.00000	0.00000	0.00000	0.00000	0.00000	.16884
39	0.00000	0.00000	0.00000	0.00000	0.00000	0.00000	0.00000	0.00000	0.00000	.08820

REMAINING MORTGAGE BALANCE TABLE FOR 9.250 PERCENT

ORIGINAL LOAN TERM

AGE OF LOAN	1	2	3	4	5	6	7	8	9	10
1	0.00000	.52302	.69687	.78342	.83506	.86925	.89346	.91145	.92528	.93620
2	0.00000	0.00000	.36448	.54594	.65421	.72588	.77664	.81434	.84334	.86624
3	0.00000	0.00000	0.00000	.28554	.45590	.56867	.64855	.70787	.75349	.78953
4	0.00000	0.00000	0.00000	0.00000	.23844	.39629	.50809	.59112	.65497	.70542
5	0.00000	0.00000	0.00000	0.00000	0.00000	.20727	.35407	.46309	.54695	.61319
6	0.00000	0.00000	0.00000	0.00000	0.00000	0.00000	.18519	.32272	.42849	.51205
7	0.00000	0.00000	0.00000	0.00000	0.00000	0.00000	0.00000	.16879	.29860	.40115
8	0.00000	0.00000	0.00000	0.00000	0.00000	0.00000	0.00000	0.00000	.15617	.27955
9	0.00000	0.00000	0.00000	0.00000	0.00000	0.00000	0.00000	0.00000	0.00000	.14621

AGE OF LOAN	11	12	13	14	15	20	25	30	35	40
1	.94502	.95225	.95627	.96334	.96765	.98184	.98929	.99351	.99600	.99752
2	.88472	.89989	.91251	.92314	.93217	.96192	.97754	.98639	.99162	.99479
3	.81861	.84248	.86234	.87906	.89327	.94009	.96466	.97858	.98682	.99181
4	.74612	.77953	.80732	.83073	.85062	.91614	.95054	.97003	.98155	.98854
5	.66663	.71050	.74700	.77773	.80385	.88989	.93505	.96064	.97577	.98495
6	.57947	.63480	.68085	.71961	.75257	.86110	.91807	.95035	.96944	.98101
7	.48390	.55180	.60831	.65589	.69633	.82953	.89945	.93907	.96249	.97670
8	.37910	.46079	.52878	.58601	.63467	.79492	.87903	.92669	.95488	.97196
9	.26418	.36099	.44156	.50939	.56705	.75696	.85664	.91313	.94652	.96677
10	.13817	.25157	.34593	.42537	.49291	.71534	.83209	.89825	.93737	.96108
11	0.00000	.13157	.24107	.33325	.41161	.66970	.80517	.88193	.92733	.95485
12	0.00000	0.00000	.12608	.23223	.32247	.61966	.77565	.86405	.91632	.94800
13	0.00000	0.00000	0.00000	.12146	.22472	.56478	.74329	.84443	.90424	.94050
14	0.00000	0.00000	0.00000	0.00000	.11753	.50461	.70779	.82292	.89100	.93228
15	0.00000	0.00000	0.00000	0.00000	0.00000	.43864	.66888	.79934	.87649	.92326
16	0.00000	0.00000	0.00000	0.00000	0.00000	.36629	.62620	.77348	.86057	.91337
17	0.00000	0.00000	0.00000	0.00000	0.00000	.28696	.57941	.74512	.84311	.90252
18	0.00000	0.00000	0.00000	0.00000	0.00000	.19997	.52810	.71403	.82397	.89063
19	0.00000	0.00000	0.00000	0.00000	0.00000	.10459	.47184	.67994	.80299	.87759
20	0.00000	0.00000	0.00000	0.00000	0.00000	0.00000	.41015	.64255	.77998	.86329
21	0.00000	0.00000	0.00000	0.00000	0.00000	0.00000	.34250	.60156	.75474	.84761
22	0.00000	0.00000	0.00000	0.00000	0.00000	0.00000	.26832	.55661	.72707	.83042
23	0.00000	0.00000	0.00000	0.00000	0.00000	0.00000	.18698	.50732	.69673	.81157
24	0.00000	0.00000	0.00000	0.00000	0.00000	0.00000	.09780	.45327	.66346	.79090
25	0.00000	0.00000	0.00000	0.00000	0.00000	0.00000	0.00000	.39400	.62698	.76823
26	0.00000	0.00000	0.00000	0.00000	0.00000	0.00000	0.00000	.32902	.58698	.74338
27	0.00000	0.00000	0.00000	0.00000	0.00000	0.00000	0.00000	.25776	.54312	.71613
28	0.00000	0.00000	0.00000	0.00000	0.00000	0.00000	0.00000	.17963	.49502	.68624
29	0.00000	0.00000	0.00000	0.00000	0.00000	0.00000	0.00000	.09395	.44229	.65348
30	0.00000	0.00000	0.00000	0.00000	0.00000	0.00000	0.00000	0.00000	.38446	.61755
31	0.00000	0.00000	0.00000	0.00000	0.00000	0.00000	0.00000	0.00000	.32105	.57815
32	0.00000	0.00000	0.00000	0.00000	0.00000	0.00000	0.00000	0.00000	.25152	.53495
33	0.00000	0.00000	0.00000	0.00000	0.00000	0.00000	0.00000	0.00000	.17527	.48757
34	0.00000	0.00000	0.00000	0.00000	0.00000	0.00000	0.00000	0.00000	.09167	.43563
35	0.00000	0.00000	0.00000	0.00000	0.00000	0.00000	0.00000	0.00000	0.00000	.37867
36	0.00000	0.00000	0.00000	0.00000	0.00000	0.00000	0.00000	0.00000	0.00000	.31621
37	0.00000	0.00000	0.00000	0.00000	0.00000	0.00000	0.00000	0.00000	0.00000	.24773
38	0.00000	0.00000	0.00000	0.00000	0.00000	0.00000	0.00000	0.00000	0.00000	.17264
39	0.00000	0.00000	0.00000	0.00000	0.00000	0.00000	0.00000	0.00000	0.00000	.09029

REMAINING MORTGAGE BALANCE TABLE FOR 9.500 PERCENT

ORIGINAL LOAN TERM

AGE OF LOAN	1	2	3	4	5	6	7	8	9	10
1	0.00000	.52364	.69767	.78429	.83596	.87015	.89435	.91232	.92613	.93703
2	0.00000	0.00000	.36532	.54717	.65563	.72740	.77822	.81593	.84492	.86781
3	0.00000	0.00000	0.00000	.28652	.45741	.57050	.65055	.70998	.75565	.79171
4	0.00000	0.00000	0.00000	0.00000	.23952	.39802	.51022	.59351	.65753	.70807
5	0.00000	0.00000	0.00000	0.00000	0.00000	.20842	.35597	.46549	.54967	.61612
6	0.00000	0.00000	0.00000	0.00000	0.00000	0.00000	.18640	.32475	.43110	.51505
7	0.00000	0.00000	0.00000	0.00000	0.00000	0.00000	0.00000	.17005	.30076	.40395
8	0.00000	0.00000	0.00000	0.00000	0.00000	0.00000	0.00000	0.00000	.15749	.28182
9	0.00000	0.00000	0.00000	0.00000	0.00000	0.00000	0.00000	0.00000	0.00000	.14757

AGE OF LOAN	11	12	13	14	15	20	25	30	35	40
1	.94582	.95302	.95902	.96406	.96834	.98239	.98972	.99383	.99625	.99769
2	.88626	.90139	.91397	.92455	.93353	.96303	.97841	.98706	.99212	.99516
3	.82079	.84463	.86445	.88112	.89527	.94176	.96599	.97960	.98758	.99237
4	.74882	.78223	.81001	.83338	.85322	.91837	.95233	.97141	.98260	.98931
5	.66970	.71364	.75017	.78050	.80699	.89265	.93731	.96241	.97712	.98594
6	.58274	.63825	.68439	.72321	.75617	.86439	.92081	.95251	.97109	.98224
7	.48715	.55537	.61209	.65980	.70031	.83332	.90266	.94163	.96447	.97817
8	.38206	.46426	.53261	.59009	.63890	.79917	.88272	.92967	.95719	.97370
9	.26655	.36412	.44524	.51346	.57140	.76163	.86079	.91653	.94918	.96878
10	.13958	.25403	.34919	.42923	.49721	.72036	.83669	.90208	.94039	.96338
11	0.00000	.13302	.24362	.33664	.41564	.67500	.81020	.88619	.93071	.95744
12	0.00000	0.00000	.12757	.23486	.32598	.62513	.78108	.86873	.92008	.95091
13	0.00000	0.00000	0.00000	.12298	.22743	.57032	.74907	.84954	.90840	.94373
14	0.00000	0.00000	0.00000	0.00000	.11909	.51007	.71388	.82844	.89555	.93584
15	0.00000	0.00000	0.00000	0.00000	0.00000	.44383	.67520	.80524	.88143	.92717
16	0.00000	0.00000	0.00000	0.00000	0.00000	.37103	.63268	.77975	.86591	.91763
17	0.00000	0.00000	0.00000	0.00000	0.00000	.29099	.58595	.75172	.84885	.90715
18	0.00000	0.00000	0.00000	0.00000	0.00000	.20301	.53457	.72091	.83009	.89563
19	0.00000	0.00000	0.00000	0.00000	0.00000	.10631	.47809	.68705	.80948	.88296
20	0.00000	0.00000	0.00000	0.00000	0.00000	0.00000	.41601	.64982	.78681	.86904
21	0.00000	0.00000	0.00000	0.00000	0.00000	0.00000	.34777	.60890	.76190	.85374
22	0.00000	0.00000	0.00000	0.00000	0.00000	0.00000	.27275	.56392	.73452	.83692
23	0.00000	0.00000	0.00000	0.00000	0.00000	0.00000	.19029	.51447	.70442	.81843
24	0.00000	0.00000	0.00000	0.00000	0.00000	0.00000	.09964	.46012	.67133	.79810
25	0.00000	0.00000	0.00000	0.00000	0.00000	0.00000	0.00000	.40037	.63495	.77575
26	0.00000	0.00000	0.00000	0.00000	0.00000	0.00000	0.00000	.33469	.59497	.75119
27	0.00000	0.00000	0.00000	0.00000	0.00000	0.00000	0.00000	.26250	.55101	.72419
28	0.00000	0.00000	0.00000	0.00000	0.00000	0.00000	0.00000	.18313	.50270	.69451
29	0.00000	0.00000	0.00000	0.00000	0.00000	0.00000	0.00000	.09590	.44959	.66189
30	0.00000	0.00000	0.00000	0.00000	0.00000	0.00000	0.00000	0.00000	.39121	.62603
31	0.00000	0.00000	0.00000	0.00000	0.00000	0.00000	0.00000	0.00000	.32703	.58660
32	0.00000	0.00000	0.00000	0.00000	0.00000	0.00000	0.00000	0.00000	.25649	.54327
33	0.00000	0.00000	0.00000	0.00000	0.00000	0.00000	0.00000	0.00000	.17894	.49563
34	0.00000	0.00000	0.00000	0.00000	0.00000	0.00000	0.00000	0.00000	.09370	.44327
35	0.00000	0.00000	0.00000	0.00000	0.00000	0.00000	0.00000	0.00000	0.00000	.38571
36	0.00000	0.00000	0.00000	0.00000	0.00000	0.00000	0.00000	0.00000	0.00000	.32244
37	0.00000	0.00000	0.00000	0.00000	0.00000	0.00000	0.00000	0.00000	0.00000	.25288
38	0.00000	0.00000	0.00000	0.00000	0.00000	0.00000	0.00000	0.00000	0.00000	.17643
39	0.00000	0.00000	0.00000	0.00000	0.00000	0.00000	0.00000	0.00000	0.00000	.09238

REMAINING MORTGAGE BALANCE TABLE FOR 9.750 PERCENT

ORIGINAL LOAN TERM

AGE OF LOAN	1	2	3	4	5	6	7	8	9	10
1	0.00000	.52426	.69846	.78516	.83685	.87104	.89523	.91318	.92697	.93785
2	0.00000	0.00000	.36617	.54840	.65705	.72892	.77978	.81751	.84649	.86936
3	0.00000	0.00000	0.00000	.28750	.45893	.57232	.65256	.71208	.75781	.79388
4	0.00000	0.00000	0.00000	0.00000	.24060	.39974	.51236	.59590	.66008	.71071
5	0.00000	0.00000	0.00000	0.00000	0.00000	.20957	.35786	.46788	.55238	.61905
6	0.00000	0.00000	0.00000	0.00000	0.00000	0.00000	.18761	.32679	.43371	.51805
7	0.00000	0.00000	0.00000	0.00000	0.00000	0.00000	0.00000	.17132	.30293	.40675
8	0.00000	0.00000	0.00000	0.00000	0.00000	0.00000	0.00000	0.00000	.15881	.28410
9	0.00000	0.00000	0.00000	0.00000	0.00000	0.00000	0.00000	0.00000	0.00000	.14894

AGE OF LOAN	11	12	13	14	15	20	25	30	35	40
1	.94661	.95379	.95975	.96476	.96902	.98293	.99013	.99414	.99647	.99786
2	.88778	.90287	.91540	.92594	.93487	.96412	.97925	.98769	.99259	.99550
3	.82294	.84675	.86653	.88315	.89725	.94339	.96727	.98058	.98831	.99290
4	.75149	.78491	.81267	.83600	.85579	.92054	.95406	.97274	.98359	.99003
5	.67276	.71677	.75332	.78404	.81009	.89537	.93951	.96411	.97839	.98688
6	.58600	.64167	.68792	.72678	.75974	.86762	.92347	.95459	.97266	.98340
7	.49039	.55892	.61585	.66368	.70426	.83705	.90579	.94411	.96635	.97956
8	.38503	.46773	.53643	.59415	.64312	.80336	.88632	.93255	.95939	.97534
9	.26893	.36724	.44891	.51753	.57574	.76624	.86485	.91982	.95173	.97068
10	.14099	.25650	.35246	.43309	.50149	.72533	.84120	.90579	.94328	.96555
11	0.00000	.13447	.24618	.34004	.41967	.68025	.81514	.89032	.93397	.95990
12	0.00000	0.00000	.12906	.23751	.32951	.63057	.78642	.87328	.92371	.95367
13	0.00000	0.00000	0.00000	.12451	.23015	.57583	.75477	.85451	.91240	.94680
14	0.00000	0.00000	0.00000	0.00000	.12066	.51550	.71989	.83381	.89994	.93924
15	0.00000	0.00000	0.00000	0.00000	0.00000	.44902	.68145	.81101	.88621	.93090
16	0.00000	0.00000	0.00000	0.00000	0.00000	.37576	.63910	.78588	.87109	.92171
17	0.00000	0.00000	0.00000	0.00000	0.00000	.29503	.59242	.75819	.85441	.91159
18	0.00000	0.00000	0.00000	0.00000	0.00000	.20607	.54099	.72768	.83604	.90043
19	0.00000	0.00000	0.00000	0.00000	0.00000	.10803	.48431	.69405	.81580	.88813
20	0.00000	0.00000	0.00000	0.00000	0.00000	0.00000	.42186	.65700	.79349	.87458
21	0.00000	0.00000	0.00000	0.00000	0.00000	0.00000	.35303	.61616	.76890	.85965
22	0.00000	0.00000	0.00000	0.00000	0.00000	0.00000	.27718	.57116	.74181	.84320
23	0.00000	0.00000	0.00000	0.00000	0.00000	0.00000	.19360	.52158	.71195	.82507
24	0.00000	0.00000	0.00000	0.00000	0.00000	0.00000	.10150	.46693	.67905	.80509
25	0.00000	0.00000	0.00000	0.00000	0.00000	0.00000	0.00000	.40671	.64280	.78307
26	0.00000	0.00000	0.00000	0.00000	0.00000	0.00000	0.00000	.34036	.60285	.75881
27	0.00000	0.00000	0.00000	0.00000	0.00000	0.00000	0.00000	.26723	.55882	.73207
28	0.00000	0.00000	0.00000	0.00000	0.00000	0.00000	0.00000	.18665	.51030	.70261
29	0.00000	0.00000	0.00000	0.00000	0.00000	0.00000	0.00000	.09785	.45684	.67014
30	0.00000	0.00000	0.00000	0.00000	0.00000	0.00000	0.00000	0.00000	.39793	.63436
31	0.00000	0.00000	0.00000	0.00000	0.00000	0.00000	0.00000	0.00000	.33300	.59494
32	0.00000	0.00000	0.00000	0.00000	0.00000	0.00000	0.00000	0.00000	.26146	.55149
33	0.00000	0.00000	0.00000	0.00000	0.00000	0.00000	0.00000	0.00000	.18262	.50361
34	0.00000	0.00000	0.00000	0.00000	0.00000	0.00000	0.00000	0.00000	.09574	.45085
35	0.00000	0.00000	0.00000	0.00000	0.00000	0.00000	0.00000	0.00000	0.00000	.39270
36	0.00000	0.00000	0.00000	0.00000	0.00000	0.00000	0.00000	0.00000	0.00000	.32863
37	0.00000	0.00000	0.00000	0.00000	0.00000	0.00000	0.00000	0.00000	0.00000	.25803
38	0.00000	0.00000	0.00000	0.00000	0.00000	0.00000	0.00000	0.00000	0.00000	.18022
39	0.00000	0.00000	0.00000	0.00000	0.00000	0.00000	0.00000	0.00000	0.00000	.09448

REMAINING MORTGAGE BALANCE TABLE FOR 10.000 PERCENT

ORIGINAL LOAN TERM

AGE OF LOAN	1	2	3	4	5	6	7	8	9	10
1	0.00000	.52488	.69926	.78602	.83773	.87193	.89611	.91404	.92781	.93866
2	0.00000	0.00000	.36702	.54963	.65847	.73044	.78134	.81908	.84805	.87089
3	0.00000	0.00000	0.00000	.28849	.46044	.57414	.65455	.71418	.75995	.79603
4	0.00000	0.00000	0.00000	0.00000	.24167	.40147	.51449	.59829	.66262	.71333
5	0.00000	0.00000	0.00000	0.00000	0.00000	.21072	.35976	.47027	.55510	.62197
6	0.00000	0.00000	0.00000	0.00000	0.00000	0.00000	.18883	.32884	.43632	.52105
7	0.00000	0.00000	0.00000	0.00000	0.00000	0.00000	0.00000	.17260	.30510	.40955
8	0.00000	0.00000	0.00000	0.00000	0.00000	0.00000	0.00000	0.00000	.16014	.28638
9	0.00000	0.00000	0.00000	0.00000	0.00000	0.00000	0.00000	0.00000	0.00000	.15031

AGE OF LOAN	11	12	13	14	15	20	25	30	35	40
1	.94739	.95454	.96048	.96546	.96968	.98345	.99053	.99444	.99669	.99801
2	.88928	.90433	.91682	.92731	.93619	.96517	.98007	.98830	.99303	.99582
3	.82508	.84886	.86859	.88515	.89919	.94498	.96851	.98152	.98900	.99339
4	.75416	.78757	.81531	.83859	.85832	.92267	.95574	.97402	.98453	.99071
5	.67581	.71988	.75645	.78715	.81317	.89802	.94164	.96574	.97960	.98776
6	.58925	.64509	.69143	.73032	.76329	.87080	.92606	.95660	.97416	.98449
7	.49364	.56247	.61959	.66754	.70818	.84072	.90884	.94649	.96814	.98087
8	.38801	.47120	.54024	.59819	.64731	.80750	.88983	.93533	.96150	.97689
9	.27132	.37037	.45258	.52158	.58006	.77079	.86882	.92300	.95416	.97248
10	.14241	.25898	.35573	.43654	.50577	.73024	.84561	.90938	.94605	.96761
11	0.00000	.13593	.24875	.34345	.42370	.68545	.81998	.89433	.93709	.96223
12	0.00000	0.00000	.13056	.24016	.33303	.63596	.79166	.87771	.92719	.95629
13	0.00000	0.00000	0.00000	.12605	.23288	.58130	.76037	.85934	.91625	.94972
14	0.00000	0.00000	0.00000	0.00000	.12223	.52091	.72581	.83906	.90418	.94247
15	0.00000	0.00000	0.00000	0.00000	0.00000	.45419	.68762	.81665	.89083	.93446
16	0.00000	0.00000	0.00000	0.00000	0.00000	.38049	.64544	.79189	.87609	.92561
17	0.00000	0.00000	0.00000	0.00000	0.00000	.29907	.59885	.76454	.85981	.91584
18	0.00000	0.00000	0.00000	0.00000	0.00000	.20913	.54737	.73432	.84182	.90504
19	0.00000	0.00000	0.00000	0.00000	0.00000	.10977	.49050	.70094	.82194	.89310
20	0.00000	0.00000	0.00000	0.00000	0.00000	0.00000	.42768	.66407	.79999	.87992
21	0.00000	0.00000	0.00000	0.00000	0.00000	0.00000	.35828	.62333	.77574	.86536
22	0.00000	0.00000	0.00000	0.00000	0.00000	0.00000	.28162	.57833	.74894	.84928
23	0.00000	0.00000	0.00000	0.00000	0.00000	0.00000	.19692	.52862	.71934	.83151
24	0.00000	0.00000	0.00000	0.00000	0.00000	0.00000	.10336	.47370	.68665	.81188
25	0.00000	0.00000	0.00000	0.00000	0.00000	0.00000	0.00000	.41303	.65052	.79019
26	0.00000	0.00000	0.00000	0.00000	0.00000	0.00000	0.00000	.34601	.61062	.76624
27	0.00000	0.00000	0.00000	0.00000	0.00000	0.00000	0.00000	.27197	.56654	.73977
28	0.00000	0.00000	0.00000	0.00000	0.00000	0.00000	0.00000	.19018	.51784	.71054
29	0.00000	0.00000	0.00000	0.00000	0.00000	0.00000	0.00000	.09982	.46404	.67824
30	0.00000	0.00000	0.00000	0.00000	0.00000	0.00000	0.00000	0.00000	.40461	.64256
31	0.00000	0.00000	0.00000	0.00000	0.00000	0.00000	0.00000	0.00000	.33895	.60314
32	0.00000	0.00000	0.00000	0.00000	0.00000	0.00000	0.00000	0.00000	.26642	.55960
33	0.00000	0.00000	0.00000	0.00000	0.00000	0.00000	0.00000	0.00000	.18630	.51150
34	0.00000	0.00000	0.00000	0.00000	0.00000	0.00000	0.00000	0.00000	.09778	.45836
35	0.00000	0.00000	0.00000	0.00000	0.00000	0.00000	0.00000	0.00000	0.00000	.39965
36	0.00000	0.00000	0.00000	0.00000	0.00000	0.00000	0.00000	0.00000	0.00000	.33480
37	0.00000	0.00000	0.00000	0.00000	0.00000	0.00000	0.00000	0.00000	0.00000	.26316
38	0.00000	0.00000	0.00000	0.00000	0.00000	0.00000	0.00000	0.00000	0.00000	.18402
39	0.00000	0.00000	0.00000	0.00000	0.00000	0.00000	0.00000	0.00000	0.00000	.09659

REMAINING MORTGAGE BALANCE TABLE FOR 10.250 PERCENT

ORIGINAL LOAN TERM

AGE OF LOAN	1	2	3	4	5	6	7	8	9	10
1	0.00000	.52549	.70005	.78688	.83861	.87281	.89698	.91489	.92864	.93946
2	0.00000	0.00000	.36787	.55086	.65989	.73195	.78289	.82064	.84960	.87242
3	0.00000	0.00000	0.00000	.28947	.46196	.57596	.65655	.71626	.76208	.79817
4	0.00000	0.00000	0.00000	0.00000	.24276	.40320	.51662	.60067	.66515	.71594
5	0.00000	0.00000	0.00000	0.00000	0.00000	.21188	.36166	.47265	.55780	.62488
6	0.00000	0.00000	0.00000	0.00000	0.00000	0.00000	.19005	.33088	.43892	.52404
7	0.00000	0.00000	0.00000	0.00000	0.00000	0.00000	0.00000	.17388	.30727	.41235
8	0.00000	0.00000	0.00000	0.00000	0.00000	0.00000	0.00000	0.00000	.16147	.28867
9	0.00000	0.00000	0.00000	0.00000	0.00000	0.00000	0.00000	0.00000	0.00000	.15169

	11	12	13	14	15	20	25	30	35	40
1	.94817	.95529	.96120	.96615	.97034	.98396	.99092	.99472	.99689	.99816
2	.89077	.90578	.91822	.92866	.93749	.96620	.98085	.98888	.99345	.99612
3	.82720	.85094	.87063	.88714	.90111	.94653	.96971	.98241	.98965	.99385
4	.75680	.79022	.81792	.84115	.86082	.92475	.95737	.97525	.98543	.99135
5	.67884	.72296	.75955	.79023	.81620	.90063	.94371	.96731	.98075	.98858
6	.59249	.64849	.69491	.73384	.76679	.87392	.92857	.95852	.97558	.98551
7	.49687	.56600	.62332	.67138	.71207	.84433	.91181	.94879	.96985	.98211
8	.39098	.47466	.54404	.60222	.65147	.81157	.89325	.93801	.96351	.97834
9	.27371	.37350	.45624	.52562	.58436	.77528	.87270	.92608	.95648	.97417
10	.14383	.26147	.35901	.44079	.51003	.73510	.84993	.91286	.94870	.96955
11	0.00000	.13740	.25132	.34685	.42772	.69060	.82472	.89822	.94008	.96444
12	0.00000	0.00000	.13207	.24281	.33656	.64131	.79680	.88201	.93053	.95877
13	0.00000	0.00000	0.00000	.12760	.23561	.58673	.76588	.86405	.91996	.95250
14	0.00000	0.00000	0.00000	0.00000	.12381	.52629	.73164	.84417	.90825	.94555
15	0.00000	0.00000	0.00000	0.00000	0.00000	.45935	.69372	.82215	.89529	.93786
16	0.00000	0.00000	0.00000	0.00000	0.00000	.38522	.65172	.79776	.88093	.92934
17	0.00000	0.00000	0.00000	0.00000	0.00000	.30312	.60521	.77075	.86503	.91990
18	0.00000	0.00000	0.00000	0.00000	0.00000	.21220	.55370	.74085	.84742	.90945
19	0.00000	0.00000	0.00000	0.00000	0.00000	.11151	.49666	.70772	.82792	.89788
20	0.00000	0.00000	0.00000	0.00000	0.00000	0.00000	.43349	.67104	.80633	.88506
21	0.00000	0.00000	0.00000	0.00000	0.00000	0.00000	.36353	.63042	.78241	.87087
22	0.00000	0.00000	0.00000	0.00000	0.00000	0.00000	.28606	.58543	.75592	.85515
23	0.00000	0.00000	0.00000	0.00000	0.00000	0.00000	.20025	.53560	.72659	.83774
24	0.00000	0.00000	0.00000	0.00000	0.00000	0.00000	.10523	.48043	.69410	.81847
25	0.00000	0.00000	0.00000	0.00000	0.00000	0.00000	0.00000	.41932	.65813	.79712
26	0.00000	0.00000	0.00000	0.00000	0.00000	0.00000	0.00000	.35165	.61828	.77347
27	0.00000	0.00000	0.00000	0.00000	0.00000	0.00000	0.00000	.27671	.57416	.74729
28	0.00000	0.00000	0.00000	0.00000	0.00000	0.00000	0.00000	.19371	.52530	.71829
29	0.00000	0.00000	0.00000	0.00000	0.00000	0.00000	0.00000	.10179	.47118	.68618
30	0.00000	0.00000	0.00000	0.00000	0.00000	0.00000	0.00000	0.00000	.41125	.65061
31	0.00000	0.00000	0.00000	0.00000	0.00000	0.00000	0.00000	0.00000	.34488	.61122
32	0.00000	0.00000	0.00000	0.00000	0.00000	0.00000	0.00000	0.00000	.27138	.56760
33	0.00000	0.00000	0.00000	0.00000	0.00000	0.00000	0.00000	0.00000	.18998	.51930
34	0.00000	0.00000	0.00000	0.00000	0.00000	0.00000	0.00000	0.00000	.09983	.46580
35	0.00000	0.00000	0.00000	0.00000	0.00000	0.00000	0.00000	0.00000	0.00000	.40655
36	0.00000	0.00000	0.00000	0.00000	0.00000	0.00000	0.00000	0.00000	0.00000	.34094
37	0.00000	0.00000	0.00000	0.00000	0.00000	0.00000	0.00000	0.00000	0.00000	.26828
38	0.00000	0.00000	0.00000	0.00000	0.00000	0.00000	0.00000	0.00000	0.00000	.18781
39	0.00000	0.00000	0.00000	0.00000	0.00000	0.00000	0.00000	0.00000	0.00000	.09869

REMAINING MORTGAGE BALANCE TABLE FOR 10.500 PERCENT

ORIGINAL LOAN TERM

AGE OF LOAN	1	2	3	4	5	6	7	8	9	10
1	0.00000	.52611	.70085	.78774	.83949	.87369	.89785	.91574	.92946	.94026
2	0.00000	0.00000	.36872	.55208	.66130	.73346	.78444	.82220	.85114	.87393
3	0.00000	0.00000	0.00000	.29046	.46347	.57777	.65853	.71834	.76420	.80029
4	0.00000	0.00000	0.00000	0.00000	.24384	.40493	.51875	.60305	.66767	.71854
5	0.00000	0.00000	0.00000	0.00000	0.00000	.21304	.36356	.47504	.56051	.62778
6	0.00000	0.00000	0.00000	0.00000	0.00000	0.00000	.19128	.33293	.44153	.52702
7	0.00000	0.00000	0.00000	0.00000	0.00000	0.00000	0.00000	.17516	.30945	.41515
8	0.00000	0.00000	0.00000	0.00000	0.00000	0.00000	0.00000	0.00000	.16280	.29096
9	0.00000	0.00000	0.00000	0.00000	0.00000	0.00000	0.00000	0.00000	0.00000	.15308

AGE OF LOAN	11	12	13	14	15	20	25	30	35	40
1	.94894	.95603	.96190	.96682	.97098	.98446	.99129	.99499	.99709	.99829
2	.89224	.90721	.91960	.92999	.93877	.96721	.98161	.98944	.99385	.99639
3	.82930	.85301	.87264	.88909	.90300	.94806	.97087	.98327	.99026	.99429
4	.75943	.79284	.82051	.84369	.86329	.92679	.95895	.97642	.98627	.99195
5	.68185	.72603	.76263	.79329	.81921	.90319	.94571	.96882	.98185	.98935
6	.59573	.65187	.69837	.73733	.77027	.87698	.93102	.96038	.97693	.98647
7	.50011	.56953	.62703	.67520	.71593	.84788	.91470	.95100	.97148	.98327
8	.39395	.47812	.54783	.60623	.65561	.81558	.89659	.94060	.96542	.97972
9	.27610	.37663	.45990	.52965	.58864	.77971	.87648	.92905	.95870	.97577
10	.14526	.26396	.36228	.44464	.51428	.73990	.85415	.91622	.95123	.97139
11	0.00000	.13887	.25390	.35026	.43174	.69569	.82937	.90199	.94294	.96653
12	0.00000	0.00000	.13358	.24548	.34010	.64662	.80185	.88618	.93374	.96113
13	0.00000	0.00000	0.00000	.12915	.23836	.59214	.77130	.86863	.92352	.95514
14	0.00000	0.00000	0.00000	0.00000	.12540	.53165	.73739	.84915	.91218	.94849
15	0.00000	0.00000	0.00000	0.00000	0.00000	.46449	.69973	.82752	.89959	.94110
16	0.00000	0.00000	0.00000	0.00000	0.00000	.38994	.65793	.80351	.88561	.93290
17	0.00000	0.00000	0.00000	0.00000	0.00000	.30717	.61152	.77685	.87009	.92380
18	0.00000	0.00000	0.00000	0.00000	0.00000	.21528	.55999	.74725	.85286	.91369
19	0.00000	0.00000	0.00000	0.00000	0.00000	.11326	.50279	.71439	.83373	.90247
20	0.00000	0.00000	0.00000	0.00000	0.00000	0.00000	.43928	.67791	.81250	.89001
21	0.00000	0.00000	0.00000	0.00000	0.00000	0.00000	.36877	.63741	.78892	.87618
22	0.00000	0.00000	0.00000	0.00000	0.00000	0.00000	.29050	.59245	.76275	.86083
23	0.00000	0.00000	0.00000	0.00000	0.00000	0.00000	.20359	.54253	.73369	.84378
24	0.00000	0.00000	0.00000	0.00000	0.00000	0.00000	.10711	.48711	.70142	.82486
25	0.00000	0.00000	0.00000	0.00000	0.00000	0.00000	0.00000	.42558	.66560	.80385
26	0.00000	0.00000	0.00000	0.00000	0.00000	0.00000	0.00000	.35727	.62584	.78052
27	0.00000	0.00000	0.00000	0.00000	0.00000	0.00000	0.00000	.28144	.58169	.75462
28	0.00000	0.00000	0.00000	0.00000	0.00000	0.00000	0.00000	.19724	.53268	.72587
29	0.00000	0.00000	0.00000	0.00000	0.00000	0.00000	0.00000	.10377	.47827	.69395
30	0.00000	0.00000	0.00000	0.00000	0.00000	0.00000	0.00000	0.00000	.41786	.65852
31	0.00000	0.00000	0.00000	0.00000	0.00000	0.00000	0.00000	0.00000	.35079	.61918
32	0.00000	0.00000	0.00000	0.00000	0.00000	0.00000	0.00000	0.00000	.27633	.57550
33	0.00000	0.00000	0.00000	0.00000	0.00000	0.00000	0.00000	0.00000	.19366	.52701
34	0.00000	0.00000	0.00000	0.00000	0.00000	0.00000	0.00000	0.00000	.10189	.47317
35	0.00000	0.00000	0.00000	0.00000	0.00000	0.00000	0.00000	0.00000	0.00000	.41341
36	0.00000	0.00000	0.00000	0.00000	0.00000	0.00000	0.00000	0.00000	0.00000	.34705
37	0.00000	0.00000	0.00000	0.00000	0.00000	0.00000	0.00000	0.00000	0.00000	.27339
38	0.00000	0.00000	0.00000	0.00000	0.00000	0.00000	0.00000	0.00000	0.00000	.19160
39	0.00000	0.00000	0.00000	0.00000	0.00000	0.00000	0.00000	0.00000	0.00000	.10080

REMAINING MORTGAGE BALANCE TABLE FOR 10.750 PERCENT

ORIGINAL LOAN TERM

AGE OF LOAN	1	2	3	4	5	6	7	8	9	10
1	0.00000	.52673	.70164	.78859	.84037	.87456	.89871	.91658	.93027	.94104
2	0.00000	0.00000	.36957	.55331	.66271	.73496	.78598	.82374	.85267	.87543
3	0.00000	0.00000	0.00000	.29144	.46498	.57958	.66051	.72042	.76631	.80240
4	0.00000	0.00000	0.00000	0.00000	.24492	.40666	.52088	.60542	.67018	.72113
5	0.00000	0.00000	0.00000	0.00000	0.00000	.21420	.36547	.47743	.56320	.63067
6	0.00000	0.00000	0.00000	0.00000	0.00000	0.00000	.19250	.33498	.44414	.53000
7	0.00000	0.00000	0.00000	0.00000	0.00000	0.00000	0.00000	.17644	.31162	.41795
8	0.00000	0.00000	0.00000	0.00000	0.00000	0.00000	0.00000	0.00000	.16414	.29325
9	0.00000	0.00000	0.00000	0.00000	0.00000	0.00000	0.00000	0.00000	0.00000	.15447

AGE OF LOAN	11	12	13	14	15	20	25	30	35	40
1	.94969	.95675	.96260	.96749	.97161	.98495	.99165	.99525	.99727	.99842
2	.89370	.90862	.92097	.93130	.94002	.96819	.98235	.98997	.99423	.99665
3	.83139	.85505	.87464	.89102	.90486	.94954	.97200	.98409	.99084	.99469
4	.76204	.79544	.82307	.84620	.86573	.92879	.96048	.97754	.98708	.99251
5	.68485	.72908	.76568	.79631	.82218	.90569	.94766	.97026	.98288	.99008
6	.59895	.65523	.70181	.74079	.77371	.87998	.93339	.96215	.97822	.98737
7	.50334	.57304	.63073	.67899	.71976	.85137	.91752	.95313	.97302	.98436
8	.39693	.48157	.55161	.61022	.65972	.81952	.89984	.94309	.96724	.98101
9	.27850	.37976	.46356	.53367	.59290	.78408	.88017	.93192	.96081	.97728
10	.14669	.26646	.36556	.44849	.51853	.74464	.85828	.91948	.95365	.97313
11	0.00000	.14035	.25649	.35367	.43575	.70074	.83392	.90564	.94569	.96851
12	0.00000	0.00000	.13510	.24815	.34363	.65188	.80681	.89023	.93682	.96337
13	0.00000	0.00000	0.00000	.13071	.24111	.59750	.77663	.87308	.92695	.95765
14	0.00000	0.00000	0.00000	0.00000	.12700	.53698	.74304	.85400	.91596	.95128
15	0.00000	0.00000	0.00000	0.00000	0.00000	.46962	.70566	.83276	.90374	.94419
16	0.00000	0.00000	0.00000	0.00000	0.00000	.39466	.66406	.80912	.89013	.93630
17	0.00000	0.00000	0.00000	0.00000	0.00000	.31122	.61776	.78281	.87499	.92752
18	0.00000	0.00000	0.00000	0.00000	0.00000	.21837	.56623	.75353	.85814	.91775
19	0.00000	0.00000	0.00000	0.00000	0.00000	.11502	.50887	.72095	.83938	.90687
20	0.00000	0.00000	0.00000	0.00000	0.00000	0.00000	.44504	.68468	.81851	.89477
21	0.00000	0.00000	0.00000	0.00000	0.00000	0.00000	.37400	.64431	.79527	.88130
22	0.00000	0.00000	0.00000	0.00000	0.00000	0.00000	.29494	.59939	.76941	.86631
23	0.00000	0.00000	0.00000	0.00000	0.00000	0.00000	.20694	.54939	.74064	.84962
24	0.00000	0.00000	0.00000	0.00000	0.00000	0.00000	.10900	.49374	.70861	.83105
25	0.00000	0.00000	0.00000	0.00000	0.00000	0.00000	0.00000	.43181	.67296	.81038
26	0.00000	0.00000	0.00000	0.00000	0.00000	0.00000	0.00000	.36288	.63328	.78738
27	0.00000	0.00000	0.00000	0.00000	0.00000	0.00000	0.00000	.28616	.58913	.76178
28	0.00000	0.00000	0.00000	0.00000	0.00000	0.00000	0.00000	.20078	.53998	.73329
29	0.00000	0.00000	0.00000	0.00000	0.00000	0.00000	0.00000	.10576	.48529	.70157
30	0.00000	0.00000	0.00000	0.00000	0.00000	0.00000	0.00000	0.00000	.42442	.66628
31	0.00000	0.00000	0.00000	0.00000	0.00000	0.00000	0.00000	0.00000	.35667	.62700
32	0.00000	0.00000	0.00000	0.00000	0.00000	0.00000	0.00000	0.00000	.28127	.58328
33	0.00000	0.00000	0.00000	0.00000	0.00000	0.00000	0.00000	0.00000	.19735	.53463
34	0.00000	0.00000	0.00000	0.00000	0.00000	0.00000	0.00000	0.00000	.10395	.48047
35	0.00000	0.00000	0.00000	0.00000	0.00000	0.00000	0.00000	0.00000	0.00000	.42021
36	0.00000	0.00000	0.00000	0.00000	0.00000	0.00000	0.00000	0.00000	0.00000	.35313
37	0.00000	0.00000	0.00000	0.00000	0.00000	0.00000	0.00000	0.00000	0.00000	.27847
38	0.00000	0.00000	0.00000	0.00000	0.00000	0.00000	0.00000	0.00000	0.00000	.19539
39	0.00000	0.00000	0.00000	0.00000	0.00000	0.00000	0.00000	0.00000	0.00000	.10292

REMAINING MORTGAGE BALANCE TABLE FOR 11.000 PERCENT

ORIGINAL LOAN TERM

AGE OF LOAN	1	2	3	4	5	6	7	8	9	10
1	0.00000	.52735	.70243	.78945	.84125	.87544	.89957	.91742	.93108	.94182
2	0.00000	0.00000	.37042	.55453	.66412	.73646	.78751	.82528	.85419	.87692
3	0.00000	0.00000	0.00000	.29243	.46650	.58139	.66249	.72248	.76840	.80450
4	0.00000	0.00000	0.00000	0.00000	.24601	.40839	.52300	.60778	.67269	.72370
5	0.00000	0.00000	0.00000	0.00000	0.00000	.21536	.36737	.47981	.56590	.63355
6	0.00000	0.00000	0.00000	0.00000	0.00000	0.00000	.19373	.33703	.44675	.53297
7	0.00000	0.00000	0.00000	0.00000	0.00000	0.00000	0.00000	.17773	.31381	.42076
8	0.00000	0.00000	0.00000	0.00000	0.00000	0.00000	0.00000	0.00000	.16549	.29555
9	0.00000	0.00000	0.00000	0.00000	0.00000	0.00000	0.00000	0.00000	0.00000	.15586

AGE OF LOAN	11	12	13	14	15	20	25	30	35	40
1	.95044	.95747	.96328	.96814	.97224	.98542	.99199	.99550	.99744	.99853
2	.89515	.91002	.92232	.93259	.94126	.96915	.98305	.99048	.99458	.99689
3	.83346	.85708	.87661	.89293	.90670	.95099	.97308	.98487	.99139	.99507
4	.76463	.79801	.82561	.84868	.86814	.93074	.96196	.97862	.98783	.99303
5	.68784	.73211	.76871	.79931	.82512	.90814	.94955	.97165	.98386	.99075
6	.60216	.65858	.70523	.74422	.77711	.88293	.93570	.96386	.97944	.98822
7	.50656	.57655	.63440	.68276	.72356	.85480	.92025	.95518	.97450	.98538
8	.39990	.48502	.55538	.61419	.66381	.82341	.90301	.94549	.96898	.98223
9	.28090	.38290	.46721	.53768	.59714	.78839	.88378	.93468	.96283	.97870
10	.14813	.26896	.36884	.45232	.52276	.74932	.86232	.92263	.95597	.97477
11	0.00000	.14183	.25908	.35709	.43977	.70573	.83838	.90917	.94831	.97038
12	0.00000	0.00000	.13663	.25083	.34717	.65709	.81167	.89416	.93977	.96548
13	0.00000	0.00000	0.00000	.13227	.24386	.60283	.78187	.87741	.93024	.96002
14	0.00000	0.00000	0.00000	0.00000	.12860	.54228	.74862	.85872	.91960	.95393
15	0.00000	0.00000	0.00000	0.00000	0.00000	.47473	.71152	.83787	.90774	.94713
16	0.00000	0.00000	0.00000	0.00000	0.00000	.39937	.67012	.81461	.89450	.93954
17	0.00000	0.00000	0.00000	0.00000	0.00000	.31528	.62394	.78866	.87973	.93108
18	0.00000	0.00000	0.00000	0.00000	0.00000	.22146	.57241	.75970	.86325	.92164
19	0.00000	0.00000	0.00000	0.00000	0.00000	.11679	.51493	.72739	.84487	.91110
20	0.00000	0.00000	0.00000	0.00000	0.00000	0.00000	.45078	.69134	.82435	.89935
21	0.00000	0.00000	0.00000	0.00000	0.00000	0.00000	.37922	.65112	.80147	.88623
22	0.00000	0.00000	0.00000	0.00000	0.00000	0.00000	.29937	.60625	.77593	.87160
23	0.00000	0.00000	0.00000	0.00000	0.00000	0.00000	.21029	.55618	.74744	.85527
24	0.00000	0.00000	0.00000	0.00000	0.00000	0.00000	.11090	.50033	.71565	.83706
25	0.00000	0.00000	0.00000	0.00000	0.00000	0.00000	0.00000	.43800	.68019	.81673
26	0.00000	0.00000	0.00000	0.00000	0.00000	0.00000	0.00000	.36847	.64062	.79406
27	0.00000	0.00000	0.00000	0.00000	0.00000	0.00000	0.00000	.29089	.59647	.76876
28	0.00000	0.00000	0.00000	0.00000	0.00000	0.00000	0.00000	.20433	.54721	.74053
29	0.00000	0.00000	0.00000	0.00000	0.00000	0.00000	0.00000	.10775	.49225	.70904
30	0.00000	0.00000	0.00000	0.00000	0.00000	0.00000	0.00000	0.00000	.43094	.67390
31	0.00000	0.00000	0.00000	0.00000	0.00000	0.00000	0.00000	0.00000	.36252	.63469
32	0.00000	0.00000	0.00000	0.00000	0.00000	0.00000	0.00000	0.00000	.28619	.59095
33	0.00000	0.00000	0.00000	0.00000	0.00000	0.00000	0.00000	0.00000	.20103	.54215
34	0.00000	0.00000	0.00000	0.00000	0.00000	0.00000	0.00000	0.00000	.10601	.48770
35	0.00000	0.00000	0.00000	0.00000	0.00000	0.00000	0.00000	0.00000	0.00000	.42695
36	0.00000	0.00000	0.00000	0.00000	0.00000	0.00000	0.00000	0.00000	0.00000	.35917
37	0.00000	0.00000	0.00000	0.00000	0.00000	0.00000	0.00000	0.00000	0.00000	.28355
38	0.00000	0.00000	0.00000	0.00000	0.00000	0.00000	0.00000	0.00000	0.00000	.19917
39	0.00000	0.00000	0.00000	0.00000	0.00000	0.00000	0.00000	0.00000	0.00000	.10503

REMAINING MORTGAGE BALANCE TABLE FOR 11.250 PERCENT

ORIGINAL LOAN TERM

AGE OF LOAN	1	2	3	4	5	6	7	8	9	10
1	0.00000	.52796	.70322	.79030	.84212	.87630	.90042	.91825	.93189	.94260
2	0.00000	0.00000	.37128	.55576	.66552	.73795	.78904	.82681	.85570	.87839
3	0.00000	0.00000	0.00000	.29342	.46801	.58320	.66446	.72453	.77049	.80658
4	0.00000	0.00000	0.00000	0.00000	.24709	.41012	.52513	.61014	.67518	.72626
5	0.00000	0.00000	0.00000	0.00000	0.00000	.21653	.36928	.48219	.56858	.63642
6	0.00000	0.00000	0.00000	0.00000	0.00000	0.00000	.19497	.33909	.44935	.53594
7	0.00000	0.00000	0.00000	0.00000	0.00000	0.00000	0.00000	.17903	.31599	.42356
8	0.00000	0.00000	0.00000	0.00000	0.00000	0.00000	0.00000	0.00000	.16683	.29785
9	0.00000	0.00000	0.00000	0.00000	0.00000	0.00000	0.00000	0.00000	0.00000	.15726

AGE OF LOAN	11	12	13	14	15	20	25	30	35	40
1	.95118	.95818	.96396	.96878	.97285	.98588	.99232	.99573	.99760	.99864
2	.89658	.91141	.92365	.93386	.94248	.97008	.98374	.99096	.99491	.99712
3	.83551	.85909	.87856	.89481	.90851	.95241	.97413	.98562	.99191	.99542
4	.76721	.80057	.82812	.85113	.87051	.93265	.96339	.97965	.98855	.99352
5	.69081	.73512	.77172	.80227	.82802	.91054	.95138	.97297	.98480	.99139
6	.60536	.66192	.70863	.74763	.78049	.88582	.93794	.96551	.98059	.98901
7	.50978	.58004	.63806	.68651	.72733	.85816	.92291	.95715	.97589	.98635
8	.40288	.48846	.55913	.61814	.66786	.82723	.90610	.94781	.97064	.98337
9	.28331	.38603	.47086	.54168	.60136	.79264	.88730	.93736	.96476	.98004
10	.14958	.27147	.37212	.45616	.52697	.75394	.86627	.92567	.95818	.97632
11	0.00000	.14332	.26168	.36050	.44377	.71067	.84275	.91259	.95083	.97215
12	0.00000	0.00000	.13816	.25351	.35071	.66226	.81644	.89797	.94260	.96749
13	0.00000	0.00000	0.00000	.13385	.24663	.60812	.78701	.88161	.93340	.96228
14	0.00000	0.00000	0.00000	0.00000	.13021	.54756	.75410	.86332	.92310	.95645
15	0.00000	0.00000	0.00000	0.00000	0.00000	.47983	.71729	.84286	.91159	.94993
16	0.00000	0.00000	0.00000	0.00000	0.00000	.40407	.67611	.81997	.89872	.94264
17	0.00000	0.00000	0.00000	0.00000	0.00000	.31934	.63006	.79437	.88432	.93448
18	0.00000	0.00000	0.00000	0.00000	0.00000	.22456	.57855	.76574	.86821	.92536
19	0.00000	0.00000	0.00000	0.00000	0.00000	.11856	.52094	.73372	.85019	.91516
20	0.00000	0.00000	0.00000	0.00000	0.00000	0.00000	.45650	.69790	.83004	.90374
21	0.00000	0.00000	0.00000	0.00000	0.00000	0.00000	.38442	.65784	.80750	.89098
22	0.00000	0.00000	0.00000	0.00000	0.00000	0.00000	.30381	.61303	.78229	.87670
23	0.00000	0.00000	0.00000	0.00000	0.00000	0.00000	.21365	.56291	.75410	.86073
24	0.00000	0.00000	0.00000	0.00000	0.00000	0.00000	.11280	.50686	.72256	.84287
25	0.00000	0.00000	0.00000	0.00000	0.00000	0.00000	0.00000	.44416	.68729	.82289
26	0.00000	0.00000	0.00000	0.00000	0.00000	0.00000	0.00000	.37404	.64784	.80055
27	0.00000	0.00000	0.00000	0.00000	0.00000	0.00000	0.00000	.29560	.60371	.77556
28	0.00000	0.00000	0.00000	0.00000	0.00000	0.00000	0.00000	.20787	.55436	.74761
29	0.00000	0.00000	0.00000	0.00000	0.00000	0.00000	0.00000	.10975	.49915	.71634
30	0.00000	0.00000	0.00000	0.00000	0.00000	0.00000	0.00000	0.00000	.43741	.68137
31	0.00000	0.00000	0.00000	0.00000	0.00000	0.00000	0.00000	0.00000	.36835	.64226
32	0.00000	0.00000	0.00000	0.00000	0.00000	0.00000	0.00000	0.00000	.29111	.59851
33	0.00000	0.00000	0.00000	0.00000	0.00000	0.00000	0.00000	0.00000	.20471	.54958
34	0.00000	0.00000	0.00000	0.00000	0.00000	0.00000	0.00000	0.00000	.10808	.49485
35	0.00000	0.00000	0.00000	0.00000	0.00000	0.00000	0.00000	0.00000	0.00000	.43364
36	0.00000	0.00000	0.00000	0.00000	0.00000	0.00000	0.00000	0.00000	0.00000	.36518
37	0.00000	0.00000	0.00000	0.00000	0.00000	0.00000	0.00000	0.00000	0.00000	.28860
38	0.00000	0.00000	0.00000	0.00000	0.00000	0.00000	0.00000	0.00000	0.00000	.20295
39	0.00000	0.00000	0.00000	0.00000	0.00000	0.00000	0.00000	0.00000	0.00000	.10715

REMAINING MORTGAGE BALANCE TABLE FOR 11.500 PERCENT

ORIGINAL LOAN TERM

AGE OF LOAN	1	2	3	4	5	6	7	8	9	10
1	0.00000	.52858	.70401	.79115	.84298	.87717	.90127	.91907	.93268	.94336
2	0.00000	0.00000	.37213	.55659	.66693	.73944	.79056	.82833	.85720	.87986
3	0.00000	0.00000	0.00000	.29441	.46952	.58501	.66643	.72658	.77256	.80865
4	0.00000	0.00000	0.00000	0.00000	.24818	.41185	.52725	.61249	.67767	.72881
5	0.00000	0.00000	0.00000	0.00000	0.00000	.21770	.37119	.48458	.57126	.63929
6	0.00000	0.00000	0.00000	0.00000	0.00000	0.00000	.19620	.34115	.45195	.53891
7	0.00000	0.00000	0.00000	0.00000	0.00000	0.00000	0.00000	.18032	.31818	.42636
8	0.00000	0.00000	0.00000	0.00000	0.00000	0.00000	0.00000	0.00000	.16818	.30016
9	0.00000	0.00000	0.00000	0.00000	0.00000	0.00000	0.00000	0.00000	0.00000	.15866

AGE OF LOAN	11	12	13	14	15	20	25	30	35	40
1	.95192	.95888	.96462	.96941	.97345	.98632	.99264	.99596	.99775	.99874
2	.89800	.91277	.92496	.93512	.94367	.97099	.98440	.99142	.99523	.99733
3	.83755	.86107	.88048	.89667	.91029	.95379	.97515	.98634	.99240	.99575
4	.76977	.80311	.83061	.85355	.87286	.93451	.96478	.98064	.98923	.99397
5	.69376	.73811	.77470	.80521	.83089	.91289	.95315	.97425	.98568	.99198
6	.60855	.66524	.71200	.75100	.78383	.88865	.94011	.96708	.98169	.98975
7	.51299	.58352	.64170	.69022	.73106	.86147	.92550	.95904	.97722	.98725
8	.40586	.49190	.56288	.62208	.67190	.83099	.90911	.95003	.97221	.98445
9	.28573	.38917	.47450	.54566	.60556	.79682	.89073	.93993	.96659	.98130
10	.15103	.27398	.37540	.45999	.53117	.75851	.87012	.92860	.96029	.97777
11	0.00000	.14482	.26428	.36392	.44777	.71555	.84702	.91590	.95323	.97382
12	0.00000	0.00000	.13970	.25620	.35425	.66738	.82111	.90166	.94531	.96939
13	0.00000	0.00000	0.00000	.13542	.24940	.61337	.79206	.88569	.93643	.96442
14	0.00000	0.00000	0.00000	0.00000	.13183	.55281	.75949	.86779	.92647	.95884
15	0.00000	0.00000	0.00000	0.00000	0.00000	.48490	.72297	.84771	.91530	.95259
16	0.00000	0.00000	0.00000	0.00000	0.00000	.40877	.68203	.82520	.90278	.94559
17	0.00000	0.00000	0.00000	0.00000	0.00000	.32340	.63611	.79997	.88875	.93773
18	0.00000	0.00000	0.00000	0.00000	0.00000	.22767	.58463	.77167	.87301	.92892
19	0.00000	0.00000	0.00000	0.00000	0.00000	.12034	.52691	.73993	.85536	.91904
20	0.00000	0.00000	0.00000	0.00000	0.00000	0.00000	.46219	.70436	.83557	.90797
21	0.00000	0.00000	0.00000	0.00000	0.00000	0.00000	.38962	.66446	.81339	.89555
22	0.00000	0.00000	0.00000	0.00000	0.00000	0.00000	.30825	.61973	.78851	.88162
23	0.00000	0.00000	0.00000	0.00000	0.00000	0.00000	.21701	.56958	.76061	.86601
24	0.00000	0.00000	0.00000	0.00000	0.00000	0.00000	.11471	.51334	.72934	.84850
25	0.00000	0.00000	0.00000	0.00000	0.00000	0.00000	0.00000	.45028	.69427	.82887
26	0.00000	0.00000	0.00000	0.00000	0.00000	0.00000	0.00000	.37958	.65494	.80686
27	0.00000	0.00000	0.00000	0.00000	0.00000	0.00000	0.00000	.30031	.61085	.78219
28	0.00000	0.00000	0.00000	0.00000	0.00000	0.00000	0.00000	.21142	.56142	.75452
29	0.00000	0.00000	0.00000	0.00000	0.00000	0.00000	0.00000	.11175	.50599	.72349
30	0.00000	0.00000	0.00000	0.00000	0.00000	0.00000	0.00000	0.00000	.44383	.68870
31	0.00000	0.00000	0.00000	0.00000	0.00000	0.00000	0.00000	0.00000	.37415	.64969
32	0.00000	0.00000	0.00000	0.00000	0.00000	0.00000	0.00000	0.00000	.29601	.60596
33	0.00000	0.00000	0.00000	0.00000	0.00000	0.00000	0.00000	0.00000	.20839	.55692
34	0.00000	0.00000	0.00000	0.00000	0.00000	0.00000	0.00000	0.00000	.11015	.50193
35	0.00000	0.00000	0.00000	0.00000	0.00000	0.00000	0.00000	0.00000	0.00000	.44028
36	0.00000	0.00000	0.00000	0.00000	0.00000	0.00000	0.00000	0.00000	0.00000	.37115
37	0.00000	0.00000	0.00000	0.00000	0.00000	0.00000	0.00000	0.00000	0.00000	.29363
38	0.00000	0.00000	0.00000	0.00000	0.00000	0.00000	0.00000	0.00000	0.00000	.20672
39	0.00000	0.00000	0.00000	0.00000	0.00000	0.00000	0.00000	0.00000	0.00000	.10927

REMAINING MORTGAGE BALANCE TABLE FOR 11.750 PERCENT

ORIGINAL LOAN TERM

AGE OF LOAN	1	2	3	4	5	6	7	8	9	10
1	0.00000	.52920	.70480	.79200	.84385	.87802	.90211	.91989	.93347	.94412
2	0.00000	0.00000	.37298	.55820	.66833	.74092	.79207	.82984	.85869	.88131
3	0.00000	0.00000	0.00000	.29540	.47104	.58681	.66839	.72862	.77463	.81070
4	0.00000	0.00000	0.00000	0.00000	.24927	.41358	.52936	.61484	.68014	.73134
5	0.00000	0.00000	0.00000	0.00000	0.00000	.21887	.37309	.48696	.57394	.64213
6	0.00000	0.00000	0.00000	0.00000	0.00000	0.00000	.19744	.34320	.45456	.54186
7	0.00000	0.00000	0.00000	0.00000	0.00000	0.00000	0.00000	.18162	.32037	.42916
8	0.00000	0.00000	0.00000	0.00000	0.00000	0.00000	0.00000	0.00000	.16954	.30247
9	0.00000	0.00000	0.00000	0.00000	0.00000	0.00000	0.00000	0.00000	0.00000	.16007

AGE OF LOAN	11	12	13	14	15	20	25	30	35	40
1	.95264	.95957	.96528	.97004	.97404	.98676	.99295	.99617	.99789	.99883
2	.89941	.91412	.92625	.93636	.94485	.97187	.98503	.99186	.99553	.99753
3	.83957	.86304	.88239	.89850	.91205	.95514	.97613	.98702	.99286	.99605
4	.77231	.80562	.83308	.85595	.87517	.93633	.96612	.98158	.98987	.99440
5	.69670	.74108	.77765	.80812	.83372	.91519	.95487	.97547	.98651	.99254
6	.61172	.66854	.71535	.75435	.78713	.89143	.94222	.96859	.98273	.99045
7	.51620	.58699	.64532	.69392	.73476	.86472	.92801	.96086	.97848	.98810
8	.40883	.49533	.56661	.62599	.67590	.83470	.91203	.95218	.97371	.98546
9	.28814	.39230	.47613	.54963	.60973	.80095	.89407	.94242	.96834	.98249
10	.15249	.27649	.37868	.46381	.53536	.76302	.87389	.93144	.96231	.97915
11	0.00000	.14632	.26689	.36734	.45176	.72038	.85120	.91911	.95553	.97540
12	0.00000	0.00000	.14124	.25859	.35780	.67245	.82569	.90524	.94790	.97118
13	0.00000	0.00000	0.00000	.13701	.25217	.61858	.79703	.88966	.93933	.96644
14	0.00000	0.00000	0.00000	0.00000	.13345	.55802	.76480	.87214	.92970	.96112
15	0.00000	0.00000	0.00000	0.00000	0.00000	.48996	.72858	.85245	.91888	.95513
16	0.00000	0.00000	0.00000	0.00000	0.00000	.41345	.68787	.83031	.90671	.94840
17	0.00000	0.00000	0.00000	0.00000	0.00000	.32745	.64210	.80544	.89303	.94083
18	0.00000	0.00000	0.00000	0.00000	0.00000	.23079	.59066	.77747	.87766	.93233
19	0.00000	0.00000	0.00000	0.00000	0.00000	.12213	.53284	.74604	.86037	.92277
20	0.00000	0.00000	0.00000	0.00000	0.00000	0.00000	.46785	.71070	.84095	.91202
21	0.00000	0.00000	0.00000	0.00000	0.00000	0.00000	.39479	.67099	.81911	.89994
22	0.00000	0.00000	0.00000	0.00000	0.00000	0.00000	.31267	.62635	.79457	.88637
23	0.00000	0.00000	0.00000	0.00000	0.00000	0.00000	.22037	.57617	.76698	.87111
24	0.00000	0.00000	0.00000	0.00000	0.00000	0.00000	.11662	.51977	.73597	.85395
25	0.00000	0.00000	0.00000	0.00000	0.00000	0.00000	0.00000	.45637	.70112	.83467
26	0.00000	0.00000	0.00000	0.00000	0.00000	0.00000	0.00000	.38511	.66194	.81300
27	0.00000	0.00000	0.00000	0.00000	0.00000	0.00000	0.00000	.30500	.61790	.78864
28	0.00000	0.00000	0.00000	0.00000	0.00000	0.00000	0.00000	.21497	.56840	.76126
29	0.00000	0.00000	0.00000	0.00000	0.00000	0.00000	0.00000	.11376	.51276	.73048
30	0.00000	0.00000	0.00000	0.00000	0.00000	0.00000	0.00000	0.00000	.45021	.69589
31	0.00000	0.00000	0.00000	0.00000	0.00000	0.00000	0.00000	0.00000	.37991	.65700
32	0.00000	0.00000	0.00000	0.00000	0.00000	0.00000	0.00000	0.00000	.30089	.61329
33	0.00000	0.00000	0.00000	0.00000	0.00000	0.00000	0.00000	0.00000	.21207	.56416
34	0.00000	0.00000	0.00000	0.00000	0.00000	0.00000	0.00000	0.00000	.11223	.50893
35	0.00000	0.00000	0.00000	0.00000	0.00000	0.00000	0.00000	0.00000	0.00000	.44685
36	0.00000	0.00000	0.00000	0.00000	0.00000	0.00000	0.00000	0.00000	0.00000	.37708
37	0.00000	0.00000	0.00000	0.00000	0.00000	0.00000	0.00000	0.00000	0.00000	.29864
38	0.00000	0.00000	0.00000	0.00000	0.00000	0.00000	0.00000	0.00000	0.00000	.21048
39	0.00000	0.00000	0.00000	0.00000	0.00000	0.00000	0.00000	0.00000	0.00000	.11139

REMAINING MORTGAGE BALANCE TABLE FOR 12.000 PERCENT

ORIGINAL LOAN TERM

AGE OF LOAN	1	2	3	4	5	6	7	8	9	10
1	0.00000	.52982	.70558	.79285	.84471	.87888	.90294	.92070	.93425	.94487
2	0.00000	0.00000	.37383	.55942	.66972	.74240	.79358	.83134	.86016	.88274
3	0.00000	0.00000	0.00000	.29639	.47255	.58861	.67034	.73065	.77668	.81274
4	0.00000	0.00000	0.00000	0.00000	.25036	.41531	.53148	.61718	.68261	.73386
5	0.00000	0.00000	0.00000	0.00000	0.00000	.22004	.37500	.48933	.57661	.64497
6	0.00000	0.00000	0.00000	0.00000	0.00000	0.00000	.19868	.34527	.45716	.54482
7	0.00000	0.00000	0.00000	0.00000	0.00000	0.00000	0.00000	.18293	.32256	.43196
8	0.00000	0.00000	0.00000	0.00000	0.00000	0.00000	0.00000	0.00000	.17090	.30478
9	0.00000	0.00000	0.00000	0.00000	0.00000	0.00000	0.00000	0.00000	0.00000	.16148

AGE OF LOAN	11	12	13	14	15	20	25	30	35	40
1	.95336	.96025	.96593	.97065	.97461	.98718	.99325	.99637	.99803	.99892
2	.90079	.91546	.92753	.93758	.94601	.97273	.98564	.99228	.99581	.99771
3	.84157	.86499	.88427	.90031	.91377	.95646	.97707	.98767	.99330	.99634
4	.77483	.80812	.83552	.85831	.87745	.93811	.96741	.98248	.99048	.99480
5	.69963	.74403	.78058	.81099	.83652	.91744	.95653	.97663	.98730	.99306
6	.61489	.67182	.71868	.75767	.79040	.89415	.94427	.97004	.98372	.99110
7	.51940	.59045	.64893	.69759	.73844	.86791	.93045	.96261	.97968	.98889
8	.41181	.49876	.57033	.62988	.67988	.83834	.91488	.95424	.97513	.98641
9	.29056	.39544	.48176	.55359	.61389	.80501	.89733	.94481	.97001	.98360
10	.15395	.27901	.38196	.46762	.53954	.76746	.87756	.93418	.96423	.98045
11	0.00000	.14783	.26951	.37075	.45575	.72515	.85529	.92220	.95772	.97689
12	0.00000	0.00000	.14279	.26160	.36134	.67747	.83018	.90871	.95039	.97288
13	0.00000	0.00000	0.00000	.13860	.25496	.62375	.80189	.89350	.94212	.96836
14	0.00000	0.00000	0.00000	0.00000	.13508	.56321	.77002	.87637	.93281	.96327
15	0.00000	0.00000	0.00000	0.00000	0.00000	.49499	.73410	.85706	.92232	.95754
16	0.00000	0.00000	0.00000	0.00000	0.00000	.41813	.69363	.83530	.91049	.95107
17	0.00000	0.00000	0.00000	0.00000	0.00000	.33151	.64802	.81078	.89717	.94379
18	0.00000	0.00000	0.00000	0.00000	0.00000	.23391	.59664	.78316	.88215	.93558
19	0.00000	0.00000	0.00000	0.00000	0.00000	.12393	.53873	.75203	.86524	.92633
20	0.00000	0.00000	0.00000	0.00000	0.00000	0.00000	.47348	.71695	.84617	.91591
21	0.00000	0.00000	0.00000	0.00000	0.00000	0.00000	.39995	.67742	.82469	.90417
22	0.00000	0.00000	0.00000	0.00000	0.00000	0.00000	.31710	.63288	.80049	.89094
23	0.00000	0.00000	0.00000	0.00000	0.00000	0.00000	.22374	.58269	.77321	.87603
24	0.00000	0.00000	0.00000	0.00000	0.00000	0.00000	.11854	.52614	.74248	.85923
25	0.00000	0.00000	0.00000	0.00000	0.00000	0.00000	0.00000	.46241	.70784	.84030
26	0.00000	0.00000	0.00000	0.00000	0.00000	0.00000	0.00000	.39060	.66882	.81897
27	0.00000	0.00000	0.00000	0.00000	0.00000	0.00000	0.00000	.30969	.62484	.79493
28	0.00000	0.00000	0.00000	0.00000	0.00000	0.00000	0.00000	.21851	.57529	.76784
29	0.00000	0.00000	0.00000	0.00000	0.00000	0.00000	0.00000	.11577	.51946	.73732
30	0.00000	0.00000	0.00000	0.00000	0.00000	0.00000	0.00000	0.00000	.45654	.70293
31	0.00000	0.00000	0.00000	0.00000	0.00000	0.00000	0.00000	0.00000	.38564	.66418
32	0.00000	0.00000	0.00000	0.00000	0.00000	0.00000	0.00000	0.00000	.30576	.62051
33	0.00000	0.00000	0.00000	0.00000	0.00000	0.00000	0.00000	0.00000	.21574	.57130
34	0.00000	0.00000	0.00000	0.00000	0.00000	0.00000	0.00000	0.00000	.11430	.51585
35	0.00000	0.00000	0.00000	0.00000	0.00000	0.00000	0.00000	0.00000	0.00000	.45337
36	0.00000	0.00000	0.00000	0.00000	0.00000	0.00000	0.00000	0.00000	0.00000	.38297
37	0.00000	0.00000	0.00000	0.00000	0.00000	0.00000	0.00000	0.00000	0.00000	.30363
38	0.00000	0.00000	0.00000	0.00000	0.00000	0.00000	0.00000	0.00000	0.00000	.21424
39	0.00000	0.00000	0.00000	0.00000	0.00000	0.00000	0.00000	0.00000	0.00000	.11351

REMAINING MORTGAGE BALANCE TABLE FOR 12.250 PERCENT

AGE OF LOAN	ORIGINAL LOAN TERM 1	2	3	4	5	6	7	8	9	10
1	0.00000	.53043	.70637	.79369	.84557	.87973	.90378	.92150	.93503	.94561
2	0.00000	0.00000	.37468	.56064	.67112	.74387	.79508	.83283	.86163	.88417
3	0.00000	0.00000	0.00000	.29738	.47406	.59040	.67229	.73267	.77872	.81477
4	0.00000	0.00000	0.00000	0.00000	.25146	.41704	.53359	.61952	.68506	.73636
5	0.00000	0.00000	0.00000	0.00000	0.00000	.22121	.37691	.49171	.57927	.64780
6	0.00000	0.00000	0.00000	0.00000	0.00000	0.00000	.19993	.34733	.45976	.54776
7	0.00000	0.00000	0.00000	0.00000	0.00000	0.00000	0.00000	.18423	.32476	.43475
8	0.00000	0.00000	0.00000	0.00000	0.00000	0.00000	0.00000	0.00000	.17226	.30710
9	0.00000	0.00000	0.00000	0.00000	0.00000	0.00000	0.00000	0.00000	0.00000	.16289

AGE OF LOAN	11	12	13	14	15	20	25	30	35	40
1	.95406	.96092	.96656	.97125	.97518	.98759	.99354	.99656	.99815	.99930
2	.90217	.91678	.92879	.93878	.94715	.97357	.98623	.99268	.99607	.99788
3	.84355	.86692	.88613	.90209	.91548	.95774	.97799	.98830	.99371	.99660
4	.77734	.81059	.83793	.86065	.87970	.93985	.96867	.98334	.99105	.99517
5	.70254	.74696	.78349	.81384	.83929	.91965	.95814	.97775	.98805	.99354
6	.61804	.67508	.72198	.76096	.79364	.89682	.94625	.97143	.98465	.99171
7	.52260	.59389	.65251	.70123	.74207	.87104	.93282	.96429	.98082	.98964
8	.41478	.50218	.57403	.63375	.68382	.84191	.91765	.95622	.97648	.98730
9	.29299	.39857	.48539	.55753	.61802	.80901	.90051	.94711	.97159	.98465
10	.15541	.28154	.38525	.47143	.54369	.77185	.88115	.93682	.96606	.98167
11	0.00000	.14934	.27213	.37417	.45973	.72987	.85928	.92520	.95982	.97829
12	0.00000	0.00000	.14434	.26430	.36488	.68245	.83458	.91207	.95276	.97448
13	0.00000	0.00000	0.00000	.14019	.25774	.62888	.80667	.89723	.94479	.97018
14	0.00000	0.00000	0.00000	0.00000	.13672	.56836	.77515	.88047	.93579	.96532
15	0.00000	0.00000	0.00000	0.00000	0.00000	.50001	.73954	.86155	.92562	.95982
16	0.00000	0.00000	0.00000	0.00000	0.00000	.42279	.69932	.84016	.91414	.95362
17	0.00000	0.00000	0.00000	0.00000	0.00000	.33556	.65388	.81601	.90116	.94661
18	0.00000	0.00000	0.00000	0.00000	0.00000	.23703	.60255	.78872	.88651	.93869
19	0.00000	0.00000	0.00000	0.00000	0.00000	.12573	.54457	.75790	.86995	.92975
20	0.00000	0.00000	0.00000	0.00000	0.00000	0.00000	.47908	.72309	.85125	.91965
21	0.00000	0.00000	0.00000	0.00000	0.00000	0.00000	.40509	.68376	.83012	.90824
22	0.00000	0.00000	0.00000	0.00000	0.00000	0.00000	.32152	.63933	.80626	.89535
23	0.00000	0.00000	0.00000	0.00000	0.00000	0.00000	.22711	.58915	.77930	.88078
24	0.00000	0.00000	0.00000	0.00000	0.00000	0.00000	.12047	.53246	.74884	.86433
25	0.00000	0.00000	0.00000	0.00000	0.00000	0.00000	0.00000	.46842	.71444	.84575
26	0.00000	0.00000	0.00000	0.00000	0.00000	0.00000	0.00000	.39608	.67558	.82476
27	0.00000	0.00000	0.00000	0.00000	0.00000	0.00000	0.00000	.31436	.63169	.80105
28	0.00000	0.00000	0.00000	0.00000	0.00000	0.00000	0.00000	.22206	.58210	.77427
29	0.00000	0.00000	0.00000	0.00000	0.00000	0.00000	0.00000	.11779	.52609	.74401
30	0.00000	0.00000	0.00000	0.00000	0.00000	0.00000	0.00000	0.00000	.46282	.70983
31	0.00000	0.00000	0.00000	0.00000	0.00000	0.00000	0.00000	0.00000	.39134	.67122
32	0.00000	0.00000	0.00000	0.00000	0.00000	0.00000	0.00000	0.00000	.31061	.62761
33	0.00000	0.00000	0.00000	0.00000	0.00000	0.00000	0.00000	0.00000	.21940	.57835
34	0.00000	0.00000	0.00000	0.00000	0.00000	0.00000	0.00000	0.00000	.11638	.52269
35	0.00000	0.00000	0.00000	0.00000	0.00000	0.00000	0.00000	0.00000	0.00000	.45983
36	0.00000	0.00000	0.00000	0.00000	0.00000	0.00000	0.00000	0.00000	0.00000	.38882
37	0.00000	0.00000	0.00000	0.00000	0.00000	0.00000	0.00000	0.00000	0.00000	.30860
38	0.00000	0.00000	0.00000	0.00000	0.00000	0.00000	0.00000	0.00000	0.00000	.21799
39	0.00000	0.00000	0.00000	0.00000	0.00000	0.00000	0.00000	0.00000	0.00000	.11563

REMAINING MORTGAGE BALANCE TABLE FOR 12.500 PERCENT

ORIGINAL LOAN TERM

AGE OF LOAN	1	2	3	4	5	6	7	8	9	10
1	0.00000	.53105	.70716	.79453	.84642	.88058	.90460	.92230	.93579	.94634
2	0.00000	0.00000	.37553	.56186	.67251	.74534	.79657	.83432	.86308	.88558
3	0.00000	0.00000	0.00000	.29837	.47557	.59220	.67424	.73468	.78075	.81677
4	0.00000	0.00000	0.00000	0.00000	.25255	.41878	.53570	.62185	.68751	.73886
5	0.00000	0.00000	0.00000	0.00000	0.00000	.22239	.37883	.49408	.58192	.65062
6	0.00000	0.00000	0.00000	0.00000	0.00000	0.00000	.20117	.34939	.46236	.55070
7	0.00000	0.00000	0.00000	0.00000	0.00000	0.00000	0.00000	.18554	.32696	.43755
8	0.00000	0.00000	0.00000	0.00000	0.00000	0.00000	0.00000	0.00000	.17363	.30942
9	0.00000	0.00000	0.00000	0.00000	0.00000	0.00000	0.00000	0.00000	0.00000	.16431

AGE OF LOAN	11	12	13	14	15	20	25	30	35	40
1	.95476	.96159	.96719	.97184	.97574	.98799	.99381	.99675	.99827	.99908
2	.90353	.91808	.93004	.93996	.94826	.97439	.98680	.99306	.99632	.99803
3	.84552	.86882	.88796	.90385	.91715	.95899	.97887	.98889	.99410	.99685
4	.77982	.81304	.84032	.86296	.88192	.94155	.96988	.98417	.99159	.99551
5	.70543	.74987	.78636	.81666	.84202	.92180	.95970	.97882	.98875	.99400
6	.62119	.67833	.72527	.76422	.79684	.89944	.94817	.97276	.98554	.99228
7	.52579	.59732	.65608	.70484	.74568	.87411	.93512	.96590	.98189	.99034
8	.41776	.50559	.57773	.63760	.68774	.84543	.92034	.95813	.97777	.98813
9	.29542	.40171	.48900	.56146	.62213	.81296	.90361	.94933	.97310	.98564
10	.15688	.28407	.38853	.47523	.54784	.77618	.88465	.93937	.96781	.98282
11	0.00000	.15085	.27475	.37759	.46370	.73453	.86319	.92809	.96182	.97962
12	0.00000	0.00000	.14591	.26701	.36843	.68737	.83888	.91531	.95504	.97600
13	0.00000	0.00000	0.00000	.14180	.26054	.63396	.81136	.90085	.94735	.97190
14	0.00000	0.00000	0.00000	0.00000	.13836	.57348	.78019	.88447	.93866	.96726
15	0.00000	0.00000	0.00000	0.00000	0.00000	.50500	.74490	.86591	.92881	.96200
16	0.00000	0.00000	0.00000	0.00000	0.00000	.42744	.70493	.84491	.91765	.95604
17	0.00000	0.00000	0.00000	0.00000	0.00000	.33962	.65967	.82112	.90502	.94930
18	0.00000	0.00000	0.00000	0.00000	0.00000	.24016	.60841	.79417	.89072	.94167
19	0.00000	0.00000	0.00000	0.00000	0.00000	.12754	.55037	.76367	.87452	.93302
20	0.00000	0.00000	0.00000	0.00000	0.00000	0.00000	.48465	.72912	.85617	.92323
21	0.00000	0.00000	0.00000	0.00000	0.00000	0.00000	.41022	.69000	.83540	.91214
22	0.00000	0.00000	0.00000	0.00000	0.00000	0.00000	.32593	.64570	.81188	.89959
23	0.00000	0.00000	0.00000	0.00000	0.00000	0.00000	.23048	.59553	.78524	.88537
24	0.00000	0.00000	0.00000	0.00000	0.00000	0.00000	.12240	.53871	.75508	.86927
25	0.00000	0.00000	0.00000	0.00000	0.00000	0.00000	0.00000	.47438	.72092	.85103
26	0.00000	0.00000	0.00000	0.00000	0.00000	0.00000	0.00000	.40153	.68224	.83039
27	0.00000	0.00000	0.00000	0.00000	0.00000	0.00000	0.00000	.31903	.63843	.80701
28	0.00000	0.00000	0.00000	0.00000	0.00000	0.00000	0.00000	.22560	.58883	.78053
29	0.00000	0.00000	0.00000	0.00000	0.00000	0.00000	0.00000	.11981	.53266	.75055
30	0.00000	0.00000	0.00000	0.00000	0.00000	0.00000	0.00000	0.00000	.46904	.71659
31	0.00000	0.00000	0.00000	0.00000	0.00000	0.00000	0.00000	0.00000	.39701	.67814
32	0.00000	0.00000	0.00000	0.00000	0.00000	0.00000	0.00000	0.00000	.31544	.63460
33	0.00000	0.00000	0.00000	0.00000	0.00000	0.00000	0.00000	0.00000	.22306	.58529
34	0.00000	0.00000	0.00000	0.00000	0.00000	0.00000	0.00000	0.00000	.11846	.52946
35	0.00000	0.00000	0.00000	0.00000	0.00000	0.00000	0.00000	0.00000	0.00000	.46623
36	0.00000	0.00000	0.00000	0.00000	0.00000	0.00000	0.00000	0.00000	0.00000	.39463
37	0.00000	0.00000	0.00000	0.00000	0.00000	0.00000	0.00000	0.00000	0.00000	.31354
38	0.00000	0.00000	0.00000	0.00000	0.00000	0.00000	0.00000	0.00000	0.00000	.22172
39	0.00000	0.00000	0.00000	0.00000	0.00000	0.00000	0.00000	0.00000	0.00000	.11775

REMAINING MORTGAGE BALANCE TABLE FOR 12.750 PERCENT

ORIGINAL LOAN TERM

AGE OF LOAN	1	2	3	4	5	6	7	8	9	10
1	0.00000	.53166	.70794	.79537	.84728	.88142	.90542	.92310	.93655	.94707
2	0.00000	0.00000	.37639	.56308	.67390	.74681	.79806	.83579	.86453	.88698
3	0.00000	0.00000	0.00000	.29937	.47708	.59399	.67618	.73669	.78277	.81977
4	0.00000	0.00000	0.00000	0.00000	.25365	.42051	.53781	.62418	.68995	.74133
5	0.00000	0.00000	0.00000	0.00000	0.00000	.22357	.38074	.49645	.58457	.65343
6	0.00000	0.00000	0.00000	0.00000	0.00000	0.00000	.20243	.35146	.46495	.55363
7	0.00000	0.00000	0.00000	0.00000	0.00000	0.00000	0.00000	.18686	.32916	.44034
8	0.00000	0.00000	0.00000	0.00000	0.00000	0.00000	0.00000	0.00000	.17500	.31174
9	0.00000	0.00000	0.00000	0.00000	0.00000	0.00000	0.00000	0.00000	0.00000	.16574

AGE OF LOAN	11	12	13	14	15	20	25	30	35	40
1	.95545	.96224	.96781	.97242	.97629	.98838	.99408	.99692	.99838	.99915
2	.90488	.91937	.93126	.94112	.94936	.97519	.98735	.99343	.99655	.99818
3	.84747	.87071	.88978	.90558	.91880	.96021	.97971	.98946	.99447	.99708
4	.78230	.81547	.84268	.86524	.88411	.94321	.97105	.98495	.99210	.99584
5	.70831	.75276	.78922	.81944	.84472	.92391	.96121	.97984	.98942	.99442
6	.62432	.68156	.72852	.76745	.80001	.90200	.95004	.97403	.98637	.99281
7	.52897	.60074	.65962	.70843	.74925	.87713	.93736	.96744	.98292	.99099
8	.42073	.50900	.58140	.64143	.69163	.84889	.92296	.95996	.97899	.98892
9	.29785	.40484	.49261	.56537	.62622	.81684	.90662	.95147	.97453	.98657
10	.15836	.28660	.39181	.47903	.55196	.78045	.88807	.94183	.96947	.98390
11	0.00000	.15238	.27738	.38100	.46767	.73914	.86701	.93088	.96373	.98087
12	0.00000	0.00000	.14747	.26973	.37197	.69224	.84310	.91846	.95721	.97743
13	0.00000	0.00000	0.00000	.14340	.26333	.63901	.81596	.90435	.94981	.97353
14	0.00000	0.00000	0.00000	0.00000	.14000	.57857	.78515	.88834	.94140	.96909
15	0.00000	0.00000	0.00000	0.00000	0.00000	.50997	.75017	.87016	.93186	.96406
16	0.00000	0.00000	0.00000	0.00000	0.00000	.43208	.71046	.84953	.92104	.95835
17	0.00000	0.00000	0.00000	0.00000	0.00000	.34367	.66539	.82610	.90874	.95187
18	0.00000	0.00000	0.00000	0.00000	0.00000	.24329	.61422	.79951	.89479	.94451
19	0.00000	0.00000	0.00000	0.00000	0.00000	.12935	.55613	.76932	.87894	.93615
20	0.00000	0.00000	0.00000	0.00000	0.00000	0.00000	.49018	.73505	.86096	.92666
21	0.00000	0.00000	0.00000	0.00000	0.00000	0.00000	.41532	.69614	.84054	.91590
22	0.00000	0.00000	0.00000	0.00000	0.00000	0.00000	.33033	.65197	.81736	.90367
23	0.00000	0.00000	0.00000	0.00000	0.00000	0.00000	.23386	.60184	.79105	.88979
24	0.00000	0.00000	0.00000	0.00000	0.00000	0.00000	.12433	.54492	.76118	.87404
25	0.00000	0.00000	0.00000	0.00000	0.00000	0.00000	0.00000	.48030	.72727	.85615
26	0.00000	0.00000	0.00000	0.00000	0.00000	0.00000	0.00000	.40695	.68878	.83585
27	0.00000	0.00000	0.00000	0.00000	0.00000	0.00000	0.00000	.32367	.64508	.81280
28	0.00000	0.00000	0.00000	0.00000	0.00000	0.00000	0.00000	.22914	.59547	.78664
29	0.00000	0.00000	0.00000	0.00000	0.00000	0.00000	0.00000	.12183	.53915	.75693
30	0.00000	0.00000	0.00000	0.00000	0.00000	0.00000	0.00000	0.00000	.47522	.72321
31	0.00000	0.00000	0.00000	0.00000	0.00000	0.00000	0.00000	0.00000	.40264	.68493
32	0.00000	0.00000	0.00000	0.00000	0.00000	0.00000	0.00000	0.00000	.32025	.64148
33	0.00000	0.00000	0.00000	0.00000	0.00000	0.00000	0.00000	0.00000	.22672	.59215
34	0.00000	0.00000	0.00000	0.00000	0.00000	0.00000	0.00000	0.00000	.12054	.53614
35	0.00000	0.00000	0.00000	0.00000	0.00000	0.00000	0.00000	0.00000	0.00000	.47257
36	0.00000	0.00000	0.00000	0.00000	0.00000	0.00000	0.00000	0.00000	0.00000	.40039
37	0.00000	0.00000	0.00000	0.00000	0.00000	0.00000	0.00000	0.00000	0.00000	.31846
38	0.00000	0.00000	0.00000	0.00000	0.00000	0.00000	0.00000	0.00000	0.00000	.22545
39	0.00000	0.00000	0.00000	0.00000	0.00000	0.00000	0.00000	0.00000	0.00000	.11987

REMAINING MORTGAGE BALANCE TABLE FOR 13.000 PERCENT

ORIGINAL LOAN TERM

AGE OF LOAN	1	2	3	4	5	6	7	8	9	10
1	0.00000	.53228	.70872	.79621	.84813	.88226	.90624	.92388	.93731	.94779
2	0.00000	0.00000	.37724	.56429	.67529	.74827	.79954	.83726	.86596	.88837
3	0.00000	0.00000	0.00000	.30036	.47859	.59578	.67811	.73868	.78477	.82075
4	0.00000	0.00000	0.00000	0.00000	.25474	.42224	.53992	.62649	.69237	.74380
5	0.00000	0.00000	0.00000	0.00000	0.00000	.22475	.38265	.49882	.58722	.65622
6	0.00000	0.00000	0.00000	0.00000	0.00000	0.00000	.20368	.35353	.46755	.55656
7	0.00000	0.00000	0.00000	0.00000	0.00000	0.00000	0.00000	.18817	.33136	.44314
8	0.00000	0.00000	0.00000	0.00000	0.00000	0.00000	0.00000	0.00000	.17638	.31406
9	0.00000	0.00000	0.00000	0.00000	0.00000	0.00000	0.00000	0.00000	0.00000	.16717

AGE OF LOAN	11	12	13	14	15	20	25	30	35	40
1	.95613	.96289	.96842	.97300	.97682	.98876	.99433	.99709	.99849	.99921
2	.90621	.92065	.93247	.94227	.95045	.97596	.98788	.99377	.99677	.99832
3	.84940	.87258	.89157	.90729	.92043	.96140	.98053	.99000	.99481	.99730
4	.78475	.81788	.84502	.86750	.88627	.94483	.97218	.98570	.99258	.99614
5	.71117	.75562	.79205	.82220	.84739	.92597	.96267	.98082	.99005	.99481
6	.62744	.68478	.73176	.77066	.80315	.90451	.95184	.97526	.98717	.99331
7	.53214	.60415	.66315	.71200	.75280	.88008	.93952	.96893	.98388	.99160
8	.42370	.51239	.58507	.64524	.69550	.85229	.92551	.96172	.98015	.98965
9	.30029	.40797	.49621	.56927	.63029	.82065	.90955	.95353	.97590	.98744
10	.15984	.28914	.39509	.48281	.55608	.78466	.89140	.94420	.97106	.98492
11	0.00000	.15390	.28001	.38442	.47162	.74369	.87074	.93358	.96555	.98205
12	0.00000	0.00000	.14904	.27245	.37551	.69707	.84723	.92150	.95929	.97878
13	0.00000	0.00000	0.00000	.14502	.26613	.64401	.82047	.90775	.95215	.97506
14	0.00000	0.00000	0.00000	0.00000	.14166	.58363	.79002	.89211	.94404	.97084
15	0.00000	0.00000	0.00000	0.00000	0.00000	.51491	.75536	.87430	.93480	.96602
16	0.00000	0.00000	0.00000	0.00000	0.00000	.43671	.71592	.85403	.92429	.96054
17	0.00000	0.00000	0.00000	0.00000	0.00000	.34771	.67104	.83097	.91233	.95431
18	0.00000	0.00000	0.00000	0.00000	0.00000	.24643	.61996	.80473	.89872	.94722
19	0.00000	0.00000	0.00000	0.00000	0.00000	.13117	.56184	.77486	.88323	.93914
20	0.00000	0.00000	0.00000	0.00000	0.00000	0.00000	.49568	.74087	.86560	.92996
21	0.00000	0.00000	0.00000	0.00000	0.00000	0.00000	.42040	.70219	.84554	.91950
22	0.00000	0.00000	0.00000	0.00000	0.00000	0.00000	.33473	.65817	.82270	.90760
23	0.00000	0.00000	0.00000	0.00000	0.00000	0.00000	.23723	.60807	.79672	.89406
24	0.00000	0.00000	0.00000	0.00000	0.00000	0.00000	.12627	.55106	.76715	.87865
25	0.00000	0.00000	0.00000	0.00000	0.00000	0.00000	0.00000	.48618	.73350	.86111
26	0.00000	0.00000	0.00000	0.00000	0.00000	0.00000	0.00000	.41234	.69520	.84115
27	0.00000	0.00000	0.00000	0.00000	0.00000	0.00000	0.00000	.32831	.65162	.81844
28	0.00000	0.00000	0.00000	0.00000	0.00000	0.00000	0.00000	.23268	.60202	.79259
29	0.00000	0.00000	0.00000	0.00000	0.00000	0.00000	0.00000	.12385	.54558	.76317
30	0.00000	0.00000	0.00000	0.00000	0.00000	0.00000	0.00000	0.00000	.48134	.72970
31	0.00000	0.00000	0.00000	0.00000	0.00000	0.00000	0.00000	0.00000	.40824	.69160
32	0.00000	0.00000	0.00000	0.00000	0.00000	0.00000	0.00000	0.00000	.32504	.64824
33	0.00000	0.00000	0.00000	0.00000	0.00000	0.00000	0.00000	0.00000	.23036	.59890
34	0.00000	0.00000	0.00000	0.00000	0.00000	0.00000	0.00000	0.00000	.12262	.54275
35	0.00000	0.00000	0.00000	0.00000	0.00000	0.00000	0.00000	0.00000	0.00000	.47884
36	0.00000	0.00000	0.00000	0.00000	0.00000	0.00000	0.00000	0.00000	0.00000	.40612
37	0.00000	0.00000	0.00000	0.00000	0.00000	0.00000	0.00000	0.00000	0.00000	.32336
38	0.00000	0.00000	0.00000	0.00000	0.00000	0.00000	0.00000	0.00000	0.00000	.22917
39	0.00000	0.00000	0.00000	0.00000	0.00000	0.00000	0.00000	0.00000	0.00000	.12198

REMAINING MORTGAGE BALANCE TABLE FOR 13.250 PERCENT

ORIGINAL LOAN TERM

AGE OF LOAN	1	2	3	4	5	6	7	8	9	10
1	0.00000	.53290	.70950	.79705	.84897	.88309	.90705	.92466	.93806	.94850
2	0.00000	0.00000	.37809	.56551	.67667	.74972	.80101	.83872	.86739	.88975
3	0.00000	0.00000	0.00000	.30136	.48010	.59756	.68004	.74067	.78677	.82272
4	0.00000	0.00000	0.00000	0.00000	.25584	.42397	.54202	.62881	.69479	.74625
5	0.00000	0.00000	0.00000	0.00000	0.00000	.22593	.38457	.50119	.58985	.65901
6	0.00000	0.00000	0.00000	0.00000	0.00000	0.00000	.20493	.35559	.47014	.55948
7	0.00000	0.00000	0.00000	0.00000	0.00000	0.00000	0.00000	.18949	.33357	.44593
8	0.00000	0.00000	0.00000	0.00000	0.00000	0.00000	0.00000	0.00000	.17776	.31639
9	0.00000	0.00000	0.00000	0.00000	0.00000	0.00000	0.00000	0.00000	0.00000	.16860

AGE OF LOAN	11	12	13	14	15	20	25	30	35	40
1	.95681	.96352	.96902	.97356	.97735	.98912	.99457	.99724	.99859	.99927
2	.90753	.92191	.93367	.94339	.95151	.97672	.98838	.99410	.99698	.99844
3	.85132	.87443	.89334	.90898	.92203	.96256	.98132	.99051	.99514	.99750
4	.78718	.82026	.84733	.86972	.88839	.94641	.97327	.98642	.99304	.99642
5	.71402	.75847	.79485	.82493	.85002	.92798	.96407	.98175	.99065	.99518
6	.63054	.68797	.73497	.77383	.80624	.90696	.95359	.97642	.98791	.99378
7	.53531	.60754	.66665	.71553	.75630	.88298	.94163	.97035	.98480	.99217
8	.42667	.51579	.58872	.64903	.69933	.85562	.92798	.96341	.98125	.99034
9	.30272	.41111	.49980	.57315	.63433	.82441	.91241	.95550	.97719	.98826
10	.16132	.29168	.39837	.48659	.56017	.78881	.89465	.94648	.97257	.98587
11	0.00000	.15544	.28264	.38783	.47557	.74818	.87438	.93619	.96729	.98316
12	0.00000	0.00000	.15062	.27517	.37905	.70184	.85126	.92444	.96127	.98006
13	0.00000	0.00000	0.00000	.14664	.26894	.64896	.82489	.91104	.95440	.97652
14	0.00000	0.00000	0.00000	0.00000	.14332	.58864	.79480	.89576	.94657	.97248
15	0.00000	0.00000	0.00000	0.00000	0.00000	.51983	.76047	.87832	.93763	.96788
16	0.00000	0.00000	0.00000	0.00000	0.00000	.44132	.72130	.85842	.92743	.96263
17	0.00000	0.00000	0.00000	0.00000	0.00000	.35175	.67662	.83573	.91579	.95664
18	0.00000	0.00000	0.00000	0.00000	0.00000	.24957	.62565	.80983	.90252	.94980
19	0.00000	0.00000	0.00000	0.00000	0.00000	.13299	.56750	.78029	.88738	.94201
20	0.00000	0.00000	0.00000	0.00000	0.00000	0.00000	.50115	.74659	.87010	.93311
21	0.00000	0.00000	0.00000	0.00000	0.00000	0.00000	.42546	.70814	.85039	.92296
22	0.00000	0.00000	0.00000	0.00000	0.00000	0.00000	.33912	.66428	.82791	.91138
23	0.00000	0.00000	0.00000	0.00000	0.00000	0.00000	.24060	.61423	.80226	.89817
24	0.00000	0.00000	0.00000	0.00000	0.00000	0.00000	.12822	.55714	.77299	.88310
25	0.00000	0.00000	0.00000	0.00000	0.00000	0.00000	0.00000	.49201	.73960	.86591
26	0.00000	0.00000	0.00000	0.00000	0.00000	0.00000	0.00000	.41770	.70152	.84630
27	0.00000	0.00000	0.00000	0.00000	0.00000	0.00000	0.00000	.33293	.65806	.82392
28	0.00000	0.00000	0.00000	0.00000	0.00000	0.00000	0.00000	.23621	.60849	.79839
29	0.00000	0.00000	0.00000	0.00000	0.00000	0.00000	0.00000	.12588	.55193	.76927
30	0.00000	0.00000	0.00000	0.00000	0.00000	0.00000	0.00000	0.00000	.48740	.73604
31	0.00000	0.00000	0.00000	0.00000	0.00000	0.00000	0.00000	0.00000	.41379	.69814
32	0.00000	0.00000	0.00000	0.00000	0.00000	0.00000	0.00000	0.00000	.32981	.65489
33	0.00000	0.00000	0.00000	0.00000	0.00000	0.00000	0.00000	0.00000	.23400	.60555
34	0.00000	0.00000	0.00000	0.00000	0.00000	0.00000	0.00000	0.00000	.12470	.54927
35	0.00000	0.00000	0.00000	0.00000	0.00000	0.00000	0.00000	0.00000	0.00000	.48506
36	0.00000	0.00000	0.00000	0.00000	0.00000	0.00000	0.00000	0.00000	0.00000	.41180
37	0.00000	0.00000	0.00000	0.00000	0.00000	0.00000	0.00000	0.00000	0.00000	.32822
38	0.00000	0.00000	0.00000	0.00000	0.00000	0.00000	0.00000	0.00000	0.00000	.23288
39	0.00000	0.00000	0.00000	0.00000	0.00000	0.00000	0.00000	0.00000	0.00000	.12410

REMAINING MORTGAGE BALANCE TABLE FOR 13.500 PERCENT

ORIGINAL LOAN TERM

AGE OF LOAN	1	2	3	4	5	6	7	8	9	10
1	0.00000	.53351	.71028	.79788	.84981	.88392	.90786	.92544	.93880	.94920
2	0.00000	0.00000	.37894	.56672	.67805	.75117	.80248	.84017	.86880	.89111
3	0.00000	0.00000	0.00000	.30235	.48161	.59935	.68196	.74265	.78875	.82467
4	0.00000	0.00000	0.00000	0.00000	.25694	.42571	.54412	.63111	.69719	.74868
5	0.00000	0.00000	0.00000	0.00000	0.00000	.22712	.38648	.50355	.59248	.66178
6	0.00000	0.00000	0.00000	0.00000	0.00000	0.00000	.20619	.35766	.47273	.56239
7	0.00000	0.00000	0.00000	0.00000	0.00000	0.00000	0.00000	.19082	.33577	.44872
8	0.00000	0.00000	0.00000	0.00000	0.00000	0.00000	0.00000	0.00000	.17914	.31872
9	0.00000	0.00000	0.00000	0.00000	0.00000	0.00000	0.00000	0.00000	0.00000	.17004

AGE OF LOAN	11	12	13	14	15	20	25	30	35	40
1	.95747	.96415	.96961	.97411	.97787	.98948	.99481	.99739	.99868	.99933
2	.90884	.92315	.93485	.94450	.95255	.97745	.98887	.99441	.99717	.99856
3	.85321	.87626	.89509	.91064	.92360	.96369	.98208	.99100	.99544	.99768
4	.78960	.82263	.84962	.87192	.89049	.94795	.97432	.98710	.99347	.99668
5	.71684	.76129	.79762	.82763	.85262	.92995	.96544	.98264	.99121	.99553
6	.63364	.69114	.73815	.77697	.80931	.90937	.95528	.97754	.98862	.99421
7	.53847	.61092	.67014	.71904	.75978	.88583	.94367	.97171	.98567	.99271
8	.42964	.51917	.59235	.65279	.70313	.85890	.93038	.96504	.98229	.99099
9	.30516	.41423	.50339	.57702	.63834	.82811	.91519	.95741	.97842	.98902
10	.16281	.29422	.40164	.49036	.56424	.79289	.89781	.94868	.97400	.98677
11	0.00000	.15697	.28528	.39125	.47950	.75262	.87794	.93870	.96895	.98420
12	0.00000	0.00000	.15220	.27790	.38259	.70656	.85521	.92729	.96316	.98126
13	0.00000	0.00000	0.00000	.14826	.27175	.65388	.82922	.91423	.95655	.97789
14	0.00000	0.00000	0.00000	0.00000	.14498	.59363	.79949	.89930	.94899	.97405
15	0.00000	0.00000	0.00000	0.00000	0.00000	.52472	.76549	.88223	.94034	.96964
16	0.00000	0.00000	0.00000	0.00000	0.00000	.44592	.72661	.86270	.93045	.96461
17	0.00000	0.00000	0.00000	0.00000	0.00000	.35579	.68214	.84037	.91913	.95885
18	0.00000	0.00000	0.00000	0.00000	0.00000	.25271	.63128	.81482	.90619	.95227
19	0.00000	0.00000	0.00000	0.00000	0.00000	.13482	.57311	.78561	.89139	.94474
20	0.00000	0.00000	0.00000	0.00000	0.00000	0.00000	.50659	.75220	.87447	.93613
21	0.00000	0.00000	0.00000	0.00000	0.00000	0.00000	.43050	.71399	.85511	.92628
22	0.00000	0.00000	0.00000	0.00000	0.00000	0.00000	.34349	.67030	.83298	.91502
23	0.00000	0.00000	0.00000	0.00000	0.00000	0.00000	.24398	.62032	.80766	.90214
24	0.00000	0.00000	0.00000	0.00000	0.00000	0.00000	.13016	.56316	.77870	.88741
25	0.00000	0.00000	0.00000	0.00000	0.00000	0.00000	0.00000	.49779	.74559	.87056
26	0.00000	0.00000	0.00000	0.00000	0.00000	0.00000	0.00000	.42303	.70772	.85129
27	0.00000	0.00000	0.00000	0.00000	0.00000	0.00000	0.00000	.33753	.66440	.82925
28	0.00000	0.00000	0.00000	0.00000	0.00000	0.00000	0.00000	.23974	.61486	.80405
29	0.00000	0.00000	0.00000	0.00000	0.00000	0.00000	0.00000	.12790	.55821	.77522
30	0.00000	0.00000	0.00000	0.00000	0.00000	0.00000	0.00000	0.00000	.49342	.74225
31	0.00000	0.00000	0.00000	0.00000	0.00000	0.00000	0.00000	0.00000	.41931	.70455
32	0.00000	0.00000	0.00000	0.00000	0.00000	0.00000	0.00000	0.00000	.33456	.66143
33	0.00000	0.00000	0.00000	0.00000	0.00000	0.00000	0.00000	0.00000	.23763	.61211
34	0.00000	0.00000	0.00000	0.00000	0.00000	0.00000	0.00000	0.00000	.12678	.55571
35	0.00000	0.00000	0.00000	0.00000	0.00000	0.00000	0.00000	0.00000	0.00000	.49121
36	0.00000	0.00000	0.00000	0.00000	0.00000	0.00000	0.00000	0.00000	0.00000	.41744
37	0.00000	0.00000	0.00000	0.00000	0.00000	0.00000	0.00000	0.00000	0.00000	.33306
38	0.00000	0.00000	0.00000	0.00000	0.00000	0.00000	0.00000	0.00000	0.00000	.23657
39	0.00000	0.00000	0.00000	0.00000	0.00000	0.00000	0.00000	0.00000	0.00000	.12621

REMAINING MORTGAGE BALANCE TABLE FOR 13.750 PERCENT

ORIGINAL LOAN TERM

AGE OF LOAN	1	2	3	4	5	6	7	8	9	10
1	0.00000	.53413	.71106	.79871	.85065	.88475	.90866	.92621	.93953	.94990
2	0.00000	0.00000	.37980	.56794	.67943	.75262	.80394	.84161	.87020	.89246
3	0.00000	0.00000	0.00000	.30335	.48312	.60112	.68387	.74461	.79072	.82661
4	0.00000	0.00000	0.00000	0.00000	.25805	.42744	.54622	.63341	.69959	.75110
5	0.00000	0.00000	0.00000	0.00000	0.00000	.22831	.38840	.50591	.59511	.66454
6	0.00000	0.00000	0.00000	0.00000	0.00000	0.00000	.20745	.35974	.47532	.56529
7	0.00000	0.00000	0.00000	0.00000	0.00000	0.00000	0.00000	.19214	.33798	.45151
8	0.00000	0.00000	0.00000	0.00000	0.00000	0.00000	0.00000	0.00000	.18053	.32105
9	0.00000	0.00000	0.00000	0.00000	0.00000	0.00000	0.00000	0.00000	0.00000	.17148

AGE OF LOAN	11	12	13	14	15	20	25	30	35	40
1	.95813	.96477	.97019	.97466	.97837	.98983	.99503	.99753	.99877	.99938
2	.91013	.92438	.93601	.94560	.95358	.97816	.98934	.99471	.99735	.99867
3	.85510	.87806	.89682	.91228	.92515	.96479	.98282	.99147	.99573	.99785
4	.79200	.82497	.85189	.87409	.89255	.94946	.97533	.98775	.99387	.99692
5	.71966	.76409	.80037	.83030	.85518	.93188	.96675	.98349	.99174	.99585
6	.63672	.69430	.74131	.78009	.81234	.91172	.95692	.97861	.98929	.99462
7	.54163	.61428	.67360	.72253	.76322	.88861	.94564	.97301	.98649	.99321
8	.43260	.52254	.59597	.65653	.70690	.86212	.93271	.96659	.98328	.99159
9	.30761	.41736	.50696	.58087	.64233	.83175	.91789	.95923	.97959	.98974
10	.16430	.29677	.40492	.49412	.56830	.79692	.90090	.95080	.97537	.98762
11	0.00000	.15851	.28792	.39466	.48343	.75700	.88141	.94112	.97053	.98518
12	0.00000	0.00000	.15379	.28063	.38612	.71122	.85907	.93003	.96497	.98239
13	0.00000	0.00000	0.00000	.14989	.27456	.65874	.83346	.91732	.95861	.97919
14	0.00000	0.00000	0.00000	0.00000	.14665	.59857	.80410	.90274	.95131	.97552
15	0.00000	0.00000	0.00000	0.00000	0.00000	.52959	.77043	.88603	.94294	.97132
16	0.00000	0.00000	0.00000	0.00000	0.00000	.45050	.73183	.86686	.93335	.96649
17	0.00000	0.00000	0.00000	0.00000	0.00000	.35982	.68758	.84489	.92235	.96096
18	0.00000	0.00000	0.00000	0.00000	0.00000	.25585	.63684	.81970	.90974	.95463
19	0.00000	0.00000	0.00000	0.00000	0.00000	.13666	.57867	.79082	.89528	.94736
20	0.00000	0.00000	0.00000	0.00000	0.00000	0.00000	.51198	.75771	.87870	.93902
21	0.00000	0.00000	0.00000	0.00000	0.00000	0.00000	.43552	.71975	.85970	.92947
22	0.00000	0.00000	0.00000	0.00000	0.00000	0.00000	.34785	.67623	.83791	.91852
23	0.00000	0.00000	0.00000	0.00000	0.00000	0.00000	.24735	.62633	.81293	.90596
24	0.00000	0.00000	0.00000	0.00000	0.00000	0.00000	.13211	.56912	.78429	.89156
25	0.00000	0.00000	0.00000	0.00000	0.00000	0.00000	0.00000	.50353	.75145	.87505
26	0.00000	0.00000	0.00000	0.00000	0.00000	0.00000	0.00000	.42833	.71381	.85613
27	0.00000	0.00000	0.00000	0.00000	0.00000	0.00000	0.00000	.34211	.67064	.83443
28	0.00000	0.00000	0.00000	0.00000	0.00000	0.00000	0.00000	.24326	.62116	.80955
29	0.00000	0.00000	0.00000	0.00000	0.00000	0.00000	0.00000	.12993	.56442	.78103
30	0.00000	0.00000	0.00000	0.00000	0.00000	0.00000	0.00000	0.00000	.49937	.74833
31	0.00000	0.00000	0.00000	0.00000	0.00000	0.00000	0.00000	0.00000	.42479	.71084
32	0.00000	0.00000	0.00000	0.00000	0.00000	0.00000	0.00000	0.00000	.33929	.66786
33	0.00000	0.00000	0.00000	0.00000	0.00000	0.00000	0.00000	0.00000	.24125	.61858
34	0.00000	0.00000	0.00000	0.00000	0.00000	0.00000	0.00000	0.00000	.12886	.56207
35	0.00000	0.00000	0.00000	0.00000	0.00000	0.00000	0.00000	0.00000	0.00000	.49730
36	0.00000	0.00000	0.00000	0.00000	0.00000	0.00000	0.00000	0.00000	0.00000	.42303
37	0.00000	0.00000	0.00000	0.00000	0.00000	0.00000	0.00000	0.00000	0.00000	.33788
38	0.00000	0.00000	0.00000	0.00000	0.00000	0.00000	0.00000	0.00000	0.00000	.24025
39	0.00000	0.00000	0.00000	0.00000	0.00000	0.00000	0.00000	0.00000	0.00000	.12833

REMAINING MORTGAGE BALANCE TABLE FOR 14.000 PERCENT

ORIGINAL LOAN TERM

AGE OF LOAN	1	2	3	4	5	6	7	8	9	10
1	0.00000	.53474	.71184	.79954	.85149	.88557	.90946	.92697	.94026	.95059
2	0.00000	0.00000	.38065	.56915	.68080	.75406	.80539	.84304	.87160	.89380
3	0.00000	0.00000	0.00000	.30435	.48463	.60290	.68578	.74658	.79268	.82853
4	0.00000	0.00000	0.00000	0.00000	.25915	.42917	.54831	.63570	.70197	.75351
5	0.00000	0.00000	0.00000	0.00000	0.00000	.22950	.39031	.50827	.59772	.66729
6	0.00000	0.00000	0.00000	0.00000	0.00000	0.00000	.20872	.36181	.47791	.56819
7	0.00000	0.00000	0.00000	0.00000	0.00000	0.00000	0.00000	.19347	.34019	.45429
8	0.00000	0.00000	0.00000	0.00000	0.00000	0.00000	0.00000	0.00000	.18192	.32338
9	0.00000	0.00000	0.00000	0.00000	0.00000	0.00000	0.00000	0.00000	0.00000	.17293

AGE OF LOAN	11	12	13	14	15	20	25	30	35	40
1	.95878	.96538	.97076	.97519	.97887	.99016	.99525	.99767	.99885	.99943
2	.91141	.92559	.93715	.94667	.95458	.97885	.98979	.99499	.99752	.99877
3	.85696	.87985	.89852	.91390	.92567	.96586	.98352	.99191	.99600	.99801
4	.79438	.82729	.85413	.87623	.89459	.95092	.97631	.98837	.99425	.99714
5	.72245	.76688	.80310	.83293	.85771	.93376	.96803	.98431	.99224	.99614
6	.63978	.69744	.74445	.78317	.81533	.91402	.95850	.97963	.98992	.99500
7	.54477	.61763	.67705	.72598	.76662	.89135	.94756	.97426	.98727	.99368
8	.43557	.52591	.59957	.66025	.71064	.86528	.93498	.96809	.98421	.99216
9	.31006	.42049	.51053	.58470	.64630	.83533	.92052	.96099	.98070	.99041
10	.16580	.29932	.40819	.49786	.57234	.80089	.90390	.95284	.97667	.98841
11	0.00000	.16006	.29057	.39806	.48734	.76132	.88480	.94346	.97203	.98611
12	0.00000	0.00000	.15538	.28336	.38965	.71584	.86285	.93269	.96670	.98346
13	0.00000	0.00000	0.00000	.15152	.27737	.66356	.83762	.92031	.96057	.98042
14	0.00000	0.00000	0.00000	0.00000	.14832	.60348	.80862	.90607	.95353	.97692
15	0.00000	0.00000	0.00000	0.00000	0.00000	.53443	.77529	.88972	.94544	.97290
16	0.00000	0.00000	0.00000	0.00000	0.00000	.45506	.73698	.87092	.93614	.96828
17	0.00000	0.00000	0.00000	0.00000	0.00000	.36384	.69295	.84931	.92545	.96297
18	0.00000	0.00000	0.00000	0.00000	0.00000	.25900	.64235	.82447	.91316	.95687
19	0.00000	0.00000	0.00000	0.00000	0.00000	.13850	.58419	.79593	.89904	.94986
20	0.00000	0.00000	0.00000	0.00000	0.00000	0.00000	.51734	.76312	.88281	.94179
21	0.00000	0.00000	0.00000	0.00000	0.00000	0.00000	.44051	.72542	.86415	.93253
22	0.00000	0.00000	0.00000	0.00000	0.00000	0.00000	.35221	.68208	.84271	.92188
23	0.00000	0.00000	0.00000	0.00000	0.00000	0.00000	.25072	.63227	.81807	.90964
24	0.00000	0.00000	0.00000	0.00000	0.00000	0.00000	.13407	.57502	.78975	.89557
25	0.00000	0.00000	0.00000	0.00000	0.00000	0.00000	0.00000	.50922	.75720	.87941
26	0.00000	0.00000	0.00000	0.00000	0.00000	0.00000	0.00000	.43360	.71978	.86082
27	0.00000	0.00000	0.00000	0.00000	0.00000	0.00000	0.00000	.34668	.67678	.83946
28	0.00000	0.00000	0.00000	0.00000	0.00000	0.00000	0.00000	.24678	.62736	.81492
29	0.00000	0.00000	0.00000	0.00000	0.00000	0.00000	0.00000	.13196	.57056	.78670
30	0.00000	0.00000	0.00000	0.00000	0.00000	0.00000	0.00000	0.00000	.50527	.75428
31	0.00000	0.00000	0.00000	0.00000	0.00000	0.00000	0.00000	0.00000	.43023	.71701
32	0.00000	0.00000	0.00000	0.00000	0.00000	0.00000	0.00000	0.00000	.34399	.67417
33	0.00000	0.00000	0.00000	0.00000	0.00000	0.00000	0.00000	0.00000	.24487	.62494
34	0.00000	0.00000	0.00000	0.00000	0.00000	0.00000	0.00000	0.00000	.13094	.56836
35	0.00000	0.00000	0.00000	0.00000	0.00000	0.00000	0.00000	0.00000	0.00000	.50332
36	0.00000	0.00000	0.00000	0.00000	0.00000	0.00000	0.00000	0.00000	0.00000	.42857
37	0.00000	0.00000	0.00000	0.00000	0.00000	0.00000	0.00000	0.00000	0.00000	.34266
38	0.00000	0.00000	0.00000	0.00000	0.00000	0.00000	0.00000	0.00000	0.00000	.24392
39	0.00000	0.00000	0.00000	0.00000	0.00000	0.00000	0.00000	0.00000	0.00000	.13044

REMAINING MORTGAGE BALANCE TABLE FOR 14.250 PERCENT

ORIGINAL LOAN TERM

AGE OF LOAN	1	2	3	4	5	6	7	8	9	10
1	0.00000	.53536	.71262	.80037	.85232	.88639	.91025	.92773	.94098	.95127
2	0.00000	0.00000	.38151	.57036	.68218	.75549	.80684	.84447	.87298	.89513
3	0.00000	0.00000	0.00000	.30535	.48613	.60467	.68769	.74853	.79462	.83044
4	0.00000	0.00000	0.00000	0.00000	.26025	.43090	.55040	.63799	.70435	.75590
5	0.00000	0.00000	0.00000	0.00000	0.00000	.23069	.39223	.51063	.60033	.67003
6	0.00000	0.00000	0.00000	0.00000	0.00000	0.00000	.20998	.36388	.48049	.57108
7	0.00000	0.00000	0.00000	0.00000	0.00000	0.00000	0.00000	.19481	.34241	.45708
8	0.00000	0.00000	0.00000	0.00000	0.00000	0.00000	0.00000	0.00000	.18331	.32572
9	0.00000	0.00000	0.00000	0.00000	0.00000	0.00000	0.00000	0.00000	0.00000	.17438

AGE OF LOAN	11	12	13	14	15	20	25	30	35	40
1	.95942	.96598	.97132	.97571	.97936	.99049	.99546	.99780	.99892	.99947
2	.91267	.92678	.93828	.94773	.95557	.97953	.99023	.99526	.99768	.99886
3	.85881	.88162	.90021	.91549	.92817	.96690	.98420	.99234	.99625	.99816
4	.79674	.82959	.85634	.87834	.89659	.95235	.97726	.98897	.99461	.99735
5	.72523	.76964	.80580	.83554	.86021	.93559	.96926	.98508	.99271	.99642
6	.64284	.70056	.74756	.78623	.81829	.91628	.96004	.98061	.99052	.99535
7	.54791	.62097	.68047	.72941	.77000	.89402	.94941	.97546	.98800	.99411
8	.43853	.52927	.60316	.66394	.71435	.86838	.93717	.96952	.98510	.99269
9	.31250	.42361	.51409	.58851	.65024	.83884	.92307	.96268	.98175	.99105
10	.16730	.30187	.41146	.50160	.57636	.80481	.90683	.95480	.97790	.98916
11	0.00000	.16161	.29322	.40147	.49125	.76559	.88811	.94572	.97346	.98698
12	0.00000	0.00000	.15698	.28609	.39318	.72040	.86654	.93525	.96835	.98447
13	0.00000	0.00000	0.00000	.15316	.28019	.66834	.84169	.92320	.96245	.98157
14	0.00000	0.00000	0.00000	0.00000	.15000	.60836	.81305	.90931	.95566	.97824
15	0.00000	0.00000	0.00000	0.00000	0.00000	.53924	.78006	.89330	.94784	.97440
16	0.00000	0.00000	0.00000	0.00000	0.00000	.45961	.74205	.87486	.93882	.96998
17	0.00000	0.00000	0.00000	0.00000	0.00000	.36786	.69825	.85361	.92843	.96488
18	0.00000	0.00000	0.00000	0.00000	0.00000	.26214	.64779	.82913	.91646	.95901
19	0.00000	0.00000	0.00000	0.00000	0.00000	.14034	.58965	.80093	.90268	.95224
20	0.00000	0.00000	0.00000	0.00000	0.00000	0.00000	.52266	.76843	.88679	.94444
21	0.00000	0.00000	0.00000	0.00000	0.00000	0.00000	.44548	.73098	.86848	.93546
22	0.00000	0.00000	0.00000	0.00000	0.00000	0.00000	.35655	.68784	.84739	.92511
23	0.00000	0.00000	0.00000	0.00000	0.00000	0.00000	.25408	.63813	.82309	.91319
24	0.00000	0.00000	0.00000	0.00000	0.00000	0.00000	.13602	.58086	.79509	.89945
25	0.00000	0.00000	0.00000	0.00000	0.00000	0.00000	0.00000	.51487	.76282	.88361
26	0.00000	0.00000	0.00000	0.00000	0.00000	0.00000	0.00000	.43883	.72565	.86537
27	0.00000	0.00000	0.00000	0.00000	0.00000	0.00000	0.00000	.35123	.68282	.84436
28	0.00000	0.00000	0.00000	0.00000	0.00000	0.00000	0.00000	.25029	.63348	.82014
29	0.00000	0.00000	0.00000	0.00000	0.00000	0.00000	0.00000	.13400	.57662	.79224
30	0.00000	0.00000	0.00000	0.00000	0.00000	0.00000	0.00000	0.00000	.51111	.76009
31	0.00000	0.00000	0.00000	0.00000	0.00000	0.00000	0.00000	0.00000	.43563	.72306
32	0.00000	0.00000	0.00000	0.00000	0.00000	0.00000	0.00000	0.00000	.34867	.68038
33	0.00000	0.00000	0.00000	0.00000	0.00000	0.00000	0.00000	0.00000	.24847	.63121
34	0.00000	0.00000	0.00000	0.00000	0.00000	0.00000	0.00000	0.00000	.13302	.57456
35	0.00000	0.00000	0.00000	0.00000	0.00000	0.00000	0.00000	0.00000	0.00000	.50928
36	0.00000	0.00000	0.00000	0.00000	0.00000	0.00000	0.00000	0.00000	0.00000	.43407
37	0.00000	0.00000	0.00000	0.00000	0.00000	0.00000	0.00000	0.00000	0.00000	.34742
38	0.00000	0.00000	0.00000	0.00000	0.00000	0.00000	0.00000	0.00000	0.00000	.24758
39	0.00000	0.00000	0.00000	0.00000	0.00000	0.00000	0.00000	0.00000	0.00000	.13254

REMAINING MORTGAGE BALANCE TABLE FOR 14.500 PERCENT

ORIGINAL LOAN TERM

AGE OF LOAN	1	2	3	4	5	6	7	8	9	10
1	0.00000	.53597	.71340	.80120	.85316	.88721	.91103	.92848	.94169	.95195
2	0.00000	0.00000	.38236	.57157	.68354	.75692	.80827	.84588	.87435	.89644
3	0.00000	0.00000	0.00000	.30634	.48764	.60644	.68958	.75047	.79656	.83233
4	0.00000	0.00000	0.00000	0.00000	.26136	.43264	.55249	.64027	.70671	.75828
5	0.00000	0.00000	0.00000	0.00000	0.00000	.23188	.39415	.51298	.60294	.67275
6	0.00000	0.00000	0.00000	0.00000	0.00000	0.00000	.21125	.36596	.48307	.57396
7	0.00000	0.00000	0.00000	0.00000	0.00000	0.00000	0.00000	.19614	.34462	.45986
8	0.00000	0.00000	0.00000	0.00000	0.00000	0.00000	0.00000	0.00000	.18471	.32806
9	0.00000	0.00000	0.00000	0.00000	0.00000	0.00000	0.00000	0.00000	0.00000	.17583

AGE OF LOAN	11	12	13	14	15	20	25	30	35	40
1	.96006	.96657	.97187	.97623	.97983	.99081	.99566	.99792	.99899	.99951
2	.91392	.92797	.93939	.94877	.95654	.98018	.99065	.99551	.99783	.99895
3	.86063	.88337	.90187	.91706	.92964	.96792	.98486	.99274	.99649	.99830
4	.79908	.83187	.85853	.88043	.89857	.95375	.97817	.98953	.99494	.99755
5	.72799	.77237	.80847	.83812	.86268	.93738	.97044	.98583	.99315	.99668
6	.64588	.70366	.75065	.78925	.82122	.91848	.96152	.98155	.99109	.99568
7	.55104	.62429	.68387	.73281	.77334	.89665	.95121	.97660	.98870	.99452
8	.44149	.53262	.60673	.66761	.71803	.87143	.93931	.97090	.98594	.99318
9	.31496	.42673	.51764	.59231	.65415	.84230	.92556	.96430	.98275	.99164
10	.16881	.30443	.41473	.50533	.58037	.80866	.90968	.95669	.97907	.98986
11	0.00000	.16316	.29587	.40487	.49514	.76980	.89133	.94789	.97483	.98779
12	0.00000	0.00000	.15858	.28883	.39671	.72491	.87014	.93773	.96992	.98542
13	0.00000	0.00000	0.00000	.15481	.28301	.67307	.84567	.92599	.96425	.98267
14	0.00000	0.00000	0.00000	0.00000	.15168	.61319	.81740	.91244	.95770	.97949
15	0.00000	0.00000	0.00000	0.00000	0.00000	.54403	.78475	.89678	.95013	.97582
16	0.00000	0.00000	0.00000	0.00000	0.00000	.46414	.74704	.87870	.94140	.97159
17	0.00000	0.00000	0.00000	0.00000	0.00000	.37187	.70349	.85781	.93131	.96670
18	0.00000	0.00000	0.00000	0.00000	0.00000	.26529	.65318	.83368	.91965	.96105
19	0.00000	0.00000	0.00000	0.00000	0.00000	.14219	.59506	.80582	.90619	.95452
20	0.00000	0.00000	0.00000	0.00000	0.00000	0.00000	.52794	.77363	.89064	.94698
21	0.00000	0.00000	0.00000	0.00000	0.00000	0.00000	.45042	.73645	.87268	.93827
22	0.00000	0.00000	0.00000	0.00000	0.00000	0.00000	.36087	.69351	.85194	.92822
23	0.00000	0.00000	0.00000	0.00000	0.00000	0.00000	.25745	.64392	.82798	.91660
24	0.00000	0.00000	0.00000	0.00000	0.00000	0.00000	.13798	.58663	.80030	.90318
25	0.00000	0.00000	0.00000	0.00000	0.00000	0.00000	0.00000	.52046	.76833	.88768
26	0.00000	0.00000	0.00000	0.00000	0.00000	0.00000	0.00000	.44403	.73141	.86978
27	0.00000	0.00000	0.00000	0.00000	0.00000	0.00000	0.00000	.35576	.68877	.84911
28	0.00000	0.00000	0.00000	0.00000	0.00000	0.00000	0.00000	.25380	.63951	.82523
29	0.00000	0.00000	0.00000	0.00000	0.00000	0.00000	0.00000	.13603	.58261	.79764
30	0.00000	0.00000	0.00000	0.00000	0.00000	0.00000	0.00000	0.00000	.51690	.76578
31	0.00000	0.00000	0.00000	0.00000	0.00000	0.00000	0.00000	0.00000	.44099	.72898
32	0.00000	0.00000	0.00000	0.00000	0.00000	0.00000	0.00000	0.00000	.35332	.68648
33	0.00000	0.00000	0.00000	0.00000	0.00000	0.00000	0.00000	0.00000	.25206	.63738
34	0.00000	0.00000	0.00000	0.00000	0.00000	0.00000	0.00000	0.00000	.13510	.58068
35	0.00000	0.00000	0.00000	0.00000	0.00000	0.00000	0.00000	0.00000	0.00000	.51518
36	0.00000	0.00000	0.00000	0.00000	0.00000	0.00000	0.00000	0.00000	0.00000	.43953
37	0.00000	0.00000	0.00000	0.00000	0.00000	0.00000	0.00000	0.00000	0.00000	.35215
38	0.00000	0.00000	0.00000	0.00000	0.00000	0.00000	0.00000	0.00000	0.00000	.25122
39	0.00000	0.00000	0.00000	0.00000	0.00000	0.00000	0.00000	0.00000	0.00000	.13465

REMAINING MORTGAGE BALANCE TABLE FOR 14.750 PERCENT

ORIGINAL LOAN TERM

AGE OF LOAN	1	2	3	4	5	6	7	8	9	10
1	0.00000	.53658	.71417	.80202	.85398	.88802	.91181	.92923	.94240	.95261
2	0.00000	0.00000	.38321	.57278	.68491	.75835	.80971	.84729	.87571	.89774
3	0.00000	0.00000	0.00000	.30734	.48914	.60821	.69148	.75240	.79848	.83421
4	0.00000	0.00000	0.00000	0.00000	.26247	.43437	.55458	.64254	.70907	.76064
5	0.00000	0.00000	0.00000	0.00000	0.00000	.23308	.39606	.51533	.60553	.67546
6	0.00000	0.00000	0.00000	0.00000	0.00000	0.00000	.21252	.36803	.48565	.57683
7	0.00000	0.00000	0.00000	0.00000	0.00000	0.00000	0.00000	.19748	.34684	.46263
8	0.00000	0.00000	0.00000	0.00000	0.00000	0.00000	0.00000	0.00000	.18611	.33040
9	0.00000	0.00000	0.00000	0.00000	0.00000	0.00000	0.00000	0.00000	0.00000	.17729

AGE OF LOAN	11	12	13	14	15	20	25	30	35	40
1	.96068	.96716	.97242	.97673	.98030	.99111	.99585	.99803	.99906	.99955
2	.91516	.92913	.94049	.94980	.95750	.98082	.99105	.99576	.99797	.99903
3	.86245	.88510	.90351	.91860	.93109	.96891	.98548	.99312	.99672	.99843
4	.80141	.83412	.86069	.88249	.90351	.95511	.97904	.99007	.99526	.99773
5	.73074	.77509	.81112	.84067	.86511	.93913	.97159	.98653	.99357	.99692
6	.64891	.70674	.75371	.79225	.82411	.92064	.96295	.98244	.99162	.99598
7	.55416	.62760	.68725	.73619	.77664	.89922	.95295	.97770	.98935	.99490
8	.44444	.53596	.61029	.67126	.72168	.87442	.94138	.97221	.98674	.99365
9	.31741	.42985	.52118	.59609	.65804	.84570	.92797	.96586	.98370	.99219
10	.17032	.30699	.41799	.50905	.58435	.81245	.91245	.95850	.98019	.99051
11	0.00000	.16472	.29852	.40827	.49902	.77395	.89448	.94998	.97612	.98856
12	0.00000	0.00000	.16018	.29157	.40023	.72937	.87367	.94012	.97141	.98631
13	0.00000	0.00000	0.00000	.15645	.28583	.67775	.84957	.92870	.96596	.98370
14	0.00000	0.00000	0.00000	0.00000	.15337	.61799	.82167	.91547	.95965	.98067
15	0.00000	0.00000	0.00000	0.00000	0.00000	.54878	.78937	.90016	.95234	.97717
16	0.00000	0.00000	0.00000	0.00000	0.00000	.46865	.75196	.88243	.94388	.97312
17	0.00000	0.00000	0.00000	0.00000	0.00000	.37587	.70865	.86190	.93407	.96842
18	0.00000	0.00000	0.00000	0.00000	0.00000	.26843	.65850	.83813	.92273	.96299
19	0.00000	0.00000	0.00000	0.00000	0.00000	.14404	.60043	.81061	.90959	.95669
20	0.00000	0.00000	0.00000	0.00000	0.00000	0.00000	.53319	.77873	.89437	.94941
21	0.00000	0.00000	0.00000	0.00000	0.00000	0.00000	.45533	.74183	.87676	.94097
22	0.00000	0.00000	0.00000	0.00000	0.00000	0.00000	.36519	.69910	.85636	.93120
23	0.00000	0.00000	0.00000	0.00000	0.00000	0.00000	.26081	.64963	.83274	.91989
24	0.00000	0.00000	0.00000	0.00000	0.00000	0.00000	.13994	.59234	.80539	.90679
25	0.00000	0.00000	0.00000	0.00000	0.00000	0.00000	0.00000	.52601	.77373	.89162
26	0.00000	0.00000	0.00000	0.00000	0.00000	0.00000	0.00000	.44920	.73706	.87406
27	0.00000	0.00000	0.00000	0.00000	0.00000	0.00000	0.00000	.36027	.69461	.85372
28	0.00000	0.00000	0.00000	0.00000	0.00000	0.00000	0.00000	.25729	.64545	.83018
29	0.00000	0.00000	0.00000	0.00000	0.00000	0.00000	0.00000	.13806	.58853	.80291
30	0.00000	0.00000	0.00000	0.00000	0.00000	0.00000	0.00000	0.00000	.52263	.77135
31	0.00000	0.00000	0.00000	0.00000	0.00000	0.00000	0.00000	0.00000	.44631	.73479
32	0.00000	0.00000	0.00000	0.00000	0.00000	0.00000	0.00000	0.00000	.35795	.69247
33	0.00000	0.00000	0.00000	0.00000	0.00000	0.00000	0.00000	0.00000	.25564	.64346
34	0.00000	0.00000	0.00000	0.00000	0.00000	0.00000	0.00000	0.00000	.13717	.58672
35	0.00000	0.00000	0.00000	0.00000	0.00000	0.00000	0.00000	0.00000	0.00000	.52102
36	0.00000	0.00000	0.00000	0.00000	0.00000	0.00000	0.00000	0.00000	0.00000	.44494
37	0.00000	0.00000	0.00000	0.00000	0.00000	0.00000	0.00000	0.00000	0.00000	.35685
38	0.00000	0.00000	0.00000	0.00000	0.00000	0.00000	0.00000	0.00000	0.00000	.25485
39	0.00000	0.00000	0.00000	0.00000	0.00000	0.00000	0.00000	0.00000	0.00000	.13675

REMAINING MORTGAGE BALANCE TABLE FOR 15.000 PERCENT

ORIGINAL LOAN TERM

AGE OF LOAN	1	2	3	4	5	6	7	8	9	10
1	0.00000	.53720	.71495	.80284	.85481	.88882	.91259	.92997	.94310	.95327
2	0.00000	0.00000	.38407	.57359	.68627	.75977	.81113	.84868	.87706	.89903
3	0.00000	0.00000	0.00000	.30835	.49065	.60998	.69336	.75433	.80039	.83607
4	0.00000	0.00000	0.00000	0.00000	.26358	.43610	.55666	.64480	.71141	.76299
5	0.00000	0.00000	0.00000	0.00000	0.00000	.23427	.39798	.51768	.60812	.67816
6	0.00000	0.00000	0.00000	0.00000	0.00000	0.00000	.21379	.37011	.48822	.57970
7	0.00000	0.00000	0.00000	0.00000	0.00000	0.00000	0.00000	.19882	.34905	.46541
8	0.00000	0.00000	0.00000	0.00000	0.00000	0.00000	0.00000	0.00000	.18751	.33274
9	0.00000	0.00000	0.00000	0.00000	0.00000	0.00000	0.00000	0.00000	0.00000	.17875

AGE OF LOAN	11	12	13	14	15	20	25	30	35	40
1	.96130	.96774	.97296	.97723	.98076	.99141	.99604	.99814	.99912	.99959
2	.91638	.93029	.94157	.95080	.95843	.98144	.99143	.99599	.99811	.99910
3	.86424	.88682	.90513	.92013	.93251	.96987	.98609	.99348	.99693	.99855
4	.80372	.83636	.86283	.88452	.90243	.95643	.97989	.99058	.99556	.99790
5	.73347	.77779	.81374	.84319	.86750	.94084	.97269	.98721	.99397	.99714
6	.65192	.70980	.75675	.79521	.82697	.92274	.96434	.98329	.99212	.99627
7	.55727	.63089	.69061	.73952	.77991	.90173	.95464	.97875	.98998	.99526
8	.44740	.53929	.61383	.67488	.72530	.87735	.94338	.97347	.98749	.99408
9	.31986	.43296	.52470	.59985	.66190	.84904	.93032	.96735	.98460	.99271
10	.17183	.30954	.42125	.51276	.58831	.81618	.91515	.96325	.98125	.99113
11	0.00000	.16629	.30117	.41166	.50289	.77804	.89754	.95200	.97736	.98929
12	0.00000	0.00000	.16179	.29432	.40374	.73378	.87711	.94243	.97284	.98715
13	0.00000	0.00000	0.00000	.15811	.28865	.68239	.85339	.93131	.96760	.98467
14	0.00000	0.00000	0.00000	0.00000	.15506	.62274	.82585	.91841	.96152	.98179
15	0.00000	0.00000	0.00000	0.00000	0.00000	.55351	.79390	.90344	.95445	.97845
16	0.00000	0.00000	0.00000	0.00000	0.00000	.47314	.75680	.88606	.94625	.97457
17	0.00000	0.00000	0.00000	0.00000	0.00000	.37986	.71374	.86589	.93674	.97006
18	0.00000	0.00000	0.00000	0.00000	0.00000	.27158	.66375	.84247	.92569	.96484
19	0.00000	0.00000	0.00000	0.00000	0.00000	.14589	.60574	.81529	.91287	.95877
20	0.00000	0.00000	0.00000	0.00000	0.00000	0.00000	.53839	.78374	.89799	.95173
21	0.00000	0.00000	0.00000	0.00000	0.00000	0.00000	.46022	.74712	.88071	.94355
22	0.00000	0.00000	0.00000	0.00000	0.00000	0.00000	.36948	.70461	.86066	.93406
23	0.00000	0.00000	0.00000	0.00000	0.00000	0.00000	.26416	.65526	.83739	.92305
24	0.00000	0.00000	0.00000	0.00000	0.00000	0.00000	.14191	.59799	.81037	.91026
25	0.00000	0.00000	0.00000	0.00000	0.00000	0.00000	0.00000	.53150	.77901	.89542
26	0.00000	0.00000	0.00000	0.00000	0.00000	0.00000	0.00000	.45433	.74261	.87820
27	0.00000	0.00000	0.00000	0.00000	0.00000	0.00000	0.00000	.36476	.70035	.85820
28	0.00000	0.00000	0.00000	0.00000	0.00000	0.00000	0.00000	.26078	.65131	.83499
29	0.00000	0.00000	0.00000	0.00000	0.00000	0.00000	0.00000	.14309	.59438	.80805
30	0.00000	0.00000	0.00000	0.00000	0.00000	0.00000	0.00000	0.00000	.52830	.77678
31	0.00000	0.00000	0.00000	0.00000	0.00000	0.00000	0.00000	0.00000	.45159	.74049
32	0.00000	0.00000	0.00000	0.00000	0.00000	0.00000	0.00000	0.00000	.36256	.69835
33	0.00000	0.00000	0.00000	0.00000	0.00000	0.00000	0.00000	0.00000	.25921	.64945
34	0.00000	0.00000	0.00000	0.00000	0.00000	0.00000	0.00000	0.00000	.13925	.59268
35	0.00000	0.00000	0.00000	0.00000	0.00000	0.00000	0.00000	0.00000	0.00000	.52679
36	0.00000	0.00000	0.00000	0.00000	0.00000	0.00000	0.00000	0.00000	0.00000	.45030
37	0.00000	0.00000	0.00000	0.00000	0.00000	0.00000	0.00000	0.00000	0.00000	.36152
38	0.00000	0.00000	0.00000	0.00000	0.00000	0.00000	0.00000	0.00000	0.00000	.25847
39	0.00000	0.00000	0.00000	0.00000	0.00000	0.00000	0.00000	0.00000	0.00000	.13885

REMAINING MORTGAGE BALANCE TABLE FOR 15.250 PERCENT

ORIGINAL LOAN TERM

AGE OF LOAN	1	2	3	4	5	6	7	8	9	10
1	0.00000	.53781	.71572	.80366	.85563	.88962	.91336	.93070	.94380	.95392
2	0.00000	0.00000	.38492	.57519	.68763	.76119	.81255	.85007	.87839	.90031
3	0.00000	0.00000	0.00000	.30935	.49215	.61174	.69524	.75624	.80229	.83792
4	0.00000	0.00000	0.00000	0.00000	.26469	.43783	.55874	.64706	.71374	.76533
5	0.00000	0.00000	0.00000	0.00000	0.00000	.23547	.39990	.52002	.61070	.68085
6	0.00000	0.00000	0.00000	0.00000	0.00000	0.00000	.21507	.37219	.49079	.58256
7	0.00000	0.00000	0.00000	0.00000	0.00000	0.00000	0.00000	.20017	.35127	.46818
8	0.00000	0.00000	0.00000	0.00000	0.00000	0.00000	0.00000	0.00000	.18892	.33508
9	0.00000	0.00000	0.00000	0.00000	0.00000	0.00000	0.00000	0.00000	0.00000	.18021

AGE OF LOAN	11	12	13	14	15	20	25	30	35	40
1	.96191	.96830	.97348	.97772	.98121	.99170	.99621	.99825	.99918	.99962
2	.91759	.93142	.94263	.95179	.95935	.98204	.99180	.99620	.99823	.99917
3	.86602	.88851	.90673	.92163	.93391	.97080	.98667	.99383	.99712	.99866
4	.80601	.83857	.86495	.88652	.90431	.95773	.98070	.99107	.99584	.99805
5	.73618	.78046	.81633	.84568	.86987	.94251	.97376	.98785	.99434	.99735
6	.65492	.71284	.75977	.79815	.82979	.92480	.96568	.98411	.99259	.99654
7	.56037	.63416	.69394	.74284	.78315	.90420	.95627	.97975	.99056	.99559
8	.45035	.54261	.61735	.67848	.72888	.88022	.94533	.97468	.98820	.99448
9	.32232	.43607	.52822	.60359	.66573	.85232	.93259	.96879	.98545	.99320
10	.17335	.31211	.42451	.51645	.59225	.81986	.91778	.96193	.98225	.99170
11	0.00000	.16785	.30383	.41505	.50675	.78208	.90053	.95394	.97853	.98996
12	0.00000	0.00000	.16340	.29706	.40725	.73813	.88047	.94465	.97420	.98794
13	0.00000	0.00000	0.00000	.15976	.29148	.68698	.85712	.93384	.96916	.98558
14	0.00000	0.00000	0.00000	0.00000	.15676	.62746	.82996	.92126	.96330	.98284
15	0.00000	0.00000	0.00000	0.00000	0.00000	.55820	.79834	.90662	.95648	.97965
16	0.00000	0.00000	0.00000	0.00000	0.00000	.47761	.76156	.88959	.94854	.97594
17	0.00000	0.00000	0.00000	0.00000	0.00000	.38384	.71876	.86977	.93930	.97162
18	0.00000	0.00000	0.00000	0.00000	0.00000	.27472	.66895	.84671	.92855	.96660
19	0.00000	0.00000	0.00000	0.00000	0.00000	.14775	.61099	.81987	.91604	.96075
20	0.00000	0.00000	0.00000	0.00000	0.00000	0.00000	.54356	.78864	.90149	.95395
21	0.00000	0.00000	0.00000	0.00000	0.00000	0.00000	.46508	.75231	.88455	.94603
22	0.00000	0.00000	0.00000	0.00000	0.00000	0.00000	.37377	.71002	.86484	.93681
23	0.00000	0.00000	0.00000	0.00000	0.00000	0.00000	.26751	.66082	.84191	.92609
24	0.00000	0.00000	0.00000	0.00000	0.00000	0.00000	.14387	.60357	.81523	.91362
25	0.00000	0.00000	0.00000	0.00000	0.00000	0.00000	0.00000	.53695	.78418	.89910
26	0.00000	0.00000	0.00000	0.00000	0.00000	0.00000	0.00000	.45943	.74805	.88221
27	0.00000	0.00000	0.00000	0.00000	0.00000	0.00000	0.00000	.36923	.70600	.86255
28	0.00000	0.00000	0.00000	0.00000	0.00000	0.00000	0.00000	.26426	.65708	.83968
29	0.00000	0.00000	0.00000	0.00000	0.00000	0.00000	0.00000	.14212	.60015	.81307
30	0.00000	0.00000	0.00000	0.00000	0.00000	0.00000	0.00000	0.00000	.53391	.78210
31	0.00000	0.00000	0.00000	0.00000	0.00000	0.00000	0.00000	0.00000	.45683	.74606
32	0.00000	0.00000	0.00000	0.00000	0.00000	0.00000	0.00000	0.00000	.36713	.70413
33	0.00000	0.00000	0.00000	0.00000	0.00000	0.00000	0.00000	0.00000	.26277	.65534
34	0.00000	0.00000	0.00000	0.00000	0.00000	0.00000	0.00000	0.00000	.14132	.59856
35	0.00000	0.00000	0.00000	0.00000	0.00000	0.00000	0.00000	0.00000	0.00000	.53250
36	0.00000	0.00000	0.00000	0.00000	0.00000	0.00000	0.00000	0.00000	0.00000	.45562
37	0.00000	0.00000	0.00000	0.00000	0.00000	0.00000	0.00000	0.00000	0.00000	.36616
38	0.00000	0.00000	0.00000	0.00000	0.00000	0.00000	0.00000	0.00000	0.00000	.26207
39	0.00000	0.00000	0.00000	0.00000	0.00000	0.00000	0.00000	0.00000	0.00000	.14094

REMAINING MORTGAGE BALANCE TABLE FOR 15.500 PERCENT

ORIGINAL LOAN TERM

AGE OF LOAN	1	2	3	4	5	6	7	8	9	10
1	0.00000	.53843	.71649	.80448	.85645	.89042	.91413	.93143	.94448	.95457
2	0.00000	0.00000	.38578	.57640	.68899	.76260	.81396	.85145	.87972	.90158
3	0.00000	0.00000	0.00000	.31035	.49366	.61349	.69711	.75815	.80418	.83976
4	0.00000	0.00000	0.00000	0.00000	.26580	.43956	.56081	.64932	.71606	.76765
5	0.00000	0.00000	0.00000	0.00000	0.00000	.23667	.40182	.52236	.61327	.68353
6	0.00000	0.00000	0.00000	0.00000	0.00000	0.00000	.21635	.37427	.49336	.58541
7	0.00000	0.00000	0.00000	0.00000	0.00000	0.00000	0.00000	.20151	.35349	.47095
8	0.00000	0.00000	0.00000	0.00000	0.00000	0.00000	0.00000	0.00000	.19033	.33743
9	0.00000	0.00000	0.00000	0.00000	0.00000	0.00000	0.00000	0.00000	0.00000	.18168

AGE OF LOAN	11	12	13	14	15	20	25	30	35	40
1	.96251	.96887	.97400	.97820	.98165	.99198	.99638	.99834	.99924	.99965
2	.91879	.93255	.94368	.95277	.96025	.98263	.99216	.99641	.99835	.99924
3	.86778	.89018	.90830	.92310	.93529	.97171	.98723	.99416	.99731	.99876
4	.80828	.84076	.86704	.88850	.90617	.95898	.98149	.99153	.99610	.99820
5	.73887	.78311	.81890	.84814	.87220	.94414	.97479	.98846	.99469	.99755
6	.65791	.71587	.76275	.80105	.83258	.92681	.96697	.98488	.99304	.99678
7	.56346	.63742	.69726	.74613	.78635	.90661	.95785	.98071	.99112	.99590
8	.45329	.54592	.62085	.68205	.73244	.88304	.94721	.97584	.98887	.99486
9	.32478	.43918	.53173	.60732	.66954	.85555	.93480	.97016	.98626	.99365
10	.17487	.31467	.42776	.52013	.59617	.82348	.92033	.96354	.98321	.99224
11	0.00000	.16943	.30649	.41844	.51059	.78606	.90345	.95581	.97965	.99060
12	0.00000	0.00000	.16502	.29981	.41076	.74243	.88375	.94680	.97550	.98868
13	0.00000	0.00000	0.00000	.16142	.29431	.69152	.86078	.93628	.97066	.98645
14	0.00000	0.00000	0.00000	0.00000	.15846	.63214	.83398	.92402	.96501	.98384
15	0.00000	0.00000	0.00000	0.00000	0.00000	.56287	.80271	.90971	.95842	.98080
16	0.00000	0.00000	0.00000	0.00000	0.00000	.48207	.76625	.89302	.95073	.97725
17	0.00000	0.00000	0.00000	0.00000	0.00000	.38781	.72371	.87355	.94177	.97310
18	0.00000	0.00000	0.00000	0.00000	0.00000	.27786	.67408	.85084	.93131	.96827
19	0.00000	0.00000	0.00000	0.00000	0.00000	.14961	.61620	.82435	.91911	.96264
20	0.00000	0.00000	0.00000	0.00000	0.00000	0.00000	.54868	.79345	.90488	.95607
21	0.00000	0.00000	0.00000	0.00000	0.00000	0.00000	.46991	.75740	.88828	.94840
22	0.00000	0.00000	0.00000	0.00000	0.00000	0.00000	.37803	.71536	.86891	.93946
23	0.00000	0.00000	0.00000	0.00000	0.00000	0.00000	.27086	.66631	.84632	.92902
24	0.00000	0.00000	0.00000	0.00000	0.00000	0.00000	.14584	.60909	.81997	.91685
25	0.00000	0.00000	0.00000	0.00000	0.00000	0.00000	0.00000	.54235	.78923	.90266
26	0.00000	0.00000	0.00000	0.00000	0.00000	0.00000	0.00000	.46449	.75338	.88610
27	0.00000	0.00000	0.00000	0.00000	0.00000	0.00000	0.00000	.37367	.71155	.86678
28	0.00000	0.00000	0.00000	0.00000	0.00000	0.00000	0.00000	.26773	.66277	.84424
29	0.00000	0.00000	0.00000	0.00000	0.00000	0.00000	0.00000	.14415	.60585	.81796
30	0.00000	0.00000	0.00000	0.00000	0.00000	0.00000	0.00000	0.00000	.53946	.78730
31	0.00000	0.00000	0.00000	0.00000	0.00000	0.00000	0.00000	0.00000	.46202	.75153
32	0.00000	0.00000	0.00000	0.00000	0.00000	0.00000	0.00000	0.00000	.37169	.70981
33	0.00000	0.00000	0.00000	0.00000	0.00000	0.00000	0.00000	0.00000	.26631	.66114
34	0.00000	0.00000	0.00000	0.00000	0.00000	0.00000	0.00000	0.00000	.14339	.60437
35	0.00000	0.00000	0.00000	0.00000	0.00000	0.00000	0.00000	0.00000	0.00000	.53814
36	0.00000	0.00000	0.00000	0.00000	0.00000	0.00000	0.00000	0.00000	0.00000	.46089
37	0.00000	0.00000	0.00000	0.00000	0.00000	0.00000	0.00000	0.00000	0.00000	.37077
38	0.00000	0.00000	0.00000	0.00000	0.00000	0.00000	0.00000	0.00000	0.00000	.26566
39	0.00000	0.00000	0.00000	0.00000	0.00000	0.00000	0.00000	0.00000	0.00000	.14304

REMAINING MORTGAGE BALANCE TABLE FOR 15.750 PERCENT

ORIGINAL LOAN TERM

AGE OF LOAN	1	2	3	4	5	6	7	8	9	10
1	0.00000	.53904	.71726	.80529	.85726	.89122	.91489	.93216	.94516	.95521
2	0.00000	0.00000	.38663	.57761	.69035	.76401	.81536	.85282	.88104	.90283
3	0.00000	0.00000	0.00000	.31135	.49516	.61525	.69898	.76005	.80606	.84158
4	0.00000	0.00000	0.00000	0.00000	.26691	.44129	.56288	.65156	.71837	.76995
5	0.00000	0.00000	0.00000	0.00000	0.00000	.23787	.40374	.52470	.61583	.68619
6	0.00000	0.00000	0.00000	0.00000	0.00000	0.00000	.21763	.37634	.49592	.58825
7	0.00000	0.00000	0.00000	0.00000	0.00000	0.00000	0.00000	.20286	.35571	.47371
8	0.00000	0.00000	0.00000	0.00000	0.00000	0.00000	0.00000	0.00000	.19174	.33977
9	0.00000	0.00000	0.00000	0.00000	0.00000	0.00000	0.00000	0.00000	0.00000	.18315

AGE OF LOAN	11	12	13	14	15	20	25	30	35	40
1	.96311	.96942	.97451	.97867	.98209	.99225	.99654	.99844	.99929	.99968
2	.91997	.93365	.94471	.95373	.96114	.98319	.99250	.99661	.99846	.99930
3	.86952	.89183	.90986	.92456	.93664	.97260	.98777	.99447	.99748	.99885
4	.81053	.84293	.86910	.89045	.90800	.96021	.98224	.99197	.99635	.99833
5	.74155	.78574	.82145	.85057	.87450	.94572	.97578	.98904	.99501	.99773
6	.66088	.71887	.76572	.80393	.83533	.92878	.96822	.98563	.99346	.99702
7	.56655	.64067	.70055	.74938	.78952	.90897	.95938	.98163	.99164	.99619
8	.45623	.54922	.62434	.68560	.73596	.88580	.94904	.97695	.98951	.99521
9	.32724	.44228	.53522	.61102	.67332	.85871	.93695	.97148	.98702	.99408
10	.17639	.31723	.43101	.52381	.60008	.82703	.92282	.96509	.98411	.99275
11	0.00000	.17100	.30915	.42182	.51442	.78999	.90628	.95761	.93071	.99120
12	0.00000	0.00000	.16664	.30255	.41426	.74667	.88695	.94887	.97673	.98938
13	0.00000	0.00000	0.00000	.16309	.29713	.69601	.86435	.93864	.97208	.98726
14	0.00000	0.00000	0.00000	0.00000	.16017	.63678	.83791	.92669	.96664	.98478
15	0.00000	0.00000	0.00000	0.00000	0.00000	.56750	.80700	.91271	.96028	.98188
16	0.00000	0.00000	0.00000	0.00000	0.00000	.48650	.77086	.89636	.95284	.97848
17	0.00000	0.00000	0.00000	0.00000	0.00000	.39177	.72859	.87724	.94414	.97451
18	0.00000	0.00000	0.00000	0.00000	0.00000	.28101	.67915	.85488	.93396	.96987
19	0.00000	0.00000	0.00000	0.00000	0.00000	.15147	.62135	.82873	.92207	.96444
20	0.00000	0.00000	0.00000	0.00000	0.00000	0.00000	.55376	.79816	.90816	.95809
21	0.00000	0.00000	0.00000	0.00000	0.00000	0.00000	.47472	.76241	.89189	.95067
22	0.00000	0.00000	0.00000	0.00000	0.00000	0.00000	.38229	.72060	.87286	.94199
23	0.00000	0.00000	0.00000	0.00000	0.00000	0.00000	.27420	.67171	.85062	.93184
24	0.00000	0.00000	0.00000	0.00000	0.00000	0.00000	.14780	.61455	.82460	.91997
25	0.00000	0.00000	0.00000	0.00000	0.00000	0.00000	0.00000	.54769	.79418	.90609
26	0.00000	0.00000	0.00000	0.00000	0.00000	0.00000	0.00000	.46952	.75861	.88986
27	0.00000	0.00000	0.00000	0.00000	0.00000	0.00000	0.00000	.37810	.71701	.87088
28	0.00000	0.00000	0.00000	0.00000	0.00000	0.00000	0.00000	.27119	.66837	.84868
29	0.00000	0.00000	0.00000	0.00000	0.00000	0.00000	0.00000	.14618	.61148	.82273
30	0.00000	0.00000	0.00000	0.00000	0.00000	0.00000	0.00000	0.00000	.54496	.79238
31	0.00000	0.00000	0.00000	0.00000	0.00000	0.00000	0.00000	0.00000	.46718	.75688
32	0.00000	0.00000	0.00000	0.00000	0.00000	0.00000	0.00000	0.00000	.37621	.71538
33	0.00000	0.00000	0.00000	0.00000	0.00000	0.00000	0.00000	0.00000	.26984	.66685
34	0.00000	0.00000	0.00000	0.00000	0.00000	0.00000	0.00000	0.00000	.14546	.61009
35	0.00000	0.00000	0.00000	0.00000	0.00000	0.00000	0.00000	0.00000	0.00000	.54372
36	0.00000	0.00000	0.00000	0.00000	0.00000	0.00000	0.00000	0.00000	0.00000	.46611
37	0.00000	0.00000	0.00000	0.00000	0.00000	0.00000	0.00000	0.00000	0.00000	.37536
38	0.00000	0.00000	0.00000	0.00000	0.00000	0.00000	0.00000	0.00000	0.00000	.26923
39	0.00000	0.00000	0.00000	0.00000	0.00000	0.00000	0.00000	0.00000	0.00000	.14513

REMAINING MORTGAGE BALANCE TABLE FOR 16.000 PERCENT

ORIGINAL LOAN TERM

AGE OF LOAN	1	2	3	4	5	6	7	8	9	10
1	0.00000	.53965	.71803	.80611	.85807	.89201	.91565	.93287	.94584	.95584
2	0.00000	0.00000	.38749	.57881	.69170	.76541	.81676	.85418	.88235	.90407
3	0.00000	0.00000	0.00000	.31236	.49566	.61700	.70084	.76194	.80792	.84338
4	0.00000	0.00000	0.00000	0.00000	.26802	.44302	.56495	.65380	.72067	.77224
5	0.00000	0.00000	0.00000	0.00000	0.00000	.23908	.40565	.52703	.61839	.68884
6	0.00000	0.00000	0.00000	0.00000	0.00000	0.00000	.21891	.37842	.49848	.59108
7	0.00000	0.00000	0.00000	0.00000	0.00000	0.00000	0.00000	.20422	.35793	.47647
8	0.00000	0.00000	0.00000	0.00000	0.00000	0.00000	0.00000	0.00000	.19316	.34212
9	0.00000	0.00000	0.00000	0.00000	0.00000	0.00000	0.00000	0.00000	0.00000	.18463

AGE OF LOAN	11	12	13	14	15	20	25	30	35	40
1	.96370	.96996	.97502	.97913	.98251	.99252	.99670	.99852	.99934	.99970
2	.92114	.93475	.94573	.95467	.96201	.98374	.99283	.99679	.99856	.99935
3	.87125	.89347	.91139	.92599	.93797	.97346	.98829	.99477	.99765	.99894
4	.81276	.84508	.87115	.89238	.90980	.96140	.98297	.99239	.99658	.99846
5	.74420	.78835	.82396	.85297	.87677	.94727	.97674	.98960	.99532	.99789
6	.66383	.72185	.76865	.80677	.83805	.93070	.96943	.98633	.99386	.99723
7	.56962	.64389	.70382	.75261	.79266	.91128	.96086	.98250	.99213	.99645
8	.45917	.55251	.62781	.68913	.73945	.88851	.95081	.97801	.99011	.99554
9	.32970	.44538	.53870	.61471	.67708	.86182	.93904	.97275	.98775	.99448
10	.17792	.31980	.43425	.52746	.60395	.83054	.92523	.96658	.98497	.99323
11	0.00000	.17258	.31181	.42519	.51824	.79386	.90905	.95934	.98172	.99176
12	0.00000	0.00000	.16827	.30530	.41775	.75086	.89008	.95086	.97791	.99004
13	0.00000	0.00000	0.00000	.16476	.29996	.70046	.86784	.94092	.97344	.98803
14	0.00000	0.00000	0.00000	0.00000	.16187	.64137	.84177	.92927	.96820	.98567
15	0.00000	0.00000	0.00000	0.00000	0.00000	.57211	.81121	.91561	.96206	.98290
16	0.00000	0.00000	0.00000	0.00000	0.00000	.49091	.77539	.89960	.95486	.97965
17	0.00000	0.00000	0.00000	0.00000	0.00000	.39573	.73339	.88082	.94642	.97585
18	0.00000	0.00000	0.00000	0.00000	0.00000	.28414	.68416	.85882	.93652	.97139
19	0.00000	0.00000	0.00000	0.00000	0.00000	.15334	.62645	.83302	.92493	.96616
20	0.00000	0.00000	0.00000	0.00000	0.00000	0.00000	.55880	.80278	.91133	.96003
21	0.00000	0.00000	0.00000	0.00000	0.00000	0.00000	.47949	.76733	.89539	.95285
22	0.00000	0.00000	0.00000	0.00000	0.00000	0.00000	.38652	.72577	.87670	.94442
23	0.00000	0.00000	0.00000	0.00000	0.00000	0.00000	.27753	.67705	.85480	.93455
24	0.00000	0.00000	0.00000	0.00000	0.00000	0.00000	.14977	.61994	.82912	.92298
25	0.00000	0.00000	0.00000	0.00000	0.00000	0.00000	0.00000	.55299	.79902	.90941
26	0.00000	0.00000	0.00000	0.00000	0.00000	0.00000	0.00000	.47450	.76374	.89350
27	0.00000	0.00000	0.00000	0.00000	0.00000	0.00000	0.00000	.38250	.72237	.87486
28	0.00000	0.00000	0.00000	0.00000	0.00000	0.00000	0.00000	.27465	.67388	.85300
29	0.00000	0.00000	0.00000	0.00000	0.00000	0.00000	0.00000	.14521	.61704	.82738
30	0.00000	0.00000	0.00000	0.00000	0.00000	0.00000	0.00000	0.00000	.55040	.79734
31	0.00000	0.00000	0.00000	0.00000	0.00000	0.00000	0.00000	0.00000	.47229	.76213
32	0.00000	0.00000	0.00000	0.00000	0.00000	0.00000	0.00000	0.00000	.38071	.72085
33	0.00000	0.00000	0.00000	0.00000	0.00000	0.00000	0.00000	0.00000	.27336	.67246
34	0.00000	0.00000	0.00000	0.00000	0.00000	0.00000	0.00000	0.00000	.14752	.61574
35	0.00000	0.00000	0.00000	0.00000	0.00000	0.00000	0.00000	0.00000	0.00000	.54924
36	0.00000	0.00000	0.00000	0.00000	0.00000	0.00000	0.00000	0.00000	0.00000	.47129
37	0.00000	0.00000	0.00000	0.00000	0.00000	0.00000	0.00000	0.00000	0.00000	.37991
38	0.00000	0.00000	0.00000	0.00000	0.00000	0.00000	0.00000	0.00000	0.00000	.27279
39	0.00000	0.00000	0.00000	0.00000	0.00000	0.00000	0.00000	0.00000	0.00000	.14721

REMAINING MORTGAGE BALANCE TABLE FOR 16.250 PERCENT

ORIGINAL LOAN TERM

AGE OF LOAN	1	2	3	4	5	6	7	8	9	10
1	0.00000	.54027	.71880	.80692	.85888	.89279	.91640	.93358	.94651	.95646
2	0.00000	0.00000	.38834	.58001	.69305	.76680	.81815	.85554	.88364	.90530
3	0.00000	0.00000	0.00000	.31336	.49816	.61875	.70270	.76381	.80977	.84517
4	0.00000	0.00000	0.00000	0.00000	.26914	.44475	.56702	.65603	.72296	.77451
5	0.00000	0.00000	0.00000	0.00000	0.00000	.24029	.40757	.52936	.62093	.69148
6	0.00000	0.00000	0.00000	0.00000	0.00000	0.00000	.22020	.38050	.50104	.59390
7	0.00000	0.00000	0.00000	0.00000	0.00000	0.00000	0.00000	.20557	.36015	.47923
8	0.00000	0.00000	0.00000	0.00000	0.00000	0.00000	0.00000	0.00000	.19458	.34447
9	0.00000	0.00000	0.00000	0.00000	0.00000	0.00000	0.00000	0.00000	0.00000	.18610

AGE OF LOAN	11	12	13	14	15	20	25	30	35	40
1	.96428	.97050	.97551	.97959	.98293	.99277	.99685	.99861	.99938	.99972
2	.92229	.93583	.94673	.95560	.96286	.98428	.99314	.99697	.99865	.99940
3	.87296	.89508	.91291	.92740	.93928	.97430	.98879	.99505	.99780	.99902
4	.81498	.84720	.87316	.89427	.91157	.96256	.98367	.99279	.99680	.99857
5	.74685	.79094	.82645	.85534	.87900	.94878	.97766	.99013	.99562	.99805
6	.66678	.72481	.77157	.80958	.84073	.93258	.97059	.98701	.99423	.99743
7	.57268	.64711	.70706	.75581	.79576	.91354	.96229	.98334	.99260	.99670
8	.46211	.55579	.63126	.69263	.74291	.89117	.95253	.97903	.99068	.99585
9	.33216	.44847	.54218	.61837	.68080	.86488	.94106	.97396	.98843	.99485
10	.17946	.32236	.43749	.53111	.60781	.83398	.92758	.96801	.98579	.99367
11	0.00000	.17416	.31447	.42856	.52204	.79767	.91174	.96101	.98268	.99229
12	0.00000	0.00000	.16990	.30805	.42124	.75500	.89313	.95279	.97903	.99066
13	0.00000	0.00000	0.00000	.16643	.30279	.70486	.87126	.94313	.97474	.98875
14	0.00000	0.00000	0.00000	0.00000	.16359	.64593	.84555	.93177	.96969	.98650
15	0.00000	0.00000	0.00000	0.00000	0.00000	.57668	.81535	.91843	.96376	.98386
16	0.00000	0.00000	0.00000	0.00000	0.00000	.49530	.77985	.90274	.95680	.98076
17	0.00000	0.00000	0.00000	0.00000	0.00000	.39967	.73813	.88431	.94861	.97712
18	0.00000	0.00000	0.00000	0.00000	0.00000	.28728	.68911	.86266	.93899	.97283
19	0.00000	0.00000	0.00000	0.00000	0.00000	.15521	.63150	.83721	.92768	.96780
20	0.00000	0.00000	0.00000	0.00000	0.00000	0.00000	.56380	.80730	.91440	.96188
21	0.00000	0.00000	0.00000	0.00000	0.00000	0.00000	.48423	.77215	.89879	.95493
22	0.00000	0.00000	0.00000	0.00000	0.00000	0.00000	.39074	.73085	.88044	.94676
23	0.00000	0.00000	0.00000	0.00000	0.00000	0.00000	.28086	.68231	.85888	.93716
24	0.00000	0.00000	0.00000	0.00000	0.00000	0.00000	.15174	.62526	.83354	.92587
25	0.00000	0.00000	0.00000	0.00000	0.00000	0.00000	0.00000	.55823	.80376	.91261
26	0.00000	0.00000	0.00000	0.00000	0.00000	0.00000	0.00000	.47945	.76876	.89703
27	0.00000	0.00000	0.00000	0.00000	0.00000	0.00000	0.00000	.38688	.72764	.87872
28	0.00000	0.00000	0.00000	0.00000	0.00000	0.00000	0.00000	.27809	.67931	.85720
29	0.00000	0.00000	0.00000	0.00000	0.00000	0.00000	0.00000	.15024	.62252	.83191
30	0.00000	0.00000	0.00000	0.00000	0.00000	0.00000	0.00000	0.00000	.55578	.80219
31	0.00000	0.00000	0.00000	0.00000	0.00000	0.00000	0.00000	0.00000	.47735	.76726
32	0.00000	0.00000	0.00000	0.00000	0.00000	0.00000	0.00000	0.00000	.38518	.72622
33	0.00000	0.00000	0.00000	0.00000	0.00000	0.00000	0.00000	0.00000	.27687	.67799
34	0.00000	0.00000	0.00000	0.00000	0.00000	0.00000	0.00000	0.00000	.14958	.62131
35	0.00000	0.00000	0.00000	0.00000	0.00000	0.00000	0.00000	0.00000	0.00000	.55470
36	0.00000	0.00000	0.00000	0.00000	0.00000	0.00000	0.00000	0.00000	0.00000	.47642
37	0.00000	0.00000	0.00000	0.00000	0.00000	0.00000	0.00000	0.00000	0.00000	.38443
38	0.00000	0.00000	0.00000	0.00000	0.00000	0.00000	0.00000	0.00000	0.00000	.27633
39	0.00000	0.00000	0.00000	0.00000	0.00000	0.00000	0.00000	0.00000	0.00000	.14929

REMAINING MORTGAGE BALANCE TABLE FOR 16.500 PERCENT

AGE OF LOAN	ORIGINAL LOAN TERM 1	2	3	4	5	6	7	8	9	10
1	0.00000	.54088	.71957	.80773	.85969	.89357	.91714	.93429	.94717	.95708
2	0.00000	0.00000	.38920	.58121	.69439	.76819	.81954	.85688	.88493	.90652
3	0.00000	0.00000	0.00000	.31436	.49966	.62049	.70455	.76568	.81161	.84695
4	0.00000	0.00000	0.00000	0.00000	.27026	.44648	.56908	.65825	.72523	.77677
5	0.00000	0.00000	0.00000	0.00000	0.00000	.24149	.40949	.53168	.62347	.69410
6	0.00000	0.00000	0.00000	0.00000	0.00000	0.00000	.22148	.38258	.50360	.59671
7	0.00000	0.00000	0.00000	0.00000	0.00000	0.00000	0.00000	.20693	.36237	.48198
8	0.00000	0.00000	0.00000	0.00000	0.00000	0.00000	0.00000	0.00000	.19600	.34682
9	0.00000	0.00000	0.00000	0.00000	0.00000	0.00000	0.00000	0.00000	0.00000	.18759

AGE OF LOAN	11	12	13	14	15	20	25	30	35	40
1	.96485	.97103	.97600	.98003	.98333	.99302	.99699	.99869	.99942	.99975
2	.92344	.93689	.94772	.95651	.96370	.98480	.99344	.99714	.99874	.99945
3	.87465	.89668	.91440	.92879	.94056	.97511	.98927	.99531	.99794	.99910
4	.81718	.84931	.87516	.89614	.91331	.96370	.98434	.99316	.99700	.99868
5	.74947	.79350	.82892	.85768	.88121	.95025	.97855	.99063	.99589	.99819
6	.66971	.72775	.77445	.81237	.84338	.93441	.97172	.98765	.99458	.99762
7	.57574	.65030	.71028	.75899	.79883	.91575	.96367	.98414	.99304	.99694
8	.46504	.55906	.63469	.69610	.74634	.89377	.95419	.98000	.99122	.99614
9	.33463	.45156	.54564	.62202	.68450	.86787	.94302	.97512	.98908	.99520
10	.18099	.32493	.44072	.53474	.61165	.83737	.92986	.96938	.98656	.99409
11	0.00000	.17575	.31713	.43192	.52583	.80143	.91436	.96261	.98359	.99278
12	0.00000	0.00000	.17153	.31080	.42472	.75909	.89611	.95464	.98009	.99124
13	0.00000	0.00000	0.00000	.16810	.30562	.70921	.87460	.94525	.97597	.98943
14	0.00000	0.00000	0.00000	0.00000	.16530	.65044	.84925	.93419	.97112	.98729
15	0.00000	0.00000	0.00000	0.00000	0.00000	.58122	.81940	.92115	.96540	.98478
16	0.00000	0.00000	0.00000	0.00000	0.00000	.49967	.78423	.90580	.95866	.98181
17	0.00000	0.00000	0.00000	0.00000	0.00000	.40359	.74230	.88771	.95072	.97832
18	0.00000	0.00000	0.00000	0.00000	0.00000	.29041	.69399	.86640	.94137	.97421
19	0.00000	0.00000	0.00000	0.00000	0.00000	.15708	.63649	.84130	.93035	.96936
20	0.00000	0.00000	0.00000	0.00000	0.00000	0.00000	.56875	.81173	.91737	.96365
21	0.00000	0.00000	0.00000	0.00000	0.00000	0.00000	.48895	.77689	.90208	.95692
22	0.00000	0.00000	0.00000	0.00000	0.00000	0.00000	.39494	.73584	.88406	.94900
23	0.00000	0.00000	0.00000	0.00000	0.00000	0.00000	.28418	.68749	.86284	.93966
24	0.00000	0.00000	0.00000	0.00000	0.00000	0.00000	.15371	.63053	.83784	.92867
25	0.00000	0.00000	0.00000	0.00000	0.00000	0.00000	0.00000	.56342	.80839	.91571
26	0.00000	0.00000	0.00000	0.00000	0.00000	0.00000	0.00000	.48437	.77369	.90045
27	0.00000	0.00000	0.00000	0.00000	0.00000	0.00000	0.00000	.39124	.73282	.88246
28	0.00000	0.00000	0.00000	0.00000	0.00000	0.00000	0.00000	.28152	.68466	.86128
29	0.00000	0.00000	0.00000	0.00000	0.00000	0.00000	0.00000	.15227	.62794	.83633
30	0.00000	0.00000	0.00000	0.00000	0.00000	0.00000	0.00000	0.00000	.56111	.80693
31	0.00000	0.00000	0.00000	0.00000	0.00000	0.00000	0.00000	0.00000	.48238	.77229
32	0.00000	0.00000	0.00000	0.00000	0.00000	0.00000	0.00000	0.00000	.38963	.73149
33	0.00000	0.00000	0.00000	0.00000	0.00000	0.00000	0.00000	0.00000	.28036	.68343
34	0.00000	0.00000	0.00000	0.00000	0.00000	0.00000	0.00000	0.00000	.15164	.62680
35	0.00000	0.00000	0.00000	0.00000	0.00000	0.00000	0.00000	0.00000	0.00000	.56009
36	0.00000	0.00000	0.00000	0.00000	0.00000	0.00000	0.00000	0.00000	0.00000	.48150
37	0.00000	0.00000	0.00000	0.00000	0.00000	0.00000	0.00000	0.00000	0.00000	.38892
38	0.00000	0.00000	0.00000	0.00000	0.00000	0.00000	0.00000	0.00000	0.00000	.27986
39	0.00000	0.00000	0.00000	0.00000	0.00000	0.00000	0.00000	0.00000	0.00000	.15137

REMAINING MORTGAGE BALANCE TABLE FOR 16.750 PERCENT

ORIGINAL LOAN TERM

AGE OF LOAN	1	2	3	4	5	6	7	8	9	10
1	0.00000	.54149	.72033	.80853	.86049	.89435	.91789	.93499	.94782	.95769
2	0.00000	0.00000	.39005	.58241	.69573	.76958	.82091	.85821	.88621	.90772
3	0.00000	0.00000	0.00000	.31537	.50116	.62223	.70639	.76754	.81344	.84871
4	0.00000	0.00000	0.00000	0.00000	.27137	.44821	.57114	.66046	.72750	.77932
5	0.00000	0.00000	0.00000	0.00000	0.00000	.24270	.41141	.53401	.62600	.69672
6	0.00000	0.00000	0.00000	0.00000	0.00000	0.00000	.22277	.38466	.50614	.59952
7	0.00000	0.00000	0.00000	0.00000	0.00000	0.00000	0.00000	.20829	.36459	.48473
8	0.00000	0.00000	0.00000	0.00000	0.00000	0.00000	0.00000	0.00000	.19742	.34917
9	0.00000	0.00000	0.00000	0.00000	0.00000	0.00000	0.00000	0.00000	0.00000	.18907

AGE OF LOAN	11	12	13	14	15	20	25	30	35	40
1	.96541	.97155	.97647	.98047	.98373	.99326	.99713	.99876	.99946	.99977
2	.92456	.93794	.94869	.95740	.96452	.98530	.99373	.99730	.99883	.99949
3	.87633	.89826	.91588	.93016	.94182	.97590	.98972	.99557	.99808	.99916
4	.81936	.85139	.87712	.89799	.91502	.96480	.98499	.99352	.99719	.99878
5	.75207	.79604	.83136	.85999	.88338	.95169	.97940	.99111	.99615	.99833
6	.67262	.73068	.77731	.81512	.84600	.93620	.97280	.98827	.99491	.99779
7	.57878	.65348	.71348	.76213	.80186	.91792	.96500	.98490	.99345	.99715
8	.46796	.56231	.63811	.69955	.74973	.89632	.95580	.98093	.99173	.99641
9	.33709	.45465	.54908	.62564	.68817	.87082	.94492	.97624	.98970	.99552
10	.18253	.32750	.44395	.53836	.61546	.84070	.93208	.97070	.98729	.99448
11	0.00000	.17734	.31979	.43528	.52960	.80513	.91692	.96416	.98446	.99325
12	0.00000	0.00000	.17316	.31355	.42820	.76312	.89901	.95643	.98111	.99179
13	0.00000	0.00000	0.00000	.16978	.30845	.71351	.87786	.94730	.97715	.99007
14	0.00000	0.00000	0.00000	0.00000	.16702	.65492	.85288	.93653	.97248	.98804
15	0.00000	0.00000	0.00000	0.00000	0.00000	.58573	.82338	.92380	.96696	.98564
16	0.00000	0.00000	0.00000	0.00000	0.00000	.50401	.78854	.90877	.96044	.98281
17	0.00000	0.00000	0.00000	0.00000	0.00000	.40751	.74740	.89102	.95274	.97946
18	0.00000	0.00000	0.00000	0.00000	0.00000	.29354	.69881	.87006	.94365	.97551
19	0.00000	0.00000	0.00000	0.00000	0.00000	.15895	.64143	.84530	.93292	.97085
20	0.00000	0.00000	0.00000	0.00000	0.00000	0.00000	.57366	.81606	.92024	.96534
21	0.00000	0.00000	0.00000	0.00000	0.00000	0.00000	.49363	.78153	.90527	.95883
22	0.00000	0.00000	0.00000	0.00000	0.00000	0.00000	.39912	.74076	.88759	.95115
23	0.00000	0.00000	0.00000	0.00000	0.00000	0.00000	.28750	.69260	.86670	.94207
24	0.00000	0.00000	0.00000	0.00000	0.00000	0.00000	.15568	.63573	.84204	.93136
25	0.00000	0.00000	0.00000	0.00000	0.00000	0.00000	0.00000	.56856	.81292	.91870
26	0.00000	0.00000	0.00000	0.00000	0.00000	0.00000	0.00000	.48924	.77852	.90375
27	0.00000	0.00000	0.00000	0.00000	0.00000	0.00000	0.00000	.39557	.73790	.88610
28	0.00000	0.00000	0.00000	0.00000	0.00000	0.00000	0.00000	.28494	.68993	.86525
29	0.00000	0.00000	0.00000	0.00000	0.00000	0.00000	0.00000	.15429	.63328	.84063
30	0.00000	0.00000	0.00000	0.00000	0.00000	0.00000	0.00000	0.00000	.56637	.81156
31	0.00000	0.00000	0.00000	0.00000	0.00000	0.00000	0.00000	0.00000	.48736	.77722
32	0.00000	0.00000	0.00000	0.00000	0.00000	0.00000	0.00000	0.00000	.39404	.73667
33	0.00000	0.00000	0.00000	0.00000	0.00000	0.00000	0.00000	0.00000	.28384	.68878
34	0.00000	0.00000	0.00000	0.00000	0.00000	0.00000	0.00000	0.00000	.15370	.63222
35	0.00000	0.00000	0.00000	0.00000	0.00000	0.00000	0.00000	0.00000	0.00000	.56542
36	0.00000	0.00000	0.00000	0.00000	0.00000	0.00000	0.00000	0.00000	0.00000	.48654
37	0.00000	0.00000	0.00000	0.00000	0.00000	0.00000	0.00000	0.00000	0.00000	.39339
38	0.00000	0.00000	0.00000	0.00000	0.00000	0.00000	0.00000	0.00000	0.00000	.28337
39	0.00000	0.00000	0.00000	0.00000	0.00000	0.00000	0.00000	0.00000	0.00000	.15344

REMAINING MORTGAGE BALANCE TABLE FOR 17.000 PERCENT

ORIGINAL LOAN TERM

AGE OF LOAN	1	2	3	4	5	6	7	8	9	10
1	0.00000	.54210	.72110	.80934	.86129	.89512	.91862	.93568	.94847	.95829
2	0.00000	0.00000	.39091	.58361	.69707	.77096	.82228	.85954	.88747	.90891
3	0.00000	0.00000	0.00000	.31638	.50266	.62397	.70822	.76940	.81525	.85046
4	0.00000	0.00000	0.00000	0.00000	.27249	.44994	.57319	.66267	.72975	.78125
5	0.00000	0.00000	0.00000	0.00000	0.00000	.24391	.41333	.53633	.62853	.69931
6	0.00000	0.00000	0.00000	0.00000	0.00000	0.00000	.22407	.38674	.50869	.60231
7	0.00000	0.00000	0.00000	0.00000	0.00000	0.00000	0.00000	.20965	.36682	.48747
8	0.00000	0.00000	0.00000	0.00000	0.00000	0.00000	0.00000	0.00000	.19885	.35152
9	0.00000	0.00000	0.00000	0.00000	0.00000	0.00000	0.00000	0.00000	0.00000	.19056

AGE OF LOAN	11	12	13	14	15	20	25	30	35	40
1	.96597	.97206	.97694	.98090	.98412	.99349	.99726	.99883	.99950	.99978
2	.92568	.93898	.94965	.95828	.96532	.98579	.99401	.99745	.99891	.99953
3	.87798	.89982	.91733	.93150	.94306	.97667	.99017	.99581	.99820	.99923
4	.82152	.85345	.87907	.89980	.91671	.96587	.98561	.99387	.99737	.99887
5	.75466	.79856	.83377	.86228	.88552	.95308	.98023	.99157	.99639	.99845
6	.67552	.73358	.78015	.81784	.84858	.93795	.97385	.98885	.99522	.99795
7	.58182	.65664	.71666	.76524	.80486	.92003	.96630	.98563	.99384	.99736
8	.47088	.56556	.64150	.70297	.75309	.89882	.95735	.98182	.99221	.99666
9	.33955	.45773	.55252	.62925	.69181	.87370	.94677	.97731	.99028	.99583
10	.18407	.33007	.44717	.54196	.61925	.84397	.93424	.97196	.98799	.99484
11	0.00000	.17893	.32246	.43863	.53336	.80877	.91940	.96564	.98528	.99368
12	0.00000	0.00000	.17480	.31630	.43167	.76710	.90184	.95815	.98207	.99230
13	0.00000	0.00000	0.00000	.17146	.31127	.71776	.88104	.94928	.97827	.99067
14	0.00000	0.00000	0.00000	0.00000	.16874	.65935	.85643	.93879	.97378	.98874
15	0.00000	0.00000	0.00000	0.00000	0.00000	.59020	.82728	.92636	.96845	.98646
16	0.00000	0.00000	0.00000	0.00000	0.00000	.50833	.79278	.91165	.96215	.98375
17	0.00000	0.00000	0.00000	0.00000	0.00000	.41141	.75193	.89424	.95469	.98055
18	0.00000	0.00000	0.00000	0.00000	0.00000	.29667	.70357	.87362	.94586	.97676
19	0.00000	0.00000	0.00000	0.00000	0.00000	.16083	.64631	.84921	.93540	.97227
20	0.00000	0.00000	0.00000	0.00000	0.00000	0.00000	.57853	.82031	.92302	.96695
21	0.00000	0.00000	0.00000	0.00000	0.00000	0.00000	.49828	.78609	.90836	.96066
22	0.00000	0.00000	0.00000	0.00000	0.00000	0.00000	.40328	.74559	.89101	.95321
23	0.00000	0.00000	0.00000	0.00000	0.00000	0.00000	.29080	.69764	.87046	.94439
24	0.00000	0.00000	0.00000	0.00000	0.00000	0.00000	.15764	.64086	.84614	.93395
25	0.00000	0.00000	0.00000	0.00000	0.00000	0.00000	0.00000	.57365	.81734	.92159
26	0.00000	0.00000	0.00000	0.00000	0.00000	0.00000	0.00000	.49408	.78326	.90695
27	0.00000	0.00000	0.00000	0.00000	0.00000	0.00000	0.00000	.39988	.74290	.88962
28	0.00000	0.00000	0.00000	0.00000	0.00000	0.00000	0.00000	.28835	.69512	.86911
29	0.00000	0.00000	0.00000	0.00000	0.00000	0.00000	0.00000	.15632	.63855	.84483
30	0.00000	0.00000	0.00000	0.00000	0.00000	0.00000	0.00000	0.00000	.57158	.81608
31	0.00000	0.00000	0.00000	0.00000	0.00000	0.00000	0.00000	0.00000	.49230	.78204
32	0.00000	0.00000	0.00000	0.00000	0.00000	0.00000	0.00000	0.00000	.39843	.74174
33	0.00000	0.00000	0.00000	0.00000	0.00000	0.00000	0.00000	0.00000	.28731	.69404
34	0.00000	0.00000	0.00000	0.00000	0.00000	0.00000	0.00000	0.00000	.15575	.63756
35	0.00000	0.00000	0.00000	0.00000	0.00000	0.00000	0.00000	0.00000	0.00000	.57069
36	0.00000	0.00000	0.00000	0.00000	0.00000	0.00000	0.00000	0.00000	0.00000	.49153
37	0.00000	0.00000	0.00000	0.00000	0.00000	0.00000	0.00000	0.00000	0.00000	.39782
38	0.00000	0.00000	0.00000	0.00000	0.00000	0.00000	0.00000	0.00000	0.00000	.28686
39	0.00000	0.00000	0.00000	0.00000	0.00000	0.00000	0.00000	0.00000	0.00000	.15551

REMAINING MORTGAGE BALANCE TABLE FOR 17.250 PERCENT

ORIGINAL LOAN TERM

AGE OF LOAN	1	2	3	4	5	6	7	8	9	10
1	0.00000	.54271	.72186	.81014	.86209	.89589	.91935	.93637	.94912	.95889
2	0.00000	0.00000	.39176	.58481	.69841	.77234	.82364	.86086	.88873	.91010
3	0.00000	0.00000	0.00000	.31738	.50416	.62570	.71005	.77124	.81705	.85219
4	0.00000	0.00000	0.00000	0.00000	.27361	.45167	.57524	.66487	.73199	.78346
5	0.00000	0.00000	0.00000	0.00000	0.00000	.24513	.41524	.53864	.63104	.70190
6	0.00000	0.00000	0.00000	0.00000	0.00000	0.00000	.22536	.38882	.51123	.60510
7	0.00000	0.00000	0.00000	0.00000	0.00000	0.00000	0.00000	.21102	.36904	.49021
8	0.00000	0.00000	0.00000	0.00000	0.00000	0.00000	0.00000	0.00000	.20028	.35387
9	0.00000	0.00000	0.00000	0.00000	0.00000	0.00000	0.00000	0.00000	0.00000	.19205

AGE OF LOAN	11	12	13	14	15	20	25	30	35	40
1	.96652	.97256	.97740	.98132	.98450	.99372	.99738	.99890	.99953	.99980
2	.92678	.94000	.95059	.95914	.96611	.98626	.99428	.99759	.99898	.99957
3	.87963	.90136	.91876	.93283	.94428	.97741	.99059	.99604	.99832	.99929
4	.82366	.85549	.88099	.90160	.91837	.96691	.98621	.99419	.99754	.99896
5	.75723	.80106	.83616	.86453	.88762	.95445	.98102	.99200	.99662	.99856
6	.67840	.73646	.78296	.82054	.85113	.93965	.97486	.98941	.99552	.99810
7	.58484	.65979	.71982	.76833	.80782	.92210	.96754	.98633	.99421	.99755
8	.47380	.56879	.64488	.70637	.75642	.90126	.95886	.98267	.99266	.99689
9	.34202	.46080	.55594	.63283	.69542	.87654	.94856	.97833	.99083	.99611
10	.18562	.33263	.45039	.54555	.62302	.84719	.93633	.97318	.98865	.99518
11	0.00000	.18053	.32512	.44197	.53710	.81236	.92182	.96706	.98606	.99409
12	0.00000	0.00000	.17645	.31904	.43512	.77102	.90460	.95981	.98299	.99278
13	0.00000	0.00000	0.00000	.17315	.31410	.72196	.88416	.95119	.97934	.99124
14	0.00000	0.00000	0.00000	0.00000	.17047	.66374	.85990	.94097	.97502	.98940
15	0.00000	0.00000	0.00000	0.00000	0.00000	.59464	.83111	.92884	.96988	.98723
16	0.00000	0.00000	0.00000	0.00000	0.00000	.51263	.79694	.91445	.96379	.98464
17	0.00000	0.00000	0.00000	0.00000	0.00000	.41530	.75639	.89736	.95656	.98158
18	0.00000	0.00000	0.00000	0.00000	0.00000	.29979	.70826	.87709	.94798	.97794
19	0.00000	0.00000	0.00000	0.00000	0.00000	.16270	.65114	.85302	.93779	.97362
20	0.00000	0.00000	0.00000	0.00000	0.00000	0.00000	.58336	.82446	.92570	.96849
21	0.00000	0.00000	0.00000	0.00000	0.00000	0.00000	.50290	.79057	.91135	.96241
22	0.00000	0.00000	0.00000	0.00000	0.00000	0.00000	.40742	.75034	.89433	.95518
23	0.00000	0.00000	0.00000	0.00000	0.00000	0.00000	.29410	.70260	.87412	.94661
24	0.00000	0.00000	0.00000	0.00000	0.00000	0.00000	.15961	.64594	.85014	.93644
25	0.00000	0.00000	0.00000	0.00000	0.00000	0.00000	0.00000	.57869	.82167	.92437
26	0.00000	0.00000	0.00000	0.00000	0.00000	0.00000	0.00000	.49888	.78789	.91005
27	0.00000	0.00000	0.00000	0.00000	0.00000	0.00000	0.00000	.40416	.74780	.89304
28	0.00000	0.00000	0.00000	0.00000	0.00000	0.00000	0.00000	.29175	.70022	.87286
29	0.00000	0.00000	0.00000	0.00000	0.00000	0.00000	0.00000	.15834	.64375	.84892
30	0.00000	0.00000	0.00000	0.00000	0.00000	0.00000	0.00000	0.00000	.57673	.82049
31	0.00000	0.00000	0.00000	0.00000	0.00000	0.00000	0.00000	0.00000	.49719	.78676
32	0.00000	0.00000	0.00000	0.00000	0.00000	0.00000	0.00000	0.00000	.40280	.74673
33	0.00000	0.00000	0.00000	0.00000	0.00000	0.00000	0.00000	0.00000	.29076	.69922
34	0.00000	0.00000	0.00000	0.00000	0.00000	0.00000	0.00000	0.00000	.15780	.64283
35	0.00000	0.00000	0.00000	0.00000	0.00000	0.00000	0.00000	0.00000	0.00000	.57590
36	0.00000	0.00000	0.00000	0.00000	0.00000	0.00000	0.00000	0.00000	0.00000	.49648
37	0.00000	0.00000	0.00000	0.00000	0.00000	0.00000	0.00000	0.00000	0.00000	.40222
38	0.00000	0.00000	0.00000	0.00000	0.00000	0.00000	0.00000	0.00000	0.00000	.29035
39	0.00000	0.00000	0.00000	0.00000	0.00000	0.00000	0.00000	0.00000	0.00000	.15757

REMAINING MORTGAGE BALANCE TABLE FOR 17.500 PERCENT

ORIGINAL LOAN TERM

AGE OF LOAN	1	2	3	4	5	6	7	8	9	10
1	0.00000	.54333	.72262	.81094	.86288	.89666	.92008	.93706	.94975	.95948
2	0.00000	0.00000	.39262	.58600	.69974	.77371	.82500	.86217	.88997	.91127
3	0.00000	0.00000	0.00000	.31839	.50565	.62743	.71187	.77307	.81884	.85391
4	0.00000	0.00000	0.00000	0.00000	.27473	.45340	.57729	.66707	.73422	.78566
5	0.00000	0.00000	0.00000	0.00000	0.00000	.24634	.41716	.54095	.63355	.70447
6	0.00000	0.00000	0.00000	0.00000	0.00000	0.00000	.22665	.39090	.51377	.60787
7	0.00000	0.00000	0.00000	0.00000	0.00000	0.00000	0.00000	.21239	.37126	.49295
8	0.00000	0.00000	0.00000	0.00000	0.00000	0.00000	0.00000	0.00000	.20172	.35622
9	0.00000	0.00000	0.00000	0.00000	0.00000	0.00000	0.00000	0.00000	0.00000	.19354

AGE OF LOAN	11	12	13	14	15	20	25	30	35	40
1	.96706	.97306	.97786	.98173	.98488	.99394	.99750	.99896	.99957	.99982
2	.92787	.94101	.95152	.95999	.96688	.98672	.99453	.99772	.99905	.99960
3	.88125	.90288	.92017	.93413	.94547	.97814	.99100	.99625	.99843	.99934
4	.82578	.85751	.88289	.90336	.92000	.96792	.98679	.99450	.99770	.99904
5	.75978	.80353	.83852	.86676	.88970	.95577	.98179	.99242	.99683	.99867
6	.68127	.73932	.78574	.82320	.85365	.94132	.97583	.98994	.99579	.99824
7	.58785	.66291	.72295	.77139	.81075	.92412	.96875	.98699	.99456	.99772
8	.47671	.57202	.64824	.70974	.75972	.90366	.96032	.98348	.99309	.99711
9	.34448	.46387	.55935	.63639	.69900	.87931	.95029	.97931	.99135	.99637
10	.18717	.33520	.45360	.54913	.62677	.85035	.93837	.97434	.98927	.99550
11	0.00000	.18212	.32778	.44531	.54083	.81589	.92417	.96843	.98680	.99447
12	0.00000	0.00000	.17809	.32179	.43858	.77490	.90729	.96140	.98386	.99324
13	0.00000	0.00000	0.00000	.17484	.31693	.72612	.88720	.95304	.98036	.99177
14	0.00000	0.00000	0.00000	0.00000	.17219	.66809	.86330	.94309	.97620	.99003
15	0.00000	0.00000	0.00000	0.00000	0.00000	.59905	.83486	.93125	.97125	.98796
16	0.00000	0.00000	0.00000	0.00000	0.00000	.51691	.80103	.91716	.96536	.98549
17	0.00000	0.00000	0.00000	0.00000	0.00000	.41918	.76078	.90041	.95835	.98255
18	0.00000	0.00000	0.00000	0.00000	0.00000	.30291	.71289	.88047	.95002	.97906
19	0.00000	0.00000	0.00000	0.00000	0.00000	.16458	.65592	.85675	.94010	.97490
20	0.00000	0.00000	0.00000	0.00000	0.00000	0.00000	.58814	.82853	.92830	.96996
21	0.00000	0.00000	0.00000	0.00000	0.00000	0.00000	.50749	.79496	.91426	.96408
22	0.00000	0.00000	0.00000	0.00000	0.00000	0.00000	.41154	.75501	.89755	.95708
23	0.00000	0.00000	0.00000	0.00000	0.00000	0.00000	.29739	.70749	.87768	.94875
24	0.00000	0.00000	0.00000	0.00000	0.00000	0.00000	.16158	.65095	.85403	.93885
25	0.00000	0.00000	0.00000	0.00000	0.00000	0.00000	0.00000	.58368	.82590	.92706
26	0.00000	0.00000	0.00000	0.00000	0.00000	0.00000	0.00000	.50364	.79244	.91304
27	0.00000	0.00000	0.00000	0.00000	0.00000	0.00000	0.00000	.40842	.75262	.89636
28	0.00000	0.00000	0.00000	0.00000	0.00000	0.00000	0.00000	.29514	.70524	.87651
29	0.00000	0.00000	0.00000	0.00000	0.00000	0.00000	0.00000	.16036	.64888	.85290
30	0.00000	0.00000	0.00000	0.00000	0.00000	0.00000	0.00000	0.00000	.58183	.82481
31	0.00000	0.00000	0.00000	0.00000	0.00000	0.00000	0.00000	0.00000	.50205	.79138
32	0.00000	0.00000	0.00000	0.00000	0.00000	0.00000	0.00000	0.00000	.40713	.75162
33	0.00000	0.00000	0.00000	0.00000	0.00000	0.00000	0.00000	0.00000	.29420	.70431
34	0.00000	0.00000	0.00000	0.00000	0.00000	0.00000	0.00000	0.00000	.15985	.64802
35	0.00000	0.00000	0.00000	0.00000	0.00000	0.00000	0.00000	0.00000	0.00000	.58105
36	0.00000	0.00000	0.00000	0.00000	0.00000	0.00000	0.00000	0.00000	0.00000	.50138
37	0.00000	0.00000	0.00000	0.00000	0.00000	0.00000	0.00000	0.00000	0.00000	.40659
38	0.00000	0.00000	0.00000	0.00000	0.00000	0.00000	0.00000	0.00000	0.00000	.29381
39	0.00000	0.00000	0.00000	0.00000	0.00000	0.00000	0.00000	0.00000	0.00000	.15963

REMAINING MORTGAGE BALANCE TABLE FOR 17.750 PERCENT

ORIGINAL LOAN TERM

AGE OF LOAN	1	2	3	4	5	6	7	8	9	10
1	0.00000	.54394	.72339	.81174	.86367	.89742	.92080	.93773	.95038	.96006
2	0.00000	0.00000	.39348	.58720	.70107	.77507	.82635	.86347	.89120	.91242
3	0.00000	0.00000	0.00000	.31940	.50715	.62916	.71369	.77489	.82062	.85561
4	0.00000	0.00000	0.00000	0.00000	.27586	.45512	.57933	.66925	.73644	.78785
5	0.00000	0.00000	0.00000	0.00000	0.00000	.24756	.41908	.54326	.63604	.70703
6	0.00000	0.00000	0.00000	0.00000	0.00000	0.00000	.22795	.39298	.51630	.61064
7	0.00000	0.00000	0.00000	0.00000	0.00000	0.00000	0.00000	.21376	.37348	.49568
8	0.00000	0.00000	0.00000	0.00000	0.00000	0.00000	0.00000	0.00000	.20315	.35857
9	0.00000	0.00000	0.00000	0.00000	0.00000	0.00000	0.00000	0.00000	0.00000	.19504

AGE OF LOAN	11	12	13	14	15	20	25	30	35	40
1	.96760	.97355	.97830	.98213	.98524	.99415	.99762	.99902	.99960	.99983
2	.92895	.94200	.95243	.96083	.96764	.98717	.99478	.99785	.99911	.99963
3	.88286	.90438	.92157	.93541	.94665	.97884	.99139	.99646	.99854	.99939
4	.82788	.85951	.88476	.90510	.92161	.96891	.98734	.99479	.99785	.99911
5	.76232	.80599	.84086	.86895	.89174	.95707	.98252	.99281	.99703	.99877
6	.68412	.74216	.78850	.82584	.85613	.94294	.97677	.99044	.99605	.99837
7	.59085	.66602	.72605	.77441	.81365	.92610	.96991	.98762	.99489	.99788
8	.47962	.57523	.65157	.71308	.76298	.90600	.96173	.98426	.99350	.99731
9	.34695	.46693	.56275	.63993	.70256	.88204	.95198	.98024	.99184	.99662
10	.18872	.33777	.45680	.55269	.63049	.85346	.94034	.97546	.98986	.99580
11	0.00000	.18373	.33044	.44864	.54453	.81937	.92646	.96975	.98750	.99483
12	0.00000	0.00000	.17974	.32454	.44202	.77872	.90991	.96294	.98469	.99366
13	0.00000	0.00000	0.00000	.17653	.31975	.73023	.89017	.95482	.98133	.99227
14	0.00000	0.00000	0.00000	0.00000	.17392	.67240	.86662	.94513	.97733	.99062
15	0.00000	0.00000	0.00000	0.00000	0.00000	.60342	.83854	.93358	.97256	.98864
16	0.00000	0.00000	0.00000	0.00000	0.00000	.52116	.80505	.91980	.96687	.98629
17	0.00000	0.00000	0.00000	0.00000	0.00000	.42304	.76511	.90337	.96008	.98348
18	0.00000	0.00000	0.00000	0.00000	0.00000	.30602	.71746	.88377	.95198	.98013
19	0.00000	0.00000	0.00000	0.00000	0.00000	.16646	.66064	.86039	.94232	.97613
20	0.00000	0.00000	0.00000	0.00000	0.00000	0.00000	.59287	.83251	.93080	.97136
21	0.00000	0.00000	0.00000	0.00000	0.00000	0.00000	.51205	.79926	.91707	.96568
22	0.00000	0.00000	0.00000	0.00000	0.00000	0.00000	.41565	.75960	.90068	.95890
23	0.00000	0.00000	0.00000	0.00000	0.00000	0.00000	.30067	.71231	.88114	.95081
24	0.00000	0.00000	0.00000	0.00000	0.00000	0.00000	.16355	.65589	.85784	.94116
25	0.00000	0.00000	0.00000	0.00000	0.00000	0.00000	0.00000	.58861	.83004	.92966
26	0.00000	0.00000	0.00000	0.00000	0.00000	0.00000	0.00000	.50837	.79689	.91594
27	0.00000	0.00000	0.00000	0.00000	0.00000	0.00000	0.00000	.41266	.75735	.89958
28	0.00000	0.00000	0.00000	0.00000	0.00000	0.00000	0.00000	.29851	.71019	.88006
29	0.00000	0.00000	0.00000	0.00000	0.00000	0.00000	0.00000	.16237	.65394	.85678
30	0.00000	0.00000	0.00000	0.00000	0.00000	0.00000	0.00000	0.00000	.58686	.82902
31	0.00000	0.00000	0.00000	0.00000	0.00000	0.00000	0.00000	0.00000	.50686	.79591
32	0.00000	0.00000	0.00000	0.00000	0.00000	0.00000	0.00000	0.00000	.41143	.75642
33	0.00000	0.00000	0.00000	0.00000	0.00000	0.00000	0.00000	0.00000	.29763	.70932
34	0.00000	0.00000	0.00000	0.00000	0.00000	0.00000	0.00000	0.00000	.16189	.65314
35	0.00000	0.00000	0.00000	0.00000	0.00000	0.00000	0.00000	0.00000	0.00000	.58614
36	0.00000	0.00000	0.00000	0.00000	0.00000	0.00000	0.00000	0.00000	0.00000	.50623
37	0.00000	0.00000	0.00000	0.00000	0.00000	0.00000	0.00000	0.00000	0.00000	.41093
38	0.00000	0.00000	0.00000	0.00000	0.00000	0.00000	0.00000	0.00000	0.00000	.29726
39	0.00000	0.00000	0.00000	0.00000	0.00000	0.00000	0.00000	0.00000	0.00000	.16169

REMAINING MORTGAGE BALANCE TABLE FOR 18.000 PERCENT

ORIGINAL LOAN TERM

AGE OF LOAN	1	2	3	4	5	6	7	8	9	10
1	0.00000	.54455	.72415	.81253	.86446	.89818	.92152	.93840	.95101	.96063
2	0.00000	0.00000	.39433	.58839	.70240	.77644	.82769	.86476	.89243	.91357
3	0.00000	0.00000	0.00000	.32041	.50864	.63088	.71550	.77671	.82239	.85730
4	0.00000	0.00000	0.00000	0.00000	.27698	.45685	.58137	.67143	.73865	.79002
5	0.00000	0.00000	0.00000	0.00000	0.00000	.24878	.42100	.54556	.63853	.70957
6	0.00000	0.00000	0.00000	0.00000	0.00000	0.00000	.22925	.39506	.51883	.61340
7	0.00000	0.00000	0.00000	0.00000	0.00000	0.00000	0.00000	.21513	.37571	.49840
8	0.00000	0.00000	0.00000	0.00000	0.00000	0.00000	0.00000	0.00000	.20459	.36092
9	0.00000	0.00000	0.00000	0.00000	0.00000	0.00000	0.00000	0.00000	0.00000	.19654

AGE OF LOAN	11	12	13	14	15	20	25	30	35	40
1	.96812	.97403	.97874	.98253	.98560	.99435	.99773	.99908	.99962	.99985
2	.93001	.94299	.95333	.96165	.96838	.98760	.99501	.99797	.99917	.99966
3	.88445	.90586	.92294	.93667	.94780	.97952	.99176	.99665	.99863	.99944
4	.82997	.86148	.88661	.90682	.92319	.96987	.98787	.99507	.99799	.99918
5	.76483	.80842	.84317	.87112	.89376	.95833	.98323	.99318	.99722	.99886
6	.68696	.74497	.79123	.82844	.85858	.94453	.97768	.99093	.99630	.99849
7	.59384	.66912	.72914	.77741	.81651	.92803	.97104	.98823	.99519	.99804
8	.48252	.57842	.65489	.71640	.76622	.90830	.96310	.98500	.99388	.99750
9	.34941	.46999	.56613	.64345	.70608	.88471	.95361	.98114	.99230	.99685
10	.19027	.34034	.46000	.55624	.63419	.85651	.94226	.97653	.99042	.99608
11	0.00000	.18533	.33311	.45196	.54823	.82280	.92869	.97101	.98817	.99516
12	0.00000	0.00000	.18139	.32729	.44545	.78248	.91246	.96442	.98548	.99406
13	0.00000	0.00000	0.00000	.17822	.32257	.73429	.89307	.95653	.98226	.99275
14	0.00000	0.00000	0.00000	0.00000	.17566	.67666	.86988	.94710	.97841	.99117
15	0.00000	0.00000	0.00000	0.00000	0.00000	.60776	.84215	.93583	.97381	.98929
16	0.00000	0.00000	0.00000	0.00000	0.00000	.52538	.80900	.92236	.96831	.98704
17	0.00000	0.00000	0.00000	0.00000	0.00000	.42689	.76936	.90624	.96173	.98436
18	0.00000	0.00000	0.00000	0.00000	0.00000	.30913	.72197	.88698	.95387	.98114
19	0.00000	0.00000	0.00000	0.00000	0.00000	.16834	.66531	.86395	.94447	.97730
20	0.00000	0.00000	0.00000	0.00000	0.00000	0.00000	.59757	.83641	.93323	.97270
21	0.00000	0.00000	0.00000	0.00000	0.00000	0.00000	.51657	.80348	.91979	.96721
22	0.00000	0.00000	0.00000	0.00000	0.00000	0.00000	.41973	.76412	.90372	.96064
23	0.00000	0.00000	0.00000	0.00000	0.00000	0.00000	.30395	.71705	.88451	.95279
24	0.00000	0.00000	0.00000	0.00000	0.00000	0.00000	.16551	.66078	.86154	.94339
25	0.00000	0.00000	0.00000	0.00000	0.00000	0.00000	0.00000	.59349	.83408	.93217
26	0.00000	0.00000	0.00000	0.00000	0.00000	0.00000	0.00000	.51305	.80125	.91874
27	0.00000	0.00000	0.00000	0.00000	0.00000	0.00000	0.00000	.41687	.76199	.90269
28	0.00000	0.00000	0.00000	0.00000	0.00000	0.00000	0.00000	.30188	.71506	.88351
29	0.00000	0.00000	0.00000	0.00000	0.00000	0.00000	0.00000	.16439	.65894	.86056
30	0.00000	0.00000	0.00000	0.00000	0.00000	0.00000	0.00000	0.00000	.59184	.83313
31	0.00000	0.00000	0.00000	0.00000	0.00000	0.00000	0.00000	0.00000	.51162	.80034
32	0.00000	0.00000	0.00000	0.00000	0.00000	0.00000	0.00000	0.00000	.41571	.76112
33	0.00000	0.00000	0.00000	0.00000	0.00000	0.00000	0.00000	0.00000	.30104	.71424
34	0.00000	0.00000	0.00000	0.00000	0.00000	0.00000	0.00000	0.00000	.16393	.65819
35	0.00000	0.00000	0.00000	0.00000	0.00000	0.00000	0.00000	0.00000	0.00000	.59117
36	0.00000	0.00000	0.00000	0.00000	0.00000	0.00000	0.00000	0.00000	0.00000	.51104
37	0.00000	0.00000	0.00000	0.00000	0.00000	0.00000	0.00000	0.00000	0.00000	.41524
38	0.00000	0.00000	0.00000	0.00000	0.00000	0.00000	0.00000	0.00000	0.00000	.30069
39	0.00000	0.00000	0.00000	0.00000	0.00000	0.00000	0.00000	0.00000	0.00000	.16374

REMAINING MORTGAGE BALANCE TABLE FOR 18.250 PERCENT

ORIGINAL LOAN TERM

AGE OF LOAN	1	2	3	4	5	6	7	8	9	10
1	0.00000	.54516	.72491	.81333	.86524	.89893	.92223	.93907	.95162	.96120
2	0.00000	0.00000	.39519	.58959	.70372	.77779	.82902	.86604	.89364	.91470
3	0.00000	0.00000	0.00000	.32142	.51013	.63260	.71730	.77851	.82414	.85897
4	0.00000	0.00000	0.00000	0.00000	.27810	.45857	.58340	.67360	.74085	.79217
5	0.00000	0.00000	0.00000	0.00000	0.00000	.25000	.42291	.54786	.64101	.71211
6	0.00000	0.00000	0.00000	0.00000	0.00000	0.00000	.23055	.39714	.52135	.61614
7	0.00000	0.00000	0.00000	0.00000	0.00000	0.00000	0.00000	.21651	.37793	.50113
8	0.00000	0.00000	0.00000	0.00000	0.00000	0.00000	0.00000	0.00000	.20603	.36327
9	0.00000	0.00000	0.00000	0.00000	0.00000	0.00000	0.00000	0.00000	0.00000	.19804

AGE OF LOAN	11	12	13	14	15	20	25	30	35	40
1	.96865	.97451	.97917	.98292	.98595	.99455	.99783	.99913	.99965	.99986
2	.93107	.94395	.95421	.96245	.96911	.98802	.99523	.99809	.99923	.99969
3	.88602	.90733	.92429	.93791	.94893	.98019	.99212	.99683	.99872	.99948
4	.83204	.86344	.88643	.90851	.92474	.97080	.98839	.99533	.99812	.99924
5	.76733	.81083	.84545	.87326	.89574	.95955	.98391	.99354	.99739	.99895
6	.68978	.74777	.79394	.83101	.86099	.94607	.97855	.99138	.99653	.99860
7	.59682	.67219	.73220	.78038	.81934	.92992	.97212	.98880	.99548	.99818
8	.48541	.58161	.65819	.71969	.76942	.91055	.96442	.98571	.99424	.99767
9	.35188	.47304	.56950	.64695	.70958	.88734	.95518	.98200	.99274	.99707
10	.19183	.34291	.46319	.55977	.63786	.85951	.94412	.97755	.99095	.99634
11	0.00000	.18694	.33577	.45528	.55191	.82617	.93085	.97223	.98880	.99548
12	0.00000	0.00000	.18305	.33003	.44888	.78620	.91495	.96584	.98623	.99444
13	0.00000	0.00000	0.00000	.17992	.32540	.73830	.89590	.95819	.98314	.99319
14	0.00000	0.00000	0.00000	0.00000	.17739	.68088	.87306	.94901	.97944	.99170
15	0.00000	0.00000	0.00000	0.00000	0.00000	.61206	.84569	.93802	.97501	.98991
16	0.00000	0.00000	0.00000	0.00000	0.00000	.52958	.81288	.92484	.96969	.98776
17	0.00000	0.00000	0.00000	0.00000	0.00000	.43072	.77355	.90904	.96332	.98519
18	0.00000	0.00000	0.00000	0.00000	0.00000	.31223	.72642	.89011	.95569	.98210
19	0.00000	0.00000	0.00000	0.00000	0.00000	.17022	.66993	.86742	.94654	.97841
20	0.00000	0.00000	0.00000	0.00000	0.00000	0.00000	.60222	.84022	.93557	.97398
21	0.00000	0.00000	0.00000	0.00000	0.00000	0.00000	.52106	.80762	.92243	.96867
22	0.00000	0.00000	0.00000	0.00000	0.00000	0.00000	.42379	.76855	.90667	.96231
23	0.00000	0.00000	0.00000	0.00000	0.00000	0.00000	.30721	.72172	.88779	.95468
24	0.00000	0.00000	0.00000	0.00000	0.00000	0.00000	.16748	.66560	.86516	.94554
25	0.00000	0.00000	0.00000	0.00000	0.00000	0.00000	0.00000	.59833	.83803	.93459
26	0.00000	0.00000	0.00000	0.00000	0.00000	0.00000	0.00000	.51770	.80552	.92146
27	0.00000	0.00000	0.00000	0.00000	0.00000	0.00000	0.00000	.42106	.76655	.90572
28	0.00000	0.00000	0.00000	0.00000	0.00000	0.00000	0.00000	.30523	.71984	.88686
29	0.00000	0.00000	0.00000	0.00000	0.00000	0.00000	0.00000	.16640	.66386	.86425
30	0.00000	0.00000	0.00000	0.00000	0.00000	0.00000	0.00000	0.00000	.59677	.83715
31	0.00000	0.00000	0.00000	0.00000	0.00000	0.00000	0.00000	0.00000	.51635	.80467
32	0.00000	0.00000	0.00000	0.00000	0.00000	0.00000	0.00000	0.00000	.41996	.76574
33	0.00000	0.00000	0.00000	0.00000	0.00000	0.00000	0.00000	0.00000	.30443	.71909
34	0.00000	0.00000	0.00000	0.00000	0.00000	0.00000	0.00000	0.00000	.16596	.66316
35	0.00000	0.00000	0.00000	0.00000	0.00000	0.00000	0.00000	0.00000	0.00000	.59614
36	0.00000	0.00000	0.00000	0.00000	0.00000	0.00000	0.00000	0.00000	0.00000	.51580
37	0.00000	0.00000	0.00000	0.00000	0.00000	0.00000	0.00000	0.00000	0.00000	.41952
38	0.00000	0.00000	0.00000	0.00000	0.00000	0.00000	0.00000	0.00000	0.00000	.30411
39	0.00000	0.00000	0.00000	0.00000	0.00000	0.00000	0.00000	0.00000	0.00000	.16579

REMAINING MORTGAGE BALANCE TABLE FOR 18.500 PERCENT

ORIGINAL LOAN TERM

AGE OF LOAN	1	2	3	4	5	6	7	8	9	10
1	0.00000	.54577	.72566	.81412	.86602	.89968	.92294	.93973	.95223	.96177
2	0.00000	0.00000	.39605	.59078	.70504	.77914	.83035	.86731	.89484	.91583
3	0.00000	0.00000	0.00000	.32243	.51163	.63431	.71910	.78030	.82589	.86063
4	0.00000	0.00000	0.00000	0.00000	.27923	.46030	.58543	.67576	.74303	.79431
5	0.00000	0.00000	0.00000	0.00000	0.00000	.25122	.42483	.55015	.64348	.71462
6	0.00000	0.00000	0.00000	0.00000	0.00000	0.00000	.23186	.39922	.52387	.61888
7	0.00000	0.00000	0.00000	0.00000	0.00000	0.00000	0.00000	.21788	.38015	.50384
8	0.00000	0.00000	0.00000	0.00000	0.00000	0.00000	0.00000	0.00000	.20748	.36562
9	0.00000	0.00000	0.00000	0.00000	0.00000	0.00000	0.00000	0.00000	0.00000	.19954

AGE OF LOAN	11	12	13	14	15	20	25	30	35	40
1	.96916	.97497	.97960	.98330	.98629	.99474	.99793	.99918	.99967	.99987
2	.93210	.94491	.95508	.96324	.96982	.98842	.99545	.99819	.99928	.99971
3	.88758	.90678	.92563	.93913	.95004	.98083	.99246	.99701	.99881	.99952
4	.83409	.86537	.89024	.91017	.92626	.97171	.98888	.99559	.99824	.99930
5	.76981	.81321	.84771	.87537	.89770	.96075	.98457	.99387	.99756	.99903
6	.69258	.75055	.79662	.83356	.86337	.94758	.97939	.99182	.99674	.99870
7	.59979	.67525	.73523	.78332	.82213	.93176	.97317	.98935	.99576	.99831
8	.48830	.58478	.66147	.72296	.77258	.91275	.96569	.98638	.99458	.99784
9	.35434	.47608	.57285	.65043	.71305	.88991	.95671	.98282	.99316	.99727
10	.19339	.34548	.46637	.56329	.64151	.86246	.94592	.97854	.99145	.99659
11	0.00000	.18855	.33843	.45858	.55557	.82949	.93296	.97339	.98940	.99577
12	0.00000	0.00000	.18470	.33278	.45230	.78986	.91738	.96721	.98694	.99479
13	0.00000	0.00000	0.00000	.18162	.32821	.74226	.89866	.95978	.98398	.99361
14	0.00000	0.00000	0.00000	0.00000	.17913	.68506	.87617	.95085	.98042	.99219
15	0.00000	0.00000	0.00000	0.00000	0.00000	.61633	.84915	.94013	.97615	.99048
16	0.00000	0.00000	0.00000	0.00000	0.00000	.53376	.81668	.92724	.97102	.98844
17	0.00000	0.00000	0.00000	0.00000	0.00000	.43454	.77768	.91176	.96485	.98598
18	0.00000	0.00000	0.00000	0.00000	0.00000	.31533	.73080	.89316	.95744	.98302
19	0.00000	0.00000	0.00000	0.00000	0.00000	.17210	.67449	.87081	.94853	.97947
20	0.00000	0.00000	0.00000	0.00000	0.00000	0.00000	.60682	.84395	.93784	.97520
21	0.00000	0.00000	0.00000	0.00000	0.00000	0.00000	.52552	.81168	.92498	.97007
22	0.00000	0.00000	0.00000	0.00000	0.00000	0.00000	.42784	.77291	.90954	.96391
23	0.00000	0.00000	0.00000	0.00000	0.00000	0.00000	.31047	.72633	.89098	.95651
24	0.00000	0.00000	0.00000	0.00000	0.00000	0.00000	.16944	.67036	.86868	.94761
25	0.00000	0.00000	0.00000	0.00000	0.00000	0.00000	0.00000	.60311	.84189	.93692
26	0.00000	0.00000	0.00000	0.00000	0.00000	0.00000	0.00000	.52230	.80970	.92408
27	0.00000	0.00000	0.00000	0.00000	0.00000	0.00000	0.00000	.42522	.77103	.90865
28	0.00000	0.00000	0.00000	0.00000	0.00000	0.00000	0.00000	.30856	.72456	.89011
29	0.00000	0.00000	0.00000	0.00000	0.00000	0.00000	0.00000	.16840	.66872	.86784
30	0.00000	0.00000	0.00000	0.00000	0.00000	0.00000	0.00000	0.00000	.60163	.84107
31	0.00000	0.00000	0.00000	0.00000	0.00000	0.00000	0.00000	0.00000	.52103	.80891
32	0.00000	0.00000	0.00000	0.00000	0.00000	0.00000	0.00000	0.00000	.42418	.77028
33	0.00000	0.00000	0.00000	0.00000	0.00000	0.00000	0.00000	0.00000	.30781	.72385
34	0.00000	0.00000	0.00000	0.00000	0.00000	0.00000	0.00000	0.00000	.16799	.66807
35	0.00000	0.00000	0.00000	0.00000	0.00000	0.00000	0.00000	0.00000	0.00000	.60105
36	0.00000	0.00000	0.00000	0.00000	0.00000	0.00000	0.00000	0.00000	0.00000	.52052
37	0.00000	0.00000	0.00000	0.00000	0.00000	0.00000	0.00000	0.00000	0.00000	.42377
38	0.00000	0.00000	0.00000	0.00000	0.00000	0.00000	0.00000	0.00000	0.00000	.30751
39	0.00000	0.00000	0.00000	0.00000	0.00000	0.00000	0.00000	0.00000	0.00000	.16783

REMAINING MORTGAGE BALANCE TABLE FOR 18.750 PERCENT

ORIGINAL LOAN TERM

AGE OF LOAN	1	2	3	4	5	6	7	8	9	10
1	0.00000	.54638	.72642	.81491	.86680	.90042	.92364	.94038	.95284	.96232
2	0.00000	0.00000	.39690	.59197	.70636	.78049	.83167	.86858	.89604	.91694
3	0.00000	0.00000	0.00000	.32344	.51312	.63602	.72089	.78209	.82762	.86227
4	0.00000	0.00000	0.00000	0.00000	.28036	.46202	.58746	.67791	.74520	.79643
5	0.00000	0.00000	0.00000	0.00000	0.00000	.25244	.42674	.55244	.64594	.71713
6	0.00000	0.00000	0.00000	0.00000	0.00000	0.00000	.23316	.40130	.52638	.62160
7	0.00000	0.00000	0.00000	0.00000	0.00000	0.00000	0.00000	.21926	.38238	.50655
8	0.00000	0.00000	0.00000	0.00000	0.00000	0.00000	0.00000	0.00000	.20892	.36797
9	0.00000	0.00000	0.00000	0.00000	0.00000	0.00000	0.00000	0.00000	0.00000	.20105

AGE OF LOAN	11	12	13	14	15	20	25	30	35	40
1	.96967	.97543	.98001	.98368	.98663	.99493	.99803	.99923	.99970	.99988
2	.93313	.94585	.95594	.96402	.97352	.98882	.99565	.99830	.99933	.99974
3	.88912	.91021	.92694	.94033	.95113	.98146	.99279	.99717	.99889	.99956
4	.83612	.86728	.89202	.91181	.92776	.97259	.98935	.99582	.99836	.99935
5	.77227	.81558	.84995	.87746	.89962	.96191	.98520	.99420	.99772	.99910
6	.69537	.75330	.79928	.83607	.86572	.94905	.98020	.99224	.99694	.99880
7	.60275	.67829	.73825	.78623	.82489	.93356	.97418	.98987	.99602	.99843
8	.49118	.58794	.66473	.72620	.77572	.91490	.96693	.98703	.99490	.99799
9	.35681	.47912	.57619	.65388	.71649	.89243	.95819	.98361	.99355	.99746
10	.19495	.34804	.46954	.56679	.64514	.86536	.94767	.97948	.99192	.99682
11	0.00000	.19016	.34109	.46188	.55921	.83275	.93500	.97451	.98997	.99605
12	0.00000	0.00000	.18636	.33552	.45570	.79348	.91974	.96853	.98761	.99512
13	0.00000	0.00000	0.00000	.18332	.33103	.74617	.90136	.96132	.98478	.99400
14	0.00000	0.00000	0.00000	0.00000	.18087	.68920	.87922	.95263	.98136	.99265
15	0.00000	0.00000	0.00000	0.00000	0.00000	.62057	.85255	.94217	.97724	.99103
16	0.00000	0.00000	0.00000	0.00000	0.00000	.53791	.82042	.92958	.97228	.98908
17	0.00000	0.00000	0.00000	0.00000	0.00000	.43835	.78173	.91440	.96631	.98672
18	0.00000	0.00000	0.00000	0.00000	0.00000	.31842	.73513	.89613	.95912	.98389
19	0.00000	0.00000	0.00000	0.00000	0.00000	.17398	.67900	.87411	.95046	.98048
20	0.00000	0.00000	0.00000	0.00000	0.00000	0.00000	.61138	.84760	.94002	.97636
21	0.00000	0.00000	0.00000	0.00000	0.00000	0.00000	.52995	.81566	.92745	.97141
22	0.00000	0.00000	0.00000	0.00000	0.00000	0.00000	.43186	.77719	.91231	.96544
23	0.00000	0.00000	0.00000	0.00000	0.00000	0.00000	.31371	.73086	.89408	.95826
24	0.00000	0.00000	0.00000	0.00000	0.00000	0.00000	.17140	.67505	.87212	.94960
25	0.00000	0.00000	0.00000	0.00000	0.00000	0.00000	0.00000	.60784	.84566	.93918
26	0.00000	0.00000	0.00000	0.00000	0.00000	0.00000	0.00000	.52687	.81380	.92662
27	0.00000	0.00000	0.00000	0.00000	0.00000	0.00000	0.00000	.42935	.77542	.91149
28	0.00000	0.00000	0.00000	0.00000	0.00000	0.00000	0.00000	.31189	.72919	.89327
29	0.00000	0.00000	0.00000	0.00000	0.00000	0.00000	0.00000	.17041	.67351	.87133
30	0.00000	0.00000	0.00000	0.00000	0.00000	0.00000	0.00000	0.00000	.60645	.84490
31	0.00000	0.00000	0.00000	0.00000	0.00000	0.00000	0.00000	0.00000	.52567	.81307
32	0.00000	0.00000	0.00000	0.00000	0.00000	0.00000	0.00000	0.00000	.42837	.77472
33	0.00000	0.00000	0.00000	0.00000	0.00000	0.00000	0.00000	0.00000	.31118	.72854
34	0.00000	0.00000	0.00000	0.00000	0.00000	0.00000	0.00000	0.00000	.17002	.67291
35	0.00000	0.00000	0.00000	0.00000	0.00000	0.00000	0.00000	0.00000	0.00000	.60590
36	0.00000	0.00000	0.00000	0.00000	0.00000	0.00000	0.00000	0.00000	0.00000	.52519
37	0.00000	0.00000	0.00000	0.00000	0.00000	0.00000	0.00000	0.00000	0.00000	.42798
38	0.00000	0.00000	0.00000	0.00000	0.00000	0.00000	0.00000	0.00000	0.00000	.31090
39	0.00000	0.00000	0.00000	0.00000	0.00000	0.00000	0.00000	0.00000	0.00000	.16987

REMAINING MORTGAGE BALANCE TABLE FOR 19.000 PERCENT

ORIGINAL LOAN TERM

AGE OF LOAN	1	2	3	4	5	6	7	8	9	10
1	0.00000	.54699	.72718	.81569	.86757	.90117	.92434	.94103	.95344	.96287
2	0.00000	0.00000	.39776	.59315	.70768	.78183	.83298	.86983	.89722	.91804
3	0.00000	0.00000	0.00000	.32445	.51461	.63773	.72267	.78386	.82933	.86390
4	0.00000	0.00000	0.00000	0.00000	.28148	.46374	.58948	.68006	.74737	.79854
5	0.00000	0.00000	0.00000	0.00000	0.00000	.25366	.42866	.55472	.64839	.71962
6	0.00000	0.00000	0.00000	0.00000	0.00000	0.00000	.23447	.40338	.52889	.62432
7	0.00000	0.00000	0.00000	0.00000	0.00000	0.00000	0.00000	.22064	.38460	.50925
8	0.00000	0.00000	0.00000	0.00000	0.00000	0.00000	0.00000	0.00000	.21037	.37032
9	0.00000	0.00000	0.00000	0.00000	0.00000	0.00000	0.00000	0.00000	0.00000	.20256

AGE OF LOAN	11	12	13	14	15	20	25	30	35	40
1	.97017	.97589	.98042	.98404	.98696	.99511	.99812	.99927	.99972	.99989
2	.93414	.94677	.95678	.96478	.97121	.98920	.99585	.99839	.99937	.99976
3	.89065	.91162	.92824	.94152	.95220	.98206	.99311	.99733	.99896	.99960
4	.83813	.86917	.89377	.91343	.92924	.97345	.98980	.99605	.99846	.99940
5	.77472	.81792	.85216	.87951	.90151	.96304	.98581	.99450	.99786	.99917
6	.69815	.75604	.80191	.83856	.86804	.95048	.98098	.99263	.99713	.99888
7	.60569	.68131	.74123	.78911	.82762	.93532	.97516	.99037	.99626	.99854
8	.49406	.59109	.66797	.72941	.77882	.91701	.96812	.98765	.99520	.99813
9	.35927	.48215	.57952	.65732	.71989	.89490	.95963	.98436	.99392	.99763
10	.19652	.35061	.47271	.57027	.64874	.86820	.94937	.98038	.99237	.99703
11	0.00000	.19178	.34374	.46517	.56283	.83596	.93699	.97559	.99051	.99630
12	0.00000	0.00000	.18802	.33826	.45910	.79704	.92204	.96979	.98826	.99543
13	0.00000	0.00000	0.00000	.18502	.33385	.75004	.90399	.96280	.98554	.99437
14	0.00000	0.00000	0.00000	0.00000	.18261	.69329	.88219	.95435	.98225	.99309
15	0.00000	0.00000	0.00000	0.00000	0.00000	.62477	.85587	.94415	.97829	.99155
16	0.00000	0.00000	0.00000	0.00000	0.00000	.54203	.82410	.93184	.97350	.98968
17	0.00000	0.00000	0.00000	0.00000	0.00000	.44213	.78572	.91697	.96772	.98743
18	0.00000	0.00000	0.00000	0.00000	0.00000	.32151	.73939	.89902	.96074	.98472
19	0.00000	0.00000	0.00000	0.00000	0.00000	.17586	.68345	.87734	.95231	.98143
20	0.00000	0.00000	0.00000	0.00000	0.00000	0.00000	.61590	.85117	.94213	.97747
21	0.00000	0.00000	0.00000	0.00000	0.00000	0.00000	.53434	.81956	.92985	.97269
22	0.00000	0.00000	0.00000	0.00000	0.00000	0.00000	.43586	.78140	.91501	.96691
23	0.00000	0.00000	0.00000	0.00000	0.00000	0.00000	.31695	.73533	.89710	.95994
24	0.00000	0.00000	0.00000	0.00000	0.00000	0.00000	.17337	.67969	.87546	.95152
25	0.00000	0.00000	0.00000	0.00000	0.00000	0.00000	0.00000	.61251	.84935	.94135
26	0.00000	0.00000	0.00000	0.00000	0.00000	0.00000	0.00000	.53140	.81781	.92907
27	0.00000	0.00000	0.00000	0.00000	0.00000	0.00000	0.00000	.43346	.77973	.91425
28	0.00000	0.00000	0.00000	0.00000	0.00000	0.00000	0.00000	.31520	.73375	.89635
29	0.00000	0.00000	0.00000	0.00000	0.00000	0.00000	0.00000	.17241	.67824	.87474
30	0.00000	0.00000	0.00000	0.00000	0.00000	0.00000	0.00000	0.00000	.61120	.84864
31	0.00000	0.00000	0.00000	0.00000	0.00000	0.00000	0.00000	0.00000	.53026	.81713
32	0.00000	0.00000	0.00000	0.00000	0.00000	0.00000	0.00000	0.00000	.43253	.77908
33	0.00000	0.00000	0.00000	0.00000	0.00000	0.00000	0.00000	0.00000	.31453	.73314
34	0.00000	0.00000	0.00000	0.00000	0.00000	0.00000	0.00000	0.00000	.17204	.67767
35	0.00000	0.00000	0.00000	0.00000	0.00000	0.00000	0.00000	0.00000	0.00000	.61069
36	0.00000	0.00000	0.00000	0.00000	0.00000	0.00000	0.00000	0.00000	0.00000	.52982
37	0.00000	0.00000	0.00000	0.00000	0.00000	0.00000	0.00000	0.00000	0.00000	.43217
38	0.00000	0.00000	0.00000	0.00000	0.00000	0.00000	0.00000	0.00000	0.00000	.31427
39	0.00000	0.00000	0.00000	0.00000	0.00000	0.00000	0.00000	0.00000	0.00000	.17190

REMAINING MORTGAGE BALANCE TABLE FOR 19.250 PERCENT

ORIGINAL LOAN TERM

AGE OF LOAN	1	2	3	4	5	6	7	8	9	10
1	0.00000	.54760	.72793	.81648	.86834	.90190	.92503	.94168	.95403	.96341
2	0.00000	0.00000	.39861	.59434	.70899	.78316	.83429	.87108	.89839	.91912
3	0.00000	0.00000	0.00000	.32546	.51609	.63944	.72445	.78563	.83104	.86552
4	0.00000	0.00000	0.00000	0.00000	.28261	.46547	.59150	.68220	.74952	.80063
5	0.00000	0.00000	0.00000	0.00000	0.00000	.25489	.43057	.55700	.65084	.72209
6	0.00000	0.00000	0.00000	0.00000	0.00000	0.00000	.23578	.40546	.53140	.62702
7	0.00000	0.00000	0.00000	0.00000	0.00000	0.00000	0.00000	.22203	.38682	.51195
8	0.00000	0.00000	0.00000	0.00000	0.00000	0.00000	0.00000	0.00000	.21182	.37267
9	0.00000	0.00000	0.00000	0.00000	0.00000	0.00000	0.00000	0.00000	0.00000	.20407

AGE OF LOAN	11	12	13	14	15	20	25	30	35	40
1	.97066	.97633	.98082	.98440	.98728	.99528	.99821	.99931	.99974	.99990
2	.93514	.94769	.95761	.96553	.97188	.98957	.99604	.99848	.99942	.99978
3	.89216	.91301	.92951	.94268	.95324	.98265	.99341	.99748	.99903	.99963
4	.84012	.87104	.89550	.91502	.93068	.97428	.99024	.99626	.99856	.99945
5	.77714	.82024	.85434	.88154	.90338	.96415	.98639	.99479	.99800	.99923
6	.70091	.75875	.80451	.84101	.87032	.95188	.98173	.99301	.99731	.99897
7	.60863	.68432	.74420	.79196	.83032	.93704	.97610	.99085	.99648	.99865
8	.49693	.59422	.67119	.73259	.78189	.91907	.96928	.98824	.99548	.99826
9	.36173	.48517	.58283	.66073	.72327	.89732	.96102	.98508	.99427	.99780
10	.19808	.35317	.47587	.57374	.65232	.87099	.95102	.98125	.99280	.99723
11	0.00000	.19340	.34640	.46845	.56644	.83912	.93893	.97662	.99102	.99655
12	0.00000	0.00000	.18969	.34100	.46249	.80055	.92428	.97101	.98887	.99572
13	0.00000	0.00000	0.00000	.18673	.33666	.75386	.90656	.96422	.98626	.99472
14	0.00000	0.00000	0.00000	0.00000	.18435	.69734	.88510	.95601	.98310	.99350
15	0.00000	0.00000	0.00000	0.00000	0.00000	.62893	.85913	.94607	.97928	.99203
16	0.00000	0.00000	0.00000	0.00000	0.00000	.54613	.82770	.93403	.97466	.99026
17	0.00000	0.00000	0.00000	0.00000	0.00000	.44590	.78965	.91947	.96907	.98810
18	0.00000	0.00000	0.00000	0.00000	0.00000	.32459	.74360	.90183	.96229	.98550
19	0.00000	0.00000	0.00000	0.00000	0.00000	.17774	.68785	.88049	.95410	.98235
20	0.00000	0.00000	0.00000	0.00000	0.00000	0.00000	.62037	.85466	.94417	.97853
21	0.00000	0.00000	0.00000	0.00000	0.00000	0.00000	.53870	.82339	.93216	.97391
22	0.00000	0.00000	0.00000	0.00000	0.00000	0.00000	.43984	.78554	.91763	.96832
23	0.00000	0.00000	0.00000	0.00000	0.00000	0.00000	.32017	.73972	.90003	.96155
24	0.00000	0.00000	0.00000	0.00000	0.00000	0.00000	.17532	.68427	.87873	.95336
25	0.00000	0.00000	0.00000	0.00000	0.00000	0.00000	0.00000	.61714	.85295	.94345
26	0.00000	0.00000	0.00000	0.00000	0.00000	0.00000	0.00000	.53589	.82174	.93145
27	0.00000	0.00000	0.00000	0.00000	0.00000	0.00000	0.00000	.43754	.78396	.91692
28	0.00000	0.00000	0.00000	0.00000	0.00000	0.00000	0.00000	.31850	.73824	.89934
29	0.00000	0.00000	0.00000	0.00000	0.00000	0.00000	0.00000	.17441	.68290	.87805
30	0.00000	0.00000	0.00000	0.00000	0.00000	0.00000	0.00000	0.00000	.61590	.85229
31	0.00000	0.00000	0.00000	0.00000	0.00000	0.00000	0.00000	0.00000	.53482	.82111
32	0.00000	0.00000	0.00000	0.00000	0.00000	0.00000	0.00000	0.00000	.43667	.78336
33	0.00000	0.00000	0.00000	0.00000	0.00000	0.00000	0.00000	0.00000	.31786	.73767
34	0.00000	0.00000	0.00000	0.00000	0.00000	0.00000	0.00000	0.00000	.17406	.68237
35	0.00000	0.00000	0.00000	0.00000	0.00000	0.00000	0.00000	0.00000	0.00000	.61543
36	0.00000	0.00000	0.00000	0.00000	0.00000	0.00000	0.00000	0.00000	0.00000	.53441
37	0.00000	0.00000	0.00000	0.00000	0.00000	0.00000	0.00000	0.00000	0.00000	.43633
38	0.00000	0.00000	0.00000	0.00000	0.00000	0.00000	0.00000	0.00000	0.00000	.31762
39	0.00000	0.00000	0.00000	0.00000	0.00000	0.00000	0.00000	0.00000	0.00000	.17393

REMAINING MORTGAGE BALANCE TABLE FOR 19.500 PERCENT

ORIGINAL LOAN TERM

AGE OF LOAN	1	2	3	4	5	6	7	8	9	10
1	0.00000	.54821	.72869	.81726	.86911	.90264	.92572	.94231	.95462	.96395
2	0.00000	0.00000	.39947	.59553	.71029	.78449	.83559	.87232	.89955	.92020
3	0.00000	0.00000	0.00000	.32647	.51758	.64114	.72622	.78739	.83273	.86712
4	0.00000	0.00000	0.00000	0.00000	.28374	.46719	.59351	.68433	.75165	.80271
5	0.00000	0.00000	0.00000	0.00000	0.00000	.25612	.43248	.55928	.65327	.72455
6	0.00000	0.00000	0.00000	0.00000	0.00000	0.00000	.23709	.40754	.53389	.62972
7	0.00000	0.00000	0.00000	0.00000	0.00000	0.00000	0.00000	.22341	.38904	.51465
8	0.00000	0.00000	0.00000	0.00000	0.00000	0.00000	0.00000	0.00000	.21328	.37502
9	0.00000	0.00000	0.00000	0.00000	0.00000	0.00000	0.00000	0.00000	0.00000	.20559

AGE OF LOAN	11	12	13	14	15	20	25	30	35	40
1	.97115	.97677	.98122	.98476	.98759	.99545	.99829	.99935	.99975	.99991
2	.93613	.94859	.95843	.96626	.97254	.98992	.99622	.99857	.99946	.99979
3	.89365	.91439	.93077	.94382	.95427	.98322	.99370	.99762	.99910	.99966
4	.84210	.87289	.89722	.91658	.93211	.97509	.99065	.99646	.99866	.99949
5	.77955	.82254	.85650	.88354	.90521	.96522	.98695	.99506	.99813	.99929
6	.70365	.76144	.80709	.84344	.87258	.95324	.98246	.99336	.99748	.99904
7	.61155	.68730	.74714	.79479	.83298	.93871	.97701	.99130	.99670	.99875
8	.49980	.59734	.67439	.73575	.78493	.92108	.97039	.98880	.99575	.99839
9	.36419	.48819	.58612	.66411	.72662	.89969	.96236	.98576	.99460	.99795
10	.19965	.35574	.47902	.57719	.65587	.87373	.95262	.98208	.99320	.99742
11	0.00000	.19502	.34905	.47172	.57003	.84223	.94080	.97761	.99150	.99677
12	0.00000	0.00000	.19135	.34373	.46586	.80401	.92646	.97218	.98944	.99599
13	0.00000	0.00000	0.00000	.18844	.33947	.75763	.90906	.96560	.98695	.99504
14	0.00000	0.00000	0.00000	0.00000	.18610	.70135	.88795	.95761	.98392	.99389
15	0.00000	0.00000	0.00000	0.00000	0.00000	.63306	.86233	.94792	.98024	.99249
16	0.00000	0.00000	0.00000	0.00000	0.00000	.55020	.83124	.93616	.97578	.99080
17	0.00000	0.00000	0.00000	0.00000	0.00000	.44966	.79351	.92189	.97036	.98874
18	0.00000	0.00000	0.00000	0.00000	0.00000	.32766	.74774	.90457	.96379	.98624
19	0.00000	0.00000	0.00000	0.00000	0.00000	.17963	.69220	.88356	.95582	.98322
20	0.00000	0.00000	0.00000	0.00000	0.00000	0.00000	.62480	.85807	.94614	.97954
21	0.00000	0.00000	0.00000	0.00000	0.00000	0.00000	.54302	.82713	.93441	.97508
22	0.00000	0.00000	0.00000	0.00000	0.00000	0.00000	.44379	.78960	.92016	.96967
23	0.00000	0.00000	0.00000	0.00000	0.00000	0.00000	.32339	.74405	.90288	.96310
24	0.00000	0.00000	0.00000	0.00000	0.00000	0.00000	.17728	.68878	.88191	.95514
25	0.00000	0.00000	0.00000	0.00000	0.00000	0.00000	0.00000	.62172	.85646	.94547
26	0.00000	0.00000	0.00000	0.00000	0.00000	0.00000	0.00000	.54034	.82558	.93374
27	0.00000	0.00000	0.00000	0.00000	0.00000	0.00000	0.00000	.44160	.78812	.91951
28	0.00000	0.00000	0.00000	0.00000	0.00000	0.00000	0.00000	.32179	.74265	.90224
29	0.00000	0.00000	0.00000	0.00000	0.00000	0.00000	0.00000	.17641	.68749	.88128
30	0.00000	0.00000	0.00000	0.00000	0.00000	0.00000	0.00000	0.00000	.62055	.85585
31	0.00000	0.00000	0.00000	0.00000	0.00000	0.00000	0.00000	0.00000	.53933	.82500
32	0.00000	0.00000	0.00000	0.00000	0.00000	0.00000	0.00000	0.00000	.44077	.78756
33	0.00000	0.00000	0.00000	0.00000	0.00000	0.00000	0.00000	0.00000	.32119	.74213
34	0.00000	0.00000	0.00000	0.00000	0.00000	0.00000	0.00000	0.00000	.17608	.68700
35	0.00000	0.00000	0.00000	0.00000	0.00000	0.00000	0.00000	0.00000	0.00000	.62011
36	0.00000	0.00000	0.00000	0.00000	0.00000	0.00000	0.00000	0.00000	0.00000	.53895
37	0.00000	0.00000	0.00000	0.00000	0.00000	0.00000	0.00000	0.00000	0.00000	.44046
38	0.00000	0.00000	0.00000	0.00000	0.00000	0.00000	0.00000	0.00000	0.00000	.32096
39	0.00000	0.00000	0.00000	0.00000	0.00000	0.00000	0.00000	0.00000	0.00000	.17595

REMAINING MORTGAGE BALANCE TABLE FOR 19.750 PERCENT

ORIGINAL LOAN TERM

AGE OF LOAN	1	2	3	4	5	6	7	8	9	10
1	0.00000	.54882	.72944	.81804	.86988	.90336	.92640	.94295	.95520	.96448
2	0.00000	0.00000	.40033	.59671	.71160	.78582	.83688	.87355	.90070	.92127
3	0.00000	0.00000	0.00000	.32749	.51907	.64283	.72798	.78913	.83441	.86871
4	0.00000	0.00000	0.00000	0.00000	.28487	.46891	.59552	.68645	.75378	.80477
5	0.00000	0.00000	0.00000	0.00000	0.00000	.25734	.43440	.56155	.65569	.72700
6	0.00000	0.00000	0.00000	0.00000	0.00000	0.00000	.23840	.40961	.53639	.63240
7	0.00000	0.00000	0.00000	0.00000	0.00000	0.00000	0.00000	.22480	.39126	.51733
8	0.00000	0.00000	0.00000	0.00000	0.00000	0.00000	0.00000	0.00000	.21473	.37736
9	0.00000	0.00000	0.00000	0.00000	0.00000	0.00000	0.00000	0.00000	0.00000	.20710

AGE OF LOAN	11	12	13	14	15	20	25	30	35	40
1	.97163	.97720	.98160	.98510	.98790	.99561	.99837	.99939	.99977	.99991
2	.93711	.94948	.95923	.96658	.97318	.99027	.99639	.99865	.99949	.99981
3	.89513	.91575	.93201	.94454	.95528	.98377	.99398	.99775	.99916	.99968
4	.84406	.87472	.89890	.91813	.93351	.97587	.99105	.99666	.99875	.99953
5	.78194	.82482	.85863	.88551	.90702	.96626	.98749	.99532	.99825	.99934
6	.70637	.76411	.80964	.84584	.87480	.95457	.98315	.99370	.99764	.99911
7	.61446	.69027	.75006	.79758	.83560	.94035	.97788	.99173	.99690	.99884
8	.50265	.60045	.67757	.73888	.78793	.92305	.97147	.98934	.99600	.99850
9	.36665	.49120	.58941	.66748	.72994	.90201	.96366	.98642	.99491	.99809
10	.20123	.35830	.48216	.58063	.65940	.87642	.95417	.98287	.99358	.99759
11	0.00000	.19664	.35171	.47498	.57360	.84528	.94263	.97856	.99196	.99698
12	0.00000	0.00000	.19302	.34647	.46923	.80741	.92859	.97331	.98999	.99625
13	0.00000	0.00000	0.00000	.19015	.34227	.76135	.91150	.96692	.98760	.99535
14	0.00000	0.00000	0.00000	0.00000	.18785	.70531	.89073	.95916	.98469	.99425
15	0.00000	0.00000	0.00000	0.00000	0.00000	.63716	.86545	.94971	.98115	.99293
16	0.00000	0.00000	0.00000	0.00000	0.00000	.55425	.83471	.93822	.97684	.99131
17	0.00000	0.00000	0.00000	0.00000	0.00000	.45340	.79731	.92424	.97160	.98934
18	0.00000	0.00000	0.00000	0.00000	0.00000	.33073	.75182	.90724	.96523	.98695
19	0.00000	0.00000	0.00000	0.00000	0.00000	.18151	.69649	.88656	.95748	.98404
20	0.00000	0.00000	0.00000	0.00000	0.00000	0.00000	.62918	.86141	.94805	.98050
21	0.00000	0.00000	0.00000	0.00000	0.00000	0.00000	.54731	.83081	.93658	.97620
22	0.00000	0.00000	0.00000	0.00000	0.00000	0.00000	.44773	.79358	.92262	.97096
23	0.00000	0.00000	0.00000	0.00000	0.00000	0.00000	.32659	.74831	.90565	.96459
24	0.00000	0.00000	0.00000	0.00000	0.00000	0.00000	.17924	.69323	.88501	.95685
25	0.00000	0.00000	0.00000	0.00000	0.00000	0.00000	0.00000	.62624	.85990	.94742
26	0.00000	0.00000	0.00000	0.00000	0.00000	0.00000	0.00000	.54475	.82935	.93596
27	0.00000	0.00000	0.00000	0.00000	0.00000	0.00000	0.00000	.44563	.79219	.92202
28	0.00000	0.00000	0.00000	0.00000	0.00000	0.00000	0.00000	.32506	.74700	.90506
29	0.00000	0.00000	0.00000	0.00000	0.00000	0.00000	0.00000	.17840	.69202	.88443
30	0.00000	0.00000	0.00000	0.00000	0.00000	0.00000	0.00000	0.00000	.62515	.85933
31	0.00000	0.00000	0.00000	0.00000	0.00000	0.00000	0.00000	0.00000	.54380	.82880
32	0.00000	0.00000	0.00000	0.00000	0.00000	0.00000	0.00000	0.00000	.44485	.79167
33	0.00000	0.00000	0.00000	0.00000	0.00000	0.00000	0.00000	0.00000	.32449	.74650
34	0.00000	0.00000	0.00000	0.00000	0.00000	0.00000	0.00000	0.00000	.17809	.69156
35	0.00000	0.00000	0.00000	0.00000	0.00000	0.00000	0.00000	0.00000	0.00000	.62473
36	0.00000	0.00000	0.00000	0.00000	0.00000	0.00000	0.00000	0.00000	0.00000	.54344
37	0.00000	0.00000	0.00000	0.00000	0.00000	0.00000	0.00000	0.00000	0.00000	.44456
38	0.00000	0.00000	0.00000	0.00000	0.00000	0.00000	0.00000	0.00000	0.00000	.32428
39	0.00000	0.00000	0.00000	0.00000	0.00000	0.00000	0.00000	0.00000	0.00000	.17797

REMAINING MORTGAGE BALANCE TABLE FOR 20.000 PERCENT

ORIGINAL LOAN TERM

AGE OF LOAN	1	2	3	4	5	6	7	8	9	10
1	0.00000	.54943	.73019	.81882	.87064	.90409	.92708	.94357	.95577	.96500
2	0.00000	0.00000	.40119	.59759	.71290	.78714	.83816	.87477	.90184	.92232
3	0.00000	0.00000	0.00000	.32850	.52055	.64452	.72974	.79087	.83608	.87028
4	0.00000	0.00000	0.00000	0.00000	.28600	.47062	.59753	.68856	.75589	.80682
5	0.00000	0.00000	0.00000	0.00000	0.00000	.25857	.43631	.56381	.65811	.72944
6	0.00000	0.00000	0.00000	0.00000	0.00000	0.00000	.23972	.41169	.53887	.63508
7	0.00000	0.00000	0.00000	0.00000	0.00000	0.00000	0.00000	.22619	.39348	.52001
8	0.00000	0.00000	0.00000	0.00000	0.00000	0.00000	0.00000	0.00000	.21619	.37971
9	0.00000	0.00000	0.00000	0.00000	0.00000	0.00000	0.00000	0.00000	0.00000	.20862

AGE OF LOAN	11	12	13	14	15	20	25	30	35	40
1	.97210	.97763	.98199	.98544	.98820	.99577	.99845	.99943	.99979	.99992
2	.93807	.95035	.96002	.96769	.97381	.99061	.99656	.99873	.99953	.99983
3	.89659	.91709	.93323	.94604	.95627	.98431	.99425	.99788	.99921	.99971
4	.84600	.87653	.90057	.91964	.93488	.97664	.99144	.99684	.99883	.99957
5	.78431	.82707	.86074	.88746	.90879	.96728	.98801	.99557	.99836	.99939
6	.70908	.76676	.81217	.84821	.87699	.95586	.98383	.99403	.99779	.99918
7	.61736	.69322	.75295	.80035	.83820	.94195	.97873	.99214	.99709	.99892
8	.50550	.60354	.68073	.74159	.79090	.92498	.97251	.98985	.99624	.99861
9	.36911	.49420	.59267	.67082	.73323	.90429	.96492	.98705	.99520	.99822
10	.20280	.36086	.48529	.58404	.66291	.87906	.95568	.98363	.99394	.99775
11	0.00000	.19826	.35436	.47823	.57715	.84829	.94440	.97947	.99240	.99718
12	0.00000	0.00000	.19469	.34920	.47259	.81077	.93065	.97439	.99052	.99648
13	0.00000	0.00000	0.00000	.19186	.34508	.76502	.91389	.96820	.98822	.99563
14	0.00000	0.00000	0.00000	0.00000	.18959	.70924	.89344	.96065	.98543	.99460
15	0.00000	0.00000	0.00000	0.00000	0.00000	.64121	.86851	.95144	.98202	.99333
16	0.00000	0.00000	0.00000	0.00000	0.00000	.55827	.83812	.94022	.97786	.99179
17	0.00000	0.00000	0.00000	0.00000	0.00000	.45712	.80105	.92653	.97279	.98991
18	0.00000	0.00000	0.00000	0.00000	0.00000	.33378	.75585	.90984	.96661	.98762
19	0.00000	0.00000	0.00000	0.00000	0.00000	.18339	.70073	.88949	.95907	.98483
20	0.00000	0.00000	0.00000	0.00000	0.00000	0.00000	.63352	.86467	.94988	.98142
21	0.00000	0.00000	0.00000	0.00000	0.00000	0.00000	.55157	.83440	.93868	.97727
22	0.00000	0.00000	0.00000	0.00000	0.00000	0.00000	.45164	.79750	.92501	.97220
23	0.00000	0.00000	0.00000	0.00000	0.00000	0.00000	.32978	.75250	.90835	.96602
24	0.00000	0.00000	0.00000	0.00000	0.00000	0.00000	.18119	.69763	.88803	.95849
25	0.00000	0.00000	0.00000	0.00000	0.00000	0.00000	0.00000	.63072	.86325	.94931
26	0.00000	0.00000	0.00000	0.00000	0.00000	0.00000	0.00000	.54913	.83304	.93811
27	0.00000	0.00000	0.00000	0.00000	0.00000	0.00000	0.00000	.44964	.79619	.92445
28	0.00000	0.00000	0.00000	0.00000	0.00000	0.00000	0.00000	.32832	.75127	.90780
29	0.00000	0.00000	0.00000	0.00000	0.00000	0.00000	0.00000	.18039	.69648	.88749
30	0.00000	0.00000	0.00000	0.00000	0.00000	0.00000	0.00000	0.00000	.62968	.86272
31	0.00000	0.00000	0.00000	0.00000	0.00000	0.00000	0.00000	0.00000	.54823	.83253
32	0.00000	0.00000	0.00000	0.00000	0.00000	0.00000	0.00000	0.00000	.44890	.79571
33	0.00000	0.00000	0.00000	0.00000	0.00000	0.00000	0.00000	0.00000	.32778	.75081
34	0.00000	0.00000	0.00000	0.00000	0.00000	0.00000	0.00000	0.00000	.18009	.69606
35	0.00000	0.00000	0.00000	0.00000	0.00000	0.00000	0.00000	0.00000	0.00000	.62930
36	0.00000	0.00000	0.00000	0.00000	0.00000	0.00000	0.00000	0.00000	0.00000	.54789
37	0.00000	0.00000	0.00000	0.00000	0.00000	0.00000	0.00000	0.00000	0.00000	.44863
38	0.00000	0.00000	0.00000	0.00000	0.00000	0.00000	0.00000	0.00000	0.00000	.32758
39	0.00000	0.00000	0.00000	0.00000	0.00000	0.00000	0.00000	0.00000	0.00000	.17998

REMAINING MORTGAGE BALANCE TABLE FOR 20.250 PERCENT

ORIGINAL LOAN TERM

AGE OF LOAN	1	2	3	4	5	6	7	8	9	10
1	0.00000	.55003	.73094	.81960	.87140	.90481	.92775	.94420	.95634	.96552
2	0.00000	0.00000	.40204	.59908	.71420	.78845	.83944	.87598	.90297	.92336
3	0.00000	0.00000	0.00000	.32951	.52203	.64621	.73149	.79260	.83774	.87184
4	0.00000	0.00000	0.00000	0.00000	.28714	.47234	.59953	.69067	.75799	.80885
5	0.00000	0.00000	0.00000	0.00000	0.00000	.25980	.43822	.56607	.66051	.73185
6	0.00000	0.00000	0.00000	0.00000	0.00000	0.00000	.24103	.41376	.54136	.63774
7	0.00000	0.00000	0.00000	0.00000	0.00000	0.00000	0.00000	.22758	.39570	.52269
8	0.00000	0.00000	0.00000	0.00000	0.00000	0.00000	0.00000	0.00000	.21765	.38205
9	0.00000	0.00000	0.00000	0.00000	0.00000	0.00000	0.00000	0.00000	0.00000	.21014

AGE OF LOAN	11	12	13	14	15	20	25	30	35	40
1	.97256	.97805	.98236	.98577	.98850	.99592	.99852	.99946	.99980	.99993
2	.93903	.95121	.96079	.96838	.97443	.99093	.99671	.99880	.99956	.99984
3	.89803	.91841	.93443	.94713	.95724	.98483	.99451	.99800	.99927	.99973
4	.84792	.87832	.90221	.92114	.93623	.97738	.99181	.99701	.99891	.99960
5	.78666	.82930	.86282	.88938	.91054	.96826	.98851	.99581	.99847	.99944
6	.71178	.76939	.81467	.85055	.87914	.95712	.98447	.99433	.99793	.99924
7	.62024	.69615	.75582	.80308	.84076	.94351	.97954	.99253	.99727	.99900
8	.50835	.60662	.68387	.74506	.79384	.92686	.97351	.99034	.99646	.99871
9	.37157	.49719	.59592	.67414	.73649	.90652	.96614	.98765	.99548	.99835
10	.20438	.36341	.48842	.58744	.66638	.88165	.95713	.98436	.99428	.99790
11	0.00000	.19989	.35700	.48147	.58069	.85124	.94612	.98034	.99281	.99737
12	0.00000	0.00000	.19636	.35152	.47593	.81408	.93266	.97543	.99101	.99671
13	0.00000	0.00000	0.00000	.19357	.34788	.76865	.91621	.96943	.98882	.99590
14	0.00000	0.00000	0.00000	0.00000	.19134	.71312	.89610	.96209	.98613	.99492
15	0.00000	0.00000	0.00000	0.00000	0.00000	.64524	.87151	.95312	.98285	.99372
16	0.00000	0.00000	0.00000	0.00000	0.00000	.56226	.84146	.94216	.97884	.99225
17	0.00000	0.00000	0.00000	0.00000	0.00000	.46083	.80472	.92875	.97394	.99046
18	0.00000	0.00000	0.00000	0.00000	0.00000	.33684	.75981	.91237	.96794	.98826
19	0.00000	0.00000	0.00000	0.00000	0.00000	.18527	.70492	.89234	.96061	.98558
20	0.00000	0.00000	0.00000	0.00000	0.00000	0.00000	.63782	.86786	.95166	.98230
21	0.00000	0.00000	0.00000	0.00000	0.00000	0.00000	.55580	.83793	.94071	.97829
22	0.00000	0.00000	0.00000	0.00000	0.00000	0.00000	.45553	.80135	.92733	.97339
23	0.00000	0.00000	0.00000	0.00000	0.00000	0.00000	.33296	.75663	.91097	.96740
24	0.00000	0.00000	0.00000	0.00000	0.00000	0.00000	.18314	.70196	.89097	.96007
25	0.00000	0.00000	0.00000	0.00000	0.00000	0.00000	0.00000	.63514	.86653	.95112
26	0.00000	0.00000	0.00000	0.00000	0.00000	0.00000	0.00000	.55346	.83664	.94018
27	0.00000	0.00000	0.00000	0.00000	0.00000	0.00000	0.00000	.45362	.80012	.92681
28	0.00000	0.00000	0.00000	0.00000	0.00000	0.00000	0.00000	.33157	.75547	.91046
29	0.00000	0.00000	0.00000	0.00000	0.00000	0.00000	0.00000	.18237	.70089	.89047
30	0.00000	0.00000	0.00000	0.00000	0.00000	0.00000	0.00000	0.00000	.63417	.86604
31	0.00000	0.00000	0.00000	0.00000	0.00000	0.00000	0.00000	0.00000	.55262	.83617
32	0.00000	0.00000	0.00000	0.00000	0.00000	0.00000	0.00000	0.00000	.45292	.79967
33	0.00000	0.00000	0.00000	0.00000	0.00000	0.00000	0.00000	0.00000	.33106	.75504
34	0.00000	0.00000	0.00000	0.00000	0.00000	0.00000	0.00000	0.00000	.18209	.70049
35	0.00000	0.00000	0.00000	0.00000	0.00000	0.00000	0.00000	0.00000	0.00000	.63381
36	0.00000	0.00000	0.00000	0.00000	0.00000	0.00000	0.00000	0.00000	0.00000	.55230
37	0.00000	0.00000	0.00000	0.00000	0.00000	0.00000	0.00000	0.00000	0.00000	.45267
38	0.00000	0.00000	0.00000	0.00000	0.00000	0.00000	0.00000	0.00000	0.00000	.33087
39	0.00000	0.00000	0.00000	0.00000	0.00000	0.00000	0.00000	0.00000	0.00000	.18199

REMAINING MORTGAGE BALANCE TABLE FOR 20.500 PERCENT

AGE OF LOAN	ORIGINAL LOAN TERM 1	2	3	4	5	6	7	8	9	10
1	0.00000	.55064	.73169	.82037	.87215	.90553	.92842	.94481	.95690	.96603
2	0.00000	0.00000	.40290	.60026	.71549	.78976	.84071	.87718	.90409	.92439
3	0.00000	0.00000	0.00000	.33053	.52352	.64790	.73323	.79431	.83938	.87338
4	0.00000	0.00000	0.00000	0.00000	.28827	.47406	.60152	.69276	.76008	.81086
5	0.00000	0.00000	0.00000	0.00000	0.00000	.26104	.44013	.56832	.66291	.73426
6	0.00000	0.00000	0.00000	0.00000	0.00000	0.00000	.24235	.41584	.54383	.64039
7	0.00000	0.00000	0.00000	0.00000	0.00000	0.00000	0.00000	.22898	.39792	.52536
8	0.00000	0.00000	0.00000	0.00000	0.00000	0.00000	0.00000	0.00000	.21911	.38440
9	0.00000	0.00000	0.00000	0.00000	0.00000	0.00000	0.00000	0.00000	0.00000	.21167

AGE OF LOAN	11	12	13	14	15	20	25	30	35	40
1	.97302	.97846	.98273	.98610	.98878	.99607	.99859	.99949	.99982	.99993
2	.93997	.95206	.96156	.96906	.97504	.99124	.99687	.99887	.99959	.99985
3	.89946	.91972	.93562	.94819	.95819	.98534	.99475	.99811	.99932	.99975
4	.84982	.88008	.90383	.92261	.93755	.97810	.99216	.99717	.99898	.99963
5	.78899	.83151	.86488	.89127	.91226	.96922	.98898	.99603	.99856	.99948
6	.71445	.77200	.81715	.85286	.88127	.95835	.98509	.99463	.99806	.99930
7	.62311	.69906	.75866	.80579	.84329	.94503	.98032	.99291	.99744	.99907
8	.51118	.60969	.68699	.74811	.79675	.92870	.97448	.99080	.99668	.99880
9	.37403	.50017	.59916	.67744	.73972	.90870	.96732	.98822	.99574	.99846
10	.20596	.36597	.49153	.59083	.66984	.88419	.95855	.98506	.99460	.99805
11	0.00000	.20152	.35965	.48470	.58420	.85415	.94780	.98118	.99320	.99754
12	0.00000	0.00000	.19804	.35465	.47926	.81734	.93462	.97643	.99148	.99692
13	0.00000	0.00000	0.00000	.19529	.35067	.77223	.91847	.97061	.98938	.99616
14	0.00000	0.00000	0.00000	0.00000	.19309	.71696	.89869	.96348	.98680	.99523
15	0.00000	0.00000	0.00000	0.00000	0.00000	.64922	.87445	.95474	.98364	.99408
16	0.00000	0.00000	0.00000	0.00000	0.00000	.56622	.84474	.94403	.97977	.99268
17	0.00000	0.00000	0.00000	0.00000	0.00000	.46451	.80833	.93091	.97503	.99097
18	0.00000	0.00000	0.00000	0.00000	0.00000	.33988	.76372	.91483	.96922	.98887
19	0.00000	0.00000	0.00000	0.00000	0.00000	.18715	.70906	.89512	.96210	.98629
20	0.00000	0.00000	0.00000	0.00000	0.00000	0.00000	.64207	.87097	.95337	.98313
21	0.00000	0.00000	0.00000	0.00000	0.00000	0.00000	.55998	.84138	.94268	.97926
22	0.00000	0.00000	0.00000	0.00000	0.00000	0.00000	.45940	.80512	.92957	.97452
23	0.00000	0.00000	0.00000	0.00000	0.00000	0.00000	.33613	.76069	.91351	.96872
24	0.00000	0.00000	0.00000	0.00000	0.00000	0.00000	.18509	.70624	.89384	.96160
25	0.00000	0.00000	0.00000	0.00000	0.00000	0.00000	0.00000	.63952	.86972	.95288
26	0.00000	0.00000	0.00000	0.00000	0.00000	0.00000	0.00000	.55776	.84018	.94219
27	0.00000	0.00000	0.00000	0.00000	0.00000	0.00000	0.00000	.45757	.80397	.92909
28	0.00000	0.00000	0.00000	0.00000	0.00000	0.00000	0.00000	.33480	.75960	.91304
29	0.00000	0.00000	0.00000	0.00000	0.00000	0.00000	0.00000	.18436	.70523	.89337
30	0.00000	0.00000	0.00000	0.00000	0.00000	0.00000	0.00000	0.00000	.63860	.86927
31	0.00000	0.00000	0.00000	0.00000	0.00000	0.00000	0.00000	0.00000	.55696	.83974
32	0.00000	0.00000	0.00000	0.00000	0.00000	0.00000	0.00000	0.00000	.45692	.80355
33	0.00000	0.00000	0.00000	0.00000	0.00000	0.00000	0.00000	0.00000	.33432	.75920
34	0.00000	0.00000	0.00000	0.00000	0.00000	0.00000	0.00000	0.00000	.18409	.70486
35	0.00000	0.00000	0.00000	0.00000	0.00000	0.00000	0.00000	0.00000	0.00000	.63827
36	0.00000	0.00000	0.00000	0.00000	0.00000	0.00000	0.00000	0.00000	0.00000	.55667
37	0.00000	0.00000	0.00000	0.00000	0.00000	0.00000	0.00000	0.00000	0.00000	.45668
38	0.00000	0.00000	0.00000	0.00000	0.00000	0.00000	0.00000	0.00000	0.00000	.33415
39	0.00000	0.00000	0.00000	0.00000	0.00000	0.00000	0.00000	0.00000	0.00000	.18400

REMAINING MORTGAGE BALANCE TABLE FOR 20.750 PERCENT

AGE OF LOAN	ORIGINAL LOAN TERM 1	2	3	4	5	6	7	8	9	10
1	0.00000	.55125	.73244	.82114	.87291	.90624	.92909	.94542	.95746	.96653
2	0.00000	0.00000	.40376	.60144	.71678	.79106	.84197	.87838	.90521	.92541
3	0.00000	0.00000	0.00000	.33154	.52500	.64958	.73497	.79602	.84101	.87491
4	0.00000	0.00000	0.00000	0.00000	.28941	.47577	.60351	.69485	.76216	.81287
5	0.00000	0.00000	0.00000	0.00000	0.00000	.26227	.44203	.57057	.66529	.73665
6	0.00000	0.00000	0.00000	0.00000	0.00000	0.00000	.24367	.41791	.54630	.64303
7	0.00000	0.00000	0.00000	0.00000	0.00000	0.00000	0.00000	.23037	.40013	.52802
8	0.00000	0.00000	0.00000	0.00000	0.00000	0.00000	0.00000	0.00000	.22057	.38674
9	0.00000	0.00000	0.00000	0.00000	0.00000	0.00000	0.00000	0.00000	0.00000	.21319

AGE OF LOAN	11	12	13	14	15	20	25	30	35	40
1	.97348	.97886	.98309	.98642	.98906	.99621	.99866	.99952	.99983	.99994
2	.94089	.95290	.96231	.96973	.97563	.99155	.99701	.99894	.99962	.99986
3	.90087	.92101	.93678	.94924	.95913	.98582	.99499	.99821	.99936	.99977
4	.85170	.88183	.90543	.92406	.93886	.97879	.99250	.99733	.99905	.99966
5	.79131	.83370	.86691	.89313	.91395	.97016	.98944	.99624	.99866	.99952
6	.71711	.77458	.81960	.85514	.88336	.95955	.98569	.99490	.99818	.99935
7	.62597	.70196	.76148	.80847	.84579	.94651	.98108	.99326	.99759	.99914
8	.51401	.61274	.69008	.75114	.79963	.93051	.97542	.99125	.99687	.99888
9	.37648	.50315	.60238	.68071	.74292	.91084	.96846	.98877	.99599	.99857
10	.20754	.36852	.49464	.59420	.67327	.88668	.95992	.98572	.99490	.99818
11	0.00000	.20315	.36229	.48792	.58770	.85700	.94942	.98199	.99357	.99770
12	0.00000	0.00000	.19971	.35737	.48258	.82055	.93652	.97739	.99193	.99712
13	0.00000	0.00000	0.00000	.19700	.35346	.77576	.92068	.97175	.98991	.99640
14	0.00000	0.00000	0.00000	0.00000	.19485	.72075	.90122	.96482	.98744	.99551
15	0.00000	0.00000	0.00000	0.00000	0.00000	.65317	.87732	.95631	.98440	.99443
16	0.00000	0.00000	0.00000	0.00000	0.00000	.57016	.84796	.94585	.98067	.99309
17	0.00000	0.00000	0.00000	0.00000	0.00000	.46818	.81188	.93300	.97608	.99145
18	0.00000	0.00000	0.00000	0.00000	0.00000	.34291	.76757	.91722	.97045	.98944
19	0.00000	0.00000	0.00000	0.00000	0.00000	.18903	.71314	.89784	.96353	.98697
20	0.00000	0.00000	0.00000	0.00000	0.00000	0.00000	.64628	.87402	.95502	.98393
21	0.00000	0.00000	0.00000	0.00000	0.00000	0.00000	.56414	.84477	.94458	.98020
22	0.00000	0.00000	0.00000	0.00000	0.00000	0.00000	.46324	.80883	.93175	.97561
23	0.00000	0.00000	0.00000	0.00000	0.00000	0.00000	.33929	.76469	.91599	.96998
24	0.00000	0.00000	0.00000	0.00000	0.00000	0.00000	.18704	.71046	.89663	.96306
25	0.00000	0.00000	0.00000	0.00000	0.00000	0.00000	0.00000	.64385	.87285	.95457
26	0.00000	0.00000	0.00000	0.00000	0.00000	0.00000	0.00000	.56202	.84363	.94413
27	0.00000	0.00000	0.00000	0.00000	0.00000	0.00000	0.00000	.46150	.80775	.93130
28	0.00000	0.00000	0.00000	0.00000	0.00000	0.00000	0.00000	.33802	.76366	.91555
29	0.00000	0.00000	0.00000	0.00000	0.00000	0.00000	0.00000	.18633	.70951	.89620
30	0.00000	0.00000	0.00000	0.00000	0.00000	0.00000	0.00000	0.00000	.64298	.87243
31	0.00000	0.00000	0.00000	0.00000	0.00000	0.00000	0.00000	0.00000	.56127	.84323
32	0.00000	0.00000	0.00000	0.00000	0.00000	0.00000	0.00000	0.00000	.46088	.80736
33	0.00000	0.00000	0.00000	0.00000	0.00000	0.00000	0.00000	0.00000	.33757	.76330
34	0.00000	0.00000	0.00000	0.00000	0.00000	0.00000	0.00000	0.00000	.18608	.70917
35	0.00000	0.00000	0.00000	0.00000	0.00000	0.00000	0.00000	0.00000	0.00000	.64268
36	0.00000	0.00000	0.00000	0.00000	0.00000	0.00000	0.00000	0.00000	0.00000	.56100
37	0.00000	0.00000	0.00000	0.00000	0.00000	0.00000	0.00000	0.00000	0.00000	.46066
38	0.00000	0.00000	0.00000	0.00000	0.00000	0.00000	0.00000	0.00000	0.00000	.33740
39	0.00000	0.00000	0.00000	0.00000	0.00000	0.00000	0.00000	0.00000	0.00000	.18599

REMAINING MORTGAGE BALANCE TABLE FOR 21.000 PERCENT

ORIGINAL LOAN TERM

AGE OF LOAN	1	2	3	4	5	6	7	8	9	10
1	0.00000	.55186	.73318	.82151	.87366	.90695	.92975	.94603	.95801	.96703
2	0.00000	0.00000	.40461	.60261	.71807	.79236	.84323	.87957	.90631	.92642
3	0.00000	0.00000	0.00000	.33256	.52648	.65125	.73669	.79772	.84263	.87642
4	0.00000	0.00000	0.00000	0.00000	.29054	.47749	.60550	.69693	.76423	.81485
5	0.00000	0.00000	0.00000	0.00000	0.00000	.26351	.44394	.57282	.66767	.73903
6	0.00000	0.00000	0.00000	0.00000	0.00000	0.00000	.24499	.41998	.54877	.64566
7	0.00000	0.00000	0.00000	0.00000	0.00000	0.00000	0.00000	.23177	.40235	.53067
8	0.00000	0.00000	0.00000	0.00000	0.00000	0.00000	0.00000	0.00000	.22204	.38908
9	0.00000	0.00000	0.00000	0.00000	0.00000	0.00000	0.00000	0.00000	0.00000	.21472

AGE OF LOAN	11	12	13	14	15	20	25	30	35	40
1	.97392	.97926	.98344	.98673	.93934	.99634	.99872	.99955	.99984	.99994
2	.94181	.95373	.96305	.97039	.97621	.99184	.99715	.99900	.99965	.99988
3	.90227	.92228	.93793	.95027	.96004	.98630	.99521	.99831	.99941	.99979
4	.85357	.88356	.90701	.92549	.94014	.97947	.99282	.99747	.99911	.99969
5	.79360	.83587	.86892	.89497	.91562	.97106	.98989	.99644	.99874	.99956
6	.71976	.77714	.82203	.85739	.88543	.96071	.98627	.99517	.99830	.99940
7	.62882	.70483	.76427	.81112	.84825	.94796	.98181	.99360	.99774	.99920
8	.51684	.61578	.69316	.75413	.80247	.93226	.97632	.99167	.99706	.99896
9	.37893	.50612	.60558	.68396	.74609	.91293	.96956	.98929	.99622	.99867
10	.20912	.37108	.49774	.59754	.67667	.88913	.96124	.98636	.99519	.99830
11	0.00000	.20478	.36493	.49113	.59117	.85981	.95099	.98276	.99392	.99785
12	0.00000	0.00000	.20139	.36009	.48589	.82371	.93838	.97832	.99235	.99730
13	0.00000	0.00000	0.00000	.19872	.35625	.77925	.92283	.97285	.99042	.99662
14	0.00000	0.00000	0.00000	0.00000	.19660	.72450	.90370	.96611	.98805	.99578
15	0.00000	0.00000	0.00000	0.00000	0.00000	.65709	.88013	.95782	.98512	.99475
16	0.00000	0.00000	0.00000	0.00000	0.00000	.57407	.85111	.94761	.98152	.99348
17	0.00000	0.00000	0.00000	0.00000	0.00000	.47184	.81538	.93504	.97709	.99191
18	0.00000	0.00000	0.00000	0.00000	0.00000	.34594	.77137	.91955	.97163	.98998
19	0.00000	0.00000	0.00000	0.00000	0.00000	.19091	.71718	.90048	.96490	.98761
20	0.00000	0.00000	0.00000	0.00000	0.00000	0.00000	.65044	.87700	.95662	.98469
21	0.00000	0.00000	0.00000	0.00000	0.00000	0.00000	.56826	.84808	.94642	.98109
22	0.00000	0.00000	0.00000	0.00000	0.00000	0.00000	.46706	.81247	.93386	.97665
23	0.00000	0.00000	0.00000	0.00000	0.00000	0.00000	.34244	.76862	.91840	.97120
24	0.00000	0.00000	0.00000	0.00000	0.00000	0.00000	.18898	.71462	.89935	.96447
25	0.00000	0.00000	0.00000	0.00000	0.00000	0.00000	0.00000	.64813	.87590	.95620
26	0.00000	0.00000	0.00000	0.00000	0.00000	0.00000	0.00000	.56624	.84702	.94630
27	0.00000	0.00000	0.00000	0.00000	0.00000	0.00000	0.00000	.46540	.81145	.93345
28	0.00000	0.00000	0.00000	0.00000	0.00000	0.00000	0.00000	.34122	.76766	.91799
29	0.00000	0.00000	0.00000	0.00000	0.00000	0.00000	0.00000	.18831	.71373	.89895
30	0.00000	0.00000	0.00000	0.00000	0.00000	0.00000	0.00000	0.00000	.64731	.87551
31	0.00000	0.00000	0.00000	0.00000	0.00000	0.00000	0.00000	0.00000	.56553	.84664
32	0.00000	0.00000	0.00000	0.00000	0.00000	0.00000	0.00000	0.00000	.46482	.81109
33	0.00000	0.00000	0.00000	0.00000	0.00000	0.00000	0.00000	0.00000	.34080	.76732
34	0.00000	0.00000	0.00000	0.00000	0.00000	0.00000	0.00000	0.00000	.18807	.71341
35	0.00000	0.00000	0.00000	0.00000	0.00000	0.00000	0.00000	0.00000	0.00000	.64703
36	0.00000	0.00000	0.00000	0.00000	0.00000	0.00000	0.00000	0.00000	0.00000	.56528
37	0.00000	0.00000	0.00000	0.00000	0.00000	0.00000	0.00000	0.00000	0.00000	.46461
38	0.00000	0.00000	0.00000	0.00000	0.00000	0.00000	0.00000	0.00000	0.00000	.34064
39	0.00000	0.00000	0.00000	0.00000	0.00000	0.00000	0.00000	0.00000	0.00000	.18799

REMAINING MORTGAGE BALANCE TABLE FOR 21.250 PERCENT

ORIGINAL LOAN TERM

AGE OF LOAN	1	2	3	4	5	6	7	8	9	10
1	0.00000	.55247	.73393	.82268	.87440	.90765	.93040	.94663	.95856	.96752
2	0.00000	0.00000	.40547	.60379	.71936	.79365	.84448	.88074	.90740	.92742
3	0.00000	0.00000	0.00000	.33357	.52795	.65292	.73841	.79941	.84424	.87792
4	0.00000	0.00000	0.00000	0.00000	.29168	.47920	.60748	.69900	.76628	.81682
5	0.00000	0.00000	0.00000	0.00000	0.00000	.26474	.44585	.57506	.67004	.74139
6	0.00000	0.00000	0.00000	0.00000	0.00000	0.00000	.24632	.42205	.55123	.64827
7	0.00000	0.00000	0.00000	0.00000	0.00000	0.00000	0.00000	.23317	.40456	.53332
8	0.00000	0.00000	0.00000	0.00000	0.00000	0.00000	0.00000	0.00000	.22351	.39142
9	0.00000	0.00000	0.00000	0.00000	0.00000	0.00000	0.00000	0.00000	0.00000	.21625

AGE OF LOAN	11	12	13	14	15	20	25	30	35	40
1	.97436	.97965	.98379	.98704	.98961	.99648	.99878	.99958	.99985	.99995
2	.94271	.95454	.96377	.97103	.97678	.99213	.99728	.99905	.99967	.99989
3	.90365	.92353	.93906	.95128	.96094	.98676	.99543	.99841	.99945	.99981
4	.85542	.88526	.90856	.92689	.94139	.98013	.99314	.99761	.99917	.99971
5	.79588	.83801	.87091	.89678	.91726	.97195	.99031	.99663	.99883	.99959
6	.72238	.77969	.82443	.85962	.88746	.96185	.98682	.99542	.99840	.99944
7	.63165	.70769	.76705	.81374	.85068	.94938	.98251	.99392	.99788	.99926
8	.51965	.61880	.69621	.75710	.80528	.93398	.97720	.99207	.99724	.99904
9	.38139	.50908	.60877	.68719	.74923	.91498	.97063	.98979	.99644	.99876
10	.21070	.37363	.50082	.60088	.68004	.89152	.96253	.98697	.99546	.99842
11	0.00000	.20642	.36757	.49433	.59463	.86257	.95253	.98350	.99425	.99800
12	0.00000	0.00000	.20307	.36280	.48919	.82682	.94018	.97920	.99275	.99747
13	0.00000	0.00000	0.00000	.20044	.35903	.78769	.92493	.97390	.99091	.99683
14	0.00000	0.00000	0.00000	0.00000	.19835	.72821	.90611	.96736	.98863	.99603
15	0.00000	0.00000	0.00000	0.00000	0.00000	.66097	.88288	.95929	.98581	.99505
16	0.00000	0.00000	0.00000	0.00000	0.00000	.57795	.85421	.94932	.98234	.99384
17	0.00000	0.00000	0.00000	0.00000	0.00000	.47547	.81881	.93701	.97805	.99235
18	0.00000	0.00000	0.00000	0.00000	0.00000	.34896	.77511	.92182	.97276	.99050
19	0.00000	0.00000	0.00000	0.00000	0.00000	.19279	.72116	.90306	.96623	.98822
20	0.00000	0.00000	0.00000	0.00000	0.00000	0.00000	.65456	.87991	.95816	.98541
21	0.00000	0.00000	0.00000	0.00000	0.00000	0.00000	.57235	.85133	.94820	.98194
22	0.00000	0.00000	0.00000	0.00000	0.00000	0.00000	.47086	.81605	.93591	.97765
23	0.00000	0.00000	0.00000	0.00000	0.00000	0.00000	.34558	.77249	.92073	.97236
24	0.00000	0.00000	0.00000	0.00000	0.00000	0.00000	.19092	.71873	.90200	.96583
25	0.00000	0.00000	0.00000	0.00000	0.00000	0.00000	0.00000	.65236	.87888	.95777
26	0.00000	0.00000	0.00000	0.00000	0.00000	0.00000	0.00000	.57042	.85033	.94781
27	0.00000	0.00000	0.00000	0.00000	0.00000	0.00000	0.00000	.46928	.81509	.93553
28	0.00000	0.00000	0.00000	0.00000	0.00000	0.00000	0.00000	.34441	.77159	.92036
29	0.00000	0.00000	0.00000	0.00000	0.00000	0.00000	0.00000	.19028	.71788	.90163
30	0.00000	0.00000	0.00000	0.00000	0.00000	0.00000	0.00000	0.00000	.65159	.87852
31	0.00000	0.00000	0.00000	0.00000	0.00000	0.00000	0.00000	0.00000	.56975	.84998
32	0.00000	0.00000	0.00000	0.00000	0.00000	0.00000	0.00000	0.00000	.46872	.81476
33	0.00000	0.00000	0.00000	0.00000	0.00000	0.00000	0.00000	0.00000	.34401	.77127
34	0.00000	0.00000	0.00000	0.00000	0.00000	0.00000	0.00000	0.00000	.19005	.71759
35	0.00000	0.00000	0.00000	0.00000	0.00000	0.00000	0.00000	0.00000	0.00000	.65132
36	0.00000	0.00000	0.00000	0.00000	0.00000	0.00000	0.00000	0.00000	0.00000	.56952
37	0.00000	0.00000	0.00000	0.00000	0.00000	0.00000	0.00000	0.00000	0.00000	.46853
38	0.00000	0.00000	0.00000	0.00000	0.00000	0.00000	0.00000	0.00000	0.00000	.34387
39	0.00000	0.00000	0.00000	0.00000	0.00000	0.00000	0.00000	0.00000	0.00000	.18998

REMAINING MORTGAGE BALANCE TABLE FOR 21.500 PERCENT

ORIGINAL LOAN TERM

AGE OF LOAN	1	2	3	4	5	6	7	8	9	10
1	0.00000	.55307	.73467	.82345	.87515	.90835	.93105	.94722	.95910	.96800
2	0.00000	0.00000	.40633	.60456	.72064	.79494	.84572	.88191	.90848	.92841
3	0.00000	0.00000	0.00000	.33459	.52943	.65459	.74013	.80109	.84584	.87941
4	0.00000	0.00000	0.00000	0.00000	.29281	.48091	.60946	.70107	.76832	.81877
5	0.00000	0.00000	0.00000	0.00000	0.00000	.26598	.44775	.57729	.67239	.74374
6	0.00000	0.00000	0.00000	0.00000	0.00000	0.00000	.24764	.42412	.55368	.65088
7	0.00000	0.00000	0.00000	0.00000	0.00000	0.00000	0.00000	.23457	.40677	.53596
8	0.00000	0.00000	0.00000	0.00000	0.00000	0.00000	0.00000	0.00000	.22498	.39376
9	0.00000	0.00000	0.00000	0.00000	0.00000	0.00000	0.00000	0.00000	0.00000	.21778

AGE OF LOAN	11	12	13	14	15	20	25	30	35	40
1	.97480	.98004	.98413	.98734	.98987	.99660	.99884	.99960	.99986	.99995
2	.94361	.95534	.96448	.97166	.97733	.99240	.99741	.99911	.99969	.99989
3	.90501	.92477	.94018	.95227	.96182	.98720	.99563	.99850	.99948	.99982
4	.85725	.88695	.91009	.92827	.94262	.98077	.99343	.99775	.99922	.99973
5	.79814	.84014	.87287	.89857	.91887	.97280	.99072	.99681	.99890	.99962
6	.72499	.78221	.82680	.86181	.88947	.96295	.98735	.99566	.99850	.99949
7	.63447	.71052	.76979	.81633	.85308	.95075	.98319	.99423	.99801	.99932
8	.52246	.62181	.69924	.76004	.80806	.93566	.97804	.99246	.99740	.99911
9	.38383	.51203	.61194	.69039	.75234	.91699	.97166	.99027	.99665	.99885
10	.21229	.37617	.50390	.60419	.68339	.89388	.96377	.98756	.99572	.99852
11	0.00000	.20805	.37020	.49752	.59807	.86528	.95401	.98420	.99456	.99813
12	0.00000	0.00000	.20475	.36551	.49248	.82988	.94193	.98005	.99314	.99764
13	0.00000	0.00000	0.00000	.20216	.36181	.78608	.92698	.97492	.99137	.99703
14	0.00000	0.00000	0.00000	0.00000	.20011	.73188	.90848	.96856	.98918	.99627
15	0.00000	0.00000	0.00000	0.00000	0.00000	.66481	.88558	.96070	.98647	.99534
16	0.00000	0.00000	0.00000	0.00000	0.00000	.58180	.85724	.95097	.98312	.99419
17	0.00000	0.00000	0.00000	0.00000	0.00000	.47909	.82218	.93893	.97898	.99276
18	0.00000	0.00000	0.00000	0.00000	0.00000	.35197	.77879	.92402	.97385	.99099
19	0.00000	0.00000	0.00000	0.00000	0.00000	.19467	.72509	.90558	.96750	.98881
20	0.00000	0.00000	0.00000	0.00000	0.00000	0.00000	.65864	.88275	.95965	.98610
21	0.00000	0.00000	0.00000	0.00000	0.00000	0.00000	.57640	.85451	.94992	.98275
22	0.00000	0.00000	0.00000	0.00000	0.00000	0.00000	.47464	.81956	.93789	.97861
23	0.00000	0.00000	0.00000	0.00000	0.00000	0.00000	.34870	.77630	.92301	.97348
24	0.00000	0.00000	0.00000	0.00000	0.00000	0.00000	.19286	.72278	.90458	.96714
25	0.00000	0.00000	0.00000	0.00000	0.00000	0.00000	0.00000	.65654	.88179	.95928
26	0.00000	0.00000	0.00000	0.00000	0.00000	0.00000	0.00000	.57457	.85357	.94957
27	0.00000	0.00000	0.00000	0.00000	0.00000	0.00000	0.00000	.47312	.81866	.93754
28	0.00000	0.00000	0.00000	0.00000	0.00000	0.00000	0.00000	.34759	.77545	.92266
29	0.00000	0.00000	0.00000	0.00000	0.00000	0.00000	0.00000	.19224	.72198	.90424
30	0.00000	0.00000	0.00000	0.00000	0.00000	0.00000	0.00000	0.00000	.65582	.88145
31	0.00000	0.00000	0.00000	0.00000	0.00000	0.00000	0.00000	0.00000	.57393	.85325
32	0.00000	0.00000	0.00000	0.00000	0.00000	0.00000	0.00000	0.00000	.47261	.81835
33	0.00000	0.00000	0.00000	0.00000	0.00000	0.00000	0.00000	0.00000	.34721	.77516
34	0.00000	0.00000	0.00000	0.00000	0.00000	0.00000	0.00000	0.00000	.19203	.72171
35	0.00000	0.00000	0.00000	0.00000	0.00000	0.00000	0.00000	0.00000	0.00000	.65557
36	0.00000	0.00000	0.00000	0.00000	0.00000	0.00000	0.00000	0.00000	0.00000	.57372
37	0.00000	0.00000	0.00000	0.00000	0.00000	0.00000	0.00000	0.00000	0.00000	.47243
38	0.00000	0.00000	0.00000	0.00000	0.00000	0.00000	0.00000	0.00000	0.00000	.34708
39	0.00000	0.00000	0.00000	0.00000	0.00000	0.00000	0.00000	0.00000	0.00000	.19196

REMAINING MORTGAGE BALANCE TABLE FOR 21.750 PERCENT

ORIGINAL LOAN TERM

AGE OF LOAN	1	2	3	4	5	6	7	8	9	10
1	0.00000	.55368	.73542	.82421	.87588	.90905	.93169	.94781	.95963	.96848
2	0.00000	0.00000	.40718	.60614	.72191	.79622	.84696	.88307	.90955	.92939
3	0.00000	0.00000	0.00000	.33561	.53091	.65626	.74184	.80276	.84742	.88088
4	0.00000	0.00000	0.00000	0.00000	.29395	.48262	.61143	.70312	.77035	.82071
5	0.00000	0.00000	0.00000	0.00000	0.00000	.26722	.44966	.57952	.67474	.74607
6	0.00000	0.00000	0.00000	0.00000	0.00000	0.00000	.24897	.42619	.55613	.65347
7	0.00000	0.00000	0.00000	0.00000	0.00000	0.00000	0.00000	.23597	.40898	.53860
8	0.00000	0.00000	0.00000	0.00000	0.00000	0.00000	0.00000	0.00000	.22645	.39609
9	0.00000	0.00000	0.00000	0.00000	0.00000	0.00000	0.00000	0.00000	0.00000	.21931

AGE OF LOAN	11	12	13	14	15	20	25	30	35	40
1	.97522	.98042	.98446	.98763	.99013	.99673	.99890	.99963	.99987	.99996
2	.94449	.95613	.96518	.97228	.97788	.99267	.99753	.99916	.99971	.99990
3	.90636	.92599	.94127	.95324	.96268	.98763	.99583	.99858	.99952	.99984
4	.85906	.88861	.91161	.92963	.94383	.98139	.99372	.99787	.99928	.99975
5	.80038	.84224	.87480	.90033	.92045	.97364	.99111	.99698	.99897	.99965
6	.72759	.78471	.82915	.86358	.89144	.96402	.98786	.99588	.99860	.99952
7	.63728	.71334	.77251	.81889	.85545	.95210	.98384	.99452	.99814	.99937
8	.52525	.62480	.70225	.76256	.81081	.93730	.97885	.99282	.99756	.99917
9	.38628	.51497	.61509	.69357	.75542	.91895	.97266	.99072	.99685	.99893
10	.21388	.37872	.50697	.60749	.68672	.89618	.96498	.98812	.99596	.99863
11	0.00000	.20969	.37283	.50070	.60149	.86794	.95545	.98488	.99486	.99825
12	0.00000	0.00000	.20643	.36822	.49575	.83290	.94363	.98087	.99350	.99779
13	0.00000	0.00000	0.00000	.20388	.36458	.78943	.92897	.97590	.99180	.99721
14	0.00000	0.00000	0.00000	0.00000	.20186	.73551	.91078	.96972	.98971	.99650
15	0.00000	0.00000	0.00000	0.00000	0.00000	.66862	.88821	.96207	.98710	.99561
16	0.00000	0.00000	0.00000	0.00000	0.00000	.58563	.86022	.95257	.98387	.99451
17	0.00000	0.00000	0.00000	0.00000	0.00000	.48268	.82549	.94078	.97987	.99315
18	0.00000	0.00000	0.00000	0.00000	0.00000	.35497	.78241	.92617	.97490	.99146
19	0.00000	0.00000	0.00000	0.00000	0.00000	.19654	.72897	.90803	.96873	.98936
20	0.00000	0.00000	0.00000	0.00000	0.00000	0.00000	.66267	.88553	.96108	.98676
21	0.00000	0.00000	0.00000	0.00000	0.00000	0.00000	.58042	.85763	.95159	.98353
22	0.00000	0.00000	0.00000	0.00000	0.00000	0.00000	.47839	.82300	.93982	.97952
23	0.00000	0.00000	0.00000	0.00000	0.00000	0.00000	.35182	.78005	.92522	.97456
24	0.00000	0.00000	0.00000	0.00000	0.00000	0.00000	.19479	.72677	.90710	.96839
25	0.00000	0.00000	0.00000	0.00000	0.00000	0.00000	0.00000	.66067	.88463	.96075
26	0.00000	0.00000	0.00000	0.00000	0.00000	0.00000	0.00000	.57867	.85675	.95126
27	0.00000	0.00000	0.00000	0.00000	0.00000	0.00000	0.00000	.47695	.82216	.93949
28	0.00000	0.00000	0.00000	0.00000	0.00000	0.00000	0.00000	.35075	.77925	.92489
29	0.00000	0.00000	0.00000	0.00000	0.00000	0.00000	0.00000	.19421	.72602	.90678
30	0.00000	0.00000	0.00000	0.00000	0.00000	0.00000	0.00000	0.00000	.65999	.88432
31	0.00000	0.00000	0.00000	0.00000	0.00000	0.00000	0.00000	0.00000	.57808	.85645
32	0.00000	0.00000	0.00000	0.00000	0.00000	0.00000	0.00000	0.00000	.47646	.82187
33	0.00000	0.00000	0.00000	0.00000	0.00000	0.00000	0.00000	0.00000	.35039	.77898
34	0.00000	0.00000	0.00000	0.00000	0.00000	0.00000	0.00000	0.00000	.19401	.72577
35	0.00000	0.00000	0.00000	0.00000	0.00000	0.00000	0.00000	0.00000	0.00000	.65976
36	0.00000	0.00000	0.00000	0.00000	0.00000	0.00000	0.00000	0.00000	0.00000	.57788
37	0.00000	0.00000	0.00000	0.00000	0.00000	0.00000	0.00000	0.00000	0.00000	.47629
38	0.00000	0.00000	0.00000	0.00000	0.00000	0.00000	0.00000	0.00000	0.00000	.35027
39	0.00000	0.00000	0.00000	0.00000	0.00000	0.00000	0.00000	0.00000	0.00000	.19394

REMAINING MORTGAGE BALANCE TABLE FOR 22.000 PERCENT

ORIGINAL LOAN TERM

AGE OF LOAN	1	2	3	4	5	6	7	8	9	10
1	0.00000	.55429	.73616	.82457	.87662	.90974	.93233	.94840	.96016	.96896
2	0.00000	0.00000	.40804	.60731	.72319	.79750	.84818	.88422	.91061	.93035
3	0.00000	0.00000	0.00000	.33662	.53238	.65792	.74354	.80442	.84899	.88234
4	0.00000	0.00000	0.00000	0.00000	.29509	.48433	.61340	.70517	.77237	.82264
5	0.00000	0.00000	0.00000	0.00000	0.00000	.26846	.45156	.58174	.67707	.74839
6	0.00000	0.00000	0.00000	0.00000	0.00000	0.00000	.25029	.42826	.55857	.65605
7	0.00000	0.00000	0.00000	0.00000	0.00000	0.00000	0.00000	.23738	.41119	.54123
8	0.00000	0.00000	0.00000	0.00000	0.00000	0.00000	0.00000	0.00000	.22792	.39843
9	0.00000	0.00000	0.00000	0.00000	0.00000	0.00000	0.00000	0.00000	0.00000	.22084

AGE OF LOAN	11	12	13	14	15	20	25	30	35	40
1	.97565	.98079	.98479	.98792	.99038	.99685	.99895	.99965	.99988	.99996
2	.94536	.95691	.96587	.97289	.97841	.99293	.99764	.99921	.99973	.99991
3	.90769	.92720	.94235	.95420	.96353	.98805	.99602	.99866	.99955	.99985
4	.86085	.89026	.91310	.93096	.94502	.98199	.99400	.99799	.99932	.99977
5	.80260	.84432	.87672	.90206	.92201	.97445	.99148	.99714	.99904	.99968
6	.73016	.78719	.83148	.86612	.89338	.96507	.98836	.99610	.99869	.99956
7	.64008	.71614	.77521	.82143	.85779	.95341	.98447	.99479	.99825	.99941
8	.52805	.62778	.70524	.76585	.81352	.93891	.97964	.99317	.99771	.99923
9	.38872	.51790	.61823	.69672	.75848	.92087	.97362	.99116	.99703	.99900
10	.21546	.38126	.51003	.61076	.69002	.89845	.96615	.98865	.99619	.99872
11	0.00000	.21133	.37546	.50386	.60489	.87056	.95685	.98553	.99514	.99837
12	0.00000	0.00000	.20811	.37052	.49901	.83587	.94529	.98166	.99384	.99793
13	0.00000	0.00000	0.00000	.20560	.36735	.79274	.93091	.97684	.99222	.99739
14	0.00000	0.00000	0.00000	0.00000	.20362	.73910	.91303	.97084	.99021	.99671
15	0.00000	0.00000	0.00000	0.00000	0.00000	.67239	.89079	.96339	.98770	.99587
16	0.00000	0.00000	0.00000	0.00000	0.00000	.58943	.86314	.95412	.98459	.99482
17	0.00000	0.00000	0.00000	0.00000	0.00000	.48626	.82875	.94259	.98072	.99352
18	0.00000	0.00000	0.00000	0.00000	0.00000	.35797	.78598	.92825	.97590	.99190
19	0.00000	0.00000	0.00000	0.00000	0.00000	.19842	.73280	.91042	.96991	.98989
20	0.00000	0.00000	0.00000	0.00000	0.00000	0.00000	.66666	.88825	.96247	.98738
21	0.00000	0.00000	0.00000	0.00000	0.00000	0.00000	.58441	.86068	.95320	.98427
22	0.00000	0.00000	0.00000	0.00000	0.00000	0.00000	.48212	.82638	.94169	.98040
23	0.00000	0.00000	0.00000	0.00000	0.00000	0.00000	.35492	.78374	.92736	.97559
24	0.00000	0.00000	0.00000	0.00000	0.00000	0.00000	.19673	.73071	.90955	.96960
25	0.00000	0.00000	0.00000	0.00000	0.00000	0.00000	0.00000	.66476	.88740	.96215
26	0.00000	0.00000	0.00000	0.00000	0.00000	0.00000	0.00000	.58274	.85985	.95290
27	0.00000	0.00000	0.00000	0.00000	0.00000	0.00000	0.00000	.48074	.82559	.94138
28	0.00000	0.00000	0.00000	0.00000	0.00000	0.00000	0.00000	.35390	.78299	.92706
29	0.00000	0.00000	0.00000	0.00000	0.00000	0.00000	0.00000	.19616	.73001	.90926
30	0.00000	0.00000	0.00000	0.00000	0.00000	0.00000	0.00000	0.00000	.66412	.88711
31	0.00000	0.00000	0.00000	0.00000	0.00000	0.00000	0.00000	0.00000	.58218	.85957
32	0.00000	0.00000	0.00000	0.00000	0.00000	0.00000	0.00000	0.00000	.48028	.82533
33	0.00000	0.00000	0.00000	0.00000	0.00000	0.00000	0.00000	0.00000	.35356	.78274
34	0.00000	0.00000	0.00000	0.00000	0.00000	0.00000	0.00000	0.00000	.19598	.72977
35	0.00000	0.00000	0.00000	0.00000	0.00000	0.00000	0.00000	0.00000	0.00000	.66390
36	0.00000	0.00000	0.00000	0.00000	0.00000	0.00000	0.00000	0.00000	0.00000	.58199
37	0.00000	0.00000	0.00000	0.00000	0.00000	0.00000	0.00000	0.00000	0.00000	.48013
38	0.00000	0.00000	0.00000	0.00000	0.00000	0.00000	0.00000	0.00000	0.00000	.35345
39	0.00000	0.00000	0.00000	0.00000	0.00000	0.00000	0.00000	0.00000	0.00000	.19591

REMAINING MORTGAGE BALANCE TABLE FOR 22.250 PERCENT

AGE OF LOAN	ORIGINAL LOAN TERM 1	2	3	4	5	6	7	8	9	10
1	0.00000	.55489	.73690	.82573	.87736	.91043	.93297	.94898	.96068	.96942
2	0.00000	0.00000	.40890	.60848	.72446	.79877	.84941	.88536	.91166	.93131
3	0.00000	0.00000	0.00000	.33764	.53385	.65957	.74523	.80606	.85055	.88379
4	0.00000	0.00000	0.00000	0.00000	.29623	.48604	.61536	.70721	.77437	.82455
5	0.00000	0.00000	0.00000	0.00000	0.00000	.26970	.45346	.58396	.67940	.75069
6	0.00000	0.00000	0.00000	0.00000	0.00000	0.00000	.25162	.43032	.56100	.65862
7	0.00000	0.00000	0.00000	0.00000	0.00000	0.00000	0.00000	.23878	.41340	.54385
8	0.00000	0.00000	0.00000	0.00000	0.00000	0.00000	0.00000	0.00000	.22939	.40076
9	0.00000	0.00000	0.00000	0.00000	0.00000	0.00000	0.00000	0.00000	0.00000	.22238

AGE OF LOAN	11	12	13	14	15	20	25	30	35	40
1	.97606	.98116	.98511	.98820	.99062	.99696	.99900	.99967	.99989	.99996
2	.94622	.95767	.96655	.97349	.97893	.99318	.99775	.99926	.99975	.99992
3	.90901	.92839	.94341	.95514	.96436	.98846	.99620	.99874	.99958	.99986
4	.86263	.89188	.91457	.93228	.94619	.98257	.99426	.99810	.99937	.99979
5	.80481	.84638	.87861	.90377	.92354	.97523	.99184	.99730	.99910	.99970
6	.73272	.78964	.83377	.86824	.89530	.96609	.98883	.99630	.99877	.99959
7	.64286	.71892	.77789	.82393	.86009	.95469	.98507	.99506	.99836	.99946
8	.53083	.63075	.70821	.76871	.81621	.94047	.98039	.99351	.99785	.99928
9	.39117	.52083	.62135	.69985	.76150	.92275	.97456	.99157	.99720	.99907
10	.21706	.38380	.51307	.61402	.69329	.90066	.96728	.98916	.99640	.99881
11	0.00000	.21297	.37808	.50702	.60826	.87313	.95821	.98616	.99541	.99848
12	0.00000	0.00000	.20979	.37362	.50226	.83879	.94690	.98241	.99416	.99806
13	0.00000	0.00000	0.00000	.20732	.37012	.79599	.93280	.97774	.99262	.99755
14	0.00000	0.00000	0.00000	0.00000	.20537	.74264	.91523	.97192	.99068	.99691
15	0.00000	0.00000	0.00000	0.00000	0.00000	.67612	.89332	.96467	.98828	.99611
16	0.00000	0.00000	0.00000	0.00000	0.00000	.59320	.86600	.95562	.98527	.99511
17	0.00000	0.00000	0.00000	0.00000	0.00000	.48982	.83195	.94434	.98153	.99387
18	0.00000	0.00000	0.00000	0.00000	0.00000	.36095	.78950	.93028	.97687	.99232
19	0.00000	0.00000	0.00000	0.00000	0.00000	.20029	.73658	.91275	.97105	.99039
20	0.00000	0.00000	0.00000	0.00000	0.00000	0.00000	.67061	.89090	.96380	.98798
21	0.00000	0.00000	0.00000	0.00000	0.00000	0.00000	.58836	.86366	.95476	.98498
22	0.00000	0.00000	0.00000	0.00000	0.00000	0.00000	.48583	.82970	.94349	.98124
23	0.00000	0.00000	0.00000	0.00000	0.00000	0.00000	.35801	.78737	.92945	.97658
24	0.00000	0.00000	0.00000	0.00000	0.00000	0.00000	.19865	.73459	.91194	.97076
25	0.00000	0.00000	0.00000	0.00000	0.00000	0.00000	0.00000	.66879	.89010	.96351
26	0.00000	0.00000	0.00000	0.00000	0.00000	0.00000	0.00000	.58677	.86289	.95448
27	0.00000	0.00000	0.00000	0.00000	0.00000	0.00000	0.00000	.48452	.82896	.94321
28	0.00000	0.00000	0.00000	0.00000	0.00000	0.00000	0.00000	.35704	.78666	.92917
29	0.00000	0.00000	0.00000	0.00000	0.00000	0.00000	0.00000	.19812	.73393	.91166
30	0.00000	0.00000	0.00000	0.00000	0.00000	0.00000	0.00000	0.00000	.66820	.88984
31	0.00000	0.00000	0.00000	0.00000	0.00000	0.00000	0.00000	0.00000	.58624	.86263
32	0.00000	0.00000	0.00000	0.00000	0.00000	0.00000	0.00000	0.00000	.48408	.82871
33	0.00000	0.00000	0.00000	0.00000	0.00000	0.00000	0.00000	0.00000	.35672	.78643
34	0.00000	0.00000	0.00000	0.00000	0.00000	0.00000	0.00000	0.00000	.19794	.73371
35	0.00000	0.00000	0.00000	0.00000	0.00000	0.00000	0.00000	0.00000	0.00000	.66800
36	0.00000	0.00000	0.00000	0.00000	0.00000	0.00000	0.00000	0.00000	0.00000	.58607
37	0.00000	0.00000	0.00000	0.00000	0.00000	0.00000	0.00000	0.00000	0.00000	.48394
38	0.00000	0.00000	0.00000	0.00000	0.00000	0.00000	0.00000	0.00000	0.00000	.35661
39	0.00000	0.00000	0.00000	0.00000	0.00000	0.00000	0.00000	0.00000	0.00000	.19788

REMAINING MORTGAGE BALANCE TABLE FOR 22.500 PERCENT

ORIGINAL LOAN TERM

AGE OF LOAN	1	2	3	4	5	6	7	8	9	10
1	0.00000	.55550	.73764	.82649	.87809	.91112	.93360	.94955	.96120	.96989
2	0.00000	0.00000	.40976	.60965	.72573	.80004	.85062	.88650	.91270	.93225
3	0.00000	0.00000	0.00000	.33866	.53532	.66122	.74692	.80770	.85210	.88522
4	0.00000	0.00000	0.00000	0.00000	.29737	.48774	.61732	.70923	.77636	.82644
5	0.00000	0.00000	0.00000	0.00000	0.00000	.27094	.45536	.58617	.68171	.75298
6	0.00000	0.00000	0.00000	0.00000	0.00000	0.00000	.25295	.43238	.56343	.66118
7	0.00000	0.00000	0.00000	0.00000	0.00000	0.00000	0.00000	.24019	.41561	.54646
8	0.00000	0.00000	0.00000	0.00000	0.00000	0.00000	0.00000	0.00000	.23087	.40309
9	0.00000	0.00000	0.00000	0.00000	0.00000	0.00000	0.00000	0.00000	0.00000	.22392

AGE OF LOAN	11	12	13	14	15	20	25	30	35	40
1	.97647	.98152	.98543	.98847	.99086	.99707	.99905	.99969	.99990	.99997
2	.94706	.95842	.96722	.97407	.97944	.99342	.99786	.99930	.99977	.99992
3	.91031	.92956	.94446	.95607	.96517	.98885	.99637	.99881	.99961	.99987
4	.86439	.89349	.91602	.93357	.94733	.98314	.99451	.99820	.99941	.99981
5	.80699	.84841	.88047	.90546	.92504	.97600	.99219	.99744	.99916	.99973
6	.73526	.79208	.83605	.87032	.89718	.96708	.98928	.99649	.99885	.99962
7	.64563	.72168	.78054	.82641	.86237	.95593	.98566	.99531	.99846	.99950
8	.53360	.63369	.71116	.77154	.81886	.94200	.98112	.99382	.99798	.99934
9	.39360	.52374	.62446	.70296	.76449	.92459	.97546	.99197	.99737	.99914
10	.21865	.38633	.51611	.61726	.69654	.90284	.96837	.98965	.99661	.99889
11	0.00000	.21461	.38070	.51016	.61162	.87565	.95953	.98676	.99566	.99858
12	0.00000	0.00000	.21148	.37631	.50550	.84167	.94847	.98314	.99447	.99819
13	0.00000	0.00000	0.00000	.20904	.37287	.79921	.93464	.97861	.99299	.99770
14	0.00000	0.00000	0.00000	0.00000	.20713	.74614	.91737	.97296	.99114	.99709
15	0.00000	0.00000	0.00000	0.00000	0.00000	.67982	.89579	.96590	.98882	.99633
16	0.00000	0.00000	0.00000	0.00000	0.00000	.59694	.86881	.95707	.98593	.99539
17	0.00000	0.00000	0.00000	0.00000	0.00000	.49337	.83510	.94604	.98231	.99420
18	0.00000	0.00000	0.00000	0.00000	0.00000	.36392	.79296	.93226	.97779	.99272
19	0.00000	0.00000	0.00000	0.00000	0.00000	.20216	.74031	.91503	.97215	.99087
20	0.00000	0.00000	0.00000	0.00000	0.00000	0.00000	.67451	.89350	.96509	.98855
21	0.00000	0.00000	0.00000	0.00000	0.00000	0.00000	.59228	.86659	.95627	.98566
22	0.00000	0.00000	0.00000	0.00000	0.00000	0.00000	.48951	.83296	.94525	.98204
23	0.00000	0.00000	0.00000	0.00000	0.00000	0.00000	.36108	.79094	.93147	.97753
24	0.00000	0.00000	0.00000	0.00000	0.00000	0.00000	.20058	.73842	.91426	.97188
25	0.00000	0.00000	0.00000	0.00000	0.00000	0.00000	0.00000	.67279	.89275	.96483
26	0.00000	0.00000	0.00000	0.00000	0.00000	0.00000	0.00000	.59076	.86586	.95601
27	0.00000	0.00000	0.00000	0.00000	0.00000	0.00000	0.00000	.48826	.83226	.94499
28	0.00000	0.00000	0.00000	0.00000	0.00000	0.00000	0.00000	.36016	.79027	.93122
29	0.00000	0.00000	0.00000	0.00000	0.00000	0.00000	0.00000	.20007	.73780	.91401
30	0.00000	0.00000	0.00000	0.00000	0.00000	0.00000	0.00000	0.00000	.67222	.89250
31	0.00000	0.00000	0.00000	0.00000	0.00000	0.00000	0.00000	0.00000	.59027	.86562
32	0.00000	0.00000	0.00000	0.00000	0.00000	0.00000	0.00000	0.00000	.48785	.83203
33	0.00000	0.00000	0.00000	0.00000	0.00000	0.00000	0.00000	0.00000	.35986	.79006
34	0.00000	0.00000	0.00000	0.00000	0.00000	0.00000	0.00000	0.00000	.19990	.73760
35	0.00000	0.00000	0.00000	0.00000	0.00000	0.00000	0.00000	0.00000	0.00000	.67204
36	0.00000	0.00000	0.00000	0.00000	0.00000	0.00000	0.00000	0.00000	0.00000	.59011
37	0.00000	0.00000	0.00000	0.00000	0.00000	0.00000	0.00000	0.00000	0.00000	.48772
38	0.00000	0.00000	0.00000	0.00000	0.00000	0.00000	0.00000	0.00000	0.00000	.35976
39	0.00000	0.00000	0.00000	0.00000	0.00000	0.00000	0.00000	0.00000	0.00000	.19985

REMAINING MORTGAGE BALANCE TABLE FOR 22.750 PERCENT

ORIGINAL LOAN TERM

AGE OF LOAN	1	2	3	4	5	6	7	8	9	10
1	0.00000	.55611	.73837	.82724	.87881	.91180	.93423	.95012	.96171	.97034
2	0.00000	0.00000	.41061	.61082	.72699	.80130	.85183	.88762	.91373	.93318
3	0.00000	0.00000	0.00000	.33968	.53679	.66287	.74860	.80933	.85363	.88663
4	0.00000	0.00000	0.00000	0.00000	.29851	.48945	.61927	.71125	.77834	.82832
5	0.00000	0.00000	0.00000	0.00000	0.00000	.27218	.45725	.58838	.68402	.75526
6	0.00000	0.00000	0.00000	0.00000	0.00000	0.00000	.25428	.43444	.56585	.66373
7	0.00000	0.00000	0.00000	0.00000	0.00000	0.00000	0.00000	.24160	.41781	.54907
8	0.00000	0.00000	0.00000	0.00000	0.00000	0.00000	0.00000	0.00000	.23235	.40542
9	0.00000	0.00000	0.00000	0.00000	0.00000	0.00000	0.00000	0.00000	0.00000	.22545

AGE OF LOAN	11	12	13	14	15	20	25	30	35	40
1	.97687	.98187	.98574	.98874	.99110	.99718	.99909	.99971	.99991	.99997
2	.94790	.95917	.96787	.97464	.97994	.99365	.99796	.99934	.99979	.99993
3	.91160	.93072	.94549	.95698	.96596	.98923	.99654	.99888	.99964	.99988
4	.86613	.89508	.91744	.93484	.94845	.98368	.99475	.99830	.99945	.99982
5	.80916	.85043	.88231	.90712	.92652	.97674	.99252	.99758	.99922	.99975
6	.73779	.79449	.83830	.87238	.89904	.96804	.98972	.99668	.99892	.99965
7	.64838	.72442	.78316	.82886	.86461	.95715	.98622	.99554	.99856	.99953
8	.53637	.63663	.71409	.77435	.82148	.94350	.98183	.99413	.99810	.99938
9	.39604	.52665	.62755	.70605	.76745	.92639	.97633	.99235	.99752	.99920
10	.22024	.38886	.51913	.62048	.69976	.90497	.96944	.99012	.99680	.99896
11	0.00000	.21625	.38332	.51329	.61496	.87813	.96080	.98733	.99590	.99867
12	0.00000	0.00000	.21316	.37900	.50872	.84450	.94999	.98383	.99477	.99830
13	0.00000	0.00000	0.00000	.21076	.37563	.80238	.93644	.97945	.99335	.99784
14	0.00000	0.00000	0.00000	0.00000	.20889	.74960	.91946	.97397	.99157	.99727
15	0.00000	0.00000	0.00000	0.00000	0.00000	.68348	.89820	.96709	.98934	.99655
16	0.00000	0.00000	0.00000	0.00000	0.00000	.60066	.87156	.95848	.98656	.99564
17	0.00000	0.00000	0.00000	0.00000	0.00000	.49689	.83819	.94769	.98306	.99451
18	0.00000	0.00000	0.00000	0.00000	0.00000	.36689	.79637	.93417	.97869	.99309
19	0.00000	0.00000	0.00000	0.00000	0.00000	.20403	.74399	.91724	.97320	.99132
20	0.00000	0.00000	0.00000	0.00000	0.00000	0.00000	.67837	.89603	.96633	.98909
21	0.00000	0.00000	0.00000	0.00000	0.00000	0.00000	.59616	.86945	.95773	.98631
22	0.00000	0.00000	0.00000	0.00000	0.00000	0.00000	.49317	.83616	.94695	.98281
23	0.00000	0.00000	0.00000	0.00000	0.00000	0.00000	.36415	.79445	.93344	.97844
24	0.00000	0.00000	0.00000	0.00000	0.00000	0.00000	.20250	.74219	.91652	.97296
25	0.00000	0.00000	0.00000	0.00000	0.00000	0.00000	0.00000	.67673	.89533	.96609
26	0.00000	0.00000	0.00000	0.00000	0.00000	0.00000	0.00000	.59472	.86877	.95749
27	0.00000	0.00000	0.00000	0.00000	0.00000	0.00000	0.00000	.49198	.83550	.94671
28	0.00000	0.00000	0.00000	0.00000	0.00000	0.00000	0.00000	.36326	.79383	.93321
29	0.00000	0.00000	0.00000	0.00000	0.00000	0.00000	0.00000	.20201	.74161	.91629
30	0.00000	0.00000	0.00000	0.00000	0.00000	0.00000	0.00000	0.00000	.67620	.89510
31	0.00000	0.00000	0.00000	0.00000	0.00000	0.00000	0.00000	0.00000	.59426	.86855
32	0.00000	0.00000	0.00000	0.00000	0.00000	0.00000	0.00000	0.00000	.49159	.83529
33	0.00000	0.00000	0.00000	0.00000	0.00000	0.00000	0.00000	0.00000	.36298	.79362
34	0.00000	0.00000	0.00000	0.00000	0.00000	0.00000	0.00000	0.00000	.20186	.74143
35	0.00000	0.00000	0.00000	0.00000	0.00000	0.00000	0.00000	0.00000	0.00000	.67603
36	0.00000	0.00000	0.00000	0.00000	0.00000	0.00000	0.00000	0.00000	0.00000	.59410
37	0.00000	0.00000	0.00000	0.00000	0.00000	0.00000	0.00000	0.00000	0.00000	.49147
38	0.00000	0.00000	0.00000	0.00000	0.00000	0.00000	0.00000	0.00000	0.00000	.36289
39	0.00000	0.00000	0.00000	0.00000	0.00000	0.00000	0.00000	0.00000	0.00000	.20180

REMAINING MORTGAGE BALANCE TABLE FOR 23.000 PERCENT

ORIGINAL LOAN TERM

AGE OF LOAN	1	2	3	4	5	6	7	8	9	10
1	0.00000	.55671	.73911	.82800	.87954	.91248	.93485	.95068	.96221	.97079
2	0.00000	0.00000	.41147	.61198	.72825	.80256	.85303	.88874	.91476	.93411
3	0.00000	0.00000	0.00000	.34070	.53826	.66451	.75027	.81095	.85516	.88804
4	0.00000	0.00000	0.00000	0.00000	.29966	.49115	.62122	.71326	.78031	.83018
5	0.00000	0.00000	0.00000	0.00000	0.00000	.27343	.45915	.59058	.68631	.75752
6	0.00000	0.00000	0.00000	0.00000	0.00000	0.00000	.25561	.43650	.56826	.66627
7	0.00000	0.00000	0.00000	0.00000	0.00000	0.00000	0.00000	.24301	.42001	.55166
8	0.00000	0.00000	0.00000	0.00000	0.00000	0.00000	0.00000	0.00000	.23382	.40774
9	0.00000	0.00000	0.00000	0.00000	0.00000	0.00000	0.00000	0.00000	0.00000	.22699

AGE OF LOAN	11	12	13	14	15	20	25	30	35	40
1	.97727	.98222	.98604	.98901	.99132	.99729	.99914	.99972	.99991	.99997
2	.94872	.95990	.96851	.97520	.98043	.99388	.99805	.99938	.99980	.99994
3	.91287	.93186	.94650	.95787	.96674	.98959	.99669	.99894	.99966	.99989
4	.86785	.89665	.91885	.93609	.94956	.98422	.99498	.99840	.99949	.99984
5	.81131	.85242	.88413	.90875	.92797	.97746	.99284	.99771	.99927	.99977
6	.74030	.79689	.84052	.87441	.90087	.96898	.99014	.99685	.99899	.99968
7	.65112	.72714	.78576	.83129	.86682	.95833	.98676	.99577	.99865	.99957
8	.53913	.63955	.71699	.77713	.82407	.94495	.98251	.99441	.99821	.99943
9	.39847	.52954	.63062	.70911	.77038	.92816	.97717	.99271	.99767	.99925
10	.22183	.39139	.52215	.62369	.70296	.90706	.97046	.99057	.99698	.99903
11	0.00000	.21789	.38593	.51641	.61828	.88056	.96204	.98788	.99612	.99876
12	0.00000	0.00000	.21485	.38168	.51193	.84729	.95147	.98450	.99504	.99841
13	0.00000	0.00000	0.00000	.21249	.37837	.80550	.93819	.98026	.99369	.99798
14	0.00000	0.00000	0.00000	0.00000	.21064	.75302	.92151	.97493	.99198	.99743
15	0.00000	0.00000	0.00000	0.00000	0.00000	.68711	.90056	.96824	.98984	.99675
16	0.00000	0.00000	0.00000	0.00000	0.00000	.60434	.87426	.95984	.98715	.99589
17	0.00000	0.00000	0.00000	0.00000	0.00000	.50039	.84122	.94929	.98378	.99481
18	0.00000	0.00000	0.00000	0.00000	0.00000	.36985	.79973	.93604	.97954	.99345
19	0.00000	0.00000	0.00000	0.00000	0.00000	.20590	.74763	.91940	.97422	.99175
20	0.00000	0.00000	0.00000	0.00000	0.00000	0.00000	.68219	.89850	.96753	.98961
21	0.00000	0.00000	0.00000	0.00000	0.00000	0.00000	.60001	.87226	.95914	.98692
22	0.00000	0.00000	0.00000	0.00000	0.00000	0.00000	.49681	.83930	.94860	.98355
23	0.00000	0.00000	0.00000	0.00000	0.00000	0.00000	.36720	.79790	.93536	.97931
24	0.00000	0.00000	0.00000	0.00000	0.00000	0.00000	.20442	.74592	.91873	.97399
25	0.00000	0.00000	0.00000	0.00000	0.00000	0.00000	0.00000	.68063	.89784	.96731
26	0.00000	0.00000	0.00000	0.00000	0.00000	0.00000	0.00000	.59864	.87162	.95891
27	0.00000	0.00000	0.00000	0.00000	0.00000	0.00000	0.00000	.49567	.83868	.94837
28	0.00000	0.00000	0.00000	0.00000	0.00000	0.00000	0.00000	.36636	.79732	.93514
29	0.00000	0.00000	0.00000	0.00000	0.00000	0.00000	0.00000	.20395	.74537	.91851
30	0.00000	0.00000	0.00000	0.00000	0.00000	0.00000	0.00000	0.00000	.68013	.89763
31	0.00000	0.00000	0.00000	0.00000	0.00000	0.00000	0.00000	0.00000	.59820	.87141
32	0.00000	0.00000	0.00000	0.00000	0.00000	0.00000	0.00000	0.00000	.49531	.83849
33	0.00000	0.00000	0.00000	0.00000	0.00000	0.00000	0.00000	0.00000	.36609	.79713
34	0.00000	0.00000	0.00000	0.00000	0.00000	0.00000	0.00000	0.00000	.20381	.74520
35	0.00000	0.00000	0.00000	0.00000	0.00000	0.00000	0.00000	0.00000	0.00000	.67997
36	0.00000	0.00000	0.00000	0.00000	0.00000	0.00000	0.00000	0.00000	0.00000	.59806
37	0.00000	0.00000	0.00000	0.00000	0.00000	0.00000	0.00000	0.00000	0.00000	.49519
38	0.00000	0.00000	0.00000	0.00000	0.00000	0.00000	0.00000	0.00000	0.00000	.36600
39	0.00000	0.00000	0.00000	0.00000	0.00000	0.00000	0.00000	0.00000	0.00000	.20376

REMAINING MORTGAGE BALANCE TABLE FOR 23.250 PERCENT

ORIGINAL LOAN TERM

AGE OF LOAN	1	2	3	4	5	6	7	8	9	10
1	0.00000	.55732	.73985	.82875	.88026	.91315	.93546	.95124	.96271	.97123
2	0.00000	0.00000	.41233	.61315	.72951	.80381	.85422	.88985	.91577	.93502
3	0.00000	0.00000	0.00000	.34172	.53973	.66615	.75193	.81256	.85667	.88943
4	0.00000	0.00000	0.00000	0.00000	.30080	.49285	.62316	.71527	.78227	.83203
5	0.00000	0.00000	0.00000	0.00000	0.00000	.27467	.46104	.59277	.68860	.75976
6	0.00000	0.00000	0.00000	0.00000	0.00000	0.00000	.25695	.43856	.57067	.66879
7	0.00000	0.00000	0.00000	0.00000	0.00000	0.00000	0.00000	.24442	.42221	.55426
8	0.00000	0.00000	0.00000	0.00000	0.00000	0.00000	0.00000	0.00000	.23530	.41006
9	0.00000	0.00000	0.00000	0.00000	0.00000	0.00000	0.00000	0.00000	0.00000	.22854

AGE OF LOAN	11	12	13	14	15	20	25	30	35	40
1	.97766	.98257	.98634	.98927	.99155	.99739	.99918	.99974	.99992	.99997
2	.94954	.96062	.96914	.97575	.98090	.99409	.99815	.99941	.99982	.99994
3	.91413	.93298	.94749	.95874	.96750	.98995	.99684	.99900	.99969	.99990
4	.86956	.89819	.92024	.93732	.95064	.98473	.99521	.99849	.99952	.99985
5	.81344	.85440	.88592	.91036	.92940	.97816	.99314	.99784	.99932	.99978
6	.74279	.79926	.84273	.87642	.90266	.96989	.99055	.99702	.99906	.99970
7	.65385	.72984	.78834	.83368	.86901	.95948	.98728	.99599	.99873	.99960
8	.54187	.64245	.71987	.77988	.82663	.94638	.98316	.99469	.99832	.99947
9	.40090	.53243	.63367	.71214	.77329	.92988	.97798	.99305	.99780	.99931
10	.22343	.39391	.52515	.62687	.70612	.90911	.97146	.99099	.99715	.99910
11	0.00000	.21953	.38853	.51952	.62157	.88295	.96324	.98840	.99634	.99884
12	0.00000	0.00000	.21654	.38436	.51512	.85003	.95290	.98514	.99530	.99852
13	0.00000	0.00000	0.00000	.21421	.38111	.80858	.93989	.98103	.99401	.99811
14	0.00000	0.00000	0.00000	0.00000	.21240	.75640	.92350	.97586	.99237	.99759
15	0.00000	0.00000	0.00000	0.00000	0.00000	.69071	.90287	.96935	.99032	.99694
16	0.00000	0.00000	0.00000	0.00000	0.00000	.60800	.87690	.96116	.98773	.99612
17	0.00000	0.00000	0.00000	0.00000	0.00000	.50388	.84420	.95084	.98447	.99509
18	0.00000	0.00000	0.00000	0.00000	0.00000	.37279	.80304	.93786	.98036	.99379
19	0.00000	0.00000	0.00000	0.00000	0.00000	.20776	.75121	.92150	.97520	.99216
20	0.00000	0.00000	0.00000	0.00000	0.00000	0.00000	.68597	.90092	.96869	.99010
21	0.00000	0.00000	0.00000	0.00000	0.00000	0.00000	.60383	.87500	.96050	.98751
22	0.00000	0.00000	0.00000	0.00000	0.00000	0.00000	.50042	.84238	.95019	.98425
23	0.00000	0.00000	0.00000	0.00000	0.00000	0.00000	.37024	.80130	.93721	.98015
24	0.00000	0.00000	0.00000	0.00000	0.00000	0.00000	.20634	.74959	.92087	.97499
25	0.00000	0.00000	0.00000	0.00000	0.00000	0.00000	0.00000	.68448	.90030	.96848
26	0.00000	0.00000	0.00000	0.00000	0.00000	0.00000	0.00000	.60252	.87440	.96030
27	0.00000	0.00000	0.00000	0.00000	0.00000	0.00000	0.00000	.49934	.84180	.94999
28	0.00000	0.00000	0.00000	0.00000	0.00000	0.00000	0.00000	.36943	.80075	.93701
29	0.00000	0.00000	0.00000	0.00000	0.00000	0.00000	0.00000	.20589	.74907	.92067
30	0.00000	0.00000	0.00000	0.00000	0.00000	0.00000	0.00000	0.00000	.68402	.90011
31	0.00000	0.00000	0.00000	0.00000	0.00000	0.00000	0.00000	0.00000	.60211	.87422
32	0.00000	0.00000	0.00000	0.00000	0.00000	0.00000	0.00000	0.00000	.49900	.84162
33	0.00000	0.00000	0.00000	0.00000	0.00000	0.00000	0.00000	0.00000	.36918	.80058
34	0.00000	0.00000	0.00000	0.00000	0.00000	0.00000	0.00000	0.00000	.20575	.74891
35	0.00000	0.00000	0.00000	0.00000	0.00000	0.00000	0.00000	0.00000	0.00000	.68387
36	0.00000	0.00000	0.00000	0.00000	0.00000	0.00000	0.00000	0.00000	0.00000	.60198
37	0.00000	0.00000	0.00000	0.00000	0.00000	0.00000	0.00000	0.00000	0.00000	.49889
38	0.00000	0.00000	0.00000	0.00000	0.00000	0.00000	0.00000	0.00000	0.00000	.36910
39	0.00000	0.00000	0.00000	0.00000	0.00000	0.00000	0.00000	0.00000	0.00000	.20571

REMAINING MORTGAGE BALANCE TABLE FOR 23.500 PERCENT

ORIGINAL LOAN TERM

AGE OF LOAN	1	2	3	4	5	6	7	8	9	10
1	0.00000	.55792	.74058	.82949	.88098	.91382	.93608	.95179	.96321	.97167
2	0.00000	0.00000	.41319	.61431	.73076	.80505	.85540	.89095	.91677	.93592
3	0.00000	0.00000	0.00000	.34274	.54119	.66779	.75359	.81417	.85817	.89080
4	0.00000	0.00000	0.00000	0.00000	.30194	.49455	.62510	.71726	.78421	.83386
5	0.00000	0.00000	0.00000	0.00000	0.00000	.27592	.46294	.59496	.69087	.76199
6	0.00000	0.00000	0.00000	0.00000	0.00000	0.00000	.25828	.44062	.57307	.67130
7	0.00000	0.00000	0.00000	0.00000	0.00000	0.00000	0.00000	.24583	.42441	.55684
8	0.00000	0.00000	0.00000	0.00000	0.00000	0.00000	0.00000	0.00000	.23679	.41238
9	0.00000	0.00000	0.00000	0.00000	0.00000	0.00000	0.00000	0.00000	0.00000	.23008

AGE OF LOAN	11	12	13	14	15	20	25	30	35	40
1	.97805	.98290	.98663	.98952	.99176	.99748	.99922	.99976	.99992	.99998
2	.95034	.96132	.96976	.97629	.98137	.99430	.99823	.99945	.99983	.99995
3	.91537	.93409	.94847	.95960	.96825	.99029	.99699	.99906	.99971	.99991
4	.87124	.89972	.92161	.93853	.95170	.98523	.99542	.99857	.99955	.99986
5	.81555	.85635	.88770	.91155	.93080	.97884	.99344	.99795	.99936	.99980
6	.74527	.80161	.84490	.87839	.90444	.97078	.99093	.99717	.99912	.99972
7	.65656	.73252	.79089	.83605	.87116	.96061	.98778	.99619	.99881	.99963
8	.54461	.64534	.72273	.78260	.82916	.94777	.98379	.99495	.99842	.99951
9	.40333	.53530	.63671	.71516	.77616	.93156	.97876	.99338	.99793	.99935
10	.22503	.39643	.52815	.63004	.70927	.91111	.97242	.99140	.99732	.99916
11	0.00000	.22118	.39114	.52261	.62485	.88530	.96441	.98891	.99654	.99892
12	0.00000	0.00000	.21822	.38704	.51831	.85273	.95430	.98576	.99555	.99861
13	0.00000	0.00000	0.00000	.21594	.38385	.81162	.94155	.98178	.99431	.99822
14	0.00000	0.00000	0.00000	0.00000	.21416	.75974	.92545	.97676	.99275	.99773
15	0.00000	0.00000	0.00000	0.00000	0.00000	.69426	.90513	.97043	.99077	.99712
16	0.00000	0.00000	0.00000	0.00000	0.00000	.61163	.87949	.96244	.98827	.99634
17	0.00000	0.00000	0.00000	0.00000	0.00000	.50734	.84713	.95235	.98513	.99536
18	0.00000	0.00000	0.00000	0.00000	0.00000	.37573	.80629	.93962	.98115	.99411
19	0.00000	0.00000	0.00000	0.00000	0.00000	.20963	.75475	.92355	.97614	.99255
20	0.00000	0.00000	0.00000	0.00000	0.00000	0.00000	.68970	.90328	.96981	.99057
21	0.00000	0.00000	0.00000	0.00000	0.00000	0.00000	.60761	.87769	.96182	.98808
22	0.00000	0.00000	0.00000	0.00000	0.00000	0.00000	.50401	.84540	.95174	.98493
23	0.00000	0.00000	0.00000	0.00000	0.00000	0.00000	.37326	.80464	.93902	.98096
24	0.00000	0.00000	0.00000	0.00000	0.00000	0.00000	.20825	.75321	.92296	.97594
25	0.00000	0.00000	0.00000	0.00000	0.00000	0.00000	0.00000	.68829	.90270	.96962
26	0.00000	0.00000	0.00000	0.00000	0.00000	0.00000	0.00000	.60637	.87713	.96163
27	0.00000	0.00000	0.00000	0.00000	0.00000	0.00000	0.00000	.50298	.84486	.95155
28	0.00000	0.00000	0.00000	0.00000	0.00000	0.00000	0.00000	.37250	.80413	.93883
29	0.00000	0.00000	0.00000	0.00000	0.00000	0.00000	0.00000	.20782	.75272	.92278
30	0.00000	0.00000	0.00000	0.00000	0.00000	0.00000	0.00000	0.00000	.68785	.90252
31	0.00000	0.00000	0.00000	0.00000	0.00000	0.00000	0.00000	0.00000	.60598	.87695
32	0.00000	0.00000	0.00000	0.00000	0.00000	0.00000	0.00000	0.00000	.50266	.84469
33	0.00000	0.00000	0.00000	0.00000	0.00000	0.00000	0.00000	0.00000	.37226	.80397
34	0.00000	0.00000	0.00000	0.00000	0.00000	0.00000	0.00000	0.00000	.20769	.75257
35	0.00000	0.00000	0.00000	0.00000	0.00000	0.00000	0.00000	0.00000	0.00000	.68772
36	0.00000	0.00000	0.00000	0.00000	0.00000	0.00000	0.00000	0.00000	0.00000	.60586
37	0.00000	0.00000	0.00000	0.00000	0.00000	0.00000	0.00000	0.00000	0.00000	.50256
38	0.00000	0.00000	0.00000	0.00000	0.00000	0.00000	0.00000	0.00000	0.00000	.37219
39	0.00000	0.00000	0.00000	0.00000	0.00000	0.00000	0.00000	0.00000	0.00000	.20765

REMAINING MORTGAGE BALANCE TABLE FOR 23.750 PERCENT

ORIGINAL LOAN TERM

AGE OF LOAN	1	2	3	4	5	6	7	8	9	10
1	0.00000	.55853	.74132	.83024	.88169	.91448	.93668	.95234	.96370	.97210
2	0.00000	0.00000	.41404	.61547	.73202	.80629	.85658	.89204	.91776	.93681
3	0.00000	0.00000	0.00000	.34376	.54265	.66942	.75524	.81576	.85966	.89216
4	0.00000	0.00000	0.00000	0.00000	.30309	.49625	.62703	.71925	.78614	.83567
5	0.00000	0.00000	0.00000	0.00000	0.00000	.27717	.46483	.59715	.69313	.76421
6	0.00000	0.00000	0.00000	0.00000	0.00000	0.00000	.25962	.44267	.57547	.67380
7	0.00000	0.00000	0.00000	0.00000	0.00000	0.00000	0.00000	.24724	.42660	.55941
8	0.00000	0.00000	0.00000	0.00000	0.00000	0.00000	0.00000	0.00000	.23827	.41470
9	0.00000	0.00000	0.00000	0.00000	0.00000	0.00000	0.00000	0.00000	0.00000	.23162

AGE OF LOAN	11	12	13	14	15	20	25	30	35	40
1	.97843	.98323	.98692	.98977	.99198	.99758	.99926	.99977	.99993	.99998
2	.95113	.96202	.97037	.97682	.98183	.99451	.99832	.99948	.99984	.99995
3	.91660	.93518	.94944	.96044	.96898	.99063	.99713	.99911	.99973	.99992
4	.87291	.90123	.92295	.93972	.95274	.98572	.99562	.99865	.99958	.99987
5	.81765	.85828	.88944	.91351	.93218	.97950	.99372	.99806	.99940	.99982
6	.74772	.80394	.84705	.88034	.90618	.97165	.99131	.99732	.99917	.99975
7	.65926	.73519	.79342	.83839	.87328	.96170	.98826	.99638	.99889	.99966
8	.54734	.64821	.72557	.78530	.83166	.94912	.98440	.99520	.99852	.99954
9	.40575	.53817	.63973	.71815	.77900	.93321	.97952	.99369	.99806	.99940
10	.22662	.39895	.53113	.63318	.71238	.91308	.97335	.99179	.99747	.99922
11	0.00000	.22282	.39373	.52569	.62810	.88761	.96554	.98939	.99673	.99899
12	0.00000	0.00000	.21991	.38970	.52148	.85538	.95566	.98635	.99579	.99870
13	0.00000	0.00000	0.00000	.21766	.38658	.81461	.94316	.98250	.99460	.99834
14	0.00000	0.00000	0.00000	0.00000	.21591	.76304	.92735	.97763	.99310	.99787
15	0.00000	0.00000	0.00000	0.00000	0.00000	.69778	.90734	.97147	.99120	.99729
16	0.00000	0.00000	0.00000	0.00000	0.00000	.61523	.88203	.96367	.98880	.99654
17	0.00000	0.00000	0.00000	0.00000	0.00000	.51079	.85001	.95381	.98576	.99561
18	0.00000	0.00000	0.00000	0.00000	0.00000	.37865	.80949	.94133	.98191	.99442
19	0.00000	0.00000	0.00000	0.00000	0.00000	.21149	.75824	.92555	.97704	.99292
20	0.00000	0.00000	0.00000	0.00000	0.00000	0.00000	.69340	.90558	.97089	.99102
21	0.00000	0.00000	0.00000	0.00000	0.00000	0.00000	.61136	.88032	.96310	.98862
22	0.00000	0.00000	0.00000	0.00000	0.00000	0.00000	.50758	.84836	.95324	.98558
23	0.00000	0.00000	0.00000	0.00000	0.00000	0.00000	.37628	.80793	.94077	.98173
24	0.00000	0.00000	0.00000	0.00000	0.00000	0.00000	.21016	.75677	.92500	.97686
25	0.00000	0.00000	0.00000	0.00000	0.00000	0.00000	0.00000	.69206	.90504	.97071
26	0.00000	0.00000	0.00000	0.00000	0.00000	0.00000	0.00000	.61018	.87980	.96292
27	0.00000	0.00000	0.00000	0.00000	0.00000	0.00000	0.00000	.50660	.84786	.95307
28	0.00000	0.00000	0.00000	0.00000	0.00000	0.00000	0.00000	.37555	.80745	.94060
29	0.00000	0.00000	0.00000	0.00000	0.00000	0.00000	0.00000	.20975	.75632	.92483
30	0.00000	0.00000	0.00000	0.00000	0.00000	0.00000	0.00000	0.00000	.69164	.90488
31	0.00000	0.00000	0.00000	0.00000	0.00000	0.00000	0.00000	0.00000	.60982	.87963
32	0.00000	0.00000	0.00000	0.00000	0.00000	0.00000	0.00000	0.00000	.50629	.84770
33	0.00000	0.00000	0.00000	0.00000	0.00000	0.00000	0.00000	0.00000	.37532	.80730
34	0.00000	0.00000	0.00000	0.00000	0.00000	0.00000	0.00000	0.00000	.20963	.75618
35	0.00000	0.00000	0.00000	0.00000	0.00000	0.00000	0.00000	0.00000	0.00000	.69152
36	0.00000	0.00000	0.00000	0.00000	0.00000	0.00000	0.00000	0.00000	0.00000	.60970
37	0.00000	0.00000	0.00000	0.00000	0.00000	0.00000	0.00000	0.00000	0.00000	.50620
38	0.00000	0.00000	0.00000	0.00000	0.00000	0.00000	0.00000	0.00000	0.00000	.37525
39	0.00000	0.00000	0.00000	0.00000	0.00000	0.00000	0.00000	0.00000	0.00000	.20959

REMAINING MORTGAGE BALANCE TABLE FOR 24.000 PERCENT

ORIGINAL LOAN TERM

AGE OF LOAN	1	2	3	4	5	6	7	8	9	10
1	0.00000	.55913	.74205	.83098	.88240	.91514	.93729	.95288	.96418	.97253
2	0.00000	0.00000	.41490	.61663	.73326	.80753	.85775	.89312	.91875	.93769
3	0.00000	0.00000	0.00000	.34478	.54412	.67104	.75688	.81734	.86113	.89351
4	0.00000	0.00000	0.00000	0.00000	.30423	.49794	.62896	.72122	.78806	.83748
5	0.00000	0.00000	0.00000	0.00000	0.00000	.27842	.46672	.59932	.69539	.76641
6	0.00000	0.00000	0.00000	0.00000	0.00000	0.00000	.26096	.44473	.57785	.67628
7	0.00000	0.00000	0.00000	0.00000	0.00000	0.00000	0.00000	.24866	.42879	.56198
8	0.00000	0.00000	0.00000	0.00000	0.00000	0.00000	0.00000	0.00000	.23975	.41702
9	0.00000	0.00000	0.00000	0.00000	0.00000	0.00000	0.00000	0.00000	0.00000	.23317

AGE OF LOAN	11	12	13	14	15	20	25	30	35	40
1	.97880	.98356	.98720	.99001	.99218	.99767	.99929	.99978	.99993	.99998
2	.95191	.96271	.97097	.97734	.98227	.99470	.99840	.99951	.99985	.99995
3	.91781	.93626	.95039	.96127	.96970	.99095	.99726	.99917	.99975	.99992
4	.87457	.90272	.92428	.94089	.95376	.98619	.99582	.99873	.99961	.99988
5	.81972	.86019	.89117	.91505	.93354	.98015	.99399	.99817	.99944	.99983
6	.75016	.80624	.84918	.88227	.90789	.97249	.99166	.99746	.99923	.99976
7	.66195	.73783	.79593	.84070	.87537	.96277	.98872	.99657	.99895	.99968
8	.55007	.65106	.72839	.78797	.83413	.95045	.98499	.99543	.99861	.99958
9	.40818	.54102	.64273	.72111	.78182	.93482	.98025	.99399	.99817	.99944
10	.22822	.40146	.53410	.63631	.71547	.91500	.97425	.99217	.99761	.99927
11	0.00000	.22447	.39633	.52876	.63134	.88987	.96664	.98985	.99691	.99906
12	0.00000	0.00000	.22160	.39237	.52463	.85799	.95698	.98691	.99601	.99879
13	0.00000	0.00000	0.00000	.21938	.38930	.81757	.94473	.98319	.99488	.99844
14	0.00000	0.00000	0.00000	0.00000	.21767	.76629	.92920	.97846	.99344	.99800
15	0.00000	0.00000	0.00000	0.00000	0.00000	.70127	.90950	.97247	.99161	.99744
16	0.00000	0.00000	0.00000	0.00000	0.00000	.61880	.88452	.96487	.98930	.99674
17	0.00000	0.00000	0.00000	0.00000	0.00000	.51421	.85283	.95523	.98636	.99584
18	0.00000	0.00000	0.00000	0.00000	0.00000	.38157	.81265	.94300	.98264	.99471
19	0.00000	0.00000	0.00000	0.00000	0.00000	.21335	.76168	.92750	.97792	.99327
20	0.00000	0.00000	0.00000	0.00000	0.00000	0.00000	.69705	.90784	.97193	.99144
21	0.00000	0.00000	0.00000	0.00000	0.00000	0.00000	.61508	.88290	.96433	.98913
22	0.00000	0.00000	0.00000	0.00000	0.00000	0.00000	.51112	.85127	.95470	.98619
23	0.00000	0.00000	0.00000	0.00000	0.00000	0.00000	.37928	.81116	.94248	.98247
24	0.00000	0.00000	0.00000	0.00000	0.00000	0.00000	.21206	.76029	.92698	.97775
25	0.00000	0.00000	0.00000	0.00000	0.00000	0.00000	0.00000	.69578	.90733	.97176
26	0.00000	0.00000	0.00000	0.00000	0.00000	0.00000	0.00000	.61395	.88241	.96417
27	0.00000	0.00000	0.00000	0.00000	0.00000	0.00000	0.00000	.51019	.85080	.95453
28	0.00000	0.00000	0.00000	0.00000	0.00000	0.00000	0.00000	.37858	.81071	.94232
29	0.00000	0.00000	0.00000	0.00000	0.00000	0.00000	0.00000	.21168	.75987	.92682
30	0.00000	0.00000	0.00000	0.00000	0.00000	0.00000	0.00000	0.00000	.69539	.90718
31	0.00000	0.00000	0.00000	0.00000	0.00000	0.00000	0.00000	0.00000	.61361	.88226
32	0.00000	0.00000	0.00000	0.00000	0.00000	0.00000	0.00000	0.00000	.50990	.85065
33	0.00000	0.00000	0.00000	0.00000	0.00000	0.00000	0.00000	0.00000	.37837	.81057
34	0.00000	0.00000	0.00000	0.00000	0.00000	0.00000	0.00000	0.00000	.21156	.75974
35	0.00000	0.00000	0.00000	0.00000	0.00000	0.00000	0.00000	0.00000	0.00000	.69527
36	0.00000	0.00000	0.00000	0.00000	0.00000	0.00000	0.00000	0.00000	0.00000	.61351
37	0.00000	0.00000	0.00000	0.00000	0.00000	0.00000	0.00000	0.00000	0.00000	.50981
38	0.00000	0.00000	0.00000	0.00000	0.00000	0.00000	0.00000	0.00000	0.00000	.37831
39	0.00000	0.00000	0.00000	0.00000	0.00000	0.00000	0.00000	0.00000	0.00000	.21152

REMAINING MORTGAGE BALANCE TABLE FOR 24.250 PERCENT

ORIGINAL LOAN TERM

AGE OF LOAN	1	2	3	4	5	6	7	8	9	10
1	0.00000	.55973	.74278	.83172	.88311	.91580	.93789	.95342	.96466	.97295
2	0.00000	0.00000	.41576	.61779	.73451	.80876	.85892	.89420	.91972	.93856
3	0.00000	0.00000	0.00000	.34580	.54557	.67266	.75852	.81891	.86259	.89485
4	0.00000	0.00000	0.00000	0.00000	.30538	.49964	.63088	.72319	.78997	.83926
5	0.00000	0.00000	0.00000	0.00000	0.00000	.27966	.46860	.60149	.69763	.76860
6	0.00000	0.00000	0.00000	0.00000	0.00000	0.00000	.26229	.44678	.58023	.67876
7	0.00000	0.00000	0.00000	0.00000	0.00000	0.00000	0.00000	.25008	.43099	.56454
8	0.00000	0.00000	0.00000	0.00000	0.00000	0.00000	0.00000	0.00000	.24124	.41933
9	0.00000	0.00000	0.00000	0.00000	0.00000	0.00000	0.00000	0.00000	0.00000	.23471

AGE OF LOAN	11	12	13	14	15	20	25	30	35	40
1	.97917	.98388	.98748	.99025	.99239	.99775	.99933	.99980	.99994	.99998
2	.95268	.96338	.97156	.97785	.98271	.99489	.99847	.99954	.99986	.99996
3	.91901	.93732	.95132	.96208	.97040	.99126	.99738	.99921	.99976	.99993
4	.87620	.90420	.92559	.94204	.95476	.98664	.99600	.99880	.99964	.99989
5	.82178	.86208	.89287	.91656	.93487	.98077	.99424	.99827	.99948	.99984
6	.75259	.80853	.85128	.88417	.90958	.97330	.99201	.99760	.99928	.99978
7	.66462	.74045	.79841	.84298	.87743	.96381	.98917	.99674	.99902	.99971
8	.55278	.65390	.73118	.79062	.83656	.95174	.98555	.99566	.99869	.99961
9	.41059	.54387	.64572	.72405	.78460	.93640	.98096	.99428	.99828	.99948
10	.22982	.40397	.53706	.63942	.71854	.91689	.97512	.99252	.99775	.99932
11	0.00000	.22612	.39891	.53182	.63455	.89209	.96770	.99029	.99708	.99912
12	0.00000	0.00000	.22329	.39502	.52777	.86056	.95826	.98746	.99623	.99886
13	0.00000	0.00000	0.00000	.22111	.39202	.82047	.94626	.98385	.99514	.99854
14	0.00000	0.00000	0.00000	0.00000	.21942	.76951	.93101	.97926	.99376	.99812
15	0.00000	0.00000	0.00000	0.00000	0.00000	.70472	.91161	.97343	.99201	.99759
16	0.00000	0.00000	0.00000	0.00000	0.00000	.62235	.88695	.96602	.98978	.99692
17	0.00000	0.00000	0.00000	0.00000	0.00000	.51762	.85561	.95660	.98694	.99607
18	0.00000	0.00000	0.00000	0.00000	0.00000	.38448	.81575	.94462	.98334	.99498
19	0.00000	0.00000	0.00000	0.00000	0.00000	.21521	.76508	.92940	.97875	.99360
20	0.00000	0.00000	0.00000	0.00000	0.00000	0.00000	.70066	.91003	.97293	.99185
21	0.00000	0.00000	0.00000	0.00000	0.00000	0.00000	.61876	.88542	.96552	.98962
22	0.00000	0.00000	0.00000	0.00000	0.00000	0.00000	.51464	.85413	.95610	.98679
23	0.00000	0.00000	0.00000	0.00000	0.00000	0.00000	.38226	.81434	.94413	.98318
24	0.00000	0.00000	0.00000	0.00000	0.00000	0.00000	.21397	.76376	.92891	.97860
25	0.00000	0.00000	0.00000	0.00000	0.00000	0.00000	0.00000	.69945	.90956	.97278
26	0.00000	0.00000	0.00000	0.00000	0.00000	0.00000	0.00000	.61769	.88496	.96537
27	0.00000	0.00000	0.00000	0.00000	0.00000	0.00000	0.00000	.51375	.85368	.95595
28	0.00000	0.00000	0.00000	0.00000	0.00000	0.00000	0.00000	.38160	.81392	.94398
29	0.00000	0.00000	0.00000	0.00000	0.00000	0.00000	0.00000	.21360	.76336	.92877
30	0.00000	0.00000	0.00000	0.00000	0.00000	0.00000	0.00000	0.00000	.69909	.90942
31	0.00000	0.00000	0.00000	0.00000	0.00000	0.00000	0.00000	0.00000	.61737	.88482
32	0.00000	0.00000	0.00000	0.00000	0.00000	0.00000	0.00000	0.00000	.51348	.85355
33	0.00000	0.00000	0.00000	0.00000	0.00000	0.00000	0.00000	0.00000	.38140	.81379
34	0.00000	0.00000	0.00000	0.00000	0.00000	0.00000	0.00000	0.00000	.21348	.76324
35	0.00000	0.00000	0.00000	0.00000	0.00000	0.00000	0.00000	0.00000	0.00000	.69898
36	0.00000	0.00000	0.00000	0.00000	0.00000	0.00000	0.00000	0.00000	0.00000	.61727
37	0.00000	0.00000	0.00000	0.00000	0.00000	0.00000	0.00000	0.00000	0.00000	.51340
38	0.00000	0.00000	0.00000	0.00000	0.00000	0.00000	0.00000	0.00000	0.00000	.38134
39	0.00000	0.00000	0.00000	0.00000	0.00000	0.00000	0.00000	0.00000	0.00000	.21345

REMAINING MORTGAGE BALANCE TABLE FOR 24.500 PERCENT

ORIGINAL LOAN TERM

AGE OF LOAN	1	2	3	4	5	6	7	8	9	10
1	0.00000	.56034	.74351	.83246	.88382	.91645	.93848	.95395	.96513	.97337
2	0.00000	0.00000	.41662	.61854	.73575	.80998	.86007	.89526	.92069	.93942
3	0.00000	0.00000	0.00000	.34682	.54703	.67428	.76015	.82047	.86405	.89617
4	0.00000	0.00000	0.00000	0.00000	.30652	.50133	.63280	.72515	.79186	.84103
5	0.00000	0.00000	0.00000	0.00000	0.00000	.28091	.47049	.60366	.69986	.77077
6	0.00000	0.00000	0.00000	0.00000	0.00000	0.00000	.26363	.44882	.58261	.68122
7	0.00000	0.00000	0.00000	0.00000	0.00000	0.00000	0.00000	.25149	.43317	.56709
8	0.00000	0.00000	0.00000	0.00000	0.00000	0.00000	0.00000	0.00000	.24272	.42164
9	0.00000	0.00000	0.00000	0.00000	0.00000	0.00000	0.00000	0.00000	0.00000	.23626

AGE OF LOAN	11	12	13	14	15	20	25	30	35	40
1	.97953	.98419	.98775	.99048	.99258	.99784	.99936	.99981	.99994	.99998
2	.95344	.96405	.97214	.97834	.98313	.99508	.99854	.99957	.99987	.99996
3	.92020	.93837	.95224	.96288	.97109	.99156	.99750	.99926	.99978	.99993
4	.87782	.90565	.92688	.94317	.95574	.98708	.99618	.99887	.99966	.99990
5	.82382	.86395	.89456	.91805	.93618	.98137	.99449	.99836	.99951	.99986
6	.75499	.81080	.85336	.88604	.91124	.97410	.99234	.99773	.99932	.99980
7	.66728	.74306	.80086	.84524	.87947	.96482	.98960	.99691	.99908	.99973
8	.55548	.65673	.73396	.79324	.83897	.95300	.98610	.99587	.99877	.99964
9	.41301	.54670	.64868	.72697	.78736	.93794	.98164	.99455	.99838	.99952
10	.23142	.40648	.54000	.64251	.72158	.91874	.97597	.99286	.99788	.99937
11	0.00000	.22776	.40150	.53486	.63774	.89427	.96873	.99071	.99724	.99918
12	0.00000	0.00000	.22497	.39767	.53090	.86309	.95951	.98798	.99643	.99894
13	0.00000	0.00000	0.00000	.22283	.39473	.82334	.94775	.98449	.99539	.99863
14	0.00000	0.00000	0.00000	0.00000	.22118	.77269	.93277	.98004	.99407	.99824
15	0.00000	0.00000	0.00000	0.00000	0.00000	.70814	.91368	.97437	.99238	.99773
16	0.00000	0.00000	0.00000	0.00000	0.00000	.62586	.88934	.96714	.99023	.99710
17	0.00000	0.00000	0.00000	0.00000	0.00000	.52101	.85833	.95794	.98750	.99628
18	0.00000	0.00000	0.00000	0.00000	0.00000	.38737	.81881	.94620	.98401	.99524
19	0.00000	0.00000	0.00000	0.00000	0.00000	.21706	.76843	.93124	.97956	.99392
20	0.00000	0.00000	0.00000	0.00000	0.00000	0.00000	.70423	.91218	.97390	.99224
21	0.00000	0.00000	0.00000	0.00000	0.00000	0.00000	.62241	.88789	.96667	.99009
22	0.00000	0.00000	0.00000	0.00000	0.00000	0.00000	.51814	.85693	.95747	.98735
23	0.00000	0.00000	0.00000	0.00000	0.00000	0.00000	.38524	.81747	.94574	.98387
24	0.00000	0.00000	0.00000	0.00000	0.00000	0.00000	.21586	.76718	.93079	.97942
25	0.00000	0.00000	0.00000	0.00000	0.00000	0.00000	0.00000	.70308	.91174	.97375
26	0.00000	0.00000	0.00000	0.00000	0.00000	0.00000	0.00000	.62140	.88746	.96653
27	0.00000	0.00000	0.00000	0.00000	0.00000	0.00000	0.00000	.51729	.85651	.95733
28	0.00000	0.00000	0.00000	0.00000	0.00000	0.00000	0.00000	.38461	.81707	.94560
29	0.00000	0.00000	0.00000	0.00000	0.00000	0.00000	0.00000	.21551	.76680	.93066
30	0.00000	0.00000	0.00000	0.00000	0.00000	0.00000	0.00000	0.00000	.70274	.91161
31	0.00000	0.00000	0.00000	0.00000	0.00000	0.00000	0.00000	0.00000	.62109	.88733
32	0.00000	0.00000	0.00000	0.00000	0.00000	0.00000	0.00000	0.00000	.51704	.85639
33	0.00000	0.00000	0.00000	0.00000	0.00000	0.00000	0.00000	0.00000	.38442	.81695
34	0.00000	0.00000	0.00000	0.00000	0.00000	0.00000	0.00000	0.00000	.21541	.76669
35	0.00000	0.00000	0.00000	0.00000	0.00000	0.00000	0.00000	0.00000	0.00000	.70264
36	0.00000	0.00000	0.00000	0.00000	0.00000	0.00000	0.00000	0.00000	0.00000	.62100
37	0.00000	0.00000	0.00000	0.00000	0.00000	0.00000	0.00000	0.00000	0.00000	.51696
38	0.00000	0.00000	0.00000	0.00000	0.00000	0.00000	0.00000	0.00000	0.00000	.38437
39	0.00000	0.00000	0.00000	0.00000	0.00000	0.00000	0.00000	0.00000	0.00000	.21537

REMAINING MORTGAGE BALANCE TABLE FOR 24.750 PERCENT

ORIGINAL LOAN TERM

AGE OF LOAN	1	2	3	4	5	6	7	8	9	10
1	0.00000	.56094	.74424	.83320	.88452	.91710	.93907	.95448	.96560	.97378
2	0.00000	0.00000	.41747	.62010	.73698	.81120	.86122	.89632	.92164	.94028
3	0.00000	0.00000	0.00000	.34784	.54849	.67589	.76177	.82202	.86549	.89747
4	0.00000	0.00000	0.00000	0.00000	.30767	.50302	.63471	.72709	.79374	.84279
5	0.00000	0.00000	0.00000	0.00000	0.00000	.28217	.47237	.60582	.70208	.77293
6	0.00000	0.00000	0.00000	0.00000	0.00000	0.00000	.26497	.45087	.58497	.68367
7	0.00000	0.00000	0.00000	0.00000	0.00000	0.00000	0.00000	.25291	.43536	.56963
8	0.00000	0.00000	0.00000	0.00000	0.00000	0.00000	0.00000	0.00000	.24421	.42394
9	0.00000	0.00000	0.00000	0.00000	0.00000	0.00000	0.00000	0.00000	0.00000	.23781

AGE OF LOAN	11	12	13	14	15	20	25	30	35	40
1	.97989	.98450	.98801	.99071	.99278	.99792	.99939	.99982	.99995	.99998
2	.95419	.96470	.97270	.97883	.98355	.99525	.99861	.99959	.99988	.99996
3	.92136	.93940	.95314	.96366	.97176	.99185	.99762	.99930	.99979	.99994
4	.87942	.90709	.92815	.94428	.95670	.98751	.99635	.99893	.99969	.99991
5	.82584	.86579	.89621	.91952	.93746	.98196	.99473	.99845	.99955	.99987
6	.75738	.81304	.85542	.88788	.91288	.97487	.99266	.99785	.99937	.99981
7	.66992	.74564	.80330	.84747	.88147	.96581	.99001	.99707	.99914	.99975
8	.55818	.65954	.73671	.79583	.84135	.95423	.98662	.99608	.99885	.99966
9	.41542	.54953	.65163	.72986	.79008	.93944	.98230	.99481	.99848	.99955
10	.23302	.40898	.54294	.64558	.72459	.92055	.97678	.99319	.99800	.99941
11	0.00000	.22941	.40408	.53789	.64991	.89641	.96973	.99112	.99739	.99923
12	0.00000	0.00000	.22666	.40032	.53401	.86557	.96071	.98848	.99662	.99901
13	0.00000	0.00000	0.00000	.22456	.39743	.82617	.94920	.98510	.99562	.99871
14	0.00000	0.00000	0.00000	0.00000	.22293	.77583	.93449	.98078	.99436	.99834
15	0.00000	0.00000	0.00000	0.00000	0.00000	.71152	.91570	.97527	.99274	.99787
16	0.00000	0.00000	0.00000	0.00000	0.00000	.62935	.89168	.96823	.99067	.99726
17	0.00000	0.00000	0.00000	0.00000	0.00000	.52438	.86101	.95923	.98803	.99648
18	0.00000	0.00000	0.00000	0.00000	0.00000	.39026	.82181	.94773	.98465	.99549
19	0.00000	0.00000	0.00000	0.00000	0.00000	.21891	.77174	.93304	.98034	.99422
20	0.00000	0.00000	0.00000	0.00000	0.00000	0.00000	.70777	.91428	.97483	.99261
21	0.00000	0.00000	0.00000	0.00000	0.00000	0.00000	.62603	.89030	.96779	.99054
22	0.00000	0.00000	0.00000	0.00000	0.00000	0.00000	.52161	.85967	.95879	.98790
23	0.00000	0.00000	0.00000	0.00000	0.00000	0.00000	.38820	.82054	.94730	.98452
24	0.00000	0.00000	0.00000	0.00000	0.00000	0.00000	.21776	.77055	.93262	.98021
25	0.00000	0.00000	0.00000	0.00000	0.00000	0.00000	0.00000	.70667	.91386	.97470
26	0.00000	0.00000	0.00000	0.00000	0.00000	0.00000	0.00000	.62506	.88990	.96766
27	0.00000	0.00000	0.00000	0.00000	0.00000	0.00000	0.00000	.52080	.85928	.95867
28	0.00000	0.00000	0.00000	0.00000	0.00000	0.00000	0.00000	.38760	.82017	.94718
29	0.00000	0.00000	0.00000	0.00000	0.00000	0.00000	0.00000	.21742	.77020	.93250
30	0.00000	0.00000	0.00000	0.00000	0.00000	0.00000	0.00000	0.00000	.70635	.91374
31	0.00000	0.00000	0.00000	0.00000	0.00000	0.00000	0.00000	0.00000	.62478	.88978
32	0.00000	0.00000	0.00000	0.00000	0.00000	0.00000	0.00000	0.00000	.52057	.85917
33	0.00000	0.00000	0.00000	0.00000	0.00000	0.00000	0.00000	0.00000	.38742	.82006
34	0.00000	0.00000	0.00000	0.00000	0.00000	0.00000	0.00000	0.00000	.21732	.77009
35	0.00000	0.00000	0.00000	0.00000	0.00000	0.00000	0.00000	0.00000	0.00000	.70626
36	0.00000	0.00000	0.00000	0.00000	0.00000	0.00000	0.00000	0.00000	0.00000	.62470
37	0.00000	0.00000	0.00000	0.00000	0.00000	0.00000	0.00000	0.00000	0.00000	.52050
38	0.00000	0.00000	0.00000	0.00000	0.00000	0.00000	0.00000	0.00000	0.00000	.38737
39	0.00000	0.00000	0.00000	0.00000	0.00000	0.00000	0.00000	0.00000	0.00000	.21729

REMAINING MORTGAGE BALANCE TABLE FOR 25.000 PERCENT

ORIGINAL LOAN TERM

AGE OF LOAN	1	2	3	4	5	6	7	8	9	10
1	0.00000	.56154	.74496	.83394	.88522	.91775	.93965	.95500	.96606	.97418
2	0.00000	0.00000	.41833	.62125	.73822	.81241	.86237	.89737	.92259	.94112
3	0.00000	0.00000	0.00000	.34886	.54994	.67750	.76338	.82356	.86691	.89877
4	0.00000	0.00000	0.00000	0.00000	.30882	.50471	.63661	.72903	.79561	.84453
5	0.00000	0.00000	0.00000	0.00000	0.00000	.28342	.47425	.60797	.70429	.77507
6	0.00000	0.00000	0.00000	0.00000	0.00000	0.00000	.26631	.45291	.58733	.68611
7	0.00000	0.00000	0.00000	0.00000	0.00000	0.00000	0.00000	.25433	.43754	.57217
8	0.00000	0.00000	0.00000	0.00000	0.00000	0.00000	0.00000	0.00000	.24570	.42624
9	0.00000	0.00000	0.00000	0.00000	0.00000	0.00000	0.00000	0.00000	0.00000	.23935

AGE OF LOAN	11	12	13	14	15	20	25	30	35	40
1	.98024	.98481	.98828	.99093	.99297	.99799	.99942	.99983	.99995	.99999
2	.95493	.96535	.97326	.97931	.98396	.99543	.99868	.99962	.99989	.99997
3	.92252	.94042	.95403	.96443	.97242	.99214	.99773	.99934	.99981	.99994
4	.88101	.90850	.92940	.94537	.95765	.98792	.99651	.99899	.99971	.99991
5	.82784	.86762	.89785	.92096	.93872	.98253	.99495	.99854	.99958	.99988
6	.75975	.81526	.85745	.88971	.91449	.97562	.99296	.99796	.99941	.99983
7	.67255	.74821	.80571	.84967	.88345	.96677	.99040	.99722	.99919	.99977
8	.56086	.66233	.73944	.79840	.84369	.95543	.98713	.99627	.99892	.99969
9	.41782	.55234	.65456	.73273	.79278	.94091	.98294	.99506	.99857	.99958
10	.23463	.41147	.54586	.64863	.72758	.92232	.97757	.99350	.99811	.99945
11	0.00000	.23106	.40665	.54091	.64406	.89851	.97070	.99151	.99754	.99929
12	0.00000	0.00000	.22835	.40296	.53711	.86801	.96189	.98896	.99680	.99907
13	0.00000	0.00000	0.00000	.22628	.40013	.82895	.95061	.98569	.99585	.99880
14	0.00000	0.00000	0.00000	0.00000	.22469	.77893	.93617	.98150	.99463	.99844
15	0.00000	0.00000	0.00000	0.00000	0.00000	.71486	.91767	.97614	.99308	.99799
16	0.00000	0.00000	0.00000	0.00000	0.00000	.63281	.89398	.96928	.99109	.99741
17	0.00000	0.00000	0.00000	0.00000	0.00000	.52772	.86363	.96048	.98854	.99667
18	0.00000	0.00000	0.00000	0.00000	0.00000	.39313	.82477	.94922	.98527	.99573
19	0.00000	0.00000	0.00000	0.00000	0.00000	.22076	.77500	.93480	.98109	.99451
20	0.00000	0.00000	0.00000	0.00000	0.00000	0.00000	.71126	.91633	.97573	.99296
21	0.00000	0.00000	0.00000	0.00000	0.00000	0.00000	.62962	.89267	.96886	.99097
22	0.00000	0.00000	0.00000	0.00000	0.00000	0.00000	.52506	.86237	.96008	.98842
23	0.00000	0.00000	0.00000	0.00000	0.00000	0.00000	.39115	.82357	.94882	.98515
24	0.00000	0.00000	0.00000	0.00000	0.00000	0.00000	.21965	.77387	.93440	.98097
25	0.00000	0.00000	0.00000	0.00000	0.00000	0.00000	0.00000	.71022	.91594	.97561
26	0.00000	0.00000	0.00000	0.00000	0.00000	0.00000	0.00000	.62870	.89229	.96875
27	0.00000	0.00000	0.00000	0.00000	0.00000	0.00000	0.00000	.52429	.86200	.95996
28	0.00000	0.00000	0.00000	0.00000	0.00000	0.00000	0.00000	.39058	.82322	.94870
29	0.00000	0.00000	0.00000	0.00000	0.00000	0.00000	0.00000	.21933	.77354	.93429
30	0.00000	0.00000	0.00000	0.00000	0.00000	0.00000	0.00000	0.00000	.70992	.91583
31	0.00000	0.00000	0.00000	0.00000	0.00000	0.00000	0.00000	0.00000	.62843	.89218
32	0.00000	0.00000	0.00000	0.00000	0.00000	0.00000	0.00000	0.00000	.52407	.86190
33	0.00000	0.00000	0.00000	0.00000	0.00000	0.00000	0.00000	0.00000	.39041	.82311
34	0.00000	0.00000	0.00000	0.00000	0.00000	0.00000	0.00000	0.00000	.21923	.77344
35	0.00000	0.00000	0.00000	0.00000	0.00000	0.00000	0.00000	0.00000	0.00000	.70983
36	0.00000	0.00000	0.00000	0.00000	0.00000	0.00000	0.00000	0.00000	0.00000	.62835
37	0.00000	0.00000	0.00000	0.00000	0.00000	0.00000	0.00000	0.00000	0.00000	.52401
38	0.00000	0.00000	0.00000	0.00000	0.00000	0.00000	0.00000	0.00000	0.00000	.39037
39	0.00000	0.00000	0.00000	0.00000	0.00000	0.00000	0.00000	0.00000	0.00000	.21921

REMAINING MORTGAGE BALANCE TABLE FOR 26.000 PERCENT

ORIGINAL LOAN TERM

AGE OF LOAN	1	2	3	4	5	6	7	8	9	10
1	0.00000	.56395	.74786	.83685	.88799	.92029	.94195	.95704	.96785	.97575
2	0.00000	0.00000	.42176	.62585	.74311	.81721	.86687	.90149	.92628	.94438
3	0.00000	0.00000	0.00000	.35295	.55574	.68388	.76977	.82963	.87251	.90381
4	0.00000	0.00000	0.00000	0.00000	.31341	.51145	.64418	.73670	.80296	.85135
5	0.00000	0.00000	0.00000	0.00000	0.00000	.28843	.48176	.61651	.71302	.78349
6	0.00000	0.00000	0.00000	0.00000	0.00000	0.00000	.27169	.46106	.59669	.69573
7	0.00000	0.00000	0.00000	0.00000	0.00000	0.00000	0.00000	.26002	.44624	.58222
8	0.00000	0.00000	0.00000	0.00000	0.00000	0.00000	0.00000	0.00000	.25166	.43542
9	0.00000	0.00000	0.00000	0.00000	0.00000	0.00000	0.00000	0.00000	0.00000	.24556

AGE OF LOAN	11	12	13	14	15	20	25	30	35	40
1	.98159	.98597	.98927	.99177	.99368	.99828	.99953	.99987	.99996	.99999
2	.95779	.96782	.97539	.98112	.98550	.99605	.99891	.99970	.99992	.99998
3	.92700	.94435	.95743	.96736	.97492	.99318	.99812	.99948	.99986	.99996
4	.88718	.91399	.93421	.94955	.96124	.98945	.99710	.99920	.99978	.99994
5	.83568	.87473	.90418	.92652	.94355	.98464	.99577	.99883	.99968	.99991
6	.76907	.82395	.86534	.89674	.92066	.97841	.99406	.99836	.99955	.99987
7	.68292	.75828	.81511	.85822	.89107	.97036	.99184	.99775	.99938	.99983
8	.57150	.67334	.75014	.80840	.85279	.95994	.98898	.99696	.99916	.99977
9	.42740	.56348	.66611	.74396	.80329	.94647	.98527	.99593	.99888	.99969
10	.24104	.42141	.55744	.66063	.73926	.92905	.98048	.99461	.99851	.99959
11	0.00000	.23765	.41688	.55285	.65645	.90652	.97428	.99290	.99804	.99946
12	0.00000	0.00000	.23510	.41345	.54935	.87738	.96626	.99069	.99743	.99929
13	0.00000	0.00000	0.00000	.23317	.41084	.83969	.95589	.98782	.99664	.99907
14	0.00000	0.00000	0.00000	0.00000	.23169	.79095	.94247	.98412	.99561	.99879
15	0.00000	0.00000	0.00000	0.00000	0.00000	.72790	.92513	.97933	.99429	.99842
16	0.00000	0.00000	0.00000	0.00000	0.00000	.64637	.90269	.97314	.99258	.99795
17	0.00000	0.00000	0.00000	0.00000	0.00000	.54091	.87367	.96513	.99037	.99734
18	0.00000	0.00000	0.00000	0.00000	0.00000	.40453	.83614	.95477	.98751	.99655
19	0.00000	0.00000	0.00000	0.00000	0.00000	.22813	.78760	.94137	.98380	.99552
20	0.00000	0.00000	0.00000	0.00000	0.00000	0.00000	.72483	.92405	.97902	.99420
21	0.00000	0.00000	0.00000	0.00000	0.00000	0.00000	.64364	.90164	.97283	.99249
22	0.00000	0.00000	0.00000	0.00000	0.00000	0.00000	.53863	.87265	.96482	.99028
23	0.00000	0.00000	0.00000	0.00000	0.00000	0.00000	.40282	.83517	.95446	.98742
24	0.00000	0.00000	0.00000	0.00000	0.00000	0.00000	.22717	.78668	.94107	.98372
25	0.00000	0.00000	0.00000	0.00000	0.00000	0.00000	0.00000	.72398	.92375	.97893
26	0.00000	0.00000	0.00000	0.00000	0.00000	0.00000	0.00000	.64288	.90135	.97274
27	0.00000	0.00000	0.00000	0.00000	0.00000	0.00000	0.00000	.53800	.87237	.96473
28	0.00000	0.00000	0.00000	0.00000	0.00000	0.00000	0.00000	.40235	.83490	.95438
29	0.00000	0.00000	0.00000	0.00000	0.00000	0.00000	0.00000	.22691	.78643	.94099
30	0.00000	0.00000	0.00000	0.00000	0.00000	0.00000	0.00000	0.00000	.72375	.92367
31	0.00000	0.00000	0.00000	0.00000	0.00000	0.00000	0.00000	0.00000	.64268	.90127
32	0.00000	0.00000	0.00000	0.00000	0.00000	0.00000	0.00000	0.00000	.53783	.87229
33	0.00000	0.00000	0.00000	0.00000	0.00000	0.00000	0.00000	0.00000	.40222	.83482
34	0.00000	0.00000	0.00000	0.00000	0.00000	0.00000	0.00000	0.00000	.22683	.78636
35	0.00000	0.00000	0.00000	0.00000	0.00000	0.00000	0.00000	0.00000	0.00000	.72368
36	0.00000	0.00000	0.00000	0.00000	0.00000	0.00000	0.00000	0.00000	0.00000	.64262
37	0.00000	0.00000	0.00000	0.00000	0.00000	0.00000	0.00000	0.00000	0.00000	.53778
38	0.00000	0.00000	0.00000	0.00000	0.00000	0.00000	0.00000	0.00000	0.00000	.40218
39	0.00000	0.00000	0.00000	0.00000	0.00000	0.00000	0.00000	0.00000	0.00000	.22681

REMAINING MORTGAGE BALANCE TABLE FOR 27.000 PERCENT

ORIGINAL LOAN TERM

AGE OF LOAN	1	2	3	4	5	6	7	8	9	10
1	0.00000	.56636	.75074	.83973	.89070	.92278	.94417	.95901	.96957	.97723
2	0.00000	0.00000	.42519	.63042	.74795	.82192	.87126	.90547	.92982	.94749
3	0.00000	0.00000	0.00000	.35704	.56152	.69019	.77603	.83555	.87791	.90865
4	0.00000	0.00000	0.00000	0.00000	.31802	.51815	.65166	.74422	.81012	.85792
5	0.00000	0.00000	0.00000	0.00000	0.00000	.29346	.48923	.62495	.72157	.79167
6	0.00000	0.00000	0.00000	0.00000	0.00000	0.00000	.27708	.46917	.60593	.70514
7	0.00000	0.00000	0.00000	0.00000	0.00000	0.00000	0.00000	.26572	.45489	.59213
8	0.00000	0.00000	0.00000	0.00000	0.00000	0.00000	0.00000	0.00000	.25763	.44454
9	0.00000	0.00000	0.00000	0.00000	0.00000	0.00000	0.00000	0.00000	0.00000	.25177

AGE OF LOAN	11	12	13	14	15	20	25	30	35	40
1	.98286	.98705	.99018	.99254	.99432	.99853	.99961	.99990	.99997	.99999
2	.96048	.97014	.97736	.98279	.98690	.99660	.99911	.99977	.99994	.99998
3	.93126	.94805	.96061	.97007	.97721	.99408	.99845	.99959	.99989	.99997
4	.89308	.91920	.93874	.95344	.96456	.99080	.99759	.99937	.99983	.99996
5	.84322	.88152	.91017	.93173	.94803	.98651	.99646	.99907	.99976	.99994
6	.77811	.83230	.87286	.90338	.92644	.98090	.99499	.99868	.99965	.99991
7	.69306	.76803	.82413	.86635	.89825	.97359	.99307	.99818	.99952	.99987
8	.58199	.68409	.76049	.81758	.86143	.96403	.99057	.99752	.99935	.99983
9	.43692	.57445	.67737	.75482	.81334	.95154	.98729	.99666	.99912	.99977
10	.24745	.43126	.56881	.67232	.75053	.93524	.98302	.99554	.99883	.99969
11	0.00000	.24425	.42703	.56457	.66850	.91394	.97743	.99407	.99844	.99959
12	0.00000	0.00000	.24185	.42384	.56136	.88613	.97014	.99215	.99793	.99946
13	0.00000	0.00000	0.00000	.24005	.42143	.84980	.96062	.98965	.99728	.99928
14	0.00000	0.00000	0.00000	0.00000	.23868	.80236	.94818	.98638	.99642	.99906
15	0.00000	0.00000	0.00000	0.00000	0.00000	.74040	.93193	.98210	.99529	.99876
16	0.00000	0.00000	0.00000	0.00000	0.00000	.65948	.91071	.97653	.99382	.99837
17	0.00000	0.00000	0.00000	0.00000	0.00000	.55379	.88299	.96924	.99191	.99787
18	0.00000	0.00000	0.00000	0.00000	0.00000	.41575	.84680	.95972	.98940	.99721
19	0.00000	0.00000	0.00000	0.00000	0.00000	.23546	.79952	.94729	.98613	.99635
20	0.00000	0.00000	0.00000	0.00000	0.00000	0.00000	.73778	.93106	.98186	.99523
21	0.00000	0.00000	0.00000	0.00000	0.00000	0.00000	.65714	.90986	.97629	.99376
22	0.00000	0.00000	0.00000	0.00000	0.00000	0.00000	.55183	.88217	.96900	.99184
23	0.00000	0.00000	0.00000	0.00000	0.00000	0.00000	.41428	.84601	.95949	.98934
24	0.00000	0.00000	0.00000	0.00000	0.00000	0.00000	.23463	.79878	.94706	.98607
25	0.00000	0.00000	0.00000	0.00000	0.00000	0.00000	0.00000	.73710	.93083	.98180
26	0.00000	0.00000	0.00000	0.00000	0.00000	0.00000	0.00000	.65653	.90964	.97622
27	0.00000	0.00000	0.00000	0.00000	0.00000	0.00000	0.00000	.55131	.88196	.96894
28	0.00000	0.00000	0.00000	0.00000	0.00000	0.00000	0.00000	.41389	.84580	.95943
29	0.00000	0.00000	0.00000	0.00000	0.00000	0.00000	0.00000	.23441	.79859	.94700
30	0.00000	0.00000	0.00000	0.00000	0.00000	0.00000	0.00000	0.00000	.73692	.93077
31	0.00000	0.00000	0.00000	0.00000	0.00000	0.00000	0.00000	0.00000	.65637	.90958
32	0.00000	0.00000	0.00000	0.00000	0.00000	0.00000	0.00000	0.00000	.55118	.88190
33	0.00000	0.00000	0.00000	0.00000	0.00000	0.00000	0.00000	0.00000	.41379	.84575
34	0.00000	0.00000	0.00000	0.00000	0.00000	0.00000	0.00000	0.00000	.23435	.79853
35	0.00000	0.00000	0.00000	0.00000	0.00000	0.00000	0.00000	0.00000	0.00000	.73687
36	0.00000	0.00000	0.00000	0.00000	0.00000	0.00000	0.00000	0.00000	0.00000	.65633
37	0.00000	0.00000	0.00000	0.00000	0.00000	0.00000	0.00000	0.00000	0.00000	.55114
38	0.00000	0.00000	0.00000	0.00000	0.00000	0.00000	0.00000	0.00000	0.00000	.41376
39	0.00000	0.00000	0.00000	0.00000	0.00000	0.00000	0.00000	0.00000	0.00000	.23434

REMAINING MORTGAGE BALANCE TABLE FOR 28.000 PERCENT

ORIGINAL LOAN TERM

AGE OF LOAN	1	2	3	4	5	6	7	8	9	10
1	0.00000	.56876	.75359	.84258	.89337	.92520	.94633	.96090	.97120	.97863
2	0.00000	0.00000	.42861	.63496	.75274	.82654	.87554	.90932	.93323	.95045
3	0.00000	0.00000	0.00000	.36114	.56726	.69643	.78218	.84130	.88314	.91329
4	0.00000	0.00000	0.00000	0.00000	.32263	.52482	.65905	.75159	.81708	.86427
5	0.00000	0.00000	0.00000	0.00000	0.00000	.29850	.49666	.63328	.72995	.79962
6	0.00000	0.00000	0.00000	0.00000	0.00000	0.00000	.28248	.47723	.61504	.71435
7	0.00000	0.00000	0.00000	0.00000	0.00000	0.00000	0.00000	.27143	.46349	.60190
8	0.00000	0.00000	0.00000	0.00000	0.00000	0.00000	0.00000	0.00000	.26361	.45359
9	0.00000	0.00000	0.00000	0.00000	0.00000	0.00000	0.00000	0.00000	0.00000	.25798

AGE OF LOAN	11	12	13	14	15	20	25	30	35	40
1	.98406	.98806	.99103	.99324	.99490	.99874	.99968	.99992	.99998	1.00000
2	.96303	.97230	.97919	.98433	.98818	.99707	.99927	.99982	.99995	.99999
3	.93530	.95153	.96358	.97257	.97931	.99488	.99872	.99968	.99992	.99998
4	.89873	.92413	.94299	.95707	.96761	.99198	.99800	.99950	.99987	.99997
5	.85049	.88799	.91584	.93662	.95219	.98816	.99704	.99926	.99981	.99995
6	.78687	.84033	.88002	.90965	.93184	.98312	.99578	.99894	.99974	.99993
7	.70297	.77747	.83279	.87408	.90501	.97648	.99412	.99853	.99963	.99991
8	.59231	.69457	.77050	.82716	.86962	.96771	.99193	.99798	.99949	.99987
9	.44636	.58523	.68834	.76529	.82294	.95616	.98905	.99726	.99931	.99983
10	.25387	.44103	.57998	.68368	.76139	.94091	.98524	.99630	.99907	.99977
11	0.00000	.25084	.43707	.57606	.68020	.92081	.98021	.99505	.99876	.99969
12	0.00000	0.00000	.24859	.43411	.57312	.89429	.97359	.99339	.99834	.99958
13	0.00000	0.00000	0.00000	.24691	.43190	.85932	.96485	.99120	.99779	.99945
14	0.00000	0.00000	0.00000	0.00000	.24565	.81320	.95333	.98831	.99707	.99927
15	0.00000	0.00000	0.00000	0.00000	0.00000	.75237	.93813	.98451	.99612	.99903
16	0.00000	0.00000	0.00000	0.00000	0.00000	.67215	.91808	.97949	.99486	.99871
17	0.00000	0.00000	0.00000	0.00000	0.00000	.56634	.89165	.97287	.99320	.99830
18	0.00000	0.00000	0.00000	0.00000	0.00000	.42679	.85678	.96414	.99101	.99775
19	0.00000	0.00000	0.00000	0.00000	0.00000	.24274	.81080	.95262	.98813	.99703
20	0.00000	0.00000	0.00000	0.00000	0.00000	0.00000	.75015	.93743	.98432	.99607
21	0.00000	0.00000	0.00000	0.00000	0.00000	0.00000	.67016	.91740	.97931	.99481
22	0.00000	0.00000	0.00000	0.00000	0.00000	0.00000	.56466	.89099	.97269	.99316
23	0.00000	0.00000	0.00000	0.00000	0.00000	0.00000	.42552	.85615	.96396	.99097
24	0.00000	0.00000	0.00000	0.00000	0.00000	0.00000	.24202	.81019	.95244	.98808
25	0.00000	0.00000	0.00000	0.00000	0.00000	0.00000	0.00000	.74959	.93726	.98428
26	0.00000	0.00000	0.00000	0.00000	0.00000	0.00000	0.00000	.66966	.91723	.97926
27	0.00000	0.00000	0.00000	0.00000	0.00000	0.00000	0.00000	.56424	.89082	.97264
28	0.00000	0.00000	0.00000	0.00000	0.00000	0.00000	0.00000	.42521	.85599	.96391
29	0.00000	0.00000	0.00000	0.00000	0.00000	0.00000	0.00000	.24184	.81004	.95240
30	0.00000	0.00000	0.00000	0.00000	0.00000	0.00000	0.00000	0.00000	.74945	.93722
31	0.00000	0.00000	0.00000	0.00000	0.00000	0.00000	0.00000	0.00000	.66954	.91719
32	0.00000	0.00000	0.00000	0.00000	0.00000	0.00000	0.00000	0.00000	.56414	.89078
33	0.00000	0.00000	0.00000	0.00000	0.00000	0.00000	0.00000	0.00000	.42513	.85595
34	0.00000	0.00000	0.00000	0.00000	0.00000	0.00000	0.00000	0.00000	.24180	.81001
35	0.00000	0.00000	0.00000	0.00000	0.00000	0.00000	0.00000	0.00000	0.00000	.74942
36	0.00000	0.00000	0.00000	0.00000	0.00000	0.00000	0.00000	0.00000	0.00000	.66951
37	0.00000	0.00000	0.00000	0.00000	0.00000	0.00000	0.00000	0.00000	0.00000	.56411
38	0.00000	0.00000	0.00000	0.00000	0.00000	0.00000	0.00000	0.00000	0.00000	.42511
39	0.00000	0.00000	0.00000	0.00000	0.00000	0.00000	0.00000	0.00000	0.00000	.24178

REMAINING MORTGAGE BALANCE TABLE FOR 29.000 PERCENT

ORIGINAL LOAN TERM

AGE OF LOAN	1	2	3	4	5	6	7	8	9	10
1	0.00000	.57115	.75643	.84539	.89599	.92756	.94841	.96271	.97276	.97996
2	0.00000	0.00000	.43204	.63948	.75746	.83108	.87971	.91305	.93649	.95327
3	0.00000	0.00000	0.00000	.36524	.57296	.70259	.78821	.84691	.88818	.91772
4	0.00000	0.00000	0.00000	0.00000	.32725	.53146	.66634	.75882	.82384	.87038
5	0.00000	0.00000	0.00000	0.00000	0.00000	.30354	.50404	.64150	.73815	.80733
6	0.00000	0.00000	0.00000	0.00000	0.00000	0.00000	.28788	.48525	.62403	.72336
7	0.00000	0.00000	0.00000	0.00000	0.00000	0.00000	0.00000	.27715	.47203	.61152
8	0.00000	0.00000	0.00000	0.00000	0.00000	0.00000	0.00000	0.00000	.26960	.46257
9	0.00000	0.00000	0.00000	0.00000	0.00000	0.00000	0.00000	0.00000	0.00000	.26420

AGE OF LOAN	11	12	13	14	15	20	25	30	35	40
1	.98518	.98899	.99180	.99388	.99543	.99892	.99974	.99994	.99999	1.00000
2	.96543	.97433	.98088	.98573	.98934	.99748	.99940	.99986	.99997	.99999
3	.93914	.95481	.96634	.97488	.98123	.99557	.99894	.99975	.99994	.99999
4	.90412	.92880	.94698	.96043	.97043	.99302	.99834	.99960	.99991	.99998
5	.85748	.89417	.92119	.94118	.95604	.98962	.99753	.99941	.99986	.99997
6	.79536	.84804	.88684	.91555	.93688	.98509	.99645	.99915	.99980	.99995
7	.71263	.78661	.84109	.88141	.91136	.97907	.99502	.99881	.99972	.99993
8	.60245	.70479	.78016	.83594	.87739	.97104	.99311	.99836	.99961	.99991
9	.45571	.59582	.69901	.77539	.83212	.96035	.99056	.99775	.99946	.99987
10	.26028	.45070	.59094	.69474	.77184	.94612	.98717	.99694	.99927	.99983
11	0.00000	.25742	.44700	.58732	.69156	.92715	.98266	.99586	.99901	.99976
12	0.00000	0.00000	.25531	.44427	.58464	.90190	.97665	.99443	.99867	.99968
13	0.00000	0.00000	0.00000	.25374	.44224	.86827	.96864	.99252	.99822	.99957
14	0.00000	0.00000	0.00000	0.00000	.25258	.82348	.95798	.98998	.99761	.99943
15	0.00000	0.00000	0.00000	0.00000	0.00000	.76383	.94378	.98659	.99680	.99924
16	0.00000	0.00000	0.00000	0.00000	0.00000	.68438	.92486	.98208	.99572	.99898
17	0.00000	0.00000	0.00000	0.00000	0.00000	.57857	.89967	.97607	.99429	.99864
18	0.00000	0.00000	0.00000	0.00000	0.00000	.43765	.86613	.96807	.99238	.99818
19	0.00000	0.00000	0.00000	0.00000	0.00000	.24996	.82145	.95741	.98984	.99757
20	0.00000	0.00000	0.00000	0.00000	0.00000	0.00000	.76194	.94322	.98645	.99677
21	0.00000	0.00000	0.00000	0.00000	0.00000	0.00000	.68269	.92432	.98194	.99569
22	0.00000	0.00000	0.00000	0.00000	0.00000	0.00000	.57714	.89914	.97593	.99426
23	0.00000	0.00000	0.00000	0.00000	0.00000	0.00000	.43656	.86562	.96793	.99235
24	0.00000	0.00000	0.00000	0.00000	0.00000	0.00000	.24934	.82096	.95728	.98980
25	0.00000	0.00000	0.00000	0.00000	0.00000	0.00000	0.00000	.76149	.94309	.98642
26	0.00000	0.00000	0.00000	0.00000	0.00000	0.00000	0.00000	.68229	.92419	.98191
27	0.00000	0.00000	0.00000	0.00000	0.00000	0.00000	0.00000	.57680	.89902	.97590
28	0.00000	0.00000	0.00000	0.00000	0.00000	0.00000	0.00000	.43631	.86549	.96790
29	0.00000	0.00000	0.00000	0.00000	0.00000	0.00000	0.00000	.24920	.82085	.95725
30	0.00000	0.00000	0.00000	0.00000	0.00000	0.00000	0.00000	0.00000	.76138	.94306
31	0.00000	0.00000	0.00000	0.00000	0.00000	0.00000	0.00000	0.00000	.68219	.92416
32	0.00000	0.00000	0.00000	0.00000	0.00000	0.00000	0.00000	0.00000	.57672	.89899
33	0.00000	0.00000	0.00000	0.00000	0.00000	0.00000	0.00000	0.00000	.43625	.86546
34	0.00000	0.00000	0.00000	0.00000	0.00000	0.00000	0.00000	0.00000	.24916	.82082
35	0.00000	0.00000	0.00000	0.00000	0.00000	0.00000	0.00000	0.00000	0.00000	.76136
36	0.00000	0.00000	0.00000	0.00000	0.00000	0.00000	0.00000	0.00000	0.00000	.68217
37	0.00000	0.00000	0.00000	0.00000	0.00000	0.00000	0.00000	0.00000	0.00000	.57670
38	0.00000	0.00000	0.00000	0.00000	0.00000	0.00000	0.00000	0.00000	0.00000	.43623
39	0.00000	0.00000	0.00000	0.00000	0.00000	0.00000	0.00000	0.00000	0.00000	.24915

REMAINING MORTGAGE BALANCE TABLE FOR 30.000 PERCENT

ORIGINAL LOAN TERM

AGE OF LOAN	1	2	3	4	5	6	7	8	9	10
1	0.00000	.57354	.75925	.84817	.89856	.92986	.95043	.96445	.97425	.98121
2	0.00000	0.00000	.43546	.64397	.76212	.83553	.88377	.91665	.93962	.95595
3	0.00000	0.00000	0.00000	.36934	.57864	.70867	.79412	.85236	.89305	.92197
4	0.00000	0.00000	0.00000	0.00000	.33187	.53805	.67354	.76589	.83041	.87627
5	0.00000	0.00000	0.00000	0.00000	0.00000	.30860	.51139	.64960	.74617	.81481
6	0.00000	0.00000	0.00000	0.00000	0.00000	0.00000	.29330	.49321	.63287	.73215
7	0.00000	0.00000	0.00000	0.00000	0.00000	0.00000	0.00000	.28287	.48051	.62099
8	0.00000	0.00000	0.00000	0.00000	0.00000	0.00000	0.00000	0.00000	.27559	.47148
9	0.00000	0.00000	0.00000	0.00000	0.00000	0.00000	0.00000	0.00000	0.00000	.27041

AGE OF LOAN	11	12	13	14	15	20	25	30	35	40
1	.98622	.98986	.99252	.99447	.99590	.99908	.99979	.99995	.99999	1.00000
2	.96770	.97622	.98245	.98703	.99039	.99784	.99951	.99989	.99997	.99999
3	.94278	.95788	.96892	.97702	.98298	.99617	.99913	.99980	.99996	.99999
4	.90927	.93322	.95072	.96356	.97301	.99392	.99862	.99969	.99993	.99998
5	.86420	.90005	.92623	.94545	.95961	.99090	.99794	.99953	.99989	.99998
6	.80358	.85543	.89331	.92111	.94158	.98684	.99702	.99932	.99985	.99996
7	.72206	.79543	.84903	.88837	.91734	.98138	.99578	.99904	.99978	.99995
8	.61243	.71474	.78948	.84433	.88473	.97404	.99411	.99866	.99970	.99993
9	.46498	.60622	.70939	.78511	.84087	.96416	.99187	.99815	.99958	.99990
10	.26669	.46027	.60168	.70547	.78190	.95088	.98886	.99747	.99942	.99987
11	0.00000	.26398	.45683	.59835	.70258	.93302	.98481	.99655	.99922	.99982
12	0.00000	0.00000	.26201	.45430	.59590	.90899	.97936	.99531	.99893	.99976
13	0.00000	0.00000	0.00000	.26056	.45244	.87668	.97203	.99365	.99856	.99967
14	0.00000	0.00000	0.00000	0.00000	.25949	.83323	.96217	.99141	.99805	.99956
15	0.00000	0.00000	0.00000	0.00000	0.00000	.77478	.94892	.98840	.99736	.99940
16	0.00000	0.00000	0.00000	0.00000	0.00000	.69619	.93109	.98435	.99644	.99919
17	0.00000	0.00000	0.00000	0.00000	0.00000	.59048	.90712	.97890	.99520	.99891
18	0.00000	0.00000	0.00000	0.00000	0.00000	.44832	.87487	.97157	.99354	.99853
19	0.00000	0.00000	0.00000	0.00000	0.00000	.25713	.83151	.96172	.99130	.99802
20	0.00000	0.00000	0.00000	0.00000	0.00000	0.00000	.77319	.94847	.98829	.99734
21	0.00000	0.00000	0.00000	0.00000	0.00000	0.00000	.69475	.93065	.98424	.99642
22	0.00000	0.00000	0.00000	0.00000	0.00000	0.00000	.58926	.90669	.97879	.99518
23	0.00000	0.00000	0.00000	0.00000	0.00000	0.00000	.44740	.87446	.97147	.99352
24	0.00000	0.00000	0.00000	0.00000	0.00000	0.00000	.25660	.83112	.96162	.99128
25	0.00000	0.00000	0.00000	0.00000	0.00000	0.00000	0.00000	.77282	.94837	.98827
26	0.00000	0.00000	0.00000	0.00000	0.00000	0.00000	0.00000	.69442	.93056	.98422
27	0.00000	0.00000	0.00000	0.00000	0.00000	0.00000	0.00000	.58899	.90659	.97877
28	0.00000	0.00000	0.00000	0.00000	0.00000	0.00000	0.00000	.44719	.87437	.97145
29	0.00000	0.00000	0.00000	0.00000	0.00000	0.00000	0.00000	.25648	.83103	.96160
30	0.00000	0.00000	0.00000	0.00000	0.00000	0.00000	0.00000	0.00000	.77274	.94835
31	0.00000	0.00000	0.00000	0.00000	0.00000	0.00000	0.00000	0.00000	.69435	.93053
32	0.00000	0.00000	0.00000	0.00000	0.00000	0.00000	0.00000	0.00000	.58892	.90657
33	0.00000	0.00000	0.00000	0.00000	0.00000	0.00000	0.00000	0.00000	.44714	.87435
34	0.00000	0.00000	0.00000	0.00000	0.00000	0.00000	0.00000	0.00000	.25645	.83101
35	0.00000	0.00000	0.00000	0.00000	0.00000	0.00000	0.00000	0.00000	0.00000	.77272
36	0.00000	0.00000	0.00000	0.00000	0.00000	0.00000	0.00000	0.00000	0.00000	.69433
37	0.00000	0.00000	0.00000	0.00000	0.00000	0.00000	0.00000	0.00000	0.00000	.58891
38	0.00000	0.00000	0.00000	0.00000	0.00000	0.00000	0.00000	0.00000	0.00000	.44713
39	0.00000	0.00000	0.00000	0.00000	0.00000	0.00000	0.00000	0.00000	0.00000	.25645

DISCOUNT POINT TABLE

Description:

The Discount Point table may be used to find the amount of points, where each point is 1% of the initial loan amount, necessary to raise the contract interest rate to a desired effective yield. To use the table, find the factor corresponding to the contract rate, effective yield, original loan term, and assumed prepayment period; then multiply the initial loan amount to arrive at the dollar value of points necessary to be charged.

Table Calculation Formula:

$$\text{Percentage points} = 1 - \left[\frac{1-1/(1+r)^{j}}{r}\right]\left[\frac{1-1/(1+i)^{n}}{i}\right]^{-1} - \frac{1}{(1+r)^{j}}\left[\frac{1-1/(1+i)^{n-j}}{1-1/(1+i)^{n}}\right],$$

where:

r = effective (desired) yield,

i = contract rate,

n = full term, and

j = prepayment period.

Table Range:

Annual contract and effective interest rates, with monthly compounding, from 7.00% to 20.75% in .25% increments. Original loan terms of 15, 20, 25, 30, and 35 years, with prepayment periods of 5, 7, 9, 12, 15, and/or full-term years.

Example:

How many points should a lender charge on a $55,000, 11.5% contract rate loan, with monthly payments for 30 years, to have an effective yield of 12.25%, assuming prepayment in year 12?

Solution:

Finding the table factor corresponding to 11.50% contract rate, 12.25% desired effective yield, with a 30-year term and 12-year prepayment yields the percentage points to be charged:

Discount points = \$55,000 × table factor *DP*, 11.50% contract, 12.25% effective, 30-year term, 12-year prepayment,

= \$55,000(.04577),

= \$2,517.35.

To raise the yield from 11.50% to 12.25% effective yield on a 30-year term \$55,000 loan with a 12-year assumed prepayment, the lender needs to charge 4.577 discount points at closing. The dollar value of the discount points is \$2,517.35.

Secondary Mortgage Market Application

To use the Discount Point table to price mortgages with various contract rates, one must treat the remaining mortgage term as the original loan term and the prepayment assumption at the present point in time. The formula for valuing or pricing mortgages is:

\$ Mortgage value = Mortgage principal balance(1 – discount points),

where the discount points are derived from the Discount Point table.

Note that, if the discount points are positive, (1 – discount points) becomes less than 100%, so that the value of the mortgage is a fraction less than the face value of the mortgage. If the discount points are negative, then [1 – (– discount points)] becomes (1 + discount points). In this case an effective yield *less* than the contract rate is desired, and the mortgage will have a premium value equal to the negative discount points in the table.

Example:

A \$100,000 mortgage with a contract rate of 12.0% for a 30-year term (360 months) with a 9-year prepayment is worth how much if only an 11.5% effective yield is required by the mortgage investor?

Solution:

$$\begin{aligned}\$\text{ Mortgage value} &= \$100{,}000(1 - \text{table value } DP,\ 12.0\%\text{ contract,}\\ &\quad 11.5\%\text{ effective, 9-year prepayment,}\\ &\quad 30\text{-year term}),\\ &= \$100{,}000[1 - (-.02745)],\\ &= \$100{,}000(1 + .02745),\\ &= \$100{,}000(1.02745),\\ &= \$102{,}745.\end{aligned}$$

A mortgage investor requiring an 11.5% effective yield would have to pay $102,745 for the 12.0%, 30-year mortgage if a 9-year prepayment is assumed.

Example:

A $1,000,000 mortgage package has 25 years left to maturity, with prepayment assumed in 7 years and a contract rate of 12.00%. With a desired effective yield of 13.75%, what is the value of the package?

Solution:

$$\begin{aligned}\$\text{ Mortgage value} &= \$1{,}000{,}000(1 - \text{table value } DP,\ 12.00\%\\ &\quad \text{contract, } 13.75\%\text{ desired, 25-year term,}\\ &\quad 7\text{-year prepayment}),\\ &= \$1{,}000{,}000(1 - .07649),\\ &= \$1{,}000{,}000(.92351),\\ &= \$923{,}510.\end{aligned}$$

To earn a yield of 13.75% on the $1,000,000, 25-year mortgage package, $923,510 should be paid, assuming a 7-year prepayment.

POINT TABLES: ORIGINAL LOAN TERM: 180 MONTHS LOAN PREPAID IN: 60 MONTHS

EFFECTIVE YIELD	CONTRACT RATE .07000	.07250	.07500	.07750	.08000	.08250	.08500	.08750	.09000	.09250
.07000	-.00000	-.00951	-.01905	-.02863	-.03824	-.04789	-.05757	-.06728	-.07703	-.08680
.07250	.00944	.00000	-.00947	-.01898	-.02852	-.03809	-.04770	-.05734	-.06701	-.07672
.07500	.01877	.00940	.00000	-.00944	-.01891	-.02841	-.03794	-.04751	-.05711	-.06674
.07750	.02799	.01870	.00936	.00000	-.00940	-.01883	-.02830	-.03779	-.04732	-.05688
.08000	.03711	.02788	.01862	.00933	.00000	-.00936	-.01876	-.02819	-.03764	-.04713
.08250	.04613	.03697	.02778	.01855	.00929	.00000	-.00933	-.01868	-.02807	-.03749
.08500	.05504	.04595	.03683	.02767	.01848	.00926	.00000	-.00929	-.01861	-.02796
.08750	.06385	.05483	.04578	.03669	.02757	.01841	.00922	-.00000	-.00925	-.01854
.09000	.07257	.06362	.05463	.04561	.03655	.02746	.01834	.00919	.00000	-.00922
.09250	.08119	.07230	.06338	.05442	.04543	.03641	.02735	.01827	.00915	.00000
.09500	.08970	.08088	.07203	.06314	.05422	.04526	.03627	.02725	.01820	.00911
.09750	.09813	.08937	.08058	.07176	.06290	.05401	.04508	.03613	.02714	.01812
.10000	.10646	.09777	.08904	.08028	.07149	.06266	.05380	.04491	.03599	.02704
.10250	.11469	.10607	.09740	.08871	.07998	.07121	.06242	.05359	.04474	.03585
.10500	.12284	.11427	.10567	.09704	.08837	.07967	.07094	.06218	.05339	.04456
.10750	.13089	.12239	.11385	.10528	.09668	.08804	.07937	.07067	.06194	.05318
.11000	.13885	.13041	.12193	.11343	.10488	.09631	.08770	.07907	.07040	.06170
.11250	.14672	.13834	.12993	.12148	.11300	.10449	.09595	.08737	.07876	.07012
.11500	.15450	.14619	.13783	.12945	.12103	.11258	.10409	.09558	.08703	.07846
.11750	.16220	.15394	.14565	.13733	.12897	.12058	.11215	.10370	.09521	.08670
.12000	.16981	.16161	.15338	.14512	.13682	.12849	.12012	.11173	.10330	.09485
.12250	.17734	.16920	.16103	.15282	.14458	.13631	.12800	.11967	.11130	.10291
.12500	.18478	.17670	.16859	.16044	.15226	.14404	.13580	.12752	.11921	.11088
.12750	.19214	.18412	.17606	.16797	.15985	.15169	.14350	.13529	.12704	.11876
.13000	.19942	.19145	.18345	.17542	.16735	.15926	.15113	.14297	.13477	.12655
.13250	.20662	.19871	.19076	.18279	.17478	.16674	.15866	.15056	.14243	.13426
.13500	.21373	.20588	.19799	.19007	.18212	.17413	.16612	.15807	.14999	.14189
.13750	.22077	.21297	.20514	.19728	.18938	.18145	.17349	.16550	.15748	.14943
.14000	.22773	.21999	.21221	.20440	.19656	.18869	.18078	.17284	.16488	.15688
.14250	.23461	.22692	.21920	.21145	.20366	.19584	.18799	.18011	.17220	.16426
.14500	.24142	.23378	.22612	.21842	.21068	.20292	.19512	.18730	.17944	.17155
.14750	.24815	.24057	.23295	.22531	.21763	.20992	.20217	.19440	.18660	.17877
.15000	.25481	.24728	.23972	.23212	.22450	.21684	.20915	.20143	.19368	.18590
.15250	.26139	.25391	.24640	.23886	.23129	.22368	.21605	.20838	.20068	.19296
.15500	.26790	.26047	.25302	.24553	.23801	.23045	.22287	.21526	.20761	.19994
.15750	.27434	.26696	.25956	.25212	.24465	.23715	.22962	.22206	.21446	.20684
.16000	.28070	.27338	.26603	.25864	.25122	.24377	.23629	.22878	.22124	.21367
.16250	.28700	.27973	.27243	.26509	.25772	.25032	.24289	.23543	.22794	.22042
.16500	.29323	.28601	.27876	.27147	.26415	.25680	.24942	.24201	.23457	.22710
.16750	.29939	.29222	.28501	.27778	.27051	.26321	.25588	.24852	.24113	.23371
.17000	.30548	.29836	.29120	.28402	.27680	.26955	.26227	.25496	.24762	.24025
.17250	.31151	.30443	.29733	.29019	.28302	.27582	.26859	.26132	.25403	.24671
.17500	.31747	.31044	.30338	.29629	.28917	.28202	.27483	.26762	.26038	.25311
.17750	.32336	.31638	.30937	.30233	.29526	.28815	.28102	.27385	.26666	.25943
.18000	.32919	.32226	.31530	.30830	.30127	.29422	.28713	.28001	.27286	.26569
.18250	.33496	.32807	.32116	.31421	.30723	.30022	.29318	.28611	.27901	.27188
.18500	.34066	.33382	.32695	.32005	.31312	.30615	.29916	.29213	.28508	.27800
.18750	.34630	.33951	.33268	.32583	.31894	.31202	.30507	.29810	.29109	.28405
.19000	.35188	.34513	.33835	.33154	.32470	.31783	.31093	.30400	.29703	.29005
.19250	.35740	.35070	.34396	.33720	.33040	.32357	.31672	.30983	.30292	.29597
.19500	.36286	.35620	.34951	.34279	.33604	.32926	.32244	.31560	.30873	.30183
.19750	.36826	.36164	.35500	.34832	.34161	.33488	.32811	.32131	.31449	.30763
.20000	.37360	.36703	.36043	.35379	.34713	.34044	.33371	.32696	.32018	.31337
.20250	.37888	.37235	.36580	.35921	.35259	.34594	.33926	.33255	.32581	.31904
.20500	.38411	.37762	.37111	.36456	.35798	.35138	.34474	.33807	.33138	.32466
.20750	.38928	.38283	.37636	.36986	.36332	.35676	.35017	.34354	.33689	.33021

POINT TABLES: ORIGINAL LOAN TERM: 180 MONTHS LOAN PREPAID IN: 60 MONTHS

EFFECTIVE YIELD	CONTRACT RATE .09500	.09750	.10000	.10250	.10500	.10750	.11000	.11250	.11500	.11750
.07000	-.09661	-.10644	-.11631	-.12620	-.13612	-.14607	-.15604	-.16605	-.17607	-.18612
.07250	-.08645	-.09621	-.10601	-.11583	-.12567	-.13555	-.14545	-.15538	-.16533	-.17531
.07500	-.07641	-.08610	-.09582	-.10557	-.11534	-.12515	-.13498	-.14483	-.15472	-.16462
.07750	-.06648	-.07610	-.08574	-.09542	-.10513	-.11486	-.12462	-.13441	-.14422	-.15405
.08000	-.05666	-.06621	-.07578	-.08539	-.09503	-.10469	-.11438	-.12409	-.13383	-.14360
.08250	-.04695	-.05643	-.06593	-.07547	-.08504	-.09463	-.10425	-.11390	-.12357	-.13326
.08500	-.03734	-.04676	-.05620	-.06566	-.07516	-.08468	-.09424	-.10381	-.11341	-.12304
.08750	-.02785	-.03719	-.04657	-.05597	-.06539	-.07485	-.08433	-.09384	-.10337	-.11293
.09000	-.01846	-.02774	-.03704	-.04638	-.05574	-.06512	-.07454	-.08398	-.09344	-.10293
.09250	-.00918	-.01839	-.02763	-.03689	-.04619	-.05551	-.06485	-.07423	-.08363	-.09305
.09500	.00000	-.00914	-.01831	-.02751	-.03674	-.04600	-.05528	-.06458	-.07392	-.08327
.09750	.00908	.00000	-.00911	-.01824	-.02740	-.03659	-.04581	-.05505	-.06431	-.07360
.10000	.01805	.00904	.00000	-.00907	-.01817	-.02729	-.03644	-.04562	-.05482	-.06404
.10250	.02693	.01798	.00900	.00000	-.00903	-.01809	-.02718	-.03629	-.04543	-.05459
.10500	.03571	.02682	.01791	.00897	0.00000	-.00900	-.01802	-.02706	-.03614	-.04524
.10750	.04439	.03556	.02672	.01784	.00893	.00000	-.00896	-.01794	-.02695	-.03599
.11000	.05297	.04421	.03542	.02661	.01777	.00890	.00000	-.00892	-.01787	-.02684
.11250	.06146	.05276	.04404	.03528	.02650	.01769	.00886	.00000	-.00889	-.01779
.11500	.06985	.06122	.05255	.04386	.03514	.02639	.01762	.00882	.00000	-.00885
.11750	.07815	.06958	.06097	.05234	.04368	.03500	.02629	.01755	.00879	.00000
.12000	.08636	.07785	.06930	.06073	.05213	.04351	.03486	.02618	.01748	.00875
.12250	.09448	.08602	.07754	.06903	.06049	.05193	.04333	.03472	.02607	.01741
.12500	.10251	.09411	.08569	.07724	.06876	.06025	.05172	.04316	.03457	.02597
.12750	.11045	.10211	.09375	.08535	.07693	.06848	.06001	.05151	.04298	.03443
.13000	.11830	.11002	.10171	.09338	.08501	.07662	.06821	.05977	.05130	.04281
.13250	.12607	.11785	.10959	.10132	.09301	.08468	.07632	.06793	.05952	.05109
.13500	.13375	.12558	.11739	.10917	.10092	.09264	.08434	.07601	.06766	.05928
.13750	.14134	.13323	.12510	.11693	.10874	.10052	.09227	.08400	.07571	.06739
.14000	.14886	.14080	.13272	.12461	.11647	.10831	.10012	.09191	.08367	.07540
.14250	.15629	.14829	.14026	.13221	.12412	.11602	.10788	.09972	.09154	.08333
.14500	.16364	.15569	.14772	.13972	.13169	.12364	.11556	.10745	.09932	.09117
.14750	.17090	.16301	.15510	.14715	.13918	.13118	.12315	.11510	.10703	.09893
.15000	.17809	.17026	.16239	.15450	.14658	.13863	.13066	.12267	.11464	.10660
.15250	.18520	.17742	.16961	.16177	.15390	.14601	.13809	.13015	.12218	.11419
.15500	.19224	.18450	.17675	.16896	.16115	.15331	.14544	.13755	.12963	.12169
.15750	.19919	.19151	.18381	.17607	.16831	.16052	.15271	.14487	.13701	.12912
.16000	.20607	.19844	.19079	.18311	.17540	.16766	.15990	.15211	.14430	.13646
.16250	.21288	.20530	.19770	.19006	.18241	.17472	.16701	.15927	.15151	.14373
.16500	.21961	.21208	.20453	.19695	.18934	.18170	.17405	.16636	.15865	.15092
.16750	.22626	.21879	.21129	.20375	.19620	.18861	.18100	.17337	.16571	.15803
.17000	.23285	.22542	.21797	.21049	.20298	.19545	.18789	.18030	.17269	.16506
.17250	.23936	.23199	.22458	.21715	.20969	.20221	.19470	.18716	.17960	.17202
.17500	.24581	.23848	.23112	.22374	.21633	.20889	.20143	.19395	.18644	.17890
.17750	.25218	.24490	.23759	.23026	.22290	.21551	.20810	.20066	.19320	.18571
.18000	.25848	.25125	.24399	.23671	.22939	.22205	.21469	.20730	.19988	.19245
.18250	.26472	.25754	.25032	.24308	.23582	.22853	.22121	.21387	.20650	.19911
.18500	.27089	.26375	.25659	.24939	.24217	.23493	.22766	.22037	.21305	.20570
.18750	.27699	.26990	.26278	.25564	.24846	.24127	.23404	.22679	.21952	.21223
.19000	.28303	.27598	.26891	.26181	.25468	.24753	.24036	.23315	.22593	.21868
.19250	.28900	.28200	.27497	.26792	.26084	.25373	.24660	.23945	.23227	.22506
.19500	.29491	.28795	.28097	.27396	.26693	.25987	.25278	.24567	.23854	.23138
.19750	.30075	.29384	.28690	.27994	.27295	.26593	.25889	.25183	.24474	.23763
.20000	.30653	.29966	.29277	.28585	.27891	.27194	.26494	.25792	.25088	.24381
.20250	.31225	.30543	.29858	.29170	.28480	.27788	.27092	.26395	.25695	.24992
.20500	.31791	.31113	.30432	.29749	.29063	.28375	.27684	.26991	.26295	.25597
.20750	.32350	.31677	.31001	.30322	.29640	.28957	.28270	.27581	.26890	.26196

POINT TABLES: ORIGINAL LOAN TERM: 180 MONTHS LOAN PREPAID IN: 60 MONTHS

EFFECTIVE YIELD	CONTRACT RATE .12000	.12250	.12500	.12750	.13000	.13250	.13500	.13750	.14000	.14250
.07000	-.19620	-.20629	-.21642	-.22656	-.23672	-.24691	-.25712	-.26735	-.27759	-.28786
.07250	-.18531	-.19534	-.20539	-.21546	-.22555	-.23567	-.24580	-.25596	-.26613	-.27632
.07500	-.17455	-.18451	-.19448	-.20448	-.21450	-.22455	-.23461	-.24469	-.25480	-.26492
.07750	-.16391	-.17379	-.18370	-.19363	-.20358	-.21355	-.22354	-.23355	-.24359	-.25364
.08000	-.15339	-.16320	-.17304	-.18289	-.19277	-.20267	-.21260	-.22254	-.23250	-.24248
.08250	-.14298	-.15272	-.16249	-.17228	-.18209	-.19192	-.20177	-.21164	-.22154	-.23145
.08500	-.13269	-.14236	-.15206	-.16178	-.17152	-.18128	-.19107	-.20087	-.21069	-.22054
.08750	-.12251	-.13212	-.14175	-.15140	-.16107	-.17077	-.18048	-.19022	-.19997	-.20975
.09000	-.11245	-.12199	-.13155	-.14113	-.15074	-.16036	-.17001	-.17968	-.18937	-.19907
.09250	-.10250	-.11197	-.12146	-.13098	-.14052	-.15008	-.15966	-.16926	-.17888	-.18852
.09500	-.09265	-.10206	-.11149	-.12094	-.13041	-.13990	-.14942	-.15895	-.16850	-.17808
.09750	-.08292	-.09226	-.10162	-.11100	-.12041	-.12984	-.13929	-.14876	-.15824	-.16775
.10000	-.07329	-.08257	-.09186	-.10118	-.11052	-.11989	-.12927	-.13867	-.14810	-.15754
.10250	-.06377	-.07298	-.08221	-.09147	-.10075	-.11004	-.11936	-.12870	-.13806	-.14744
.10500	-.05436	-.06350	-.07267	-.08186	-.09108	-.10031	-.10956	-.11884	-.12814	-.13745
.10750	-.04505	-.05413	-.06323	-.07236	-.08151	-.09068	-.09987	-.10909	-.11832	-.12757
.11000	-.03584	-.04486	-.05390	-.06296	-.07205	-.08116	-.09029	-.09944	-.10861	-.11780
.11250	-.02673	-.03569	-.04467	-.05367	-.06269	-.07174	-.08081	-.08990	-.09900	-.10813
.11500	-.01772	-.02662	-.03554	-.04448	-.05344	-.06243	-.07143	-.08046	-.08950	-.09857
.11750	-.00881	-.01765	-.02650	-.03539	-.04429	-.05321	-.06216	-.07112	-.08011	-.08911
.12000	.00000	-.00877	-.01757	-.02639	-.03523	-.04410	-.05298	-.06189	-.07081	-.07976
.12250	.00871	.00000	-.00874	-.01750	-.02628	-.03508	-.04391	-.05275	-.06162	-.07050
.12500	.01733	.00868	.00000	-.00870	-.01742	-.02617	-.03493	-.04372	-.05253	-.06135
.12750	.02586	.01726	.00864	-.00000	-.00866	-.01735	-.02606	-.03479	-.04353	-.05230
.13000	.03429	.02575	.01719	.00861	-.00000	-.00863	-.01728	-.02595	-.03464	-.04334
.13250	.04263	.03415	.02565	.01712	.00857	.00000	-.00859	-.01720	-.02583	-.03449
.13500	.05088	.04246	.03401	.02554	.01705	.00853	0.00000	-.00855	-.01713	-.02572
.13750	.05904	.05067	.04228	.03387	.02543	.01698	.00850	0.00000	-.00852	-.01706
.14000	.06711	.05880	.05046	.04211	.03373	.02533	.01690	.00846	.00000	-.00848
.14250	.07509	.06684	.05856	.05026	.04193	.03359	.02522	.01683	.00843	0.00000
.14500	.08299	.07479	.06656	.05832	.05005	.04176	.03345	.02511	.01676	.00839
.14750	.09080	.08265	.07448	.06629	.05808	.04984	.04158	.03331	.02501	.01669
.15000	.09853	.09043	.08232	.07418	.06602	.05784	.04963	.04141	.03316	.02490
.15250	.10617	.09813	.09007	.08198	.07387	.06574	.05759	.04942	.04123	.03302
.15500	.11373	.10574	.09773	.08970	.08164	.07357	.06547	.05735	.04922	.04106
.15750	.12121	.11327	.10531	.09733	.08933	.08131	.07326	.06520	.05711	.04901
.16000	.12860	.12072	.11281	.10489	.09694	.08896	.08097	.07296	.06493	.05687
.16250	.13592	.12809	.12023	.11236	.10446	.09654	.08860	.08064	.07266	.06466
.16500	.14316	.13538	.12758	.11975	.11190	.10403	.09614	.08823	.08030	.07235
.16750	.15032	.14259	.13484	.12706	.11926	.11145	.10361	.09575	.08787	.07997
.17000	.15740	.14972	.14202	.13429	.12655	.11878	.11099	.10318	.09535	.08750
.17250	.16441	.15678	.14913	.14145	.13375	.12603	.11829	.11053	.10275	.09496
.17500	.17134	.16376	.15616	.14853	.14088	.13321	.12552	.11781	.11008	.10233
.17750	.17820	.17067	.16311	.15553	.14793	.14031	.13267	.12501	.11733	.10963
.18000	.18498	.17750	.16999	.16246	.15491	.14734	.13975	.13213	.12450	.11684
.18250	.19170	.18426	.17680	.16932	.16181	.15429	.14674	.13918	.13159	.12399
.18500	.19834	.19095	.18353	.17610	.16864	.16117	.15367	.14615	.13861	.13105
.18750	.20491	.19756	.19020	.18281	.17540	.16797	.16052	.15305	.14556	.13805
.19000	.21140	.20411	.19679	.18945	.18209	.17470	.16730	.15987	.15243	.14496
.19250	.21783	.21058	.20331	.19602	.18870	.18136	.17400	.16662	.15923	.15181
.19500	.22420	.21699	.20976	.20251	.19524	.18795	.18064	.17330	.16595	.15858
.19750	.23049	.22333	.21615	.20894	.20172	.19447	.18720	.17992	.17261	.16528
.20000	.23672	.22960	.22246	.21530	.20812	.20092	.19370	.18646	.17919	.17191
.20250	.24288	.23581	.22871	.22160	.21446	.20730	.20013	.19293	.18571	.17847
.20500	.24897	.24194	.23490	.22782	.22073	.21362	.20649	.19933	.19216	.18496
.20750	.25500	.24802	.24101	.23399	.22694	.21987	.21278	.20567	.19854	.19139

POINT TABLES: ORIGINAL LOAN TERM: 180 MONTHS LOAN PREPAID IN: 60 MONTHS

EFFECTIVE YIELD	CONTRACT RATE .14500	.14750	.15000	.15250	.15500	.15750	.16000	.16250	.16500	.16750
.07000	-.29814	-.30844	-.31876	-.32910	-.33945	-.34982	-.36020	-.37060	-.38101	-.39144
.07250	-.28653	-.29676	-.30701	-.31727	-.32755	-.33785	-.34816	-.35849	-.36883	-.37918
.07500	-.27506	-.28522	-.29539	-.30558	-.31579	-.32602	-.33626	-.34651	-.35678	-.36706
.07750	-.26371	-.27379	-.28390	-.29402	-.30416	-.31431	-.32448	-.33467	-.34486	-.35508
.08000	-.25248	-.26250	-.27253	-.28258	-.29265	-.30274	-.31284	-.32295	-.33308	-.34322
.08250	-.24138	-.25133	-.26129	-.27127	-.28127	-.29129	-.30132	-.31136	-.32142	-.33150
.08500	-.23040	-.24028	-.25017	-.26009	-.27002	-.27996	-.28993	-.29990	-.30989	-.31990
.08750	-.21954	-.22935	-.23918	-.24902	-.25889	-.26876	-.27866	-.28857	-.29849	-.30843
.09000	-.20880	-.21854	-.22830	-.23808	-.24788	-.25769	-.26751	-.27736	-.28721	-.29708
.09250	-.19818	-.20785	-.21755	-.22726	-.23699	-.24673	-.25649	-.26627	-.27606	-.28586
.09500	-.18767	-.19728	-.20691	-.21655	-.22622	-.23589	-.24559	-.25530	-.26502	-.27476
.09750	-.17728	-.18682	-.19639	-.20597	-.21556	-.22518	-.23481	-.24445	-.25411	-.26378
.10000	-.16700	-.17648	-.18598	-.19549	-.20503	-.21457	-.22414	-.23372	-.24331	-.25292
.10250	-.15684	-.16625	-.17569	-.18514	-.19460	-.20409	-.21359	-.22310	-.23263	-.24218
.10500	-.14678	-.15614	-.16551	-.17489	-.18430	-.19372	-.20315	-.21260	-.22207	-.23155
.10750	-.13684	-.14613	-.15544	-.16476	-.17410	-.18346	-.19283	-.20222	-.21162	-.22104
.11000	-.12700	-.13623	-.14547	-.15474	-.16401	-.17331	-.18262	-.19195	-.20129	-.21064
.11250	-.11728	-.12644	-.13562	-.14482	-.15404	-.16327	-.17252	-.18178	-.19106	-.20036
.11500	-.10765	-.11676	-.12588	-.13501	-.14417	-.15334	-.16253	-.17173	-.18095	-.19018
.11750	-.09814	-.10718	-.11624	-.12531	-.13441	-.14352	-.15265	-.16179	-.17095	-.18012
.12000	-.08872	-.09770	-.10670	-.11572	-.12475	-.13380	-.14287	-.15195	-.16105	-.17016
.12250	-.07941	-.08833	-.09727	-.10623	-.11520	-.12419	-.13320	-.14222	-.15126	-.16032
.12500	-.07020	-.07906	-.08794	-.09684	-.10575	-.11469	-.12364	-.13260	-.14158	-.15057
.12750	-.06109	-.06989	-.07871	-.08755	-.09641	-.10528	-.11417	-.12308	-.13200	-.14093
.13000	-.05207	-.06082	-.06958	-.07836	-.08716	-.09598	-.10481	-.11366	-.12252	-.13140
.13250	-.04316	-.05185	-.06055	-.06928	-.07802	-.08678	-.09555	-.10434	-.11315	-.12197
.13500	-.03434	-.04297	-.05162	-.06029	-.06897	-.07767	-.08639	-.09512	-.10387	-.11264
.13750	-.02561	-.03419	-.04278	-.05139	-.06002	-.06867	-.07733	-.08600	-.09470	-.10340
.14000	-.01698	-.02550	-.03404	-.04259	-.05117	-.05976	-.06836	-.07698	-.08562	-.09427
.14250	-.00845	-.01691	-.02539	-.03389	-.04241	-.05094	-.05949	-.06806	-.07664	-.08524
.14500	.00000	-.00841	-.01684	-.02528	-.03374	-.04222	-.05072	-.05923	-.06775	-.07630
.14750	.00835	.00000	-.00837	-.01676	-.02517	-.03360	-.04204	-.05049	-.05897	-.06745
.15000	.01662	.00832	.00000	-.00834	-.01669	-.02506	-.03345	-.04185	-.05027	-.05870
.15250	.02480	.01655	.00828	.00000	-.00830	-.01662	-.02495	-.03330	-.04167	-.05005
.15500	.03288	.02469	.01648	.00825	.00000	-.00826	-.01654	-.02484	-.03315	-.04148
.15750	.04089	.03274	.02458	.01641	.00821	.00000	-.00823	-.01647	-.02473	-.03301
.16000	.04880	.04071	.03261	.02448	.01634	.00818	0.00000	-.00819	-.01640	-.02462
.16250	.05664	.04860	.04054	.03247	.02437	.01627	.00814	.00000	-.00816	-.01633
.16500	.06438	.05640	.04839	.04037	.03233	.02427	.01620	.00811	0.00000	-.00812
.16750	.07205	.06411	.05616	.04818	.04019	.03219	.02416	.01613	.00807	0.00000
.17000	.07963	.07175	.06384	.05592	.04798	.04002	.03205	.02406	.01606	.00804
.17250	.08714	.07930	.07144	.06357	.05568	.04777	.03985	.03191	.02396	.01599
.17500	.09456	.08677	.07897	.07114	.06330	.05544	.04757	.03968	.03177	.02385
.17750	.10191	.09417	.08641	.07863	.07084	.06303	.05521	.04737	.03951	.03164
.18000	.10917	.10148	.09377	.08605	.07830	.07054	.06276	.05497	.04716	.03934
.18250	.11636	.10872	.10106	.09338	.08568	.07797	.07024	.06250	.05474	.04696
.18500	.12348	.11588	.10827	.10064	.09299	.08532	.07764	.06994	.06223	.05450
.18750	.13052	.12297	.11540	.10782	.10021	.09260	.08496	.07731	.06964	.06196
.19000	.13748	.12998	.12246	.11492	.10737	.09979	.09221	.08460	.07698	.06935
.19250	.14437	.13691	.12944	.12195	.11444	.10692	.09937	.09182	.08424	.07665
.19500	.15119	.14378	.13635	.12891	.12144	.11396	.10647	.09895	.09143	.08388
.19750	.15794	.15057	.14319	.13579	.12837	.12094	.11349	.10602	.09854	.09104
.20000	.16461	.15729	.14995	.14260	.13523	.12784	.12043	.11301	.10557	.09812
.20250	.17122	.16394	.15665	.14934	.14201	.13467	.12730	.11993	.11253	.10513
.20500	.17775	.17052	.16327	.15601	.14872	.14142	.13411	.12677	.11942	.11206
.20750	.18422	.17703	.16983	.16261	.15537	.14811	.14084	.13355	.12624	.11892

POINT TABLES: ORIGINAL LOAN TERM: 180 MONTHS LOAN PREPAID IN: 60 MONTHS

EFFECTIVE YIELD	CONTRACT RATE .17000	.17250	.17500	.17750	.18000	.18250	.18500	.18750	.19000	.19250
.07000	-.40187	-.41233	-.42279	-.43327	-.44376	-.45426	-.46477	-.47529	-.48582	-.49636
.07250	-.38955	-.39993	-.41032	-.42073	-.43115	-.44157	-.45201	-.46246	-.47292	-.48339
.07500	-.37736	-.38767	-.39799	-.40833	-.41867	-.42903	-.43940	-.44978	-.46017	-.47057
.07750	-.36530	-.37554	-.38580	-.39606	-.40634	-.41662	-.42692	-.43723	-.44755	-.45788
.08000	-.35338	-.36355	-.37373	-.38393	-.39413	-.40435	-.41458	-.42482	-.43507	-.44533
.08250	-.34159	-.35169	-.36180	-.37193	-.38207	-.39221	-.40238	-.41255	-.42273	-.43292
.08500	-.32992	-.33995	-.35000	-.36006	-.37013	-.38021	-.39030	-.40041	-.41052	-.42064
.08750	-.31838	-.32835	-.33832	-.34832	-.35832	-.36833	-.37836	-.38839	-.39844	-.40850
.09000	-.30697	-.31687	-.32678	-.33670	-.34664	-.35659	-.36654	-.37651	-.38649	-.39648
.09250	-.29568	-.30551	-.31536	-.32521	-.33508	-.34497	-.35486	-.36476	-.37468	-.38460
.09500	-.28451	-.29428	-.30406	-.31385	-.32365	-.33347	-.34330	-.35314	-.36299	-.37285
.09750	-.27347	-.28317	-.29288	-.30261	-.31235	-.32210	-.33186	-.34164	-.35142	-.36122
.10000	-.26254	-.27218	-.28183	-.29149	-.30117	-.31085	-.32055	-.33026	-.33998	-.34971
.10250	-.25174	-.26131	-.27090	-.28049	-.29010	-.29973	-.30936	-.31901	-.32866	-.33833
.10500	-.24105	-.25056	-.26008	-.26961	-.27916	-.28872	-.29829	-.30788	-.31747	-.32707
.10750	-.23047	-.23992	-.24938	-.25885	-.26834	-.27783	-.28734	-.29686	-.30639	-.31594
.11000	-.22001	-.22940	-.23880	-.24821	-.25763	-.26706	-.27651	-.28597	-.29544	-.30492
.11250	-.20967	-.21899	-.22833	-.23767	-.24704	-.25641	-.26580	-.27519	-.28460	-.29402
.11500	-.19943	-.20869	-.21797	-.22726	-.23656	-.24587	-.25519	-.26453	-.27388	-.28324
.11750	-.18931	-.19851	-.20772	-.21695	-.22619	-.23544	-.24471	-.25398	-.26327	-.27257
.12000	-.17929	-.18843	-.19759	-.20675	-.21593	-.22513	-.23433	-.24355	-.25278	-.26201
.12250	-.16938	-.17846	-.18756	-.19667	-.20579	-.21492	-.22407	-.23322	-.24239	-.25157
.12500	-.15958	-.16860	-.17764	-.18669	-.19575	-.20483	-.21391	-.22301	-.23212	-.24124
.12750	-.14988	-.15885	-.16783	-.17682	-.18582	-.19484	-.20387	-.21291	-.22196	-.23102
.13000	-.14029	-.14920	-.15812	-.16705	-.17600	-.18496	-.19393	-.20291	-.21191	-.22091
.13250	-.13080	-.13965	-.14851	-.15739	-.16628	-.17518	-.18410	-.19302	-.20196	-.21091
.13500	-.12141	-.13021	-.13901	-.14783	-.15666	-.16551	-.17437	-.18324	-.19212	-.20101
.13750	-.11213	-.12086	-.12961	-.13838	-.14715	-.15594	-.16474	-.17356	-.18238	-.19122
.14000	-.10294	-.11162	-.12031	-.12902	-.13774	-.14647	-.15522	-.16398	-.17275	-.18153
.14250	-.09385	-.10247	-.11111	-.11976	-.12843	-.13711	-.14580	-.15450	-.16321	-.17194
.14500	-.08485	-.09342	-.10201	-.11061	-.11922	-.12784	-.13648	-.14512	-.15378	-.16245
.14750	-.07595	-.08447	-.09300	-.10154	-.11010	-.11867	-.12725	-.13585	-.14445	-.15307
.15000	-.06715	-.07561	-.08409	-.09258	-.10108	-.10960	-.11813	-.12667	-.13522	-.14378
.15250	-.05844	-.06685	-.07527	-.08371	-.09216	-.10062	-.10910	-.11758	-.12608	-.13459
.15500	-.04982	-.05818	-.06655	-.07493	-.08333	-.09174	-.10016	-.10860	-.11704	-.12550
.15750	-.04130	-.04960	-.05792	-.06625	-.07460	-.08295	-.09132	-.09971	-.10810	-.11651
.16000	-.03286	-.04111	-.04938	-.05766	-.06595	-.07426	-.08258	-.09091	-.09925	-.10760
.16250	-.02451	-.03272	-.04093	-.04916	-.05740	-.06566	-.07392	-.08220	-.09049	-.09880
.16500	-.01626	-.02441	-.03257	-.04075	-.04894	-.05714	-.06536	-.07359	-.08183	-.09008
.16750	-.00809	-.01618	-.02430	-.03243	-.04057	-.04872	-.05689	-.06506	-.07325	-.08146
.17000	0.00000	-.00805	-.01611	-.02419	-.03228	-.04038	-.04850	-.05663	-.06477	-.07292
.17250	.00800	0.00000	-.00801	-.01604	-.02408	-.03214	-.04020	-.04828	-.05637	-.06448
.17500	.01592	.00796	.00000	-.00798	-.01597	-.02398	-.03199	-.04002	-.04806	-.05612
.17750	.02375	.01585	.00793	.00000	-.00794	-.01590	-.02387	-.03185	-.03984	-.04785
.18000	.03150	.02364	.01578	.00790	.00000	-.00791	-.01583	-.02376	-.03171	-.03966
.18250	.03917	.03136	.02354	.01571	.00786	0.00000	-.00787	-.01576	-.02366	-.03156
.18500	.04676	.03900	.03122	.02344	.01564	.00783	.00000	-.00784	-.01569	-.02355
.18750	.05426	.04655	.03883	.03109	.02334	.01557	.00779	.00000	-.00780	-.01562
.19000	.06170	.05403	.04635	.03866	.03095	.02323	.01550	.00776	.00000	-.00777
.19250	.06905	.06143	.05380	.04615	.03849	.03082	.02313	.01543	.00772	0.00000
.19500	.07632	.06875	.06116	.05356	.04595	.03832	.03068	.02303	.01536	.00769
.19750	.08353	.07600	.06846	.06090	.05333	.04575	.03815	.03055	.02293	.01530
.20000	.09065	.08317	.07567	.06816	.06064	.05310	.04555	.03799	.03041	.02283
.20250	.09770	.09026	.08281	.07535	.06787	.06037	.05287	.04535	.03782	.03028
.20500	.10468	.09729	.08988	.08246	.07502	.06757	.06011	.05264	.04515	.03765
.20750	.11159	.10424	.09687	.08949	.08210	.07470	.06728	.05985	.05241	.04495

EFFECTIVE YIELD	CONTRACT RATE .19500	.19750	.20000	.20250	.20500	.20750
.07000	-.50691	-.51747	-.52803	-.53861	-.54919	-.55978
.07250	-.49387	-.50436	-.51485	-.52536	-.53587	-.54639
.07500	-.48098	-.49139	-.50182	-.51225	-.52270	-.53315
.07750	-.46822	-.47857	-.48892	-.49929	-.50966	-.52004
.08000	-.45560	-.46588	-.47617	-.48647	-.49677	-.50708
.08250	-.44312	-.45333	-.46355	-.47378	-.48402	-.49426
.08500	-.43078	-.44092	-.45107	-.46123	-.47140	-.48158
.08750	-.41857	-.42864	-.43873	-.44882	-.45892	-.46903
.09000	-.40649	-.41650	-.42651	-.43654	-.44658	-.45662
.09250	-.39454	-.40448	-.41443	-.42439	-.43436	-.44434
.09500	-.38271	-.39259	-.40248	-.41238	-.42228	-.43220
.09750	-.37102	-.38083	-.39066	-.40049	-.41033	-.42018
.10000	-.35945	-.36920	-.37896	-.38873	-.39851	-.40829
.10250	-.34801	-.35770	-.36739	-.37710	-.38681	-.39653
.10500	-.33669	-.34631	-.35595	-.36559	-.37524	-.38490
.10750	-.32549	-.33505	-.34462	-.35420	-.36379	-.37339
.11000	-.31441	-.32391	-.33342	-.34294	-.35246	-.36200
.11250	-.30345	-.31289	-.32233	-.33179	-.34126	-.35073
.11500	-.29260	-.30198	-.31137	-.32077	-.33017	-.33959
.11750	-.28188	-.29119	-.30052	-.30986	-.31921	-.32856
.12000	-.27126	-.28052	-.28979	-.29907	-.30835	-.31765
.12250	-.26076	-.26996	-.27917	-.28839	-.29762	-.30686
.12500	-.25037	-.25951	-.26867	-.27783	-.28700	-.29617
.12750	-.24009	-.24918	-.25827	-.26737	-.27649	-.28561
.13000	-.22993	-.23895	-.24799	-.25703	-.26609	-.27515
.13250	-.21986	-.22883	-.23781	-.24680	-.25580	-.26481
.13500	-.20991	-.21882	-.22775	-.23668	-.24562	-.25457
.13750	-.20006	-.20892	-.21779	-.22666	-.23555	-.24444
.14000	-.19032	-.19912	-.20793	-.21675	-.22558	-.23442
.14250	-.18068	-.18942	-.19818	-.20695	-.21572	-.22451
.14500	-.17114	-.17983	-.18853	-.19724	-.20596	-.21470
.14750	-.16170	-.17033	-.17898	-.18764	-.19631	-.20499
.15000	-.15236	-.16094	-.16954	-.17814	-.18676	-.19538
.15250	-.14312	-.15165	-.16019	-.16874	-.17730	-.18587
.15500	-.13397	-.14245	-.15094	-.15944	-.16795	-.17647
.15750	-.12492	-.13335	-.14179	-.15024	-.15869	-.16716
.16000	-.11597	-.12434	-.13273	-.14113	-.14953	-.15795
.16250	-.10711	-.11543	-.12377	-.13211	-.14047	-.14883
.16500	-.09834	-.10662	-.11490	-.12320	-.13150	-.13981
.16750	-.08967	-.09789	-.10613	-.11437	-.12262	-.13089
.17000	-.08108	-.08926	-.09744	-.10564	-.11384	-.12206
.17250	-.07259	-.08071	-.08885	-.09699	-.10515	-.11331
.17500	-.06418	-.07226	-.08034	-.08844	-.09655	-.10466
.17750	-.05586	-.06389	-.07193	-.07998	-.08803	-.09610
.18000	-.04763	-.05561	-.06360	-.07160	-.07961	-.08763
.18250	-.03948	-.04742	-.05536	-.06331	-.07127	-.07925
.18500	-.03142	-.03931	-.04720	-.05511	-.06302	-.07095
.18750	-.02344	-.03128	-.03913	-.04699	-.05486	-.06273
.19000	-.01555	-.02334	-.03114	-.03895	-.04677	-.05461
.19250	-.00773	-.01548	-.02323	-.03100	-.03878	-.04656
.19500	.00000	-.00770	-.01541	-.02313	-.03086	-.03860
.19750	.00765	0.00000	-.00766	-.01534	-.02303	-.03072
.20000	.01523	.00762	.00000	-.00763	-.01527	-.02292
.20250	.02273	.01516	.00759	0.00000	-.00760	-.01520
.20500	.03015	.02263	.01509	.00755	.00000	-.00756
.20750	.03749	.03001	.02253	.01503	.00752	.00000

POINT TABLES: ORIGINAL LOAN TERM: 180 MONTHS LOAN PREPAID IN: 84 MONTHS

EFFECTIVE YIELD	CONTRACT RATE .07000	.07250	.07500	.07750	.08000	.08250	.08500	.08750	.09000	.09250
.07000	.00000	-.01189	-.02384	-.03585	-.04792	-.06005	-.07223	-.08447	-.09676	-.10911
.07250	.01177	0.00000	-.01183	-.02372	-.03567	-.04768	-.05974	-.07186	-.08403	-.09626
.07500	.02336	.01171	.00000	-.01177	-.02360	-.03549	-.04743	-.05943	-.07148	-.08359
.07750	.03479	.02325	.01165	.00000	-.01171	-.02348	-.03531	-.04719	-.05912	-.07111
.08000	.04604	.03462	.02314	.01160	.00000	-.01165	-.02336	-.03513	-.04694	-.05881
.08250	.05712	.04581	.03445	.02302	.01154	.00000	-.01159	-.02324	-.03494	-.04670
.08500	.06804	.05684	.04559	.03428	.02291	.01148	.00000	-.01153	-.02312	-.03476
.08750	.07880	.06771	.05657	.04536	.03411	.02279	.01142	0.00000	-.01148	-.02300
.09000	.08940	.07842	.06738	.05629	.04514	.03394	.02268	.01136	.00000	-.01142
.09250	.09984	.08897	.07804	.06705	.05601	.04492	.03377	.02256	.01131	.00000
.09500	.11012	.09936	.08854	.07766	.06672	.05573	.04469	.03360	.02245	.01125
.09750	.12026	.10960	.09888	.08811	.07728	.06639	.05546	.04447	.03343	.02233
.10000	.13024	.11968	.10907	.09840	.08768	.07690	.06606	.05518	.04424	.03326
.10250	.14008	.12962	.11911	.10854	.09792	.08725	.07652	.06574	.05490	.04402
.10500	.14977	.13942	.12901	.11854	.10802	.09744	.08682	.07614	.06541	.05463
.10750	.15932	.14907	.13876	.12839	.11797	.10749	.09697	.08639	.07576	.06508
.11000	.16874	.15858	.14836	.13809	.12777	.11739	.10697	.09649	.08596	.07538
.11250	.17801	.16795	.15783	.14766	.13743	.12715	.11682	.10644	.09601	.08553
.11500	.18715	.17718	.16716	.15708	.14695	.13677	.12654	.11625	.10592	.09553
.11750	.19615	.18628	.17635	.16637	.15633	.14625	.13611	.12592	.11568	.10539
.12000	.20502	.19524	.18541	.17552	.16558	.15558	.14554	.13545	.12530	.11511
.12250	.21377	.20408	.19433	.18454	.17469	.16479	.15484	.14483	.13478	.12468
.12500	.22239	.21279	.20313	.19343	.18367	.17386	.16400	.15409	.14413	.13412
.12750	.23088	.22137	.21180	.20219	.19252	.18280	.17303	.16321	.15334	.14343
.13000	.23925	.22982	.22035	.21082	.20124	.19161	.18193	.17220	.16242	.15259
.13250	.24749	.23816	.22877	.21933	.20984	.20029	.19070	.18106	.17137	.16163
.13500	.25562	.24637	.23707	.22771	.21831	.20885	.19935	.18979	.18019	.17054
.13750	.26363	.25447	.24525	.23598	.22666	.21729	.20787	.19840	.18888	.17932
.14000	.27153	.26245	.25331	.24413	.23489	.22560	.21627	.20689	.19746	.18798
.14250	.27931	.27031	.26126	.25216	.24300	.23380	.22455	.21525	.20590	.19651
.14500	.28698	.27806	.26909	.26007	.25100	.24188	.23271	.22349	.21423	.20492
.14750	.29455	.28571	.27682	.26787	.25888	.24984	.24076	.23162	.22244	.21321
.15000	.30200	.29324	.28443	.27557	.26665	.25770	.24869	.23963	.23053	.22139
.15250	.30934	.30066	.29193	.28315	.27431	.26543	.25651	.24753	.23851	.22944
.15500	.31659	.30798	.29932	.29062	.28187	.27306	.26421	.25532	.24638	.23739
.15750	.32372	.31519	.30662	.29799	.28931	.28059	.27181	.26300	.25413	.24522
.16000	.33076	.32231	.31380	.30525	.29665	.28800	.27931	.27056	.26178	.25294
.16250	.33770	.32932	.32089	.31241	.30388	.29531	.28669	.27802	.26931	.26056
.16500	.34454	.33623	.32787	.31947	.31102	.30252	.29397	.28538	.27674	.26806
.16750	.35128	.34304	.33476	.32643	.31805	.30962	.30115	.29263	.28407	.27547
.17000	.35792	.34976	.34155	.33329	.32498	.31663	.30823	.29979	.29130	.28276
.17250	.36448	.35638	.34824	.34005	.33182	.32354	.31521	.30684	.29842	.28996
.17500	.37094	.36291	.35484	.34672	.33856	.33035	.32209	.31379	.30544	.29705
.17750	.37731	.36935	.36135	.35330	.34521	.33706	.32888	.32065	.31237	.30405
.18000	.38359	.37570	.36777	.35979	.35176	.34369	.33557	.32741	.31920	.31095
.18250	.38978	.38196	.37409	.36618	.35822	.35022	.34217	.33407	.32593	.31775
.18500	.39589	.38813	.38033	.37248	.36459	.35665	.34867	.34065	.33258	.32446
.18750	.40191	.39422	.38648	.37870	.37088	.36300	.35509	.34713	.33913	.33108
.19000	.40784	.40022	.39255	.38483	.37707	.36927	.36142	.35352	.34559	.33761
.19250	.41370	.40614	.39853	.39088	.38318	.37544	.36765	.35983	.35196	.34404
.19500	.41947	.41197	.40443	.39684	.38921	.38153	.37381	.36604	.35824	.35039
.19750	.42516	.41773	.41025	.40272	.39515	.38753	.37988	.37218	.36443	.35665
.20000	.43078	.42340	.41598	.40852	.40101	.39346	.38586	.37822	.37054	.36282
.20250	.43631	.42900	.42164	.41424	.40679	.39930	.39177	.38419	.37657	.36891
.20500	.44177	.43452	.42722	.41988	.41249	.40506	.39759	.39007	.38252	.37492
.20750	.44716	.43996	.43272	.42544	.41811	.41074	.40333	.39588	.38838	.38084

POINT TABLES: ORIGINAL LOAN TERM: 180 MONTHS LOAN PREPAID IN: 84 MONTHS

EFFECTIVE YIELD	CONTRACT RATE .09500	.09750	.10000	.10250	.10500	.10750	.11000	.11250	.11500	.11750
.07000	-.12151	-.13397	-.14647	-.15903	-.17163	-.18428	-.19698	-.20973	-.22252	-.23535
.07250	-.10853	-.12087	-.13325	-.14568	-.15816	-.17069	-.18326	-.19588	-.20855	-.22126
.07500	-.09575	-.10796	-.12022	-.13253	-.14489	-.15729	-.16974	-.18224	-.19479	-.20738
.07750	-.08315	-.09524	-.10738	-.11957	-.13181	-.14409	-.15643	-.16881	-.18123	-.19369
.08000	-.07073	-.08271	-.09473	-.10680	-.11892	-.13109	-.14330	-.15556	-.16787	-.18021
.08250	-.05850	-.07036	-.08227	-.09422	-.10623	-.11828	-.13037	-.14252	-.15470	-.16693
.08500	-.04645	-.05820	-.06999	-.08183	-.09372	-.10565	-.11763	-.12966	-.14173	-.15384
.08750	-.03458	-.04621	-.05789	-.06962	-.08139	-.09321	-.10508	-.11699	-.12895	-.14095
.09000	-.02288	-.03440	-.04597	-.05758	-.06925	-.08095	-.09271	-.10451	-.11635	-.12824
.09250	-.01136	-.02277	-.03422	-.04573	-.05728	-.06888	-.08052	-.09221	-.10394	-.11571
.09500	.00000	-.01130	-.02265	-.03404	-.04548	-.05697	-.06851	-.08008	-.09170	-.10337
.09750	.01119	.00000	-.01124	-.02253	-.03386	-.04524	-.05667	-.06814	-.07965	-.09120
.10000	.02222	.01113	.00000	-.01118	-.02241	-.03368	-.04500	-.05636	-.06777	-.07921
.10250	.03309	.02211	.01108	.00000	-.01112	-.02229	-.03350	-.04476	-.05606	-.06740
.10500	.04380	.03292	.02199	.01102	.00000	-.01106	-.02217	-.03332	-.04452	-.05576
.10750	.05435	.04357	.03275	.02188	.01096	.00000	-.01101	-.02205	-.03315	-.04428
.11000	.06475	.05407	.04335	.03258	.02176	.01090	0.00000	-.01095	-.02194	-.03297
.11250	.07500	.06442	.05380	.04313	.03241	.02165	.01085	.00000	-.01089	-.02182
.11500	.08510	.07462	.06409	.05352	.04291	.03224	.02154	.01079	.00000	-.01083
.11750	.09506	.08467	.07424	.06377	.05325	.04268	.03208	.02143	.01073	.00000
.12000	.10487	.09458	.08425	.07387	.06344	.05297	.04246	.03191	.02131	.01068
.12250	.11454	.10434	.09410	.08382	.07349	.06312	.05270	.04224	.03174	.02120
.12500	.12407	.11397	.10382	.09363	.08339	.07311	.06279	.05243	.04202	.03157
.12750	.13346	.12345	.11340	.10330	.09315	.08297	.07274	.06246	.05215	.04180
.13000	.14272	.13280	.12284	.11283	.10278	.09268	.08254	.07236	.06214	.05188
.13250	.15185	.14202	.13214	.12222	.11226	.10226	.09221	.08212	.07199	.06182
.13500	.16084	.15110	.14132	.13149	.12161	.11169	.10173	.09173	.08169	.07161
.13750	.16971	.16006	.15036	.14061	.13083	.12100	.11113	.10122	.09126	.08127
.14000	.17845	.16889	.15927	.14961	.13991	.13017	.12039	.11056	.10070	.09079
.14250	.18707	.17759	.16806	.15849	.14887	.13921	.12952	.11978	.11000	.10018
.14500	.19557	.18617	.17672	.16723	.15770	.14813	.13852	.12886	.11917	.10943
.14750	.20394	.19462	.18526	.17586	.16641	.15692	.14739	.13782	.12821	.11856
.15000	.21219	.20296	.19368	.18436	.17499	.16558	.15614	.14665	.13712	.12756
.15250	.22033	.21118	.20198	.19274	.18345	.17413	.16476	.15536	.14591	.13643
.15500	.22836	.21928	.21016	.20100	.19180	.18255	.17327	.16394	.15458	.14517
.15750	.23627	.22727	.21823	.20915	.20002	.19086	.18165	.17241	.16312	.15380
.16000	.24407	.23515	.22618	.21718	.20813	.19905	.18992	.18075	.17155	.16230
.16250	.25176	.24291	.23403	.22510	.21613	.20712	.19807	.18898	.17985	.17069
.16500	.25934	.25057	.24176	.23291	.22402	.21508	.20611	.19710	.18805	.17896
.16750	.26681	.25812	.24939	.24061	.23179	.22293	.21404	.20510	.19613	.18711
.17000	.27419	.26557	.25691	.24820	.23946	.23068	.22185	.21299	.20409	.19516
.17250	.28145	.27291	.26432	.25569	.24702	.23831	.22956	.22077	.21195	.20309
.17500	.28862	.28015	.27163	.26307	.25448	.24584	.23716	.22845	.21970	.21091
.17750	.29569	.28729	.27884	.27036	.26183	.25326	.24466	.23602	.22734	.21862
.18000	.30266	.29433	.28595	.27754	.26908	.26059	.25205	.24348	.23487	.22623
.18250	.30953	.30127	.29296	.28462	.27623	.26781	.25934	.25084	.24231	.23373
.18500	.31631	.30811	.29988	.29160	.28328	.27493	.26654	.25810	.24964	.24113
.18750	.32299	.31487	.30670	.29849	.29024	.28195	.27363	.26527	.25687	.24843
.19000	.32959	.32152	.31342	.30528	.29710	.28888	.28062	.27233	.26400	.25563
.19250	.33609	.32809	.32006	.31198	.30387	.29571	.28752	.27930	.27103	.26273
.19500	.34250	.33457	.32660	.31859	.31054	.30245	.29433	.28617	.27797	.26974
.19750	.34882	.34096	.33305	.32511	.31712	.30910	.30104	.29295	.28481	.27665
.20000	.35506	.34726	.33942	.33154	.32362	.31566	.30766	.29963	.29157	.28346
.20250	.36121	.35347	.34570	.33788	.33002	.32213	.31420	.30623	.29823	.29019
.20500	.36728	.35960	.35189	.34413	.33634	.32851	.32064	.31274	.30480	.29682
.20750	.37327	.36565	.35800	.35030	.34257	.33480	.32700	.31915	.31128	.30336

POINT TABLES: ORIGINAL LOAN TERM: 180 MONTHS LOAN PREPAID IN: 84 MONTHS

EFFECTIVE YIELD	CONTRACT RATE .12000	.12250	.12500	.12750	.13000	.13250	.13500	.13750	.14000	.14250
.07000	-.24823	-.26115	-.27411	-.28711	-.30015	-.31323	-.32635	-.33951	-.35270	-.36593
.07250	-.23401	-.24681	-.25965	-.27252	-.28544	-.29840	-.31139	-.32442	-.33748	-.35058
.07500	-.22001	-.23268	-.24539	-.25815	-.27094	-.28377	-.29664	-.30955	-.32249	-.33547
.07750	-.20620	-.21876	-.23135	-.24398	-.25665	-.26936	-.28211	-.29489	-.30771	-.32057
.08000	-.19260	-.20504	-.21751	-.23002	-.24257	-.25516	-.26779	-.28045	-.29315	-.30589
.08250	-.17920	-.19152	-.20387	-.21627	-.22870	-.24117	-.25368	-.26622	-.27880	-.29142
.08500	-.16600	-.17820	-.19043	-.20271	-.21503	-.22738	-.23977	-.25220	-.26466	-.27716
.08750	-.15299	-.16507	-.17719	-.18935	-.20155	-.21379	-.22607	-.23838	-.25072	-.26311
.09000	-.14016	-.15213	-.16414	-.17619	-.18827	-.20040	-.21256	-.22476	-.23699	-.24926
.09250	-.12753	-.13938	-.15128	-.16321	-.17519	-.18720	-.19925	-.21133	-.22345	-.23560
.09500	-.11507	-.12682	-.13860	-.15043	-.16229	-.17419	-.18613	-.19810	-.21011	-.22215
.09750	-.10280	-.11444	-.12611	-.13783	-.14958	-.16137	-.17320	-.18506	-.19696	-.20889
.10000	-.09070	-.10223	-.11380	-.12541	-.13705	-.14874	-.16045	-.17221	-.18400	-.19582
.10250	-.07878	-.09020	-.10167	-.11317	-.12471	-.13628	-.14789	-.15954	-.17122	-.18294
.10500	-.06703	-.07835	-.08971	-.10110	-.11254	-.12401	-.13551	-.14705	-.15863	-.17024
.10750	-.05545	-.06667	-.07792	-.08921	-.10054	-.11191	-.12331	-.13474	-.14622	-.15772
.11000	-.04404	-.05515	-.06630	-.07749	-.08872	-.09998	-.11128	-.12261	-.13398	-.14538
.11250	-.03279	-.04380	-.05485	-.06594	-.07706	-.08822	-.09942	-.11065	-.12192	-.13322
.11500	-.02170	-.03261	-.04356	-.05455	-.06558	-.07664	-.08773	-.09886	-.11003	-.12123
.11750	-.01077	-.02159	-.03244	-.04333	-.05425	-.06521	-.07621	-.08724	-.09831	-.10941
.12000	.00000	-.01072	-.02147	-.03226	-.04309	-.05395	-.06485	-.07579	-.08675	-.09776
.12250	.01062	.00000	-.01066	-.02135	-.03208	-.04285	-.05366	-.06449	-.07536	-.08627
.12500	.02109	.01056	0.00000	-.01060	-.02124	-.03191	-.04262	-.05336	-.06413	-.07494
.12750	.03141	.02098	.01051	-.00000	-.01054	-.02112	-.03173	-.04238	-.05306	-.06378
.13000	.04158	.03124	.02086	.01045	0.00000	-.01049	-.02101	-.03156	-.04215	-.05277
.13250	.05161	.04136	.03107	.02075	.01039	0.00000	-.01043	-.02089	-.03139	-.04191
.13500	.06149	.05134	.04114	.03091	.02064	.01034	.00000	-.01037	-.02078	-.03121
.13750	.07124	.06117	.05107	.04092	.03074	.02053	.01028	0.00000	-.01031	-.02066
.14000	.08085	.07087	.06085	.05080	.04070	.03058	.02042	.01023	.00000	-.01026
.14250	.09032	.08043	.07050	.06053	.05053	.04049	.03042	.02031	.01017	-.00000
.14500	.09966	.08985	.08001	.07013	.06021	.05026	.04027	.03025	.02020	.01012
.14750	.10887	.09915	.08939	.07959	.06976	.05989	.04999	.04006	.03009	.02009
.15000	.11795	.10831	.09863	.08892	.07917	.06939	.05957	.04972	.03984	.02993
.15250	.12691	.11735	.10775	.09812	.08846	.07876	.06902	.05926	.04946	.03963
.15500	.13573	.12626	.11674	.10719	.09761	.08799	.07834	.06866	.05894	.04919
.15750	.14444	.13504	.12561	.11614	.10664	.09710	.08753	.07793	.06829	.05862
.16000	.15302	.14370	.13435	.12496	.11554	.10608	.09659	.08707	.07751	.06793
.16250	.16149	.15225	.14297	.13366	.12432	.11494	.10553	.09608	.08661	.07710
.16500	.16983	.16067	.15147	.14224	.13298	.12367	.11434	.10498	.09558	.08615
.16750	.17806	.16898	.15986	.15070	.14151	.13229	.12303	.11374	.10442	.09507
.17000	.18618	.17717	.16813	.15905	.14993	.14079	.13161	.12239	.11315	.10388
.17250	.19419	.18525	.17628	.16728	.15824	.14917	.14006	.13092	.12176	.11256
.17500	.20208	.19322	.18432	.17539	.16643	.15743	.14840	.13934	.13024	.12112
.17750	.20987	.20108	.19226	.18340	.17451	.16558	.15663	.14764	.13862	.12957
.18000	.21755	.20883	.20008	.19129	.18247	.17362	.16474	.15582	.14688	.13790
.18250	.22512	.21648	.20780	.19908	.19033	.18155	.17274	.16390	.15502	.14612
.18500	.23259	.22402	.21541	.20676	.19809	.18938	.18063	.17186	.16306	.15422
.18750	.23996	.23145	.22291	.21434	.20573	.19709	.18842	.17972	.17098	.16222
.19000	.24723	.23879	.23032	.22181	.21327	.20470	.19610	.18747	.17880	.17011
.19250	.25440	.24603	.23762	.22919	.22072	.21221	.20368	.19511	.18652	.17789
.19500	.26147	.25317	.24483	.23646	.22805	.21962	.21115	.20266	.19413	.18557
.19750	.26844	.26021	.25194	.24363	.23530	.22693	.21853	.21010	.20164	.19315
.20000	.27533	.26715	.25895	.25071	.24244	.23414	.22580	.21744	.20904	.20062
.20250	.28211	.27401	.26587	.25769	.24949	.24125	.23298	.22468	.21635	.20799
.20500	.28881	.28077	.27269	.26458	.25644	.24826	.24006	.23183	.22356	.21527
.20750	.29542	.28744	.27942	.27138	.26330	.25519	.24705	.23888	.23067	.22244

POINT TABLES: ORIGINAL LOAN TERM: 180 MONTHS LOAN PREPAID IN: 84 MONTHS

CONTRACT RATE

EFFECTIVE YIELD	.14500	.14750	.15000	.15250	.15500	.15750	.16000	.16250	.16500	.16750
.07000	-.37919	-.39248	-.40580	-.41916	-.43255	-.44597	-.45942	-.47289	-.48640	-.49993
.07250	-.36372	-.37689	-.39009	-.40332	-.41658	-.42987	-.44319	-.45654	-.46992	-.48333
.07500	-.34848	-.36152	-.37460	-.38770	-.40084	-.41401	-.42721	-.44043	-.45369	-.46697
.07750	-.33346	-.34638	-.35933	-.37232	-.38533	-.39838	-.41145	-.42455	-.43768	-.45084
.08000	-.31865	-.33145	-.34429	-.35715	-.37005	-.38297	-.39592	-.40891	-.42191	-.43495
.08250	-.30407	-.31675	-.32946	-.34221	-.35498	-.36779	-.38062	-.39348	-.40637	-.41929
.08500	-.28969	-.30225	-.31485	-.32748	-.34013	-.35282	-.36553	-.37828	-.39105	-.40385
.08750	-.27552	-.28797	-.30045	-.31296	-.32550	-.33807	-.35067	-.36329	-.37595	-.38863
.09000	-.26156	-.27389	-.28625	-.29865	-.31107	-.32353	-.33601	-.34852	-.36106	-.37363
.09250	-.24779	-.26001	-.27226	-.28454	-.29686	-.30920	-.32157	-.33397	-.34639	-.35884
.09500	-.23423	-.24633	-.25847	-.27064	-.28284	-.29507	-.30733	-.31962	-.33193	-.34427
.09750	-.22085	-.23285	-.24488	-.25694	-.26903	-.28115	-.29330	-.30547	-.31767	-.32990
.10000	-.20768	-.21956	-.23148	-.24343	-.25541	-.26742	-.27946	-.29153	-.30362	-.31574
.10250	-.19468	-.20647	-.21828	-.23012	-.24199	-.25390	-.26583	-.27778	-.28977	-.30178
.10500	-.18188	-.19355	-.20526	-.21700	-.22876	-.24056	-.25238	-.26423	-.27611	-.28802
.10750	-.16926	-.18083	-.19243	-.20406	-.21572	-.22741	-.23913	-.25088	-.26265	-.27445
.11000	-.15682	-.16828	-.17978	-.19131	-.20286	-.21445	-.22606	-.23771	-.24938	-.26107
.11250	-.14455	-.15591	-.16731	-.17873	-.19019	-.20167	-.21319	-.22472	-.23629	-.24788
.11500	-.13246	-.14372	-.15502	-.16634	-.17769	-.18908	-.20049	-.21193	-.22339	-.23488
.11750	-.12054	-.13170	-.14290	-.15412	-.16538	-.17666	-.18797	-.19931	-.21067	-.22206
.12000	-.10879	-.11985	-.13095	-.14208	-.15323	-.16441	-.17563	-.18687	-.19813	-.20942
.12250	-.09720	-.10817	-.11917	-.13020	-.14126	-.15234	-.16346	-.17460	-.18577	-.19696
.12500	-.08578	-.09665	-.10756	-.11849	-.12945	-.14044	-.15146	-.16250	-.17358	-.18467
.12750	-.07452	-.08530	-.09611	-.10694	-.11781	-.12871	-.13963	-.15058	-.16156	-.17256
.13000	-.06342	-.07410	-.08482	-.09556	-.10633	-.11714	-.12796	-.13882	-.14970	-.16061
.13250	-.05247	-.06307	-.07369	-.08434	-.09502	-.10573	-.11646	-.12723	-.13802	-.14883
.13500	-.04168	-.05218	-.06271	-.07327	-.08386	-.09448	-.10512	-.11579	-.12649	-.13721
.13750	-.03104	-.04145	-.05189	-.06236	-.07286	-.08338	-.09394	-.10452	-.11513	-.12576
.14000	-.02055	-.03087	-.04122	-.05160	-.06201	-.07245	-.08291	-.09340	-.10392	-.11446
.14250	-.01020	-.02043	-.03070	-.04099	-.05131	-.06166	-.07204	-.08244	-.09287	-.10332
.14500	.00000	-.01015	-.02032	-.03053	-.04076	-.05102	-.06131	-.07163	-.08197	-.09234
.14750	.01006	.00000	-.01009	-.02021	-.03036	-.04053	-.05074	-.06096	-.07122	-.08150
.15000	.01998	.01001	0.00000	-.01003	-.02010	-.03019	-.04031	-.05045	-.06062	-.07081
.15250	.02976	.01987	.00995	.00000	-.00998	-.01999	-.03002	-.04008	-.05016	-.06028
.15500	.03941	.02960	.01976	.00990	0.00000	-.00992	-.01987	-.02985	-.03985	-.04988
.15750	.04893	.03920	.02944	.01966	.00984	0.00000	-.00987	-.01976	-.02968	-.03963
.16000	.05831	.04866	.03899	.02928	.01955	.00979	.00000	-.00981	-.01965	-.02952
.16250	.06756	.05800	.04840	.03877	.02912	.01944	.00973	.00000	-.00976	-.01954
.16500	.07669	.06720	.05768	.04814	.03856	.02896	.01933	.00968	.00000	-.00970
.16750	.08569	.07628	.06684	.05737	.04788	.03835	.02880	.01923	.00963	0.00000
.17000	.09457	.08524	.07587	.06648	.05706	.04762	.03814	.02865	.01912	.00957
.17250	.10333	.09407	.08478	.07547	.06612	.05675	.04736	.03794	.02849	.01902
.17500	.11197	.10278	.09357	.08433	.07506	.06577	.05645	.04710	.03773	.02833
.17750	.12049	.11138	.10224	.09307	.08388	.07466	.06541	.05614	.04684	.03752
.18000	.12889	.11985	.11079	.10170	.09258	.08343	.07426	.06506	.05584	.04659
.18250	.13718	.12822	.11923	.11021	.10116	.09208	.08298	.07386	.06471	.05553
.18500	.14536	.13647	.12755	.11860	.10962	.10062	.09159	.08254	.07346	.06436
.18750	.15343	.14461	.13576	.12688	.11797	.10904	.10008	.09110	.08209	.07306
.19000	.16139	.15263	.14385	.13505	.12621	.11735	.10846	.09955	.09061	.08165
.19250	.16924	.16055	.15184	.14310	.13434	.12555	.11673	.10789	.09902	.09013
.19500	.17698	.16837	.15973	.15105	.14236	.13363	.12488	.11611	.10731	.09849
.19750	.18463	.17608	.16750	.15890	.15027	.14161	.13293	.12423	.11549	.10674
.20000	.19217	.18368	.17517	.16664	.15808	.14949	.14087	.13223	.12357	.11488
.20250	.19960	.19119	.18275	.17427	.16578	.15726	.14871	.14013	.13154	.12291
.20500	.20694	.19859	.19022	.18181	.17338	.16492	.15644	.14793	.13940	.13084
.20750	.21419	.20590	.19759	.18924	.18088	.17248	.16407	.15562	.14716	.13866

POINT TABLES: ORIGINAL LOAN TERM: 180 MONTHS LOAN PREPAID IN: 84 MONTHS

CONTRACT RATE

EFFECTIVE YIELD	.17000	.17250	.17500	.17750	.18000	.18250	.18500	.18750	.19000	.19250
.07000	-.51348	-.52706	-.54067	-.55430	-.56795	-.58162	-.59532	-.60904	-.62277	-.63653
.07250	-.49676	-.51021	-.52369	-.53719	-.55072	-.56427	-.57784	-.59143	-.60504	-.61867
.07500	-.48027	-.49360	-.50696	-.52034	-.53374	-.54716	-.56061	-.57407	-.58756	-.60107
.07750	-.46402	-.47723	-.49046	-.50372	-.51700	-.53030	-.54362	-.55697	-.57033	-.58371
.08000	-.44801	-.46110	-.47421	-.48734	-.50050	-.51368	-.52688	-.54010	-.55335	-.56661
.08250	-.43223	-.44519	-.45819	-.47120	-.48424	-.49730	-.51038	-.52348	-.53660	-.54975
.08500	-.41667	-.42952	-.44239	-.45529	-.46821	-.48115	-.49411	-.50710	-.52010	-.53313
.08750	-.40134	-.41407	-.42682	-.43960	-.45241	-.46523	-.47808	-.49095	-.50383	-.51674
.09000	-.38622	-.39884	-.41148	-.42414	-.43683	-.44954	-.46227	-.47502	-.48780	-.50059
.09250	-.37132	-.38383	-.39635	-.40890	-.42148	-.43407	-.44669	-.45933	-.47199	-.48467
.09500	-.35664	-.36903	-.38144	-.39388	-.40634	-.41882	-.43133	-.44385	-.45640	-.46897
.09750	-.34216	-.35444	-.36674	-.37907	-.39142	-.40379	-.41619	-.42860	-.44104	-.45349
.10000	-.32789	-.34006	-.35225	-.36447	-.37671	-.38897	-.40126	-.41356	-.42589	-.43823
.10250	-.31382	-.32588	-.33796	-.35007	-.36221	-.37436	-.38654	-.39873	-.41095	-.42319
.10500	-.29995	-.31190	-.32388	-.33588	-.34791	-.35996	-.37203	-.38412	-.39623	-.40836
.10750	-.28627	-.29812	-.31000	-.32189	-.33381	-.34576	-.35772	-.36970	-.38171	-.39373
.11000	-.27279	-.28454	-.29631	-.30810	-.31992	-.33175	-.34361	-.35549	-.36739	-.37932
.11250	-.25950	-.27114	-.28281	-.29450	-.30621	-.31795	-.32971	-.34148	-.35328	-.36510
.11500	-.24640	-.25794	-.26950	-.28109	-.29270	-.30434	-.31599	-.32767	-.33936	-.35108
.11750	-.23348	-.24492	-.25638	-.26787	-.27938	-.29092	-.30247	-.31405	-.32564	-.33726
.12000	-.22074	-.23208	-.24345	-.25484	-.26625	-.27768	-.28914	-.30061	-.31211	-.32363
.12250	-.20818	-.21942	-.23069	-.24198	-.25330	-.26463	-.27599	-.28737	-.29877	-.31019
.12500	-.19580	-.20694	-.21811	-.22931	-.24053	-.25177	-.26303	-.27431	-.28561	-.29693
.12750	-.18359	-.19464	-.20571	-.21681	-.22793	-.23908	-.25024	-.26143	-.27263	-.28386
.13000	-.17154	-.18250	-.19348	-.20449	-.21552	-.22656	-.23764	-.24873	-.25984	-.27097
.13250	-.15967	-.17054	-.18142	-.19234	-.20327	-.21423	-.22520	-.23620	-.24722	-.25826
.13500	-.14796	-.15873	-.16953	-.18035	-.19119	-.20206	-.21294	-.22385	-.23477	-.24572
.13750	-.13642	-.14710	-.15780	-.16853	-.17928	-.19006	-.20085	-.21167	-.22250	-.23335
.14000	-.12503	-.13562	-.14624	-.15688	-.16754	-.17822	-.18893	-.19965	-.21040	-.22116
.14250	-.11380	-.12430	-.13483	-.14538	-.15595	-.16655	-.17716	-.18780	-.19846	-.20913
.14500	-.10273	-.11314	-.12358	-.13404	-.14453	-.15504	-.16556	-.17611	-.18668	-.19727
.14750	-.09181	-.10214	-.11249	-.12286	-.13326	-.14368	-.15412	-.16458	-.17507	-.18557
.15000	-.08103	-.09128	-.10155	-.11184	-.12215	-.13248	-.14284	-.15321	-.16361	-.17403
.15250	-.07041	-.08057	-.09075	-.10096	-.11119	-.12144	-.13171	-.14200	-.15231	-.16264
.15500	-.05993	-.07001	-.08011	-.09023	-.10038	-.11054	-.12073	-.13094	-.14116	-.15141
.15750	-.04960	-.05959	-.06961	-.07965	-.08971	-.09980	-.10990	-.12002	-.13017	-.14033
.16000	-.03941	-.04932	-.05925	-.06921	-.07919	-.08919	-.09922	-.10926	-.11932	-.12941
.16250	-.02935	-.03918	-.04904	-.05892	-.06882	-.07874	-.08868	-.09864	-.10862	-.11863
.16500	-.01943	-.02919	-.03896	-.04876	-.05858	-.06842	-.07828	-.08817	-.09807	-.10799
.16750	-.00965	-.01932	-.02902	-.03874	-.04848	-.05825	-.06803	-.07783	-.08766	-.09750
.17000	0.00000	-.00960	-.01922	-.02886	-.03852	-.04821	-.05791	-.06764	-.07739	-.08715
.17250	.00952	0.00000	-.00954	-.01911	-.02869	-.03830	-.04793	-.05758	-.06725	-.07694
.17500	.01891	.00947	.00000	-.00949	-.01900	-.02853	-.03809	-.04766	-.05725	-.06686
.17750	.02818	.01881	.00941	.00000	-.00944	-.01889	-.02837	-.03787	-.04739	-.05692
.18000	.03732	.02802	.01870	.00936	.00000	-.00938	-.01879	-.02821	-.03765	-.04712
.18250	.04633	.03711	.02787	.01860	.00931	0.00000	-.00933	-.01868	-.02805	-.03744
.18500	.05523	.04608	.03691	.02771	.01850	.00926	.00000	-.00928	-.01858	-.02789
.18750	.06401	.05493	.04583	.03670	.02756	.01839	.00921	.00000	-.00923	-.01847
.19000	.07267	.06366	.05463	.04558	.03650	.02741	.01829	.00915	.00000	-.00917
.19250	.08121	.07227	.06331	.05433	.04532	.03630	.02725	.01819	.00910	.00000
.19500	.08964	.08077	.07188	.06297	.05403	.04508	.03610	.02710	.01809	.00905
.19750	.09796	.08916	.08034	.07149	.06262	.05374	.04483	.03590	.02695	.01799
.20000	.10617	.09744	.08868	.07990	.07110	.06228	.05344	.04458	.03570	.02680
.20250	.11427	.10560	.09691	.08820	.07947	.07072	.06194	.05315	.04434	.03550
.20500	.12226	.11366	.10504	.09639	.08773	.07904	.07033	.06160	.05286	.04409
.20750	.13015	.12161	.11306	.10447	.09587	.08725	.07861	.06995	.06127	.05257

POINT TABLES: ORIGINAL LOAN TERM: 180 MONTHS LOAN PREPAID IN: 84 MONTHS

EFFECTIVE YIELD	CONTRACT RATE .19500	.19750	.20000	.20250	.20500	.20750
.07000	-.65031	-.66410	-.67791	-.69174	-.70558	-.71944
.07250	-.63232	-.64599	-.65967	-.67337	-.68709	-.70083
.07500	-.61459	-.62813	-.64169	-.65527	-.66887	-.68248
.07750	-.59711	-.61054	-.62397	-.63743	-.65090	-.66439
.08000	-.57989	-.59319	-.60650	-.61984	-.63319	-.64656
.08250	-.56291	-.57609	-.58928	-.60250	-.61573	-.62898
.08500	-.54617	-.55923	-.57231	-.58541	-.59852	-.61165
.08750	-.52967	-.54261	-.55557	-.56855	-.58155	-.59456
.09000	-.51340	-.52623	-.53908	-.55194	-.56482	-.57772
.09250	-.49736	-.51008	-.52281	-.53556	-.54833	-.56111
.09500	-.48155	-.49416	-.50678	-.51942	-.53207	-.54474
.09750	-.46596	-.47846	-.49097	-.50350	-.51604	-.52860
.10000	-.45060	-.46298	-.47538	-.48780	-.50023	-.51269
.10250	-.43545	-.44772	-.46001	-.47232	-.48465	-.49699
.10500	-.42051	-.43268	-.44486	-.45706	-.46928	-.48152
.10750	-.40578	-.41784	-.42992	-.44202	-.45413	-.46626
.11000	-.39126	-.40321	-.41519	-.42718	-.43919	-.45122
.11250	-.37694	-.38879	-.40066	-.41255	-.42446	-.43639
.11500	-.36281	-.37457	-.38634	-.39813	-.40993	-.42176
.11750	-.34889	-.36054	-.37222	-.38390	-.39561	-.40733
.12000	-.33516	-.34672	-.35829	-.36988	-.38148	-.39311
.12250	-.32162	-.33308	-.34455	-.35604	-.36755	-.37908
.12500	-.30827	-.31963	-.33101	-.34240	-.35381	-.36524
.12750	-.29510	-.30637	-.31765	-.32895	-.34026	-.35160
.13000	-.28212	-.29329	-.30448	-.31568	-.32690	-.33814
.13250	-.26931	-.28039	-.29148	-.30259	-.31372	-.32487
.13500	-.25668	-.26767	-.27867	-.28969	-.30072	-.31173
.13750	-.24423	-.25512	-.26603	-.27696	-.28790	-.29886
.14000	-.23194	-.24275	-.25357	-.26440	-.27526	-.28613
.14250	-.21983	-.23054	-.24127	-.25202	-.26279	-.27357
.14500	-.20788	-.21850	-.22914	-.23981	-.25048	-.26118
.14750	-.19609	-.20663	-.21718	-.22776	-.23835	-.24896
.15000	-.18446	-.19491	-.20538	-.21587	-.22638	-.23690
.15250	-.17299	-.18336	-.19375	-.20415	-.21457	-.22501
.15500	-.16168	-.17196	-.18226	-.19258	-.20292	-.21327
.15750	-.15052	-.16072	-.17094	-.18118	-.19143	-.20170
.16000	-.13951	-.14963	-.15977	-.16992	-.18009	-.19028
.16250	-.12865	-.13869	-.14874	-.15882	-.16891	-.17902
.16500	-.11793	-.12789	-.13787	-.14786	-.15788	-.16790
.16750	-.10736	-.11724	-.12714	-.13706	-.14699	-.15694
.17000	-.09694	-.10674	-.11656	-.12640	-.13625	-.14612
.17250	-.08665	-.09637	-.10612	-.11588	-.12565	-.13545
.17500	-.07650	-.08615	-.09581	-.10550	-.11520	-.12491
.17750	-.06648	-.07605	-.08565	-.09526	-.10488	-.11452
.18000	-.05660	-.06610	-.07562	-.08515	-.09470	-.10427
.18250	-.04685	-.05627	-.06572	-.07518	-.08466	-.09415
.18500	-.03723	-.04658	-.05595	-.06534	-.07474	-.08417
.18750	-.02773	-.03702	-.04631	-.05563	-.06496	-.07431
.19000	-.01837	-.02758	-.03681	-.04605	-.05531	-.06459
.19250	-.00912	-.01826	-.02742	-.03660	-.04579	-.05499
.19500	0.00000	-.00907	-.01816	-.02726	-.03639	-.04553
.19750	.00900	.00000	-.00902	-.01806	-.02711	-.03618
.20000	.01789	.00895	.00000	-.00897	-.01795	-.02696
.20250	.02665	.01779	.00890	.00000	-.00892	-.01785
.20500	.03531	.02651	.01769	.00885	0.00000	-.00887
.20750	.04385	.03511	.02636	.01759	.00880	.00000

POINT TABLES: ORIGINAL LOAN TERM: 180 MONTHS LOAN PREPAID IN: 108 MONTHS

EFFECTIVE YIELD	CONTRACT RATE .07000	.07250	.07500	.07750	.08000	.08250	.08500	.08750	.09000	.09250
.07000	.00000	-.01361	-.02731	-.04109	-.05496	-.06891	-.08294	-.09705	-.11124	-.12550
.07250	.01345	0.00000	-.01353	-.02715	-.04085	-.05463	-.06849	-.08242	-.09644	-.11054
.07500	.02665	.01337	.00000	-.01345	-.02698	-.04060	-.05429	-.06806	-.08191	-.09584
.07750	.03962	.02650	.01329	0.00000	-.01337	-.02682	-.04035	-.05396	-.06764	-.08140
.08000	.05236	.03939	.02634	.01321	.00000	-.01329	-.02666	-.04010	-.05363	-.06722
.08250	.06487	.05205	.03916	.02619	.01313	.00000	-.01321	-.02650	-.03986	-.05329
.08500	.07715	.06449	.05175	.03893	.02603	.01305	.00000	-.01313	-.02633	-.03961
.08750	.08922	.07671	.06412	.05145	.03870	.02588	.01298	0.00000	-.01305	-.02617
.09000	.10107	.08871	.07627	.06375	.05115	.03847	.02572	.01290	.00000	-.01297
.09250	.11271	.10050	.08820	.07583	.06337	.05085	.03825	.02557	.01282	0.00000
.09500	.12415	.11208	.09992	.08769	.07538	.06300	.05055	.03802	.02542	.01274
.09750	.13539	.12345	.11144	.09935	.08718	.07495	.06263	.05025	.03779	.02526
.10000	.14642	.13463	.12275	.11080	.09878	.08668	.07451	.06226	.04995	.03756
.10250	.15727	.14560	.13387	.12205	.11017	.09821	.08617	.07407	.06189	.04965
.10500	.16792	.15639	.14479	.13311	.12136	.10953	.09764	.08567	.07363	.06153
.10750	.17839	.16699	.15552	.14397	.13235	.12066	.10890	.09707	.08517	.07320
.11000	.18867	.17740	.16606	.15465	.14316	.13160	.11997	.10827	.09650	.08466
.11250	.19878	.18764	.17642	.16513	.15377	.14234	.13084	.11928	.10764	.09593
.11500	.20871	.19769	.18660	.17544	.16421	.15290	.14153	.13009	.11858	.10701
.11750	.21846	.20757	.19660	.18557	.17446	.16328	.15204	.14072	.12934	.11789
.12000	.22805	.21728	.20644	.19552	.18454	.17348	.16236	.15117	.13991	.12859
.12250	.23748	.22682	.21610	.20530	.19444	.18351	.17251	.16144	.15031	.13911
.12500	.24674	.23620	.22559	.21492	.20417	.19336	.18248	.17153	.16052	.14944
.12750	.25584	.24542	.23493	.22437	.21374	.20304	.19228	.18145	.17056	.15960
.13000	.26479	.25448	.24410	.23365	.22314	.21256	.20191	.19120	.18043	.16959
.13250	.27358	.26338	.25312	.24278	.23238	.22192	.21139	.20079	.19013	.17941
.13500	.28222	.27214	.26198	.25176	.24147	.23112	.22070	.21021	.19967	.18906
.13750	.29072	.28074	.27069	.26058	.25040	.24016	.22985	.21948	.20904	.19854
.14000	.29907	.28920	.27926	.26925	.25918	.24905	.23885	.22858	.21826	.20787
.14250	.30728	.29751	.28768	.27778	.26781	.25779	.24769	.23754	.22732	.21704
.14500	.31535	.30569	.29596	.28616	.27630	.26638	.25639	.24634	.23623	.22606
.14750	.32329	.31373	.30410	.29440	.28465	.27483	.26494	.25500	.24499	.23493
.15000	.33109	.32163	.31210	.30251	.29285	.28313	.27335	.26351	.25361	.24365
.15250	.33877	.32940	.31997	.31048	.30092	.29130	.28162	.27188	.26208	.25222
.15500	.34631	.33704	.32771	.31831	.30885	.29933	.28975	.28011	.27041	.26065
.15750	.35373	.34455	.33532	.32602	.31666	.30723	.29775	.28821	.27861	.26895
.16000	.36102	.35194	.34280	.33359	.32433	.31500	.30561	.29617	.28666	.27710
.16250	.36819	.35921	.35016	.34105	.33187	.32264	.31335	.30400	.29459	.28512
.16500	.37525	.36635	.35739	.34837	.33929	.33015	.32096	.31170	.30238	.29301
.16750	.38219	.37338	.36451	.35558	.34659	.33754	.32844	.31927	.31005	.30077
.17000	.38901	.38029	.37151	.36267	.35377	.34481	.33580	.32672	.31759	.30841
.17250	.39572	.38709	.37840	.36964	.36083	.35196	.34304	.33405	.32501	.31592
.17500	.40232	.39378	.38517	.37650	.36778	.35900	.35016	.34126	.33231	.32330
.17750	.40882	.40035	.39183	.38325	.37461	.36592	.35716	.34836	.33949	.33057
.18000	.41521	.40683	.39839	.38989	.38134	.37272	.36406	.35533	.34655	.33772
.18250	.42149	.41319	.40484	.39642	.38795	.37942	.37084	.36220	.35350	.34476
.18500	.42767	.41945	.41118	.40285	.39446	.38601	.37751	.36895	.36034	.35168
.18750	.43375	.42562	.41742	.40917	.40086	.39249	.38407	.37560	.36707	.35849
.19000	.43974	.43168	.42356	.41539	.40716	.39887	.39053	.38214	.37369	.36519
.19250	.44563	.43764	.42960	.42151	.41336	.40515	.39689	.38857	.38021	.37179
.19500	.45142	.44351	.43555	.42753	.41945	.41133	.40314	.39491	.38662	.37828
.19750	.45712	.44929	.44140	.43346	.42546	.41740	.40930	.40114	.39293	.38466
.20000	.46273	.45497	.44716	.43929	.43136	.42339	.41535	.40727	.39914	.39095
.20250	.46825	.46057	.45282	.44503	.43718	.42927	.42132	.41331	.40525	.39714
.20500	.47369	.46607	.45840	.45068	.44290	.43507	.42718	.41925	.41126	.40323
.20750	.47903	.47149	.46389	.45624	.44853	.44077	.43296	.42510	.41719	.40922

POINT TABLES: ORIGINAL LOAN TERM: 180 MONTHS LOAN PREPAID IN: 108 MONTHS

EFFECTIVE YIELD	CONTRACT RATE .09500	.09750	.10000	.10250	.10500	.10750	.11000	.11250	.11500	.11750
.07000	-.13984	-.15426	-.16875	-.18332	-.19795	-.21266	-.22743	-.24228	-.25719	-.27216
.07250	-.12471	-.13895	-.15327	-.16766	-.18212	-.19665	-.21125	-.22592	-.24065	-.25545
.07500	-.10984	-.12391	-.13806	-.15228	-.16657	-.18093	-.19535	-.20985	-.22441	-.23903
.07750	-.09524	-.10914	-.12312	-.13717	-.15129	-.16548	-.17974	-.19406	-.20845	-.22290
.08000	-.08089	-.09464	-.10845	-.12234	-.13629	-.15031	-.16440	-.17856	-.19278	-.20706
.08250	-.06680	-.08039	-.09404	-.10776	-.12155	-.13541	-.14933	-.16332	-.17738	-.19150
.08500	-.05296	-.06639	-.07988	-.09344	-.10707	-.12077	-.13453	-.14836	-.16225	-.17621
.08750	-.03937	-.05263	-.06597	-.07937	-.09285	-.10639	-.11999	-.13366	-.14739	-.16118
.09000	-.02601	-.03912	-.05231	-.06556	-.07887	-.09225	-.10570	-.11921	-.13279	-.14642
.09250	-.01289	-.02585	-.03888	-.05198	-.06514	-.07837	-.09166	-.10502	-.11844	-.13192
.09500	.00000	-.01281	-.02569	-.03864	-.05165	-.06473	-.07787	-.09108	-.10434	-.11767
.09750	.01267	0.00000	-.01273	-.02553	-.03840	-.05133	-.06432	-.07737	-.09049	-.10367
.10000	.02511	.01259	.00000	-.01265	-.02537	-.03816	-.05100	-.06391	-.07688	-.08991
.10250	.03734	.02496	.01251	.00000	-.01258	-.02522	-.03792	-.05068	-.06350	-.07639
.10500	.04935	.03711	.02481	.01243	.00000	-.01250	-.02506	-.03768	-.05036	-.06310
.10750	.06116	.04906	.03689	.02465	.01236	.00000	-.01242	-.02490	-.03744	-.05004
.11000	.07276	.06079	.04876	.03666	.02450	.01228	0.00000	-.01234	-.02474	-.03720
.11250	.08416	.07233	.06043	.04847	.03644	.02435	.01221	.00000	-.01226	-.02459
.11500	.09537	.08366	.07190	.06006	.04817	.03622	.02420	.01213	.00000	-.01219
.11750	.10638	.09481	.08317	.07146	.05970	.04788	.03600	.02405	.01206	0.00000
.12000	.11721	.10576	.09424	.08267	.07104	.05934	.04759	.03577	.02391	.01198
.12250	.12785	.11652	.10513	.09368	.08218	.07061	.05898	.04730	.03555	.02376
.12500	.13830	.12710	.11584	.10451	.09313	.08168	.07018	.05862	.04701	.03533
.12750	.14858	.13750	.12636	.11515	.10389	.09257	.08119	.06975	.05826	.04672
.13000	.15869	.14772	.13670	.12562	.11447	.10327	.09201	.08070	.06933	.05791
.13250	.16862	.15777	.14687	.13590	.12488	.11379	.10266	.09146	.08021	.06891
.13500	.17839	.16765	.15686	.14601	.13510	.12414	.11312	.10204	.09091	.07972
.13750	.18799	.17737	.16669	.15595	.14516	.13431	.12340	.11244	.10143	.09036
.14000	.19743	.18692	.17635	.16573	.15505	.14431	.13352	.12267	.11177	.10082
.14250	.20671	.19631	.18585	.17534	.16477	.15415	.14347	.13273	.12194	.11110
.14500	.21583	.20554	.19520	.18479	.17433	.16382	.15325	.14262	.13194	.12122
.14750	.22480	.21462	.20438	.19409	.18373	.17333	.16286	.15235	.14178	.13116
.15000	.23363	.22355	.21342	.20322	.19298	.18268	.17232	.16191	.15145	.14094
.15250	.24231	.23233	.22230	.21221	.20207	.19187	.18162	.17132	.16097	.15056
.15500	.25084	.24097	.23104	.22105	.21101	.20092	.19077	.18057	.17032	.16002
.15750	.25923	.24946	.23963	.22974	.21981	.20981	.19977	.18967	.17953	.16933
.16000	.26748	.25781	.24808	.23829	.22846	.21856	.20862	.19863	.18858	.17848
.16250	.27560	.26602	.25639	.24670	.23696	.22717	.21733	.20743	.19748	.18749
.16500	.28359	.27410	.26457	.25498	.24533	.23564	.22589	.21609	.20624	.19635
.16750	.29144	.28205	.27261	.26311	.25357	.24397	.23431	.22461	.21486	.20506
.17000	.29917	.28987	.28052	.27112	.26166	.25216	.24260	.23299	.22334	.21363
.17250	.30677	.29756	.28830	.27899	.26963	.26022	.25075	.24124	.23168	.22207
.17500	.31424	.30513	.29596	.28674	.27747	.26815	.25878	.24936	.23989	.23037
.17750	.32160	.31257	.30349	.29436	.28518	.27595	.26667	.25734	.24796	.23853
.18000	.32884	.31990	.31091	.30186	.29277	.28363	.27443	.26519	.25590	.24657
.18250	.33596	.32710	.31820	.30924	.30024	.29118	.28208	.27292	.26372	.25448
.18500	.34296	.33419	.32537	.31650	.30758	.29861	.28960	.28053	.27142	.26226
.18750	.34986	.34117	.33243	.32365	.31481	.30593	.29699	.28801	.27899	.26991
.19000	.35664	.34804	.33938	.33068	.32193	.31313	.30428	.29538	.28644	.27745
.19250	.36332	.35479	.34622	.33760	.32893	.32021	.31144	.30263	.29377	.28487
.19500	.36989	.36144	.35295	.34441	.33582	.32718	.31850	.30977	.30099	.29217
.19750	.37635	.36799	.35957	.35111	.34260	.33404	.32544	.31679	.30809	.29935
.20000	.38271	.37443	.36609	.35771	.34928	.34080	.33227	.32370	.31508	.30642
.20250	.38898	.38077	.37251	.36420	.35585	.34745	.33900	.33051	.32197	.31339
.20500	.39514	.38701	.37882	.37059	.36232	.35399	.34562	.33720	.32874	.32024
.20750	.40121	39315	.38504	.37689	.36868	.36043	.35214	.34380	.33541	.32699

POINT TABLES: ORIGINAL LOAN TERM: 180 MONTHS LOAN PREPAID IN: 108 MONTHS

EFFECTIVE YIELD	CONTRACT RATE .12000	.12250	.12500	.12750	.13000	.13250	.13500	.13750	.14000	.14250
.07000	-.28720	-.30231	-.31747	-.33270	-.34799	-.36333	-.37873	-.39419	-.40970	-.42527
.07250	-.27031	-.28524	-.30022	-.31527	-.33038	-.34554	-.36076	-.37604	-.39137	-.40675
.07500	-.25372	-.26847	-.28328	-.29815	-.31308	-.32807	-.34311	-.35821	-.37336	-.38856
.07750	-.23742	-.25200	-.26663	-.28133	-.29609	-.31090	-.32577	-.34069	-.35567	-.37070
.08000	-.22141	-.23581	-.25028	-.26481	-.27939	-.29403	-.30873	-.32348	-.33828	-.35314
.08250	-.20568	-.21992	-.23422	-.24857	-.26299	-.27746	-.29199	-.30657	-.32120	-.33589
.08500	-.19022	-.20430	-.21843	-.23262	-.24687	-.26118	-.27554	-.28996	-.30442	-.31894
.08750	-.17504	-.18895	-.20292	-.21695	-.23104	-.24518	-.25938	-.27363	-.28793	-.30229
.09000	-.16012	-.17387	-.18769	-.20156	-.21548	-.22947	-.24350	-.25759	-.27173	-.28592
.09250	-.14546	-.15906	-.17271	-.18643	-.20020	-.21402	-.22790	-.24183	-.25581	-.26984
.09500	-.13106	-.14450	-.15800	-.17156	-.18517	-.19884	-.21256	-.22634	-.24016	-.25404
.09750	-.11690	-.13020	-.14355	-.15695	-.17041	-.18393	-.19750	-.21111	-.22479	-.23851
.10000	-.10299	-.11614	-.12934	-.14259	-.15591	-.16927	-.18269	-.19616	-.20967	-.22324
.10250	-.08933	-.10232	-.11538	-.12849	-.14165	-.15487	-.16813	-.18145	-.19482	-.20824
.10500	-.07589	-.08875	-.10166	-.11462	-.12764	-.14071	-.15383	-.16700	-.18022	-.19349
.10750	-.06269	-.07540	-.08817	-.10099	-.11387	-.12679	-.13977	-.15280	-.16588	-.17900
.11000	-.04972	-.06229	-.07492	-.08760	-.10033	-.11312	-.12595	-.13884	-.15177	-.16476
.11250	-.03697	-.04940	-.06189	-.07443	-.08703	-.09967	-.11237	-.12511	-.13791	-.15075
.11500	-.02443	-.03673	-.04908	-.06149	-.07395	-.08646	-.09902	-.11163	-.12428	-.13699
.11750	-.01211	-.02428	-.03650	-.04877	-.06109	-.07347	-.08589	-.09836	-.11089	-.12345
.12000	.00000	-.01203	-.02412	-.03626	-.04845	-.06070	-.07299	-.08533	-.09772	-.11015
.12250	.01191	.00000	-.01196	-.02397	-.03603	-.04814	-.06030	-.07251	-.08477	-.09707
.12500	.02361	.01183	-.00000	-.01188	-.02382	-.03580	-.04783	-.05991	-.07204	-.08421
.12750	.03512	.02346	.01176	.00000	-.01181	-.02366	-.03557	-.04752	-.05952	-.07156
.13000	.04643	.03490	.02332	.01168	-.00000	-.01173	-.02351	-.03534	-.04721	-.05913
.13250	.05755	.04614	.03468	.02317	.01161	.00000	-.01166	-.02336	-.03511	-.04691
.13500	.06849	.05720	.04586	.03446	.02302	.01154	-.00000	-.01158	-.02321	-.03488
.13750	.07924	.06807	.05684	.04557	.03425	.02288	.01146	.00000	-.01151	-.02306
.14000	.08981	.07876	.06765	.05649	.04529	.03404	.02274	.01139	.00000	-.01143
.14250	.10021	.08927	.07827	.06723	.05614	.04501	.03382	.02259	.01132	0.00000
.14500	.11044	.09960	.08872	.07780	.06682	.05579	.04472	.03361	.02245	.01125
.14750	.12049	.10977	.09900	.08818	.07732	.06641	.05545	.04444	.03340	.02231
.15000	.13038	.11977	.10911	.09840	.08764	.07684	.06599	.05510	.04417	.03319
.15250	.14011	.12960	.11905	.10845	.09780	.08711	.07637	.06559	.05476	.04389
.15500	.14967	.13927	.12883	.11833	.10779	.09720	.08657	.07590	.06518	.05442
.15750	.15908	.14879	.13845	.12806	.11762	.10714	.09661	.08604	.07543	.06477
.16000	.16834	.15815	.14791	.13762	.12729	.11691	.10649	.09602	.08551	.07496
.16250	.17744	.16735	.15721	.14703	.13680	.12652	.11620	.10584	.09543	.08498
.16500	.18640	.17641	.16637	.15628	.14615	.13598	.12576	.11550	.10519	.09485
.16750	.19521	.18532	.17538	.16539	.15536	.14528	.13516	.12500	.11479	.10455
.17000	.20388	.19408	.18424	.17435	.16441	.15443	.14441	.13435	.12424	.11410
.17250	.21241	.20271	.19296	.18316	.17332	.16344	.15352	.14355	.13354	.12349
.17500	.22080	.21119	.20154	.19184	.18209	.17230	.16247	.15260	.14259	.13273
.17750	.22906	.21954	.20998	.20037	.19072	.18102	.17129	.16151	.15169	.14183
.18000	.23719	.22776	.21829	.20877	.19921	.18961	.17996	.17028	.16055	.15078
.18250	.24518	.23584	.22646	.21703	.20756	.19805	.18850	.17890	.16927	.15959
.18500	.25305	.24380	.23451	.22517	.21579	.20636	.19690	.18739	.17785	.16827
.18750	.26079	.25163	.24242	.23317	.22388	.21454	.20517	.19575	.18630	.17680
.19000	.26842	.25934	.25022	.24105	.23184	.22260	.21331	.20398	.19461	.18520
.19250	.27592	.26692	.25789	.24881	.23968	.23052	.22132	.21207	.20279	.19347
.19500	.28330	.27439	.26543	.25644	.24740	.23832	.22920	.22004	.21085	.20161
.19750	.29057	.28174	.27286	.26395	.25500	.24600	.23696	.22789	.21878	.20962
.20000	.29772	.28897	.28018	.27135	.26247	.25356	.24461	.23561	.22658	.21751
.20250	.30476	.29609	.28738	.27863	.26983	.26100	.25213	.24322	.23427	.22528
.20500	.31169	.30310	.29447	.28580	.27708	.26833	.25953	.25070	.24183	.23293
.20750	.31852	.31000	.30145	.29285	.28422	.27554	.26683	.25807	.24928	.24046

POINT TABLES: ORIGINAL LOAN TERM: 180 MONTHS LOAN PREPAID IN: 108 MONTHS

CONTRACT RATE

EFFECTIVE YIELD	.14500	.14750	.15000	.15250	.15500	.15750	.16000	.16250	.16500	.16750
.07000	-.44089	-.45656	-.47228	-.48805	-.50386	-.51973	-.53564	-.55159	-.56759	-.58363
.07250	-.42219	-.43768	-.45321	-.46880	-.48443	-.50011	-.51584	-.53161	-.54742	-.56328
.07500	-.40382	-.41913	-.43449	-.44989	-.46535	-.48085	-.49639	-.51198	-.52761	-.54328
.07750	-.38578	-.40091	-.41609	-.43132	-.44659	-.46191	-.47728	-.49269	-.50814	-.52364
.08000	-.36805	-.38300	-.39801	-.41306	-.42816	-.44331	-.45850	-.47374	-.48901	-.50433
.08250	-.35063	-.36541	-.38025	-.39513	-.41006	-.42503	-.44005	-.45511	-.47022	-.48536
.08500	-.33351	-.34813	-.36279	-.37751	-.39227	-.40707	-.42192	-.43681	-.45175	-.46672
.08750	-.31669	-.33114	-.34564	-.36019	-.37478	-.38942	-.40410	-.41883	-.43359	-.44840
.09000	-.30016	-.31445	-.32879	-.34317	-.35760	-.37208	-.38659	-.40115	-.41576	-.43040
.09250	-.28392	-.29805	-.31223	-.32645	-.34072	-.35503	-.36939	-.38378	-.39822	-.41270
.09500	-.26796	-.28193	-.29595	-.31001	-.32412	-.33828	-.35247	-.36671	-.38099	-.39531
.09750	-.25227	-.26609	-.27995	-.29386	-.30782	-.32181	-.33585	-.34993	-.36406	-.37822
.10000	-.23686	-.25052	-.26423	-.27799	-.29179	-.30563	-.31952	-.33344	-.34741	-.36142
.10250	-.22171	-.23522	-.24878	-.26238	-.27603	-.28972	-.30346	-.31723	-.33105	-.34490
.10500	-.20681	-.22018	-.23359	-.24705	-.26055	-.27409	-.28767	-.30130	-.31496	-.32867
.10750	-.19218	-.20540	-.21866	-.23197	-.24532	-.25872	-.27216	-.28563	-.29915	-.31271
.11000	-.17779	-.19086	-.20398	-.21715	-.23036	-.24361	-.25690	-.27024	-.28361	-.29702
.11250	-.16364	-.17658	-.18956	-.20258	-.21565	-.22876	-.24191	-.25510	-.26833	-.28160
.11500	-.14974	-.16253	-.17538	-.18826	-.20119	-.21416	-.22717	-.24022	-.25331	-.26643
.11750	-.13607	-.14873	-.16143	-.17418	-.18697	-.19980	-.21267	-.22558	-.23853	-.25152
.12000	-.12263	-.13516	-.14772	-.16034	-.17299	-.18569	-.19842	-.21120	-.22401	-.23686
.12250	-.10942	-.12181	-.13425	-.14673	-.15925	-.17181	-.18441	-.19705	-.20973	-.22245
.12500	-.09643	-.10869	-.12100	-.13334	-.14573	-.15816	-.17063	-.18314	-.19569	-.20828
.12750	-.08365	-.09579	-.10797	-.12018	-.13244	-.14475	-.15709	-.16947	-.18188	-.19434
.13000	-.07110	-.08310	-.09515	-.10724	-.11938	-.13155	-.14376	-.15602	-.16830	-.18063
.13250	-.05875	-.07063	-.08255	-.09452	-.10653	-.11858	-.13066	-.14279	-.15495	-.16715
.13500	-.04660	-.05836	-.07016	-.08201	-.09389	-.10582	-.11778	-.12978	-.14182	-.15389
.13750	-.03466	-.04630	-.05798	-.06970	-.08146	-.09327	-.10511	-.11699	-.12890	-.14085
.14000	-.02291	-.03443	-.04600	-.05760	-.06924	-.08092	-.09265	-.10440	-.11620	-.12803
.14250	-.01136	-.02276	-.03421	-.04570	-.05722	-.06878	-.08039	-.09203	-.10370	-.11542
.14500	.00000	-.01129	-.02262	-.03399	-.04540	-.05684	-.06833	-.07985	-.09141	-.10301
.14750	.01117	.00000	-.01122	-.02247	-.03377	-.04510	-.05647	-.06788	-.07932	-.09080
.15000	.02217	.01110	.00000	-.01114	-.02233	-.03355	-.04480	-.05610	-.06743	-.07880
.15250	.03298	.02203	.01103	0.00000	-.01107	-.02218	-.03333	-.04451	-.05573	-.06698
.15500	.04361	.03277	.02189	.01096	0.00000	-.01100	-.02204	-.03311	-.04422	-.05536
.15750	.05408	.04334	.03256	.02175	.01089	.00000	-.01093	-.02189	-.03289	-.04393
.16000	.06437	.05374	.04307	.03236	.02161	.01082	.00000	-.01086	-.02175	-.03268
.16250	.07450	.06397	.05340	.04279	.03215	.02147	.01075	.00000	-.01079	-.02161
.16500	.08446	.07403	.06357	.05307	.04252	.03195	.02133	.01068	.00000	-.01072
.16750	.09426	.08394	.07357	.06317	.05273	.04226	.03174	.02120	.01062	0.00000
.17000	.10391	.09368	.08342	.07312	.06278	.05240	.04199	.03154	.02106	.01055
.17250	.11340	.10327	.09311	.08290	.07266	.06238	.05207	.04172	.03134	.02093
.17500	.12274	.11271	.10264	.09253	.08239	.07221	.06199	.05174	.04146	.03114
.17750	.13193	.12200	.11202	.10201	.09196	.08188	.07176	.06160	.05142	.04120
.18000	.14098	.13113	.12125	.11134	.10138	.09139	.08137	.07131	.06122	.05109
.18250	.14988	.14013	.13034	.12051	.11065	.10076	.09083	.08086	.07086	.06083
.18500	.15864	.14898	.13928	.12955	.11978	.10998	.10014	.09026	.08036	.07042
.18750	.16727	.15770	.14809	.13844	.12876	.11905	.10930	.09952	.08970	.07986
.19000	.17576	.16627	.15675	.14720	.13761	.12798	.11832	.10863	.09890	.08915
.19250	.18411	.17472	.16528	.15582	.14631	.13677	.12720	.11760	.10796	.09829
.19500	.19234	.18303	.17368	.16430	.15488	.14543	.13595	.12643	.11688	.10730
.19750	.20043	.19121	.18195	.17265	.16332	.15395	.14455	.13512	.12566	.11616
.20000	.20841	.19926	.19009	.18087	.17163	.16234	.15303	.14368	.13430	.12489
.20250	.21626	.20719	.19810	.18897	.17980	.17060	.16137	.15211	.14281	.13349
.20500	.22398	.21500	.20599	.19694	.18786	.17874	.16959	.16041	.15120	.14195
.20750	.23159	.22269	.21376	.20479	.19579	.18675	.17768	.16858	.15945	.15029

POINT TABLES: ORIGINAL LOAN TERM: 180 MONTHS LOAN PREPAID IN: 108 MONTHS

CONTRACT RATE

EFFECTIVE YIELD	.17000	.17250	.17500	.17750	.18000	.18250	.18500	.18750	.19000	.19250
.07000	-.59971	-.61583	-.63200	-.64820	-.66443	-.68071	-.69702	-.71336	-.72974	-.74615
.07250	-.57918	-.59511	-.61109	-.62710	-.64316	-.65924	-.67537	-.69152	-.70771	-.72394
.07500	-.55900	-.57475	-.59055	-.60638	-.62225	-.63815	-.65409	-.67007	-.68607	-.70211
.07750	-.53917	-.55475	-.57036	-.58601	-.60170	-.61743	-.63319	-.64898	-.66481	-.68066
.08000	-.51969	-.53509	-.55053	-.56600	-.58151	-.59706	-.61264	-.62826	-.64391	-.65959
.08250	-.50055	-.51577	-.53104	-.54634	-.56167	-.57705	-.59245	-.60790	-.62337	-.63887
.08500	-.48174	-.49679	-.51188	-.52701	-.54218	-.55738	-.57261	-.58788	-.60318	-.61852
.08750	-.46325	-.47813	-.49306	-.50802	-.52302	-.53805	-.55311	-.56821	-.58334	-.59851
.09000	-.44508	-.45980	-.47456	-.48935	-.50418	-.51905	-.53395	-.54888	-.56385	-.57884
.09250	-.42722	-.44178	-.45637	-.47101	-.48567	-.50037	-.51511	-.52988	-.54468	-.55951
.09500	-.40967	-.42407	-.43850	-.45297	-.46748	-.48202	-.49659	-.51120	-.52584	-.54051
.09750	-.39242	-.40666	-.42094	-.43525	-.44960	-.46398	-.47839	-.49284	-.50732	-.52183
.10000	-.37546	-.38955	-.40367	-.41782	-.43202	-.44624	-.46050	-.47479	-.48912	-.50347
.10250	-.35880	-.37273	-.38669	-.40070	-.41474	-.42881	-.44291	-.45705	-.47122	-.48542
.10500	-.34241	-.35619	-.37001	-.38386	-.39775	-.41167	-.42562	-.43961	-.45363	-.46767
.10750	-.32630	-.33994	-.35361	-.36731	-.38105	-.39482	-.40862	-.42246	-.43633	-.45023
.11000	-.31047	-.32396	-.33748	-.35104	-.36463	-.37825	-.39191	-.40560	-.41932	-.43307
.11250	-.29490	-.30825	-.32162	-.33504	-.34848	-.36197	-.37548	-.38902	-.40260	-.41621
.11500	-.27960	-.29280	-.30604	-.31931	-.33261	-.34595	-.35932	-.37272	-.38616	-.39962
.11750	-.26455	-.27761	-.29071	-.30384	-.31701	-.33020	-.34344	-.35670	-.36999	-.38331
.12000	-.24975	-.26268	-.27564	-.28863	-.30166	-.31472	-.32781	-.34094	-.35409	-.36728
.12250	-.23520	-.24799	-.26082	-.27368	-.28657	-.29950	-.31245	-.32544	-.33846	-.35151
.12500	-.22090	-.23355	-.24625	-.25897	-.27173	-.28452	-.29735	-.31020	-.32308	-.33600
.12750	-.20683	-.21935	-.23191	-.24451	-.25714	-.26980	-.28249	-.29521	-.30796	-.32074
.13000	-.19299	-.20539	-.21782	-.23029	-.24278	-.25532	-.26788	-.28047	-.29309	-.30574
.13250	-.17939	-.19166	-.20396	-.21630	-.22867	-.24107	-.25351	-.26597	-.27846	-.29099
.13500	-.16600	-.17815	-.19033	-.20254	-.21479	-.22706	-.23937	-.25171	-.26408	-.27647
.13750	-.15284	-.16486	-.17692	-.18901	-.20113	-.21328	-.22547	-.23768	-.24993	-.26220
.14000	-.13990	-.15180	-.16373	-.17570	-.18770	-.19973	-.21179	-.22388	-.23600	-.24815
.14250	-.12716	-.13894	-.15076	-.16261	-.17449	-.18640	-.19834	-.21031	-.22231	-.23434
.14500	-.11464	-.12630	-.13800	-.14973	-.16149	-.17328	-.18511	-.19696	-.20884	-.22075
.14750	-.10232	-.11386	-.12545	-.13706	-.14870	-.16038	-.17209	-.18382	-.19559	-.20738
.15000	-.09020	-.10163	-.11310	-.12459	-.13613	-.14769	-.15928	-.17090	-.18255	-.19422
.15250	-.07827	-.08959	-.10095	-.11233	-.12375	-.13520	-.14668	-.15818	-.16972	-.18128
.15500	-.06654	-.07775	-.08899	-.10027	-.11157	-.12291	-.13428	-.14567	-.15709	-.16855
.15750	-.05500	-.06610	-.07723	-.08840	-.09959	-.11082	-.12208	-.13336	-.14467	-.15601
.16000	-.04364	-.05463	-.06566	-.07672	-.08780	-.09892	-.11007	-.12125	-.13245	-.14368
.16250	-.03246	-.04335	-.05427	-.06522	-.07621	-.08722	-.09826	-.10933	-.12042	-.13155
.16500	-.02147	-.03225	-.04307	-.05391	-.06479	-.07570	-.08663	-.09760	-.10859	-.11961
.16750	-.01065	-.02133	-.03204	-.04278	-.05356	-.06436	-.07519	-.08605	-.09694	-.10785
.17000	0.00000	-.01058	-.02119	-.03183	-.04250	-.05320	-.06393	-.07469	-.08548	-.09629
.17250	.01048	-.00000	-.01051	-.02105	-.03162	-.04222	-.05285	-.06351	-.07419	-.08490
.17500	.02079	.01041	.00000	-.01044	-.02091	-.03142	-.04195	-.05250	-.06309	-.07370
.17750	.03094	.02066	.01034	.00000	-.01037	-.02078	-.03121	-.04167	-.05216	-.06267
.18000	.04093	.03075	.02053	.01028	.00000	-.01031	-.02064	-.03101	-.04139	-.05181
.18250	.05077	.04067	.03055	.02040	.01021	0.00000	-.01024	-.02051	-.03080	-.04112
.18500	.06045	.05045	.04042	.03036	.02026	.01015	.00000	-.01017	-.02037	-.03060
.18750	.06998	.06007	.05013	.04016	.03016	.02014	.01008	.00000	-.01011	-.02024
.19000	.07936	.06954	.05969	.04981	.03990	.02997	.02001	.01002	.00000	-.01004
.19250	.08859	.07886	.06910	.05931	.04950	.03965	.02978	.01988	.00995	.00000
.19500	.09769	.08804	.07837	.06867	.05894	.04918	.03940	.02959	.01975	.00989
.19750	.10664	.09708	.08750	.07788	.06824	.05857	.04887	.03915	.02940	.01962
.20000	.11545	.10598	.09648	.08695	.07740	.06781	.05820	.04856	.03890	.02921
.20250	.12413	.11474	.10533	.09588	.08641	.07691	.06739	.05783	.04826	.03865
.20500	.13268	.12337	.11404	.10468	.09529	.08587	.07643	.06696	.05747	.04795
.20750	.14109	.13187	.12262	.11334	.10403	.09470	.08534	.07595	.06654	.05711

CONTRACT RATE

EFFECTIVE YIELD	.19500	.19750	.20000	.20250	.20500	.20750
.07000	-.76259	-.77906	-.79556	-.81209	-.82865	-.84523
.07250	-.74019	-.75648	-.77279	-.78913	-.80550	-.82190
.07500	-.71818	-.73428	-.75041	-.76657	-.78276	-.79897
.07750	-.69655	-.71247	-.72842	-.74440	-.76041	-.77644
.08000	-.67530	-.69104	-.70681	-.72261	-.73844	-.75429
.08250	-.65441	-.66998	-.68557	-.70119	-.71685	-.73252
.08500	-.63388	-.64927	-.66470	-.68015	-.69562	-.71113
.08750	-.61370	-.62892	-.64418	-.65946	-.67477	-.69010
.09000	-.59387	-.60892	-.62401	-.63912	-.65426	-.66943
.09250	-.57437	-.58927	-.60419	-.61913	-.63411	-.64911
.09500	-.55521	-.56994	-.58470	-.59948	-.61430	-.62914
.09750	-.53637	-.55094	-.56554	-.58017	-.59482	-.60950
.10000	-.51785	-.53227	-.54671	-.56118	-.57567	-.59020
.10250	-.49965	-.51391	-.52820	-.54251	-.55685	-.57122
.10500	-.48175	-.49586	-.50999	-.52415	-.53834	-.55256
.10750	-.46415	-.47811	-.49210	-.50611	-.52015	-.53421
.11000	-.44685	-.46066	-.47450	-.48836	-.50225	-.51617
.11250	-.42984	-.44351	-.45720	-.47092	-.48466	-.49843
.11500	-.41311	-.42663	-.44018	-.45376	-.46736	-.48099
.11750	-.39667	-.41004	-.42345	-.43689	-.45035	-.46383
.12000	-.38049	-.39373	-.40700	-.42029	-.43362	-.44696
.12250	-.36458	-.37769	-.39082	-.40398	-.41716	-.43037
.12500	-.34894	-.36191	-.37491	-.38793	-.40098	-.41405
.12750	-.33355	-.34639	-.35926	-.37215	-.38506	-.39800
.13000	-.31842	-.33113	-.34386	-.35662	-.36941	-.38222
.13250	-.30354	-.31612	-.32872	-.34135	-.35401	-.36669
.13500	-.28890	-.30135	-.31383	-.32633	-.33886	-.35142
.13750	-.27450	-.28682	-.29918	-.31156	-.32396	-.33639
.14000	-.26033	-.27254	-.28477	-.29702	-.30930	-.32161
.14250	-.24640	-.25848	-.27059	-.28272	-.29488	-.30707
.14500	-.23269	-.24465	-.25664	-.26866	-.28070	-.29276
.14750	-.21920	-.23104	-.24292	-.25481	-.26674	-.27868
.15000	-.20593	-.21766	-.22941	-.24120	-.25300	-.26483
.15250	-.19287	-.20449	-.21613	-.22780	-.23949	-.25121
.15500	-.18002	-.19153	-.20306	-.21461	-.22619	-.23779
.15750	-.16738	-.17878	-.19019	-.20164	-.21311	-.22460
.16000	-.15494	-.16623	-.17754	-.18887	-.20023	-.21161
.16250	-.14270	-.15388	-.16508	-.17631	-.18756	-.19883
.16500	-.13065	-.14172	-.15282	-.16394	-.17508	-.18625
.16750	-.11880	-.12976	-.14075	-.15177	-.16281	-.17387
.17000	-.10713	-.11799	-.12888	-.13979	-.15073	-.16169
.17250	-.09564	-.10640	-.11719	-.12800	-.13884	-.14969
.17500	-.08433	-.09500	-.10568	-.11639	-.12713	-.13789
.17750	-.07321	-.08377	-.09436	-.10497	-.11561	-.12626
.18000	-.06225	-.07272	-.08321	-.09372	-.10426	-.11482
.18250	-.05147	-.06184	-.07223	-.08265	-.09309	-.10356
.18500	-.04085	-.05113	-.06143	-.07175	-.08210	-.09247
.18750	-.03040	-.04058	-.05079	-.06102	-.07127	-.08155
.19000	-.02011	-.03020	-.04032	-.05045	-.06062	-.07080
.19250	-.00998	-.01998	-.03000	-.04005	-.05012	-.06021
.19500	.00000	-.00991	-.01985	-.02981	-.03979	-.04979
.19750	.00982	.00000	-.00985	-.01972	-.02961	-.03953
.20000	.01950	.00976	.00000	-.00978	-.01959	-.02942
.20250	.02902	.01937	.00970	.00000	-.00972	-.01946
.20500	.03841	.02884	.01925	.00964	0.00000	-.00966
.20750	.04765	.03816	.02866	.01913	.00957	.00000

POINT TABLES: ORIGINAL LOAN TERM: 180 MONTHS LOAN PREPAID IN: 144 MONTHS

EFFECTIVE YIELD	CONTRACT RATE .07000	.07250	.07500	.07750	.08000	.08250	.08500	.08750	.09000	.09250
.07000	.00000	-.01514	-.03040	-.04577	-.06126	-.07685	-.09256	-.10833	-.12431	-.14034
.07250	.01492	.00000	-.01504	-.03019	-.04545	-.06082	-.07630	-.09189	-.10759	-.12339
.07500	.02953	.01482	.00000	-.01493	-.02997	-.04513	-.06039	-.07575	-.09122	-.10680
.07750	.04383	.02933	.01472	-.00000	-.01483	-.02976	-.04481	-.05995	-.07521	-.09056
.08000	.05782	.04353	.02913	.01462	.00000	-.01472	-.02955	-.04449	-.05952	-.07466
.08250	.07152	.05743	.04323	.02893	.01452	.00000	-.01462	-.02934	-.04417	-.05909
.08500	.08494	.07105	.05705	.04294	.02873	.01442	.00000	-.01452	-.02914	-.04385
.08750	.09807	.08437	.07057	.05666	.04265	.02853	.01432	0.00000	-.01442	-.02893
.09000	.11093	.09742	.08381	.07009	.05627	.04235	.02834	.01422	0.00000	-.01431
.09250	.12353	.11021	.09678	.08325	.06962	.05589	.04206	.02814	.01412	.00000
.09500	.13586	.12272	.10948	.09613	.08269	.06915	.05551	.04177	.02794	.01402
.09750	.14794	.13498	.12192	.10875	.09549	.08213	.06868	.05513	.04149	.02775
.10000	.15978	.14699	.13410	.12111	.10803	.09485	.08158	.06821	.05475	.04120
.10250	.17137	.15875	.14603	.13322	.12031	.10731	.09422	.08103	.06775	.05437
.10500	.18272	.17027	.15773	.14508	.13235	.11952	.10660	.09358	.08048	.06728
.10750	.19385	.18156	.16918	.15671	.14414	.13148	.11872	.10588	.09295	.07993
.11000	.20474	.19262	.18040	.16809	.15569	.14319	.13061	.11793	.10517	.09232
.11250	.21542	.20346	.19140	.17925	.16701	.15467	.14225	.12974	.11715	.10446
.11500	.22589	.21408	.20217	.19018	.17810	.16592	.15366	.14132	.12888	.11636
.11750	.23614	.22448	.21273	.20090	.18897	.17695	.16485	.15266	.14038	.12802
.12000	.24619	.23468	.22308	.21140	.19962	.18776	.17581	.16377	.15165	.13945
.12250	.25604	.24468	.23323	.22169	.21006	.19835	.18655	.17467	.16270	.15066
.12500	.26570	.25448	.24317	.23178	.22030	.20873	.19708	.18535	.17353	.16164
.12750	.27516	.26408	.25292	.24167	.23033	.21891	.20741	.19582	.18415	.17240
.13000	.28444	.27350	.26247	.25136	.24017	.22889	.21753	.20608	.19456	.18296
.13250	.29354	.28273	.27184	.26087	.24981	.23867	.22745	.21615	.20477	.19331
.13500	.30246	.29179	.28103	.27019	.25927	.24826	.23718	.22602	.21478	.20346
.13750	.31121	.30066	.29004	.27933	.26854	.25767	.24672	.23569	.22459	.21341
.14000	.31978	.30937	.29887	.28829	.27763	.26690	.25608	.24519	.23421	.22317
.14250	.32819	.31790	.30753	.29708	.28655	.27594	.26526	.25449	.24365	.23274
.14500	.33644	.32628	.31603	.30570	.29530	.28482	.27426	.26362	.25291	.24213
.14750	.34454	.33449	.32436	.31416	.30388	.29352	.28309	.27258	.26199	.25134
.15000	.35247	.34254	.33254	.32245	.31229	.30206	.29175	.28136	.27090	.26037
.15250	.36026	.35045	.34056	.33059	.32055	.31044	.30024	.28998	.27954	.26923
.15500	.36790	.35820	.34843	.33858	.32865	.31865	.30858	.29844	.28822	.27793
.15750	.37539	.36581	.35615	.34641	.33660	.32672	.31676	.30673	.29663	.28646
.16000	.38275	.37327	.36372	.35410	.34440	.33463	.32479	.31487	.30489	.29484
.16250	.38997	.38060	.37116	.36164	.35205	.34240	.33266	.32286	.31299	.30305
.16500	.39705	.38779	.37845	.36905	.35957	.35002	.34040	.33070	.32095	.31112
.16750	.40400	.39484	.38561	.37631	.36694	.35750	.34798	.33840	.32875	.31903
.17000	.41082	.40177	.39264	.38344	.37418	.36484	.35543	.34596	.33641	.32680
.17250	.41752	.40857	.39954	.39044	.38128	.37204	.36274	.35337	.34393	.33443
.17500	.42410	.41524	.40631	.39732	.38825	.37912	.36992	.36065	.35132	.34192
.17750	.43055	.42179	.41296	.40407	.39510	.38607	.37697	.36780	.35857	.34927
.18000	.43689	.42823	.41949	.41069	.40182	.39289	.38388	.37482	.36569	.35649
.18250	.44311	.43454	.42590	.41720	.40842	.39958	.39068	.38171	.37267	.36358
.18500	.44922	.44074	.43220	.42358	.41490	.40616	.39735	.38848	.37954	.37054
.18750	.45522	.44684	.43838	.42986	.42127	.41262	.40390	.39512	.38628	.37738
.19000	.46112	.45282	.44445	.43602	.42752	.41896	.41034	.40165	.39290	.38409
.19250	.46691	.45869	.45042	.44207	.43366	.42519	.41666	.40806	.39941	.39069
.19500	.47259	.46447	.45627	.44802	.43970	.43131	.42287	.41436	.40579	.39717
.19750	.47818	.47014	.46203	.45386	.44562	.43733	.42897	.42055	.41207	.40353
.20000	.48367	.47571	.46768	.45960	.45145	.44323	.43496	.42663	.41824	.40979
.20250	.48906	.48118	.47324	.46523	.45717	.44904	.44085	.43260	.42430	.41593
.20500	.49436	.48656	.47870	.47077	.46279	.45474	.44664	.43847	.43025	.42197
.20750	.49957	.49184	.48406	.47622	.46831	.46035	.45232	.44424	.43610	.42790

POINT TABLES: ORIGINAL LOAN TERM: 180 MONTHS LOAN PREPAID IN: 144 MONTHS

EFFECTIVE YIELD	CONTRACT RATE .09500	.09750	.10000	.10250	.10500	.10750	.11000	.11250	.11500	.11750
.07000	-.15648	-.17273	-.18907	-.20552	-.22207	-.23872	-.25547	-.27232	-.28926	-.30629
.07250	-.13930	-.15531	-.17142	-.18764	-.20395	-.22036	-.23687	-.25347	-.27017	-.28696
.07500	-.12248	-.13826	-.15415	-.17013	-.18621	-.20238	-.21866	-.23502	-.25148	-.26804
.07750	-.10602	-.12158	-.13723	-.15299	-.16884	-.18479	-.20083	-.21696	-.23319	-.24951
.08000	-.08990	-.10524	-.12067	-.13621	-.15183	-.16756	-.18337	-.19928	-.21528	-.23137
.08250	-.07412	-.08924	-.10446	-.11978	-.13519	-.15069	-.16628	-.18197	-.19774	-.21361
.08500	-.05867	-.07358	-.08859	-.10369	-.11888	-.13417	-.14955	-.16502	-.18057	-.19622
.08750	-.04354	-.05824	-.07304	-.08794	-.10292	-.11800	-.13316	-.14842	-.16376	-.17919
.09000	-.02872	-.04322	-.05782	-.07251	-.08729	-.10216	-.11711	-.13216	-.14729	-.16251
.09250	-.01421	-.02852	-.04291	-.05740	-.07198	-.08664	-.10140	-.11624	-.13116	-.14617
.09500	.00000	-.01411	-.02831	-.04260	-.05698	-.07145	-.08600	-.10064	-.11536	-.13017
.09750	.01392	.00000	-.01401	-.02811	-.04229	-.05657	-.07092	-.08537	-.09989	-.11450
.10000	.02755	.01382	.00000	-.01391	-.02791	-.04199	-.05615	-.07040	-.08473	-.09914
.10250	.04091	.02736	.01372	.00000	-.01381	-.02770	-.04168	-.05574	-.06988	-.08410
.10500	.05400	.04063	.02717	.01363	0.00000	-.01371	-.02750	-.04138	-.05533	-.06936
.10750	.06682	.05362	.04034	.02698	.01353	.00000	-.01361	-.02730	-.04108	-.05492
.11000	.07938	.06636	.05325	.04006	.02679	.01343	.00000	-.01351	-.02711	-.04078
.11250	.09169	.07884	.06590	.05288	.03978	.02660	.01334	.00000	-.01342	-.02691
.11500	.10376	.09107	.07830	.06545	.05251	.03950	.02641	.01324	.00000	-.01332
.11750	.11558	.10305	.09045	.07776	.06499	.05215	.03922	.02622	.01315	.00000
.12000	.12717	.11480	.10235	.08983	.07722	.06454	.05178	.03895	.02604	.01306
.12250	.13853	.12632	.11403	.10166	.08921	.07669	.06409	.05142	.03857	.02585
.12500	.14966	.13760	.12547	.11326	.10097	.08860	.07616	.06365	.05106	.03840
.12750	.16058	.14867	.13669	.12463	.11249	.10028	.08799	.07563	.06320	.05070
.13000	.17128	.15952	.14768	.13577	.12379	.11172	.09959	.08738	.07511	.06276
.13250	.18177	.17016	.15847	.14670	.13486	.12295	.11096	.09891	.08678	.07458
.13500	.19206	.18059	.16904	.15742	.14572	.13396	.12212	.11021	.09823	.08618
.13750	.20215	.19082	.17941	.16793	.15638	.14475	.13306	.12129	.10946	.09755
.14000	.21205	.20085	.18958	.17824	.16682	.15534	.14378	.13216	.12047	.10871
.14250	.22175	.21069	.19955	.18835	.17707	.16572	.15430	.14282	.13127	.11965
.14500	.23127	.22034	.20934	.19826	.18712	.17591	.16462	.15328	.14186	.13038
.14750	.24061	.22981	.21893	.20799	.19698	.18590	.17475	.16353	.15225	.14091
.15000	.24977	.23909	.22835	.21753	.20665	.19570	.18468	.17360	.16245	.15123
.15250	.25875	.24820	.23758	.22690	.21614	.20531	.19442	.18347	.17245	.16137
.15500	.26757	.25714	.24665	.23608	.22545	.21475	.20399	.19316	.18226	.17131
.15750	.27622	.26592	.25554	.24509	.23458	.22401	.21337	.20266	.19190	.18107
.16000	.28471	.27452	.26426	.25394	.24355	.23309	.22258	.21199	.20135	.19064
.16250	.29305	.28297	.27283	.26262	.25235	.24201	.23161	.22115	.21062	.20004
.16500	.30122	.29126	.28123	.27114	.26098	.25076	.24048	.23013	.21973	.20926
.16750	.30925	.29940	.28948	.27950	.26946	.25935	.24918	.23895	.22866	.21831
.17000	.31713	.30739	.29758	.28771	.27778	.26779	.25773	.24761	.23744	.22720
.17250	.32486	.31523	.30553	.29577	.28595	.27606	.26612	.25611	.24605	.23593
.17500	.33245	.32293	.31334	.30368	.29397	.28419	.27435	.26446	.25450	.24449
.17750	.33991	.33049	.32100	.31145	.30184	.29217	.28244	.27265	.26281	.25290
.18000	.34723	.33791	.32852	.31908	.30957	.30001	.29038	.28070	.27096	.26116
.18250	.35442	.34520	.33591	.32657	.31716	.30770	.29818	.28860	.27896	.26927
.18500	.36148	.35235	.34317	.33392	.32462	.31526	.30584	.29636	.28683	.27724
.18750	.36841	.35938	.35030	.34115	.33194	.32268	.31336	.30398	.29455	.28506
.19000	.37522	.36629	.35730	.34824	.33914	.32997	.32075	.31147	.30213	.29275
.19250	.38191	.37307	.36417	.35522	.34620	.33713	.32800	.31882	.30959	.30029
.19500	.38848	.37973	.37093	.36206	.35314	.34417	.33513	.32605	.31690	.30771
.19750	.39493	.38628	.37756	.36879	.35996	.35108	.34214	.33314	.32410	.31500
.20000	.40128	.39271	.38408	.37540	.36666	.35787	.34902	.34012	.33116	.32215
.20250	.40751	.39903	.39049	.38189	.37324	.36454	.35578	.34697	.33811	.32919
.20500	.41363	.40523	.39678	.38828	.37971	.37110	.36243	.35370	.34493	.33610
.20750	.41965	.41134	.40297	.39455	.38607	.37754	.36896	.36032	.35163	.34290

POINT TABLES: ORIGINAL LOAN TERM: 180 MONTHS LOAN PREPAID IN: 144 MONTHS

EFFECTIVE YIELD	CONTRACT RATE .12000	.12250	.12500	.12750	.13000	.13250	.13500	.13750	.14000	.14250
.07000	-.32342	-.34064	-.35795	-.37535	-.39283	-.41040	-.42806	-.44580	-.46362	-.48152
.07250	-.30384	-.32082	-.33788	-.35503	-.37226	-.38958	-.40698	-.42447	-.44204	-.45968
.07500	-.28468	-.30141	-.31823	-.33513	-.35212	-.36920	-.38635	-.40359	-.42091	-.43830
.07750	-.26592	-.28241	-.29899	-.31566	-.33241	-.34924	-.36616	-.38315	-.40022	-.41737
.08000	-.24755	-.26381	-.28016	-.29659	-.31311	-.32970	-.34638	-.36314	-.37997	-.39688
.08250	-.22956	-.24559	-.26171	-.27792	-.29420	-.31057	-.32702	-.34354	-.36014	-.37682
.08500	-.21195	-.22776	-.24366	-.25964	-.27570	-.29184	-.30805	-.32435	-.34072	-.35717
.08750	-.19470	-.21029	-.22597	-.24173	-.25757	-.27349	-.28948	-.30555	-.32170	-.33792
.09000	-.17781	-.19319	-.20865	-.22420	-.23982	-.25552	-.27130	-.28715	-.30307	-.31907
.09250	-.16126	-.17644	-.19169	-.20702	-.22243	-.23792	-.25348	-.26912	-.28483	-.30061
.09500	-.14506	-.16003	-.17507	-.19020	-.20540	-.22068	-.23603	-.25146	-.26696	-.28253
.09750	-.12918	-.14395	-.15880	-.17372	-.18872	-.20379	-.21894	-.23416	-.24945	-.26481
.10000	-.11364	-.12821	-.14285	-.15758	-.17238	-.18725	-.20220	-.21721	-.23230	-.24746
.10250	-.09840	-.11278	-.12723	-.14176	-.15636	-.17104	-.18579	-.20061	-.21550	-.23046
.10500	-.08348	-.09766	-.11193	-.12626	-.14068	-.15516	-.16971	-.18434	-.19903	-.21379
.10750	-.06885	-.08285	-.09693	-.11108	-.12530	-.13960	-.15396	-.16840	-.18290	-.19747
.11000	-.05452	-.06834	-.08223	-.09620	-.11024	-.12435	-.13853	-.15277	-.16709	-.18147
.11250	-.04048	-.05412	-.06783	-.08162	-.09548	-.10940	-.12340	-.13746	-.15159	-.16579
.11500	-.02671	-.04018	-.05372	-.06733	-.08101	-.09476	-.10858	-.12246	-.13641	-.15042
.11750	-.01322	-.02652	-.03988	-.05332	-.06683	-.08040	-.09404	-.10775	-.12152	-.13536
.12000	0.00000	-.01313	-.02632	-.03959	-.05293	-.06633	-.07980	-.09333	-.10693	-.12059
.12250	.01296	.00000	-.01303	-.02613	-.03930	-.05253	-.06583	-.07920	-.09263	-.10612
.12500	.02567	.01287	.00000	-.01294	-.02594	-.03901	-.05214	-.06534	-.07860	-.09193
.12750	.03813	.02549	.01278	.00000	-.01284	-.02575	-.03872	-.05176	-.06486	-.07801
.13000	.05034	.03786	.02530	.01268	0.00000	-.01275	-.02556	-.03844	-.05137	-.06437
.13250	.06232	.04999	.03759	.02512	.01259	.00000	-.01266	-.02537	-.03815	-.05099
.13500	.07407	.06188	.04963	.03732	.02494	.01250	.00000	-.01256	-.02519	-.03787
.13750	.08558	.07355	.06145	.04928	.03705	.02476	.01241	.00000	-.01247	-.02500
.14000	.09688	.08499	.07303	.06102	.04893	.03679	.02459	.01232	.00000	-.01238
.14250	.10796	.09621	.08440	.07252	.06059	.04859	.03653	.02441	.01223	0.00000
.14500	.11883	.10722	.09555	.08381	.07202	.06016	.04824	.03627	.02423	.01215
.14750	.12949	.11802	.10648	.09489	.08323	.07151	.05973	.04790	.03601	.02406
.15000	.13996	.12862	.11721	.10575	.09423	.08265	.07101	.05931	.04756	.03575
.15250	.15022	.13901	.12774	.11641	.10502	.09358	.08207	.07051	.05889	.04722
.15500	.16029	.14921	.13807	.12687	.11562	.10430	.09293	.08150	.07001	.05848
.15750	.17017	.15922	.14821	.13714	.12601	.11482	.10358	.09228	.08093	.06952
.16000	.17987	.16904	.15816	.14721	.13621	.12515	.11403	.10286	.09164	.08036
.16250	.18939	.17869	.16792	.15710	.14622	.13529	.12430	.11325	.10215	.09100
.16500	.19873	.18815	.17750	.16680	.15605	.14523	.13437	.12345	.11247	.10145
.16750	.20790	.19744	.18691	.17633	.16569	.15500	.14425	.13345	.12260	.11170
.17000	.21691	.20655	.19615	.18568	.17516	.16459	.15396	.14328	.13255	.12176
.17250	.22574	.21551	.20521	.19486	.18446	.17400	.16349	.15293	.14231	.13164
.17500	.23442	.22429	.21411	.20388	.19359	.18324	.17284	.16240	.15190	.14135
.17750	.24294	.23292	.22285	.21273	.20255	.19232	.18203	.17170	.16131	.15087
.18000	.25131	.24140	.23144	.22142	.21135	.20123	.19105	.18083	.17055	.16023
.18250	.25952	.24972	.23986	.22995	.21999	.20998	.19991	.18980	.17963	.16942
.18500	.26759	.25789	.24814	.23834	.22848	.21857	.20861	.19860	.18855	.17844
.18750	.27552	.26592	.25627	.24657	.23682	.22701	.21716	.20726	.19731	.18731
.19000	.28330	.27381	.26426	.25466	.24501	.23531	.22556	.21576	.20591	.19601
.19250	.29095	.28155	.27210	.26260	.25305	.24345	.23380	.22410	.21436	.20457
.19500	.29846	.28916	.27981	.27041	.26096	.25146	.24191	.23231	.22266	.21297
.19750	.30584	.29664	.28738	.27808	.26872	.25932	.24987	.24037	.23082	.22123
.20000	.31310	.30398	.29482	.28561	.27635	.26704	.25769	.24829	.23884	.22934
.20250	.32022	.31120	.30213	.29302	.28385	.27464	.26538	.25607	.24671	.23731
.20500	.32722	.31830	.30932	.30029	.29122	.28210	.27293	.26371	.25445	.24515
.20750	.33411	.32527	.31638	.30744	.29846	.28943	.28035	.27123	.26206	.25285

POINT TABLES: ORIGINAL LOAN TERM: 180 MONTHS LOAN PREPAID IN: 144 MONTHS

CONTRACT RATE

EFFECTIVE YIELD	.14500	.14750	.15000	.15250	.15500	.15750	.16000	.16250	.16500	.16750
.07000	-.49950	-.51755	-.53569	-.55390	-.57218	-.59053	-.60896	-.62745	-.64602	-.66465
.07250	-.47740	-.49521	-.51308	-.53103	-.54905	-.56715	-.58531	-.60354	-.62184	-.64021
.07500	-.45578	-.47333	-.49095	-.50864	-.52641	-.54425	-.56216	-.58013	-.59817	-.61628
.07750	-.43460	-.45190	-.46928	-.48673	-.50424	-.52183	-.53949	-.55721	-.57500	-.59286
.08000	-.41387	-.43093	-.44806	-.46527	-.48254	-.49988	-.51729	-.53477	-.55231	-.56992
.08250	-.39357	-.41039	-.42728	-.44425	-.46128	-.47839	-.49556	-.51279	-.53009	-.54745
.08500	-.37368	-.39028	-.40694	-.42367	-.44047	-.45734	-.47427	-.49127	-.50833	-.52545
.08750	-.35421	-.37058	-.38701	-.40351	-.42008	-.43672	-.45342	-.47019	-.48702	-.50391
.09000	-.33514	-.35129	-.36750	-.38377	-.40012	-.41653	-.43300	-.44954	-.46614	-.48280
.09250	-.31647	-.33239	-.34838	-.36444	-.38056	-.39675	-.41300	-.42932	-.44569	-.46213
.09500	-.29817	-.31388	-.32965	-.34550	-.36140	-.37738	-.39341	-.40951	-.42566	-.44188
.09750	-.28024	-.29574	-.31131	-.32694	-.34264	-.35839	-.37422	-.39010	-.40604	-.42204
.10000	-.26268	-.27798	-.29334	-.30876	-.32425	-.33980	-.35541	-.37108	-.38681	-.40260
.10250	-.24548	-.26057	-.27573	-.29095	-.30623	-.32158	-.33698	-.35245	-.36797	-.38356
.10500	-.22862	-.24352	-.25847	-.27350	-.28858	-.30372	-.31893	-.33419	-.34952	-.36489
.10750	-.21210	-.22680	-.24157	-.25639	-.27128	-.28623	-.30124	-.31630	-.33143	-.34661
.11000	-.19592	-.21043	-.22500	-.23963	-.25433	-.26908	-.28390	-.29877	-.31370	-.32868
.11250	-.18005	-.19437	-.20876	-.22321	-.23771	-.25228	-.26690	-.28159	-.29632	-.31111
.11500	-.16450	-.17864	-.19284	-.20711	-.22143	-.23581	-.25025	-.26474	-.27929	-.29390
.11750	-.14926	-.16322	-.17724	-.19133	-.20547	-.21967	-.23392	-.24823	-.26250	-.27702
.12000	-.13432	-.14810	-.16195	-.17586	-.18982	-.20384	-.21792	-.23205	-.24623	-.26047
.12250	-.11967	-.13329	-.14696	-.16069	-.17448	-.18832	-.20222	-.21618	-.23019	-.24425
.12500	-.10531	-.11876	-.13226	-.14582	-.15944	-.17311	-.18684	-.20062	-.21446	-.22834
.12750	-.09123	-.10451	-.11785	-.13124	-.14469	-.15819	-.17175	-.18537	-.19903	-.21275
.13000	-.07743	-.09054	-.10371	-.11694	-.13023	-.14357	-.15696	-.17041	-.18391	-.19745
.13250	-.06389	-.07684	-.08986	-.10292	-.11605	-.12923	-.14246	-.15574	-.16907	-.18246
.13500	-.05061	-.06341	-.07627	-.08918	-.10214	-.11516	-.12823	-.14135	-.15453	-.16775
.13750	-.03759	-.05024	-.06294	-.07569	-.08850	-.10136	-.11428	-.12724	-.14026	-.15332
.14000	-.02482	-.03731	-.04986	-.06246	-.07512	-.08783	-.10059	-.11340	-.12626	-.13917
.14250	-.01229	-.02464	-.03704	-.04949	-.06200	-.07455	-.08716	-.09982	-.11253	-.12529
.14500	.00000	-.01220	-.02445	-.03676	-.04912	-.06153	-.07399	-.08650	-.09906	-.11167
.14750	.01206	.00000	-.01211	-.02427	-.03649	-.04875	-.06107	-.07343	-.08585	-.09831
.15000	.02389	.01197	.00000	-.01202	-.02410	-.03622	-.04839	-.06061	-.07238	-.08520
.15250	.03549	.02372	.01188	0.00000	-.01193	-.02392	-.03595	-.04803	-.06016	-.07233
.15500	.04688	.03524	.02354	.01180	0.00000	-.01185	-.02374	-.03568	-.04767	-.05971
.15750	.05806	.04655	.03499	.02337	.01171	-.00000	-.01176	-.02357	-.03542	-.04732
.16000	.06903	.05765	.04622	.03474	.02321	.01163	.00000	-.01167	-.02339	-.03516
.16250	.07980	.06855	.05724	.04589	.03449	.02304	.01154	0.00000	-.01159	-.02322
.16500	.09037	.07924	.06806	.05684	.04556	.03424	.02287	.01146	0.00000	-.01150
.16750	.10074	.08974	.07869	.06758	.05643	.04524	.03400	.02271	.01138	0.00000
.17000	.11093	.10005	.08911	.07813	.06711	.05603	.04492	.03375	.02254	.01129
.17250	.12093	.11017	.09935	.08849	.07759	.06663	.05564	.04459	.03351	.02238
.17500	.13075	.12010	.10941	.09866	.08788	.07704	.06616	.05524	.04428	.03327
.17750	.14039	.12986	.11928	.10865	.09798	.08726	.07650	.06570	.05485	.04396
.18000	.14986	.13944	.12897	.11846	.10790	.09730	.08665	.07597	.06523	.05446
.18250	.15916	.14885	.13849	.12809	.11765	.10716	.09663	.08605	.07543	.06477
.18500	.16829	.15809	.14784	.13755	.12722	.11684	.10642	.09595	.08545	.07490
.18750	.17726	.16717	.15703	.14685	.13662	.12635	.11604	.10568	.09529	.08485
.19000	.18607	.17609	.16605	.15598	.14586	.13569	.12549	.11524	.10495	.09463
.19250	.19473	.18485	.17492	.16495	.15493	.14487	.13477	.12463	.11445	.10423
.19500	.20323	.19345	.18363	.17376	.16384	.15389	.14389	.13386	.12378	.11367
.19750	.21159	.20191	.19218	.18241	.17260	.16275	.15286	.14292	.13295	.12294
.20000	.21980	.21022	.20059	.19092	.18121	.17146	.16166	.15183	.14196	.13205
.20250	.22787	.21838	.20885	.19928	.18967	.18001	.17032	.16058	.15081	.14100
.20500	.23580	.22641	.21698	.20750	.19798	.18842	.17883	.16919	.15951	.14980
.20750	.24360	.23430	.22496	.21557	.20615	.19669	.18719	.17764	.16806	.15845

POINT TABLES: ORIGINAL LOAN TERM: 180 MONTHS LOAN PREPAID IN: 144 MONTHS

CONTRACT RATE

EFFECTIVE YIELD	.17000	.17250	.17500	.17750	.18000	.18250	.18500	.18750	.19000	.19250
.07000	-.68334	-.70210	-.72092	-.73981	-.75875	-.77776	-.79682	-.81594	-.83511	-.85434
.07250	-.65864	-.67713	-.69569	-.71431	-.73298	-.75172	-.77051	-.78936	-.80827	-.82723
.07500	-.63445	-.65269	-.67098	-.68934	-.70775	-.72623	-.74476	-.76334	-.78198	-.80067
.07750	-.61077	-.62875	-.64679	-.66489	-.68305	-.70126	-.71954	-.73786	-.75624	-.77467
.08000	-.58758	-.60531	-.62310	-.64095	-.65886	-.67682	-.69484	-.71291	-.73103	-.74921
.08250	-.56488	-.58236	-.59990	-.61751	-.63517	-.65288	-.67065	-.68847	-.70635	-.72428
.08500	-.54264	-.55988	-.57719	-.59455	-.61196	-.62944	-.64696	-.66454	-.68217	-.69986
.08750	-.52086	-.53787	-.55493	-.57206	-.58924	-.60647	-.62376	-.64110	-.65849	-.67594
.09000	-.49952	-.51630	-.53314	-.55003	-.56698	-.58398	-.60104	-.61814	-.63530	-.65251
.09250	-.47863	-.49518	-.51179	-.52845	-.54517	-.56195	-.57877	-.59565	-.61258	-.62955
.09500	-.45815	-.47449	-.49087	-.50732	-.52381	-.54036	-.55696	-.57362	-.59032	-.60707
.09750	-.43810	-.45421	-.47038	-.48661	-.50289	-.51922	-.53560	-.55203	-.56851	-.58504
.10000	-.41845	-.43435	-.45031	-.46632	-.48238	-.49850	-.51466	-.53088	-.54714	-.56345
.10250	-.39919	-.41489	-.43064	-.44644	-.46229	-.47819	-.49415	-.51015	-.52620	-.54230
.10500	-.38033	-.39582	-.41136	-.42695	-.44260	-.45830	-.47404	-.48984	-.50568	-.52157
.10750	-.36184	-.37713	-.39247	-.40786	-.42331	-.43880	-.45434	-.46993	-.48557	-.50126
.11000	-.34372	-.35881	-.37396	-.38915	-.40440	-.41969	-.43504	-.45043	-.46586	-.48135
.11250	-.32596	-.34086	-.35581	-.37081	-.38586	-.40096	-.41611	-.43131	-.44655	-.46183
.11500	-.30855	-.32326	-.33802	-.35283	-.36770	-.38260	-.39756	-.41256	-.42761	-.44270
.11750	-.29149	-.30601	-.32059	-.33521	-.34989	-.36461	-.37937	-.39419	-.40905	-.42395
.12000	-.27476	-.28910	-.30350	-.31794	-.33243	-.34696	-.36155	-.37618	-.39085	-.40556
.12250	-.25836	-.27253	-.28674	-.30100	-.31531	-.32967	-.34407	-.35851	-.37301	-.38754
.12500	-.24228	-.25627	-.27031	-.28439	-.29853	-.31270	-.32693	-.34120	-.35551	-.36986
.12750	-.22651	-.24033	-.25420	-.26811	-.28207	-.29607	-.31012	-.32422	-.33835	-.35253
.13000	-.21105	-.22470	-.23840	-.25214	-.26593	-.27976	-.29364	-.30756	-.32153	-.33554
.13250	-.19589	-.20937	-.22290	-.23648	-.25010	-.26377	-.27748	-.29123	-.30503	-.31887
.13500	-.18102	-.19434	-.20771	-.22112	-.23453	-.24808	-.26163	-.27522	-.28885	-.30252
.13750	-.16643	-.17959	-.19280	-.20605	-.21935	-.23269	-.24608	-.25950	-.27297	-.28648
.14000	-.15213	-.16513	-.17818	-.19128	-.20442	-.21760	-.23082	-.24409	-.25740	-.27075
.14250	-.13809	-.15094	-.16384	-.17678	-.18976	-.20279	-.21586	-.22897	-.24212	-.25532
.14500	-.12432	-.13702	-.14977	-.16256	-.17539	-.18826	-.20118	-.21414	-.22714	-.24017
.14750	-.11081	-.12336	-.13596	-.14860	-.16128	-.17401	-.18678	-.19958	-.21243	-.22532
.15000	-.09756	-.10996	-.12242	-.13491	-.14745	-.16002	-.17264	-.18530	-.19800	-.21074
.15250	-.08455	-.09681	-.10912	-.12147	-.13387	-.14630	-.15877	-.17129	-.18384	-.19643
.15500	-.07179	-.08391	-.09608	-.10829	-.12054	-.13283	-.14516	-.15754	-.16995	-.18239
.15750	-.05926	-.07125	-.08328	-.09535	-.10746	-.11961	-.13181	-.14404	-.15631	-.16861
.16000	-.04696	-.05882	-.07071	-.08264	-.09462	-.10664	-.11869	-.13079	-.14292	-.15509
.16250	-.03490	-.04661	-.05838	-.07018	-.08202	-.09390	-.10582	-.11778	-.12978	-.14181
.16500	-.02305	-.03464	-.04627	-.05794	-.06965	-.08140	-.09319	-.10502	-.11688	-.12878
.16750	-.01142	-.02288	-.03438	-.04592	-.05750	-.06913	-.08078	-.09248	-.10421	-.11598
.17000	.00000	-.01133	-.02271	-.03413	-.04558	-.05707	-.06861	-.08017	-.09178	-.10342
.17250	.01121	0.00000	-.01125	-.02254	-.03387	-.04524	-.05665	-.06809	-.07957	-.09108
.17500	.02222	.01113	.00000	-.01117	-.02238	-.03362	-.04491	-.05623	-.06758	-.07897
.17750	.03303	.02206	.01105	.00000	-.01109	-.02221	-.03337	-.04457	-.05581	-.06707
.18000	.04365	.03279	.02190	.01097	.00000	-.01101	-.02205	-.03313	-.04424	-.05539
.18250	.05407	.04334	.03256	.02174	.01089	0.00000	-.01093	-.02189	-.03288	-.04391
.18500	.06432	.05369	.04303	.03233	.02159	.01081	.00000	-.01085	-.02173	-.03264
.18750	.07438	.06386	.05331	.04272	.03209	.02143	.01073	.00000	-.01077	-.02157
.19000	.08426	.07386	.06341	.05293	.04242	.03186	.02128	.01066	.00000	-.01069
.19250	.09397	.08367	.07334	.06297	.05256	.04212	.03164	.02112	.01058	.00000
.19500	.10351	.09332	.08309	.07282	.06252	.05219	.04182	.03141	.02097	.01050
.19750	.11289	.10280	.09267	.08251	.07231	.06208	.05182	.04152	.03119	.02082
.20000	.12210	.11211	.10209	.09203	.08194	.07181	.06165	.05145	.04122	.03096
.20250	.13115	.12127	.11134	.10139	.09139	.08137	.07131	.06121	.05109	.04093
.20500	.14005	.13026	.12044	.11058	.10069	.09076	.08080	.07081	.06078	.05073
.20750	.14879	.13910	.12938	.11962	.10982	.09999	.09013	.08024	.07031	.06036

EFFECTIVE YIELD	CONTRACT RATE .19500	.19750	.20000	.20250	.20500	.20750
.07000	-.87363	-.89296	-.91235	-.93178	-.95126	-.97079
.07250	-.84624	-.86530	-.88441	-.90357	-.92278	-.94204
.07500	-.81942	-.83821	-.85706	-.87595	-.89489	-.91388
.07750	-.79316	-.81169	-.83027	-.84890	-.86758	-.88630
.08000	-.76744	-.78572	-.80404	-.82242	-.84084	-.85930
.08250	-.74225	-.76028	-.77835	-.79648	-.81464	-.83286
.08500	-.71759	-.73537	-.75320	-.77107	-.78899	-.80695
.08750	-.69343	-.71097	-.72855	-.74618	-.76386	-.78158
.09000	-.66976	-.68706	-.70441	-.72181	-.73925	-.75673
.09250	-.64658	-.66365	-.68077	-.69793	-.71513	-.73238
.09500	-.62386	-.64071	-.65760	-.67453	-.69151	-.70853
.09750	-.60161	-.61823	-.63490	-.65161	-.66836	-.68516
.10000	-.57981	-.59621	-.61266	-.62915	-.64568	-.66226
.10250	-.55844	-.57463	-.59086	-.60714	-.62346	-.63982
.10500	-.53750	-.55348	-.56951	-.58557	-.60168	-.61782
.10750	-.51699	-.53276	-.54857	-.56443	-.58033	-.59627
.11000	-.49687	-.51244	-.52806	-.54371	-.55941	-.57514
.11250	-.47716	-.49253	-.50795	-.52340	-.53890	-.55444
.11500	-.45784	-.47302	-.48824	-.50350	-.51880	-.53414
.11750	-.43890	-.45388	-.46891	-.48398	-.49909	-.51424
.12000	-.42032	-.43512	-.44997	-.46485	-.47977	-.49473
.12250	-.40212	-.41673	-.43139	-.44609	-.46082	-.47560
.12500	-.38426	-.39870	-.41318	-.42769	-.44225	-.45684
.12750	-.36675	-.38101	-.39532	-.40965	-.42403	-.43845
.13000	-.34958	-.36367	-.37780	-.39196	-.40617	-.42041
.13250	-.33275	-.34666	-.36062	-.37461	-.38865	-.40271
.13500	-.31623	-.32998	-.34377	-.35760	-.37146	-.38536
.13750	-.30003	-.31362	-.32724	-.34090	-.35460	-.36834
.14000	-.28414	-.29756	-.31103	-.32453	-.33806	-.35164
.14250	-.26855	-.28181	-.29512	-.30846	-.32184	-.33525
.14500	-.25325	-.26636	-.27951	-.29270	-.30592	-.31918
.14750	-.23824	-.25120	-.26420	-.27723	-.29030	-.30341
.15000	-.22351	-.23633	-.24917	-.26206	-.27498	-.28793
.15250	-.20906	-.22173	-.23443	-.24717	-.25994	-.27274
.15500	-.19488	-.20740	-.21996	-.23255	-.24517	-.25783
.15750	-.18096	-.19334	-.20575	-.21820	-.23069	-.24320
.16000	-.16729	-.17954	-.19181	-.20412	-.21646	-.22884
.16250	-.15388	-.16599	-.17813	-.19030	-.20250	-.21474
.16500	-.14071	-.15269	-.16469	-.17673	-.18880	-.20090
.16750	-.12779	-.13963	-.15150	-.16341	-.17534	-.18731
.17000	-.11510	-.12681	-.13855	-.15032	-.16213	-.17397
.17250	-.10263	-.11422	-.12583	-.13748	-.14916	-.16087
.17500	-.09039	-.10185	-.11334	-.12487	-.13642	-.14801
.17750	-.07838	-.08971	-.10108	-.11248	-.12391	-.13537
.18000	-.06657	-.07779	-.08903	-.10031	-.11162	-.12296
.18250	-.05498	-.06607	-.07720	-.08836	-.09955	-.11077
.18500	-.04359	-.05457	-.06558	-.07662	-.08770	-.09880
.18750	-.03240	-.04327	-.05416	-.06509	-.07605	-.08704
.19000	-.02141	-.03216	-.04295	-.05376	-.06461	-.07548
.19250	-.01061	-.02125	-.03193	-.04263	-.05336	-.06412
.19500	.00000	-.01053	-.02110	-.03169	-.04232	-.05297
.19750	.01043	.00000	-.01046	-.02094	-.03146	-.04200
.20000	.02067	.01035	.00000	-.01038	-.02079	-.03123
.20250	.03074	.02053	.01028	.00000	-.01031	-.02064
.20500	.04064	.03052	.02038	.01020	0.00000	-.01023
.20750	.05037	.04035	.03031	.02023	.01013	.00000

POINT TABLES: ORIGINAL LOAN TERM: 180 MONTHS LOAN PREPAID IN: 180 MONTHS

EFFECTIVE YIELD	CONTRACT RATE .07000	.07250	.07500	.07750	.08000	.08250	.08500	.08750	.09000	.09250
.07000	.00000	-.01561	-.03136	-.04723	-.06322	-.07934	-.09558	-.11195	-.12843	-.14504
.07250	.01537	0.00000	-.01550	-.03113	-.04687	-.06274	-.07874	-.09485	-.11108	-.12743
.07500	.03040	.01526	.00000	-.01539	-.03089	-.04652	-.06227	-.07814	-.09412	-.11022
.07750	.04510	.03019	.01515	0.00000	-.01527	-.03067	-.04618	-.06180	-.07754	-.09340
.08000	.05946	.04477	.02997	.01504	.00000	-.01516	-.03044	-.04583	-.06133	-.07695
.08250	.07351	.05904	.04446	.02975	.01493	.00000	-.01505	-.03021	-.04548	-.06087
.08500	.08724	.07299	.05862	.04414	.02954	.01483	.00000	-.01494	-.02998	-.04514
.08750	.10068	.08663	.07248	.05820	.04382	.02932	.01472	.00000	-.01483	-.02976
.09000	.11381	.09998	.08603	.07196	.05779	.04351	.02911	.01461	.00000	-.01472
.09250	.12667	.11303	.09928	.08542	.07145	.05738	.04319	.02890	.01450	.00000
.09500	.13924	.12580	.11225	.09859	.08482	.07095	.05697	.04288	.02859	.01440
.09750	.15154	.13829	.12493	.11147	.09790	.08422	.07044	.05656	.04257	.02848
.10000	.16357	.15051	.13735	.12407	.11069	.09721	.08363	.06994	.05615	.04226
.10250	.17535	.16247	.14949	.13641	.12322	.10992	.09653	.08303	.06944	.05574
.10500	.18687	.17418	.16138	.14847	.13547	.12236	.10915	.09585	.08244	.06894
.10750	.19815	.18563	.17301	.16029	.14746	.13454	.12151	.10839	.09517	.08186
.11000	.20919	.19685	.18440	.17185	.15920	.14645	.13361	.12067	.10763	.09450
.11250	.22000	.20782	.19554	.18316	.17069	.15812	.14545	.13268	.11982	.10687
.11500	.23058	.21857	.20645	.19424	.18194	.16954	.15704	.14445	.13176	.11899
.11750	.24094	.22909	.21714	.20509	.19295	.18072	.16839	.15596	.14345	.13085
.12000	.25108	.23939	.22760	.21571	.20373	.19166	.17950	.16724	.15490	.14246
.12250	.26101	.24947	.23784	.22611	.21429	.20238	.19038	.17829	.16610	.15383
.12500	.27074	.25935	.24787	.23630	.22464	.21288	.20104	.18910	.17708	.16497
.12750	.28027	.26903	.25770	.24628	.23477	.22316	.21147	.19970	.18783	.17588
.13000	.28960	.27851	.26732	.25605	.24469	.23324	.22170	.21007	.19836	.18656
.13250	.29874	.28779	.27675	.26562	.25441	.24310	.23171	.22024	.20868	.19703
.13500	.30770	.29689	.28599	.27500	.26393	.25277	.24153	.23020	.21878	.20729
.13750	.31647	.30580	.29504	.28419	.27326	.26224	.25114	.23996	.22869	.21734
.14000	.32507	.31453	.30391	.29320	.28240	.27152	.26056	.24952	.23839	.22718
.14250	.33350	.32309	.31260	.30202	.29136	.28062	.26980	.25889	.24790	.23683
.14500	.34176	.33148	.32112	.31067	.30015	.28954	.27884	.26807	.25722	.24629
.14750	.34985	.33970	.32947	.31915	.30875	.29827	.28771	.27707	.26636	.25556
.15000	.35779	.34776	.33765	.32746	.31719	.30684	.29641	.28590	.27531	.26465
.15250	.36557	.35566	.34568	.33561	.32546	.31524	.30493	.29455	.28409	.27355
.15500	.37320	.36341	.35354	.34360	.33357	.32347	.31329	.30303	.29270	.28229
.15750	.38068	.37101	.36126	.35143	.34152	.33154	.32148	.31135	.30114	.29085
.16000	.38801	.37846	.36882	.35911	.34932	.33946	.32952	.31950	.30941	.29925
.16250	.39520	.38576	.37624	.36664	.35697	.34722	.33740	.32750	.31753	.30749
.16500	.40226	.39293	.38352	.37403	.36447	.35483	.34513	.33534	.32549	.31556
.16750	.40918	.39995	.39065	.38128	.37183	.36230	.35271	.34304	.33330	.32349
.17000	.41597	.40685	.39765	.38839	.37905	.36963	.36015	.35059	.34096	.33126
.17250	.42263	.41361	.40452	.39536	.38613	.37682	.36744	.35799	.34847	.33889
.17500	.42916	.42025	.41126	.40220	.39307	.38387	.37460	.36526	.35585	.34637
.17750	.43557	.42676	.41788	.40892	.39989	.39079	.38163	.37239	.36308	.35371
.18000	.44187	.43315	.42437	.41551	.40658	.39759	.38852	.37939	.37019	.36092
.18250	.44804	.43943	.43074	.42198	.41315	.40425	.39529	.38625	.37715	.36799
.18500	.45411	.44558	.43699	.42833	.41959	.41079	.40193	.39299	.38430	.37493
.18750	.46006	.45162	.44313	.43456	.42592	.41722	.40845	.39961	.39071	.38174
.19000	.46590	.45756	.44915	.44067	.43213	.42352	.41485	.40611	.39730	.38843
.19250	.47163	.46338	.45507	.44668	.43823	.42971	.42113	.41248	.40377	.39500
.19500	.47726	.46910	.46087	.45258	.44422	.43579	.42730	.41875	.41013	.40145
.19750	.48279	.47472	.46658	.45837	.45010	.44176	.43336	.42490	.41637	.40778
.20000	.48823	.48023	.47218	.46406	.45587	.44762	.43931	.43093	.42250	.41400
.20250	.49356	.48565	.47768	.46964	.46154	.45338	.44515	.43687	.42852	.42011
.20500	.49880	.49097	.48308	.47513	.46711	.45903	.45089	.44269	.43443	.42611
.20750	.50395	.49620	.48839	.48052	.47258	.46459	.45653	.44841	.44024	.43200

CONTRACT RATE

EFFECTIVE YIELD	.09500	.09750	.10000	.10250	.10500	.10750	.11000	.11250	.11500	.11750
.07000	-.16176	-.17860	-.19556	-.21264	-.22982	-.24712	-.26453	-.28205	-.29958	-.31742
.07250	-.14390	-.16048	-.17718	-.19399	-.21091	-.22795	-.24509	-.26234	-.27970	-.29716
.07500	-.12644	-.14277	-.15921	-.17577	-.19243	-.20921	-.22609	-.24307	-.26017	-.27736
.07750	-.10937	-.12545	-.14165	-.15795	-.17436	-.19088	-.20751	-.22424	-.24107	-.25801
.08000	-.09268	-.10852	-.12447	-.14053	-.15670	-.17297	-.18934	-.20582	-.22240	-.23908
.08250	-.07636	-.09197	-.10768	-.12350	-.13942	-.15545	-.17158	-.18781	-.20415	-.22058
.08500	-.06041	-.07578	-.09126	-.10684	-.12253	-.13832	-.15421	-.17020	-.18629	-.20248
.08750	-.04480	-.05995	-.07520	-.09055	-.10601	-.12157	-.13722	-.15298	-.16883	-.18478
.09000	-.02954	-.04446	-.05949	-.07462	-.08985	-.10518	-.12061	-.13614	-.15176	-.16748
.09250	-.01461	-.02931	-.04412	-.05904	-.07405	-.08915	-.10436	-.11966	-.13505	-.15054
.09500	.00000	-.01450	-.02909	-.04379	-.05858	-.07347	-.08846	-.10354	-.11871	-.13398
.09750	.01429	.00000	-.01439	-.02887	-.04346	-.05813	-.07291	-.08777	-.10273	-.11778
.10000	.02827	.01418	.00000	-.01428	-.02866	-.04313	-.05769	-.07234	-.08709	-.10192
.10250	.04195	.02806	.01408	.00000	-.01417	-.02844	-.04280	-.05724	-.07178	-.08641
.10500	.05534	.04165	.02786	.01398	0.00000	-.01407	-.02822	-.04247	-.05680	-.07123
.10750	.06845	.05494	.04134	.02765	.01387	.00000	-.01396	-.02801	-.04214	-.05637
.11000	.08127	.06795	.05454	.04104	.02745	.01377	.00000	-.01386	-.02780	-.04182
.11250	.09383	.08069	.06746	.05414	.04074	.02725	.01367	.00000	-.01375	-.02758
.11500	.10612	.09316	.08011	.06697	.05375	.04044	.02704	.01356	.00000	-.01365
.11750	.11815	.10537	.09250	.07954	.06649	.05336	.04014	.02684	.01346	.00000
.12000	.12993	.11732	.10462	.09183	.07896	.06601	.05297	.03985	.02664	.01336
.12250	.14147	.12903	.11650	.10388	.09118	.07839	.06553	.05258	.03955	.02645
.12500	.15277	.14049	.12813	.11567	.10314	.09053	.07783	.06505	.05220	.03926
.12750	.16384	.15172	.13952	.12723	.11486	.10241	.08988	.07727	.06458	.05181
.13000	.17468	.16272	.15067	.13854	.12633	.11404	.10168	.08923	.07671	.06411
.13250	.18530	.17349	.16160	.14963	.13758	.12545	.11324	.10095	.08859	.07615
.13500	.19571	.18405	.17231	.16049	.14859	.13662	.12456	.11243	.10023	.08795
.13750	.20591	.19439	.18280	.17113	.15938	.14756	.13566	.12368	.11163	.09951
.14000	.21590	.20453	.19308	.18156	.16996	.15828	.14653	.13471	.12281	.11084
.14250	.22569	.21446	.20316	.19178	.18032	.16879	.15719	.14551	.13376	.12194
.14500	.23528	.22419	.21303	.20179	.19048	.17909	.16763	.15610	.14450	.13282
.14750	.24469	.23374	.22271	.21161	.20044	.18919	.17787	.16648	.15502	.14349
.15000	.25391	.24309	.23220	.22123	.21020	.19909	.18791	.17665	.16533	.15394
.15250	.26294	.25226	.24150	.23067	.21976	.20879	.19774	.18663	.17544	.16419
.15500	.27180	.26125	.25062	.23992	.22914	.21830	.20739	.19641	.18536	.17424
.15750	.28049	.27006	.25956	.24899	.23834	.22763	.21685	.20600	.19508	.18409
.16000	.28901	.27871	.26833	.25788	.24736	.23678	.22612	.21540	.20461	.19376
.16250	.29737	.28719	.27693	.26660	.25621	.24575	.23522	.22462	.21396	.20323
.16500	.30557	.29550	.28536	.27516	.26488	.25454	.24414	.23366	.22313	.21253
.16750	.31361	.30366	.29364	.28355	.27340	.26317	.25289	.24254	.23212	.22164
.17000	.32149	.31166	.30175	.29178	.28174	.27164	.26147	.25124	.24094	.23059
.17250	.32923	.31951	.30972	.29986	.28993	.27995	.26989	.25978	.24960	.23936
.17500	.33682	.32721	.31753	.30778	.29797	.28810	.27816	.26816	.25809	.24797
.17750	.34427	.33477	.32519	.31556	.30586	.29609	.28627	.27638	.26643	.25642
.18000	.35158	.34218	.33272	.32319	.31360	.30394	.29422	.28445	.27461	.26471
.18250	.35876	.34946	.34010	.33068	.32119	.31164	.30203	.29236	.28263	.27284
.18500	.36580	.35661	.34735	.33803	.32865	.31920	.30970	.30013	.29051	.28083
.18750	.37271	.36362	.35446	.34524	.33596	.32662	.31722	.30776	.29824	.28867
.19000	.37950	.37050	.36145	.35233	.34315	.33391	.32461	.31525	.30584	.29636
.19250	.38616	.37726	.36830	.35928	.35020	.34106	.33186	.32261	.31329	.30392
.19500	.39271	.38390	.37504	.36611	.35713	.34809	.33898	.32983	.32061	.31134
.19750	.39913	.39042	.38165	.37282	.36393	.35498	.34598	.33692	.32780	.31862
.20000	.40544	.39682	.38814	.37940	.37061	.36175	.35284	.34388	.33486	.32578
.20250	.41164	.40311	.39452	.38587	.37717	.36841	.35959	.35072	.34179	.33281
.20500	.41772	.40928	.40078	.39223	.38361	.37494	.36621	.35743	.34860	.33971
.20750	.42370	.41535	.40694	.39847	.38994	.38136	.37272	.36403	.35529	.34649

POINT TABLES: ORIGINAL LOAN TERM: 180 MONTHS LOAN PREPAID IN: 180 MONTHS

CONTRACT RATE

EFFECTIVE YIELD	.12000	.12250	.12500	.12750	.13000	.13250	.13500	.13750	.14000	.14250
.07000	-.33526	-.35320	-.37125	-.38941	-.40766	-.42601	-.44446	-.46300	-.48154	-.50038
.07250	-.31473	-.33240	-.35017	-.36804	-.38602	-.40408	-.42225	-.44051	-.45886	-.47731
.07500	-.29466	-.31206	-.32956	-.34716	-.36486	-.38265	-.40054	-.41852	-.43660	-.45476
.07750	-.27504	-.29218	-.30942	-.32675	-.34418	-.36170	-.37932	-.39703	-.41483	-.43271
.08000	-.25586	-.27274	-.28972	-.30679	-.32396	-.34122	-.35857	-.37601	-.39354	-.41116
.08250	-.23711	-.25373	-.27046	-.28727	-.30418	-.32119	-.33828	-.35546	-.37273	-.39009
.08500	-.21877	-.23515	-.25162	-.26819	-.28485	-.30160	-.31844	-.33537	-.35238	-.36948
.08750	-.20083	-.21697	-.23320	-.24953	-.26594	-.28244	-.29903	-.31571	-.33248	-.34932
.09000	-.18329	-.19919	-.21519	-.23127	-.24745	-.26371	-.28006	-.29649	-.31301	-.32961
.09250	-.16613	-.18180	-.19756	-.21341	-.22935	-.24538	-.26149	-.27769	-.29397	-.31033
.09500	-.14934	-.16479	-.18032	-.19595	-.21166	-.22745	-.24333	-.25930	-.27534	-.29147
.09750	-.13292	-.14814	-.16346	-.17886	-.19434	-.20991	-.22557	-.24130	-.25712	-.27301
.10000	-.11685	-.13186	-.14695	-.16214	-.17740	-.19275	-.20818	-.22369	-.23928	-.25495
.10250	-.10112	-.11592	-.13081	-.14577	-.16082	-.17596	-.19117	-.20646	-.22184	-.23728
.10500	-.08573	-.10033	-.11500	-.12976	-.14460	-.15952	-.17452	-.18960	-.20476	-.21999
.10750	-.07067	-.08506	-.09954	-.11409	-.12873	-.14344	-.15823	-.17310	-.18805	-.20307
.11000	-.05593	-.07012	-.08440	-.09875	-.11318	-.12770	-.14229	-.15695	-.17169	-.18651
.11250	-.04150	-.05550	-.06958	-.08374	-.09797	-.11229	-.12668	-.14114	-.15568	-.17029
.11500	-.02737	-.04118	-.05507	-.06904	-.08308	-.09720	-.11139	-.12566	-.14000	-.15442
.11750	-.01354	-.02717	-.04087	-.05464	-.06850	-.08243	-.09643	-.11051	-.12456	-.13888
.12000	.00000	-.01344	-.02696	-.04055	-.05422	-.06796	-.08178	-.09567	-.10963	-.12366
.12250	.01326	.00000	-.01334	-.02675	-.04024	-.05380	-.06743	-.08114	-.09491	-.10876
.12500	.02625	.01316	0.00000	-.01324	-.02655	-.03993	-.05338	-.06691	-.08050	-.09416
.12750	.03897	.02605	.01306	0.00000	-.01314	-.02634	-.03962	-.05297	-.06639	-.07987
.13000	.05143	.03868	.02586	.01297	0.00000	-.01304	-.02614	-.03932	-.05256	-.06587
.13250	.06364	.05105	.03840	.02567	.01287	0.00000	-.01294	-.02594	-.03901	-.05215
.13500	.07560	.06317	.05068	.03811	.02548	.01277	.00000	-.01284	-.02574	-.03871
.13750	.08732	.07505	.06271	.05030	.03783	.02529	.01268	.00000	-.01274	-.02555
.14000	.09880	.08669	.07450	.06225	.04993	.03755	.02510	.01258	0.00000	-.01264
.14250	.11005	.09809	.08606	.07396	.06180	.04957	.03727	.02491	.01249	0.00000
.14500	.12108	.10927	.09738	.08544	.07342	.06134	.04920	.03699	.02472	.01239
.14750	.13189	.12022	.10849	.09668	.08482	.07289	.06089	.04884	.03672	.02454
.15000	.14248	.13096	.11937	.10771	.09599	.08420	.07236	.06045	.04848	.03644
.15250	.15287	.14149	.13004	.11852	.10694	.09530	.08359	.07183	.06000	.04812
.15500	.16306	.15181	.14049	.12912	.11768	.10617	.09461	.08299	.07130	.05956
.15750	.17304	.16193	.15075	.13951	.12821	.11684	.10541	.09393	.08239	.07078
.16000	.18284	.17185	.16081	.14970	.13853	.12730	.11601	.10466	.09325	.08179
.16250	.19244	.18159	.17067	.15969	.14865	.13756	.12640	.11518	.10391	.09258
.16500	.20186	.19113	.18035	.16950	.15859	.14762	.13659	.12550	.11436	.10316
.16750	.21110	.20050	.18983	.17911	.16833	.15748	.14658	.13563	.12462	.11355
.17000	.22017	.20968	.19914	.18854	.17788	.16717	.15639	.14556	.13467	.12373
.17250	.22906	.21870	.20828	.19780	.18726	.17666	.16601	.15530	.14454	.13373
.17500	.23778	.22754	.21724	.20688	.19646	.18598	.17545	.16486	.15422	.14353
.17750	.24635	.23622	.22603	.21578	.20548	.19513	.18471	.17425	.16372	.15315
.18000	.25475	.24473	.23466	.22453	.21434	.20410	.19380	.18345	.17305	.16259
.18250	.26300	.25309	.24313	.23311	.22303	.21291	.20272	.19249	.18220	.17186
.18500	.27109	.26129	.25144	.24153	.23157	.22155	.21148	.20136	.19118	.18095
.18750	.27904	.26934	.25960	.24980	.23994	.23004	.22007	.21006	.20000	.18988
.19000	.28684	.27725	.26761	.25792	.24817	.23837	.22851	.21861	.20865	.19865
.19250	.29449	.28501	.27547	.26588	.25624	.24654	.23680	.22700	.21715	.20725
.19500	.30201	.29263	.28320	.27371	.26417	.25457	.24493	.23524	.22549	.21570
.19750	.30940	.30011	.29078	.28139	.27195	.26246	.25292	.24333	.23369	.22400
.20000	.31665	.30746	.29823	.28894	.27960	.27020	.26076	.25127	.24173	.23215
.20250	.32377	.31468	.30554	.29635	.28710	.27781	.26847	.25908	.24964	.24015
.20500	.33077	.32177	.31273	.30363	.29448	.28528	.27604	.26674	.25740	.24801
.20750	.33764	.32874	.31978	.31078	.30172	.29262	.28347	.27427	.26502	.25573

EFFECTIVE YIELD	CONTRACT RATE .14500	.14750	.15000	.15250	.15500	.15750	.16000	.16250	.16500	.16750
.07000	-.51920	-.53812	-.55712	-.57622	-.59540	-.61467	-.63402	-.65345	-.67297	-.69256
.07250	-.49584	-.51447	-.53318	-.55199	-.57087	-.58984	-.60890	-.62803	-.64724	-.66654
.07500	-.47301	-.49135	-.50978	-.52830	-.54689	-.56558	-.58434	-.60318	-.62210	-.64110
.07750	-.45069	-.46876	-.48690	-.50514	-.52345	-.54185	-.56033	-.57889	-.59752	-.61623
.08000	-.42887	-.44666	-.46454	-.48250	-.50054	-.51866	-.53686	-.55514	-.57349	-.59192
.08250	-.40753	-.42506	-.44266	-.46036	-.47813	-.49598	-.51391	-.53191	-.54999	-.56815
.08500	-.38666	-.40393	-.42128	-.43870	-.45621	-.47380	-.49146	-.50920	-.52701	-.54490
.08750	-.36625	-.38327	-.40036	-.41753	-.43478	-.45211	-.46951	-.48699	-.50454	-.52216
.09000	-.34629	-.36306	-.37990	-.39682	-.41382	-.43089	-.44804	-.46526	-.48256	-.49992
.09250	-.32677	-.34329	-.35989	-.37656	-.39332	-.41014	-.42704	-.44401	-.46106	-.47817
.09500	-.30767	-.32395	-.34031	-.35675	-.37326	-.38984	-.40650	-.42323	-.44002	-.45689
.09750	-.28898	-.30503	-.32116	-.33736	-.35363	-.36998	-.38640	-.40289	-.41945	-.43607
.10000	-.27070	-.28652	-.30242	-.31839	-.33443	-.35055	-.36674	-.38299	-.39931	-.41570
.10250	-.25281	-.26841	-.28408	-.29983	-.31565	-.33153	-.34749	-.36352	-.37961	-.39577
.10500	-.23530	-.25068	-.26614	-.28166	-.29726	-.31293	-.32866	-.34446	-.36033	-.37626
.10750	-.21817	-.23333	-.24857	-.26389	-.27927	-.29471	-.31023	-.32581	-.34146	-.35717
.11000	-.20139	-.21635	-.23138	-.24648	-.26165	-.27689	-.29219	-.30756	-.32299	-.33849
.11250	-.18498	-.19973	-.21456	-.22945	-.24441	-.25944	-.27453	-.28969	-.30491	-.32020
.11500	-.16890	-.18346	-.19808	-.21277	-.22753	-.24236	-.25724	-.27220	-.28721	-.30229
.11750	-.15317	-.16753	-.18195	-.19645	-.21101	-.22563	-.24032	-.25507	-.26988	-.28476
.12000	-.13776	-.15193	-.16616	-.18046	-.19482	-.20925	-.22375	-.23830	-.25292	-.26759
.12250	-.12267	-.13665	-.15069	-.16480	-.17898	-.19322	-.20752	-.22188	-.23630	-.25078
.12500	-.10789	-.12169	-.13555	-.14947	-.16346	-.17751	-.19162	-.20579	-.22003	-.23432
.12750	-.09342	-.10703	-.12071	-.13446	-.14826	-.16213	-.17605	-.19004	-.20409	-.21819
.13000	-.07924	-.09268	-.10618	-.11975	-.13337	-.14706	-.16081	-.17461	-.18847	-.20240
.13250	-.06535	-.07862	-.09195	-.10534	-.11879	-.13230	-.14587	-.15950	-.17318	-.18692
.13500	-.05175	-.06484	-.07800	-.09122	-.10450	-.11784	-.13123	-.14469	-.15820	-.17176
.13750	-.03841	-.05134	-.06434	-.07739	-.09050	-.10367	-.11689	-.13018	-.14352	-.15691
.14000	-.02535	-.03812	-.05095	-.06383	-.07678	-.08978	-.10284	-.11596	-.12913	-.14235
.14250	-.01255	-.02516	-.03782	-.05055	-.06333	-.07618	-.08907	-.10202	-.11503	-.12809
.14500	.00000	-.01245	-.02496	-.03753	-.05016	-.06284	-.07558	-.08837	-.10121	-.11411
.14750	.01230	.00000	-.01236	-.02477	-.03724	-.04977	-.06235	-.07498	-.08767	-.10041
.15000	.02435	.01221	.00000	-.01226	-.02458	-.03695	-.04938	-.06186	-.07439	-.08698
.15250	.03617	.02417	.01211	.00000	-.01217	-.02439	-.03667	-.04900	-.06138	-.07381
.15500	.04776	.03590	.02399	.01202	.00000	-.01208	-.02421	-.03639	-.04862	-.06090
.15750	.05912	.04741	.03564	.02381	.01193	.00000	-.01198	-.02402	-.03611	-.04824
.16000	.07027	.05869	.04706	.03537	.02363	.01184	0.00000	-.01189	-.02384	-.03583
.16250	.08119	.06975	.05826	.04671	.03511	.02346	.01175	.00000	-.01180	-.02365
.16500	.09191	.08060	.06924	.05783	.04636	.03485	.02328	.01166	.00000	-.01171
.16750	.10242	.09125	.08002	.06874	.05740	.04602	.03459	.02311	.01158	.00000
.17000	.11274	.10169	.09059	.07944	.06823	.05698	.04568	.03433	.02293	.01149
.17250	.12286	.11193	.10096	.08994	.07886	.06774	.05656	.04534	.03408	.02276
.17500	.13278	.12198	.11114	.10024	.08929	.07829	.06724	.05615	.04501	.03382
.17750	.14252	.13185	.12112	.11034	.09952	.08864	.07772	.06675	.05574	.04468
.18000	.15208	.14153	.13092	.12026	.10956	.09880	.08800	.07716	.06626	.05533
.18250	.16147	.15103	.14054	.13000	.11941	.10877	.09809	.08737	.07650	.06578
.18500	.17068	.16035	.14997	.13955	.12908	.11856	.10800	.09739	.08674	.07604
.18750	.17972	.16950	.15924	.14893	.13857	.12817	.11772	.10723	.09669	.08611
.19000	.18859	.17849	.16834	.15814	.14789	.13760	.12727	.11689	.10647	.09600
.19250	.19730	.18731	.17727	.16718	.15704	.14686	.13664	.12637	.11606	.10571
.19500	.20586	.19597	.18604	.17605	.16603	.15596	.14584	.13568	.12548	.11524
.19750	.21426	.20448	.19465	.18477	.17485	.16489	.15488	.14483	.13473	.12460
.20000	.22251	.21283	.20310	.19333	.18351	.17365	.16375	.15381	.14382	.13379
.20250	.23061	.22103	.21141	.20174	.19202	.18227	.17247	.16263	.15274	.14282
.20500	.23857	.22909	.21957	.21000	.20038	.19073	.18103	.17129	.16151	.15169
.20750	.24639	.23701	.22758	.21811	.20859	.19904	.18944	.17980	.17012	.16040

POINT TABLES: ORIGINAL LOAN TERM: 180 MONTHS LOAN PREPAID IN: 180 MONTHS

CONTRACT RATE

EFFECTIVE YIELD	.17000	.17250	.17500	.17750	.18000	.18250	.18500	.18750	.19000	.19250
.07000	-.71223	-.73198	-.75181	-.77171	-.79169	-.81174	-.83186	-.85204	-.87230	-.89262
.07250	-.68591	-.70536	-.72488	-.74448	-.76414	-.78388	-.80369	-.82357	-.84351	-.86353
.07500	-.66018	-.67933	-.69855	-.71785	-.73722	-.75665	-.77616	-.79574	-.81538	-.83508
.07750	-.63502	-.65388	-.67281	-.69182	-.71089	-.73004	-.74925	-.76852	-.78787	-.80727
.08000	-.61042	-.62900	-.64765	-.66637	-.68515	-.70401	-.72293	-.74192	-.76097	-.78009
.08250	-.58637	-.60467	-.62304	-.64148	-.65999	-.67856	-.69720	-.71591	-.73467	-.75350
.08500	-.56285	-.58088	-.59898	-.61714	-.63538	-.65368	-.67204	-.69047	-.70896	-.72751
.08750	-.53985	-.55762	-.57545	-.59335	-.61131	-.62934	-.64743	-.66559	-.68380	-.70208
.09000	-.51736	-.53486	-.55243	-.57007	-.58777	-.60553	-.62336	-.64125	-.65920	-.67722
.09250	-.49535	-.51260	-.52992	-.54730	-.56474	-.58225	-.59982	-.61745	-.63514	-.65289
.09500	-.47382	-.49083	-.50789	-.52502	-.54222	-.55947	-.57679	-.59417	-.61160	-.62910
.09750	-.45276	-.46952	-.48634	-.50323	-.52018	-.53719	-.55426	-.57139	-.58857	-.60582
.10000	-.43216	-.44868	-.46526	-.48191	-.49862	-.51538	-.53221	-.54910	-.56604	-.58304
.10250	-.41199	-.42828	-.44463	-.46104	-.47752	-.49405	-.51064	-.52729	-.54399	-.56075
.10500	-.39226	-.40832	-.42444	-.44063	-.45687	-.47317	-.48953	-.50594	-.52242	-.53894
.10750	-.37295	-.38879	-.40468	-.42064	-.43666	-.45273	-.46887	-.48505	-.50130	-.51759
.11000	-.35405	-.36967	-.38534	-.40108	-.41688	-.43273	-.44864	-.46461	-.48063	-.49670
.11250	-.33554	-.35095	-.36641	-.38194	-.39752	-.41315	-.42885	-.44459	-.46039	-.47625
.11500	-.31743	-.33262	-.34788	-.36319	-.37856	-.39399	-.40947	-.42500	-.44058	-.45622
.11750	-.29969	-.31468	-.32973	-.34484	-.36000	-.37522	-.39049	-.40581	-.42119	-.43662
.12000	-.28232	-.29712	-.31196	-.32687	-.34183	-.35684	-.37191	-.38703	-.40220	-.41742
.12250	-.26532	-.27991	-.29457	-.30927	-.32403	-.33885	-.35372	-.36863	-.38360	-.39862
.12500	-.24866	-.26307	-.27753	-.29204	-.30661	-.32123	-.33590	-.35062	-.36539	-.38021
.12750	-.23235	-.24657	-.26084	-.27516	-.28954	-.30397	-.31845	-.33298	-.34755	-.36218
.13000	-.21637	-.23040	-.24449	-.25863	-.27282	-.28706	-.30135	-.31569	-.33008	-.34452
.13250	-.20072	-.21457	-.22847	-.24243	-.25644	-.27050	-.28460	-.29876	-.31297	-.32722
.13500	-.18538	-.19906	-.21278	-.22656	-.24039	-.25427	-.26820	-.28217	-.29620	-.31027
.13750	-.17036	-.18386	-.19741	-.21101	-.22467	-.23837	-.25212	-.26592	-.27977	-.29366
.14000	-.15563	-.16896	-.18235	-.19578	-.20926	-.22279	-.23637	-.24999	-.26367	-.27738
.14250	-.14120	-.15437	-.16758	-.18085	-.19416	-.20752	-.22093	-.23439	-.24789	-.26143
.14500	-.12706	-.14006	-.15311	-.16621	-.17936	-.19256	-.20580	-.21909	-.23242	-.24580
.14750	-.11320	-.12604	-.13893	-.15187	-.16486	-.17789	-.19097	-.20410	-.21727	-.23048
.15000	-.09961	-.11230	-.12503	-.13781	-.15064	-.16351	-.17644	-.18940	-.20241	-.21546
.15250	-.08629	-.09882	-.11140	-.12403	-.13670	-.14942	-.16218	-.17499	-.18784	-.20074
.15500	-.07323	-.08561	-.09804	-.11051	-.12303	-.13560	-.14821	-.16086	-.17356	-.18630
.15750	-.06043	-.07266	-.08494	-.09726	-.10963	-.12205	-.13451	-.14701	-.15956	-.17215
.16000	-.04787	-.05996	-.07209	-.08427	-.09649	-.10876	-.12107	-.13343	-.14583	-.15826
.16250	-.03555	-.04750	-.05949	-.07153	-.08361	-.09573	-.10790	-.12011	-.13236	-.14465
.16500	-.02347	-.03528	-.04713	-.05903	-.07097	-.08295	-.09498	-.10704	-.11915	-.13130
.16750	-.01162	-.02329	-.03501	-.04677	-.05857	-.07041	-.08230	-.09423	-.10619	-.11820
.17000	.00000	-.01154	-.02311	-.03474	-.04640	-.05811	-.06986	-.08165	-.09348	-.10535
.17250	.01140	.00000	-.01145	-.02294	-.03447	-.04605	-.05766	-.06932	-.08101	-.09275
.17500	.02259	.01132	.00000	-.01136	-.02276	-.03421	-.04569	-.05722	-.06878	-.08038
.17750	.03357	.02242	.01123	.00000	-.01127	-.02259	-.03395	-.04534	-.05677	-.06824
.18000	.04435	.03332	.02226	.01115	.00000	-.01119	-.02242	-.03369	-.04499	-.05633
.18250	.05492	.04402	.03308	.02209	.01107	.00000	-.01110	-.02225	-.03343	-.04465
.18500	.06530	.05452	.04370	.03283	.02193	.01098	.00000	-.01102	-.02208	-.03317
.18750	.07549	.06482	.05412	.04337	.03259	.02176	.01090	.00000	-.01094	-.02191
.19000	.08549	.07494	.06435	.05372	.04305	.03235	.02160	.01082	.00000	-.01085
.19250	.09531	.08488	.07440	.06388	.05333	.04274	.03211	.02144	.01074	.00000
.19500	.10495	.09463	.08427	.07386	.06342	.05294	.04242	.03187	.02128	.01066
.19750	.11442	.10421	.09395	.08366	.07333	.06296	.05255	.04211	.03164	.02112
.20000	.12372	.11361	.10347	.09328	.08306	.07280	.06250	.05217	.04180	.03140
.20250	.13285	.12285	.11281	.10273	.09262	.08246	.07227	.06205	.05179	.04150
.20500	.14183	.13193	.12199	.11201	.10200	.09195	.08187	.07175	.06160	.05141
.20750	.15064	.14084	.13100	.12113	.11122	.10128	.09130	.08128	.07124	.06115

CONTRACT RATE

EFFECTIVE YIELD	.19500	.19750	.20000	.20250	.20500	.20750
.07000	-.91301	-.93347	-.95398	-.97456	-.99521	-1.01591
.07250	-.88360	-.90374	-.92394	-.94421	-.96453	-.98491
.07500	-.85485	-.87468	-.89458	-.91453	-.93454	-.95462
.07750	-.82674	-.84628	-.86587	-.88552	-.90523	-.92500
.08000	-.79926	-.81850	-.83780	-.85716	-.87657	-.89604
.08250	-.77239	-.79134	-.81035	-.82942	-.84854	-.86772
.08500	-.74612	-.76479	-.78351	-.80230	-.82114	-.84003
.08750	-.72042	-.73881	-.75727	-.77577	-.79434	-.81295
.09000	-.69528	-.71341	-.73159	-.74983	-.76812	-.78647
.09250	-.67070	-.68856	-.70648	-.72445	-.74248	-.76056
.09500	-.64665	-.66425	-.68191	-.69963	-.71740	-.73521
.09750	-.62312	-.64047	-.65788	-.67534	-.69285	-.71042
.10000	-.60009	-.61720	-.63436	-.65158	-.66884	-.68616
.10250	-.57757	-.59443	-.61135	-.62832	-.64535	-.66242
.10500	-.55552	-.57215	-.58884	-.60557	-.62235	-.63918
.10750	-.53394	-.55034	-.56680	-.58330	-.59985	-.61645
.11000	-.51282	-.52900	-.54522	-.56150	-.57782	-.59419
.11250	-.49215	-.50810	-.52411	-.54016	-.55626	-.57241
.11500	-.47191	-.48765	-.50343	-.51927	-.53515	-.55108
.11750	-.45209	-.46762	-.48319	-.49882	-.51448	-.53020
.12000	-.43269	-.44801	-.46338	-.47879	-.49425	-.50975
.12250	-.41369	-.42881	-.44397	-.45918	-.47443	-.48973
.12500	-.39508	-.41000	-.42496	-.43997	-.45502	-.47012
.12750	-.37686	-.39158	-.40635	-.42116	-.43601	-.45091
.13000	-.35900	-.37354	-.38811	-.40273	-.41739	-.43210
.13250	-.34152	-.35586	-.37025	-.38468	-.39915	-.41367
.13500	-.32438	-.33854	-.35275	-.36699	-.38128	-.39562
.13750	-.30759	-.32158	-.33560	-.34967	-.36377	-.37792
.14000	-.29114	-.30495	-.31880	-.33269	-.34662	-.36059
.14250	-.27502	-.28866	-.30233	-.31605	-.32980	-.34360
.14500	-.25922	-.27269	-.28619	-.29974	-.31333	-.32695
.14750	-.24374	-.25703	-.27037	-.28375	-.29717	-.31063
.15000	-.22856	-.24169	-.25487	-.26808	-.28134	-.29463
.15250	-.21367	-.22665	-.23967	-.25272	-.26582	-.27895
.15500	-.19908	-.21190	-.22476	-.23766	-.25060	-.26357
.15750	-.18477	-.19744	-.21015	-.22289	-.23568	-.24850
.16000	-.17074	-.18326	-.19582	-.20841	-.22104	-.23371
.16250	-.15698	-.16935	-.18176	-.19421	-.20669	-.21921
.16500	-.14349	-.15571	-.16798	-.18028	-.19262	-.20499
.16750	-.13025	-.14233	-.15445	-.16661	-.17881	-.19104
.17000	-.11726	-.12921	-.14119	-.15321	-.16526	-.17735
.17250	-.10452	-.11633	-.12818	-.14006	-.15198	-.16393
.17500	-.09202	-.10370	-.11541	-.12716	-.13894	-.15075
.17750	-.07975	-.09130	-.10288	-.11449	-.12614	-.13783
.18000	-.06771	-.07913	-.09058	-.10207	-.11359	-.12514
.18250	-.05590	-.06719	-.07851	-.08987	-.10127	-.11269
.18500	-.04430	-.05547	-.06667	-.07790	-.08917	-.10047
.18750	-.03292	-.04396	-.05504	-.06615	-.07730	-.08848
.19000	-.02174	-.03267	-.04363	-.05462	-.06564	-.07670
.19250	-.01077	-.02158	-.03242	-.04329	-.05420	-.06514
.19500	.00000	-.01069	-.02142	-.03218	-.04296	-.05379
.19750	.01058	.00000	-.01061	-.02126	-.03193	-.04264
.20000	.02097	.01050	.00000	-.01053	-.02110	-.03169
.20250	.03117	.02081	.01042	.00000	-.01045	-.02094
.20500	.04119	.03094	.02066	.01035	.00000	-.01038
.20750	.05104	.04089	.03072	.02051	.01027	.00000

POINT TABLES: ORIGINAL LOAN TERM: 240 MONTHS LOAN PREPAID IN: 60 MONTHS

CONTRACT RATE

EFFECTIVE YIELD	.07000	.07250	.07500	.07750	.08000	.08250	.08500	.08750	.09000	.09250
.07000	-.00000	-.00991	-.01985	-.02983	-.03983	-.04986	-.05992	-.07001	-.08012	-.09026
.07250	.00984	.00000	-.00987	-.01977	-.02970	-.03966	-.04964	-.05966	-.06970	-.07977
.07500	.01956	.00980	.00000	-.00983	-.01968	-.02957	-.03949	-.04943	-.05940	-.06939
.07750	.02917	.01948	.00976	-.00000	-.00979	-.01960	-.02944	-.03931	-.04921	-.05913
.08000	.03867	.02905	.01940	.00971	.00000	-.00974	-.01952	-.02932	-.03914	-.04899
.08250	.04806	.03851	.02893	.01932	.00967	.00000	-.00970	-.01943	-.02919	-.03897
.08500	.05734	.04787	.03835	.02881	.01924	.00963	0.00000	-.00966	-.01935	-.02906
.08750	.06652	.05711	.04767	.03819	.02869	.01915	.00959	-.00000	-.00962	-.01926
.09000	.07559	.06625	.05688	.04747	.03803	.02857	.01907	.00955	.00000	-.00958
.09250	.08456	.07528	.06598	.05664	.04727	.03787	.02845	.01899	.00951	0.00000
.09500	.09342	.08421	.07498	.06570	.05640	.04707	.03771	.02832	.01891	.00947
.09750	.10218	.09304	.08387	.07467	.06543	.05617	.04687	.03755	.02820	.01883
.10000	.11084	.10177	.09266	.08353	.07436	.06516	.05593	.04667	.03739	.02808
.10250	.11941	.11040	.10136	.09228	.08318	.07405	.06488	.05569	.04647	.03723
.10500	.12787	.11893	.10995	.10094	.09190	.08283	.07373	.06461	.05545	.04627
.10750	.13624	.12736	.11845	.10950	.10053	.09152	.08248	.07342	.06433	.05521
.11000	.14451	.13569	.12684	.11796	.10905	.10011	.09114	.08214	.07311	.06406
.11250	.15269	.14393	.13515	.12633	.11748	.10860	.09969	.09075	.08179	.07280
.11500	.16077	.15208	.14336	.13460	.12581	.11699	.10815	.09927	.09037	.08144
.11750	.16876	.16013	.15147	.14278	.13405	.12529	.11651	.10769	.09885	.08998
.12000	.17666	.16810	.15949	.15086	.14219	.13350	.12477	.11602	.10724	.09843
.12250	.18448	.17597	.16742	.15885	.15025	.14161	.13295	.12425	.11553	.10679
.12500	.19220	.18375	.17527	.16675	.15821	.14963	.14103	.13239	.12373	.11505
.12750	.19983	.19144	.18302	.17456	.16608	.15756	.14902	.14044	.13184	.12321
.13000	.20738	.19905	.19068	.18229	.17386	.16540	.15692	.14840	.13986	.13129
.13250	.21484	.20657	.19826	.18992	.18155	.17315	.16473	.15627	.14778	.13927
.13500	.22222	.21400	.20575	.19747	.18916	.18082	.17245	.16405	.15562	.14716
.13750	.22951	.22135	.21316	.20494	.19668	.18840	.18008	.17174	.16337	.15497
.14000	.23672	.22862	.22048	.21232	.20412	.19589	.18763	.17934	.17103	.16269
.14250	.24385	.23581	.22773	.21961	.21147	.20330	.19510	.18687	.17861	.17032
.14500	.25090	.24291	.23489	.22683	.21874	.21062	.20248	.19430	.18610	.17787
.14750	.25787	.24993	.24196	.23396	.22593	.21787	.20977	.20165	.19350	.18533
.15000	.26476	.25688	.24896	.24102	.23304	.22503	.21699	.20892	.20083	.19271
.15250	.27157	.26374	.25588	.24799	.24007	.23211	.22413	.21611	.20807	.20000
.15500	.27831	.27053	.26273	.25489	.24701	.23911	.23118	.22322	.21523	.20722
.15750	.28497	.27725	.26949	.26170	.25389	.24604	.23816	.23025	.22232	.21435
.16000	.29155	.28388	.27618	.26845	.26068	.25288	.24506	.23720	.22932	.22141
.16250	.29806	.29045	.28279	.27511	.26740	.25965	.25188	.24407	.23624	.22838
.16500	.30450	.29693	.28934	.28170	.27404	.26635	.25862	.25087	.24309	.23528
.16750	.31087	.30335	.29580	.28822	.28061	.27297	.26529	.25759	.24986	.24211
.17000	.31716	.30970	.30220	.29467	.28710	.27951	.27189	.26424	.25656	.24885
.17250	.32338	.31597	.30852	.30104	.29353	.28598	.27841	.27081	.26318	.25552
.17500	.32954	.32217	.31477	.30734	.29988	.29238	.28486	.27731	.26973	.26212
.17750	.33562	.32831	.32095	.31357	.30616	.29871	.29124	.28374	.27621	.26865
.18000	.34164	.33437	.32707	.31973	.31237	.30497	.29755	.29009	.28261	.27510
.18250	.34759	.34037	.33311	.32583	.31851	.31116	.30379	.29638	.28894	.28148
.18500	.35347	.34630	.33909	.33185	.32458	.31728	.30995	.30260	.29521	.28779
.18750	.35929	.35216	.34500	.33781	.33059	.32334	.31605	.30874	.30140	.29404
.19000	.36504	.35796	.35085	.34370	.33653	.32932	.32209	.31482	.30753	.30021
.19250	.37073	.36370	.35663	.34953	.34240	.33524	.32805	.32083	.31359	.30631
.19500	.37636	.36937	.36235	.35529	.34821	.34110	.33395	.32678	.31958	.31235
.19750	.38192	.37498	.36800	.36099	.35396	.34689	.33979	.33266	.32551	.31832
.20000	.38742	.38052	.37359	.36663	.35964	.35261	.34556	.33848	.33137	.32423
.20250	.39286	.38601	.37912	.37220	.36525	.35827	.35127	.34423	.33716	.33007
.20500	.39824	.39143	.38459	.37771	.37081	.36388	.35691	.34992	.34290	.33585
.20750	.40356	.39679	.39000	.38317	.37630	.36941	.36249	.35554	.34857	.34156

POINT TABLES: ORIGINAL LOAN TERM: 240 MONTHS LOAN PREPAID IN: 60 MONTHS

CONTRACT RATE

EFFECTIVE YIELD	.09500	.09750	.10000	.10250	.10500	.10750	.11000	.11250	.11500	.11750
.07000	-.10043	-.11062	-.12083	-.13106	-.14131	-.15159	-.16188	-.17219	-.18253	-.19287
.07250	-.08986	-.09997	-.11011	-.12027	-.13045	-.14066	-.15088	-.16112	-.17138	-.18166
.07500	-.07941	-.08945	-.09952	-.10961	-.11972	-.12985	-.14000	-.15017	-.16036	-.17056
.07750	-.06908	-.07905	-.08905	-.09907	-.10911	-.11917	-.12924	-.13934	-.14946	-.15960
.08000	-.05887	-.06877	-.07870	-.08864	-.09861	-.10860	-.11861	-.12864	-.13869	-.14875
.08250	-.04878	-.05861	-.06846	-.07834	-.08824	-.09816	-.10810	-.11806	-.12804	-.13803
.08500	-.03880	-.04856	-.05834	-.06815	-.07798	-.08783	-.09771	-.10760	-.11751	-.12743
.08750	-.02893	-.03862	-.04834	-.05808	-.06784	-.07763	-.08743	-.09725	-.10709	-.11695
.09000	-.01918	-.02880	-.03845	-.04812	-.05782	-.06753	-.07727	-.08702	-.09680	-.10659
.09250	-.00953	-.01909	-.02867	-.03828	-.04791	-.05755	-.06722	-.07691	-.08662	-.09635
.09500	.00000	-.00949	-.01901	-.02855	-.03811	-.04769	-.05729	-.06691	-.07655	-.08621
.09750	.00943	.00000	-.00945	-.01892	-.02842	-.03793	-.04747	-.05703	-.06660	-.07620
.10000	.01874	.00938	0.00000	-.00941	-.01884	-.02829	-.03776	-.04725	-.05676	-.06629
.10250	.02796	.01866	.00934	.00000	-.00937	-.01875	-.02816	-.03759	-.04703	-.05650
.10500	.03707	.02783	.01858	.00930	.00000	-.00932	-.01867	-.02803	-.03741	-.04682
.10750	.04607	.03690	.02771	.01850	.00926	0.00000	-.00928	-.01858	-.02790	-.03724
.11000	.05498	.04587	.03674	.02759	.01842	.00922	.00000	-.00924	-.01850	-.02777
.11250	.06378	.05474	.04567	.03658	.02747	.01833	.00918	.00000	-.00920	-.01841
.11500	.07248	.06350	.05450	.04547	.03642	.02735	.01825	.00914	.00000	-.00915
.11750	.08109	.07217	.06323	.05426	.04527	.03626	.02722	.01817	.00909	.00000
.12000	.08960	.08074	.07186	.06295	.05402	.04507	.03609	.02710	.01809	.00905
.12250	.09801	.08921	.08039	.07154	.06267	.05378	.04487	.03593	.02698	.01800
.12500	.10633	.09759	.08883	.08004	.07123	.06240	.05354	.04467	.03577	.02686
.12750	.11456	.10588	.09717	.08844	.07969	.07092	.06212	.05330	.04447	.03561
.13000	.12269	.11407	.10542	.09675	.08806	.07934	.07060	.06184	.05306	.04426
.13250	.13073	.12217	.11358	.10496	.09633	.08767	.07899	.07029	.06157	.05282
.13500	.13868	.13018	.12164	.11309	.10451	.09591	.08728	.07864	.06997	.06129
.13750	.14654	.13809	.12962	.12112	.11260	.10405	.09549	.08690	.07829	.06966
.14000	.15432	.14593	.13751	.12906	.12060	.11211	.10360	.09506	.08651	.07794
.14250	.16201	.15367	.14530	.13692	.12851	.12007	.11162	.10314	.09464	.08613
.14500	.16961	.16133	.15302	.14468	.13633	.12795	.11955	.11113	.10268	.09422
.14750	.17713	.16890	.16064	.15236	.14406	.13574	.12739	.11903	.11064	.10223
.15000	.18456	.17638	.16818	.15996	.15171	.14344	.13515	.12684	.11850	.11015
.15250	.19191	.18379	.17564	.16747	.15928	.15106	.14282	.13456	.12628	.11798
.15500	.19918	.19111	.18302	.17490	.16676	.15859	.15041	.14220	.13397	.12572
.15750	.20636	.19835	.19031	.18224	.17416	.16604	.15791	.14976	.14158	.13338
.16000	.21347	.20551	.19752	.18951	.18147	.17341	.16533	.15723	.14910	.14096
.16250	.22050	.21259	.20465	.19669	.18871	.18070	.17267	.16462	.15654	.14845
.16500	.22745	.21959	.21170	.20379	.19586	.18790	.17993	.17193	.16390	.15586
.16750	.23432	.22651	.21868	.21082	.20294	.19503	.18710	.17915	.17118	.16319
.17000	.24112	.23336	.22558	.21777	.20993	.20208	.19420	.18630	.17838	.17044
.17250	.24784	.24013	.23240	.22464	.21686	.20905	.20122	.19337	.18550	.17761
.17500	.25449	.24683	.23914	.23143	.22370	.21594	.20816	.20036	.19254	.18470
.17750	.26106	.25345	.24582	.23815	.23047	.22276	.21503	.20728	.19951	.19171
.18000	.26756	.26000	.25241	.24480	.23717	.22951	.22182	.21412	.20639	.19865
.18250	.27399	.26648	.25894	.25138	.24379	.23618	.22854	.22089	.21321	.20551
.18500	.28035	.27289	.26539	.25788	.25034	.24277	.23519	.22758	.21995	.21230
.18750	.28664	.27922	.27178	.26431	.25681	.24930	.24176	.23420	.22661	.21901
.19000	.29286	.28549	.27809	.27067	.26322	.25575	.24826	.24074	.23321	.22565
.19250	.29901	.29169	.28433	.27696	.26956	.26213	.25469	.24722	.23973	.23222
.19500	.30510	.29782	.29051	.28318	.27582	.26844	.26104	.25362	.24618	.23871
.19750	.31111	.30388	.29662	.28933	.28202	.27469	.26733	.25996	.25256	.24514
.20000	.31706	.30987	.30266	.29542	.28815	.28086	.27355	.26622	.25887	.25149
.20250	.32295	.31580	.30863	.30144	.29422	.28697	.27971	.27242	.26511	.25778
.20500	.32877	.32167	.31454	.30739	.30022	.29302	.28579	.27855	.27129	.26400
.20750	.33453	.32747	.32039	.31328	.30615	.29899	.29182	.28462	.27739	.27015

POINT TABLES: ORIGINAL LOAN TERM: 240 MONTHS LOAN PREPAID IN: 60 MONTHS

CONTRACT RATE

EFFECTIVE YIELD	.12000	.12250	.12500	.12750	.13000	.13250	.13500	.13750	.14000	.14250
.07000	-.20324	-.21362	-.22402	-.23443	-.24485	-.25529	-.26574	-.27620	-.28668	-.29716
.07250	-.19195	-.20226	-.21258	-.22292	-.23328	-.24364	-.25402	-.26442	-.27482	-.28523
.07500	-.18079	-.19102	-.20128	-.21155	-.22183	-.23213	-.24244	-.25276	-.26309	-.27344
.07750	-.16975	-.17992	-.19010	-.20030	-.21051	-.22074	-.23098	-.24123	-.25150	-.26177
.08000	-.15884	-.16893	-.17905	-.18918	-.19932	-.20948	-.21965	-.22984	-.24003	-.25024
.08250	-.14805	-.15808	-.16812	-.17818	-.18826	-.19835	-.20845	-.21857	-.22869	-.23883
.08500	-.13738	-.14734	-.15732	-.16731	-.17732	-.18734	-.19738	-.20742	-.21748	-.22755
.08750	-.12683	-.13672	-.14663	-.15656	-.16650	-.17646	-.18642	-.19640	-.20640	-.21640
.09000	-.11640	-.12623	-.13607	-.14593	-.15580	-.16569	-.17559	-.18551	-.19544	-.20537
.09250	-.10609	-.11585	-.12563	-.13542	-.14523	-.15505	-.16488	-.17473	-.18460	-.19447
.09500	-.09589	-.10559	-.11530	-.12503	-.13477	-.14453	-.15430	-.16408	-.17388	-.18368
.09750	-.08581	-.09544	-.10509	-.11475	-.12443	-.13412	-.14382	-.15354	-.16328	-.17302
.10000	-.07584	-.08541	-.09499	-.10459	-.11420	-.12383	-.13347	-.14313	-.15279	-.16247
.10250	-.06598	-.07549	-.08500	-.09454	-.10409	-.11365	-.12323	-.13282	-.14243	-.15205
.10500	-.05624	-.06568	-.07513	-.08460	-.09409	-.10359	-.11311	-.12263	-.13218	-.14173
.10750	-.04660	-.05598	-.06537	-.07478	-.08420	-.09364	-.10309	-.11256	-.12204	-.13153
.11000	-.03707	-.04638	-.05571	-.06506	-.07442	-.08380	-.09319	-.10260	-.11201	-.12145
.11250	-.02765	-.03690	-.04617	-.05545	-.06475	-.07407	-.08340	-.09274	-.10210	-.11147
.11500	-.01833	-.02752	-.03673	-.04595	-.05519	-.06444	-.07371	-.08300	-.09230	-.10161
.11750	-.00911	-.01824	-.02739	-.03655	-.04573	-.05493	-.06414	-.07336	-.08260	-.09185
.12000	0.00000	-.00907	-.01816	-.02726	-.03638	-.04552	-.05467	-.06383	-.07301	-.08220
.12250	.00901	.00000	-.00903	-.01807	-.02713	-.03621	-.04530	-.05441	-.06353	-.07266
.12500	.01792	.00897	.00000	-.00899	-.01799	-.02701	-.03604	-.04509	-.05415	-.06322
.12750	.02673	.01784	.00893	0.00000	-.00894	-.01790	-.02688	-.03587	-.04487	-.05389
.13000	.03545	.02661	.01776	.00889	0.00000	-.00890	-.01782	-.02675	-.03570	-.04466
.13250	.04406	.03529	.02649	.01768	.00885	0.00000	-.00886	-.01774	-.02663	-.03553
.13500	.05259	.04386	.03512	.02637	.01759	.00880	0.00000	-.00882	-.01765	-.02650
.13750	.06101	.05235	.04366	.03496	.02625	.01751	.00876	0.00000	-.00878	-.01757
.14000	.06935	.06074	.05211	.04346	.03480	.02612	.01743	.00872	.00000	-.00874
.14250	.07759	.06903	.06046	.05187	.04326	.03464	.02600	.01735	.00868	.00000
.14500	.08574	.07724	.06872	.06019	.05163	.04307	.03448	.02588	.01727	.00864
.14750	.09380	.08536	.07689	.06841	.05991	.05140	.04287	.03432	.02576	.01719
.15000	.10177	.09338	.08497	.07654	.06810	.05964	.05116	.04267	.03416	.02564
.15250	.10966	.10132	.09296	.08459	.07619	.06779	.05936	.05092	.04247	.03400
.15500	.11746	.10917	.10086	.09254	.08420	.07585	.06748	.05909	.05069	.04227
.15750	.12517	.11693	.10868	.10041	.09212	.08382	.07550	.06717	.05882	.05045
.16000	.13280	.12461	.11641	.10819	.09996	.09171	.08344	.07515	.06686	.05854
.16250	.14034	.13221	.12406	.11589	.10771	.09951	.09129	.08306	.07481	.06655
.16500	.14780	.13972	.13162	.12350	.11537	.10722	.09905	.09087	.08267	.07446
.16750	.15518	.14715	.13910	.13103	.12295	.11485	.10673	.09860	.09046	.08229
.17000	.16248	.15450	.14650	.13848	.13045	.12240	.11433	.10625	.09815	.09004
.17250	.16970	.16177	.15382	.14585	.13787	.12986	.12185	.11381	.10577	.09770
.17500	.17684	.16896	.16105	.15314	.14520	.13725	.12928	.12130	.11330	.10528
.17750	.18390	.17607	.16821	.16034	.15246	.14455	.13663	.12870	.12075	.11278
.18000	.19088	.18310	.17530	.16747	.15963	.15178	.14391	.13602	.12812	.12020
.18250	.19779	.19006	.18230	.17453	.16673	.15893	.15110	.14326	.13541	.12754
.18500	.20463	.19694	.18923	.18150	.17376	.16600	.15822	.15043	.14262	.13479
.18750	.21139	.20374	.19608	.18840	.18070	.17299	.16526	.15751	.14975	.14197
.19000	.21807	.21048	.20286	.19523	.18758	.17991	.17222	.16452	.15681	.14908
.19250	.22468	.21713	.20957	.20198	.19437	.18675	.17911	.17146	.16379	.15610
.19500	.23123	.22372	.21620	.20866	.20110	.19352	.18593	.17832	.17069	.16306
.19750	.23770	.23024	.22276	.21526	.20775	.20022	.19267	.18511	.17753	.16993
.20000	.24410	.23668	.22925	.22180	.21433	.20684	.19934	.19182	.18429	.17674
.20250	.25043	.24306	.23567	.22826	.22084	.21340	.20594	.19846	.19097	.18347
.20500	.25669	.24937	.24202	.23466	.22728	.21988	.21247	.20503	.19759	.19013
.20750	.26289	.25561	.24831	.24099	.23365	.22629	.21892	.21154	.20413	.19671

CONTRACT RATE

EFFECTIVE YIELD	.14500	.14750	.15000	.15250	.15500	.15750	.16000	.16250	.16500	.16750
.07000	-.30766	-.31816	-.32868	-.33920	-.34973	-.36027	-.37082	-.38137	-.39194	-.40250
.07250	-.29566	-.30609	-.31654	-.32699	-.33745	-.34792	-.35840	-.36889	-.37938	-.38987
.07500	-.28379	-.29416	-.30453	-.31492	-.32531	-.33571	-.34612	-.35653	-.36696	-.37739
.07750	-.27206	-.28236	-.29266	-.30298	-.31330	-.32363	-.33397	-.34432	-.35468	-.36504
.08000	-.26046	-.27068	-.28092	-.29117	-.30143	-.31169	-.32196	-.33224	-.34253	-.35282
.08250	-.24898	-.25914	-.26931	-.27949	-.28968	-.29988	-.31009	-.32030	-.33052	-.34075
.08500	-.23764	-.24773	-.25783	-.26795	-.27807	-.28820	-.29834	-.30849	-.31864	-.32880
.08750	-.22642	-.23645	-.24648	-.25653	-.26659	-.27665	-.28672	-.29680	-.30689	-.31699
.09000	-.21532	-.22529	-.23526	-.24524	-.25523	-.26523	-.27524	-.28525	-.29527	-.30530
.09250	-.20435	-.21425	-.22416	-.23407	-.24400	-.25393	-.26388	-.27383	-.28378	-.29375
.09500	-.19350	-.20334	-.21318	-.22303	-.23289	-.24276	-.25264	-.26253	-.27242	-.28232
.09750	-.18278	-.19254	-.20232	-.21211	-.22191	-.23171	-.24153	-.25135	-.26118	-.27102
.10000	-.17217	-.18187	-.19158	-.20131	-.21104	-.22079	-.23054	-.24030	-.25007	-.25985
.10250	-.16167	-.17132	-.18097	-.19063	-.20030	-.20998	-.21967	-.22937	-.23908	-.24879
.10500	-.15130	-.16088	-.17047	-.18007	-.18968	-.19929	-.20892	-.21856	-.22820	-.23786
.10750	-.14104	-.15055	-.16008	-.16962	-.17917	-.18873	-.19829	-.20787	-.21745	-.22704
.11000	-.13089	-.14035	-.14981	-.15929	-.16878	-.17827	-.18778	-.19729	-.20682	-.21635
.11250	-.12085	-.13025	-.13965	-.14907	-.15850	-.16793	-.17738	-.18684	-.19630	-.20577
.11500	-.11093	-.12026	-.12961	-.13897	-.14833	-.15771	-.16710	-.17649	-.18590	-.19531
.11750	-.10111	-.11039	-.11967	-.12897	-.13828	-.14760	-.15692	-.16626	-.17561	-.18496
.12000	-.09141	-.10062	-.10985	-.11909	-.12834	-.13760	-.14686	-.15614	-.16543	-.17472
.12250	-.08181	-.09096	-.10013	-.10931	-.11850	-.12770	-.13691	-.14613	-.15536	-.16460
.12500	-.07231	-.08141	-.09052	-.09964	-.10878	-.11792	-.12707	-.13623	-.14540	-.15458
.12750	-.06292	-.07196	-.08101	-.09008	-.09916	-.10824	-.11734	-.12644	-.13556	-.14468
.13000	-.05363	-.06262	-.07161	-.08062	-.08964	-.09867	-.10771	-.11676	-.12582	-.13488
.13250	-.04444	-.05337	-.06231	-.07127	-.08023	-.08920	-.09818	-.10718	-.11618	-.12519
.13500	-.03536	-.04423	-.05312	-.06201	-.07092	-.07984	-.08876	-.09770	-.10665	-.11560
.13750	-.02637	-.03519	-.04402	-.05286	-.06171	-.07057	-.07945	-.08833	-.09722	-.10612
.14000	-.01749	-.02625	-.03502	-.04381	-.05260	-.06141	-.07023	-.07906	-.08790	-.09674
.14250	-.00869	-.01740	-.02612	-.03485	-.04360	-.05235	-.06111	-.06989	-.07867	-.08746
.14500	0.00000	-.00865	-.01732	-.02600	-.03469	-.04339	-.05210	-.06082	-.06955	-.07828
.14750	.00860	.00000	-.00861	-.01724	-.02587	-.03452	-.04318	-.05184	-.06052	-.06921
.15000	.01711	.00856	.00000	-.00857	-.01715	-.02575	-.03435	-.04297	-.05159	-.06022
.15250	.02552	.01703	.00852	-.00000	-.00853	-.01707	-.02562	-.03419	-.04276	-.05134
.15500	.03384	.02540	.01695	.00848	0.00000	-.00849	-.01699	-.02550	-.03402	-.04255
.15750	.04207	.03368	.02528	.01687	.00844	.00000	-.00845	-.01691	-.02538	-.03386
.16000	.05022	.04188	.03353	.02516	.01679	.00840	.00000	-.00841	-.01683	-.02525
.16250	.05827	.04998	.04168	.03337	.02504	.01671	.00836	-.00000	-.00837	-.01675
.16500	.06624	.05800	.04975	.04149	.03321	.02492	.01663	.00832	.00000	-.00833
.16750	.07412	.06593	.05773	.04952	.04129	.03305	.02481	.01655	.00828	0.00000
.17000	.08192	.07378	.06562	.05746	.04928	.04110	.03290	.02469	.01647	.00824
.17250	.08963	.08154	.07343	.06532	.05719	.04905	.04090	.03274	.02457	.01639
.17500	.09726	.08921	.08116	.07309	.06501	.05692	.04882	.04071	.03259	.02445
.17750	.10480	.09681	.08880	.08078	.07275	.06471	.05666	.04859	.04052	.03243
.18000	.11227	.10432	.09636	.08839	.08041	.07241	.06441	.05639	.04836	.04032
.18250	.11965	.11175	.10384	.09592	.08798	.08003	.07207	.06410	.05612	.04813
.18500	.12696	.11910	.11124	.10336	.09547	.08757	.07966	.07174	.06380	.05586
.18750	.13418	.12638	.11856	.11073	.10289	.09503	.08717	.07929	.07140	.06350
.19000	.14133	.13357	.12580	.11802	.11022	.10241	.09459	.08676	.07892	.07106
.19250	.14840	.14069	.13297	.12523	.11748	.10971	.10194	.09415	.08635	.07855
.19500	.15540	.14773	.14005	.13236	.12465	.11694	.10921	.10146	.09371	.08595
.19750	.16232	.15470	.14707	.13942	.13176	.12408	.11640	.10870	.10099	.09328
.20000	.16917	.16159	.15400	.14640	.13878	.13115	.12351	.11586	.10820	.10052
.20250	.17595	.16841	.16087	.15331	.14573	.13815	.13055	.12294	.11532	.10770
.20500	.18265	.17516	.16766	.16014	.15261	.14507	.13752	.12995	.12238	.11479
.20750	.18928	.18184	.17438	.16690	.15942	.15192	.14441	.13689	.12935	.12181

POINT TABLES: ORIGINAL LOAN TERM: 240 MONTHS LOAN PREPAID IN: 60 MONTHS

EFFECTIVE YIELD	CONTRACT RATE .17000	.17250	.17500	.17750	.18000	.18250	.18500	.18750	.19000	.19250
.07000	-.41307	-.42365	-.43423	-.44482	-.45541	-.46601	-.47661	-.48721	-.49781	-.50842
.07250	-.40038	-.41089	-.42140	-.43192	-.44244	-.45297	-.46350	-.47403	-.48457	-.49511
.07500	-.38782	-.39826	-.40871	-.41916	-.42961	-.44007	-.45053	-.46100	-.47147	-.48194
.07750	-.37540	-.38578	-.39615	-.40654	-.41692	-.42732	-.43771	-.44811	-.45852	-.46892
.08000	-.36312	-.37343	-.38374	-.39406	-.40438	-.41470	-.42503	-.43537	-.44570	-.45604
.08250	-.35098	-.36122	-.37146	-.38171	-.39197	-.40223	-.41249	-.42276	-.43303	-.44330
.08500	-.33897	-.34914	-.35932	-.36950	-.37969	-.38989	-.40009	-.41029	-.42049	-.43070
.08750	-.32709	-.33720	-.34731	-.35743	-.36755	-.37768	-.38782	-.39796	-.40810	-.41824
.09000	-.31534	-.32539	-.33543	-.34549	-.35555	-.36561	-.37568	-.38576	-.39583	-.40592
.09250	-.30372	-.31370	-.32369	-.33368	-.34367	-.35368	-.36368	-.37369	-.38371	-.39372
.09500	-.29223	-.30215	-.31207	-.32200	-.33193	-.34187	-.35181	-.36176	-.37171	-.38167
.09750	-.28087	-.29072	-.30058	-.31044	-.32031	-.33019	-.34007	-.34996	-.35985	-.36974
.10000	-.26963	-.27942	-.28922	-.29902	-.30883	-.31864	-.32846	-.33828	-.34811	-.35794
.10250	-.25851	-.26824	-.27798	-.28772	-.29746	-.30721	-.31697	-.32673	-.33650	-.34627
.10500	-.24752	-.25718	-.26686	-.27654	-.28622	-.29591	-.30561	-.31531	-.32502	-.33473
.10750	-.23664	-.24625	-.25586	-.26548	-.27511	-.28474	-.29437	-.30401	-.31366	-.32331
.11000	-.22589	-.23543	-.24499	-.25454	-.26411	-.27368	-.28326	-.29284	-.30242	-.31202
.11250	-.21525	-.22474	-.23423	-.24373	-.25323	-.26275	-.27226	-.28178	-.29131	-.30084
.11500	-.20473	-.21415	-.22359	-.23303	-.24248	-.25193	-.26139	-.27085	-.28032	-.28979
.11750	-.19432	-.20369	-.21306	-.22245	-.23183	-.24123	-.25063	-.26003	-.26944	-.27886
.12000	-.18403	-.19334	-.20265	-.21198	-.22131	-.23064	-.23999	-.24933	-.25869	-.26804
.12250	-.17384	-.18310	-.19236	-.20162	-.21090	-.22017	-.22946	-.23875	-.24805	-.25735
.12500	-.16377	-.17297	-.18217	-.19138	-.20060	-.20982	-.21905	-.22828	-.23752	-.24676
.12750	-.15381	-.16295	-.17210	-.18125	-.19041	-.19957	-.20875	-.21792	-.22711	-.23630
.13000	-.14396	-.15304	-.16213	-.17123	-.18033	-.18944	-.19856	-.20768	-.21681	-.22594
.13250	-.13421	-.14324	-.15227	-.16131	-.17036	-.17942	-.18848	-.19754	-.20662	-.21569
.13500	-.12457	-.13354	-.14252	-.15151	-.16050	-.16950	-.17851	-.18752	-.19654	-.20556
.13750	-.11503	-.12395	-.13287	-.14180	-.15074	-.15969	-.16864	-.17760	-.18656	-.19553
.14000	-.10560	-.11446	-.12333	-.13221	-.14109	-.14998	-.15888	-.16779	-.17670	-.18561
.14250	-.09626	-.10507	-.11389	-.12271	-.13155	-.14038	-.14923	-.15808	-.16694	-.17580
.14500	-.08703	-.09579	-.10455	-.11332	-.12210	-.13089	-.13968	-.14848	-.15728	-.16609
.14750	-.07790	-.08660	-.09531	-.10403	-.11276	-.12149	-.13023	-.13898	-.14773	-.15649
.15000	-.06887	-.07752	-.08618	-.09484	-.10352	-.11220	-.12088	-.12958	-.13828	-.14698
.15250	-.05993	-.06853	-.07714	-.08575	-.09437	-.10300	-.11164	-.12028	-.12893	-.13758
.15500	-.05109	-.05964	-.06819	-.07676	-.08533	-.09390	-.10249	-.11108	-.11968	-.12828
.15750	-.04234	-.05084	-.05934	-.06786	-.07638	-.08490	-.09344	-.10198	-.11053	-.11908
.16000	-.03369	-.04214	-.05059	-.05905	-.06752	-.07600	-.08448	-.09297	-.10147	-.10997
.16250	-.02513	-.03353	-.04193	-.05034	-.05876	-.06719	-.07562	-.08407	-.09251	-.10097
.16500	-.01666	-.02501	-.03336	-.04173	-.05010	-.05847	-.06686	-.07525	-.08365	-.09205
.16750	-.00829	-.01658	-.02489	-.03320	-.04152	-.04985	-.05819	-.06653	-.07488	-.08323
.17000	.00000	-.00825	-.01650	-.02477	-.03304	-.04132	-.04961	-.05790	-.06620	-.07451
.17250	.00820	0.00000	-.00821	-.01642	-.02465	-.03288	-.04112	-.04936	-.05762	-.06587
.17500	.01631	.00816	0.00000	-.00817	-.01634	-.02453	-.03272	-.04092	-.04912	-.05733
.17750	.02434	.01623	.00812	.00000	-.00813	-.01627	-.02441	-.03256	-.04072	-.04888
.18000	.03228	.02422	.01616	.00808	-.00000	-.00809	-.01619	-.02429	-.03240	-.04052
.18250	.04013	.03212	.02410	.01608	.00804	.00000	-.00805	-.01611	-.02417	-.03224
.18500	.04790	.03994	.03197	.02399	.01600	.00800	.00000	-.00801	-.01603	-.02405
.18750	.05559	.04768	.03975	.03182	.02387	.01592	.00797	.00000	-.00797	-.01595
.19000	.06320	.05533	.04745	.03956	.03166	.02376	.01585	.00793	0.00000	-.00793
.19250	.07073	.06290	.05507	.04723	.03937	.03151	.02365	.01577	.00789	.00000
.19500	.07818	.07040	.06261	.05481	.04700	.03919	.03136	.02353	.01569	.00785
.19750	.08555	.07781	.07007	.06231	.05455	.04678	.03900	.03121	.02342	.01562
.20000	.09284	.08515	.07745	.06974	.06202	.05429	.04656	.03881	.03106	.02331
.20250	.10006	.09241	.08475	.07708	.06941	.06172	.05403	.04633	.03863	.03091
.20500	.10720	.09959	.09198	.08435	.07672	.06908	.06143	.05378	.04611	.03844
.20750	.11426	.10670	.09913	.09154	.08396	.07636	.06875	.06114	.05352	.04589

POINT TABLES: ORIGINAL LOAN TERM: 240 MONTHS LOAN PREPAID IN: 60 MONTHS

EFFECTIVE YIELD	CONTRACT RATE .19500	.19750	.20000	.20250	.20500	.20750
.07000	-.51903	-.52965	-.54026	-.55088	-.56150	-.57212
.07250	-.50565	-.51620	-.52675	-.53730	-.54785	-.55840
.07500	-.49242	-.50290	-.51338	-.52386	-.53435	-.54483
.07750	-.47933	-.48974	-.50016	-.51057	-.52099	-.53141
.08000	-.46639	-.47673	-.48708	-.49743	-.50778	-.51814
.08250	-.45358	-.46386	-.47415	-.48443	-.49472	-.50501
.08500	-.44092	-.45113	-.46135	-.47157	-.48180	-.49202
.08750	-.42839	-.43854	-.44870	-.45885	-.46901	-.47918
.09000	-.41600	-.42609	-.43618	-.44627	-.45637	-.46647
.09250	-.40375	-.41377	-.42380	-.43383	-.44386	-.45390
.09500	-.39163	-.40159	-.41155	-.42152	-.43149	-.44147
.09750	-.37964	-.38954	-.39944	-.40935	-.41926	-.42917
.10000	-.36778	-.37762	-.38746	-.39730	-.40715	-.41700
.10250	-.35605	-.36582	-.37561	-.38539	-.39518	-.40497
.10500	-.34444	-.35416	-.36388	-.37361	-.38333	-.39306
.10750	-.33296	-.34262	-.35228	-.36195	-.37162	-.38129
.11000	-.32161	-.33121	-.34081	-.35042	-.36003	-.36964
.11250	-.31038	-.31992	-.32946	-.33901	-.34856	-.35811
.11500	-.29927	-.30875	-.31824	-.32773	-.33722	-.34671
.11750	-.28828	-.29770	-.30713	-.31656	-.32600	-.33544
.12000	-.27741	-.28677	-.29614	-.30552	-.31490	-.32428
.12250	-.26665	-.27596	-.28528	-.29459	-.30392	-.31324
.12500	-.25601	-.26527	-.27452	-.28379	-.29305	-.30232
.12750	-.24549	-.25469	-.26389	-.27309	-.28230	-.29152
.13000	-.23508	-.24422	-.25337	-.26252	-.27167	-.28083
.13250	-.22478	-.23386	-.24296	-.25205	-.26115	-.27026
.13500	-.21459	-.22362	-.23266	-.24170	-.25075	-.25980
.13750	-.20451	-.21349	-.22247	-.23146	-.24045	-.24945
.14000	-.19453	-.20346	-.21239	-.22132	-.23026	-.23921
.14250	-.18467	-.19354	-.20242	-.21130	-.22019	-.22907
.14500	-.17491	-.18373	-.19255	-.20138	-.21021	-.21905
.14750	-.16525	-.17402	-.18279	-.19157	-.20035	-.20913
.15000	-.15569	-.16441	-.17313	-.18186	-.19059	-.19932
.15250	-.14624	-.15491	-.16358	-.17225	-.18093	-.18961
.15500	-.13689	-.14550	-.15412	-.16275	-.17138	-.18001
.15750	-.12764	-.13620	-.14477	-.15334	-.16192	-.17050
.16000	-.11848	-.12700	-.13551	-.14404	-.15257	-.16110
.16250	-.10942	-.11789	-.12636	-.13483	-.14331	-.15180
.16500	-.10046	-.10888	-.11730	-.12572	-.13415	-.14259
.16750	-.09159	-.09996	-.10833	-.11671	-.12509	-.13348
.17000	-.08282	-.09114	-.09946	-.10779	-.11612	-.12446
.17250	-.07414	-.08241	-.09069	-.09897	-.10725	-.11554
.17500	-.06555	-.07377	-.08200	-.09023	-.09847	-.10672
.17750	-.05705	-.06523	-.07341	-.08159	-.08979	-.09798
.18000	-.04864	-.05677	-.06490	-.07304	-.08119	-.08934
.18250	-.04032	-.04840	-.05649	-.06458	-.07268	-.08079
.18500	-.03208	-.04012	-.04816	-.05621	-.06426	-.07232
.18750	-.02394	-.03193	-.03992	-.04793	-.05593	-.06395
.19000	-.01587	-.02382	-.03177	-.03973	-.04769	-.05566
.19250	-.00790	-.01580	-.02370	-.03162	-.03953	-.04746
.19500	.00000	-.00786	-.01572	-.02359	-.03146	-.03934
.19750	.00781	.00000	-.00782	-.01564	-.02347	-.03131
.20000	.01554	.00778	0.00000	-.00778	-.01557	-.02336
.20250	.02319	.01547	.00774	.00000	-.00774	-.01549
.20500	.03077	.02308	.01539	.00770	.00000	-.00771
.20750	.03826	.03062	.02297	.01532	.00766	.00000

POINT TABLES: ORIGINAL LOAN TERM: 240 MONTHS LOAN PREPAID IN: 84 MONTHS

CONTRACT RATE

EFFECTIVE YIELD	.07000	.07250	.07500	.07750	.08000	.08250	.08500	.08750	.09000	.09250
.07000	.00000	-.01265	-.02535	-.03812	-.05093	-.06379	-.07671	-.08968	-.10269	-.11575
.07250	.01252	.00000	-.01258	-.02521	-.03790	-.05064	-.06343	-.07627	-.08915	-.10208
.07500	.02485	.01245	.00000	-.01251	-.02507	-.03769	-.05035	-.06306	-.07582	-.08863
.07750	.03699	.02472	.01239	.00000	-.01244	-.02493	-.03747	-.05006	-.06270	-.07538
.08000	.04895	.03679	.02458	.01232	.00000	-.01237	-.02479	-.03726	-.04977	-.06233
.08250	.06072	.04868	.03659	.02445	.01225	-.00000	-.01230	-.02465	-.03734	-.04948
.08500	.07230	.06039	.04842	.03639	.02431	.01218	.00000	-.01223	-.02450	-.03683
.08750	.08372	.07192	.06006	.04815	.03619	.02417	.01211	-.00000	-.01216	-.02436
.09000	.09495	.08327	.07153	.05973	.04789	.03599	.02404	.01204	0.00000	-.01209
.09250	.10602	.09445	.08282	.07114	.05940	.04762	.03579	.02390	.01197	0.00000
.09500	.11691	.10545	.09394	.08237	.07075	.05908	.04735	.03558	.02377	.01191
.09750	.12764	.11629	.10489	.09343	.08192	.07036	.05875	.04709	.03538	.02363
.10000	.13821	.12697	.11567	.10432	.09292	.08147	.06997	.05842	.04682	.03518
.10250	.14861	.13748	.12629	.11505	.10376	.09241	.08102	.06958	.05809	.04656
.10500	.15886	.14783	.13675	.12562	.11443	.10319	.09191	.08057	.06919	.05776
.10750	.16895	.15803	.14705	.13602	.12494	.11381	.10263	.09140	.08012	.06880
.11000	.17889	.16807	.15720	.14627	.13529	.12426	.11319	.10206	.09089	.07967
.11250	.18868	.17796	.16719	.15637	.14549	.13456	.12359	.11257	.10150	.09038
.11500	.19832	.18770	.17703	.16631	.15553	.14471	.13383	.12291	.11194	.10093
.11750	.20782	.19730	.18673	.17610	.16543	.15470	.14393	.13310	.12224	.11132
.12000	.21717	.20675	.19627	.18575	.17517	.16454	.15387	.14314	.13237	.12156
.12250	.22638	.21605	.20568	.19525	.18477	.17424	.16366	.15303	.14236	.13165
.12500	.23545	.22522	.21494	.20461	.19422	.18379	.17330	.16278	.15220	.14158
.12750	.24438	.23425	.22406	.21382	.20353	.19319	.18281	.17237	.16189	.15137
.13000	.25319	.24314	.23305	.22290	.21271	.20246	.19217	.18183	.17144	.16101
.13250	.26185	.25191	.24190	.23185	.22174	.21159	.20139	.19114	.18085	.17051
.13500	.27039	.26054	.25062	.24066	.23065	.22058	.21047	.20032	.19011	.17987
.13750	.27881	.26904	.25921	.24934	.23942	.22944	.21942	.20936	.19925	.18909
.14000	.28709	.27741	.26768	.25789	.24806	.23817	.22824	.21826	.20824	.19817
.14250	.29526	.28566	.27601	.26632	.25657	.24677	.23693	.22704	.21710	.20713
.14500	.30330	.29379	.28423	.27462	.26496	.25525	.24549	.23569	.22584	.21595
.14750	.31122	.30180	.29232	.28279	.27322	.26359	.25392	.24420	.23444	.22464
.15000	.31902	.30968	.30029	.29085	.28136	.27182	.26223	.25260	.24292	.23320
.15250	.32671	.31745	.30815	.29879	.28938	.27992	.27042	.26087	.25127	.24164
.15500	.33429	.32511	.31588	.30661	.29728	.28790	.27848	.26902	.25951	.24995
.15750	.34175	.33265	.32351	.31431	.30507	.29577	.28643	.27705	.26762	.25814
.16000	.34910	.34009	.33102	.32190	.31274	.30352	.29426	.28496	.27561	.26622
.16250	.35635	.34741	.33842	.32938	.32030	.31116	.30198	.29276	.28349	.27417
.16500	.36348	.35462	.34571	.33675	.32774	.31869	.30959	.30044	.29125	.28201
.16750	[illegible]	.36173	.35290	.34402	.33508	.32611	.31708	.30801	.29890	.28974
.17000	.37745	.36874	.35998	.35117	.34232	.33341	.32447	.31547	.30644	.29736
.17250	.38427	.37564	.36696	.35822	.34944	.34062	.33174	.32283	.31386	.30486
.17500	.39100	.38244	.37383	.36517	.35647	.34771	.33892	.33007	.32119	.31226
.17750	.39763	.38914	.38061	.37202	.36339	.35471	.34598	.33722	.32840	.31955
.18000	.40416	.39575	.38728	.37877	.37021	.36160	.35295	.34425	.33551	.32673
.18250	.41060	.40226	.39386	.38542	.37693	.36840	.35982	.35119	.34252	.33381
.18500	.41694	.40867	.40035	.39198	.38356	.37509	.36658	.35803	.34943	.34079
.18750	.42320	.41499	.40674	.39844	.39009	.38169	.37325	.36477	.35624	.34767
.19000	.42936	.42122	.41304	.40480	.39652	.38820	.37983	.37141	.36295	.35445
.19250	.43543	.42736	.41924	.41108	.40287	.39461	.38631	.37796	.36957	.36114
.19500	.44141	.43341	.42536	.41726	.40912	.40093	.39269	.38441	.37609	.36773
.19750	.44731	.43937	.43139	.42336	.41528	.40716	.39899	.39078	.38252	.37423
.20000	.45312	.44525	.43733	.42937	.42135	.41329	.40519	.39705	.38886	.38063
.20250	.45885	.45105	.44319	.43529	.42734	.41935	.41131	.40323	.39511	.38694
.20500	.46450	.45676	.44896	.44113	.43324	.42531	.41734	.40932	.40126	.39316
.20750	.47006	.46238	.45465	.44688	.43906	.43119	.42328	.41533	.40734	.39930

POINT TABLES: ORIGINAL LOAN TERM: 240 MONTHS LOAN PREPAID IN: 84 MONTHS

EFFECTIVE YIELD	CONTRACT RATE .09500	.09750	.10000	.10250	.10500	.10750	.11000	.11250	.11500	.11750
.07000	-.12885	-.14199	-.15518	-.16841	-.18167	-.19498	-.20832	-.22169	-.23510	-.24854
.07250	-.11506	-.12808	-.14114	-.15424	-.16738	-.18055	-.19377	-.20701	-.22029	-.23361
.07500	-.10148	-.11437	-.12731	-.14028	-.15330	-.16635	-.17943	-.19256	-.20571	-.21890
.07750	-.08811	-.10087	-.11369	-.12654	-.13943	-.15236	-.16532	-.17832	-.19135	-.20442
.08000	-.07494	-.08758	-.10027	-.11300	-.12577	-.13858	-.15142	-.16430	-.17721	-.19015
.08250	-.06197	-.07449	-.08706	-.09967	-.11232	-.12501	-.13773	-.15048	-.16328	-.17610
.08500	-.04919	-.06160	-.07405	-.08654	-.09907	-.11164	-.12424	-.13688	-.14955	-.16226
.08750	-.03661	-.04890	-.06124	-.07361	-.08602	-.09847	-.11096	-.12348	-.13604	-.14862
.09000	-.02422	-.03640	-.04861	-.06087	-.07317	-.08550	-.09787	-.11028	-.12272	-.13519
.09250	-.01202	-.02408	-.03618	-.04833	-.06051	-.07273	-.08499	-.09728	-.10960	-.12196
.09500	.00000	-.01195	-.02394	-.03597	-.04804	-.06015	-.07229	-.08447	-.09668	-.10893
.09750	.01184	0.00000	-.01188	-.02380	-.03576	-.04775	-.05979	-.07185	-.08396	-.09609
.10000	.02350	.01177	.00000	-.01181	-.02366	-.03554	-.04747	-.05943	-.07142	-.08344
.10250	.03498	.02336	.01170	.00000	-.01174	-.02352	-.03533	-.04718	-.05907	-.07098
.10500	.04629	.03478	.02323	.01163	.00000	-.01167	-.02338	-.03512	-.04690	-.05871
.10750	.05744	.04603	.03458	.02309	.01157	.00000	-.01160	-.02324	-.03491	-.04661
.11000	.06841	.05711	.04577	.03438	.02296	.01150	.00000	-.01153	-.02310	-.03470
.11250	.07923	.06803	.05678	.04550	.03418	.02282	.01143	.00000	-.01146	-.02296
.11500	.08988	.07876	.06764	.05646	.04524	.03398	.02269	.01136	0.00000	-.01140
.11750	.10037	.08937	.07833	.06725	.05613	.04498	.03378	.02256	.01129	0.00000
.12000	.11070	.09980	.08886	.07788	.06686	.05581	.04471	.03359	.02242	.01123
.12250	.12089	.11008	.09924	.08836	.07744	.06648	.05548	.04445	.03339	.02229
.12500	.13092	.12021	.10947	.09868	.08785	.07699	.06609	.05516	.04419	.03319
.12750	.14080	.13019	.11954	.10885	.09812	.08735	.07655	.06571	.05484	.04393
.13000	.15054	.14002	.12946	.11887	.10823	.09756	.08685	.07611	.06533	.05452
.13250	.16013	.14970	.13924	.12874	.11819	.10762	.09700	.08635	.07566	.06494
.13500	.16958	.15925	.14887	.13846	.12801	.11752	.10700	.09644	.08585	.07522
.13750	.17889	.16865	.15837	.14805	.13769	.12729	.11686	.10639	.09589	.08535
.14000	.18806	.17791	.16772	.15749	.14722	.13691	.12657	.11619	.10578	.09533
.14250	.19710	.18704	.17694	.16679	.15661	.14639	.13614	.12585	.11552	.10517
.14500	.20601	.19603	.18602	.17596	.16587	.15573	.14557	.13536	.12513	.11486
.14750	.21479	.20490	.19497	.18500	.17499	.16494	.15486	.14474	.13459	.12441
.15000	.22343	.21363	.20378	.19390	.18398	.17402	.16402	.15399	.14392	.13383
.15250	.23196	.22223	.21247	.20267	.19283	.18296	.17305	.16310	.15312	.14310
.15500	.24035	.23071	.22104	.21132	.20156	.19177	.18194	.17208	.16218	.15225
.15750	.24863	.23907	.22947	.21984	.21016	.20045	.19071	.18093	.17111	.16126
.16000	.25678	.24731	.23779	.22824	.21864	.20901	.19935	.18965	.17991	.17015
.16250	.26482	.25542	.24599	.23651	.22700	.21745	.20786	.19824	.18859	.17890
.16500	.27274	.26342	.25406	.24467	.23523	.22576	.21626	.20672	.19714	.18754
.16750	.28054	.27130	.26202	.25271	.24335	.23396	.22453	.21507	.20557	.19604
.17000	.28823	.27907	.26987	.26063	.25135	.24203	.23268	.22330	.21388	.20443
.17250	.29581	.28673	.27760	.26844	.25923	.25000	.24072	.23141	.22207	.21270
.17500	.30329	.29427	.28522	.27613	.26701	.25784	.24865	.23941	.23015	.22085
.17750	.31065	.30171	.29274	.28372	.27467	.26558	.25645	.24730	.23810	.22888
.18000	.31791	.30904	.30014	.29120	.28222	.27320	.26415	.25507	.24595	.23680
.18250	.32506	.31627	.30744	.29857	.28966	.28072	.27174	.26273	.25369	.24461
.18500	.33211	.32339	.31463	.30584	.29700	.28813	.27922	.27028	.26131	.25231
.18750	.33906	.33041	.32172	.31300	.30423	.29543	.28660	.27773	.26883	.25989
.19000	.34591	.33733	.32872	.32006	.31137	.30264	.29387	.28507	.27624	.26738
.19250	.35267	.34416	.33561	.32702	.31839	.30973	.30104	.29231	.28355	.27475
.19500	.35933	.35088	.34240	.33388	.32533	.31673	.30811	.29945	.29075	.28203
.19750	.36589	.35751	.34910	.34065	.33216	.32363	.31507	.30648	.29786	.28920
.20000	.37236	.36405	.35570	.34732	.33889	.33044	.32194	.31342	.30486	.29627
.20250	.37874	.37049	.36221	.35389	.34554	.33714	.32872	.32026	.31176	.30324
.20500	.38502	.37685	.36863	.36037	.35208	.34376	.33540	.32700	.31857	.31012
.20750	.39122	.38311	.37496	.36677	.35854	.35028	.34198	.33365	.32529	.31689

POINT TABLES: ORIGINAL LOAN TERM: 240 MONTHS LOAN PREPAID IN: 84 MONTHS

CONTRACT RATE

EFFECTIVE YIELD	.12000	.12250	.12500	.12750	.13000	.13250	.13500	.13750	.14000	.14250
.07000	-.26201	-.27551	-.28904	-.30260	-.31618	-.32979	-.34343	-.35708	-.37076	-.38446
.07250	-.24695	-.26033	-.27373	-.28716	-.30062	-.31411	-.32761	-.34115	-.35470	-.36827
.07500	-.23212	-.24537	-.25865	-.27196	-.28529	-.29865	-.31204	-.32544	-.33887	-.35232
.07750	-.21752	-.23064	-.24380	-.25698	-.27019	-.28343	-.29669	-.30998	-.32328	-.33661
.08000	-.20313	-.21613	-.22917	-.24223	-.25532	-.26844	-.28158	-.29474	-.30793	-.32113
.08250	-.18896	-.20184	-.21476	-.22770	-.24067	-.25366	-.26669	-.27973	-.29280	-.30589
.08500	-.17500	-.18776	-.20056	-.21338	-.22624	-.23911	-.25202	-.26494	-.27789	-.29086
.08750	-.16124	-.17389	-.18657	-.19928	-.21202	-.22478	-.23756	-.25037	-.26321	-.27606
.09000	-.14770	-.16023	-.17280	-.18539	-.19801	-.21065	-.22333	-.23602	-.24874	-.26148
.09250	-.13435	-.14677	-.15922	-.17170	-.18421	-.19674	-.20930	-.22188	-.23448	-.24711
.09500	-.12121	-.13352	-.14585	-.15822	-.17061	-.18303	-.19548	-.20795	-.22044	-.23296
.09750	-.10826	-.12046	-.13268	-.14494	-.15722	-.16953	-.18186	-.19422	-.20660	-.21901
.10000	-.09550	-.10759	-.11971	-.13185	-.14402	-.15622	-.16845	-.18070	-.19297	-.20527
.10250	-.08293	-.09491	-.10692	-.11896	-.13102	-.14311	-.15523	-.16737	-.17954	-.19173
.10500	-.07055	-.08242	-.09432	-.10625	-.11821	-.13020	-.14221	-.15424	-.16630	-.17838
.10750	-.05835	-.07012	-.08191	-.09374	-.10559	-.11747	-.12938	-.14131	-.15326	-.16524
.11000	-.04633	-.05799	-.06969	-.08141	-.09316	-.10493	-.11673	-.12856	-.14041	-.15228
.11250	-.03449	-.04605	-.05764	-.06926	-.08090	-.09258	-.10427	-.11600	-.12774	-.13951
.11500	-.02282	-.03428	-.04577	-.05728	-.06883	-.08040	-.09200	-.10362	-.11526	-.12693
.11750	-.01133	-.02268	-.03407	-.04549	-.05693	-.06840	-.07990	-.09142	-.10297	-.11454
.12000	0.00000	-.01126	-.02255	-.03386	-.04521	-.05658	-.06798	-.07940	-.09085	-.10232
.12250	.01116	.00000	-.01119	-.02241	-.03366	-.04493	-.05623	-.06756	-.07891	-.09028
.12500	.02216	.01109	.00000	-.01112	-.02227	-.03345	-.04465	-.05588	-.06714	-.07841
.12750	.03299	.02203	.01103	.00000	-.01106	-.02214	-.03325	-.04438	-.05554	-.06672
.13000	.04367	.03280	.02189	.01096	0.00000	-.01099	-.02200	-.03304	-.04410	-.05519
.13250	.05419	.04341	.03260	.02176	.01089	.00000	-.01092	-.02187	-.03284	-.04383
.13500	.06456	.05387	.04316	.03241	.02163	.01083	0.00000	-.01085	-.02173	-.03263
.13750	.07478	.06418	.05356	.04290	.03221	.02150	.01076	-.00000	-.01079	-.02160
.14000	.08485	.07434	.06381	.05324	.04264	.03202	.02137	.01070	0.00000	-.01072
.14250	.09478	.08436	.07391	.06343	.05292	.04239	.03183	.02124	.01063	0.00000
.14500	.10456	.09422	.08386	.07347	.06305	.05261	.04213	.03164	.02111	.01057
.14750	.11420	.10395	.09367	.08337	.07304	.06268	.05229	.04188	.03144	.02099
.15000	.12370	.11354	.10335	.09313	.08288	.07260	.06230	.05198	.04163	.03125
.15250	.13306	.12298	.11288	.10274	.09258	.08239	.07217	.06193	.05157	.04138
.15500	.14229	.13229	.12227	.11222	.10214	.09203	.08190	.07174	.06156	.05136
.15750	.15138	.14147	.13153	.12156	.11157	.10154	.09149	.08142	.07132	.06119
.16000	.16035	.15052	.14066	.13077	.12086	.11091	.10095	.09095	.08093	.07089
.16250	.16919	.15944	.14966	.13985	.13002	.12015	.11027	.10035	.09041	.08045
.16500	.17790	.16823	.15853	.14880	.13904	.12926	.11945	.10962	.09976	.08988
.16750	.18648	.17689	.16727	.15762	.14795	.13824	.12851	.11875	.10897	.09917
.17000	.19495	.18543	.17589	.16632	.15672	.14709	.13744	.12776	.11836	.10833
.17250	.20329	.19385	.18439	.17489	.16537	.15582	.14624	.13664	.12702	.11737
.17500	.21152	.20216	.19276	.18334	.17390	.16442	.15492	.14540	.13585	.12627
.17750	.21962	.21034	.20102	.19168	.18231	.17291	.16348	.15403	.14455	.13505
.18000	.22762	.21841	.20916	.19989	.19059	.18127	.17192	.16254	.15314	.14371
.18250	.23550	.22636	.21719	.20799	.19877	.18951	.18024	.17093	.16160	.15225
.18500	.24327	.23420	.22510	.21598	.20683	.19765	.18844	.17921	.16995	.16067
.18750	.25093	.24193	.23291	.22385	.21477	.20566	.19653	.18737	.17818	.16897
.19000	.25848	.24956	.24060	.23162	.22261	.21357	.20450	.19541	.18630	.17716
.19250	.26593	.25707	.24819	.23927	.23033	.22136	.21237	.20335	.19430	.18524
.19500	.27327	.26448	.25567	.24682	.23795	.22905	.22012	.21117	.20220	.19320
.19750	.28051	.27179	.26304	.25426	.24546	.23663	.22777	.21889	.20998	.20105
.20000	.28765	.27899	.27031	.26160	.25287	.24410	.23531	.22650	.21766	.20879
.20250	.29468	.28610	.27748	.26884	.26017	.25147	.24275	.23400	.22523	.21643
.20500	.30163	.29311	.28456	.27598	.26737	.25874	.25008	.24140	.23270	.22396
.20750	.30847	.30001	.29153	.28302	.27448	.26591	.25732	.24870	.24006	.23139

POINT TABLES: ORIGINAL LOAN TERM: 240 MONTHS LOAN PREPAID IN: 84 MONTHS

EFFECTIVE YIELD	CONTRACT RATE .14500	.14750	.15000	.15250	.15500	.15750	.16000	.16250	.16500	.16750
.07000	-.39818	-.41192	-.42568	-.43946	-.45325	-.46706	-.48088	-.49471	-.50856	-.52243
.07250	-.38187	-.39548	-.40912	-.42277	-.43643	-.45012	-.46381	-.47753	-.49125	-.50499
.07500	-.36580	-.37929	-.39280	-.40632	-.41987	-.43343	-.44700	-.46059	-.47420	-.48781
.07750	-.34996	-.36333	-.37672	-.39012	-.40355	-.41699	-.43044	-.44391	-.45739	-.47089
.08000	-.33436	-.34761	-.36088	-.37416	-.38747	-.40079	-.41412	-.42747	-.44083	-.45421
.08250	-.31899	-.33212	-.34527	-.35844	-.37162	-.38482	-.39804	-.41127	-.42452	-.43777
.08500	-.30385	-.31687	-.32990	-.34295	-.35601	-.36910	-.38220	-.39531	-.40844	-.42158
.08750	-.28894	-.30183	-.31475	-.32768	-.34063	-.35360	-.36659	-.37958	-.39260	-.40563
.09000	-.27424	-.28702	-.29982	-.31264	-.32548	-.33833	-.35120	-.36409	-.37699	-.38990
.09250	-.25976	-.27243	-.28512	-.29782	-.31055	-.32329	-.33605	-.34882	-.36161	-.37441
.09500	-.24549	-.25805	-.27063	-.28322	-.29583	-.30846	-.32111	-.33377	-.34645	-.35914
.09750	-.23143	-.24388	-.25635	-.26883	-.28134	-.29386	-.30639	-.31894	-.33151	-.34409
.10000	-.21758	-.22992	-.24228	-.25465	-.26705	-.27946	-.29189	-.30433	-.31679	-.32927
.10250	-.20393	-.21616	-.22841	-.24068	-.25297	-.26528	-.27760	-.28993	-.30229	-.31465
.10500	-.19049	-.20261	-.21475	-.22692	-.23910	-.25130	-.26351	-.27574	-.28799	-.30025
.10750	-.17723	-.18925	-.20129	-.21335	-.22543	-.23752	-.24963	-.26176	-.27390	-.28606
.11000	-.16417	-.17609	-.18802	-.19998	-.21195	-.22394	-.23595	-.24798	-.26001	-.27207
.11250	-.15131	-.16312	-.17495	-.18680	-.19867	-.21056	-.22247	-.23439	-.24633	-.25828
.11500	-.13862	-.15034	-.16207	-.17382	-.18559	-.19738	-.20918	-.22100	-.23284	-.24469
.11750	-.12613	-.13774	-.14937	-.16102	-.17269	-.18438	-.19609	-.20781	-.21955	-.23130
.12000	-.11381	-.12532	-.13686	-.14841	-.15998	-.17157	-.18318	-.19480	-.20644	-.21810
.12250	-.10167	-.11309	-.12452	-.13598	-.14745	-.15895	-.17046	-.18198	-.19353	-.20509
.12500	-.08971	-.10103	-.11237	-.12373	-.13511	-.14650	-.15792	-.16935	-.18080	-.19226
.12750	-.07792	-.08914	-.10039	-.11165	-.12294	-.13424	-.14556	-.15690	-.16825	-.17962
.13000	-.06630	-.07743	-.08858	-.09975	-.11094	-.12215	-.13338	-.14462	-.15588	-.16715
.13250	-.05485	-.06588	-.07694	-.08802	-.09912	-.11023	-.12137	-.13252	-.14368	-.15487
.13500	-.04356	-.05450	-.06547	-.07646	-.08746	-.09849	-.10953	-.12059	-.13156	-.14276
.13750	-.03243	-.04329	-.05416	-.06506	-.07598	-.08691	-.09786	-.10883	-.11982	-.13082
.14000	-.02147	-.03223	-.04302	-.05382	-.06465	-.07550	-.08636	-.09724	-.10813	-.11905
.14250	-.01066	-.02133	-.03203	-.04275	-.05349	-.06424	-.07502	-.08581	-.09662	-.10744
.14500	0.00000	-.01059	-.02120	-.03183	-.04248	-.05315	-.06384	-.07454	-.08526	-.09600
.14750	.01050	.00000	-.01052	-.02107	-.03163	-.04222	-.05282	-.06344	-.07407	-.08472
.15000	.02086	.01044	.00000	-.01046	-.02094	-.03144	-.04195	-.05249	-.06304	-.07360
.15250	.03106	.02073	.01038	.00000	-.01040	-.02081	-.03124	-.04169	-.05216	-.06264
.15500	.04113	.03088	.02060	.01031	-.00000	-.01033	-.02068	-.03105	-.04143	-.05183
.15750	.05105	.04088	.03069	.02048	.01025	.00000	-.01027	-.02055	-.03085	-.04117
.16000	.06083	.05074	.04063	.03050	.02035	.01019	.00000	-.01020	-.02042	-.03066
.16250	.07047	.06046	.05043	.04038	.03032	.02023	.01012	0.00000	-.01014	-.02030
.16500	.07997	.07004	.06010	.05013	.04014	.03013	.02010	.01006	.00000	-.01008
.16750	.08934	.07949	.06962	.05973	.04982	.03989	.02995	.01998	.01000	0.00000
.17000	.09858	.08881	.07902	.06921	.05937	.04952	.03965	.02976	.01986	.00994
.17250	.10769	.09800	.08828	.07855	.06879	.05901	.04922	.03941	.02958	.01974
.17500	.11668	.10706	.09742	.08776	.07808	.06838	.05866	.04892	.03917	.02940
.17750	.12553	.11599	.10642	.09684	.08723	.07761	.06796	.05830	.04862	.03893
.18000	.13427	.12480	.11530	.10579	.09626	.08671	.07714	.06755	.05795	.04833
.18250	.14288	.13348	.12406	.11462	.10517	.09569	.08619	.07668	.06715	.05760
.18500	.15137	.14205	.13270	.12333	.11395	.10454	.09512	.08568	.07622	.06674
.18750	.15974	.15049	.14122	.13192	.12261	.11327	.10392	.09455	.08516	.07576
.19000	.16800	.15882	.14962	.14039	.13115	.12188	.11260	.10330	.09399	.08465
.19250	.17615	.16703	.15790	.14874	.13957	.13038	.12116	.11193	.10269	.09342
.19500	.18418	.17513	.16607	.15698	.14788	.13875	.12961	.12045	.11127	.10208
.19750	.19210	.18312	.17413	.16511	.15607	.14701	.13794	.12885	.11974	.11061
.20000	.19991	.19100	.18207	.17312	.16415	.15516	.14616	.13713	.12809	.11903
.20250	.20761	.19877	.18991	.18103	.17212	.16320	.15426	.14530	.13633	.12733
.20500	.21521	.20644	.19764	.18882	.17999	.17113	.16225	.15336	.14445	.13553
.20750	.22271	.21400	.20526	.19651	.18774	.17895	.17014	.16131	.15247	.14361

POINT TABLES: ORIGINAL LOAN TERM: 240 MONTHS LOAN PREPAID IN: 84 MONTHS

EFFECTIVE YIELD	CONTRACT RATE .17000	.17250	.17500	.17750	.18000	.18250	.18500	.18750	.19000	.19250
.07000	-.53630	-.55019	-.56408	-.57799	-.59190	-.60582	-.61975	-.63369	-.64764	-.66159
.07250	-.51874	-.53250	-.54627	-.56006	-.57385	-.58765	-.60146	-.61527	-.62910	-.64293
.07500	-.50144	-.51508	-.52873	-.54239	-.55606	-.56974	-.58343	-.59712	-.61083	-.62453
.07750	-.48439	-.49791	-.51144	-.52498	-.53853	-.55209	-.56566	-.57924	-.59282	-.60641
.08000	-.46760	-.48100	-.49441	-.50783	-.52126	-.53470	-.54815	-.56161	-.57508	-.58855
.08250	-.45104	-.46433	-.47762	-.49093	-.50424	-.51757	-.53090	-.54424	-.55759	-.57095
.08500	-.43474	-.44790	-.46108	-.47427	-.48747	-.50068	-.51390	-.52712	-.54036	-.55360
.08750	-.41867	-.43172	-.44478	-.45786	-.47094	-.48404	-.49714	-.51025	-.52337	-.53650
.09000	-.40283	-.41577	-.42872	-.44168	-.45465	-.46763	-.48063	-.49363	-.50664	-.51965
.09250	-.38722	-.40005	-.41289	-.42574	-.43860	-.45147	-.46435	-.47724	-.49014	-.50304
.09500	-.37184	-.38456	-.39729	-.41003	-.42278	-.43554	-.44831	-.46109	-.47388	-.48668
.09750	-.35669	-.36930	-.38192	-.39455	-.40719	-.41984	-.43250	-.44518	-.45786	-.47054
.10000	-.34175	-.35425	-.36676	-.37929	-.39182	-.40437	-.41692	-.42949	-.44206	-.45464
.10250	-.32703	-.33943	-.35183	-.36425	-.37668	-.38912	-.40157	-.41403	-.42649	-.43897
.10500	-.31253	-.32481	-.33712	-.34943	-.36175	-.37409	-.38643	-.39879	-.41115	-.42352
.10750	-.29823	-.31041	-.32261	-.33482	-.34704	-.35927	-.37151	-.38376	-.39602	-.40829
.11000	-.28414	-.29622	-.30831	-.32042	-.33254	-.34467	-.35681	-.36896	-.38111	-.39328
.11250	-.27025	-.28223	-.29422	-.30623	-.31824	-.33027	-.34231	-.35436	-.36642	-.37848
.11500	-.25656	-.26844	-.28033	-.29224	-.30415	-.31608	-.32802	-.33997	-.35193	-.36390
.11750	-.24307	-.25485	-.26664	-.27845	-.29027	-.30210	-.31394	-.32579	-.33765	-.34952
.12000	-.22977	-.24145	-.25315	-.26486	-.27658	-.28831	-.30005	-.31181	-.32357	-.33534
.12250	-.21666	-.22824	-.23984	-.25146	-.26308	-.27472	-.28636	-.29802	-.30969	-.32136
.12500	-.20374	-.21523	-.22673	-.23825	-.24978	-.26132	-.27287	-.28443	-.29600	-.30759
.12750	-.19100	-.20240	-.21381	-.22523	-.23666	-.24811	-.25957	-.27104	-.28251	-.29400
.13000	-.17844	-.18975	-.20106	-.21239	-.22373	-.23509	-.24645	-.25783	-.26921	-.28061
.13250	-.16606	-.17728	-.18850	-.19974	-.21099	-.22225	-.23352	-.24481	-.25610	-.26741
.13500	-.15386	-.16498	-.17612	-.18726	-.19842	-.20959	-.22078	-.23197	-.24317	-.25439
.13750	-.14183	-.15286	-.16391	-.17496	-.18603	-.19712	-.20821	-.21931	-.23043	-.24155
.14000	-.12997	-.14091	-.15187	-.16284	-.17382	-.18481	-.19582	-.20683	-.21786	-.22889
.14250	-.11828	-.12913	-.14000	-.15088	-.16178	-.17268	-.18360	-.19453	-.20547	-.21641
.14500	-.10675	-.11752	-.12830	-.13910	-.14990	-.16072	-.17155	-.18239	-.19325	-.20411
.14750	-.09539	-.10607	-.11676	-.12747	-.13819	-.14893	-.15967	-.17043	-.18120	-.19197
.15000	-.08418	-.09478	-.10539	-.11601	-.12665	-.13730	-.14796	-.15863	-.16931	-.18001
.15250	-.07314	-.08365	-.09417	-.10471	-.11527	-.12583	-.13641	-.14700	-.15760	-.16821
.15500	-.06224	-.07267	-.08312	-.09357	-.10404	-.11453	-.12502	-.13553	-.14604	-.15657
.15750	-.05150	-.06185	-.07221	-.08259	-.09298	-.10338	-.11379	-.12421	-.13465	-.14510
.16000	-.04091	-.05118	-.06146	-.07175	-.08206	-.09238	-.10271	-.11306	-.12341	-.13378
.16250	-.03047	-.04065	-.05086	-.06107	-.07130	-.08154	-.09179	-.10206	-.11233	-.12262
.16500	-.02017	-.03028	-.04040	-.05053	-.06068	-.07085	-.08102	-.09120	-.10140	-.11161
.16750	-.01001	-.02004	-.03009	-.04015	-.05022	-.06030	-.07040	-.08050	-.09062	-.10075
.17000	.00000	-.00995	-.01992	-.02990	-.03989	-.04990	-.05992	-.06995	-.07999	-.09004
.17250	.00988	0.00000	-.00989	-.01979	-.02971	-.03964	-.04959	-.05954	-.06951	-.07948
.17500	.01961	.00981	.00000	-.00983	-.01967	-.02953	-.03939	-.04927	-.05916	-.06907
.17750	.02922	.01949	.00975	.00000	-.00977	-.01955	-.02934	-.03915	-.04896	-.05879
.18000	.03869	.02904	.01937	.00969	.00000	-.00971	-.01943	-.02916	-.03890	-.04865
.18250	.04804	.03846	.02886	.01926	.00963	0.00000	-.00965	-.01931	-.02898	-.03866
.18500	.05725	.04774	.03822	.02869	.01914	.00957	.00000	-.00959	-.01918	-.02879
.18750	.06634	.05690	.04745	.03799	.02851	.01902	.00952	0.00000	-.00953	-.01907
.19000	.07530	.06594	.05656	.04716	.03776	.02834	.01890	.00946	0.00000	-.00947
.19250	.08414	.07485	.06554	.05621	.04688	.03753	.02816	.01879	.00940	.00000
.19500	.09286	.08364	.07440	.06514	.05587	.04659	.03730	.02799	.01867	.00934
.19750	.10147	.09231	.08314	.07395	.06475	.05553	.04631	.03707	.02782	.01856
.20000	.10995	.10086	.09176	.08264	.07350	.06436	.05520	.04603	.03684	.02765
.20250	.11832	.10930	.10026	.09121	.08214	.07306	.06397	.05486	.04575	.03662
.20500	.12658	.11762	.10865	.09966	.09066	.08165	.07262	.06358	.05453	.04547
.20750	.13473	.12584	.11693	.10801	.09907	.09012	.08116	.07218	.06320	.05420

POINT TABLES: ORIGINAL LOAN TERM: 240 MONTHS LOAN PREPAID IN: 84 MONTHS

EFFECTIVE YIELD	CONTRACT RATE .19500	.19750	.20000	.20250	.20500	.20750
.07000	-.67555	-.68951	-.70348	-.71745	-.73143	-.74541
.07250	-.65676	-.67060	-.68445	-.69830	-.71216	-.72602
.07500	-.63825	-.65197	-.66570	-.67943	-.69317	-.70691
.07750	-.62001	-.63361	-.64722	-.66083	-.67445	-.68807
.08000	-.60203	-.61551	-.62900	-.64250	-.65600	-.66951
.08250	-.58431	-.59768	-.61105	-.62443	-.63782	-.65121
.08500	-.56685	-.58010	-.59336	-.60663	-.61990	-.63318
.08750	-.54964	-.56276	-.57593	-.58908	-.60224	-.61540
.09000	-.53267	-.54571	-.55874	-.57178	-.58483	-.59788
.09250	-.51596	-.52888	-.54180	-.55474	-.56767	-.58062
.09500	-.49948	-.51229	-.52511	-.53793	-.55076	-.56360
.09750	-.48324	-.49594	-.50865	-.52137	-.53409	-.54682
.10000	-.46723	-.47983	-.49243	-.50504	-.51766	-.53028
.10250	-.45145	-.46394	-.47644	-.48895	-.50146	-.51398
.10500	-.43590	-.44829	-.46068	-.47308	-.48549	-.49790
.10750	-.42057	-.43285	-.44515	-.45744	-.46975	-.48206
.11000	-.40546	-.41764	-.42983	-.44203	-.45423	-.46644
.11250	-.39056	-.40264	-.41473	-.42683	-.43893	-.45104
.11500	-.37587	-.38786	-.39985	-.41185	-.42385	-.43586
.11750	-.36139	-.37328	-.38517	-.39707	-.40898	-.42090
.12000	-.34712	-.35891	-.37071	-.38251	-.39432	-.40614
.12250	-.33305	-.34474	-.35644	-.36815	-.37987	-.39159
.12500	-.31918	-.33078	-.34238	-.35400	-.36562	-.37725
.12750	-.30550	-.31701	-.32852	-.34004	-.35157	-.36310
.13000	-.29201	-.30343	-.31485	-.32628	-.33772	-.34916
.13250	-.27872	-.29004	-.30137	-.31271	-.32406	-.33541
.13500	-.26561	-.27684	-.28808	-.29933	-.31059	-.32185
.13750	-.25268	-.26383	-.27498	-.28614	-.29730	-.30848
.14000	-.23994	-.25099	-.26206	-.27313	-.28421	-.29529
.14250	-.22737	-.23834	-.24932	-.26030	-.27129	-.28229
.14500	-.21498	-.22586	-.23675	-.24765	-.25856	-.26947
.14750	-.20276	-.21356	-.22436	-.23518	-.24600	-.25683
.15000	-.19071	-.20142	-.21214	-.22287	-.23361	-.24436
.15250	-.17883	-.18946	-.20009	-.21074	-.22139	-.23206
.15500	-.16711	-.17766	-.18821	-.19878	-.20935	-.21993
.15750	-.15555	-.16602	-.17649	-.18697	-.19747	-.20797
.16000	-.14415	-.15454	-.16493	-.17534	-.18575	-.19617
.16250	-.13291	-.14322	-.15353	-.16386	-.17419	-.18453
.16500	-.12183	-.13205	-.14229	-.15253	-.16279	-.17305
.16750	-.11089	-.12104	-.13120	-.14137	-.15154	-.16173
.17000	-.10011	-.11018	-.12026	-.13035	-.14045	-.15056
.17250	-.08947	-.09947	-.10947	-.11949	-.12951	-.13954
.17500	-.07898	-.08890	-.09883	-.10877	-.11872	-.12868
.17750	-.06863	-.07848	-.08833	-.09820	-.10807	-.11796
.18000	-.05842	-.06819	-.07798	-.08777	-.09757	-.10738
.18250	-.04835	-.05805	-.06776	-.07748	-.08721	-.09695
.18500	-.03841	-.04804	-.05768	-.06733	-.07699	-.08666
.18750	-.02861	-.03817	-.04774	-.05732	-.06691	-.07650
.19000	-.01895	-.02844	-.03793	-.04744	-.05696	-.06648
.19250	-.00941	-.01883	-.02826	-.03770	-.04714	-.05660
.19500	0.00000	-.00935	-.01871	-.02808	-.03746	-.04685
.19750	.00928	.00000	-.00929	-.01860	-.02791	-.03723
.20000	.01844	.00923	.00000	-.00924	-.01848	-.02773
.20250	.02748	.01833	.00917	.00000	-.00918	-.01837
.20500	.03639	.02731	.01822	.00911	0.00000	-.00912
.20750	.04519	.03617	.02714	.01810	.00906	.00000

POINT TABLES: ORIGINAL LOAN TERM: 240 MONTHS LOAN PREPAID IN: 108 MONTHS

EFFECTIVE YIELD	CONTRACT RATE .07000	.07250	.07500	.07750	.08000	.08250	.08500	.08750	.09000	.09250
.07000	.00000	-.01482	-.02973	-.04471	-.05978	-.07492	-.09013	-.10542	-.12078	-.13621
.07250	.01464	.00000	-.01472	-.02952	-.04440	-.05936	-.07439	-.08950	-.10467	-.11992
.07500	.02900	.01454	.00000	-.01462	-.02932	-.04410	-.05895	-.07387	-.08887	-.10393
.07750	.04309	.02881	.01444	.00000	-.01452	-.02912	-.04379	-.05854	-.07335	-.08823
.08000	.05692	.04281	.02862	.01435	.00000	-.01442	-.02892	-.04349	-.05813	-.07283
.08250	.07049	.05655	.04253	.02843	.01425	0.00000	-.01432	-.02872	-.04318	-.05772
.08500	.08380	.07003	.05617	.04224	.02824	.01415	.00000	-.01423	-.02852	-.04288
.08750	.09686	.08326	.06957	.05580	.04196	.02805	.01406	0.00000	-.01413	-.02832
.09000	.10968	.09624	.08271	.06911	.05543	.04168	.02786	.01396	.00000	-.01403
.09250	.12226	.10898	.09561	.08217	.06865	.05506	.04140	.02767	.01387	.00000
.09500	.13461	.12148	.10827	.09499	.08163	.06820	.05469	.04112	.02748	.01377
.09750	.14673	.13375	.12070	.10757	.09436	.08109	.06774	.05432	.04084	.02729
.10000	.15862	.14580	.13289	.11992	.10686	.09374	.08055	.06728	.05395	.04056
.10250	.17029	.15762	.14486	.13204	.11914	.10616	.09312	.08001	.06683	.05359
.10500	.18175	.16922	.15661	.14393	.13118	.11836	.10546	.09250	.07947	.06638
.10750	.19299	.18061	.16815	.15561	.14301	.13033	.11758	.10476	.09188	.07893
.11000	.20403	.19179	.17947	.16708	.15461	.14208	.12947	.11680	.10406	.09126
.11250	.21487	.20277	.19059	.17833	.16601	.15362	.14115	.12862	.11603	.10337
.11500	.22551	.21354	.20150	.18938	.17720	.16494	.15262	.14023	.12777	.11526
.11750	.23595	.22412	.21221	.20023	.18818	.17607	.16388	.15163	.13931	.12693
.12000	.24620	.23450	.22273	.21089	.19897	.18699	.17493	.16282	.15063	.13839
.12250	.25627	.24470	.23306	.22134	.20956	.19771	.18579	.17380	.16175	.14964
.12500	.26615	.25471	.24320	.23161	.21996	.20824	.19645	.18459	.17268	.16070
.12750	.27585	.26454	.25315	.24170	.23017	.21858	.20692	.19519	.18340	.17155
.13000	.28538	.27419	.26293	.25160	.24020	.22873	.21720	.20560	.19393	.18221
.13250	.29474	.28367	.27253	.26132	.25005	.23870	.22729	.21582	.20428	.19268
.13500	.30392	.29298	.28196	.27087	.25972	.24849	.23721	.22586	.21444	.20297
.13750	.31295	.30212	.29122	.28025	.26921	.25811	.24695	.23571	.22442	.21307
.14000	.32181	.31109	.30031	.28946	.27854	.26756	.25651	.24540	.23423	.22299
.14250	.33051	.31991	.30924	.29851	.28771	.27684	.26591	.25491	.24385	.23274
.14500	.33905	.32857	.31801	.30739	.29670	.28595	.27513	.26425	.25331	.24231
.14750	.34744	.33707	.32663	.31612	.30554	.29490	.28420	.27343	.26261	.25172
.15000	.35569	.34543	.33509	.32469	.31423	.30370	.29311	.28245	.27174	.26096
.15250	.36379	.35363	.34341	.33312	.32276	.31234	.30185	.29131	.28071	.27004
.15500	.37174	.36169	.35157	.34139	.33114	.32083	.31045	.30001	.28952	.27896
.15750	.37955	.36961	.35959	.34952	.33937	.32916	.31890	.30857	.29818	.28773
.16000	.38723	.37739	.36748	.35750	.34746	.33736	.32719	.31697	.30668	.29634
.16250	.39477	.38503	.37522	.36534	.35541	.34541	.33535	.32522	.31504	.30481
.16500	.40218	.39253	.38283	.37305	.36322	.35332	.34336	.33334	.32326	.31312
.16750	.40945	.39991	.39030	.38063	.37089	.36109	.35123	.34131	.33133	.32130
.17000	.41660	.40716	.39764	.38807	.37843	.36872	.35896	.34914	.33926	.32933
.17250	.42363	.41428	.40486	.39538	.38583	.37623	.36656	.35684	.34706	.33722
.17500	.43053	.42128	.41195	.40256	.39312	.38361	.37404	.36441	.35472	.34498
.17750	.43732	.42815	.41892	.40963	.40027	.39085	.38138	.37184	.36225	.35261
.18000	.44399	.43491	.42577	.41657	.40730	.39798	.38859	.37915	.36966	.36010
.18250	.45054	.44155	.43250	.42339	.41421	.40498	.39569	.38634	.37693	.36747
.18500	.45698	.44808	.43911	.43009	.42101	.41186	.40266	.39340	.38408	.37471
.18750	.46330	.45449	.44562	.43668	.42768	.41863	.40951	.40034	.39112	.38183
.19000	.46952	.46080	.45201	.44316	.43425	.42528	.41625	.40717	.39803	.38883
.19250	.47564	.46699	.45829	.44952	.44070	.43181	.42287	.41387	.40482	.39572
.19500	.48164	.47308	.46446	.45578	.44704	.43824	.42938	.42047	.41150	.40248
.19750	.48755	.47907	.47053	.46193	.45327	.44456	.43578	.42696	.41807	.40914
.20000	.49336	.48496	.47650	.46798	.45940	.45077	.44208	.43333	.42453	.41568
.20250	.49907	.49075	.48237	.47393	.46543	.45688	.44827	.43960	.43088	.42211
.20500	.50468	.49644	.48814	.47977	.47136	.46288	.45435	.44577	.43713	.42844
.20750	.51019	.50203	.49381	.48552	.47718	.46879	.46033	.45183	.44327	.43466

EFFECTIVE YIELD	CONTRACT RATE .09500	.09750	.10000	.10250	.10500	.10750	.11000	.11250	.11500	.11750
.07000	-.15171	-.16727	-.18290	-.19859	-.21433	-.23014	-.24600	-.26191	-.27787	-.29389
.07250	-.13523	-.15061	-.16605	-.18155	-.19711	-.21272	-.22839	-.24412	-.25990	-.27573
.07500	-.11906	-.13425	-.14951	-.16482	-.18020	-.19563	-.21112	-.22666	-.24225	-.25790
.07750	-.10318	-.11820	-.13327	-.14841	-.16360	-.17886	-.19416	-.20952	-.22494	-.24040
.08000	-.08760	-.10244	-.11734	-.13230	-.14732	-.16239	-.17752	-.19270	-.20793	-.22322
.08250	-.07232	-.08698	-.10170	-.11649	-.13133	-.14623	-.16118	-.17619	-.19125	-.20635
.08500	-.05731	-.07180	-.08635	-.10096	-.11564	-.13036	-.14514	-.15998	-.17486	-.18980
.08750	-.04258	-.05690	-.07129	-.08573	-.10023	-.11479	-.12940	-.14407	-.15878	-.17355
.09000	-.02812	-.04228	-.05650	-.07077	-.08511	-.09950	-.11395	-.12844	-.14299	-.15759
.09250	-.01393	-.02792	-.04198	-.05609	-.07026	-.08449	-.09877	-.11311	-.12749	-.14192
.09500	.00000	-.01383	-.02773	-.04168	-.05569	-.06976	-.08388	-.09805	-.11227	-.12654
.09750	.01368	0.00000	-.01374	-.02753	-.04138	-.05529	-.06925	-.08326	-.09733	-.11144
.10000	.02710	.01358	.00000	-.01364	-.02733	-.04109	-.05489	-.06875	-.08265	-.09661
.10250	.04028	.02691	.01349	.00000	-.01354	-.02714	-.04079	-.05449	-.06824	-.08205
.10500	.05322	.04000	.02673	.01339	0.00000	-.01345	-.02695	-.04050	-.05410	-.06775
.10750	.06593	.05286	.03973	.02654	.01330	.00000	-.01335	-.02675	-.04020	-.05370
.11000	.07840	.06548	.05249	.03945	.02635	.01320	0.00000	-.01325	-.02656	-.03991
.11250	.09065	.07787	.06503	.05213	.03918	.02617	.01311	.00000	-.01316	-.02637
.11500	.10267	.09003	.07734	.06458	.05177	.03890	.02599	.01302	0.00000	-.01307
.11750	.11448	.10198	.08942	.07681	.06413	.05141	.03863	.02580	.01292	0.00000
.12000	.12608	.11372	.10129	.08881	.07628	.06369	.05105	.03836	.02562	.01283
.12250	.13747	.12524	.11295	.10061	.08821	.07575	.06325	.05069	.03809	.02544
.12500	.14866	.13656	.12440	.11219	.09992	.08760	.07523	.06281	.05034	.03782
.12750	.15964	.14767	.13564	.12356	.11143	.09924	.08700	.07471	.06237	.04998
.13000	.17043	.15859	.14669	.13474	.12273	.11067	.09856	.08640	.07419	.06193
.13250	.18103	.16931	.15754	.14571	.13383	.12190	.10991	.09788	.08580	.07367
.13500	.19143	.17984	.16819	.15649	.14474	.13293	.12107	.10916	.09720	.08520
.13750	.20166	.19019	.17866	.16708	.15545	.14376	.13203	.12024	.10841	.09653
.14000	.21170	.20035	.18895	.17749	.16597	.15441	.14280	.13113	.11942	.10767
.14250	.22157	.21033	.19905	.18771	.17631	.16487	.15337	.14183	.13024	.11860
.14500	.23126	.22014	.20897	.19775	.18647	.17514	.16377	.15234	.14087	.12935
.14750	.24078	.22978	.21872	.20761	.19645	.18524	.17398	.16267	.15132	.13991
.15000	.25013	.23924	.22830	.21731	.20626	.19516	.18402	.17282	.16158	.15029
.15250	.25932	.24855	.23772	.22683	.21590	.20491	.19388	.18279	.17167	.16049
.15500	.26835	.25769	.24697	.23619	.22537	.21449	.20357	.19260	.18158	.17052
.15750	.27723	.26667	.25605	.24539	.23467	.22391	.21309	.20223	.19132	.18037
.16000	.28594	.27549	.26499	.25443	.24382	.23316	.22245	.21170	.20089	.19005
.16250	.29451	.28416	.27376	.26331	.25280	.24225	.23165	.22100	.21031	.19957
.16500	.30293	.29269	.28239	.27204	.26164	.25119	.24069	.23015	.21956	.20892
.16750	.31121	.30106	.29087	.28062	.27032	.25997	.24958	.23913	.22865	.21812
.17000	.31934	.30929	.29920	.28905	.27885	.26860	.25831	.24797	.23758	.22716
.17250	.32733	.31738	.30739	.29734	.28724	.27709	.26690	.25666	.24637	.23604
.17500	.33519	.32534	.31544	.30548	.29548	.28543	.27534	.26519	.25501	.24478
.17750	.34291	.33315	.32335	.31349	.30359	.29363	.28363	.27359	.26350	.25337
.18000	.35050	.34084	.33113	.32136	.31155	.30170	.29179	.28184	.27185	.26181
.18250	.35796	.34839	.33877	.32910	.31939	.30962	.29981	.28996	.28006	.27011
.18500	.36529	.35582	.34629	.33671	.32709	.31742	.30770	.29793	.28813	.27828
.18750	.37250	.36312	.35368	.34419	.33466	.32508	.31545	.30578	.29606	.28630
.19000	.37959	.37029	.36094	.35155	.34210	.33261	.32307	.31349	.30387	.29420
.19250	.38656	.37735	.36809	.35878	.34942	.34002	.33057	.32108	.31154	.30196
.19500	.39341	.38429	.37511	.36589	.35662	.34730	.33794	.32854	.31909	.30960
.19750	.40015	.39111	.38202	.37288	.36370	.35447	.34519	.33587	.32651	.31710
.20000	.40677	.39782	.38881	.37976	.37066	.36151	.35232	.34309	.33381	.32449
.20250	.41329	.40441	.39549	.38652	.37750	.36844	.35933	.35018	.34099	.33175
.20500	.41969	.41090	.40206	.39317	.38424	.37526	.36623	.35716	.34805	.33890
.20750	.42599	.41728	.40852	.39971	.39086	.38196	.37301	.36403	.35500	.34593

POINT TABLES: ORIGINAL LOAN TERM: 240 MONTHS LOAN PREPAID IN: 108 MONTHS

EFFECTIVE YIELD	CONTRACT RATE .12000	.12250	.12500	.12750	.13000	.13250	.13500	.13750	.14000	.14250
.07000	-.30996	-.32607	-.34222	-.35842	-.37466	-.39095	-.40727	-.42363	-.44002	-.45645
.07250	-.29160	-.30753	-.32350	-.33951	-.35556	-.37166	-.38779	-.40396	-.42017	-.43641
.07500	-.27359	-.28933	-.30511	-.32094	-.33681	-.35272	-.36867	-.38465	-.40067	-.41673
.07750	-.25591	-.27147	-.28707	-.30271	-.31840	-.33413	-.34989	-.36570	-.38154	-.39741
.08000	-.23855	-.25393	-.26935	-.28482	-.30033	-.31588	-.33146	-.34709	-.36275	-.37844
.08250	-.22151	-.23671	-.25196	-.26725	-.28258	-.29796	-.31337	-.32882	-.34430	-.35982
.08500	-.20478	-.21981	-.23489	-.25000	-.26516	-.28036	-.29560	-.31088	-.32619	-.34153
.08750	-.18836	-.20322	-.21812	-.23307	-.24806	-.26309	-.27816	-.29326	-.30840	-.32357
.09000	-.17224	-.18693	-.20166	-.21644	-.23126	-.24613	-.26102	-.27596	-.29093	-.30594
.09250	-.15640	-.17093	-.18550	-.20012	-.21477	-.22947	-.24420	-.25898	-.27378	-.28862
.09500	-.14086	-.15523	-.16963	-.18409	-.19858	-.21311	-.22769	-.24229	-.25694	-.27162
.09750	-.12560	-.13980	-.15405	-.16834	-.18268	-.19705	-.21146	-.22591	-.24040	-.25492
.10000	-.11061	-.12466	-.13875	-.15289	-.16706	-.18128	-.19553	-.20982	-.22415	-.23851
.10250	-.09589	-.10979	-.12373	-.13771	-.15173	-.16579	-.17989	-.19402	-.20820	-.22240
.10500	-.08144	-.09518	-.10897	-.12280	-.13667	-.15057	-.16452	-.17850	-.19252	-.20658
.10750	-.06725	-.08084	-.09448	-.10815	-.12187	-.13563	-.14943	-.16326	-.17713	-.19103
.11000	-.05331	-.06676	-.08024	-.09377	-.10734	-.12096	-.13460	-.14829	-.16201	-.17577
.11250	-.03962	-.05292	-.06626	-.07965	-.09307	-.10654	-.12004	-.13358	-.14716	-.16077
.11500	-.02618	-.03933	-.05253	-.06578	-.07906	-.09238	-.10574	-.11914	-.13257	-.14603
.11750	-.01297	-.02599	-.03905	-.05215	-.06529	-.07847	-.09169	-.10494	-.11824	-.13156
.12000	.00000	-.01288	-.02580	-.03876	-.05176	-.06481	-.07789	-.09100	-.10415	-.11734
.12250	.01274	.00000	-.01278	-.02561	-.03848	-.05138	-.06433	-.07730	-.09032	-.10337
.12500	.02526	.01265	.00000	-.01269	-.02542	-.03819	-.05100	-.06385	-.07673	-.08964
.12750	.03755	.02508	.01256	.00000	-.01260	-.02524	-.03791	-.05063	-.06337	-.07615
.13000	.04963	.03729	.02490	.01247	0.00000	-.01251	-.02505	-.03763	-.05025	-.06290
.13250	.06150	.04928	.03702	.02472	.01238	-.00000	-.01242	-.02487	-.03736	-.04988
.13500	.07316	.06106	.04893	.03676	.02454	.01229	-.00000	-.01233	-.02469	-.03708
.13750	.08461	.07264	.06063	.04858	.03649	.02437	.01220	0.00000	-.01224	-.02451
.14000	.09586	.08402	.07213	.06021	.04824	.03623	.02419	.01211	0.00000	-.01215
.14250	.10692	.09520	.08343	.07163	.05978	.04790	.03597	.02402	.01203	0.00000
.14500	.11779	.10618	.09454	.08285	.07112	.05936	.04755	.03572	.02384	.01194
.14750	.12847	.11698	.10545	.09388	.08227	.07062	.05894	.04721	.03546	.02367
.15000	.13896	.12759	.11617	.10472	.09322	.08169	.07012	.05852	.04688	.03521
.15250	.14927	.13801	.12671	.11537	.10399	.09257	.08112	.06962	.05810	.04654
.15500	.15941	.14826	.13707	.12584	.11457	.10326	.09192	.08054	.06913	.05769
.15750	.16937	.15833	.14725	.13613	.12497	.11378	.10254	.09128	.07998	.06864
.16000	.17916	.16823	.15726	.14625	.13520	.12411	.11299	.10183	.09064	.07941
.16250	.18878	.17796	.16710	.15619	.14525	.13427	.12325	.11220	.10112	.09000
.16500	.19824	.18753	.17677	.16597	.15513	.14426	.13334	.12240	.11142	.10041
.16750	.20754	.19693	.18627	.17558	.16484	.15407	.14327	.13243	.12155	.11064
.17000	.21668	.20617	.19562	.18502	.17439	.16373	.15302	.14228	.13151	.12071
.17250	.22567	.21526	.20480	.19431	.18378	.17322	.16261	.15198	.14131	.13060
.17500	.23450	.22419	.21384	.20344	.19301	.18255	.17204	.16151	.15094	.14034
.17750	.24319	.23297	.22272	.21242	.20209	.19172	.18132	.17088	.16041	.14990
.18000	.25173	.24161	.23145	.22125	.21102	.20075	.19044	.18010	.16972	.15932
.18250	.26013	.25010	.24004	.22993	.21979	.20962	.19941	.18916	.17888	.16857
.18500	.26838	.25845	.24848	.23847	.22843	.21834	.20823	.19807	.18789	.17767
.18750	.27650	.26666	.25679	.24687	.23691	.22692	.21690	.20684	.19675	.18663
.19000	.28449	.27474	.26495	.25513	.24526	.23536	.22543	.21546	.20546	.19543
.19250	.29234	.28268	.27298	.26325	.25347	.24366	.23382	.22394	.21404	.20409
.19500	.30006	.29049	.28088	.27123	.26155	.25183	.24207	.23229	.22247	.21261
.19750	.30766	.29817	.28865	.27909	.26949	.25986	.25019	.24049	.23076	.22100
.20000	.31513	.30573	.29629	.28682	.27731	.26776	.25818	.24857	.23892	.22924
.20250	.32248	.31316	.30381	.29442	.28499	.27553	.26604	.25651	.24695	.23736
.20500	.32970	.32047	.31120	.30190	.29255	.28318	.27377	.26432	.25485	.24534
.20750	.33681	.32766	.31848	.30925	.29999	.29070	.28137	.27201	.26262	.25319

POINT TABLES: ORIGINAL LOAN TERM: 240 MONTHS LOAN PREPAID IN: 108 MONTHS

CONTRACT RATE

EFFECTIVE YIELD	.14500	.14750	.15000	.15250	.15500	.15750	.16000	.16250	.16500	.16750
.07000	-.47291	-.48940	-.50592	-.52247	-.53905	-.55566	-.57229	-.58894	-.60562	-.62231
.07250	-.45268	-.46898	-.48532	-.50168	-.51807	-.53449	-.55093	-.56740	-.58389	-.60040
.07500	-.43282	-.44894	-.46509	-.48127	-.49747	-.51371	-.52996	-.54625	-.56255	-.57888
.07750	-.41332	-.42926	-.44522	-.46122	-.47725	-.49330	-.50938	-.52548	-.54160	-.55775
.08000	-.39417	-.40993	-.42572	-.44154	-.45739	-.47326	-.48916	-.50508	-.52102	-.53699
.08250	-.37537	-.39095	-.40657	-.42221	-.43788	-.45358	-.46930	-.48505	-.50082	-.51661
.08500	-.35691	-.37232	-.38776	-.40323	-.41873	-.43425	-.44980	-.46538	-.48097	-.49659
.08750	-.33878	-.35402	-.36929	-.38459	-.39992	-.41527	-.43065	-.44606	-.46148	-.47693
.09000	-.32098	-.33605	-.35116	-.36629	-.38145	-.39663	-.41184	-.42708	-.44234	-.45762
.09250	-.30350	-.31841	-.33334	-.34831	-.36330	-.37832	-.39337	-.40844	-.42354	-.43866
.09500	-.28633	-.30107	-.31585	-.33065	-.34548	-.36034	-.37523	-.39014	-.40507	-.42003
.09750	-.26947	-.28405	-.29867	-.31331	-.32798	-.34268	-.35741	-.37216	-.38693	-.40172
.10000	-.25291	-.26733	-.28179	-.29628	-.31079	-.32533	-.33990	-.35449	-.36911	-.38375
.10250	-.23664	-.25091	-.26521	-.27955	-.29391	-.30829	-.32270	-.33714	-.35160	-.36609
.10500	-.22066	-.23478	-.24893	-.26311	-.27732	-.29155	-.30581	-.32010	-.33440	-.34874
.10750	-.20497	-.21894	-.23294	-.24697	-.26102	-.27511	-.28922	-.30335	-.31751	-.33169
.11000	-.18955	-.20337	-.21723	-.23111	-.24501	-.25895	-.27291	-.28690	-.30091	-.31494
.11250	-.17441	-.18809	-.20179	-.21552	-.22929	-.24308	-.25689	-.27073	-.28450	-.29849
.11500	-.15953	-.17306	-.18663	-.20022	-.21384	-.22748	-.24115	-.25485	-.26857	-.28232
.11750	-.14492	-.15831	-.17173	-.18518	-.19865	-.21216	-.22569	-.23925	-.25283	-.26643
.12000	-.13056	-.14381	-.15709	-.17040	-.18374	-.19710	-.21050	-.22391	-.23735	-.25082
.12250	-.11645	-.12956	-.14271	-.15588	-.16908	-.18231	-.19557	-.20885	-.22215	-.23548
.12500	-.10259	-.11557	-.12858	-.14161	-.15468	-.16777	-.18089	-.19404	-.20721	-.22040
.12750	-.08897	-.10181	-.11469	-.12759	-.14053	-.15349	-.16648	-.17949	-.19252	-.20558
.13000	-.07558	-.08830	-.10104	-.11382	-.12662	-.13945	-.15231	-.16519	-.17809	-.19102
.13250	-.06243	-.07502	-.08763	-.10028	-.11295	-.12565	-.13838	-.15113	-.16391	-.17671
.13500	-.04951	-.06197	-.07446	-.08697	-.09952	-.11209	-.12469	-.13732	-.14997	-.16264
.13750	-.03681	-.04914	-.06150	-.07390	-.08632	-.09877	-.11124	-.12374	-.13626	-.14881
.14000	-.02433	-.03654	-.04878	-.06105	-.07334	-.08567	-.09802	-.11040	-.12280	-.13522
.14250	-.01206	-.02415	-.03627	-.04841	-.06059	-.07279	-.08502	-.09728	-.10956	-.12186
.14500	0.00000	-.01197	-.02397	-.03600	-.04805	-.06014	-.07225	-.08438	-.09654	-.10872
.14750	.01185	0.00000	-.01188	-.02379	-.03573	-.04770	-.05969	-.07170	-.08374	-.09581
.15000	.02350	.01177	.00000	-.01179	-.02362	-.03547	-.04734	-.05924	-.07117	-.08311
.15250	.03495	.02333	.01168	0.00000	-.01171	-.02344	-.03520	-.04699	-.05880	-.07063
.15500	.04621	.03470	.02316	.01159	.00000	-.01162	-.02327	-.03494	-.04664	-.05836
.15750	.05727	.04588	.03445	.02299	.01151	.00000	-.01154	-.02310	-.03468	-.04629
.16000	.06815	.05687	.04555	.03420	.02283	.01143	0.00000	-.01145	-.02293	-.03443
.16250	.07885	.06767	.05646	.04522	.03396	.02266	.01134	0.00000	-.01137	-.02276
.16500	.08937	.07829	.06719	.05606	.04490	.03371	.02250	.01126	.00000	-.01128
.16750	.09971	.08874	.07774	.06671	.05566	.04457	.03347	.02234	.01118	.00000
.17000	.10987	.09901	.08811	.07719	.06624	.05526	.04425	.03323	.02217	.01110
.17250	.11987	.10911	.09831	.08749	.07664	.06576	.05486	.04394	.03299	.02201
.17500	.12970	.11904	.10834	.09762	.08687	.07610	.06530	.05447	.04362	.03275
.17750	.13937	.12880	.11821	.10759	.09694	.08626	.07556	.06483	.05408	.04331
.18000	.14888	.13841	.12791	.11739	.10683	.09626	.08565	.07502	.06437	.05369
.18250	.15823	.14786	.13746	.12703	.11657	.10609	.09558	.08505	.07449	.06391
.18500	.16743	.15715	.14684	.13651	.12615	.11576	.10535	.09491	.08445	.07396
.18750	.17647	.16629	.15607	.14583	.13557	.12527	.11495	.10461	.09424	.08385
.19000	.18537	.17528	.16516	.15501	.14483	.13463	.12440	.11415	.10388	.09358
.19250	.19412	.18412	.17409	.16403	.15395	.14384	.13370	.12354	.11336	.10315
.19500	.20273	.19282	.18288	.17291	.16292	.15290	.14285	.13278	.12268	.11257
.19750	.21120	.20138	.19153	.18165	.17174	.16181	.15185	.14187	.13186	.12183
.20000	.21954	.20980	.20003	.19024	.18042	.17058	.16070	.15081	.14089	.13095
.20250	.22773	.21808	.20840	.19870	.18896	.17920	.16942	.15961	.14978	.13992
.20500	.23580	.22623	.21664	.20702	.19737	.18769	.17799	.16827	.15852	.14875
.20750	.24374	.23425	.22474	.21520	.20564	.19605	.18643	.17679	.16713	.15744

POINT TABLES: ORIGINAL LOAN TERM: 240 MONTHS LOAN PREPAID IN: 108 MONTHS

CONTRACT RATE

EFFECTIVE YIELD	.17000	.17250	.17500	.17750	.18000	.18250	.18500	.18750	.19000	.19250
.07000	-.63903	-.65577	-.67252	-.68930	-.70608	-.72289	-.73971	-.75654	-.77338	-.79024
.07250	-.61693	-.63348	-.65005	-.66663	-.68324	-.69986	-.71649	-.73314	-.74980	-.76647
.07500	-.59523	-.61159	-.62798	-.64438	-.66080	-.67724	-.69369	-.71015	-.72663	-.74312
.07750	-.57391	-.59010	-.60630	-.62253	-.63877	-.65502	-.67129	-.68758	-.70387	-.72018
.08000	-.55298	-.56899	-.58502	-.60106	-.61712	-.63320	-.64929	-.66540	-.68152	-.69766
.08250	-.53242	-.54826	-.56411	-.57998	-.59587	-.61177	-.62769	-.64362	-.65957	-.67553
.08500	-.51223	-.52789	-.54357	-.55927	-.57499	-.59072	-.60647	-.62223	-.63800	-.65379
.08750	-.49240	-.50790	-.52341	-.53893	-.55448	-.57004	-.58562	-.60121	-.61682	-.63244
.09000	-.47293	-.48825	-.50359	-.51896	-.53434	-.54973	-.56514	-.58057	-.59601	-.61146
.09250	-.45380	-.46895	-.48413	-.49933	-.51455	-.52978	-.54503	-.56029	-.57557	-.59086
.09500	-.43500	-.45000	-.46502	-.48005	-.49511	-.51018	-.52526	-.54036	-.55548	-.57061
.09750	-.41654	-.43138	-.44624	-.46111	-.47601	-.49092	-.50585	-.52079	-.53575	-.55072
.10000	-.39841	-.41309	-.42779	-.44251	-.45725	-.47200	-.48677	-.50156	-.51636	-.53117
.10250	-.38059	-.39512	-.40966	-.42423	-.43881	-.45341	-.46803	-.48266	-.49731	-.51197
.10500	-.36309	-.37746	-.39186	-.40627	-.42070	-.43515	-.44961	-.46409	-.47859	-.49310
.10750	-.34589	-.36012	-.37436	-.38862	-.40290	-.41720	-.43152	-.44585	-.46020	-.47456
.11000	-.32900	-.34307	-.35717	-.37128	-.38542	-.39957	-.41374	-.42792	-.44212	-.45633
.11250	-.31240	-.32633	-.34028	-.35425	-.36824	-.38224	-.39627	-.41030	-.42436	-.43843
.11500	-.29608	-.30987	-.32368	-.33751	-.35135	-.36521	-.37909	-.39299	-.40690	-.42083
.11750	-.28005	-.29370	-.30737	-.32105	-.33476	-.34848	-.36222	-.37598	-.38975	-.40353
.12000	-.26430	-.27781	-.29134	-.30489	-.31845	-.33204	-.34564	-.35925	-.37288	-.38653
.12250	-.24883	-.26220	-.27559	-.28900	-.30243	-.31587	-.32934	-.34282	-.35631	-.36982
.12500	-.23361	-.24685	-.26010	-.27338	-.28667	-.29999	-.31332	-.32666	-.34002	-.35340
.12750	-.21866	-.23177	-.24489	-.25803	-.27119	-.28437	-.29757	-.31078	-.32401	-.33725
.13000	-.20397	-.21694	-.22993	-.24295	-.25598	-.26903	-.28209	-.29517	-.30827	-.32138
.13250	-.18953	-.20237	-.21523	-.22812	-.24102	-.25394	-.26688	-.27983	-.29280	-.30578
.13500	-.17533	-.18805	-.20079	-.21354	-.22632	-.23911	-.25192	-.26475	-.27759	-.29045
.13750	-.16138	-.17397	-.18658	-.19921	-.21186	-.22453	-.23722	-.24992	-.26263	-.27537
.14000	-.14766	-.16013	-.17262	-.18513	-.19765	-.21020	-.22276	-.23534	-.24793	-.26054
.14250	-.13418	-.14653	-.15889	-.17128	-.18368	-.19611	-.20855	-.22100	-.23348	-.24597
.14500	-.12093	-.13315	-.14540	-.15766	-.16995	-.18225	-.19457	-.20691	-.21927	-.23163
.14750	-.10790	-.12000	-.13213	-.14428	-.15645	-.16863	-.18083	-.19305	-.20529	-.21754
.15000	-.09508	-.10707	-.11909	-.13112	-.14317	-.15524	-.16733	-.17943	-.19155	-.20368
.15250	-.08249	-.09436	-.10626	-.11818	-.13011	-.14207	-.15404	-.16603	-.17804	-.19006
.15500	-.07010	-.08187	-.09365	-.10545	-.11728	-.12912	-.14098	-.15285	-.16475	-.17665
.15750	-.05792	-.06958	-.08125	-.09294	-.10465	-.11638	-.12813	-.13990	-.15168	-.16347
.16000	-.04595	-.05749	-.06905	-.08064	-.09224	-.10386	-.11550	-.12715	-.13882	-.15051
.16250	-.03417	-.04561	-.05706	-.06854	-.08003	-.09154	-.10307	-.11462	-.12618	-.13776
.16500	-.02259	-.03392	-.04527	-.05664	-.06802	-.07943	-.09085	-.10229	-.11375	-.12522
.16750	-.01120	-.02242	-.03367	-.04493	-.05621	-.06751	-.07883	-.09017	-.10152	-.11289
.17000	-.00000	-.01112	-.02226	-.03342	-.04460	-.05579	-.06701	-.07824	-.08949	-.10075
.17250	.01102	-.00000	-.01104	-.02209	-.03317	-.04427	-.05538	-.06651	-.07765	-.08881
.17500	.02185	.01094	.00000	-.01096	-.02193	-.03293	-.04394	-.05497	-.06601	-.07707
.17750	.03251	.02169	.01086	0.00000	-.01088	-.02177	-.03268	-.04361	-.05456	-.06552
.18000	.04300	.03228	.02154	.01078	.00000	-.01080	-.02161	-.03244	-.04329	-.05415
.18250	.05331	.04269	.03204	.02138	.01070	0.00000	-.01072	-.02145	-.03220	-.04297
.18500	.06346	.05293	.04238	.03181	.02123	.01062	.00000	-.01064	-.02130	-.03197
.18750	.07344	.06301	.05255	.04208	.03158	.02107	.01055	0.00000	-.01056	-.02114
.19000	.08326	.07292	.06256	.05218	.04178	.03136	.02092	.01047	.00000	-.01048
.19250	.09292	.08267	.07240	.06211	.05180	.04148	.03113	.02077	.01039	.00000
.19500	.10243	.09227	.08209	.07189	.06167	.05143	.04118	.03091	.02062	.01032
.19750	.11178	.10171	.09162	.08151	.07138	.06123	.05107	.04089	.03069	.02047
.20000	.12099	.11101	.10100	.09098	.08094	.07088	.06080	.05070	.04059	.03047
.20250	.13005	.12015	.11023	.10030	.09034	.08037	.07038	.06037	.05034	.04030
.20500	.13896	.12915	.11932	.10947	.09960	.08971	.07980	.06988	.05994	.04999
.20750	.14774	.13801	.12826	.11849	.10871	.09890	.08908	.07924	.06939	.05952

EFFECTIVE YIELD	CONTRACT RATE .19500	.19750	.20000	.20250	.20500	.20750
.07000	-.80711	-.82399	-.84088	-.85777	-.87468	-.89159
.07250	-.78315	-.79984	-.81655	-.83326	-.84998	-.86671
.07500	-.75962	-.77613	-.79265	-.80918	-.82572	-.84227
.07750	-.73651	-.75284	-.76918	-.78553	-.80190	-.81827
.08000	-.71380	-.72996	-.74613	-.76230	-.77849	-.79468
.08250	-.69150	-.70748	-.72348	-.73948	-.75550	-.77152
.08500	-.66959	-.68541	-.70123	-.71706	-.73291	-.74876
.08750	-.64807	-.66372	-.67937	-.69504	-.71071	-.72640
.09000	-.62693	-.64241	-.65790	-.67340	-.68891	-.70443
.09250	-.60616	-.62147	-.63680	-.65214	-.66749	-.68284
.09500	-.58575	-.60091	-.61607	-.63125	-.64644	-.66163
.09750	-.56570	-.58070	-.59571	-.61072	-.62575	-.64079
.10000	-.54600	-.56084	-.57569	-.59056	-.60543	-.62031
.10250	-.52664	-.54133	-.55603	-.57074	-.58546	-.60019
.10500	-.50762	-.52216	-.53670	-.55126	-.56583	-.58041
.10750	-.48893	-.50332	-.51771	-.53212	-.54655	-.56098
.11000	-.47056	-.48480	-.49905	-.51332	-.52759	-.54187
.11250	-.45251	-.46660	-.48071	-.49483	-.50896	-.52310
.11500	-.43477	-.44872	-.46268	-.47666	-.49065	-.50465
.11750	-.41733	-.43114	-.44497	-.45880	-.47265	-.48651
.12000	-.40019	-.41387	-.42755	-.44125	-.45496	-.46868
.12250	-.38335	-.39688	-.41043	-.42400	-.43757	-.45116
.12500	-.36679	-.38019	-.39361	-.40704	-.42048	-.43393
.12750	-.35051	-.36378	-.37707	-.39036	-.40367	-.41699
.13000	-.33451	-.34765	-.36081	-.37397	-.38715	-.40034
.13250	-.31878	-.33179	-.34482	-.35786	-.37091	-.38397
.13500	-.30332	-.31620	-.32910	-.34201	-.35494	-.36787
.13750	-.28811	-.30088	-.31365	-.32644	-.33923	-.35204
.14000	-.27317	-.28580	-.29846	-.31112	-.32380	-.33648
.14250	-.25847	-.27099	-.28352	-.29606	-.30861	-.32118
.14500	-.24402	-.25641	-.26883	-.28125	-.29368	-.30613
.14750	-.22981	-.24209	-.25438	-.26669	-.27900	-.29133
.15000	-.21583	-.22800	-.24017	-.25236	-.26457	-.27678
.15250	-.20209	-.21414	-.22620	-.23828	-.25037	-.26247
.15500	-.18858	-.20051	-.21246	-.22443	-.23640	-.24839
.15750	-.17528	-.18711	-.19895	-.21080	-.22267	-.23454
.16000	-.16221	-.17393	-.18566	-.19740	-.20915	-.22092
.16250	-.14935	-.16096	-.17258	-.18422	-.19586	-.20752
.16500	-.13671	-.14821	-.15972	-.17125	-.18279	-.19434
.16750	-.12427	-.13566	-.14707	-.15850	-.16993	-.18138
.17000	-.11203	-.12332	-.13463	-.14595	-.15728	-.16862
.17250	-.09999	-.11118	-.12239	-.13360	-.14483	-.15608
.17500	-.08815	-.09924	-.11034	-.12146	-.13259	-.14373
.17750	-.07650	-.08749	-.09849	-.10951	-.12054	-.13158
.18000	-.06503	-.07592	-.08683	-.09775	-.10868	-.11963
.18250	-.05375	-.06455	-.07536	-.08618	-.09702	-.10786
.18500	-.04265	-.05335	-.06407	-.07480	-.08554	-.09629
.18750	-.03173	-.04234	-.05296	-.06359	-.07424	-.08490
.19000	-.02098	-.03150	-.04203	-.05257	-.06312	-.07369
.19250	-.01041	-.02083	-.03127	-.04172	-.05218	-.06266
.19500	.00000	-.01033	-.02068	-.03104	-.04141	-.05180
.19750	.01024	.00000	-.01026	-.02053	-.03081	-.04111
.20000	.02033	.01017	.00000	-.01018	-.02038	-.03059
.20250	.03025	.02018	.01010	.00000	-.01011	-.02023
.20500	.04002	.03003	.02004	.01002	.00000	-.01004
.20750	.04963	.03973	.02982	.01989	.00995	.00000

POINT TABLES: ORIGINAL LOAN TERM: 240 MONTHS LOAN PREPAID IN: 144 MONTHS

EFFECTIVE YIELD	CONTRACT RATE .07000	.07250	.07500	.07750	.08000	.08250	.08500	.08750	.09000	.09250
.07000	.00000	-.01717	-.03447	-.05188	-.06942	-.08706	-.10482	-.12270	-.14067	-.15876
.07250	.01691	.00000	-.01703	-.03418	-.05145	-.06883	-.08632	-.10392	-.12153	-.13944
.07500	.03343	.01677	0.00000	-.01689	-.03390	-.05102	-.06825	-.08559	-.10333	-.12057
.07750	.04956	.03316	.01664	.00000	-.01675	-.03362	-.05059	-.06767	-.08485	-.10214
.08000	.06533	.04917	.03289	.01650	.00000	-.01661	-.03333	-.05016	-.06739	-.08412
.08250	.08073	.06481	.04877	.03263	.01637	.00000	-.01648	-.03305	-.04974	-.06652
.08500	.09577	.08009	.06429	.04838	.03236	.01623	.00000	-.01634	-.03278	-.04931
.08750	.11047	.09502	.07946	.06378	.04799	.03210	.01610	0.00000	-.01620	-.03250
.09000	.12484	.10961	.09427	.07883	.06327	.04760	.03184	.01597	0.00000	-.01606
.09250	.13888	.12388	.10876	.09353	.07820	.06276	.04722	.03158	.01584	.00000
.09500	.15260	.13781	.12291	.10790	.09279	.07757	.06225	.04683	.03132	.01570
.09750	.16602	.15144	.13675	.12195	.10705	.09205	.07695	.06175	.04645	.03106
.10000	.17913	.16475	.15027	.13569	.12100	.10621	.09131	.07633	.06124	.04607
.10250	.19194	.17777	.16349	.14911	.13463	.12004	.10536	.09058	.07571	.06074
.10500	.20447	.19050	.17642	.16224	.14796	.13358	.11910	.10452	.08985	.07509
.10750	.21672	.20294	.18906	.17507	.16099	.14681	.13253	.11815	.10369	.08913
.11000	.22869	.21511	.20142	.18762	.17373	.15974	.14566	.13148	.11721	.10285
.11250	.24040	.22700	.21350	.19990	.18620	.17240	.15850	.14452	.13044	.11628
.11500	.25186	.23864	.22532	.21190	.19838	.18477	.17107	.15727	.14338	.12941
.11750	.26306	.25002	.23688	.22364	.21031	.19688	.18335	.16974	.15604	.14225
.12000	.27401	.26115	.24818	.23512	.22197	.20872	.19537	.18194	.16842	.15482
.12250	.28472	.27203	.25924	.24635	.23337	.22030	.20713	.19388	.18054	.16711
.12500	.29521	.28268	.27006	.25734	.24453	.23163	.21864	.20556	.19239	.17914
.12750	.30546	.29310	.28064	.26809	.25545	.24272	.22989	.21698	.20399	.19091
.13000	.31549	.30329	.29100	.27861	.26613	.25356	.24091	.22816	.21534	.20242
.13250	.32530	.31326	.30113	.28890	.27659	.26418	.25169	.23911	.22644	.21370
.13500	.33491	.32302	.31105	.29898	.28682	.27457	.26223	.24981	.23731	.22473
.13750	.34430	.33257	.32075	.30883	.29683	.28474	.27256	.26029	.24795	.23552
.14000	.35350	.34192	.33024	.31848	.30663	.29469	.28266	.27055	.25836	.24609
.14250	.36250	.35107	.33954	.32792	.31622	.30443	.29255	.28060	.26856	.25644
.14500	.37131	.36002	.34864	.33717	.32561	.31396	.30224	.29043	.27854	.26657
.14750	.37994	.36879	.35754	.34621	.33480	.32330	.31172	.30005	.28831	.27649
.15000	.38838	.37737	.36626	.35507	.34380	.33244	.32100	.30948	.29788	.28620
.15250	.39665	.38577	.37480	.36375	.35261	.34139	.33009	.31871	.30725	.29571
.15500	.40474	.39399	.38316	.37224	.36124	.35015	.33899	.32774	.31642	.30503
.15750	.41267	.40205	.39135	.38056	.36969	.35874	.34770	.33660	.32541	.31415
.16000	.42043	.40994	.39936	.38870	.37796	.36714	.35624	.34526	.33421	.32308
.16250	.42803	.41766	.40721	.39668	.38607	.37538	.36460	.35376	.34283	.33184
.16500	.43547	.42523	.41490	.40450	.39401	.38344	.37280	.36208	.35128	.34041
.16750	.44277	.43264	.42244	.41215	.40179	.39134	.38082	.37023	.35956	.34881
.17000	.44991	.43990	.42982	.41965	.40941	.39908	.38868	.37821	.36766	.35705
.17250	.45691	.44702	.43705	.42700	.41687	.40667	.39639	.38604	.37561	.36511
.17500	.46376	.45399	.44413	.43420	.42419	.41410	.40394	.39370	.38340	.37302
.17750	.47048	.46082	.45108	.44125	.43136	.42138	.41134	.40122	.39103	.38076
.18000	.47706	.46751	.45788	.44817	.43838	.42852	.41859	.40858	.39850	.38836
.18250	.48352	.47407	.46455	.45494	.44527	.43552	.42569	.41580	.40584	.39580
.18500	.48984	.48050	.47108	.46159	.45202	.44238	.43266	.42288	.41302	.40310
.18750	.49604	.48680	.47749	.46810	.45863	.44910	.43949	.42981	.42007	.41025
.19000	.50211	.49298	.48377	.47448	.46512	.45569	.44619	.43661	.42697	.41727
.19250	.50807	.49903	.48992	.48074	.47148	.46215	.45275	.44328	.43375	.42414
.19500	.51391	.50497	.49596	.48687	.47771	.46849	.45919	.44982	.44039	.43089
.19750	.51963	.51079	.50188	.49289	.48383	.47470	.46550	.45623	.44690	.43750
.20000	.52525	.51650	.50768	.49879	.48983	.48079	.47169	.46252	.45329	.44399
.20250	.53075	.52210	.51337	.50457	.49571	.48677	.47776	.46869	.45955	.45035
.20500	.53615	.52759	.51895	.51025	.50147	.49263	.48372	.47474	.46570	.45660
.20750	.54145	.53297	.52443	.51582	.50713	.49838	.48956	.48068	.47173	.46272

POINT TABLES: ORIGINAL LOAN TERM: 240 MONTHS LOAN PREPAID IN: 144 MONTHS

EFFECTIVE YIELD	CONTRACT RATE .09500	.09750	.10000	.10250	.10500	.10750	.11000	.11250	.11500	.11750
.07000	-.17694	-.19523	-.21361	-.23209	-.25066	-.26932	-.28807	-.30690	-.32582	-.34481
.07250	-.15736	-.17537	-.19348	-.21168	-.22997	-.24836	-.26683	-.28538	-.30402	-.32273
.07500	-.13822	-.15597	-.17381	-.19174	-.20976	-.22787	-.24607	-.26435	-.28271	-.30115
.07750	-.11952	-.13701	-.15458	-.17225	-.19001	-.20786	-.22579	-.24380	-.26189	-.28007
.08000	-.10125	-.11848	-.13580	-.15321	-.17071	-.18829	-.20596	-.22372	-.24155	-.25946
.08250	-.08340	-.10037	-.11744	-.13460	-.15184	-.16917	-.18659	-.20408	-.22166	-.23931
.08500	-.06595	-.08268	-.09950	-.11641	-.13340	-.15049	-.16765	-.18490	-.20222	-.21962
.08750	-.04889	-.06538	-.08196	-.09863	-.11538	-.13222	-.14914	-.16614	-.18322	-.20037
.09000	-.03222	-.04848	-.06482	-.08125	-.09776	-.11436	-.13104	-.14780	-.16464	-.18155
.09250	-.01593	-.03195	-.04806	-.06426	-.08054	-.09690	-.11335	-.12987	-.14647	-.16315
.09500	.00000	-.01579	-.03168	-.04765	-.06370	-.07984	-.09605	-.11234	-.12871	-.14516
.09750	.01557	.00000	-.01566	-.03141	-.04724	-.06315	-.07914	-.09520	-.11135	-.12756
.10000	.03080	.01544	0.00000	-.01553	-.03114	-.04683	-.06260	-.07844	-.09436	-.11036
.10250	.04569	.03054	.01531	.00000	-.01540	-.03087	-.04642	-.06205	-.07776	-.09353
.10500	.06025	.04531	.03029	.01519	-.00000	-.01526	-.03061	-.04602	-.06151	-.07707
.10750	.07448	.05975	.04493	.03004	.01506	.00000	-.01513	-.03034	-.04562	-.06097
.11000	.08841	.07388	.05926	.04456	.02978	.01493	.00000	-.01500	-.03008	-.04523
.11250	.10203	.08769	.07327	.05877	.04419	.02954	.01480	.00000	-.01488	-.02982
.11500	.11535	.10120	.08698	.07267	.05828	.04382	.02929	.01468	.00000	-.01475
.11750	.12838	.11442	.10038	.08627	.07207	.05780	.04346	.02904	.01455	.00000
.12000	.14113	.12735	.11350	.09957	.08556	.07148	.05732	.04309	.02880	.01443
.12250	.15360	.14001	.12634	.11259	.09876	.08486	.07089	.05684	.04273	.02855
.12500	.16580	.15239	.13889	.12532	.11168	.09795	.08416	.07030	.05637	.04237
.12750	.17775	.16450	.15118	.13779	.12431	.11077	.09715	.08347	.06972	.05590
.13000	.18943	.17636	.16321	.14998	.13668	.12331	.10987	.09636	.08278	.06914
.13250	.20087	.18796	.17498	.16192	.14879	.13559	.12232	.10898	.09557	.08210
.13500	.21206	.19932	.18650	.17361	.16064	.14761	.13450	.12133	.10809	.09479
.13750	.22302	.21044	.19778	.18505	.17225	.15937	.14643	.13342	.12035	.10721
.14000	.23375	.22132	.20882	.19625	.18360	.17089	.15811	.14526	.13235	.11937
.14250	.24425	.23198	.21963	.20721	.19472	.18217	.16954	.15685	.14410	.13128
.14500	.25453	.24241	.23021	.21795	.20561	.19321	.18074	.16820	.15560	.14294
.14750	.26459	.25262	.24058	.22846	.21628	.20402	.19170	.17932	.16687	.15436
.15000	.27445	.26262	.25072	.23876	.22672	.21461	.20244	.19021	.17791	.16555
.15250	.28410	.27242	.26066	.24884	.23694	.22498	.21296	.20087	.18872	.17651
.15500	.29355	.28201	.27040	.25871	.24696	.23514	.22326	.21131	.19931	.18724
.15750	.30281	.29141	.27993	.26839	.25677	.24509	.23335	.22155	.20968	.19775
.16000	.31188	.30061	.28927	.27786	.26638	.25484	.24324	.23157	.21984	.20806
.16250	.32077	.30963	.29842	.28714	.27580	.26439	.25292	.24139	.22980	.21815
.16500	.32947	.31846	.30738	.29624	.28503	.27375	.26241	.25102	.23956	.22804
.16750	.33800	.32712	.31617	.30515	.29407	.28292	.27172	.26045	.24912	.23773
.17000	.34636	.33560	.32477	.31388	.30293	.29191	.28083	.26969	.25849	.24723
.17250	.35455	.34391	.33321	.32244	.31161	.30072	.28976	.27875	.26767	.25655
.17500	.36257	.35206	.34147	.33083	.32012	.30935	.29852	.28763	.27668	.26567
.17750	.37043	.36004	.34958	.33905	.32846	.31781	.30710	.29633	.28550	.27462
.18000	.37814	.36786	.35752	.34711	.33664	.32610	.31551	.30486	.29415	.28339
.18250	.38570	.37553	.36530	.35501	.34465	.33424	.32376	.31323	.30264	.29199
.18500	.39311	.38305	.37293	.36275	.35251	.34221	.33185	.32143	.31095	.30042
.18750	.40037	.39043	.38042	.37035	.36022	.35002	.33978	.32947	.31911	.30869
.19000	.40749	.39766	.38776	.37779	.36777	.35769	.34755	.33736	.32711	.31680
.19250	.41448	.40474	.39495	.38510	.37518	.36521	.35518	.34509	.33495	.32476
.19500	.42132	.41170	.40201	.39226	.38245	.37258	.36266	.35268	.34264	.33256
.19750	.42804	.41852	.40893	.39928	.38958	.37981	.36999	.36012	.35019	.34021
.20000	.43463	.42520	.41572	.40617	.39657	.38691	.37719	.36742	.35760	.34772
.20250	.44109	.43176	.42238	.41293	.40343	.39387	.38425	.37458	.36486	.35509
.20500	.44743	.43820	.42891	.41956	.41016	.40070	.39118	.38161	.37199	.36231
.20750	.45365	.44451	.43532	.42607	.41676	.40740	.39798	.38850	.37898	.36940

POINT TABLES: ORIGINAL LOAN TERM: 240 MONTHS LOAN PREPAID IN: 144 MONTHS

CONTRACT RATE

EFFECTIVE YIELD	.12000	.12250	.12500	.12750	.13000	.13250	.13500	.13750	.14000	.14250
.07000	-.36389	-.38303	-.40226	-.42155	-.44091	-.46034	-.47983	-.49938	-.51899	-.53866
.07250	-.34152	-.36039	-.37933	-.39834	-.41742	-.43656	-.45577	-.47504	-.49437	-.51375
.07500	-.31967	-.33826	-.35693	-.37566	-.39446	-.41333	-.43226	-.45125	-.47029	-.48940
.07750	-.29832	-.31664	-.33503	-.35349	-.37202	-.39062	-.40927	-.42799	-.44677	-.46560
.08000	-.27744	-.29550	-.31363	-.33182	-.35009	-.36842	-.38681	-.40526	-.42376	-.44233
.08250	-.25704	-.27484	-.29271	-.31064	-.32865	-.34671	-.36484	-.38303	-.40128	-.41958
.08500	-.23709	-.25464	-.27225	-.28994	-.30768	-.32550	-.34337	-.36130	-.37929	-.39734
.08750	-.21759	-.23489	-.25226	-.26969	-.28719	-.30475	-.32237	-.34006	-.35779	-.37559
.09000	-.19853	-.21559	-.23271	-.24990	-.26715	-.28447	-.30185	-.31928	-.33677	-.35432
.09250	-.17989	-.19671	-.21359	-.23054	-.24756	-.26464	-.28177	-.29897	-.31622	-.33352
.09500	-.16167	-.17825	-.19490	-.21162	-.22840	-.24524	-.26214	-.27910	-.29611	-.31318
.09750	-.14385	-.16020	-.17662	-.19311	-.20966	-.22627	-.24294	-.25967	-.27645	-.29329
.10000	-.12642	-.14255	-.15875	-.17501	-.19133	-.20772	-.22416	-.24066	-.25722	-.27383
.10250	-.10937	-.12528	-.14126	-.15730	-.17341	-.18957	-.20579	-.22207	-.23840	-.25479
.10500	-.09270	-.10840	-.12416	-.13998	-.15587	-.17182	-.18782	-.20388	-.22000	-.23617
.10750	-.07639	-.09188	-.10743	-.12304	-.13872	-.15445	-.17024	-.18609	-.20199	-.21795
.11000	-.06044	-.07572	-.09106	-.10647	-.12194	-.13746	-.15304	-.16868	-.18437	-.20012
.11250	-.04483	-.05991	-.07505	-.09025	-.10552	-.12084	-.13622	-.15165	-.16714	-.18267
.11500	-.02956	-.04444	-.05938	-.07439	-.08945	-.10457	-.11975	-.13498	-.15027	-.16560
.11750	-.01462	-.02931	-.04405	-.05886	-.07373	-.08865	-.10364	-.11867	-.13376	-.14890
.12000	-.00000	-.01449	-.02905	-.04367	-.05834	-.07308	-.08787	-.10271	-.11760	-.13255
.12250	.01431	.00000	-.01437	-.02880	-.04329	-.05783	-.07243	-.08708	-.10179	-.11654
.12500	.02831	.01419	.00000	-.01425	-.02855	-.04291	-.05732	-.07179	-.08631	-.10087
.12750	.04202	.02807	.01406	0.00000	-.01412	-.02830	-.04253	-.05682	-.07115	-.08554
.13000	.05543	.04166	.02783	.01394	.00000	-.01400	-.02805	-.04216	-.05632	-.07052
.13250	.06856	.05497	.04131	.02760	.01383	.00000	-.01388	-.02781	-.04179	-.05582
.13500	.08142	.06799	.05451	.04096	.02736	.01371	0.00000	-.01376	-.02757	-.04142
.13750	.09401	.08075	.06743	.05405	.04062	.02713	.01359	.00000	-.01364	-.02733
.14000	.10633	.09323	.08008	.06686	.05359	.04027	.02690	.01347	.00000	-.01352
.14250	.11840	.10546	.09246	.07941	.06631	.05314	.03993	.02667	.01336	0.00000
.14500	.13022	.11744	.10460	.09170	.07875	.06575	.05270	.03959	.02644	.01324
.14750	.14179	.12916	.11648	.10374	.09095	.07810	.06520	.05225	.03926	.02622
.15000	.15313	.14065	.12812	.11553	.10289	.09019	.07745	.06466	.05182	.03893
.15250	.16423	.15191	.13952	.12708	.11459	.10204	.08945	.07681	.06412	.05138
.15500	.17511	.16293	.15069	.13840	.12605	.11365	.10121	.08871	.07617	.06358
.15750	.18577	.17373	.16163	.14948	.13728	.12503	.11273	.10037	.08798	.07553
.16000	.19621	.18431	.17235	.16035	.14828	.13617	.12401	.11180	.09955	.08725
.16250	.20644	.19468	.18286	.17099	.15907	.14710	.13507	.12301	.11089	.09873
.16500	.21647	.20484	.19316	.18142	.16963	.15780	.14591	.13398	.12201	.10998
.16750	.22629	.21480	.20325	.19164	.17999	.16829	.15654	.14474	.13290	.12102
.17000	.23592	.22456	.21314	.20166	.19014	.17857	.16695	.15529	.14358	.13183
.17250	.24536	.23412	.22283	.21149	.20009	.18865	.17716	.16563	.15405	.14243
.17500	.25461	.24350	.23233	.22112	.20985	.19854	.18717	.17577	.16432	.15282
.17750	.26368	.25269	.24165	.23056	.21941	.20822	.19699	.18571	.17438	.16301
.18000	.27257	.26170	.25078	.23981	.22879	.21772	.20661	.19545	.18425	.17300
.18250	.28129	.27054	.25974	.24889	.23799	.22704	.21605	.20501	.19393	.18280
.18500	.28984	.27921	.26852	.25779	.24700	.23618	.22530	.21438	.20342	.19241
.18750	.29822	.28770	.27713	.26652	.25585	.24513	.23438	.22357	.21273	.20184
.19000	.30645	.29604	.28558	.27508	.26452	.25392	.24328	.23259	.22186	.21109
.19250	.31451	.30421	.29387	.28347	.27303	.26254	.25201	.24144	.23082	.22016
.19500	.32242	.31223	.30199	.29171	.28138	.27100	.26058	.25011	.23961	.22906
.19750	.33018	.32010	.30997	.29979	.28956	.27930	.26898	.25863	.24823	.23779
.20000	.33779	.32781	.31779	.30772	.29760	.28744	.27723	.26698	.25669	.24636
.20250	.34526	.33539	.32546	.31550	.30548	.29542	.28532	.27518	.26499	.25477
.20500	.35259	.34282	.33300	.32313	.31322	.30326	.29326	.28322	.27314	.26302
.20750	.35978	.35011	.34039	.33062	.32081	.31095	.30105	.29112	.28114	.27112

POINT TABLES: ORIGINAL LOAN TERM: 240 MONTHS LOAN PREPAID IN: 144 MONTHS

EFFECTIVE YIELD	CONTRACT RATE .14500	.14750	.15000	.15250	.15500	.15750	.16000	.16250	.16500	.16750
.07000	-.55839	-.57817	-.59800	-.61788	-.63781	-.65779	-.67781	-.69787	-.71797	-.73811
.07250	-.53319	-.55269	-.57223	-.59183	-.61147	-.63116	-.65089	-.67067	-.69048	-.71034
.07500	-.50856	-.52778	-.54704	-.56636	-.58572	-.60513	-.62458	-.64407	-.66360	-.68318
.07750	-.48449	-.50343	-.52242	-.54146	-.56054	-.57968	-.59885	-.61807	-.63733	-.65662
.08000	-.46095	-.47962	-.49834	-.51711	-.53593	-.55479	-.57370	-.59265	-.61163	-.63066
.08250	-.43794	-.45634	-.47480	-.49331	-.51186	-.53046	-.54910	-.56779	-.58651	-.60527
.08500	-.41543	-.43359	-.45179	-.47004	-.48833	-.50667	-.52505	-.54348	-.56194	-.58044
.08750	-.39343	-.41133	-.42928	-.44728	-.46532	-.48340	-.50153	-.51970	-.53791	-.55616
.09000	-.37192	-.38957	-.40727	-.42502	-.44281	-.46065	-.47853	-.49645	-.51441	-.53241
.09250	-.35088	-.36829	-.38575	-.40325	-.42080	-.43840	-.45603	-.47371	-.49143	-.50918
.09500	-.33030	-.34747	-.36469	-.38196	-.39927	-.41663	-.43403	-.45146	-.46894	-.48646
.09750	-.31017	-.32711	-.34410	-.36113	-.37821	-.39533	-.41250	-.42970	-.44695	-.46423
.10000	-.29049	-.30720	-.32395	-.34076	-.35761	-.37450	-.39144	-.40841	-.42543	-.44248
.10250	-.27123	-.28771	-.30425	-.32083	-.33745	-.35412	-.37083	-.38758	-.40437	-.42120
.10500	-.25238	-.26865	-.28497	-.30133	-.31773	-.33418	-.35067	-.36720	-.38377	-.40037
.10750	-.23395	-.25000	-.26610	-.28225	-.29844	-.31467	-.33094	-.34726	-.36361	-.38000
.11000	-.21591	-.23175	-.24764	-.26358	-.27956	-.29558	-.31164	-.32774	-.34388	-.36006
.11250	-.19826	-.21390	-.22958	-.24531	-.26108	-.27689	-.29275	-.30864	-.32457	-.34054
.11500	-.18099	-.19642	-.21190	-.22743	-.24300	-.25861	-.27426	-.28995	-.30567	-.32144
.11750	-.16408	-.17932	-.19460	-.20993	-.22530	-.24071	-.25616	-.27165	-.28717	-.30274
.12000	-.14754	-.16258	-.17767	-.19280	-.20797	-.22318	-.23844	-.25373	-.26906	-.28443
.12250	-.13134	-.14619	-.16109	-.17603	-.19101	-.20603	-.22110	-.23620	-.25133	-.26651
.12500	-.11549	-.13015	-.14486	-.15961	-.17441	-.18924	-.20412	-.21903	-.23398	-.24896
.12750	-.09997	-.11445	-.12897	-.14354	-.15815	-.17280	-.18749	-.20222	-.21698	-.23178
.13000	-.08478	-.09907	-.11342	-.12780	-.14223	-.15670	-.17121	-.18576	-.20034	-.21496
.13250	-.06990	-.08402	-.09819	-.11240	-.12665	-.14094	-.15527	-.16964	-.18404	-.19848
.13500	-.05533	-.06928	-.08327	-.09731	-.11138	-.12550	-.13966	-.15385	-.16808	-.18234
.13750	-.04106	-.05484	-.06866	-.08253	-.09644	-.11038	-.12437	-.13839	-.15245	-.16654
.14000	-.02709	-.04070	-.05436	-.06806	-.08180	-.09557	-.10939	-.12324	-.13713	-.15106
.14250	-.01340	-.02685	-.04035	-.05388	-.06745	-.08107	-.09472	-.10841	-.12213	-.13589
.14500	.00000	-.01329	-.02662	-.03999	-.05341	-.06686	-.08035	-.09387	-.10743	-.12103
.14750	.01313	-.00000	-.01317	-.02639	-.03964	-.05294	-.06627	-.07963	-.09304	-.10647
.15000	.02599	.01302	.00000	-.01306	-.02616	-.03930	-.05247	-.06568	-.07893	-.09221
.15250	.03860	.02577	.01291	.00000	-.01295	-.02593	-.03895	-.05201	-.06510	-.07823
.15500	.05095	.03827	.02555	.01280	0.00000	-.01283	-.02571	-.03861	-.05155	-.06453
.15750	.06305	.05052	.03795	.02534	.01269	0.00000	-.01272	-.02548	-.03828	-.05110
.16000	.07491	.06252	.05009	.03763	.02512	.01258	.00000	-.01261	-.02526	-.03794
.16250	.08653	.07428	.06200	.04967	.03731	.02491	.01247	-.00000	-.01251	-.02504
.16500	.09792	.08581	.07367	.06148	.04926	.03699	.02470	.01237	.00000	-.01240
.16750	.10909	.09712	.08510	.07306	.06097	.04884	.03668	.02449	.01226	-.00000
.17000	.12003	.10820	.09632	.08440	.07245	.06046	.04843	.03637	.02428	.01216
.17250	.13076	.11906	.10731	.09553	.08371	.07185	.05995	.04803	.03607	.02408
.17500	.14128	.12971	.11809	.10644	.09474	.08302	.07125	.05946	.04763	.03576
.17750	.15160	.14015	.12866	.11713	.10557	.09397	.08233	.07066	.05896	.04723
.18000	.16172	.15039	.13903	.12762	.11618	.10471	.09320	.08165	.07008	.05847
.18250	.17164	.16043	.14919	.13791	.12659	.11524	.10385	.09243	.08098	.06950
.18500	.18137	.17028	.15916	.14800	.13680	.12557	.11431	.10301	.09168	.08032
.18750	.19091	.17995	.16894	.15790	.14682	.13571	.12456	.11338	.10217	.09093
.19000	.20028	.18942	.17854	.16761	.15665	.14565	.13462	.12356	.11247	.10134
.19250	.20946	.19872	.18795	.17714	.16629	.15541	.14449	.13355	.12257	.11156
.19500	.21847	.20785	.19718	.18648	.17575	.16498	.15418	.14334	.13248	.12158
.19750	.22731	.21680	.20624	.19565	.18503	.17437	.16368	.15296	.14221	.13142
.20000	.23599	.22558	.21514	.20466	.19414	.18359	.17301	.16240	.15175	.14108
.20250	.24450	.23420	.22386	.21349	.20308	.19264	.18216	.17166	.16112	.15055
.20500	.25286	.24266	.23243	.22216	.21185	.20152	.19115	.18075	.17032	.15986
.20750	.26106	.25096	.24083	.23067	.22047	.21023	.19997	.18967	.17934	.16899

POINT TABLES: ORIGINAL LOAN TERM: 240 MONTHS LOAN PREPAID IN: 144 MONTHS

CONTRACT RATE

EFFECTIVE YIELD	.17000	.17250	.17500	.17750	.18000	.18250	.18500	.18750	.19000	.19250
.07000	-.75829	-.77851	-.79876	-.81904	-.83935	-.85969	-.88007	-.90046	-.92089	-.94134
.07250	-.73023	-.75015	-.77012	-.79011	-.81013	-.83019	-.85027	-.87038	-.89052	-.91068
.07500	-.70279	-.72243	-.74211	-.76182	-.78157	-.80134	-.82114	-.84097	-.86082	-.88070
.07750	-.67596	-.69533	-.71473	-.73417	-.75363	-.77313	-.79266	-.81221	-.83179	-.85139
.08000	-.64972	-.66882	-.68796	-.70712	-.72632	-.74554	-.76480	-.78408	-.80339	-.82272
.08250	-.62407	-.64291	-.66177	-.68067	-.69960	-.71857	-.73755	-.75657	-.77561	-.79468
.08500	-.59898	-.61756	-.63617	-.65481	-.67348	-.69218	-.71091	-.72966	-.74845	-.76725
.08750	-.57445	-.59277	-.61112	-.62951	-.64792	-.66637	-.68484	-.70335	-.72187	-.74042
.09000	-.55045	-.56852	-.58662	-.60476	-.62293	-.64112	-.65935	-.67760	-.69588	-.71418
.09250	-.52697	-.54480	-.56266	-.58055	-.59847	-.61642	-.63441	-.65241	-.67044	-.68850
.09500	-.50401	-.52160	-.53922	-.55687	-.57455	-.59226	-.61000	-.62777	-.64556	-.66338
.09750	-.48154	-.49890	-.51628	-.53370	-.55115	-.56862	-.58613	-.60366	-.62122	-.63880
.10000	-.45956	-.47669	-.49384	-.51103	-.52824	-.54549	-.56276	-.58007	-.59739	-.61474
.10250	-.43806	-.45495	-.47188	-.48884	-.50583	-.52286	-.53990	-.55698	-.57408	-.59120
.10500	-.41701	-.43369	-.45040	-.46714	-.48391	-.50070	-.51753	-.53438	-.55126	-.56817
.10750	-.39642	-.41288	-.42937	-.44589	-.46244	-.47902	-.49563	-.51227	-.52893	-.54562
.11000	-.37627	-.39251	-.40879	-.42510	-.44144	-.45781	-.47420	-.49062	-.50707	-.52354
.11250	-.35654	-.37258	-.38865	-.40475	-.42088	-.43704	-.45322	-.46944	-.48567	-.50194
.11500	-.33723	-.35307	-.36893	-.38482	-.40075	-.41670	-.43269	-.44869	-.46473	-.48078
.11750	-.31833	-.33396	-.34963	-.36532	-.38105	-.39680	-.41258	-.42839	-.44422	-.46008
.12000	-.29983	-.31527	-.33073	-.34623	-.36176	-.37731	-.39290	-.40850	-.42414	-.43980
.12250	-.28172	-.29696	-.31223	-.32754	-.34287	-.35823	-.37362	-.38904	-.40448	-.41994
.12500	-.26398	-.27903	-.29412	-.30923	-.32438	-.33955	-.35475	-.36997	-.38522	-.40050
.12750	-.24661	-.26148	-.27638	-.29131	-.30626	-.32125	-.33626	-.35130	-.36637	-.38145
.13000	-.22961	-.24429	-.25901	-.27375	-.28853	-.30333	-.31816	-.33302	-.34790	-.36280
.13250	-.21295	-.22746	-.24199	-.25656	-.27116	-.28578	-.30043	-.31511	-.32981	-.34453
.13500	-.19664	-.21097	-.22533	-.23972	-.25414	-.26859	-.28306	-.29756	-.31209	-.32664
.13750	-.18066	-.19482	-.20901	-.22323	-.23747	-.25175	-.26605	-.28038	-.29473	-.30911
.14000	-.16501	-.17900	-.19302	-.20707	-.22115	-.23525	-.24938	-.26354	-.27772	-.29193
.14250	-.14968	-.16350	-.17736	-.19124	-.20515	-.21909	-.23305	-.24705	-.26106	-.27510
.14500	-.13466	-.14832	-.16201	-.17573	-.18948	-.20325	-.21705	-.23088	-.24473	-.25861
.14750	-.11994	-.13344	-.14697	-.16053	-.17412	-.18773	-.20138	-.21504	-.22873	-.24245
.15000	-.10552	-.11886	-.13224	-.14564	-.15907	-.17253	-.18601	-.19952	-.21305	-.22661
.15250	-.09139	-.10458	-.11779	-.13104	-.14432	-.15762	-.17095	-.18431	-.19768	-.21109
.15500	-.07754	-.09057	-.10364	-.11674	-.12986	-.14301	-.15619	-.16939	-.18262	-.19587
.15750	-.06396	-.07685	-.08977	-.10272	-.11569	-.12870	-.14172	-.15478	-.16785	-.18095
.16000	-.05066	-.06340	-.07617	-.08897	-.10180	-.11466	-.12754	-.14045	-.15338	-.16633
.16250	-.03761	-.05021	-.06284	-.07550	-.08819	-.10090	-.11364	-.12640	-.13919	-.15200
.16500	-.02483	-.03729	-.04978	-.06229	-.07484	-.08741	-.10001	-.11263	-.12527	-.13794
.16750	-.01229	-.02461	-.03696	-.04934	-.06175	-.07418	-.08664	-.09912	-.11163	-.12415
.17000	.00000	-.01219	-.02440	-.03664	-.04891	-.06121	-.07353	-.08588	-.09825	-.11064
.17250	.01205	-.00000	-.01208	-.02419	-.03633	-.04849	-.06068	-.07289	-.08512	-.09738
.17500	.02387	.01195	.00000	-.01198	-.02398	-.03601	-.04807	-.06015	-.07225	-.08438
.17750	.03546	.02367	.01185	.00000	-.01188	-.02378	-.03570	-.04765	-.05963	-.07162
.18000	.04683	.03517	.02347	.01175	.00000	-.01177	-.02357	-.03540	-.04724	-.05911
.18250	.05799	.04644	.03487	.02327	.01165	.00000	-.01167	-.02337	-.03509	-.04684
.18500	.06892	.05750	.04606	.03458	.02308	.01155	.00000	-.01158	-.02317	-.03479
.18750	.07966	.06836	.05703	.04567	.03429	.02289	.01145	.00000	-.01148	-.02298
.19000	.09019	.07900	.06779	.05656	.04529	.03401	.02269	.01136	0.00000	-.01138
.19250	.10052	.08945	.07836	.06724	.05609	.04492	.03372	.02250	.01126	.00000
.19500	.11066	.09971	.08873	.07772	.06669	.05563	.04455	.03344	.02232	.01117
.19750	.12061	.10977	.09890	.08800	.07708	.06614	.05517	.04418	.03317	.02213
.20000	.13037	.11964	.10889	.09810	.08729	.07646	.06560	.05472	.04382	.03289
.20250	.13996	.12934	.11869	.10801	.09731	.08658	.07584	.06506	.05427	.04346
.20500	.14937	.13885	.12831	.11774	.10715	.09653	.08589	.07522	.06454	.05383
.20750	.15860	.14819	.13775	.12729	.11680	.10629	.09575	.08519	.07461	.06401

EFFECTIVE YIELD	CONTRACT RATE .19500	.19750	.20000	.20250	.20500	.20750
.07000	-.96181	-.98230	-1.00281	-1.02335	-1.04390	-1.06447
.07250	-.93086	-.95107	-.97130	-.99154	-1.01181	-1.03209
.07500	-.90061	-.92053	-.94047	-.96044	-.98042	-1.00042
.07750	-.87101	-.89066	-.91033	-.93002	-.94973	-.96945
.08000	-.84207	-.86145	-.88085	-.90027	-.91971	-.93916
.08250	-.81377	-.83288	-.85202	-.87117	-.89034	-.90953
.08500	-.78608	-.80494	-.82381	-.84270	-.86162	-.88055
.08750	-.75900	-.77760	-.79622	-.81486	-.83351	-.85219
.09000	-.73250	-.75085	-.76922	-.78761	-.80602	-.82445
.09250	-.70658	-.72469	-.74281	-.76096	-.77912	-.79730
.09500	-.68122	-.69908	-.71697	-.73487	-.75280	-.77074
.09750	-.65640	-.67403	-.69168	-.70935	-.72704	-.74475
.10000	-.63212	-.64952	-.66693	-.68437	-.70183	-.71931
.10250	-.60835	-.62552	-.64272	-.65993	-.67716	-.69441
.10500	-.58509	-.60204	-.61901	-.63600	-.65301	-.67004
.10750	-.56233	-.57906	-.59581	-.61258	-.62938	-.64619
.11000	-.54004	-.55656	-.57310	-.58966	-.60624	-.62283
.11250	-.51822	-.53453	-.55086	-.56721	-.58358	-.59997
.11500	-.49687	-.51297	-.52909	-.54524	-.56140	-.57759
.11750	-.47595	-.49186	-.50778	-.52372	-.53969	-.55567
.12000	-.45548	-.47118	-.48691	-.50266	-.51842	-.53421
.12250	-.43543	-.45094	-.46647	-.48202	-.49760	-.51319
.12500	-.41580	-.43112	-.44646	-.46182	-.47720	-.49260
.12750	-.39657	-.41170	-.42685	-.44203	-.45722	-.47244
.13000	-.37773	-.39268	-.40765	-.42264	-.43766	-.45269
.13250	-.35928	-.37405	-.38884	-.40366	-.41849	-.43334
.13500	-.34121	-.35580	-.37042	-.38505	-.39971	-.41438
.13750	-.32351	-.33793	-.35237	-.36683	-.38131	-.39581
.14000	-.30616	-.32041	-.33468	-.34897	-.36328	-.37761
.14250	-.28916	-.30325	-.31735	-.33147	-.34562	-.35978
.14500	-.27251	-.28643	-.30037	-.31433	-.32831	-.34231
.14750	-.25619	-.26994	-.28372	-.29752	-.31134	-.32518
.15000	-.24019	-.25379	-.26741	-.28105	-.29471	-.30839
.15250	-.22451	-.23796	-.25142	-.26491	-.27841	-.29194
.15500	-.20914	-.22244	-.23575	-.24908	-.26244	-.27581
.15750	-.19408	-.20722	-.22038	-.23357	-.24677	-.25999
.16000	-.17931	-.19230	-.20532	-.21836	-.23141	-.24449
.16250	-.16483	-.17768	-.19055	-.20344	-.21635	-.22928
.16500	-.15063	-.16334	-.17607	-.18882	-.20159	-.21438
.16750	-.13670	-.14928	-.16187	-.17448	-.18711	-.19976
.17000	-.12305	-.13548	-.14794	-.16041	-.17291	-.18542
.17250	-.10966	-.12196	-.13428	-.14662	-.15898	-.17135
.17500	-.09652	-.10869	-.12088	-.13309	-.14531	-.15755
.17750	-.08364	-.09568	-.10774	-.11981	-.13191	-.14402
.18000	-.07100	-.08291	-.09484	-.10679	-.11876	-.13074
.18250	-.05860	-.07039	-.08219	-.09401	-.10585	-.11771
.18500	-.04643	-.05810	-.06978	-.08148	-.09319	-.10493
.18750	-.03450	-.04604	-.05760	-.06917	-.08077	-.09239
.19000	-.02278	-.03420	-.04564	-.05710	-.06858	-.08007
.19250	-.01128	-.02259	-.03391	-.04525	-.05661	-.06799
.19500	0.00000	-.01119	-.02240	-.03362	-.04487	-.05613
.19750	.01108	0.00000	-.01109	-.02221	-.03334	-.04449
.20000	.02195	.01098	.00000	-.01100	-.02202	-.03306
.20250	.03262	.02177	.01089	.00000	-.01091	-.02184
.20500	.04310	.03235	.02159	.01080	-.00000	-.01082
.20750	.05339	.04275	.03209	.02141	.01071	.00000

POINT TABLES: ORIGINAL LOAN TERM: 240 MONTHS LOAN PREPAID IN: 180 MONTHS

EFFECTIVE YIELD	CONTRACT RATE .07000	.07250	.07500	.07750	.08000	.08250	.08500	.08750	.09000	.09250
.07000	.00000	-.01862	-.03739	-.05631	-.07539	-.09461	-.11398	-.13349	-.15314	-.17292
.07250	.01829	0.00000	-.01844	-.03704	-.05578	-.07467	-.09370	-.11287	-.13218	-.15162
.07500	.03610	.01812	-.00000	-.01827	-.03669	-.05525	-.07396	-.09280	-.11177	-.13088
.07750	.05344	.03577	.01796	.00000	-.01810	-.03635	-.05473	-.07325	-.09190	-.11068
.08000	.07032	.05296	.03545	.01780	.00000	-.01793	-.03601	-.05421	-.07255	-.09101
.08250	.08677	.06970	.05248	.03513	.01763	0.00000	-.01777	-.03567	-.05369	-.07185
.08500	.10278	.08600	.06908	.05201	.03481	.01747	.00000	-.01760	-.03533	-.05318
.08750	.11839	.10188	.08524	.06846	.05154	.03449	.01731	0.00000	-.01743	-.03499
.09000	.13359	.11736	.10099	.08448	.06784	.05107	.03417	.01715	.00000	-.01727
.09250	.14840	.13244	.11633	.10010	.08373	.06723	.05061	.03386	.01699	.00000
.09500	.16284	.14713	.13129	.11532	.09921	.08298	.06663	.05015	.03355	.01683
.09750	.17691	.16145	.14586	.13015	.11430	.09833	.08224	.06602	.04969	.03324
.10000	.19062	.17541	.16007	.14460	.12901	.11329	.09746	.08150	.06542	.04923
.10250	.20398	.18902	.17392	.15870	.14335	.12788	.11229	.09659	.08076	.06483
.10500	.21702	.20228	.18742	.17244	.15733	.14211	.12676	.11130	.09572	.08004
.10750	.22972	.21522	.20059	.18584	.17097	.15597	.14087	.12564	.11031	.09486
.11000	.24211	.22783	.21343	.19891	.18426	.16950	.15462	.13964	.12454	.10933
.11250	.25420	.24014	.22595	.21165	.19723	.18269	.16804	.15328	.13841	.12343
.11500	.26599	.25214	.23817	.22408	.20988	.19556	.18113	.16660	.15195	.13720
.11750	.27749	.26385	.25009	.23621	.22222	.20812	.19391	.17959	.16516	.15062
.12000	.28871	.27527	.26171	.24804	.23426	.22037	.20637	.19226	.17804	.16373
.12250	.29965	.28641	.27306	.25959	.24601	.23232	.21853	.20463	.19062	.17651
.12500	.31034	.29729	.28413	.27086	.25748	.24399	.23040	.21670	.20290	.18899
.12750	.32076	.30791	.29494	.28186	.26867	.25538	.24198	.22848	.21488	.20118
.13000	.33094	.31827	.30549	.29260	.27960	.26650	.25329	.23998	.22657	.21307
.13250	.34087	.32838	.31579	.30308	.29027	.27735	.26433	.25121	.23799	.22468
.13500	.35058	.33826	.32584	.31331	.30068	.28795	.27511	.26218	.24915	.23602
.13750	.36005	.34791	.33566	.32331	.31085	.29830	.28564	.27289	.26004	.24709
.14000	.36930	.35733	.34525	.33307	.32079	.30840	.29592	.28335	.27067	.25791
.14250	.37833	.36653	.35462	.34260	.33049	.31828	.30597	.29356	.28106	.26847
.14500	.38716	.37551	.36376	.35192	.33997	.32792	.31578	.30354	.29121	.27879
.14750	.39578	.38429	.37270	.36101	.34923	.33734	.32537	.31330	.30113	.28888
.15000	.40420	.39287	.38144	.36991	.35828	.34655	.33473	.32282	.31082	.29874
.15250	.41244	.40125	.38997	.37859	.36712	.35555	.34389	.33214	.32030	.30837
.15500	.42048	.40945	.39831	.38709	.37576	.36435	.35284	.34124	.32955	.31778
.15750	.42834	.41745	.40647	.39539	.38421	.37294	.36158	.35014	.33860	.32698
.16000	.43603	.42528	.41444	.40350	.39247	.38135	.37014	.35884	.34745	.33598
.16250	.44355	.43294	.42223	.41143	.40054	.38956	.37850	.36734	.35610	.34478
.16500	.45090	.44042	.42985	.41919	.40844	.39760	.38667	.37566	.36456	.35338
.16750	.45808	.44774	.43730	.42678	.41616	.40546	.39467	.38379	.37284	.36180
.17000	.46511	.45490	.44459	.43420	.42371	.41314	.40249	.39175	.38093	.37003
.17250	.47198	.46190	.45172	.44145	.43110	.42066	.41014	.39954	.38885	.37808
.17500	.47871	.46875	.45869	.44856	.43833	.42802	.41763	.40715	.39659	.38596
.17750	.48529	.47545	.46552	.45550	.44540	.43522	.42495	.41460	.40417	.39367
.18000	.49173	.48201	.47220	.46230	.45232	.44226	.43212	.42189	.41159	.40121
.18250	.49803	.48842	.47873	.46896	.45910	.44915	.43913	.42903	.41885	.40860
.18500	.50419	.49470	.48513	.47547	.46573	.45590	.44600	.43602	.42596	.41582
.18750	.51023	.50085	.49139	.48184	.47222	.46251	.45272	.44286	.43291	.42290
.19000	.51614	.50687	.49752	.48808	.47857	.46897	.45930	.44955	.43973	.42983
.19250	.52193	.51277	.50352	.49420	.48479	.47531	.46575	.45611	.44640	.43661
.19500	.52759	.51854	.50940	.50018	.49088	.48151	.47206	.46253	.45293	.44326
.19750	.53314	.52419	.51516	.50604	.49685	.48758	.47824	.46882	.45933	.44976
.20000	.53858	.52973	.52079	.51178	.50270	.49353	.48429	.47498	.46559	.45614
.20250	.54390	.53515	.52632	.51741	.50842	.49936	.49022	.48102	.47173	.46238
.20500	.54912	.54046	.53173	.52292	.51403	.50507	.49604	.48693	.47775	.46850
.20750	.55423	.54567	.53703	.52832	.51953	.51067	.50173	.49272	.48365	.47450

POINT TABLES: ORIGINAL LOAN TERM: 240 MONTHS LOAN PREPAID IN: 180 MONTHS

EFFECTIVE YIELD	CONTRACT RATE .09500	.09750	.10000	.10250	.10500	.10750	.11000	.11250	.11500	.11750
.07000	-.19284	-.21289	-.23307	-.25337	-.27380	-.29434	-.31501	-.33578	-.35667	-.37767
.07250	-.17120	-.19090	-.21073	-.23068	-.25075	-.27095	-.29125	-.31167	-.33220	-.35284
.07500	-.15012	-.16948	-.18897	-.20858	-.22831	-.24816	-.26812	-.28819	-.30837	-.32866
.07750	-.12959	-.14863	-.16779	-.18706	-.20646	-.22597	-.24559	-.26532	-.28516	-.30510
.08000	-.10960	-.12831	-.14715	-.16610	-.18517	-.20435	-.22365	-.24305	-.26255	-.28216
.08250	-.09013	-.10853	-.12705	-.14568	-.16443	-.18330	-.20227	-.22134	-.24052	-.25981
.08500	-.07116	-.08925	-.10746	-.12579	-.14423	-.16278	-.18144	-.20020	-.21906	-.23803
.08750	-.05267	-.07047	-.08838	-.10641	-.12454	-.14279	-.16114	-.17960	-.19815	-.21681
.09000	-.03466	-.05217	-.06979	-.08752	-.10536	-.12331	-.14136	-.15952	-.17777	-.19612
.09250	-.01711	-.03433	-.05167	-.06911	-.08666	-.10432	-.12208	-.13995	-.15791	-.17596
.09500	.00000	-.01695	-.03400	-.05117	-.06844	-.08582	-.10329	-.12087	-.13854	-.15631
.09750	.01668	.00000	-.01679	-.03368	-.05068	-.06778	-.08498	-.10227	-.11967	-.13716
.10000	.03293	.01652	-.00000	-.01663	-.03336	-.05019	-.06712	-.08414	-.10126	-.11848
.10250	.04878	.03263	.01637	.00000	-.01647	-.03304	-.04970	-.06646	-.08332	-.10026
.10500	.06424	.04833	.03233	.01621	-.00000	-.01631	-.03272	-.04922	-.06532	-.08250
.10750	.07931	.06365	.04789	.03202	.01606	.00000	-.01616	-.03241	-.04874	-.06517
.11000	.09401	.07859	.06307	.04745	.03173	.01591	.00000	-.01600	-.03209	-.04827
.11250	.10835	.09317	.07788	.06249	.04701	.03143	.01576	.00000	-.01585	-.03179
.11500	.12234	.10738	.09233	.07717	.06192	.04657	.03114	.01561	.00000	-.01570
.11750	.13599	.12125	.10642	.09149	.07647	.06135	.04614	.03085	.01547	.00000
.12000	.14931	.13479	.12018	.10547	.09066	.07577	.06079	.04571	.03056	.01532
.12250	.16231	.14800	.13360	.11911	.10452	.08984	.07508	.06023	.04529	.03027
.12500	.17499	.16090	.14670	.13242	.11804	.10358	.08903	.07439	.05967	.04487
.12750	.18738	.17348	.15949	.14542	.13125	.11699	.10265	.08822	.07371	.05912
.13000	.19947	.18577	.17198	.15810	.14414	.13008	.11594	.10172	.08742	.07304
.13250	.21127	.19777	.18418	.17049	.15672	.14287	.12893	.11490	.10080	.08662
.13500	.22280	.20949	.19608	.18259	.16901	.15535	.14161	.12778	.11388	.09989
.13750	.23406	.22093	.20771	.19441	.18102	.16755	.15399	.14036	.12664	.11285
.14000	.24505	.23210	.21907	.20595	.19274	.17946	.16609	.15264	.13912	.12552
.14250	.25579	.24302	.23017	.21722	.20420	.19109	.17791	.16464	.15130	.13789
.14500	.26629	.25369	.24101	.22824	.21539	.20246	.18945	.17637	.16321	.14997
.14750	.27654	.26411	.25160	.23900	.22633	.21357	.20074	.18783	.17484	.16178
.15000	.28656	.27430	.26195	.24952	.23702	.22443	.21177	.19903	.18621	.17333
.15250	.29635	.28425	.27207	.25981	.24746	.23504	.22254	.20997	.19733	.18461
.15500	.30592	.29398	.28196	.26986	.25767	.24542	.23308	.22067	.20819	.19564
.15750	.31528	.30349	.29163	.27968	.26766	.25556	.24338	.23113	.21882	.20643
.16000	.32443	.31279	.30108	.28929	.27742	.26547	.25345	.24136	.22920	.21697
.16250	.33337	.32189	.31032	.29868	.28696	.27517	.26330	.25137	.23936	.22729
.16500	.34212	.33078	.31936	.30787	.29630	.28465	.27294	.26115	.24930	.23737
.16750	.35068	.33948	.32820	.31685	.30543	.29393	.28236	.27072	.25901	.24724
.17000	.35905	.34799	.33685	.32564	.31436	.30300	.29158	.28008	.26852	.25689
.17250	.36724	.35631	.34531	.33424	.32310	.31188	.30059	.28924	.27782	.26634
.17500	.37525	.36446	.35359	.34266	.33165	.32057	.30942	.29820	.28692	.27558
.17750	.38308	.37243	.36169	.35089	.34001	.32907	.31805	.30697	.29583	.28462
.18000	.39076	.38023	.36962	.35895	.34820	.33739	.32651	.31556	.30455	.29347
.18250	.39826	.38786	.37738	.36683	.35622	.34553	.33478	.32396	.31308	.30214
.18500	.40561	.39533	.38498	.37456	.36406	.35350	.34288	.33219	.32143	.31062
.18750	.41281	.40265	.39242	.38211	.37174	.36131	.35081	.34024	.32961	.31892
.19000	.41986	.40981	.39970	.38952	.37927	.36895	.35857	.34813	.33762	.32706
.19250	.42675	.41683	.40683	.39676	.38663	.37644	.36618	.35585	.34547	.33502
.19500	.43351	.42370	.41381	.40386	.39385	.38377	.37362	.36342	.35315	.34282
.19750	.44013	.43043	.42066	.41082	.40091	.39095	.38092	.37083	.36068	.35047
.20000	.44661	.43702	.42736	.41763	.40784	.39798	.38807	.37809	.36805	.35795
.20250	.45296	.44348	.43392	.42430	.41462	.40488	.39507	.38520	.37527	.36529
.20500	.45919	.44981	.44036	.43084	.42127	.41163	.40193	.39217	.38235	.37248
.20750	.46529	.45601	.44666	.43725	.42778	.41825	.40865	.39900	.38929	.37953

POINT TABLES: ORIGINAL LOAN TERM: 240 MONTHS LOAN PREPAID IN: 180 MONTHS

EFFECTIVE YIELD	CONTRACT RATE .12000	.12250	.12500	.12750	.13000	.13250	.13500	.13750	.14000	.14250
.07000	-.39877	-.41998	-.44128	-.46269	-.48418	-.50578	-.52746	-.54923	-.57108	-.59301
.07250	-.37358	-.39442	-.41536	-.43640	-.45753	-.47875	-.50007	-.52146	-.54294	-.56451
.07500	-.34904	-.36953	-.39012	-.41080	-.43157	-.45243	-.47339	-.49442	-.51554	-.53674
.07750	-.32515	-.34529	-.36553	-.38586	-.40628	-.42680	-.44740	-.46808	-.48884	-.50969
.08000	-.30187	-.32167	-.34157	-.36157	-.38165	-.40182	-.42208	-.44242	-.46284	-.48333
.08250	-.27919	-.29866	-.31824	-.33790	-.35765	-.37749	-.39741	-.41741	-.43749	-.45766
.08500	-.25709	-.27625	-.29549	-.31483	-.33426	-.35377	-.37337	-.39305	-.41280	-.43263
.08750	-.23556	-.25440	-.27333	-.29236	-.31147	-.33066	-.34994	-.36930	-.38873	-.40824
.09000	-.21457	-.23311	-.25174	-.27045	-.28926	-.30814	-.32711	-.34615	-.36527	-.38447
.09250	-.19411	-.21235	-.23068	-.24910	-.26760	-.28619	-.30485	-.32359	-.34241	-.36130
.09500	-.17417	-.19212	-.21016	-.22829	-.24649	-.26478	-.28315	-.30159	-.32011	-.33870
.09750	-.15473	-.17240	-.19015	-.20799	-.22591	-.24391	-.26199	-.28015	-.29838	-.31668
.10000	-.13578	-.15317	-.17065	-.18821	-.20585	-.22357	-.24136	-.25923	-.27718	-.29519
.10250	-.11730	-.13442	-.15162	-.16891	-.18628	-.20372	-.22124	-.23884	-.25651	-.27424
.10500	-.09927	-.11613	-.13307	-.15009	-.16719	-.18437	-.20162	-.21895	-.23634	-.25381
.10750	-.08169	-.09829	-.11497	-.13173	-.14857	-.16549	-.18248	-.19954	-.21667	-.23388
.11000	-.06454	-.08089	-.09731	-.11382	-.13041	-.14707	-.16380	-.18061	-.19748	-.21443
.11250	-.04781	-.06391	-.08009	-.09635	-.11269	-.12910	-.14558	-.16214	-.17876	-.19545
.11500	-.03148	-.04734	-.06328	-.07930	-.09540	-.11157	-.12781	-.14411	-.16049	-.17693
.11750	-.01555	-.03118	-.04688	-.06267	-.07852	-.09445	-.11045	-.12652	-.14266	-.15886
.12000	0.00000	-.01540	-.03088	-.04643	-.06205	-.07775	-.09352	-.10935	-.12526	-.14122
.12250	.01518	.00000	-.01525	-.03058	-.04598	-.06145	-.07699	-.09259	-.10827	-.12400
.12500	.02999	.01503	.00000	-.01511	-.03028	-.04553	-.06085	-.07623	-.09168	-.10719
.12750	.04445	.02971	.01489	0.00000	-.01496	-.02999	-.04509	-.06026	-.07548	-.09077
.13000	.05858	.04404	.02943	.01475	-.00000	-.01482	-.02970	-.04466	-.05967	-.07474
.13250	.07237	.05804	.04363	.02916	.01461	0.00000	-.01468	-.02942	-.04422	-.05909
.13500	.08583	.07170	.05750	.04323	.02888	.01447	.00000	-.01454	-.02914	-.04380
.13750	.09899	.08505	.07105	.05697	.04282	.02861	.01434	0.00000	-.01440	-.02886
.14000	.11184	.09810	.08428	.07039	.05644	.04243	.02835	.01420	-.00000	-.01426
.14250	.12440	.11084	.09721	.08351	.06975	.05592	.04203	.02808	.01407	.00000
.14500	.13667	.12329	.10984	.09633	.08275	.06911	.05541	.04164	.02782	.01394
.14750	.14866	.13546	.12219	.10886	.09546	.08200	.06848	.05490	.04126	.02756
.15000	.16037	.14735	.13426	.12110	.10788	.09460	.08125	.06785	.05439	.04087
.15250	.17183	.15897	.14605	.13307	.12002	.10691	.09374	.08051	.06723	.05389
.15500	.18302	.17034	.15759	.14477	.13189	.11895	.10595	.09290	.07978	.06661
.15750	.19397	.18145	.16886	.15621	.14350	.13072	.11789	.10500	.09206	.07906
.16000	.20468	.19231	.17989	.16740	.15485	.14224	.12957	.11684	.10406	.09123
.16250	.21515	.20294	.19067	.17834	.16595	.15349	.14099	.12842	.11580	.10313
.16500	.22538	.21333	.20122	.18904	.17680	.16451	.15216	.13975	.12729	.11477
.16750	.23540	.22350	.21153	.19951	.18742	.17528	.16308	.15083	.13852	.12616
.17000	.24520	.23344	.22163	.20975	.19781	.18582	.17377	.16167	.14951	.13731
.17250	.25479	.24317	.23150	.21977	.20798	.19613	.18423	.17228	.16027	.14821
.17500	.26417	.25270	.24117	.22958	.21793	.20623	.19447	.18266	.17080	.15888
.17750	.27335	.26202	.25062	.23917	.22767	.21610	.20449	.19282	.18110	.16933
.18000	.28233	.27114	.25988	.24857	.23720	.22577	.21430	.20277	.19118	.17955
.18250	.29113	.28007	.26894	.25776	.24653	.23524	.22390	.21250	.20106	.18957
.18500	.29974	.28881	.27782	.26677	.25566	.24451	.23330	.22204	.21073	.19937
.18750	.30818	.29737	.28650	.27558	.26461	.25358	.24250	.23137	.22019	.20896
.19000	.31643	.30575	.29501	.28422	.27337	.26247	.25152	.24051	.22946	.21836
.19250	.32452	.31396	.30334	.29267	.28195	.27117	.26034	.24947	.23854	.22757
.19500	.33244	.32200	.31150	.30095	.29035	.27970	.26899	.25824	.24744	.23659
.19750	.34020	.32988	.31950	.30907	.29858	.28805	.27747	.26683	.25615	.24543
.20000	.34780	.33759	.32733	.31702	.30665	.29623	.28577	.27525	.26469	.25408
.20250	.35525	.34516	.33501	.32481	.31455	.30425	.29390	.28350	.27306	.26257
.20500	.36255	.35257	.34253	.33244	.32230	.31211	.30187	.29159	.28126	.27088
.20750	.36971	.35983	.34990	.33992	.32989	.31981	.30969	.29951	.28929	.27903

POINT TABLES: ORIGINAL LOAN TERM: 240 MONTHS LOAN PREPAID IN: 180 MONTHS

EFFECTIVE YIELD		CONTRACT RATE .14500	.14750	.15000	.15250	.15500	.15750	.16000	.16250	.16500	.16750
.07000	*	-.61503	-.63712	-.65929	-.68153	-.70384	-.72622	-.74867	-.77118	-.79375	-.81638
.07250	*	-.58615	-.60787	-.62966	-.65152	-.67346	-.69546	-.71752	-.73965	-.76184	-.78409
.07500	*	-.55802	-.57937	-.60079	-.62229	-.64386	-.66549	-.68718	-.70894	-.73076	-.75264
.07750	*	-.53061	-.55161	-.57267	-.59381	-.61502	-.63629	-.65762	-.67902	-.70048	-.72199
.08000	*	-.50391	-.52456	-.54527	-.56606	-.58692	-.60784	-.62882	-.64987	-.67097	-.69213
.08250	*	-.47789	-.49820	-.51858	-.53902	-.55954	-.58012	-.60075	-.62145	-.64221	-.66303
.08500	*	-.45254	-.47251	-.49256	-.51267	-.53285	-.55310	-.57340	-.59377	-.61419	-.63466
.08750	*	-.42783	-.44748	-.46720	-.48699	-.50684	-.52676	-.54674	-.56678	-.58687	-.60702
.09000	*	-.40374	-.42308	-.44248	-.46196	-.48149	-.50109	-.52075	-.54047	-.56024	-.58007
.09250	*	-.38026	-.39929	-.41839	-.43755	-.45678	-.47606	-.49541	-.51482	-.53427	-.55379
.09500	*	-.35737	-.37610	-.39489	-.41375	-.43268	-.45166	-.47070	-.48980	-.50896	-.52817
.09750	*	-.33505	-.35348	-.37199	-.39055	-.40918	-.42787	-.44661	-.46542	-.48427	-.50318
.10000	*	-.31328	-.33143	-.34964	-.36792	-.38626	-.40466	-.42312	-.44163	-.46019	-.47881
.10250	*	-.29205	-.30992	-.32786	-.34585	-.36391	-.38203	-.40020	-.41843	-.43671	-.45504
.10500	*	-.27134	-.28894	-.30660	-.32433	-.34211	-.35995	-.37785	-.39580	-.41380	-.43185
.10750	*	-.25114	-.26847	-.28587	-.30332	-.32084	-.33841	-.35604	-.37372	-.39145	-.40923
.11000	*	-.23144	-.24851	-.26564	-.28283	-.30009	-.31739	-.33476	-.35217	-.36964	-.38716
.11250	*	-.21221	-.22902	-.24590	-.26284	-.27983	-.29689	-.31399	-.33115	-.34836	-.36562
.11500	*	-.19344	-.21001	-.22664	-.24333	-.26007	-.27687	-.29373	-.31063	-.32759	-.34459
.11750	*	-.17513	-.19145	-.20784	-.22428	-.24078	-.25734	-.27394	-.29060	-.30731	-.32407
.12000	*	-.15725	-.17334	-.18949	-.20569	-.22195	-.23827	-.25464	-.27105	-.28752	-.30404
.12250	*	-.13980	-.15566	-.17157	-.18754	-.20357	-.21965	-.23578	-.25197	-.26820	-.28448
.12500	*	-.12276	-.13839	-.15408	-.16982	-.18562	-.20148	-.21738	-.23333	-.24933	-.26538
.12750	*	-.10612	-.12153	-.13700	-.15252	-.16810	-.18373	-.19940	-.21513	-.23091	-.24673
.13000	*	-.08988	-.10507	-.12032	-.13563	-.15098	-.16639	-.18185	-.19736	-.21291	-.22851
.13250	*	-.07401	-.08899	-.10403	-.11912	-.13427	-.14946	-.16471	-.18000	-.19534	-.21072
.13500	*	-.05851	-.07329	-.08812	-.10300	-.11794	-.13292	-.14796	-.16304	-.17817	-.19334
.13750	*	-.04337	-.05794	-.07257	-.08725	-.10198	-.11676	-.13159	-.14647	-.16139	-.17636
.14000	*	-.02858	-.04295	-.05738	-.07186	-.08639	-.10098	-.11560	-.13028	-.14500	-.15977
.14250	*	-.01413	-.02831	-.04254	-.05683	-.07116	-.08555	-.09998	-.11446	-.12898	-.14355
.14500	*	.00000	-.01399	-.02804	-.04213	-.05628	-.07047	-.08471	-.09900	-.11333	-.12770
.14750	*	.01381	0.00000	-.01386	-.02777	-.04173	-.05573	-.06978	-.08388	-.09802	-.11221
.15000	*	.02730	.01368	.00000	-.01373	-.02750	-.04133	-.05519	-.06911	-.08306	-.09706
.15250	*	.04049	.02705	.01355	.00000	-.01360	-.02724	-.04093	-.05466	-.06844	-.08226
.15500	*	.05339	.04012	.02679	.01342	0.00000	-.01347	-.02698	-.04054	-.05414	-.06778
.15750	*	.06601	.05290	.03975	.02655	.01330	.00000	-.01334	-.02672	-.04015	-.05362
.16000	*	.07834	.06540	.05242	.03938	.02630	.01317	-.00000	-.01321	-.02647	-.03977
.16250	*	.09041	.07763	.06481	.05194	.03902	.02606	.01305	0.00000	-.01309	-.02622
.16500	*	.10221	.08959	.07693	.06422	.05146	.03866	.02581	.01293	.00000	-.01297
.16750	*	.11375	.10129	.08879	.07623	.06363	.05099	.03830	.02558	.01281	.00000
.17000	*	.12505	.11274	.10039	.08799	.07554	.06306	.05052	.03795	.02534	.01269
.17250	*	.13610	.12395	.11174	.09949	.08720	.07486	.06248	.05006	.03761	.02511
.17500	*	.14692	.13491	.12286	.11075	.09861	.08642	.07419	.06192	.04961	.03726
.17750	*	.15751	.14564	.13373	.12178	.10977	.09773	.08565	.07352	.06136	.04916
.18000	*	.16788	.15615	.14438	.13256	.12071	.10881	.09686	.08488	.07286	.06081
.18250	*	.17802	.16644	.15480	.14313	.13141	.11965	.10785	.09601	.08413	.07221
.18500	*	.18796	.17651	.16501	.15347	.14189	.13026	.11860	.10690	.09516	.08338
.18750	*	.19769	.18637	.17501	.16360	.15215	.14066	.12913	.11756	.10596	.09432
.19000	*	.20722	.19603	.18480	.17352	.16220	.15084	.13945	.12801	.11654	.10503
.19250	*	.21655	.20549	.19438	.18324	.17205	.16082	.14955	.13824	.12690	.11552
.19500	*	.22570	.21476	.20378	.19276	.18169	.17059	.15945	.14827	.13705	.12580
.19750	*	.23465	.22384	.21298	.20208	.19114	.18016	.16915	.15809	.14700	.13588
.20000	*	.24343	.23274	.22200	.21122	.20040	.18955	.17865	.16772	.15675	.14575
.20250	*	.25203	.24146	.23084	.22018	.20948	.19874	.18796	.17715	.16630	.15542
.20500	*	.26046	.25000	.23950	.22895	.21837	.20775	.19709	.18640	.17567	.16491
.20750	*	.26873	.25838	.24799	.23756	.22709	.21658	.20604	.19546	.18485	.17420

POINT TABLES: ORIGINAL LOAN TERM: 240 MONTHS LOAN PREPAID IN: 180 MONTHS

EFFECTIVE YIELD	CONTRACT RATE .17000	.17250	.17500	.17750	.18000	.18250	.18500	.18750	.19000	.19250
.07000	-.83907	-.86181	-.88461	-.90746	-.93035	-.95330	-.97629	-.99933	-1.02241	-1.04553
.07250	-.80640	-.82876	-.85117	-.87364	-.89615	-.91871	-.94132	-.96397	-.98666	-1.00939
.07500	-.77457	-.79656	-.81860	-.84069	-.86283	-.88501	-.90724	-.92952	-.95183	-.97419
.07750	-.74356	-.76518	-.78686	-.80858	-.83036	-.85218	-.87404	-.89595	-.91790	-.93988
.08000	-.71334	-.73461	-.75593	-.77730	-.79871	-.82018	-.84168	-.86323	-.88482	-.90645
.08250	-.68390	-.70482	-.72579	-.74681	-.76788	-.78899	-.81015	-.83135	-.85259	-.87387
.08500	-.65519	-.67578	-.69641	-.71709	-.73782	-.75859	-.77941	-.80027	-.82117	-.84210
.08750	-.62722	-.64747	-.66777	-.68812	-.70852	-.72896	-.74945	-.76997	-.79054	-.81114
.09000	-.59995	-.61988	-.63986	-.65988	-.67996	-.70007	-.72023	-.74043	-.76067	-.78095
.09250	-.57335	-.59297	-.61263	-.63235	-.65210	-.67190	-.69175	-.71163	-.73155	-.75151
.09500	-.54743	-.56673	-.58609	-.60550	-.62494	-.64444	-.66397	-.68354	-.70315	-.72280
.09750	-.52214	-.54115	-.56021	-.57931	-.59846	-.61765	-.63688	-.65615	-.67546	-.69480
.10000	-.49748	-.51620	-.53496	-.55377	-.57262	-.59152	-.61045	-.62943	-.64844	-.66749
.10250	-.47342	-.49186	-.51033	-.52885	-.54742	-.56603	-.58468	-.60336	-.62209	-.64085
.10500	-.44996	-.46811	-.48631	-.50455	-.52283	-.54116	-.55953	-.57793	-.59637	-.61485
.10750	-.42706	-.44494	-.46287	-.48083	-.49884	-.51690	-.53499	-.55312	-.57129	-.58949
.11000	-.40472	-.42233	-.43999	-.45769	-.47544	-.49322	-.51104	-.52890	-.54680	-.56473
.11250	-.38292	-.40027	-.41767	-.43511	-.45259	-.47011	-.48767	-.50527	-.52291	-.54058
.11500	-.36164	-.37874	-.39588	-.41307	-.43029	-.44756	-.46486	-.48220	-.49958	-.51699
.11750	-.34087	-.35772	-.37462	-.39155	-.40853	-.42554	-.44260	-.45969	-.47681	-.49397
.12000	-.32060	-.33720	-.35385	-.37055	-.38728	-.40405	-.42086	-.43770	-.45458	-.47150
.12250	-.30080	-.31717	-.33358	-.35004	-.36653	-.38306	-.39963	-.41624	-.43288	-.44955
.12500	-.28147	-.29761	-.31379	-.33001	-.34627	-.36257	-.37890	-.39527	-.41168	-.42812
.12750	-.26260	-.27851	-.29446	-.31045	-.32648	-.34255	-.35866	-.37480	-.39098	-.40719
.13000	-.24416	-.25985	-.27558	-.29135	-.30716	-.32300	-.33888	-.35480	-.37075	-.38674
.13250	-.22615	-.24162	-.25713	-.27269	-.28828	-.30390	-.31957	-.33527	-.35100	-.36676
.13500	-.20856	-.22382	-.23912	-.25446	-.26983	-.28525	-.30070	-.31618	-.33170	-.34725
.13750	-.19137	-.20642	-.22151	-.23664	-.25181	-.26702	-.28226	-.29753	-.31284	-.32818
.14000	-.17457	-.18942	-.20431	-.21924	-.23420	-.24920	-.26424	-.27931	-.29441	-.30954
.14250	-.15816	-.17281	-.18750	-.20223	-.21699	-.23179	-.24663	-.26150	-.27640	-.29133
.14500	-.14212	-.15657	-.17107	-.18560	-.20017	-.21477	-.22941	-.24409	-.25879	-.27352
.14750	-.12643	-.14070	-.15500	-.16935	-.18372	-.19814	-.21259	-.22707	-.24158	-.25612
.15000	-.11110	-.12518	-.13930	-.15346	-.16765	-.18187	-.19613	-.21042	-.22475	-.23910
.15250	-.09611	-.11001	-.12395	-.13792	-.15193	-.16597	-.18005	-.19415	-.20829	-.22246
.15500	-.08146	-.09518	-.10893	-.12273	-.13656	-.15042	-.16431	-.17824	-.19220	-.20619
.15750	-.06712	-.08067	-.09425	-.10787	-.12152	-.13521	-.14893	-.16268	-.17646	-.19027
.16000	-.05310	-.06648	-.07989	-.09334	-.10682	-.12033	-.13388	-.14746	-.16107	-.17470
.16250	-.03939	-.05260	-.06584	-.07912	-.09243	-.10578	-.11916	-.13257	-.14600	-.15947
.16500	-.02597	-.03902	-.05210	-.06521	-.07836	-.09154	-.10475	-.11799	-.13127	-.14457
.16750	-.01285	-.02573	-.03865	-.05160	-.06459	-.07761	-.09066	-.10374	-.11685	-.12999
.17000	.00000	-.01273	-.02549	-.03828	-.05111	-.06397	-.07686	-.08979	-.10274	-.11572
.17250	.01257	0.00000	-.01261	-.02525	-.03792	-.05063	-.06336	-.07613	-.08893	-.10175
.17500	.02488	.01246	-.00000	-.01249	-.02501	-.03757	-.05015	-.06276	-.07541	-.08808
.17750	.03692	.02465	.01234	.00000	-.01237	-.02478	-.03721	-.04968	-.06217	-.07469
.18000	.04871	.03659	.02442	.01223	0.00000	-.01226	-.02455	-.03687	-.04921	-.06159
.18250	.06026	.04827	.03625	.02420	.01212	.00000	-.01215	-.02432	-.03652	-.04875
.18500	.07157	.05972	.04784	.03593	.02398	.01200	.00000	-.01203	-.02409	-.03618
.18750	.08264	.07093	.05918	.04741	.03560	.02376	.01190	0.00000	-.01192	-.02387
.19000	.09349	.08191	.07030	.05866	.04698	.03528	.02355	.01179	0.00000	-.01181
.19250	.10411	.09266	.08119	.06967	.05813	.04656	.03496	.02334	.01168	0.00000
.19500	.11452	.10320	.09185	.08047	.06906	.05762	.04615	.03465	.02313	.01158
.19750	.12472	.11353	.10230	.09105	.07976	.06845	.05711	.04574	.03434	.02292
.20000	.13471	.12364	.11254	.10141	.09025	.07906	.06785	.05660	.04533	.03403
.20250	.14451	.13356	.12258	.11157	.10053	.08947	.07837	.06725	.05610	.04493
.20500	.15411	.14328	.13242	.12153	.11061	.09967	.08869	.07769	.06666	.05561
.20750	.16352	.15281	.14207	.13129	.12049	.10966	.09881	.08792	.07701	.06608

POINT TABLES: ORIGINAL LOAN TERM: 240 MONTHS LOAN PREPAID IN: 180 MONTHS

EFFECTIVE YIELD	CONTRACT RATE .19500	.19750	.20000	.20250	.20500	.20750
.07000	-1.06869	-1.09188	-1.11511	-1.13838	-1.16168	-1.18501
.07250	-1.03217	-1.05497	-1.07782	-1.10070	-1.12361	-1.14656
.07500	-.99658	-1.01901	-1.04148	-1.06398	-1.08652	-1.10908
.07750	-.96191	-.98397	-1.00607	-1.02820	-1.05037	-1.07256
.08000	-.92812	-.94982	-.97156	-.99333	-1.01514	-1.03697
.08250	-.89518	-.91654	-.93792	-.95934	-.98080	-1.00228
.08500	-.86308	-.88409	-.90513	-.92621	-.94732	-.96846
.08750	-.83178	-.85246	-.87317	-.89391	-.91468	-.93549
.09000	-.80126	-.82161	-.84200	-.86241	-.88286	-.90334
.09250	-.77151	-.79154	-.81160	-.83170	-.85183	-.87198
.09500	-.74249	-.76221	-.78196	-.80175	-.82156	-.84141
.09750	-.71419	-.73360	-.75305	-.77253	-.79204	-.81158
.10000	-.68658	-.70570	-.72485	-.74403	-.76325	-.78249
.10250	-.65964	-.67847	-.69734	-.71623	-.73515	-.75410
.10500	-.63337	-.65191	-.67049	-.68910	-.70774	-.72641
.10750	-.60773	-.62600	-.64430	-.66263	-.68099	-.69938
.11000	-.58270	-.60070	-.61873	-.63679	-.65489	-.67300
.11250	-.55828	-.57601	-.59378	-.61158	-.62941	-.64726
.11500	-.53444	-.55192	-.56943	-.58696	-.60453	-.62213
.11750	-.51117	-.52839	-.54565	-.56293	-.58025	-.59759
.12000	-.48844	-.50542	-.52243	-.53947	-.55654	-.57363
.12250	-.46626	-.48299	-.49976	-.51656	-.53339	-.55024
.12500	-.44459	-.46109	-.47762	-.49418	-.51077	-.52739
.12750	-.42343	-.43970	-.45600	-.47233	-.48869	-.50507
.13000	-.40275	-.41880	-.43488	-.45098	-.46711	-.48327
.13250	-.38256	-.39839	-.41424	-.43012	-.44604	-.46197
.13500	-.36283	-.37844	-.39408	-.40975	-.42544	-.44116
.13750	-.34355	-.35895	-.37438	-.38983	-.40532	-.42082
.14000	-.32471	-.33990	-.35512	-.37037	-.38565	-.40095
.14250	-.30629	-.32128	-.33630	-.35135	-.36642	-.38152
.14500	-.28829	-.30308	-.31791	-.33276	-.34763	-.36253
.14750	-.27069	-.28529	-.29992	-.31458	-.32926	-.34396
.15000	-.25349	-.26790	-.28234	-.29680	-.31129	-.32581
.15250	-.23666	-.25089	-.26514	-.27942	-.29373	-.30806
.15500	-.22021	-.23425	-.24832	-.26242	-.27655	-.29069
.15750	-.20411	-.21798	-.23188	-.24580	-.25974	-.27371
.16000	-.18837	-.20206	-.21578	-.22953	-.24330	-.25710
.16250	-.17297	-.18649	-.20004	-.21362	-.22722	-.24084
.16500	-.15790	-.17126	-.18464	-.19805	-.21148	-.22494
.16750	-.14316	-.15635	-.16957	-.18281	-.19608	-.20937
.17000	-.12872	-.14176	-.15482	-.16790	-.18101	-.19414
.17250	-.11460	-.12748	-.14038	-.15331	-.16626	-.17923
.17500	-.10077	-.11350	-.12625	-.13902	-.15182	-.16463
.17750	-.08724	-.09981	-.11241	-.12503	-.13768	-.15034
.18000	-.07398	-.08641	-.09886	-.11133	-.12383	-.13635
.18250	-.06101	-.07329	-.08559	-.09792	-.11027	-.12265
.18500	-.04830	-.06044	-.07260	-.08479	-.09700	-.10923
.18750	-.03585	-.04785	-.05987	-.07192	-.08399	-.09608
.19000	-.02365	-.03552	-.04740	-.05932	-.07125	-.08320
.19250	-.01171	-.02344	-.03519	-.04697	-.05877	-.07059
.19500	.00000	-.01160	-.02322	-.03487	-.04654	-.05822
.19750	.01147	.00000	-.01149	-.02301	-.03455	-.04611
.20000	.02271	.01137	.00000	-.01139	-.02280	-.03423
.20250	.03373	.02251	.01127	.00000	-.01129	-.02260
.20500	.04453	.03343	.02231	.01117	.00000	-.01119
.20750	.05512	.04414	.03314	.02211	.01107	.00000

POINT TABLES: ORIGINAL LOAN TERM: 240 MONTHS LOAN PREPAID IN: 240 MONTHS

EFFECTIVE YIELD	CONTRACT RATE .07000	.07250	.07500	.07750	.08000	.08250	.08500	.08750	.09000	.09250
.07000	.00000	-.01945	-.03907	-.05888	-.07886	-.09902	-.11934	-.13983	-.16049	-.18131
.07250	.01908	.00000	-.01925	-.03868	-.05828	-.07805	-.09799	-.11809	-.13835	-.15877
.07500	.03760	.01889	0.00000	-.01906	-.03829	-.05769	-.07725	-.09697	-.11685	-.13689
.07750	.05561	.03724	.01870	.00000	-.01887	-.03790	-.05710	-.07645	-.09596	-.11562
.08000	.07310	.05507	.03688	.01852	.00000	-.01868	-.03752	-.05651	-.07566	-.09496
.08250	.09009	.07240	.05454	.03652	.01834	0.00000	-.01849	-.03714	-.05594	-.07488
.08500	.10662	.08924	.07171	.05401	.03616	.01816	.00000	-.01831	-.03676	-.05536
.08750	.12268	.10562	.08840	.07102	.05349	.03581	.01798	0.00000	-.01812	-.03639
.09000	.13829	.12154	.10462	.08756	.07034	.05297	.03546	.01780	.00000	-.01794
.09250	.15348	.13702	.12040	.10364	.08672	.06966	.05246	.03511	.01762	0.00000
.09500	.16825	.15208	.13575	.11928	.10266	.08590	.06899	.05195	.03476	.01745
.09750	.18262	.16672	.15068	.13449	.11816	.10169	.08507	.06832	.05144	.03442
.10000	.19660	.18098	.16521	.14930	.13324	.11705	.10072	.08426	.06766	.05094
.10250	.21020	.19484	.17934	.16370	.14792	.13200	.11595	.09976	.08345	.06701
.10500	.22344	.20834	.19310	.17772	.16220	.14655	.13077	.11486	.09881	.08265
.10750	.23633	.22148	.20649	.19137	.17611	.16072	.14519	.12955	.11377	.09787
.11000	.24888	.23427	.21953	.20465	.18964	.17451	.15924	.14385	.12833	.11269
.11250	.26110	.24673	.23222	.21759	.20283	.18793	.17292	.15777	.14251	.12713
.11500	.27300	.25886	.24459	.23019	.21566	.20101	.18623	.17134	.15632	.14118
.11750	.28459	.27067	.25663	.24246	.22817	.21375	.19921	.18455	.16977	.15488
.12000	.29588	.28219	.26836	.25442	.24035	.22616	.21185	.19742	.18287	.16822
.12250	.30688	.29340	.27980	.26607	.25222	.23825	.22416	.20996	.19564	.18121
.12500	.31760	.30433	.29094	.27742	.26379	.25003	.23617	.22218	.20809	.19388
.12750	.32805	.31499	.30180	.28849	.27506	.26152	.24786	.23409	.22021	.20622
.13000	.33824	.32537	.31238	.29928	.28606	.27272	.25927	.24571	.23204	.21826
.13250	.34818	.33550	.32271	.30980	.29677	.28364	.27039	.25703	.24357	.23000
.13500	.35786	.34538	.33277	.32005	.30722	.29428	.28123	.26807	.25481	.24144
.13750	.36731	.35501	.34259	.33006	.31742	.30467	.29181	.27884	.26577	.25260
.14000	.37653	.36440	.35217	.33982	.32736	.31480	.30212	.28935	.27647	.26349
.14250	.38552	.37357	.36151	.34934	.33706	.32468	.31219	.29960	.28690	.27411
.14500	.39430	.38252	.37063	.35863	.34653	.33432	.32201	.30960	.29709	.28448
.14750	.40286	.39125	.37953	.36770	.35577	.34373	.33160	.31936	.30703	.29459
.15000	.41122	.39977	.38821	.37655	.36479	.35292	.34096	.32889	.31673	.30447
.15250	.41938	.40809	.39669	.38519	.37359	.36189	.35009	.33819	.32620	.31411
.15500	.42735	.41621	.40497	.39363	.38219	.37065	.35901	.34728	.33545	.32352
.15750	.43513	.42415	.41306	.40187	.39059	.37920	.36772	.35615	.34448	.33272
.16000	.44273	.43190	.42096	.40992	.39879	.38756	.37623	.36481	.35330	.34170
.16250	.45016	.43947	.42868	.41779	.40680	.39572	.38454	.37328	.36192	.35047
.16500	.45742	.44686	.43621	.42547	.41463	.40369	.39266	.38155	.37034	.35904
.16750	.46451	.45409	.44358	.43298	.42228	.41148	.40060	.38963	.37856	.36742
.17000	.47144	.46116	.45078	.44031	.42975	.41910	.40836	.39752	.38661	.37560
.17250	.47821	.46806	.45782	.44749	.43706	.42654	.41594	.40525	.39447	.38360
.17500	.48483	.47481	.46470	.45450	.44420	.43382	.42335	.41279	.40215	.39143
.17750	.49131	.48141	.47143	.46135	.45119	.44094	.43060	.42017	.40967	.39908
.18000	.49764	.48787	.47801	.46806	.45802	.44790	.43769	.42739	.41702	.40656
.18250	.50383	.49418	.48445	.47462	.46471	.45471	.44462	.43445	.42420	.41387
.18500	.50989	.50036	.49074	.48104	.47124	.46136	.45140	.44136	.43124	.42103
.18750	.51582	.50641	.49690	.48731	.47764	.46788	.45804	.44812	.43812	.42804
.19000	.52162	.51232	.50293	.49346	.48390	.47426	.46453	.45473	.44485	.43489
.19250	.52730	.51811	.50883	.49947	.49002	.48050	.47089	.46120	.45144	.44160
.19500	.53286	.52377	.51460	.50535	.49602	.48660	.47711	.46754	.45789	.44816
.19750	.53830	.52932	.52026	.51111	.50189	.49258	.48320	.47374	.46420	.45459
.20000	.54363	.53475	.52579	.51675	.50764	.49844	.48916	.47981	.47038	.46088
.20250	.54884	.54007	.53121	.52228	.51326	.50417	.49500	.48576	.47644	.46704
.20500	.55395	.54528	.53652	.52769	.51878	.50979	.50072	.49158	.48237	.47308
.20750	.55896	.55038	.54172	.53299	.52418	.51529	.50632	.49729	.48818	.47899

POINT TABLES: ORIGINAL LOAN TERM: 240 MONTHS LOAN PREPAID IN: 240 MONTHS

EFFECTIVE YIELD	CONTRACT RATE .09500	.09750	.10000	.10250	.10500	.10750	.11000	.11250	.11500	.11750
.07000	-.20229	-.22342	-.24471	-.26615	-.28774	-.30947	-.33134	-.35336	-.37551	-.39779
.07250	-.17935	-.20008	-.22097	-.24200	-.26317	-.28449	-.30595	-.32754	-.34927	-.37113
.07500	-.15707	-.17741	-.19790	-.21853	-.23931	-.26023	-.28128	-.30246	-.32378	-.34523
.07750	-.13543	-.15539	-.17550	-.19574	-.21613	-.23665	-.25731	-.27810	-.29902	-.32007
.08000	-.11440	-.13399	-.15372	-.17360	-.19361	-.21375	-.23403	-.25443	-.27496	-.29562
.08250	-.09397	-.11320	-.13257	-.15207	-.17172	-.19149	-.21140	-.23143	-.25158	-.27186
.08500	-.07410	-.09298	-.11200	-.13116	-.15044	-.16986	-.18940	-.20907	-.22886	-.24876
.08750	-.05479	-.07333	-.09201	-.11082	-.12976	-.14882	-.16802	-.18733	-.20676	-.22631
.09000	-.03602	-.05423	-.07257	-.09105	-.10965	-.12838	-.14723	-.16620	-.18528	-.20449
.09250	-.01776	-.03565	-.05367	-.07182	-.09009	-.10849	-.12701	-.14564	-.16439	-.18326
.09500	.00000	-.01758	-.03529	-.05312	-.07107	-.08915	-.10734	-.12565	-.14408	-.16261
.09750	.01728	.00000	-.01740	-.03492	-.05257	-.07033	-.08821	-.10621	-.12431	-.14253
.10000	.03408	.01710	.00000	-.01722	-.03457	-.05203	-.06960	-.08729	-.10508	-.12299
.10250	.05044	.03375	.01693	.00000	-.01705	-.03421	-.05149	-.06888	-.08637	-.10397
.10500	.06636	.04994	.03341	.01676	0.00000	-.01688	-.03386	-.05096	-.06816	-.08547
.10750	.08185	.06571	.04945	.03308	.01660	0.00000	-.01671	-.03352	-.05043	-.06745
.11000	.09694	.08106	.06507	.04897	.03275	.01643	.00000	-.01654	-.03317	-.04991
.11250	.11163	.09601	.08028	.06444	.04849	.03243	.01627	.00000	-.01637	-.03283
.11500	.12593	.11057	.09509	.07950	.06381	.04801	.03211	.01610	0.00000	-.01620
.11750	.13987	.12475	.10952	.09418	.07874	.06319	.04754	.03179	.01594	0.00000
.12000	.15344	.13856	.12357	.10848	.09328	.07797	.06257	.04707	.03147	.01578
.12250	.16667	.15202	.13727	.12241	.10745	.09238	.07722	.06196	.04661	.03116
.12500	.17956	.16514	.15061	.13598	.12125	.10642	.09150	.07647	.06136	.04615
.12750	.19213	.17793	.16362	.14922	.13471	.12011	.10541	.09062	.07573	.06076
.13000	.20438	.19039	.17630	.16212	.14783	.13345	.11897	.10441	.08975	.07500
.13250	.21632	.20255	.18867	.17469	.16062	.14646	.13220	.11785	.10341	.08889
.13500	.22797	.21440	.20073	.18696	.17310	.15914	.14510	.13096	.11674	.10243
.13750	.23933	.22596	.21249	.19892	.18527	.17152	.15768	.14375	.12973	.11563
.14000	.25041	.23723	.22396	.21059	.19713	.18359	.16995	.15622	.14241	.12852
.14250	.26122	.24823	.23515	.22198	.20871	.19536	.18192	.16839	.15478	.14109
.14500	.27177	.25897	.24608	.23309	.22001	.20685	.19360	.18027	.16685	.15335
.14750	.28207	.26945	.25674	.24393	.23104	.21807	.20500	.19186	.17863	.16532
.15000	.29212	.27967	.26714	.25452	.24181	.22901	.21613	.20317	.19013	.17701
.15250	.30193	.28966	.27730	.26485	.25232	.23970	.22700	.21422	.20135	.18842
.15500	.31151	.29941	.28722	.27494	.26258	.25013	.23761	.22500	.21232	.19955
.15750	.32087	.30893	.29690	.28479	.27260	.26032	.24797	.23553	.22302	.21043
.16000	.33001	.31823	.30637	.29442	.28239	.27028	.25809	.24582	.23348	.22106
.16250	.33894	.32731	.31561	.30382	.29195	.28000	.26798	.25587	.24369	.23144
.16500	.34766	.33619	.32464	.31301	.30130	.28950	.27763	.26569	.25367	.24158
.16750	.35618	.34487	.33347	.32198	.31043	.29879	.28707	.27529	.26342	.25149
.17000	.36451	.35334	.34209	.33076	.31935	.30786	.29630	.28466	.27296	.26118
.17250	.37266	.36163	.35052	.33934	.32807	.31673	.30532	.29383	.28227	.27064
.17500	.38062	.36973	.35876	.34772	.33660	.32540	.31413	.30279	.29138	.27990
.17750	.38841	.37765	.36682	.35592	.34494	.33388	.32276	.31156	.30029	.28895
.18000	.39602	.38540	.37471	.36394	.35309	.34217	.33119	.32013	.30900	.29780
.18250	.40347	.39298	.38242	.37178	.36107	.35029	.33943	.32851	.31752	.30646
.18500	.41075	.40039	.38996	.37945	.36887	.35822	.34750	.33671	.32585	.31493
.18750	.41788	.40765	.39734	.38696	.37651	.36598	.35539	.34473	.33401	.32322
.19000	.42485	.41474	.40456	.39430	.38398	.37358	.36312	.35258	.34199	.33133
.19250	.43168	.42169	.41163	.40149	.39129	.38102	.37067	.36027	.34980	.33926
.19500	.43836	.42849	.41854	.40853	.39844	.38829	.37807	.36779	.35744	.34703
.19750	.44490	.43515	.42532	.41542	.40545	.39542	.38532	.37515	.36493	.35464
.20000	.45131	.44166	.43195	.42216	.41231	.40239	.39241	.38236	.37225	.36208
.20250	.45758	.44805	.43844	.42877	.41903	.40922	.39936	.38942	.37943	.36938
.20500	.46372	.45430	.44480	.43524	.42561	.41592	.40616	.39634	.38646	.37652
.20750	.46974	.46042	.45103	.44158	.43205	.42247	.41282	.40311	.39334	.38351

POINT TABLES: ORIGINAL LOAN TERM: 240 MONTHS LOAN PREPAID IN: 240 MONTHS

EFFECTIVE YIELD	CONTRACT RATE .12000	.12250	.12500	.12750	.13000	.13250	.13500	.13750	.14000	.14250
.07000	-.42021	-.44275	-.46542	-.48822	-.51113	-.53416	-.55730	-.58056	-.60392	-.62740
.07250	-.39312	-.41523	-.43747	-.45983	-.48230	-.50489	-.52760	-.55041	-.57333	-.59635
.07500	-.36680	-.38850	-.41032	-.43225	-.45430	-.47647	-.49874	-.52112	-.54361	-.56620
.07750	-.34124	-.36253	-.38394	-.40546	-.42710	-.44885	-.47071	-.49267	-.51474	-.53690
.08000	-.31640	-.33729	-.35830	-.37943	-.40067	-.42202	-.44347	-.46502	-.48668	-.50844
.08250	-.29226	-.31277	-.33340	-.35413	-.37498	-.39594	-.41700	-.43816	-.45942	-.48078
.08500	-.26879	-.28893	-.30918	-.32955	-.35002	-.37059	-.39127	-.41204	-.43292	-.45389
.08750	-.24598	-.26576	-.28565	-.30564	-.32575	-.34595	-.36626	-.38666	-.40716	-.42775
.09000	-.22380	-.24323	-.26276	-.28240	-.30215	-.32199	-.34194	-.36198	-.38211	-.40234
.09250	-.20223	-.22132	-.24051	-.25980	-.27920	-.29869	-.31829	-.33797	-.35775	-.37762
.09500	-.18126	-.20001	-.21886	-.23782	-.25688	-.27603	-.29528	-.31463	-.33406	-.35359
.09750	-.16085	-.17928	-.19781	-.21644	-.23517	-.25399	-.27291	-.29192	-.31102	-.33020
.10000	-.14100	-.15911	-.17732	-.19563	-.21404	-.23254	-.25114	-.26982	-.28859	-.30745
.10250	-.12168	-.13948	-.15739	-.17539	-.19348	-.21167	-.22995	-.24832	-.26677	-.28531
.10500	-.10287	-.12038	-.13798	-.15568	-.17348	-.19136	-.20933	-.22739	-.24554	-.26377
.10750	-.08457	-.10179	-.11910	-.13650	-.15400	-.17159	-.18926	-.20702	-.22487	-.24279
.11000	-.06675	-.08368	-.10071	-.11783	-.13504	-.15234	-.16972	-.18719	-.20474	-.22237
.11250	-.04940	-.06606	-.08281	-.09965	-.11658	-.13359	-.15070	-.16788	-.18515	-.20249
.11500	-.03250	-.04889	-.06537	-.08194	-.09860	-.11534	-.13217	-.14907	-.16606	-.18312
.11750	-.01604	-.03217	-.04838	-.06469	-.08108	-.09756	-.11412	-.13075	-.14747	-.16426
.12000	0.00000	-.01587	-.03184	-.04788	-.06402	-.08023	-.09653	-.11291	-.12936	-.14589
.12250	.01563	.00000	-.01571	-.03151	-.04739	-.06335	-.07940	-.09552	-.11171	-.12798
.12500	.03085	.01547	.00000	-.01555	-.03119	-.04690	-.06270	-.07857	-.09451	-.11053
.12750	.04570	.03055	.01532	0.00000	-.01540	-.03087	-.04642	-.06205	-.07775	-.09352
.13000	.06017	.04525	.03025	.01516	.00000	-.01524	-.03056	-.04595	-.06141	-.07694
.13250	.07427	.05958	.04480	.02995	.01501	.00000	-.01509	-.03025	-.04548	-.06078
.13500	.08803	.07356	.05900	.04436	.02965	.01486	.00000	-.01493	-.02994	-.04501
.13750	.10145	.08719	.07285	.05842	.04393	.02936	.01471	.00000	-.01478	-.02963
.14000	.11454	.10049	.08635	.07214	.05786	.04350	.02907	.01457	0.00000	-.01463
.14250	.12731	.11346	.09953	.08552	.07144	.05729	.04307	.02878	.01442	.00000
.14500	.13977	.12612	.11239	.09858	.08470	.07076	.05674	.04265	.02850	.01428
.14750	.15194	.13848	.12494	.11133	.09765	.08389	.07007	.05619	.04223	.02822
.15000	.16381	.15054	.13719	.12377	.11028	.09672	.08309	.06940	.05564	.04182
.15250	.17540	.16231	.14915	.13591	.12261	.10924	.09580	.08230	.06873	.05510
.15500	.18672	.17381	.16083	.14777	.13465	.12147	.10821	.09489	.08151	.06807
.15750	.19777	.18504	.17223	.15936	.14641	.13341	.12033	.10719	.09400	.08074
.16000	.20857	.19600	.18337	.17067	.15790	.14507	.13217	.11921	.10619	.09311
.16250	.21911	.20672	.19425	.18172	.16912	.15646	.14373	.13095	.11810	.10519
.16500	.22942	.21719	.20488	.19252	.18009	.16759	.15503	.14241	.12974	.11700
.16750	.23949	.22741	.21527	.20307	.19080	.17847	.16607	.15362	.14111	.12854
.17000	.24933	.23741	.22543	.21338	.20127	.18910	.17687	.16457	.15222	.13982
.17250	.25895	.24718	.23536	.22346	.21151	.19949	.18741	.17528	.16309	.15084
.17500	.26835	.25674	.24506	.23332	.22151	.20965	.19773	.18575	.17371	.16162
.17750	.27755	.26608	.25455	.24295	.23130	.21958	.20781	.19598	.18409	.17215
.18000	.28654	.27522	.26383	.25238	.24087	.22930	.21767	.20599	.19425	.18246
.18250	.29534	.28415	.27291	.26160	.25023	.23880	.22732	.21578	.20419	.19254
.18500	.30395	.29290	.28179	.27062	.25939	.24810	.23675	.22536	.21391	.20240
.18750	.31237	.30145	.29047	.27944	.26834	.25719	.24599	.23473	.22341	.21205
.19000	.32060	.30982	.29898	.28807	.27711	.26609	.25502	.24390	.23272	.22149
.19250	.32867	.31801	.30730	.29652	.28569	.27480	.26386	.25287	.24183	.23073
.19500	.33656	.32603	.31544	.30479	.29409	.28333	.27252	.26165	.25074	.23977
.19750	.34429	.33388	.32341	.31289	.30231	.29168	.28099	.27025	.25947	.24863
.20000	.35185	.34157	.33122	.32082	.31036	.29985	.28929	.27867	.26801	.25730
.20250	.35926	.34909	.33886	.32858	.31824	.30785	.29741	.28692	.27638	.26579
.20500	.36652	.35646	.34635	.33619	.32597	.31569	.30537	.29500	.28457	.27410
.20750	.37363	.36369	.35369	.34363	.33353	.32337	.31316	.30291	.29260	.28225

POINT TABLES: ORIGINAL LOAN TERM: 240 MONTHS LOAN PREPAID IN: 240 MONTHS

EFFECTIVE YIELD	CONTRACT RATE .14500	.14750	.15000	.15250	.15500	.15750	.16000	.16250	.16500	.16750
.07000	-.65097	-.67465	-.69843	-.72230	-.74627	-.77033	-.79448	-.81871	-.84303	-.86743
.07250	-.61948	-.64271	-.66603	-.68945	-.71296	-.73656	-.76025	-.78402	-.80787	-.83181
.07500	-.58889	-.61168	-.63456	-.65753	-.68060	-.70376	-.72700	-.75032	-.77372	-.79721
.07750	-.55917	-.58153	-.60399	-.62653	-.64917	-.67189	-.69469	-.71758	-.74055	-.76359
.08000	-.53029	-.55224	-.57428	-.59641	-.61862	-.64092	-.66331	-.68577	-.70831	-.73093
.08250	-.50223	-.52377	-.54541	-.56713	-.58894	-.61083	-.63280	-.65486	-.67698	-.69919
.08500	-.47495	-.49611	-.51735	-.53868	-.56009	-.58158	-.60316	-.62481	-.64653	-.66833
.08750	-.44844	-.46921	-.49007	-.51101	-.53204	-.55315	-.57433	-.59560	-.61693	-.63834
.09000	-.42265	-.44306	-.46355	-.48412	-.50477	-.52550	-.54631	-.56719	-.58815	-.60918
.09250	-.39758	-.41762	-.43775	-.45796	-.47825	-.49862	-.51906	-.53957	-.56016	-.58082
.09500	-.37319	-.39289	-.41267	-.43252	-.45246	-.47247	-.49255	-.51271	-.53294	-.55324
.09750	-.34947	-.36883	-.38826	-.40778	-.42737	-.44703	-.46677	-.48658	-.50646	-.52640
.10000	-.32639	-.34542	-.36452	-.38370	-.40295	-.42228	-.44168	-.46115	-.48069	-.50030
.10250	-.30393	-.32263	-.34141	-.36027	-.37920	-.39820	-.41727	-.43641	-.45562	-.47489
.10500	-.28207	-.30046	-.31893	-.33747	-.35608	-.37476	-.39351	-.41233	-.43122	-.45017
.10750	-.26080	-.27888	-.29704	-.31527	-.33357	-.35195	-.37039	-.38889	-.40747	-.42610
.11000	-.24008	-.25787	-.27573	-.29366	-.31166	-.32973	-.34787	-.36607	-.38434	-.40267
.11250	-.21991	-.23741	-.25497	-.27261	-.29032	-.30810	-.32595	-.34385	-.36182	-.37985
.11500	-.20026	-.21748	-.23476	-.25212	-.26955	-.28704	-.30459	-.32221	-.33989	-.35763
.11750	-.18113	-.19807	-.21508	-.23216	-.24931	-.26652	-.28379	-.30113	-.31853	-.33599
.12000	-.16249	-.17916	-.19590	-.21271	-.22959	-.24653	-.26353	-.28060	-.29772	-.31490
.12250	-.14432	-.16073	-.17721	-.19376	-.21037	-.22705	-.24379	-.26058	-.27744	-.29435
.12500	-.12662	-.14278	-.15900	-.17529	-.19165	-.20807	-.22455	-.24108	-.25768	-.27433
.12750	-.10936	-.12527	-.14125	-.15729	-.17340	-.18956	-.20579	-.22208	-.23842	-.25481
.13000	-.09254	-.10821	-.12395	-.13975	-.15561	-.17153	-.18751	-.20355	-.21964	-.23579
.13250	-.07614	-.09158	-.10708	-.12264	-.13826	-.15394	-.16968	-.18548	-.20133	-.21724
.13500	-.06015	-.07535	-.09062	-.10595	-.12134	-.13679	-.15230	-.16786	-.18348	-.19915
.13750	-.04455	-.05953	-.07457	-.08968	-.10484	-.12007	-.13534	-.15068	-.16606	-.18150
.14000	-.02933	-.04410	-.05892	-.07380	-.08875	-.10375	-.11880	-.13391	-.14908	-.16429
.14250	-.01449	-.02904	-.04365	-.05832	-.07304	-.08783	-.10267	-.11756	-.13250	-.14750
.14500	0.00000	-.01434	-.02874	-.04320	-.05772	-.07229	-.08692	-.10160	-.11633	-.13111
.14750	.01414	.00000	-.01420	-.02845	-.04277	-.05713	-.07155	-.08602	-.10055	-.11512
.15000	.02794	.01400	.00000	-.01406	-.02817	-.04233	-.05655	-.07082	-.08514	-.09951
.15250	.04141	.02767	.01386	0.00000	-.01392	-.02789	-.04191	-.05598	-.07010	-.08427
.15500	.05457	.04101	.02740	.01372	0.00000	-.01378	-.02761	-.04148	-.05541	-.06938
.15750	.06742	.05404	.04061	.02713	.01359	.00000	-.01364	-.02733	-.04107	-.05485
.16000	.07997	.06677	.05352	.04022	.02686	.01346	0.00000	-.01351	-.02706	-.04066
.16250	.09223	.07921	.06614	.05301	.03983	.02660	.01333	0.00000	-.01337	-.02679
.16500	.10421	.09136	.07846	.06551	.05250	.03945	.02635	.01320	.00000	-.01324
.16750	.11591	.10323	.09050	.07772	.06488	.05200	.03907	.02609	.01307	.00000
.17000	.12735	.11484	.10227	.08965	.07698	.06427	.05150	.03869	.02584	.01294
.17250	.13854	.12618	.11378	.10132	.08881	.07626	.06366	.05101	.03832	.02559
.17500	.14947	.13727	.12502	.11272	.10038	.08798	.07554	.06306	.05053	.03796
.17750	.16016	.14812	.13602	.12388	.11168	.09945	.08716	.07483	.06246	.05005
.18000	.17062	.15872	.14678	.13478	.12274	.11066	.09853	.08635	.07413	.06187
.18250	.18084	.16909	.15730	.14545	.13356	.12162	.10964	.09762	.08555	.07344
.18500	.19085	.17924	.16759	.15589	.14414	.13235	.12051	.10864	.09672	.08476
.18750	.20063	.18917	.17766	.16610	.15449	.14284	.13115	.11942	.10764	.09583
.19000	.21021	.19888	.18751	.17609	.16462	.15311	.14156	.12997	.11834	.10666
.19250	.21959	.20839	.19715	.18587	.17454	.16317	.15175	.14030	.12880	.11726
.19500	.22876	.21770	.20659	.19544	.18424	.17301	.16172	.15040	.13904	.12764
.19750	.23774	.22681	.21583	.20481	.19375	.18264	.17149	.16030	.14907	.13780
.20000	.24654	.23573	.22488	.21399	.20305	.19207	.18105	.16999	.15889	.14775
.20250	.25515	.24447	.23374	.22297	.21216	.20130	.19041	.17948	.16850	.15749
.20500	.26359	.25303	.24242	.23177	.22108	.21035	.19958	.18877	.17792	.16704
.20750	.27185	.26141	.25092	.24039	.22982	.21921	.20856	.19787	.18715	.17638

POINT TABLES: ORIGINAL LOAN TERM: 240 MONTHS LOAN PREPAID IN: 240 MONTHS

EFFECTIVE YIELD	CONTRACT RATE .17000	.17250	.17500	.17750	.18000	.18250	.18500	.18750	.19000	.19250
.07000	-.89192	-.91648	-.94111	-.96582	-.99060	-1.01545	-1.04037	-1.06535	-1.09040	-1.11551
.07250	-.85583	-.87992	-.90408	-.92832	-.95263	-.97701	-1.00145	-1.02595	-1.05052	-1.07515
.07500	-.82077	-.84441	-.86812	-.89190	-.91575	-.93966	-.96364	-.98769	-1.01179	-1.03596
.07750	-.78671	-.80991	-.83317	-.85651	-.87991	-.90338	-.92691	-.95051	-.97416	-.99787
.08000	-.75362	-.77639	-.79922	-.82213	-.84510	-.86813	-.89123	-.91438	-.93760	-.96087
.08250	-.72146	-.74381	-.76623	-.78871	-.81126	-.83387	-.85654	-.87928	-.90207	-.92491
.08500	-.69021	-.71215	-.73416	-.75623	-.77837	-.80057	-.82283	-.84515	-.86753	-.88996
.08750	-.65982	-.68137	-.70298	-.72466	-.74640	-.76820	-.79006	-.81198	-.83395	-.85598
.09000	-.63027	-.65144	-.67267	-.69396	-.71531	-.73673	-.75820	-.77973	-.80131	-.82295
.09250	-.60154	-.62233	-.64319	-.66411	-.68508	-.70612	-.72721	-.74836	-.76956	-.79082
.09500	-.57360	-.59403	-.61452	-.63507	-.65568	-.67635	-.69708	-.71785	-.73869	-.75957
.09750	-.54641	-.56649	-.58663	-.60682	-.62708	-.64739	-.66776	-.68818	-.70865	-.72917
.10000	-.51997	-.53970	-.55949	-.57934	-.59925	-.61922	-.63923	-.65931	-.67943	-.69960
.10250	-.49423	-.51363	-.53308	-.55260	-.57217	-.59180	-.61148	-.63121	-.65099	-.67082
.10500	-.46918	-.48825	-.50738	-.52657	-.54582	-.56511	-.58446	-.60386	-.62331	-.64281
.10750	-.44480	-.46355	-.48237	-.50124	-.52016	-.53914	-.55817	-.57725	-.59637	-.61555
.11000	-.42106	-.43951	-.45801	-.47657	-.49518	-.51385	-.53257	-.55133	-.57014	-.58900
.11250	-.39794	-.41609	-.43429	-.45255	-.47086	-.48922	-.50764	-.52610	-.54460	-.56316
.11500	-.37543	-.39329	-.41120	-.42916	-.44718	-.46524	-.48336	-.50152	-.51973	-.53798
.11750	-.35350	-.37107	-.38870	-.40638	-.42410	-.44188	-.45971	-.47758	-.49550	-.51346
.12000	-.33214	-.34943	-.36678	-.38418	-.40163	-.41912	-.43667	-.45426	-.47190	-.48958
.12250	-.31132	-.32835	-.34542	-.36255	-.37972	-.39695	-.41422	-.43154	-.44890	-.46630
.12500	-.29104	-.30780	-.32461	-.34147	-.35838	-.37534	-.39234	-.40939	-.42648	-.44362
.12750	-.27127	-.28777	-.30432	-.32093	-.33758	-.35427	-.37102	-.38781	-.40464	-.42151
.13000	-.25199	-.26824	-.28455	-.30090	-.31730	-.33374	-.35023	-.36676	-.38334	-.39995
.13250	-.23320	-.24920	-.26526	-.28137	-.29752	-.31372	-.32996	-.34625	-.36257	-.37894
.13500	-.21487	-.23064	-.24646	-.26232	-.27824	-.29419	-.31020	-.32624	-.34232	-.35844
.13750	-.19699	-.21253	-.22812	-.24375	-.25943	-.27515	-.29092	-.30672	-.32257	-.33846
.14000	-.17955	-.19487	-.21023	-.22563	-.24108	-.25658	-.27211	-.28769	-.30330	-.31896
.14250	-.16254	-.17763	-.19277	-.20795	-.22318	-.23845	-.25376	-.26911	-.28451	-.29993
.14500	-.14594	-.16082	-.17574	-.19070	-.20571	-.22077	-.23586	-.25099	-.26616	-.28137
.14750	-.12974	-.14440	-.15911	-.17387	-.18867	-.20351	-.21838	-.23330	-.24826	-.26325
.15000	-.11392	-.12838	-.14289	-.15744	-.17203	-.18666	-.20133	-.21604	-.23078	-.24557
.15250	-.09848	-.11274	-.12705	-.14139	-.15578	-.17021	-.18468	-.19918	-.21372	-.22830
.15500	-.08340	-.09747	-.11158	-.12573	-.13992	-.15415	-.16842	-.18272	-.19707	-.21144
.15750	-.06868	-.08255	-.09647	-.11043	-.12443	-.13846	-.15254	-.16665	-.18080	-.19498
.16000	-.05430	-.06799	-.08171	-.09548	-.10929	-.12314	-.13703	-.15095	-.16491	-.17890
.16250	-.04025	-.05375	-.06730	-.08089	-.09451	-.10818	-.12188	-.13561	-.14938	-.16319
.16500	-.02652	-.03985	-.05322	-.06662	-.08007	-.09355	-.10707	-.12063	-.13422	-.14784
.16750	-.01311	-.02626	-.03945	-.05269	-.06596	-.07926	-.09261	-.10598	-.11940	-.13284
.17000	0.00000	-.01298	-.02600	-.03906	-.05216	-.06530	-.07847	-.09167	-.10491	-.11818
.17250	.01282	0.00000	-.01285	-.02575	-.03868	-.05164	-.06465	-.07768	-.09075	-.10385
.17500	.02534	.01269	.00000	-.01273	-.02550	-.03830	-.05113	-.06401	-.07691	-.08984
.17750	.03759	.02510	.01257	.00000	-.01261	-.02525	-.03792	-.05063	-.06337	-.07614
.18000	.04958	.03724	.02486	.01245	0.00000	-.01248	-.02500	-.03755	-.05013	-.06275
.18250	.06129	.04911	.03689	.02463	.01233	.00000	-.01236	-.02476	-.03719	-.04964
.18500	.07276	.06072	.04865	.03654	.02439	.01221	.00000	-.01224	-.02452	-.03683
.18750	.08397	.07208	.06015	.04819	.03619	.02416	.01210	0.00000	-.01213	-.02428
.19000	.09495	.08320	.07142	.05960	.04774	.03585	.02393	.01198	0.00000	-.01201
.19250	.10569	.09408	.08244	.07076	.05904	.04730	.03552	.02371	.01187	.00000
.19500	.11621	.10473	.09323	.08168	.07011	.05850	.04686	.03519	.02349	.01176
.19750	.12650	.11516	.10379	.09238	.08094	.06946	.05796	.04642	.03486	.02327
.20000	.13658	.12537	.11413	.10285	.09154	.08020	.06883	.05743	.04630	.03454
.20250	.14645	.13537	.12425	.11311	.10193	.09072	.07947	.06820	.05690	.04557
.20500	.15612	.14516	.13417	.12315	.11210	.10101	.08990	.07875	.06758	.05638
.20750	.16559	.15475	.14389	.13299	.12206	.11110	.10011	.08909	.07805	.06697

CONTRACT RATE

EFFECTIVE YIELD	.19500	.19750	.20000	.20250	.20500	.20750
.07000	-1.14068	-1.16590	-1.19119	-1.21652	-1.24191	-1.26736
.07250	-1.09984	-1.12459	-1.14939	-1.17424	-1.19915	-1.22411
.07500	-1.06018	-1.08445	-1.10879	-1.13317	-1.15761	-1.18209
.07750	-1.02164	-1.04547	-1.06934	-1.09327	-1.11725	-1.14128
.08000	-.98420	-1.00758	-1.03102	-1.05450	-1.07804	-1.10162
.08250	-.94781	-.97077	-.99377	-1.01683	-1.03993	-1.06308
.08500	-.91245	-.93498	-.95757	-.98021	-1.00289	-1.02562
.08750	-.87806	-.90020	-.92238	-.94461	-.96688	-.98920
.09000	-.84463	-.86637	-.88816	-.90999	-.93187	-.95379
.09250	-.81212	-.83348	-.85488	-.87633	-.89782	-.91936
.09500	-.78051	-.80149	-.82252	-.84359	-.86471	-.88587
.09750	-.74975	-.77037	-.79103	-.81174	-.83250	-.85329
.10000	-.71982	-.74009	-.76040	-.78076	-.80116	-.82160
.10250	-.69070	-.71062	-.73059	-.75060	-.77066	-.79075
.10500	-.66236	-.68195	-.70158	-.72126	-.74097	-.76073
.10750	-.63477	-.65403	-.67334	-.69269	-.71208	-.73151
.11000	-.60791	-.62686	-.64585	-.66488	-.68395	-.70306
.11250	-.58175	-.60039	-.61908	-.63780	-.65656	-.67536
.11500	-.55628	-.57462	-.59300	-.61142	-.62988	-.64838
.11750	-.53147	-.54952	-.56760	-.58573	-.60390	-.62210
.12000	-.50730	-.52506	-.54286	-.56070	-.57858	-.59650
.12250	-.48374	-.50123	-.51875	-.53632	-.55391	-.57155
.12500	-.46079	-.47801	-.49526	-.51255	-.52988	-.54724
.12750	-.43842	-.45537	-.47236	-.48938	-.50645	-.52354
.13000	-.41661	-.43330	-.45003	-.46680	-.48360	-.50044
.13250	-.39534	-.41179	-.42827	-.44478	-.46133	-.47792
.13500	-.37461	-.39081	-.40704	-.42331	-.43961	-.45595
.13750	-.35438	-.37034	-.38634	-.40237	-.41843	-.43453
.14000	-.33465	-.35038	-.36614	-.38194	-.39777	-.41363
.14250	-.31540	-.33090	-.34644	-.36201	-.37761	-.39324
.14500	-.29662	-.31190	-.32721	-.34256	-.35794	-.37335
.14750	-.27828	-.29335	-.30844	-.32357	-.33874	-.35393
.15000	-.26039	-.27524	-.29013	-.30504	-.31999	-.33497
.15250	-.24292	-.25756	-.27224	-.28695	-.30170	-.31647
.15500	-.22586	-.24030	-.25478	-.26929	-.28383	-.29840
.15750	-.20920	-.22345	-.23773	-.25204	-.26638	-.28075
.16000	-.19293	-.20698	-.22107	-.23519	-.24934	-.26352
.16250	-.17703	-.19090	-.20480	-.21873	-.23269	-.24668
.16500	-.16150	-.17519	-.18890	-.20265	-.21643	-.23023
.16750	-.14632	-.15983	-.17337	-.18694	-.20053	-.21416
.17000	-.13149	-.14482	-.15818	-.17158	-.18500	-.19844
.17250	-.11699	-.13015	-.14334	-.15656	-.16981	-.18309
.17500	-.10281	-.11581	-.12883	-.14188	-.15496	-.16807
.17750	-.08895	-.10178	-.11464	-.12753	-.14045	-.15339
.18000	-.07539	-.08806	-.10077	-.11349	-.12625	-.13903
.18250	-.06213	-.07465	-.08719	-.09977	-.11236	-.12499
.18500	-.04916	-.06152	-.07392	-.08633	-.09878	-.11125
.18750	-.03647	-.04868	-.06093	-.07319	-.08549	-.09781
.19000	-.02405	-.03612	-.04821	-.06033	-.07248	-.08465
.19250	-.01190	-.02382	-.03577	-.04775	-.05975	-.07178
.19500	.00000	-.01178	-.02360	-.03543	-.04729	-.05918
.19750	.01165	.00000	-.01167	-.02337	-.03509	-.04684
.20000	.02305	.01154	.00000	-.01156	-.02315	-.03476
.20250	.03422	.02284	.01143	.00000	-.01146	-.02293
.20500	.04516	.03390	.02263	.01133	.00000	-.01135
.20750	.05587	.04475	.03359	.02242	.01122	.00000

POINT TABLES: ORIGINAL LOAN TERM: 300 MONTHS LOAN PREPAID IN: 60 MONTHS

EFFECTIVE YIELD	CONTRACT RATE .07000	.07250	.07500	.07750	.08000	.08250	.08500	.08750	.09000	.09250
.07000	.00000	-.01013	-.02029	-.03048	-.04069	-.05092	-.06118	-.07146	-.08176	-.09208
.07250	.01006	.00000	-.01009	-.02020	-.03034	-.04050	-.05068	-.06089	-.07112	-.08137
.07500	.02000	.01001	.00000	-.01004	-.02011	-.03020	-.04031	-.05045	-.06060	-.07078
.07750	.02983	.01991	.00997	-.00000	-.00999	-.02001	-.03006	-.04012	-.05021	-.06032
.08000	.03954	.02969	.01982	.00992	.00000	-.00995	-.01992	-.02992	-.03993	-.04997
.08250	.04914	.03936	.02956	.01973	.00988	.00000	-.00990	-.01983	-.02978	-.03974
.08500	.05862	.04892	.03919	.02943	.01964	.00983	.00000	-.00986	-.01974	-.02963
.08750	.06800	.05837	.04870	.03901	.02930	.01955	.00979	.00000	-.00981	-.01964
.09000	.07727	.06770	.05811	.04849	.03884	.02916	.01946	.00974	.00000	-.00976
.09250	.08643	.07693	.06740	.05785	.04827	.03866	.02903	.01937	.00970	.00000
.09500	.09548	.08605	.07659	.06710	.05759	.04805	.03848	.02890	.01928	.00965
.09750	.10443	.09507	.08567	.07625	.06680	.05733	.04783	.03831	.02876	.01919
.10000	.11328	.10398	.09465	.08529	.07591	.06650	.05707	.04761	.03813	.02863
.10250	.12202	.11279	.10352	.09423	.08491	.07557	.06620	.05681	.04739	.03795
.10500	.13066	.12150	.11230	.10307	.09381	.08453	.07523	.06590	.05655	.04717
.10750	.13921	.13010	.12097	.11180	.10261	.09339	.08415	.07489	.06560	.05628
.11000	.14765	.13861	.12954	.12044	.11131	.10215	.09297	.08377	.07454	.06529
.11250	.15600	.14702	.13801	.12897	.11991	.11081	.10170	.09255	.08339	.07420
.11500	.16425	.15533	.14638	.13741	.12840	.11937	.11032	.10124	.09213	.08300
.11750	.17240	.16355	.15466	.14575	.13680	.12783	.11884	.10982	.10078	.09171
.12000	.18047	.17167	.16284	.15399	.14511	.13620	.12726	.11830	.10932	.10031
.12250	.18843	.17970	.17093	.16214	.15332	.14447	.13559	.12669	.11777	.10882
.12500	.19631	.18764	.17893	.17020	.16143	.15264	.14383	.13499	.12612	.11723
.12750	.20410	.19548	.18684	.17816	.16946	.16072	.15197	.14319	.13438	.12555
.13000	.21180	.20324	.19465	.18603	.17739	.16871	.16002	.15129	.14254	.13377
.13250	.21940	.21090	.20237	.19382	.18523	.17661	.16797	.15930	.15061	.14190
.13500	.22693	.21848	.21001	.20151	.19298	.18442	.17584	.16723	.15859	.14993
.13750	.23436	.22598	.21756	.20912	.20064	.19214	.18361	.17506	.16648	.15788
.14000	.24171	.23338	.22502	.21663	.20822	.19977	.19130	.18280	.17428	.16574
.14250	.24898	.24071	.23240	.22407	.21571	.20732	.19890	.19046	.18199	.17350
.14500	.25616	.24794	.23970	.23142	.22311	.21478	.20641	.19803	.18962	.18118
.14750	.26326	.25510	.24691	.23868	.23043	.22215	.21384	.20551	.19715	.18877
.15000	.27028	.26217	.25404	.24587	.23767	.22944	.22119	.21291	.20461	.19628
.15250	.27722	.26917	.26108	.25297	.24482	.23665	.22845	.22023	.21198	.20370
.15500	.28408	.27608	.26805	.25999	.25190	.24378	.23563	.22746	.21926	.21104
.15750	.29087	.28292	.27494	.26693	.25889	.25082	.24273	.23461	.22646	.21829
.16000	.29757	.28968	.28175	.27379	.26580	.25779	.24975	.24168	.23359	.22547
.16250	.30420	.29636	.28848	.28058	.27264	.26468	.25669	.24867	.24063	.23256
.16500	.31075	.30296	.29514	.28728	.27940	.27149	.26355	.25558	.24759	.23958
.16750	.31723	.30949	.30172	.29392	.28608	.27822	.27033	.26242	.25448	.24651
.17000	.32364	.31595	.30823	.30047	.29269	.28488	.27704	.26918	.26128	.25337
.17250	.32997	.32233	.31466	.30696	.29922	.29146	.28367	.27586	.26802	.26015
.17500	.33623	.32864	.32102	.31337	.30568	.29797	.29023	.28246	.27467	.26686
.17750	.34242	.33488	.32731	.31970	.31207	.30441	.29671	.28900	.28125	.27349
.18000	.34855	.34105	.33353	.32597	.31838	.31077	.30313	.29546	.28776	.28004
.18250	.35460	.34715	.33967	.33216	.32463	.31706	.30947	.30184	.29420	.28653
.18500	.36058	.35318	.34575	.33829	.33080	.32328	.31573	.30816	.30056	.29294
.18750	.36650	.35914	.35176	.34435	.33690	.32943	.32193	.31441	.30685	.29928
.19000	.37234	.36504	.35770	.35034	.34294	.33551	.32806	.32058	.31308	.30554
.19250	.37813	.37087	.36358	.35626	.34891	.34153	.33412	.32669	.31923	.31174
.19500	.38384	.37663	.36939	.36211	.35481	.34748	.34012	.33273	.32531	.31787
.19750	.38950	.38233	.37513	.36790	.36065	.35336	.34604	.33870	.33133	.32393
.20000	.39509	.38797	.38081	.37363	.36642	.35917	.35190	.34460	.33728	.32993
.20250	.40061	.39354	.38643	.37929	.37212	.36492	.35770	.35044	.34316	.33586
.20500	.40608	.39905	.39198	.38489	.37776	.37061	.36343	.35622	.34898	.34172
.20750	.41148	.40449	.39747	.39042	.38334	.37623	.36909	.36193	.35474	.34752

POINT TABLES: ORIGINAL LOAN TERM: 300 MONTHS LOAN PREPAID IN: 60 MONTHS

EFFECTIVE YIELD	.09500	.09750	.10000	.10250	.10500	.10750	.11000	.11250	.11500	.11750
				CONTRACT RATE						
.07000	-.10242	-.11277	-.12315	-.13354	-.14394	-.15436	-.16479	-.17524	-.18569	-.19616
.07250	-.09164	-.10192	-.11222	-.12254	-.13287	-.14322	-.15359	-.16396	-.17435	-.18474
.07500	-.08098	-.09119	-.10142	-.11167	-.12193	-.13221	-.14251	-.15281	-.16313	-.17346
.07750	-.07044	-.08059	-.09075	-.10093	-.11112	-.12133	-.13155	-.14179	-.15204	-.16230
.08000	-.06003	-.07010	-.08019	-.09030	-.10043	-.11057	-.12072	-.13089	-.14107	-.15126
.08250	-.04973	-.05974	-.06976	-.07980	-.08986	-.09993	-.11002	-.12012	-.13023	-.14036
.08500	-.03955	-.04949	-.05945	-.06942	-.07941	-.08942	-.09944	-.10947	-.11951	-.12957
.08750	-.02949	-.03936	-.04925	-.05916	-.06908	-.07902	-.08897	-.09894	-.10892	-.11891
.09000	-.01955	-.02935	-.03918	-.04902	-.05887	-.06874	-.07863	-.08853	-.09844	-.10837
.09250	-.00972	-.01946	-.02921	-.03899	-.04878	-.05858	-.06840	-.07824	-.08809	-.09795
.09500	.00000	-.00967	-.01936	-.02907	-.03880	-.04854	-.05829	-.06807	-.07785	-.08765
.09750	.00961	0.00000	-.00963	-.01927	-.02893	-.03861	-.04830	-.05801	-.06773	-.07746
.10000	.01910	.00956	.00000	-.00958	-.01918	-.02879	-.03842	-.04806	-.05772	-.06739
.10250	.02849	.01901	.00952	-.00000	-.00953	-.01908	-.02865	-.03823	-.04782	-.05743
.10500	.03778	.02836	.01892	.00947	.00000	-.00949	-.01899	-.02851	-.03804	-.04759
.10750	.04695	.03760	.02823	.01883	.00943	.00000	-.00944	-.01890	-.02837	-.03785
.11000	.05602	.04673	.03742	.02809	.01874	.00938	.00000	-.00940	-.01881	-.02823
.11250	.06499	.05576	.04651	.03724	.02796	.01865	.00933	.00000	-.00935	-.01871
.11500	.07386	.06469	.05550	.04629	.03707	.02782	.01856	.00929	.00000	-.00930
.11750	.08262	.07351	.06438	.05524	.04607	.03689	.02769	.01847	.00924	.00000
.12000	.09129	.08224	.07317	.06408	.05497	.04585	.03671	.02756	.01838	.00920
.12250	.09985	.09086	.08185	.07283	.06378	.05471	.04563	.03653	.02742	.01829
.12500	.10832	.09939	.09044	.08147	.07248	.06348	.05445	.04541	.03636	.02729
.12750	.11670	.10782	.09893	.09002	.08109	.07214	.06317	.05419	.04519	.03618
.13000	.12498	.11616	.10733	.09847	.08960	.08070	.07180	.06287	.05393	.04497
.13250	.13316	.12440	.11562	.10683	.09801	.08917	.08032	.07145	.06257	.05367
.13500	.14125	.13255	.12383	.11509	.10633	.09755	.08875	.07994	.07111	.06227
.13750	.14926	.14061	.13194	.12326	.11455	.10583	.09709	.08833	.07956	.07077
.14000	.15717	.14858	.13997	.13133	.12268	.11402	.10533	.09663	.08791	.07918
.14250	.16499	.15645	.14790	.13932	.13073	.12211	.11348	.10483	.09617	.08749
.14500	.17272	.16424	.15574	.14722	.13868	.13012	.12154	.11295	.10433	.09571
.14750	.18037	.17194	.16349	.15503	.14654	.13803	.12951	.12097	.11241	.10384
.15000	.18793	.17955	.17116	.16275	.15431	.14586	.13739	.12890	.12040	.11188
.15250	.19540	.18708	.17874	.17038	.16200	.15360	.14518	.13675	.12829	.11983
.15500	.20279	.19453	.18624	.17793	.16960	.16125	.15289	.14450	.13610	.12769
.15750	.21010	.20189	.19365	.18539	.17712	.16882	.16051	.15217	.14383	.13546
.16000	.21733	.20916	.20098	.19277	.18455	.17630	.16804	.15976	.15146	.14315
.16250	.22447	.21636	.20823	.20007	.19190	.18370	.17549	.16726	.15901	.15075
.16500	.23154	.22348	.21539	.20729	.19916	.19102	.18286	.17468	.16648	.15827
.16750	.23852	.23051	.22248	.21442	.20635	.19826	.19014	.18201	.17387	.16571
.17000	.24543	.23747	.22949	.22148	.21346	.20541	.19735	.18927	.18117	.17306
.17250	.25226	.24435	.23641	.22846	.22048	.21249	.20448	.19644	.18840	.18033
.17500	.25902	.25115	.24327	.23536	.22743	.21949	.21152	.20354	.19554	.18752
.17750	.26569	.25788	.25004	.24218	.23431	.22641	.21849	.21056	.20260	.19464
.18000	.27230	.26453	.25674	.24893	.24110	.23325	.22538	.21750	.20959	.20167
.18250	.27883	.27111	.26337	.25561	.24782	.24002	.23220	.22436	.21650	.20863
.18500	.28529	.27762	.26992	.26221	.25447	.24671	.23894	.23115	.22333	.21551
.18750	.29167	.28405	.27640	.26873	.26104	.25333	.24560	.23786	.23009	.22231
.19000	.29799	.29041	.28281	.27519	.26754	.25988	.25220	.24450	.23678	.22904
.19250	.30423	.29670	.28915	.28157	.27397	.26635	.25872	.25106	.24339	.23570
.19500	.31041	.30292	.29541	.28788	.28033	.27276	.26517	.25756	.24993	.24228
.19750	.31652	.30907	.30161	.29412	.28662	.27909	.27154	.26398	.25640	.24880
.20000	.32256	.31516	.30774	.30030	.29283	.28535	.27785	.27033	.26279	.25524
.20250	.32853	.32118	.31380	.30640	.29898	.29155	.28409	.27661	.26912	.26161
.20500	.33444	.32713	.31980	.31244	.30507	.29767	.29026	.28283	.27538	.26791
.20750	.34028	.33301	.32572	.31841	.31108	.30373	.29636	.28897	.28156	.27414

POINT TABLES: ORIGINAL LOAN TERM: 300 MONTHS LOAN PREPAID IN: 60 MONTHS

EFFECTIVE YIELD	CONTRACT RATE .12000	.12250	.12500	.12750	.13000	.13250	.13500	.13750	.14000	.14250
.07000	-.20664	-.21713	-.22763	-.23813	-.24865	-.25917	-.26970	-.28023	-.29077	-.30132
.07250	-.19515	-.20557	-.21600	-.22644	-.23688	-.24734	-.25780	-.26826	-.27874	-.28921
.07500	-.18380	-.19415	-.20451	-.21487	-.22525	-.23564	-.24603	-.25643	-.26683	-.27724
.07750	-.17257	-.18285	-.19314	-.20344	-.21375	-.22407	-.23439	-.24472	-.25506	-.26541
.08000	-.16147	-.17168	-.18191	-.19214	-.20238	-.21263	-.22289	-.23315	-.24343	-.25370
.08250	-.15049	-.16064	-.17080	-.18096	-.19114	-.20132	-.21152	-.22171	-.23192	-.24213
.08500	-.13964	-.14972	-.15982	-.16992	-.18003	-.19014	-.20027	-.21040	-.22054	-.23069
.08750	-.12892	-.13893	-.14896	-.15899	-.16904	-.17909	-.18915	-.19922	-.20929	-.21938
.09000	-.11831	-.12826	-.13822	-.14819	-.15817	-.16816	-.17816	-.18816	-.19817	-.20819
.09250	-.10782	-.11771	-.12761	-.13751	-.14743	-.15735	-.16728	-.17722	-.18717	-.19713
.09500	-.09746	-.10728	-.11711	-.12695	-.13680	-.14667	-.15653	-.16641	-.17630	-.18619
.09750	-.08721	-.09697	-.10673	-.11651	-.12630	-.13610	-.14591	-.15572	-.16554	-.17537
.10000	-.07707	-.08677	-.09647	-.10619	-.11592	-.12565	-.13540	-.14515	-.15491	-.16468
.10250	-.06705	-.07669	-.08633	-.09598	-.10565	-.11532	-.12501	-.13470	-.14440	-.15410
.10500	-.05715	-.06672	-.07630	-.08589	-.09550	-.10511	-.11473	-.12436	-.13400	-.14364
.10750	-.04735	-.05686	-.06638	-.07591	-.08546	-.09501	-.10457	-.11414	-.12372	-.13330
.11000	-.03767	-.04711	-.05657	-.06605	-.07553	-.08502	-.09452	-.10403	-.11355	-.12308
.11250	-.02809	-.03748	-.04688	-.05629	-.06571	-.07514	-.08459	-.09404	-.10350	-.11296
.11500	-.01862	-.02795	-.03729	-.04664	-.05601	-.06538	-.07476	-.08415	-.09355	-.10296
.11750	-.00926	-.01853	-.02781	-.03710	-.04641	-.05572	-.06505	-.07438	-.08372	-.09307
.12000	.00000	-.00921	-.01844	-.02767	-.03692	-.04617	-.05544	-.06472	-.07400	-.08329
.12250	.00915	.00000	-.00917	-.01834	-.02753	-.03673	-.04594	-.05516	-.06439	-.07362
.12500	.01820	.00911	.00000	-.00912	-.01825	-.02739	-.03655	-.04571	-.05488	-.06406
.12750	.02715	.01812	.00906	.00000	-.00908	-.01816	-.02726	-.03636	-.04548	-.05460
.13000	.03600	.02702	.01803	.00902	.00000	-.00903	-.01807	-.02712	-.03618	-.04525
.13250	.04476	.03583	.02689	.01794	.00897	0.00000	-.00898	-.01798	-.02698	-.03599
.13500	.05341	.04454	.03565	.02676	.01785	.00893	.00000	-.00894	-.01789	-.02685
.13750	.06197	.05315	.04432	.03548	.02662	.01776	.00889	0.00000	-.00889	-.01780
.14000	.07043	.06167	.05289	.04410	.03530	.02649	.01767	.00884	.00000	-.00885
.14250	.07879	.07009	.06137	.05263	.04389	.03513	.02636	.01758	.00880	0.00000
.14500	.08707	.07841	.06975	.06107	.05237	.04367	.03496	.02623	.01750	.00875
.14750	.09525	.08665	.07804	.06941	.06077	.05212	.04345	.03478	.02610	.01741
.15000	.10334	.09479	.08623	.07766	.06907	.06047	.05186	.04324	.03461	.02597
.15250	.11134	.10285	.09434	.08581	.07728	.06873	.06017	.05160	.04303	.03444
.15500	.11926	.11081	.10235	.09388	.08540	.07690	.06840	.05988	.05135	.04281
.15750	.12708	.11869	.11028	.10186	.09343	.08498	.07653	.06806	.05958	.05110
.16000	.13482	.12648	.11812	.10975	.10137	.09297	.08457	.07615	.06773	.05929
.16250	.14247	.13418	.12587	.11756	.10922	.10088	.09252	.08416	.07578	.06739
.16500	.15004	.14180	.13354	.12527	.11699	.10870	.10039	.09207	.08374	.07541
.16750	.15753	.14933	.14113	.13291	.12467	.11643	.10817	.09990	.09162	.08333
.17000	.16493	.15679	.14863	.14046	.13227	.12407	.11587	.10765	.09942	.09117
.17250	.17225	.16415	.15605	.14792	.13979	.13164	.12348	.11531	.10712	.09893
.17500	.17949	.17144	.16338	.15531	.14722	.13912	.13100	.12288	.11475	.10660
.17750	.18665	.17865	.17064	.16261	.15457	.14652	.13845	.13037	.12229	.11419
.18000	.19373	.18578	.17781	.16983	.16184	.15383	.14582	.13779	.12975	.12170
.18250	.20074	.19283	.18491	.17698	.16903	.16107	.15310	.14512	.13712	.12912
.18500	.20766	.19981	.19193	.18405	.17615	.16823	.16031	.15237	.14442	.13646
.18750	.21452	.20670	.19888	.19104	.18318	.17531	.16743	.15954	.15164	.14373
.19000	.22129	.21353	.20574	.19795	.19014	.18232	.17448	.16664	.15878	.15091
.19250	.22799	.22027	.21254	.20479	.19702	.18925	.18146	.17366	.16585	.15802
.19500	.23462	.22695	.21926	.21155	.20383	.19610	.18836	.18060	.17283	.16505
.19750	.24118	.23355	.22590	.21824	.21057	.20288	.19518	.18747	.17974	.17201
.20000	.24766	.24008	.23247	.22486	.21723	.20958	.20193	.19426	.18658	.17889
.20250	.25408	.24654	.23898	.23140	.22382	.21622	.20861	.20098	.19335	.18570
.20500	.26042	.25292	.24541	.23788	.23034	.22278	.21521	.20763	.20004	.19243
.20750	.26670	.25924	.25177	.24428	.23678	.22927	.22174	.21420	.20665	.19909

POINT TABLES: ORIGINAL LOAN TERM: 300 MONTHS LOAN PREPAID IN: 60 MONTHS

CONTRACT RATE

EFFECTIVE YIELD	.14500	.14750	.15000	.15250	.15500	.15750	.16000	.16250	.16500	.16750
.07000	-.31187	-.32243	-.33299	-.34355	-.35412	-.36469	-.37526	-.38584	-.39641	-.40699
.07250	-.29970	-.31018	-.32068	-.33117	-.34167	-.35217	-.36268	-.37319	-.38370	-.39421
.07500	-.28766	-.29808	-.30850	-.31893	-.32937	-.33980	-.35024	-.36068	-.37113	-.38157
.07750	-.27576	-.28611	-.29647	-.30683	-.31720	-.32757	-.33794	-.34832	-.35870	-.36908
.08000	-.26399	-.27427	-.28457	-.29486	-.30516	-.31547	-.32578	-.33609	-.34640	-.35672
.08250	-.25235	-.26257	-.27280	-.28303	-.29327	-.30351	-.31375	-.32400	-.33425	-.34450
.08500	-.24084	-.25100	-.26116	-.27133	-.28150	-.29168	-.30186	-.31204	-.32222	-.33241
.08750	-.22946	-.23956	-.24966	-.25976	-.26987	-.27998	-.29009	-.30021	-.31034	-.32046
.09000	-.21821	-.22824	-.23828	-.24832	-.25836	-.26841	-.27846	-.28852	-.29858	-.30864
.09250	-.20709	-.21705	-.22703	-.23700	-.24699	-.25697	-.26696	-.27695	-.28695	-.29695
.09500	-.19609	-.20599	-.21590	-.22582	-.23573	-.24566	-.25559	-.26552	-.27545	-.28539
.09750	-.18521	-.19505	-.20490	-.21475	-.22461	-.23447	-.24434	-.25421	-.26408	-.27396
.10000	-.17445	-.18423	-.19402	-.20381	-.21361	-.22341	-.23321	-.24302	-.25284	-.26265
.10250	-.16381	-.17353	-.18326	-.19299	-.20273	-.21247	-.22221	-.23196	-.24172	-.25147
.10500	-.15330	-.16296	-.17262	-.18229	-.19197	-.20165	-.21133	-.22102	-.23072	-.24042
.10750	-.14289	-.15249	-.16210	-.17171	-.18133	-.19095	-.20058	-.21021	-.21984	-.22948
.11000	-.13261	-.14215	-.15170	-.16125	-.17080	-.18037	-.18994	-.19951	-.20908	-.21866
.11250	-.12244	-.13192	-.14141	-.15090	-.16040	-.16990	-.17941	-.18893	-.19844	-.20797
.11500	-.11238	-.12180	-.13123	-.14067	-.15011	-.15955	-.16900	-.17846	-.18792	-.19739
.11750	-.10243	-.11180	-.12117	-.13055	-.13993	-.14932	-.15871	-.16811	-.17751	-.18692
.12000	-.09259	-.10190	-.11122	-.12054	-.12986	-.13920	-.14853	-.15787	-.16722	-.17657
.12250	-.08287	-.09212	-.10137	-.11064	-.11991	-.12918	-.13846	-.14775	-.15704	-.16634
.12500	-.07324	-.08244	-.09164	-.10085	-.11006	-.11928	-.12851	-.13774	-.14697	-.15621
.12750	-.06373	-.07287	-.08201	-.09117	-.10033	-.10949	-.11866	-.12783	-.13701	-.14620
.13000	-.05432	-.06340	-.07249	-.08159	-.09069	-.09980	-.10892	-.11804	-.12716	-.13629
.13250	-.04502	-.05404	-.06308	-.07212	-.08117	-.09022	-.09929	-.10835	-.11742	-.12650
.13500	-.03581	-.04479	-.05377	-.06276	-.07175	-.08075	-.08976	-.09877	-.10779	-.11681
.13750	-.02671	-.03563	-.04456	-.05349	-.06243	-.07138	-.08033	-.08929	-.09826	-.10722
.14000	-.01771	-.02657	-.03545	-.04433	-.05322	-.06211	-.07101	-.07992	-.08883	-.09774
.14250	-.00881	-.01762	-.02644	-.03527	-.04410	-.05294	-.06179	-.07065	-.07950	-.08837
.14500	-.00000	-.00876	-.01753	-.02631	-.03509	-.04388	-.05267	-.06147	-.07028	-.07909
.14750	.00871	0.00000	-.00872	-.01744	-.02617	-.03491	-.04365	-.05240	-.06116	-.06992
.15000	.01732	.00866	0.00000	-.00867	-.01735	-.02604	-.03473	-.04343	-.05213	-.06084
.15250	.02584	.01724	.00862	.00000	-.00863	-.01726	-.02591	-.03455	-.04321	-.05186
.15500	.03427	.02571	.01715	.00858	.00000	-.00858	-.01718	-.02577	-.03438	-.04298
.15750	.04260	.03410	.02558	.01706	.00853	.00000	-.00854	-.01709	-.02564	-.03420
.16000	.05084	.04239	.03393	.02545	.01698	.00849	0.00000	-.00850	-.01700	-.02551
.16250	.05900	.05059	.04218	.03376	.02533	.01689	.00845	.00000	-.00845	-.01691
.16500	.06706	.05870	.05034	.04197	.03359	.02520	.01681	.00841	.00000	-.00841
.16750	.07504	.06673	.05841	.05009	.04176	.03342	.02507	.01672	.00836	0.00000
.17000	.08292	.07467	.06640	.05812	.04984	.04155	.03325	.02495	.01664	.00832
.17250	.09073	.08252	.07430	.06607	.05783	.04959	.04134	.03308	.02482	.01655
.17500	.09845	.09028	.08211	.07393	.06574	.05755	.04934	.04113	.03292	.02470
.17750	.10608	.09797	.08984	.08171	.07357	.06542	.05726	.04910	.04093	.03275
.18000	.11364	.10557	.09749	.08940	.08130	.07320	.06509	.05698	.04885	.04072
.18250	.12111	.11308	.10505	.09701	.08896	.08090	.07284	.06477	.05669	.04861
.18500	.12850	.12052	.11253	.10454	.09653	.08852	.08050	.07248	.06445	.05641
.18750	.13581	.12787	.11993	.11198	.10402	.09606	.08809	.08011	.07212	.06413
.19000	.14304	.13515	.12725	.11935	.11144	.10352	.09559	.08765	.07971	.07176
.19250	.15019	.14235	.13450	.12664	.11877	.11089	.10301	.09512	.08722	.07932
.19500	.15727	.14947	.14166	.13385	.12602	.11819	.11035	.10250	.09465	.08679
.19750	.16427	.15651	.14875	.14098	.13320	.12541	.11761	.10981	.10200	.09418
.20000	.17119	.16348	.15576	.14803	.14030	.13255	.12480	.11704	.10927	.10150
.20250	.17804	.17037	.16270	.15501	.14732	.13962	.13191	.12419	.11647	.10874
.20500	.18482	.17719	.16956	.16192	.15427	.14661	.13894	.13127	.12359	.11590
.20750	.19152	.18394	.17635	.16875	.16114	.15353	.14590	.13827	.13063	.12298

POINT TABLES: ORIGINAL LOAN TERM: 300 MONTHS LOAN PREPAID IN: 60 MONTHS

EFFECTIVE YIELD	CONTRACT RATE .17000	.17250	.17500	.17750	.18000	.18250	.18500	.18750	.19000	.19250
.07000	-.41757	-.42815	-.43874	-.44932	-.45991	-.47049	-.48108	-.49167	-.50225	-.51284
.07250	-.40473	-.41524	-.42576	-.43628	-.44680	-.45732	-.46784	-.47836	-.48888	-.49940
.07500	-.39202	-.40247	-.41292	-.42338	-.43383	-.44429	-.45474	-.46520	-.47565	-.48611
.07750	-.37946	-.38984	-.40023	-.41062	-.42101	-.43140	-.44179	-.45218	-.46257	-.47296
.08000	-.36704	-.37736	-.38768	-.39800	-.40833	-.41865	-.42898	-.43931	-.44963	-.45996
.08250	-.35475	-.36501	-.37527	-.38552	-.39579	-.40605	-.41631	-.42657	-.43684	-.44710
.08500	-.34260	-.35279	-.36299	-.37319	-.38338	-.39358	-.40378	-.41398	-.42418	-.43439
.08750	-.33059	-.34072	-.35085	-.36098	-.37112	-.38125	-.39139	-.40153	-.41167	-.42181
.09000	-.31871	-.32877	-.33884	-.34891	-.35899	-.36906	-.37914	-.38921	-.39929	-.40937
.09250	-.30695	-.31696	-.32697	-.33698	-.34699	-.35700	-.36702	-.37703	-.38705	-.39706
.09500	-.29533	-.30528	-.31522	-.32517	-.33512	-.34507	-.35503	-.36498	-.37494	-.38489
.09750	-.28384	-.29372	-.30361	-.31350	-.32339	-.33328	-.34317	-.35307	-.36296	-.37286
.10000	-.27247	-.28230	-.29212	-.30195	-.31178	-.32161	-.33144	-.34128	-.35112	-.36095
.10250	-.26123	-.27100	-.28076	-.29053	-.30030	-.31007	-.31985	-.32962	-.33940	-.34918
.10500	-.25012	-.25982	-.26953	-.27924	-.28895	-.29866	-.30837	-.31809	-.32781	-.33753
.10750	-.23912	-.24877	-.25841	-.26806	-.27772	-.28737	-.29703	-.30669	-.31635	-.32601
.11000	-.22825	-.23783	-.24742	-.25701	-.26661	-.27621	-.28581	-.29541	-.30501	-.31461
.11250	-.21749	-.22702	-.23655	-.24609	-.25562	-.26516	-.27470	-.28425	-.29379	-.30334
.11500	-.20685	-.21633	-.22580	-.23528	-.24476	-.25424	-.26373	-.27321	-.28270	-.29219
.11750	-.19633	-.20575	-.21517	-.22459	-.23401	-.24344	-.25286	-.26230	-.27173	-.28116
.12000	-.18593	-.19529	-.20465	-.21401	-.22338	-.23275	-.24212	-.25150	-.26087	-.27025
.12250	-.17564	-.18494	-.19424	-.20355	-.21286	-.22218	-.23150	-.24082	-.25014	-.25946
.12500	-.16546	-.17470	-.18395	-.19321	-.20246	-.21172	-.22099	-.23025	-.23952	-.24879
.12750	-.15539	-.16458	-.17378	-.18297	-.19218	-.20138	-.21059	-.21980	-.22901	-.23823
.13000	-.14543	-.15457	-.16371	-.17285	-.18200	-.19115	-.20031	-.20946	-.21862	-.22778
.13250	-.13558	-.14466	-.15375	-.16284	-.17193	-.18103	-.19013	-.19923	-.20834	-.21745
.13500	-.12583	-.13486	-.14390	-.15294	-.16198	-.17102	-.18007	-.18912	-.19817	-.20722
.13750	-.11620	-.12517	-.13416	-.14314	-.15213	-.16112	-.17011	-.17911	-.18811	-.19711
.14000	-.10666	-.11559	-.12452	-.13345	-.14239	-.15133	-.16027	-.16921	-.17816	-.18711
.14250	-.09724	-.10611	-.11498	-.12386	-.13275	-.14164	-.15053	-.15942	-.16831	-.17721
.14500	-.08791	-.09673	-.10555	-.11438	-.12321	-.13205	-.14089	-.14973	-.15858	-.16742
.14750	-.07868	-.08745	-.09623	-.10500	-.11378	-.12257	-.13136	-.14015	-.14894	-.15774
.15000	-.06956	-.07827	-.08700	-.09572	-.10445	-.11319	-.12193	-.13067	-.13941	-.14816
.15250	-.06053	-.06920	-.07787	-.08655	-.09523	-.10391	-.11260	-.12129	-.12998	-.13868
.15500	-.05160	-.06022	-.06884	-.07746	-.08610	-.09473	-.10337	-.11201	-.12065	-.12930
.15750	-.04276	-.05133	-.05991	-.06848	-.07706	-.08565	-.09424	-.10283	-.11142	-.12002
.16000	-.03403	-.04254	-.05107	-.05960	-.06813	-.07666	-.08520	-.09375	-.10229	-.11084
.16250	-.02538	-.03385	-.04233	-.05081	-.05929	-.06778	-.07627	-.08476	-.09326	-.10176
.16500	-.01683	-.02525	-.03368	-.04211	-.05054	-.05898	-.06743	-.07587	-.08432	-.09277
.16750	-.00837	-.01674	-.02512	-.03351	-.04189	-.05028	-.05868	-.06708	-.07548	-.08388
.17000	0.00000	-.00833	-.01666	-.02499	-.03333	-.04168	-.05003	-.05838	-.06673	-.07509
.17250	.00828	.00000	-.00828	-.01657	-.02487	-.03316	-.04146	-.04977	-.05808	-.06639
.17500	.01647	.00824	.00000	-.00824	-.01649	-.02474	-.03299	-.04125	-.04951	-.05778
.17750	.02457	.01639	.00820	.00000	-.00820	-.01640	-.02461	-.03282	-.04104	-.04926
.18000	.03259	.02445	.01630	.00815	.00000	-.00816	-.01632	-.02449	-.03266	-.04083
.18250	.04052	.03243	.02433	.01622	.00811	.00000	-.00812	-.01624	-.02436	-.03249
.18500	.04837	.04032	.03226	.02420	.01614	.00807	.00000	-.00808	-.01616	-.02424
.18750	.05613	.04812	.04012	.03210	.02408	.01606	.00803	0.00000	-.00803	-.01607
.19000	.06381	.05585	.04788	.03991	.03194	.02396	.01598	.00799	.00000	-.00799
.19250	.07141	.06349	.05557	.04764	.03971	.03178	.02384	.01590	.00795	0.00000
.19500	.07892	.07105	.06318	.05529	.04741	.03952	.03162	.02372	.01582	.00791
.19750	.08636	.07853	.07070	.06286	.05502	.04717	.03932	.03146	.02360	.01574
.20000	.09372	.08594	.07815	.07035	.06255	.05474	.04693	.03912	.03130	.02348
.20250	.10100	.09326	.08551	.07776	.07000	.06224	.05447	.04670	.03893	.03115
.20500	.10821	.10051	.09280	.08509	.07737	.06965	.06193	.05420	.04647	.03873
.20750	.11533	.10768	.10001	.09234	.08467	.07699	.06931	.06162	.05393	.04624

POINT TABLES: ORIGINAL LOAN TERM: 300 MONTHS LOAN PREPAID IN: 60 MONTHS

CONTRACT RATE

EFFECTIVE YIELD	.19500	.19750	.20000	.20250	.20500	.20750
.07000	-.52343	-.53401	-.54460	-.55518	-.56577	-.57635
.07250	-.50992	-.52044	-.53096	-.54148	-.55200	-.56252
.07500	-.49656	-.50702	-.51748	-.52793	-.53839	-.54884
.07750	-.48335	-.49375	-.50414	-.51453	-.52492	-.53531
.08000	-.47029	-.48062	-.49095	-.50128	-.51160	-.52193
.08250	-.45737	-.46763	-.47790	-.48817	-.49843	-.50870
.08500	-.44459	-.45479	-.46500	-.47520	-.48540	-.49560
.08750	-.43195	-.44209	-.45223	-.46237	-.47251	-.48266
.09000	-.41945	-.42953	-.43961	-.44969	-.45977	-.46985
.09250	-.40708	-.41710	-.42712	-.43714	-.44716	-.45718
.09500	-.39485	-.40481	-.41477	-.42473	-.43469	-.44465
.09750	-.38276	-.39265	-.40255	-.41245	-.42235	-.43225
.10000	-.37079	-.38063	-.39047	-.40031	-.41015	-.41999
.10250	-.35896	-.36874	-.37852	-.38830	-.39808	-.40786
.10500	-.34725	-.35697	-.36669	-.37642	-.38614	-.39587
.10750	-.33567	-.34533	-.35500	-.36467	-.37433	-.38400
.11000	-.32422	-.33382	-.34343	-.35304	-.36265	-.37226
.11250	-.31289	-.32244	-.33199	-.34154	-.35109	-.36065
.11500	-.30168	-.31118	-.32067	-.33017	-.33966	-.34916
.11750	-.29060	-.30003	-.30947	-.31891	-.32835	-.33779
.12000	-.27963	-.28901	-.29840	-.30778	-.31717	-.32655
.12250	-.26879	-.27811	-.28744	-.29677	-.30610	-.31543
.12500	-.25806	-.26733	-.27660	-.28588	-.29515	-.30443
.12750	-.24744	-.25666	-.26588	-.27510	-.28432	-.29355
.13000	-.23694	-.24611	-.25527	-.26444	-.27361	-.28278
.13250	-.22656	-.23567	-.24478	-.25389	-.26301	-.27213
.13500	-.21628	-.22534	-.23440	-.24346	-.25252	-.26159
.13750	-.20612	-.21512	-.22413	-.23314	-.24215	-.25116
.14000	-.19606	-.20501	-.21397	-.22293	-.23189	-.24085
.14250	-.18611	-.19502	-.20392	-.21283	-.22173	-.23064
.14500	-.17627	-.18512	-.19398	-.20283	-.21169	-.22055
.14750	-.16654	-.17534	-.18414	-.19294	-.20175	-.21056
.15000	-.15690	-.16565	-.17441	-.18316	-.19192	-.20068
.15250	-.14737	-.15608	-.16478	-.17348	-.18219	-.19090
.15500	-.13795	-.14660	-.15525	-.16391	-.17256	-.18122
.15750	-.12862	-.13722	-.14583	-.15443	-.16304	-.17165
.16000	-.11939	-.12795	-.13650	-.14506	-.15362	-.16218
.16250	-.11026	-.11877	-.12728	-.13579	-.14430	-.15281
.16500	-.10123	-.10969	-.11815	-.12661	-.13507	-.14354
.16750	-.09229	-.10070	-.10912	-.11753	-.12595	-.13437
.17000	-.08345	-.09181	-.10018	-.10855	-.11692	-.12529
.17250	-.07470	-.08302	-.09134	-.09966	-.10798	-.11631
.17500	-.06604	-.07432	-.08259	-.09086	-.09914	-.10742
.17750	-.05748	-.06570	-.07393	-.08216	-.09039	-.09863
.18000	-.04901	-.05718	-.06537	-.07355	-.08174	-.08993
.18250	-.04062	-.04875	-.05689	-.06503	-.07317	-.08132
.18500	-.03232	-.04041	-.04850	-.05660	-.06470	-.07279
.18750	-.02411	-.03216	-.04021	-.04826	-.05631	-.06436
.19000	-.01599	-.02399	-.03200	-.04000	-.04801	-.05602
.19250	-.00795	-.01591	-.02387	-.03183	-.03980	-.04776
.19500	.00000	-.00791	-.01583	-.02375	-.03167	-.03959
.19750	.00787	0.00000	-.00787	-.01575	-.02363	-.03151
.20000	.01566	.00783	.00000	-.00783	-.01567	-.02351
.20250	.02336	.01558	.00779	.00000	-.00779	-.01559
.20500	.03099	.02325	.01550	.00775	.00000	-.00775
.20750	.03854	.03084	.02313	.01542	.00771	.00000

POINT TABLES: ORIGINAL LOAN TERM: 300 MONTHS LOAN PREPAID IN: 84 MONTHS

EFFECTIVE YIELD	CONTRACT RATE .07000	.07250	.07500	.07750	.08000	.08250	.08500	.08750	.09000	.09250
.07000	.00000	-.01307	-.02619	-.03935	-.05256	-.06581	-.07911	-.09244	-.10582	-.11923
.07250	.01294	0.00000	-.01299	-.02603	-.03911	-.05224	-.06540	-.07861	-.09136	-.10514
.07500	.02568	.01286	.00000	-.01291	-.02587	-.03887	-.05191	-.06499	-.07812	-.09127
.07750	.03822	.02553	.01279	.00000	-.01283	-.02571	-.03863	-.05159	-.06459	-.07762
.08000	.05056	.03799	.02538	.01271	.00000	-.01275	-.02555	-.03839	-.05126	-.06418
.08250	.06271	.05026	.03777	.02522	.01263	0.00000	-.01268	-.02539	-.03815	-.05094
.08500	.07467	.06234	.04997	.03754	.02507	.01256	.00000	-.01260	-.02523	-.03791
.08750	.08644	.07424	.06198	.04967	.03732	.02492	.01248	.00000	-.01252	-.02508
.09000	.09804	.08594	.07380	.06161	.04937	.03709	.02477	.01240	.00000	-.01244
.09250	.10945	.09747	.08544	.07337	.06124	.04908	.03687	.02462	.01233	0.00000
.09500	.12068	.10882	.09690	.08494	.07293	.06088	.04878	.03664	.02447	.01225
.09750	.13174	.11999	.10819	.09633	.08444	.07250	.06051	.04848	.03642	.02431
.10000	.14263	.13099	.11929	.10755	.09577	.08393	.07206	.06014	.04819	.03619
.10250	.15335	.14182	.13023	.11860	.10692	.09520	.08343	.07162	.05978	.04789
.10500	.16390	.15248	.14100	.12948	.11791	.10629	.09463	.08293	.07119	.05941
.10750	.17430	.16298	.15161	.14019	.12872	.11721	.10566	.09406	.08243	.07076
.11000	.18453	.17331	.16205	.15073	.13937	.12797	.11652	.10503	.09350	.08193
.11250	.19460	.18349	.17233	.16112	.14986	.13856	.12721	.11582	.10440	.09293
.11500	.20452	.19351	.18245	.17134	.16019	.14899	.13774	.12646	.11513	.10377
.11750	.21429	.20338	.19242	.18141	.17035	.15925	.14811	.13693	.12570	.11444
.12000	.22390	.21309	.20223	.19132	.18037	.16937	.15832	.14724	.13611	.12495
.12250	.23337	.22266	.21190	.20109	.19023	.17933	.16838	.15739	.14637	.13530
.12500	.24269	.23208	.22141	.21070	.19994	.18914	.17829	.16740	.15646	.14549
.12750	.25188	.24136	.23079	.22017	.20951	.19880	.18804	.17725	.16641	.15554
.13000	.26092	.25049	.24002	.22949	.21892	.20831	.19765	.18695	.17621	.16543
.13250	.26982	.25949	.24911	.23868	.22820	.21768	.20711	.19650	.18586	.17517
.13500	.27859	.26835	.25806	.24772	.23734	.22691	.21643	.20592	.19536	.18476
.13750	.28722	.27707	.26687	.25663	.24633	.23599	.22561	.21519	.20472	.19422
.14000	.29573	.28567	.27556	.26540	.25520	.24495	.23465	.22432	.21394	.20353
.14250	.30410	.29413	.28411	.27404	.26392	.25376	.24356	.23331	.22302	.21270
.14500	.31235	.30246	.29253	.28255	.27252	.26245	.25233	.24217	.23197	.22173
.14750	.32047	.31067	.30082	.29093	.28099	.27100	.26097	.25090	.24078	.23063
.15000	.32847	.31876	.30899	.29918	.28933	.27943	.26948	.25949	.24947	.23940
.15250	.33635	.32672	.31704	.30732	.29754	.28773	.27786	.26796	.25802	.24803
.15500	.34411	.33456	.32497	.31532	.30563	.29590	.28612	.27630	.26644	.25654
.15750	.35175	.34229	.33277	.32321	.31361	.30395	.29426	.28452	.27474	.26493
.16000	.35928	.34989	.34046	.33098	.32146	.31189	.30227	.29262	.28292	.27318
.16250	.36669	.35739	.34804	.33864	.32919	.31970	.31017	.30059	.29098	.28132
.16500	.37399	.36477	.35550	.34618	.33681	.32740	.31795	.30845	.29891	.28934
.16750	.38119	.37204	.36285	.35361	.34432	.33499	.32561	.31619	.30673	.29723
.17000	.38827	.37921	.37009	.36092	.35171	.34246	.33316	.32382	.31444	.30501
.17250	.39525	.38626	.37722	.36813	.35900	.34982	.34060	.33133	.32203	.31268
.17500	.40213	.39321	.38425	.37524	.36618	.35707	.34792	.33873	.32951	.32024
.17750	.40890	.40006	.39117	.38223	.37325	.36422	.35514	.34603	.33687	.32768
.18000	.41558	.40681	.39799	.38912	.38021	.37126	.36226	.35322	.34414	.33501
.18250	.42215	.41345	.40471	.39592	.38708	.37819	.36927	.36030	.35129	.34224
.18500	.42863	.42000	.41133	.40261	.39384	.38503	.37617	.36728	.35834	.34936
.18750	.43501	.42645	.41785	.40920	.40050	.39176	.38298	.37415	.36529	.35638
.19000	.44129	.43281	.42427	.41569	.40707	.39840	.38968	.38093	.37213	.36330
.19250	.44748	.43907	.43060	.42209	.41354	.40494	.39629	.38761	.37888	.37011
.19500	.45358	.44524	.43684	.42840	.41991	.41138	.40280	.39419	.38553	.37683
.19750	.45960	.45132	.44299	.43461	.42619	.41773	.40922	.40067	.39208	.38345
.20000	.46552	.45731	.44904	.44074	.43238	.42398	.41554	.40706	.39854	.38997
.20250	.47135	.46321	.45501	.44677	.43848	.43015	.42177	.41336	.40490	.39640
.20500	.47710	.46902	.46089	.45271	.44449	.43622	.42791	.41956	.41117	.40274
.20750	.48277	.47475	.46669	.45857	.45041	.44221	.43397	.42568	.41735	.40899

POINT TABLES: ORIGINAL LOAN TERM: 300 MONTHS LOAN PREPAID IN: 84 MONTHS

EFFECTIVE YIELD	CONTRACT RATE .09500	.09750	.10000	.10250	.10500	.10750	.11000	.11250	.11500	.11750
.07000	-.13267	-.14615	-.15965	-.17319	-.18676	-.20035	-.21397	-.22761	-.24128	-.25496
.07250	-.11846	-.13181	-.14519	-.15860	-.17204	-.18551	-.19900	-.21252	-.22606	-.23962
.07500	-.10447	-.11769	-.13095	-.14424	-.15755	-.17090	-.18427	-.19766	-.21108	-.22452
.07750	-.09069	-.10379	-.11693	-.13009	-.14329	-.15651	-.16976	-.18303	-.19632	-.20964
.08000	-.07713	-.09011	-.10312	-.11617	-.12924	-.14234	-.15547	-.16862	-.18179	-.19499
.08250	-.06377	-.07663	-.08953	-.10245	-.11540	-.12839	-.14139	-.15443	-.16749	-.18057
.08500	-.05062	-.06336	-.07614	-.08895	-.10178	-.11465	-.12754	-.14045	-.15339	-.16636
.08750	-.03767	-.05030	-.06296	-.07565	-.08837	-.10112	-.11389	-.12669	-.13952	-.15236
.09000	-.02492	-.03743	-.04997	-.06255	-.07516	-.08779	-.10045	-.11314	-.12585	-.13858
.09250	-.01236	-.02476	-.03719	-.04965	-.06215	-.07467	-.08722	-.09979	-.11239	-.12501
.09500	-.00000	-.01229	-.02460	-.03695	-.04933	-.06174	-.07418	-.08664	-.09913	-.11164
.09750	.01217	.00000	-.01221	-.02445	-.03672	-.04902	-.06134	-.07369	-.08607	-.09847
.10000	.02416	.01210	-.00000	-.01213	-.02429	-.03648	-.04870	-.06094	-.07321	-.08550
.10250	.03597	.02401	.01202	0.00000	-.01205	-.02414	-.03624	-.04838	-.06054	-.07273
.10500	.04760	.03575	.02386	.01195	.00000	-.01198	-.02398	-.03601	-.04807	-.06015
.10750	.05905	.04730	.03552	.02371	.01187	.00000	-.01190	-.02382	-.03578	-.04775
.11000	.07032	.05868	.04701	.03530	.02356	.01180	.00000	-.01182	-.02367	-.03554
.11250	.08143	.06989	.05832	.04671	.03508	.02341	.01172	.00000	-.01175	-.02352
.11500	.09237	.08093	.06946	.05796	.04642	.03486	.02326	.01165	.00000	-.01167
.11750	.10314	.09180	.08043	.06903	.05759	.04613	.03464	.02312	.01157	0.00000
.12000	.11375	.10251	.09124	.07993	.06860	.05723	.04584	.03442	.02297	.01150
.12250	.12420	.11306	.10188	.09068	.07944	.06817	.05687	.04555	.03420	.02282
.12500	.13449	.12344	.11237	.10126	.09011	.07894	.06774	.05651	.04526	.03398
.12750	.14462	.13368	.12269	.11168	.10063	.08956	.07845	.06732	.05616	.04497
.13000	.15461	.14376	.13287	.12195	.11099	.10001	.08900	.07796	.06689	.05580
.13250	.16444	.15368	.14289	.13206	.12120	.11031	.09939	.08844	.07747	.06647
.13500	.17413	.16346	.15276	.14202	.13125	.12046	.10963	.09877	.08789	.07698
.13750	.18367	.17310	.16248	.15184	.14116	.13045	.11971	.10895	.09815	.08734
.14000	.19307	.18259	.17206	.16151	.15092	.14030	.12965	.11897	.10827	.09754
.14250	.20233	.19193	.18150	.17103	.16053	.15000	.13944	.12885	.11823	.10759
.14500	.21146	.20114	.19080	.18041	.17000	.15956	.14908	.13858	.12805	.11750
.14750	.22044	.21021	.19995	.18966	.17933	.16897	.15859	.14817	.13773	.12726
.15000	.22929	.21915	.20898	.19877	.18853	.17825	.16795	.15762	.14726	.13688
.15250	.23801	.22796	.21787	.20774	.19758	.18739	.17718	.16693	.15666	.14636
.15500	.24661	.23663	.22662	.21658	.20651	.19640	.18627	.17610	.16591	.15570
.15750	.25507	.24518	.23525	.22529	.21530	.20528	.19522	.18514	.17503	.16490
.16000	.26341	.25360	.24375	.23388	.22396	.21402	.20405	.19405	.18402	.17397
.16250	.27163	.26190	.25213	.24233	.23250	.22264	.21275	.20283	.19288	.18290
.16500	.27972	.27007	.26038	.25067	.24091	.23113	.22132	.21148	.20161	.19171
.16750	.28770	.27812	.26852	.25888	.24920	.23950	.22976	.22000	.21021	.20039
.17000	.29556	.28606	.27653	.26697	.25737	.24774	.23809	.22840	.21869	.20895
.17250	.30330	.29388	.28443	.27494	.26542	.25587	.24629	.23668	.22704	.21738
.17500	.31093	.30159	.29221	.28280	.27335	.26388	.25437	.24484	.23528	.22569
.17750	.31845	.30918	.29988	.29054	.28117	.27177	.26234	.25288	.24339	.23388
.18000	.32586	.31666	.30743	.29817	.28887	.27955	.27019	.26080	.25139	.24195
.18250	.33316	.32404	.31488	.30569	.29647	.28721	.27793	.26861	.25927	.24991
.18500	.34035	.33130	.32222	.31310	.30395	.29476	.28555	.27631	.26704	.25775
.18750	.34744	.33846	.32945	.32040	.31132	.30221	.29307	.28390	.27470	.26548
.19000	.35443	.34552	.33658	.32760	.31859	.30955	.30048	.29138	.28225	.27310
.19250	.36131	.35247	.34360	.33469	.32575	.31678	.30778	.29875	.28969	.28061
.19500	.36810	.35933	.35052	.34168	.33281	.32391	.31498	.30602	.29703	.28801
.19750	.37478	.36608	.35735	.34857	.33977	.33094	.32207	.31318	.30426	.29531
.20000	.38138	.37274	.36407	.35537	.34663	.33786	.32907	.32024	.31139	.30250
.20250	.38787	.37930	.37070	.36206	.35339	.34469	.33596	.32720	.31841	.30960
.20500	.39427	.38577	.37723	.36866	.36006	.35142	.34276	.33406	.32534	.31659
.20750	.40058	.39215	.38367	.37517	.36663	.35806	.34946	.34083	.33217	.32348

POINT TABLES: ORIGINAL LOAN TERM: 300 MONTHS LOAN PREPAID IN: 84 MONTHS

EFFECTIVE YIELD	CONTRACT RATE .12000	.12250	.12500	.12750	.13000	.13250	.13500	.13750	.14000	.14250
.07000	-.26867	-.28239	-.29614	-.30990	-.32367	-.33746	-.35126	-.36508	-.37891	-.39274
.07250	-.25321	-.26681	-.28043	-.29406	-.30771	-.32138	-.33506	-.34875	-.36246	-.37617
.07500	-.23798	-.25146	-.26495	-.27847	-.29200	-.30554	-.31910	-.33267	-.34626	-.35985
.07750	-.22298	-.23634	-.24971	-.26311	-.27652	-.28994	-.30338	-.31684	-.33030	-.34378
.08000	-.20821	-.22145	-.23471	-.24798	-.26127	-.27458	-.28790	-.30124	-.31458	-.32794
.08250	-.19367	-.20679	-.21993	-.23308	-.24626	-.25945	-.27265	-.28587	-.29910	-.31235
.08500	-.17934	-.19235	-.20537	-.21841	-.23147	-.24454	-.25763	-.27074	-.28385	-.29698
.08750	-.16523	-.17812	-.19103	-.20396	-.21690	-.22986	-.24284	-.25583	-.26883	-.28185
.09000	-.15134	-.16411	-.17691	-.18972	-.20255	-.21540	-.22827	-.24114	-.25403	-.26694
.09250	-.13765	-.15032	-.16300	-.17570	-.18842	-.20116	-.21391	-.22668	-.23946	-.25225
.09500	-.12417	-.13673	-.14930	-.16189	-.17450	-.18713	-.19977	-.21243	-.22510	-.23778
.09750	-.11089	-.12334	-.13580	-.14829	-.16079	-.17331	-.18584	-.19839	-.21095	-.22353
.10000	-.09782	-.11015	-.12251	-.13489	-.14728	-.15969	-.17212	-.18456	-.19702	-.20949
.10250	-.08494	-.09717	-.10942	-.12169	-.13397	-.14628	-.15860	-.17094	-.18329	-.19565
.10500	-.07225	-.08437	-.09652	-.10868	-.12086	-.13306	-.14528	-.15751	-.16976	-.18202
.10750	-.05975	-.07177	-.08381	-.09587	-.10795	-.12005	-.13216	-.14429	-.15643	-.16859
.11000	-.04744	-.05936	-.07129	-.08325	-.09523	-.10722	-.11924	-.13126	-.14330	-.15536
.11250	-.03531	-.04713	-.05896	-.07082	-.08270	-.09459	-.10650	-.11843	-.13037	-.14232
.11500	-.02336	-.03508	-.04682	-.05857	-.07035	-.08214	-.09395	-.10578	-.11762	-.12948
.11750	-.01159	-.02321	-.03485	-.04651	-.05818	-.06988	-.08159	-.09332	-.10507	-.11683
.12000	.00000	-.01152	-.02306	-.03462	-.04620	-.05780	-.06941	-.08105	-.09269	-.10436
.12250	.01142	0.00000	-.01144	-.02291	-.03439	-.04589	-.05741	-.06895	-.08050	-.09207
.12500	.02267	.01135	.00000	-.01137	-.02276	-.03416	-.04559	-.05703	-.06849	-.07996
.12750	.03376	.02253	.01127	.00000	-.01129	-.02261	-.03394	-.04529	-.05665	-.06803
.13000	.04468	.03354	.02238	.01120	.00000	-.01122	-.02246	-.03371	-.04499	-.05627
.13250	.05544	.04440	.03333	.02224	.01113	.00000	-.01115	-.02231	-.03349	-.04469
.13500	.06605	.05509	.04411	.03311	.02209	.01106	.00000	-.01107	-.02216	-.03327
.13750	.07649	.06563	.05474	.04383	.03290	.02195	.01098	.00000	-.01100	-.02202
.14000	.08679	.07601	.06521	.05439	.04355	.03269	.02181	.01091	.00000	-.01093
.14250	.09693	.08624	.07553	.06479	.05404	.04327	.03248	.02167	.01084	.00000
.14500	.10692	.09632	.08569	.07505	.06438	.05369	.04299	.03226	.02153	.01077
.14750	.11677	.10625	.09571	.08515	.07457	.06397	.05335	.04271	.03206	.02139
.15000	.12647	.11604	.10558	.09511	.08461	.07409	.06356	.05300	.04243	.03185
.15250	.13603	.12568	.11531	.10492	.09450	.08407	.07362	.06315	.05266	.04216
.15500	.14545	.13519	.12490	.11459	.10426	.09391	.08354	.07315	.06274	.05232
.15750	.15474	.14455	.13435	.12412	.11387	.10360	.09331	.08300	.07268	.06234
.16000	.16389	.15378	.14366	.13351	.12334	.11315	.10294	.09272	.08247	.07221
.16250	.17291	.16288	.15284	.14277	.13268	.12257	.11244	.10229	.09213	.08195
.16500	.18179	.17185	.16188	.15189	.14188	.13185	.12180	.11173	.10164	.09154
.16750	.19055	.18068	.17079	.16088	.15095	.14100	.13102	.12103	.11102	.10100
.17000	.19918	.18939	.17958	.16974	.15989	.15001	.14012	.13020	.12027	.11032
.17250	.20769	.19798	.18824	.17848	.16870	.15890	.14908	.13924	.12939	.11951
.17500	.21607	.20644	.19677	.18709	.17739	.16766	.15792	.14815	.13837	.12857
.17750	.22434	.21477	.20519	.15558	.18595	.17630	.16663	.15694	.14723	.13751
.18000	.23248	.22299	.21348	.20394	.19439	.18481	.17521	.16560	.15596	.14631
.18250	.24051	.23109	.22165	.21219	.20271	.19320	.18368	.17413	.16457	.15499
.18500	.24843	.23908	.22971	.22032	.21091	.20147	.19202	.18255	.17306	.16355
.18750	.25623	.24695	.23765	.22833	.21899	.20963	.20025	.19085	.18143	.17199
.19000	.26392	.25471	.24548	.23623	.22696	.21767	.20836	.19903	.18968	.18031
.19250	.27150	.26236	.25320	.24402	.23482	.22560	.21635	.20709	.19781	.18852
.19500	.27897	.26990	.26081	.25170	.24257	.23341	.22424	.21504	.20583	.19660
.19750	.28634	.27734	.26832	.25927	.25020	.24112	.23201	.22289	.21374	.20458
.20000	.29360	.28467	.27571	.26673	.25774	.24872	.23968	.23062	.22154	.21245
.20250	.30076	.29189	.28300	.27409	.26516	.25621	.24723	.23824	.22923	.22020
.20500	.30782	.29902	.29019	.28135	.27248	.26359	.25468	.24576	.23681	.22785
.20750	.31477	.30604	.29728	.28850	.27970	.27088	.26203	.25317	.24429	.23539

POINT TABLES: ORIGINAL LOAN TERM: 300 MONTHS LOAN PREPAID IN: 84 MONTHS

CONTRACT RATE

EFFECTIVE YIELD	.14500	.14750	.15000	.15250	.15500	.15750	.16000	.16250	.16500	.16750
.07000	-.40659	-.42045	-.43431	-.44819	-.46207	-.47595	-.48985	-.50375	-.51765	-.53156
.07250	-.38990	-.40364	-.41738	-.43113	-.44489	-.45866	-.47243	-.48621	-.49999	-.51378
.07500	-.37346	-.38708	-.40070	-.41433	-.42797	-.44162	-.45528	-.46894	-.48260	-.49627
.07750	-.35727	-.37076	-.38427	-.39778	-.41131	-.42484	-.43837	-.45192	-.46546	-.47902
.08000	-.34131	-.35469	-.36808	-.38148	-.39489	-.40830	-.42172	-.43515	-.44858	-.46202
.08250	-.32560	-.33887	-.35214	-.36542	-.37872	-.39201	-.40532	-.41863	-.43195	-.44528
.08500	-.31012	-.32327	-.33643	-.34960	-.36278	-.37597	-.38916	-.40236	-.41557	-.42878
.08750	-.29487	-.30791	-.32096	-.33402	-.34708	-.36016	-.37324	-.38633	-.39942	-.41252
.09000	-.27985	-.29278	-.30572	-.31866	-.33162	-.34458	-.35755	-.37053	-.38351	-.39650
.09250	-.26506	-.27787	-.29070	-.30354	-.31638	-.32924	-.34210	-.35497	-.36784	-.38072
.09500	-.25048	-.26319	-.27590	-.28863	-.30137	-.31412	-.32687	-.33963	-.35240	-.36517
.09750	-.23612	-.24872	-.26133	-.27395	-.28658	-.29922	-.31187	-.32452	-.33718	-.34985
.10000	-.22197	-.23446	-.24697	-.25948	-.27201	-.28454	-.29708	-.30963	-.32219	-.33475
.10250	-.20803	-.22042	-.23282	-.24523	-.25765	-.27008	-.28252	-.29496	-.30742	-.31988
.10500	-.19429	-.20658	-.21888	-.23118	-.24350	-.25583	-.26816	-.28051	-.29286	-.30522
.10750	-.18076	-.19295	-.20514	-.21735	-.22956	-.24179	-.25402	-.26626	-.27851	-.29077
.11000	-.16743	-.17951	-.19161	-.20371	-.21583	-.22795	-.24008	-.25222	-.26437	-.27653
.11250	-.15429	-.16628	-.17827	-.19027	-.20229	-.21432	-.22635	-.23839	-.25044	-.26250
.11500	-.14135	-.15323	-.16513	-.17704	-.18895	-.20088	-.21282	-.22476	-.23671	-.24867
.11750	-.12860	-.14038	-.15218	-.16399	-.17581	-.18764	-.19948	-.21133	-.22318	-.23505
.12000	-.11603	-.12772	-.13942	-.15113	-.16286	-.17459	-.18634	-.19809	-.20985	-.22162
.12250	-.10365	-.11524	-.12685	-.13847	-.15009	-.16173	-.17338	-.18504	-.19671	-.20838
.12500	-.09145	-.10295	-.11446	-.12598	-.13752	-.14906	-.16062	-.17218	-.18376	-.19534
.12750	-.07942	-.09083	-.10225	-.11368	-.12512	-.13657	-.14804	-.15951	-.17099	-.18248
.13000	-.06757	-.07889	-.09021	-.10155	-.11290	-.12427	-.13564	-.14702	-.15841	-.16981
.13250	-.05590	-.06712	-.07836	-.08960	-.10086	-.11214	-.12342	-.13471	-.14601	-.15732
.13500	-.04439	-.05552	-.06667	-.07783	-.08900	-.10018	-.11137	-.12257	-.13378	-.14500
.13750	-.03305	-.04409	-.05515	-.06622	-.07730	-.08840	-.09950	-.11061	-.12174	-.13287
.14000	-.02187	-.03283	-.04380	-.05478	-.06578	-.07678	-.08780	-.09883	-.10986	-.12091
.14250	-.01086	-.02173	-.03261	-.04351	-.05441	-.06533	-.07626	-.08720	-.09815	-.10911
.14500	-.00000	-.01078	-.02158	-.03239	-.04322	-.05405	-.06490	-.07575	-.08662	-.09749
.14750	.01070	.00000	-.01071	-.02144	-.03218	-.04293	-.05369	-.06446	-.07524	-.08603
.15000	.02125	.01063	0.00000	-.01064	-.02130	-.03196	-.04264	-.05333	-.06403	-.07473
.15250	.03164	.02111	.01056	.00000	-.01057	-.02116	-.03175	-.04236	-.05297	-.06360
.15500	.04189	.03143	.02097	.01049	.00000	-.01050	-.02102	-.03154	-.04207	-.05262
.15750	.05198	.04161	.03123	.02083	.01042	-.00000	-.01043	-.02088	-.03133	-.04179
.16000	.06194	.05165	.04134	.03103	.02070	.01035	.00000	-.01036	-.02074	-.03112
.16250	.07175	.06154	.05131	.04108	.03082	.02056	.01029	-.00000	-.01030	-.02060
.16500	.08142	.07129	.06114	.05098	.04081	.03062	.02043	.01022	.00000	-.01023
.16750	.09096	.08090	.07083	.06075	.05065	.04054	.03042	.02029	.01015	.00000
.17000	.10036	.09038	.08039	.07038	.06036	.05033	.04028	.03023	.02016	.01008
.17250	.10962	.09972	.08980	.07987	.06993	.05997	.05000	.04002	.03003	.02003
.17500	.11876	.10893	.09909	.08923	.07936	.06948	.05958	.04968	.03976	.02983
.17750	.12777	.11801	.10824	.09846	.08866	.07885	.06903	.05920	.04935	.03950
.18000	.13664	.12696	.11727	.10755	.09783	.08809	.07835	.06859	.05882	.04904
.18250	.14540	.13579	.12616	.11653	.10687	.09721	.08753	.07784	.06815	.05844
.18500	.15403	.14449	.13494	.12537	.11579	.10620	.09659	.08697	.07735	.06771
.18750	.16254	.15307	.14359	.13409	.12458	.11506	.10552	.09598	.08642	.07685
.19000	.17093	.16153	.15212	.14269	.13325	.12380	.11433	.10485	.09537	.08587
.19250	.17920	.16987	.16053	.15117	.14180	.13241	.12302	.11361	.10419	.09476
.19500	.18736	.17810	.16882	.15953	.15023	.14091	.13158	.12224	.11289	.10353
.19750	.19540	.18621	.17700	.16778	.15854	.14929	.14003	.13076	.12148	.11218
.20000	.20334	.19421	.18507	.17591	.16674	.15756	.14836	.13916	.12994	.12071
.20250	.21116	.20210	.19302	.18393	.17483	.16571	.15658	.14744	.13829	.12913
.20500	.21887	.20987	.20086	.19184	.18280	.17375	.16469	.15561	.14652	.13743
.20750	.22648	.21755	.20860	.19964	.19067	.18168	.17268	.16367	.15465	.14561

POINT TABLES: ORIGINAL LOAN TERM: 300 MONTHS LOAN PREPAID IN: 84 MONTHS

CONTRACT RATE

EFFECTIVE YIELD	.17000	.17250	.17500	.17750	.18000	.18250	.18500	.18750	.19000	.19250
.07000	-.54547	-.55938	-.57330	-.58722	-.60114	-.61506	-.62899	-.64291	-.65684	-.67076
.07250	-.52757	-.54137	-.55517	-.56897	-.58277	-.59657	-.61038	-.62419	-.63800	-.65181
.07500	-.50994	-.52362	-.53730	-.55098	-.56467	-.57836	-.59205	-.60574	-.61943	-.63312
.07750	-.49257	-.50614	-.51970	-.53327	-.54684	-.56041	-.57399	-.58756	-.60114	-.61472
.08000	-.47546	-.48891	-.50236	-.51581	-.52927	-.54273	-.55619	-.56965	-.58311	-.59658
.08250	-.45860	-.47194	-.48527	-.49861	-.51196	-.52530	-.53865	-.55200	-.56535	-.57870
.08500	-.44199	-.45521	-.46844	-.48167	-.49490	-.50813	-.52137	-.53461	-.54785	-.56109
.08750	-.42563	-.43874	-.45185	-.46497	-.47809	-.49121	-.50434	-.51747	-.53060	-.54373
.09000	-.40950	-.42250	-.43550	-.44851	-.46153	-.47454	-.48756	-.50058	-.51360	-.52663
.09250	-.39361	-.40650	-.41940	-.43230	-.44520	-.45811	-.47102	-.48394	-.49685	-.50977
.09500	-.37795	-.39074	-.40353	-.41632	-.42912	-.44192	-.45473	-.46754	-.48035	-.49316
.09750	-.36253	-.37520	-.38789	-.40058	-.41327	-.42597	-.43867	-.45137	-.46408	-.47679
.10000	-.34732	-.35990	-.37248	-.38506	-.39765	-.41025	-.42284	-.43544	-.44804	-.46065
.10250	-.33234	-.34481	-.35729	-.36977	-.38226	-.39475	-.40724	-.41974	-.43224	-.44474
.10500	-.31758	-.32995	-.34232	-.35470	-.36709	-.37948	-.39187	-.40427	-.41667	-.42907
.10750	-.30303	-.31530	-.32758	-.33986	-.35214	-.36443	-.37672	-.38902	-.40132	-.41362
.11000	-.28869	-.30086	-.31304	-.32522	-.33741	-.34960	-.36179	-.37399	-.38619	-.39839
.11250	-.27457	-.28664	-.29871	-.31080	-.32288	-.33498	-.34707	-.35917	-.37128	-.38338
.11500	-.26064	-.27262	-.28460	-.29658	-.30857	-.32057	-.33257	-.34457	-.35658	-.36859
.11750	-.24692	-.25880	-.27068	-.28257	-.29446	-.30636	-.31827	-.33018	-.34209	-.35400
.12000	-.23339	-.24518	-.25696	-.26876	-.28056	-.29236	-.30417	-.31599	-.32781	-.33963
.12250	-.22006	-.23175	-.24345	-.25515	-.26685	-.27857	-.29028	-.30200	-.31373	-.32546
.12500	-.20693	-.21852	-.23012	-.24173	-.25335	-.26497	-.27659	-.28822	-.29985	-.31149
.12750	-.19398	-.20548	-.21699	-.22851	-.24003	-.25156	-.26309	-.27463	-.28617	-.29772
.13000	-.18121	-.19263	-.20405	-.21547	-.22690	-.23834	-.24978	-.26123	-.27268	-.28414
.13250	-.16863	-.17996	-.19129	-.20262	-.21397	-.22531	-.23667	-.24803	-.25939	-.27076
.13500	-.15623	-.16747	-.17871	-.18996	-.20121	-.21247	-.22374	-.23501	-.24628	-.25756
.13750	-.14401	-.15515	-.16631	-.17747	-.18864	-.19981	-.21099	-.22217	-.23336	-.24455
.14000	-.13196	-.14302	-.15409	-.16516	-.17624	-.18733	-.19842	-.20952	-.22062	-.23173
.14250	-.12008	-.13105	-.14204	-.15303	-.16402	-.17502	-.18603	-.19704	-.20806	-.21908
.14500	-.10837	-.11926	-.13016	-.14106	-.15197	-.16289	-.17381	-.18474	-.19567	-.20661
.14750	-.09683	-.10763	-.11845	-.12927	-.14010	-.15093	-.16177	-.17261	-.18346	-.19432
.15000	-.08545	-.09617	-.10690	-.11764	-.12839	-.13914	-.14989	-.16066	-.17142	-.18220
.15250	-.07423	-.08487	-.09552	-.10618	-.11684	-.12751	-.13819	-.14887	-.15955	-.17025
.15500	-.06317	-.07373	-.08430	-.09487	-.10546	-.11605	-.12664	-.13724	-.14785	-.15846
.15750	-.05227	-.06275	-.07324	-.08373	-.09423	-.10474	-.11526	-.12578	-.13631	-.14684
.16000	-.04152	-.05192	-.06233	-.07274	-.08317	-.09360	-.10403	-.11448	-.12492	-.13538
.16250	-.03092	-.04124	-.05157	-.06191	-.07225	-.08261	-.09297	-.10333	-.11370	-.12408
.16500	-.02047	-.03071	-.04096	-.05123	-.06149	-.07177	-.08205	-.09234	-.10263	-.11293
.16750	-.01016	-.02033	-.03051	-.04069	-.05088	-.06108	-.07129	-.08150	-.09172	-.10194
.17000	0.00000	-.01009	-.02020	-.03030	-.04042	-.05055	-.06068	-.07081	-.08096	-.09110
.17250	.01002	.00000	-.01003	-.02006	-.03010	-.04015	-.05021	-.06027	-.07034	-.08041
.17500	.01990	.00995	.00000	-.00996	-.01993	-.02991	-.03989	-.04988	-.05987	-.06987
.17750	.02964	.01977	.00989	.00000	-.00990	-.01980	-.02971	-.03962	-.04955	-.05947
.18000	.03925	.02945	.01964	.00982	.00000	-.00983	-.01967	-.02951	-.03936	-.04922
.18250	.04872	.03899	.02926	.01951	.00976	.00000	-.00977	-.01954	-.02932	-.03910
.18500	.05806	.04840	.03874	.02907	.01938	.00970	.00000	-.00970	-.01941	-.02912
.18750	.06727	.05769	.04809	.03849	.02888	.01926	.00963	.00000	-.00964	-.01928
.19000	.07636	.06684	.05732	.04778	.03824	.02869	.01913	.00957	.00000	-.00958
.19250	.08532	.07587	.06641	.05695	.04747	.03799	.02850	.01901	.00951	.00000
.19500	.09416	.08478	.07539	.06599	.05658	.04717	.03775	.02832	.01889	.00945
.19750	.10288	.09356	.08424	.07491	.06557	.05622	.04687	.03751	.02814	.01876
.20000	.11147	.10223	.09297	.08370	.07443	.06515	.05586	.04657	.03726	.02796
.20250	.11995	.11077	.10158	.09238	.08317	.07396	.06473	.05550	.04627	.03702
.20500	.12832	.11920	.11007	.10094	.09180	.08264	.07349	.06432	.05515	.04597
.20750	.13657	.12752	.11845	.10938	.10030	.09122	.08212	.07302	.06391	.05480

EFFECTIVE YIELD	CONTRACT RATE .19500	.19750	.20000	.20250	.20500	.20750
.07000	-.68469	-.69862	-.71254	-.72647	-.74040	-.75432
.07250	-.66561	-.67942	-.69323	-.70704	-.72085	-.73466
.07500	-.64682	-.66051	-.67421	-.68790	-.70159	-.71529
.07750	-.62830	-.64188	-.65546	-.66904	-.68262	-.69620
.08000	-.61004	-.62351	-.63698	-.65045	-.66391	-.67738
.08250	-.59206	-.60541	-.61877	-.63213	-.64548	-.65884
.08500	-.57434	-.58758	-.60083	-.61407	-.62732	-.64056
.08750	-.55687	-.57000	-.58314	-.59628	-.60942	-.62255
.09000	-.53966	-.55268	-.56571	-.57874	-.59177	-.60480
.09250	-.52269	-.53561	-.54854	-.56146	-.57438	-.58731
.09500	-.50597	-.51879	-.53161	-.54442	-.55724	-.57006
.09750	-.48950	-.50221	-.51492	-.52764	-.54035	-.55307
.10000	-.47326	-.48587	-.49848	-.51109	-.52370	-.53632
.10250	-.45725	-.46976	-.48227	-.49478	-.50729	-.51980
.10500	-.44147	-.45388	-.46629	-.47870	-.49111	-.50353
.10750	-.42593	-.43823	-.45054	-.46285	-.47517	-.48748
.11000	-.41060	-.42281	-.43502	-.44723	-.45945	-.47166
.11250	-.39549	-.40760	-.41972	-.43183	-.44395	-.45607
.11500	-.38060	-.39262	-.40464	-.41666	-.42868	-.44070
.11750	-.36592	-.37784	-.38977	-.40169	-.41362	-.42555
.12000	-.35145	-.36328	-.37511	-.38694	-.39878	-.41061
.12250	-.33719	-.34892	-.36066	-.37240	-.38414	-.39589
.12500	-.32313	-.33477	-.34642	-.35806	-.36971	-.38137
.12750	-.30926	-.32082	-.33237	-.34393	-.35549	-.36705
.13000	-.29560	-.30706	-.31853	-.33000	-.34147	-.35294
.13250	-.28213	-.29350	-.30488	-.31626	-.32764	-.33903
.13500	-.26884	-.28013	-.29142	-.30271	-.31401	-.32531
.13750	-.25575	-.26695	-.27815	-.28936	-.30057	-.31178
.14000	-.24284	-.25395	-.26507	-.27619	-.28731	-.29844
.14250	-.23011	-.24113	-.25217	-.26320	-.27424	-.28529
.14500	-.21755	-.22850	-.23945	-.25040	-.26136	-.27232
.14750	-.20518	-.21604	-.22691	-.23778	-.24865	-.25953
.15000	-.19297	-.20375	-.21454	-.22533	-.23612	-.24691
.15250	-.18094	-.19164	-.20234	-.21305	-.22376	-.23448
.15500	-.16908	-.17969	-.19032	-.20095	-.21158	-.22221
.15750	-.15737	-.16791	-.17846	-.18901	-.19956	-.21012
.16000	-.14584	-.15630	-.16676	-.17723	-.18771	-.19819
.16250	-.13446	-.14484	-.15523	-.16562	-.17602	-.18642
.16500	-.12324	-.13354	-.14386	-.15417	-.16449	-.17482
.16750	-.11217	-.12240	-.13264	-.14288	-.15312	-.16337
.17000	-.10126	-.11141	-.12157	-.13174	-.14191	-.15208
.17250	-.09049	-.10057	-.11066	-.12075	-.13085	-.14095
.17500	-.07988	-.08989	-.09990	-.10992	-.11994	-.12997
.17750	-.06940	-.07934	-.08928	-.09923	-.10918	-.11914
.18000	-.05908	-.06894	-.07881	-.08869	-.09857	-.10845
.18250	-.04889	-.05869	-.06849	-.07829	-.08810	-.09791
.18500	-.03884	-.04857	-.05830	-.06803	-.07777	-.08751
.18750	-.02893	-.03859	-.04825	-.05791	-.06758	-.07725
.19000	-.01916	-.02874	-.03833	-.04793	-.05753	-.06713
.19250	-.00951	-.01903	-.02855	-.03808	-.04762	-.05715
.19500	.00000	-.00945	-.01891	-.02837	-.03783	-.04730
.19750	.00938	.00000	-.00939	-.01878	-.02818	-.03759
.20000	.01864	.00932	.00000	-.00933	-.01866	-.02800
.20250	.02778	.01852	.00926	.00000	-.00927	-.01854
.20500	.03679	.02760	.01840	.00920	.00000	-.00921
.20750	.04568	.03655	.02742	.01829	.00914	.00000

POINT TABLES: ORIGINAL LOAN TERM: 300 MONTHS LOAN PREPAID IN: 108 MONTHS

EFFECTIVE YIELD	CONTRACT RATE .07000	.07250	.07500	.07750	.08000	.08250	.08500	.08750	.09000	.09250
.07000	0.00000	-.01549	-.03105	-.04668	-.06239	-.07815	-.09399	-.10988	-.12583	-.14184
.07250	.01530	.00000	-.01537	-.03082	-.04633	-.06191	-.07756	-.09326	-.10902	-.12484
.07500	.03030	.01519	.00000	-.01526	-.03059	-.04598	-.06144	-.07696	-.09254	-.10817
.07750	.04502	.03009	.01508	.00000	-.01515	-.03036	-.04564	-.06097	-.07637	-.09182
.08000	.05945	.04470	.02987	.01497	.00000	-.01503	-.03013	-.04529	-.06051	-.07578
.08250	.07360	.05903	.04437	.02965	.01486	.00000	-.01492	-.02990	-.04494	-.06004
.08500	.08749	.07308	.05860	.04405	.02943	.01475	.00000	-.01481	-.02968	-.04460
.08750	.10110	.08687	.07256	.05818	.04373	.02921	.01464	.00000	-.01470	-.02945
.09000	.11446	.10039	.08625	.07203	.05775	.04341	.02900	.01453	.00000	-.01458
.09250	.12756	.11366	.09968	.08563	.07151	.05733	.04309	.02878	.01442	0.00000
.09500	.14041	.12667	.11285	.09897	.08501	.07099	.05691	.04277	.02857	.01431
.09750	.15302	.13943	.12578	.11205	.09826	.08440	.07047	.05649	.04245	.02835
.10000	.16538	.15196	.13846	.12489	.11125	.09755	.08378	.06996	.05607	.04213
.10250	.17752	.16424	.15090	.13748	.12400	.11045	.09684	.08317	.06944	.05565
.10500	.18942	.17630	.16310	.14984	.13651	.12311	.10965	.09613	.08256	.06892
.10750	.20110	.18812	.17508	.16196	.14878	.13553	.12222	.10886	.09543	.08195
.11000	.21255	.19973	.18683	.17386	.16082	.14773	.13456	.12134	.10806	.09473
.11250	.22380	.21111	.19836	.18553	.17264	.15969	.14667	.13360	.12046	.10727
.11500	.23483	.22228	.20967	.19699	.18424	.17143	.15856	.14562	.13263	.11958
.11750	.24565	.23325	.22077	.20823	.19562	.18295	.17022	.15742	.14457	.13167
.12000	.25627	.24400	.23167	.21926	.20679	.19426	.18166	.16901	.15630	.14353
.12250	.26669	.25456	.24236	.23009	.21776	.20536	.19290	.18038	.16780	.15517
.12500	.27692	.26492	.25285	.24072	.22852	.21625	.20393	.19154	.17910	.16660
.12750	.28696	.27509	.26315	.25115	.23908	.22695	.21475	.20250	.19019	.17782
.13000	.29681	.28507	.27326	.26139	.24944	.23744	.22538	.21325	.20107	.18884
.13250	.30647	.29486	.28318	.27143	.25962	.24774	.23581	.22381	.21176	.19965
.13500	.31596	.30448	.29292	.28130	.26961	.25786	.24605	.23418	.22225	.21027
.13750	.32527	.31391	.30248	.29098	.27941	.26779	.25610	.24435	.23255	.22069
.14000	.33442	.32317	.31186	.30048	.28904	.27753	.26597	.25434	.24266	.23093
.14250	.34339	.33226	.32107	.30981	.29849	.28710	.27566	.26415	.25259	.24098
.14500	.35220	.34119	.33011	.31897	.30777	.29650	.28517	.27378	.26234	.25085
.14750	.36084	.34995	.33899	.32796	.31687	.30572	.29451	.28324	.27192	.26054
.15000	.36933	.35855	.34770	.33679	.32582	.31478	.30368	.29253	.28132	.27005
.15250	.37766	.36700	.35626	.34546	.33460	.32367	.31269	.30165	.29055	.27940
.15500	.38585	.37529	.36466	.35397	.34322	.33240	.32153	.31060	.29961	.28857
.15750	.39388	.38343	.37291	.36233	.35169	.34098	.33022	.31939	.30852	.29759
.16000	.40176	.39142	.38101	.37054	.36000	.34940	.33875	.32803	.31726	.30644
.16250	.40951	.39927	.38896	.37860	.36816	.35767	.34712	.33651	.32585	.31514
.16500	.41711	.40698	.39678	.38651	.37618	.36579	.35535	.34485	.33429	.32368
.16750	.42458	.41454	.40445	.39428	.38406	.37377	.36343	.35303	.34257	.33207
.17000	.43191	.42198	.41198	.40192	.39179	.38161	.37137	.36107	.35071	.34031
.17250	.43911	.42928	.41938	.40941	.39939	.38930	.37916	.36896	.35871	.34841
.17500	.44618	.43644	.42664	.41678	.40685	.39686	.38682	.37672	.36657	.35636
.17750	.45313	.44349	.43378	.42401	.41418	.40429	.39434	.38434	.37428	.36417
.18000	.45995	.45040	.44079	.43111	.42138	.41158	.40173	.39182	.38186	.37185
.18250	.46665	.45719	.44767	.43809	.42845	.41875	.40899	.39918	.38931	.37939
.18500	.47323	.46387	.45444	.44495	.43540	.42579	.41612	.40640	.39663	.38681
.18750	.47969	.47042	.46108	.45168	.44222	.43271	.42313	.41350	.40382	.39409
.19000	.48604	.47686	.46761	.45830	.44893	.43950	.43002	.42048	.41089	.40125
.19250	.49228	.48318	.47402	.46480	.45552	.44618	.43678	.42733	.41783	.40828
.19500	.49841	.48940	.48032	.47119	.46199	.45274	.44343	.43407	.42466	.41519
.19750	.50443	.49550	.48651	.47746	.46835	.45919	.44997	.44069	.43136	.42198
.20000	.51035	.50150	.49260	.48363	.47461	.46552	.45639	.44719	.43795	.42866
.20250	.51616	.50740	.49857	.48969	.48075	.47175	.46270	.45359	.44443	.43522
.20500	.52187	.51319	.50445	.49564	.48678	.47787	.46890	.45987	.45079	.44167
.20750	.52748	.51888	.51022	.50150	.49272	.48388	.47499	.46605	.45705	.44801

CONTRACT RATE

EFFECTIVE YIELD	.09500	.09750	.10000	.10250	.10500	.10750	.11000	.11250	.11500	.11750
.07000	-.15790	-.17401	-.19017	-.20638	-.22263	-.23892	-.25525	-.27162	-.28803	-.30447
.07250	-.14072	-.15664	-.17261	-.18863	-.20469	-.22080	-.23695	-.25313	-.26935	-.28560
.07500	-.12386	-.13960	-.15539	-.17122	-.18710	-.20302	-.21898	-.23498	-.25102	-.26709
.07750	-.10733	-.12288	-.13849	-.15414	-.16984	-.18558	-.20136	-.21717	-.23303	-.24892
.08000	-.09110	-.10648	-.12191	-.13738	-.15290	-.16846	-.18406	-.19970	-.21538	-.23109
.08250	-.07519	-.09039	-.10564	-.12094	-.13628	-.15166	-.16709	-.18255	-.19806	-.21359
.08500	-.05957	-.07460	-.08968	-.10480	-.11997	-.13518	-.15044	-.16573	-.18106	-.19642
.08750	-.04425	-.05911	-.07402	-.08897	-.10397	-.11901	-.13409	-.14922	-.16437	-.17957
.09000	-.02922	-.04391	-.05865	-.07344	-.08827	-.10314	-.11806	-.13301	-.14800	-.16303
.09250	-.01447	-.02900	-.04357	-.05819	-.07286	-.08757	-.10232	-.11711	-.13193	-.14680
.09500	.00000	-.01436	-.02877	-.04323	-.05774	-.07228	-.08687	-.10150	-.11616	-.13086
.09750	.01420	0.00000	-.01425	-.02855	-.04289	-.05728	-.07171	-.08618	-.10068	-.11522
.10000	.02814	.01409	.00000	-.01414	-.02833	-.04256	-.05683	-.07114	-.08549	-.09987
.10250	.04182	.02793	.01399	.00000	-.01403	-.02811	-.04222	-.05638	-.07057	-.08480
.10500	.05524	.04150	.02771	.01388	-.00000	-.01392	-.02789	-.04189	-.05593	-.07001
.10750	.06841	.05482	.04119	.02750	.01377	.00000	-.01381	-.02767	-.04156	-.05549
.11000	.08134	.06790	.05441	.04087	.02729	.01367	0.00000	-.01371	-.02745	-.04123
.11250	.09403	.08073	.06739	.05400	.04056	.02708	.01356	.00000	-.01360	-.02723
.11500	.10648	.09333	.08013	.06688	.05359	.04025	.02687	.01346	.00000	-.01349
.11750	.11871	.10570	.09264	.07953	.06638	.05318	.03994	.02667	.01335	.00000
.12000	.13071	.11784	.10492	.09195	.07893	.06588	.05278	.03964	.02646	.01325
.12250	.14249	.12975	.11697	.10414	.09126	.07834	.06538	.05237	.03933	.02626
.12500	.15405	.14145	.12880	.11610	.10336	.09057	.07775	.06488	.05197	.03903
.12750	.16540	.15294	.14042	.12785	.11524	.10259	.08989	.07716	.06438	.05157
.13000	.17655	.16421	.15182	.13939	.12691	.11439	.10182	.08922	.07657	.06389
.13250	.18749	.17528	.16302	.15072	.13836	.12597	.11353	.10106	.08854	.07599
.13500	.19824	.18615	.17402	.16184	.14961	.13734	.12503	.11268	.10030	.08787
.13750	.20878	.19682	.18481	.17276	.16066	.14851	.13633	.12410	.11184	.09954
.14000	.21914	.20730	.19542	.18348	.17151	.15948	.14742	.13532	.12318	.11100
.14250	.22931	.21759	.20583	.19402	.18216	.17026	.15832	.14633	.13431	.12226
.14500	.23930	.22770	.21605	.20436	.19262	.18084	.16902	.15715	.14525	.13331
.14750	.24910	.23762	.22609	.21452	.20290	.19123	.17953	.16778	.15600	.14418
.15000	.25874	.24737	.23595	.22449	.21299	.20144	.18985	.17822	.16655	.15485
.15250	.26819	.25694	.24564	.23429	.22290	.21147	.19999	.18847	.17692	.16533
.15500	.27748	.26634	.25515	.24392	.23264	.22131	.20995	.19855	.18710	.17563
.15750	.28661	.27558	.26450	.25337	.24220	.23099	.21974	.20844	.19711	.18574
.16000	.29557	.28465	.27367	.26266	.25160	.24049	.22935	.21816	.20694	.19568
.16250	.30437	.29355	.28269	.27178	.26083	.24983	.23879	.22772	.21650	.20545
.16500	.31302	.30231	.29155	.28074	.26989	.25900	.24807	.23710	.22609	.21504
.16750	.32151	.31090	.30025	.28955	.27880	.26802	.25719	.24632	.23542	.22447
.17000	.32985	.31935	.30880	.29820	.28756	.27687	.26615	.25538	.24458	.23374
.17250	.33805	.32765	.31719	.30670	.29616	.28557	.27495	.26428	.25358	.24285
.17500	.34610	.33580	.32545	.31505	.30461	.29412	.28360	.27303	.26243	.25179
.17750	.35401	.34381	.33355	.32325	.31291	.30252	.29210	.28163	.27113	.26059
.18000	.36179	.35168	.34152	.33131	.32107	.31078	.30045	.29008	.27967	.26923
.18250	.36943	.35941	.34935	.33924	.32909	.31889	.30866	.29839	.28807	.27773
.18500	.37693	.36701	.35704	.34702	.33697	.32687	.31673	.30655	.29633	.28608
.18750	.38431	.37447	.36460	.35468	.34471	.33470	.32466	.31457	.30445	.29429
.19000	.39155	.38181	.37203	.36220	.35232	.34241	.33245	.32245	.31242	.30236
.19250	.39868	.38902	.37933	.36959	.35980	.34998	.34011	.33021	.32026	.31029
.19500	.40567	.39611	.38650	.37685	.36715	.35742	.34764	.33782	.32797	.31808
.19750	.41255	.40308	.39356	.38399	.37438	.36473	.35504	.34532	.33555	.32575
.20000	.41931	.40992	.40049	.39101	.38149	.37192	.36232	.35268	.34300	.33329
.20250	.42596	.41666	.40730	.39791	.38847	.37899	.36948	.35992	.35033	.34070
.20500	.43249	.42327	.41400	.40469	.39534	.38594	.37651	.36704	.35753	.34798
.20750	.43891	.42977	.42059	.41136	.40209	.39278	.38343	.37404	.36461	.35515

POINT TABLES: ORIGINAL LOAN TERM: 300 MONTHS LOAN PREPAID IN: 108 MONTHS

EFFECTIVE YIELD	CONTRACT RATE .12000	.12250	.12500	.12750	.13000	.13250	.13500	.13750	.14000	.14250
.07000	-.32095	-.33745	-.35398	-.37054	-.38712	-.40373	-.42036	-.43701	-.45368	-.47037
.07250	-.30189	-.31821	-.33455	-.35092	-.36732	-.38375	-.40019	-.41666	-.43314	-.44965
.07500	-.28319	-.29932	-.31549	-.33168	-.34789	-.36413	-.38040	-.39668	-.41298	-.42931
.07750	-.26484	-.28079	-.29678	-.31279	-.32882	-.34488	-.36097	-.37707	-.39320	-.40934
.08000	-.24683	-.26261	-.27841	-.29425	-.31010	-.32599	-.34190	-.35783	-.37378	-.38974
.08250	-.22916	-.24476	-.26039	-.27605	-.29173	-.30744	-.32318	-.33893	-.35471	-.37051
.08500	-.21182	-.22725	-.24270	-.25819	-.27370	-.28924	-.30481	-.32039	-.33600	-.35162
.08750	-.19480	-.21005	-.22534	-.24066	-.25601	-.27138	-.28677	-.30219	-.31762	-.33308
.09000	-.17809	-.19318	-.20830	-.22346	-.23863	-.25384	-.26907	-.28432	-.29959	-.31488
.09250	-.16169	-.17662	-.19158	-.20657	-.22158	-.23662	-.25169	-.26677	-.28188	-.29701
.09500	-.14560	-.16036	-.17516	-.18999	-.20484	-.21972	-.23462	-.24955	-.26450	-.27947
.09750	-.12980	-.14441	-.15904	-.17371	-.18841	-.20313	-.21787	-.23264	-.24743	-.26225
.10000	-.11429	-.12874	-.14322	-.15773	-.17227	-.18684	-.20143	-.21604	-.23068	-.24533
.10250	-.09907	-.11336	-.12769	-.14205	-.15643	-.17084	-.18528	-.19974	-.21422	-.22873
.10500	-.08412	-.09827	-.11244	-.12665	-.14088	-.15514	-.16943	-.18374	-.19807	-.21242
.10750	-.06945	-.08345	-.09747	-.11153	-.12561	-.13972	-.15386	-.16802	-.18220	-.19641
.11000	-.05505	-.06889	-.08277	-.09668	-.11062	-.12458	-.13857	-.15259	-.16663	-.18068
.11250	-.04090	-.05461	-.06834	-.08211	-.09590	-.10972	-.12356	-.13743	-.15133	-.16524
.11500	-.02702	-.04058	-.05417	-.06779	-.08144	-.09512	-.10882	-.12255	-.13630	-.15008
.11750	-.01339	-.02681	-.04026	-.05374	-.06725	-.08079	-.09435	-.10794	-.12155	-.13518
.12000	.00000	-.01328	-.02659	-.03994	-.05331	-.06671	-.08013	-.09358	-.10706	-.12055
.12250	.01314	.00000	-.01318	-.02638	-.03962	-.05288	-.06617	-.07949	-.09282	-.10618
.12500	.02605	.01304	0.00000	-.01307	-.02617	-.03930	-.05246	-.06564	-.07884	-.09207
.12750	.03873	.02585	.01294	.00000	-.01297	-.02597	-.03899	-.05204	-.06511	-.07820
.13000	.05118	.03843	.02565	.01284	.00000	-.01287	-.02576	-.03868	-.05162	-.06458
.13250	.06340	.05078	.03813	.02545	.01274	-.00000	-.01277	-.02556	-.03837	-.05121
.13500	.07541	.06292	.05039	.03784	.02525	.01264	.00000	-.01266	-.02535	-.03806
.13750	.08720	.07484	.06243	.05000	.03754	.02505	.01254	.00000	-.01256	-.02515
.14000	.09879	.08654	.07426	.06195	.04962	.03725	.02486	.01244	.00000	-.01246
.14250	.11017	.09804	.08588	.07370	.06148	.04923	.03696	.02466	.01234	0.00000
.14500	.12134	.10934	.09730	.08523	.07313	.06101	.04885	.03667	.02447	.01225
.14750	.13232	.12043	.10851	.09656	.08458	.07257	.06054	.04847	.03639	.02428
.15000	.14311	.13133	.11953	.10769	.09583	.08393	.07201	.06007	.04810	.03611
.15250	.15370	.14204	.13035	.11863	.10688	.09510	.08329	.07146	.05961	.04773
.15500	.16411	.15257	.14099	.12938	.11774	.10607	.09438	.08266	.07091	.05915
.15750	.17434	.16290	.15144	.13994	.12841	.11685	.10527	.09366	.08203	.07037
.16000	.18439	.17306	.16170	.15031	.13889	.12744	.11597	.10447	.09295	.08140
.16250	.19426	.18304	.17179	.16051	.14920	.13786	.12649	.11510	.10368	.09224
.16500	.20396	.19285	.18170	.17053	.15932	.14809	.13683	.12554	.11423	.10289
.16750	.21350	.20249	.19145	.18037	.16927	.15814	.14699	.13580	.12460	.11337
.17000	.22287	.21196	.20102	.19005	.17905	.16803	.15697	.14589	.13479	.12366
.17250	.23207	.22127	.21043	.19956	.18867	.17774	.16679	.15581	.14481	.13378
.17500	.24112	.23042	.21968	.20891	.19811	.18729	.17644	.16556	.15466	.14373
.17750	.25002	.23941	.22877	.21810	.20740	.19667	.18592	.17514	.16434	.15351
.18000	.25876	.24825	.23770	.22713	.21653	.20590	.19524	.18456	.17386	.16313
.18250	.26735	.25693	.24649	.23601	.22551	.21497	.20441	.19382	.18321	.17258
.18500	.27579	.26547	.25512	.24474	.23433	.22389	.21342	.20293	.19241	.18187
.18750	.28409	.27387	.26361	.25332	.24300	.23266	.22228	.21188	.20146	.19101
.19000	.29225	.28212	.27195	.26175	.25153	.24127	.23099	.22069	.21036	.20000
.19250	.30028	.29023	.28015	.27005	.25991	.24975	.23956	.22934	.21910	.20884
.19500	.30816	.29821	.28822	.27820	.26816	.25808	.24798	.23785	.22770	.21753
.19750	.31592	.30605	.29615	.28622	.27626	.26628	.25626	.24623	.23616	.22608
.20000	.32354	.31376	.30395	.29410	.28423	.27433	.26441	.25446	.24448	.23448
.20250	.33104	.32134	.31161	.30186	.29207	.28226	.27242	.26255	.25266	.24275
.20500	.33841	.32880	.31915	.30948	.29978	.29005	.28030	.27051	.26071	.25088
.20750	.34565	.33613	.32657	.31698	.30736	.29772	.28804	.27835	.26862	.25888

POINT TABLES: ORIGINAL LOAN TERM: 300 MONTHS LOAN PREPAID IN: 108 MONTHS

CONTRACT RATE

EFFECTIVE YIELD	.14500	.14750	.15000	.15250	.15500	.15750	.16000	.16250	.16500	.16750
.07000	-.48708	-.50380	-.52054	-.53729	-.55405	-.57082	-.58760	-.60440	-.62120	-.63801
.07250	-.46617	-.48271	-.49926	-.51583	-.53241	-.54900	-.56560	-.58221	-.59883	-.61546
.07500	-.44565	-.46201	-.47838	-.49476	-.51116	-.52757	-.54400	-.56043	-.57687	-.59332
.07750	-.42550	-.44168	-.45788	-.47409	-.49031	-.50654	-.52279	-.53904	-.55531	-.57158
.08000	-.40573	-.42174	-.43775	-.45379	-.46984	-.48590	-.50197	-.51805	-.53414	-.55024
.08250	-.38632	-.40215	-.41800	-.43386	-.44974	-.46563	-.48153	-.49744	-.51336	-.52929
.08500	-.36727	-.38293	-.39860	-.41430	-.43000	-.44572	-.46145	-.47720	-.49295	-.50871
.08750	-.34856	-.36405	-.37956	-.39509	-.41063	-.42618	-.44175	-.45732	-.47291	-.48851
.09000	-.33019	-.34552	-.36087	-.37623	-.39161	-.40700	-.42240	-.43781	-.45324	-.46867
.09250	-.31216	-.32733	-.34251	-.35771	-.37293	-.38816	-.40340	-.41865	-.43391	-.44919
.09500	-.29446	-.30947	-.32449	-.33953	-.35459	-.36966	-.38474	-.39983	-.41494	-.43005
.09750	-.27708	-.29193	-.30679	-.32168	-.33658	-.35149	-.36641	-.38135	-.39630	-.41126
.10000	-.26001	-.27470	-.28942	-.30415	-.31889	-.33365	-.34842	-.36320	-.37800	-.39281
.10250	-.24325	-.25779	-.27235	-.28693	-.30152	-.31613	-.33075	-.34538	-.36003	-.37468
.10500	-.22679	-.24119	-.25560	-.27002	-.28446	-.29892	-.31339	-.32788	-.34237	-.35688
.10750	-.21063	-.22488	-.23914	-.25342	-.26771	-.28202	-.29634	-.31068	-.32503	-.33939
.11000	-.19476	-.20886	-.22298	-.23711	-.25126	-.26542	-.27960	-.29379	-.30800	-.32221
.11250	-.17918	-.19313	-.20710	-.22109	-.23510	-.24912	-.26316	-.27720	-.29127	-.30534
.11500	-.16387	-.17768	-.19151	-.20536	-.21923	-.23311	-.24700	-.26091	-.27483	-.28876
.11750	-.14883	-.16251	-.17620	-.18991	-.20363	-.21738	-.23113	-.24490	-.25868	-.27248
.12000	-.13407	-.14760	-.16116	-.17473	-.18832	-.20192	-.21554	-.22917	-.24282	-.25648
.12250	-.11956	-.13296	-.14638	-.15982	-.17327	-.18674	-.20023	-.21373	-.22724	-.24076
.12500	-.10531	-.11858	-.13187	-.14517	-.15849	-.17183	-.18518	-.19855	-.21193	-.22532
.12750	-.09132	-.10445	-.11761	-.13078	-.14397	-.15718	-.17040	-.18363	-.19688	-.21014
.13000	-.07757	-.09058	-.10360	-.11665	-.12971	-.14278	-.15588	-.16898	-.18210	-.19523
.13250	-.06406	-.07694	-.08984	-.10276	-.11569	-.12864	-.14161	-.15458	-.16758	-.18058
.13500	-.05080	-.06355	-.07632	-.08911	-.10192	-.11474	-.12758	-.14044	-.15331	-.16619
.13750	-.03776	-.05039	-.06304	-.07570	-.08839	-.10109	-.11380	-.12654	-.13928	-.15204
.14000	-.02495	-.03746	-.04998	-.06253	-.07509	-.08767	-.10027	-.11287	-.12550	-.13814
.14250	-.01237	-.02475	-.03716	-.04958	-.06203	-.07448	-.08696	-.09945	-.11195	-.12447
.14500	0.00000	-.01227	-.02456	-.03686	-.04919	-.06153	-.07388	-.08626	-.09864	-.11104
.14750	.01215	-.00000	-.01217	-.02436	-.03657	-.04879	-.06103	-.07329	-.08556	-.09784
.15000	.02409	.01206	.00000	-.01207	-.02417	-.03628	-.04840	-.06054	-.07270	-.08487
.15250	.03583	.02390	.01196	.00000	-.01198	-.02398	-.03599	-.04801	-.06006	-.07211
.15500	.04736	.03555	.02372	.01187	.00000	-.01188	-.02378	-.03570	-.04763	-.05958
.15750	.05869	.04699	.03527	.02353	.01177	.00000	-.01179	-.02360	-.03542	-.04725
.16000	.06983	.05824	.04663	.03500	.02335	.01168	0.00000	-.01170	-.02341	-.03514
.16250	.08078	.06929	.05779	.04627	.03472	.02317	.01159	0.00000	-.01161	-.02322
.16500	.09154	.08016	.06876	.05734	.04591	.03445	.02299	.01150	0.00000	-.01151
.16750	.10211	.09084	.07955	.06823	.05690	.04555	.03419	.02281	.01141	0.00000
.17000	.11251	.10134	.09015	.07894	.06771	.05646	.04520	.03392	.02263	.01132
.17250	.12273	.11166	.10057	.08946	.07834	.06719	.05603	.04485	.03366	.02245
.17500	.13278	.12181	.11082	.09981	.08878	.07774	.06668	.05560	.04451	.03340
.17750	.14266	.13179	.12090	.10999	.09906	.08811	.07715	.06617	.05517	.04416
.18000	.15237	.14160	.13080	.11999	.10916	.09831	.08744	.07656	.06566	.05475
.18250	.16192	.15124	.14055	.12983	.11909	.10834	.09757	.08678	.07598	.06516
.18500	.17131	.16073	.15012	.13950	.12886	.11820	.10752	.09683	.08612	.07540
.18750	.18054	.17005	.15954	.14901	.13846	.12790	.11731	.10672	.09610	.08547
.19000	.18962	.17923	.16881	.15837	.14791	.13744	.12695	.11644	.10591	.09538
.19250	.19855	.18824	.17792	.16757	.15720	.14682	.13642	.12600	.11557	.10512
.19500	.20733	.19711	.18688	.17662	.16634	.15605	.14573	.13541	.12506	.11471
.19750	.21597	.20584	.19569	.18552	.17533	.16512	.15490	.14466	.13440	.12413
.20000	.22446	.21442	.20435	.19427	.18417	.17405	.16391	.15376	.14359	.13341
.20250	.23281	.22286	.21288	.20288	.19287	.18283	.17278	.16271	.15263	.14254
.20500	.24103	.23116	.22126	.21135	.20142	.19147	.18151	.17152	.16153	.15151
.20750	.24911	.23932	.22951	.21968	.20984	.19997	.19009	.18019	.17028	.16035

POINT TABLES: ORIGINAL LOAN TERM: 300 MONTHS LOAN PREPAID IN: 108 MONTHS

CONTRACT RATE

EFFECTIVE YIELD	.17000	.17250	.17500	.17750	.18000	.18250	.18500	.18750	.19000	.19250
.07000	-.65483	-.67165	-.68848	-.70531	-.72215	-.73899	-.75583	-.77268	-.78953	-.80638
.07250	-.63209	-.64874	-.66538	-.68204	-.69870	-.71536	-.73202	-.74869	-.76536	-.78203
.07500	-.60978	-.62624	-.64271	-.65919	-.67567	-.69215	-.70864	-.72513	-.74163	-.75813
.07750	-.58787	-.60416	-.62045	-.63675	-.65306	-.66937	-.68568	-.70200	-.71832	-.73465
.08000	-.56635	-.58247	-.59859	-.61472	-.63086	-.64700	-.66314	-.67929	-.69544	-.71159
.08250	-.54523	-.56117	-.57713	-.59309	-.60905	-.62502	-.64100	-.65698	-.67296	-.68895
.08500	-.52448	-.54026	-.55605	-.57184	-.58764	-.60345	-.61925	-.63507	-.65088	-.66670
.08750	-.50412	-.51973	-.53535	-.55098	-.56661	-.58226	-.59790	-.61355	-.62920	-.64486
.09000	-.48411	-.49956	-.51502	-.53049	-.54596	-.56144	-.57693	-.59242	-.60791	-.62340
.09250	-.46447	-.47976	-.49506	-.51037	-.52568	-.54100	-.55633	-.57166	-.58699	-.60233
.09500	-.44518	-.46031	-.47545	-.49060	-.50576	-.52092	-.53609	-.55127	-.56644	-.58163
.09750	-.42623	-.44121	-.45620	-.47119	-.48620	-.50120	-.51622	-.53124	-.54626	-.56129
.10000	-.40762	-.42245	-.43728	-.45213	-.46698	-.48183	-.49669	-.51156	-.52644	-.54131
.10250	-.38935	-.40402	-.41871	-.43340	-.44810	-.46280	-.47752	-.49224	-.50696	-.52169
.10500	-.37139	-.38592	-.40046	-.41500	-.42955	-.44411	-.45868	-.47325	-.48782	-.50240
.10750	-.35376	-.36814	-.38253	-.39693	-.41133	-.42575	-.44017	-.45459	-.46902	-.48346
.11000	-.33644	-.35067	-.36492	-.37917	-.39344	-.40771	-.42198	-.43627	-.45055	-.46485
.11250	-.31942	-.33352	-.34762	-.36173	-.37585	-.38998	-.40412	-.41826	-.43241	-.44656
.11500	-.30271	-.31666	-.33062	-.34460	-.35858	-.37257	-.38656	-.40057	-.41457	-.42859
.11750	-.28628	-.30010	-.31393	-.32776	-.34161	-.35546	-.36932	-.38318	-.39705	-.41093
.12000	-.27015	-.28383	-.29752	-.31122	-.32493	-.33864	-.35237	-.36610	-.37984	-.39358
.12250	-.25430	-.26784	-.28140	-.29497	-.30854	-.32212	-.33571	-.34931	-.36292	-.37653
.12500	-.23872	-.25214	-.26556	-.27899	-.29244	-.30589	-.31935	-.33281	-.34629	-.35977
.12750	-.22342	-.23670	-.25000	-.26330	-.27661	-.28994	-.30327	-.31660	-.32995	-.34330
.13000	-.20838	-.22154	-.23470	-.24788	-.26106	-.27426	-.28746	-.30067	-.31389	-.32711
.13250	-.19360	-.20663	-.21967	-.23272	-.24578	-.25885	-.27193	-.28501	-.29810	-.31120
.13500	-.17908	-.19199	-.20490	-.21783	-.23076	-.24371	-.25666	-.26962	-.28259	-.29556
.13750	-.16481	-.17759	-.19038	-.20319	-.21600	-.22882	-.24165	-.25449	-.26734	-.28019
.14000	-.15078	-.16345	-.17612	-.18880	-.20149	-.21419	-.22690	-.23962	-.25234	-.26508
.14250	-.13700	-.14954	-.16209	-.17466	-.18723	-.19981	-.21240	-.22500	-.23761	-.25022
.14500	-.12345	-.13588	-.14831	-.16076	-.17321	-.18568	-.19815	-.21063	-.22312	-.23562
.14750	-.11014	-.12244	-.13476	-.14709	-.15943	-.17178	-.18414	-.19651	-.20888	-.22126
.15000	-.09705	-.10924	-.12145	-.13366	-.14589	-.15812	-.17037	-.18262	-.19488	-.20715
.15250	-.08418	-.09626	-.10835	-.12046	-.13257	-.14469	-.15682	-.16896	-.18111	-.19327
.15500	-.07153	-.08350	-.09548	-.10747	-.11948	-.13149	-.14351	-.15554	-.16758	-.17962
.15750	-.05910	-.07096	-.08283	-.09471	-.10661	-.11851	-.13042	-.14234	-.15427	-.16620
.16000	-.04687	-.05863	-.07039	-.08216	-.09395	-.10574	-.11755	-.12936	-.14118	-.15301
.16250	-.03486	-.04650	-.05816	-.06983	-.08151	-.09319	-.10489	-.11660	-.12831	-.14003
.16500	-.02304	-.03458	-.04613	-.05770	-.06927	-.08085	-.09245	-.10405	-.11566	-.12728
.16750	-.01142	-.02286	-.03431	-.04577	-.05724	-.06872	-.08021	-.09170	-.10321	-.11473
.17000	-.00000	-.01133	-.02268	-.03404	-.04540	-.05678	-.06817	-.07957	-.09097	-.10238
.17250	.01123	.00000	-.01125	-.02250	-.03377	-.04505	-.05633	-.06763	-.07893	-.09025
.17500	.02228	.01115	.00000	-.01116	-.02232	-.03350	-.04469	-.05589	-.06709	-.07831
.17750	.03314	.02211	.01106	-.00000	-.01107	-.02215	-.03324	-.04434	-.05545	-.06656
.18000	.04382	.03289	.02194	.01097	.00000	-.01098	-.02198	-.03298	-.04399	-.05501
.18250	.05433	.04349	.03263	.02177	.01089	0.00000	-.01090	-.02181	-.03272	-.04365
.18500	.06466	.05392	.04316	.03238	.02160	.01080	0.00000	-.01081	-.02164	-.03247
.18750	.07483	.06417	.05350	.04282	.03213	.02143	.01072	0.00000	-.01073	-.02147
.19000	.08483	.07426	.06369	.05310	.04250	.03189	.02127	.01064	.00000	-.01065
.19250	.09466	.08419	.07370	.06320	.05269	.04217	.03164	.02110	.01056	.00000
.19500	.10433	.09395	.08355	.07314	.06272	.05229	.04185	.03140	.02094	.01048
.19750	.11385	.10355	.09325	.08293	.07259	.06225	.05190	.04154	.03116	.02078
.20000	.12321	.11300	.10278	.09255	.08230	.07205	.06178	.05151	.04122	.03093
.20250	.13243	.12230	.11217	.10202	.09186	.08169	.07151	.06132	.05112	.04091
.20500	.14149	.13145	.12140	.11133	.10126	.09117	.08108	.07097	.06086	.05073
.20750	.15041	.14045	.13048	.12050	.11051	.10051	.09049	.08047	.07044	.06040

POINT TABLES: ORIGINAL LOAN TERM: 300 MONTHS LOAN PREPAID IN: 108 MONTHS

CONTRACT RATE

EFFECTIVE YIELD	.19500	.19750	.20000	.20250	.20500	.20750
.07000	-.82323	-.84009	-.85694	-.87379	-.89065	-.90750
.07250	-.79871	-.81538	-.83206	-.84874	-.86541	-.88209
.07500	-.77463	-.79113	-.80763	-.82413	-.84063	-.85713
.07750	-.75097	-.76730	-.78363	-.79996	-.81629	-.83262
.08000	-.72775	-.74390	-.76006	-.77622	-.79238	-.80855
.08250	-.70493	-.72092	-.73692	-.75291	-.76890	-.78490
.08500	-.68253	-.69835	-.71418	-.73001	-.74584	-.76167
.08750	-.66052	-.67618	-.69185	-.70751	-.72318	-.73885
.09000	-.63890	-.65441	-.66991	-.68542	-.70093	-.71644
.09250	-.61767	-.63302	-.64836	-.66371	-.67906	-.69442
.09500	-.59681	-.61200	-.62719	-.64239	-.65759	-.67278
.09750	-.57632	-.59136	-.60640	-.62144	-.63648	-.65153
.10000	-.55619	-.57108	-.58597	-.60086	-.61575	-.63065
.10250	-.53642	-.55116	-.56590	-.58064	-.59538	-.61013
.10500	-.51699	-.53158	-.54617	-.56077	-.57537	-.58997
.10750	-.49790	-.51235	-.52680	-.54125	-.55570	-.57016
.11000	-.47915	-.49345	-.50776	-.52207	-.53638	-.55069
.11250	-.46072	-.47488	-.48905	-.50322	-.51739	-.53157
.11500	-.44261	-.45663	-.47066	-.48469	-.49873	-.51277
.11750	-.42481	-.43870	-.45259	-.46649	-.48039	-.49429
.12000	-.40733	-.42108	-.43484	-.44860	-.46236	-.47613
.12250	-.39014	-.40376	-.41739	-.43102	-.44465	-.45829
.12500	-.37325	-.38674	-.40024	-.41374	-.42724	-.44075
.12750	-.35665	-.37001	-.38338	-.39675	-.41013	-.42350
.13000	-.34034	-.35357	-.36681	-.38006	-.39330	-.40656
.13250	-.32430	-.33741	-.35053	-.36364	-.37677	-.38990
.13500	-.30854	-.32153	-.33452	-.34751	-.36051	-.37352
.13750	-.29305	-.30591	-.31878	-.33165	-.34453	-.35742
.14000	-.27781	-.29056	-.30331	-.31606	-.32882	-.34159
.14250	-.26284	-.27547	-.28810	-.30074	-.31338	-.32602
.14500	-.24812	-.26063	-.27315	-.28567	-.29819	-.31072
.14750	-.23365	-.24604	-.25844	-.27085	-.28326	-.29567
.15000	-.21942	-.23170	-.24399	-.25628	-.26858	-.28088
.15250	-.20543	-.21760	-.22977	-.24195	-.25414	-.26633
.15500	-.19167	-.20373	-.21580	-.22787	-.23994	-.25202
.15750	-.17815	-.19010	-.20205	-.21401	-.22598	-.23795
.16000	-.16485	-.17669	-.18854	-.20039	-.21225	-.22412
.16250	-.15176	-.16350	-.17524	-.18699	-.19875	-.21051
.16500	-.13890	-.15053	-.16217	-.17382	-.18547	-.19712
.16750	-.12625	-.13778	-.14931	-.16085	-.17240	-.18396
.17000	-.11381	-.12523	-.13667	-.14811	-.15955	-.17100
.17250	-.10157	-.11289	-.12423	-.13557	-.14691	-.15827
.17500	-.08953	-.10076	-.11199	-.12323	-.13448	-.14573
.17750	-.07769	-.08882	-.09995	-.11110	-.12225	-.13340
.18000	-.06604	-.07707	-.08811	-.09916	-.11022	-.12128
.18250	-.05458	-.06552	-.07646	-.08742	-.09838	-.10934
.18500	-.04331	-.05415	-.06500	-.07586	-.08673	-.09760
.18750	-.03221	-.04297	-.05373	-.06449	-.07527	-.08605
.19000	-.02130	-.03196	-.04263	-.05331	-.06399	-.07468
.19250	-.01056	-.02114	-.03172	-.04230	-.05289	-.06349
.19500	.00000	-.01048	-.02097	-.03147	-.04197	-.05248
.19750	.01040	.00000	-.01040	-.02081	-.03123	-.04165
.20000	.02063	.01032	.00000	-.01032	-.02065	-.03099
.20250	.03069	.02047	.01024	0.00000	-.01024	-.02050
.20500	.04060	.03046	.02031	.01016	.00000	-.01017
.20750	.05035	.04030	.03023	.02016	.01008	.00000

POINT TABLES: ORIGINAL LOAN TERM: 300 MONTHS LOAN PREPAID IN: 144 MONTHS

EFFECTIVE YIELD	CONTRACT RATE .07000	.07250	.07500	.07750	.08000	.08250	.08500	.08750	.09000	.09250
.07000	.00000	-.01829	-.03670	-.05521	-.07384	-.09256	-.11139	-.13031	-.14932	-.16842
.07250	.01801	.00000	-.01813	-.03636	-.05470	-.07315	-.09169	-.11032	-.12905	-.14787
.07500	.03559	.01785	.00000	-.01796	-.03603	-.05419	-.07246	-.09082	-.10927	-.12780
.07750	.05274	.03527	.01769	0.00000	-.01780	-.03569	-.05368	-.07177	-.08995	-.10821
.08000	.06949	.05228	.03496	.01753	.00000	-.01763	-.03536	-.05318	-.07109	-.08909
.08250	.08583	.06888	.05181	.03464	.01737	.00000	-.01747	-.03503	-.05268	-.07042
.08500	.10178	.08508	.06827	.05135	.03433	.01721	.00000	-.01731	-.03470	-.05218
.08750	.11735	.10090	.08433	.06766	.05089	.03402	.01706	.00000	-.01714	-.03437
.09000	.13255	.11634	.10001	.08359	.06706	.05043	.03371	.01690	.00000	-.01698
.09250	.14740	.13142	.11533	.09914	.08285	.06646	.04998	.03340	.01674	.00000
.09500	.16189	.14614	.13028	.11432	.09826	.08211	.06586	.04952	.03310	.01659
.09750	.17604	.16051	.14488	.12915	.11332	.09739	.08137	.06527	.04907	.03279
.10000	.18986	.17455	.15914	.14363	.12803	.11232	.09653	.08064	.06467	.04862
.10250	.20335	.18826	.17307	.15778	.14239	.12690	.11133	.09567	.07992	.06409
.10500	.21653	.20165	.18667	.17160	.15642	.14115	.12579	.11034	.09481	.07920
.10750	.22940	.21473	.19996	.18509	.17013	.15507	.13992	.12468	.10936	.09396
.11000	.24198	.22751	.21294	.19828	.18352	.16866	.15372	.13869	.12358	.10838
.11250	.25426	.23999	.22562	.21116	.19660	.18195	.16721	.15238	.13747	.12248
.11500	.26626	.25219	.23801	.22375	.20938	.19493	.18038	.16576	.15105	.13626
.11750	.27798	.26410	.25012	.23604	.22187	.20761	.19326	.17883	.16432	.14972
.12000	.28944	.27574	.26195	.24806	.23408	.22001	.20585	.19161	.17728	.16288
.12250	.30063	.28712	.27351	.25981	.24601	.23212	.21815	.20410	.18996	.17575
.12500	.31157	.29824	.28481	.27129	.25767	.24397	.23018	.21631	.20235	.18832
.12750	.32226	.30910	.29585	.28251	.26907	.25554	.24193	.22824	.21447	.20062
.13000	.33271	.31973	.30664	.29347	.28021	.26686	.25343	.23991	.22631	.21264
.13250	.34292	.33011	.31720	.30419	.29110	.27792	.26466	.25132	.23789	.22440
.13500	.35291	.34025	.32751	.31467	.30175	.28874	.27565	.26247	.24922	.23589
.13750	.36266	.35018	.33759	.32492	.31216	.29932	.28639	.27338	.26029	.24713
.14000	.37221	.35988	.34745	.33494	.32234	.30966	.29689	.28405	.27112	.25813
.14250	.38153	.36936	.35710	.34474	.33230	.31977	.30717	.29448	.28172	.26888
.14500	.39066	.37864	.36652	.35432	.34204	.32967	.31722	.30469	.29208	.27940
.14750	.39958	.38771	.37574	.36369	.35156	.33934	.32704	.31467	.30222	.28969
.15000	.40830	.39658	.38476	.37286	.36087	.34881	.33666	.32443	.31213	.29976
.15250	.41683	.40525	.39358	.38183	.36999	.35807	.34606	.33399	.32183	.30961
.15500	.42518	.41374	.40221	.39060	.37890	.36712	.35527	.34333	.33133	.31925
.15750	.43334	.42204	.41065	.39918	.38762	.37599	.36427	.35248	.34062	.32868
.16000	.44133	.43016	.41891	.40758	.39616	.38466	.37308	.36143	.34971	.33791
.16250	.44914	.43811	.42699	.41579	.40451	.39315	.38171	.37019	.35860	.34695
.16500	.45679	.44589	.43490	.42383	.41268	.40145	.39014	.37876	.36731	.35579
.16750	.46427	.45349	.44264	.43170	.42068	.40958	.39840	.38716	.37584	.36445
.17000	.47159	.46094	.45021	.43940	.42851	.41753	.40649	.39537	.38418	.37292
.17250	.47875	.46823	.45762	.44693	.43617	.42532	.41440	.40341	.39235	.38122
.17500	.48576	.47536	.46488	.45431	.44367	.43295	.42215	.41128	.40035	.38934
.17750	.49263	.48235	.47198	.46154	.45101	.44041	.42974	.41899	.40818	.39730
.18000	.49935	.48918	.47893	.46861	.45820	.44772	.43717	.42654	.41585	.40509
.18250	.50593	.49588	.48574	.47553	.46524	.45488	.44444	.43393	.42336	.41272
.18500	.51237	.50243	.49241	.48231	.47214	.46189	.45157	.44117	.43071	.42019
.18750	.51867	.50885	.49894	.48895	.47889	.46875	.45854	.44827	.43792	.42751
.19000	.52485	.51513	.50533	.49545	.48550	.47548	.46538	.45521	.44498	.43468
.19250	.53090	.52128	.51159	.50182	.49198	.48206	.47207	.46202	.45189	.44171
.19500	.53682	.52731	.51772	.50806	.49832	.48851	.47863	.46868	.45867	.44859
.19750	.54262	.53322	.52373	.51417	.50454	.49483	.48506	.47522	.46531	.45533
.20000	.54831	.53900	.52962	.52016	.51063	.50103	.49136	.48162	.47181	.46194
.20250	.55388	.54467	.53539	.52603	.51660	.50710	.49753	.48789	.47819	.46842
.20500	.55933	.55022	.54104	.53178	.52245	.51304	.50357	.49404	.48444	.47477
.20750	.56468	.55566	.54657	.53741	.52818	.51887	.50950	.50006	.49056	.48100

POINT TABLES: ORIGINAL LOAN TERM: 300 MONTHS LOAN PREPAID IN: 144 MONTHS

EFFECTIVE YIELD	CONTRACT RATE .09500	.09750	.10000	.10250	.10500	.10750	.11000	.11250	.11500	.11750
.07000	-.18761	-.20688	-.22622	-.24565	-.26514	-.28470	-.30433	-.32402	-.34377	-.36357
.07250	-.16677	-.18575	-.20481	-.22395	-.24315	-.26243	-.28177	-.30117	-.32063	-.34015
.07500	-.14643	-.16513	-.18391	-.20276	-.22169	-.24068	-.25974	-.27887	-.29805	-.31728
.07750	-.12656	-.14499	-.16350	-.18208	-.20073	-.21945	-.23824	-.25708	-.27599	-.29495
.08000	-.10717	-.12533	-.14357	-.16188	-.18026	-.19871	-.21723	-.23581	-.25444	-.27314
.08250	-.08823	-.10613	-.12411	-.14216	-.16028	-.17846	-.19672	-.21503	-.23340	-.25183
.08500	-.06974	-.08739	-.10510	-.12290	-.14076	-.15869	-.17668	-.19473	-.21285	-.23102
.08750	-.05169	-.06908	-.08654	-.10408	-.12169	-.13937	-.15711	-.17491	-.19277	-.21069
.09000	-.03405	-.05119	-.06841	-.08571	-.10307	-.12050	-.13799	-.15554	-.17315	-.19082
.09250	-.01682	-.03373	-.05071	-.06776	-.08488	-.10206	-.11931	-.13662	-.15399	-.17142
.09500	.00000	-.01667	-.03341	-.05022	-.06710	-.08405	-.10106	-.11814	-.13527	-.15245
.09750	.01644	0.00000	-.01651	-.03309	-.04974	-.06646	-.08323	-.10007	-.11697	-.13392
.10000	.03249	.01628	.00000	-.01635	-.03278	-.04926	-.06581	-.08242	-.09909	-.11582
.10250	.04818	.03219	.01613	.00000	-.01620	-.03246	-.04879	-.06518	-.08162	-.09812
.10500	.06350	.04773	.03189	.01598	.00000	-.01605	-.03215	-.04832	-.06454	-.08082
.10750	.07848	.06292	.04729	.03160	.01583	.00000	-.01589	-.03184	-.04785	-.06392
.11000	.09311	.07777	.06235	.04686	.03130	.01568	.00000	-.01574	-.03154	-.04739
.11250	.10741	.09227	.07706	.06177	.04642	.03101	.01553	.00000	-.01559	-.03124
.11500	.12139	.10645	.09144	.07635	.06121	.04599	.03072	.01539	.00000	-.01544
.11750	.13505	.12031	.10549	.09061	.07566	.06064	.04557	.03043	.01524	.00000
.12000	.14840	.13385	.11923	.10454	.08978	.07496	.06008	.04514	.03015	.01510
.12250	.16146	.14709	.13266	.11816	.10359	.08896	.07427	.05953	.04472	.02987
.12500	.17422	.16004	.14579	.13148	.11710	.10266	.08815	.07359	.05898	.04431
.12750	.18670	.17270	.15863	.14450	.13030	.11604	.10173	.08735	.07292	.05843
.13000	.19889	.18508	.17119	.15724	.14322	.12914	.11500	.10080	.08655	.07224
.13250	.21082	.19718	.18347	.16969	.15585	.14194	.12798	.11396	.09989	.08576
.13500	.22249	.20902	.19548	.18187	.16820	.15447	.14068	.12683	.11293	.09898
.13750	.23390	.22059	.20722	.19378	.18028	.16672	.15310	.13942	.12569	.11191
.14000	.24506	.23192	.21871	.20544	.19210	.17871	.16525	.15174	.13818	.12456
.14250	.25597	.24299	.22995	.21684	.20367	.19043	.17714	.16380	.15040	.13694
.14500	.26665	.25383	.24094	.22799	.21498	.20191	.18878	.17559	.16235	.14906
.14750	.27710	.26443	.25170	.23891	.22605	.21313	.20016	.18713	.17405	.16092
.15000	.28732	.27480	.26223	.24958	.23688	.22412	.21130	.19843	.18550	.17252
.15250	.29731	.28495	.27252	.26003	.24748	.23487	.22220	.20948	.19670	.18388
.15500	.30710	.29486	.28260	.27026	.25786	.24539	.23287	.22030	.20767	.19500
.15750	.31668	.30460	.29247	.28027	.26801	.25569	.24332	.23089	.21841	.20588
.16000	.32605	.31412	.30212	.29007	.27795	.26577	.25354	.24126	.22892	.21654
.16250	.33522	.32343	.31157	.29966	.28768	.27564	.26355	.25141	.23922	.22697
.16500	.34420	.33254	.32082	.30904	.29720	.28531	.27336	.26135	.24929	.23719
.16750	.35299	.34147	.32988	.31824	.30653	.29477	.28295	.27108	.25916	.24719
.17000	.36159	.35020	.33875	.32724	.31566	.30403	.29235	.28061	.26883	.25699
.17250	.37002	.35876	.34743	.33605	.32461	.31311	.30155	.28995	.27829	.26659
.17500	.37827	.36713	.35594	.34468	.33336	.32199	.31057	.29909	.28756	.27599
.17750	.38635	.37534	.36426	.35313	.34194	.33070	.31940	.30805	.29664	.28520
.18000	.39426	.38337	.37242	.36141	.35034	.33922	.32804	.31682	.30554	.29422
.18250	.40201	.39124	.38041	.36952	.35857	.34757	.33652	.32541	.31426	.30306
.18500	.40960	.39895	.38823	.37746	.36663	.35575	.34482	.33383	.32280	.31172
.18750	.41703	.40650	.39590	.38524	.37453	.36377	.35295	.34208	.33117	.32020
.19000	.42432	.41389	.40341	.39287	.38227	.37162	.36092	.35017	.33937	.32852
.19250	.43145	.42114	.41077	.40034	.38986	.37932	.36873	.35809	.34740	.33667
.19500	.43845	.42824	.41798	.40766	.39729	.38686	.37639	.36586	.35528	.34466
.19750	.44530	.43520	.42505	.41484	.40457	.39426	.38389	.37347	.36300	.35249
.20000	.45201	.44202	.43198	.42187	.41171	.40150	.39124	.38093	.37057	.36017
.20250	.45860	.44871	.43877	.42877	.41871	.40861	.39845	.38825	.37799	.36770
.20500	.46505	.45526	.44542	.43552	.42557	.41557	.40552	.39542	.38527	.37508
.20750	.47137	.46169	.45195	.44215	.43230	.42240	.41245	.40245	.39241	.38232

POINT TABLES: ORIGINAL LOAN TERM: 300 MONTHS LOAN PREPAID IN: 144 MONTHS

EFFECTIVE YIELD	CONTRACT RATE .12000	.12250	.12500	.12750	.13000	.13250	.13500	.13750	.14000	.14250
.07000	-.38343	-.40334	-.42330	-.44331	-.46336	-.48345	-.50358	-.52375	-.54395	-.56418
.07250	-.35973	-.37935	-.39902	-.41874	-.43851	-.45831	-.47815	-.49803	-.51795	-.53790
.07500	-.33658	-.35592	-.37531	-.39475	-.41423	-.43375	-.45332	-.47292	-.49255	-.51222
.07750	-.31397	-.33303	-.35215	-.37131	-.39052	-.40977	-.42906	-.44838	-.46774	-.48713
.08000	-.29188	-.31068	-.32953	-.34842	-.36736	-.38634	-.40535	-.42441	-.44350	-.46262
.08250	-.27031	-.28885	-.30743	-.32606	-.34473	-.36344	-.38220	-.40099	-.41982	-.43868
.08500	-.24924	-.26752	-.28584	-.30421	-.32262	-.34108	-.35957	-.37811	-.39667	-.41528
.08750	-.22866	-.24668	-.26475	-.28286	-.30102	-.31922	-.33747	-.35575	-.37406	-.39241
.09000	-.20854	-.22632	-.24414	-.26201	-.27992	-.29787	-.31586	-.33389	-.35196	-.37006
.09250	-.18889	-.20642	-.22400	-.24162	-.25929	-.27700	-.29475	-.31254	-.33036	-.34822
.09500	-.16969	-.18698	-.20432	-.22171	-.23914	-.25661	-.27412	-.29167	-.30925	-.32687
.09750	-.15093	-.16799	-.18509	-.20224	-.21944	-.23668	-.25395	-.27127	-.28862	-.30600
.10000	-.13259	-.14942	-.16630	-.18322	-.20018	-.21719	-.23424	-.25132	-.26845	-.28560
.10250	-.11467	-.13128	-.14793	-.16462	-.18137	-.19815	-.21497	-.23183	-.24873	-.26566
.10500	-.09716	-.11354	-.12997	-.14645	-.16297	-.17953	-.19613	-.21277	-.22945	-.24616
.10750	-.08004	-.09620	-.11242	-.12868	-.14498	-.16133	-.17771	-.19414	-.21060	-.22709
.11000	-.06330	-.07925	-.09526	-.11131	-.12740	-.14353	-.15971	-.17592	-.19216	-.20845
.11250	-.04694	-.06268	-.07848	-.09432	-.11021	-.12613	-.14210	-.15810	-.17414	-.19021
.11500	-.03094	-.04648	-.06207	-.07771	-.09339	-.10912	-.12488	-.14068	-.15651	-.17238
.11750	-.01530	-.03064	-.04603	-.06147	-.07695	-.09248	-.10804	-.12364	-.13927	-.15494
.12000	0.00000	-.01515	-.03035	-.04559	-.06087	-.07620	-.09157	-.10697	-.12241	-.13788
.12250	.01496	.00000	-.01500	-.03005	-.04515	-.06028	-.07546	-.09067	-.10591	-.12120
.12500	.02959	.01482	.00000	-.01486	-.02977	-.04471	-.05970	-.07472	-.08978	-.10487
.12750	.04389	.02931	.01468	.00000	-.01472	-.02948	-.04428	-.05912	-.07399	-.08890
.13000	.05789	.04348	.02903	.01454	.00000	-.01458	-.02920	-.04385	-.05854	-.07327
.13250	.07158	.05735	.04308	.02876	.01440	0.00000	-.01444	-.02892	-.04343	-.05798
.13500	.08497	.07092	.05682	.04268	.02849	.01427	.00000	-.01430	-.02864	-.04301
.13750	.09808	.08419	.07027	.05629	.04228	.02822	.01413	.00000	-.01417	-.02837
.14000	.11090	.09718	.08342	.06962	.05577	.04188	.02796	.01400	.00000	-.01403
.14250	.12344	.10989	.09630	.08266	.06898	.05525	.04149	.02770	.01387	.00000
.14500	.13572	.12233	.10890	.09542	.08190	.06834	.05474	.04111	.02744	.01374
.14750	.14773	.13450	.12123	.10791	.09455	.08115	.06771	.05424	.04073	.02718
.15000	.15949	.14642	.13330	.12014	.10693	.09369	.08041	.06709	.05373	.04035
.15250	.17100	.15808	.14512	.13211	.11905	.10596	.09284	.07967	.06647	.05324
.15500	.18227	.16950	.15668	.14382	.13092	.11798	.10500	.09199	.07894	.06586
.15750	.19330	.18068	.16801	.15530	.14254	.12975	.11692	.10405	.09115	.07822
.16000	.20410	.19162	.17910	.16653	.15392	.14128	.12859	.11587	.10311	.09033
.16250	.21468	.20234	.18996	.17753	.16507	.15256	.14002	.12744	.11483	.10218
.16500	.22503	.21283	.20059	.18831	.17598	.16362	.15121	.13878	.12630	.11380
.16750	.23518	.22311	.21101	.19886	.18667	.17444	.16218	.14988	.13754	.12518
.17000	.24511	.23318	.22121	.20919	.19714	.18505	.17292	.16075	.14855	.13632
.17250	.25484	.24304	.23120	.21932	.20740	.19544	.18344	.17141	.15934	.14724
.17500	.26437	.25270	.24099	.22924	.21745	.20562	.19375	.18185	.16991	.15795
.17750	.27370	.26216	.25058	.23895	.22729	.21559	.20385	.19208	.18027	.16843
.18000	.28285	.27143	.25997	.24848	.23694	.22536	.21375	.20210	.19042	.17871
.18250	.29181	.28052	.26918	.25781	.24639	.23494	.22345	.21193	.20037	.18878
.18500	.30059	.28942	.27820	.26695	.25566	.24432	.23296	.22156	.21012	.19865
.18750	.30919	.29814	.28705	.27591	.26474	.25352	.24228	.23099	.21968	.20833
.19000	.31763	.30669	.29571	.28469	.27364	.26254	.25141	.24025	.22905	.21782
.19250	.32589	.31507	.30421	.29330	.28236	.27138	.26037	.24932	.23823	.22712
.19500	.33399	.32328	.31253	.30174	.29091	.28005	.26915	.25821	.24724	.23624
.19750	.34194	.33134	.32070	.31002	.29930	.28854	.27775	.26693	.25607	.24519
.20000	.34972	.33923	.32870	.31813	.30752	.29687	.28619	.27548	.26473	.25396
.20250	.35736	.34697	.33655	.32608	.31558	.30505	.29447	.28387	.27323	.26256
.20500	.36484	.35456	.34424	.33389	.32349	.31306	.30259	.29209	.28156	.27100
.20750	.37218	.36201	.35179	.34154	.33124	.32092	.31055	.30016	.28973	.27927

POINT TABLES: ORIGINAL LOAN TERM: 300 MONTHS LOAN PREPAID IN: 144 MONTHS

EFFECTIVE YIELD	CONTRACT RATE .14500	.14750	.15000	.15250	.15500	.15750	.16000	.16250	.16500	.16750
.07000	-.58445	-.60474	-.62506	-.64541	-.66578	-.68617	-.70658	-.72701	-.74746	-.76792
.07250	-.55788	-.57789	-.59792	-.61798	-.63807	-.65817	-.67830	-.69845	-.71861	-.73879
.07500	-.53192	-.55165	-.57140	-.59118	-.61099	-.63082	-.65066	-.67053	-.69042	-.71032
.07750	-.50656	-.52601	-.54549	-.56500	-.58453	-.60409	-.62366	-.64326	-.66287	-.68250
.08000	-.48178	-.50096	-.52018	-.53942	-.55868	-.57797	-.59727	-.61660	-.63594	-.65531
.08250	-.45757	-.47649	-.49544	-.51441	-.53341	-.55244	-.57148	-.59055	-.60963	-.62873
.08500	-.43391	-.45257	-.47126	-.48998	-.50872	-.52749	-.54628	-.56509	-.58391	-.60276
.08750	-.41079	-.42920	-.44764	-.46610	-.48459	-.50311	-.52164	-.54020	-.55877	-.57736
.09000	-.38819	-.40635	-.42454	-.44276	-.46100	-.47927	-.49756	-.51587	-.53420	-.55254
.09250	-.36611	-.38403	-.40197	-.41995	-.43795	-.45597	-.47402	-.49208	-.51017	-.52827
.09500	-.34452	-.36220	-.37991	-.39765	-.41541	-.43319	-.45100	-.46883	-.48668	-.50455
.09750	-.32342	-.34086	-.35834	-.37584	-.39337	-.41092	-.42850	-.44609	-.46371	-.48134
.10000	-.30279	-.32001	-.33725	-.35453	-.37182	-.38915	-.40649	-.42386	-.44125	-.45866
.10250	-.28262	-.29961	-.31663	-.33368	-.35076	-.36786	-.38498	-.40212	-.41929	-.43647
.10500	-.26290	-.27967	-.29647	-.31330	-.33016	-.34704	-.36394	-.38086	-.39781	-.41477
.10750	-.24362	-.26017	-.27676	-.29337	-.31001	-.32667	-.34336	-.36007	-.37680	-.39355
.11000	-.22476	-.24110	-.25748	-.27388	-.29031	-.30676	-.32323	-.33973	-.35625	-.37279
.11250	-.20632	-.22246	-.23862	-.25482	-.27104	-.28728	-.30355	-.31984	-.33615	-.35248
.11500	-.18828	-.20422	-.22018	-.23617	-.25218	-.26823	-.28429	-.30038	-.31648	-.33261
.11750	-.17064	-.18638	-.20214	-.21793	-.23374	-.24959	-.26545	-.28134	-.29724	-.31317
.12000	-.15339	-.16893	-.18449	-.20008	-.21570	-.23135	-.24702	-.26271	-.27842	-.29415
.12250	-.13651	-.15185	-.16723	-.18263	-.19805	-.21351	-.22898	-.24448	-.26000	-.27554
.12500	-.11999	-.13515	-.15033	-.16555	-.18078	-.19605	-.21134	-.22665	-.24198	-.25733
.12750	-.10384	-.11881	-.13381	-.14883	-.16389	-.17896	-.19407	-.20919	-.22434	-.23950
.13000	-.08803	-.10281	-.11763	-.13248	-.14735	-.16225	-.17717	-.19211	-.20707	-.22206
.13250	-.07256	-.08717	-.10180	-.11647	-.13116	-.14588	-.16062	-.17539	-.19017	-.20498
.13500	-.05742	-.07185	-.08631	-.10081	-.11532	-.12987	-.14443	-.15902	-.17363	-.18826
.13750	-.04260	-.05686	-.07115	-.08547	-.09982	-.11419	-.12858	-.14300	-.15744	-.17190
.14000	-.02809	-.04219	-.05631	-.07046	-.08464	-.09884	-.11307	-.12732	-.14159	-.15588
.14250	-.01390	-.02783	-.04178	-.05577	-.06978	-.08382	-.09788	-.11196	-.12606	-.14019
.14500	0.00000	-.01377	-.02756	-.04138	-.05523	-.06911	-.08300	-.09692	-.11087	-.12483
.14750	.01361	0.00000	-.01364	-.02730	-.04099	-.05470	-.06844	-.08220	-.09598	-.10978
.15000	.02693	.01348	.00000	-.01351	-.02704	-.04060	-.05418	-.06778	-.08141	-.09505
.15250	.03997	.02668	.01335	.00000	-.01338	-.02678	-.04021	-.05366	-.06713	-.08062
.15500	.05275	.03960	.02643	.01323	.00000	-.01325	-.02653	-.03983	-.05315	-.06649
.15750	.06525	.05226	.03923	.02618	.01310	0.00000	-.01313	-.02628	-.03945	-.05264
.16000	.07751	.06466	.05178	.03887	.02594	.01298	0.00000	-.01300	-.02603	-.03907
.16250	.08951	.07680	.06406	.05130	.03851	.02570	.01286	0.00000	-.01288	-.02578
.16500	.10126	.08870	.07610	.06348	.05083	.03816	.02546	.01274	0.00000	-.01276
.16750	.11278	.10035	.08789	.07541	.06290	.05036	.03781	.02522	.01262	.00000
.17000	.12406	.11177	.09945	.08710	.07472	.06233	.04990	.03746	.02499	.01251
.17250	.13511	.12296	.11077	.09855	.08631	.07405	.06176	.04945	.03712	.02476
.17500	.14595	.13392	.12186	.10978	.09767	.08554	.07338	.06120	.04900	.03678
.17750	.15656	.14466	.13274	.12078	.10880	.09680	.08477	.07272	.06064	.04855
.18000	.16697	.15519	.14339	.13156	.11971	.10783	.09593	.08401	.07206	.06010
.18250	.17716	.16551	.15384	.14213	.13040	.11865	.10687	.09508	.08326	.07142
.18500	.18716	.17563	.16408	.15250	.14089	.12926	.11760	.10593	.09423	.08251
.18750	.19695	.18555	.17411	.16265	.15117	.13966	.12812	.11657	.10499	.09339
.19000	.20656	.19527	.18396	.17261	.16125	.14985	.13844	.12700	.11554	.10407
.19250	.21598	.20481	.19361	.18238	.17113	.15985	.14856	.13723	.12589	.11453
.19500	.22521	.21416	.20307	.19196	.18082	.16966	.15848	.14727	.13604	.12480
.19750	.23427	.22332	.21235	.20135	.19033	.17928	.16821	.15711	.14600	.13486
.20000	.24315	.23231	.22145	.21056	.19965	.18871	.17775	.16677	.15576	.14474
.20250	.25186	.24113	.23038	.21960	.20879	.19796	.18711	.17624	.16534	.15443
.20500	.26040	.24978	.23914	.22846	.21776	.20704	.19630	.18553	.17474	.16394
.20750	.26879	.25827	.24773	.23716	.22657	.21595	.20531	.19465	.18397	.17327

POINT TABLES: ORIGINAL LOAN TERM: 300 MONTHS LOAN PREPAID IN: 144 MONTHS

EFFECTIVE YIELD	CONTRACT RATE .17000	.17250	.17500	.17750	.18000	.18250	.18500	.18750	.19000	.19250
.07000	-.78840	-.80889	-.82940	-.84991	-.87044	-.89097	-.91151	-.93206	-.95262	-.97318
.07250	-.75898	-.77919	-.79941	-.81965	-.83989	-.86014	-.88040	-.90067	-.92095	-.94123
.07500	-.73024	-.75017	-.77011	-.79007	-.81003	-.83001	-.85000	-.86999	-.88999	-.91000
.07750	-.70214	-.72180	-.74148	-.76116	-.78086	-.80056	-.82028	-.84000	-.85973	-.87947
.08000	-.67469	-.69408	-.71349	-.73290	-.75234	-.77178	-.79123	-.81069	-.83015	-.84962
.08250	-.64785	-.66698	-.68613	-.70529	-.72446	-.74364	-.76283	-.78203	-.80123	-.82045
.08500	-.62162	-.64049	-.65938	-.67829	-.69720	-.71613	-.73506	-.75401	-.77296	-.79192
.08750	-.59597	-.61460	-.63324	-.65189	-.67056	-.68923	-.70792	-.72661	-.74532	-.76403
.09000	-.57090	-.58928	-.60768	-.62608	-.64450	-.66293	-.68137	-.69983	-.71828	-.73675
.09250	-.54639	-.56453	-.58268	-.60085	-.61903	-.63722	-.65542	-.67363	-.69185	-.71008
.09500	-.52243	-.54033	-.55825	-.57618	-.59412	-.61207	-.63004	-.64801	-.66600	-.68399
.09750	-.49900	-.51666	-.53435	-.55205	-.56976	-.58748	-.60521	-.62296	-.64071	-.65848
.10000	-.47608	-.49352	-.51098	-.52845	-.54593	-.56343	-.58094	-.59845	-.61598	-.63352
.10250	-.45367	-.47089	-.48812	-.50537	-.52263	-.53990	-.55719	-.57448	-.59179	-.60910
.10500	-.43175	-.44875	-.46576	-.48279	-.49983	-.51689	-.53396	-.55103	-.56812	-.58522
.10750	-.41031	-.42710	-.44389	-.46071	-.47754	-.49438	-.51123	-.52809	-.54497	-.56185
.11000	-.38934	-.40591	-.42250	-.43911	-.45572	-.47235	-.48900	-.50565	-.52231	-.53899
.11250	-.36883	-.38519	-.40157	-.41797	-.43438	-.45080	-.46724	-.48369	-.50015	-.51662
.11500	-.34875	-.36492	-.38110	-.39729	-.41350	-.42972	-.44595	-.46220	-.47846	-.49472
.11750	-.32912	-.34508	-.36106	-.37705	-.39306	-.40909	-.42512	-.44117	-.45723	-.47330
.12000	-.30990	-.32567	-.34145	-.35725	-.37307	-.38890	-.40474	-.42059	-.43645	-.45233
.12250	-.29110	-.30667	-.32227	-.33788	-.35350	-.36913	-.38478	-.40045	-.41612	-.43180
.12500	-.27270	-.28808	-.30349	-.31891	-.33434	-.34979	-.36525	-.38073	-.39621	-.41171
.12750	-.25469	-.26989	-.28511	-.30035	-.31560	-.33086	-.34614	-.36143	-.37673	-.39204
.13000	-.23706	-.25208	-.26712	-.28217	-.29724	-.31233	-.32742	-.34253	-.35765	-.37278
.13250	-.21981	-.23465	-.24951	-.26439	-.27928	-.29418	-.30910	-.32403	-.33898	-.35393
.13500	-.20291	-.21758	-.23227	-.24697	-.26169	-.27642	-.29116	-.30592	-.32069	-.33547
.13750	-.18638	-.20087	-.21539	-.22992	-.24446	-.25902	-.27360	-.28818	-.30278	-.31739
.14000	-.17019	-.18452	-.19886	-.21322	-.22760	-.24199	-.25639	-.27081	-.28524	-.29968
.14250	-.15433	-.16850	-.18268	-.19687	-.21108	-.22531	-.23955	-.25380	-.26807	-.28234
.14500	-.13881	-.15281	-.16683	-.18086	-.19491	-.20897	-.22305	-.23714	-.25124	-.26536
.14750	-.12361	-.13745	-.15130	-.16518	-.17907	-.19297	-.20689	-.22082	-.23476	-.24872
.15000	-.10872	-.12240	-.13610	-.14982	-.16355	-.17730	-.19106	-.20483	-.21862	-.23242
.15250	-.09413	-.10766	-.12121	-.13477	-.14835	-.16194	-.17555	-.18917	-.20280	-.21645
.15500	-.07985	-.09322	-.10662	-.12003	-.13346	-.14690	-.16036	-.17383	-.18731	-.20080
.15750	-.06585	-.07908	-.09233	-.10559	-.11887	-.13216	-.14547	-.15879	-.17213	-.18547
.16000	-.05214	-.06522	-.07832	-.09144	-.10457	-.11772	-.13088	-.14406	-.15725	-.17045
.16250	-.03871	-.05165	-.06460	-.07758	-.09057	-.10357	-.11659	-.12962	-.14267	-.15572
.16500	-.02554	-.03834	-.05116	-.06399	-.07684	-.08970	-.10258	-.11547	-.12838	-.14129
.16750	-.01264	-.02530	-.03798	-.05068	-.06339	-.07611	-.08885	-.10160	-.11437	-.12715
.17000	.00000	-.01252	-.02507	-.03762	-.05020	-.06279	-.07539	-.08801	-.10064	-.11328
.17250	.01239	.00000	-.01241	-.02483	-.03727	-.04973	-.06220	-.07468	-.08718	-.09968
.17500	.02454	.01228	.00000	-.01229	-.02460	-.03693	-.04926	-.06162	-.07398	-.08636
.17750	.03644	.02431	.01216	.00000	-.01218	-.02437	-.03658	-.04881	-.06104	-.07329
.18000	.04811	.03611	.02409	.01205	.00000	-.01207	-.02415	-.03624	-.04835	-.06047
.18250	.05956	.04768	.03578	.02387	.01194	.00000	-.01196	-.02393	-.03591	-.04791
.18500	.07078	.05902	.04725	.03546	.02365	.01183	.00000	-.01185	-.02371	-.03558
.18750	.08178	.07014	.05849	.04682	.03514	.02344	.01173	.00000	-.01174	-.02349
.19000	.09257	.08105	.06952	.05797	.04640	.03482	.02323	.01162	0.00000	-.01163
.19250	.10315	.09175	.08033	.06890	.05745	.04599	.03451	.02302	.01152	.00000
.19500	.11353	.10225	.09094	.07963	.06829	.05694	.04558	.03420	.02281	.01141
.19750	.12371	.11254	.10135	.09015	.07892	.06769	.05644	.04518	.03390	.02261
.20000	.13370	.12264	.11156	.10047	.08936	.07823	.06709	.05594	.04478	.03360
.20250	.14350	.13255	.12158	.11059	.09959	.08858	.07755	.06650	.05545	.04438
.20500	.15311	.14227	.13141	.12053	.10964	.09873	.08781	.07687	.06592	.05496
.20750	.16255	.15181	.14105	.13028	.11949	.10869	.09787	.08705	.07620	.06535

EFFECTIVE YIELD	CONTRACT RATE .19500	.19750	.20000	.20250	.20500	.20750
.07000	-.99374	-1.01431	-1.03488	-1.05546	-1.07604	-1.09662
.07250	-.96151	-.98180	-1.00210	-1.02239	-1.04269	-1.06299
.07500	-.93001	-.95002	-.97004	-.99007	-1.01009	-1.03012
.07750	-.89921	-.91896	-.93871	-.95847	-.97823	-.99799
.08000	-.86910	-.88859	-.90808	-.92757	-.94707	-.96657
.08250	-.83967	-.85890	-.87813	-.89736	-.91660	-.93584
.08500	-.81089	-.82986	-.84884	-.86782	-.88681	-.90580
.08750	-.78275	-.80147	-.82020	-.83894	-.85768	-.87642
.09000	-.75523	-.77371	-.79220	-.81069	-.82918	-.84769
.09250	-.72831	-.74656	-.76480	-.78306	-.80132	-.81958
.09500	-.70199	-.72000	-.73801	-.75603	-.77406	-.79209
.09750	-.67625	-.69402	-.71181	-.72960	-.74740	-.76520
.10000	-.65106	-.66862	-.68617	-.70374	-.72131	-.73889
.10250	-.62643	-.64376	-.66110	-.67844	-.69579	-.71315
.10500	-.60233	-.61944	-.63656	-.65369	-.67082	-.68796
.10750	-.57874	-.59565	-.61255	-.62947	-.64639	-.66332
.11000	-.55567	-.57236	-.58906	-.60577	-.62248	-.63920
.11250	-.53309	-.54958	-.56607	-.58258	-.59908	-.61560
.11500	-.51100	-.52728	-.54358	-.55988	-.57618	-.59250
.11750	-.48938	-.50546	-.52156	-.53766	-.55377	-.56989
.12000	-.46821	-.48410	-.50001	-.51591	-.53183	-.54775
.12250	-.44750	-.46320	-.47891	-.49463	-.51035	-.52608
.12500	-.42722	-.44273	-.45825	-.47379	-.48933	-.50487
.12750	-.40736	-.42269	-.43803	-.45338	-.46874	-.48410
.13000	-.38793	-.40308	-.41824	-.43340	-.44858	-.46376
.13250	-.36889	-.38387	-.39885	-.41384	-.42884	-.44385
.13500	-.35026	-.36506	-.37987	-.39468	-.40951	-.42434
.13750	-.33201	-.34664	-.36127	-.37592	-.39058	-.40524
.14000	-.31413	-.32860	-.34307	-.35755	-.37203	-.38653
.14250	-.29663	-.31092	-.32523	-.33955	-.35387	-.36820
.14500	-.27948	-.29362	-.30776	-.32191	-.33607	-.35024
.14750	-.26268	-.27666	-.29064	-.30464	-.31864	-.33265
.15000	-.24623	-.26005	-.27388	-.28771	-.30156	-.31541
.15250	-.23011	-.24377	-.25745	-.27113	-.28482	-.29853
.15500	-.21431	-.22782	-.24135	-.25488	-.26842	-.28197
.15750	-.19883	-.21219	-.22557	-.23896	-.25235	-.26575
.16000	-.18366	-.19688	-.21011	-.22335	-.23660	-.24986
.16250	-.16879	-.18187	-.19496	-.20805	-.22116	-.23427
.16500	-.15422	-.16716	-.18010	-.19306	-.20603	-.21900
.16750	-.13993	-.15273	-.16554	-.17836	-.19119	-.20402
.17000	-.12593	-.13859	-.15127	-.16395	-.17664	-.18934
.17250	-.11220	-.12473	-.13727	-.14982	-.16238	-.17495
.17500	-.09874	-.11114	-.12355	-.13597	-.14840	-.16083
.17750	-.08555	-.09782	-.11009	-.12238	-.13468	-.14699
.18000	-.07260	-.08475	-.09690	-.10906	-.12123	-.13341
.18250	-.05991	-.07193	-.08396	-.09599	-.10804	-.12010
.18500	-.04746	-.05936	-.07126	-.08318	-.09510	-.10703
.18750	-.03525	-.04703	-.05881	-.07061	-.08241	-.09422
.19000	-.02328	-.03493	-.04660	-.05827	-.06996	-.08165
.19250	-.01153	-.02307	-.03462	-.04617	-.05774	-.06932
.19500	.00000	-.01142	-.02286	-.03430	-.04575	-.05722
.19750	.01131	0.00000	-.01132	-.02265	-.03399	-.04534
.20000	.02241	.01121	.00000	-.01122	-.02245	-.03369
.20250	.03330	.02221	.01111	0.00000	-.01112	-.02225
.20500	.04399	.03301	.02201	.01101	.00000	-.01102
.20750	.05448	.04361	.03272	.02182	.01092	.00000

POINT TABLES: ORIGINAL LOAN TERM: 300 MONTHS LOAN PREPAID IN: 180 MONTHS

EFFECTIVE YIELD	CONTRACT RATE .07000	.07250	.07500	.07750	.08000	.08250	.08500	.08750	.09000	.09250
.07000	.00000	-.02027	-.04070	-.06127	-.08198	-.10284	-.12383	-.14494	-.16619	-.18756
.07250	.01991	0.00000	-.02006	-.04026	-.06061	-.08109	-.10171	-.12246	-.14333	-.16432
.07500	.03926	.01970	0.00000	-.01985	-.03983	-.05996	-.08021	-.10059	-.12110	-.14172
.07750	.05806	.03885	.01950	-.00000	-.01964	-.03941	-.05931	-.07934	-.09949	-.11975
.08000	.07635	.05747	.03846	.01930	.00000	-.01943	-.03899	-.05867	-.07847	-.09839
.08250	.09412	.07558	.05689	.03806	.01909	.00000	-.01922	-.03857	-.05803	-.07761
.08500	.11141	.09318	.07481	.05630	.03766	.01890	.00000	-.01902	-.03815	-.05740
.08750	.12821	.11030	.09224	.07405	.05573	.03727	.01870	.00000	-.01881	-.03774
.09000	.14456	.12695	.10920	.09131	.07329	.05515	.03688	.01850	.00000	-.01861
.09250	.16046	.14314	.12569	.10810	.09038	.07254	.05458	.03650	.01831	.00000
.09500	.17593	.15890	.14173	.12444	.10701	.08947	.07180	.05401	.03612	.01811
.09750	.19098	.17423	.15734	.14033	.12319	.10593	.08855	.07106	.05345	.03574
.10000	.20562	.18914	.17254	.15580	.13894	.12196	.10486	.08765	.07033	.05290
.10250	.21987	.20366	.18732	.17085	.15427	.13756	.12073	.10380	.08675	.06960
.10500	.23374	.21779	.20171	.18551	.16918	.15274	.13619	.11952	.10274	.08586
.10750	.24723	.23154	.21572	.19977	.18371	.16753	.15123	.13482	.11831	.10169
.11000	.26037	.24493	.22936	.21366	.19785	.18192	.16588	.14973	.13347	.11711
.11250	.27317	.25796	.24264	.22719	.21162	.19594	.18014	.16424	.14824	.13213
.11500	.28563	.27066	.25557	.24036	.22503	.20959	.19404	.17838	.16262	.14676
.11750	.29776	.28302	.26816	.25318	.23809	.22288	.20757	.19215	.17663	.16101
.12000	.30957	.29506	.28043	.26568	.25081	.23584	.22075	.20557	.19028	.17489
.12250	.32108	.30679	.29238	.27785	.26321	.24846	.23360	.21864	.20358	.18842
.12500	.33230	.31822	.30402	.28971	.27528	.26075	.24612	.23138	.21654	.20160
.12750	.34322	.32935	.31537	.30126	.28705	.27274	.25831	.24379	.22917	.21445
.13000	.35387	.34020	.32642	.31253	.29852	.28442	.27020	.25589	.24148	.22698
.13250	.36425	.35078	.33720	.32350	.30971	.29580	.28179	.26769	.25349	.23919
.13500	.37436	.36109	.34770	.33421	.32060	.30690	.29309	.27919	.26519	.25110
.13750	.38422	.37113	.35794	.34464	.33123	.31772	.30411	.29040	.27660	.26271
.14000	.39383	.38093	.36793	.35481	.34159	.32827	.31486	.30134	.28773	.27404
.14250	.40320	.39049	.37766	.36473	.35170	.33857	.32533	.31201	.29859	.28508
.14500	.41234	.39980	.38716	.37441	.36156	.34860	.33556	.32241	.30918	.29586
.14750	.42125	.40889	.39642	.38384	.37117	.35840	.34553	.33256	.31951	.30637
.15000	.42995	.41775	.40545	.39305	.38055	.36795	.35526	.34247	.32959	.31663
.15250	.43843	.42640	.41427	.40204	.38970	.37727	.36475	.35213	.33943	.32664
.15500	.44671	.43484	.42287	.41080	.39863	.38637	.37401	.36157	.34903	.33641
.15750	.45479	.44308	.43127	.41936	.40735	.39525	.38306	.37077	.35840	.34595
.16000	.46267	.45111	.43946	.42771	.41586	.40392	.39188	.37976	.36755	.35526
.16250	.47036	.45896	.44746	.43586	.42416	.41238	.40050	.38854	.37649	.36436
.16500	.47787	.46662	.45527	.44382	.43227	.42064	.40892	.39711	.38521	.37323
.16750	.48521	.47410	.46289	.45159	.44019	.42871	.41713	.40547	.39373	.38191
.17000	.49237	.48140	.47034	.45918	.44793	.43659	.42516	.41365	.40205	.39038
.17250	.49936	.48853	.47761	.46659	.45548	.44429	.43300	.42163	.41018	.39865
.17500	.50619	.49550	.48471	.47383	.46286	.45180	.44066	.42943	.41813	.40674
.17750	.51286	.50231	.49165	.48091	.47007	.45915	.44815	.43706	.42589	.41464
.18000	.51938	.50895	.49843	.48782	.47712	.46633	.45546	.44451	.43347	.42236
.18250	.52575	.51545	.50506	.49457	.48400	.47335	.46261	.45179	.44089	.42991
.18500	.53198	.52180	.51153	.50118	.49073	.48020	.46959	.45890	.44813	.43729
.18750	.53806	.52801	.51786	.50763	.49731	.48691	.47642	.46586	.45522	.44450
.19000	.54401	.53408	.52405	.51394	.50374	.49346	.48310	.47266	.46215	.45156
.19250	.54983	.54001	.53010	.52011	.51003	.49987	.48963	.47931	.46892	.45845
.19500	.55551	.54581	.53602	.52614	.51618	.50614	.49602	.48582	.47555	.46520
.19750	.56107	.55148	.54180	.53204	.52220	.51227	.50227	.49218	.48203	.47180
.20000	.56651	.55703	.54746	.53781	.52808	.51827	.50838	.49841	.48837	.47826
.20250	.57183	.56246	.55300	.54346	.53383	.52413	.51435	.50450	.49457	.48458
.20500	.57703	.56776	.55841	.54898	.53947	.52987	.52020	.51046	.50065	.49076
.20750	.58212	.57296	.56371	.55439	.54498	.53549	.52593	.51629	.50659	.49681

POINT TABLES: ORIGINAL LOAN TERM: 300 MONTHS LOAN PREPAID IN: 180 MONTHS

EFFECTIVE YIELD	CONTRACT RATE .09500	.09750	.10000	.10250	.10500	.10750	.11000	.11250	.11500	.11750
.07000	-.20904	-.23064	-.25234	-.27416	-.29607	-.31808	-.34018	-.36237	-.38465	-.40701
.07250	-.18542	-.20664	-.22797	-.24940	-.27093	-.29256	-.31428	-.33609	-.35798	-.37995
.07500	-.16246	-.18331	-.20427	-.22533	-.24649	-.26774	-.28909	-.31052	-.33204	-.35364
.07750	-.14013	-.16062	-.18122	-.20192	-.22271	-.24361	-.26459	-.28566	-.30681	-.32804
.08000	-.11842	-.13856	-.15880	-.17915	-.19959	-.22013	-.24076	-.26147	-.28226	-.30314
.08250	-.09730	-.11710	-.13700	-.15700	-.17710	-.19729	-.21757	-.23794	-.25839	-.27891
.08500	-.07676	-.09622	-.11579	-.13546	-.15522	-.17507	-.19502	-.21504	-.23515	-.25534
.08750	-.05677	-.07592	-.09516	-.11450	-.13393	-.15346	-.17307	-.19277	-.21254	-.23240
.09000	-.03733	-.05615	-.07508	-.09410	-.11322	-.13242	-.15171	-.17109	-.19054	-.21007
.09250	-.01841	-.03693	-.05554	-.07425	-.09305	-.11195	-.13093	-.14999	-.16913	-.18834
.09500	-.00000	-.01821	-.03653	-.05493	-.07343	-.09202	-.11069	-.12945	-.14828	-.16719
.09750	.01792	0.00000	-.01802	-.03613	-.05433	-.07262	-.09100	-.10945	-.12798	-.14659
.10000	.03536	.01773	0.00000	-.01782	-.03574	-.05374	-.07182	-.08998	-.10822	-.12654
.10250	.05234	.03499	.01754	.00000	-.01763	-.03535	-.05315	-.07102	-.08898	-.10701
.10500	.06888	.05180	.03462	.01735	.00000	-.01744	-.03496	-.05256	-.07024	-.08799
.10750	.08498	.06816	.05125	.03426	.01717	.00000	-.01725	-.03458	-.05199	-.06946
.11000	.10065	.08410	.06745	.05072	.03389	.01699	0.00000	-.01706	-.03420	-.05141
.11250	.11592	.09962	.08323	.06675	.05018	.03353	.01681	.00000	-.01638	-.03383
.11500	.13080	.11475	.09860	.08237	.06606	.04966	.03318	.01663	.00000	-.01670
.11750	.14529	.12948	.11358	.09759	.08152	.06537	.04914	.03283	.01645	0.00000
.12000	.15941	.14383	.12817	.11242	.09659	.08068	.06468	.04862	.03248	.01627
.12250	.17317	.15782	.14239	.12687	.11128	.09560	.07984	.06401	.04811	.03214
.12500	.18658	.17146	.15625	.14096	.12559	.11014	.09461	.07901	.06334	.04760
.12750	.19965	.18475	.16976	.15469	.13955	.12432	.10902	.09364	.07819	.06268
.13000	.21239	.19770	.18293	.16808	.15315	.13814	.12306	.10790	.09268	.07738
.13250	.22481	.21033	.19578	.18114	.16642	.15162	.13675	.12181	.10680	.09172
.13500	.23692	.22265	.20830	.19387	.17936	.16477	.15011	.13538	.12057	.10571
.13750	.24873	.23466	.22051	.20628	.19197	.17759	.16313	.14861	.13401	.11935
.14000	.26025	.24638	.23243	.21839	.20428	.19010	.17584	.16151	.14712	.13266
.14250	.27149	.25781	.24405	.23021	.21629	.20230	.18824	.17411	.15991	.14565
.14500	.28245	.26896	.25538	.24173	.22801	.21421	.20034	.18640	.17239	.15833
.14750	.29314	.27984	.26645	.25298	.23944	.22583	.21214	.19839	.18458	.17070
.15000	.30358	.29045	.27724	.26396	.25060	.23717	.22367	.21010	.19647	.18277
.15250	.31377	.30081	.28778	.27467	.26149	.24824	.23491	.22153	.20807	.19456
.15500	.32371	.31093	.29807	.28513	.27212	.25904	.24590	.23268	.21941	.20607
.15750	.33341	.32080	.30811	.29534	.28250	.26959	.25662	.24358	.23047	.21731
.16000	.34289	.33044	.31791	.30531	.29264	.27990	.26709	.25421	.24128	.22828
.16250	.35214	.33985	.32749	.31505	.30254	.28996	.27731	.26460	.25183	.23900
.16500	.36118	.34905	.33684	.32456	.31221	.29979	.28730	.27475	.26214	.24947
.16750	.37000	.35802	.34597	.33384	.32165	.30939	.29706	.28467	.27222	.25971
.17000	.37862	.36680	.35489	.34292	.33088	.31877	.30659	.29436	.28206	.26970
.17250	.38705	.37536	.36361	.35178	.33989	.32793	.31591	.30382	.29168	.27947
.17500	.39528	.38374	.37213	.36045	.34870	.33689	.32501	.31307	.30108	.28902
.17750	.40332	.39192	.38045	.36892	.35731	.34564	.33391	.32212	.31026	.29835
.18000	.41118	.39992	.38859	.37719	.36573	.35420	.34261	.33096	.31925	.30748
.18250	.41886	.40774	.39654	.38528	.37395	.36256	.35111	.33960	.32803	.31640
.18500	.42637	.41538	.40432	.39319	.38200	.37074	.35943	.34805	.33662	.32513
.18750	.43371	.42285	.41192	.40093	.38987	.37874	.36756	.35631	.34501	.33366
.19000	.44089	.43016	.41936	.40849	.39756	.38656	.37551	.36440	.35323	.34201
.19250	.44792	.43731	.42663	.41589	.40508	.39422	.38329	.37230	.36126	.35017
.19500	.45478	.44430	.43374	.42313	.41244	.40170	.39090	.38004	.36913	.35816
.19750	.46150	.45114	.44070	.43021	.41965	.40902	.39835	.38761	.37682	.36598
.20000	.46808	.45783	.44751	.43713	.42669	.41619	.40563	.39502	.38435	.37362
.20250	.47451	.46437	.45418	.44391	.43359	.42320	.41276	.40227	.39172	.38111
.20500	.48080	.47078	.46070	.45055	.44034	.43007	.41974	.40936	.39893	.38844
.20750	.48697	.47705	.46708	.45704	.44694	.43679	.42658	.41631	.40599	.39562

POINT TABLES: ORIGINAL LOAN TERM: 300 MONTHS LOAN PREPAID IN: 180 MONTHS

EFFECTIVE YIELD	CONTRACT RATE .12000	.12250	.12500	.12750	.13000	.13250	.13500	.13750	.14000	.14250
.07000	-.42945	-.45196	-.47455	-.49720	-.51992	-.54270	-.56554	-.58844	-.61139	-.63439
.07250	-.40201	-.42413	-.44633	-.46860	-.49093	-.51332	-.53577	-.55828	-.58084	-.60345
.07500	-.37531	-.39706	-.41888	-.44077	-.46272	-.48474	-.50681	-.52894	-.55112	-.57335
.07750	-.34935	-.37073	-.39218	-.41370	-.43529	-.45693	-.47863	-.50039	-.52220	-.54407
.08000	-.32409	-.34511	-.36621	-.38737	-.40859	-.42988	-.45122	-.47262	-.49407	-.51557
.08250	-.29951	-.32019	-.34093	-.36174	-.38262	-.40355	-.42454	-.44559	-.46658	-.48783
.08500	-.27560	-.29593	-.31634	-.33680	-.35734	-.37793	-.39857	-.41928	-.44003	-.46083
.08750	-.25233	-.27233	-.29240	-.31253	-.33273	-.35299	-.37330	-.39367	-.41409	-.43456
.09000	-.22968	-.24936	-.26910	-.28891	-.30878	-.32871	-.34870	-.36874	-.38883	-.40897
.09250	-.20763	-.22699	-.24642	-.26591	-.28546	-.30508	-.32474	-.34447	-.36424	-.38406
.09500	-.18617	-.20522	-.22434	-.24352	-.26276	-.28206	-.30142	-.32083	-.34029	-.35980
.09750	-.16527	-.18402	-.20284	-.22172	-.24066	-.25965	-.27871	-.29781	-.31697	-.33618
.10000	-.14493	-.16338	-.18190	-.20049	-.21913	-.23783	-.25659	-.27540	-.29426	-.31317
.10250	-.12511	-.14328	-.16151	-.17981	-.19816	-.21657	-.23504	-.25356	-.27213	-.29075
.10500	-.10581	-.12370	-.14165	-.15966	-.17774	-.19587	-.21405	-.23229	-.25058	-.26891
.10750	-.08701	-.10462	-.12230	-.14004	-.15784	-.17569	-.19360	-.21156	-.22957	-.24763
.11000	-.06870	-.08604	-.10345	-.12092	-.13845	-.15604	-.17368	-.19137	-.20911	-.22690
.11250	-.05085	-.06794	-.08508	-.10229	-.11956	-.13688	-.15426	-.17169	-.18916	-.20669
.11500	-.03346	-.05029	-.06719	-.08414	-.10115	-.11822	-.13534	-.15251	-.16972	-.18699
.11750	-.01652	-.03310	-.04974	-.06644	-.08321	-.10002	-.11689	-.13381	-.15077	-.16779
.12000	.00000	-.01634	-.03274	-.04920	-.06571	-.08228	-.09891	-.11558	-.13230	-.14906
.12250	.01610	0.00000	-.01616	-.03238	-.04866	-.06499	-.08137	-.09780	-.11428	-.13081
.12500	.03180	.01593	.00000	-.01599	-.03203	-.04813	-.06428	-.08047	-.09672	-.11301
.12750	.04710	.03146	.01576	.00000	-.01581	-.03168	-.04760	-.06357	-.07959	-.09564
.13000	.06203	.04661	.03113	.01559	.00000	-.01564	-.03134	-.04708	-.06287	-.07871
.13250	.07658	.06138	.04612	.03080	.01543	0.00000	-.01548	-.03100	-.04657	-.06219
.13500	.09078	.07579	.06074	.04563	.03047	.01526	.00000	-.01531	-.03067	-.04607
.13750	.10463	.08985	.07500	.06011	.04516	.03015	.01510	.00000	-.01515	-.03034
.14000	.11814	.10356	.08892	.07423	.05948	.04468	.02984	.01494	.00000	-.01498
.14250	.13133	.11695	.10251	.08801	.07346	.05886	.04422	.02952	.01478	0.00000
.14500	.14420	.13001	.11576	.10146	.08711	.07271	.05825	.04376	.02921	.01463
.14750	.15676	.14276	.12870	.11459	.10043	.08622	.07196	.05765	.04330	.02891
.15000	.16901	.15520	.14133	.12741	.11343	.09941	.08534	.07122	.05705	.04285
.15250	.18098	.16735	.15366	.13992	.12613	.11229	.09840	.08446	.07049	.05647
.15500	.19267	.17921	.16571	.15214	.13853	.12487	.11116	.09740	.08360	.06976
.15750	.20408	.19080	.17746	.16408	.15064	.13715	.12362	.11004	.09642	.08275
.16000	.21523	.20212	.18895	.17573	.16247	.14915	.13579	.12238	.10893	.09544
.16250	.22611	.21317	.20017	.18712	.17402	.16087	.14768	.13444	.12116	.10784
.16500	.23675	.22397	.21113	.19825	.18531	.17233	.15930	.14623	.13311	.11996
.16750	.24714	.23452	.22184	.20912	.19634	.18352	.17065	.15774	.14479	.13180
.17000	.25729	.24482	.23231	.21974	.20712	.19446	.18175	.16900	.15620	.14337
.17250	.26721	.25490	.24254	.23012	.21766	.20515	.19259	.18000	.16736	.15468
.17500	.27691	.26475	.25253	.24027	.22796	.21560	.20320	.19075	.17827	.16574
.17750	.28639	.27437	.26231	.25019	.23803	.22582	.21356	.20127	.18893	.17656
.18000	.29566	.28379	.27186	.25989	.24787	.23581	.22370	.21155	.19936	.18713
.18250	.30472	.29299	.28121	.26938	.25750	.24558	.23361	.22161	.20956	.19747
.18500	.31358	.30199	.29035	.27865	.26692	.25513	.24331	.23144	.21953	.20759
.18750	.32225	.31079	.29928	.28773	.27613	.26448	.25279	.24106	.22929	.21749
.19000	.33073	.31940	.30803	.29661	.28514	.27362	.26207	.25048	.23884	.22717
.19250	.33902	.32783	.31658	.30529	.29395	.28257	.27115	.25969	.24818	.23665
.19500	.34714	.33607	.32495	.31379	.30258	.29133	.28003	.26870	.25733	.24592
.19750	.35508	.34414	.33314	.32210	.31102	.29990	.28873	.27752	.26628	.25500
.20000	.36285	.35203	.34116	.33024	.31928	.30828	.29724	.28616	.27504	.26388
.20250	.37046	.35976	.34901	.33821	.32737	.31649	.30557	.29461	.28361	.27258
.20500	.37790	.36732	.35669	.34601	.33529	.32453	.31373	.30289	.29201	.28110
.20750	.38519	.37473	.36421	.35365	.34305	.33240	.32172	.31099	.30023	.28944

EFFECTIVE YIELD	CONTRACT RATE .14500	.14750	.15000	.15250	.15500	.15750	.16000	.16250	.16500	.16750
.07000	-.65743	-.68053	-.70366	-.72684	-.75005	-.77330	-.79659	-.81990	-.84325	-.86662
.07250	-.62611	-.64881	-.67156	-.69434	-.71717	-.74003	-.76292	-.78585	-.80880	-.83179
.07500	-.59563	-.61795	-.64032	-.66273	-.68517	-.70765	-.73017	-.75271	-.77529	-.79789
.07750	-.56597	-.58793	-.60992	-.63196	-.65403	-.67614	-.69829	-.72046	-.74267	-.76490
.08000	-.53711	-.55871	-.58034	-.60201	-.62373	-.64547	-.66726	-.68907	-.71092	-.73279
.08250	-.50903	-.53026	-.55155	-.57287	-.59423	-.61562	-.63705	-.65851	-.68000	-.70152
.08500	-.48169	-.50258	-.52352	-.54450	-.56551	-.58656	-.60765	-.62876	-.64991	-.67109
.08750	-.45507	-.47563	-.49623	-.51687	-.53755	-.55827	-.57902	-.59980	-.62061	-.64145
.09000	-.42916	-.44939	-.46966	-.48995	-.51033	-.53072	-.55114	-.57159	-.59207	-.61258
.09250	-.40393	-.42384	-.44379	-.46379	-.48382	-.50388	-.52398	-.54412	-.56428	-.58447
.09500	-.37936	-.39896	-.41860	-.43828	-.45800	-.47775	-.49754	-.51736	-.53721	-.55709
.09750	-.35543	-.37472	-.39406	-.41343	-.43285	-.45230	-.47178	-.49129	-.51084	-.53041
.10000	-.33212	-.35112	-.37015	-.38923	-.40835	-.42750	-.44668	-.46590	-.48514	-.50442
.10250	-.30941	-.32812	-.34687	-.36565	-.38448	-.40334	-.42223	-.44115	-.46011	-.47909
.10500	-.28729	-.30571	-.32418	-.34268	-.36122	-.37979	-.39840	-.41704	-.43571	-.45441
.10750	-.26573	-.28388	-.30207	-.32029	-.33855	-.35685	-.37518	-.39354	-.41193	-.43035
.11000	-.24473	-.26260	-.28052	-.29847	-.31646	-.33449	-.35255	-.37064	-.38876	-.40690
.11250	-.22425	-.24186	-.25951	-.27720	-.29493	-.31269	-.33048	-.34831	-.36616	-.38404
.11500	-.20430	-.22165	-.23904	-.25647	-.27394	-.29144	-.30897	-.32654	-.34413	-.36176
.11750	-.18484	-.20194	-.21908	-.23626	-.25347	-.27072	-.28800	-.30531	-.32265	-.34002
.12000	-.16587	-.18273	-.19962	-.21655	-.23351	-.25051	-.26755	-.28461	-.30170	-.31882
.12250	-.14738	-.16399	-.18064	-.19733	-.21405	-.23081	-.24760	-.26442	-.28127	-.29815
.12500	-.12934	-.14572	-.16213	-.17858	-.19507	-.21159	-.22814	-.24473	-.26134	-.27798
.12750	-.11175	-.12789	-.14407	-.16029	-.17655	-.19284	-.20916	-.22552	-.24190	-.25831
.13000	-.09459	-.11050	-.12646	-.14246	-.15849	-.17455	-.19065	-.20677	-.22293	-.23911
.13250	-.07784	-.09354	-.10928	-.12505	-.14086	-.15670	-.17258	-.18848	-.20442	-.22038
.13500	-.06151	-.07699	-.09251	-.10807	-.12366	-.13929	-.15495	-.17063	-.18635	-.20210
.13750	-.04557	-.06084	-.07615	-.09149	-.10688	-.12229	-.13774	-.15321	-.16872	-.18425
.14000	-.03001	-.04507	-.06018	-.07532	-.09049	-.10570	-.12094	-.13621	-.15151	-.16683
.14250	-.01482	-.02969	-.04459	-.05953	-.07450	-.08950	-.10454	-.11961	-.13470	-.14982
.14500	.00000	-.01467	-.02937	-.04411	-.05888	-.07369	-.08853	-.10340	-.11829	-.13321
.14750	.01447	0.00000	-.01451	-.02906	-.04364	-.05825	-.07289	-.08757	-.10227	-.11700
.15000	.02860	.01432	.00000	-.01436	-.02875	-.04317	-.05762	-.07211	-.08652	-.10116
.15250	.04241	.02831	.01417	0.00000	-.01420	-.02844	-.04271	-.05701	-.07133	-.08568
.15500	.05588	.04197	.02801	.01402	.00000	-.01406	-.02814	-.04226	-.05640	-.07057
.15750	.06905	.05531	.04153	.02772	.01388	.00000	-.01391	-.02784	-.04181	-.05580
.16000	.08191	.06835	.05474	.04111	.02744	.01373	.00000	-.01376	-.02755	-.04137
.16250	.09448	.08109	.06765	.05418	.04068	.02715	.01359	0.00000	-.01362	-.02726
.16500	.10676	.09353	.08027	.06697	.05363	.04027	.02687	.01345	-.00000	-.01348
.16750	.11877	.10570	.09259	.07946	.06629	.05309	.03986	.02660	.01331	.00000
.17000	.13050	.11759	.10465	.09167	.07866	.06562	.05255	.03945	.02633	.01318
.17250	.14197	.12921	.11643	.10361	.09075	.07787	.06496	.05202	.03905	.02606
.17500	.15318	.14058	.12795	.11528	.10258	.08985	.07709	.06431	.05149	.03866
.17750	.16414	.15169	.13921	.12669	.11415	.10157	.08896	.07633	.06356	.05098
.18000	.17486	.16256	.15023	.13786	.12546	.11303	.10057	.08808	.07557	.06303
.18250	.18535	.17319	.16100	.14878	.13652	.12424	.11192	.09958	.08721	.07482
.18500	.19561	.18359	.17154	.15946	.14735	.13520	.12303	.11083	.09861	.08636
.18750	.20564	.19377	.18185	.16991	.15794	.14593	.13390	.12184	.10976	.09765
.19000	.21546	.20372	.19194	.18014	.16830	.15643	.14454	.13261	.12067	.10869
.19250	.22507	.21346	.20182	.19015	.17844	.16671	.15495	.14316	.13134	.11951
.19500	.23447	.22300	.21148	.19994	.18837	.17677	.16514	.15348	.14180	.13009
.19750	.24368	.23233	.22094	.20953	.19808	.18661	.17511	.16358	.15203	.14045
.20000	.25269	.24146	.23021	.21892	.20760	.19625	.18488	.17348	.16205	.15060
.20250	.26151	.25041	.23927	.22811	.21691	.20569	.19444	.18316	.17186	.16054
.20500	.27015	.25917	.24815	.23711	.22604	.21493	.20381	.19265	.18147	.17027
.20750	.27861	.26774	.25685	.24592	.23497	.22399	.21298	.20194	.19088	.17980

POINT TABLES: ORIGINAL LOAN TERM: 300 MONTHS LOAN PREPAID IN: 180 MONTHS

EFFECTIVE YIELD	CONTRACT RATE .17000	.17250	.17500	.17750	.18000	.18250	.18500	.18750	.19000	.19250
.07000	-.89002	-.91344	-.93688	-.96035	-.98383	-1.00733	-1.03085	-1.05439	-1.07793	-1.10149
.07250	-.85480	-.87783	-.90089	-.92396	-.94706	-.97017	-.99330	-1.01645	-1.03961	-1.06278
.07500	-.82052	-.84318	-.86585	-.88855	-.91127	-.93400	-.95676	-.97953	-1.00231	-1.02510
.07750	-.78716	-.80944	-.83175	-.85408	-.87643	-.89880	-.92118	-.94358	-.96599	-.98842
.08000	-.75469	-.77661	-.79856	-.82052	-.84251	-.86452	-.88654	-.90858	-.93063	-.95270
.08250	-.72307	-.74464	-.76623	-.78785	-.80949	-.83114	-.85281	-.87450	-.89620	-.91792
.08500	-.69229	-.71351	-.73476	-.75604	-.77733	-.79864	-.81997	-.84131	-.86267	-.88405
.08750	-.66231	-.68320	-.70412	-.72505	-.74601	-.76699	-.78798	-.80899	-.83002	-.85106
.09000	-.63312	-.65368	-.67427	-.69488	-.71551	-.73616	-.75682	-.77751	-.79820	-.81892
.09250	-.60469	-.62493	-.64520	-.66549	-.68579	-.70612	-.72647	-.74683	-.76721	-.78761
.09500	-.57699	-.59692	-.61688	-.63685	-.65685	-.67686	-.69690	-.71695	-.73702	-.75710
.09750	-.55001	-.56963	-.58928	-.60895	-.62864	-.64836	-.66809	-.68783	-.70760	-.72737
.10000	-.52372	-.54305	-.56240	-.58177	-.60116	-.62058	-.64001	-.65946	-.67892	-.69840
.10250	-.49810	-.51714	-.53620	-.55528	-.57438	-.59350	-.61264	-.63180	-.65097	-.67016
.10500	-.47313	-.49189	-.51066	-.52946	-.54827	-.56711	-.58597	-.60484	-.62373	-.64264
.10750	-.44880	-.46727	-.48577	-.50429	-.52283	-.54139	-.55997	-.57856	-.59717	-.61580
.11000	-.42508	-.44328	-.46150	-.47975	-.49802	-.51631	-.53461	-.55294	-.57128	-.58964
.11250	-.40195	-.41989	-.43785	-.45583	-.47383	-.49185	-.50990	-.52795	-.54603	-.56412
.11500	-.37941	-.39708	-.41478	-.43250	-.45024	-.46801	-.48579	-.50359	-.52141	-.53924
.11750	-.35742	-.37484	-.39228	-.40975	-.42724	-.44475	-.46228	-.47982	-.49739	-.51497
.12000	-.33597	-.35315	-.37034	-.38756	-.40480	-.42207	-.43935	-.45664	-.47396	-.49129
.12250	-.31506	-.33199	-.34894	-.36592	-.38292	-.39994	-.41697	-.43403	-.45110	-.46819
.12500	-.29465	-.31135	-.32806	-.34480	-.36156	-.37835	-.39515	-.41197	-.42880	-.44565
.12750	-.27475	-.29121	-.30769	-.32420	-.34073	-.35728	-.37385	-.39043	-.40704	-.42366
.13000	-.25532	-.27156	-.28782	-.30410	-.32040	-.33672	-.35306	-.36942	-.38580	-.40219
.13250	-.23637	-.25238	-.26842	-.28448	-.30056	-.31666	-.33278	-.34891	-.36507	-.38124
.13500	-.21787	-.23366	-.24948	-.26532	-.28119	-.29707	-.31297	-.32889	-.34483	-.36078
.13750	-.19981	-.21539	-.23100	-.24663	-.26228	-.27795	-.29364	-.30935	-.32507	-.34081
.14000	-.18218	-.19756	-.21296	-.22838	-.24382	-.25928	-.27477	-.29026	-.30578	-.32131
.14250	-.16497	-.18014	-.19534	-.21056	-.22580	-.24105	-.25633	-.27163	-.28694	-.30227
.14500	-.14816	-.16314	-.17813	-.19315	-.20819	-.22325	-.23833	-.25343	-.26854	-.28367
.14750	-.13175	-.14653	-.16133	-.17616	-.19100	-.20587	-.22075	-.23565	-.25057	-.26550
.15000	-.11572	-.13031	-.14492	-.15955	-.17421	-.18888	-.20357	-.21828	-.23301	-.24776
.15250	-.10006	-.11446	-.12889	-.14333	-.15780	-.17229	-.18679	-.20132	-.21586	-.23041
.15500	-.08476	-.09898	-.11322	-.12749	-.14177	-.15607	-.17040	-.18474	-.19910	-.21347
.15750	-.06981	-.08385	-.09792	-.11200	-.12611	-.14023	-.15437	-.16854	-.18271	-.19691
.16000	-.05521	-.06907	-.08296	-.09687	-.11080	-.12475	-.13872	-.15270	-.16670	-.18072
.16250	-.04093	-.05462	-.06834	-.08208	-.09583	-.10961	-.12341	-.13722	-.15105	-.16490
.16500	-.02698	-.04050	-.05405	-.06762	-.08121	-.09482	-.10844	-.12209	-.13575	-.14943
.16750	-.01334	-.02670	-.04008	-.05348	-.06691	-.08035	-.09381	-.10729	-.12079	-.13430
.17000	.00000	-.01320	-.02642	-.03966	-.05293	-.06621	-.07951	-.09283	-.10616	-.11951
.17250	.01304	.00000	-.01306	-.02615	-.03925	-.05238	-.06552	-.07868	-.09185	-.10504
.17500	.02579	.01291	0.00000	-.01293	-.02588	-.03885	-.05183	-.06484	-.07786	-.09089
.17750	.03827	.02553	.01278	0.00000	-.01280	-.02561	-.03845	-.05130	-.06417	-.07705
.18000	.05047	.03788	.02528	.01265	.00000	-.01267	-.02535	-.03805	-.05077	-.06351
.18250	.06240	.04997	.03750	.02502	.01252	.00000	-.01254	-.02509	-.03767	-.05025
.18500	.07408	.06179	.04947	.03713	.02477	.01240	0.00000	-.01241	-.02484	-.03728
.18750	.08551	.07336	.06118	.04898	.03676	.02453	.01227	.00000	-.01229	-.02459
.19000	.09670	.08468	.07264	.06058	.04850	.03640	.02428	.01215	0.00000	-.01216
.19250	.10765	.09576	.08386	.07193	.05999	.04802	.03604	.02404	.01203	.00000
.19500	.11836	.10661	.09484	.08304	.07123	.05940	.04755	.03569	.02381	.01191
.19750	.12885	.11723	.10559	.09393	.08224	.07054	.05883	.04709	.03534	.02357
.20000	.13913	.12763	.11612	.10458	.09303	.08146	.06986	.05826	.04663	.03500
.20250	.14919	.13782	.12643	.11502	.10359	.09214	.08068	.06919	.05770	.04619
.20500	.15904	.14780	.13653	.12524	.11393	.10261	.09127	.07991	.06853	.05715
.20750	.16870	.15757	.14642	.13525	.12407	.11286	.10164	.09040	.07915	.06788

POINT TABLES: ORIGINAL LOAN TERM: 300 MONTHS LOAN PREPAID IN: 180 MONTHS

EFFECTIVE YIELD	CONTRACT RATE .19500	.19750	.20000	.20250	.20500	.20750
.07000	-1.12506	-1.14864	-1.17223	-1.19583	-1.21943	-1.24305
.07250	-1.08597	-1.10916	-1.13237	-1.15558	-1.17880	-1.20203
.07500	-1.04791	-1.07073	-1.09356	-1.11639	-1.13924	-1.16209
.07750	-1.01086	-1.03331	-1.05577	-1.07824	-1.10072	-1.12320
.08000	-.97478	-.99687	-1.01898	-1.04109	-1.06321	-1.08534
.08250	-.93965	-.96139	-.98314	-1.00491	-1.02668	-1.04846
.08500	-.90544	-.92684	-.94825	-.96967	-.99109	-1.01253
.08750	-.87211	-.89317	-.91425	-.93534	-.95643	-.97754
.09000	-.83964	-.86038	-.88113	-.90189	-.92266	-.94344
.09250	-.80802	-.82844	-.84887	-.86931	-.88976	-.91022
.09500	-.77720	-.79731	-.81743	-.83756	-.85770	-.87785
.09750	-.74717	-.76697	-.78679	-.80661	-.82645	-.84630
.10000	-.71790	-.73740	-.75692	-.77645	-.79600	-.81555
.10250	-.68937	-.70859	-.72782	-.74706	-.76631	-.78557
.10500	-.66156	-.68049	-.69944	-.71839	-.73736	-.75634
.10750	-.63445	-.65310	-.67177	-.69045	-.70914	-.72784
.11000	-.60801	-.62639	-.64479	-.66320	-.68162	-.70005
.11250	-.58223	-.60035	-.61848	-.63662	-.65478	-.67295
.11500	-.55708	-.57495	-.59282	-.61070	-.62860	-.64651
.11750	-.53256	-.55017	-.56779	-.58542	-.60306	-.62072
.12000	-.50864	-.52600	-.54337	-.56075	-.57815	-.59556
.12250	-.48529	-.50241	-.51954	-.53668	-.55384	-.57100
.12500	-.46252	-.47940	-.49629	-.51320	-.53011	-.54704
.12750	-.44029	-.45694	-.47360	-.49028	-.50696	-.52366
.13000	-.41860	-.43502	-.45145	-.46790	-.48436	-.50083
.13250	-.39742	-.41362	-.42984	-.44606	-.46230	-.47855
.13500	-.37675	-.39273	-.40873	-.42474	-.44076	-.45679
.13750	-.35657	-.37234	-.38812	-.40392	-.41973	-.43555
.14000	-.33686	-.35242	-.36800	-.38359	-.39919	-.41480
.14250	-.31762	-.33297	-.34835	-.36373	-.37913	-.39453
.14500	-.29882	-.31398	-.32915	-.34433	-.35953	-.37474
.14750	-.28045	-.29542	-.31040	-.32539	-.34039	-.35540
.15000	-.26251	-.27729	-.29207	-.30687	-.32168	-.33651
.15250	-.24499	-.25957	-.27417	-.28878	-.30341	-.31804
.15500	-.22786	-.24226	-.25668	-.27111	-.28555	-.30000
.15750	-.21112	-.22534	-.23958	-.25383	-.26809	-.28236
.16000	-.19475	-.20880	-.22286	-.23694	-.25102	-.26512
.16250	-.17876	-.19263	-.20652	-.22043	-.23434	-.24826
.16500	-.16312	-.17683	-.19055	-.20428	-.21803	-.23178
.16750	-.14783	-.16137	-.17493	-.18849	-.20207	-.21566
.17000	-.13288	-.14626	-.15965	-.17305	-.18647	-.19990
.17250	-.11825	-.13147	-.14471	-.15795	-.17121	-.18448
.17500	-.10394	-.11701	-.13009	-.14318	-.15628	-.16940
.17750	-.08995	-.10286	-.11579	-.12873	-.14168	-.15464
.18000	-.07626	-.08902	-.10180	-.11458	-.12738	-.14020
.18250	-.06286	-.07547	-.08810	-.10074	-.11340	-.12606
.18500	-.04974	-.06222	-.07470	-.08720	-.09971	-.11223
.18750	-.03691	-.04924	-.06158	-.07394	-.08631	-.09869
.19000	-.02434	-.03654	-.04874	-.06096	-.07319	-.08544
.19250	-.01204	-.02410	-.03617	-.04826	-.06035	-.07246
.19500	.00000	-.01192	-.02386	-.03581	-.04777	-.05975
.19750	.01179	.00000	-.01181	-.02363	-.03546	-.04730
.20000	.02334	.01168	.00000	-.01169	-.02339	-.03511
.20250	.03466	.02312	.01157	.00000	-.01158	-.02317
.20500	.04574	.03433	.02290	.01145	.00000	-.01146
.20750	.05660	.04531	.03400	.02268	.01134	.00000

POINT TABLES: ORIGINAL LOAN TERM: 300 MONTHS LOAN PREPAID IN: 300 MONTHS

EFFECTIVE YIELD	CONTRACT RATE .07000	.07250	.07500	.07750	.08000	.08250	.08500	.08750	.09000	.09250
.07000	.00000	-.02268	-.04558	-.06869	-.09202	-.11555	-.13929	-.16323	-.18735	-.21167
.07250	.02217	.00000	-.02239	-.04499	-.06780	-.09082	-.11403	-.13743	-.16102	-.18480
.07500	.04359	.02190	.00000	-.02211	-.04442	-.06693	-.08963	-.11252	-.13560	-.15885
.07750	.06428	.04306	.02163	.00000	-.02183	-.04385	-.06606	-.08846	-.11103	-.13379
.08000	.08426	.06350	.04253	.02136	.00000	-.02155	-.04329	-.06521	-.08730	-.10957
.08250	.10358	.08326	.06273	.04201	.02110	.00000	-.02128	-.04273	-.06436	-.08616
.08500	.12226	.10236	.08226	.06197	.04149	.02084	.00000	-.02101	-.04219	-.06353
.08750	.14032	.12083	.10114	.08127	.06121	.04098	.02058	.00000	-.02074	-.04165
.09000	.15779	.13869	.11941	.09994	.08029	.06047	.04048	.02032	.00000	-.02048
.09250	.17469	.15598	.13708	.11800	.09875	.07932	.05973	.03998	.02007	.00000
.09500	.19105	.17270	.15418	.13548	.11661	.09757	.07837	.05901	.03949	.01982
.09750	.20688	.18889	.17073	.15240	.13390	.11523	.09641	.07742	.05829	.03900
.10000	.22221	.20457	.18676	.16878	.15064	.13233	.11387	.09525	.07649	.05758
.10250	.23706	.21975	.20228	.18465	.16685	.14889	.13078	.11252	.09412	.07556
.10500	.25144	.23446	.21732	.20002	.18256	.16494	.14717	.12925	.11119	.09299
.10750	.26537	.24871	.23189	.21491	.19777	.18048	.16305	.14546	.12774	.10988
.11000	.27888	.26253	.24601	.22935	.21252	.19555	.17843	.16117	.14378	.12624
.11250	.29197	.27592	.25971	.24334	.22682	.21016	.19335	.17641	.15932	.14211
.11500	.30467	.28890	.27298	.25691	.24069	.22432	.20782	.19118	.17440	.15749
.11750	.31699	.30150	.28586	.27007	.25414	.23806	.22185	.20550	.18902	.17242
.12000	.32894	.31372	.29835	.28284	.26719	.25139	.23546	.21940	.20321	.18689
.12250	.34053	.32558	.31048	.29523	.27985	.26433	.24868	.23289	.21698	.20095
.12500	.35179	.33709	.32225	.30726	.29214	.27689	.26150	.24598	.23035	.21458
.12750	.36272	.34827	.33367	.31894	.30408	.28908	.27395	.25870	.24332	.22783
.13000	.37333	.35912	.34477	.33028	.31567	.30092	.28604	.27104	.25592	.24069
.13250	.38364	.36966	.35555	.34130	.32692	.31242	.29779	.28304	.26816	.25318
.13500	.39366	.37991	.36602	.35201	.33786	.32359	.30920	.29469	.28006	.26531
.13750	.40339	.38986	.37620	.36241	.34849	.33445	.32029	.30601	.29152	.27711
.14000	.41286	.39954	.38610	.37253	.35883	.34501	.33107	.31702	.30285	.28858
.14250	.42206	.40895	.39572	.38236	.36888	.35528	.34156	.32772	.31378	.29973
.14500	.43101	.41811	.40508	.39192	.37865	.36526	.35175	.33814	.32441	.31057
.14750	.43972	.42701	.41418	.40123	.38816	.37497	.36167	.34826	.33474	.32112
.15000	.44819	.43567	.42304	.41028	.39741	.38442	.37132	.35812	.34480	.33139
.15250	.45643	.44411	.43166	.41909	.40641	.39362	.38072	.36771	.35459	.34138
.15500	.46446	.45231	.44005	.42767	.41513	.40257	.38986	.37704	.36412	.35110
.15750	.47227	.46031	.44822	.43602	.42371	.41129	.39877	.38613	.37340	.36057
.16000	.47988	.46809	.45618	.44416	.43202	.41978	.40744	.39499	.38244	.36979
.16250	.48730	.47567	.46393	.45208	.44012	.42805	.41588	.40361	.39124	.37878
.16500	.49452	.48306	.47149	.45980	.44801	.43611	.42412	.41202	.39982	.38753
.16750	.50157	.49026	.47885	.46733	.45570	.44397	.43214	.42021	.40818	.39606
.17000	.50843	.49728	.48603	.47466	.46320	.45163	.43996	.42819	.41633	.40438
.17250	.51512	.50413	.49302	.48181	.47050	.45909	.44758	.43598	.42428	.41249
.17500	.52165	.51080	.49985	.48879	.47763	.46637	.45502	.44357	.43203	.42040
.17750	.52801	.51731	.50650	.49559	.48458	.47347	.46227	.45097	.43959	.42811
.18000	.53423	.52366	.51300	.50223	.49137	.48040	.46935	.45820	.44696	.43564
.18250	.54029	.52986	.51934	.50871	.49799	.48717	.47625	.46525	.45416	.44298
.18500	.54620	.53591	.52552	.51503	.50445	.49377	.48300	.47213	.46118	.45015
.18750	.55198	.54182	.53156	.52121	.51075	.50021	.48958	.47885	.46804	.45715
.19000	.55762	.54759	.53746	.52723	.51691	.50650	.49600	.48541	.47474	.46398
.19250	.56313	.55322	.54322	.53312	.52293	.51265	.50228	.49182	.48128	.47066
.19500	.56851	.55873	.54885	.53887	.52881	.51865	.50841	.49808	.48767	.47718
.19750	.57377	.56411	.55435	.54449	.53455	.52452	.51440	.50420	.49392	.48355
.20000	.57891	.56936	.55972	.54998	.54016	.53025	.52026	.51018	.50002	.48978
.20250	.58393	.57450	.56497	.55535	.54565	.53586	.52598	.51602	.50598	.49587
.20500	.58884	.57952	.57011	.56060	.55101	.54133	.53157	.52173	.51181	.50182
.20750	.59365	.58443	.57513	.56573	.55625	.54669	.53705	.52732	.51752	.50763

EFFECTIVE YIELD	CONTRACT RATE .09500	.09750	.10000	.10250	.10500	.10750	.11000	.11250	.11500	.11750
.07000	-.23617	-.26084	-.28569	-.31071	-.33589	-.36124	-.38673	-.41238	-.43817	-.46410
.07250	-.20876	-.23288	-.25718	-.28165	-.30627	-.33105	-.35598	-.38106	-.40628	-.43164
.07500	-.18228	-.20588	-.22965	-.25358	-.27766	-.30190	-.32629	-.35081	-.37548	-.40028
.07750	-.15671	-.17980	-.20305	-.22646	-.25003	-.27374	-.29760	-.32160	-.34573	-.37000
.08000	-.13200	-.15460	-.17735	-.20026	-.22332	-.24653	-.26988	-.29336	-.31698	-.34073
.08250	-.10812	-.13024	-.15252	-.17494	-.19752	-.22023	-.24309	-.26608	-.28920	-.31245
.08500	-.08503	-.10669	-.12850	-.15046	-.17257	-.19481	-.21719	-.23970	-.26234	-.28510
.08750	-.06271	-.08392	-.10528	-.12679	-.14844	-.17022	-.19214	-.21419	-.23636	-.25866
.09000	-.04111	-.06189	-.08282	-.10389	-.12510	-.14645	-.16792	-.18952	-.21124	-.23308
.09250	-.02022	-.04058	-.06109	-.08174	-.10252	-.12344	-.14448	-.16565	-.18693	-.20834
.09500	0.00000	-.01996	-.04006	-.06030	-.08067	-.10117	-.12180	-.14255	-.16341	-.18439
.09750	.01957	0.00000	-.01971	-.03955	-.05952	-.07962	-.09985	-.12019	-.14064	-.16121
.10000	.03852	.01933	.00000	-.01946	-.03905	-.05876	-.07859	-.09853	-.11860	-.13877
.10250	.05687	.03805	.01909	.00000	-.01921	-.03855	-.05800	-.07757	-.09724	-.11703
.10500	.07465	.05618	.03758	.01885	.00000	-.01897	-.03806	-.05725	-.07656	-.09597
.10750	.09188	.07375	.05550	.03712	.01862	0.00000	-.01873	-.03757	-.05652	-.07557
.11000	.10858	.09078	.07286	.05482	.03666	.01839	0.00000	-.01849	-.03709	-.05579
.11250	.12476	.10729	.08970	.07198	.05415	.03621	.01816	0.00000	-.01826	-.03662
.11500	.14046	.12330	.10602	.08863	.07112	.05350	.03577	.01793	.00000	-.01803
.11750	.15568	.13883	.12186	.10477	.08757	.07026	.05285	.03533	.01771	.00000
.12000	.17046	.15390	.13722	.12043	.10353	.08653	.06942	.05221	.03490	.01749
.12250	.18479	.16852	.15213	.13563	.11902	.10231	.08550	.06858	.05157	.03447
.12500	.19870	.18271	.16660	.15038	.13406	.11763	.10111	.08448	.06776	.05095
.12750	.21221	.19649	.18065	.16471	.14866	.13251	.11626	.09992	.08348	.06695
.13000	.22533	.20987	.19430	.17862	.16284	.14696	.13098	.11491	.09874	.08249
.13250	.23808	.22287	.20755	.19213	.17661	.16099	.14528	.12947	.11357	.09759
.13500	.25046	.23550	.22043	.20526	.18999	.17463	.15917	.14362	.12798	.11225
.13750	.26250	.24777	.23295	.21802	.20300	.18788	.17267	.15737	.14198	.12651
.14000	.27419	.25971	.24512	.23043	.21564	.20076	.18579	.17073	.15559	.14036
.14250	.28557	.27131	.25695	.24249	.22793	.21329	.19855	.18373	.16882	.15384
.14500	.29663	.28259	.26845	.25422	.23989	.22547	.21096	.19637	.18169	.16694
.14750	.30740	.29357	.27965	.26563	.25152	.23732	.22304	.20867	.19422	.17969
.15000	.31787	.30425	.29054	.27673	.26284	.24885	.23478	.22063	.20640	.19209
.15250	.32806	.31465	.30114	.28754	.27385	.26008	.24622	.23228	.21826	.20416
.15500	.33798	.32477	.31146	.29806	.28457	.27100	.25735	.24361	.22980	.21591
.15750	.34764	.33462	.32151	.30830	.29501	.28164	.26818	.25465	.24104	.22735
.16000	.35705	.34422	.33129	.31828	.30518	.29200	.27874	.26540	.25199	.23850
.16250	.36622	.35356	.34082	.32800	.31509	.30209	.28902	.27587	.26265	.24935
.16500	.37515	.36267	.35011	.33747	.32474	.31193	.29904	.28608	.27304	.25993
.16750	.38385	.37155	.35917	.34670	.33414	.32151	.30880	.29602	.28317	.27024
.17000	.39234	.38021	.36799	.35569	.34331	.33086	.31832	.30572	.29304	.28029
.17250	.40061	.38864	.37660	.36446	.35225	.33997	.32760	.31517	.30266	.29009
.17500	.40868	.39687	.38499	.37302	.36097	.34885	.33665	.32439	.31205	.29964
.17750	.41655	.40490	.39317	.38136	.36948	.35752	.34548	.33338	.32120	.30896
.18000	.42423	.41273	.40116	.38951	.37778	.36597	.35410	.34215	.33014	.31806
.18250	.43172	.42038	.40895	.39745	.38587	.37422	.36250	.35071	.33886	.32693
.18500	.43903	.42784	.41656	.40521	.39378	.38228	.37071	.35907	.34736	.33560
.18750	.44617	.43512	.42399	.41278	.40149	.39014	.37872	.36723	.35567	.34405
.19000	.45315	.44223	.43124	.42017	.40903	.39782	.38654	.37519	.36378	.35231
.19250	.45996	.44918	.43832	.42739	.41639	.40532	.39418	.38298	.37171	.36038
.19500	.46661	.45596	.44524	.43444	.42358	.41264	.40164	.39058	.37945	.36826
.19750	.47311	.46259	.45200	.44134	.43060	.41980	.40893	.39800	.38701	.37596
.20000	.47946	.46907	.45861	.44807	.43747	.42680	.41606	.40526	.39440	.38348
.20250	.48567	.47541	.46507	.45466	.44418	.43364	.42303	.41236	.40163	.39084
.20500	.49174	.48160	.47138	.46109	.45074	.44032	.42984	.41929	.40869	.39803
.20750	.49768	.48765	.47755	.46739	.45716	.44686	.43650	.42608	.41560	.40506

POINT TABLES: ORIGINAL LOAN TERM: 300 MONTHS LOAN PREPAID IN: 300 MONTHS

EFFECTIVE YIELD	CONTRACT RATE .12000	.12250	.12500	.12750	.13000	.13250	.13500	.13750	.14000	.14250
.07000	-.49017	-.51638	-.54271	-.56916	-.59574	-.62243	-.64923	-.67615	-.70316	-.73028
.07250	-.45713	-.48275	-.50850	-.53437	-.56035	-.58645	-.61266	-.63898	-.66540	-.69191
.07500	-.42522	-.45028	-.47546	-.50077	-.52618	-.55171	-.57735	-.60309	-.62892	-.65486
.07750	-.39439	-.41891	-.44355	-.46830	-.49317	-.51815	-.54323	-.56841	-.59369	-.61907
.08000	-.36460	-.38860	-.41271	-.43694	-.46127	-.48572	-.51026	-.53491	-.55965	-.58448
.08250	-.33582	-.35930	-.38291	-.40662	-.43045	-.45437	-.47840	-.50252	-.52674	-.55105
.08500	-.30798	-.33098	-.35410	-.37732	-.40064	-.42407	-.44760	-.47122	-.49493	-.51874
.08750	-.28107	-.30360	-.32623	-.34898	-.37182	-.39477	-.41781	-.44095	-.46417	-.48749
.09000	-.25504	-.27711	-.29928	-.32156	-.34395	-.36643	-.38900	-.41167	-.43442	-.45726
.09250	-.22985	-.25148	-.27321	-.29504	-.31698	-.33901	-.36113	-.38334	-.40564	-.42802
.09500	-.20548	-.22668	-.24798	-.26938	-.29088	-.31247	-.33415	-.35592	-.37778	-.39972
.09750	-.18189	-.20267	-.22355	-.24454	-.26561	-.28678	-.30804	-.32939	-.35081	-.37232
.10000	-.15904	-.17942	-.19990	-.22048	-.24115	-.26191	-.28276	-.30369	-.32471	-.34580
.10250	-.13692	-.15691	-.17700	-.19719	-.21746	-.23783	-.25827	-.27881	-.29942	-.32011
.10500	-.11549	-.13510	-.15481	-.17462	-.19451	-.21449	-.23456	-.25470	-.27493	-.29522
.10750	-.09472	-.11397	-.13332	-.15275	-.17227	-.19188	-.21157	-.23134	-.25119	-.27111
.11000	-.07459	-.09349	-.11248	-.13156	-.15072	-.16997	-.18930	-.20870	-.22819	-.24774
.11250	-.05508	-.07363	-.09228	-.11101	-.12982	-.14872	-.16770	-.18676	-.20588	-.22508
.11500	-.03616	-.05438	-.07269	-.09108	-.10956	-.12812	-.14676	-.16547	-.18426	-.20311
.11750	-.01781	-.03570	-.05369	-.07176	-.08991	-.10814	-.12645	-.14483	-.16328	-.18180
.12000	.00000	-.01758	-.03525	-.05301	-.07084	-.08875	-.10674	-.12480	-.14293	-.16113
.12250	.01728	.00000	-.01736	-.03481	-.05234	-.06994	-.08762	-.10536	-.12318	-.14106
.12500	.03405	.01707	.00000	-.01715	-.03438	-.05168	-.06905	-.08650	-.10401	-.12159
.12750	.05034	.03364	.01686	0.00000	-.01694	-.03395	-.05103	-.06818	-.08540	-.10268
.13000	.06615	.04973	.03323	.01665	0.00000	-.01673	-.03352	-.05039	-.06732	-.08431
.13250	.08152	.06537	.04914	.03283	.01645	.00000	-.01652	-.03311	-.04976	-.06648
.13500	.09645	.08056	.06459	.04855	.03244	.01625	.00000	-.01632	-.03270	-.04914
.13750	.11095	.09532	.07961	.06383	.04797	.03205	.01606	.00000	-.01612	-.03230
.14000	.12506	.10967	.09421	.07868	.06307	.04740	.03166	.01586	.00000	-.01592
.14250	.13877	.12362	.10841	.09312	.07776	.06233	.04684	.03129	.01567	.00000
.14500	.15210	.13720	.12221	.10716	.09204	.07685	.06160	.04629	.03092	.01549
.14750	.16508	.15040	.13564	.12082	.10593	.09098	.07596	.06088	.04574	.03055
.15000	.17770	.16324	.14871	.13411	.11945	.10472	.08993	.07508	.06017	.04521
.15250	.18999	.17575	.16143	.14705	.13261	.11810	.10353	.08890	.07421	.05947
.15500	.20195	.18792	.17381	.15965	.14541	.13112	.11677	.10235	.08788	.07336
.15750	.21359	.19977	.18587	.17191	.15789	.14380	.12965	.11545	.10119	.08688
.16000	.22494	.21131	.19761	.18385	.17003	.15615	.14221	.12821	.11416	.10005
.16250	.23599	.22255	.20905	.19549	.18186	.16818	.15444	.14064	.12679	.11288
.16500	.24675	.23351	.22020	.20683	.19339	.17990	.16635	.15275	.13909	.12538
.16750	.25725	.24418	.23106	.21787	.20463	.19132	.17796	.16455	.15108	.13757
.17000	.26747	.25459	.24165	.22864	.21558	.20246	.18928	.17605	.16277	.14944
.17250	.27745	.26474	.25197	.23915	.22626	.21332	.20032	.18727	.17417	.16102
.17500	.28717	.27464	.26204	.24939	.23668	.22391	.21109	.19821	.18529	.17232
.17750	.29666	.28429	.27186	.25938	.24683	.23424	.22159	.20888	.19613	.18333
.18000	.30592	.29371	.28145	.26912	.25675	.24431	.23183	.21929	.20671	.19408
.18250	.31495	.30290	.29080	.27864	.26642	.25415	.24183	.22945	.21703	.20457
.18500	.32377	.31187	.29993	.28792	.27586	.26375	.25158	.23937	.22711	.21481
.18750	.33237	.32063	.30884	.29698	.28508	.27312	.26111	.24905	.23695	.22480
.19000	.34078	.32919	.31754	.30584	.29408	.28227	.27041	.25851	.24656	.23456
.19250	.34899	.33754	.32604	.31448	.30287	.29121	.27950	.26774	.25594	.24409
.19500	.35701	.34570	.33434	.32293	.31146	.29994	.28838	.27676	.26511	.25340
.19750	.36484	.35368	.34245	.33118	.31985	.30847	.29705	.28558	.27406	.26250
.20000	.37250	.36147	.35038	.33924	.32805	.31681	.30552	.29419	.28281	.27140
.20250	.37999	.36909	.35813	.34712	.33607	.32496	.31381	.30261	.29137	.28009
.20500	.38731	.37653	.36571	.35483	.34390	.33293	.32191	.31084	.29973	.28858
.20750	.39446	.38382	.37312	.36237	.35157	.34072	.32983	.31889	.30791	.29689

POINT TABLES: ORIGINAL LOAN TERM: 300 MONTHS LOAN PREPAID IN: 300 MONTHS

EFFECTIVE YIELD	CONTRACT RATE .14500	.14750	.15000	.15250	.15500	.15750	.16000	.16250	.16500	.16750
.07000	-.75750	-.78481	-.81221	-.83970	-.86727	-.89492	-.92265	-.95046	-.97833	-1.00628
.07250	-.71853	-.74523	-.77202	-.79890	-.82586	-.85290	-.88002	-.90721	-.93447	-.96179
.07500	-.68089	-.70701	-.73322	-.75950	-.78587	-.81232	-.83884	-.86544	-.89210	-.91883
.07750	-.64453	-.67009	-.69573	-.72145	-.74725	-.77312	-.79907	-.82509	-.85117	-.87732
.08000	-.60940	-.63441	-.65950	-.68467	-.70992	-.73524	-.76064	-.78610	-.81163	-.83722
.08250	-.57545	-.59993	-.62449	-.64913	-.67385	-.69864	-.72349	-.74842	-.77341	-.79846
.08500	-.54262	-.56660	-.59065	-.61477	-.63897	-.66324	-.68758	-.71199	-.73646	-.76099
.08750	-.51088	-.53436	-.55792	-.58155	-.60525	-.62902	-.65286	-.67676	-.70073	-.72476
.09000	-.48018	-.50318	-.52626	-.54941	-.57263	-.59592	-.61927	-.64269	-.66617	-.68971
.09250	-.45048	-.47302	-.49563	-.51832	-.54107	-.56389	-.58678	-.60973	-.63274	-.65580
.09500	-.42173	-.44382	-.46599	-.48823	-.51053	-.53290	-.55533	-.57783	-.60038	-.62299
.09750	-.39391	-.41557	-.43730	-.45910	-.48097	-.50290	-.52489	-.54695	-.56906	-.59122
.10000	-.36697	-.38821	-.40952	-.43090	-.45234	-.47385	-.49542	-.51705	-.53873	-.56047
.10250	-.34087	-.36171	-.38261	-.40359	-.42462	-.44572	-.46688	-.48809	-.50936	-.53068
.10500	-.31560	-.33604	-.35655	-.37713	-.39777	-.41847	-.43922	-.46004	-.48091	-.50183
.10750	-.29111	-.31117	-.33130	-.35149	-.37174	-.39206	-.41243	-.43286	-.45334	-.47387
.11000	-.26737	-.28706	-.30682	-.32664	-.34652	-.36646	-.38646	-.40651	-.42662	-.44677
.11250	-.24435	-.26369	-.28309	-.30255	-.32207	-.34165	-.36129	-.38097	-.40071	-.42050
.11500	-.22204	-.24103	-.26008	-.27919	-.29836	-.31759	-.33687	-.35621	-.37559	-.39502
.11750	-.20039	-.21904	-.23776	-.25653	-.27536	-.29425	-.31319	-.33218	-.35122	-.37031
.12000	-.17939	-.19772	-.21610	-.23455	-.25305	-.27161	-.29022	-.30888	-.32759	-.34634
.12250	-.15901	-.17702	-.19509	-.21322	-.23140	-.24964	-.26792	-.28626	-.30464	-.32307
.12500	-.13923	-.15693	-.17469	-.19251	-.21038	-.22831	-.24628	-.26431	-.28238	-.30049
.12750	-.12002	-.13743	-.15489	-.17240	-.18998	-.20760	-.22527	-.24299	-.26076	-.27857
.13000	-.10137	-.11848	-.13565	-.15288	-.17016	-.18749	-.20486	-.22229	-.23976	-.25727
.13250	-.08325	-.10008	-.11697	-.13391	-.15091	-.16795	-.18504	-.20218	-.21936	-.23659
.13500	-.06564	-.08220	-.09882	-.11548	-.13220	-.14897	-.16578	-.18264	-.19955	-.21649
.13750	-.04853	-.06483	-.08117	-.09757	-.11402	-.13052	-.14707	-.16365	-.18029	-.19696
.14000	-.03190	-.04794	-.06402	-.08016	-.09635	-.11259	-.12887	-.14520	-.16156	-.17797
.14250	-.01573	-.03151	-.04735	-.06323	-.07917	-.09515	-.11118	-.12725	-.14336	-.15951
.14500	0.00000	-.01554	-.03113	-.04677	-.06246	-.07819	-.09397	-.10979	-.12565	-.14155
.14750	.01530	.00000	-.01535	-.03075	-.04620	-.06169	-.07723	-.09281	-.10843	-.12409
.15000	.03019	.01512	.00000	-.01517	-.03038	-.04564	-.06094	-.07629	-.09167	-.10709
.15250	.04468	.02984	.01494	.00000	-.01499	-.03002	-.04509	-.06021	-.07536	-.09055
.15500	.05879	.04416	.02949	.01477	.00000	-.01481	-.02966	-.04455	-.05948	-.07445
.15750	.07252	.05811	.04365	.02914	.01459	.00000	-.01463	-.02931	-.04402	-.05877
.16000	.08590	.07169	.05744	.04315	.02881	.01442	.00000	-.01446	-.02896	-.04350
.16250	.09893	.08493	.07088	.05679	.04265	.02847	.01426	0.00000	-.01429	-.02862
.16500	.11163	.09782	.08397	.07008	.05614	.04216	.02815	.01409	.00000	-.01413
.16750	.12400	.11039	.09673	.08303	.06929	.05551	.04168	.02783	.01393	.00000
.17000	.13606	.12264	.10917	.09566	.08211	.06851	.05488	.04121	.02751	.01377
.17250	.14783	.13458	.12130	.10797	.09460	.08119	.06775	.05427	.04075	.02720
.17500	.15930	.14623	.13313	.11998	.10679	.09356	.08030	.06700	.05366	.04029
.17750	.17049	.15760	.14466	.13169	.11868	.10563	.09254	.07941	.06626	.05307
.18000	.18140	.16868	.15592	.14312	.13028	.11740	.10448	.09153	.07854	.06553
.18250	.19206	.17950	.16691	.15427	.14159	.12888	.11613	.10335	.09054	.07769
.18500	.20246	.19006	.17763	.16515	.15264	.14009	.12751	.11489	.10224	.08956
.18750	.21261	.20037	.18810	.17578	.16343	.15104	.13862	.12616	.11367	.10115
.19000	.22252	.21044	.19832	.18616	.17396	.16173	.14946	.13716	.12483	.11246
.19250	.23220	.22027	.20830	.19629	.18425	.17217	.16005	.14791	.13573	.12352
.19500	.24166	.22988	.21806	.20619	.19430	.18237	.17040	.15840	.14637	.13432
.19750	.25090	.23926	.22758	.21587	.20412	.19233	.18051	.16866	.15678	.14487
.20000	.25994	.24844	.23690	.22532	.21371	.20207	.19039	.17868	.16694	.15518
.20250	.26876	.25740	.24600	.23456	.22309	.21159	.20005	.18848	.17688	.16525
.20500	.27740	.26617	.25490	.24360	.23226	.22089	.20949	.19806	.18660	.17511
.20750	.28584	.27474	.26360	.25243	.24123	.22999	.21873	.20743	.19610	.18474

POINT TABLES: ORIGINAL LOAN TERM: 300 MONTHS LOAN PREPAID IN: 300 MONTHS

EFFECTIVE YIELD	CONTRACT RATE .17000	.17250	.17500	.17750	.18000	.18250	.18500	.18750	.19000	.19250
.07000	-1.03429	-1.06237	-1.09051	-1.11871	-1.14696	-1.17527	-1.20364	-1.23205	-1.26051	-1.28901
.07250	-.98919	-1.01664	-1.04416	-1.07173	-1.09936	-1.12704	-1.15477	-1.18255	-1.21038	-1.23826
.07500	-.94562	-.97247	-.99939	-1.02636	-1.05338	-1.08046	-1.10758	-1.13476	-1.16197	-1.18924
.07750	-.90354	-.92981	-.95614	-.98253	-1.00897	-1.03546	-1.06200	-1.08858	-1.11521	-1.14189
.08000	-.86287	-.88859	-.91435	-.94018	-.96605	-.99197	-1.01795	-1.04396	-1.07003	-1.09613
.08250	-.82357	-.84874	-.87397	-.89924	-.92457	-.94995	-.97537	-1.00084	-1.02636	-1.05191
.08500	-.78558	-.81022	-.83492	-.85967	-.88447	-.90932	-.93422	-.95916	-.98414	-1.00916
.08750	-.74884	-.77298	-.79717	-.82141	-.84570	-.87004	-.89442	-.91884	-.94331	-.96782
.09000	-.71330	-.73695	-.76065	-.78440	-.80819	-.83204	-.85592	-.87985	-.90382	-.92783
.09250	-.67892	-.70209	-.72532	-.74859	-.77191	-.79527	-.81868	-.84213	-.86562	-.88914
.09500	-.64565	-.66836	-.69112	-.71394	-.73679	-.75969	-.78264	-.80562	-.82864	-.85170
.09750	-.61344	-.63571	-.65803	-.68039	-.70280	-.72525	-.74775	-.77028	-.79285	-.81546
.10000	-.58226	-.60409	-.62598	-.64791	-.66989	-.69191	-.71397	-.73607	-.75820	-.78037
.10250	-.55205	-.57348	-.59494	-.61646	-.63802	-.65961	-.68125	-.70293	-.72464	-.74639
.10500	-.52280	-.54381	-.56488	-.58599	-.60714	-.62833	-.64956	-.67083	-.69213	-.71347
.10750	-.49445	-.51507	-.53575	-.55646	-.57722	-.59801	-.61885	-.63972	-.66063	-.68157
.11000	-.46697	-.48722	-.50751	-.52784	-.54822	-.56863	-.58909	-.60957	-.63010	-.65065
.11250	-.44033	-.46021	-.48014	-.50010	-.52011	-.54015	-.56023	-.58035	-.60050	-.62068
.11500	-.41450	-.43402	-.45359	-.47320	-.49284	-.51253	-.53225	-.55201	-.57179	-.59162
.11750	-.38945	-.40862	-.42784	-.44710	-.46640	-.48574	-.50511	-.52451	-.54395	-.56342
.12000	-.36514	-.38398	-.40286	-.42179	-.44075	-.45974	-.47878	-.49784	-.51694	-.53607
.12250	-.34155	-.36007	-.37862	-.39722	-.41585	-.43452	-.45322	-.47196	-.49073	-.50953
.12500	-.31865	-.33685	-.35509	-.37337	-.39169	-.41004	-.42842	-.44684	-.46529	-.48376
.12750	-.29642	-.31431	-.33225	-.35022	-.36822	-.38626	-.40434	-.42244	-.44058	-.45875
.13000	-.27483	-.29242	-.31006	-.32773	-.34544	-.36318	-.38095	-.39875	-.41659	-.43445
.13250	-.25386	-.27116	-.28851	-.30589	-.32330	-.34075	-.35823	-.37574	-.39328	-.41085
.13500	-.23348	-.25050	-.26756	-.28466	-.30179	-.31896	-.33616	-.35338	-.37064	-.38792
.13750	-.21367	-.23042	-.24721	-.26404	-.28089	-.29778	-.31470	-.33165	-.34863	-.36564
.14000	-.19442	-.21091	-.22743	-.24398	-.26057	-.27720	-.29385	-.31053	-.32724	-.34398
.14250	-.17570	-.19193	-.20819	-.22449	-.24082	-.25718	-.27357	-.28999	-.30644	-.32291
.14500	-.15749	-.17347	-.18948	-.20553	-.22160	-.23771	-.25385	-.27001	-.28621	-.30243
.14750	-.13978	-.15551	-.17128	-.18708	-.20291	-.21877	-.23466	-.25058	-.26653	-.28250
.15000	-.12255	-.13804	-.15357	-.16913	-.18472	-.20034	-.21600	-.23167	-.24738	-.26311
.15250	-.10578	-.12104	-.13634	-.15166	-.16702	-.18241	-.19783	-.21327	-.22874	-.24424
.15500	-.08945	-.10449	-.11956	-.13466	-.14979	-.16495	-.18014	-.19536	-.21060	-.22586
.15750	-.07355	-.08837	-.10322	-.11810	-.13301	-.14795	-.16292	-.17791	-.19293	-.20797
.16000	-.05807	-.07267	-.08731	-.10197	-.11667	-.13139	-.14615	-.16092	-.17573	-.19055
.16250	-.04298	-.05738	-.07181	-.08626	-.10075	-.11526	-.12981	-.14437	-.15896	-.17358
.16500	-.02829	-.04248	-.05670	-.07096	-.08524	-.09955	-.11389	-.12825	-.14263	-.15704
.16750	-.01396	-.02796	-.04198	-.05604	-.07012	-.08423	-.09837	-.11253	-.12672	-.14092
.17000	.00000	-.01380	-.02763	-.04150	-.05539	-.06930	-.08324	-.09721	-.11120	-.12521
.17250	.01361	0.00000	-.01364	-.02732	-.04102	-.05474	-.06850	-.08227	-.09607	-.10989
.17500	.02689	.01346	.00000	-.01349	-.02700	-.04055	-.05411	-.06770	-.08132	-.09495
.17750	.03984	.02659	.01331	.00000	-.01334	-.02670	-.04008	-.05349	-.06693	-.08038
.18000	.05248	.03940	.02629	.01316	0.00000	-.01319	-.02640	-.03963	-.05289	-.06616
.18250	.06481	.05190	.03897	.02600	.01301	.00000	-.01304	-.02610	-.03918	-.05229
.18500	.07685	.06411	.05134	.03854	.02572	.01287	.00000	-.01289	-.02581	-.03874
.18750	.08860	.07602	.06341	.05078	.03812	.02544	.01273	.00000	-.01275	-.02552
.19000	.10007	.08765	.07520	.06273	.05023	.03771	.02516	.01259	.00000	-.01261
.19250	.11128	.09901	.08672	.07440	.06206	.04969	.03730	.02489	.01245	.00000
.19500	.12223	.11011	.09797	.08580	.07361	.06140	.04916	.03690	.02462	.01232
.19750	.13292	.12096	.10896	.09694	.08490	.07283	.06075	.04864	.03651	.02436
.20000	.14338	.13156	.11971	.10783	.09593	.08401	.07207	.06011	.04812	.03612
.20250	.15360	.14192	.13021	.11848	.10672	.09494	.08314	.07132	.05948	.04762
.20500	.16359	.15204	.14047	.12888	.11726	.10562	.09396	.08228	.07058	.05886
.20750	.17336	.16195	.15051	.13906	.12757	.11607	.10455	.09300	.08144	.06985

EFFECTIVE YIELD	CONTRACT RATE .19500	.19750	.20000	.20250	.20500	.20750
.07000	-1.31756	-1.34616	-1.37479	-1.40346	-1.43217	-1.46091
.07250	-1.26617	-1.29413	-1.32213	-1.35017	-1.37824	-1.40635
.07500	-1.21654	-1.24389	-1.27127	-1.29870	-1.32615	-1.35365
.07750	-1.16860	-1.19535	-1.22215	-1.24898	-1.27584	-1.30274
.08000	-1.12227	-1.14846	-1.17468	-1.20093	-1.22722	-1.25355
.08250	-1.07750	-1.10313	-1.12880	-1.15450	-1.18024	-1.20600
.08500	-1.03422	-1.05931	-1.08445	-1.10961	-1.13481	-1.16004
.08750	-.99236	-1.01694	-1.04156	-1.06620	-1.09088	-1.11559
.09000	-.95187	-.97596	-1.00007	-1.02422	-1.04840	-1.07261
.09250	-.91271	-.93630	-.95993	-.98360	-1.00729	-1.03101
.09500	-.87480	-.89793	-.92109	-.94429	-.96751	-.99076
.09750	-.83811	-.86078	-.88349	-.90623	-.92900	-.95180
.10000	-.80258	-.82482	-.84709	-.86939	-.89172	-.91408
.10250	-.76817	-.78999	-.81183	-.83371	-.85561	-.87754
.10500	-.73484	-.75625	-.77768	-.79914	-.82063	-.84215
.10750	-.70254	-.72355	-.74458	-.76565	-.78674	-.80785
.11000	-.67124	-.69186	-.71251	-.73318	-.75389	-.77461
.11250	-.64089	-.66114	-.68141	-.70171	-.72204	-.74239
.11500	-.61147	-.63135	-.65126	-.67119	-.69116	-.71114
.11750	-.58292	-.60245	-.62201	-.64159	-.66120	-.68083
.12000	-.55523	-.57442	-.59363	-.61287	-.63214	-.65143
.12250	-.52836	-.54721	-.56609	-.58500	-.60393	-.62289
.12500	-.50227	-.52080	-.53936	-.55795	-.57656	-.59519
.12750	-.47694	-.49516	-.51341	-.53168	-.54998	-.56830
.13000	-.45235	-.47026	-.48821	-.50617	-.52416	-.54218
.13250	-.42845	-.44607	-.46372	-.48140	-.49909	-.51681
.13500	-.40524	-.42257	-.43993	-.45732	-.47473	-.49216
.13750	-.38267	-.39973	-.41681	-.43392	-.45105	-.46820
.14000	-.36074	-.37753	-.39434	-.41117	-.42803	-.44491
.14250	-.33941	-.35594	-.37249	-.38906	-.40565	-.42226
.14500	-.31867	-.33494	-.35123	-.36755	-.38388	-.40024
.14750	-.29850	-.31452	-.33056	-.34662	-.36271	-.37881
.15000	-.27886	-.29464	-.31044	-.32626	-.34210	-.35796
.15250	-.25975	-.27530	-.29086	-.30645	-.32205	-.33768
.15500	-.24115	-.25647	-.27180	-.28715	-.30253	-.31792
.15750	-.22304	-.23813	-.25324	-.26837	-.28352	-.29869
.16000	-.20540	-.22027	-.23516	-.25008	-.26501	-.27996
.16250	-.18822	-.20288	-.21756	-.23226	-.24698	-.26171
.16500	-.17147	-.18593	-.20040	-.21489	-.22940	-.24393
.16750	-.15515	-.16941	-.18368	-.19797	-.21228	-.22661
.17000	-.13925	-.15330	-.16738	-.18147	-.19558	-.20971
.17250	-.12374	-.13760	-.15148	-.16539	-.17931	-.19324
.17500	-.10861	-.12229	-.13599	-.14970	-.16343	-.17718
.17750	-.09386	-.10735	-.12087	-.13440	-.14795	-.16152
.18000	-.07946	-.09278	-.10611	-.11947	-.13284	-.14623
.18250	-.06541	-.07856	-.09172	-.10490	-.11810	-.13131
.18500	-.05170	-.06468	-.07767	-.09068	-.10371	-.11675
.18750	-.03831	-.05112	-.06395	-.07680	-.08966	-.10254
.19000	-.02524	-.03789	-.05056	-.06324	-.07594	-.08866
.19250	-.01247	-.02496	-.03747	-.05000	-.06254	-.07510
.19500	.00000	-.01234	-.02469	-.03706	-.04945	-.06185
.19750	.01219	.00000	-.01220	-.02442	-.03666	-.04891
.20000	.02410	.01206	.00000	-.01207	-.02416	-.03627
.20250	.03574	.02384	.01193	0.00000	-.01194	-.02390
.20500	.04712	.03536	.02359	.01180	.00000	-.01182
.20750	.05825	.04663	.03500	.02335	.01168	0.00000

POINT TABLES: ORIGINAL LOAN TERM: 360 MONTHS LOAN PREPAID IN: 60 MONTHS

EFFECTIVE YIELD	CONTRACT RATE .07000	.07250	.07500	.07750	.08000	.08250	.08500	.08750	.09000	.09250
.07000	.00000	-.01027	-.02055	-.03086	-.04119	-.05154	-.06191	-.07229	-.08269	-.09311
.07250	.01019	.00000	-.01022	-.02045	-.03071	-.04099	-.05129	-.06160	-.07193	-.08228
.07500	.02027	.01015	0.00000	-.01017	-.02036	-.03056	-.04079	-.05103	-.06129	-.07157
.07750	.03022	.02017	.01010	.00000	-.01012	-.02026	-.03041	-.04059	-.05078	-.06098
.08000	.04006	.03008	.02008	.01005	-.00000	-.01007	-.02016	-.03026	-.04038	-.05052
.08250	.04979	.03987	.02994	.01998	.01000	.00000	-.01002	-.02006	-.03011	-.04018
.08500	.05940	.04955	.03969	.02980	.01988	.00995	0.00000	-.00997	-.01996	-.02996
.08750	.06890	.05912	.04932	.03950	.02965	.01979	.00990	.00000	-.00992	-.01986
.09000	.07828	.06858	.05884	.04909	.03931	.02951	.01969	.00986	.00000	-.00987
.09250	.08756	.07792	.06825	.05857	.04885	.03912	.02937	.01960	.00981	-.00000
.09500	.09673	.08716	.07756	.06793	.05829	.04862	.03893	.02922	.01950	.00976
.09750	.10579	.09629	.08675	.07719	.06761	.05801	.04838	.03874	.02908	.01940
.10000	.11475	.10531	.09584	.08634	.07683	.06729	.05773	.04815	.03855	.02894
.10250	.12361	.11423	.10482	.09539	.08594	.07646	.06697	.05745	.04792	.03836
.10500	.13236	.12304	.11370	.10433	.09494	.08553	.07610	.06664	.05717	.04768
.10750	.14100	.13175	.12247	.11317	.10384	.09449	.08512	.07573	.06632	.05689
.11000	.14955	.14036	.13115	.12190	.11264	.10335	.09404	.08471	.07536	.06599
.11250	.15800	.14887	.13972	.13054	.12133	.11211	.10286	.09359	.08430	.07499
.11500	.16635	.15729	.14819	.13907	.12993	.12076	.11157	.10237	.09314	.08389
.11750	.17461	.16560	.15657	.14751	.13843	.12932	.12019	.11104	.10187	.09269
.12000	.18277	.17382	.16485	.15585	.14682	.13778	.12871	.11962	.11051	.10138
.12250	.19083	.18194	.17303	.16409	.15513	.14614	.13713	.12810	.11905	.10998
.12500	.19880	.18997	.18112	.17224	.16333	.15440	.14545	.13648	.12749	.11847
.12750	.20668	.19791	.18911	.18029	.17144	.16257	.15368	.14476	.13583	.12687
.13000	.21447	.20576	.19702	.18825	.17946	.17065	.16181	.15296	.14408	.13518
.13250	.22217	.21351	.20483	.19612	.18739	.17863	.16985	.16105	.15223	.14339
.13500	.22978	.22118	.21255	.20390	.19523	.18653	.17780	.16906	.16029	.15150
.13750	.23730	.22876	.22019	.21159	.20297	.19433	.18566	.17697	.16826	.15953
.14000	.24473	.23625	.22773	.21920	.21063	.20204	.19343	.18479	.17614	.16746
.14250	.25208	.24365	.23519	.22671	.21820	.20967	.20111	.19253	.18393	.17530
.14500	.25935	.25097	.24257	.23414	.22568	.21720	.20870	.20017	.19163	.18306
.14750	.26653	.25821	.24986	.24148	.23308	.22465	.21620	.20773	.19924	.19072
.15000	.27362	.26536	.25706	.24874	.24039	.23202	.22362	.21521	.20676	.19830
.15250	.28064	.27243	.26419	.25592	.24762	.23930	.23096	.22259	.21420	.20580
.15500	.28758	.27942	.27123	.26301	.25477	.24650	.23821	.22990	.22156	.21320
.15750	.29444	.28633	.27819	.27003	.26184	.25362	.24538	.23712	.22883	.22053
.16000	.30121	.29316	.28507	.27696	.26882	.26066	.25247	.24426	.23602	.22777
.16250	.30791	.29991	.29188	.28382	.27573	.26762	.25948	.25132	.24313	.23493
.16500	.31454	.30659	.29860	.29059	.28256	.27449	.26641	.25830	.25016	.24201
.16750	.32109	.31318	.30525	.29729	.28931	.28129	.27326	.26520	.25711	.24901
.17000	.32756	.31971	.31183	.30392	.29598	.28802	.28003	.27202	.26398	.25593
.17250	.33396	.32616	.31833	.31046	.30258	.29466	.28672	.27876	.27078	.26277
.17500	.34029	.33253	.32475	.31694	.30910	.30123	.29334	.28543	.27750	.26954
.17750	.34654	.33884	.33110	.32334	.31555	.30773	.29989	.29203	.28414	.27623
.18000	.35273	.34507	.33738	.32967	.32192	.31416	.30636	.29854	.29070	.28284
.18250	.35884	.35123	.34359	.33592	.32823	.32051	.31276	.30499	.29720	.28938
.18500	.36488	.35732	.34973	.34211	.33446	.32679	.31909	.31136	.30362	.29585
.18750	.37086	.36334	.35580	.34822	.34062	.33300	.32534	.31767	.30997	.30224
.19000	.37676	.36930	.36180	.35427	.34672	.33913	.33153	.32390	.31624	.30857
.19250	.38260	.37518	.36773	.36025	.35274	.34520	.33764	.33006	.32245	.31482
.19500	.38838	.38100	.37359	.36616	.35870	.35121	.34369	.33615	.32859	.32100
.19750	.39408	.38675	.37939	.37200	.36458	.35714	.34967	.34217	.33466	.32711
.20000	.39973	.39244	.38513	.37778	.37041	.36301	.35558	.34813	.34066	.33316
.20250	.40531	.39807	.39079	.38349	.37616	.36881	.36143	.35402	.34659	.33914
.20500	.41082	.40363	.39640	.38914	.38186	.37454	.36721	.35984	.35246	.34505
.20750	.41628	.40912	.40194	.39473	.38749	.38022	.37292	.36560	.35826	.35089

EFFECTIVE YIELD	CONTRACT RATE .09500	.09750	.10000	.10250	.10500	.10750	.11000	.11250	.11500	.11750
.07000	-.10354	-.11398	-.12443	-.13490	-.14537	-.15585	-.16635	-.17685	-.18736	-.19787
.07250	-.09263	-.10301	-.11339	-.12378	-.13419	-.14461	-.15503	-.16546	-.17590	-.18635
.07500	-.08186	-.09216	-.10247	-.11280	-.12314	-.13349	-.14384	-.15421	-.16458	-.17496
.07750	-.07120	-.08144	-.09169	-.10194	-.11221	-.12249	-.13278	-.14308	-.15339	-.16370
.08000	-.06068	-.07084	-.08102	-.09121	-.10142	-.11163	-.12185	-.13208	-.14232	-.15257
.08250	-.05027	-.06037	-.07048	-.08060	-.09074	-.10089	-.11104	-.12121	-.13138	-.14156
.08500	-.03998	-.05001	-.06006	-.07012	-.08019	-.09027	-.10036	-.11046	-.12057	-.13068
.08750	-.02981	-.03978	-.04976	-.05975	-.06976	-.07977	-.08980	-.09983	-.10938	-.11993
.09000	-.01976	-.02966	-.03958	-.04950	-.05944	-.06940	-.07936	-.08933	-.09931	-.10930
.09250	-.00982	-.01966	-.02951	-.03937	-.04925	-.05914	-.06903	-.07894	-.08886	-.09878
.09500	0.00000	-.00977	-.01956	-.02936	-.03917	-.04900	-.05883	-.06868	-.07853	-.08839
.09750	.00971	.00000	-.00972	-.01946	-.02921	-.03897	-.04874	-.05853	-.06832	-.07812
.10000	.01931	.00966	-.00000	-.00967	-.01936	-.02906	-.03877	-.04849	-.05822	-.06796
.10250	.02879	.01921	.00961	.00000	-.00963	-.01926	-.02891	-.03857	-.04824	-.05792
.10500	.03817	.02865	.01911	.00956	0.00000	-.00958	-.01916	-.02876	-.03837	-.04799
.10750	.04745	.03798	.02851	.01902	.00952	.00000	-.00953	-.01906	-.02861	-.03817
.11000	.05661	.04721	.03780	.02837	.01892	.00947	.00000	-.00948	-.01897	-.02846
.11250	.06567	.05633	.04698	.03761	.02822	.01883	.00942	.00000	-.00943	-.01887
.11500	.07463	.06535	.05605	.04674	.03742	.02808	.01873	.00937	.00000	-.00938
.11750	.08348	.07426	.06502	.05577	.04651	.03723	.02794	.01864	.00932	0.00000
.12000	.09224	.08307	.07389	.06470	.05549	.04627	.03704	.02780	.01854	.00927
.12250	.10089	.09178	.08266	.07353	.06438	.05522	.04604	.03685	.02765	.01845
.12500	.10944	.10040	.09133	.08226	.07316	.06406	.05494	.04581	.03666	.02751
.12750	.11790	.10891	.09990	.09088	.08185	.07280	.06373	.05466	.04557	.03648
.13000	.12626	.11733	.10838	.09941	.09043	.08144	.07243	.06341	.05438	.04534
.13250	.13453	.12565	.11676	.10785	.09892	.08998	.08103	.07207	.06309	.05411
.13500	.14270	.13388	.12504	.11618	.10732	.09843	.08954	.08063	.07171	.06277
.13750	.15078	.14201	.13323	.12443	.11561	.10679	.09794	.08909	.08022	.07134
.14000	.15877	.15005	.14132	.13258	.12382	.11504	.10626	.09745	.08864	.07982
.14250	.16666	.15801	.14933	.14064	.13193	.12321	.11447	.10573	.09697	.08820
.14500	.17447	.16587	.15724	.14861	.13995	.13128	.12260	.11391	.10520	.09648
.14750	.18219	.17364	.16507	.15648	.14788	.13927	.13064	.12199	.11334	.10467
.15000	.18982	.18132	.17281	.16427	.15572	.14716	.13858	.12999	.12139	.11277
.15250	.19737	.18892	.18046	.17197	.16348	.15497	.14644	.13790	.12935	.12079
.15500	.20483	.19643	.18802	.17959	.17114	.16268	.15421	.14572	.13722	.12871
.15750	.21220	.20386	.19550	.18712	.17872	.17031	.16189	.15345	.14500	.13654
.16000	.21950	.21120	.20289	.19456	.18622	.17786	.16949	.16110	.15270	.14429
.16250	.22671	.21846	.21020	.20192	.19363	.18532	.17700	.16866	.16031	.15195
.16500	.23384	.22564	.21743	.20920	.20096	.19270	.18442	.17614	.16783	.15952
.16750	.24088	.23274	.22458	.21640	.20820	.19999	.19177	.18353	.17528	.16701
.17000	.24785	.23976	.23165	.22352	.21537	.20721	.19903	.19084	.18264	.17442
.17250	.25475	.24670	.23864	.23055	.22246	.21434	.20621	.19807	.18991	.18174
.17500	.26156	.25356	.24555	.23751	.22946	.22139	.21331	.20522	.19711	.18899
.17750	.26830	.26035	.25238	.24439	.23639	.22837	.22034	.21229	.20423	.19615
.18000	.27496	.26706	.25914	.25120	.24324	.23527	.22728	.21928	.21127	.20324
.18250	.28155	.27369	.26582	.25792	.25002	.24209	.23415	.22619	.21823	.21024
.18500	.28806	.28025	.27242	.26458	.25671	.24884	.24094	.23303	.22511	.21717
.18750	.29450	.28674	.27896	.27116	.26334	.25551	.24766	.23979	.23192	.22403
.19000	.30087	.29315	.28542	.27766	.26989	.26210	.25430	.24648	.23865	.23081
.19250	.30717	.29950	.29180	.28410	.27637	.26863	.26087	.25310	.24531	.23751
.19500	.31339	.30577	.29812	.29046	.28278	.27508	.26736	.25964	.25189	.24414
.19750	.31955	.31197	.30437	.29675	.28911	.28146	.27379	.26610	.25841	.25069
.20000	.32564	.31810	.31055	.30297	.29538	.28777	.28014	.27250	.26485	.25718
.20250	.33166	.32417	.31666	.30912	.30157	.29401	.28643	.27883	.27122	.26359
.20500	.33762	.33017	.32270	.31521	.30770	.30018	.29264	.28509	.27752	.26994
.20750	.34351	.33610	.32867	.32123	.31376	.30628	.29879	.29128	.28375	.27621

POINT TABLES: ORIGINAL LOAN TERM: 360 MONTHS LOAN PREPAID IN: 60 MONTHS

EFFECTIVE YIELD	CONTRACT RATE .12000	.12250	.12500	.12750	.13000	.13250	.13500	.13750	.14000	.14250
.07000	-.20839	-.21892	-.22945	-.23999	-.25053	-.26107	-.27162	-.28217	-.29272	-.30327
.07250	-.19680	-.20726	-.21773	-.22819	-.23867	-.24914	-.25963	-.27011	-.28060	-.29108
.07500	-.18534	-.19574	-.20613	-.21654	-.22694	-.23736	-.24777	-.25819	-.26861	-.27903
.07750	-.17402	-.18434	-.19468	-.20501	-.21535	-.22570	-.23605	-.24640	-.25676	-.26711
.08000	-.16282	-.17308	-.18335	-.19362	-.20389	-.21417	-.22446	-.23475	-.24504	-.25533
.08250	-.15175	-.16195	-.17215	-.18235	-.19257	-.20278	-.21300	-.22322	-.23345	-.24368
.08500	-.14081	-.15094	-.16107	-.17122	-.18136	-.19152	-.20167	-.21183	-.22200	-.23216
.08750	-.12999	-.14005	-.15013	-.16021	-.17029	-.18038	-.19047	-.20057	-.21067	-.22077
.09000	-.11929	-.12930	-.13930	-.14932	-.15934	-.16937	-.17940	-.18943	-.19947	-.20951
.09250	-.10872	-.11866	-.12860	-.13856	-.14852	-.15848	-.16845	-.17842	-.18840	-.19838
.09500	-.09826	-.10814	-.11802	-.12792	-.13781	-.14771	-.15762	-.16753	-.17745	-.18737
.09750	-.08793	-.09774	-.10756	-.11739	-.12723	-.13707	-.14692	-.15677	-.16662	-.17648
.10000	-.07771	-.08746	-.09722	-.10699	-.11677	-.12655	-.13633	-.14612	-.15592	-.16571
.10250	-.06760	-.07730	-.08700	-.09671	-.10642	-.11614	-.12587	-.13560	-.14533	-.15507
.10500	-.05761	-.06725	-.07689	-.08654	-.09619	-.10585	-.11552	-.12519	-.13486	-.14454
.10750	-.04774	-.05731	-.06689	-.07648	-.08608	-.09568	-.10529	-.11490	-.12451	-.13413
.11000	-.03797	-.04749	-.05701	-.06654	-.07608	-.08562	-.09517	-.10472	-.11428	-.12384
.11250	-.02832	-.03777	-.04724	-.05671	-.06619	-.07567	-.08516	-.09466	-.10416	-.11366
.11500	-.01877	-.02817	-.03758	-.04699	-.05641	-.06584	-.07527	-.08471	-.09415	-.10360
.11750	-.00933	-.01867	-.02802	-.03738	-.04674	-.05611	-.06549	-.07487	-.08426	-.09365
.12000	.00000	-.00928	-.01858	-.02788	-.03718	-.04650	-.05582	-.06514	-.07447	-.08381
.12250	.00923	.00000	-.00924	-.01848	-.02773	-.03699	-.04625	-.05552	-.06480	-.07407
.12500	.01835	.00918	.00000	-.00919	-.01838	-.02758	-.03679	-.04601	-.05523	-.06445
.12750	.02737	.01826	.00913	.00000	-.00914	-.01829	-.02744	-.03660	-.04576	-.05493
.13000	.03629	.02723	.01816	.00908	.00000	-.00909	-.01819	-.02730	-.03641	-.04552
.13250	.04511	.03611	.02709	.01807	.00904	.00000	-.00904	-.01810	-.02715	-.03621
.13500	.05383	.04488	.03592	.02695	.01797	.00899	0.00000	-.00900	-.01800	-.02701
.13750	.06246	.05356	.04465	.03574	.02681	.01788	.00894	0.00000	-.00895	-.01791
.14000	.07098	.06214	.05328	.04442	.03555	.02667	.01779	.00890	.00000	-.00890
.14250	.07941	.07062	.06182	.05301	.04419	.03537	.02654	.01770	.00885	.00000
.14500	.08775	.07901	.07026	.06151	.05274	.04397	.03519	.02640	.01760	.00881
.14750	.09600	.08731	.07861	.06991	.06119	.05247	.04374	.03500	.02626	.01751
.15000	.10415	.09551	.08687	.07821	.06955	.06088	.05220	.04352	.03482	.02613
.15250	.11221	.10363	.09503	.08643	.07782	.06919	.06057	.05193	.04329	.03464
.15500	.12018	.11165	.10310	.09455	.08599	.07742	.06884	.06026	.05166	.04307
.15750	.12807	.11958	.11109	.10258	.09407	.08555	.07702	.06849	.05995	.05140
.16000	.13586	.12743	.11898	.11053	.10207	.09360	.08512	.07663	.06814	.05964
.16250	.14357	.13519	.12679	.11839	.10997	.10155	.09312	.08468	.07624	.06779
.16500	.15119	.14286	.13451	.12616	.11779	.10942	.10104	.09265	.08425	.07585
.16750	.15873	.15045	.14215	.13384	.12552	.11720	.10887	.10052	.09218	.08382
.17000	.16619	.15795	.14970	.14144	.13317	.12489	.11661	.10832	.10002	.09171
.17250	.17356	.16537	.15717	.14896	.14074	.13251	.12427	.11602	.10777	.09951
.17500	.18085	.17271	.16456	.15639	.14822	.14003	.13184	.12364	.11544	.10722
.17750	.18807	.17997	.17186	.16374	.15561	.14748	.13933	.13118	.12302	.11485
.18000	.19520	.18715	.17908	.17101	.16293	.15484	.14674	.13864	.13052	.12240
.18250	.20225	.19425	.18623	.17820	.17017	.16212	.15407	.14601	.13794	.12987
.18500	.20923	.20127	.19330	.18532	.17733	.16933	.16132	.15330	.14528	.13725
.18750	.21613	.20821	.20029	.19235	.18441	.17645	.16849	.16052	.15254	.14455
.19000	.22295	.21508	.20720	.19931	.19141	.18350	.17558	.16765	.15972	.15178
.19250	.22970	.22187	.21404	.20619	.19833	.19047	.18259	.17471	.16682	.15893
.19500	.23637	.22859	.22080	.21300	.20518	.19736	.18953	.18169	.17385	.16599
.19750	.24297	.23523	.22749	.21973	.21196	.20418	.19640	.18860	.18080	.17299
.20000	.24950	.24181	.23410	.22639	.21866	.21093	.20318	.19543	.18767	.17990
.20250	.25596	.24831	.24064	.23297	.22529	.21760	.20990	.20219	.19447	.18675
.20500	.26234	.25473	.24712	.23949	.23185	.22420	.21654	.20887	.20120	.19352
.20750	.26866	.26109	.25352	.24593	.23833	.23073	.22311	.21549	.20785	.20021

POINT TABLES: ORIGINAL LOAN TERM: 360 MONTHS LOAN PREPAID IN: 60 MONTHS

EFFECTIVE YIELD	CONTRACT RATE .14500	.14750	.15000	.15250	.15500	.15750	.16000	.16250	.16500	.16750
.07000	-.31383	-.32439	-.33495	-.34551	-.35607	-.36664	-.37720	-.38776	-.39833	-.40889
.07250	-.30158	-.31207	-.32256	-.33306	-.34355	-.35405	-.36455	-.37505	-.38555	-.39604
.07500	-.28946	-.29988	-.31031	-.32074	-.33118	-.34161	-.35204	-.36247	-.37291	-.38334
.07750	-.27748	-.28784	-.29820	-.30857	-.31894	-.32930	-.33967	-.35004	-.36041	-.37078
.08000	-.26563	-.27593	-.28623	-.29653	-.30683	-.31714	-.32744	-.33775	-.34806	-.35836
.08250	-.25391	-.26415	-.27439	-.28463	-.29487	-.30511	-.31535	-.32559	-.33584	-.34608
.08500	-.24233	-.25250	-.26268	-.27285	-.28303	-.29321	-.30339	-.31357	-.32375	-.33394
.08750	-.23088	-.24099	-.25110	-.26121	-.27133	-.28145	-.29157	-.30169	-.31181	-.32193
.09000	-.21956	-.22960	-.23965	-.24971	-.25976	-.26982	-.27987	-.28993	-.29999	-.31005
.09250	-.20836	-.21835	-.22833	-.23832	-.24832	-.25831	-.26831	-.27831	-.28830	-.29830
.09500	-.19729	-.20721	-.21714	-.22707	-.23700	-.24694	-.25687	-.26681	-.27675	-.28669
.09750	-.18634	-.19621	-.20607	-.21594	-.22582	-.23569	-.24557	-.25544	-.26532	-.27520
.10000	-.17552	-.18532	-.19513	-.20494	-.21475	-.22457	-.23438	-.24420	-.25402	-.26384
.10250	-.16481	-.17456	-.18431	-.19406	-.20381	-.21357	-.22332	-.23308	-.24284	-.25261
.10500	-.15423	-.16391	-.17360	-.18330	-.19299	-.20269	-.21239	-.22209	-.23179	-.24150
.10750	-.14376	-.15339	-.16302	-.17265	-.18229	-.19193	-.20157	-.21122	-.22086	-.23051
.11000	-.13341	-.14298	-.15255	-.16213	-.17171	-.18129	-.19088	-.20046	-.21005	-.21964
.11250	-.12317	-.13269	-.14220	-.15172	-.16125	-.17077	-.18030	-.18983	-.19936	-.20889
.11500	-.11305	-.12251	-.13197	-.14143	-.15090	-.16037	-.16984	-.17931	-.18879	-.19826
.11750	-.10304	-.11244	-.12185	-.13125	-.14066	-.15008	-.15949	-.16891	-.17833	-.18775
.12000	-.09315	-.10249	-.11184	-.12119	-.13054	-.13990	-.14926	-.15862	-.16799	-.17735
.12250	-.08336	-.09265	-.10194	-.11124	-.12054	-.12984	-.13914	-.14845	-.15776	-.16707
.12500	-.07368	-.08291	-.09215	-.10139	-.11064	-.11988	-.12913	-.13839	-.14764	-.15690
.12750	-.06411	-.07329	-.08247	-.09166	-.10085	-.11004	-.11924	-.12844	-.13764	-.14684
.13000	-.05464	-.06377	-.07290	-.08203	-.09117	-.10031	-.10945	-.11859	-.12774	-.13689
.13250	-.04528	-.05435	-.06343	-.07251	-.08159	-.09068	-.09977	-.10886	-.11795	-.12705
.13500	-.03602	-.04504	-.05406	-.06309	-.07212	-.08115	-.09019	-.09923	-.10827	-.11732
.13750	-.02687	-.03583	-.04480	-.05378	-.06275	-.07174	-.08072	-.08971	-.09870	-.10769
.14000	-.01781	-.02672	-.03564	-.04456	-.05349	-.06242	-.07135	-.08029	-.08923	-.09817
.14250	-.00886	-.01772	-.02658	-.03545	-.04433	-.05321	-.06209	-.07097	-.07986	-.08875
.14500	.00000	-.00881	-.01762	-.02644	-.03527	-.04409	-.05292	-.06176	-.07059	-.07943
.14750	.00876	.00000	-.00876	-.01753	-.02630	-.03508	-.04386	-.05264	-.06143	-.07022
.15000	.01742	.00871	.00000	-.00872	-.01744	-.02617	-.03490	-.04363	-.05236	-.06110
.15250	.02599	.01733	.00867	0.00000	-.00867	-.01735	-.02603	-.03471	-.04340	-.05209
.15500	.03446	.02585	.01724	.00862	.00000	-.00863	-.01726	-.02589	-.03453	-.04317
.15750	.04284	.03429	.02572	.01715	.00858	.00000	-.00858	-.01717	-.02575	-.03435
.16000	.05113	.04262	.03411	.02559	.01706	.00853	0.00000	-.00854	-.01708	-.02562
.16250	.05933	.05087	.04240	.03393	.02545	.01697	.00849	.00000	-.00849	-.01699
.16500	.06744	.05903	.05061	.04218	.03375	.02532	.01688	.00844	.00000	-.00845
.16750	.07546	.06710	.05872	.05035	.04197	.03358	.02519	.01680	.00840	.00000
.17000	.08339	.07508	.06675	.05842	.05009	.04175	.03341	.02506	.01671	.00836
.17250	.09124	.08297	.07469	.06641	.05812	.04983	.04153	.03323	.02493	.01662
.17500	.09900	.09078	.08255	.07431	.06607	.05782	.04957	.04132	.03306	.02480
.17750	.10668	.09850	.09031	.08212	.07393	.06573	.05752	.04932	.04110	.03289
.18000	.11427	.10614	.09800	.08985	.08170	.07355	.06539	.05723	.04906	.04089
.18250	.12178	.11369	.10560	.09750	.08940	.08129	.07317	.06506	.05693	.04881
.18500	.12921	.12117	.11312	.10507	.09701	.08894	.08087	.07280	.06472	.05664
.18750	.13656	.12856	.12056	.11255	.10453	.09651	.08849	.08046	.07243	.06439
.19000	.14383	.13588	.12792	.11995	.11198	.10400	.09602	.08804	.08005	.07206
.19250	.15102	.14311	.13519	.12727	.11934	.11141	.10348	.09553	.08759	.07964
.19500	.15813	.15027	.14239	.13452	.12663	.11874	.11085	.10295	.09505	.08714
.19750	.16517	.15735	.14952	.14168	.13384	.12599	.11814	.11029	.10243	.09457
.20000	.17213	.16435	.15656	.14877	.14097	.13317	.12536	.11755	.10973	.10191
.20250	.17902	.17128	.16353	.15578	.14803	.14027	.13250	.12473	.11696	.10918
.20500	.18583	.17813	.17043	.16272	.15501	.14729	.13956	.13184	.12410	.11637
.20750	.19256	.18491	.17725	.16958	.16191	.15423	.14655	.13887	.13118	.12348

POINT TABLES: ORIGINAL LOAN TERM: 360 MONTHS LOAN PREPAID IN: 60 MONTHS

EFFECTIVE YIELD	CONTRACT RATE .17000	.17250	.17500	.17750	.18000	.18250	.18500	.18750	.19000	.19250
.07000	-.41945	-.43002	-.44058	-.45114	-.46170	-.47227	-.48283	-.49339	-.50395	-.51451
.07250	-.40654	-.41704	-.42754	-.43804	-.44854	-.45904	-.46953	-.48003	-.49052	-.50102
.07500	-.39378	-.40421	-.41465	-.42508	-.43552	-.44595	-.45638	-.46682	-.47725	-.48768
.07750	-.38116	-.39153	-.40190	-.41227	-.42264	-.43301	-.44338	-.45375	-.46412	-.47449
.08000	-.36867	-.37898	-.38929	-.39960	-.40991	-.42021	-.43052	-.44083	-.45114	-.46144
.08250	-.35633	-.36657	-.37682	-.38707	-.39731	-.40756	-.41780	-.42805	-.43829	-.44854
.08500	-.34412	-.35430	-.36449	-.37467	-.38486	-.39504	-.40523	-.41541	-.42559	-.43578
.08750	-.33205	-.34217	-.35229	-.36242	-.37254	-.38266	-.39279	-.40291	-.41303	-.42316
.09000	-.32011	-.33017	-.34023	-.35030	-.36036	-.37042	-.38048	-.39055	-.40061	-.41067
.09250	-.30831	-.31831	-.32831	-.33831	-.34831	-.35831	-.36832	-.37832	-.38832	-.39833
.09500	-.29663	-.30657	-.31651	-.32646	-.33640	-.34634	-.35628	-.36623	-.37617	-.38611
.09750	-.28508	-.29497	-.30485	-.31473	-.32461	-.33450	-.34438	-.35427	-.36415	-.37404
.10000	-.27366	-.28349	-.29331	-.30314	-.31296	-.32279	-.33261	-.34244	-.35226	-.36209
.10250	-.26237	-.27214	-.28190	-.29167	-.30143	-.31120	-.32097	-.33074	-.34051	-.35027
.10500	-.25120	-.26091	-.27062	-.28033	-.29003	-.29974	-.30945	-.31917	-.32888	-.33859
.10750	-.24016	-.24981	-.25946	-.26911	-.27876	-.28841	-.29807	-.30772	-.31737	-.32703
.11000	-.22923	-.23882	-.24842	-.25801	-.26761	-.27720	-.28680	-.29640	-.30600	-.31559
.11250	-.21843	-.22796	-.23750	-.24704	-.25658	-.26612	-.27566	-.28520	-.29474	-.30428
.11500	-.20774	-.21722	-.22670	-.23619	-.24567	-.25515	-.26464	-.27412	-.28361	-.29310
.11750	-.19717	-.20660	-.21602	-.22545	-.23488	-.24431	-.25374	-.26317	-.27260	-.28203
.12000	-.18672	-.19609	-.20546	-.21483	-.22421	-.23358	-.24296	-.25233	-.26171	-.27109
.12250	-.17638	-.18570	-.19502	-.20433	-.21365	-.22297	-.23229	-.24161	-.25094	-.26026
.12500	-.16616	-.17542	-.18468	-.19395	-.20321	-.21248	-.22174	-.23101	-.24028	-.24955
.12750	-.15605	-.16525	-.17446	-.18367	-.19288	-.20210	-.21131	-.22052	-.22974	-.23896
.13000	-.14604	-.15520	-.16435	-.17351	-.18267	-.19183	-.20099	-.21015	-.21931	-.22848
.13250	-.13615	-.14525	-.15435	-.16346	-.17256	-.18167	-.19078	-.19989	-.20900	-.21811
.13500	-.12636	-.13541	-.14446	-.15352	-.16257	-.17162	-.18068	-.18974	-.19880	-.20785
.13750	-.11668	-.12568	-.13468	-.14368	-.15268	-.16169	-.17069	-.17970	-.18870	-.19771
.14000	-.10711	-.11606	-.12500	-.13395	-.14290	-.15185	-.16081	-.16976	-.17872	-.18767
.14250	-.09764	-.10654	-.11543	-.12433	-.13323	-.14213	-.15103	-.15994	-.16884	-.17775
.14500	-.08827	-.09712	-.10596	-.11481	-.12366	-.13251	-.14136	-.15022	-.15907	-.16793
.14750	-.07901	-.08780	-.09660	-.10539	-.11419	-.12299	-.13180	-.14060	-.14940	-.15821
.15000	-.06984	-.07859	-.08733	-.09608	-.10483	-.11358	-.12233	-.13109	-.13984	-.14860
.15250	-.06078	-.06947	-.07817	-.08687	-.09557	-.10427	-.11297	-.12168	-.13038	-.13909
.15500	-.05181	-.06046	-.06910	-.07775	-.08640	-.09506	-.10371	-.11237	-.12102	-.12968
.15750	-.04294	-.05154	-.06013	-.06874	-.07734	-.08594	-.09455	-.10316	-.11177	-.12038
.16000	-.03416	-.04271	-.05126	-.05982	-.06837	-.07693	-.08549	-.09404	-.10261	-.11117
.16250	-.02548	-.03398	-.04249	-.05099	-.05950	-.06801	-.07652	-.08503	-.09354	-.10206
.16500	-.01690	-.02535	-.03381	-.04226	-.05072	-.05918	-.06765	-.07611	-.08458	-.09305
.16750	-.00840	-.01681	-.02522	-.03363	-.04204	-.05046	-.05887	-.06729	-.07571	-.08413
.17000	.00000	-.00836	-.01672	-.02508	-.03345	-.04182	-.05019	-.05856	-.06693	-.07531
.17250	.00831	.00000	-.00832	-.01663	-.02495	-.03328	-.04160	-.04992	-.05825	-.06658
.17500	.01654	.00827	.00000	-.00827	-.01655	-.02482	-.03310	-.04138	-.04966	-.05795
.17750	.02467	.01645	.00823	0.00000	-.00823	-.01646	-.02469	-.03293	-.04116	-.04940
.18000	.03272	.02454	.01637	.00818	-.00000	-.00819	-.01637	-.02456	-.03275	-.04095
.18250	.04068	.03255	.02442	.01628	.00814	.00000	-.00814	-.01629	-.02444	-.03258
.18500	.04856	.04047	.03238	.02429	.01620	.00810	0.00000	-.00810	-.01620	-.02431
.18750	.05635	.04831	.04026	.03222	.02416	.01611	.00806	.00000	-.00806	-.01612
.19000	.06406	.05606	.04806	.04006	.03205	.02404	.01603	.00802	.00000	-.00802
.19250	.07169	.06373	.05578	.04781	.03985	.03188	.02392	.01595	.00797	.00000
.19500	.07924	.07132	.06341	.05549	.04757	.03965	.03172	.02379	.01586	.00793
.19750	.08670	.07883	.07096	.06308	.05521	.04733	.03944	.03156	.02367	.01578
.20000	.09409	.08626	.07843	.07060	.06276	.05492	.04708	.03924	.03140	.02355
.20250	.10140	.09361	.08582	.07803	.07024	.06244	.05464	.04684	.03904	.03123
.20500	.10863	.10088	.09314	.08539	.07764	.06988	.06212	.05436	.04660	.03884
.20750	.11578	.10808	.10037	.09267	.08496	.07724	.06953	.06181	.05409	.04637

EFFECTIVE YIELD	CONTRACT RATE .19500	.19750	.20000	.20250	.20500	.20750
.07000	-.52506	-.53562	-.54618	-.55673	-.56729	-.57784
.07250	-.51151	-.52201	-.53250	-.54299	-.55348	-.56397
.07500	-.49811	-.50854	-.51897	-.52940	-.53983	-.55026
.07750	-.48486	-.49522	-.50559	-.51596	-.52632	-.53669
.08000	-.47175	-.48205	-.49236	-.50266	-.51297	-.52327
.08250	-.45878	-.46903	-.47927	-.48951	-.49975	-.51000
.08500	-.44596	-.45614	-.46632	-.47651	-.48669	-.49687
.08750	-.43328	-.44340	-.45352	-.46364	-.47376	-.48388
.09000	-.42073	-.43080	-.44086	-.45092	-.46098	-.47104
.09250	-.40833	-.41833	-.42833	-.43833	-.44833	-.45833
.09500	-.39606	-.40600	-.41594	-.42589	-.43583	-.44577
.09750	-.38392	-.39380	-.40369	-.41357	-.42346	-.43334
.10000	-.37192	-.38174	-.39157	-.40139	-.41122	-.42104
.10250	-.36004	-.36981	-.37958	-.38935	-.39912	-.40888
.10500	-.34830	-.35801	-.36772	-.37743	-.38714	-.39685
.10750	-.33668	-.34634	-.35599	-.36565	-.37530	-.38495
.11000	-.32519	-.33479	-.34439	-.35399	-.36358	-.37318
.11250	-.31383	-.32337	-.33291	-.34245	-.35200	-.36154
.11500	-.30258	-.31207	-.32156	-.33105	-.34053	-.35002
.11750	-.29146	-.30090	-.31033	-.31976	-.32919	-.33863
.12000	-.28046	-.28984	-.29922	-.30860	-.31798	-.32735
.12250	-.26958	-.27891	-.28823	-.29755	-.30688	-.31620
.12500	-.25882	-.26809	-.27736	-.28663	-.29590	-.30517
.12750	-.24817	-.25739	-.26661	-.27582	-.28504	-.29426
.13000	-.23764	-.24680	-.25597	-.26513	-.27430	-.28346
.13250	-.22722	-.23633	-.24544	-.25456	-.26367	-.27278
.13500	-.21691	-.22597	-.23503	-.24410	-.25316	-.26222
.13750	-.20672	-.21573	-.22474	-.23375	-.24276	-.25177
.14000	-.19663	-.20559	-.21455	-.22351	-.23247	-.24143
.14250	-.18665	-.19556	-.20447	-.21338	-.22229	-.23120
.14500	-.17678	-.18564	-.19450	-.20335	-.21221	-.22107
.14750	-.16702	-.17582	-.18463	-.19344	-.20225	-.21106
.15000	-.15736	-.16611	-.17487	-.18363	-.19239	-.20115
.15250	-.14780	-.15651	-.16522	-.17393	-.18264	-.19135
.15500	-.13834	-.14700	-.15566	-.16433	-.17299	-.18165
.15750	-.12899	-.13760	-.14621	-.15483	-.16344	-.17206
.16000	-.11973	-.12830	-.13686	-.14543	-.15399	-.16256
.16250	-.11057	-.11909	-.12761	-.13613	-.14465	-.15317
.16500	-.10152	-.10999	-.11846	-.12693	-.13540	-.14388
.16750	-.09255	-.10098	-.10940	-.11783	-.12625	-.13468
.17000	-.08368	-.09206	-.10044	-.10882	-.11720	-.12558
.17250	-.07491	-.08324	-.09157	-.09991	-.10824	-.11658
.17500	-.06623	-.07452	-.08280	-.09109	-.09938	-.10767
.17750	-.05764	-.06588	-.07412	-.08237	-.09061	-.09885
.18000	-.04914	-.05734	-.06554	-.07373	-.08193	-.09013
.18250	-.04073	-.04888	-.05704	-.06519	-.07335	-.08150
.18500	-.03241	-.04052	-.04863	-.05674	-.06485	-.07296
.18750	-.02418	-.03224	-.04031	-.04838	-.05644	-.06451
.19000	-.01604	-.02406	-.03208	-.04010	-.04812	-.05615
.19250	-.00798	-.01595	-.02393	-.03191	-.03989	-.04787
.19500	.00000	-.00793	-.01587	-.02381	-.03174	-.03968
.19750	.00789	.00000	-.00789	-.01579	-.02368	-.03158
.20000	.01570	.00785	0.00000	-.00785	-.01571	-.02356
.20250	.02343	.01562	.00781	.00000	-.00781	-.01563
.20500	.03107	.02331	.01554	.00777	0.00000	-.00777
.20750	.03864	.03092	.02319	.01546	.00773	.00000

POINT TABLES: ORIGINAL LOAN TERM: 360 MONTHS LOAN PREPAID IN: 84 MONTHS

CONTRACT RATE

EFFECTIVE YIELD	.07000	.07250	.07500	.07750	.08000	.08250	.08500	.08750	.09000	.09250
.07000	.00000	-.01332	-.02668	-.04008	-.05352	-.06699	-.08050	-.09404	-.10750	-.12120
.07250	.01319	.00000	-.01323	-.02651	-.03982	-.05317	-.06655	-.07996	-.09340	-.10687
.07500	.02618	.01311	.00000	-.01315	-.02634	-.03956	-.05282	-.06611	-.07943	-.09277
.07750	.03896	.02601	.01303	.00000	-.01306	-.02617	-.03930	-.05247	-.06566	-.07889
.08000	.05154	.03871	.02585	.01294	-.00000	-.01298	-.02599	-.03904	-.05212	-.06522
.08250	.06392	.05121	.03847	.02568	.01286	.00000	-.01290	-.02582	-.03878	-.05177
.08500	.07610	.06352	.05089	.03823	.02552	.01278	.00000	-.01281	-.02565	-.03852
.08750	.08810	.07563	.06312	.05057	.03798	.02536	.01269	.00000	-.01273	-.02548
.09000	.09990	.08755	.07516	.06272	.05025	.03774	.02519	.01261	.00000	-.01264
.09250	.11152	.09929	.08701	.07469	.06233	.04993	.03749	.02503	.01253	.00000
.09500	.12296	.11084	.09867	.08646	.07422	.06193	.04961	.03725	.02486	.01245
.09750	.13422	.12221	.11015	.09806	.08592	.07374	.06153	.04929	.03701	.02470
.10000	.14530	.13340	.12146	.10947	.09744	.08538	.07327	.06114	.04897	.03677
.10250	.15622	.14442	.13258	.12071	.10878	.09683	.08483	.07280	.06074	.04865
.10500	.16696	.15527	.14354	.13177	.11995	.10810	.09621	.08429	.07233	.06035
.10750	.17753	.16595	.15432	.14266	.13095	.11920	.10742	.09560	.08375	.07186
.11000	.18794	.17646	.16494	.15338	.14177	.13013	.11845	.10673	.09499	.08321
.11250	.19818	.18681	.17539	.16393	.15243	.14089	.12931	.11770	.10605	.09437
.11500	.20827	.19700	.18568	.17432	.16292	.15149	.14001	.12850	.11695	.10537
.11750	.21820	.20703	.19582	.18456	.17326	.16192	.15054	.13913	.12768	.11620
.12000	.22798	.21691	.20579	.19463	.18343	.17219	.16091	.14960	.13825	.12687
.12250	.23760	.22663	.21561	.20455	.19345	.18230	.17112	.15990	.14865	.13737
.12500	.24708	.23620	.22528	.21432	.20331	.19226	.18118	.17006	.15890	.14771
.12750	.25641	.24563	.23480	.22393	.21302	.20207	.19108	.18005	.16899	.15790
.13000	.26560	.25491	.24418	.23340	.22258	.21173	.20083	.18990	.17893	.16793
.13250	.27464	.26405	.25341	.24273	.23200	.22124	.21043	.19959	.18872	.17781
.13500	.28355	.27305	.26250	.25191	.24127	.23060	.21989	.20914	.19836	.18754
.13750	.29232	.28191	.27145	.26095	.25041	.23982	.22920	.21854	.20785	.19712
.14000	.30095	.29063	.28026	.26985	.25940	.24890	.23837	.22780	.21720	.20656
.14250	.30945	.29922	.28894	.27862	.26825	.25785	.24740	.23692	.22640	.21585
.14500	.31782	.30768	.29749	.28725	.27697	.26666	.25630	.24590	.23547	.22501
.14750	.32607	.31601	.30590	.29575	.28556	.27533	.26506	.25475	.24441	.23403
.15000	.33418	.32421	.31419	.30413	.29402	.28387	.27369	.26346	.25320	.24291
.15250	.34218	.33229	.32235	.31237	.30235	.29229	.28218	.27205	.26187	.25166
.15500	.35005	.34024	.33039	.32049	.31055	.30057	.29055	.28050	.27041	.26028
.15750	.35780	.34808	.33831	.32849	.31863	.30874	.29880	.28882	.27881	.26877
.16000	.36543	.35579	.34610	.33637	.32659	.31678	.30692	.29703	.28710	.27713
.16250	.37295	.36339	.35378	.34413	.33443	.32469	.31492	.30510	.29525	.28537
.16500	.38036	.37087	.36134	.35177	.34215	.33249	.32280	.31306	.30329	.29348
.16750	.38765	.37824	.36879	.35930	.34976	.34018	.33056	.32090	.31121	.30148
.17000	.39483	.38550	.37613	.36671	.35725	.34774	.33820	.32862	.31901	.30935
.17250	.40190	.39265	.38335	.37401	.36462	.35520	.34573	.33623	.32669	.31711
.17500	.40887	.39969	.39047	.38120	.37189	.36254	.35315	.34372	.33426	.32476
.17750	.41573	.40663	.39748	.38829	.37905	.36977	.36046	.35110	.34171	.33229
.18000	.42248	.41346	.40438	.39526	.38610	.37690	.36766	.35838	.34906	.33971
.18250	.42914	.42019	.41119	.40214	.39305	.38392	.37475	.36554	.35630	.34702
.18500	.43570	.42681	.41788	.40891	.39989	.39083	.38174	.37260	.36343	.35422
.18750	.44215	.43334	.42448	.41558	.40664	.39765	.38862	.37956	.37045	.36132
.19000	.44851	.43977	.43099	.42215	.41328	.40436	.39540	.38641	.37738	.36831
.19250	.45478	.44611	.43739	.42863	.41982	.41097	.40208	.39316	.38420	.37520
.19500	.46095	.45235	.44370	.43500	.42627	.41749	.40867	.39981	.39092	.38199
.19750	.46703	.45850	.44991	.44129	.43262	.42391	.41515	.40636	.39754	.38868
.20000	.47302	.46455	.45604	.44748	.43887	.43023	.42155	.41282	.40406	.39527
.20250	.47892	.47052	.46207	.45358	.44504	.43646	.42784	.41919	.41049	.40177
.20500	.48474	.47640	.46801	.45959	.45111	.44260	.43405	.42546	.41683	.40817
.20750	.49046	.48219	.47387	.46551	.45710	.44865	.44016	.43164	.42307	.41448

POINT TABLES: ORIGINAL LOAN TERM: 360 MONTHS LOAN PREPAID IN: 84 MONTHS

EFFECTIVE YIELD	CONTRACT RATE .09500	.09750	.10000	.10250	.10500	.10750	.11000	.11250	.11500	.11750
.07000	-.13482	-.14846	-.16213	-.17582	-.18952	-.20325	-.21699	-.23074	-.24451	-.25830
.07250	-.12037	-.13389	-.14743	-.16100	-.17458	-.18818	-.20180	-.21543	-.22908	-.24275
.07500	-.10615	-.11954	-.13296	-.14641	-.15987	-.17335	-.18685	-.20036	-.21389	-.22743
.07750	-.09214	-.10542	-.11872	-.13204	-.14538	-.15874	-.17212	-.18552	-.19893	-.21235
.08000	-.07836	-.09151	-.10469	-.11790	-.13112	-.14437	-.15763	-.17090	-.18420	-.19750
.08250	-.06478	-.07782	-.09089	-.10397	-.11708	-.13021	-.14335	-.15651	-.16969	-.18288
.08500	-.05142	-.06434	-.07729	-.09026	-.10325	-.11627	-.12930	-.14234	-.15541	-.16848
.08750	-.03826	-.05107	-.06391	-.07676	-.08964	-.10254	-.11546	-.12839	-.14134	-.15430
.09000	-.02531	-.03801	-.05073	-.06347	-.07624	-.08902	-.10183	-.11465	-.12749	-.14034
.09250	-.01256	-.02514	-.03775	-.05038	-.06304	-.07571	-.08840	-.10112	-.11384	-.12659
.09500	-.00000	-.01247	-.02497	-.03749	-.05004	-.06260	-.07519	-.08779	-.10041	-.11305
.09750	.01236	.00000	-.01239	-.02480	-.03724	-.04970	-.06217	-.07467	-.08718	-.09971
.10000	.02454	.01228	0.00000	-.01231	-.02463	-.03698	-.04935	-.06174	-.07415	-.08657
.10250	.03653	.02438	.01220	.00000	-.01222	-.02447	-.03673	-.04902	-.06132	-.07363
.10500	.04833	.03628	.02421	.01212	0.00000	-.01214	-.02430	-.03648	-.04868	-.06089
.10750	.05995	.04801	.03604	.02405	.01204	.00000	-.01206	-.02413	-.03623	-.04834
.11000	.07140	.05956	.04769	.03580	.02389	.01196	.00000	-.01198	-.02397	-.03598
.11250	.08267	.07093	.05917	.04738	.03557	.02373	.01188	.00000	-.01189	-.02381
.11500	.09376	.08213	.07046	.05878	.04706	.03533	.02357	.01180	0.00000	-.01181
.11750	.10469	.09316	.08159	.07000	.05839	.04675	.03509	.02341	.01172	.00000
.12000	.11546	.10402	.09255	.08106	.06954	.05800	.04644	.03486	.02325	.01164
.12250	.12606	.11471	.10334	.09194	.08052	.06908	.05761	.04613	.03462	.02310
.12500	.13649	.12525	.11397	.10267	.09134	.07999	.06862	.05723	.04582	.03439
.12750	.14677	.13562	.12444	.11323	.10200	.09074	.07946	.06817	.05685	.04551
.13000	.15690	.14584	.13475	.12363	.11249	.10133	.09014	.07894	.06771	.05647
.13250	.16687	.15590	.14490	.13388	.12283	.11176	.10067	.08955	.07841	.06726
.13500	.17669	.16581	.15491	.14397	.13302	.12203	.11103	.10000	.08896	.07789
.13750	.18636	.17557	.16476	.15391	.14305	.13215	.12124	.11030	.09934	.08837
.14000	.19589	.18519	.17446	.16371	.15293	.14212	.13129	.12044	.10958	.09869
.14250	.20527	.19466	.18402	.17335	.16266	.15194	.14120	.13044	.11956	.10885
.14500	.21452	.20399	.19344	.18285	.17225	.16162	.15096	.14028	.12959	.11887
.14750	.22362	.21318	.20271	.19221	.18169	.17115	.16058	.14998	.13937	.12874
.15000	.23259	.22223	.21185	.20143	.19100	.18053	.17005	.15954	.14901	.13846
.15250	.24142	.23115	.22085	.21052	.20016	.18978	.17938	.16896	.15851	.14804
.15500	.25012	.23993	.22971	.21947	.20919	.19890	.18858	.17823	.16787	.15748
.15750	.25869	.24858	.23845	.22828	.21809	.20787	.19763	.18737	.17709	.16679
.16000	.26713	.25711	.24705	.23697	.22686	.21672	.20656	.19638	.18617	.17595
.16250	.27545	.26551	.25553	.24552	.23549	.22543	.21535	.20525	.19513	.18498
.16500	.28365	.27378	.26388	.25395	.24400	.23402	.22402	.21399	.20395	.19388
.16750	.29172	.28193	.27211	.26226	.25238	.24248	.23256	.22261	.21264	.20265
.17000	.29967	.28996	.28021	.27044	.26064	.25082	.24097	.23110	.22121	.21129
.17250	.30751	.29787	.28820	.27850	.26878	.25903	.24926	.23946	.22965	.21981
.17500	.31523	.30566	.29607	.28645	.27680	.26713	.25743	.24771	.23796	.22820
.17750	.32283	.31334	.30382	.29428	.28470	.27510	.26548	.25583	.24616	.23647
.18000	.33032	.32091	.31146	.30199	.29249	.28296	.27341	.26384	.25424	.24462
.18250	.33771	.32836	.31899	.30959	.30016	.29071	.28123	.27172	.26220	.25265
.18500	.34498	.33571	.32641	.31708	.30772	.29834	.28893	.27950	.27005	.26057
.18750	.35215	.34295	.33372	.32446	.31517	.30586	.29652	.28716	.27778	.26837
.19000	.35921	.35008	.34092	.33173	.32251	.31327	.30400	.29471	.28540	.27607
.19250	.36617	.35711	.34802	.33890	.32975	.32058	.31138	.30216	.29291	.28365
.19500	.37303	.36403	.35501	.34596	.33688	.32777	.31864	.30949	.30031	.29112
.19750	.37978	.37086	.36190	.35292	.34391	.33487	.32581	.31672	.30761	.29848
.20000	.38644	.37759	.36870	.35978	.35083	.34186	.33287	.32385	.31481	.30574
.20250	.39301	.38421	.37539	.36654	.35766	.34876	.33983	.33087	.32190	.31290
.20500	.39947	.39075	.38199	.37320	.36439	.35555	.34668	.33779	.32888	.31995
.20750	.40585	.39718	.38849	.37977	.37102	.36224	.35344	.34462	.33577	.32691

POINT TABLES: ORIGINAL LOAN TERM: 360 MONTHS LOAN PREPAID IN: 84 MONTHS

EFFECTIVE YIELD	CONTRACT RATE .12000	.12250	.12500	.12750	.13000	.13250	.13500	.13750	.14000	.14250
.07000	-.27209	-.28590	-.29971	-.31354	-.32737	-.34121	-.35506	-.36891	-.38277	-.39664
.07250	-.25642	-.27011	-.28380	-.29751	-.31122	-.32494	-.33867	-.35240	-.36614	-.37989
.07500	-.24099	-.25455	-.26813	-.28172	-.29531	-.30892	-.32253	-.33614	-.34977	-.36339
.07750	-.22579	-.23924	-.25270	-.26617	-.27965	-.29313	-.30663	-.32013	-.33364	-.34715
.08000	-.21083	-.22416	-.23750	-.25086	-.26422	-.27759	-.29097	-.30436	-.31775	-.33115
.08250	-.19609	-.20931	-.22254	-.23577	-.24902	-.26228	-.27555	-.28882	-.30210	-.31538
.08500	-.18158	-.19468	-.20780	-.22092	-.23406	-.24720	-.26036	-.27352	-.28669	-.29986
.08750	-.16728	-.18028	-.19328	-.20629	-.21932	-.23235	-.24540	-.25845	-.27150	-.28457
.09000	-.15321	-.16609	-.17898	-.19189	-.20480	-.21773	-.23066	-.24360	-.25655	-.26950
.09250	-.13935	-.15212	-.16490	-.17770	-.19051	-.20332	-.21615	-.22898	-.24182	-.25467
.09500	-.12570	-.13836	-.15104	-.16372	-.17642	-.18913	-.20185	-.21458	-.22731	-.24005
.09750	-.11225	-.12481	-.13738	-.14996	-.16255	-.17516	-.18777	-.20039	-.21302	-.22565
.10000	-.09901	-.11146	-.12393	-.13640	-.14889	-.16139	-.17390	-.18641	-.19894	-.21147
.10250	-.08597	-.09831	-.11067	-.12305	-.13543	-.14783	-.16023	-.17264	-.18507	-.19750
.10500	-.07312	-.08537	-.09762	-.10989	-.12218	-.13447	-.14677	-.15908	-.17140	-.18373
.10750	-.06047	-.07261	-.08477	-.09694	-.10912	-.12131	-.13351	-.14572	-.15794	-.17017
.11000	-.04801	-.06005	-.07211	-.08417	-.09625	-.10835	-.12045	-.13256	-.14458	-.15681
.11250	-.03573	-.04767	-.05963	-.07160	-.08358	-.09558	-.10758	-.11959	-.13162	-.14365
.11500	-.02364	-.03549	-.04734	-.05922	-.07110	-.08300	-.09490	-.10682	-.11874	-.13068
.11750	-.01173	-.02348	-.03524	-.04702	-.05880	-.07060	-.08241	-.09423	-.10606	-.11790
.12000	0.00000	-.01165	-.02332	-.03500	-.04669	-.05839	-.07011	-.08183	-.09357	-.10531
.12250	.01156	.00000	-.01157	-.02316	-.03475	-.04636	-.05799	-.06962	-.08126	-.09291
.12500	.02294	.01148	.00000	-.01149	-.02300	-.03451	-.04604	-.05758	-.06913	-.08069
.12750	.03416	.02279	.01140	0.00000	-.01141	-.02284	-.03427	-.04572	-.05718	-.06865
.13000	.04520	.03392	.02263	.01132	.00000	-.01133	-.02268	-.03404	-.04540	-.05678
.13250	.05609	.04490	.03369	.02248	.01124	0.00000	-.01126	-.02252	-.03380	-.04509
.13500	.06681	.05571	.04460	.03347	.02232	.01117	0.00000	-.01118	-.02237	-.03357
.13750	.07737	.06636	.05534	.04429	.03324	.02217	.01109	.00000	-.01110	-.02221
.14000	.08778	.07686	.06592	.05496	.04400	.03301	.02202	.01102	.00000	-.01103
.14250	.09803	.08720	.07634	.06548	.05459	.04370	.03279	.02187	.01094	.00000
.14500	.10814	.09738	.08662	.07583	.06504	.05423	.04340	.03257	.02172	.01087
.14750	.11809	.10742	.09674	.08604	.07533	.06460	.05386	.04311	.03235	.02157
.15000	.12790	.11731	.10671	.09610	.08547	.07482	.06416	.05350	.04282	.03213
.15250	.13756	.12706	.11654	.10601	.09546	.08490	.07432	.06373	.05314	.04253
.15500	.14708	.13666	.12622	.11577	.10530	.09482	.08433	.07382	.06330	.05278
.15750	.15646	.14612	.13577	.12539	.11501	.10461	.09419	.08377	.07333	.06288
.16000	.16571	.15545	.14517	.13488	.12457	.11425	.10391	.09357	.08321	.07284
.16250	.17482	.16464	.15444	.14422	.13399	.12375	.11349	.10322	.09294	.08265
.16500	.18380	.17369	.16357	.15343	.14328	.13311	.12294	.11274	.10254	.09232
.16750	.19264	.18261	.17257	.16251	.15243	.14234	.13224	.12213	.11200	.10186
.17000	.20136	.19141	.18144	.17146	.16146	.15144	.14141	.13137	.12132	.11126
.17250	.20995	.20007	.19018	.18027	.17035	.16041	.15045	.14049	.13051	.12052
.17500	.21842	.20862	.19880	.18896	.17911	.16925	.15937	.14947	.13957	.12966
.17750	.22676	.21703	.20729	.19753	.18775	.17796	.16815	.15833	.14850	.13866
.18000	.23498	.22533	.21566	.20597	.19626	.18654	.17681	.16706	.15730	.14753
.18250	.24309	.23351	.22391	.21429	.20465	.19501	.18534	.17567	.16598	.15628
.18500	.25108	.24157	.23204	.22249	.21293	.20335	.19376	.18415	.17454	.16491
.18750	.25895	.24951	.24005	.23057	.22108	.21157	.20205	.19252	.18297	.17341
.19000	.26671	.25734	.24795	.23854	.22912	.21968	.21023	.20076	.19128	.18179
.19250	.27436	.26506	.25573	.24640	.23704	.22767	.21829	.20889	.19948	.19006
.19500	.28190	.27266	.26341	.25414	.24485	.23555	.22623	.21690	.20756	.19821
.19750	.28933	.28016	.27098	.26177	.25255	.24332	.23407	.22480	.21553	.20624
.20000	.29666	.28756	.27844	.26930	.26014	.25097	.24179	.23259	.22338	.21416
.20250	.30388	.29484	.28579	.27672	.26763	.25852	.24941	.24027	.23113	.22197
.20500	.31100	.30203	.29304	.28403	.27501	.26597	.25691	.24785	.23877	.22968
.20750	.31802	.30911	.30018	.29124	.28228	.27331	.26432	.25531	.24630	.23727

POINT TABLES: ORIGINAL LOAN TERM: 360 MONTHS LOAN PREPAID IN: 84 MONTHS

EFFECTIVE YIELD	CONTRACT RATE .14500	.14750	.15000	.15250	.15500	.15750	.16000	.16250	.16500	.16750
.07000	-.41050	-.42437	-.43825	-.45212	-.46600	-.47988	-.49376	-.50765	-.52153	-.53541
.07250	-.39364	-.40739	-.42115	-.43491	-.44867	-.46243	-.47619	-.48996	-.50373	-.51750
.07500	-.37703	-.39066	-.40430	-.41795	-.43159	-.44524	-.45889	-.47254	-.48619	-.49984
.07750	-.36066	-.37419	-.38771	-.40124	-.41477	-.42830	-.44184	-.45538	-.46891	-.48245
.08000	-.34455	-.35796	-.37137	-.38478	-.39820	-.41162	-.42504	-.43847	-.45190	-.46532
.08250	-.32868	-.34197	-.35527	-.36857	-.38188	-.39519	-.40850	-.42181	-.43513	-.44844
.08500	-.31304	-.32622	-.33941	-.35260	-.36580	-.37900	-.39220	-.40540	-.41861	-.43182
.08750	-.29764	-.31071	-.32379	-.33687	-.34996	-.36305	-.37614	-.38924	-.40234	-.41543
.09000	-.28247	-.29543	-.30840	-.32138	-.33436	-.34734	-.36032	-.37331	-.38630	-.39929
.09250	-.26752	-.28038	-.29324	-.30611	-.31898	-.33186	-.34474	-.35762	-.37050	-.38339
.09500	-.25280	-.26555	-.27831	-.29107	-.30384	-.31661	-.32938	-.34216	-.35494	-.36772
.09750	-.23830	-.25094	-.26360	-.27626	-.28892	-.30159	-.31426	-.32693	-.33961	-.35228
.10000	-.22401	-.23655	-.24910	-.26166	-.27422	-.28678	-.29935	-.31192	-.32450	-.33707
.10250	-.20993	-.22238	-.23482	-.24728	-.25974	-.27220	-.28466	-.29713	-.30961	-.32208
.10500	-.19607	-.20841	-.22075	-.23311	-.24547	-.25783	-.27019	-.28256	-.29494	-.30731
.10750	-.18240	-.19465	-.20689	-.21915	-.23141	-.24367	-.25594	-.26821	-.28048	-.29276
.11000	-.16895	-.18109	-.19324	-.20539	-.21755	-.22972	-.24189	-.25406	-.26624	-.27842
.11250	-.15569	-.16773	-.17978	-.19184	-.20390	-.21597	-.22804	-.24012	-.25220	-.26428
.11500	-.14262	-.15457	-.16652	-.17849	-.19045	-.20243	-.21440	-.22638	-.23837	-.25036
.11750	-.12975	-.14160	-.15346	-.16533	-.17720	-.18908	-.20096	-.21285	-.22474	-.23663
.12000	-.11707	-.12882	-.14059	-.15236	-.16414	-.17593	-.18771	-.19951	-.21130	-.22310
.12250	-.10457	-.11623	-.12791	-.13959	-.15127	-.16296	-.17466	-.18636	-.19807	-.20977
.12500	-.09225	-.10383	-.11541	-.12700	-.13859	-.15019	-.16180	-.17341	-.18502	-.19664
.12750	-.08012	-.09160	-.10309	-.11459	-.12610	-.13760	-.14912	-.16064	-.17216	-.18369
.13000	-.06817	-.07956	-.09096	-.10237	-.11378	-.12520	-.13663	-.14806	-.15949	-.17093
.13250	-.05638	-.06769	-.07900	-.09032	-.10164	-.11298	-.12431	-.13565	-.14700	-.15835
.13500	-.04477	-.05599	-.06721	-.07845	-.08968	-.10093	-.11218	-.12343	-.13469	-.14595
.13750	-.03333	-.04446	-.05560	-.06674	-.07790	-.08905	-.10022	-.11138	-.12256	-.13373
.14000	-.02206	-.03310	-.04415	-.05521	-.06628	-.07735	-.08843	-.09951	-.11060	-.12169
.14250	-.01095	-.02191	-.03287	-.04385	-.05483	-.06582	-.07681	-.08781	-.09881	-.10982
.14500	-.00000	-.01087	-.02176	-.03265	-.04354	-.05445	-.06536	-.07627	-.08719	-.09812
.14750	.01079	-.00000	-.01080	-.02161	-.03242	-.04324	-.05407	-.06490	-.07574	-.08658
.15000	.02143	.01072	-.00000	-.01073	-.02146	-.03220	-.04294	-.05369	-.06445	-.07521
.15250	.03191	.02128	.01064	0.00000	-.01065	-.02131	-.03197	-.04265	-.05332	-.06400
.15500	.04224	.03169	.02114	.01057	.00000	-.01058	-.02116	-.03175	-.04235	-.05295
.15750	.05242	.04195	.03148	.02099	.01050	0.00000	-.01051	-.02102	-.03154	-.04206
.16000	.06246	.05207	.04167	.03126	.02085	.01043	.00000	-.01043	-.02087	-.03132
.16250	.07235	.06204	.05172	.04139	.03105	.02071	.01036	0.00000	-.01036	-.02073
.16500	.08210	.07186	.06162	.05137	.04111	.03084	.02057	.01029	.00000	-.01029
.16750	.09171	.08155	.07138	.06121	.05102	.04083	.03063	.02043	.01022	0.00000
.17000	.10118	.09110	.08101	.07091	.06080	.05068	.04056	.03043	.02029	.01015
.17250	.11052	.10051	.09049	.08047	.07043	.06039	.05034	.04028	.03022	.02015
.17500	.11973	.10979	.09985	.08989	.07993	.06996	.05999	.05000	.04001	.03002
.17750	.12880	.11894	.10907	.09919	.08930	.07940	.06950	.05958	.04967	.03974
.18000	.13775	.12796	.11816	.10835	.09853	.08871	.07887	.06903	.05919	.04933
.18250	.14657	.13685	.12712	.11738	.10764	.09788	.08812	.07835	.06857	.05879
.18500	.15527	.14562	.13596	.12629	.11661	.10693	.09723	.08754	.07783	.06812
.18750	.16384	.15426	.14467	.13507	.12546	.11585	.10622	.09659	.08696	.07731
.19000	.17229	.16278	.15326	.14373	.13419	.12464	.11509	.10553	.09596	.08638
.19250	.18062	.17118	.16173	.15227	.14279	.13331	.12383	.11433	.10483	.09533
.19500	.18884	.17946	.17008	.16068	.15128	.14187	.13245	.12302	.11359	.10415
.19750	.19694	.18763	.17831	.16898	.15965	.15030	.14095	.13159	.12222	.11284
.20000	.20493	.19569	.18643	.17717	.16790	.15862	.14933	.14003	.13073	.12142
.20250	.21281	.20363	.19444	.18524	.17603	.16682	.15760	.14836	.13913	.12988
.20500	.22057	.21146	.20233	.19320	.18406	.17491	.16575	.15658	.14741	.13823
.20750	.22823	.21918	.21012	.20105	.19197	.18288	.17379	.16469	.15558	.14646

POINT TABLES: ORIGINAL LOAN TERM: 360 MONTHS LOAN PREPAID IN: 84 MONTHS

CONTRACT RATE

EFFECTIVE YIELD	.17000	.17250	.17500	.17750	.18000	.18250	.18500	.18750	.19000	.19250
.07000	-.54930	-.56318	-.57706	-.59095	-.60483	-.61871	-.63259	-.64647	-.66035	-.67423
.07250	-.53126	-.54503	-.55880	-.57257	-.58633	-.60010	-.61387	-.62763	-.64140	-.65516
.07500	-.51350	-.52715	-.54080	-.55446	-.56811	-.58176	-.59542	-.60907	-.62272	-.63637
.07750	-.49599	-.50953	-.52308	-.53662	-.55016	-.56370	-.57724	-.59078	-.60432	-.61785
.08000	-.47875	-.49218	-.50561	-.51904	-.53247	-.54590	-.55933	-.57276	-.58618	-.59961
.08250	-.46176	-.47508	-.48840	-.50172	-.51504	-.52836	-.54168	-.55500	-.56832	-.58164
.08500	-.44503	-.45823	-.47145	-.48466	-.49787	-.51108	-.52429	-.53750	-.55071	-.56392
.08750	-.42854	-.44164	-.45474	-.46784	-.48095	-.49405	-.50715	-.52026	-.53336	-.54647
.09000	-.41229	-.42528	-.43828	-.45128	-.46427	-.47727	-.49027	-.50327	-.51627	-.52926
.09250	-.39628	-.40917	-.42206	-.43495	-.44784	-.46074	-.47363	-.48652	-.49942	-.51231
.09500	-.38051	-.39329	-.40608	-.41887	-.43166	-.44444	-.45723	-.47003	-.48282	-.49561
.09750	-.36496	-.37765	-.39033	-.40302	-.41570	-.42839	-.44108	-.45377	-.46645	-.47914
.10000	-.34965	-.36223	-.37481	-.38740	-.39998	-.41257	-.42515	-.43774	-.45033	-.46292
.10250	-.33456	-.34704	-.35952	-.37201	-.38449	-.39698	-.40946	-.42195	-.43444	-.44693
.10500	-.31969	-.33207	-.34445	-.35684	-.36922	-.38161	-.39400	-.40639	-.41878	-.43117
.10750	-.30504	-.31732	-.32960	-.34189	-.35418	-.36647	-.37876	-.39105	-.40334	-.41563
.11000	-.29060	-.30278	-.31497	-.32716	-.33935	-.35154	-.36374	-.37593	-.38813	-.40032
.11250	-.27637	-.28846	-.30055	-.31264	-.32474	-.33683	-.34893	-.36103	-.37313	-.38523
.11500	-.26235	-.27434	-.28634	-.29834	-.31034	-.32234	-.33434	-.34635	-.35835	-.37036
.11750	-.24853	-.26043	-.27233	-.28424	-.29614	-.30805	-.31996	-.33187	-.34378	-.35570
.12000	-.23491	-.24672	-.25853	-.27034	-.28215	-.29397	-.30579	-.31760	-.32943	-.34125
.12250	-.22149	-.23320	-.24492	-.25664	-.26836	-.28009	-.29181	-.30354	-.31527	-.32700
.12500	-.20826	-.21988	-.23151	-.24314	-.25477	-.26641	-.27804	-.28968	-.30132	-.31296
.12750	-.19522	-.20676	-.21829	-.22983	-.24138	-.25292	-.26447	-.27602	-.28757	-.29912
.13000	-.18237	-.19382	-.20527	-.21672	-.22817	-.23963	-.25109	-.26255	-.27401	-.28547
.13250	-.16971	-.18106	-.19242	-.20379	-.21516	-.22652	-.23790	-.24927	-.26064	-.27202
.13500	-.15722	-.16849	-.17977	-.19104	-.20232	-.21361	-.22489	-.23618	-.24747	-.25876
.13750	-.14492	-.15610	-.16729	-.17848	-.18968	-.20087	-.21207	-.22328	-.23448	-.24568
.14000	-.13279	-.14389	-.15499	-.16610	-.17721	-.18832	-.19944	-.21055	-.22167	-.23279
.14250	-.12083	-.13185	-.14287	-.15389	-.16492	-.17595	-.18698	-.19801	-.20905	-.22009
.14500	-.10905	-.11998	-.13092	-.14186	-.15280	-.16375	-.17470	-.18565	-.19660	-.20756
.14750	-.09743	-.10828	-.11914	-.12999	-.14086	-.15172	-.16259	-.17346	-.18433	-.19520
.15000	-.08598	-.09675	-.10752	-.11830	-.12908	-.13986	-.15065	-.16144	-.17223	-.18302
.15250	-.07469	-.08538	-.09607	-.10677	-.11747	-.12817	-.13888	-.14959	-.16030	-.17101
.15500	-.06356	-.07417	-.08478	-.09540	-.10602	-.11665	-.12728	-.13791	-.14854	-.15917
.15750	-.05259	-.06312	-.07365	-.08419	-.09474	-.10528	-.11583	-.12638	-.13694	-.14750
.16000	-.04177	-.05222	-.06268	-.07314	-.08361	-.09408	-.10455	-.11503	-.12550	-.13598
.16250	-.03110	-.04148	-.05186	-.06225	-.07264	-.08303	-.09343	-.10382	-.11423	-.12463
.16500	-.02059	-.03089	-.04120	-.05151	-.06182	-.07214	-.08246	-.09278	-.10310	-.11343
.16750	-.01022	-.02045	-.03068	-.04091	-.05115	-.06139	-.07164	-.08189	-.09214	-.10239
.17000	.00000	-.01015	-.02031	-.03047	-.04063	-.05080	-.06097	-.07115	-.08132	-.09150
.17250	.01008	0.00000	-.01008	-.02017	-.03026	-.04036	-.05045	-.06055	-.07066	-.08076
.17500	.02002	.01001	.00000	-.01001	-.02003	-.03006	-.04008	-.05011	-.06014	-.07017
.17750	.02981	.01988	.00994	0.00000	-.00995	-.01990	-.02985	-.03981	-.04977	-.05973
.18000	.03948	.02961	.01975	.00988	.00000	-.00988	-.01976	-.02965	-.03954	-.04943
.18250	.04900	.03921	.02942	.01961	.00981	0.00000	-.00981	-.01963	-.02945	-.03927
.18500	.05840	.04868	.03895	.02922	.01948	.00974	.00000	-.00975	-.01950	-.02925
.18750	.06767	.05801	.04835	.03869	.02902	.01935	.00968	0.00000	-.00968	-.01937
.19000	.07680	.06722	.05763	.04803	.03843	.02883	.01922	.00961	.00000	-.00962
.19250	.08581	.07630	.06677	.05725	.04771	.03818	.02864	.01910	.00955	.00000
.19500	.09470	.08525	.07579	.06633	.05687	.04740	.03792	.02845	.01897	.00949
.19750	.10347	.09408	.08469	.07529	.06590	.05649	.04708	.03767	.02826	.01884
.20000	.11211	.10279	.09346	.08413	.07480	.06546	.05612	.04677	.03743	.02807
.20250	.12063	.11138	.10212	.09285	.08358	.07431	.06503	.05575	.04647	.03718
.20500	.12904	.11985	.11066	.10145	.09225	.08304	.07382	.06461	.05539	.04616
.20750	.13734	.12821	.11908	.10994	.10080	.09165	.08250	.07334	.06418	.05502

POINT TABLES: ORIGINAL LOAN TERM: 360 MONTHS LOAN PREPAID IN: 84 MONTHS

CONTRACT RATE

EFFECTIVE YIELD	.19500	.19750	.20000	.20250	.20500	.20750
.07000	-.68810	-.70198	-.71585	-.72972	-.74359	-.75746
.07250	-.66892	-.68268	-.69644	-.71020	-.72395	-.73771
.07500	-.65002	-.66366	-.67731	-.69096	-.70460	-.71824
.07750	-.63139	-.64493	-.65846	-.67200	-.68553	-.69906
.08000	-.61304	-.62646	-.63989	-.65331	-.66674	-.68016
.08250	-.59495	-.60827	-.62159	-.63490	-.64821	-.66153
.08500	-.57713	-.59034	-.60355	-.61676	-.62996	-.64317
.08750	-.55957	-.57267	-.58577	-.59887	-.61197	-.62507
.09000	-.54226	-.55526	-.56826	-.58125	-.59425	-.60724
.09250	-.52521	-.53810	-.55099	-.56388	-.57678	-.58967
.09500	-.50840	-.52119	-.53398	-.54677	-.55956	-.57234
.09750	-.49183	-.50452	-.51721	-.52990	-.54258	-.55527
.10000	-.47551	-.48809	-.50068	-.51327	-.52586	-.53844
.10250	-.45941	-.47190	-.48439	-.49688	-.50937	-.52186
.10500	-.44356	-.45595	-.46834	-.48073	-.49312	-.50551
.10750	-.42793	-.44022	-.45251	-.46480	-.47710	-.48939
.11000	-.41252	-.42472	-.43691	-.44911	-.46131	-.47351
.11250	-.39733	-.40944	-.42154	-.43364	-.44574	-.45785
.11500	-.38237	-.39437	-.40638	-.41839	-.43040	-.44241
.11750	-.36761	-.37953	-.39144	-.40336	-.41528	-.42719
.12000	-.35307	-.36489	-.37672	-.38854	-.40036	-.41219
.12250	-.33873	-.35047	-.36220	-.37393	-.38567	-.39740
.12500	-.32460	-.33624	-.34789	-.35953	-.37118	-.38282
.12750	-.31067	-.32222	-.33378	-.34533	-.35689	-.36845
.13000	-.29694	-.30840	-.31987	-.33134	-.34280	-.35427
.13250	-.28340	-.29478	-.30616	-.31754	-.32892	-.34030
.13500	-.27005	-.28134	-.29264	-.30393	-.31523	-.32652
.13750	-.25689	-.26810	-.27931	-.29052	-.30173	-.31294
.14000	-.24392	-.25504	-.26617	-.27729	-.28842	-.29955
.14250	-.23113	-.24217	-.25321	-.26425	-.27530	-.28634
.14500	-.21851	-.22947	-.24043	-.25139	-.26236	-.27332
.14750	-.20608	-.21696	-.22784	-.23872	-.24960	-.26048
.15000	-.19382	-.20462	-.21541	-.22621	-.23701	-.24782
.15250	-.18173	-.19245	-.20317	-.21389	-.22461	-.23533
.15500	-.16981	-.18045	-.19109	-.20173	-.21237	-.22302
.15750	-.15805	-.16862	-.17918	-.18974	-.20031	-.21087
.16000	-.14646	-.15695	-.16743	-.17792	-.18841	-.19890
.16250	-.13503	-.14544	-.15585	-.16626	-.17667	-.18709
.16500	-.12376	-.13409	-.14443	-.15476	-.16510	-.17544
.16750	-.11265	-.12290	-.13316	-.14342	-.15369	-.16395
.17000	-.10168	-.11187	-.12205	-.13224	-.14243	-.15262
.17250	-.09087	-.10098	-.11110	-.12121	-.13133	-.14145
.17500	-.08021	-.09025	-.10029	-.11033	-.12038	-.13042
.17750	-.06970	-.07966	-.08963	-.09960	-.10958	-.11955
.18000	-.05932	-.06922	-.07912	-.08902	-.09892	-.10883
.18250	-.04909	-.05892	-.06875	-.07858	-.08841	-.09825
.18500	-.03900	-.04876	-.05852	-.06828	-.07805	-.08781
.18750	-.02905	-.03874	-.04843	-.05813	-.06782	-.07752
.19000	-.01924	-.02886	-.03848	-.04811	-.05773	-.06736
.19250	-.00955	-.01911	-.02866	-.03822	-.04778	-.05735
.19500	0.00000	-.00949	-.01898	-.02847	-.03797	-.04746
.19750	.00942	.00000	-.00943	-.01885	-.02828	-.03771
.20000	.01872	.00936	.00000	-.00936	-.01873	-.02809
.20250	.02789	.01859	.00930	.00000	-.00930	-.01860
.20500	.03693	.02770	.01847	.00924	-.00000	-.00924
.20750	.04586	.03669	.02752	.01835	.00918	.00000

POINT TABLES: ORIGINAL LOAN TERM: 360 MONTHS LOAN PREPAID IN: 108 MONTHS

CONTRACT RATE

EFFECTIVE YIELD	.07000	.07250	.07500	.07750	.08000	.08250	.08500	.08750	.09000	.09250
.07000	.00000	-.01589	-.03184	-.04785	-.06392	-.08005	-.09622	-.11244	-.12871	-.14502
.07250	.01570	.00000	-.01576	-.03159	-.04747	-.06341	-.07939	-.09543	-.11151	-.12763
.07500	.03109	.01558	0.00000	-.01564	-.03134	-.04709	-.06289	-.07874	-.09464	-.11058
.07750	.04618	.03085	.01546	.00000	-.01551	-.03108	-.04671	-.06238	-.07809	-.09385
.08000	.06098	.04583	.03061	.01534	.00000	-.01539	-.03083	-.04633	-.06186	-.07745
.08250	.07549	.06052	.04548	.03037	.01521	0.00000	-.01527	-.03058	-.04595	-.06135
.08500	.08972	.07492	.06005	.04512	.03014	.01509	.00000	-.01514	-.03033	-.04557
.08750	.10367	.08904	.07434	.05959	.04477	.02990	.01497	.00000	-.01502	-.03009
.09000	.11735	.10289	.08836	.07377	.05912	.04442	.02966	.01485	.00000	-.01490
.09250	.13077	.11647	.10211	.08768	.07320	.05866	.04407	.02942	.01473	0.00000
.09500	.14392	.12979	.11559	.10133	.08700	.07263	.05820	.04372	.02919	.01462
.09750	.15683	.14285	.12881	.11471	.10055	.08633	.07206	.05774	.04337	.02896
.10000	.16948	.15566	.14178	.12783	.11383	.09977	.08566	.07149	.05728	.04302
.10250	.18189	.16823	.15450	.14071	.12686	.11295	.09900	.08499	.07093	.05682
.10500	.19406	.18055	.16698	.15334	.13964	.12589	.11208	.09822	.08432	.07037
.10750	.20600	.19264	.17922	.16573	.15218	.13858	.12492	.11121	.09746	.08365
.11000	.21771	.20450	.19122	.17788	.16448	.15103	.13752	.12396	.11035	.09669
.11250	.22920	.21613	.20300	.18980	.17655	.16324	.14987	.13646	.12299	.10948
.11500	.24047	.22754	.21455	.20150	.18839	.17522	.16200	.14873	.13540	.12204
.11750	.25152	.23874	.22589	.21298	.20000	.18698	.17390	.16076	.14758	.13435
.12000	.26236	.24972	.23701	.22423	.21140	.19851	.18557	.17258	.15953	.14644
.12250	.27300	.26049	.24792	.23528	.22258	.20983	.19703	.18417	.17126	.15831
.12500	.28344	.27106	.25862	.24612	.23356	.22094	.20827	.19554	.18277	.16995
.12750	.29368	.28143	.26912	.25675	.24432	.23184	.21930	.20671	.19406	.18138
.13000	.30372	.29161	.27943	.26719	.25489	.24253	.23012	.21766	.20515	.19259
.13250	.31358	.30159	.28954	.27743	.26526	.25303	.24075	.22841	.21603	.20360
.13500	.32325	.31139	.29946	.28748	.27543	.26333	.25117	.23897	.22671	.21441
.13750	.33274	.32100	.30920	.29734	.28542	.27344	.26141	.24933	.23719	.22501
.14000	.34205	.33044	.31876	.30702	.29522	.28336	.27145	.25949	.24748	.23542
.14250	.35119	.33969	.32813	.31652	.30484	.29310	.28131	.26947	.25758	.24565
.14500	.36015	.34878	.33734	.32584	.31428	.30266	.29099	.27927	.26750	.25568
.14750	.36895	.35769	.34637	.33499	.32354	.31204	.30049	.28889	.27723	.26553
.15000	.37759	.36645	.35524	.34397	.33264	.32126	.30982	.29833	.28679	.27520
.15250	.38607	.37503	.36394	.35278	.34157	.33030	.31897	.30760	.29617	.28470
.15500	.39438	.38346	.37248	.36144	.35033	.33917	.32796	.31670	.30538	.29402
.15750	.40255	.39174	.38087	.36993	.35894	.34789	.33678	.32563	.31443	.30317
.16000	.41056	.39986	.38910	.37827	.36738	.35644	.34545	.33440	.32331	.31216
.16250	.41843	.40783	.39718	.38645	.37568	.36484	.35395	.34301	.33203	.32099
.16500	.42615	.41566	.40511	.39449	.38382	.37309	.36231	.35147	.34059	.32966
.16750	.43373	.42335	.41289	.40238	.39181	.38119	.37051	.35978	.34900	.33817
.17000	.44118	.43089	.42054	.41013	.39966	.38914	.37856	.36793	.35726	.34653
.17250	.44848	.43830	.42805	.41774	.40737	.39695	.38647	.37594	.36537	.35474
.17500	.45566	.44557	.43542	.42520	.41494	.40461	.39424	.38381	.37333	.36281
.17750	.46270	.45271	.44265	.43254	.42237	.41214	.40186	.39153	.38115	.37073
.18000	.46961	.45972	.44976	.43974	.42967	.41954	.40935	.39912	.38884	.37851
.18250	.47640	.46660	.45674	.44681	.43683	.42680	.41671	.40657	.39638	.38615
.18500	.48307	.47336	.46359	.45376	.44387	.43393	.42394	.41389	.40380	.39366
.18750	.48962	.48000	.47032	.46058	.45079	.44094	.43103	.42108	.41108	.40103
.19000	.49604	.48652	.47693	.46728	.45758	.44782	.43801	.42814	.41823	.40828
.19250	.50236	.49292	.48342	.47386	.46425	.45458	.44485	.43508	.42526	.41540
.19500	.50856	.49921	.48980	.48032	.47080	.46122	.45158	.44190	.43217	.42239
.19750	.51465	.50538	.49606	.48667	.47723	.46774	.45819	.44860	.43895	.42926
.20000	.52063	.51145	.50221	.49291	.48356	.47415	.46469	.45518	.44562	.43601
.20250	.52650	.51741	.50825	.49904	.48977	.48044	.47107	.46164	.45217	.44265
.20500	.53227	.52326	.51419	.50506	.49587	.48663	.47733	.46799	.45860	.44917
.20750	.53794	.52901	.52002	.51097	.50186	.49270	.48349	.47423	.46493	.45557

POINT TABLES: ORIGINAL LOAN TERM: 360 MONTHS LOAN PREPAID IN: 108 MONTHS

EFFECTIVE YIELD	CONTRACT RATE .09500	.09750	.10000	.10250	.10500	.10750	.11000	.11250	.11500	.11750
.07000	-.16138	-.17776	-.19419	-.21065	-.22713	-.24365	-.26019	-.27676	-.29335	-.30996
.07250	-.14380	-.16000	-.17624	-.19251	-.20882	-.22515	-.24151	-.25789	-.27430	-.29073
.07500	-.12656	-.14258	-.15864	-.17473	-.19085	-.20700	-.22318	-.23938	-.25561	-.27186
.07750	-.10965	-.12549	-.14137	-.15728	-.17322	-.18919	-.20519	-.22122	-.23727	-.25334
.08000	-.09307	-.10873	-.12443	-.14017	-.15593	-.17173	-.18755	-.20340	-.21928	-.23517
.08250	-.07680	-.09229	-.10782	-.12338	-.13897	-.15459	-.17024	-.18592	-.20152	-.21735
.08500	-.06085	-.07616	-.09152	-.10691	-.12233	-.13778	-.15326	-.16877	-.18430	-.19986
.08750	-.04520	-.06034	-.07553	-.09075	-.10600	-.12129	-.13660	-.15194	-.16730	-.18269
.09000	-.02984	-.04482	-.05984	-.07490	-.08998	-.10510	-.12025	-.13543	-.15063	-.16585
.09250	-.01478	-.02960	-.04445	-.05934	-.07427	-.08922	-.10421	-.11922	-.13426	-.14932
.09500	.00000	-.01466	-.02935	-.04408	-.05885	-.07364	-.08847	-.10332	-.11820	-.13311
.09750	.01450	.00000	-.01454	-.02911	-.04371	-.05835	-.07302	-.08772	-.10244	-.11719
.10000	.02872	.01438	0.00000	-.01442	-.02887	-.04335	-.05786	-.07241	-.08697	-.10157
.10250	.04268	.02849	.01426	.00000	-.01430	-.02863	-.04299	-.05738	-.07179	-.08623
.10500	.05637	.04233	.02826	.01415	0.00000	-.01418	-.02839	-.04263	-.05689	-.07119
.10750	.06981	.05592	.04199	.02803	.01403	.00000	-.01406	-.02815	-.04227	-.05641
.11000	.08299	.06925	.05547	.04165	.02780	.01392	.00000	-.01395	-.02792	-.04192
.11250	.09593	.08233	.06870	.05502	.04132	.02757	.01380	.00000	-.01383	-.02768
.11500	.10862	.09517	.08168	.06815	.05458	.04098	.02735	.01369	0.00000	-.01371
.11750	.12108	.10777	.09441	.08102	.06760	.05414	.04065	.02712	.01358	.00000
.12000	.13331	.12013	.10692	.09366	.08038	.06705	.05370	.04031	.02690	.01346
.12250	.14531	.13227	.11919	.10607	.09292	.07973	.06651	.05326	.03999	.02668
.12500	.15709	.14418	.13123	.11825	.10523	.09218	.07909	.06597	.05283	.03966
.12750	.16864	.15587	.14306	.13020	.11732	.10439	.09144	.07845	.06544	.05240
.13000	.17999	.16735	.15466	.14194	.12918	.11639	.10356	.09071	.07782	.06491
.13250	.19113	.17861	.16605	.15346	.14083	.12816	.11546	.10274	.08998	.07719
.13500	.20206	.18967	.17724	.16477	.15226	.13972	.12715	.11455	.10191	.08926
.13750	.21279	.20052	.18822	.17587	.16349	.15107	.13862	.12614	.11364	.10110
.14000	.22332	.21118	.19899	.18677	.17451	.16222	.14989	.13753	.12515	.11273
.14250	.23366	.22164	.20958	.19747	.18533	.17316	.16095	.14872	.13645	.12415
.14500	.24382	.23191	.21997	.20798	.19596	.18390	.17182	.15970	.14755	.13537
.14750	.25378	.24200	.23017	.21830	.20640	.19446	.18248	.17048	.15845	.14639
.15000	.26357	.25190	.24018	.22843	.21664	.20482	.19296	.18107	.16916	.15721
.15250	.27318	.26162	.25002	.23838	.22670	.21499	.20325	.19148	.17967	.16784
.15500	.28262	.27117	.25968	.24815	.23659	.22499	.21336	.20169	.19000	.17828
.15750	.29188	.28054	.26916	.25775	.24629	.23480	.22328	.21173	.20014	.18853
.16000	.30098	.28975	.27848	.26717	.25582	.24444	.23303	.22158	.21011	.19861
.16250	.30991	.29879	.28763	.27642	.26518	.25391	.24260	.23127	.21990	.20850
.16500	.31868	.30767	.29661	.28551	.27438	.26321	.25201	.24078	.22951	.21822
.16750	.32730	.31639	.30543	.29444	.28341	.27235	.26125	.25012	.23896	.22777
.17000	.33576	.32495	.31410	.30321	.29228	.28132	.27033	.25930	.24824	.23716
.17250	.34408	.33337	.32261	.31183	.30100	.29014	.27924	.26832	.25736	.24638
.17500	.35224	.34163	.33098	.32029	.30956	.29880	.28800	.27718	.26632	.25544
.17750	.36026	.34975	.33919	.32860	.31797	.30731	.29661	.28588	.27513	.26434
.18000	.36813	.35772	.34726	.33677	.32624	.31567	.30507	.29444	.28378	.27309
.18250	.37587	.36555	.35519	.34479	.33435	.32388	.31338	.30284	.29228	.28168
.18500	.38347	.37325	.36298	.35267	.34233	.33195	.32154	.31110	.30063	.29013
.18750	.39094	.38081	.37063	.36042	.35017	.33989	.32957	.31922	.30884	.29843
.19000	.39828	.38823	.37815	.36803	.35787	.34768	.33745	.32719	.31691	.30659
.19250	.40549	.39553	.38554	.37551	.36544	.35534	.34520	.33503	.32484	.31461
.19500	.41257	.40270	.39280	.38286	.37288	.36286	.35282	.34274	.33263	.32249
.19750	.41953	.40975	.39993	.39008	.38019	.37026	.36030	.35031	.34029	.33024
.20000	.42636	.41667	.40694	.39717	.38737	.37753	.36766	.35775	.34782	.33785
.20250	.43308	.42348	.41383	.40415	.39443	.38468	.37489	.36507	.35522	.34534
.20500	.43969	.43017	.42060	.41100	.40137	.39170	.38199	.37226	.36249	.35270
.20750	.44618	.43674	.42726	.41774	.40819	.39860	.38898	.37933	.36965	.35994

POINT TABLES: ORIGINAL LOAN TERM: 360 MONTHS LOAN PREPAID IN: 108 MONTHS

CONTRACT RATE

EFFECTIVE YIELD	.12000	.12250	.12500	.12750	.13000	.13250	.13500	.13750	.14000	.14250
.07000	-.32660	-.34325	-.35991	-.37659	-.39329	-.40999	-.42671	-.44344	-.46018	-.47692
.07250	-.30718	-.32364	-.34013	-.35663	-.37314	-.38967	-.40620	-.42275	-.43931	-.45588
.07500	-.28813	-.30441	-.32072	-.33704	-.35337	-.36972	-.38608	-.40245	-.41883	-.43522
.07750	-.26943	-.28554	-.30167	-.31782	-.33398	-.35015	-.36633	-.38253	-.39874	-.41495
.08000	-.25109	-.26703	-.28298	-.29895	-.31494	-.33094	-.34695	-.36298	-.37901	-.39506
.08250	-.23309	-.24886	-.26464	-.28044	-.29626	-.31209	-.32793	-.34379	-.35966	-.37553
.08500	-.21543	-.23103	-.24665	-.26228	-.27793	-.29359	-.30927	-.32496	-.34066	-.35637
.08750	-.19810	-.21354	-.22899	-.24445	-.25994	-.27544	-.29095	-.30647	-.32201	-.33755
.09000	-.18110	-.19637	-.21165	-.22696	-.24228	-.25761	-.27296	-.28833	-.30370	-.31909
.09250	-.16441	-.17952	-.19464	-.20979	-.22495	-.24012	-.25531	-.27052	-.28573	-.30096
.09500	-.14803	-.16298	-.17795	-.19293	-.20794	-.22296	-.23799	-.25303	-.26809	-.28316
.09750	-.13196	-.14675	-.16156	-.17639	-.19124	-.20610	-.22098	-.23587	-.25078	-.26569
.10000	-.11618	-.13082	-.14548	-.16016	-.17485	-.18956	-.20429	-.21902	-.23378	-.24854
.10250	-.10070	-.11518	-.12969	-.14422	-.15876	-.17332	-.18790	-.20249	-.21709	-.23170
.10500	-.08550	-.09984	-.11420	-.12857	-.14297	-.15738	-.17181	-.18625	-.20070	-.21517
.10750	-.07058	-.08477	-.09898	-.11321	-.12746	-.14173	-.15601	-.17030	-.18461	-.19894
.11000	-.05594	-.06998	-.08405	-.09814	-.11224	-.12636	-.14050	-.15465	-.16882	-.18300
.11250	-.04156	-.05547	-.06939	-.08333	-.09730	-.11128	-.12527	-.13928	-.15331	-.16734
.11500	-.02745	-.04122	-.05500	-.06880	-.08262	-.09646	-.11032	-.12419	-.13808	-.15198
.11750	-.01360	-.02722	-.04087	-.05453	-.06822	-.08192	-.09564	-.10937	-.12312	-.13688
.12000	0.00000	-.01349	-.02700	-.04053	-.05407	-.06764	-.08122	-.09482	-.10843	-.12206
.12250	.01335	.00000	-.01337	-.02677	-.04018	-.05362	-.06707	-.08053	-.09401	-.10750
.12500	.02646	.01324	0.00000	-.01326	-.02655	-.03985	-.05316	-.06650	-.07985	-.09321
.12750	.03933	.02624	.01313	.00000	-.01315	-.02632	-.03951	-.05272	-.06593	-.07917
.13000	.05197	.03901	.02603	.01302	.00000	-.01304	-.02610	-.03918	-.05227	-.06538
.13250	.06438	.05155	.03869	.02581	.01292	.00000	-.01293	-.02588	-.03885	-.05183
.13500	.07657	.06386	.05113	.03838	.02560	.01281	.00000	-.01283	-.02567	-.03852
.13750	.08854	.07595	.06334	.05071	.03806	.02539	.01270	.00000	-.01272	-.02545
.14000	.10029	.08783	.07534	.06283	.05030	.03775	.02518	.01260	.00000	-.01261
.14250	.11183	.09949	.08712	.07473	.06232	.04989	.03744	.02498	.01250	0.00000
.14500	.12317	.11094	.09869	.08642	.07413	.06181	.04948	.03713	.02477	.01239
.14750	.13430	.12219	.11006	.09790	.08572	.07353	.06131	.04908	.03683	.02457
.15000	.14524	.13324	.12122	.10918	.09712	.08503	.07293	.06081	.04866	.03653
.15250	.15598	.14410	.13219	.12026	.10831	.09634	.08435	.07234	.06032	.04828
.15500	.16653	.15476	.14296	.13114	.11930	.10744	.09557	.08367	.07176	.05983
.15750	.17690	.16523	.15355	.14184	.13011	.11836	.10659	.09480	.08300	.07118
.16000	.18708	.17552	.16394	.15234	.14072	.12908	.11742	.10574	.09404	.08233
.16250	.19708	.18563	.17416	.16266	.15115	.13961	.12806	.11649	.10490	.09329
.16500	.20691	.19556	.18420	.17281	.16140	.14996	.13851	.12705	.11556	.10406
.16750	.21656	.20532	.19406	.18277	.17146	.16014	.14879	.13743	.12604	.11465
.17000	.22605	.21491	.20375	.19256	.18136	.17013	.15889	.14763	.13635	.12505
.17250	.23537	.22433	.21327	.20219	.19108	.17996	.16881	.15765	.14647	.13528
.17500	.24453	.23359	.22263	.21164	.20064	.18961	.17857	.16750	.15642	.14533
.17750	.25353	.24269	.23182	.22094	.21003	.19910	.18815	.17719	.16620	.15521
.18000	.26237	.25163	.24086	.23007	.21926	.20843	.19758	.18671	.17582	.16492
.18250	.27106	.26041	.24974	.23905	.22833	.21759	.20684	.19606	.18527	.17446
.18500	.27960	.26905	.25847	.24787	.23725	.22660	.21594	.20526	.19456	.18385
.18750	.28800	.27753	.26705	.25654	.24601	.23546	.22489	.21430	.20370	.19308
.19000	.29625	.28588	.27548	.26507	.25463	.24417	.23369	.22319	.21268	.20215
.19250	.30436	.29408	.28377	.27345	.26310	.25273	.24234	.23193	.22151	.21107
.19500	.31233	.30214	.29192	.28168	.27142	.26114	.25085	.24053	.23019	.21984
.19750	.32016	.31006	.29993	.28978	.27961	.26942	.25921	.24898	.23873	.22846
.20000	.32786	.31785	.30781	.29774	.28766	.27755	.26743	.25728	.24712	.23695
.20250	.33544	.32551	.31555	.30557	.29557	.28555	.27551	.26545	.25538	.24529
.20500	.34288	.33303	.32316	.31327	.30335	.29342	.28346	.27349	.26350	.25349
.20750	.35020	.34044	.33065	.32084	.31101	.30115	.29128	.28139	.27148	.26155

CONTRACT RATE

EFFECTIVE YIELD	.14500	.14750	.15000	.15250	.15500	.15750	.16000	.16250	.16500	.16750
.07000	-.49367	-.51043	-.52720	-.54396	-.56074	-.57751	-.59429	-.61107	-.62786	-.64464
.07250	-.47245	-.48903	-.50562	-.52221	-.53880	-.55540	-.57200	-.58861	-.60521	-.62182
.07500	-.45162	-.46802	-.48443	-.50085	-.51727	-.53370	-.55012	-.56655	-.58299	-.59942
.07750	-.43118	-.44741	-.46364	-.47989	-.49614	-.51239	-.52865	-.54491	-.56117	-.57743
.08000	-.41111	-.42717	-.44324	-.45931	-.47539	-.49147	-.50756	-.52365	-.53975	-.55584
.08250	-.39142	-.40731	-.42321	-.43911	-.45503	-.47094	-.48686	-.50279	-.51872	-.53465
.08500	-.37208	-.38781	-.40355	-.41929	-.43503	-.45079	-.46654	-.48230	-.49807	-.51383
.08750	-.35311	-.36867	-.38424	-.39982	-.41541	-.43100	-.44659	-.46219	-.47779	-.49340
.09000	-.33448	-.34988	-.36530	-.38071	-.39614	-.41157	-.42701	-.44245	-.45789	-.47334
.09250	-.31619	-.33144	-.34669	-.36195	-.37722	-.39249	-.40777	-.42306	-.43834	-.45364
.09500	-.29824	-.31333	-.32843	-.34353	-.35865	-.37377	-.38889	-.40402	-.41915	-.43429
.09750	-.28062	-.29555	-.31050	-.32545	-.34041	-.35538	-.37035	-.38532	-.40031	-.41529
.10000	-.26331	-.27810	-.29289	-.30769	-.32250	-.33732	-.35214	-.36697	-.38180	-.39664
.10250	-.24633	-.26096	-.27561	-.29026	-.30492	-.31959	-.33426	-.34894	-.36352	-.37831
.10500	-.22965	-.24413	-.25863	-.27314	-.28765	-.30217	-.31670	-.33124	-.34577	-.36032
.10750	-.21327	-.22761	-.24196	-.25633	-.27070	-.28507	-.29946	-.31385	-.32824	-.34264
.11000	-.19719	-.21139	-.22560	-.23982	-.25404	-.26828	-.28252	-.29677	-.31103	-.32528
.11250	-.18139	-.19545	-.20952	-.22360	-.23769	-.25179	-.26589	-.28000	-.29411	-.30823
.11500	-.16589	-.17981	-.19374	-.20768	-.22163	-.23559	-.24955	-.26352	-.27750	-.29149
.11750	-.15066	-.16444	-.17824	-.19204	-.20586	-.21968	-.23351	-.24734	-.26119	-.27503
.12000	-.13570	-.14935	-.16301	-.17668	-.19036	-.20405	-.21775	-.23145	-.24516	-.25887
.12250	-.12101	-.13453	-.14806	-.16159	-.17514	-.18870	-.20226	-.21583	-.22941	-.24299
.12500	-.10658	-.11997	-.13337	-.14678	-.16019	-.17362	-.18705	-.20049	-.21394	-.22740
.12750	-.09241	-.10567	-.11894	-.13222	-.14551	-.15881	-.17211	-.18543	-.19875	-.21207
.13000	-.07850	-.09163	-.10477	-.11792	-.13108	-.14425	-.15743	-.17062	-.18382	-.19702
.13250	-.06482	-.07783	-.09085	-.10387	-.11691	-.12996	-.14301	-.15608	-.16915	-.18222
.13500	-.05139	-.06428	-.07717	-.09007	-.10299	-.11591	-.12884	-.14179	-.15473	-.16769
.13750	-.03820	-.05096	-.06373	-.07652	-.08931	-.10211	-.11492	-.12774	-.14057	-.15340
.14000	-.02524	-.03788	-.05053	-.06320	-.07587	-.08855	-.10125	-.11395	-.12665	-.13937
.14250	-.01251	-.02503	-.03757	-.05011	-.06267	-.07523	-.08781	-.10039	-.11298	-.12557
.14500	0.00000	-.01241	-.02482	-.03725	-.04969	-.06214	-.07460	-.08706	-.09954	-.11202
.14750	.01229	.00000	-.01230	-.02462	-.03694	-.04928	-.06162	-.07397	-.08633	-.09870
.15000	.02437	.01219	.00000	-.01220	-.02441	-.03663	-.04886	-.06110	-.07335	-.08561
.15250	.03623	.02417	.01209	0.00000	-.01210	-.02421	-.03633	-.04846	-.06059	-.07274
.15500	.04789	.03594	.02397	.01199	.00000	-.01200	-.02401	-.03603	-.04806	-.06009
.15750	.05935	.04750	.03564	.02377	.01189	.00000	-.01190	-.02381	-.03573	-.04766
.16000	.07061	.05887	.04712	.03535	.02358	.01179	.00000	-.01180	-.02362	-.03544
.16250	.08167	.07004	.05839	.04674	.03507	.02339	.01170	.00000	-.01171	-.02342
.16500	.09255	.08102	.06948	.05792	.04636	.03478	.02320	.01160	.00000	-.01161
.16750	.10324	.09181	.08037	.06892	.05746	.04598	.03450	.02301	.01151	.00000
.17000	.11374	.10242	.09108	.07973	.06837	.05700	.04561	.03422	.02282	.01142
.17250	.12407	.11284	.10160	.09035	.07909	.06782	.05654	.04525	.03395	.02264
.17500	.13421	.12309	.11195	.10080	.08964	.07846	.06728	.05609	.04489	.03367
.17750	.14419	.13316	.12212	.11107	.10000	.08893	.07784	.06674	.05564	.04453
.18000	.15400	.14307	.13212	.12116	.11020	.09921	.08822	.07722	.06621	.05520
.18250	.16364	.15280	.14195	.13109	.12022	.10933	.09843	.08753	.07661	.06569
.18500	.17312	.16238	.15162	.14085	.13007	.11928	.10847	.09766	.08684	.07601
.18750	.18244	.17179	.16112	.15045	.13976	.12906	.11835	.10763	.09690	.08616
.19000	.19160	.18104	.17047	.15988	.14928	.13868	.12805	.11742	.10679	.09614
.19250	.20061	.19014	.17966	.16916	.15865	.14813	.13760	.12706	.11651	.10595
.19500	.20947	.19909	.18870	.17829	.16787	.15744	.14699	.13654	.12608	.11561
.19750	.21818	.20789	.19758	.18726	.17693	.16658	.15623	.14586	.13549	.12511
.20000	.22675	.21654	.20632	.19609	.18584	.17558	.16531	.15503	.14475	.13445
.20250	.23518	.22505	.21492	.20477	.19461	.18443	.17425	.16406	.15385	.14364
.20500	.24346	.23342	.22337	.21331	.20323	.19314	.18304	.17293	.16281	.15268
.20750	.25161	.24166	.23169	.22170	.21171	.20170	.19169	.18166	.17162	.16158

POINT TABLES: ORIGINAL LOAN TERM: 360 MONTHS LOAN PREPAID IN: 108 MONTHS

EFFECTIVE YIELD	CONTRACT RATE .17000	.17250	.17500	.17750	.18000	.18250	.18500	.18750	.19000	.19250
.07000	-.66143	-.67821	-.69500	-.71178	-.72857	-.74535	-.76213	-.77892	-.79570	-.81248
.07250	-.63843	-.65504	-.67165	-.68826	-.70487	-.72148	-.73809	-.75470	-.77131	-.78791
.07500	-.61586	-.63230	-.64873	-.66517	-.68161	-.69805	-.71449	-.73092	-.74736	-.76379
.07750	-.59370	-.60997	-.62623	-.64250	-.65877	-.67504	-.69131	-.70758	-.72384	-.74011
.08000	-.57194	-.58804	-.60414	-.62024	-.63634	-.65245	-.66855	-.68465	-.70075	-.71685
.08250	-.55058	-.56651	-.58245	-.59839	-.61432	-.63026	-.64620	-.66214	-.67808	-.69401
.08500	-.52960	-.54538	-.56115	-.57692	-.59270	-.60848	-.62425	-.64003	-.65581	-.67158
.08750	-.50901	-.52462	-.54023	-.55585	-.57146	-.58708	-.60270	-.61832	-.63393	-.64955
.09000	-.48879	-.50424	-.51970	-.53515	-.55061	-.56607	-.58153	-.59699	-.61245	-.62791
.09250	-.46893	-.48423	-.49953	-.51483	-.53013	-.54544	-.56074	-.57605	-.59136	-.60666
.09500	-.44943	-.46457	-.47972	-.49487	-.51002	-.52517	-.54032	-.55548	-.57063	-.58579
.09750	-.43028	-.44527	-.46027	-.47527	-.49027	-.50527	-.52027	-.53527	-.55023	-.56528
.10000	-.41148	-.42632	-.44117	-.45601	-.47087	-.48572	-.50057	-.51543	-.53029	-.54514
.10250	-.39301	-.40770	-.42240	-.43710	-.45181	-.46652	-.48122	-.49593	-.51064	-.52536
.10500	-.37487	-.38942	-.40397	-.41853	-.43309	-.44765	-.46222	-.47678	-.49135	-.50592
.10750	-.35705	-.37146	-.38587	-.40029	-.41470	-.42912	-.44355	-.45797	-.47240	-.48682
.11000	-.33955	-.35382	-.36809	-.38236	-.39664	-.41092	-.42520	-.43949	-.45378	-.46806
.11250	-.32236	-.33649	-.35062	-.36476	-.37890	-.39304	-.40719	-.42133	-.43548	-.44963
.11500	-.30547	-.31947	-.33346	-.34746	-.36147	-.37547	-.38948	-.40349	-.41751	-.43152
.11750	-.28889	-.30274	-.31661	-.33047	-.34434	-.35821	-.37209	-.38597	-.39984	-.41373
.12000	-.27259	-.28632	-.30005	-.31378	-.32752	-.34126	-.35500	-.36874	-.38249	-.39624
.12250	-.25658	-.27018	-.28378	-.29738	-.31098	-.32459	-.33821	-.35182	-.36544	-.37906
.12500	-.24086	-.25432	-.26779	-.28126	-.29474	-.30822	-.32171	-.33519	-.34858	-.36217
.12750	-.22540	-.23874	-.25208	-.26543	-.27878	-.29213	-.30549	-.31885	-.33221	-.34558
.13000	-.21022	-.22343	-.23665	-.24987	-.26310	-.27633	-.28956	-.30279	-.31603	-.32927
.13250	-.19530	-.20839	-.22149	-.23458	-.24769	-.26079	-.27390	-.28701	-.30013	-.31324
.13500	-.18065	-.19361	-.20658	-.21956	-.23254	-.24552	-.25851	-.27150	-.28450	-.29749
.13750	-.16624	-.17909	-.19194	-.20479	-.21765	-.23052	-.24339	-.25626	-.26913	-.28201
.14000	-.15209	-.16482	-.17755	-.19028	-.20303	-.21577	-.22852	-.24127	-.25403	-.26679
.14250	-.13818	-.15079	-.16340	-.17602	-.18865	-.20128	-.21391	-.22655	-.23919	-.25183
.14500	-.12451	-.13700	-.14950	-.16201	-.17452	-.18703	-.19955	-.21207	-.22460	-.23712
.14750	-.11107	-.12345	-.13584	-.14823	-.16063	-.17303	-.18543	-.19784	-.21025	-.22267
.15000	-.09787	-.11014	-.12241	-.13469	-.14697	-.15926	-.17155	-.18385	-.19615	-.20845
.15250	-.08489	-.09705	-.10921	-.12138	-.13355	-.14573	-.15791	-.17010	-.18229	-.19448
.15500	-.07213	-.08418	-.09623	-.10829	-.12036	-.13243	-.14450	-.15658	-.16866	-.18074
.15750	-.05959	-.07153	-.08348	-.09543	-.10739	-.11935	-.13131	-.14328	-.15526	-.16723
.16000	-.04726	-.05910	-.07094	-.08278	-.09463	-.10649	-.11835	-.13021	-.14208	-.15395
.16250	-.03514	-.04687	-.05861	-.07035	-.08209	-.09385	-.10560	-.11736	-.12913	-.14089
.16500	-.02323	-.03485	-.04649	-.05812	-.06977	-.08142	-.09307	-.10473	-.11639	-.12805
.16750	-.01152	-.02304	-.03457	-.04611	-.05765	-.06919	-.08074	-.09230	-.10386	-.11542
.17000	.00000	-.01142	-.02285	-.03429	-.04573	-.05717	-.06862	-.08008	-.09154	-.10300
.17250	.01132	-.00000	-.01133	-.02267	-.03401	-.04535	-.05671	-.06806	-.07942	-.09079
.17500	.02246	.01123	.00000	-.01124	-.02248	-.03373	-.04498	-.05624	-.06751	-.07877
.17750	.03341	.02228	.01114	.00000	-.01115	-.02230	-.03346	-.04462	-.05579	-.06696
.18000	.04417	.03314	.02210	.01105	.00000	-.01106	-.02212	-.03319	-.04426	-.05533
.18250	.05476	.04382	.03287	.02192	.01096	-.00000	-.01097	-.02194	-.03292	-.04390
.18500	.06517	.05432	.04347	.03261	.02175	.01088	.00000	-.01088	-.02177	-.03266
.18750	.07541	.06466	.05389	.04313	.03235	.02157	.01079	-.00000	-.01079	-.02159
.19000	.08548	.07482	.06415	.05347	.04279	.03210	.02140	.01070	.00000	-.01071
.19250	.09539	.08481	.07423	.06364	.05305	.04245	.03184	.02123	.01062	.00000
.19500	.10513	.09464	.08415	.07365	.06315	.05263	.04212	.03159	.02107	.01054
.19750	.11472	.10432	.09391	.08350	.07308	.06265	.05222	.04179	.03135	.02090
.20000	.12414	.11383	.10351	.09318	.08285	.07251	.06216	.05181	.04146	.03110
.20250	.13342	.12319	.11295	.10271	.09246	.08221	.07195	.06168	.05141	.04114
.20500	.14254	.13240	.12225	.11209	.10192	.09175	.08157	.07139	.06121	.05101
.20750	.15152	.14146	.13139	.12131	.11123	.10114	.09105	.08095	.07084	.06073

POINT TABLES: ORIGINAL LOAN TERM: 360 MONTHS LOAN PREPAID IN: 108 MONTHS

EFFECTIVE YIELD	CONTRACT RATE .19500	.19750	.20000	.20250	.20500	.20750
.07000	-.82925	-.84603	-.86280	-.87957	-.89634	-.91311
.07250	-.80452	-.82112	-.83772	-.85432	-.87091	-.88751
.07500	-.78023	-.79666	-.81309	-.82952	-.84594	-.86237
.07750	-.75638	-.77264	-.78890	-.80516	-.82142	-.83768
.08000	-.73295	-.74905	-.76515	-.78124	-.79734	-.81343
.08250	-.70995	-.72588	-.74182	-.75775	-.77368	-.78961
.08500	-.68736	-.70313	-.71891	-.73468	-.75045	-.76622
.08750	-.66517	-.68078	-.69640	-.71201	-.72763	-.74324
.09000	-.64337	-.65883	-.67429	-.68975	-.70521	-.72067
.09250	-.62197	-.63728	-.65258	-.66789	-.68319	-.69850
.09500	-.60094	-.61610	-.63125	-.64641	-.66156	-.67671
.09750	-.58029	-.59529	-.61030	-.62531	-.64031	-.65531
.10000	-.56000	-.57486	-.58972	-.60457	-.61943	-.63429
.10250	-.54007	-.55478	-.56950	-.58421	-.59892	-.61363
.10500	-.52049	-.53506	-.54963	-.56420	-.57877	-.59334
.10750	-.50125	-.51568	-.53011	-.54454	-.55897	-.57340
.11000	-.48235	-.49664	-.51093	-.52522	-.53951	-.55380
.11250	-.46378	-.47793	-.49209	-.50624	-.52039	-.53455
.11500	-.44554	-.45955	-.47357	-.48759	-.50161	-.51563
.11750	-.42761	-.44149	-.45538	-.46926	-.48315	-.49703
.12000	-.40999	-.42374	-.43750	-.45125	-.46500	-.47876
.12250	-.39268	-.40630	-.41992	-.43355	-.44717	-.46080
.12500	-.37567	-.38916	-.40266	-.41615	-.42965	-.44315
.12750	-.35895	-.37231	-.38568	-.39905	-.41243	-.42580
.13000	-.34251	-.35576	-.36900	-.38225	-.39550	-.40875
.13250	-.32636	-.33948	-.35261	-.36573	-.37886	-.39199
.13500	-.31049	-.32349	-.33649	-.34950	-.36250	-.37551
.13750	-.29489	-.30777	-.32065	-.33354	-.34642	-.35931
.14000	-.27955	-.29231	-.30508	-.31785	-.33061	-.34339
.14250	-.26447	-.27712	-.28977	-.30242	-.31508	-.32773
.14500	-.24965	-.26219	-.27472	-.28726	-.29980	-.31234
.14750	-.23508	-.24750	-.25993	-.27235	-.28478	-.29720
.15000	-.22076	-.23307	-.24538	-.25769	-.27001	-.28232
.15250	-.20668	-.21888	-.23108	-.24328	-.25549	-.26769
.15500	-.19283	-.20492	-.21701	-.22911	-.24121	-.25330
.15750	-.17922	-.19120	-.20318	-.21517	-.22716	-.23916
.16000	-.16583	-.17771	-.18959	-.20147	-.21335	-.22524
.16250	-.15266	-.16444	-.17621	-.18799	-.19977	-.21156
.16500	-.13972	-.15139	-.16306	-.17474	-.18642	-.19810
.16750	-.12699	-.13856	-.15013	-.16171	-.17328	-.18486
.17000	-.11447	-.12594	-.13741	-.14889	-.16036	-.17184
.17250	-.10215	-.11353	-.12490	-.13628	-.14766	-.15904
.17500	-.09004	-.10132	-.11259	-.12387	-.13516	-.14644
.17750	-.07813	-.08931	-.10049	-.11167	-.12286	-.13405
.18000	-.06641	-.07750	-.08858	-.09967	-.11076	-.12186
.18250	-.05489	-.06588	-.07687	-.08786	-.09886	-.10986
.18500	-.04355	-.05445	-.06535	-.07625	-.08715	-.09806
.18750	-.03239	-.04320	-.05401	-.06482	-.07563	-.08645
.19000	-.02142	-.03214	-.04285	-.05358	-.06430	-.07503
.19250	-.01062	-.02125	-.03188	-.04251	-.05315	-.06379
.19500	.00000	-.01054	-.02108	-.03163	-.04218	-.05273
.19750	.01045	.00000	-.01046	-.02092	-.03138	-.04184
.20000	.02074	.01037	0.00000	-.01037	-.02075	-.03113
.20250	.03086	.02058	.01029	.00000	-.01029	-.02059
.20500	.04082	.03062	.02042	.01021	.00000	-.01021
.20750	.05062	.04050	.03038	.02026	.01013	.00000

POINT TABLES: ORIGINAL LOAN TERM: 360 MONTHS LOAN PREPAID IN: 144 MONTHS

EFFECTIVE YIELD	CONTRACT RATE .07000	.07250	.07500	.07750	.08000	.08250	.08500	.08750	.09000	.09250
.07000	0.00000	-.01897	-.03803	-.05719	-.07644	-.09578	-.11520	-.13469	-.15426	-.17390
.07250	.01868	.00000	-.01878	-.03765	-.05662	-.07567	-.09480	-.11401	-.13329	-.15264
.07500	.03690	.01850	.00000	-.01859	-.03728	-.05605	-.07490	-.09383	-.11283	-.13190
.07750	.05467	.03654	.01832	.00000	-.01841	-.03690	-.05548	-.07413	-.09286	-.11166
.08000	.07201	.05415	.03619	.01814	.00000	-.01823	-.03653	-.05492	-.07338	-.09190
.08250	.08892	.07132	.05363	.03584	.01796	.00000	-.01804	-.03617	-.05436	-.07262
.08500	.10542	.08808	.07064	.05311	.03549	.01779	.00000	-.01786	-.03580	-.05381
.08750	.12152	.10443	.08724	.06996	.05260	.03514	.01761	.00000	-.01768	-.03544
.09000	.13722	.12036	.10344	.08641	.06929	.05208	.03480	.01744	.00000	-.01751
.09250	.15255	.13595	.11925	.10246	.08558	.06862	.05158	.03446	.01726	.00000
.09500	.16751	.15114	.13468	.11813	.10149	.08476	.06795	.05107	.03412	.01709
.09750	.18211	.16597	.14974	.13342	.11701	.10052	.08394	.06729	.05057	.03378
.10000	.19635	.18044	.16444	.14835	.13216	.11590	.09955	.08313	.06663	.05007
.10250	.21026	.19457	.17879	.16292	.14696	.13091	.11479	.09859	.08232	.06598
.10500	.22383	.20836	.19280	.17714	.16140	.14558	.12967	.11369	.09764	.08152
.10750	.23708	.22183	.20647	.19103	.17550	.15989	.14420	.12844	.11260	.09669
.11000	.25002	.23497	.21983	.20459	.18928	.17387	.15839	.14284	.12721	.11152
.11250	.26265	.24780	.23287	.21784	.20272	.18753	.17225	.15690	.14148	.12599
.11500	.27498	.26034	.24560	.23077	.21586	.20086	.18579	.17064	.15542	.14014
.11750	.28702	.27257	.25803	.24340	.22868	.21389	.19901	.18406	.16904	.15395
.12000	.29878	.28452	.27017	.25574	.24121	.22661	.21193	.19717	.18235	.16745
.12250	.31026	.29619	.28203	.26778	.25345	.23904	.22455	.20998	.19534	.18064
.12500	.32148	.30759	.29362	.27955	.26541	.25118	.23687	.22249	.20805	.19353
.12750	.33243	.31873	.30493	.29105	.27709	.26304	.24892	.23472	.22046	.20612
.13000	.34313	.32961	.31599	.30229	.28850	.27463	.26069	.24667	.23258	.21843
.13250	.35359	.34023	.32679	.31326	.29965	.28596	.27219	.25835	.24444	.23046
.13500	.36380	.35062	.33734	.32398	.31054	.29702	.28343	.26976	.25602	.24222
.13750	.37378	.36076	.34766	.33446	.32119	.30784	.29441	.28091	.26734	.25371
.14000	.38353	.37067	.35773	.34471	.33160	.31841	.30515	.29182	.27841	.26495
.14250	.39305	.38036	.36758	.35472	.34177	.32874	.31565	.30247	.28924	.27593
.14500	.40236	.38983	.37721	.36450	.35171	.33885	.32591	.31289	.29982	.28667
.14750	.41146	.39908	.38661	.37406	.36143	.34872	.33594	.32308	.31016	.29717
.15000	.42036	.40813	.39581	.38341	.37093	.35837	.34574	.33304	.32027	.30744
.15250	.42905	.41697	.40480	.39255	.38022	.36781	.35533	.34278	.33017	.31748
.15500	.43755	.42561	.41359	.40149	.38930	.37704	.36471	.35231	.33984	.32731
.15750	.44586	.43406	.42218	.41022	.39818	.38607	.37388	.36163	.34930	.33692
.16000	.45398	.44233	.43059	.41877	.40687	.39490	.38285	.37074	.35856	.34631
.16250	.46192	.45040	.43880	.42712	.41536	.40353	.39163	.37965	.36761	.35551
.16500	.46969	.45831	.44684	.43530	.42367	.41198	.40021	.38837	.37647	.36450
.16750	.47728	.46603	.45470	.44329	.43180	.42024	.40860	.39690	.38513	.37330
.17000	.48471	.47359	.46239	.45111	.43975	.42832	.41682	.40525	.39361	.38192
.17250	.49198	.48098	.46991	.45876	.44753	.43623	.42485	.41341	.40191	.39034
.17500	.49908	.48822	.47727	.46624	.45514	.44396	.43272	.42141	.41003	.39859
.17750	.50604	.49529	.48447	.47356	.46259	.45153	.44041	.42923	.41798	.40666
.18000	.51284	.50221	.49151	.48073	.46987	.45894	.44795	.43688	.42575	.41457
.18250	.51949	.50899	.49840	.48774	.47700	.46619	.45532	.44437	.43337	.42230
.18500	.52600	.51562	.50515	.49460	.48398	.47329	.46253	.45171	.44082	.42987
.18750	.53238	.52210	.51175	.50132	.49081	.48024	.46960	.45889	.44812	.43729
.19000	.53861	.52845	.51821	.50789	.49750	.48704	.47651	.46592	.45526	.44455
.19250	.54472	.53466	.52453	.51433	.50405	.49370	.48328	.47280	.46226	.45166
.19500	.55069	.54075	.53073	.52063	.51046	.50022	.48991	.47954	.46911	.45862
.19750	.55654	.54670	.53679	.52680	.51673	.50660	.49641	.48614	.47582	.46544
.20000	.56227	.55253	.54272	.53284	.52288	.51286	.50276	.49261	.48239	.47212
.20250	.56787	.55824	.54853	.53875	.52890	.51898	.50899	.49894	.48883	.47866
.20500	.57336	.56383	.55422	.54454	.53479	.52498	.51509	.50514	.49514	.48507
.20750	.57874	.56931	.55980	.55022	.54057	.53085	.52107	.51122	.50131	.49135

POINT TABLES: ORIGINAL LOAN TERM: 360 MONTHS LOAN PREPAID IN: 144 MONTHS

EFFECTIVE YIELD	CONTRACT RATE .09500	.09750	.10000	.10250	.10500	.10750	.11000	.11250	.11500	.11750
.07000	-.19360	-.21337	-.23319	-.25307	-.27300	-.29298	-.31300	-.33307	-.35317	-.37331
.07250	-.17206	-.19154	-.21108	-.23067	-.25031	-.27001	-.28974	-.30952	-.32934	-.34920
.07500	-.15104	-.17024	-.18949	-.20881	-.22817	-.24758	-.26704	-.28654	-.30608	-.32566
.07750	-.13052	-.14944	-.16843	-.18747	-.20656	-.22569	-.24488	-.26410	-.28337	-.30268
.08000	-.11050	-.12915	-.14787	-.16664	-.18546	-.20433	-.22324	-.24220	-.26120	-.28024
.08250	-.09095	-.10934	-.12780	-.14630	-.16486	-.18347	-.20212	-.22082	-.23955	-.25833
.08500	-.07188	-.09001	-.10820	-.12645	-.14475	-.16310	-.18150	-.19994	-.21842	-.23693
.08750	-.05325	-.07114	-.08908	-.10707	-.12512	-.14322	-.16136	-.17955	-.19777	-.21604
.09000	-.03508	-.05271	-.07040	-.08815	-.10595	-.12380	-.14170	-.15964	-.17762	-.19564
.09250	-.01733	-.03472	-.05217	-.06967	-.08723	-.10484	-.12249	-.14019	-.15793	-.17571
.09500	.00000	-.01715	-.03436	-.05163	-.06895	-.08632	-.10374	-.12120	-.13870	-.15624
.09750	.01692	.00000	-.01698	-.03401	-.05110	-.06824	-.08542	-.10265	-.11992	-.13723
.10000	.03344	.01675	.00000	-.01681	-.03366	-.05057	-.06753	-.08453	-.10157	-.11865
.10250	.04958	.03311	.01658	.00000	-.01663	-.03332	-.05005	-.06683	-.08365	-.10050
.10500	.06533	.04909	.03278	.01642	0.00000	-.01647	-.03298	-.04954	-.06613	-.08277
.10750	.08072	.06469	.04860	.03245	.01625	.00000	-.01630	-.03264	-.04902	-.06545
.11000	.09576	.07993	.06405	.04812	.03213	.01609	.00000	-.01613	-.03230	-.04852
.11250	.11044	.09482	.07915	.06342	.04764	.03180	.01592	.00000	-.01597	-.03197
.11500	.12479	.10937	.09390	.07837	.06279	.04716	.03149	.01576	.00000	-.01580
.11750	.13880	.12359	.10831	.09298	.07760	.06217	.04669	.03117	.01561	.00000
.12000	.15249	.13747	.12240	.10726	.09208	.07684	.06156	.04623	.03036	.01545
.12250	.16587	.15104	.13616	.12122	.10622	.09118	.07608	.06095	.04577	.03055
.12500	.17895	.16431	.14961	.13485	.12004	.10519	.09028	.07533	.06034	.04531
.12750	.19173	.17727	.16275	.14818	.13356	.11888	.10416	.08940	.07459	.05974
.13000	.20421	.18994	.17560	.16121	.14677	.13227	.11773	.10315	.08852	.07386
.13250	.21642	.20232	.18816	.17395	.15968	.14536	.13100	.11660	.10215	.08766
.13500	.22835	.21442	.20044	.18640	.17230	.15816	.14397	.12974	.11547	.10115
.13750	.24001	.22626	.21244	.19857	.18465	.17068	.15666	.14260	.12849	.11435
.14000	.25142	.23782	.22418	.21047	.19672	.18292	.16907	.15517	.14123	.12726
.14250	.26256	.24914	.23565	.22211	.20852	.19488	.18120	.16747	.15370	.13988
.14500	.27346	.26020	.24687	.23350	.22007	.20659	.19306	.17950	.16589	.15223
.14750	.28412	.27101	.25785	.24463	.23136	.21804	.20467	.19126	.17781	.16432
.15000	.29455	.28159	.26858	.25552	.24240	.22924	.21603	.20277	.18948	.17614
.15250	.30474	.29194	.27908	.26617	.25321	.24019	.22714	.21403	.20089	.18771
.15500	.31471	.30206	.28935	.27659	.26377	.25091	.23800	.22505	.21206	.19902
.15750	.32447	.31196	.29940	.28678	.27411	.26140	.24864	.23583	.22299	.21010
.16000	.33401	.32164	.30923	.29675	.28423	.27166	.25904	.24638	.23368	.22094
.16250	.34334	.33112	.31884	.30651	.29413	.28170	.26923	.25671	.24415	.23155
.16500	.35248	.34039	.32825	.31606	.30382	.29153	.27919	.26682	.25440	.24194
.16750	.36141	.34946	.33746	.32541	.31330	.30115	.28895	.27671	.26442	.25210
.17000	.37016	.35834	.34647	.33455	.32258	.31056	.29850	.28639	.27424	.26206
.17250	.37872	.36703	.35529	.34351	.33167	.31978	.30785	.29587	.28386	.27180
.17500	.38709	.37554	.36393	.35227	.34056	.32880	.31700	.30515	.29327	.28134
.17750	.39529	.38386	.37238	.36085	.34926	.33763	.32596	.31424	.30248	.29069
.18000	.40332	.39201	.38066	.36925	.35779	.34628	.33473	.32314	.31151	.29984
.18250	.41117	.39999	.38876	.37747	.36613	.35475	.34333	.33186	.32035	.30880
.18500	.41887	.40780	.39669	.38552	.37431	.36305	.35174	.34039	.32900	.31758
.18750	.42640	.41545	.40446	.39341	.38231	.37117	.35998	.34875	.33748	.32618
.19000	.43377	.42295	.41206	.40113	.39015	.37913	.36806	.35694	.34579	.33460
.19250	.44100	.43028	.41951	.40870	.39783	.38692	.37596	.36497	.35393	.34285
.19500	.44807	.43747	.42681	.41611	.40535	.39455	.38371	.37283	.36190	.35094
.19750	.45500	.44451	.43396	.42337	.41272	.40203	.39130	.38053	.36972	.35887
.20000	.46179	.45140	.44096	.43048	.41994	.40936	.39874	.38808	.37737	.36663
.20250	.46844	.45816	.44782	.43744	.42702	.41654	.40603	.39547	.38488	.37424
.20500	.47495	.46477	.45455	.44427	.43395	.42358	.41317	.40272	.39223	.38170
.20750	.48133	.47126	.46114	.45096	.44074	.43048	.42017	.40983	.39944	.38902

POINT TABLES: ORIGINAL LOAN TERM: 360 MONTHS LOAN PREPAID IN: 144 MONTHS

EFFECTIVE YIELD	CONTRACT RATE .12000	.12250	.12500	.12750	.13000	.13250	.13500	.13750	.14000	.14250
.07000	-.39348	-.41369	-.43392	-.45418	-.47446	-.49477	-.51510	-.53544	-.55581	-.57619
.07250	-.36909	-.38901	-.40896	-.42893	-.44894	-.46896	-.48901	-.50907	-.52916	-.54925
.07500	-.34527	-.36491	-.38458	-.40429	-.42401	-.44376	-.46353	-.48332	-.50313	-.52295
.07750	-.32201	-.34139	-.36079	-.38022	-.39967	-.41915	-.43865	-.45817	-.47771	-.49726
.08000	-.29931	-.31841	-.33755	-.35671	-.37590	-.39511	-.41435	-.43360	-.45288	-.47217
.08250	-.27714	-.29598	-.31485	-.33376	-.35269	-.37164	-.39061	-.40961	-.42862	-.44766
.08500	-.25549	-.27407	-.29269	-.31134	-.33001	-.34871	-.36743	-.38617	-.40493	-.42371
.08750	-.23434	-.25268	-.27105	-.28944	-.30786	-.32631	-.34478	-.36328	-.38179	-.40032
.09000	-.21369	-.23178	-.24990	-.26805	-.28623	-.30443	-.32266	-.34091	-.35918	-.37746
.09250	-.19352	-.21137	-.22925	-.24716	-.26510	-.28306	-.30105	-.31905	-.33708	-.35513
.09500	-.17382	-.19143	-.20907	-.22675	-.24445	-.26218	-.27993	-.29770	-.31549	-.33331
.09750	-.15457	-.17195	-.18936	-.20681	-.22428	-.24177	-.25929	-.27683	-.29440	-.31198
.10000	-.13577	-.15292	-.17011	-.18732	-.20456	-.22183	-.23913	-.25644	-.27378	-.29114
.10250	-.11740	-.13433	-.15129	-.16828	-.18530	-.20235	-.21942	-.23651	-.25363	-.27077
.10500	-.09945	-.11616	-.13290	-.14968	-.16648	-.18331	-.20016	-.21704	-.23394	-.25085
.10750	-.08191	-.09840	-.11493	-.13149	-.14808	-.16470	-.18134	-.19800	-.21468	-.23139
.11000	-.06477	-.08105	-.09737	-.11372	-.13010	-.14651	-.16294	-.17939	-.19587	-.21236
.11250	-.04802	-.06410	-.08021	-.09635	-.11252	-.12872	-.14495	-.16120	-.17747	-.19376
.11500	-.03165	-.04752	-.06343	-.07937	-.09534	-.11134	-.12736	-.14341	-.15948	-.17557
.11750	-.01564	-.03132	-.04703	-.06277	-.07855	-.09435	-.11017	-.12602	-.14189	-.15778
.12000	-.00000	-.01548	-.03100	-.04655	-.06213	-.07773	-.09336	-.10902	-.12469	-.14039
.12250	.01529	.00000	-.01533	-.03068	-.04607	-.06148	-.07692	-.09239	-.10788	-.12338
.12500	.03024	.01514	.00000	-.01517	-.03037	-.04560	-.06085	-.07613	-.09143	-.10675
.12750	.04486	.02994	.01499	.00000	-.01502	-.03006	-.04513	-.06022	-.07534	-.09048
.13000	.05915	.04441	.02964	.01483	.00000	-.01486	-.02975	-.04467	-.05960	-.07456
.13250	.07313	.05857	.04397	.02934	.01469	.00000	-.01471	-.02945	-.04421	-.05899
.13500	.08680	.07241	.05799	.04353	.02905	.01454	-.00000	-.01456	-.02915	-.04376
.13750	.10017	.08595	.07170	.05741	.04310	.02876	.01439	.00000	-.01442	-.02885
.14000	.11324	.09919	.08511	.07099	.05685	.04267	.02847	.01425	.00000	-.01427
.14250	.12603	.11215	.09823	.08428	.07030	.05629	.04225	.02819	.01411	.00000
.14500	.13855	.12482	.11106	.09728	.08346	.06961	.05573	.04183	.02791	.01397
.14750	.15079	.13722	.12362	.10999	.09633	.08264	.06893	.05519	.04142	.02763
.15000	.16277	.14936	.13591	.12244	.10893	.09540	.08184	.06825	.05464	.04101
.15250	.17448	.16123	.14794	.13462	.12126	.10788	.09448	.08104	.06759	.05411
.15500	.18595	.17285	.15971	.14654	.13333	.12010	.10685	.09356	.08026	.06693
.15750	.19718	.18422	.17123	.15820	.14515	.13207	.11896	.10582	.09266	.07948
.16000	.20816	.19535	.18250	.16962	.15671	.14377	.13081	.11782	.10481	.09177
.16250	.21891	.20624	.19354	.18080	.16803	.15524	.14242	.12957	.11670	.10381
.16500	.22944	.21691	.20434	.19175	.17912	.16646	.15378	.14107	.12834	.11559
.16750	.23974	.22735	.21492	.20246	.18997	.17745	.16491	.15234	.13975	.12713
.17000	.24983	.23757	.22528	.21295	.20060	.18822	.17581	.16337	.15092	.13844
.17250	.25971	.24758	.23542	.22323	.21101	.19876	.18648	.17418	.16186	.14951
.17500	.26938	.25738	.24535	.23329	.22120	.20908	.19694	.18477	.17257	.16035
.17750	.27885	.26698	.25508	.24315	.23119	.21920	.20718	.19514	.18307	.17098
.18000	.28813	.27639	.26461	.25280	.24097	.22910	.21721	.20529	.19335	.18139
.18250	.29721	.28560	.27394	.26226	.25055	.23881	.22704	.21525	.20343	.19159
.18500	.30611	.29462	.28309	.27153	.25993	.24832	.23667	.22500	.21330	.20159
.18750	.31483	.30346	.29204	.28060	.26913	.25763	.24611	.23456	.22298	.21138
.19000	.32337	.31211	.30082	.28950	.27814	.26676	.25535	.24392	.23246	.22099
.19250	.33174	.32060	.30942	.29821	.28697	.27571	.26442	.25310	.24176	.23040
.19500	.33994	.32891	.31785	.30675	.29563	.28448	.27330	.26210	.25087	.23962
.19750	.34798	.33706	.32611	.31512	.30411	.29307	.28201	.27092	.25980	.24866
.20000	.35586	.34505	.33420	.32333	.31243	.30150	.29054	.27956	.26856	.25753
.20250	.36358	.35287	.34214	.33137	.32058	.30976	.29891	.28804	.27714	.26622
.20500	.37114	.36055	.34992	.33926	.32857	.31786	.30711	.29635	.28556	.27475
.20750	.37856	.36807	.35754	.34699	.33641	.32580	.31516	.30450	.29381	.28311

POINT TABLES: ORIGINAL LOAN TERM: 360 MONTHS LOAN PREPAID IN: 144 MONTHS

EFFECTIVE YIELD	CONTRACT RATE .14500	.14750	.15000	.15250	.15500	.15750	.16000	.16250	.16500	.16750
.07000	-.59658	-.61698	-.63740	-.65782	-.67826	-.69870	-.71915	-.73960	-.76006	-.78052
.07250	-.56937	-.58949	-.60963	-.62978	-.64993	-.67010	-.69027	-.71044	-.73063	-.75081
.07500	-.54279	-.56264	-.58250	-.60238	-.62226	-.64216	-.66205	-.68196	-.70187	-.72179
.07750	-.51683	-.53641	-.55601	-.57562	-.59523	-.61486	-.63449	-.65413	-.67378	-.69343
.08000	-.49147	-.51080	-.53013	-.54947	-.56883	-.58819	-.60757	-.62694	-.64633	-.66572
.08250	-.46670	-.48577	-.50484	-.52393	-.54303	-.56214	-.58125	-.60038	-.61951	-.63865
.08500	-.44251	-.46132	-.48014	-.49898	-.51782	-.53668	-.55554	-.57442	-.59330	-.61218
.08750	-.41886	-.43743	-.45600	-.47459	-.49319	-.51180	-.53042	-.54905	-.56768	-.58632
.09000	-.39577	-.41408	-.43242	-.45076	-.46912	-.48749	-.50587	-.52425	-.54265	-.56105
.09250	-.37319	-.39127	-.40937	-.42748	-.44560	-.46373	-.48187	-.50002	-.51818	-.53634
.09500	-.35114	-.36898	-.38684	-.40472	-.42261	-.44050	-.45841	-.47633	-.49425	-.51219
.09750	-.32958	-.34720	-.36483	-.38247	-.40013	-.41780	-.43548	-.45317	-.47087	-.48858
.10000	-.30851	-.32590	-.34331	-.36073	-.37817	-.39561	-.41307	-.43053	-.44801	-.46549
.10250	-.28792	-.30509	-.32228	-.33948	-.35669	-.37392	-.39116	-.40840	-.42566	-.44292
.10500	-.26779	-.28475	-.30172	-.31870	-.33570	-.35271	-.36973	-.38676	-.40380	-.42085
.10750	-.24811	-.26486	-.28161	-.29839	-.31517	-.33197	-.34878	-.36560	-.38243	-.39927
.11000	-.22888	-.24541	-.26196	-.27852	-.29510	-.31169	-.32830	-.34491	-.36153	-.37816
.11250	-.21007	-.22640	-.24274	-.25910	-.27548	-.29186	-.30826	-.32467	-.34109	-.35752
.11500	-.19168	-.20781	-.22395	-.24011	-.25628	-.27247	-.28867	-.30488	-.32110	-.33733
.11750	-.17370	-.18963	-.20557	-.22154	-.23751	-.25350	-.26951	-.28552	-.30155	-.31758
.12000	-.15611	-.17185	-.18760	-.20337	-.21916	-.23495	-.25076	-.26658	-.28242	-.29826
.12250	-.13891	-.15446	-.17002	-.18560	-.20120	-.21681	-.23243	-.24806	-.26370	-.27936
.12500	-.12209	-.13745	-.15283	-.16822	-.18363	-.19905	-.21449	-.22994	-.24539	-.26086
.12750	-.10564	-.12081	-.13601	-.15122	-.16644	-.18168	-.19694	-.21220	-.22748	-.24277
.13000	-.08954	-.10454	-.11955	-.13458	-.14963	-.16469	-.17977	-.19485	-.20995	-.22506
.13250	-.07379	-.08861	-.10345	-.11831	-.13318	-.14806	-.16296	-.17787	-.19280	-.20773
.13500	-.05839	-.07303	-.08770	-.10238	-.11708	-.13179	-.14652	-.16126	-.17601	-.19077
.13750	-.04331	-.05779	-.07229	-.08680	-.10133	-.11587	-.13043	-.14499	-.15957	-.17417
.14000	-.02856	-.04287	-.05720	-.07155	-.08591	-.10028	-.11467	-.12908	-.14349	-.15792
.14250	-.01413	-.02827	-.04244	-.05662	-.07082	-.08503	-.09926	-.11349	-.12775	-.14201
.14500	0.00000	-.01399	-.02799	-.04201	-.05605	-.07010	-.08416	-.09824	-.11233	-.12643
.14750	.01383	0.00000	-.01385	-.02771	-.04159	-.05548	-.06939	-.08331	-.09724	-.11118
.15000	.02736	.01369	.00000	-.01371	-.02743	-.04117	-.05492	-.06869	-.08246	-.09625
.15250	.04061	.02709	.01355	.00000	-.01357	-.02716	-.04076	-.05437	-.06800	-.08163
.15500	.05358	.04021	.02683	.01342	.00000	-.01344	-.02689	-.04035	-.05383	-.06731
.15750	.06628	.05306	.03982	.02656	.01329	0.00000	-.01330	-.02662	-.03995	-.05329
.16000	.07872	.06564	.05254	.03943	.02630	.01316	.00000	-.01317	-.02636	-.03955
.16250	.09089	.07796	.06501	.05203	.03905	.02605	.01303	.00000	-.01304	-.02610
.16500	.10282	.09002	.07721	.06438	.05153	.03867	.02579	.01290	.00000	-.01291
.16750	.11450	.10184	.08916	.07647	.06376	.05104	.03830	.02554	.01278	.00000
.17000	.12593	.11341	.10087	.08831	.07574	.06315	.05055	.03793	.02530	.01265
.17250	.13714	.12475	.11234	.09992	.08748	.07502	.06255	.05006	.03756	.02505
.17500	.14812	.13586	.12358	.11129	.09898	.08665	.07431	.06195	.04958	.03720
.17750	.15887	.14674	.13459	.12243	.11024	.09804	.08583	.07360	.06136	.04911
.18000	.16941	.15740	.14538	.13334	.12128	.10921	.09712	.08502	.07291	.06078
.18250	.17973	.16785	.15595	.14404	.13211	.12016	.10819	.09622	.08423	.07223
.18500	.18985	.17809	.16632	.15452	.14271	.13088	.11904	.10719	.09532	.08344
.18750	.19977	.18813	.17647	.16480	.15311	.14140	.12968	.11794	.10620	.09444
.19000	.20949	.19797	.18643	.17487	.16330	.15171	.14011	.12849	.11686	.10522
.19250	.21901	.20761	.19619	.18475	.17329	.16182	.15033	.13883	.12731	.11579
.19500	.22835	.21706	.20575	.19443	.18308	.17173	.16035	.14897	.13757	.12615
.19750	.23751	.22633	.21513	.20392	.19269	.18144	.17018	.15891	.14762	.13632
.20000	.24648	.23542	.22433	.21323	.20211	.19097	.17982	.16866	.15748	.14629
.20250	.25529	.24433	.23335	.22235	.21134	.20032	.18927	.17822	.16715	.15607
.20500	.26392	.25306	.24219	.23131	.22040	.20948	.19855	.18760	.17664	.16566
.20750	.27238	.26163	.25087	.24009	.22929	.21847	.20764	.19680	.18594	.17507

POINT TABLES: ORIGINAL LOAN TERM: 360 MONTHS LOAN PREPAID IN: 144 MONTHS

EFFECTIVE YIELD	CONTRACT RATE .17000	.17250	.17500	.17750	.18000	.18250	.18500	.18750	.19000	.19250
.07000	-.80098	-.82145	-.84192	-.86239	-.88286	-.90333	-.92380	-.94427	-.96474	-.98520
.07250	-.77100	-.79119	-.81139	-.83158	-.85178	-.87198	-.89218	-.91237	-.93257	-.95276
.07500	-.74171	-.76163	-.78156	-.80148	-.82141	-.84134	-.86127	-.88120	-.90113	-.92106
.07750	-.71309	-.73275	-.75241	-.77207	-.79174	-.81140	-.83107	-.85074	-.87041	-.89007
.08000	-.68512	-.70452	-.72392	-.74333	-.76273	-.78214	-.80155	-.82096	-.84037	-.85979
.08250	-.65779	-.67693	-.69608	-.71523	-.73439	-.75355	-.77270	-.79186	-.81102	-.83018
.08500	-.63108	-.64997	-.66887	-.68778	-.70668	-.72559	-.74450	-.76341	-.78232	-.80124
.08750	-.60497	-.62362	-.64228	-.66094	-.67960	-.69827	-.71693	-.73560	-.75427	-.77294
.09000	-.57945	-.59787	-.61628	-.63470	-.65313	-.67155	-.68998	-.70841	-.72684	-.74528
.09250	-.55451	-.57269	-.59087	-.60905	-.62724	-.64544	-.66363	-.68183	-.70003	-.71823
.09500	-.53013	-.54807	-.56602	-.58398	-.60194	-.61990	-.63787	-.65583	-.67380	-.69177
.09750	-.50629	-.52401	-.54173	-.55946	-.57720	-.59493	-.61267	-.63042	-.64816	-.66591
.10000	-.48298	-.50048	-.51798	-.53549	-.55300	-.57052	-.58804	-.60556	-.62308	-.64061
.10250	-.46019	-.47747	-.49476	-.51205	-.52934	-.54664	-.56394	-.58125	-.59855	-.61586
.10500	-.43791	-.45497	-.47204	-.48912	-.50620	-.52329	-.54038	-.55747	-.57456	-.59166
.10750	-.41612	-.43297	-.44983	-.46670	-.48357	-.50045	-.51733	-.53421	-.55109	-.56798
.11000	-.39480	-.41145	-.42811	-.44477	-.46143	-.47810	-.49478	-.51146	-.52814	-.54482
.11250	-.37396	-.39040	-.40686	-.42331	-.43978	-.45625	-.47272	-.48920	-.50568	-.52216
.11500	-.35357	-.36982	-.38607	-.40233	-.41859	-.43486	-.45114	-.46742	-.48370	-.49999
.11750	-.33362	-.34967	-.36573	-.38180	-.39787	-.41394	-.43002	-.44611	-.46220	-.47829
.12000	-.31411	-.32997	-.34584	-.36171	-.37759	-.39347	-.40936	-.42526	-.44116	-.45706
.12250	-.29502	-.31069	-.32637	-.34205	-.35775	-.37344	-.38915	-.40485	-.42057	-.43628
.12500	-.27634	-.29183	-.30732	-.32282	-.33833	-.35384	-.36936	-.38488	-.40041	-.41594
.12750	-.25806	-.27337	-.28868	-.30400	-.31933	-.33466	-.35000	-.36534	-.38069	-.39604
.13000	-.24018	-.25530	-.27044	-.28558	-.30073	-.31588	-.33104	-.34621	-.36138	-.37655
.13250	-.22267	-.23762	-.25258	-.26755	-.28252	-.29750	-.31249	-.32748	-.34248	-.35748
.13500	-.20554	-.22032	-.23510	-.24990	-.26470	-.27951	-.29433	-.30915	-.32397	-.33880
.13750	-.18877	-.20338	-.21800	-.23262	-.24726	-.26190	-.27654	-.29120	-.30585	-.32052
.14000	-.17235	-.18680	-.20125	-.21571	-.23018	-.24465	-.25913	-.27362	-.28811	-.30261
.14250	-.15628	-.17056	-.18485	-.19915	-.21346	-.22777	-.24209	-.25641	-.27074	-.28508
.14500	-.14054	-.15467	-.16880	-.18293	-.19708	-.21123	-.22539	-.23956	-.25373	-.26790
.14750	-.12514	-.13910	-.15308	-.16706	-.18105	-.19504	-.20904	-.22305	-.23707	-.25109
.15000	-.11005	-.12386	-.13768	-.15151	-.16534	-.17918	-.19303	-.20689	-.22075	-.23461
.15250	-.09528	-.10894	-.12260	-.13628	-.14996	-.16365	-.17735	-.19105	-.20476	-.21847
.15500	-.08081	-.09432	-.10784	-.12136	-.13490	-.14844	-.16199	-.17554	-.18910	-.20267
.15750	-.06664	-.08000	-.09337	-.10675	-.12014	-.13353	-.14694	-.16034	-.17376	-.18718
.16000	-.05276	-.06598	-.07920	-.09244	-.10568	-.11893	-.13219	-.14545	-.15873	-.17200
.16250	-.03916	-.05224	-.06532	-.07842	-.09152	-.10463	-.11774	-.13087	-.14400	-.15713
.16500	-.02584	-.03878	-.05172	-.06468	-.07764	-.09061	-.10359	-.11657	-.12956	-.14256
.16750	-.01279	-.02559	-.03840	-.05121	-.06404	-.07687	-.08971	-.10256	-.11542	-.12827
.17000	.00000	-.01266	-.02534	-.03802	-.05071	-.06341	-.07612	-.08883	-.10155	-.11428
.17250	.01253	0.00000	-.01254	-.02509	-.03765	-.05022	-.06279	-.07537	-.08796	-.10055
.17500	.02481	.01241	.00000	-.01242	-.02485	-.03729	-.04973	-.06218	-.07464	-.08710
.17750	.03685	.02458	.01229	0.00000	-.01230	-.02461	-.03693	-.04925	-.06158	-.07392
.18000	.04865	.03650	.02434	.01218	.00000	-.01218	-.02437	-.03657	-.04878	-.06099
.18250	.06021	.04819	.03615	.02411	.01206	0.00000	-.01207	-.02414	-.03622	-.04831
.18500	.07155	.05965	.04774	.03581	.02388	.01195	.00000	-.01195	-.02391	-.03588
.18750	.08266	.07088	.05909	.04729	.03548	.02366	.01183	0.00000	-.01184	-.02369
.19000	.09356	.08190	.07022	.05854	.04685	.03515	.02344	.01172	0.00000	-.01173
.19250	.10425	.09270	.08114	.06957	.05800	.04641	.03482	.02322	.01161	.00000
.19500	.11473	.10329	.09185	.08040	.06893	.05746	.04598	.03450	.02300	.01150
.19750	.12501	.11368	.10235	.09101	.07966	.06830	.05693	.04556	.03418	.02279
.20000	.13509	.12388	.11265	.10142	.09018	.07893	.06768	.05641	.04514	.03386
.20250	.14498	.13387	.12276	.11164	.10050	.08936	.07822	.06706	.05590	.04473
.20500	.15468	.14368	.13267	.12166	.11063	.09960	.08856	.07751	.06645	.05539
.20750	.16419	.15330	.14240	.13149	.12057	.10964	.09870	.08776	.07681	.06585

EFFECTIVE YIELD	CONTRACT RATE .19500	.19750	.20000	.20250	.20500	.20750
.07000	-1.00566	-1.02613	-1.04658	-1.06704	-1.08749	-1.10794
.07250	-.97295	-.99314	-1.01333	-1.03352	-1.05370	-1.07388
.07500	-.94098	-.96091	-.98083	-1.00075	-1.02067	-1.04059
.07750	-.90974	-.92940	-.94907	-.96873	-.98839	-1.00804
.08000	-.87920	-.89860	-.91801	-.93742	-.95682	-.97623
.08250	-.84934	-.86850	-.88765	-.90681	-.92596	-.94512
.08500	-.82015	-.83906	-.85797	-.87688	-.89579	-.91470
.08750	-.79161	-.81028	-.82895	-.84762	-.86629	-.88496
.09000	-.76371	-.78214	-.80058	-.81901	-.83744	-.85587
.09250	-.73643	-.75463	-.77283	-.79103	-.80923	-.82743
.09500	-.70975	-.72772	-.74569	-.76367	-.78164	-.79961
.09750	-.68365	-.70140	-.71915	-.73690	-.75465	-.77240
.10000	-.65814	-.67566	-.69319	-.71072	-.72826	-.74579
.10250	-.63318	-.65049	-.66780	-.68512	-.70243	-.71975
.10500	-.60876	-.62586	-.64296	-.66007	-.67717	-.69428
.10750	-.58488	-.60177	-.61866	-.63556	-.65246	-.66935
.11000	-.56151	-.57820	-.59489	-.61158	-.62827	-.64497
.11250	-.53865	-.55513	-.57162	-.58812	-.60461	-.62110
.11500	-.51628	-.53257	-.54886	-.56516	-.58145	-.59775
.11750	-.49439	-.51048	-.52658	-.54269	-.55879	-.57490
.12000	-.47297	-.48887	-.50478	-.52070	-.53661	-.55253
.12250	-.45200	-.46772	-.48345	-.49917	-.51490	-.53063
.12500	-.43148	-.44702	-.46256	-.47810	-.49365	-.50920
.12750	-.41139	-.42675	-.44211	-.45748	-.47284	-.48821
.13000	-.39173	-.40691	-.42210	-.43728	-.45247	-.46767
.13250	-.37248	-.38749	-.40250	-.41751	-.43253	-.44755
.13500	-.35364	-.36847	-.38331	-.39816	-.41300	-.42785
.13750	-.33518	-.34985	-.36452	-.37920	-.39388	-.40856
.14000	-.31711	-.33162	-.34613	-.36064	-.37515	-.38967
.14250	-.29942	-.31376	-.32811	-.34246	-.35681	-.37116
.14500	-.28208	-.29627	-.31046	-.32465	-.33884	-.35304
.14750	-.26511	-.27914	-.29317	-.30720	-.32124	-.33528
.15000	-.24848	-.26236	-.27623	-.29012	-.30400	-.31789
.15250	-.23219	-.24592	-.25964	-.27338	-.28711	-.30085
.15500	-.21624	-.22981	-.24339	-.25697	-.27056	-.28415
.15750	-.20060	-.21403	-.22746	-.24090	-.25434	-.26778
.16000	-.18528	-.19857	-.21186	-.22515	-.23845	-.25175
.16250	-.17027	-.18341	-.19656	-.20972	-.22287	-.23603
.16500	-.15556	-.16856	-.18157	-.19459	-.20761	-.22063
.16750	-.14114	-.15401	-.16688	-.17976	-.19264	-.20553
.17000	-.12701	-.13974	-.15248	-.16523	-.17797	-.19073
.17250	-.11315	-.12576	-.13837	-.15098	-.16359	-.17621
.17500	-.09957	-.11205	-.12453	-.13701	-.14950	-.16199
.17750	-.08626	-.09860	-.11096	-.12331	-.13567	-.14803
.18000	-.07320	-.08542	-.09765	-.10988	-.12212	-.13435
.18250	-.06040	-.07250	-.08460	-.09671	-.10882	-.12094
.18500	-.04785	-.05983	-.07181	-.08379	-.09578	-.10778
.18750	-.03554	-.04739	-.05926	-.07112	-.08299	-.09487
.19000	-.02346	-.03520	-.04695	-.05870	-.07045	-.08221
.19250	-.01162	-.02324	-.03487	-.04651	-.05814	-.06979
.19500	0.00000	-.01151	-.02303	-.03455	-.04607	-.05760
.19750	.01140	.00000	-.01140	-.02281	-.03422	-.04564
.20000	.02258	.01129	0.00000	-.01130	-.02260	-.03391
.20250	.03356	.02238	.01119	.00000	-.01119	-.02239
.20500	.04432	.03325	.02217	.01109	0.00000	-.01109
.20750	.05489	.04392	.03295	.02197	.01099	.00000

POINT TABLES: ORIGINAL LOAN TERM: 360 MONTHS LOAN PREPAID IN: 180 MONTHS

CONTRACT RATE

EFFECTIVE YIELD	.07000	.07250	.07500	.07750	.08000	.08250	.08500	.08750	.09000	.09250
.07000	.00000	-.02127	-.04267	-.06421	-.08587	-.10764	-.12954	-.15154	-.17365	-.19585
.07250	.02089	.00000	-.02102	-.04218	-.06345	-.08485	-.10636	-.12797	-.14969	-.17151
.07500	.04117	.02065	0.00000	-.02078	-.04168	-.06271	-.08384	-.10508	-.12643	-.14787
.07750	.06086	.04071	.02042	.00000	-.02054	-.04120	-.06197	-.08284	-.10382	-.12489
.08000	.07999	.06019	.04025	.02019	.00000	-.02030	-.04072	-.06123	-.08185	-.10257
.08250	.09857	.07911	.05952	.03980	.01996	.00000	-.02007	-.04024	-.06051	-.08088
.08500	.11662	.09749	.07823	.05885	.03935	.01973	.00000	-.01983	-.03976	-.05979
.08750	.13416	.11536	.09642	.07737	.05819	.03890	.01950	.00000	-.01960	-.03930
.09000	.15120	.13271	.11410	.09536	.07650	.05753	.03846	.01928	.00000	-.01937
.09250	.16776	.14958	.13127	.11285	.09430	.07565	.05688	.03802	.01906	.00000
.09500	.18385	.16597	.14797	.12985	.11161	.09326	.07480	.05624	.03758	.01884
.09750	.19949	.18191	.16420	.14637	.12843	.11038	.09222	.07396	.05550	.03715
.10000	.21470	.19740	.17998	.16244	.14479	.12702	.10916	.09119	.07312	.05497
.10250	.22948	.21246	.19532	.17806	.16069	.14321	.12563	.10795	.09017	.07230
.10500	.24386	.22711	.21024	.19326	.17616	.15896	.14165	.12425	.10675	.08916
.10750	.25783	.24135	.22475	.20804	.19121	.17428	.15724	.14011	.12288	.10556
.11000	.27143	.25521	.23887	.22241	.20585	.18918	.17241	.15554	.13857	.12152
.11250	.28465	.26868	.25260	.23640	.22009	.20368	.18716	.17055	.15385	.13706
.11500	.29751	.28179	.26596	.25001	.23395	.21778	.20152	.18516	.16871	.15217
.11750	.31003	.29455	.27895	.26325	.24743	.23151	.21550	.19938	.18318	.16689
.12000	.32221	.30696	.29160	.27613	.26056	.24488	.22910	.21323	.19726	.18122
.12250	.33406	.31904	.30391	.28868	.27333	.25789	.24234	.22670	.21098	.19517
.12500	.34559	.33080	.31590	.30089	.28577	.27055	.25524	.23983	.22433	.20875
.12750	.35682	.34225	.32756	.31277	.29788	.28288	.26779	.25261	.23733	.22198
.13000	.36775	.35339	.33892	.32435	.30967	.29489	.28002	.26505	.25000	.23486
.13250	.37839	.36424	.34998	.33562	.32115	.30659	.29193	.27717	.26234	.24742
.13500	.38875	.37481	.36076	.34660	.33234	.31798	.30353	.28898	.27436	.25965
.13750	.39885	.38510	.37125	.35729	.34323	.32908	.31483	.30049	.28607	.27156
.14000	.40868	.39513	.38147	.36771	.35384	.33989	.32584	.31170	.29748	.28317
.14250	.41825	.40489	.39143	.37786	.36419	.35042	.33657	.32263	.30860	.29449
.14500	.42758	.41441	.40113	.38775	.37427	.36069	.34703	.33328	.31944	.30553
.14750	.43667	.42368	.41058	.39738	.38409	.37070	.35722	.34366	.33001	.31628
.15000	.44553	.43272	.41980	.40678	.39366	.38046	.36716	.35378	.34031	.32677
.15250	.45417	.44153	.42878	.41594	.40300	.38997	.37685	.36364	.35036	.33699
.15500	.46258	.45011	.43754	.42487	.41210	.39924	.38630	.37327	.36016	.34697
.15750	.47079	.45848	.44608	.43357	.42098	.40829	.39551	.38265	.36971	.35670
.16000	.47879	.46665	.45440	.44206	.42963	.41711	.40450	.39181	.37904	.36619
.16250	.48659	.47461	.46252	.45035	.43807	.42571	.41327	.40074	.38813	.37545
.16500	.49420	.48237	.47045	.45842	.44631	.43411	.42182	.40945	.39701	.38448
.16750	.50163	.48995	.47817	.46630	.45435	.44230	.43017	.41796	.40567	.39330
.17000	.50887	.49734	.48571	.47399	.46219	.45029	.43831	.42625	.41412	.40191
.17250	.51593	.50455	.49307	.48150	.46984	.45809	.44626	.43436	.42237	.41031
.17500	.52283	.51159	.50025	.48882	.47731	.46571	.45402	.44226	.43043	.41851
.17750	.52956	.51845	.50726	.49597	.48460	.47314	.46160	.44998	.43829	.42652
.18000	.53612	.52516	.51410	.50295	.49172	.48040	.46900	.45752	.44597	.43435
.18250	.54254	.53171	.52078	.50977	.49867	.48749	.47623	.46489	.45347	.44199
.18500	.54880	.53810	.52730	.51642	.50546	.49441	.48328	.47208	.46080	.44945
.18750	.55491	.54434	.53367	.52292	.51209	.50117	.49017	.47910	.46796	.45674
.19000	.56088	.55043	.53990	.52927	.51857	.50778	.49691	.48597	.47495	.46387
.19250	.56671	.55639	.54598	.53548	.52489	.51423	.50349	.49267	.48179	.47083
.19500	.57241	.56221	.55191	.54154	.53108	.52054	.50992	.49923	.48847	.47764
.19750	.57798	.56789	.55772	.54746	.53712	.52670	.51620	.50564	.49500	.48429
.20000	.58342	.57345	.56339	.55325	.54302	.53272	.52235	.51190	.50138	.49079
.20250	.58873	.57887	.56893	.55891	.54880	.53861	.52835	.51802	.50762	.49715
.20500	.59393	.58418	.57435	.56444	.55444	.54437	.53423	.52401	.51372	.50337
.20750	.59901	.58937	.57965	.56984	.55996	.55000	.53997	.52986	.51969	.50945

POINT TABLES: ORIGINAL LOAN TERM: 360 MONTHS LOAN PREPAID IN: 180 MONTHS

EFFECTIVE YIELD	CONTRACT RATE .09500	.09750	.10000	.10250	.10500	.10750	.11000	.11250	.11500	.11750
.07000	-.21815	-.24053	-.26300	-.28555	-.30817	-.33086	-.35362	-.37643	-.39931	-.42224
.07250	-.19342	-.21542	-.23750	-.25966	-.28189	-.30420	-.32656	-.34900	-.37148	-.39403
.07500	-.16940	-.19102	-.21272	-.23450	-.25636	-.27828	-.30028	-.32233	-.34444	-.36660
.07750	-.14606	-.16731	-.18865	-.21006	-.23155	-.25310	-.27472	-.29641	-.31815	-.33995
.08000	-.12338	-.14427	-.16525	-.18630	-.20743	-.22862	-.24989	-.27121	-.29259	-.31403
.08250	-.10133	-.12186	-.14250	-.16321	-.18398	-.20483	-.22574	-.24671	-.26774	-.28883
.08500	-.07991	-.10011	-.12040	-.14076	-.16119	-.18169	-.20226	-.22289	-.24358	-.26433
.08750	-.05908	-.07895	-.09890	-.11893	-.13903	-.15920	-.17944	-.19973	-.22009	-.24049
.09000	-.03883	-.05838	-.07800	-.09771	-.11748	-.13733	-.15724	-.17721	-.19723	-.21732
.09250	-.01914	-.03837	-.05768	-.07707	-.09653	-.11605	-.13564	-.15530	-.17500	-.19477
.09500	-.00000	-.01892	-.03792	-.05700	-.07614	-.09536	-.11464	-.13398	-.15338	-.17283
.09750	.01862	0.00000	-.01870	-.03747	-.05632	-.07523	-.09421	-.11325	-.13234	-.15149
.10000	.03673	.01840	-.00000	-.01848	-.03703	-.05565	-.07433	-.09307	-.11187	-.13072
.10250	.05434	.03631	.01819	.00000	-.01826	-.03659	-.05498	-.07344	-.09195	-.11051
.10500	.07148	.05373	.03589	.01798	.00000	-.01805	-.03616	-.05433	-.07256	-.09084
.10750	.08816	.07068	.05311	.03548	.01777	.00000	-.01784	-.03573	-.05368	-.07169
.11000	.10439	.08717	.06988	.05251	.03507	.01757	.00000	-.01763	-.03531	-.05305
.11250	.12018	.10322	.08619	.06908	.05191	.03467	.01736	.00000	-.01742	-.03489
.11500	.13555	.11885	.10207	.08522	.06830	.05132	.03427	.01716	.00000	-.01722
.11750	.15052	.13406	.11753	.10093	.08426	.06753	.05073	.03388	.01696	.00000
.12000	.16509	.14888	.13259	.11623	.09981	.08332	.06677	.05015	.03349	.01677
.12250	.17927	.16330	.14725	.13113	.11495	.09869	.08238	.06601	.04958	.03310
.12500	.19309	.17735	.16153	.14564	.12969	.11367	.09759	.08146	.06526	.04902
.12750	.20654	.19103	.17544	.15978	.14405	.12826	.11241	.09651	.08054	.06453
.13000	.21965	.20435	.18899	.17355	.15805	.14248	.12686	.11117	.09543	.07964
.13250	.23242	.21734	.20219	.18697	.17168	.15634	.14093	.12546	.10994	.09437
.13500	.24486	.22999	.21505	.20005	.18497	.16984	.15464	.13939	.12409	.10873
.13750	.25698	.24232	.22759	.21279	.19793	.18300	.16801	.15297	.13787	.12273
.14000	.26879	.25434	.23981	.22521	.21055	.19583	.18105	.16621	.15132	.13637
.14250	.28031	.26605	.25172	.23732	.22286	.20834	.19375	.17912	.16442	.14968
.14500	.29153	.27747	.26333	.24913	.23486	.22053	.20614	.19170	.17721	.16266
.14750	.30248	.28860	.27465	.26064	.24656	.23243	.21823	.20398	.18967	.17532
.15000	.31315	.29946	.28570	.27187	.25798	.24403	.23002	.21595	.20184	.18767
.15250	.32356	.31004	.29646	.28282	.26911	.25534	.24152	.22763	.21370	.19972
.15500	.33371	.32037	.30697	.29350	.27997	.26638	.25273	.23903	.22528	.21148
.15750	.34361	.33045	.31722	.30392	.29057	.27715	.26368	.25015	.23658	.22295
.16000	.35327	.34027	.32722	.31409	.30091	.28766	.27436	.26101	.24760	.23415
.16250	.36269	.34987	.33697	.32402	.31100	.29792	.28479	.27160	.25837	.24508
.16500	.37189	.35923	.34650	.33370	.32085	.30793	.29497	.28195	.26887	.25576
.16750	.38087	.36836	.35579	.34316	.33046	.31771	.30490	.29204	.27913	.26618
.17000	.38963	.37728	.36486	.35239	.33985	.32725	.31460	.30190	.28915	.27635
.17250	.39818	.38598	.37372	.36140	.34901	.33657	.32408	.31153	.29894	.28629
.17500	.40653	.39449	.38237	.37020	.35797	.34568	.33333	.32094	.30849	.29600
.17750	.41469	.40279	.39082	.37879	.36671	.35457	.34237	.33012	.31783	.30548
.18000	.42265	.41090	.39907	.38719	.37525	.36325	.35120	.33910	.32695	.31475
.18250	.43043	.41882	.40713	.39539	.38359	.37173	.35983	.34787	.33586	.32381
.18500	.43803	.42655	.41501	.40340	.39174	.38003	.36826	.35644	.34457	.33266
.18750	.44546	.43411	.42270	.41123	.39971	.38813	.37650	.36481	.35308	.34131
.19000	.45272	.44150	.43022	.41889	.40749	.39605	.38455	.37300	.36141	.34977
.19250	.45981	.44872	.43757	.42637	.41511	.40379	.39242	.38101	.36954	.35803
.19500	.46674	.45578	.44476	.43368	.42255	.41136	.40012	.38883	.37750	.36612
.19750	.47352	.46268	.45178	.44083	.42982	.41876	.40765	.39648	.38528	.37403
.20000	.48014	.46943	.45865	.44782	.43693	.42600	.41501	.40397	.39289	.38176
.20250	.48662	.47602	.46537	.45466	.44389	.43307	.42221	.41129	.40033	.38932
.20500	.49295	.48248	.47194	.46135	.45070	.44000	.42925	.41845	.40761	.39673
.20750	.49915	.48879	.47836	.46789	.45736	.44677	.43614	.42546	.41474	.40397

POINT TABLES: ORIGINAL LOAN TERM: 360 MONTHS LOAN PREPAID IN: 180 MONTHS

CONTRACT RATE

EFFECTIVE YIELD	.12000	.12250	.12500	.12750	.13000	.13250	.13500	.13750	.14000	.14250
.07000	-.44523	-.46826	-.49133	-.51444	-.53760	-.56079	-.58401	-.60726	-.63054	-.65384
.07250	-.41662	-.43927	-.46195	-.48468	-.50745	-.53025	-.55308	-.57595	-.59884	-.62176
.07500	-.38882	-.41109	-.43339	-.45574	-.47813	-.50056	-.52302	-.54551	-.56802	-.59057
.07750	-.36179	-.38369	-.40563	-.42761	-.44963	-.47169	-.49378	-.51590	-.53805	-.56023
.08000	-.33552	-.35705	-.37863	-.40026	-.42192	-.44362	-.46535	-.48711	-.50890	-.53072
.08250	-.30997	-.33115	-.35238	-.37365	-.39496	-.41631	-.43769	-.45911	-.48055	-.50202
.08500	-.28512	-.30596	-.32685	-.34778	-.36875	-.38975	-.41079	-.43187	-.45297	-.47410
.08750	-.26095	-.28146	-.30202	-.32261	-.34325	-.36392	-.38463	-.40536	-.42613	-.44693
.09000	-.23745	-.25763	-.27786	-.29813	-.31844	-.33878	-.35916	-.37958	-.40002	-.42049
.09250	-.21458	-.23445	-.25436	-.27431	-.29430	-.31433	-.33439	-.35448	-.37461	-.39476
.09500	-.19234	-.21189	-.23149	-.25113	-.27081	-.29053	-.31028	-.33006	-.34988	-.36972
.09750	-.17069	-.18994	-.20924	-.22857	-.24795	-.26736	-.28681	-.30629	-.32581	-.34535
.10000	-.14963	-.16858	-.18758	-.20662	-.22570	-.24482	-.26397	-.28316	-.30237	-.32162
.10250	-.12913	-.14779	-.16650	-.18525	-.20404	-.22287	-.24173	-.26063	-.27956	-.29851
.10500	-.10917	-.12755	-.14598	-.16445	-.18295	-.20150	-.22008	-.23869	-.25734	-.27601
.10750	-.08975	-.10785	-.12600	-.14419	-.16242	-.18069	-.19900	-.21734	-.23570	-.25410
.11000	-.07083	-.08867	-.10655	-.12447	-.14243	-.16043	-.17847	-.19653	-.21463	-.23276
.11250	-.05242	-.06999	-.08760	-.10526	-.12296	-.14070	-.15847	-.17627	-.19411	-.21197
.11500	-.03448	-.05180	-.06915	-.08656	-.10400	-.12147	-.13899	-.15653	-.17411	-.19172
.11750	-.01701	-.03408	-.05118	-.06833	-.08552	-.10275	-.12001	-.13730	-.15463	-.17198
.12000	0.00000	-.01682	-.03368	-.05058	-.06752	-.08450	-.10152	-.11857	-.13564	-.15275
.12250	.01658	0.00000	-.01662	-.03328	-.04998	-.06672	-.08350	-.10031	-.11714	-.13401
.12500	.03273	.01639	.00000	-.01643	-.03289	-.04940	-.06594	-.08251	-.09911	-.11574
.12750	.04846	.03235	.01620	.00000	-.01624	-.03251	-.04882	-.06516	-.08153	-.09794
.13000	.06380	.04791	.03198	.01601	0.00000	-.01605	-.03213	-.04825	-.06440	-.08057
.13250	.07875	.06308	.04737	.03162	.01583	.00000	-.01586	-.03176	-.04769	-.06364
.13500	.09332	.07787	.06237	.04684	.03126	.01565	0.00000	-.01568	-.03139	-.04713
.13750	.10753	.09229	.07700	.06168	.04631	.03091	.01547	-.00000	-.01550	-.03103
.14000	.12138	.10635	.09127	.07615	.06099	.04579	.03056	.01529	0.00000	-.01532
.14250	.13489	.12006	.10518	.09026	.07530	.06031	.04528	.03021	.01512	0.00000
.14500	.14807	.13343	.11875	.10402	.08926	.07447	.05963	.04477	.02988	.01495
.14750	.16092	.14647	.13198	.11746	.10289	.08828	.07364	.05897	.04427	.02954
.15000	.17346	.15920	.14490	.13056	.11618	.10176	.08732	.07283	.05832	.04378
.15250	.18569	.17162	.15750	.14335	.12915	.11492	.10066	.08636	.07203	.05768
.15500	.19763	.18374	.16980	.15583	.14181	.12776	.11368	.09957	.08542	.07125
.15750	.20928	.19556	.18180	.16801	.15417	.14030	.12639	.11246	.09849	.08449
.16000	.22065	.20711	.19352	.17990	.16624	.15254	.13881	.12504	.11125	.09743
.16250	.23175	.21838	.20496	.19151	.17801	.16449	.15093	.13733	.12371	.11006
.16500	.24259	.22938	.21613	.20284	.18952	.17616	.16276	.14934	.13588	.12239
.16750	.25317	.24013	.22704	.21391	.20075	.18755	.17432	.16106	.14777	.13445
.17000	.26351	.25062	.23769	.22473	.21172	.19869	.18562	.17251	.15938	.14622
.17250	.27360	.26087	.24810	.23529	.22244	.20956	.19665	.18370	.17073	.15772
.17500	.28346	.27089	.25827	.24561	.23292	.22019	.20743	.19464	.18181	.16897
.17750	.29310	.28067	.26820	.25569	.24315	.23057	.21796	.20532	.19265	.17995
.18000	.30251	.29023	.27791	.26555	.25315	.24072	.22826	.21577	.20324	.19069
.18250	.31171	.29957	.28739	.27518	.26293	.25064	.23832	.22597	.21360	.20119
.18500	.32070	.30870	.29667	.28459	.27248	.26034	.24816	.23595	.22372	.21146
.18750	.32949	.31763	.30573	.29380	.28182	.26982	.25778	.24571	.23362	.22149
.19000	.33808	.32636	.31459	.30279	.29096	.27909	.26719	.25526	.24330	.23131
.19250	.34648	.33489	.32326	.31159	.29989	.28816	.27639	.26459	.25277	.24091
.19500	.35470	.34324	.33174	.32020	.30863	.29702	.28539	.27372	.26203	.25031
.19750	.36273	.35140	.34003	.32862	.31717	.30570	.29419	.28265	.27109	.25950
.20000	.37059	.35938	.34813	.33685	.32553	.31418	.30280	.29139	.27995	.26849
.20250	.37828	.36719	.35607	.34491	.33371	.32249	.31123	.29994	.28863	.27729
.20500	.38580	.37483	.36383	.35279	.34172	.33061	.31948	.30831	.29712	.28590
.20750	.39316	.38231	.37143	.36051	.34955	.33857	.32755	.31650	.30543	.29433

EFFECTIVE YIELD	CONTRACT RATE .14500	.14750	.15000	.15250	.15500	.15750	.16000	.16250	.16500	.16750
.07000	-.67717	-.70052	-.72388	-.74727	-.77067	-.79408	-.81751	-.84094	-.86439	-.88785
.07250	-.64470	-.66767	-.69065	-.71365	-.73667	-.75970	-.78275	-.80580	-.82867	-.85194
.07500	-.61313	-.63572	-.65833	-.68096	-.70360	-.72626	-.74893	-.77162	-.79431	-.81701
.07750	-.58243	-.60465	-.62690	-.64916	-.67144	-.69373	-.71604	-.73836	-.76069	-.78303
.08000	-.55257	-.57443	-.59632	-.61822	-.64015	-.66209	-.68404	-.70600	-.72798	-.74997
.08250	-.52351	-.54503	-.56657	-.58813	-.60970	-.63129	-.65290	-.67452	-.69615	-.71779
.08500	-.49525	-.51643	-.53763	-.55884	-.58008	-.60133	-.62260	-.64388	-.66517	-.68648
.08750	-.46775	-.48859	-.50946	-.53035	-.55125	-.57217	-.59311	-.61406	-.63502	-.65599
.09000	-.44099	-.46151	-.48205	-.50261	-.52319	-.54379	-.56440	-.58503	-.60567	-.62632
.09250	-.41494	-.43515	-.45537	-.47562	-.49588	-.51616	-.53646	-.55677	-.57710	-.59743
.09500	-.38959	-.40948	-.42940	-.44934	-.46929	-.48927	-.50926	-.52926	-.54928	-.56931
.09750	-.36491	-.38450	-.40412	-.42375	-.44341	-.46308	-.48277	-.50247	-.52219	-.54191
.10000	-.34089	-.36018	-.37950	-.39884	-.41820	-.43758	-.45697	-.47638	-.49580	-.51524
.10250	-.31749	-.33650	-.35553	-.37458	-.39365	-.41274	-.43185	-.45097	-.47010	-.48925
.10500	-.29471	-.31344	-.33218	-.35095	-.36974	-.38855	-.40738	-.42622	-.44507	-.46394
.10750	-.27253	-.29097	-.30945	-.32794	-.34646	-.36499	-.38354	-.40210	-.42058	-.43928
.11000	-.25091	-.26909	-.28730	-.30552	-.32377	-.34203	-.36031	-.37861	-.39692	-.41525
.11250	-.22986	-.24778	-.26572	-.28368	-.30166	-.31966	-.33768	-.35572	-.37377	-.39183
.11500	-.20935	-.22701	-.24469	-.26240	-.28012	-.29787	-.31563	-.33341	-.35120	-.36901
.11750	-.18937	-.20677	-.22420	-.24166	-.25913	-.27662	-.29413	-.31166	-.32920	-.34676
.12000	-.16989	-.18705	-.20423	-.22144	-.23867	-.25592	-.27318	-.29046	-.30776	-.32507
.12250	-.15091	-.16783	-.18477	-.20174	-.21873	-.23573	-.25276	-.26980	-.28686	-.30393
.12500	-.13240	-.14909	-.16580	-.18253	-.19928	-.21605	-.23284	-.24965	-.26647	-.28331
.12750	-.11436	-.13082	-.14730	-.16380	-.18032	-.19686	-.21342	-.23000	-.24659	-.26320
.13000	-.09678	-.11301	-.12926	-.14554	-.16183	-.17815	-.19449	-.21084	-.22721	-.24359
.13250	-.07963	-.09564	-.11167	-.12773	-.14380	-.15990	-.17602	-.19215	-.20830	-.22446
.13500	-.06290	-.07870	-.09451	-.11035	-.12622	-.14210	-.15800	-.17391	-.18985	-.20580
.13750	-.04659	-.06217	-.07778	-.09341	-.10906	-.12473	-.14042	-.15613	-.17185	-.18759
.14000	-.03067	-.04605	-.06145	-.07688	-.09232	-.10778	-.12327	-.13877	-.15428	-.16982
.14250	-.01515	-.03032	-.04552	-.06074	-.07599	-.09125	-.10653	-.12183	-.13714	-.15247
.14500	0.00000	-.01498	-.02998	-.04500	-.06005	-.07511	-.09019	-.10530	-.12041	-.13554
.14750	.01478	0.00000	-.01481	-.02964	-.04449	-.05936	-.07425	-.08916	-.10408	-.11902
.15000	.02921	.01462	.00000	-.01464	-.02930	-.04398	-.05868	-.07340	-.08814	-.10289
.15250	.04330	.02889	.01445	0.00000	-.01448	-.02897	-.04349	-.05802	-.07257	-.08713
.15500	.05704	.04282	.02857	.01429	.00000	-.01431	-.02865	-.04300	-.05736	-.07175
.15750	.07047	.05642	.04235	.02825	.01414	.00000	-.01415	-.02833	-.04252	-.05672
.16000	.08358	.06970	.05580	.04188	.02794	.01398	.00000	-.01400	-.02801	-.04204
.16250	.09638	.08268	.06895	.05520	.04143	.02764	.01383	.00000	-.01334	-.02770
.16500	.10888	.09535	.08179	.06820	.05460	.04098	.02734	.01368	0.00000	-.01369
.16750	.12110	.10773	.09433	.08091	.06747	.05401	.04053	.02704	.01353	.00000
.17000	.13303	.11982	.10659	.09333	.08005	.06675	.05343	.04010	.02675	.01338
.17250	.14469	.13164	.11856	.10546	.09234	.07920	.06604	.05286	.03967	.02646
.17500	.15609	.14319	.13027	.11732	.10435	.09137	.07836	.06534	.05230	.03925
.17750	.16723	.15448	.14171	.12891	.11610	.10326	.09041	.07754	.06465	.05175
.18000	.17812	.16551	.15289	.14024	.12758	.11489	.10219	.08946	.07672	.06397
.18250	.18876	.17630	.16383	.15132	.13880	.12626	.11370	.10113	.08853	.07592
.18500	.19917	.18685	.17452	.16216	.14978	.13738	.12497	.11253	.10008	.08762
.18750	.20934	.19717	.18497	.17276	.16052	.14826	.13598	.12369	.11138	.09905
.19000	.21930	.20726	.19520	.18312	.17102	.15890	.14676	.13460	.12243	.11024
.19250	.22903	.21713	.20521	.19326	.18129	.16931	.15730	.14528	.13324	.12119
.19500	.23856	.22679	.21500	.20318	.19135	.17949	.16762	.15573	.14382	.13190
.19750	.24788	.23624	.22457	.21289	.20118	.18946	.17771	.16595	.15418	.14239
.20000	.25700	.24548	.23395	.22239	.21081	.19921	.18760	.17596	.16431	.15265
.20250	.26592	.25453	.24312	.23168	.22023	.20876	.19727	.18576	.17424	.16270
.20500	.27466	.26339	.25210	.24079	.22945	.21810	.20674	.19535	.18395	.17254
.20750	.28321	.27206	.26089	.24970	.23849	.22726	.21601	.20474	.19346	.18217

POINT TABLES: ORIGINAL LOAN TERM: 360 MONTHS LOAN PREPAID IN: 180 MONTHS

CONTRACT RATE

EFFECTIVE YIELD	.17000	.17250	.17500	.17750	.18000	.18250	.18500	.18750	.19000	.19250
.07000	-.91131	-.93478	-.95825	-.98173	-1.00521	-1.02869	-1.05217	-1.07566	-1.09914	-1.12263
.07250	-.87502	-.89811	-.92121	-.94431	-.96741	-.99051	-1.01362	-1.03673	-1.05984	-1.08295
.07500	-.83973	-.86244	-.88517	-.90790	-.93063	-.95337	-.97611	-.99885	-1.02159	-1.04433
.07750	-.80538	-.82774	-.85010	-.87247	-.89484	-.91722	-.93960	-.96198	-.98437	-1.00675
.08000	-.77196	-.79397	-.81598	-.83799	-.86002	-.88204	-.90407	-.92610	-.94813	-.97017
.08250	-.73944	-.76110	-.78277	-.80444	-.82612	-.84780	-.86949	-.89117	-.91287	-.93456
.08500	-.70779	-.72911	-.75044	-.77178	-.79312	-.81447	-.83582	-.85717	-.87853	-.89989
.08750	-.67698	-.69797	-.71897	-.73998	-.76100	-.78201	-.80304	-.82407	-.84510	-.86613
.09000	-.64699	-.66766	-.68834	-.70902	-.72972	-.75042	-.77112	-.79183	-.81254	-.83326
.09250	-.61778	-.63814	-.65851	-.67888	-.69926	-.71965	-.74004	-.76044	-.78084	-.80124
.09500	-.58935	-.60940	-.62946	-.64953	-.66960	-.68968	-.70977	-.72986	-.74995	-.77005
.09750	-.56166	-.58141	-.60117	-.62093	-.64071	-.66049	-.68028	-.70007	-.71987	-.73967
.10000	-.53469	-.55414	-.57361	-.59309	-.61257	-.63206	-.65156	-.67106	-.69057	-.71008
.10250	-.50841	-.52759	-.54677	-.56596	-.58515	-.60436	-.62357	-.64279	-.66201	-.68124
.10500	-.48282	-.50171	-.52061	-.53952	-.55844	-.57737	-.59630	-.61524	-.63418	-.65313
.10750	-.45788	-.47650	-.49513	-.51377	-.53241	-.55107	-.56973	-.58839	-.60706	-.62574
.11000	-.43359	-.45194	-.47030	-.48867	-.50705	-.52543	-.54383	-.56223	-.58063	-.59904
.11250	-.40991	-.42800	-.44609	-.46420	-.48232	-.50045	-.51858	-.53672	-.55486	-.57301
.11500	-.38683	-.40466	-.42250	-.44036	-.45822	-.47609	-.49397	-.51185	-.52974	-.54764
.11750	-.36433	-.38191	-.39951	-.41711	-.43472	-.45234	-.46997	-.48761	-.50525	-.52289
.12000	-.34240	-.35974	-.37708	-.39444	-.41181	-.42919	-.44657	-.46396	-.48136	-.49876
.12250	-.32101	-.33811	-.35522	-.37234	-.38947	-.40661	-.42375	-.44090	-.45806	-.47523
.12500	-.30016	-.31702	-.33390	-.35078	-.36768	-.38458	-.40149	-.41841	-.43534	-.45227
.12750	-.27982	-.29646	-.31310	-.32976	-.34643	-.36310	-.37978	-.39648	-.41317	-.42988
.13000	-.25999	-.27640	-.29282	-.30925	-.32569	-.34214	-.35860	-.37507	-.39155	-.40803
.13250	-.24064	-.25683	-.27303	-.28924	-.30546	-.32170	-.33794	-.35419	-.37044	-.38670
.13500	-.22176	-.23773	-.25372	-.26972	-.28573	-.30174	-.31777	-.33381	-.34985	-.36590
.13750	-.20334	-.21910	-.23488	-.25067	-.26646	-.28227	-.29809	-.31391	-.32975	-.34559
.14000	-.18536	-.20092	-.21649	-.23207	-.24767	-.26327	-.27888	-.29450	-.31013	-.32576
.14250	-.16782	-.18317	-.19854	-.21392	-.22931	-.24472	-.26013	-.27554	-.29097	-.30640
.14500	-.15069	-.16585	-.18102	-.19621	-.21140	-.22660	-.24182	-.25704	-.27227	-.28750
.14750	-.13397	-.14894	-.16392	-.17891	-.19391	-.20892	-.22394	-.23897	-.25400	-.26905
.15000	-.11765	-.13243	-.14722	-.16202	-.17683	-.19165	-.20648	-.22132	-.23617	-.25102
.15250	-.10171	-.11630	-.13091	-.14552	-.16015	-.17478	-.18943	-.20408	-.21875	-.23342
.15500	-.08614	-.10055	-.11498	-.12941	-.14385	-.15831	-.17277	-.18725	-.20173	-.21622
.15750	-.07094	-.08517	-.09942	-.11367	-.12794	-.14222	-.15650	-.17080	-.18510	-.19941
.16000	-.05609	-.07014	-.08421	-.09830	-.11239	-.12649	-.14060	-.15473	-.16886	-.18299
.16250	-.04158	-.05546	-.06936	-.08327	-.09720	-.11113	-.12507	-.13902	-.15298	-.16695
.16500	-.02740	-.04112	-.05485	-.06859	-.08235	-.09611	-.10989	-.12367	-.13746	-.15126
.16750	-.01354	-.02710	-.04067	-.05424	-.06784	-.08144	-.09505	-.10867	-.12230	-.13593
.17000	.00000	-.01339	-.02680	-.04022	-.05365	-.06709	-.08054	-.09400	-.10747	-.12094
.17250	.01324	.00000	-.01325	-.02651	-.03978	-.05307	-.06636	-.07966	-.09297	-.10629
.17500	.02618	.01309	0.00000	-.01311	-.02622	-.03935	-.05249	-.06564	-.07879	-.09196
.17750	.03883	.02590	.01296	0.00000	-.01297	-.02594	-.03893	-.05193	-.06493	-.07794
.18000	.05120	.03842	.02562	.01282	0.00000	-.01283	-.02567	-.03851	-.05137	-.06423
.18250	.06330	.05066	.03802	.02535	.01268	0.00000	-.01269	-.02539	-.03810	-.05082
.18500	.07514	.06264	.05014	.03762	.02509	.01255	0.00000	-.01256	-.02513	-.03770
.18750	.08671	.07436	.06199	.04962	.03723	.02483	.01242	-.00000	-.01243	-.02486
.19000	.09804	.08582	.07360	.06136	.04910	.03684	.02457	.01229	-.00000	-.01230
.19250	.10912	.09704	.08495	.07284	.06073	.04860	.03646	.02432	.01216	.00000
.19500	.11997	.10802	.09606	.08409	.07210	.06011	.04810	.03609	.02407	.01204
.19750	.13058	.11876	.10693	.09509	.08324	.07137	.05950	.04761	.03572	.02382
.20000	.14097	.12928	.11758	.10586	.09414	.08240	.07065	.05890	.04713	.03536
.20250	.15115	.13958	.12800	.11641	.10481	.09320	.08158	.06995	.05831	.04666
.20500	.16111	.14966	.13821	.12674	.11526	.10377	.09227	.08077	.06925	.05773
.20750	.17086	.15954	.14820	.13685	.12550	.11413	.10275	.09136	.07997	.06856

POINT TABLES: ORIGINAL LOAN TERM: 360 MONTHS LOAN PREPAID IN: 180 MONTHS

EFFECTIVE YIELD	CONTRACT RATE .19500	.19750	.20000	.20250	.20500	.20750
.07000	-1.14611	-1.16959	-1.19307	-1.21655	-1.24002	-1.26350
.07250	-1.10605	-1.12916	-1.15227	-1.17537	-1.19847	-1.22157
.07500	-1.06707	-1.08982	-1.11256	-1.13530	-1.15803	-1.18077
.07750	-1.02914	-1.05152	-1.07390	-1.09629	-1.11867	-1.14105
.08000	-.99221	-1.01424	-1.03628	-1.05831	-1.08035	-1.10238
.08250	-.95625	-.97795	-.99964	-1.02134	-1.04303	-1.06473
.08500	-.92125	-.94261	-.96398	-.98534	-1.00670	-1.02806
.08750	-.88717	-.90820	-.92924	-.95028	-.97132	-.99235
.09000	-.85397	-.87469	-.89541	-.91613	-.93685	-.95758
.09250	-.82165	-.84205	-.86246	-.88287	-.90329	-.92370
.09500	-.79016	-.81026	-.83037	-.85047	-.87058	-.89069
.09750	-.75948	-.77929	-.79910	-.81891	-.83872	-.85853
.10000	-.72959	-.74911	-.76863	-.78815	-.80767	-.82720
.10250	-.70047	-.71970	-.73894	-.75817	-.77741	-.79666
.10500	-.67208	-.69104	-.71000	-.72896	-.74792	-.76689
.10750	-.64442	-.66311	-.68179	-.70048	-.71918	-.73787
.11000	-.61746	-.63588	-.65430	-.67272	-.69115	-.70958
.11250	-.59117	-.60933	-.62749	-.64566	-.66383	-.68200
.11500	-.56554	-.58344	-.60135	-.61927	-.63718	-.65510
.11750	-.54055	-.55820	-.57587	-.59353	-.61120	-.62887
.12000	-.51617	-.53359	-.55101	-.56843	-.58585	-.60328
.12250	-.49240	-.50958	-.52676	-.54394	-.56113	-.57832
.12500	-.46921	-.48615	-.50310	-.52005	-.53701	-.55397
.12750	-.44659	-.46330	-.48002	-.49675	-.51348	-.53021
.13000	-.42451	-.44101	-.45750	-.47401	-.49051	-.50702
.13250	-.40297	-.41925	-.43553	-.45181	-.46810	-.48439
.13500	-.38195	-.39801	-.41408	-.43015	-.44622	-.46230
.13750	-.36143	-.37728	-.39314	-.40900	-.42486	-.44073
.14000	-.34140	-.35705	-.37270	-.38835	-.40401	-.41968
.14250	-.32184	-.33729	-.35274	-.36820	-.38366	-.39912
.14500	-.30275	-.31800	-.33325	-.34851	-.36377	-.37904
.14750	-.28410	-.29916	-.31422	-.32928	-.34436	-.35943
.15000	-.26589	-.28075	-.29563	-.31051	-.32539	-.34028
.15250	-.24809	-.26278	-.27747	-.29216	-.30686	-.32156
.15500	-.23071	-.24522	-.25972	-.27424	-.28876	-.30328
.15750	-.21373	-.22806	-.24239	-.25672	-.27106	-.28541
.16000	-.19714	-.21129	-.22545	-.23961	-.25378	-.26795
.16250	-.18092	-.19490	-.20889	-.22288	-.23688	-.25088
.16500	-.16507	-.17888	-.19270	-.20653	-.22036	-.23419
.16750	-.14957	-.16322	-.17688	-.19054	-.20421	-.21788
.17000	-.13443	-.14792	-.16141	-.17491	-.18842	-.20193
.17250	-.11961	-.13295	-.14628	-.15963	-.17298	-.18633
.17500	-.10513	-.11831	-.13149	-.14468	-.15787	-.17108
.17750	-.09096	-.10399	-.11702	-.13006	-.14310	-.15615
.18000	-.07710	-.08998	-.10287	-.11576	-.12865	-.14155
.18250	-.06355	-.07628	-.08902	-.10176	-.11451	-.12727
.18500	-.05028	-.06287	-.07547	-.08807	-.10068	-.11329
.18750	-.03730	-.04975	-.06221	-.07467	-.08714	-.09961
.19000	-.02460	-.03691	-.04923	-.06156	-.07389	-.08622
.19250	-.01217	-.02435	-.03653	-.04872	-.06092	-.07312
.19500	.00000	-.01204	-.02410	-.03615	-.04822	-.06028
.19750	.01191	.00000	-.01192	-.02385	-.03578	-.04772
.20000	.02358	.01179	.00000	-.01180	-.02361	-.03542
.20250	.03500	.02334	.01167	.00000	-.01168	-.02337
.20500	.04619	.03465	.02311	.01156	.00000	-.01156
.20750	.05715	.04573	.03431	.02288	.01144	.00000

POINT TABLES: ORIGINAL LOAN TERM: 360 MONTHS LOAN PREPAID IN: 360 MONTHS

CONTRACT RATE

EFFECTIVE YIELD	.07000	.07250	.07500	.07750	.08000	.08250	.08500	.08750	.09000	.09250
.07000	0.00000	-.02536	-.05097	-.07682	-.10290	-.12921	-.15574	-.18247	-.20941	-.23654
.07250	.02474	.00000	-.02498	-.05019	-.07562	-.10128	-.12715	-.15322	-.17949	-.20596
.07500	.04850	.02437	.00000	-.02460	-.04941	-.07444	-.09968	-.12512	-.15075	-.17657
.07750	.07134	.04779	.02401	0.00000	-.02422	-.04865	-.07328	-.09811	-.12313	-.14833
.08000	.09330	.07031	.04709	.02365	.00000	-.02385	-.04790	-.07214	-.09657	-.12117
.08250	.11443	.09197	.06929	.04639	.02330	0.00000	-.02349	-.04717	-.07102	-.09505
.08500	.13475	.11280	.09065	.06828	.04571	.02295	.00000	-.02313	-.04644	-.06992
.08750	.15431	.13286	.11121	.08935	.06729	.04504	.02261	.00000	-.02278	-.04573
.09000	.17315	.15218	.13100	.10963	.08806	.06631	.04438	.02227	.00000	-.02244
.09250	.19129	.17078	.15007	.12917	.10808	.08680	.06535	.04373	.02194	0.00000
.09500	.20878	.18871	.16845	.14799	.12736	.10654	.08556	.06440	.04309	.02162
.09750	.22563	.20599	.18616	.16614	.14595	.12557	.10503	.08433	.06347	.04246
.10000	.24188	.22265	.20324	.18364	.16387	.14393	.12382	.10355	.08313	.06255
.10250	.25756	.23873	.21971	.20052	.18116	.16163	.14193	.12209	.10209	.08194
.10500	.27269	.25424	.23561	.21681	.19784	.17871	.15942	.13997	.12038	.10064
.10750	.28729	.26921	.25096	.23254	.21395	.19520	.17629	.15724	.13804	.11870
.11000	.30139	.28367	.26578	.24772	.22950	.21112	.19259	.17391	.15510	.13614
.11250	.31501	.29764	.28010	.26239	.24452	.22650	.20834	.19002	.17157	.15298
.11500	.32818	.31114	.29393	.27656	.25904	.24137	.22355	.20559	.18749	.16926
.11750	.34090	.32416	.30730	.29027	.27308	.25574	.23825	.22063	.20288	.18499
.12000	.35320	.33680	.32024	.30352	.28665	.26963	.25248	.23518	.21776	.20021
.12250	.36511	.34900	.33274	.31633	.29977	.28307	.26623	.24926	.23215	.21493
.12500	.37662	.36081	.34485	.32874	.31248	.29608	.27954	.26288	.24608	.22917
.12750	.38777	.37225	.35657	.34074	.32477	.30867	.29243	.27606	.25957	.24296
.13000	.39857	.38332	.36791	.35237	.33668	.32086	.30491	.28883	.27262	.25630
.13250	.40903	.39404	.37890	.36363	.34821	.33267	.31699	.30119	.28527	.26924
.13500	.41916	.40443	.38955	.37454	.35939	.34411	.32870	.31317	.29753	.28176
.13750	.42898	.41450	.39987	.38511	.37022	.35520	.34005	.32479	.30940	.29391
.14000	.43850	.42426	.40988	.39537	.38072	.36595	.35106	.33605	.32092	.30568
.14250	.44774	.43373	.41959	.40531	.39091	.37638	.36173	.34697	.33209	.31710
.14500	.45670	.44292	.42901	.41496	.40079	.38650	.37209	.35756	.34293	.32818
.14750	.46540	.45184	.43815	.42433	.41038	.39632	.38214	.36785	.35344	.33894
.15000	.47384	.46049	.44702	.43342	.41969	.40585	.39190	.37783	.36366	.34938
.15250	.48204	.46890	.45563	.44225	.42874	.41511	.40137	.38752	.37357	.35952
.15500	.49000	.47707	.46401	.45082	.43752	.42410	.41058	.39694	.38320	.36936
.15750	.49774	.48500	.47214	.45916	.44606	.43284	.41952	.40609	.39256	.37893
.16000	.50526	.49271	.48004	.46726	.45435	.44134	.42821	.41499	.40166	.38823
.16250	.51258	.50021	.48773	.47513	.46242	.44960	.43667	.42364	.41050	.39728
.16500	.51969	.50751	.49521	.48279	.47026	.45763	.44489	.43205	.41911	.40607
.16750	.52661	.51460	.50248	.49024	.47789	.46544	.45288	.44023	.42748	.41463
.17000	.53334	.52151	.50956	.49749	.48532	.47305	.46067	.44819	.43562	.42296
.17250	.53990	.52823	.51644	.50455	.49255	.48045	.46824	.45594	.44355	.43106
.17500	.54628	.53477	.52315	.51142	.49959	.48765	.47562	.46349	.45127	.43895
.17750	.55249	.54114	.52968	.51812	.50644	.49467	.48280	.47084	.45878	.44664
.18000	.55855	.54735	.53605	.52464	.51312	.50151	.48980	.47800	.46611	.45413
.18250	.56445	.55340	.54225	.53099	.51963	.50817	.49662	.48498	.47324	.46142
.18500	.57020	.55930	.54829	.53718	.52597	.51467	.50327	.49178	.48020	.46854
.18750	.57581	.56505	.55419	.54322	.53216	.52100	.50975	.49841	.48698	.47547
.19000	.58128	.57066	.55994	.54911	.53819	.52718	.51607	.50487	.49360	.48223
.19250	.58661	.57613	.56554	.55486	.54407	.53320	.52224	.51118	.50005	.48883
.19500	.59182	.58147	.57101	.56046	.54982	.53908	.52825	.51734	.50634	.49527
.19750	.59690	.58668	.57635	.56593	.55542	.54481	.53412	.52335	.51249	.50155
.20000	.60186	.59176	.58156	.57127	.56089	.55041	.53985	.52921	.51848	.50768
.20250	.60670	.59673	.58665	.57649	.56623	.55588	.54545	.53493	.52434	.51367
.20500	.61143	.60157	.59162	.58158	.57144	.56122	.55092	.54053	.53006	.51952
.20750	.61605	.60631	.59648	.58655	.57654	.56644	.55626	.54599	.53565	.52523

POINT TABLES: ORIGINAL LOAN TERM: 360 MONTHS LOAN PREPAID IN: 360 MONTHS

EFFECTIVE YIELD	CONTRACT RATE .09500	.09750	.10000	.10250	.10500	.10750	.11000	.11250	.11500	.11750
.07000	-.26387	-.29137	-.31906	-.34691	-.37492	-.40309	-.43141	-.45988	-.48848	-.51722
.07250	-.23261	-.25943	-.28643	-.31359	-.34091	-.36839	-.39601	-.42377	-.45167	-.47969
.07500	-.20257	-.22874	-.25508	-.28158	-.30824	-.33504	-.36199	-.38907	-.41629	-.44363
.07750	-.17370	-.19925	-.22495	-.25082	-.27683	-.30299	-.32930	-.35573	-.38229	-.40898
.08000	-.14595	-.17089	-.19599	-.22124	-.24664	-.27218	-.29786	-.32367	-.34960	-.37566
.08250	-.11925	-.14361	-.16812	-.19279	-.21760	-.24254	-.26762	-.29283	-.31816	-.34361
.08500	-.09356	-.11736	-.14131	-.16541	-.18965	-.21403	-.23853	-.26316	-.28791	-.31277
.08750	-.06884	-.09210	-.11551	-.13906	-.16275	-.18658	-.21053	-.23460	-.25879	-.28309
.09000	-.04503	-.06777	-.09066	-.11369	-.13686	-.16015	-.18357	-.20710	-.23075	-.25451
.09250	-.02210	-.04434	-.06673	-.08925	-.11191	-.13469	-.15759	-.18061	-.20375	-.22698
.09500	.00000	-.02176	-.04367	-.06570	-.08787	-.11016	-.13257	-.15509	-.17772	-.20046
.09750	.02130	.00000	-.02144	-.04300	-.06470	-.08651	-.10844	-.13049	-.15263	-.17489
.10000	.04184	.02099	0.00000	-.02111	-.04235	-.06371	-.08518	-.10676	-.12845	-.15023
.10250	.06165	.04123	.02068	0.00000	-.02080	-.04171	-.06274	-.08387	-.10511	-.12645
.10500	.08077	.06077	.04063	.02038	.00000	-.02049	-.04109	-.06179	-.08259	-.10349
.10750	.09923	.07962	.05989	.04004	.02008	.00000	-.02018	-.04047	-.06086	-.08134
.11000	.11705	.09783	.07849	.05904	.03947	.01979	.00000	-.01989	-.03987	-.05994
.11250	.13427	.11542	.09646	.07738	.05819	.03890	.01950	.00000	-.01959	-.03928
.11500	.15090	.13242	.11382	.09511	.07629	.05737	.03834	.01922	.00000	-.01931
.11750	.16698	.14885	.13061	.11225	.09379	.07522	.05655	.03779	.01894	.00000
.12000	.18254	.16474	.14684	.12883	.11071	.09248	.07417	.05576	.03726	.01867
.12250	.19758	.18012	.16254	.14486	.12707	.10919	.09120	.07313	.05497	.03673
.12500	.21214	.19499	.17773	.16037	.14291	.12535	.10769	.08995	.07212	.05420
.12750	.22623	.20939	.19244	.17539	.15824	.14099	.12365	.10622	.08871	.07112
.13000	.23987	.22333	.20668	.18993	.17308	.15614	.13910	.12198	.10478	.08750
.13250	.25309	.23683	.22047	.20401	.18746	.17081	.15407	.13725	.12035	.10336
.13500	.26589	.24992	.23384	.21766	.20139	.18503	.16858	.15204	.13543	.11874
.13750	.27831	.26260	.24679	.23089	.21489	.19881	.18263	.16638	.15005	.13364
.14000	.29034	.27490	.25935	.24371	.22798	.21217	.19626	.18028	.16422	.14809
.14250	.30201	.28682	.27154	.25615	.24068	.22513	.20948	.19376	.17797	.16210
.14500	.31334	.29840	.28336	.26822	.25300	.23770	.22231	.20685	.19131	.17569
.14750	.32433	.30963	.29483	.27994	.26496	.24990	.23476	.21954	.20425	.18889
.15000	.33500	.32053	.30596	.29131	.27657	.26175	.24684	.23187	.21682	.20170
.15250	.34536	.33112	.31678	.30235	.28784	.27325	.25858	.24384	.22902	.21414
.15500	.35543	.34140	.32728	.31308	.29879	.28442	.26998	.25546	.24087	.22622
.15750	.36521	.35139	.33749	.32350	.30943	.29528	.28106	.26676	.25239	.23796
.16000	.37472	.36111	.34741	.33363	.31977	.30584	.29182	.27774	.26359	.24937
.16250	.38396	.37055	.35706	.34348	.32983	.31610	.30229	.28842	.27448	.26047
.16500	.39295	.37974	.36644	.35306	.33961	.32608	.31248	.29880	.28506	.27126
.16750	.40170	.38867	.37557	.36238	.34912	.33579	.32238	.30891	.29536	.28176
.17000	.41021	.39737	.38445	.37145	.35838	.34524	.33202	.31874	.30539	.29198
.17250	.41849	.40583	.39310	.38028	.36739	.35443	.34140	.32831	.31514	.30192
.17500	.42656	.41408	.40152	.38888	.37617	.36339	.35054	.33762	.32464	.31161
.17750	.43441	.42210	.40972	.39725	.38472	.37211	.35943	.34670	.33390	.32104
.18000	.44207	.42992	.41770	.40541	.39304	.38060	.36810	.35554	.34291	.33022
.18250	.44952	.43754	.42549	.41336	.40115	.38888	.37655	.36415	.35169	.33918
.18500	.45679	.44497	.43307	.42110	.40906	.39695	.38478	.37255	.36025	.34790
.18750	.46388	.45221	.44047	.42866	.41677	.40482	.39281	.38073	.36860	.35641
.19000	.47079	.45927	.44768	.43602	.42429	.41250	.40064	.38872	.37674	.36471
.19250	.47753	.46616	.45472	.44321	.43163	.41998	.40827	.39651	.38468	.37280
.19500	.48411	.47289	.46159	.45022	.43878	.42728	.41572	.40410	.39243	.38070
.19750	.49053	.47945	.46829	.45706	.44577	.43441	.42300	.41152	.39999	.38841
.20000	.49680	.48585	.47483	.46374	.45259	.44137	.43009	.41876	.40737	.39593
.20250	.50292	.49210	.48122	.47026	.45924	.44816	.43703	.42583	.41458	.40328
.20500	.50890	.49821	.48745	.47663	.46575	.45480	.44380	.43273	.42162	.41045
.20750	.51474	.50418	.49355	.48285	.47210	.46128	.45041	.43948	.42850	.41746

POINT TABLES: ORIGINAL LOAN TERM: 360 MONTHS LOAN PREPAID IN: 360 MONTHS

EFFECTIVE YIELD	CONTRACT RATE .12000	.12250	.12500	.12750	.13000	.13250	.13500	.13750	.14000	.14250
.07000	-.54608	-.57507	-.60417	-.63338	-.66270	-.69212	-.72164	-.75125	-.78095	-.81074
.07250	-.50784	-.53611	-.56449	-.59298	-.62157	-.65027	-.67906	-.70793	-.73690	-.76595
.07500	-.47110	-.49868	-.52637	-.55416	-.58206	-.61005	-.63814	-.66632	-.69458	-.72291
.07750	-.43578	-.46270	-.48973	-.51685	-.54408	-.57140	-.59882	-.62632	-.65390	-.68156
.08000	-.40183	-.42811	-.45450	-.48098	-.50757	-.53424	-.56101	-.58786	-.61478	-.64179
.08250	-.36917	-.39484	-.42061	-.44648	-.47245	-.49850	-.52464	-.55086	-.57717	-.60354
.08500	-.33775	-.36283	-.38801	-.41328	-.43865	-.46411	-.48965	-.51527	-.54097	-.56674
.08750	-.30750	-.33201	-.35663	-.38133	-.40613	-.43101	-.45597	-.48101	-.50613	-.53132
.09000	-.27838	-.30235	-.32641	-.35056	-.37481	-.39913	-.42354	-.44802	-.47258	-.49721
.09250	-.25033	-.27377	-.29730	-.32093	-.34464	-.36843	-.39230	-.41625	-.44027	-.46435
.09500	-.22329	-.24623	-.26925	-.29237	-.31557	-.33885	-.36220	-.38563	-.40913	-.43269
.09750	-.19724	-.21968	-.24222	-.26484	-.28754	-.31033	-.33319	-.35612	-.37911	-.40218
.10000	-.17211	-.19409	-.21615	-.23830	-.26052	-.28283	-.30521	-.32766	-.35017	-.37275
.10250	-.14788	-.16940	-.19100	-.21269	-.23446	-.25630	-.27822	-.30020	-.32225	-.34436
.10500	-.12449	-.14557	-.16673	-.18798	-.20931	-.23070	-.25217	-.27371	-.29531	-.31697
.10750	-.10191	-.12257	-.14331	-.16413	-.18503	-.20599	-.22703	-.24814	-.26930	-.29053
.11000	-.08011	-.10036	-.12069	-.14110	-.16158	-.18213	-.20276	-.22344	-.24419	-.26500
.11250	-.05905	-.07890	-.09884	-.11885	-.13893	-.15908	-.17930	-.19959	-.21993	-.24033
.11500	-.03870	-.05817	-.07772	-.09735	-.11704	-.13681	-.15664	-.17654	-.19649	-.21650
.11750	-.01902	-.03813	-.05731	-.07656	-.09589	-.11528	-.13473	-.15425	-.17383	-.19346
.12000	0.00000	-.01875	-.03757	-.05647	-.07543	-.09446	-.11355	-.13270	-.15191	-.17118
.12250	.01840	0.00000	-.01848	-.03702	-.05564	-.07432	-.09306	-.11186	-.13071	-.14962
.12500	.03621	.01814	.00000	-.01821	-.03649	-.05483	-.07323	-.09169	-.11020	-.12877
.12750	.05345	.03570	.01788	0.00000	-.01795	-.03596	-.05403	-.07216	-.09035	-.10858
.13000	.07014	.05271	.03520	.01763	.00000	-.01769	-.03545	-.05326	-.07112	-.08903
.13250	.08631	.06918	.05198	.03471	.01739	0.00000	-.01744	-.03494	-.05250	-.07010
.13500	.10197	.08514	.06823	.05126	.03423	.01715	0.00000	-.01720	-.03445	-.05175
.13750	.11716	.10060	.08399	.06731	.05056	.03376	.01691	0.00000	-.01696	-.03397
.14000	.13188	.11560	.09926	.08286	.06640	.04988	.03330	.01668	.00000	-.01672
.14250	.14616	.13015	.11408	.09795	.08175	.06551	.04920	.03285	.01645	0.00000
.14500	.16001	.14426	.12845	.11258	.09665	.08067	.06463	.04854	.03241	.01623
.14750	.17346	.15796	.14240	.12679	.11111	.09538	.07960	.06377	.04789	.03197
.15000	.18651	.17126	.15595	.14058	.12515	.10967	.09414	.07856	.06293	.04726
.15250	.19919	.18417	.16910	.15397	.13878	.12354	.10825	.09292	.07753	.06211
.15500	.21150	.19672	.18188	.16698	.15202	.13702	.12196	.10686	.09172	.07653
.15750	.22346	.20891	.19429	.17962	.16489	.15011	.13529	.12042	.10550	.09054
.16000	.23509	.22075	.20636	.19190	.17740	.16284	.14824	.13359	.11890	.10416
.16250	.24640	.23227	.21809	.20385	.18956	.17522	.16083	.14640	.13192	.11740
.16500	.25740	.24348	.22950	.21547	.20139	.18725	.17308	.15885	.14459	.13028
.16750	.26810	.25438	.24060	.22677	.21289	.19896	.18499	.17097	.15691	.14281
.17000	.27851	.26498	.25140	.23777	.22409	.21036	.19658	.18276	.16890	.15501
.17250	.28864	.27531	.26192	.24848	.23499	.22145	.20787	.19424	.18058	.16687
.17500	.29851	.28536	.27215	.25890	.24560	.23225	.21886	.20542	.19194	.17843
.17750	.30812	.29515	.28213	.26905	.25593	.24277	.22956	.21631	.20301	.18969
.18000	.31748	.30469	.29184	.27894	.26600	.25301	.23998	.22691	.21380	.20065
.18250	.32661	.31398	.30131	.28858	.27581	.26300	.25014	.23724	.22431	.21134
.18500	.33550	.32304	.31053	.29798	.28538	.27273	.26004	.24732	.23455	.22175
.18750	.34417	.33187	.31953	.30714	.29470	.28222	.26970	.25714	.24454	.23190
.19000	.35262	.34049	.32830	.31607	.30379	.29147	.27911	.26671	.25428	.24181
.19250	.36087	.34889	.33686	.32478	.31266	.30050	.28830	.27606	.26378	.25147
.19500	.36892	.35709	.34521	.33328	.32132	.30931	.29726	.28517	.27305	.26089
.19750	.37677	.36509	.35336	.34158	.32976	.31790	.30600	.29407	.28210	.27009
.20000	.38444	.37290	.36131	.34968	.33801	.32630	.31454	.30275	.29093	.27907
.20250	.39193	.38053	.36908	.35759	.34606	.33449	.32288	.31123	.29955	.28784
.20500	.39924	.38798	.37667	.36532	.35392	.34249	.33102	.31952	.30798	.29640
.20750	.40638	.39525	.38408	.37286	.36161	.35031	.33898	.32761	.31620	.30477

EFFECTIVE YIELD	CONTRACT RATE .14500	.14750	.15000	.15250	.15500	.15750	.16000	.16250	.16500	.16750
.07000	-.84060	-.87054	-.90056	-.93064	-.96079	-.99100	-1.02127	-1.05160	-1.08198	-1.11242
.07250	-.79507	-.82427	-.85354	-.88288	-.91229	-.94175	-.97127	-1.00085	-1.03048	-1.06016
.07500	-.75133	-.77982	-.80838	-.83700	-.86569	-.89444	-.92324	-.95210	-.98131	-1.00996
.07750	-.70929	-.73709	-.76497	-.79290	-.82090	-.84896	-.87707	-.90524	-.93345	-.96171
.08000	-.66887	-.69601	-.72323	-.75050	-.77784	-.80523	-.83268	-.86018	-.88773	-.91532
.08250	-.62999	-.65650	-.68308	-.70972	-.73642	-.76318	-.78999	-.81684	-.84375	-.87070
.08500	-.59258	-.61849	-.64446	-.67049	-.69657	-.72271	-.74891	-.77515	-.80144	-.82777
.08750	-.55657	-.58189	-.60728	-.63272	-.65821	-.68376	-.70936	-.73501	-.76071	-.78644
.09000	-.52190	-.54666	-.57147	-.59635	-.62128	-.64626	-.67129	-.69637	-.72149	-.74665
.09250	-.48850	-.51272	-.53699	-.56132	-.58570	-.61013	-.63461	-.65914	-.68371	-.70832
.09500	-.45632	-.48001	-.50376	-.52756	-.55142	-.57532	-.59927	-.62327	-.64731	-.67139
.09750	-.42530	-.44849	-.47173	-.49503	-.51837	-.54177	-.56521	-.58870	-.61222	-.63579
.10000	-.39539	-.41809	-.44084	-.46365	-.48651	-.50941	-.53236	-.55535	-.57839	-.60146
.10250	-.36654	-.38877	-.41105	-.43339	-.45577	-.47820	-.50068	-.52319	-.54575	-.56834
.10500	-.33869	-.36047	-.38230	-.40418	-.42611	-.44808	-.47010	-.49216	-.51425	-.53639
.10750	-.31182	-.33316	-.35455	-.37599	-.39748	-.41901	-.44058	-.46220	-.48385	-.50554
.11000	-.28586	-.30678	-.32775	-.34876	-.36983	-.39093	-.41208	-.43327	-.45449	-.47575
.11250	-.26079	-.28130	-.30186	-.32246	-.34312	-.36381	-.38455	-.40532	-.42613	-.44698
.11500	-.23656	-.25668	-.27684	-.29705	-.31731	-.33760	-.35794	-.37832	-.39873	-.41917
.11750	-.21314	-.23287	-.25266	-.27248	-.29236	-.31227	-.33222	-.35221	-.37224	-.39229
.12000	-.19049	-.20986	-.22927	-.24873	-.26823	-.28777	-.30735	-.32697	-.34662	-.36630
.12250	-.16858	-.18759	-.20665	-.22575	-.24489	-.26407	-.28329	-.30255	-.32184	-.34116
.12500	-.14739	-.16605	-.18476	-.20351	-.22231	-.24114	-.26001	-.27892	-.29786	-.31683
.12750	-.12686	-.14520	-.16357	-.18199	-.20045	-.21894	-.23748	-.25604	-.27465	-.29328
.13000	-.10699	-.12500	-.14305	-.16115	-.17928	-.19745	-.21566	-.23390	-.25217	-.27047
.13250	-.08775	-.10544	-.12318	-.14096	-.15877	-.17663	-.19452	-.21244	-.23040	-.24838
.13500	-.06910	-.08649	-.10392	-.12139	-.13891	-.15645	-.17404	-.19165	-.20930	-.22698
.13750	-.05102	-.06812	-.08525	-.10243	-.11965	-.13690	-.15419	-.17150	-.18885	-.20623
.14000	-.03349	-.05030	-.06716	-.08405	-.10098	-.11794	-.13494	-.15197	-.16903	-.18612
.14250	-.01649	-.03303	-.04960	-.06622	-.08287	-.09955	-.11627	-.13302	-.14980	-.16661
.14500	.00000	-.01627	-.03257	-.04892	-.06530	-.08171	-.09816	-.11464	-.13114	-.14768
.14750	.01601	0.00000	-.01605	-.03213	-.04825	-.06440	-.08058	-.09679	-.11304	-.12931
.15000	.03155	.01579	0.00000	-.01583	-.03169	-.04759	-.06352	-.07947	-.09546	-.11147
.15250	.04664	.03113	.01558	.00000	-.01562	-.03127	-.04694	-.06265	-.07839	-.09415
.15500	.06130	.04603	.03072	.01536	.00000	-.01541	-.03085	-.04631	-.06181	-.07733
.15750	.07554	.06050	.04543	.03032	.01517	.00000	-.01520	-.03044	-.04570	-.06098
.16000	.08938	.07457	.05972	.04484	.02992	.01498	0.00000	-.01500	-.03004	-.04509
.16250	.10285	.08825	.07362	.05896	.04426	.02954	.01478	0.00000	-.01481	-.02964
.16500	.11594	.10156	.08714	.07269	.05821	.04370	.02916	.01459	0.00000	-.01462
.16750	.12868	.11450	.10029	.08605	.07178	.05748	.04315	.02879	.01441	.00000
.17000	.14107	.12710	.11309	.09905	.08498	.07088	.05676	.04260	.02843	.01422
.17250	.15313	.13936	.12555	.11171	.09784	.08393	.07001	.05605	.04207	.02807
.17500	.16488	.15130	.13768	.12403	.11035	.09664	.08291	.06915	.05536	.04155
.17750	.17632	.16292	.14949	.13603	.12254	.10902	.09547	.08190	.06830	.05468
.18000	.18747	.17425	.16100	.14772	.13441	.12107	.10771	.09432	.08091	.06747
.18250	.19833	.18529	.17222	.15911	.14598	.13282	.11964	.10643	.09319	.07994
.18500	.20891	.19605	.18315	.17022	.15726	.14427	.13126	.11823	.10517	.09209
.18750	.21924	.20654	.19380	.18104	.16825	.15544	.14260	.12973	.11684	.10393
.19000	.22930	.21677	.20420	.19160	.17898	.16633	.15365	.14095	.12823	.11549
.19250	.23912	.22674	.21434	.20190	.18944	.17695	.16443	.15190	.13934	.12676
.19500	.24870	.23648	.22423	.21195	.19964	.18731	.17496	.16258	.15017	.13775
.19750	.25805	.24598	.23388	.22176	.20960	.19743	.18522	.17300	.16075	.14848
.20000	.26718	.25526	.24331	.23133	.21933	.20730	.19525	.18317	.17108	.15896
.20250	.27609	.26432	.25251	.24068	.22882	.21694	.20503	.19311	.18116	.16919
.20500	.28480	.27316	.26150	.24981	.23810	.22636	.21459	.20281	.19100	.17918
.20750	.29330	.28181	.27028	.25873	.24716	.23556	.22393	.21229	.20062	.18894

POINT TABLES: ORIGINAL LOAN TERM: 360 MONTHS LOAN PREPAID IN: 360 MONTHS

EFFECTIVE YIELD	CONTRACT RATE .17000	.17250	.17500	.17750	.18000	.18250	.18500	.18750	.19000	.19250
.07000	-1.14290	-1.17343	-1.20400	-1.23461	-1.26526	-1.29595	-1.32668	-1.35744	-1.38823	-1.41905
.07250	-1.08989	-1.11967	-1.14948	-1.17934	-1.20923	-1.23916	-1.26913	-1.29912	-1.32915	-1.35921
.07500	-1.03897	-1.06801	-1.09710	-1.12623	-1.15540	-1.18460	-1.21383	-1.24310	-1.27240	-1.30172
.07750	-.99002	-1.01837	-1.04676	-1.07519	-1.10366	-1.13216	-1.16069	-1.18925	-1.21785	-1.24647
.08000	-.94296	-.97064	-.99836	-1.02612	-1.05391	-1.08173	-1.10959	-1.13748	-1.16540	-1.19334
.08250	-.89770	-.92473	-.95180	-.97891	-1.00606	-1.03324	-1.06045	-1.08768	-1.11495	-1.14224
.08500	-.85414	-.88056	-.90701	-.93350	-.96002	-.98657	-1.01316	-1.03977	-1.06641	-1.09308
.08750	-.81222	-.83804	-.86389	-.88978	-.91570	-.94166	-.96764	-.99365	-1.01969	-1.04576
.09000	-.77186	-.79710	-.82238	-.84769	-.87303	-.89841	-.92381	-.94925	-.97471	-1.00019
.09250	-.73297	-.75766	-.78239	-.80714	-.83193	-.85675	-.88160	-.90647	-.93137	-.95630
.09500	-.69551	-.71966	-.74385	-.76807	-.79233	-.81661	-.84092	-.86526	-.88962	-.91400
.09750	-.65939	-.68303	-.70671	-.73041	-.75415	-.77791	-.80171	-.82553	-.84937	-.87323
.10000	-.62457	-.64771	-.67089	-.69410	-.71734	-.74060	-.76390	-.78721	-.81056	-.83392
.10250	-.59098	-.61364	-.63634	-.65907	-.68182	-.70461	-.72742	-.75026	-.77312	-.79600
.10500	-.55856	-.58076	-.60300	-.62526	-.64756	-.66988	-.69222	-.71460	-.73699	-.75940
.10750	-.52727	-.54902	-.57081	-.59263	-.61448	-.63635	-.65825	-.68017	-.70211	-.72408
.11000	-.49705	-.51838	-.53973	-.56112	-.58254	-.60398	-.62544	-.64693	-.66844	-.68997
.11250	-.46786	-.48877	-.50971	-.53068	-.55168	-.57270	-.59375	-.61482	-.63591	-.65702
.11500	-.43965	-.46016	-.48070	-.50127	-.52186	-.54248	-.56312	-.58378	-.60447	-.62517
.11750	-.41239	-.43251	-.45266	-.47283	-.49304	-.51326	-.53351	-.55379	-.57408	-.59439
.12000	-.38602	-.40576	-.42554	-.44534	-.46516	-.48501	-.50489	-.52478	-.54469	-.56463
.12250	-.36051	-.37989	-.39930	-.41874	-.43820	-.45769	-.47719	-.49672	-.51627	-.53584
.12500	-.33583	-.35486	-.37392	-.39300	-.41211	-.43124	-.45039	-.46957	-.48876	-.50797
.12750	-.31194	-.33063	-.34935	-.36809	-.38685	-.40564	-.42445	-.44328	-.46214	-.48100
.13000	-.28880	-.30717	-.32555	-.34396	-.36240	-.38086	-.39934	-.41783	-.43635	-.45489
.13250	-.26640	-.28444	-.30250	-.32060	-.33871	-.35685	-.37501	-.39318	-.41138	-.42959
.13500	-.24468	-.26242	-.28017	-.29795	-.31576	-.33358	-.35143	-.36930	-.38718	-.40508
.13750	-.22364	-.24107	-.25853	-.27601	-.29351	-.31103	-.32858	-.34614	-.36372	-.38132
.14000	-.20323	-.22037	-.23754	-.25473	-.27194	-.28917	-.30642	-.32369	-.34098	-.35829
.14250	-.18344	-.20030	-.21718	-.23409	-.25102	-.26797	-.28493	-.30192	-.31893	-.33595
.14500	-.16424	-.18082	-.19743	-.21407	-.23072	-.24739	-.26409	-.28080	-.29753	-.31427
.14750	-.14560	-.16192	-.17827	-.19463	-.21102	-.22743	-.24385	-.26030	-.27676	-.29323
.15000	-.12751	-.14357	-.15966	-.17577	-.19190	-.20804	-.22421	-.24039	-.25659	-.27281
.15250	-.10994	-.12576	-.14159	-.15745	-.17332	-.18922	-.20513	-.22107	-.23701	-.25298
.15500	-.09288	-.10845	-.12404	-.13965	-.15528	-.17093	-.18660	-.20229	-.21799	-.23371
.15750	-.07629	-.09163	-.10698	-.12236	-.13775	-.15317	-.16860	-.18405	-.19951	-.21499
.16000	-.06017	-.07528	-.09040	-.10555	-.12071	-.13590	-.15110	-.16631	-.18155	-.19679
.16250	-.04450	-.05938	-.07428	-.08920	-.10414	-.11910	-.13408	-.14907	-.16408	-.17910
.16500	-.02926	-.04392	-.05861	-.07331	-.08803	-.10277	-.11753	-.13230	-.14709	-.16190
.16750	-.01443	-.02888	-.04335	-.05785	-.07236	-.08688	-.10143	-.11599	-.13057	-.14516
.17000	.00000	-.01425	-.02851	-.04280	-.05710	-.07142	-.08576	-.10012	-.11448	-.12887
.17250	.01405	0.00000	-.01407	-.02815	-.04225	-.05638	-.07051	-.08466	-.09883	-.11301
.17500	.02772	.01387	.00000	-.01389	-.02780	-.04172	-.05566	-.06962	-.08359	-.09757
.17750	.04104	.02738	.01370	0.00000	-.01372	-.02745	-.04120	-.05496	-.06874	-.08254
.18000	.05402	.04054	.02705	.01353	0.00000	-.01355	-.02711	-.04069	-.05428	-.06789
.18250	.06666	.05337	.04005	.02672	.01337	.00000	-.01338	-.02678	-.04019	-.05361
.18500	.07899	.06587	.05273	.03957	.02640	.01321	.00000	-.01322	-.02645	-.03970
.18750	.09100	.07806	.06509	.05210	.03910	.02608	.01305	0.00000	-.01306	-.02613
.19000	.10272	.08994	.07714	.06432	.05149	.03864	.02577	.01289	0.00000	-.01290
.19250	.11416	.10154	.08890	.07624	.06357	.05088	.03818	.02547	.01274	.00000
.19500	.12531	.11285	.10037	.08787	.07536	.06284	.05029	.03774	.02517	.01259
.19750	.13620	.12389	.11157	.09923	.08687	.07450	.06211	.04972	.03730	.02488
.20000	.14682	.13467	.12250	.11031	.09810	.08589	.07365	.06141	.04915	.03688
.20250	.15720	.14519	.13317	.12113	.10907	.09700	.08492	.07282	.06071	.04859
.20500	.16733	.15547	.14359	.13170	.11979	.10786	.09592	.08397	.07201	.06003
.20750	.17723	.16551	.15377	.14202	.13025	.11847	.10667	.09486	.08304	.07121

POINT TABLES: ORIGINAL LOAN TERM: 360 MONTHS LOAN PREPAID IN: 360 MONTHS

EFFECTIVE YIELD	CONTRACT RATE .19500	.19750	.20000	.20250	.20500	.20750
.07000	-1.44989	-1.48077	-1.51167	-1.54259	-1.57354	-1.60451
.07250	-1.38929	-1.41941	-1.44954	-1.47970	-1.50988	-1.54008
.07500	-1.33107	-1.36045	-1.38985	-1.41928	-1.44872	-1.47819
.07750	-1.27511	-1.30379	-1.33248	-1.36120	-1.38994	-1.41870
.08000	-1.22131	-1.24931	-1.27732	-1.30536	-1.33342	-1.36150
.08250	-1.16956	-1.19690	-1.22427	-1.25165	-1.27906	-1.30648
.08500	-1.11977	-1.14648	-1.17322	-1.19998	-1.22675	-1.25355
.08750	-1.07184	-1.09795	-1.12409	-1.15024	-1.17641	-1.20260
.09000	-1.02569	-1.05122	-1.07677	-1.10234	-1.12793	-1.15354
.09250	-.98124	-1.00621	-1.03120	-1.05621	-1.08124	-1.10628
.09500	-.93841	-.96284	-.98729	-1.01175	-1.03624	-1.06074
.09750	-.89712	-.92103	-.94496	-.96890	-.99287	-1.01685
.10000	-.85731	-.88071	-.90414	-.92758	-.95104	-.97452
.10250	-.81890	-.84182	-.86477	-.88772	-.91070	-.93369
.10500	-.78184	-.80430	-.82677	-.84926	-.87177	-.89429
.10750	-.74607	-.76807	-.79009	-.81213	-.83419	-.85626
.11000	-.71152	-.73309	-.75468	-.77628	-.79790	-.81953
.11250	-.67815	-.69930	-.72046	-.74164	-.76284	-.78406
.11500	-.64590	-.66664	-.68740	-.70818	-.72897	-.74977
.11750	-.61473	-.63508	-.65544	-.67582	-.69622	-.71663
.12000	-.58458	-.60455	-.62454	-.64454	-.66455	-.68458
.12250	-.55542	-.57502	-.59464	-.61427	-.63392	-.65358
.12500	-.52720	-.54645	-.56571	-.58499	-.60428	-.62359
.12750	-.49989	-.51879	-.53771	-.55664	-.57559	-.59455
.13000	-.47344	-.49201	-.51059	-.52919	-.54780	-.56643
.13250	-.44782	-.46607	-.48433	-.50260	-.52089	-.53919
.13500	-.42300	-.44093	-.45888	-.47684	-.49482	-.51280
.13750	-.39894	-.41657	-.43421	-.45187	-.46954	-.48722
.14000	-.37561	-.39294	-.41029	-.42766	-.44503	-.46242
.14250	-.35298	-.37003	-.38710	-.40418	-.42127	-.43837
.14500	-.33103	-.34780	-.36459	-.38139	-.39821	-.41503
.14750	-.30972	-.32623	-.34275	-.35928	-.37583	-.39238
.15000	-.28904	-.30529	-.32154	-.33782	-.35410	-.37039
.15250	-.26895	-.28495	-.30095	-.31697	-.33300	-.34904
.15500	-.24944	-.26519	-.28095	-.29672	-.31250	-.32830
.15750	-.23048	-.24599	-.26151	-.27704	-.29259	-.30814
.16000	-.21206	-.22733	-.24262	-.25792	-.27323	-.28855
.16250	-.19414	-.20919	-.22425	-.23932	-.25441	-.26950
.16500	-.17671	-.19154	-.20638	-.22124	-.23610	-.25097
.16750	-.15976	-.17437	-.18900	-.20364	-.21829	-.23295
.17000	-.14326	-.15767	-.17209	-.18652	-.20096	-.21541
.17250	-.12720	-.14141	-.15563	-.16985	-.18409	-.19834
.17500	-.11157	-.12558	-.13960	-.15363	-.16767	-.18172
.17750	-.09634	-.11016	-.12398	-.13782	-.15167	-.16553
.18000	-.08150	-.09513	-.10878	-.12243	-.13609	-.14976
.18250	-.06705	-.08050	-.09395	-.10742	-.12090	-.13439
.18500	-.05296	-.06623	-.07951	-.09280	-.10610	-.11941
.18750	-.03922	-.05232	-.06542	-.07854	-.09167	-.10480
.19000	-.02582	-.03875	-.05169	-.06464	-.07759	-.09056
.19250	-.01275	-.02552	-.03829	-.05107	-.06387	-.07667
.19500	.00000	-.01260	-.02522	-.03784	-.05047	-.06311
.19750	.01245	.00000	-.01246	-.02492	-.03740	-.04988
.20000	.02459	.01230	0.00000	-.01231	-.02463	-.03696
.20250	.03646	.02432	.01216	0.00000	-.01217	-.02435
.20500	.04804	.03605	.02404	.01202	.00000	-.01203
.20750	.05936	.04751	.03565	.02377	.01189	.00000

CONTRACT RATE

EFFECTIVE YIELD	.07000	.07250	.07500	.07750	.08000	.08250	.08500	.08750	.09000	.09250
.07000	0.00000	-.01035	-.02072	-.03110	-.04151	-.05192	-.06235	-.07280	-.08325	-.09372
.07250	.01028	-.00000	-.01030	-.02061	-.03095	-.04129	-.05165	-.06203	-.07241	-.08281
.07500	.02044	.01023	0.00000	-.01025	-.02051	-.03079	-.04108	-.05139	-.06170	-.07203
.07750	.03048	.02034	.01018	0.00000	-.01019	-.02040	-.03063	-.04087	-.05112	-.06138
.08000	.04040	.03033	.02024	.01013	.00000	-.01014	-.02030	-.03047	-.04065	-.05085
.08250	.05020	.04020	.03018	.02013	.01008	.00000	-.01009	-.02019	-.03031	-.04044
.08500	.05989	.04996	.04000	.03003	.02003	.01002	.00000	-.01004	-.02009	-.03015
.08750	.06947	.05960	.04971	.03980	.02988	.01993	.00997	.00000	-.00999	-.01999
.09000	.07893	.06913	.05931	.04946	.03960	.02972	.01983	.00992	-.00000	-.00993
.09250	.08828	.07855	.06879	.05901	.04922	.03940	.02957	.01973	.00987	.00000
.09500	.09753	.08786	.07816	.06845	.05872	.04897	.03920	.02942	.01963	.00982
.09750	.10666	.09706	.08743	.07778	.06811	.05842	.04872	.03900	.02927	.01953
.10000	.11569	.10615	.09658	.08700	.07739	.06777	.05813	.04848	.03881	.02912
.10250	.12461	.11513	.10563	.09611	.08657	.07701	.06743	.05784	.04823	.03861
.10500	.13343	.12402	.11458	.10512	.09564	.08614	.07662	.06709	.05754	.04798
.10750	.14215	.13280	.12342	.11402	.10460	.09516	.08571	.07624	.06675	.05725
.11000	.15076	.14147	.13216	.12282	.11346	.10408	.09469	.08528	.07585	.06641
.11250	.15928	.15005	.14079	.13151	.12222	.11290	.10356	.09421	.08485	.07546
.11500	.16769	.15852	.14933	.14011	.13087	.12161	.11234	.10305	.09374	.08442
.11750	.17601	.16690	.15776	.14861	.13943	.13023	.12101	.11178	.10253	.09326
.12000	.18423	.17518	.16610	.15700	.14788	.13874	.12959	.12041	.11122	.10201
.12250	.19236	.18336	.17435	.16531	.15624	.14716	.13806	.12894	.11981	.11066
.12500	.20039	.19145	.18249	.17351	.16451	.15548	.14644	.13738	.12830	.11921
.12750	.20833	.19945	.19055	.18162	.17267	.16371	.15472	.14572	.13669	.12766
.13000	.21617	.20735	.19851	.18964	.18075	.17184	.16291	.15396	.14499	.13601
.13250	.22393	.21516	.20637	.19756	.18873	.17987	.17100	.16210	.15319	.14427
.13500	.23159	.22288	.21415	.20539	.19661	.18782	.17900	.17016	.16130	.15243
.13750	.23917	.23052	.22184	.21314	.20441	.19567	.18690	.17812	.16932	.16050
.14000	.24666	.23806	.22944	.22079	.21212	.20343	.19472	.18599	.17725	.16848
.14250	.25406	.24552	.23695	.22836	.21974	.21110	.20245	.19377	.18508	.17637
.14500	.26138	.25289	.24437	.23583	.22727	.21869	.21009	.20146	.19282	.18417
.14750	.26861	.26017	.25171	.24323	.23472	.22619	.21764	.20907	.20048	.19188
.15000	.27576	.26737	.25897	.25053	.24208	.23360	.22510	.21659	.20805	.19950
.15250	.28282	.27449	.26614	.25776	.24935	.24093	.23248	.22402	.21554	.20703
.15500	.28981	.28153	.27323	.26490	.25655	.24817	.23978	.23137	.22293	.21448
.15750	.29671	.28849	.28023	.27196	.26366	.25534	.24699	.23863	.23025	.22185
.16000	.30354	.29536	.28716	.27894	.27069	.26242	.25412	.24581	.23746	.22913
.16250	.31028	.30216	.29401	.28583	.27764	.26941	.26117	.25291	.24463	.23633
.16500	.31695	.30888	.30078	.29265	.28451	.27633	.26814	.25993	.25170	.24345
.16750	.32354	.31552	.30747	.29940	.29130	.28318	.27503	.26687	.25869	.25048
.17000	.33006	.32209	.31409	.30606	.29801	.28994	.28184	.27373	.26559	.25744
.17250	.33650	.32858	.32063	.31265	.30465	.29662	.28858	.28051	.27243	.26432
.17500	.34287	.33500	.32709	.31916	.31121	.30323	.29524	.28722	.27918	.27112
.17750	.34917	.34134	.33348	.32560	.31770	.30977	.30182	.29385	.28586	.27785
.18000	.35539	.34761	.33980	.33197	.32411	.31623	.30833	.30040	.29246	.28450
.18250	.36154	.35381	.34605	.33826	.33045	.32262	.31476	.30688	.29899	.29107
.18500	.36762	.35994	.35223	.34449	.33672	.32893	.32112	.31329	.30544	.29757
.18750	.37364	.36600	.35833	.35064	.34292	.33518	.32741	.31963	.31182	.30400
.19000	.37958	.37199	.36437	.35672	.34905	.34135	.33363	.32589	.31813	.31035
.19250	.38546	.37791	.37033	.36273	.35511	.34745	.33978	.33209	.32437	.31664
.19500	.39127	.38376	.37623	.36868	.36110	.35349	.34586	.33821	.33054	.32285
.19750	.39701	.38955	.38207	.37455	.36702	.35946	.35187	.34427	.33654	.32900
.20000	.40269	.39527	.38783	.38037	.37287	.36536	.35782	.35025	.34267	.33507
.20250	.40830	.40093	.39353	.38611	.37866	.37119	.36369	.35617	.34864	.34108
.20500	.41385	.40652	.39917	.39179	.38439	.37696	.36950	.36203	.35453	.34702
.20750	.41934	.41205	.40474	.39741	.39004	.38266	.37525	.36782	.36036	.35289

CONTRACT RATE

EFFECTIVE YIELD	.09500	.09750	.10000	.10250	.10500	.10750	.11000	.11250	.11500	.11750
.07000	-.10419	-.11468	-.12517	-.13567	-.14618	-.15669	-.16721	-.17773	-.18826	-.19879
.07250	-.09322	-.10364	-.11406	-.12449	-.13493	-.14538	-.15583	-.16628	-.17674	-.18721
.07500	-.08237	-.09272	-.10308	-.11344	-.12382	-.13420	-.14458	-.15497	-.16537	-.17576
.07750	-.07165	-.08193	-.09223	-.10252	-.11283	-.12314	-.13346	-.14379	-.15412	-.16445
.08000	-.06106	-.07127	-.08150	-.09173	-.10197	-.11222	-.12247	-.13273	-.14300	-.15327
.08250	-.05058	-.06073	-.07089	-.08106	-.09124	-.10142	-.11161	-.12180	-.13200	-.14221
.08500	-.04023	-.05032	-.06041	-.07051	-.08063	-.09074	-.10087	-.11100	-.12114	-.13128
.08750	-.03000	-.04002	-.05005	-.06009	-.07014	-.08019	-.09025	-.10032	-.11040	-.12047
.09000	-.01988	-.02984	-.03981	-.04978	-.05977	-.06976	-.07976	-.08976	-.09976	-.10979
.09250	-.00988	-.01978	-.02968	-.03959	-.04952	-.05945	-.06938	-.07933	-.08928	-.09923
.09500	.00000	-.00983	-.01967	-.02952	-.03938	-.04925	-.05913	-.06901	-.07890	-.08879
.09750	.00977	.00000	-.00978	-.01957	-.02937	-.03917	-.04899	-.05881	-.06864	-.07847
.10000	.01943	.00972	.00000	-.00973	-.01947	-.02921	-.03896	-.04872	-.05849	-.06826
.10250	.02897	.01932	.00967	0.00000	-.00968	-.01936	-.02906	-.03876	-.04846	-.05818
.10500	.03841	.02882	.01922	.00962	.00000	-.00963	-.01926	-.02890	-.03855	-.04820
.10750	.04773	.03821	.02867	.01912	.00957	.00000	-.00957	-.01916	-.02875	-.03834
.11000	.05696	.04749	.03801	.02852	.01902	.00952	.00000	-.00952	-.01905	-.02859
.11250	.06607	.05666	.04724	.03781	.02837	.01892	.00947	.00000	-.00947	-.01895
.11500	.07508	.06573	.05637	.04700	.03762	.02822	.01882	.00942	0.00000	-.00942
.11750	.08399	.07470	.06539	.05608	.04675	.03742	.02808	.01872	.00937	.00000
.12000	.09279	.08356	.07431	.06505	.05579	.04651	.03722	.02793	.01863	.00932
.12250	.10150	.09232	.08313	.07393	.06472	.05550	.04627	.03703	.02778	.01853
.12500	.11010	.10098	.09185	.08270	.07355	.06438	.05521	.04602	.03683	.02763
.12750	.11861	.10954	.10046	.09138	.08228	.07317	.06405	.05492	.04578	.03664
.13000	.12702	.11801	.10898	.09995	.09091	.08185	.07278	.06371	.05463	.04554
.13250	.13533	.12637	.11741	.10843	.09944	.09044	.08143	.07241	.06338	.05434
.13500	.14355	.13465	.12573	.11681	.10787	.09893	.08997	.08100	.07203	.06305
.13750	.15167	.14283	.13397	.12510	.11621	.10732	.09842	.08950	.08058	.07165
.14000	.15970	.15091	.14211	.13329	.12446	.11562	.10677	.09791	.08904	.08016
.14250	.16765	.15891	.15015	.14139	.13261	.12382	.11502	.10622	.09740	.08858
.14500	.17550	.16681	.15811	.14940	.14067	.13194	.12319	.11443	.10567	.09690
.14750	.18326	.17462	.16598	.15731	.14864	.13996	.13126	.12256	.11384	.10512
.15000	.19093	.18235	.17375	.16514	.15652	.14789	.13924	.13059	.12193	.11326
.15250	.19852	.18999	.18144	.17288	.16431	.15573	.14714	.13853	.12992	.12130
.15500	.20602	.19754	.18904	.18053	.17201	.16348	.15494	.14639	.13782	.12925
.15750	.21343	.20500	.19656	.18810	.17963	.17115	.16266	.15415	.14564	.13712
.16000	.22077	.21239	.20399	.19558	.18716	.17873	.17028	.16183	.15337	.14490
.16250	.22801	.21968	.21134	.20298	.19461	.18622	.17783	.16942	.16101	.15259
.16500	.23518	.22690	.21860	.21029	.20197	.19364	.18529	.17693	.16857	.16019
.16750	.24227	.23403	.22579	.21752	.20925	.20096	.19267	.18436	.17604	.16771
.17000	.24927	.24109	.23289	.22468	.21645	.20821	.19996	.19170	.18343	.17515
.17250	.25620	.24806	.23991	.23175	.22357	.21538	.20717	.19896	.19073	.18250
.17500	.26305	.25496	.24686	.23874	.23060	.22246	.21430	.20614	.19796	.18977
.17750	.26982	.26178	.25372	.24565	.23756	.22947	.22136	.21324	.20511	.19697
.18000	.27652	.26852	.26051	.25249	.24445	.23639	.22833	.22026	.21217	.20408
.18250	.28314	.27519	.26722	.25924	.25125	.24325	.23523	.22720	.21916	.21111
.18500	.28968	.28178	.27386	.26593	.25798	.25002	.24205	.23407	.22607	.21807
.18750	.29616	.28830	.28043	.27254	.26463	.25672	.24879	.24085	.23291	.22495
.19000	.30256	.29474	.28692	.27907	.27122	.26334	.25546	.24757	.23966	.23175
.19250	.30889	.30112	.29333	.28553	.27772	.26990	.26206	.25421	.24635	.23848
.19500	.31514	.30742	.29968	.29193	.28416	.27637	.26858	.26078	.25296	.24513
.19750	.32133	.31365	.30596	.29825	.29052	.28278	.27503	.26727	.25950	.25171
.20000	.32745	.31981	.31216	.30449	.29681	.28912	.28141	.27369	.26596	.25822
.20250	.33350	.32591	.31830	.31067	.30304	.29538	.28772	.28004	.27236	.26466
.20500	.33948	.33193	.32437	.31679	.30919	.30158	.29396	.28632	.27868	.27102
.20750	.34540	.33789	.33037	.32283	.31528	.30771	.30013	.29254	.28493	.27732

POINT TABLES: ORIGINAL LOAN TERM: 420 MONTHS LOAN PREPAID IN: 60 MONTHS

EFFECTIVE YIELD	CONTRACT RATE .12000	.12250	.12500	.12750	.13000	.13250	.13500	.13750	.14000	.14250
.07000	-.20932	-.21986	-.23040	-.24094	-.25148	-.26203	-.27257	-.28312	-.29367	-.30422
.07250	-.19768	-.20815	-.21862	-.22910	-.23958	-.25005	-.26054	-.27102	-.28150	-.29199
.07500	-.18617	-.19657	-.20698	-.21739	-.22781	-.23822	-.24864	-.25905	-.26947	-.27989
.07750	-.17479	-.18513	-.19547	-.20582	-.21617	-.22652	-.23687	-.24723	-.25758	-.26794
.08000	-.16354	-.17382	-.18410	-.19438	-.20466	-.21495	-.22524	-.23553	-.24582	-.25612
.08250	-.15242	-.16263	-.17285	-.18307	-.19329	-.20351	-.21374	-.22397	-.23420	-.24443
.08500	-.14143	-.15158	-.16173	-.17189	-.18205	-.19221	-.20237	-.21254	-.22270	-.23287
.08750	-.13056	-.14065	-.15074	-.16083	-.17093	-.18103	-.19113	-.20123	-.21134	-.22145
.09000	-.11981	-.12984	-.13987	-.14990	-.15994	-.16997	-.18002	-.19006	-.20010	-.21015
.09250	-.10919	-.11915	-.12912	-.13909	-.14907	-.15905	-.16903	-.17901	-.18899	-.19898
.09500	-.09869	-.10859	-.11850	-.12841	-.13832	-.14824	-.15816	-.16808	-.17801	-.18793
.09750	-.08831	-.09815	-.10800	-.11785	-.12770	-.13756	-.14742	-.15728	-.16715	-.17701
.10000	-.07804	-.08783	-.09761	-.10740	-.11720	-.12700	-.13680	-.14660	-.15641	-.16621
.10250	-.06789	-.07762	-.08735	-.09708	-.10681	-.11655	-.12629	-.13604	-.14579	-.15553
.10500	-.05786	-.06753	-.07719	-.08687	-.09655	-.10623	-.11591	-.12560	-.13528	-.14498
.10750	-.04794	-.05755	-.06716	-.07677	-.08639	-.09602	-.10564	-.11527	-.12490	-.13454
.11000	-.03813	-.04766	-.05724	-.06679	-.07635	-.08592	-.09549	-.10506	-.11463	-.12421
.11250	-.02844	-.03793	-.04742	-.05692	-.06643	-.07594	-.08545	-.09496	-.10448	-.11400
.11500	-.01885	-.02828	-.03772	-.04717	-.05662	-.06607	-.07552	-.08498	-.09444	-.10391
.11750	-.00937	-.01875	-.02813	-.03752	-.04691	-.05631	-.06571	-.07511	-.08452	-.09393
.12000	.00000	-.00932	-.01865	-.02798	-.03732	-.04666	-.05600	-.06535	-.07470	-.08405
.12250	.00927	.00000	-.00927	-.01855	-.02783	-.03712	-.04640	-.05570	-.06499	-.07429
.12500	.01843	.00922	.00000	-.00922	-.01845	-.02768	-.03691	-.04615	-.05540	-.06464
.12750	.02749	.01833	.00917	.00000	-.00917	-.01835	-.02753	-.03672	-.04590	-.05509
.13000	.03644	.02734	.01823	.00912	0.00000	-.00912	-.01825	-.02738	-.03652	-.04565
.13250	.04530	.03625	.02720	.01814	.00907	.00000	-.00907	-.01815	-.02723	-.03632
.13500	.05406	.04506	.03606	.02705	.01804	.00902	.00000	-.00903	-.01805	-.02709
.13750	.06272	.05377	.04482	.03587	.02691	.01794	.00897	.00000	-.00898	-.01796
.14000	.07128	.06239	.05349	.04459	.03568	.02676	.01785	.00893	.00000	-.00893
.14250	.07974	.07090	.06206	.05321	.04435	.03549	.02662	.01775	.00888	.00000
.14500	.08811	.07933	.07053	.06173	.05293	.04412	.03530	.02648	.01766	.00883
.14750	.09639	.08766	.07891	.07016	.06141	.05265	.04388	.03511	.02634	.01756
.15000	.10458	.09589	.08720	.07850	.06979	.06108	.05237	.04365	.03493	.02620
.15250	.11267	.10403	.09539	.08674	.07809	.06943	.06076	.05209	.04342	.03474
.15500	.12067	.11209	.10349	.09490	.08629	.07768	.06906	.06044	.05182	.04319
.15750	.12859	.12005	.11151	.10296	.09440	.08584	.07727	.06870	.06012	.05154
.16000	.13641	.12793	.11943	.11093	.10242	.09391	.08539	.07687	.06834	.05981
.16250	.14415	.13571	.12727	.11881	.11035	.10189	.09342	.08494	.07646	.06798
.16500	.15181	.14342	.13502	.12661	.11820	.10978	.10136	.09293	.08450	.07606
.16750	.15937	.15103	.14268	.13432	.12596	.11759	.10921	.10083	.09245	.08406
.17000	.16686	.15856	.15026	.14195	.13363	.12531	.11698	.10865	.10031	.09196
.17250	.17426	.16601	.15775	.14949	.14122	.13294	.12466	.11637	.10808	.09979
.17500	.18158	.17338	.16517	.15695	.14872	.14049	.13226	.12402	.11577	.10752
.17750	.18882	.18066	.17250	.16432	.15615	.14796	.13977	.13158	.12338	.11517
.18000	.19598	.18786	.17975	.17162	.16349	.15535	.14720	.13905	.13090	.12274
.18250	.20305	.19499	.18692	.17883	.17075	.16265	.15455	.14645	.13834	.13022
.18500	.21006	.20203	.19401	.18597	.17793	.16988	.16182	.15376	.14570	.13763
.18750	.21698	.20900	.20102	.19303	.18503	.17702	.16901	.16100	.15298	.14495
.19000	.22383	.21589	.20795	.20001	.19205	.18409	.17613	.16815	.16018	.15219
.19250	.23060	.22271	.21481	.20691	.19900	.19108	.18316	.17523	.16730	.15936
.19500	.23730	.22945	.22160	.21374	.20587	.19800	.19012	.18223	.17434	.16645
.19750	.24392	.23612	.22831	.22049	.21267	.20484	.19700	.18916	.18131	.17346
.20000	.25047	.24271	.23495	.22717	.21939	.21160	.20381	.19601	.18820	.18039
.20250	.25695	.24924	.24151	.23378	.22604	.21829	.21054	.20278	.19502	.18725
.20500	.26336	.25569	.24800	.24031	.23262	.22491	.21720	.20949	.20176	.19404
.20750	.26970	.26207	.25443	.24678	.23912	.23146	.22379	.21612	.20844	.20075

POINT TABLES: ORIGINAL LOAN TERM: 420 MONTHS LOAN PREPAID IN: 60 MONTHS

EFFECTIVE YIELD	CONTRACT RATE .14500	.14750	.15000	.15250	.15500	.15750	.16000	.16250	.16500	.16750
.07000	-.31476	-.32531	-.33586	-.34641	-.35696	-.36751	-.37806	-.38861	-.39916	-.40970
.07250	-.30247	-.31295	-.32344	-.33393	-.34441	-.35490	-.36538	-.37586	-.38635	-.39683
.07500	-.29031	-.30073	-.31116	-.32158	-.33200	-.34242	-.35284	-.36326	-.37368	-.38410
.07750	-.27829	-.28865	-.29901	-.30937	-.31973	-.33009	-.34044	-.35080	-.36116	-.37152
.08000	-.26641	-.27671	-.28700	-.29730	-.30759	-.31789	-.32818	-.33848	-.34878	-.35907
.08250	-.25466	-.26489	-.27513	-.28536	-.29559	-.30583	-.31606	-.32630	-.33653	-.34676
.08500	-.24304	-.25321	-.26338	-.27356	-.28373	-.29390	-.30407	-.31425	-.32442	-.33459
.08750	-.23155	-.24166	-.25177	-.26189	-.27200	-.28211	-.29222	-.30233	-.31245	-.32256
.09000	-.22020	-.23025	-.24029	-.25034	-.26040	-.27045	-.28050	-.29055	-.30060	-.31066
.09250	-.20897	-.21895	-.22894	-.23893	-.24892	-.25892	-.26891	-.27890	-.28889	-.29889
.09500	-.19786	-.20779	-.21772	-.22765	-.23758	-.24751	-.25745	-.26738	-.27731	-.28725
.09750	-.18688	-.19675	-.20662	-.21649	-.22636	-.23624	-.24611	-.25599	-.26586	-.27574
.10000	-.17602	-.18583	-.19564	-.20546	-.21527	-.22509	-.23490	-.24472	-.25454	-.26435
.10250	-.16529	-.17504	-.18479	-.19455	-.20430	-.21406	-.22382	-.23358	-.24334	-.25309
.10500	-.15467	-.16436	-.17406	-.18376	-.19346	-.20316	-.21286	-.22256	-.23226	-.24196
.10750	-.14417	-.15381	-.16345	-.17309	-.18273	-.19237	-.20202	-.21166	-.22131	-.23095
.11000	-.13379	-.14337	-.15295	-.16254	-.17212	-.18171	-.19130	-.20088	-.21047	-.22006
.11250	-.12353	-.13305	-.14258	-.15210	-.16163	-.17116	-.18069	-.19023	-.19976	-.20929
.11500	-.11337	-.12284	-.13231	-.14179	-.15126	-.16073	-.17021	-.17969	-.18916	-.19864
.11750	-.10334	-.11275	-.12216	-.13158	-.14100	-.15042	-.15984	-.16926	-.17868	-.18811
.12000	-.09341	-.10277	-.11213	-.12149	-.13085	-.14022	-.14959	-.15895	-.16832	-.17769
.12250	-.08359	-.09290	-.10220	-.11151	-.12082	-.13013	-.13944	-.14876	-.15807	-.16739
.12500	-.07389	-.08314	-.09239	-.10164	-.11090	-.12016	-.12941	-.13867	-.14793	-.15720
.12750	-.06429	-.07348	-.08268	-.09188	-.10108	-.11029	-.11949	-.12870	-.13791	-.14712
.13000	-.05479	-.06394	-.07308	-.08223	-.09138	-.10053	-.10968	-.11884	-.12799	-.13715
.13250	-.04541	-.05450	-.06359	-.07268	-.08178	-.09088	-.09998	-.10908	-.11818	-.12729
.13500	-.03612	-.04516	-.05420	-.06324	-.07229	-.08134	-.09038	-.09943	-.10848	-.11754
.13750	-.02694	-.03593	-.04492	-.05391	-.06290	-.07190	-.08089	-.08989	-.09889	-.10789
.14000	-.01786	-.02680	-.03573	-.04467	-.05362	-.06256	-.07150	-.08045	-.08940	-.09835
.14250	-.00888	-.01776	-.02665	-.03554	-.04443	-.05332	-.06222	-.07112	-.08001	-.08891
.14500	.00000	-.00883	-.01767	-.02651	-.03535	-.04419	-.05304	-.06188	-.07073	-.07958
.14750	.00878	0.00000	-.00879	-.01757	-.02637	-.03516	-.04395	-.05275	-.06155	-.07035
.15000	.01747	.00874	.00000	-.00874	-.01748	-.02622	-.03497	-.04372	-.05246	-.06121
.15250	.02606	.01738	.00869	.00000	-.00869	-.01739	-.02608	-.03478	-.04348	-.05218
.15500	.03456	.02592	.01728	.00864	0.00000	-.00865	-.01729	-.02594	-.03459	-.04325
.15750	.04296	.03437	.02578	.01719	.00860	.00000	-.00860	-.01720	-.02580	-.03441
.16000	.05127	.04273	.03419	.02565	.01710	.00855	.00000	-.00855	-.01711	-.02567
.16250	.05949	.05100	.04251	.03401	.02551	.01701	.00851	-.00000	-.00851	-.01702
.16500	.06762	.05918	.05073	.04228	.03383	.02538	.01692	.00846	.00000	-.00846
.16750	.07566	.06727	.05887	.05047	.04206	.03365	.02524	.01683	.00842	0.00000
.17000	.08362	.07527	.06692	.05856	.05020	.04184	.03347	.02511	.01674	.00837
.17250	.09149	.08318	.07487	.06656	.05825	.04994	.04162	.03330	.02498	.01665
.17500	.09927	.09101	.08275	.07448	.06622	.05795	.04967	.04140	.03312	.02484
.17750	.10696	.09875	.09053	.08232	.07409	.06587	.05764	.04941	.04118	.03295
.18000	.11458	.10641	.09824	.09006	.08189	.07371	.06552	.05734	.04915	.04097
.18250	.12211	.11398	.10586	.09773	.08960	.08146	.07332	.06518	.05704	.04890
.18500	.12955	.12148	.11339	.10531	.09722	.08913	.08104	.07294	.06484	.05674
.18750	.13692	.12889	.12085	.11281	.10476	.09672	.08867	.08062	.07256	.06450
.19000	.14421	.13622	.12822	.12023	.11223	.10422	.09622	.08821	.08020	.07218
.19250	.15142	.14347	.13552	.12756	.11961	.11165	.10368	.09572	.08775	.07978
.19500	.15855	.15064	.14274	.13482	.12691	.11899	.11107	.10315	.09522	.08730
.19750	.16560	.15774	.14987	.14201	.13413	.12626	.11838	.11050	.10262	.09473
.20000	.17258	.16476	.15694	.14911	.14128	.13345	.12561	.11777	.10993	.10209
.20250	.17948	.17170	.16392	.15614	.14835	.14056	.13276	.12497	.11717	.10937
.20500	.18631	.17857	.17083	.16309	.15534	.14759	.13984	.13209	.12433	.11657
.20750	.19306	.18537	.17767	.16997	.16226	.15455	.14684	.13913	.13141	.12369

POINT TABLES: ORIGINAL LOAN TERM: 420 MONTHS LOAN PREPAID IN: 60 MONTHS

EFFECTIVE YIELD	CONTRACT RATE .17000	.17250	.17500	.17750	.18000	.18250	.18500	.18750	.19000	.19250
.07000	-.42025	-.43080	-.44134	-.45189	-.46243	-.47298	-.48352	-.49406	-.50460	-.51514
.07250	-.40732	-.41780	-.42828	-.43876	-.44924	-.45972	-.47020	-.48068	-.49116	-.50164
.07500	-.39452	-.40494	-.41536	-.42578	-.43620	-.44662	-.45703	-.46745	-.47787	-.48828
.07750	-.38188	-.39223	-.40259	-.41295	-.42330	-.43366	-.44401	-.45437	-.46472	-.47507
.08000	-.36937	-.37966	-.38996	-.40025	-.41055	-.42084	-.43113	-.44142	-.45172	-.46201
.08250	-.35700	-.36723	-.37747	-.38770	-.39793	-.40816	-.41839	-.42863	-.43886	-.44909
.08500	-.34477	-.35494	-.36511	-.37528	-.38546	-.39563	-.40580	-.41597	-.42614	-.43631
.08750	-.33267	-.34278	-.35289	-.36301	-.37312	-.38323	-.39334	-.40345	-.41356	-.42367
.09000	-.32071	-.33076	-.34081	-.35086	-.36092	-.37097	-.38102	-.39107	-.40112	-.41117
.09250	-.30888	-.31887	-.32886	-.33886	-.34885	-.35884	-.36883	-.37883	-.38832	-.39881
.09500	-.29718	-.30711	-.31705	-.32698	-.33692	-.34685	-.35678	-.36671	-.37665	-.38658
.09750	-.28561	-.29549	-.30536	-.31524	-.32511	-.33499	-.34486	-.35474	-.36461	-.37449
.10000	-.27417	-.28399	-.29380	-.30362	-.31344	-.32326	-.33307	-.34289	-.35271	-.36252
.10250	-.26285	-.27261	-.28237	-.29213	-.30189	-.31165	-.32141	-.33117	-.34093	-.35069
.10500	-.25166	-.26137	-.27107	-.28077	-.29048	-.30018	-.30988	-.31959	-.32929	-.33899
.10750	-.24060	-.25024	-.25989	-.26954	-.27918	-.28883	-.29848	-.30812	-.31777	-.32742
.11000	-.22965	-.23924	-.24883	-.25842	-.26801	-.27760	-.28720	-.29679	-.30638	-.31597
.11250	-.21883	-.22836	-.23790	-.24743	-.25697	-.26650	-.27604	-.28557	-.29511	-.30464
.11500	-.20812	-.21760	-.22708	-.23656	-.24604	-.25552	-.26500	-.27448	-.28396	-.29344
.11750	-.19753	-.20696	-.21638	-.22581	-.23523	-.24466	-.25408	-.26351	-.27294	-.28236
.12000	-.18706	-.19643	-.20580	-.21517	-.22454	-.23392	-.24329	-.25266	-.26203	-.27140
.12250	-.17670	-.18602	-.19534	-.20465	-.21397	-.22329	-.23261	-.24193	-.25125	-.26056
.12500	-.16646	-.17572	-.18498	-.19425	-.20351	-.21278	-.22204	-.23131	-.24058	-.24984
.12750	-.15633	-.16554	-.17475	-.18396	-.19317	-.20238	-.21159	-.22081	-.23002	-.23923
.13000	-.14630	-.15546	-.16462	-.17378	-.18294	-.19210	-.20126	-.21042	-.21958	-.22874
.13250	-.13639	-.14550	-.15460	-.16371	-.17282	-.18193	-.19103	-.20014	-.20925	-.21836
.13500	-.12659	-.13564	-.14470	-.15375	-.16281	-.17186	-.18092	-.18998	-.19904	-.20809
.13750	-.11689	-.12589	-.13490	-.14390	-.15291	-.16191	-.17092	-.17992	-.18893	-.19794
.14000	-.10730	-.11625	-.12520	-.13416	-.14311	-.15207	-.16102	-.16998	-.17893	-.18789
.14250	-.09781	-.10671	-.11562	-.12452	-.13342	-.14233	-.15123	-.16014	-.16904	-.17795
.14500	-.08843	-.09728	-.10613	-.11499	-.12384	-.13269	-.14155	-.15041	-.15926	-.16812
.14750	-.07915	-.08795	-.09675	-.10556	-.11436	-.12316	-.13197	-.14078	-.14958	-.15839
.15000	-.06997	-.07872	-.08747	-.09623	-.10498	-.11374	-.12249	-.13125	-.14001	-.14877
.15250	-.06088	-.06959	-.07829	-.08700	-.09570	-.10441	-.11312	-.12183	-.13054	-.13925
.15500	-.05190	-.06056	-.06921	-.07787	-.08653	-.09519	-.10385	-.11251	-.12117	-.12983
.15750	-.04301	-.05162	-.06023	-.06884	-.07745	-.08606	-.09467	-.10328	-.11190	-.12051
.16000	-.03422	-.04278	-.05134	-.05991	-.06847	-.07703	-.08560	-.09416	-.10273	-.11129
.16250	-.02553	-.03404	-.04255	-.05107	-.05958	-.06810	-.07662	-.08514	-.09365	-.10217
.16500	-.01693	-.02539	-.03386	-.04233	-.05080	-.05926	-.06774	-.07621	-.08468	-.09315
.16750	-.00842	-.01684	-.02526	-.03368	-.04210	-.05052	-.05895	-.06737	-.07580	-.08422
.17000	.00000	-.00837	-.01675	-.02512	-.03350	-.04188	-.05025	-.05863	-.06701	-.07539
.17250	.00833	0.00000	-.00833	-.01666	-.02499	-.03332	-.04165	-.04999	-.05832	-.06665
.17500	.01656	.00828	.00000	-.00828	-.01657	-.02486	-.03314	-.04143	-.04972	-.05801
.17750	.02471	.01648	.00824	.00000	-.00824	-.01648	-.02472	-.03297	-.04121	-.04946
.18000	.03278	.02458	.01639	.00820	0.00000	-.00820	-.01639	-.02459	-.03279	-.04099
.18250	.04075	.03260	.02445	.01630	.00815	.00000	-.00815	-.01631	-.02446	-.03262
.18500	.04864	.04054	.03243	.02433	.01622	.00811	.00000	-.00811	-.01622	-.02433
.18750	.05645	.04839	.04033	.03226	.02420	.01613	.00807	.00000	-.00807	-.01614
.19000	.06417	.05615	.04813	.04011	.03209	.02407	.01605	.00802	.00000	-.00803
.19250	.07181	.06384	.05586	.04788	.03991	.03193	.02395	.01597	.00798	.00000
.19500	.07937	.07144	.06350	.05557	.04763	.03970	.03176	.02382	.01588	.00794
.19750	.08685	.07896	.07107	.06318	.05528	.04739	.03949	.03160	.02370	.01580
.20000	.09424	.08640	.07855	.07070	.06285	.05500	.04714	.03929	.03143	.02357
.20250	.10156	.09376	.08595	.07814	.07033	.06252	.05471	.04690	.03908	.03127
.20500	.10881	.10104	.09328	.08551	.07774	.06997	.06220	.05443	.04666	.03888
.20750	.11597	.10825	.10053	.09280	.08507	.07734	.06961	.06188	.05415	.04642

POINT TABLES: ORIGINAL LOAN TERM: 420 MONTHS LOAN PREPAID IN: 60 MONTHS

EFFECTIVE YIELD	CONTRACT RATE .19500	.19750	.20000	.20250	.20500	.20750
.07000	-.52568	-.53622	-.54676	-.55730	-.56784	-.57837
.07250	-.51212	-.52259	-.53307	-.54354	-.55402	-.56449
.07500	-.49870	-.50911	-.51952	-.52994	-.54035	-.55076
.07750	-.48542	-.49578	-.50613	-.51648	-.52683	-.53718
.08000	-.47230	-.48259	-.49288	-.50317	-.51346	-.52374
.08250	-.45932	-.46955	-.47977	-.49000	-.50023	-.51046
.08500	-.44648	-.45665	-.46681	-.47698	-.48715	-.49732
.08750	-.43378	-.44389	-.45400	-.46410	-.47421	-.48432
.09000	-.42122	-.43127	-.44132	-.45137	-.46141	-.47146
.09250	-.40880	-.41879	-.42878	-.43877	-.44876	-.45875
.09500	-.39651	-.40644	-.41638	-.42631	-.43624	-.44617
.09750	-.38436	-.39423	-.40411	-.41398	-.42385	-.43373
.10000	-.37234	-.38216	-.39197	-.40179	-.41160	-.42142
.10250	-.36045	-.37021	-.37997	-.38973	-.39949	-.40925
.10500	-.34869	-.35840	-.36810	-.37780	-.38750	-.39720
.10750	-.33706	-.34671	-.35636	-.36600	-.37565	-.38529
.11000	-.32556	-.33515	-.34474	-.35433	-.36392	-.37351
.11250	-.31418	-.32372	-.33325	-.34279	-.35232	-.36186
.11500	-.30292	-.31240	-.32189	-.33137	-.34085	-.35033
.11750	-.29179	-.30122	-.31064	-.32007	-.32950	-.33892
.12000	-.28078	-.29015	-.29952	-.30889	-.31827	-.32764
.12250	-.26988	-.27920	-.28852	-.29784	-.30716	-.31648
.12500	-.25911	-.26837	-.27764	-.28690	-.29617	-.30544
.12750	-.24845	-.25766	-.26687	-.27609	-.28530	-.29451
.13000	-.23790	-.24706	-.25622	-.26539	-.27455	-.28371
.13250	-.22747	-.23658	-.24569	-.25480	-.26391	-.27302
.13500	-.21715	-.22621	-.23527	-.24433	-.25339	-.26244
.13750	-.20694	-.21595	-.22496	-.23397	-.24297	-.25198
.14000	-.19685	-.20580	-.21476	-.22372	-.23267	-.24163
.14250	-.18686	-.19576	-.20467	-.21358	-.22248	-.23139
.14500	-.17697	-.18583	-.19469	-.20355	-.21240	-.22126
.14750	-.16720	-.17601	-.18481	-.19362	-.20243	-.21124
.15000	-.15753	-.16628	-.17504	-.18380	-.19256	-.20132
.15250	-.14796	-.15667	-.16538	-.17409	-.18280	-.19151
.15500	-.13849	-.14715	-.15582	-.16448	-.17314	-.18180
.15750	-.12913	-.13774	-.14635	-.15497	-.16358	-.17220
.16000	-.11986	-.12843	-.13699	-.14556	-.15413	-.16270
.16250	-.11069	-.11921	-.12773	-.13625	-.14478	-.15330
.16500	-.10162	-.11010	-.11857	-.12705	-.13552	-.14399
.16750	-.09265	-.10108	-.10951	-.11793	-.12636	-.13479
.17000	-.08377	-.09215	-.10054	-.10892	-.11730	-.12568
.17250	-.07499	-.08333	-.09166	-.10000	-.10834	-.11667
.17500	-.06630	-.07459	-.08288	-.09117	-.09947	-.10776
.17750	-.05770	-.06595	-.07419	-.08244	-.09069	-.09894
.18000	-.04919	-.05740	-.06560	-.07380	-.08200	-.09021
.18250	-.04078	-.04893	-.05709	-.06525	-.07341	-.08157
.18500	-.03245	-.04056	-.04868	-.05679	-.06490	-.07302
.18750	-.02421	-.03228	-.04035	-.04842	-.05649	-.06456
.19000	-.01605	-.02408	-.03211	-.04014	-.04816	-.05619
.19250	-.00798	-.01597	-.02395	-.03194	-.03992	-.04791
.19500	.00000	-.00794	-.01588	-.02383	-.03177	-.03972
.19750	.00790	0.00000	-.00790	-.01580	-.02370	-.03161
.20000	.01572	.00786	.00000	-.00786	-.01572	-.02358
.20250	.02345	.01564	.00782	.00000	-.00782	-.01564
.20500	.03111	.02333	.01555	.00778	.00000	-.00778
.20750	.03868	.03095	.02321	.01547	.00774	0.00000

POINT TABLES: ORIGINAL LOAN TERM: 420 MONTHS LOAN PREPAID IN: 84 MONTHS

EFFECTIVE YIELD	CONTRACT RATE .07000	.07250	.07500	.07750	.08000	.08250	.08500	.08750	.09000	.09250
.07000	.00000	-.01348	-.02699	-.04054	-.05411	-.06772	-.08135	-.09500	-.10867	-.12236
.07250	.01335	.00000	-.01339	-.02681	-.04026	-.05374	-.06725	-.08078	-.09433	-.10790
.07500	.02650	.01327	.00000	-.01330	-.02663	-.03998	-.05337	-.06678	-.08021	-.09366
.07750	.03943	.02632	.01318	.00000	-.01321	-.02645	-.03971	-.05300	-.06631	-.07964
.08000	.05216	.03917	.02615	.01309	0.00000	-.01312	-.02626	-.03943	-.05263	-.06584
.08250	.06469	.05182	.03891	.02597	.01300	.00000	-.01303	-.02608	-.03916	-.05226
.08500	.07701	.06426	.05147	.03865	.02580	.01291	0.00000	-.01294	-.02590	-.03888
.08750	.08915	.07651	.06384	.05113	.03839	.02562	.01282	.00000	-.01285	-.02572
.09000	.10109	.08857	.07601	.06342	.05079	.03813	.02545	.01274	0.00000	-.01276
.09250	.11285	.10044	.08799	.07551	.06300	.05045	.03788	.02528	.01265	.00000
.09500	.12442	.11212	.09978	.08741	.07501	.06257	.05011	.03762	.02510	.01256
.09750	.13580	.12362	.11139	.09913	.08683	.07451	.06215	.04977	.03736	.02493
.10000	.14701	.13493	.12282	.11066	.09848	.08626	.07401	.06173	.04943	.03711
.10250	.15804	.14607	.13406	.12202	.10994	.09782	.08568	.07351	.06131	.04909
.10500	.16890	.15704	.14513	.13319	.12122	.10921	.09717	.08511	.07301	.06090
.10750	.17959	.16783	.15603	.14419	.13232	.12042	.10849	.09652	.08453	.07252
.11000	.19011	.17845	.16676	.15502	.14326	.13145	.11962	.10776	.09587	.08396
.11250	.20047	.18891	.17732	.16569	.15402	.14232	.13059	.11883	.10704	.09523
.11500	.21066	.19921	.18772	.17618	.16462	.15302	.14138	.12972	.11804	.10632
.11750	.22070	.20934	.19795	.18652	.17505	.16355	.15201	.14045	.12886	.11725
.12000	.23058	.21932	.20803	.19669	.18532	.17392	.16248	.15102	.13952	.12800
.12250	.24030	.22914	.21794	.20671	.19543	.18413	.17279	.16142	.15002	.13859
.12500	.24988	.23881	.22771	.21657	.20539	.19418	.18293	.17166	.16035	.14902
.12750	.25930	.24833	.23733	.22628	.21519	.20407	.19292	.18174	.17053	.15930
.13000	.26858	.25771	.24679	.23584	.22485	.21382	.20276	.19167	.18055	.16941
.13250	.27772	.26693	.25611	.24525	.23435	.22341	.21245	.20145	.19042	.17937
.13500	.28671	.27602	.26529	.25452	.24371	.23286	.22199	.21108	.20014	.18918
.13750	.29556	.28496	.27432	.26364	.25292	.24217	.23138	.22056	.20971	.19884
.14000	.30428	.29377	.28322	.27262	.26199	.25133	.24063	.22990	.21914	.20835
.14250	.31287	.30244	.29198	.28147	.27093	.26035	.24974	.23909	.22842	.21772
.14500	.32132	.31098	.30060	.29018	.27973	.26923	.25871	.24815	.23756	.22695
.14750	.32964	.31939	.30909	.29876	.28839	.27798	.26754	.25707	.24657	.23604
.15000	.33783	.32766	.31745	.30721	.29692	.28660	.27624	.26585	.25543	.24499
.15250	.34590	.33581	.32569	.31552	.30532	.29508	.28481	.27450	.26417	.25380
.15500	.35384	.34384	.33380	.32371	.31359	.30344	.29325	.28302	.27277	.26249
.15750	.36166	.35174	.34178	.33178	.32174	.31167	.30156	.29141	.28124	.27104
.16000	.36936	.35952	.34964	.33972	.32977	.31977	.30974	.29968	.28959	.27947
.16250	.37694	.36719	.35739	.34755	.33767	.32775	.31780	.30782	.29781	.28776
.16500	.38441	.37473	.36501	.35525	.34545	.33561	.32574	.31584	.30590	.29594
.16750	.39177	.38217	.37252	.36284	.35311	.34336	.33356	.32373	.31388	.30399
.17000	.39901	.38948	.37992	.37031	.36066	.35098	.34126	.33151	.32173	.31192
.17250	.40614	.39669	.38720	.37767	.36810	.35849	.34885	.33918	.32947	.31973
.17500	.41316	.40379	.39437	.38492	.37542	.36589	.35632	.34672	.33709	.32743
.17750	.42008	.41078	.40144	.39206	.38264	.37318	.36368	.35416	.34460	.33501
.18000	.42689	.41767	.40840	.39909	.38974	.38036	.37094	.36148	.35200	.34248
.18250	.43360	.42445	.41525	.40601	.39674	.38743	.37808	.36870	.35929	.34984
.18500	.44020	.43112	.42200	.41284	.40363	.39439	.38512	.37581	.36646	.35709
.18750	.44671	.43770	.42865	.41956	.41042	.40125	.39205	.38281	.37354	.36424
.19000	.45312	.44418	.43520	.42618	.41711	.40801	.39888	.38971	.38050	.37127
.19250	.45943	.45056	.44165	.43270	.42370	.41467	.40560	.39650	.38737	.37821
.19500	.46565	.45685	.44800	.43912	.43019	.42123	.41223	.40320	.39413	.38504
.19750	.47177	.46304	.45426	.44544	.43659	.42769	.41876	.40979	.40080	.39177
.20000	.47781	.46914	.46043	.45168	.44289	.43406	.42519	.41629	.40736	.39840
.20250	.48375	.47515	.46650	.45782	.44909	.44033	.43153	.42270	.41383	.40494
.20500	.48960	.48107	.47249	.46387	.45521	.44651	.43777	.42901	.42021	.41138
.20750	.49537	.48690	.47838	.46982	.46123	.45259	.44393	.43522	.42649	.41772

POINT TABLES: ORIGINAL LOAN TERM: 420 MONTHS LOAN PREPAID IN: 84 MONTHS

EFFECTIVE YIELD	CONTRACT RATE .09500	.09750	.10000	.10250	.10500	.10750	.11000	.11250	.11500	.11750
.07000	-.13608	-.14981	-.16355	-.17731	-.19108	-.20486	-.21865	-.23246	-.24627	-.26008
.07250	-.12149	-.13510	-.14872	-.16236	-.17601	-.18967	-.20335	-.21703	-.23072	-.24442
.07500	-.10713	-.12062	-.13412	-.14764	-.16117	-.17472	-.18827	-.20184	-.21541	-.22900
.07750	-.09299	-.10636	-.11975	-.13315	-.14657	-.15999	-.17343	-.18688	-.20034	-.21381
.08000	-.07908	-.09233	-.10560	-.11889	-.13218	-.14550	-.15882	-.17216	-.18550	-.19885
.08250	-.06538	-.07851	-.09167	-.10484	-.11803	-.13122	-.14443	-.15766	-.17089	-.18413
.08500	-.05189	-.06491	-.07796	-.09101	-.10409	-.11717	-.13027	-.14338	-.15650	-.16963
.08750	-.03861	-.05152	-.06445	-.07740	-.09036	-.10333	-.11632	-.12932	-.14233	-.15535
.09000	-.02554	-.03834	-.05116	-.06399	-.07684	-.08971	-.10259	-.11548	-.12837	-.14128
.09250	-.01267	-.02536	-.03807	-.05080	-.06354	-.07629	-.08906	-.10184	-.11463	-.12744
.09500	0.00000	-.01258	-.02518	-.03780	-.05043	-.06308	-.07574	-.08842	-.10110	-.11380
.09750	.01247	.00000	-.01249	-.02501	-.03753	-.05008	-.06263	-.07520	-.08778	-.10037
.10000	.02476	.01239	.00000	-.01241	-.02483	-.03727	-.04972	-.06218	-.07466	-.08714
.10250	.03685	.02459	.01230	.00000	-.01232	-.02465	-.03700	-.04936	-.06174	-.07412
.10500	.04876	.03660	.02442	.01222	0.00000	-.01223	-.02448	-.03674	-.04901	-.06129
.10750	.06048	.04842	.03634	.02425	.01213	.00000	-.01215	-.02430	-.03648	-.04866
.11000	.07203	.06007	.04809	.03609	.02408	.01205	.00000	-.01206	-.02413	-.03622
.11250	.08339	.07153	.05965	.04776	.03584	.02391	.01196	0.00000	-.01197	-.02396
.11500	.09458	.08282	.07104	.05924	.04743	.03559	.02374	.01188	0.00000	-.01189
.11750	.10561	.09394	.08226	.07056	.05883	.04710	.03534	.02357	.01179	0.00000
.12000	.11646	.10489	.09330	.08170	.07007	.05843	.04677	.03510	.02341	.01171
.12250	.12715	.11567	.10418	.09267	.08114	.06959	.05802	.04644	.03485	.02325
.12500	.13767	.12629	.11489	.10347	.09203	.08058	.06911	.05762	.04612	.03461
.12750	.14803	.13675	.12544	.11411	.10277	.09140	.08003	.06863	.05722	.04580
.13000	.15824	.14705	.13583	.12460	.11334	.10207	.09078	.07947	.06816	.05682
.13250	.16829	.15719	.14606	.13492	.12375	.11257	.10137	.09016	.07893	.06768
.13500	.17819	.16718	.15614	.14508	.13401	.12291	.11180	.10068	.08954	.07838
.13750	.18794	.17701	.16607	.15510	.14411	.13310	.12208	.11104	.09999	.08892
.14000	.19754	.18670	.17584	.16496	.15406	.14314	.13220	.12125	.11028	.09930
.14250	.20700	.19624	.18547	.17468	.16386	.15303	.14218	.13131	.12043	.10953
.14500	.21631	.20564	.19495	.18424	.17351	.16277	.15200	.14122	.13042	.11961
.14750	.22548	.21490	.20430	.19367	.18302	.17236	.16168	.15098	.14026	.12953
.15000	.23452	.22402	.21350	.20295	.19239	.18181	.17121	.16059	.14996	.13931
.15250	.24341	.23300	.22256	.21210	.20162	.19112	.18060	.17007	.15951	.14895
.15500	.25218	.24185	.23149	.22111	.21071	.20029	.18985	.17940	.16893	.15844
.15750	.26081	.25056	.24028	.22998	.21966	.20932	.19897	.18859	.17820	.16780
.16000	.26932	.25914	.24895	.23873	.22849	.21823	.20795	.19765	.18734	.17701
.16250	.27769	.26760	.25748	.24734	.23718	.22700	.21680	.20658	.19634	.18610
.16500	.28595	.27593	.26589	.25583	.24574	.23564	.22551	.21537	.20522	.19504
.16750	.29408	.28414	.27417	.26418	.25418	.24415	.23410	.22404	.21396	.20386
.17000	.30208	.29222	.28233	.27242	.26249	.25253	.24256	.23257	.22257	.21255
.17250	.30997	.30018	.29037	.28053	.27068	.26080	.25090	.24099	.23106	.22111
.17500	.31774	.30803	.29829	.28853	.27874	.26894	.25912	.24928	.23942	.22955
.17750	.32540	.31576	.30609	.29640	.28669	.27696	.26721	.25745	.24766	.23786
.18000	.33294	.32337	.31378	.30416	.29453	.28487	.27519	.26549	.25578	.24605
.18250	.34037	.33088	.32136	.31181	.30224	.29266	.28305	.27343	.26379	.25413
.18500	.34769	.33827	.32882	.31934	.30985	.30033	.29080	.28124	.27167	.26209
.18750	.35491	.34555	.33617	.32677	.31734	.30790	.29843	.28895	.27945	.26993
.19000	.36201	.35273	.34342	.33408	.32473	.31535	.30595	.29654	.28711	.27766
.19250	.36902	.35980	.35056	.34129	.33200	.32269	.31337	.30402	.29466	.28528
.19500	.37592	.36677	.35759	.34839	.33917	.32993	.32067	.31139	.30210	.29278
.19750	.38271	.37363	.36453	.35539	.34624	.33707	.32787	.31866	.30943	.30018
.20000	.38941	.38040	.37136	.36229	.35320	.34410	.33497	.32582	.31666	.30748
.20250	.39601	.38706	.37809	.36909	.36007	.35102	.34196	.33288	.32378	.31467
.20500	.40252	.39363	.38472	.37579	.36683	.35785	.34886	.33984	.33080	.32175
.20750	.40893	.40011	.39126	.38239	.37350	.36458	.35565	.34670	.33773	.32874

POINT TABLES: ORIGINAL LOAN TERM: 420 MONTHS LOAN PREPAID IN: 84 MONTHS

EFFECTIVE YIELD	*	CONTRACT RATE .12000	.12250	.12500	.12750	.13000	.13250	.13500	.13750	.14000	.14250
.07000	*	-.27391	-.28774	-.30157	-.31541	-.32926	-.34310	-.35695	-.37080	-.38466	-.39851
.07250	*	-.25813	-.27184	-.28556	-.29928	-.31300	-.32673	-.34047	-.35420	-.36794	-.38168
.07500	*	-.24258	-.25618	-.26978	-.28339	-.29700	-.31061	-.32423	-.33785	-.35147	-.36510
.07750	*	-.22728	-.24076	-.25425	-.26774	-.28124	-.29474	-.30824	-.32175	-.33526	-.34877
.08000	*	-.21221	-.22558	-.23895	-.25233	-.26572	-.27910	-.29250	-.30589	-.31929	-.33269
.08250	*	-.19737	-.21063	-.22389	-.23716	-.25043	-.26371	-.27699	-.29027	-.30356	-.31685
.08500	*	-.18276	-.19591	-.20906	-.22221	-.23538	-.24854	-.26171	-.27489	-.28807	-.30125
.08750	*	-.16837	-.18141	-.19445	-.20750	-.22055	-.23361	-.24667	-.25974	-.27281	-.28588
.09000	*	-.15420	-.16713	-.18006	-.19300	-.20595	-.21890	-.23185	-.24481	-.25778	-.27074
.09250	*	-.14025	-.15307	-.16589	-.17873	-.19157	-.20441	-.21726	-.23011	-.24297	-.25583
.09500	*	-.12650	-.13922	-.15194	-.16467	-.17740	-.19014	-.20289	-.21563	-.22839	-.24114
.09750	*	-.11297	-.12558	-.13820	-.15082	-.16345	-.17609	-.18873	-.20137	-.21402	-.22668
.10000	*	-.09964	-.11215	-.12466	-.13718	-.14971	-.16224	-.17478	-.18732	-.19987	-.21242
.10250	*	-.08651	-.09892	-.11133	-.12375	-.13617	-.14861	-.16104	-.17349	-.18593	-.19839
.10500	*	-.07359	-.08589	-.09820	-.11052	-.12284	-.13517	-.14751	-.15986	-.17220	-.18455
.10750	*	-.06085	-.07305	-.08527	-.09748	-.10971	-.12194	-.13418	-.14643	-.15868	-.17093
.11000	*	-.04831	-.06041	-.07253	-.08465	-.09678	-.10891	-.12105	-.13320	-.14535	-.15751
.11250	*	-.03596	-.04796	-.05998	-.07200	-.08403	-.09607	-.10812	-.12017	-.13222	-.14428
.11500	*	-.02379	-.03570	-.04762	-.05955	-.07148	-.08343	-.09538	-.10733	-.11929	-.13126
.11750	*	-.01180	-.02362	-.03544	-.04728	-.05912	-.07097	-.08282	-.09468	-.10655	-.11842
.12000	*	.00000	-.01172	-.02345	-.03519	-.04694	-.05869	-.07046	-.08222	-.09400	-.10577
.12250	*	.01163	.00000	-.01164	-.02326	-.03494	-.04660	-.05827	-.06995	-.08153	-.09332
.12500	*	.02308	.01155	.00000	-.01156	-.02312	-.03469	-.04627	-.05785	-.06944	-.08104
.12750	*	.03436	.02292	.01146	0.00000	-.01147	-.02295	-.03444	-.04594	-.05744	-.06894
.13000	*	.04548	.03412	.02276	.01138	0.00000	-.01139	-.02279	-.03420	-.04561	-.05703
.13250	*	.05643	.04516	.03389	.02260	.01130	0.00000	-.01131	-.02263	-.03395	-.04528
.13500	*	.06721	.05604	.04485	.03365	.02244	.01122	0.00000	-.01123	-.02247	-.03371
.13750	*	.07784	.06675	.05565	.04453	.03341	.02228	.01114	0.00000	-.01115	-.02231
.14000	*	.08831	.07730	.06629	.05526	.04422	.03318	.02213	.01107	.00000	-.01107
.14250	*	.09862	.08770	.07677	.06583	.05487	.04391	.03295	.02197	.01099	.00000
.14500	*	.10878	.09794	.08710	.07624	.06537	.05449	.04361	.03272	.02182	.01091
.14750	*	.11879	.10804	.09727	.08650	.07571	.06492	.05411	.04330	.03249	.02166
.15000	*	.12865	.11798	.10730	.09660	.08590	.07519	.06447	.05374	.04300	.03226
.15250	*	.13837	.12778	.11718	.10656	.09594	.08531	.07467	.06402	.05337	.04270
.15500	*	.14795	.13743	.12691	.11638	.10584	.09528	.08472	.07415	.06358	.05300
.15750	*	.15738	.14695	.13650	.12605	.11559	.10511	.09463	.08414	.07364	.06314
.16000	*	.16667	.15632	.14596	.13558	.12519	.11480	.10439	.09398	.08356	.07314
.16250	*	.17583	.16556	.15527	.14497	.13466	.12434	.11402	.10368	.09334	.08299
.16500	*	.18486	.17466	.16445	.15423	.14399	.13375	.12350	.11324	.10298	.09270
.16750	*	.19375	.18363	.17349	.16335	.15319	.14302	.13285	.12266	.11247	.10227
.17000	*	.20251	.19247	.18241	.17234	.16225	.15216	.14206	.13195	.12183	.11171
.17250	*	.21115	.20118	.19119	.18119	.17119	.16117	.15114	.14110	.13106	.12101
.17500	*	.21966	.20976	.19985	.18992	.17999	.17004	.16009	.15013	.14015	.13018
.17750	*	.22805	.21822	.20838	.19853	.18866	.17879	.16891	.15902	.14912	.13921
.18000	*	.23631	.22656	.21679	.20701	.19722	.18741	.17760	.16778	.15796	.14812
.18250	*	.24446	.23477	.22508	.21537	.20564	.19591	.18617	.17642	.16667	.15690
.18500	*	.25249	.24287	.23324	.22360	.21395	.20429	.19462	.18494	.17525	.16556
.18750	*	.26040	.25085	.24129	.23172	.22214	.21255	.20295	.19334	.18372	.17409
.19000	*	.26820	.25872	.24923	.23973	.23021	.22069	.21116	.20162	.19206	.18251
.19250	*	.27588	.26647	.25705	.24762	.23817	.22872	.21925	.20977	.20029	.19080
.19500	*	.28346	.27411	.26476	.25539	.24601	.23663	.22723	.21782	.20840	.19898
.19750	*	.29092	.28165	.27236	.26306	.25375	.24442	.23509	.22575	.21640	.20704
.20000	*	.29828	.28907	.27985	.27062	.26137	.25211	.24284	.23357	.22428	.21499
.20250	*	.30554	.29639	.28724	.27807	.26888	.25969	.25049	.24128	.23206	.22283
.20500	*	.31269	.30361	.29451	.28541	.27629	.26716	.25802	.24888	.23972	.23056
.20750	*	.31974	.31072	.30169	.29265	.28359	.27453	.26545	.25637	.24728	.23818

POINT TABLES: ORIGINAL LOAN TERM: 420 MONTHS LOAN PREPAID IN: 84 MONTHS

EFFECTIVE YIELD		CONTRACT RATE .14500	.14750	.15000	.15250	.15500	.15750	.16000	.16250	.16500	.16750
.07000	*	-.41237	-.42622	-.44008	-.45394	-.46779	-.48165	-.49551	-.50936	-.52322	-.53707
.07250	*	-.39542	-.40916	-.42290	-.43664	-.45038	-.46413	-.47787	-.49161	-.50535	-.51909
.07500	*	-.37872	-.39235	-.40598	-.41961	-.43324	-.44687	-.46049	-.47412	-.48775	-.50138
.07750	*	-.36228	-.37580	-.38931	-.40283	-.41635	-.42986	-.44338	-.45690	-.47041	-.48393
.08000	*	-.34609	-.35949	-.37290	-.38630	-.39971	-.41311	-.42652	-.43993	-.45334	-.46674
.08250	*	-.33014	-.34343	-.35673	-.37002	-.38332	-.39662	-.40991	-.42321	-.43651	-.44981
.08500	*	-.31443	-.32761	-.34080	-.35399	-.36717	-.38036	-.39355	-.40674	-.41993	-.43312
.08750	*	-.29895	-.31203	-.32511	-.33819	-.35127	-.36435	-.37744	-.39052	-.40360	-.41669
.09000	*	-.28371	-.29668	-.30965	-.32263	-.33560	-.34858	-.36156	-.37454	-.38751	-.40049
.09250	*	-.26869	-.28156	-.29443	-.30730	-.32017	-.33304	-.34591	-.35879	-.37166	-.38454
.09500	*	-.25390	-.26667	-.27943	-.29220	-.30496	-.31773	-.33050	-.34327	-.35605	-.36882
.09750	*	-.23933	-.25199	-.26465	-.27732	-.28998	-.30265	-.31532	-.32799	-.34066	-.35333
.10000	*	-.22498	-.23754	-.25010	-.26266	-.27523	-.28779	-.30036	-.31293	-.32550	-.33807
.10250	*	-.21084	-.22330	-.23576	-.24822	-.26069	-.27315	-.28562	-.29809	-.31056	-.32303
.10500	*	-.19691	-.20927	-.22163	-.23399	-.24636	-.25873	-.27110	-.28347	-.29584	-.30821
.10750	*	-.18319	-.19545	-.20771	-.21998	-.23225	-.24452	-.25679	-.26906	-.28134	-.29361
.11000	*	-.16967	-.18183	-.19400	-.20617	-.21834	-.23051	-.24269	-.25487	-.26705	-.27923
.11250	*	-.15635	-.16842	-.18049	-.19256	-.20464	-.21672	-.22880	-.24088	-.25296	-.26505
.11500	*	-.14323	-.15520	-.16717	-.17915	-.19114	-.20312	-.21511	-.22710	-.23909	-.25108
.11750	*	-.13030	-.14218	-.15406	-.16594	-.17783	-.18973	-.20162	-.21352	-.22541	-.23731
.12000	*	-.11756	-.12934	-.14114	-.15293	-.16473	-.17653	-.18833	-.20013	-.21194	-.22374
.12250	*	-.10501	-.11670	-.12840	-.14010	-.15181	-.16352	-.17523	-.18694	-.19866	-.21037
.12500	*	-.09264	-.10424	-.11585	-.12747	-.13908	-.15070	-.16232	-.17394	-.18557	-.19720
.12750	*	-.08045	-.09197	-.10349	-.11501	-.12654	-.13807	-.14960	-.16113	-.17257	-.18421
.13000	*	-.06845	-.07987	-.09131	-.10274	-.11418	-.12562	-.13706	-.14851	-.15996	-.17141
.13250	*	-.05662	-.06796	-.07930	-.09065	-.10200	-.11335	-.12471	-.13607	-.14743	-.15880
.13500	*	-.04496	-.05621	-.06747	-.07873	-.09000	-.10126	-.11253	-.12381	-.13508	-.14636
.13750	*	-.03347	-.04464	-.05581	-.06699	-.07817	-.08935	-.10053	-.11172	-.12291	-.13411
.14000	*	-.02215	-.03323	-.04432	-.05541	-.06651	-.07761	-.08871	-.09981	-.11092	-.12203
.14250	*	-.01099	-.02199	-.03300	-.04400	-.05502	-.06603	-.07705	-.08807	-.09910	-.11012
.14500	*	0.00000	-.01092	-.02184	-.03276	-.04369	-.05463	-.06556	-.07650	-.08744	-.09839
.14750	*	.01083	.00000	-.01084	-.02168	-.03253	-.04338	-.05424	-.06510	-.07596	-.08682
.15000	*	.02151	.01076	.00000	-.01076	-.02153	-.03230	-.04308	-.05385	-.06463	-.07542
.15250	*	.03204	.02136	.01068	0.00000	-.01069	-.02138	-.03207	-.04277	-.05347	-.06418
.15500	*	.04241	.03181	.02121	.01061	-.00000	-.01061	-.02123	-.03185	-.04247	-.05310
.15750	*	.05263	.04211	.03159	.02107	.01053	0.00000	-.01054	-.02108	-.03162	-.04217
.16000	*	.06270	.05226	.04182	.03137	.02092	.01046	.00000	-.01046	-.02093	-.03140
.16250	*	.07263	.06227	.05190	.04153	.03115	.02077	.01039	0.00000	-.01039	-.02079
.16500	*	.08242	.07213	.06184	.05155	.04124	.03094	.02063	.01032	.00000	-.01032
.16750	*	.09207	.08186	.07164	.06142	.05119	.04096	.03073	.02049	.01024	.00000
.17000	*	.10158	.09144	.08130	.07115	.06100	.05084	.04068	.03051	.02035	.01017
.17250	*	.11095	.10089	.09082	.08074	.07066	.06058	.05049	.04040	.03030	.02021
.17500	*	.12019	.11020	.10020	.09020	.08019	.07018	.06016	.05014	.04012	.03010
.17750	*	.12930	.11938	.10945	.09952	.08959	.07965	.06970	.05975	.04980	.03985
.18000	*	.13828	.12843	.11858	.10872	.09885	.08898	.07911	.06923	.05935	.04946
.18250	*	.14713	.13735	.12757	.11778	.10798	.09818	.08838	.07857	.06876	.05894
.18500	*	.15586	.14615	.13643	.12671	.11699	.10726	.09752	.08778	.07804	.06829
.18750	*	.16446	.15482	.14517	.13552	.12586	.11620	.10653	.09686	.08719	.07751
.19000	*	.17294	.16337	.15379	.14421	.13462	.12502	.11542	.10582	.09621	.08660
.19250	*	.18130	.17180	.16229	.15277	.14325	.13372	.12419	.11465	.10511	.09557
.19500	*	.18955	.18011	.17066	.16121	.15176	.14230	.13283	.12336	.11389	.10441
.19750	*	.19767	.18830	.17892	.16954	.16015	.15075	.14135	.13195	.12254	.11313
.20000	*	.20569	.19638	.18707	.17775	.16842	.15909	.14976	.14042	.13108	.12173
.20250	*	.21359	.20435	.19510	.18584	.17658	.16732	.15805	.14877	.13949	.13021
.20500	*	.22138	.21220	.20302	.19383	.18463	.17543	.16622	.15701	.14779	.13857
.20750	*	.22907	.21995	.21083	.20170	.19256	.18343	.17428	.16513	.15598	.14682

POINT TABLES: ORIGINAL LOAN TERM: 420 MONTHS LOAN PREPAID IN: 84 MONTHS

CONTRACT RATE

EFFECTIVE YIELD	.17000	.17250	.17500	.17750	.18000	.18250	.18500	.18750	.19000	.19250
.07000	-.55092	-.56478	-.57863	-.59248	-.60633	-.62017	-.63402	-.64787	-.66171	-.67555
.07250	-.53283	-.54657	-.56031	-.57404	-.58778	-.60151	-.61525	-.62898	-.64271	-.65644
.07500	-.51501	-.52863	-.54226	-.55588	-.56951	-.58313	-.59675	-.61037	-.62399	-.63761
.07750	-.49745	-.51096	-.52448	-.53799	-.55150	-.56502	-.57853	-.59204	-.60555	-.61905
.08000	-.48015	-.49355	-.50696	-.52036	-.53377	-.54717	-.56057	-.57397	-.58737	-.60077
.08250	-.46310	-.47640	-.48970	-.50299	-.51629	-.52958	-.54288	-.55617	-.56946	-.58275
.08500	-.44631	-.45950	-.47269	-.48588	-.49907	-.51226	-.52545	-.53863	-.55182	-.56500
.08750	-.42977	-.44285	-.45594	-.46902	-.48210	-.49519	-.50827	-.52135	-.53443	-.54751
.09000	-.41347	-.42645	-.43943	-.45241	-.46539	-.47836	-.49134	-.50432	-.51729	-.53027
.09250	-.39741	-.41029	-.42316	-.43604	-.44891	-.46179	-.47466	-.48754	-.50041	-.51328
.09500	-.38159	-.39436	-.40714	-.41991	-.43268	-.44546	-.45823	-.47100	-.48377	-.49654
.09750	-.36600	-.37867	-.39134	-.40402	-.41669	-.42936	-.44203	-.45470	-.46737	-.48004
.10000	-.35064	-.36321	-.37578	-.38835	-.40093	-.41350	-.42607	-.43864	-.45121	-.46378
.10250	-.33550	-.34798	-.36045	-.37292	-.38539	-.39787	-.41034	-.42281	-.43529	-.44776
.10500	-.32059	-.33296	-.34534	-.35771	-.37009	-.38246	-.39484	-.40722	-.41959	-.43197
.10750	-.30589	-.31817	-.33045	-.34273	-.35500	-.36728	-.37956	-.39184	-.40412	-.41640
.11000	-.29141	-.30359	-.31577	-.32796	-.34014	-.35232	-.36451	-.37669	-.38888	-.40106
.11250	-.27714	-.28922	-.30131	-.31340	-.32549	-.33758	-.34967	-.36176	-.37385	-.38594
.11500	-.26307	-.27507	-.28706	-.29906	-.31105	-.32305	-.33504	-.34704	-.35904	-.37104
.11750	-.24921	-.26111	-.27302	-.28492	-.29682	-.30873	-.32063	-.33254	-.34444	-.35635
.12000	-.23555	-.24736	-.25917	-.27098	-.28280	-.29461	-.30642	-.31824	-.33005	-.34187
.12250	-.22209	-.23381	-.24553	-.25725	-.26897	-.28070	-.29242	-.30414	-.31587	-.32759
.12500	-.20882	-.22045	-.23209	-.24372	-.25535	-.26698	-.27862	-.29025	-.30189	-.31352
.12750	-.19575	-.20729	-.21883	-.23038	-.24192	-.25347	-.26501	-.27656	-.28811	-.29965
.13000	-.18286	-.19432	-.20577	-.21723	-.22868	-.24014	-.25160	-.26306	-.27452	-.28598
.13250	-.17016	-.18153	-.19290	-.20427	-.21564	-.22701	-.23838	-.24976	-.26113	-.27250
.13500	-.15764	-.16892	-.18021	-.19149	-.20278	-.21406	-.22535	-.23664	-.24793	-.25922
.13750	-.14530	-.15650	-.16770	-.17890	-.19010	-.20130	-.21250	-.22371	-.23491	-.24612
.14000	-.13314	-.14425	-.15537	-.16648	-.17760	-.18872	-.19984	-.21096	-.22208	-.23320
.14250	-.12115	-.13218	-.14321	-.15425	-.16528	-.17632	-.18736	-.19839	-.20943	-.22047
.14500	-.10933	-.12028	-.13123	-.14218	-.15314	-.16409	-.17505	-.18600	-.19696	-.20792
.14750	-.09769	-.10855	-.11942	-.13029	-.14116	-.15204	-.16291	-.17379	-.18467	-.19554
.15000	-.08620	-.09699	-.10778	-.11857	-.12936	-.14016	-.15095	-.16175	-.17254	-.18334
.15250	-.07488	-.08559	-.09630	-.10701	-.11772	-.12844	-.13916	-.14987	-.16059	-.17131
.15500	-.06372	-.07435	-.08498	-.09562	-.10625	-.11689	-.12753	-.13816	-.14880	-.15945
.15750	-.05272	-.06327	-.07383	-.08438	-.09494	-.10550	-.11606	-.12662	-.13718	-.14775
.16000	-.04188	-.05235	-.06283	-.07331	-.08379	-.09427	-.10475	-.11524	-.12573	-.13621
.16250	-.03118	-.04158	-.05198	-.06239	-.07279	-.08320	-.09361	-.10402	-.11443	-.12484
.16500	-.02064	-.03097	-.04129	-.05162	-.06195	-.07228	-.08262	-.09295	-.10329	-.11362
.16750	-.01025	-.02050	-.03075	-.04100	-.05126	-.06152	-.07178	-.08204	-.09230	-.10256
.17000	0.00000	-.01018	-.02036	-.03054	-.04072	-.05090	-.06109	-.07128	-.08147	-.09166
.17250	.01010	.00000	-.01011	-.02021	-.03032	-.04044	-.05055	-.06067	-.07078	-.08090
.17500	.02007	.01003	.00000	-.01004	-.02007	-.03012	-.04016	-.05020	-.06024	-.07029
.17750	.02989	.01993	.00997	-.00000	-.00997	-.01994	-.02991	-.03988	-.04985	-.05983
.18000	.03958	.02968	.01979	.00990	0.00000	-.00990	-.01980	-.02970	-.03961	-.04951
.18250	.04913	.03931	.02948	.01966	.00983	.00000	-.00983	-.01966	-.02950	-.03933
.18500	.05854	.04879	.03904	.02928	.01952	.00976	.00000	-.00976	-.01953	-.02930
.18750	.06783	.05815	.04846	.03877	.02908	.01939	.00970	.00000	-.00970	-.01940
.19000	.07699	.06737	.05776	.04814	.03851	.02889	.01926	.00963	.00000	-.00963
.19250	.08602	.07647	.06692	.05737	.04781	.03825	.02869	.01913	.00957	.00000
.19500	.09493	.08545	.07596	.06647	.05698	.04749	.03799	.02850	.01900	.00950
.19750	.10372	.09430	.08488	.07545	.06603	.05660	.04717	.03774	.02831	.01887
.20000	.11238	.10303	.09367	.08431	.07495	.06559	.05622	.04686	.03749	.02812
.20250	.12092	.11163	.10234	.09305	.08375	.07445	.06515	.05585	.04654	.03724
.20500	.12935	.12013	.11090	.10167	.09243	.08320	.07396	.06472	.05548	.04623
.20750	.13766	.12850	.11933	.11017	.10099	.09182	.08265	.07347	.06429	.05511

POINT TABLES: ORIGINAL LOAN TERM: 420 MONTHS LOAN PREPAID IN: 84 MONTHS

CONTRACT RATE

EFFECTIVE YIELD	.19500	.19750	.20000	.20250	.20500	.20750
.07000	-.68939	-.70323	-.71707	-.73091	-.74474	-.75858
.07250	-.67017	-.68389	-.69762	-.71135	-.72507	-.73879
.07500	-.65123	-.66484	-.67846	-.69207	-.70568	-.71929
.07750	-.63256	-.64607	-.65957	-.67307	-.68658	-.70008
.08000	-.61417	-.62757	-.64096	-.65436	-.66775	-.68114
.08250	-.59605	-.60933	-.62262	-.63591	-.64920	-.66248
.08500	-.57819	-.59137	-.60455	-.61773	-.63091	-.64409
.08750	-.56059	-.57367	-.58674	-.59982	-.61290	-.62597
.09000	-.54325	-.55622	-.56919	-.58217	-.59514	-.60811
.09250	-.52615	-.53903	-.55190	-.56477	-.57764	-.59051
.09500	-.50931	-.52208	-.53485	-.54762	-.56039	-.57316
.09750	-.49271	-.50538	-.51805	-.53072	-.54339	-.55605
.10000	-.47635	-.48892	-.50149	-.51406	-.52663	-.53920
.10250	-.46023	-.47270	-.48518	-.49765	-.51012	-.52259
.10500	-.44434	-.45672	-.46909	-.48146	-.49384	-.50621
.10750	-.42868	-.44096	-.45324	-.46552	-.47779	-.49007
.11000	-.41324	-.42543	-.43761	-.44979	-.46198	-.47416
.11250	-.39803	-.41012	-.42221	-.43430	-.44639	-.45848
.11500	-.38303	-.39503	-.40703	-.41902	-.43102	-.44302
.11750	-.36825	-.38016	-.39206	-.40397	-.41587	-.42777
.12000	-.35368	-.36549	-.37731	-.38912	-.40094	-.41275
.12250	-.33932	-.35104	-.36277	-.37449	-.38621	-.39794
.12500	-.32516	-.33679	-.34843	-.36006	-.37170	-.38334
.12750	-.31120	-.32275	-.33430	-.34584	-.35739	-.36894
.13000	-.29744	-.30890	-.32036	-.33182	-.34329	-.35475
.13250	-.28388	-.29525	-.30663	-.31800	-.32938	-.34075
.13500	-.27051	-.28180	-.29309	-.30438	-.31567	-.32696
.13750	-.25732	-.26853	-.27973	-.29094	-.30215	-.31335
.14000	-.24433	-.25545	-.26657	-.27769	-.28882	-.29994
.14250	-.23151	-.24255	-.25359	-.26463	-.27567	-.28672
.14500	-.21888	-.22984	-.24080	-.25175	-.26272	-.27368
.14750	-.20642	-.21730	-.22818	-.23906	-.24994	-.26082
.15000	-.19414	-.20494	-.21574	-.22654	-.23734	-.24814
.15250	-.18203	-.19275	-.20347	-.21419	-.22491	-.23563
.15500	-.17009	-.18073	-.19137	-.20201	-.21266	-.22330
.15750	-.15831	-.16888	-.17944	-.19001	-.20058	-.21114
.16000	-.14670	-.15719	-.16768	-.17817	-.18866	-.19915
.16250	-.13525	-.14566	-.15608	-.16649	-.17691	-.18732
.16500	-.12396	-.13430	-.14464	-.15498	-.16532	-.17566
.16750	-.11283	-.12309	-.13336	-.14362	-.15389	-.16416
.17000	-.10185	-.11204	-.12223	-.13242	-.14262	-.15281
.17250	-.09102	-.10114	-.11126	-.12138	-.13150	-.14162
.17500	-.08034	-.09039	-.10043	-.11048	-.12053	-.13058
.17750	-.06980	-.07978	-.08976	-.09974	-.10972	-.11970
.18000	-.05942	-.06932	-.07923	-.08914	-.09905	-.10896
.18250	-.04917	-.05901	-.06885	-.07869	-.08853	-.09837
.18500	-.03906	-.04883	-.05860	-.06838	-.07815	-.08792
.18750	-.02910	-.03880	-.04850	-.05820	-.06791	-.07761
.19000	-.01926	-.02890	-.03853	-.04817	-.05781	-.06745
.19250	-.00957	-.01913	-.02870	-.03827	-.04784	-.05741
.19500	.00000	-.00950	-.01901	-.02851	-.03801	-.04752
.19750	.00944	.00000	-.00944	-.01888	-.02832	-.03776
.20000	.01875	.00937	.00000	-.00937	-.01875	-.02813
.20250	.02793	.01862	.00931	0.00000	-.00931	-.01862
.20500	.03699	.02774	.01850	.00925	-.00000	-.00925
.20750	.04593	.03674	.02756	.01837	.00919	.00000

POINT TABLES: ORIGINAL LOAN TERM: 420 MONTHS LOAN PREPAID IN: 108 MONTHS

EFFECTIVE YIELD	CONTRACT RATE .07000	.07250	.07500	.07750	.08000	.08250	.08500	.08750	.09000	.09250
.07000	.00000	-.01614	-.03234	-.04858	-.06487	-.08121	-.09758	-.11399	-.13043	-.14691
.07250	.01596	.00000	-.01601	-.03207	-.04817	-.06432	-.08051	-.09673	-.11299	-.12928
.07500	.03160	.01582	.00000	-.01587	-.03180	-.04776	-.06377	-.07981	-.09589	-.11200
.07750	.04693	.03134	.01569	.00000	-.01574	-.03153	-.04735	-.06322	-.07912	-.09505
.08000	.06196	.04655	.03108	.01556	.00000	-.01561	-.03126	-.04695	-.06267	-.07843
.08250	.07670	.06146	.04617	.03083	.01544	.00000	-.01548	-.03099	-.04655	-.06213
.08500	.09114	.07608	.06096	.04579	.03057	.01531	.00000	-.01535	-.03073	-.04615
.08750	.10531	.09041	.07546	.06046	.04541	.03032	.01518	.00000	-.01522	-.03046
.09000	.11919	.10447	.08969	.07485	.05997	.04504	.03006	.01505	.00000	-.01509
.09250	.13281	.11825	.10363	.08896	.07424	.05947	.04466	.02981	.01492	.00000
.09500	.14616	.13176	.11730	.10279	.08824	.07363	.05898	.04429	.02956	.01480
.09750	.15925	.14501	.13071	.11636	.10196	.08751	.07302	.05849	.04392	.02931
.10000	.17209	.15801	.14386	.12967	.11542	.10113	.08680	.07242	.05830	.04355
.10250	.18468	.17075	.15676	.14272	.12863	.11449	.10031	.08608	.07182	.05752
.10500	.19702	.18324	.16941	.15552	.14158	.12759	.11356	.09948	.08537	.07122
.10750	.20913	.19550	.18181	.16807	.15428	.14044	.12656	.11263	.09867	.08466
.11000	.22100	.20752	.19398	.18039	.16674	.15305	.13931	.12553	.11171	.09785
.11250	.23265	.21931	.20591	.19246	.17896	.16541	.15182	.13818	.12450	.11079
.11500	.24406	.23087	.21762	.20431	.19095	.17754	.16409	.15059	.13706	.12349
.11750	.25526	.24221	.22910	.21593	.20271	.18944	.17613	.16277	.14938	.13594
.12000	.26625	.25333	.24036	.22733	.21425	.20112	.18794	.17472	.16146	.14817
.12250	.27702	.26424	.25141	.23851	.22557	.21257	.19953	.18645	.17332	.16016
.12500	.28759	.27495	.26224	.24948	.23667	.22381	.21090	.19795	.18496	.17193
.12750	.29796	.28545	.27287	.26024	.24756	.23483	.22206	.20924	.19638	.18348
.13000	.30813	.29575	.28330	.27080	.25825	.24565	.23301	.22031	.20758	.19481
.13250	.31811	.30585	.29353	.28116	.26874	.25627	.24375	.23118	.21858	.20594
.13500	.32789	.31576	.30357	.29133	.27903	.26668	.25429	.24185	.22937	.21685
.13750	.33750	.32549	.31342	.30130	.28913	.27690	.26463	.25232	.23996	.22757
.14000	.34692	.33503	.32309	.31109	.29904	.28693	.27479	.26259	.25036	.23808
.14250	.35616	.34439	.33257	.32069	.30876	.29678	.28475	.27268	.26056	.24841
.14500	.36523	.35358	.34187	.33011	.31830	.30644	.29453	.28257	.27057	.25854
.14750	.37412	.36259	.35101	.33936	.32766	.31592	.30412	.29228	.28040	.26848
.15000	.38286	.37144	.35997	.34844	.33685	.32522	.31354	.30182	.29005	.27825
.15250	.39142	.38012	.36876	.35734	.34587	.33435	.32279	.31118	.29952	.28783
.15500	.39983	.38864	.37739	.36608	.35473	.34332	.33186	.32036	.30882	.29724
.15750	.40808	.39700	.38586	.37466	.36342	.35212	.34077	.32938	.31795	.30648
.16000	.41617	.40520	.39417	.38308	.37194	.36075	.34952	.33824	.32691	.31555
.16250	.42412	.41325	.40233	.39135	.38032	.36923	.35810	.34693	.33571	.32445
.16500	.43192	.42116	.41034	.39946	.38853	.37756	.36653	.35546	.34435	.33320
.16750	.43957	.42891	.41820	.40743	.39660	.38573	.37481	.36384	.35283	.34178
.17000	.44708	.43653	.42591	.41524	.40452	.39375	.38293	.37207	.36116	.35021
.17250	.45446	.44400	.43349	.42292	.41230	.40163	.39091	.38014	.36934	.35849
.17500	.46169	.45134	.44092	.43045	.41993	.40936	.39874	.38807	.37737	.36662
.17750	.46880	.45854	.44822	.43785	.42743	.41695	.40643	.39586	.38525	.37460
.18000	.47577	.46561	.45539	.44511	.43479	.42441	.41398	.40351	.39300	.38244
.18250	.48262	.47255	.46243	.45225	.44201	.43173	.42140	.41102	.40060	.39014
.18500	.48934	.47937	.46934	.45925	.44911	.43892	.42868	.41840	.40807	.39771
.18750	.49594	.48606	.47612	.46612	.45608	.44598	.43583	.42564	.41541	.40514
.19000	.50242	.49263	.48278	.47287	.46292	.45291	.44286	.43276	.42262	.41244
.19250	.50878	.49908	.48932	.47950	.46964	.45972	.44976	.43975	.42970	.41960
.19500	.51503	.50541	.49574	.48602	.47624	.46641	.45653	.44661	.43665	.42665
.19750	.52116	.51163	.50205	.49241	.48272	.47298	.46319	.45336	.44348	.43356
.20000	.52718	.51774	.50824	.49869	.48908	.47943	.46973	.45998	.45019	.44036
.20250	.53310	.52374	.51433	.50486	.49534	.48577	.47615	.46649	.45678	.44704
.20500	.53891	.52963	.52030	.51092	.50148	.49199	.48246	.47288	.46326	.45360
.20750	.54461	.53542	.52617	.51687	.50751	.49811	.48866	.47916	.46962	.46005

POINT TABLES: ORIGINAL LOAN TERM: 420 MONTHS LOAN PREPAID IN: 108 MONTHS

EFFECTIVE YIELD	CONTRACT RATE .09500	.09750	.10000	.10250	.10500	.10750	.11000	.11250	.11500	.11750
.07000	-.16341	-.17994	-.19650	-.21308	-.22968	-.24629	-.26293	-.27957	-.29624	-.31291
.07250	-.14561	-.16195	-.17833	-.19472	-.21114	-.22758	-.24403	-.26050	-.27698	-.29348
.07500	-.12814	-.14431	-.16051	-.17672	-.19296	-.20922	-.22550	-.24179	-.25810	-.27441
.07750	-.11102	-.12701	-.14303	-.15907	-.17513	-.19122	-.20732	-.22343	-.23957	-.25571
.08000	-.09422	-.11004	-.12588	-.14175	-.15764	-.17355	-.18948	-.20543	-.22139	-.23736
.08250	-.07775	-.09340	-.10907	-.12477	-.14049	-.15623	-.17199	-.18776	-.20356	-.21936
.08500	-.06159	-.07707	-.09258	-.10810	-.12366	-.13923	-.15482	-.17043	-.18606	-.20170
.08750	-.04575	-.06106	-.07640	-.09176	-.10715	-.12256	-.13798	-.15343	-.16889	-.18437
.09000	-.03020	-.04535	-.06053	-.07573	-.09095	-.10620	-.12146	-.13675	-.15205	-.16737
.09250	-.01496	-.02994	-.04496	-.06000	-.07506	-.09015	-.10525	-.12038	-.13552	-.15068
.09500	.00000	-.01483	-.02968	-.04457	-.05947	-.07440	-.08935	-.10432	-.11931	-.13431
.09750	.01467	.00000	-.01470	-.02943	-.04418	-.05895	-.07375	-.08856	-.10339	-.11824
.10000	.02906	.01455	.00000	-.01457	-.02917	-.04379	-.05844	-.07310	-.08778	-.10247
.10250	.04318	.02882	.01442	.00000	-.01445	-.02892	-.04341	-.05792	-.07245	-.08700
.10500	.05704	.04282	.02857	.01430	0.00000	-.01432	-.02867	-.04303	-.05742	-.07182
.10750	.07063	.05656	.04246	.02833	.01418	.00000	-.01420	-.02842	-.04266	-.05691
.11000	.08396	.07003	.05608	.04210	.02809	.01406	.00000	-.01408	-.02817	-.04228
.11250	.09704	.08326	.06945	.05561	.04174	.02785	.01393	.00000	-.01395	-.02793
.11500	.10988	.09624	.08256	.06886	.05514	.04139	.02761	.01382	0.00000	-.01383
.11750	.12247	.10897	.09544	.08187	.06829	.05467	.04103	.02738	.01370	.00000
.12000	.13483	.12147	.10807	.09464	.08119	.06771	.05421	.04068	.02714	.01358
.12250	.14696	.13373	.12047	.10717	.09385	.08051	.06714	.05375	.04034	.02691
.12500	.15886	.14576	.13263	.11947	.10628	.09307	.07983	.06657	.05329	.04000
.12750	.17054	.15757	.14457	.13154	.11848	.10540	.09229	.07916	.06601	.05284
.13000	.18201	.16917	.15629	.14339	.13046	.11750	.10452	.09152	.07850	.06546
.13250	.19326	.18054	.16780	.15502	.14222	.12939	.11653	.10365	.09076	.07784
.13500	.20430	.19171	.17909	.16644	.15376	.14105	.12832	.11557	.10279	.09000
.13750	.21514	.20267	.19017	.17764	.16508	.15250	.13989	.12726	.11461	.10194
.14000	.22577	.21343	.20105	.18864	.17621	.16374	.15126	.13874	.12621	.11366
.14250	.23622	.22399	.21173	.19944	.18712	.17478	.16241	.15002	.13760	.12517
.14500	.24646	.23436	.22222	.21004	.19784	.18562	.17337	.16109	.14879	.13647
.14750	.25653	.24453	.23251	.22045	.20837	.19626	.18412	.17196	.15978	.14758
.15000	.26640	.25453	.24262	.23067	.21870	.20671	.19468	.18264	.17057	.15848
.15250	.27610	.26434	.25254	.24071	.22885	.21696	.20505	.19312	.18116	.16918
.15500	.28562	.27397	.26228	.25056	.23881	.22704	.21524	.20341	.19157	.17970
.15750	.29497	.28342	.27185	.26024	.24860	.23693	.22524	.21353	.20179	.19003
.16000	.30415	.29271	.28124	.26974	.25821	.24665	.23506	.22346	.21183	.20017
.16250	.31316	.30183	.29046	.27907	.26764	.25619	.24471	.23321	.22169	.21014
.16500	.32201	.31078	.29952	.28823	.27691	.26556	.25419	.24279	.23137	.21993
.16750	.33069	.31957	.30842	.29723	.28601	.27477	.26350	.25220	.24088	.22954
.17000	.33923	.32821	.31715	.30607	.29495	.28381	.27264	.26145	.25023	.23899
.17250	.34761	.33669	.32573	.31475	.30373	.29269	.28162	.27053	.25941	.24827
.17500	.35583	.34501	.33416	.32327	.31236	.30141	.29044	.27945	.26843	.25739
.17750	.36392	.35319	.34244	.33165	.32083	.30998	.29911	.28821	.27729	.26635
.18000	.37185	.36123	.35056	.33987	.32915	.31840	.30762	.29682	.28600	.27515
.18250	.37965	.36912	.35855	.34795	.33733	.32667	.31599	.30528	.29455	.28380
.18500	.38731	.37687	.36640	.35589	.34536	.33480	.32421	.31359	.30296	.29230
.18750	.39483	.38448	.37410	.36369	.35325	.34278	.33228	.32176	.31122	.30065
.19000	.40222	.39196	.38167	.37135	.36100	.35062	.34022	.32979	.31934	.30886
.19250	.40948	.39931	.38911	.37888	.36862	.35833	.34802	.33768	.32731	.31693
.19500	.41661	.40653	.39642	.38628	.37610	.36590	.35568	.34543	.33515	.32485
.19750	.42361	.41362	.40360	.39354	.38346	.37335	.36321	.35304	.34286	.33265
.20000	.43049	.42059	.41065	.40069	.39069	.38066	.37061	.36053	.35043	.34030
.20250	.43726	.42744	.41759	.40770	.39779	.38785	.37788	.36789	.35787	.34783
.20500	.44390	.43417	.42440	.41460	.40477	.39491	.38503	.37512	.36519	.35523
.20750	.45043	.44078	.43109	.42138	.41163	.40186	.39205	.38223	.37238	.36250

POINT TABLES: ORIGINAL LOAN TERM: 420 MONTHS LOAN PREPAID IN: 108 MONTHS

EFFECTIVE YIELD	CONTRACT RATE .12000	.12250	.12500	.12750	.13000	.13250	.13500	.13750	.14000	.14250
.07000	-.32960	-.34629	-.36299	-.37970	-.39642	-.41314	-.42987	-.44660	-.46334	-.48007
.07250	-.30998	-.32650	-.34303	-.35956	-.37610	-.39265	-.40920	-.42575	-.44231	-.45888
.07500	-.29075	-.30709	-.32344	-.33980	-.35616	-.37253	-.38891	-.40529	-.42168	-.43807
.07750	-.27187	-.28804	-.30422	-.32040	-.33660	-.35280	-.36901	-.38522	-.40143	-.41765
.08000	-.25335	-.26935	-.28536	-.30138	-.31740	-.33343	-.34947	-.36552	-.38156	-.39762
.08250	-.23518	-.25101	-.26685	-.28270	-.29856	-.31443	-.33030	-.34618	-.36206	-.37795
.08500	-.21735	-.23302	-.24870	-.26438	-.28008	-.29578	-.31149	-.32720	-.34293	-.35865
.08750	-.19986	-.21536	-.23088	-.24640	-.26194	-.27748	-.29303	-.30858	-.32414	-.33971
.09000	-.18270	-.19804	-.21339	-.22876	-.24413	-.25952	-.27491	-.29030	-.30570	-.32111
.09250	-.16585	-.18104	-.19624	-.21144	-.22666	-.24189	-.25712	-.27236	-.28761	-.30286
.09500	-.14933	-.16435	-.17940	-.19445	-.20951	-.22458	-.23966	-.25475	-.26984	-.28494
.09750	-.13310	-.14798	-.16287	-.17777	-.19268	-.20760	-.22253	-.23746	-.25240	-.26735
.10000	-.11719	-.13191	-.14665	-.16140	-.17616	-.19093	-.20571	-.22049	-.23529	-.25008
.10250	-.10156	-.11614	-.13073	-.14533	-.15995	-.17457	-.18920	-.20384	-.21848	-.23313
.10500	-.08623	-.10066	-.11511	-.12956	-.14403	-.15850	-.17299	-.18748	-.20198	-.21649
.10750	-.07118	-.08547	-.09977	-.11408	-.12840	-.14274	-.15708	-.17143	-.18579	-.20015
.11000	-.05641	-.07056	-.08471	-.09888	-.11307	-.12726	-.14146	-.15567	-.16988	-.18411
.11250	-.04191	-.05592	-.06994	-.08397	-.09801	-.11206	-.12612	-.14019	-.15427	-.16836
.11500	-.02768	-.04155	-.05543	-.06932	-.08322	-.09714	-.11106	-.12500	-.13894	-.15289
.11750	-.01371	-.02744	-.04119	-.05494	-.06871	-.08249	-.09628	-.11008	-.12339	-.13770
.12000	.00000	-.01359	-.02720	-.04083	-.05446	-.06811	-.08177	-.09543	-.10911	-.12279
.12250	.01346	.00000	-.01348	-.02697	-.04047	-.05399	-.06751	-.08105	-.09459	-.10814
.12500	.02668	.01335	.00000	-.01336	-.02673	-.04012	-.05352	-.06692	-.08034	-.09376
.12750	.03966	.02645	.01323	.00000	-.01325	-.02650	-.03977	-.05305	-.06634	-.07963
.13000	.05240	.03932	.02623	.01312	0.00000	-.01313	-.02627	-.03943	-.05259	-.06576
.13250	.06490	.05195	.03898	.02600	.01301	.00000	-.01302	-.02605	-.03908	-.05213
.13500	.07719	.06436	.05151	.03865	.02578	.01290	0.00000	-.01291	-.02582	-.03875
.13750	.08925	.07654	.06382	.05108	.03833	.02556	.01279	.00000	-.01280	-.02560
.14000	.10109	.08850	.07590	.06328	.05065	.03800	.02534	.01268	0.00000	-.01269
.14250	.11272	.10025	.08776	.07526	.06275	.05022	.03768	.02513	.01257	.00000
.14500	.12414	.11178	.09941	.08703	.07463	.06222	.04980	.03736	.02492	.01246
.14750	.13535	.12312	.11086	.09859	.08630	.07401	.06170	.04938	.03705	.02471
.15000	.14637	.13424	.12210	.10994	.09777	.08559	.07339	.06118	.04896	.03673
.15250	.15719	.14517	.13314	.12110	.10904	.09696	.08487	.07278	.06067	.04855
.15500	.16781	.15591	.14399	.13205	.12010	.10814	.09616	.08417	.07217	.06016
.15750	.17825	.16646	.15464	.14281	.13097	.11911	.10724	.09536	.08347	.07157
.16000	.18850	.17681	.16511	.15339	.14165	.12990	.11814	.10636	.09458	.08278
.16250	.19857	.18699	.17539	.16377	.15214	.14050	.12884	.11717	.10549	.09380
.16500	.20847	.19699	.18549	.17398	.16245	.15091	.13935	.12779	.11621	.10462
.16750	.21819	.20681	.19541	.18400	.17258	.16114	.14969	.13822	.12675	.11526
.17000	.22773	.21646	.20516	.19386	.18253	.17119	.15984	.14848	.13710	.12572
.17250	.23712	.22594	.21475	.20354	.19231	.18107	.16982	.15856	.14728	.13600
.17500	.24633	.23525	.22416	.21305	.20192	.19078	.17963	.16846	.15728	.14609
.17750	.25539	.24441	.23341	.22239	.21136	.20032	.18926	.17819	.16711	.15602
.18000	.26429	.25340	.24250	.23158	.22065	.20970	.19874	.18776	.17678	.16578
.18250	.27303	.26224	.25143	.24061	.22977	.21891	.20805	.19717	.18627	.17537
.18500	.28162	.27093	.26021	.24948	.23873	.22797	.21720	.20641	.19561	.18480
.18750	.29007	.27946	.26884	.25820	.24754	.23687	.22619	.21550	.20479	.19407
.19000	.29837	.28785	.27732	.26677	.25620	.24563	.23503	.22443	.21381	.20318
.19250	.30652	.29610	.28565	.27519	.26472	.25423	.24373	.23321	.22268	.21214
.19500	.31454	.30420	.29385	.28347	.27309	.26269	.25227	.24184	.23140	.22095
.19750	.32242	.31217	.30190	.29161	.28131	.27100	.26067	.25033	.23998	.22961
.20000	.33016	.32000	.30981	.29962	.28940	.27917	.26893	.25868	.24841	.23813
.20250	.33777	.32769	.31760	.30748	.29735	.28721	.27705	.26688	.25670	.24651
.20500	.34526	.33526	.32525	.31522	.30517	.29511	.28504	.27495	.26485	.25474
.20750	.35261	.34270	.33277	.32282	.31286	.30288	.29289	.28289	.27287	.26284

POINT TABLES: ORIGINAL LOAN TERM: 420 MONTHS LOAN PREPAID IN: 108 MONTHS

EFFECTIVE YIELD	CONTRACT RATE .14500	.14750	.15000	.15250	.15500	.15750	.16000	.16250	.16500	.16750
.07000	-.49681	-.51355	-.53030	-.54704	-.56378	-.58053	-.59727	-.61401	-.63075	-.64749
.07250	-.47544	-.49201	-.50857	-.52514	-.54171	-.55828	-.57485	-.59142	-.60799	-.62456
.07500	-.45446	-.47086	-.48725	-.50365	-.52005	-.53645	-.55285	-.56925	-.58565	-.60205
.07750	-.43388	-.45010	-.46633	-.48256	-.49879	-.51502	-.53125	-.54748	-.56371	-.57994
.08000	-.41367	-.42973	-.44579	-.46186	-.47792	-.49398	-.51005	-.52612	-.54218	-.55825
.08250	-.39384	-.40974	-.42563	-.44153	-.45743	-.47334	-.48924	-.50514	-.52104	-.53695
.08500	-.37438	-.39011	-.40585	-.42158	-.43732	-.45306	-.46881	-.48455	-.50029	-.51604
.08750	-.35527	-.37085	-.38642	-.40200	-.41758	-.43316	-.44875	-.46433	-.47992	-.49550
.09000	-.33652	-.35194	-.36736	-.38278	-.39820	-.41363	-.42906	-.44448	-.45991	-.47534
.09250	-.31811	-.33337	-.34864	-.36391	-.37918	-.39445	-.40972	-.42500	-.44027	-.45555
.09500	-.30004	-.31515	-.33026	-.34538	-.36050	-.37562	-.39074	-.40586	-.42099	-.43611
.09750	-.28230	-.29726	-.31222	-.32719	-.34215	-.35713	-.37210	-.38707	-.40205	-.41702
.10000	-.26489	-.27970	-.29451	-.30933	-.32415	-.33897	-.35379	-.36862	-.38345	-.39828
.10250	-.24779	-.26245	-.27712	-.29179	-.30647	-.32114	-.33582	-.35050	-.36519	-.37987
.10500	-.23100	-.24552	-.26005	-.27457	-.28910	-.30364	-.31817	-.33271	-.34725	-.36180
.10750	-.21452	-.22890	-.24328	-.25767	-.27205	-.28645	-.30084	-.31524	-.32964	-.34404
.11000	-.19834	-.21258	-.22682	-.24106	-.25531	-.26957	-.28382	-.29808	-.31234	-.32661
.11250	-.18245	-.19655	-.21065	-.22476	-.23887	-.25299	-.26711	-.28123	-.29535	-.30948
.11500	-.16685	-.18081	-.19478	-.20875	-.22272	-.23670	-.25069	-.26468	-.27866	-.29266
.11750	-.15152	-.16535	-.17919	-.19302	-.20687	-.22071	-.23456	-.24842	-.26227	-.27613
.12000	-.13648	-.15017	-.16387	-.17758	-.19129	-.20501	-.21873	-.23245	-.24617	-.25990
.12250	-.12170	-.13527	-.14884	-.16241	-.17599	-.18958	-.20317	-.21676	-.23036	-.24395
.12500	-.10719	-.12062	-.13407	-.14751	-.16097	-.17443	-.18789	-.20135	-.21482	-.22829
.12750	-.09293	-.10624	-.11956	-.13288	-.14621	-.15954	-.17287	-.18621	-.19956	-.21290
.13000	-.07894	-.09212	-.10531	-.11851	-.13171	-.14492	-.15813	-.17134	-.18456	-.19778
.13250	-.06519	-.07825	-.09131	-.10439	-.11747	-.13055	-.14364	-.15673	-.16983	-.18293
.13500	-.05168	-.06462	-.07757	-.09052	-.10348	-.11644	-.12941	-.14238	-.15535	-.16833
.13750	-.03841	-.05123	-.06406	-.07689	-.08973	-.10257	-.11542	-.12827	-.14113	-.15399
.14000	-.02538	-.03808	-.05079	-.06351	-.07623	-.08895	-.10168	-.11442	-.12716	-.13990
.14250	-.01258	-.02516	-.03775	-.05035	-.06296	-.07557	-.08818	-.10080	-.11342	-.12605
.14500	.00000	-.01247	-.02495	-.03743	-.04992	-.06242	-.07492	-.08742	-.09993	-.11244
.14750	.01236	.00000	-.01236	-.02473	-.03711	-.04949	-.06188	-.07427	-.08667	-.09907
.15000	.02450	.01225	.00000	-.01226	-.02452	-.03679	-.04907	-.06135	-.07364	-.08592
.15250	.03643	.02429	.01215	.00000	-.01216	-.02432	-.03648	-.04865	-.06083	-.07301
.15500	.04815	.03612	.02409	.01205	.00000	-.01205	-.02411	-.03617	-.04824	-.06031
.15750	.05966	.04774	.03582	.02388	.01195	0.00000	-.01195	-.02391	-.03587	-.04783
.16000	.07098	.05917	.04735	.03552	.02369	.01185	.00000	-.01185	-.02371	-.03556
.16250	.08210	.07039	.05868	.04695	.03522	.02349	.01175	.00000	-.01175	-.02351
.16500	.09303	.08142	.06981	.05819	.04656	.03493	.02329	.01165	.00000	-.01165
.16750	.10377	.09227	.08075	.06924	.05771	.04618	.03464	.02310	.01155	.00000
.17000	.11432	.10292	.09151	.08009	.06867	.05724	.04580	.03436	.02291	.01146
.17250	.12470	.11340	.10208	.09076	.07944	.06810	.05677	.04542	.03407	.02272
.17500	.13490	.12369	.11248	.10125	.09003	.07879	.06755	.05630	.04505	.03379
.17750	.14492	.13381	.12269	.11157	.10043	.08929	.07815	.06700	.05584	.04468
.18000	.15477	.14376	.13274	.12171	.11067	.09962	.08857	.07752	.06645	.05539
.18250	.16446	.15354	.14261	.13167	.12073	.10978	.09882	.08786	.07689	.06592
.18500	.17398	.16315	.15232	.14147	.13062	.11976	.10890	.09803	.08715	.07627
.18750	.18334	.17261	.16186	.15111	.14035	.12958	.11880	.10803	.09724	.08645
.19000	.19255	.18190	.17124	.16058	.14991	.13923	.12855	.11786	.10716	.09646
.19250	.20160	.19104	.18047	.16990	.15931	.14873	.13813	.12753	.11692	.10631
.19500	.21049	.20002	.18954	.17906	.16856	.15806	.14755	.13704	.12652	.11600
.19750	.21924	.20886	.19847	.18807	.17766	.16724	.15682	.14639	.13596	.12552
.20000	.22784	.21755	.20724	.19692	.18660	.17627	.16594	.15560	.14525	.13490
.20250	.23630	.22609	.21587	.20564	.19540	.18515	.17490	.16465	.15438	.14411
.20500	.24462	.23449	.22435	.21421	.20405	.19389	.18372	.17355	.16337	.15318
.20750	.25280	.24276	.23270	.22263	.21256	.20248	.19240	.18230	.17221	.16210

POINT TABLES: ORIGINAL LOAN TERM: 420 MONTHS LOAN PREPAID IN: 108 MONTHS

EFFECTIVE YIELD	CONTRACT RATE .17000	.17250	.17500	.17750	.18000	.18250	.18500	.18750	.19000	.19250
.07000	-.66423	-.68097	-.69770	-.71444	-.73117	-.74790	-.76463	-.78136	-.79808	-.81480
.07250	-.64112	-.65769	-.67425	-.69082	-.70738	-.72394	-.74050	-.75705	-.77361	-.79016
.07500	-.61844	-.63484	-.65123	-.66763	-.68402	-.70041	-.71680	-.73319	-.74958	-.76596
.07750	-.59618	-.61240	-.62863	-.64486	-.66109	-.67731	-.69354	-.70976	-.72598	-.74220
.08000	-.57431	-.59038	-.60644	-.62251	-.63857	-.65463	-.67069	-.68675	-.70281	-.71886
.08250	-.55285	-.56875	-.58466	-.60056	-.61646	-.63236	-.64826	-.66416	-.68005	-.69595
.08500	-.53178	-.54752	-.56327	-.57901	-.59475	-.61049	-.62623	-.64197	-.65771	-.67344
.08750	-.51109	-.52668	-.54226	-.55785	-.57343	-.58902	-.60460	-.62018	-.63576	-.65134
.09000	-.49077	-.50620	-.52164	-.53707	-.55250	-.56793	-.58335	-.59878	-.61421	-.62964
.09250	-.47083	-.48610	-.50138	-.51666	-.53194	-.54721	-.56249	-.57777	-.59304	-.60832
.09500	-.45124	-.46636	-.48149	-.49662	-.51175	-.52687	-.54200	-.55713	-.57225	-.58738
.09750	-.43200	-.44698	-.46196	-.47694	-.49192	-.50690	-.52188	-.53685	-.55183	-.56681
.10000	-.41311	-.42794	-.44278	-.45761	-.47244	-.48727	-.50211	-.51694	-.53177	-.54661
.10250	-.39456	-.40925	-.42394	-.43862	-.45331	-.46800	-.48269	-.49738	-.51207	-.52676
.10500	-.37634	-.39089	-.40543	-.41998	-.43452	-.44907	-.46362	-.47817	-.49271	-.50726
.10750	-.35845	-.37285	-.38726	-.40166	-.41607	-.43048	-.44488	-.45929	-.47370	-.48811
.11000	-.34087	-.35514	-.36940	-.38367	-.39794	-.41221	-.42648	-.44075	-.45502	-.46929
.11250	-.32361	-.33774	-.35187	-.36600	-.38013	-.39427	-.40840	-.42253	-.43667	-.45080
.11500	-.30665	-.32064	-.33464	-.34864	-.36264	-.37664	-.39064	-.40464	-.41864	-.43264
.11750	-.28999	-.30385	-.31772	-.33158	-.34545	-.35932	-.37319	-.38705	-.40092	-.41479
.12000	-.27363	-.28736	-.30109	-.31483	-.32857	-.34230	-.35604	-.36978	-.38352	-.39726
.12250	-.25756	-.27116	-.28476	-.29837	-.31198	-.32558	-.33919	-.35280	-.36641	-.38002
.12500	-.24176	-.25524	-.26872	-.28219	-.29568	-.30916	-.32264	-.33612	-.34961	-.36309
.12750	-.22625	-.23960	-.25295	-.26630	-.27966	-.29302	-.30637	-.31973	-.33309	-.34645
.13000	-.21101	-.22423	-.23746	-.25069	-.26392	-.27715	-.29039	-.30362	-.31686	-.33010
.13250	-.19603	-.20913	-.22224	-.23535	-.24846	-.26157	-.27468	-.28779	-.30091	-.31403
.13500	-.18131	-.19430	-.20728	-.22027	-.23326	-.24625	-.25924	-.27224	-.28523	-.29823
.13750	-.16685	-.17972	-.19258	-.20545	-.21833	-.23120	-.24407	-.25695	-.26983	-.28270
.14000	-.15264	-.16539	-.17814	-.19089	-.20365	-.21640	-.22916	-.24192	-.25468	-.26744
.14250	-.13868	-.15131	-.16395	-.17658	-.18922	-.20186	-.21451	-.22715	-.23980	-.25244
.14500	-.12496	-.13748	-.15000	-.16252	-.17505	-.18757	-.20010	-.21263	-.22516	-.23770
.14750	-.11147	-.12388	-.13629	-.14870	-.16111	-.17353	-.18594	-.19836	-.21078	-.22320
.15000	-.09822	-.11051	-.12281	-.13511	-.14741	-.15972	-.17202	-.18433	-.19664	-.20895
.15250	-.08519	-.09737	-.10956	-.12175	-.13395	-.14614	-.15834	-.17054	-.18274	-.19494
.15500	-.07238	-.08446	-.09654	-.10863	-.12071	-.13280	-.14489	-.15698	-.16908	-.18117
.15750	-.05980	-.07177	-.08374	-.09572	-.10770	-.11968	-.13167	-.14365	-.15564	-.16763
.16000	-.04743	-.05929	-.07116	-.08303	-.09491	-.10679	-.11867	-.13055	-.14243	-.15431
.16250	-.03527	-.04703	-.05879	-.07056	-.08233	-.09411	-.10588	-.11766	-.12944	-.14122
.16500	-.02331	-.03497	-.04663	-.05830	-.06997	-.08164	-.09331	-.10499	-.11667	-.12835
.16750	-.01156	-.02312	-.03468	-.04624	-.05781	-.06938	-.08096	-.09253	-.10411	-.11569
.17000	-.00000	-.01146	-.02292	-.03439	-.04586	-.05733	-.06880	-.08028	-.09176	-.10324
.17250	.01136	.00000	-.01136	-.02273	-.03410	-.04548	-.05685	-.06823	-.07961	-.09099
.17500	.02253	.01127	.00000	-.01127	-.02255	-.03382	-.04510	-.05638	-.06767	-.07895
.17750	.03352	.02235	.01118	-.00000	-.01118	-.02236	-.03354	-.04473	-.05592	-.06711
.18000	.04432	.03324	.02217	.01108	.00000	-.01109	-.02218	-.03327	-.04436	-.05546
.18250	.05494	.04396	.03297	.02199	.01099	.00000	-.01100	-.02200	-.03300	-.04400
.18500	.06538	.05450	.04360	.03271	.02181	.01090	.00000	-.01091	-.02182	-.03273
.18750	.07566	.06486	.05406	.04325	.03244	.02163	.01082	.00000	-.01082	-.02164
.19000	.08576	.07505	.06434	.05362	.04290	.03218	.02146	.01073	.00000	-.01073
.19250	.09570	.08508	.07445	.06382	.05319	.04256	.03192	.02128	.01064	.00000
.19500	.10547	.09494	.08440	.07386	.06332	.05277	.04222	.03167	.02111	.01056
.19750	.11508	.10464	.09419	.08373	.07327	.06281	.05235	.04188	.03142	.02095
.20000	.12454	.11418	.10381	.09344	.08307	.07269	.06232	.05194	.04155	.03117
.20250	.13384	.12356	.11328	.10300	.09271	.08242	.07212	.06183	.05153	.04122
.20500	.14299	.13280	.12260	.11240	.10219	.09198	.08177	.07156	.06134	.05112
.20750	.15200	.14188	.13177	.12165	.11152	.10140	.09127	.08113	.07100	.06086

EFFECTIVE YIELD	CONTRACT RATE .19500	.19750	.20000	.20250	.20500	.20750
.07000	-.83153	-.84824	-.86496	-.88168	-.89839	-.91510
.07250	-.80671	-.82326	-.83981	-.85635	-.87289	-.88944
.07500	-.78234	-.79872	-.81510	-.83148	-.84786	-.86423
.07750	-.75842	-.77463	-.79085	-.80706	-.82327	-.83948
.08000	-.73492	-.75097	-.76702	-.78307	-.79912	-.81517
.08250	-.71184	-.72773	-.74363	-.75952	-.77540	-.79129
.08500	-.68918	-.70491	-.72065	-.73638	-.75211	-.76784
.08750	-.66692	-.68250	-.69808	-.71365	-.72923	-.74480
.09000	-.64506	-.66049	-.67591	-.69133	-.70675	-.72217
.09250	-.62359	-.63886	-.65414	-.66941	-.68468	-.69995
.09500	-.60250	-.61763	-.63275	-.64787	-.66299	-.67811
.09750	-.58179	-.59676	-.61174	-.62671	-.64169	-.65666
.10000	-.56144	-.57627	-.59110	-.60593	-.62076	-.63559
.10250	-.54145	-.55613	-.57082	-.58551	-.60019	-.61488
.10500	-.52181	-.53636	-.55090	-.56545	-.57999	-.59454
.10750	-.50252	-.51692	-.53133	-.54574	-.56014	-.57455
.11000	-.48356	-.49783	-.51210	-.52637	-.54064	-.55491
.11250	-.46494	-.47907	-.49321	-.50734	-.52148	-.53561
.11500	-.44664	-.46064	-.47464	-.48864	-.50265	-.51665
.11750	-.42866	-.44253	-.45640	-.47027	-.48414	-.49801
.12000	-.41100	-.42474	-.43848	-.45222	-.46595	-.47969
.12250	-.39364	-.40725	-.42086	-.43447	-.44808	-.46169
.12500	-.37658	-.39006	-.40355	-.41703	-.43052	-.44400
.12750	-.35981	-.37317	-.38653	-.39989	-.41326	-.42662
.13000	-.34333	-.35657	-.36981	-.38305	-.39629	-.40953
.13250	-.32714	-.34026	-.35338	-.36649	-.37961	-.39273
.13500	-.31123	-.32422	-.33722	-.35022	-.36322	-.37622
.13750	-.29558	-.30846	-.32134	-.33422	-.34710	-.35998
.14000	-.28021	-.29297	-.30573	-.31850	-.33126	-.34402
.14250	-.26509	-.27774	-.29039	-.30304	-.31569	-.32834
.14500	-.25023	-.26277	-.27530	-.28784	-.30038	-.31291
.14750	-.23563	-.24805	-.26047	-.27290	-.28532	-.29775
.15000	-.22127	-.23358	-.24589	-.25821	-.27052	-.28284
.15250	-.20715	-.21935	-.23156	-.24376	-.25597	-.26818
.15500	-.19327	-.20536	-.21746	-.22956	-.24166	-.25376
.15750	-.17962	-.19161	-.20360	-.21560	-.22759	-.23958
.16000	-.16620	-.17809	-.18997	-.20186	-.21375	-.22564
.16250	-.15300	-.16479	-.17657	-.18836	-.20014	-.21193
.16500	-.14003	-.15171	-.16339	-.17508	-.18676	-.19845
.16750	-.12727	-.13885	-.15043	-.16202	-.17360	-.18519
.17000	-.11472	-.12620	-.13768	-.14917	-.16066	-.17214
.17250	-.10238	-.11376	-.12515	-.13653	-.14792	-.15931
.17500	-.09024	-.10153	-.11282	-.12411	-.13540	-.14669
.17750	-.07830	-.08949	-.10069	-.11188	-.12308	-.13428
.18000	-.06656	-.07765	-.08875	-.09986	-.11096	-.12206
.18250	-.05500	-.06601	-.07702	-.08803	-.09904	-.11005
.18500	-.04364	-.05456	-.06547	-.07639	-.08731	-.09823
.18750	-.03246	-.04329	-.05411	-.06494	-.07577	-.08660
.19000	-.02146	-.03220	-.04294	-.05367	-.06441	-.07515
.19250	-.01065	-.02129	-.03194	-.04259	-.05324	-.06389
.19500	.00000	-.01056	-.02112	-.03168	-.04225	-.05281
.19750	.01047	0.00000	-.01048	-.02095	-.03143	-.04191
.20000	.02078	.01039	.00000	-.01039	-.02079	-.03118
.20250	.03092	.02062	.01031	.00000	-.01031	-.02062
.20500	.04090	.03068	.02045	.01023	-.00000	-.01023
.20750	.05072	.04058	.03044	.02029	.01015	.00000

POINT TABLES: ORIGINAL LOAN TERM: 420 MONTHS LOAN PREPAID IN: 144 MONTHS

EFFECTIVE YIELD	CONTRACT RATE .07000	.07250	.07500	.07750	.08000	.08250	.08500	.08750	.09000	.09250
.07000	.00000	-.01939	-.03887	-.05842	-.07805	-.09775	-.11751	-.13733	-.15721	-.17714
.07250	.01911	.00000	-.01919	-.03846	-.05780	-.07721	-.09669	-.11623	-.13582	-.15547
.07500	.03773	.01891	.00000	-.01899	-.03805	-.05718	-.07638	-.09564	-.11495	-.13432
.07750	.05590	.03735	.01871	.00000	-.01879	-.03765	-.05657	-.07556	-.09460	-.11369
.08000	.07361	.05533	.03697	.01852	.00000	-.01859	-.03725	-.05596	-.07474	-.09357
.08250	.09089	.07287	.05477	.03659	.01833	.00000	-.01839	-.03685	-.05536	-.07393
.08500	.10774	.08998	.07213	.05421	.03621	.01814	0.00000	-.01820	-.03646	-.05477
.08750	.12417	.10666	.08907	.07140	.05365	.03583	.01795	0.00000	-.01801	-.03606
.09000	.14020	.12294	.10560	.08817	.07067	.05310	.03546	.01776	.00000	-.01781
.09250	.15584	.13882	.12172	.10453	.08727	.06994	.05255	.03509	.01757	.00000
.09500	.17109	.15431	.13744	.12050	.10348	.08638	.06923	.05200	.03472	.01739
.09750	.18597	.16943	.15279	.13608	.11929	.10243	.08550	.06851	.05146	.03436
.10000	.20050	.18417	.16777	.15128	.13472	.11809	.10139	.08463	.06780	.05093
.10250	.21466	.19856	.18238	.16612	.14978	.13337	.11689	.10035	.08376	.06710
.10500	.22849	.21261	.19664	.18060	.16448	.14829	.13203	.11571	.09933	.08289
.10750	.24198	.22631	.21056	.19473	.17883	.16285	.14681	.13070	.11453	.09831
.11000	.25515	.23969	.22415	.20853	.19283	.17707	.16123	.14534	.12938	.11337
.11250	.26800	.25275	.23741	.22200	.20651	.19095	.17532	.15963	.14388	.12807
.11500	.28054	.26549	.25036	.23514	.21986	.20450	.18907	.17358	.15804	.14243
.11750	.29278	.27793	.26300	.24798	.23289	.21773	.20250	.18721	.17186	.15646
.12000	.30474	.29008	.27534	.26051	.24562	.23065	.21562	.20052	.18537	.17015
.12250	.31640	.30194	.28738	.27275	.25805	.24327	.22843	.21352	.19856	.18354
.12500	.32780	.31351	.29915	.28470	.27018	.25560	.24094	.22622	.21144	.19661
.12750	.33892	.32482	.31064	.29637	.28204	.26763	.25316	.23862	.22403	.20938
.13000	.34978	.33586	.32186	.30777	.29362	.27939	.26510	.25074	.23633	.22185
.13250	.36039	.34664	.33281	.31891	.30493	.29088	.27676	.26258	.24834	.23405
.13500	.37075	.35717	.34352	.32978	.31598	.30210	.28815	.27415	.26008	.24596
.13750	.38086	.36746	.35397	.34041	.32677	.31306	.29929	.28545	.27155	.25760
.14000	.39075	.37751	.36419	.35079	.33731	.32377	.31016	.29649	.28276	.26898
.14250	.40040	.38732	.37416	.36093	.34762	.33424	.32079	.30729	.29372	.28010
.14500	.40983	.39691	.38391	.37084	.35769	.34447	.33118	.31784	.30443	.29097
.14750	.41904	.40628	.39344	.38052	.36753	.35446	.34134	.32815	.31490	.30160
.15000	.42804	.41544	.40275	.38998	.37714	.36423	.35126	.33823	.32513	.31198
.15250	.43684	.42438	.41184	.39923	.38654	.37378	.36096	.34808	.33514	.32214
.15500	.44544	.43312	.42073	.40827	.39573	.38312	.37045	.35771	.34492	.33207
.15750	.45384	.44167	.42942	.41710	.40471	.39225	.37972	.36713	.35449	.34178
.16000	.46205	.45002	.43792	.42574	.41349	.40117	.38879	.37634	.36384	.35128
.16250	.47007	.45818	.44622	.43418	.42207	.40989	.39765	.38535	.37299	.36057
.16500	.47791	.46616	.45434	.44244	.43046	.41842	.40632	.39415	.38193	.36965
.16750	.48558	.47397	.46227	.45051	.43867	.42677	.41480	.40277	.39068	.37854
.17000	.49308	.48160	.47004	.45840	.44670	.43493	.42309	.41119	.39924	.38723
.17250	.50041	.48905	.47762	.46612	.45455	.44291	.43120	.41944	.40761	.39574
.17500	.50757	.49635	.48505	.47367	.46222	.45071	.43914	.42750	.41581	.40406
.17750	.51458	.50348	.49230	.48105	.46973	.45835	.44690	.43539	.42382	.41220
.18000	.52144	.51046	.49940	.48828	.47708	.46582	.45449	.44311	.43167	.42017
.18250	.52814	.51728	.50635	.49534	.48427	.47313	.46192	.45066	.43934	.42797
.18500	.53470	.52396	.51314	.50226	.49130	.48028	.46919	.45805	.44685	.43560
.18750	.54111	.53049	.51979	.50902	.49818	.48728	.47631	.46528	.45420	.44307
.19000	.54739	.53688	.52629	.51564	.50491	.49413	.48327	.47237	.46140	.45038
.19250	.55353	.54313	.53266	.52212	.51150	.50083	.49009	.47930	.46844	.45754
.19500	.55954	.54925	.53889	.52845	.51795	.50739	.49676	.48608	.47534	.46455
.19750	.56541	.55524	.54498	.53466	.52427	.51381	.50330	.49272	.48209	.47141
.20000	.57117	.56109	.55095	.54073	.53045	.52010	.50969	.49923	.48871	.47813
.20250	.57680	.56683	.55679	.54668	.53650	.52626	.51595	.50559	.49518	.48471
.20500	.58231	.57244	.56250	.55250	.54242	.53228	.52209	.51183	.50152	.49116
.20750	.58770	.57794	.56810	.55819	.54822	.53819	.52809	.51794	.50773	.49747

EFFECTIVE YIELD	CONTRACT RATE .09500	.09750	.10000	.10250	.10500	.10750	.11000	.11250	.11500	.11750
.07000	-.19712	-.21714	-.23720	-.25730	-.27744	-.29760	-.31780	-.33802	-.35827	-.37853
.07250	-.17516	-.19490	-.21468	-.23450	-.25435	-.27424	-.29415	-.31409	-.33406	-.35405
.07500	-.15374	-.17320	-.19270	-.21225	-.23182	-.25143	-.27107	-.29074	-.31043	-.33015
.07750	-.13284	-.15203	-.17126	-.19053	-.20984	-.22918	-.24855	-.26795	-.28737	-.30682
.08000	-.11245	-.13137	-.15034	-.16934	-.18838	-.20746	-.22657	-.24570	-.26486	-.28405
.08250	-.09255	-.11121	-.12992	-.14866	-.16744	-.18626	-.20511	-.22398	-.24289	-.26181
.08500	-.07313	-.09153	-.10998	-.12848	-.14700	-.16557	-.18416	-.20278	-.22143	-.24011
.08750	-.05417	-.07233	-.09053	-.10877	-.12705	-.14537	-.16371	-.18209	-.20049	-.21891
.09000	-.03568	-.05359	-.07154	-.08954	-.10757	-.12564	-.14375	-.16188	-.18003	-.19822
.09250	-.01762	-.03529	-.05301	-.07077	-.08856	-.10639	-.12425	-.14214	-.16006	-.17801
.09500	.00000	-.01743	-.03491	-.05243	-.06999	-.08759	-.10522	-.12288	-.14056	-.15827
.09750	.01720	.00000	-.01725	-.03454	-.05187	-.06923	-.08663	-.10406	-.12152	-.13900
.10000	.03400	.01702	.00000	-.01706	-.03417	-.05131	-.06848	-.08568	-.10291	-.12017
.10250	.05040	.03364	.01684	.00000	-.01688	-.03380	-.05075	-.06773	-.08474	-.10178
.10500	.06641	.04987	.03329	.01666	.00000	-.01670	-.03343	-.05020	-.06700	-.08382
.10750	.08204	.06572	.04935	.03294	.01649	.00000	-.01652	-.03307	-.04966	-.06627
.11000	.09731	.08119	.06503	.04883	.03259	.01631	.00000	-.01634	-.03272	-.04912
.11250	.11221	.09631	.08035	.06436	.04832	.03225	.01614	0.00000	-.01617	-.03237
.11500	.12678	.11107	.09532	.07952	.06369	.04782	.03191	.01597	0.00000	-.01600
.11750	.14100	.12549	.10994	.09434	.07870	.06303	.04732	.03157	.01580	.00000
.12000	.15489	.13958	.12422	.10881	.09337	.07789	.06237	.04682	.03124	.01563
.12250	.16846	.15334	.13817	.12295	.10770	.09241	.07708	.06172	.04633	.03091
.12500	.18172	.16678	.15180	.13677	.12171	.10660	.09146	.07629	.06108	.04585
.12750	.19467	.17992	.16512	.15028	.13539	.12047	.10551	.09052	.07550	.06045
.13000	.20733	.19276	.17814	.16347	.14877	.13403	.11925	.10444	.08959	.07472
.13250	.21970	.20530	.19086	.17637	.16184	.14727	.13267	.11804	.10337	.08868
.13500	.23178	.21756	.20329	.18897	.17462	.16023	.14580	.13133	.11684	.10232
.13750	.24360	.22954	.21544	.20130	.18711	.17289	.15863	.14434	.13001	.11566
.14000	.25514	.24125	.22732	.21334	.19932	.18527	.17117	.15705	.14289	.12870
.14250	.26642	.25270	.23893	.22512	.21126	.19737	.18344	.16948	.15548	.14146
.14500	.27746	.26389	.25028	.23663	.22294	.20920	.19544	.18163	.16780	.15394
.14750	.28824	.27484	.26138	.24789	.23435	.22078	.20717	.19352	.17985	.16614
.15000	.29878	.28553	.27224	.25890	.24552	.23210	.21864	.20515	.19163	.17808
.15250	.30909	.29599	.28285	.26966	.25643	.24317	.22986	.21653	.20316	.18976
.15500	.31917	.30622	.29323	.28019	.26711	.25399	.24084	.22765	.21443	.20118
.15750	.32903	.31623	.30338	.29049	.27756	.26459	.25158	.23854	.22547	.21236
.16000	.33867	.32601	.31331	.30056	.28777	.27495	.26208	.24919	.23626	.22330
.16250	.34810	.33559	.32302	.31042	.29777	.28509	.27236	.25961	.24682	.23401
.16500	.35733	.34495	.33252	.32006	.30755	.29500	.28242	.26981	.25716	.24448
.16750	.36635	.35411	.34182	.32949	.31712	.30471	.29227	.27979	.26728	.25474
.17000	.37518	.36307	.35092	.33872	.32648	.31421	.30190	.28955	.27718	.26477
.17250	.38381	.37184	.35982	.34775	.33565	.32350	.31133	.29911	.28687	.27460
.17500	.39226	.38042	.36852	.35659	.34462	.33260	.32055	.30847	.29636	.28421
.17750	.40053	.38881	.37705	.36524	.35339	.34151	.32959	.31763	.30565	.29363
.18000	.40862	.39703	.38539	.37371	.36199	.35023	.33843	.32660	.31474	.30285
.18250	.41654	.40507	.39356	.38200	.37040	.35876	.34709	.33538	.32365	.31188
.18500	.42430	.41295	.40155	.39011	.37864	.36712	.35557	.34398	.33237	.32072
.18750	.43189	.42065	.40938	.39806	.38670	.37530	.36387	.35240	.34091	.32938
.19000	.43931	.42820	.41704	.40584	.39459	.38332	.37200	.36065	.34927	.33786
.19250	.44659	.43559	.42454	.41345	.40233	.39116	.37996	.36873	.35747	.34617
.19500	.45371	.44282	.43189	.42091	.40990	.39885	.38776	.37664	.36549	.35431
.19750	.46068	.44991	.43908	.42822	.41732	.40638	.39540	.38439	.37335	.36229
.20000	.46751	.45684	.44613	.43538	.42458	.41375	.40289	.39199	.38106	.37010
.20250	.47420	.46364	.45303	.44239	.43170	.42098	.41022	.39943	.38861	.37775
.20500	.48075	.47030	.45980	.44925	.43867	.42806	.41740	.40672	.39600	.38526
.20750	.48717	.47682	.46642	.45598	.44551	.43499	.42444	.41386	.40325	.39261

POINT TABLES: ORIGINAL LOAN TERM: 420 MONTHS LOAN PREPAID IN: 144 MONTHS

EFFECTIVE YIELD	CONTRACT RATE .12000	.12250	.12500	.12750	.13000	.13250	.13500	.13750	.14000	.14250
.07000	-.39882	-.41912	-.43944	-.45977	-.48011	-.50047	-.52083	-.54120	-.56158	-.58196
.07250	-.37405	-.39408	-.41412	-.43418	-.45424	-.47432	-.49441	-.51451	-.53461	-.55472
.07500	-.34988	-.36963	-.38940	-.40919	-.42899	-.44879	-.46861	-.48844	-.50828	-.52812
.07750	-.32629	-.34577	-.36528	-.38479	-.40432	-.42387	-.44342	-.46299	-.48256	-.50214
.08000	-.30325	-.32248	-.34172	-.36097	-.38025	-.39953	-.41882	-.43813	-.45744	-.47676
.08250	-.28076	-.29973	-.31871	-.33772	-.35673	-.37576	-.39480	-.41385	-.43291	-.45198
.08500	-.25880	-.27752	-.29625	-.31500	-.33377	-.35255	-.37134	-.39014	-.40895	-.42777
.08750	-.23736	-.25583	-.27432	-.29282	-.31135	-.32988	-.34843	-.36698	-.38555	-.40413
.09000	-.21642	-.23465	-.25290	-.27116	-.28944	-.30774	-.32604	-.34436	-.36269	-.38103
.09250	-.19598	-.21397	-.23198	-.25001	-.26805	-.28611	-.30418	-.32226	-.34035	-.35846
.09500	-.17601	-.19377	-.21154	-.22934	-.24715	-.26498	-.28282	-.30067	-.31853	-.33641
.09750	-.15651	-.17403	-.19158	-.20915	-.22674	-.24434	-.26195	-.27957	-.29721	-.31486
.10000	-.13745	-.15476	-.17209	-.18943	-.20679	-.22417	-.24156	-.25896	-.27638	-.29380
.10250	-.11884	-.13593	-.15304	-.17016	-.18730	-.20446	-.22164	-.23882	-.25602	-.27323
.10500	-.10066	-.11753	-.13443	-.15134	-.16826	-.18521	-.20217	-.21914	-.23612	-.25312
.10750	-.08290	-.09956	-.11624	-.13294	-.14966	-.16639	-.18314	-.19990	-.21668	-.23346
.11000	-.06555	-.08200	-.09847	-.11496	-.13147	-.14800	-.16454	-.18110	-.19767	-.21425
.11250	-.04859	-.06484	-.08111	-.09740	-.11370	-.13003	-.14637	-.16272	-.17909	-.19547
.11500	-.03202	-.04807	-.06414	-.08023	-.09633	-.11246	-.12860	-.14476	-.16092	-.17711
.11750	-.01583	-.03168	-.04755	-.06345	-.07936	-.09529	-.11123	-.12719	-.14317	-.15915
.12000	0.00000	-.01566	-.03134	-.04704	-.06276	-.07850	-.09425	-.11002	-.12581	-.14160
.12250	.01547	.00000	-.01549	-.03101	-.04654	-.06209	-.07765	-.09323	-.10883	-.12444
.12500	.03059	.01531	.00000	-.01533	-.03068	-.04604	-.06142	-.07682	-.09223	-.10765
.12750	.04537	.03027	.01515	.00000	-.01517	-.03035	-.04555	-.06077	-.07600	-.09124
.13000	.05982	.04490	.02995	.01499	.00000	-.01501	-.03003	-.04507	-.06012	-.07518
.13250	.07395	.05921	.04443	.02964	.01483	.00000	-.01485	-.02971	-.04459	-.05948
.13500	.08777	.07319	.05859	.04397	.02933	.01468	.00000	-.01469	-.02940	-.04412
.13750	.10128	.08687	.07244	.05799	.04352	.02903	.01452	.00000	-.01454	-.02909
.14000	.11449	.10025	.08599	.07170	.05740	.04307	.02873	.01437	.00000	-.01439
.14250	.12741	.11333	.09923	.08511	.07097	.05681	.04263	.02843	.01422	.00000
.14500	.14005	.12613	.11219	.09823	.08425	.07025	.05623	.04219	.02814	.01408
.14750	.15241	.13865	.12487	.11106	.09724	.08339	.06953	.05565	.04176	.02785
.15000	.16450	.15090	.13727	.12362	.10995	.09626	.08255	.06883	.05509	.04133
.15250	.17633	.16288	.14940	.13591	.12239	.10885	.09529	.08172	.06813	.05453
.15500	.18791	.17460	.16128	.14793	.13456	.12117	.10776	.09434	.08090	.06745
.15750	.19923	.18608	.17290	.15970	.14647	.13323	.11997	.10669	.09340	.08009
.16000	.21032	.19730	.18427	.17121	.15813	.14503	.13192	.11878	.10563	.09247
.16250	.22116	.20829	.19540	.18248	.16954	.15659	.14361	.13062	.11761	.10459
.16500	.23178	.21905	.20629	.19351	.18072	.16790	.15506	.14221	.12934	.11645
.16750	.24217	.22957	.21696	.20431	.19165	.17897	.16627	.15355	.14082	.12807
.17000	.25234	.23988	.22739	.21489	.20236	.18981	.17725	.16467	.15207	.13945
.17250	.26229	.24997	.23762	.22524	.21285	.20043	.18800	.17555	.16308	.15060
.17500	.27204	.25985	.24762	.23538	.22311	.21083	.19852	.18620	.17387	.16151
.17750	.28159	.26952	.25742	.24531	.23317	.22101	.20883	.19664	.18443	.17221
.18000	.29093	.27899	.26702	.25503	.24302	.23098	.21893	.20687	.19478	.18268
.18250	.30008	.28826	.27642	.26455	.25266	.24075	.22883	.21688	.20492	.19295
.18500	.30905	.29735	.28562	.27388	.26211	.25032	.23852	.22669	.21486	.20300
.18750	.31783	.30625	.29464	.28302	.27137	.25970	.24801	.23631	.22459	.21285
.19000	.32643	.31496	.30348	.29197	.28044	.26889	.25732	.24573	.23413	.22251
.19250	.33485	.32350	.31213	.30074	.28932	.27789	.26643	.25496	.24347	.23197
.19500	.34310	.33187	.32061	.30933	.29803	.28671	.27537	.26401	.25264	.24125
.19750	.35119	.34007	.32892	.31775	.30656	.29535	.28412	.27288	.26162	.25034
.20000	.35911	.34810	.33706	.32600	.31492	.30382	.29271	.28157	.27042	.25925
.20250	.36688	.35597	.34504	.33409	.32312	.31213	.30112	.29009	.27905	.26799
.20500	.37449	.36369	.35287	.34202	.33116	.32027	.30937	.29845	.28751	.27656
.20750	.38194	.37125	.36053	.34979	.33903	.32825	.31745	.30664	.29580	.28496

CONTRACT RATE

EFFECTIVE YIELD	.14500	.14750	.15000	.15250	.15500	.15750	.16000	.16250	.16500	.16750
.07000	-.60235	-.62275	-.64314	-.66354	-.68394	-.70434	-.72474	-.74514	-.76553	-.78593
.07250	-.57484	-.59496	-.61508	-.63521	-.65533	-.67546	-.69559	-.71572	-.73585	-.75598
.07500	-.54797	-.56782	-.58767	-.60753	-.62739	-.64726	-.66712	-.68699	-.70685	-.72672
.07750	-.52172	-.54131	-.56091	-.58051	-.60011	-.61971	-.63931	-.65892	-.67852	-.69813
.08000	-.49609	-.51542	-.53476	-.55410	-.57345	-.59280	-.61214	-.63149	-.65085	-.67020
.08250	-.47106	-.49014	-.50922	-.52831	-.54741	-.56650	-.58560	-.60470	-.62380	-.64291
.08500	-.44660	-.46543	-.48427	-.50312	-.52196	-.54081	-.55967	-.57852	-.59738	-.61624
.08750	-.42271	-.44130	-.45990	-.47850	-.49710	-.51571	-.53433	-.55294	-.57156	-.59017
.09000	-.39937	-.41772	-.43608	-.45445	-.47281	-.49119	-.50956	-.52794	-.54632	-.56470
.09250	-.37657	-.39469	-.41281	-.43094	-.44908	-.46722	-.48536	-.50351	-.52166	-.53981
.09500	-.35429	-.37218	-.39007	-.40797	-.42588	-.44379	-.46171	-.47963	-.49755	-.51547
.09750	-.33252	-.35018	-.36785	-.38553	-.40321	-.42090	-.43859	-.45629	-.47398	-.49169
.10000	-.31124	-.32868	-.34613	-.36359	-.38105	-.39852	-.41599	-.43347	-.45095	-.46843
.10250	-.29045	-.30767	-.32491	-.34215	-.35939	-.37665	-.39390	-.41116	-.42843	-.44570
.10500	-.27012	-.28714	-.30416	-.32119	-.33822	-.35526	-.37231	-.38936	-.40641	-.42347
.10750	-.25026	-.26706	-.28388	-.30070	-.31752	-.33436	-.35119	-.36804	-.38488	-.40173
.11000	-.23084	-.24744	-.26405	-.28066	-.29729	-.31391	-.33055	-.34719	-.36383	-.38048
.11250	-.21186	-.22825	-.24466	-.26108	-.27750	-.29393	-.31036	-.32680	-.34324	-.35969
.11500	-.19330	-.20950	-.22571	-.24193	-.25815	-.27438	-.29062	-.30686	-.32311	-.33936
.11750	-.17515	-.19116	-.20717	-.22320	-.23923	-.25527	-.27131	-.28736	-.30342	-.31948
.12000	-.15741	-.17322	-.18905	-.20488	-.22073	-.23657	-.25243	-.26829	-.28415	-.30002
.12250	-.14006	-.15569	-.17132	-.18697	-.20263	-.21829	-.23396	-.24963	-.26531	-.28100
.12500	-.12309	-.13853	-.15399	-.16945	-.18493	-.20041	-.21589	-.23138	-.24688	-.26238
.12750	-.10649	-.12176	-.13703	-.15232	-.16761	-.18291	-.19822	-.21353	-.22885	-.24417
.13000	-.09026	-.10535	-.12045	-.13555	-.15067	-.16579	-.18092	-.19606	-.21120	-.22635
.13250	-.07438	-.08930	-.10422	-.11915	-.13410	-.14905	-.16400	-.17897	-.19393	-.20891
.13500	-.05885	-.07359	-.08835	-.10311	-.11788	-.13266	-.14745	-.16224	-.17704	-.19184
.13750	-.04365	-.05823	-.07281	-.08741	-.10201	-.11663	-.13124	-.14587	-.16050	-.17514
.14000	-.02878	-.04320	-.05762	-.07205	-.08649	-.10093	-.11539	-.12985	-.14432	-.15879
.14250	-.01424	-.02848	-.04274	-.05701	-.07129	-.08558	-.09987	-.11417	-.12848	-.14279
.14500	0.00000	-.01409	-.02819	-.04230	-.05642	-.07054	-.08468	-.09882	-.11297	-.12712
.14750	.01393	.00000	-.01394	-.02790	-.04186	-.05583	-.06981	-.08380	-.09779	-.11179
.15000	.02757	.01379	.00000	-.01380	-.02761	-.04143	-.05525	-.06909	-.08292	-.09677
.15250	.04092	.02729	.01365	.00000	-.01366	-.02733	-.04100	-.05468	-.06837	-.08207
.15500	.05398	.04050	.02701	.01351	0.00000	-.01352	-.02705	-.04058	-.05412	-.06767
.15750	.06677	.05344	.04009	.02674	.01337	.00000	-.01338	-.02677	-.04017	-.05357
.16000	.07929	.06610	.05290	.03969	.02647	.01324	0.00000	-.01325	-.02650	-.03976
.16250	.09155	.07850	.06544	.05237	.03929	.02620	.01311	0.00000	-.01311	-.02623
.16500	.10356	.09065	.07773	.06479	.05185	.03890	.02594	.01297	.00000	-.01298
.16750	.11531	.10254	.08975	.07696	.06415	.05134	.03851	.02568	.01284	0.00000
.17000	.12683	.11419	.10154	.08887	.07620	.06352	.05083	.03813	.02543	.01272
.17250	.13810	.12560	.11308	.10055	.08801	.07546	.06290	.05033	.03776	.02518
.17500	.14915	.13677	.12438	.11198	.09957	.08715	.07472	.06228	.04984	.03739
.17750	.15997	.14772	.13546	.12318	.11090	.09861	.08630	.07399	.06168	.04935
.18000	.17057	.15845	.14631	.13416	.12200	.10983	.09766	.08547	.07328	.06108
.18250	.18096	.16895	.15694	.14492	.13288	.12083	.10878	.09672	.08465	.07257
.18500	.19113	.17925	.16736	.15546	.14354	.13162	.11968	.10774	.09580	.08384
.18750	.20111	.18934	.17757	.16579	.15399	.14219	.13037	.11855	.10672	.09488
.19000	.21088	.19923	.18758	.17591	.16423	.15254	.14085	.12914	.11743	.10571
.19250	.22046	.20893	.19739	.18583	.17427	.16270	.15112	.13953	.12793	.11633
.19500	.22985	.21843	.20700	.19556	.18411	.17266	.16119	.14971	.13823	.12674
.19750	.23905	.22774	.21643	.20510	.19376	.18242	.17106	.15970	.14832	.13694
.20000	.24807	.23688	.22567	.21445	.20323	.19199	.18074	.16949	.15822	.14695
.20250	.25692	.24583	.23473	.22362	.21250	.20137	.19024	.17909	.16793	.15677
.20500	.26559	.25461	.24362	.23262	.22160	.21058	.19955	.18851	.17746	.16640
.20750	.27409	.26322	.25233	.24143	.23053	.21961	.20868	.19774	.18680	.17585

POINT TABLES: ORIGINAL LOAN TERM: 420 MONTHS LOAN PREPAID IN: 144 MONTHS

EFFECTIVE YIELD	CONTRACT RATE .17000	.17250	.17500	.17750	.18000	.18250	.18500	.18750	.19000	.19250
.07000	-.80633	-.82672	-.84712	-.86751	-.88790	-.90828	-.92866	-.94904	-.96942	-.98980
.07250	-.77611	-.79623	-.81636	-.83648	-.85660	-.87672	-.89684	-.91695	-.93706	-.95717
.07500	-.74658	-.76644	-.78631	-.80617	-.82603	-.84588	-.86574	-.88559	-.90544	-.92529
.07750	-.71773	-.73734	-.75694	-.77655	-.79615	-.81575	-.83534	-.85494	-.87453	-.89412
.08000	-.68955	-.70890	-.72825	-.74760	-.76695	-.78630	-.80564	-.82499	-.84433	-.86367
.08250	-.66201	-.68111	-.70021	-.71931	-.73842	-.75751	-.77661	-.79571	-.81480	-.83390
.08500	-.63509	-.65395	-.67281	-.69167	-.71053	-.72938	-.74824	-.76709	-.78595	-.80480
.08750	-.60879	-.62741	-.64603	-.66465	-.68327	-.70189	-.72050	-.73912	-.75773	-.77635
.09000	-.58309	-.60147	-.61985	-.63824	-.65662	-.67501	-.69339	-.71177	-.73015	-.74853
.09250	-.55796	-.57611	-.59427	-.61242	-.63057	-.64873	-.66688	-.68504	-.70319	-.72134
.09500	-.53340	-.55132	-.56925	-.58718	-.60511	-.62304	-.64097	-.65889	-.67682	-.69475
.09750	-.50939	-.52709	-.54480	-.56250	-.58021	-.59792	-.61563	-.63333	-.65104	-.66875
.10000	-.48592	-.50340	-.52089	-.53838	-.55587	-.57336	-.59085	-.60834	-.62583	-.64332
.10250	-.46297	-.48024	-.49751	-.51479	-.53206	-.54934	-.56662	-.58389	-.60117	-.61845
.10500	-.44053	-.45759	-.47465	-.49172	-.50878	-.52585	-.54292	-.55998	-.57705	-.59412
.10750	-.41858	-.43544	-.45230	-.46915	-.48601	-.50288	-.51974	-.53660	-.55346	-.57033
.11000	-.39713	-.41378	-.43043	-.44709	-.46375	-.48041	-.49707	-.51373	-.53039	-.54705
.11250	-.37614	-.39259	-.40905	-.42551	-.44197	-.45843	-.47489	-.49135	-.50781	-.52428
.11500	-.35561	-.37187	-.38813	-.40439	-.42066	-.43692	-.45319	-.46946	-.48573	-.50200
.11750	-.33554	-.35160	-.36767	-.38374	-.39981	-.41589	-.43197	-.44804	-.46412	-.48020
.12000	-.31590	-.33177	-.34765	-.36354	-.37942	-.39531	-.41120	-.42709	-.44298	-.45887
.12250	-.29669	-.31238	-.32807	-.34377	-.35947	-.37517	-.39087	-.40658	-.42229	-.43799
.12500	-.27789	-.29340	-.30891	-.32443	-.33994	-.35546	-.37099	-.38651	-.40204	-.41756
.12750	-.25950	-.27483	-.29016	-.30550	-.32084	-.33618	-.35152	-.36687	-.38222	-.39757
.13000	-.24150	-.25665	-.27181	-.28697	-.30214	-.31731	-.33248	-.34765	-.36282	-.37799
.13250	-.22389	-.23887	-.25386	-.26885	-.28384	-.29883	-.31383	-.32883	-.34383	-.35883
.13500	-.20665	-.22146	-.23628	-.25110	-.26592	-.28075	-.29558	-.31041	-.32524	-.34008
.13750	-.18978	-.20443	-.21908	-.23373	-.24839	-.26305	-.27771	-.29238	-.30704	-.32171
.14000	-.17327	-.18775	-.20224	-.21673	-.23122	-.24572	-.26022	-.27472	-.28922	-.30373
.14250	-.15711	-.17143	-.18575	-.20008	-.21442	-.22875	-.24309	-.25743	-.27178	-.28612
.14500	-.14128	-.15545	-.16961	-.18379	-.19796	-.21214	-.22632	-.24050	-.25469	-.26888
.14750	-.12579	-.13980	-.15381	-.16783	-.18185	-.19587	-.20990	-.22393	-.23796	-.25199
.15000	-.11062	-.12448	-.13834	-.15220	-.16607	-.17994	-.19381	-.20769	-.22157	-.23545
.15250	-.09577	-.10947	-.12318	-.13690	-.15061	-.16434	-.17806	-.19179	-.20552	-.21925
.15500	-.08122	-.09478	-.10834	-.12191	-.13548	-.14905	-.16263	-.17621	-.18979	-.20338
.15750	-.06698	-.08039	-.09381	-.10723	-.12065	-.13408	-.14752	-.16095	-.17439	-.18783
.16000	-.05302	-.06629	-.07957	-.09285	-.10613	-.11942	-.13271	-.14600	-.15930	-.17259
.16250	-.03936	-.05249	-.06562	-.07876	-.09190	-.10505	-.11820	-.13135	-.14451	-.15767
.16500	-.02597	-.03896	-.05196	-.06496	-.07796	-.09097	-.10399	-.11700	-.13002	-.14304
.16750	-.01285	-.02571	-.03857	-.05143	-.06430	-.07718	-.09006	-.10294	-.11582	-.12871
.17000	.00000	-.01272	-.02545	-.03818	-.05092	-.06366	-.07641	-.08915	-.10190	-.11466
.17250	.01259	.00000	-.01260	-.02520	-.03780	-.05041	-.06303	-.07565	-.08826	-.10089
.17500	.02493	.01247	.00000	-.01247	-.02495	-.03743	-.04992	-.06240	-.07490	-.08739
.17750	.03702	.02469	.01235	.00000	-.01235	-.02470	-.03706	-.04942	-.06179	-.07416
.18000	.04887	.03666	.02445	.01223	.00000	-.01223	-.02446	-.03670	-.04894	-.06118
.18250	.06049	.04840	.03631	.02421	.01211	0.00000	-.01211	-.02423	-.03634	-.04846
.18500	.07188	.05981	.04794	.03596	.02398	.01199	.00000	-.01199	-.02399	-.03599
.18750	.08304	.07119	.05934	.04748	.03562	.02375	.01188	.00000	-.01188	-.02376
.19000	.09399	.08225	.07052	.05877	.04703	.03528	.02352	.01176	.00000	-.01177
.19250	.10472	.09310	.08148	.06985	.05822	.04658	.03494	.02330	.01165	.00000
.19500	.11524	.10374	.09223	.08071	.06919	.05767	.04614	.03461	.02308	.01154
.19750	.12556	.11417	.10277	.09137	.07996	.06855	.05713	.04571	.03429	.02286
.20000	.13568	.12440	.11311	.10181	.09052	.07921	.06791	.05660	.04528	.03397
.20250	.14560	.13443	.12325	.11206	.10087	.08968	.07848	.06728	.05607	.04486
.20500	.15534	.14427	.13320	.12212	.11104	.09995	.08885	.07776	.06666	.05555
.20750	.16489	.15393	.14296	.13198	.12100	.11002	.09903	.08804	.07705	.06605

EFFECTIVE YIELD	CONTRACT RATE .19500	.19750	.20000	.20250	.20500	.20750
.07000	-1.01017	-1.03053	-1.05090	-1.07126	-1.09162	-1.11197
.07250	-.97727	-.99738	-1.01748	-1.03757	-1.05767	-1.07776
.07500	-.94513	-.96497	-.98481	-1.00465	-1.02448	-1.04431
.07750	-.91371	-.93330	-.95288	-.97246	-.99204	-1.01162
.08000	-.88301	-.90234	-.92167	-.94101	-.96033	-.97966
.08250	-.85299	-.87208	-.89117	-.91025	-.92933	-.94841
.08500	-.82365	-.84249	-.86134	-.88018	-.89903	-.91787
.08750	-.79496	-.81357	-.83218	-.85079	-.86939	-.88800
.09000	-.76691	-.78529	-.80367	-.82204	-.84042	-.85879
.09250	-.73949	-.75764	-.77579	-.79393	-.81208	-.83022
.09500	-.71267	-.73060	-.74852	-.76645	-.78437	-.80229
.09750	-.68645	-.70416	-.72186	-.73956	-.75726	-.77497
.10000	-.66081	-.67829	-.69578	-.71327	-.73075	-.74824
.10250	-.63572	-.65300	-.67027	-.68755	-.70482	-.72210
.10500	-.61119	-.62826	-.64532	-.66239	-.67946	-.69652
.10750	-.58719	-.60405	-.62092	-.63778	-.65464	-.67150
.11000	-.56371	-.58037	-.59704	-.61370	-.63036	-.64702
.11250	-.54074	-.55721	-.57367	-.59014	-.60660	-.62306
.11500	-.51827	-.53454	-.55081	-.56708	-.58335	-.59962
.11750	-.49628	-.51236	-.52844	-.54452	-.56060	-.57668
.12000	-.47476	-.49065	-.50655	-.52244	-.53833	-.55422
.12250	-.45370	-.46941	-.48512	-.50083	-.51654	-.53225
.12500	-.43309	-.44862	-.46415	-.47967	-.49520	-.51073
.12750	-.41292	-.42827	-.44362	-.45897	-.47432	-.48967
.13000	-.39317	-.40834	-.42352	-.43870	-.45388	-.46905
.13250	-.37384	-.38884	-.40385	-.41885	-.43386	-.44887
.13500	-.35491	-.36975	-.38458	-.39942	-.41426	-.42910
.13750	-.33638	-.35105	-.36572	-.38040	-.39507	-.40974
.14000	-.31824	-.33274	-.34725	-.36176	-.37627	-.39079
.14250	-.30047	-.31482	-.32917	-.34352	-.35787	-.37222
.14500	-.28307	-.29726	-.31145	-.32564	-.33984	-.35403
.14750	-.26603	-.28006	-.29410	-.30814	-.32218	-.33622
.15000	-.24933	-.26322	-.27710	-.29099	-.30488	-.31877
.15250	-.23298	-.24672	-.26045	-.27419	-.28793	-.30167
.15500	-.21696	-.23055	-.24414	-.25773	-.27133	-.28492
.15750	-.20127	-.21472	-.22816	-.24161	-.25506	-.26851
.16000	-.18590	-.19920	-.21250	-.22581	-.23911	-.25242
.16250	-.17083	-.18399	-.19716	-.21032	-.22349	-.23666
.16500	-.15606	-.16909	-.18212	-.19515	-.20818	-.22121
.16750	-.14159	-.15449	-.16738	-.18027	-.19317	-.20606
.17000	-.12741	-.14017	-.15293	-.16569	-.17845	-.19122
.17250	-.11351	-.12614	-.13877	-.15140	-.16403	-.17667
.17500	-.09989	-.11238	-.12488	-.13739	-.14989	-.16240
.17750	-.08653	-.09890	-.11127	-.12365	-.13603	-.14841
.18000	-.07343	-.08568	-.09793	-.11018	-.12243	-.13469
.18250	-.06059	-.07271	-.08484	-.09697	-.10910	-.12123
.18500	-.04799	-.06000	-.07201	-.08402	-.09603	-.10804
.18750	-.03564	-.04753	-.05942	-.07131	-.08320	-.09510
.19000	-.02353	-.03530	-.04708	-.05885	-.07063	-.08240
.19250	-.01165	-.02331	-.03497	-.04663	-.05829	-.06995
.19500	.00000	-.01154	-.02309	-.03463	-.04618	-.05773
.19750	.01143	0.00000	-.01143	-.02287	-.03431	-.04575
.20000	.02265	.01132	.00000	-.01133	-.02266	-.03399
.20250	.03365	.02244	.01122	.00000	-.01122	-.02244
.20500	.04445	.03334	.02223	.01112	-.00000	-.01112
.20750	.05504	.04404	.03303	.02202	.01101	.00000

POINT TABLES: ORIGINAL LOAN TERM: 420 MONTHS LOAN PREPAID IN: 180 MONTHS

EFFECTIVE YIELD	CONTRACT RATE .07000	.07250	.07500	.07750	.08000	.08250	.08500	.08750	.09000	.09250
.07000	.00000	-.02190	-.04391	-.06604	-.08826	-.11059	-.13301	-.15551	-.17810	-.20075
.07250	.02151	-.00000	-.02163	-.04337	-.06521	-.08715	-.10918	-.13130	-.15349	-.17576
.07500	.04239	.02125	0.00000	-.02136	-.04283	-.06439	-.08604	-.10778	-.12960	-.15150
.07750	.06265	.04188	.02100	.00000	-.02110	-.04229	-.06358	-.08495	-.10641	-.12793
.08000	.08232	.06191	.04138	.02074	.00000	-.02084	-.04177	-.06278	-.08387	-.10504
.08250	.10141	.08135	.06117	.04088	.02049	0.00000	-.02058	-.04124	-.06199	-.08281
.08500	.11995	.10023	.08039	.06044	.04039	.02024	0.00000	-.02032	-.04073	-.06120
.08750	.13795	.11856	.09905	.07943	.05971	.03990	.01999	0.00000	-.02007	-.04022
.09000	.15543	.13636	.11717	.09788	.07848	.05899	.03941	.01975	.00000	-.01982
.09250	.17241	.15365	.13478	.11580	.09672	.07755	.05828	.03893	.01950	.00000
.09500	.18890	.17045	.15189	.13322	.11444	.09558	.07662	.05758	.03846	.01926
.09750	.20492	.18677	.16851	.15013	.13166	.11310	.09444	.07570	.05688	.03799
.10000	.22049	.20263	.18465	.16658	.14840	.13013	.11176	.09332	.07480	.05620
.10250	.23561	.21803	.20035	.18255	.16466	.14668	.12860	.11045	.09221	.07390
.10500	.25031	.23301	.21560	.19809	.18047	.16277	.14497	.12710	.10914	.09111
.10750	.26459	.24756	.23043	.21318	.19584	.17841	.16089	.14329	.12561	.10785
.11000	.27848	.26171	.24484	.22786	.21079	.19362	.17637	.15903	.14162	.12413
.11250	.29197	.27547	.25885	.24214	.22532	.20842	.19142	.17435	.15719	.13997
.11500	.30510	.28884	.27248	.25602	.23946	.22280	.20607	.18925	.17235	.15538
.11750	.31785	.30185	.28573	.26951	.25320	.23680	.22031	.20374	.18709	.17037
.12000	.33026	.31449	.29862	.28265	.26658	.25041	.23417	.21784	.20143	.18496
.12250	.34233	.32680	.31116	.29542	.27959	.26366	.24765	.23156	.21539	.19915
.12500	.35407	.33876	.32336	.30785	.29224	.27655	.26077	.24491	.22898	.21297
.12750	.36549	.35041	.33522	.31994	.30456	.28910	.27354	.25791	.24221	.22643
.13000	.37660	.36174	.34677	.33171	.31655	.30131	.28598	.27057	.25508	.23953
.13250	.38741	.37276	.35801	.34316	.32822	.31319	.29808	.28288	.26762	.25228
.13500	.39793	.38349	.36895	.35431	.33958	.32476	.30986	.29488	.27982	.26470
.13750	.40818	.39394	.37960	.36517	.35064	.33603	.32133	.30656	.29171	.27680
.14000	.41815	.40411	.38997	.37574	.36141	.34700	.33251	.31794	.30329	.28858
.14250	.42785	.41401	.40007	.38603	.37190	.35769	.34339	.32902	.31457	.30006
.14500	.43730	.42365	.40990	.39605	.38212	.36810	.35399	.33982	.32556	.31124
.14750	.44651	.43304	.41947	.40582	.39207	.37824	.36432	.35033	.33627	.32214
.15000	.45547	.44218	.42880	.41533	.40176	.38812	.37439	.36058	.34671	.33276
.15250	.46420	.45109	.43789	.42460	.41121	.39774	.38420	.37057	.35688	.34312
.15500	.47271	.45977	.44675	.43363	.42042	.40713	.39376	.38031	.36680	.35321
.15750	.48100	.46823	.45538	.44243	.42939	.41627	.40308	.38980	.37646	.36305
.16000	.48907	.47648	.46379	.45100	.43814	.42519	.41216	.39906	.38589	.37265
.16250	.49694	.48451	.47198	.45937	.44666	.43388	.42102	.40808	.39508	.38201
.16500	.50462	.49234	.47998	.46752	.45498	.44236	.42966	.41689	.40404	.39113
.16750	.51210	.49998	.48777	.47547	.46309	.45062	.43808	.42547	.41279	.40004
.17000	.51939	.50742	.49537	.48322	.47099	.45868	.44630	.43384	.42132	.40873
.17250	.52650	.51468	.50278	.49078	.47871	.46655	.45432	.44201	.42964	.41720
.17500	.53343	.52177	.51001	.49816	.48623	.47422	.46214	.44999	.43776	.42548
.17750	.54020	.52867	.51706	.50536	.49357	.48171	.46977	.45777	.44569	.43355
.18000	.54680	.53541	.52394	.51238	.50074	.48902	.47722	.46536	.45343	.44143
.18250	.55324	.54199	.53065	.51923	.50773	.49615	.48450	.47277	.46098	.44913
.18500	.55952	.54841	.53721	.52592	.51455	.50311	.49159	.48001	.46836	.45664
.18750	.56565	.55467	.54360	.53245	.52122	.50991	.49853	.48708	.47556	.46398
.19000	.57164	.56078	.54985	.53882	.52772	.51654	.50529	.49398	.48259	.47115
.19250	.57748	.56675	.55594	.54505	.53407	.52302	.51190	.50072	.48946	.47815
.19500	.58319	.57258	.56189	.55112	.54028	.52935	.51836	.50730	.49618	.48499
.19750	.58876	.57827	.56771	.55706	.54634	.53554	.52467	.51373	.50273	.49167
.20000	.59420	.58383	.57339	.56286	.55226	.54158	.53083	.52002	.50914	.49820
.20250	.59951	.58926	.57894	.56853	.55804	.54748	.53685	.52616	.51540	.50459
.20500	.60470	.59457	.58436	.57406	.56369	.55325	.54274	.53216	.52153	.51083
.20750	.60977	.59975	.58965	.57947	.56922	.55889	.54849	.53803	.52751	.51693

EFFECTIVE YIELD	CONTRACT RATE .09500	.09750	.10000	.10250	.10500	.10750	.11000	.11250	.11500	.11750
.07000	-.22348	-.24627	-.26913	-.29203	-.31499	-.33800	-.36104	-.38413	-.40726	-.43041
.07250	-.19811	-.22051	-.24298	-.26550	-.28807	-.31069	-.33336	-.35606	-.37880	-.40158
.07500	-.17346	-.19549	-.21758	-.23973	-.26193	-.28417	-.30646	-.32879	-.35116	-.37356
.07750	-.14953	-.17119	-.19292	-.21469	-.23653	-.25840	-.28033	-.30229	-.32430	-.34633
.08000	-.12628	-.14759	-.16895	-.19037	-.21185	-.23337	-.25493	-.27654	-.29819	-.31987
.08250	-.10370	-.12465	-.14567	-.16674	-.18786	-.20904	-.23026	-.25152	-.27281	-.29415
.08500	-.08175	-.10237	-.12304	-.14377	-.16456	-.18539	-.20627	-.22719	-.24815	-.26915
.08750	-.06043	-.08071	-.10106	-.12145	-.14191	-.16241	-.18296	-.20354	-.22417	-.24484
.09000	-.03971	-.05967	-.07969	-.09976	-.11989	-.14007	-.16029	-.18055	-.20086	-.22120
.09250	-.01957	-.03921	-.05891	-.07867	-.09848	-.11835	-.13825	-.15820	-.17819	-.19822
.09500	.00000	-.01933	-.03872	-.05817	-.07767	-.09723	-.11682	-.13646	-.15614	-.17586
.09750	.01903	.00000	-.01909	-.03824	-.05744	-.07669	-.09598	-.11532	-.13470	-.15412
.10000	.03753	.01879	0.00000	-.01885	-.03776	-.05671	-.07572	-.09476	-.11385	-.13297
.10250	.05552	.03707	.01856	.00000	-.01862	-.03729	-.05600	-.07476	-.09356	-.11239
.10500	.07301	.05485	.03662	.01834	.00000	-.01839	-.03682	-.05530	-.07381	-.09237
.10750	.09002	.07213	.05418	.03617	.01811	.00000	-.01816	-.03636	-.05450	-.07288
.11000	.10657	.08895	.07127	.05353	.03573	.01789	.00000	-.01793	-.03591	-.05392
.11250	.12267	.10531	.08789	.07041	.05288	.03530	.01767	.00000	-.01771	-.03546
.11500	.13834	.12123	.10407	.08685	.06957	.05224	.03487	.01746	.00000	-.01749
.11750	.15358	.13672	.11981	.10284	.08581	.06874	.05162	.03445	.01724	0.00000
.12000	.16841	.15180	.13513	.11840	.10162	.08479	.06792	.05099	.03403	.01703
.12250	.18285	.16648	.15004	.13356	.11702	.10042	.08379	.06711	.05038	.03362
.12500	.19690	.18076	.16456	.14831	.13200	.11565	.09924	.08279	.06631	.04978
.12750	.21058	.19467	.17870	.16268	.14660	.13047	.11429	.09808	.08182	.06552
.13000	.22390	.20822	.19247	.17667	.16081	.14491	.12895	.11296	.09692	.08085
.13250	.23687	.22140	.20588	.19029	.17466	.15897	.14324	.12746	.11164	.09579
.13500	.24951	.23425	.21894	.20357	.18814	.17267	.15715	.14159	.12599	.11035
.13750	.26181	.24676	.23166	.21650	.20128	.18602	.17071	.15536	.13997	.12453
.14000	.27380	.25895	.24405	.22910	.21409	.19903	.18392	.16878	.15359	.13836
.14250	.28548	.27083	.25613	.24137	.22656	.21171	.19680	.18186	.16687	.15184
.14500	.29686	.28241	.26790	.25334	.23873	.22406	.20936	.19461	.17981	.16499
.14750	.30795	.29369	.27937	.26500	.25058	.23611	.22160	.20704	.19244	.17780
.15000	.31875	.30468	.29056	.27637	.26214	.24786	.23353	.21916	.20475	.19030
.15250	.32929	.31540	.30146	.28746	.27341	.25931	.24517	.23098	.21675	.20249
.15500	.33956	.32585	.31209	.29827	.28440	.27048	.25651	.24251	.22846	.21438
.15750	.34958	.33605	.32245	.30881	.29512	.28137	.26759	.25376	.23989	.22598
.16000	.35935	.34598	.33257	.31909	.30557	.29200	.27839	.26473	.25103	.23730
.16250	.36887	.35568	.34243	.32912	.31577	.30237	.28892	.27543	.26191	.24834
.16500	.37816	.36513	.35205	.33891	.32572	.31249	.29920	.28588	.27252	.25912
.16750	.38723	.37436	.36144	.34846	.33543	.32236	.30924	.29608	.28288	.26965
.17000	.39607	.38336	.37060	.35778	.34491	.33199	.31903	.30603	.29300	.27992
.17250	.40471	.39215	.37954	.36687	.35416	.34140	.32860	.31575	.30287	.28995
.17500	.41313	.40072	.38826	.37575	.36319	.35058	.33793	.32524	.31251	.29974
.17750	.42135	.40909	.39678	.38442	.37201	.35955	.34705	.33451	.32193	.30931
.18000	.42938	.41727	.40510	.39288	.38062	.36831	.35595	.34355	.33112	.31865
.18250	.43722	.42525	.41322	.40115	.38902	.37686	.36465	.35239	.34010	.32778
.18500	.44487	.43304	.42115	.40922	.39724	.38521	.37314	.36103	.34888	.33670
.18750	.45234	.44065	.42890	.41711	.40526	.39337	.38144	.36947	.35746	.34541
.19000	.45964	.44808	.43647	.42481	.41310	.40134	.38955	.37771	.36584	.35393
.19250	.46678	.45535	.44387	.43234	.42076	.40914	.39747	.38577	.37403	.36225
.19500	.47374	.46244	.45109	.43969	.42824	.41675	.40522	.39364	.38203	.37039
.19750	.48055	.46938	.45815	.44688	.43556	.42419	.41279	.40134	.38986	.37834
.20000	.48721	.47616	.46506	.45391	.44271	.43147	.42019	.40887	.39751	.38612
.20250	.49371	.48278	.47181	.46078	.44970	.43859	.42743	.41623	.40500	.39373
.20500	.50007	.48926	.47840	.46749	.45654	.44554	.43451	.42343	.41232	.40117
.20750	.50629	.49560	.48485	.47406	.46323	.45235	.44143	.43047	.41948	.40845

POINT TABLES: ORIGINAL LOAN TERM: 420 MONTHS LOAN PREPAID IN: 180 MONTHS

CONTRACT RATE

EFFECTIVE YIELD	.12000	.12250	.12500	.12750	.13000	.13250	.13500	.13750	.14000	.14250
.07000	-.45360	-.47681	-.50005	-.52331	-.54659	-.56989	-.59320	-.61652	-.63986	-.66321
.07250	-.42438	-.44721	-.47007	-.49295	-.51585	-.53877	-.56170	-.58465	-.60761	-.63058
.07500	-.39599	-.41845	-.44094	-.46344	-.48597	-.50852	-.53108	-.55366	-.57625	-.59886
.07750	-.36840	-.39050	-.41262	-.43476	-.45693	-.47912	-.50132	-.52354	-.54577	-.56801
.08000	-.34158	-.36332	-.38509	-.40688	-.42870	-.45053	-.47238	-.49425	-.51613	-.53802
.08250	-.31551	-.33691	-.35833	-.37978	-.40125	-.42274	-.44424	-.46577	-.48730	-.50885
.08500	-.29017	-.31123	-.33231	-.35342	-.37455	-.39571	-.41688	-.43807	-.45927	-.48048
.08750	-.26553	-.28626	-.30701	-.32779	-.34860	-.36942	-.39026	-.41112	-.43200	-.45289
.09000	-.24157	-.26198	-.28241	-.30287	-.32335	-.34385	-.36438	-.38491	-.40547	-.42604
.09250	-.21827	-.23836	-.25848	-.27863	-.29879	-.31898	-.33919	-.35942	-.37966	-.39992
.09500	-.19561	-.21539	-.23521	-.25504	-.27490	-.29479	-.31469	-.33461	-.35455	-.37450
.09750	-.17357	-.19305	-.21256	-.23210	-.25166	-.27124	-.29085	-.31047	-.33011	-.34976
.10000	-.15212	-.17131	-.19053	-.20977	-.22904	-.24833	-.26764	-.28698	-.30632	-.32569
.10250	-.13126	-.15016	-.16909	-.18805	-.20703	-.22604	-.24506	-.26411	-.28317	-.30225
.10500	-.11096	-.12958	-.14823	-.16691	-.18561	-.20433	-.22308	-.24185	-.26063	-.27943
.10750	-.09120	-.10955	-.12792	-.14633	-.16476	-.18321	-.20168	-.22018	-.23869	-.25722
.11000	-.07197	-.09005	-.10816	-.12629	-.14446	-.16264	-.18085	-.19908	-.21732	-.23558
.11250	-.05325	-.07107	-.08891	-.10679	-.12469	-.14262	-.16056	-.17853	-.19651	-.21452
.11500	-.03502	-.05259	-.07018	-.08780	-.10544	-.12311	-.14080	-.15852	-.17625	-.19399
.11750	-.01728	-.03459	-.05193	-.06930	-.08670	-.10412	-.12156	-.13902	-.15651	-.17400
.12000	.00000	-.01707	-.03416	-.05129	-.06844	-.08562	-.10282	-.12004	-.13727	-.15453
.12250	.01683	.00000	-.01686	-.03375	-.05066	-.06760	-.08456	-.10154	-.11854	-.13555
.12500	.03322	.01662	.00000	-.01665	-.03333	-.05004	-.06676	-.08351	-.10028	-.11706
.12750	.04919	.03282	.01642	.00000	-.01645	-.03293	-.04942	-.06594	-.08248	-.09904
.13000	.06474	.04860	.03243	.01623	-.00000	-.01625	-.03253	-.04882	-.06514	-.08147
.13250	.07990	.06398	.04802	.03204	.01603	0.00000	-.01606	-.03213	-.04823	-.06434
.13500	.09467	.07896	.06322	.04746	.03166	.01584	.00000	-.01586	-.03175	-.04765
.13750	.10907	.09357	.07804	.06248	.04690	.03129	.01565	.00000	-.01557	-.03137
.14000	.12310	.10781	.09248	.07713	.06175	.04635	.03092	.01547	.00000	-.01549
.14250	.13678	.12169	.10657	.09141	.07623	.06103	.04580	.03056	.01529	.00000
.14500	.15012	.13523	.12030	.10534	.09036	.07535	.06032	.04527	.03020	.01511
.14750	.16313	.14843	.13369	.11893	.10414	.08932	.07448	.05962	.04474	.02985
.15000	.17582	.16130	.14675	.13218	.11758	.10295	.08830	.07363	.05894	.04423
.15250	.18819	.17386	.15950	.14511	.13069	.11625	.10178	.08729	.07279	.05826
.15500	.20026	.18611	.17193	.15772	.14348	.12922	.11494	.10063	.08630	.07196
.15750	.21204	.19806	.18406	.17003	.15597	.14188	.12778	.11365	.09950	.08533
.16000	.22353	.20973	.19590	.18204	.16815	.15424	.14031	.12635	.11238	.09838
.16250	.23475	.22111	.20745	.19376	.18005	.16631	.15254	.13876	.12495	.11112
.16500	.24569	.23223	.21873	.20521	.19166	.17808	.16449	.15087	.13723	.12357
.16750	.25638	.24308	.22974	.21638	.20300	.18958	.17615	.16269	.14922	.13572
.17000	.26681	.25367	.24049	.22729	.21407	.20081	.18754	.17424	.16093	.14759
.17250	.27700	.26401	.25099	.23795	.22488	.21178	.19867	.18553	.17237	.15919
.17500	.28694	.27411	.26125	.24836	.23544	.22250	.20953	.19655	.18354	.17052
.17750	.29666	.28398	.27126	.25852	.24576	.23297	.22015	.20732	.19446	.18159
.18000	.30615	.29361	.28105	.26846	.25584	.24319	.23053	.21784	.20513	.19241
.18250	.31542	.30303	.29061	.27816	.26569	.25319	.24067	.22813	.21556	.20298
.18500	.32448	.31223	.29995	.28765	.27531	.26296	.25058	.23818	.22576	.21332
.18750	.33333	.32122	.30908	.29691	.28472	.27250	.26027	.24800	.23572	.22342
.19000	.34198	.33001	.31801	.30598	.29392	.28184	.26974	.25761	.24547	.23330
.19250	.35044	.33860	.32673	.31483	.30291	.29096	.27900	.26701	.25530	.24297
.19500	.35871	.34700	.33526	.32350	.31170	.29989	.28805	.27619	.26431	.25242
.19750	.36679	.35521	.34360	.33197	.32030	.30862	.29691	.28518	.27343	.26166
.20000	.37470	.36324	.35176	.34025	.32871	.31715	.30557	.29397	.28235	.27071
.20250	.38243	.37110	.35974	.34835	.33694	.32550	.31405	.30257	.29107	.27955
.20500	.38999	.37878	.36754	.35628	.34499	.33367	.32234	.31098	.29961	.28821
.20750	.39739	.38630	.37518	.36403	.35286	.34167	.33045	.31922	.30796	.29669

POINT TABLES: ORIGINAL LOAN TERM: 420 MONTHS LOAN PREPAID IN: 180 MONTHS

EFFECTIVE YIELD	CONTRACT RATE .14500	.14750	.15000	.15250	.15500	.15750	.16000	.16250	.16500	.16750
.07000	-.68657	-.70993	-.73330	-.75667	-.78005	-.80343	-.82682	-.85020	-.87359	-.89697
.07250	-.65356	-.67655	-.69954	-.72254	-.74555	-.76855	-.79156	-.81458	-.83759	-.86060
.07500	-.62147	-.64409	-.66672	-.68935	-.71199	-.73464	-.75728	-.77993	-.80258	-.82523
.07750	-.59027	-.61253	-.63480	-.65708	-.67936	-.70165	-.72394	-.74623	-.76853	-.79082
.08000	-.55993	-.58184	-.60376	-.62569	-.64762	-.66956	-.69150	-.71345	-.73540	-.75735
.08250	-.53041	-.55199	-.57357	-.59515	-.61675	-.63835	-.65995	-.68156	-.70317	-.72478
.08500	-.50171	-.52295	-.54420	-.56545	-.58671	-.60798	-.62925	-.65053	-.67181	-.69309
.08750	-.47379	-.49470	-.51562	-.53655	-.55749	-.57843	-.59938	-.62033	-.64129	-.66225
.09000	-.44662	-.46721	-.48782	-.50843	-.52905	-.54967	-.57031	-.59094	-.61158	-.63223
.09250	-.42019	-.44047	-.46076	-.48106	-.50137	-.52169	-.54201	-.56234	-.58257	-.60301
.09500	-.39446	-.41444	-.43443	-.45443	-.47443	-.49445	-.51447	-.53449	-.55452	-.57456
.09750	-.36943	-.38911	-.40880	-.42850	-.44821	-.46793	-.48765	-.50738	-.52712	-.54686
.10000	-.34506	-.36445	-.38365	-.40326	-.42268	-.44211	-.46155	-.48099	-.50044	-.51989
.10250	-.32134	-.34045	-.35956	-.37869	-.39783	-.41697	-.43613	-.45529	-.47445	-.49362
.10500	-.29825	-.31707	-.33591	-.35476	-.37362	-.39249	-.41137	-.43025	-.44914	-.46804
.10750	-.27576	-.29432	-.31288	-.33146	-.35005	-.36865	-.38726	-.40587	-.42449	-.44311
.11000	-.25386	-.27215	-.29045	-.30877	-.32709	-.34543	-.36377	-.38212	-.40047	-.41883
.11250	-.23253	-.25056	-.26861	-.28666	-.30473	-.32280	-.34089	-.35898	-.37707	-.39518
.11500	-.21176	-.22953	-.24732	-.26513	-.28294	-.30076	-.31859	-.33643	-.35427	-.37212
.11750	-.19152	-.20905	-.22659	-.24414	-.26171	-.27928	-.29686	-.31446	-.33205	-.34966
.12000	-.17180	-.18909	-.20638	-.22370	-.24102	-.25835	-.27569	-.29304	-.31040	-.32776
.12250	-.15259	-.16963	-.18670	-.20377	-.22085	-.23795	-.25505	-.27216	-.28928	-.30641
.12500	-.13386	-.15068	-.16751	-.18435	-.20120	-.21806	-.23493	-.25181	-.26870	-.28560
.12750	-.11561	-.13220	-.14880	-.16541	-.18204	-.19867	-.21532	-.23197	-.24864	-.26531
.13000	-.09782	-.11418	-.13056	-.14695	-.16336	-.17977	-.19619	-.21263	-.22907	-.24551
.13250	-.08048	-.09662	-.11278	-.12896	-.14514	-.16134	-.17754	-.19376	-.20998	-.22621
.13500	-.06357	-.07950	-.09545	-.11141	-.12738	-.14336	-.15935	-.17536	-.19137	-.20739
.13750	-.04707	-.06280	-.07854	-.09429	-.11005	-.12583	-.14161	-.15741	-.17321	-.18902
.14000	-.03099	-.04651	-.06205	-.07759	-.09315	-.10872	-.12430	-.13989	-.15549	-.17110
.14250	-.01530	-.03062	-.04596	-.06130	-.07666	-.09203	-.10742	-.12281	-.13820	-.15361
.14500	.00000	-.01512	-.03026	-.04541	-.06058	-.07575	-.09094	-.10613	-.12133	-.13655
.14750	.01493	.00000	-.01495	-.02990	-.04488	-.05986	-.07485	-.08986	-.10487	-.11989
.15000	.02950	.01476	.00000	-.01477	-.02955	-.04435	-.05916	-.07397	-.08880	-.10363
.15250	.04372	.02916	.01459	.00000	-.01460	-.02921	-.04383	-.05846	-.07310	-.08775
.15500	.05760	.04322	.02883	.01442	.00000	-.01443	-.02887	-.04332	-.05778	-.07225
.15750	.07114	.05694	.04273	.02850	.01425	.00000	-.01426	-.02854	-.04282	-.05712
.16000	.08437	.07034	.05630	.04224	.02817	.01409	-.00000	-.01410	-.02821	-.04233
.16250	.09728	.08342	.06955	.05567	.04177	.02785	.01393	.00000	-.01394	-.02789
.16500	.10989	.09620	.08250	.06878	.05504	.04130	.02754	.01378	.00000	-.01378
.16750	.12221	.10868	.09514	.08158	.06801	.05443	.04084	.02723	.01362	.00000
.17000	.13424	.12087	.10749	.09409	.08068	.06726	.05383	.04038	.02693	.01347
.17250	.14599	.13278	.11956	.10631	.09306	.07980	.06652	.05323	.03994	.02663
.17500	.15748	.14442	.13135	.11826	.10516	.09205	.07893	.06579	.05265	.03950
.17750	.16870	.15579	.14287	.12993	.11698	.10402	.09105	.07807	.06508	.05208
.18000	.17966	.16691	.15413	.14134	.12854	.11573	.10290	.09007	.07723	.06437
.18250	.19038	.17777	.16514	.15250	.13984	.12717	.11449	.10180	.08911	.07640
.18500	.20086	.18839	.17590	.16340	.15089	.13836	.12583	.11328	.10072	.08816
.18750	.21111	.19878	.18643	.17407	.16169	.14931	.13691	.12450	.11208	.09966
.19000	.22113	.20893	.19672	.18449	.17226	.16001	.14775	.13548	.12320	.11091
.19250	.23092	.21886	.20678	.19469	.18259	.17048	.15835	.14621	.13407	.12191
.19500	.24050	.22857	.21663	.20467	.19270	.18072	.16872	.15672	.14470	.13268
.19750	.24988	.23808	.22626	.21443	.20259	.19074	.17887	.16700	.15511	.14322
.20000	.25905	.24737	.23569	.22398	.21227	.20054	.18881	.17706	.16530	.15353
.20250	.26802	.25647	.24491	.23333	.22174	.21014	.19853	.18690	.17527	.16363
.20500	.27680	.26538	.25393	.24248	.23101	.21953	.20804	.19654	.18503	.17351
.20750	.28540	.27409	.26277	.25143	.24009	.22873	.21736	.20597	.19458	.18318

POINT TABLES: ORIGINAL LOAN TERM: 420 MONTHS LOAN PREPAID IN: 180 MONTHS

EFFECTIVE YIELD	CONTRACT RATE .17000	.17250	.17500	.17750	.18000	.18250	.18500	.18750	.19000	.19250
.07000	-.92035	-.94374	-.96712	-.99049	-1.01387	-1.03724	-1.06061	-1.08398	-1.10734	-1.13070
.07250	-.88362	-.90663	-.92964	-.95265	-.97566	-.99866	-1.02166	-1.04466	-1.06766	-1.09065
.07500	-.84788	-.87053	-.89318	-.91583	-.93848	-.96112	-.98377	-1.00641	-1.02904	-1.05168
.07750	-.81312	-.83542	-.85772	-.88001	-.90231	-.92460	-.94689	-.96918	-.99147	-1.01375
.08000	-.77930	-.80126	-.82321	-.84516	-.86711	-.88906	-.91101	-.93296	-.95490	-.97684
.08250	-.74640	-.76801	-.78963	-.81124	-.83286	-.85447	-.87609	-.89770	-.91931	-.94092
.08500	-.71437	-.73566	-.75695	-.77823	-.79952	-.82081	-.84209	-.86338	-.88466	-.90594
.08750	-.68321	-.70417	-.72514	-.74610	-.76707	-.78804	-.80900	-.82997	-.85093	-.87189
.09000	-.65287	-.67352	-.69417	-.71483	-.73548	-.75613	-.77678	-.79743	-.81809	-.83874
.09250	-.62335	-.64369	-.66403	-.68437	-.70472	-.72507	-.74541	-.76576	-.78610	-.80645
.09500	-.59460	-.61464	-.63468	-.65472	-.67477	-.69482	-.71486	-.73491	-.75496	-.77500
.09750	-.56660	-.58635	-.60610	-.62585	-.64560	-.66536	-.68511	-.70486	-.72462	-.74437
.10000	-.53934	-.55880	-.57826	-.59773	-.61719	-.63666	-.65613	-.67560	-.69507	-.71454
.10250	-.51279	-.53197	-.55115	-.57034	-.58952	-.60871	-.62790	-.64709	-.66628	-.68547
.10500	-.48694	-.50584	-.52474	-.54365	-.56256	-.58148	-.60039	-.61931	-.63822	-.65714
.10750	-.46174	-.48038	-.49902	-.51766	-.53630	-.55494	-.57359	-.59224	-.61089	-.62954
.11000	-.43720	-.45557	-.47395	-.49232	-.51070	-.52909	-.54747	-.56586	-.58425	-.60263
.11250	-.41329	-.43140	-.44952	-.46764	-.48576	-.50389	-.52202	-.54015	-.55828	-.57641
.11500	-.38998	-.40784	-.42571	-.44358	-.46145	-.47933	-.49720	-.51508	-.53297	-.55085
.11750	-.36727	-.38488	-.40250	-.42013	-.43775	-.45538	-.47302	-.49065	-.50829	-.52592
.12000	-.34513	-.36250	-.37988	-.39726	-.41465	-.43204	-.44943	-.46683	-.48422	-.50162
.12250	-.32354	-.34068	-.35783	-.37497	-.39212	-.40928	-.42643	-.44359	-.46076	-.47792
.12500	-.30250	-.31941	-.33632	-.35324	-.37016	-.38708	-.40401	-.42094	-.43787	-.45480
.12750	-.28198	-.29866	-.31535	-.33204	-.34873	-.36543	-.38213	-.39884	-.41555	-.43225
.13000	-.26197	-.27843	-.29489	-.31136	-.32784	-.34432	-.36080	-.37728	-.39377	-.41026
.13250	-.24245	-.25869	-.27494	-.29120	-.30745	-.32372	-.33998	-.35625	-.37252	-.38879
.13500	-.22341	-.23944	-.25548	-.27152	-.28757	-.30362	-.31967	-.33573	-.35179	-.36785
.13750	-.20484	-.22066	-.23649	-.25232	-.26816	-.28400	-.29985	-.31570	-.33155	-.34741
.14000	-.18671	-.20233	-.21796	-.23359	-.24922	-.26486	-.28051	-.29615	-.31181	-.32746
.14250	-.16903	-.18445	-.19987	-.21530	-.23074	-.24618	-.26163	-.27708	-.29253	-.30798
.14500	-.15176	-.16699	-.18222	-.19746	-.21270	-.22795	-.24320	-.25845	-.27371	-.28897
.14750	-.13492	-.14995	-.16499	-.18004	-.19509	-.21014	-.22520	-.24027	-.25533	-.27040
.15000	-.11847	-.13332	-.14817	-.16303	-.17789	-.19276	-.20763	-.22251	-.23739	-.25227
.15250	-.10241	-.11707	-.13174	-.14642	-.16110	-.17578	-.19047	-.20517	-.21986	-.23456
.15500	-.08673	-.10121	-.11570	-.13020	-.14470	-.15921	-.17372	-.18823	-.20275	-.21727
.15750	-.07142	-.08572	-.10004	-.11436	-.12868	-.14301	-.15735	-.17168	-.18603	-.20037
.16000	-.05646	-.07059	-.08473	-.09888	-.11303	-.12719	-.14135	-.15552	-.16969	-.18386
.16250	-.04185	-.05581	-.06979	-.08376	-.09775	-.11173	-.12573	-.13972	-.15373	-.16773
.16500	-.02758	-.04137	-.05518	-.06899	-.08281	-.09663	-.11046	-.12429	-.13813	-.15196
.16750	-.01363	-.02727	-.04091	-.05456	-.06821	-.08187	-.09554	-.10921	-.12288	-.13655
.17000	.00000	-.01348	-.02696	-.04045	-.05394	-.06745	-.08095	-.09446	-.10797	-.12149
.17250	.01332	.00000	-.01333	-.02666	-.04000	-.05334	-.06669	-.08005	-.09340	-.10676
.17500	.02634	.01317	.00000	-.01318	-.02637	-.03956	-.05275	-.06595	-.07916	-.09236
.17750	.03907	.02605	.01303	0.00000	-.01304	-.02608	-.03912	-.05217	-.06522	-.07828
.18000	.05151	.03864	.02577	.01289	.00000	-.01289	-.02579	-.03869	-.05160	-.06451
.18250	.06368	.05096	.03823	.02549	.01275	0.00000	-.01275	-.02551	-.03827	-.05104
.18500	.07558	.06300	.05041	.03782	.02522	.01261	-.00000	-.01262	-.02524	-.03786
.18750	.08722	.07478	.06233	.04988	.03742	.02495	.01248	.00000	-.01248	-.02497
.19000	.09861	.08630	.07399	.06167	.04935	.03702	.02468	.01234	.00000	-.01235
.19250	.10975	.09758	.08540	.07322	.06103	.04883	.03663	.02442	.01221	0.00000
.19500	.12065	.10861	.09657	.08451	.07245	.06039	.04832	.03625	.02417	.01209
.19750	.13132	.11941	.10749	.09557	.08364	.07170	.05976	.04782	.03587	.02392
.20000	.14176	.12997	.11819	.10639	.09459	.08278	.07097	.05915	.04733	.03550
.20250	.15198	.14032	.12865	.11698	.10530	.09362	.08193	.07024	.05854	.04684
.20500	.16198	.15045	.13890	.12735	.11580	.10424	.09267	.08110	.06953	.05795
.20750	.17178	.16036	.14894	.13751	.12608	.11463	.10319	.09174	.08028	.06882

EFFECTIVE YIELD	CONTRACT RATE .19500	.19750	.20000	.20250	.20500	.20750
.07000	-1.15406	-1.17741	-1.20075	-1.22410	-1.24744	-1.27077
.07250	-1.11364	-1.13662	-1.15961	-1.18258	-1.20556	-1.22853
.07500	-1.07431	-1.09694	-1.11956	-1.14218	-1.16480	-1.18741
.07750	-1.03604	-1.05831	-1.08059	-1.10286	-1.12513	-1.14740
.08000	-.99878	-1.02072	-1.04265	-1.06459	-1.08652	-1.10844
.08250	-.96252	-.98413	-1.00573	-1.02733	-1.04892	-1.07051
.08500	-.92722	-.94850	-.96977	-.99105	-1.01232	-1.03359
.08750	-.89285	-.91381	-.93477	-.95572	-.97667	-.99763
.09000	-.85938	-.88003	-.90068	-.92132	-.94196	-.96260
.09250	-.82679	-.84713	-.86748	-.88782	-.90815	-.92849
.09500	-.79505	-.81509	-.83514	-.85518	-.87522	-.89526
.09750	-.76413	-.78388	-.80363	-.82339	-.84314	-.86288
.10000	-.73401	-.75347	-.77294	-.79241	-.81187	-.83134
.10250	-.70466	-.72385	-.74304	-.76222	-.78141	-.80060
.10500	-.67606	-.69498	-.71389	-.73281	-.75172	-.77064
.10750	-.64819	-.66684	-.68549	-.70414	-.72279	-.74144
.11000	-.62102	-.63941	-.65780	-.67619	-.69458	-.71297
.11250	-.59455	-.61268	-.63081	-.64895	-.66708	-.68522
.11500	-.56873	-.58662	-.60450	-.62239	-.64027	-.65816
.11750	-.54356	-.56120	-.57884	-.59648	-.61413	-.63177
.12000	-.51902	-.53642	-.55382	-.57122	-.58863	-.60603
.12250	-.49508	-.51225	-.52942	-.54659	-.56375	-.58092
.12500	-.47174	-.48868	-.50561	-.52255	-.53949	-.55643
.12750	-.44897	-.46568	-.48239	-.49911	-.51582	-.53254
.13000	-.42675	-.44324	-.45973	-.47623	-.49272	-.50922
.13250	-.40507	-.42135	-.43762	-.45390	-.47018	-.48647
.13500	-.38391	-.39998	-.41605	-.43212	-.44819	-.46426
.13750	-.36327	-.37913	-.39499	-.41085	-.42671	-.44258
.14000	-.34311	-.35877	-.37443	-.39009	-.40575	-.42142
.14250	-.32344	-.33890	-.35436	-.36982	-.38529	-.40075
.14500	-.30423	-.31950	-.33476	-.35003	-.36530	-.38057
.14750	-.28547	-.30055	-.31563	-.33070	-.34579	-.36087
.15000	-.26716	-.28205	-.29694	-.31183	-.32672	-.34162
.15250	-.24927	-.26397	-.27868	-.29339	-.30810	-.32282
.15500	-.23179	-.24632	-.26085	-.27538	-.28991	-.30445
.15750	-.21472	-.22907	-.24342	-.25778	-.27214	-.28650
.16000	-.19804	-.21222	-.22640	-.24058	-.25477	-.26895
.16250	-.18174	-.19575	-.20976	-.22377	-.23779	-.25181
.16500	-.16581	-.17965	-.19350	-.20735	-.22120	-.23505
.16750	-.15023	-.16392	-.17760	-.19129	-.20498	-.21867
.17000	-.13501	-.14853	-.16206	-.17559	-.18912	-.20265
.17250	-.12013	-.13350	-.14687	-.16024	-.17361	-.18699
.17500	-.10558	-.11879	-.13201	-.14523	-.15845	-.17167
.17750	-.09134	-.10441	-.11747	-.13054	-.14362	-.15669
.18000	-.07742	-.09034	-.10326	-.11618	-.12911	-.14203
.18250	-.06381	-.07658	-.08936	-.10213	-.11491	-.12770
.18500	-.05049	-.06312	-.07575	-.08839	-.10103	-.11367
.18750	-.03745	-.04995	-.06244	-.07494	-.08744	-.09994
.19000	-.02470	-.03705	-.04941	-.06177	-.07414	-.08650
.19250	-.01222	-.02444	-.03666	-.04889	-.06112	-.07335
.19500	.00000	-.01209	-.02418	-.03628	-.04837	-.06047
.19750	.01196	.00000	-.01196	-.02393	-.03590	-.04787
.20000	.02367	.01184	.00000	-.01184	-.02368	-.03553
.20250	.03514	.02343	.01171	.00000	-.01172	-.02344
.20500	.04636	.03478	.02319	.01160	-.00000	-.01160
.20750	.05736	.04589	.03443	.02295	.01148	.00000

POINT TABLES: ORIGINAL LOAN TERM: 420 MONTHS LOAN PREPAID IN: 420 MONTHS

EFFECTIVE YIELD	CONTRACT RATE .07000	.07250	.07500	.07750	.08000	.08250	.08500	.08750	.09000	.09250
.07000	0.00000	-.02757	-.05539	-.08346	-.11177	-.14031	-.16906	-.19802	-.22718	-.25653
.07250	.02683	.00000	-.02708	-.05440	-.08194	-.10971	-.13770	-.16588	-.19426	-.22282
.07500	.05248	.02636	.00000	-.02660	-.05342	-.08046	-.10770	-.13515	-.16278	-.19059
.07750	.07703	.05159	.02591	.00000	-.02613	-.05247	-.07900	-.10573	-.13265	-.15974
.08000	.10053	.07574	.05071	.02546	.00000	-.02567	-.05153	-.07758	-.10381	-.13021
.08250	.12304	.09887	.07447	.04985	.02502	.00000	-.02522	-.05061	-.07619	-.10193
.08500	.14461	.12103	.09723	.07322	.04900	.02460	0.00000	-.02477	-.04972	-.07482
.08750	.16529	.14228	.11906	.09562	.07199	.04818	.02417	0.00000	-.02434	-.04884
.09000	.18512	.16266	.13999	.11711	.09405	.07079	.04736	.02376	0.00000	-.02392
.09250	.20416	.18222	.16008	.13774	.11521	.09250	.06962	.04657	.02336	.00000
.09500	.22244	.20100	.17937	.15754	.13553	.11334	.09098	.06846	.04579	.02296
.09750	.23999	.21904	.19789	.17656	.15504	.13336	.11150	.08949	.06733	.04502
.10000	.25686	.23638	.21570	.19484	.17380	.15259	.13123	.10970	.08803	.06622
.10250	.27308	.25304	.23282	.21241	.19183	.17109	.15019	.12914	.10794	.08660
.10500	.28868	.26908	.24929	.22932	.20918	.18888	.16843	.14783	.12709	.10621
.10750	.30370	.28451	.26513	.24559	.22588	.20601	.18599	.16582	.14551	.12508
.11000	.31816	.29936	.28039	.26125	.24195	.22249	.20289	.18314	.16326	.14324
.11250	.33209	.31367	.29509	.27634	.25743	.23837	.21917	.19982	.18035	.16074
.11500	.34551	.32746	.30925	.29088	.27235	.25368	.23486	.21590	.19682	.17761
.11750	.35845	.34076	.32291	.30490	.28674	.26843	.24998	.23140	.21270	.19387
.12000	.37093	.35358	.33608	.31842	.30061	.28266	.26458	.24636	.22801	.20955
.12250	.38297	.36596	.34879	.33147	.31400	.29640	.27865	.26078	.24279	.22468
.12500	.39459	.37791	.36106	.34407	.32693	.30965	.29225	.27471	.25706	.23929
.12750	.40582	.38944	.37291	.35623	.33941	.32246	.30537	.28816	.27084	.25340
.13000	.41667	.40059	.38436	.36799	.35147	.33483	.31806	.30116	.28415	.26703
.13250	.42716	.41137	.39543	.37935	.36313	.34679	.33032	.31372	.29702	.28021
.13500	.43730	.42179	.40613	.39034	.37441	.35835	.34217	.32587	.30946	.29295
.13750	.44711	.43187	.41649	.40097	.38531	.36954	.35364	.33763	.32150	.30528
.14000	.45660	.44162	.42651	.41125	.39587	.38036	.36474	.34900	.33315	.31720
.14250	.46580	.45107	.43621	.42121	.40609	.39084	.37548	.36001	.34443	.32875
.14500	.47470	.46022	.44560	.43086	.41599	.40100	.38589	.37068	.35536	.33994
.14750	.48332	.46908	.45471	.44020	.42558	.41083	.39598	.38101	.36595	.35078
.15000	.49169	.47767	.46353	.44926	.43487	.42037	.40575	.39103	.37621	.36129
.15250	.49979	.48600	.47209	.45805	.44389	.42961	.41523	.40074	.38615	.37147
.15500	.50766	.49409	.48039	.46657	.45263	.43858	.42442	.41016	.39581	.38135
.15750	.51529	.50193	.48844	.47483	.46111	.44728	.43334	.41931	.40517	.39094
.16000	.52270	.50954	.49626	.48286	.46935	.45573	.44200	.42818	.41426	.40025
.16250	.52989	.51693	.50385	.49065	.47735	.46393	.45041	.43680	.42309	.40929
.16500	.53688	.52411	.51122	.49822	.48511	.47190	.45858	.44517	.43166	.41807
.16750	.54367	.53109	.51839	.50558	.49266	.47964	.46652	.45330	.44000	.42660
.17000	.55027	.53787	.52536	.51273	.50000	.48717	.47424	.46121	.44810	.43490
.17250	.55669	.54447	.53213	.51969	.50714	.49449	.48174	.46890	.45597	.44296
.17500	.56293	.55088	.53872	.52645	.51408	.50161	.48904	.47638	.46363	.45081
.17750	.56900	.55712	.54513	.53303	.52083	.50853	.49614	.48366	.47109	.45844
.18000	.57492	.56320	.55137	.53944	.52740	.51527	.50305	.49074	.47834	.46587
.18250	.58067	.56911	.55745	.54567	.53380	.52184	.50978	.49764	.48541	.47310
.18500	.58628	.57487	.56336	.55175	.54004	.52823	.51633	.50435	.49229	.48014
.18750	.59174	.58049	.56913	.55767	.54611	.53446	.52272	.51090	.49899	.48701
.19000	.59706	.58595	.57474	.56343	.55203	.54053	.52894	.51727	.50552	.49369
.19250	.60225	.59129	.58022	.56905	.55779	.54644	.53501	.52349	.51189	.50021
.19500	.60731	.59648	.58556	.57453	.56342	.55221	.54092	.52955	.51810	.50657
.19750	.61224	.60155	.59076	.57988	.56890	.55784	.54669	.53546	.52415	.51277
.20000	.61706	.60650	.59585	.58510	.57426	.56333	.55232	.54123	.53006	.51882
.20250	.62175	.61133	.60080	.59019	.57948	.56868	.55781	.54685	.53582	.52472
.20500	.62634	.61604	.60564	.59515	.58458	.57391	.56317	.55235	.54145	.53048
.20750	.63082	.62064	.61037	.60000	.58955	.57902	.56840	.55771	.54694	.53611

POINT TABLES: ORIGINAL LOAN TERM: 420 MONTHS LOAN PREPAID IN: 420 MONTHS

EFFECTIVE YIELD	CONTRACT RATE .09500	.09750	.10000	.10250	.10500	.10750	.11000	.11250	.11500	.11750
.07000	-.28607	-.31577	-.34564	-.37567	-.40585	-.43616	-.46662	-.49720	-.52790	-.55871
.07250	-.25157	-.28047	-.30954	-.33877	-.36813	-.39764	-.42727	-.45703	-.48691	-.51690
.07500	-.21857	-.24672	-.27502	-.30347	-.33206	-.36079	-.38964	-.41862	-.44771	-.47691
.07750	-.18700	-.21442	-.24199	-.26970	-.29755	-.32553	-.35364	-.38187	-.41020	-.43864
.08000	-.15677	-.18349	-.21036	-.23737	-.26451	-.29178	-.31917	-.34668	-.37429	-.40201
.08250	-.12783	-.15388	-.18007	-.20641	-.23287	-.25946	-.28616	-.31298	-.33990	-.36693
.08500	-.10009	-.12550	-.15105	-.17673	-.20255	-.22848	-.25453	-.28069	-.30695	-.33331
.08750	-.07349	-.09829	-.12322	-.14829	-.17347	-.19878	-.22420	-.24973	-.27535	-.30107
.09000	-.04798	-.07219	-.09653	-.12100	-.14559	-.17029	-.19511	-.22003	-.24505	-.27016
.09250	-.02350	-.04714	-.07092	-.09481	-.11883	-.14296	-.16719	-.19153	-.21596	-.24049
.09500	.00000	-.02310	-.04632	-.06967	-.09314	-.11671	-.14039	-.16417	-.18804	-.21200
.09750	.02258	.00000	-.02270	-.04552	-.06846	-.09150	-.11464	-.13788	-.16122	-.18464
.10000	.04427	.02220	.00000	-.02231	-.04474	-.06727	-.08990	-.11263	-.13544	-.15834
.10250	.06513	.04354	.02183	0.00000	-.02194	-.04397	-.06611	-.08834	-.11066	-.13306
.10500	.08520	.06407	.04282	.02146	.00000	-.02157	-.04323	-.06498	-.08682	-.10874
.10750	.10451	.08383	.06303	.04212	.02111	.00000	-.02120	-.04250	-.06387	-.08533
.11000	.12311	.10285	.08249	.06201	.04144	.02076	.00000	-.02085	-.04178	-.06280
.11250	.14102	.12118	.10123	.08117	.06101	.04076	.02042	0.00000	-.02051	-.04109
.11500	.15828	.13884	.11928	.09963	.07988	.06004	.04011	.02009	.00000	-.02017
.11750	.17492	.15586	.13670	.11743	.09807	.07862	.05908	.03947	.01977	0.00000
.12000	.19097	.17228	.15349	.13460	.11562	.09655	.07739	.05815	.03884	.01945
.12250	.20646	.18813	.16970	.15117	.13255	.11384	.09505	.07618	.05724	.03823
.12500	.22141	.20342	.18534	.16716	.14889	.13054	.11210	.09359	.07500	.05635
.12750	.23585	.21820	.20045	.18261	.16468	.14666	.12857	.11040	.09216	.07385
.13000	.24980	.23247	.21505	.19753	.17993	.16225	.14448	.12664	.10873	.09076
.13250	.26329	.24627	.22916	.21196	.19467	.17731	.15986	.14234	.12476	.10711
.13500	.27633	.25961	.24281	.22591	.20893	.19187	.17473	.15753	.14025	.12291
.13750	.28895	.27252	.25601	.23941	.22272	.20596	.18912	.17221	.15524	.13820
.14000	.30116	.28501	.26878	.25247	.23607	.21959	.20305	.18643	.16975	.15300
.14250	.31298	.29711	.28115	.26511	.24899	.23279	.21653	.20019	.18379	.16733
.14500	.32443	.30882	.29313	.27736	.26151	.24558	.22958	.21352	.19739	.18121
.14750	.33552	.32017	.30474	.28922	.27363	.25797	.24223	.22643	.21057	.19465
.15000	.34627	.33117	.31599	.30073	.28539	.26998	.25450	.23895	.22335	.20768
.15250	.35670	.34184	.32690	.31188	.29679	.28162	.26639	.25109	.23573	.22032
.15500	.36681	.35219	.33748	.32270	.30784	.29291	.27792	.26287	.24775	.23258
.15750	.37663	.36223	.34775	.33320	.31857	.30387	.28911	.27429	.25941	.24447
.16000	.38616	.37198	.35772	.34339	.32898	.31451	.29998	.28538	.27073	.25602
.16250	.39541	.38144	.36740	.35328	.33910	.32484	.31053	.29615	.28172	.26723
.16500	.40439	.39064	.37680	.36290	.34892	.33488	.32078	.30661	.29240	.27812
.16750	.41313	.39957	.38594	.37224	.35847	.34463	.33073	.31678	.30277	.28871
.17000	.42161	.40825	.39482	.38132	.36775	.35411	.34042	.32666	.31286	.29900
.17250	.42987	.41670	.40346	.39015	.37677	.36333	.34983	.33627	.32266	.30900
.17500	.43790	.42491	.41186	.39873	.38554	.37229	.35898	.34562	.33220	.31873
.17750	.44571	.43291	.42003	.40709	.39408	.38102	.36789	.35471	.34148	.32820
.18000	.45331	.44069	.42799	.41522	.40240	.38951	.37656	.36356	.35051	.33741
.18250	.46072	.44826	.43573	.42314	.41049	.39778	.38501	.37218	.35931	.34639
.18500	.46793	.45564	.44328	.43085	.41837	.40583	.39323	.38058	.36787	.35513
.18750	.47495	.46282	.45063	.43837	.42605	.41367	.40124	.38875	.37622	.36364
.19000	.48179	.46983	.45779	.44569	.43353	.42131	.40904	.39672	.38435	.37193
.19250	.48847	.47665	.46477	.45283	.44082	.42877	.41665	.40449	.39228	.38002
.19500	.49497	.48331	.47158	.45979	.44794	.43603	.42407	.41206	.40001	.38791
.19750	.50132	.48980	.47822	.46657	.45487	.44312	.43131	.41945	.40755	.39560
.20000	.50751	.49613	.48469	.47320	.46164	.45003	.43837	.42666	.41490	.40310
.20250	.51355	.50231	.49102	.47966	.46824	.45678	.44526	.43369	.42208	.41042
.20500	.51945	.50835	.49719	.48597	.47469	.46336	.45198	.44056	.42908	.41757
.20750	.52521	.51424	.50321	.49213	.48098	.46979	.45855	.44726	.43593	.42455

POINT TABLES: ORIGINAL LOAN TERM: 420 MONTHS LOAN PREPAID IN: 420 MONTHS

EFFECTIVE YIELD	CONTRACT RATE .12000	.12250	.12500	.12750	.13000	.13250	.13500	.13750	.14000	.14250
.07000	-.58964	-.62066	-.65179	-.68300	-.71430	-.74569	-.77715	-.80868	-.84028	-.87194
.07250	-.54699	-.57719	-.60747	-.63785	-.66831	-.69885	-.72947	-.76016	-.79091	-.82172
.07500	-.50621	-.53561	-.56510	-.59467	-.62433	-.65407	-.68388	-.71375	-.74369	-.77370
.07750	-.46718	-.49582	-.52455	-.55336	-.58225	-.61121	-.64025	-.66935	-.69852	-.72774
.08000	-.42983	-.45773	-.48573	-.51380	-.54196	-.57019	-.59848	-.62685	-.65527	-.68375
.08250	-.39405	-.42125	-.44855	-.47592	-.50337	-.53089	-.55848	-.58613	-.61385	-.64162
.08500	-.35976	-.38630	-.41292	-.43962	-.46640	-.49324	-.52015	-.54712	-.57415	-.60124
.08750	-.32689	-.35278	-.37876	-.40482	-.43095	-.45714	-.48340	-.50972	-.53610	-.56253
.09000	-.29536	-.32064	-.34600	-.37144	-.39694	-.42252	-.44815	-.47385	-.49960	-.52540
.09250	-.26510	-.28979	-.31456	-.33940	-.36431	-.38929	-.41432	-.43942	-.46457	-.48977
.09500	-.23605	-.26017	-.28437	-.30864	-.33298	-.35738	-.38185	-.40636	-.43094	-.45556
.09750	-.20814	-.23172	-.25537	-.27910	-.30289	-.32674	-.35065	-.37461	-.39863	-.42270
.10000	-.18132	-.20438	-.22751	-.25070	-.27397	-.29729	-.32067	-.34410	-.36758	-.39111
.10250	-.15554	-.17809	-.20071	-.22340	-.24616	-.26897	-.29184	-.31476	-.33773	-.36075
.10500	-.13073	-.15280	-.17494	-.19714	-.21941	-.24173	-.26411	-.28654	-.30902	-.33154
.10750	-.10686	-.12847	-.15014	-.17187	-.19367	-.21552	-.23742	-.25938	-.28138	-.30343
.11000	-.08388	-.10504	-.12626	-.14754	-.16888	-.19028	-.21173	-.23323	-.25478	-.27637
.11250	-.06174	-.08246	-.10325	-.12410	-.14501	-.16597	-.18698	-.20804	-.22915	-.25030
.11500	-.04041	-.06071	-.08108	-.10151	-.12200	-.14254	-.16313	-.18377	-.20445	-.22518
.11750	-.01984	-.03974	-.05971	-.07974	-.09982	-.11995	-.14014	-.16037	-.18064	-.20095
.12000	.00000	-.01952	-.03910	-.05873	-.07842	-.09817	-.11796	-.13779	-.15767	-.17759
.12250	.01914	.00000	-.01920	-.03846	-.05778	-.07714	-.09655	-.11601	-.13551	-.15505
.12500	.03763	.01884	.00000	-.01890	-.03785	-.05685	-.07589	-.09498	-.11411	-.13328
.12750	.05547	.03704	.01855	.00000	-.01860	-.03725	-.05594	-.07467	-.09345	-.11226
.13000	.07272	.05462	.03647	.01826	.00000	-.01831	-.03666	-.05505	-.07348	-.09196
.13250	.08939	.07162	.05379	.03591	.01798	.00000	-.01802	-.03608	-.05419	-.07233
.13500	.10551	.08805	.07054	.05297	.03536	.01770	0.00000	-.01774	-.03552	-.05334
.13750	.12111	.10395	.08674	.06949	.05218	.03483	.01743	.00000	-.01747	-.03498
.14000	.13620	.11934	.10243	.08546	.06845	.05140	.03431	.01717	.00000	-.01721
.14250	.15081	.13423	.11761	.10093	.08421	.06745	.05064	.03380	.01692	.00000
.14500	.16496	.14866	.13231	.11592	.09947	.08299	.06646	.04990	.03330	.01667
.14750	.17867	.16264	.14656	.13043	.11426	.09805	.08179	.06550	.04917	.03281
.15000	.19196	.17619	.16037	.14451	.12860	.11264	.09665	.08062	.06456	.04846
.15250	.20485	.18933	.17376	.15815	.14249	.12680	.11106	.09529	.07948	.06364
.15500	.21735	.20208	.18675	.17139	.15598	.14052	.12504	.10951	.09395	.07836
.15750	.22948	.21445	.19936	.18423	.16906	.15385	.13860	.12331	.10830	.09265
.16000	.24126	.22645	.21160	.19670	.18176	.16678	.15176	.13671	.12163	.10651
.16250	.25270	.23811	.22348	.20880	.19409	.17934	.16455	.14972	.13487	.11998
.16500	.26380	.24943	.23502	.22056	.20607	.19153	.17696	.16236	.14773	.13306
.16750	.27460	.26044	.24624	.23199	.21771	.20339	.18903	.17464	.16022	.14577
.17000	.28509	.27114	.25714	.24310	.22902	.21491	.20076	.18658	.17237	.15813
.17250	.29529	.28154	.26774	.25390	.24003	.22611	.21217	.19819	.18418	.17014
.17500	.30522	.29165	.27805	.26441	.25073	.23701	.22326	.20948	.19567	.18183
.17750	.31487	.30150	.28808	.27463	.26114	.24761	.23406	.22047	.20685	.19320
.18000	.32427	.31108	.29785	.28458	.27128	.25794	.24456	.23116	.21773	.20427
.18250	.33342	.32041	.30736	.29427	.28114	.26798	.25479	.24157	.22832	.21504
.18500	.34233	.32950	.31662	.30370	.29075	.27777	.26476	.25171	.23864	.22554
.18750	.35101	.33835	.32564	.31290	.30012	.28731	.27446	.26159	.24869	.23576
.19000	.35947	.34697	.33443	.32185	.30924	.29660	.28392	.27121	.25848	.24572
.19250	.36772	.35538	.34300	.33059	.31814	.30565	.29314	.28060	.26803	.25543
.19500	.37576	.36358	.35136	.33910	.32681	.31448	.30213	.28975	.27734	.26490
.19750	.38361	.37158	.35951	.34740	.33527	.32310	.31090	.29867	.28642	.27414
.20000	.39126	.37938	.36746	.35551	.34352	.33150	.31945	.30738	.29528	.28315
.20250	.39873	.38699	.37522	.36341	.35157	.33970	.32780	.31588	.30392	.29195
.20500	.40602	.39442	.38279	.37113	.35943	.34771	.33595	.32417	.31236	.30053
.20750	.41313	.40168	.39019	.37866	.36711	.35552	.34391	.33227	.32060	.30891

EFFECTIVE YIELD	CONTRACT RATE .14500	.14750	.15000	.15250	.15500	.15750	.16000	.16250	.16500	.16750
.07000	-.90367	-.93545	-.96729	-.99917	-1.03111	-1.06308	-1.09510	-1.12716	-1.15926	-1.19138
.07250	-.85260	-.88353	-.91451	-.94554	-.97662	-1.00774	-1.03890	-1.07010	-1.10133	-1.13260
.07500	-.80376	-.83387	-.86404	-.89425	-.92451	-.95481	-.98515	-1.01552	-1.04593	-1.07637
.07750	-.75703	-.78636	-.81574	-.84517	-.87465	-.90416	-.93371	-.96330	-.99292	-1.02258
.08000	-.71229	-.74087	-.76951	-.79819	-.82691	-.85568	-.88448	-.91331	-.94218	-.97108
.08250	-.66944	-.69731	-.72523	-.75319	-.78119	-.80924	-.83732	-.86543	-.89358	-.92175
.08500	-.62838	-.65556	-.68280	-.71007	-.73739	-.76474	-.79213	-.81955	-.84700	-.87449
.08750	-.58901	-.61554	-.64211	-.66873	-.69538	-.72208	-.74880	-.77556	-.80235	-.82917
.09000	-.55125	-.57715	-.60309	-.62908	-.65510	-.68116	-.70725	-.73337	-.75952	-.78570
.09250	-.51502	-.54031	-.56565	-.59102	-.61644	-.64188	-.66737	-.69288	-.71842	-.74399
.09500	-.48023	-.50494	-.52969	-.55449	-.57932	-.60418	-.62908	-.65401	-.67896	-.70394
.09750	-.44681	-.47096	-.49516	-.51939	-.54366	-.56796	-.59230	-.61666	-.64106	-.66547
.10000	-.41469	-.43831	-.46197	-.48566	-.50939	-.53316	-.55695	-.58078	-.60463	-.62850
.10250	-.38381	-.40691	-.43006	-.45324	-.47645	-.49969	-.52297	-.54627	-.56960	-.59296
.10500	-.35411	-.37672	-.39936	-.42204	-.44476	-.46750	-.49028	-.51308	-.53591	-.55876
.10750	-.32552	-.34765	-.36982	-.39202	-.41426	-.43652	-.45882	-.48114	-.50349	-.52586
.11000	-.29800	-.31967	-.34138	-.36312	-.38489	-.40670	-.42853	-.45039	-.47227	-.49418
.11250	-.27149	-.29272	-.31398	-.33528	-.35661	-.37796	-.39935	-.42076	-.44220	-.46366
.11500	-.24594	-.26674	-.28758	-.30845	-.32935	-.35028	-.37123	-.39221	-.41322	-.43425
.11750	-.22131	-.24170	-.26212	-.28258	-.30307	-.32358	-.34412	-.36469	-.38528	-.40589
.12000	-.19755	-.21754	-.23757	-.25763	-.27772	-.29783	-.31798	-.33814	-.35833	-.37854
.12250	-.17462	-.19423	-.21388	-.23355	-.25326	-.27299	-.29274	-.31252	-.33233	-.35215
.12500	-.15249	-.17173	-.19101	-.21031	-.22964	-.24900	-.26839	-.28779	-.30722	-.32668
.12750	-.13112	-.15000	-.16892	-.18786	-.20684	-.22584	-.24486	-.26391	-.28298	-.30207
.13000	-.11046	-.12900	-.14757	-.16617	-.18480	-.20345	-.22213	-.24083	-.25955	-.27829
.13250	-.09050	-.10871	-.12694	-.14521	-.16350	-.18182	-.20016	-.21852	-.23691	-.25531
.13500	-.07119	-.08908	-.10699	-.12493	-.14290	-.16090	-.17891	-.19695	-.21501	-.23309
.13750	-.05252	-.07009	-.08769	-.10532	-.12298	-.14066	-.15836	-.17609	-.19383	-.21159
.14000	-.03445	-.05172	-.06902	-.08634	-.10369	-.12107	-.13847	-.15589	-.17333	-.19079
.14250	-.01695	-.03393	-.05093	-.06797	-.08503	-.10211	-.11921	-.13634	-.15348	-.17065
.14500	.00000	-.01670	-.03342	-.05017	-.06694	-.08374	-.10056	-.11740	-.13426	-.15114
.14750	.01642	0.00000	-.01645	-.03292	-.04942	-.06594	-.08249	-.09905	-.11563	-.13223
.15000	.03234	.01618	.00000	-.01621	-.03244	-.04869	-.06497	-.08127	-.09758	-.11391
.15250	.04777	.03187	.01595	.00000	-.01597	-.03197	-.04798	-.06402	-.08007	-.09615
.15500	.06274	.04710	.03142	.01572	0.00000	-.01574	-.03151	-.04729	-.06309	-.07891
.15750	.07727	.06187	.04643	.03098	.01550	.00000	-.01552	-.03106	-.04662	-.06219
.16000	.09137	.07620	.06101	.04579	.03055	.01528	.00000	-.01530	-.03062	-.04596
.16250	.10507	.09012	.07516	.06017	.04516	.03012	.01507	0.00000	-.01509	-.03019
.16500	.11837	.10365	.08891	.07414	.05935	.04454	.02971	.01486	.00000	-.01488
.16750	.13129	.11679	.10226	.08771	.07314	.05855	.04394	.02931	.01456	.00000
.17000	.14386	.12957	.11525	.10091	.08655	.07217	.05777	.04335	.02891	.01446
.17250	.15608	.14199	.12787	.11374	.09958	.08541	.07121	.05700	.04277	.02853
.17500	.16796	.15407	.14016	.12622	.11226	.09829	.08429	.07028	.05625	.04221
.17750	.17952	.16583	.15211	.13836	.12460	.11082	.09702	.08320	.06937	.05552
.18000	.19078	.17727	.16374	.15018	.13661	.12301	.10940	.09578	.08213	.06848
.18250	.20174	.18841	.17506	.16169	.14830	.13489	.12146	.10802	.09456	.08109
.18500	.21241	.19926	.18609	.17290	.15969	.14646	.13321	.11995	.10667	.09338
.18750	.22281	.20983	.19683	.18382	.17078	.15772	.14465	.13156	.11846	.10534
.19000	.23294	.22013	.20731	.19446	.18159	.16871	.15580	.14289	.12995	.11701
.19250	.24282	.23017	.21751	.20483	.19213	.17941	.16667	.15392	.14116	.12838
.19500	.25245	.23997	.22746	.21494	.20240	.18985	.17727	.16468	.15208	.13946
.19750	.26184	.24952	.23717	.22481	.21242	.20002	.18761	.17518	.16273	.15027
.20000	.27100	.25883	.24664	.23443	.22220	.20996	.19769	.18542	.17313	.16082
.20250	.27995	.26792	.25588	.24382	.23174	.21965	.20754	.19541	.18327	.17112
.20500	.28867	.27680	.26490	.25299	.24106	.22911	.21714	.20516	.19317	.18117
.20750	.29720	.28546	.27371	.26194	.25015	.23834	.22652	.21469	.20284	.19098

POINT TABLES: ORIGINAL LOAN TERM: 420 MONTHS LOAN PREPAID IN: 420 MONTHS

EFFECTIVE YIELD	CONTRACT RATE .17000	.17250	.17500	.17750	.18000	.18250	.18500	.18750	.19000	.19250
.07000	-1.22355	-1.25574	-1.28796	-1.32020	-1.35247	-1.38477	-1.41708	-1.44942	-1.48177	-1.51414
.07250	-1.16389	-1.19522	-1.22658	-1.25796	-1.28936	-1.32079	-1.35224	-1.38371	-1.41519	-1.44670
.07500	-1.10685	-1.13735	-1.16788	-1.19843	-1.22901	-1.25961	-1.29023	-1.32086	-1.35152	-1.38219
.07750	-1.05226	-1.08197	-1.11171	-1.14147	-1.17126	-1.20106	-1.23089	-1.26073	-1.29059	-1.32047
.08000	-1.00001	-1.02896	-1.05794	-1.08695	-1.11597	-1.14502	-1.17409	-1.20317	-1.23227	-1.26139
.08250	-.94996	-.97819	-1.00644	-1.03472	-1.06302	-1.09134	-1.11968	-1.14804	-1.17641	-1.20480
.08500	-.90200	-.92953	-.95709	-.98468	-1.01228	-1.03990	-1.06754	-1.09520	-1.12288	-1.15057
.08750	-.85602	-.88289	-.90978	-.93670	-.96363	-.99059	-1.01756	-1.04455	-1.07156	-1.09858
.09000	-.81191	-.83814	-.86440	-.89067	-.91697	-.94329	-.96962	-.99597	-1.02233	-1.04871
.09250	-.76959	-.79521	-.82085	-.84651	-.87219	-.89789	-.92361	-.94934	-.97509	-1.00086
.09500	-.72895	-.75398	-.77903	-.80411	-.82920	-.85431	-.87944	-.90458	-.92974	-.95491
.09750	-.68992	-.71438	-.73887	-.76338	-.78790	-.81245	-.83701	-.86158	-.88617	-.91077
.10000	-.65240	-.67633	-.70027	-.72423	-.74821	-.77221	-.79623	-.82026	-.84430	-.86836
.10250	-.61634	-.63974	-.66316	-.68660	-.71006	-.73353	-.75702	-.78053	-.80404	-.82758
.10500	-.58164	-.60454	-.62746	-.65039	-.67335	-.69632	-.71931	-.74231	-.76532	-.78835
.10750	-.54825	-.57067	-.59310	-.61555	-.63802	-.66051	-.68301	-.70553	-.72805	-.75059
.11000	-.51610	-.53805	-.56002	-.58201	-.60401	-.62603	-.64807	-.67011	-.69217	-.71425
.11250	-.48514	-.50664	-.52816	-.54970	-.57125	-.59282	-.61440	-.63600	-.65761	-.67923
.11500	-.45530	-.47637	-.49745	-.51856	-.53968	-.56081	-.58196	-.60313	-.62430	-.64549
.11750	-.42653	-.44718	-.46785	-.48854	-.50924	-.52996	-.55069	-.57143	-.59219	-.61296
.12000	-.39878	-.41903	-.43929	-.45958	-.47988	-.50020	-.52052	-.54087	-.56122	-.58158
.12250	-.37200	-.39186	-.41174	-.43164	-.45155	-.47148	-.49141	-.51137	-.53133	-.55130
.12500	-.34615	-.36563	-.38514	-.40466	-.42420	-.44375	-.46331	-.48289	-.50248	-.52207
.12750	-.32118	-.34031	-.35945	-.37861	-.39778	-.41697	-.43617	-.45539	-.47461	-.49384
.13000	-.29706	-.31583	-.33463	-.35344	-.37226	-.39110	-.40995	-.42881	-.44769	-.46657
.13250	-.27374	-.29218	-.31063	-.32911	-.34759	-.36609	-.38460	-.40313	-.42166	-.44020
.13500	-.25119	-.26930	-.28743	-.30558	-.32374	-.34191	-.36009	-.37829	-.39649	-.41471
.13750	-.22938	-.24717	-.26499	-.28282	-.30066	-.31851	-.33638	-.35426	-.37215	-.39004
.14000	-.20827	-.22576	-.24327	-.26079	-.27832	-.29587	-.31343	-.33100	-.34858	-.36618
.14250	-.18783	-.20502	-.22224	-.23946	-.25670	-.27395	-.29122	-.30849	-.32577	-.34307
.14500	-.16803	-.18494	-.20187	-.21881	-.23576	-.25272	-.26970	-.28668	-.30368	-.32068
.14750	-.14885	-.16548	-.18213	-.19879	-.21547	-.23215	-.24885	-.26555	-.28227	-.29900
.15000	-.13026	-.14662	-.16300	-.17939	-.19580	-.21221	-.22864	-.24507	-.26152	-.27797
.15250	-.11223	-.12834	-.14445	-.16058	-.17672	-.19288	-.20904	-.22522	-.24140	-.25759
.15500	-.09475	-.11060	-.12646	-.14233	-.15822	-.17412	-.19003	-.20595	-.22188	-.23782
.15750	-.07778	-.09338	-.10900	-.12463	-.14027	-.15592	-.17159	-.18726	-.20294	-.21863
.16000	-.06131	-.07667	-.09205	-.10744	-.12284	-.13826	-.15368	-.16912	-.18456	-.20001
.16250	-.04531	-.06045	-.07559	-.09075	-.10592	-.12110	-.13629	-.15150	-.16671	-.18192
.16500	-.02977	-.04466	-.05960	-.07454	-.08948	-.10444	-.11940	-.13438	-.14936	-.16436
.16750	-.01468	-.02937	-.04407	-.05878	-.07351	-.08825	-.10299	-.11775	-.13251	-.14728
.17000	0.00000	-.01448	-.02897	-.04347	-.05798	-.07251	-.08704	-.10158	-.11613	-.13069
.17250	.01427	.00000	-.01428	-.02858	-.04288	-.05720	-.07153	-.08586	-.10020	-.11455
.17500	.02815	.01408	.00000	-.01409	-.02820	-.04231	-.05644	-.07057	-.08471	-.09886
.17750	.04166	.02778	.01390	0.00000	-.01391	-.02783	-.04175	-.05569	-.06964	-.08359
.18000	.05480	.04112	.02742	.01372	.00000	-.01373	-.02746	-.04121	-.05496	-.06872
.18250	.06760	.05411	.04060	.02707	.01354	.00000	-.01355	-.02711	-.04068	-.05425
.18500	.08007	.06675	.05342	.04008	.02673	.01337	0.00000	-.01338	-.02676	-.04016
.18750	.09221	.07907	.06592	.05275	.03958	.02639	.01320	.00000	-.01321	-.02642
.19000	.10405	.09108	.07810	.06510	.05210	.03909	.02607	.01304	.00000	-.01304
.19250	.11558	.10278	.08997	.07714	.06430	.05146	.03861	.02574	.01288	.00000
.19500	.12683	.11419	.10154	.08888	.07620	.06352	.05083	.03814	.02543	.01272
.19750	.13780	.12532	.11283	.10032	.08781	.07529	.06276	.05022	.03768	.02512
.20000	.14851	.13618	.12384	.11149	.09914	.08677	.07439	.06201	.04962	.03723
.20250	.15895	.14678	.13459	.12239	.11019	.09797	.08575	.07352	.06128	.04904
.20500	.16915	.15712	.14508	.13303	.12097	.10891	.09683	.08475	.07266	.06056
.20750	.17910	.16722	.15532	.14342	.13151	.11958	.10765	.09572	.08377	.07182

EFFECTIVE YIELD	CONTRACT RATE .19500	.19750	.20000	.20250	.20500	.20750
.07000	-1.54653	-1.57893	-1.61135	-1.64378	-1.67623	-1.70868
.07250	-1.47821	-1.50975	-1.54130	-1.57286	-1.60443	-1.63602
.07500	-1.41288	-1.44358	-1.47430	-1.50503	-1.53577	-1.56652
.07750	-1.35037	-1.38027	-1.41019	-1.44013	-1.47007	-1.50003
.08000	-1.29052	-1.31967	-1.34882	-1.37800	-1.40718	-1.43637
.08250	-1.23320	-1.26162	-1.29005	-1.31849	-1.34694	-1.37540
.08500	-1.17827	-1.20599	-1.23372	-1.26146	-1.28921	-1.31698
.08750	-1.12561	-1.15266	-1.17972	-1.20679	-1.23387	-1.26096
.09000	-1.07510	-1.10151	-1.12793	-1.15435	-1.18079	-1.20724
.09250	-1.02663	-1.05242	-1.07822	-1.10403	-1.12985	-1.15568
.09500	-.98009	-1.00529	-1.03050	-1.05571	-1.08094	-1.10618
.09750	-.93539	-.96002	-.98465	-1.00930	-1.03396	-1.05862
.10000	-.89243	-.91651	-.94060	-.96470	-.98881	-1.01293
.10250	-.85112	-.87467	-.89824	-.92181	-.94540	-.96899
.10500	-.81139	-.83443	-.85749	-.88056	-.90364	-.92673
.10750	-.77315	-.79571	-.81828	-.84086	-.86345	-.88605
.11000	-.73633	-.75842	-.78053	-.80264	-.82476	-.84689
.11250	-.70086	-.72251	-.74416	-.76582	-.78749	-.80917
.11500	-.66669	-.68790	-.70911	-.73034	-.75157	-.77282
.11750	-.63374	-.65453	-.67532	-.69613	-.71695	-.73777
.12000	-.60196	-.62234	-.64273	-.66314	-.68355	-.70396
.12250	-.57129	-.59128	-.61129	-.63130	-.65131	-.67134
.12500	-.54168	-.56130	-.58093	-.60056	-.62020	-.63985
.12750	-.51309	-.53234	-.55160	-.57087	-.59015	-.60943
.13000	-.48546	-.50436	-.52327	-.54219	-.56112	-.58005
.13250	-.45876	-.47732	-.49589	-.51447	-.53305	-.55164
.13500	-.43293	-.45117	-.46941	-.48766	-.50591	-.52418
.13750	-.40795	-.42587	-.44379	-.46172	-.47966	-.49760
.14000	-.38377	-.40138	-.41900	-.43662	-.45425	-.47189
.14250	-.36037	-.37768	-.39500	-.41232	-.42965	-.44699
.14500	-.33770	-.35472	-.37175	-.38878	-.40583	-.42287
.14750	-.31573	-.33247	-.34922	-.36598	-.38274	-.39951
.15000	-.29444	-.31091	-.32739	-.34387	-.36036	-.37686
.15250	-.27379	-.29000	-.30622	-.32244	-.33867	-.35490
.15500	-.25377	-.26972	-.28568	-.30165	-.31762	-.33360
.15750	-.23433	-.25004	-.26575	-.28147	-.29720	-.31293
.16000	-.21547	-.23093	-.24641	-.26189	-.27737	-.29286
.16250	-.19715	-.21238	-.22762	-.24287	-.25812	-.27338
.16500	-.17936	-.19436	-.20938	-.22440	-.23942	-.25445
.16750	-.16206	-.17685	-.19164	-.20644	-.22125	-.23606
.17000	-.14526	-.15983	-.17441	-.18899	-.20358	-.21818
.17250	-.12891	-.14328	-.15765	-.17203	-.18641	-.20080
.17500	-.11302	-.12718	-.14135	-.15552	-.16970	-.18389
.17750	-.09755	-.11151	-.12548	-.13946	-.15345	-.16743
.18000	-.08249	-.09627	-.11005	-.12383	-.13762	-.15142
.18250	-.06783	-.08142	-.09501	-.10861	-.12222	-.13583
.18500	-.05356	-.06696	-.08037	-.09379	-.10721	-.12064
.18750	-.03965	-.05288	-.06611	-.07935	-.09260	-.10585
.19000	-.02609	-.03915	-.05221	-.06528	-.07835	-.09143
.19250	-.01288	-.02577	-.03866	-.05156	-.06447	-.07738
.19500	.00000	-.01272	-.02545	-.03819	-.05093	-.06368
.19750	.01256	.00000	-.01257	-.02515	-.03773	-.05031
.20000	.02482	.01241	0.00000	-.01242	-.02484	-.03727
.20250	.03679	.02453	.01227	.00000	-.01227	-.02455
.20500	.04846	.03635	.02424	.01212	0.00000	-.01213
.20750	.05986	.04790	.03593	.02396	.01198	0.00000

ANNUAL PERCENTAGE RATE TABLE

Description:

The Annual Percentage Rate table can be used to find the effective interest rate being charged on a mortgage loan, which must be disclosed to the borrower, after all costs at closing are added to the contract rate. To use the table, the total amount of points, where one point is 1% of the loan amount, is calculated, and the table factor corresponding to the contract rate, total point charge, and original loan term is derived. This factor is the annual percentage rate that must be disclosed to the borrower at the loan closing.

Table Range:

Annual contract interest rates from 7.00% to 20.75%, in .25% increments. Percentage points from .25% to 15.00% in .25% increments, with all points expressed as percentages. Loan terms from 5 to 35 years in 5-year increments as well as 29 years are included.

Example:

What is the annual percentage rate on a 12% contract rate, $45,000, 30-year term loan, if the lender charges $1,350 in discount points, $450 origination fee, and $788 in prepaid interest?

Solution:

Adding the total charges incurred at closing yields $2,588. Dividing this by the initial loan amount gives the percentage points charged at closing:

$$\text{Percentage points} = \frac{\$2{,}588}{\$45{,}000}$$

$$= .0575.$$

Looking in the Annual Percentage Rate table under 30 years, 12% contract rate, and .0575 percentage points yields an annual percentage rate of 12.81%.

ANNUAL PERCENTAGE RATE TABLES: TERM OF MORTGAGE: 60 MONTHS

INTEREST RATE	POINTS CHARGED .00250	.00500	.00750	.01000	.01250	.01500	.01750	.02000	.02250	.02500
.07000	.07105	.07211	.07316	.07423	.07529	.07636	.07744	.07851	.07959	.08068
.07250	.07355	.07461	.07567	.07674	.07780	.07888	.07995	.08103	.08212	.08320
.07500	.07606	.07712	.07818	.07925	.08032	.08139	.08247	.08355	.08464	.08573
.07750	.07856	.07962	.08069	.08176	.08283	.08391	.08499	.08607	.08716	.08826
.08000	.08106	.08213	.08319	.08427	.08534	.08642	.08751	.08859	.08969	.09078
.08250	.08356	.08463	.08570	.08678	.08786	.08894	.09002	.09111	.09221	.09331
.08500	.08607	.08714	.08821	.08929	.09037	.09145	.09254	.09364	.09473	.09583
.08750	.08857	.08964	.09072	.09180	.09288	.09397	.09506	.09616	.09726	.09836
.09000	.09107	.09215	.09322	.09431	.09539	.09648	.09758	.09868	.09978	.10089
.09250	.09357	.09465	.09573	.09682	.09791	.09900	.10010	.10120	.10230	.10341
.09500	.09608	.09716	.09824	.09933	.10042	.10152	.10261	.10372	.10483	.10594
.09750	.09858	.09966	.10075	.10184	.10293	.10403	.10513	.10624	.10735	.10846
.10000	.10108	.10217	.10326	.10435	.10545	.10655	.10765	.10876	.10987	.11099
.10250	.10358	.10467	.10576	.10686	.10796	.10906	.11017	.11128	.11240	.11352
.10500	.10609	.10718	.10827	.10937	.11047	.11158	.11269	.11380	.11492	.11604
.10750	.10859	.10968	.11078	.11188	.11299	.11409	.11521	.11632	.11745	.11857
.11000	.11109	.11219	.11329	.11439	.11550	.11661	.11773	.11885	.11997	.12110
.11250	.11359	.11469	.11580	.11690	.11801	.11913	.12024	.12137	.12249	.12362
.11500	.11610	.11720	.11830	.11941	.12053	.12164	.12276	.12389	.12502	.12615
.11750	.11860	.11970	.12081	.12192	.12304	.12416	.12528	.12641	.12754	.12868
.12000	.12110	.12221	.12332	.12443	.12555	.12667	.12780	.12893	.13007	.13121
.12250	.12361	.12471	.12583	.12694	.12807	.12919	.13032	.13145	.13259	.13373
.12500	.12611	.12722	.12834	.12946	.13058	.13171	.13284	.13398	.13512	.13626
.12750	.12861	.12972	.13084	.13197	.13309	.13422	.13536	.13650	.13764	.13879
.13000	.13111	.13223	.13335	.13448	.13561	.13674	.13788	.13902	.14016	.14132
.13250	.13362	.13474	.13586	.13699	.13812	.13926	.14040	.14154	.14269	.14384
.13500	.13612	.13724	.13837	.13950	.14063	.14177	.14292	.14406	.14521	.14637
.13750	.13862	.13975	.14088	.14201	.14315	.14429	.14544	.14659	.14774	.14890
.14000	.14112	.14225	.14338	.14452	.14566	.14681	.14795	.14911	.15026	.15143
.14250	.14363	.14476	.14589	.14703	.14818	.14932	.15047	.15163	.15279	.15395
.14500	.14613	.14726	.14840	.14954	.15069	.15184	.15299	.15415	.15532	.15648
.14750	.14863	.14977	.15091	.15205	.15320	.15436	.15551	.15667	.15784	.15901
.15000	.15114	.15227	.15342	.15457	.15572	.15687	.15803	.15920	.16037	.16154
.15250	.15364	.15478	.15593	.15708	.15823	.15939	.16055	.16172	.16289	.16407
.15500	.15614	.15729	.15843	.15959	.16075	.16191	.16307	.16424	.16542	.16660
.15750	.15864	.15979	.16094	.16210	.16326	.16442	.16559	.16677	.16794	.16913
.16000	.16115	.16230	.16345	.16461	.16577	.16694	.16811	.16929	.17047	.17165
.16250	.16365	.16480	.16596	.16712	.16829	.16946	.17063	.17181	.17300	.17418
.16500	.16615	.16731	.16847	.16963	.17080	.17198	.17315	.17433	.17552	.17671
.16750	.16865	.16981	.17098	.17214	.17332	.17449	.17567	.17686	.17805	.17924
.17000	.17116	.17232	.17349	.17466	.17583	.17701	.17819	.17938	.18057	.18177
.17250	.17366	.17483	.17599	.17717	.17835	.17953	.18071	.18190	.18310	.18430
.17500	.17616	.17733	.17850	.17968	.18086	.18204	.18323	.18443	.18563	.18683
.17750	.17867	.17984	.18101	.18219	.18337	.18456	.18575	.18695	.18815	.18936
.18000	.18117	.18234	.18352	.18470	.18589	.18708	.18828	.18947	.19068	.19189
.18250	.18367	.18485	.18603	.18721	.18840	.18960	.19080	.19200	.19321	.19442
.18500	.18617	.18735	.18854	.18973	.19092	.19211	.19332	.19452	.19573	.19695
.18750	.18868	.18986	.19105	.19224	.19343	.19463	.19584	.19705	.19826	.19948
.19000	.19118	.19237	.19356	.19475	.19595	.19715	.19836	.19957	.20079	.20201
.19250	.19368	.19487	.19606	.19726	.19846	.19967	.20088	.20209	.20331	.20454
.19500	.19619	.19738	.19857	.19977	.20098	.20219	.20340	.20462	.20584	.20707
.19750	.19869	.19988	.20108	.20228	.20349	.20470	.20592	.20714	.20837	.20960
.20000	.20119	.20239	.20359	.20480	.20601	.20722	.20844	.20967	.21089	.21213
.20250	.20370	.20490	.20610	.20731	.20852	.20974	.21096	.21219	.21342	.21466
.20500	.20620	.20740	.20861	.20982	.21104	.21226	.21348	.21471	.21595	.21719
.20750	.20870	.20991	.21112	.21233	.21355	.21478	.21601	.21724	.21848	.21972

ANNUAL PERCENTAGE RATE TABLES: TERM OF MORTGAGE: 60 MONTHS

INTEREST RATE	POINTS CHARGED .02750	.03000	.03250	.03500	.03750	.04000	.04250	.04500	.04750	.05000
.07000	.08177	.08286	.08396	.08506	.08616	.08727	.08839	.08950	.09062	.09175
.07250	.08430	.08539	.08649	.08759	.08870	.08981	.09093	.09205	.09317	.09430
.07500	.08682	.08792	.08902	.09013	.09124	.09236	.09347	.09460	.09572	.09685
.07750	.08935	.09045	.09156	.09267	.09378	.09490	.09602	.09714	.09827	.09941
.08000	.09188	.09298	.09409	.09520	.09632	.09744	.09856	.09969	.10082	.10196
.08250	.09441	.09552	.09663	.09774	.09886	.09998	.10111	.10224	.10337	.10451
.08500	.09694	.09805	.09916	.10028	.10140	.10252	.10365	.10479	.10592	.10707
.08750	.09947	.10058	.10169	.10281	.10394	.10506	.10620	.10733	.10847	.10962
.09000	.10200	.10311	.10423	.10535	.10648	.10761	.10874	.10988	.11102	.11217
.09250	.10452	.10564	.10676	.10789	.10902	.11015	.11129	.11243	.11358	.11473
.09500	.10705	.10817	.10930	.11042	.11156	.11269	.11383	.11498	.11613	.11728
.09750	.10958	.11070	.11183	.11296	.11410	.11524	.11638	.11753	.11868	.11983
.10000	.11211	.11324	.11437	.11550	.11664	.11778	.11892	.12007	.12123	.12239
.10250	.11464	.11577	.11690	.11804	.11918	.12032	.12147	.12262	.12378	.12494
.10500	.11717	.11830	.11944	.12057	.12172	.12286	.12402	.12517	.12633	.12750
.10750	.11970	.12083	.12197	.12311	.12426	.12541	.12656	.12772	.12888	.13005
.11000	.12223	.12337	.12451	.12565	.12680	.12795	.12911	.13027	.13144	.13261
.11250	.12476	.12590	.12704	.12819	.12934	.13050	.13166	.13282	.13399	.13516
.11500	.12729	.12843	.12958	.13073	.13188	.13304	.13420	.13537	.13654	.13772
.11750	.12982	.13096	.13211	.13326	.13442	.13558	.13675	.13792	.13909	.14027
.12000	.13235	.13350	.13465	.13580	.13696	.13813	.13930	.14047	.14165	.14283
.12250	.13488	.13603	.13718	.13834	.13950	.14067	.14184	.14302	.14420	.14539
.12500	.13741	.13856	.13972	.14088	.14205	.14322	.14439	.14557	.14675	.14794
.12750	.13994	.14109	.14225	.14342	.14459	.14576	.14694	.14812	.14931	.15050
.13000	.14247	.14363	.14479	.14596	.14713	.14831	.14949	.15067	.15186	.15306
.13250	.14500	.14616	.14733	.14850	.14967	.15085	.15203	.15322	.15442	.15561
.13500	.14753	.14870	.14986	.15104	.15221	.15340	.15458	.15577	.15697	.15817
.13750	.15006	.15123	.15240	.15358	.15476	.15594	.15713	.15833	.15952	.16073
.14000	.15259	.15376	.15494	.15612	.15730	.15849	.15968	.16088	.16208	.16328
.14250	.15512	.15630	.15747	.15866	.15984	.16103	.16223	.16343	.16463	.16584
.14500	.15765	.15883	.16001	.16120	.16239	.16358	.16478	.16598	.16719	.16840
.14750	.16019	.16136	.16255	.16374	.16493	.16612	.16733	.16853	.16974	.17096
.15000	.16272	.16390	.16509	.16628	.16747	.16867	.16988	.17108	.17230	.17352
.15250	.16525	.16643	.16762	.16882	.17001	.17122	.17242	.17364	.17485	.17607
.15500	.16778	.16897	.17016	.17136	.17256	.17376	.17497	.17619	.17741	.17863
.15750	.17031	.17150	.17270	.17390	.17510	.17631	.17752	.17874	.17996	.18119
.16000	.17284	.17404	.17524	.17644	.17765	.17886	.18007	.18130	.18252	.18375
.16250	.17538	.17657	.17777	.17898	.18019	.18140	.18262	.18385	.18508	.18631
.16500	.17791	.17911	.18031	.18152	.18273	.18395	.18517	.18640	.18763	.18887
.16750	.18044	.18164	.18285	.18406	.18528	.18650	.18772	.18896	.19019	.19143
.17000	.18297	.18418	.18539	.18660	.18782	.18905	.19028	.19151	.19275	.19399
.17250	.18550	.18671	.18793	.18914	.19037	.19159	.19283	.19406	.19530	.19655
.17500	.18804	.18925	.19046	.19169	.19291	.19414	.19538	.19662	.19786	.19911
.17750	.19057	.19178	.19300	.19423	.19546	.19669	.19793	.19917	.20042	.20167
.18000	.19310	.19432	.19554	.19677	.19800	.19924	.20048	.20173	.20298	.20423
.18250	.19563	.19686	.19808	.19931	.20055	.20179	.20303	.20428	.20553	.20679
.18500	.19817	.19939	.20062	.20185	.20309	.20433	.20558	.20683	.20809	.20935
.18750	.20070	.20193	.20316	.20440	.20564	.20688	.20813	.20939	.21065	.21192
.19000	.20323	.20446	.20570	.20694	.20818	.20943	.21069	.21194	.21321	.21448
.19250	.20577	.20700	.20824	.20948	.21073	.21198	.21324	.21450	.21577	.21704
.19500	.20830	.20954	.21078	.21202	.21327	.21453	.21579	.21706	.21833	.21960
.19750	.21083	.21207	.21332	.21457	.21582	.21708	.21834	.21961	.22089	.22216
.20000	.21337	.21461	.21586	.21711	.21837	.21963	.22090	.22217	.22344	.22473
.20250	.21590	.21715	.21840	.21965	.22091	.22218	.22345	.22472	.22600	.22729
.20500	.21843	.21968	.22094	.22220	.22346	.22473	.22600	.22728	.22856	.22985
.20750	.22097	.22222	.22348	.22474	.22601	.22728	.22855	.22984	.23112	.23241

ANNUAL PERCENTAGE RATE TABLES: TERM OF MORTGAGE: 60 MONTHS

POINTS CHARGED

INTEREST RATE	.05250	.05500	.05750	.06000	.06250	.06500	.06750	.07000	.07250	.07500
.07000	.09288	.09401	.09515	.09629	.09744	.09859	.09975	.10091	.10207	.10324
.07250	.09543	.09657	.09771	.09886	.10001	.10116	.10232	.10348	.10465	.10582
.07500	.09799	.09913	.10027	.10142	.10257	.10373	.10489	.10605	.10722	.10840
.07750	.10054	.10169	.10283	.10398	.10514	.10630	.10746	.10863	.10980	.11098
.08000	.10310	.10424	.10539	.10655	.10771	.10887	.11003	.11121	.11238	.11356
.08250	.10566	.10680	.10796	.10911	.11027	.11144	.11261	.11378	.11496	.11614
.08500	.10821	.10936	.11052	.11168	.11284	.11401	.11518	.11636	.11754	.11872
.08750	.11077	.11192	.11308	.11424	.11541	.11658	.11775	.11893	.12012	.12131
.09000	.11332	.11448	.11564	.11681	.11797	.11915	.12033	.12151	.12270	.12389
.09250	.11588	.11704	.11820	.11937	.12054	.12172	.12290	.12409	.12528	.12647
.09500	.11844	.11960	.12077	.12194	.12311	.12429	.12547	.12666	.12786	.12905
.09750	.12099	.12216	.12333	.12450	.12568	.12686	.12805	.12924	.13044	.13164
.10000	.12355	.12472	.12589	.12707	.12825	.12943	.13062	.13182	.13302	.13422
.10250	.12611	.12728	.12845	.12963	.13082	.13201	.13320	.13440	.13560	.13681
.10500	.12867	.12984	.13102	.13220	.13339	.13458	.13577	.13697	.13818	.13939
.10750	.13122	.13240	.13358	.13477	.13596	.13715	.13835	.13955	.14076	.14197
.11000	.13378	.13496	.13615	.13733	.13853	.13972	.14093	.14213	.14334	.14456
.11250	.13634	.13752	.13871	.13990	.14110	.14230	.14350	.14471	.14593	.14715
.11500	.13890	.14008	.14127	.14247	.14367	.14487	.14608	.14729	.14851	.14973
.11750	.14146	.14265	.14384	.14504	.14624	.14744	.14865	.14987	.15109	.15232
.12000	.14402	.14521	.14640	.14760	.14881	.15002	.15123	.15245	.15367	.15490
.12250	.14658	.14777	.14897	.15017	.15138	.15259	.15381	.15503	.15626	.15749
.12500	.14913	.15033	.15153	.15274	.15395	.15517	.15639	.15761	.15884	.16008
.12750	.15169	.15289	.15410	.15531	.15652	.15774	.15896	.16019	.16143	.16266
.13000	.15425	.15546	.15666	.15788	.15909	.16032	.16154	.16277	.16401	.16525
.13250	.15681	.15802	.15923	.16045	.16167	.16289	.16412	.16535	.16659	.16784
.13500	.15937	.16058	.16180	.16302	.16424	.16547	.16670	.16794	.16918	.17043
.13750	.16193	.16315	.16436	.16558	.16681	.16804	.16928	.17052	.17176	.17301
.14000	.16449	.16571	.16693	.16815	.16938	.17062	.17186	.17310	.17435	.17560
.14250	.16706	.16827	.16950	.17072	.17196	.17319	.17444	.17568	.17694	.17819
.14500	.16962	.17084	.17206	.17329	.17453	.17577	.17702	.17827	.17952	.18078
.14750	.17218	.17340	.17463	.17587	.17710	.17835	.17960	.18085	.18211	.18337
.15000	.17474	.17597	.17720	.17844	.17968	.18093	.18218	.18343	.18469	.18596
.15250	.17730	.17853	.17977	.18101	.18225	.18350	.18476	.18602	.18728	.18855
.15500	.17986	.18110	.18234	.18358	.18483	.18608	.18734	.18860	.18987	.19114
.15750	.18242	.18366	.18490	.18615	.18740	.18866	.18992	.19119	.19246	.19373
.16000	.18499	.18623	.18747	.18872	.18998	.19124	.19250	.19377	.19504	.19632
.16250	.18755	.18879	.19004	.19129	.19255	.19381	.19508	.19636	.19763	.19892
.16500	.19011	.19136	.19261	.19387	.19513	.19639	.19766	.19894	.20022	.20151
.16750	.19268	.19392	.19518	.19644	.19770	.19897	.20025	.20153	.20281	.20410
.17000	.19524	.19649	.19775	.19901	.20028	.20155	.20283	.20411	.20540	.20669
.17250	.19780	.19906	.20032	.20158	.20286	.20413	.20541	.20670	.20799	.20929
.17500	.20037	.20162	.20289	.20416	.20543	.20671	.20800	.20928	.21058	.21188
.17750	.20293	.20419	.20546	.20673	.20801	.20929	.21058	.21187	.21317	.21447
.18000	.20549	.20676	.20803	.20931	.21059	.21187	.21316	.21446	.21576	.21707
.18250	.20806	.20933	.21060	.21188	.21316	.21445	.21575	.21705	.21835	.21966
.18500	.21062	.21189	.21317	.21445	.21574	.21703	.21833	.21963	.22094	.22225
.18750	.21319	.21446	.21574	.21703	.21832	.21961	.22092	.22222	.22353	.22485
.19000	.21575	.21703	.21831	.21960	.22090	.22220	.22350	.22481	.22612	.22744
.19250	.21832	.21960	.22089	.22218	.22348	.22478	.22609	.22740	.22872	.23004
.19500	.22088	.22217	.22346	.22475	.22605	.22736	.22867	.22999	.23131	.23264
.19750	.22345	.22474	.22603	.22733	.22863	.22994	.23126	.23258	.23390	.23523
.20000	.22601	.22731	.22860	.22990	.23121	.23252	.23384	.23517	.23649	.23783
.20250	.22858	.22987	.23117	.23248	.23379	.23511	.23643	.23776	.23909	.24042
.20500	.23115	.23244	.23375	.23506	.23637	.23769	.23902	.24035	.24168	.24302
.20750	.23371	.23501	.23632	.23763	.23895	.24027	.24160	.24294	.24427	.24562

ANNUAL PERCENTAGE RATE TABLES: TERM OF MORTGAGE: 60 MONTHS

POINTS CHARGED

INTEREST RATE	.07750	.08000	.08250	.08500	.08750	.09000	.09250	.09500	.09750	.10000
.07000	.10441	.10559	.10677	.10796	.10915	.11034	.11154	.11275	.11396	.11517
.07250	.10699	.10817	.10936	.11055	.11174	.11294	.11415	.11535	.11657	.11778
.07500	.10958	.11076	.11195	.11314	.11434	.11554	.11675	.11796	.11917	.12039
.07750	.11216	.11335	.11454	.11573	.11693	.11814	.11935	.12056	.12178	.12301
.08000	.11475	.11593	.11713	.11833	.11953	.12074	.12195	.12317	.12439	.12562
.08250	.11733	.11852	.11972	.12092	.12213	.12334	.12455	.12577	.12700	.12823
.08500	.11991	.12111	.12231	.12351	.12472	.12594	.12716	.12838	.12961	.13084
.08750	.12250	.12370	.12490	.12611	.12732	.12854	.12976	.13099	.13222	.13345
.09000	.12509	.12629	.12749	.12870	.12992	.13114	.13236	.13359	.13483	.13607
.09250	.12767	.12888	.13008	.13130	.13252	.13374	.13497	.13620	.13744	.13868
.09500	.13026	.13146	.13268	.13389	.13511	.13634	.13757	.13881	.14005	.14129
.09750	.13284	.13405	.13527	.13649	.13771	.13894	.14018	.14142	.14266	.14391
.10000	.13543	.13664	.13786	.13908	.14031	.14154	.14278	.14402	.14527	.14652
.10250	.13802	.13923	.14045	.14168	.14291	.14415	.14539	.14663	.14788	.14914
.10500	.14060	.14182	.14305	.14428	.14551	.14675	.14799	.14924	.15050	.15175
.10750	.14319	.14442	.14564	.14687	.14811	.14935	.15060	.15185	.15311	.15437
.11000	.14578	.14701	.14824	.14947	.15071	.15196	.15321	.15446	.15572	.15699
.11250	.14837	.14960	.15083	.15207	.15331	.15456	.15581	.15707	.15834	.15960
.11500	.15096	.15219	.15343	.15467	.15591	.15717	.15842	.15968	.16095	.16222
.11750	.15355	.15478	.15602	.15727	.15852	.15977	.16103	.16229	.16356	.16484
.12000	.15614	.15737	.15862	.15986	.16112	.16238	.16364	.16491	.16618	.16746
.12250	.15873	.15997	.16121	.16246	.16372	.16498	.16625	.16752	.16879	.17008
.12500	.16132	.16256	.16381	.16506	.16632	.16759	.16886	.17013	.17141	.17269
.12750	.16391	.16515	.16641	.16766	.16893	.17019	.17147	.17274	.17403	.17531
.13000	.16650	.16775	.16900	.17026	.17153	.17280	.17408	.17536	.17664	.17793
.13250	.16909	.17034	.17160	.17286	.17413	.17541	.17669	.17797	.17926	.18055
.13500	.17168	.17294	.17420	.17547	.17674	.17801	.17930	.18058	.18188	.18318
.13750	.17427	.17553	.17680	.17807	.17934	.18062	.18191	.18320	.18450	.18580
.14000	.17686	.17813	.17939	.18067	.18195	.18323	.18452	.18581	.18711	.18842
.14250	.17945	.18072	.18199	.18327	.18455	.18584	.18713	.18843	.18973	.19104
.14500	.18205	.18332	.18459	.18587	.18716	.18845	.18974	.19105	.19235	.19366
.14750	.18464	.18591	.18719	.18848	.18976	.19106	.19236	.19366	.19497	.19629
.15000	.18723	.18851	.18979	.19108	.19237	.19367	.19497	.19628	.19759	.19891
.15250	.18983	.19111	.19239	.19368	.19498	.19628	.19758	.19890	.20021	.20153
.15500	.19242	.19370	.19499	.19629	.19758	.19889	.20020	.20151	.20283	.20416
.15750	.19501	.19630	.19759	.19889	.20019	.20150	.20281	.20413	.20545	.20678
.16000	.19761	.19890	.20019	.20149	.20280	.20411	.20543	.20675	.20808	.20941
.16250	.20020	.20150	.20280	.20410	.20541	.20672	.20804	.20937	.21070	.21203
.16500	.20280	.20410	.20540	.20670	.20802	.20933	.21066	.21199	.21332	.21466
.16750	.20539	.20669	.20800	.20931	.21063	.21195	.21327	.21461	.21594	.21729
.17000	.20799	.20929	.21060	.21192	.21324	.21456	.21589	.21723	.21857	.21991
.17250	.21059	.21189	.21321	.21452	.21585	.21717	.21851	.21985	.22119	.22254
.17500	.21318	.21449	.21581	.21713	.21846	.21979	.22112	.22247	.22381	.22517
.17750	.21578	.21709	.21841	.21974	.22107	.22240	.22374	.22509	.22644	.22780
.18000	.21838	.21969	.22102	.22234	.22368	.22502	.22636	.22771	.22906	.23043
.18250	.22098	.22230	.22362	.22495	.22629	.22763	.22898	.23033	.23169	.23305
.18500	.22357	.22490	.22623	.22756	.22890	.23025	.23160	.23295	.23432	.23568
.18750	.22617	.22750	.22883	.23017	.23151	.23286	.23422	.23558	.23694	.23831
.19000	.22877	.23010	.23144	.23278	.23413	.23548	.23684	.23820	.23957	.24094
.19250	.23137	.23270	.23404	.23539	.23674	.23809	.23946	.24082	.24220	.24358
.19500	.23397	.23531	.23665	.23800	.23935	.24071	.24208	.24345	.24482	.24621
.19750	.23657	.23791	.23926	.24061	.24197	.24333	.24470	.24607	.24745	.24884
.20000	.23917	.24051	.24186	.24322	.24458	.24595	.24732	.24870	.25008	.25147
.20250	.24177	.24312	.24447	.24583	.24719	.24856	.24994	.25132	.25271	.25410
.20500	.24437	.24572	.24708	.24844	.24981	.25118	.25256	.25395	.25534	.25674
.20750	.24697	.24832	.24969	.25105	.25242	.25380	.25519	.25657	.25797	.25937

ANNUAL PERCENTAGE RATE TABLES: TERM OF MORTGAGE: 60 MONTHS

POINTS CHARGED

INTEREST RATE	.10250	.10500	.10750	.11000	.11250	.11500	.11750	.12000	.12250	.12500
.07000	.11639	.11762	.11885	.12008	.12132	.12256	.12381	.12507	.12633	.12759
.07250	.11901	.12023	.12147	.12270	.12395	.12519	.12645	.12770	.12897	.13023
.07500	.12162	.12285	.12409	.12533	.12657	.12782	.12908	.13034	.13160	.13287
.07750	.12423	.12547	.12671	.12795	.12920	.13045	.13171	.13297	.13424	.13552
.08000	.12685	.12809	.12933	.13057	.13183	.13308	.13434	.13561	.13688	.13816
.08250	.12946	.13070	.13195	.13320	.13445	.13571	.13698	.13825	.13952	.14080
.08500	.13208	.13332	.13457	.13582	.13708	.13834	.13961	.14089	.14217	.14345
.08750	.13469	.13594	.13719	.13845	.13971	.14098	.14225	.14352	.14481	.14609
.09000	.13731	.13856	.13982	.14107	.14234	.14361	.14488	.14616	.14745	.14874
.09250	.13993	.14118	.14244	.14370	.14497	.14624	.14752	.14880	.15009	.15139
.09500	.14254	.14380	.14506	.14633	.14760	.14887	.15016	.15144	.15274	.15403
.09750	.14516	.14642	.14769	.14895	.15023	.15151	.15279	.15408	.15538	.15668
.10000	.14778	.14904	.15031	.15158	.15286	.15414	.15543	.15672	.15802	.15933
.10250	.15040	.15166	.15294	.15421	.15549	.15678	.15807	.15937	.16067	.16198
.10500	.15302	.15429	.15556	.15684	.15812	.15941	.16071	.16201	.16331	.16462
.10750	.15564	.15691	.15819	.15947	.16076	.16205	.16335	.16465	.16596	.16727
.11000	.15826	.15953	.16081	.16210	.16339	.16469	.16599	.16729	.16861	.16992
.11250	.16088	.16216	.16344	.16473	.16602	.16732	.16863	.16994	.17125	.17257
.11500	.16350	.16478	.16607	.16736	.16866	.16996	.17127	.17258	.17390	.17523
.11750	.16612	.16740	.16869	.16999	.17129	.17260	.17391	.17523	.17655	.17788
.12000	.16874	.17003	.17132	.17262	.17393	.17524	.17655	.17787	.17920	.18053
.12250	.17136	.17265	.17395	.17525	.17656	.17787	.17919	.18052	.18185	.18318
.12500	.17398	.17528	.17658	.17789	.17920	.18051	.18184	.18316	.18450	.18584
.12750	.17661	.17791	.17921	.18052	.18183	.18315	.18448	.18581	.18715	.18849
.13000	.17923	.18053	.18184	.18315	.18447	.18579	.18712	.18846	.18980	.19114
.13250	.18185	.18316	.18447	.18579	.18711	.18844	.18977	.19111	.19245	.19380
.13500	.18448	.18579	.18710	.18842	.18975	.19108	.19241	.19375	.19510	.19645
.13750	.18710	.18842	.18973	.19106	.19238	.19372	.19506	.19640	.19775	.19911
.14000	.18973	.19104	.19237	.19369	.19502	.19636	.19770	.19905	.20041	.20177
.14250	.19235	.19367	.19500	.19633	.19766	.19900	.20035	.20170	.20306	.20442
.14500	.19498	.19630	.19763	.19896	.20030	.20165	.20300	.20435	.20571	.20708
.14750	.19761	.19893	.20026	.20160	.20294	.20429	.20564	.20700	.20837	.20974
.15000	.20023	.20156	.20290	.20424	.20558	.20694	.20829	.20966	.21102	.21240
.15250	.20286	.20419	.20553	.20688	.20823	.20958	.21094	.21231	.21368	.21506
.15500	.20549	.20683	.20817	.20951	.21087	.21223	.21359	.21496	.21634	.21772
.15750	.20812	.20946	.21080	.21215	.21351	.21487	.21624	.21761	.21899	.22038
.16000	.21075	.21209	.21344	.21479	.21615	.21752	.21889	.22027	.22165	.22304
.16250	.21337	.21472	.21607	.21743	.21880	.22017	.22154	.22292	.22431	.22570
.16500	.21600	.21736	.21871	.22007	.22144	.22281	.22419	.22558	.22697	.22836
.16750	.21863	.21999	.22135	.22271	.22408	.22546	.22684	.22823	.22963	.23103
.17000	.22127	.22262	.22399	.22536	.22673	.22811	.22950	.23089	.23229	.23369
.17250	.22390	.22526	.22662	.22800	.22938	.23076	.23215	.23355	.23495	.23636
.17500	.22653	.22789	.22926	.23064	.23202	.23341	.23480	.23620	.23761	.23902
.17750	.22916	.23053	.23190	.23328	.23467	.23606	.23746	.23886	.24027	.24169
.18000	.23179	.23316	.23454	.23593	.23731	.23871	.24011	.24152	.24293	.24435
.18250	.23442	.23580	.23718	.23857	.23996	.24136	.24277	.24418	.24559	.24702
.18500	.23706	.23844	.23982	.24121	.24261	.24401	.24542	.24684	.24826	.24968
.18750	.23969	.24107	.24246	.24386	.24526	.24667	.24808	.24950	.25092	.25235
.19000	.24233	.24371	.24511	.24650	.24791	.24932	.25073	.25216	.25359	.25502
.19250	.24496	.24635	.24775	.24915	.25056	.25197	.25339	.25482	.25625	.25769
.19500	.24760	.24899	.25039	.25180	.25321	.25463	.25605	.25748	.25892	.26036
.19750	.25023	.25163	.25303	.25444	.25586	.25728	.25871	.26014	.26158	.26303
.20000	.25287	.25427	.25568	.25709	.25851	.25993	.26137	.26280	.26425	.26570
.20250	.25550	.25691	.25832	.25974	.26116	.26259	.26403	.26547	.26691	.26837
.20500	.25814	.25955	.26096	.26239	.26381	.26525	.26669	.26813	.26958	.27104
.20750	.26078	.26219	.26361	.26503	.26647	.26790	.26935	.27080	.27225	.27371

ANNUAL PERCENTAGE RATE TABLES: TERM OF MORTGAGE: 60 MONTHS

POINTS CHARGED

INTEREST RATE	.12750	.13000	.13250	.13500	.13750	.14000	.14250	.14500	.14750	.15000
.07000	.12886	.13014	.13142	.13270	.13399	.13529	.13659	.13790	.13921	.14053
.07250	.13151	.13278	.13407	.13536	.13665	.13795	.13925	.14056	.14188	.14320
.07500	.13415	.13543	.13672	.13801	.13931	.14061	.14192	.14323	.14455	.14588
.07750	.13680	.13808	.13937	.14067	.14197	.14327	.14459	.14590	.14723	.14855
.08000	.13944	.14073	.14202	.14332	.14463	.14594	.14725	.14857	.14990	.15123
.08250	.14209	.14338	.14468	.14598	.14729	.14860	.14992	.15124	.15257	.15391
.08500	.14474	.14603	.14733	.14864	.14995	.15127	.15259	.15392	.15525	.15659
.08750	.14739	.14868	.14999	.15130	.15261	.15393	.15526	.15659	.15792	.15927
.09000	.15004	.15134	.15264	.15396	.15527	.15660	.15793	.15926	.16060	.16195
.09250	.15269	.15399	.15530	.15662	.15794	.15926	.16060	.16193	.16328	.16463
.09500	.15534	.15664	.15796	.15928	.16060	.16193	.16327	.16461	.16596	.16731
.09750	.15799	.15930	.16061	.16194	.16326	.16460	.16594	.16728	.16863	.16999
.10000	.16064	.16195	.16327	.16460	.16593	.16727	.16861	.16996	.17131	.17267
.10250	.16329	.16461	.16593	.16726	.16860	.16994	.17128	.17263	.17399	.17536
.10500	.16594	.16726	.16859	.16992	.17126	.17261	.17396	.17531	.17667	.17804
.10750	.16859	.16992	.17125	.17259	.17393	.17528	.17663	.17799	.17935	.18073
.11000	.17125	.17258	.17391	.17525	.17660	.17795	.17930	.18067	.18204	.18341
.11250	.17390	.17523	.17657	.17791	.17926	.18062	.18198	.18335	.18472	.18610
.11500	.17656	.17789	.17923	.18058	.18193	.18329	.18466	.18603	.18740	.18878
.11750	.17921	.18055	.18189	.18325	.18460	.18596	.18733	.18871	.19009	.19147
.12000	.18187	.18321	.18456	.18591	.18727	.18864	.19001	.19139	.19277	.19416
.12250	.18452	.18587	.18722	.18858	.18994	.19131	.19269	.19407	.19545	.19685
.12500	.18718	.18853	.18988	.19125	.19261	.19399	.19537	.19675	.19814	.19954
.12750	.18984	.19119	.19255	.19391	.19529	.19666	.19804	.19943	.20083	.20223
.13000	.19249	.19385	.19521	.19658	.19796	.19934	.20072	.20212	.20351	.20492
.13250	.19515	.19651	.19788	.19925	.20063	.20201	.20340	.20480	.20620	.20761
.13500	.19781	.19918	.20055	.20192	.20330	.20469	.20609	.20749	.20889	.21030
.13750	.20047	.20184	.20321	.20459	.20598	.20737	.20877	.21017	.21158	.21300
.14000	.20313	.20450	.20588	.20726	.20865	.21005	.21145	.21286	.21427	.21569
.14250	.20579	.20717	.20855	.20994	.21133	.21273	.21413	.21554	.21696	.21838
.14500	.20845	.20983	.21122	.21261	.21401	.21541	.21682	.21823	.21965	.22108
.14750	.21112	.21250	.21389	.21528	.21668	.21809	.21950	.22092	.22234	.22378
.15000	.21378	.21517	.21656	.21796	.21936	.22077	.22219	.22361	.22504	.22647
.15250	.21644	.21783	.21923	.22063	.22204	.22345	.22487	.22630	.22773	.22917
.15500	.21911	.22050	.22190	.22331	.22472	.22613	.22756	.22899	.23042	.23187
.15750	.22177	.22317	.22457	.22598	.22740	.22882	.23025	.23168	.23312	.23457
.16000	.22444	.22584	.22724	.22866	.23008	.23150	.23293	.23437	.23582	.23727
.16250	.22710	.22851	.22992	.23133	.23276	.23419	.23562	.23706	.23851	.23997
.16500	.22977	.23118	.23259	.23401	.23544	.23687	.23831	.23976	.24121	.24267
.16750	.23243	.23385	.23526	.23669	.23812	.23956	.24100	.24245	.24391	.24537
.17000	.23510	.23652	.23794	.23937	.24080	.24224	.24369	.24514	.24660	.24807
.17250	.23777	.23919	.24062	.24205	.24349	.24493	.24638	.24784	.24930	.25077
.17500	.24044	.24186	.24329	.24473	.24617	.24762	.24907	.25054	.25200	.25348
.17750	.24311	.24453	.24597	.24741	.24885	.25031	.25177	.25323	.25470	.25618
.18000	.24578	.24721	.24865	.25009	.25154	.25300	.25446	.25593	.25740	.25889
.18250	.24845	.24988	.25132	.25277	.25423	.25569	.25715	.25863	.26011	.26159
.18500	.25112	.25256	.25400	.25545	.25691	.25838	.25985	.26132	.26281	.26430
.18750	.25379	.25523	.25668	.25814	.25960	.26107	.26254	.26402	.26551	.26701
.19000	.25646	.25791	.25936	.26082	.26229	.26376	.26524	.26672	.26822	.26971
.19250	.25913	.26058	.26204	.26351	.26498	.26645	.26793	.26942	.27092	.27242
.19500	.26181	.26326	.26472	.26619	.26766	.26914	.27063	.27213	.27363	.27513
.19750	.26448	.26594	.26740	.26888	.27035	.27184	.27333	.27483	.27633	.27784
.20000	.26715	.26862	.27009	.27156	.27304	.27453	.27603	.27753	.27904	.28055
.20250	.26983	.27130	.27277	.27425	.27574	.27723	.27873	.28023	.28175	.28327
.20500	.27250	.27398	.27545	.27694	.27843	.27992	.28143	.28294	.28445	.28598
.20750	.27518	.27666	.27814	.27962	.28112	.28262	.28413	.28564	.28716	.28869

ANNUAL PERCENTAGE RATE TABLES: TERM OF MORTGAGE: 120 MONTHS

INTEREST RATE	POINTS CHARGED .00250	.00500	.00750	.01000	.01250	.01500	.01750	.02000	.02250	.02500
.07000	.07056	.07113	.07170	.07227	.07284	.07342	.07399	.07457	.07515	.07573
.07250	.07307	.07364	.07421	.07478	.07535	.07593	.07651	.07709	.07768	.07826
.07500	.07557	.07614	.07671	.07729	.07787	.07845	.07903	.07961	.08020	.08079
.07750	.07807	.07865	.07922	.07980	.08038	.08097	.08155	.08214	.08273	.08332
.08000	.08058	.08115	.08173	.08231	.08290	.08348	.08407	.08466	.08525	.08585
.08250	.08308	.08366	.08424	.08482	.08541	.08600	.08659	.08718	.08778	.08837
.08500	.08558	.08616	.08675	.08734	.08792	.08852	.08911	.08970	.09030	.09090
.08750	.08808	.08867	.08926	.08985	.09044	.09103	.09163	.09223	.09283	.09343
.09000	.09059	.09117	.09177	.09236	.09295	.09355	.09415	.09475	.09535	.09596
.09250	.09309	.09368	.09427	.09487	.09547	.09607	.09667	.09727	.09788	.09849
.09500	.09559	.09619	.09678	.09738	.09798	.09858	.09919	.09980	.10041	.10102
.09750	.09809	.09869	.09929	.09989	.10050	.10110	.10171	.10232	.10293	.10355
.10000	.10060	.10120	.10180	.10240	.10301	.10362	.10423	.10484	.10546	.10608
.10250	.10310	.10370	.10431	.10492	.10553	.10614	.10675	.10737	.10799	.10861
.10500	.10560	.10621	.10682	.10743	.10804	.10866	.10927	.10989	.11051	.11114
.10750	.10811	.10872	.10933	.10994	.11056	.11117	.11179	.11242	.11304	.11367
.11000	.11061	.11122	.11184	.11245	.11307	.11369	.11431	.11494	.11557	.11620
.11250	.11311	.11373	.11434	.11496	.11559	.11621	.11684	.11746	.11810	.11873
.11500	.11562	.11623	.11685	.11748	.11810	.11873	.11936	.11999	.12062	.12126
.11750	.11812	.11874	.11936	.11999	.12062	.12125	.12188	.12251	.12315	.12379
.12000	.12062	.12125	.12187	.12250	.12313	.12376	.12440	.12504	.12568	.12632
.12250	.12312	.12375	.12438	.12501	.12565	.12628	.12692	.12756	.12821	.12885
.12500	.12563	.12626	.12689	.12753	.12816	.12880	.12944	.13009	.13074	.13139
.12750	.12813	.12876	.12940	.13004	.13068	.13132	.13197	.13261	.13327	.13392
.13000	.13063	.13127	.13191	.13255	.13319	.13384	.13449	.13514	.13579	.13645
.13250	.13314	.13378	.13442	.13506	.13571	.13636	.13701	.13767	.13832	.13898
.13500	.13564	.13628	.13693	.13758	.13823	.13888	.13953	.14019	.14085	.14152
.13750	.13814	.13879	.13944	.14009	.14074	.14140	.14206	.14272	.14338	.14405
.14000	.14065	.14130	.14195	.14260	.14326	.14392	.14458	.14524	.14591	.14658
.14250	.14315	.14380	.14446	.14512	.14578	.14644	.14710	.14777	.14844	.14911
.14500	.14565	.14631	.14697	.14763	.14829	.14896	.14963	.15030	.15097	.15165
.14750	.14816	.14882	.14948	.15014	.15081	.15148	.15215	.15282	.15350	.15418
.15000	.15066	.15132	.15199	.15265	.15332	.15400	.15467	.15535	.15603	.15672
.15250	.15316	.15383	.15450	.15517	.15584	.15652	.15720	.15788	.15856	.15925
.15500	.15567	.15634	.15701	.15768	.15836	.15904	.15972	.16041	.16109	.16178
.15750	.15817	.15884	.15952	.16020	.16088	.16156	.16224	.16293	.16362	.16432
.16000	.16067	.16135	.16203	.16271	.16339	.16408	.16477	.16546	.16616	.16685
.16250	.16318	.16386	.16454	.16522	.16591	.16660	.16729	.16799	.16869	.16939
.16500	.16568	.16636	.16705	.16774	.16843	.16912	.16982	.17052	.17122	.17192
.16750	.16818	.16887	.16956	.17025	.17094	.17164	.17234	.17304	.17375	.17446
.17000	.17069	.17138	.17207	.17276	.17346	.17416	.17487	.17557	.17628	.17699
.17250	.17319	.17388	.17458	.17528	.17598	.17668	.17739	.17810	.17881	.17953
.17500	.17569	.17639	.17709	.17779	.17850	.17921	.17992	.18063	.18135	.18206
.17750	.17820	.17890	.17960	.18031	.18102	.18173	.18244	.18316	.18388	.18460
.18000	.18070	.18140	.18211	.18282	.18353	.18425	.18497	.18569	.18641	.18714
.18250	.18320	.18391	.18462	.18534	.18605	.18677	.18749	.18822	.18894	.18967
.18500	.18571	.18642	.18713	.18785	.18857	.18929	.19002	.19075	.19148	.19221
.18750	.18821	.18893	.18964	.19036	.19109	.19181	.19254	.19327	.19401	.19475
.19000	.19072	.19143	.19215	.19288	.19361	.19434	.19507	.19580	.19654	.19728
.19250	.19322	.19394	.19467	.19539	.19612	.19686	.19759	.19833	.19908	.19982
.19500	.19572	.19645	.19718	.19791	.19864	.19938	.20012	.20086	.20161	.20236
.19750	.19823	.19896	.19969	.20042	.20116	.20190	.20265	.20339	.20414	.20490
.20000	.20073	.20146	.20220	.20294	.20368	.20443	.20517	.20592	.20668	.20744
.20250	.20323	.20397	.20471	.20545	.20620	.20695	.20770	.20845	.20921	.20997
.20500	.20574	.20648	.20722	.20797	.20872	.20947	.21023	.21099	.21175	.21251
.20750	.20824	.20899	.20973	.21048	.21124	.21199	.21275	.21352	.21428	.21505

ANNUAL PERCENTAGE RATE TABLES: TERM OF MORTGAGE: 120 MONTHS

POINTS CHARGED

INTEREST RATE	.02750	.03000	.03250	.03500	.03750	.04000	.04250	.04500	.04750	.05000
.07000	.07632	.07691	.07750	.07809	.07868	.07928	.07988	.08048	.08108	.08168
.07250	.07885	.07944	.08003	.08063	.08122	.08182	.08242	.08303	.08363	.08424
.07500	.08138	.08197	.08257	.08317	.08377	.08437	.08497	.08558	.08619	.08680
.07750	.08391	.08451	.08511	.08571	.08631	.08691	.08752	.08813	.08874	.08936
.08000	.08644	.08704	.08764	.08825	.08885	.08946	.09007	.09068	.09130	.09191
.08250	.08897	.08958	.09018	.09079	.09139	.09200	.09262	.09323	.09385	.09447
.08500	.09151	.09211	.09272	.09333	.09394	.09455	.09517	.09579	.09641	.09703
.08750	.09404	.09464	.09525	.09587	.09648	.09710	.09772	.09834	.09896	.09959
.09000	.09657	.09718	.09779	.09841	.09902	.09964	.10027	.10089	.10152	.10215
.09250	.09910	.09971	.10033	.10095	.10157	.10219	.10282	.10344	.10407	.10471
.09500	.10163	.10225	.10287	.10349	.10411	.10474	.10537	.10600	.10663	.10727
.09750	.10417	.10479	.10541	.10603	.10666	.10729	.10792	.10855	.10919	.10983
.10000	.10670	.10732	.10795	.10857	.10920	.10984	.11047	.11111	.11175	.11239
.10250	.10923	.10986	.11049	.11112	.11175	.11238	.11302	.11366	.11431	.11495
.10500	.11176	.11239	.11302	.11366	.11429	.11493	.11557	.11622	.11686	.11751
.10750	.11430	.11493	.11556	.11620	.11684	.11748	.11813	.11877	.11942	.12008
.11000	.11683	.11747	.11810	.11874	.11939	.12003	.12068	.12133	.12198	.12264
.11250	.11937	.12000	.12064	.12129	.12193	.12258	.12323	.12389	.12454	.12520
.11500	.12190	.12254	.12319	.12383	.12448	.12513	.12579	.12644	.12710	.12776
.11750	.12443	.12508	.12573	.12638	.12703	.12768	.12834	.12900	.12966	.13033
.12000	.12697	.12762	.12827	.12892	.12958	.13023	.13090	.13156	.13222	.13289
.12250	.12950	.13015	.13081	.13146	.13212	.13279	.13345	.13412	.13479	.13546
.12500	.13204	.13269	.13335	.13401	.13467	.13534	.13600	.13667	.13735	.13802
.12750	.13457	.13523	.13589	.13656	.13722	.13789	.13856	.13923	.13991	.14059
.13000	.13711	.13777	.13843	.13910	.13977	.14044	.14112	.14179	.14247	.14316
.13250	.13964	.14031	.14098	.14165	.14232	.14299	.14367	.14435	.14504	.14572
.13500	.14218	.14285	.14352	.14419	.14487	.14555	.14623	.14691	.14760	.14829
.13750	.14472	.14539	.14606	.14674	.14742	.14810	.14879	.14947	.15016	.15086
.14000	.14725	.14793	.14861	.14929	.14997	.15065	.15134	.15203	.15273	.15342
.14250	.14979	.15047	.15115	.15183	.15252	.15321	.15390	.15459	.15529	.15599
.14500	.15233	.15301	.15369	.15438	.15507	.15576	.15646	.15716	.15786	.15856
.14750	.15486	.15555	.15624	.15693	.15762	.15832	.15902	.15972	.16042	.16113
.15000	.15740	.15809	.15878	.15948	.16017	.16087	.16158	.16228	.16299	.16370
.15250	.15994	.16063	.16133	.16202	.16272	.16343	.16413	.16484	.16556	.16627
.15500	.16248	.16317	.16387	.16457	.16528	.16598	.16669	.16741	.16812	.16884
.15750	.16501	.16571	.16642	.16712	.16783	.16854	.16925	.16997	.17069	.17141
.16000	.16755	.16826	.16896	.16967	.17038	.17110	.17181	.17253	.17326	.17398
.16250	.17009	.17080	.17151	.17222	.17293	.17365	.17437	.17510	.17582	.17655
.16500	.17263	.17334	.17405	.17477	.17549	.17621	.17693	.17766	.17839	.17913
.16750	.17517	.17588	.17660	.17732	.17804	.17877	.17950	.18023	.18096	.18170
.17000	.17771	.17843	.17915	.17987	.18060	.18133	.18206	.18279	.18353	.18427
.17250	.18025	.18097	.18169	.18242	.18315	.18388	.18462	.18536	.18610	.18685
.17500	.18279	.18351	.18424	.18497	.18570	.18644	.18718	.18792	.18867	.18942
.17750	.18533	.18606	.18679	.18752	.18826	.18900	.18974	.19049	.19124	.19199
.18000	.18787	.18860	.18933	.19007	.19082	.19156	.19231	.19306	.19381	.19457
.18250	.19041	.19114	.19188	.19263	.19337	.19412	.19487	.19563	.19638	.19714
.18500	.19295	.19369	.19443	.19518	.19593	.19668	.19743	.19819	.19895	.19972
.18750	.19549	.19623	.19698	.19773	.19848	.19924	.20000	.20076	.20153	.20230
.19000	.19803	.19878	.19953	.20028	.20104	.20180	.20256	.20333	.20410	.20487
.19250	.20057	.20132	.20208	.20284	.20360	.20436	.20513	.20590	.20667	.20745
.19500	.20311	.20387	.20463	.20539	.20615	.20692	.20769	.20847	.20925	.21003
.19750	.20565	.20641	.20718	.20794	.20871	.20948	.21026	.21104	.21182	.21260
.20000	.20820	.20896	.20973	.21050	.21127	.21204	.21282	.21361	.21439	.21518
.20250	.21074	.21151	.21228	.21305	.21383	.21461	.21539	.21618	.21697	.21776
.20500	.21328	.21405	.21483	.21560	.21639	.21717	.21796	.21875	.21954	.22034
.20750	.21582	.21660	.21738	.21816	.21894	.21973	.22052	.22132	.22212	.22292

ANNUAL PERCENTAGE RATE TABLES: TERM OF MORTGAGE: 120 MONTHS

INTEREST RATE	POINTS CHARGED .05250	.05500	.05750	.06000	.06250	.06500	.06750	.07000	.07250	.07500
.07000	.08229	.08290	.08351	.08413	.08474	.08536	.08599	.08661	.08724	.08786
.07250	.08485	.08546	.08608	.08670	.08732	.08794	.08856	.08919	.08982	.09045
.07500	.08741	.08803	.08864	.08927	.08989	.09051	.09114	.09177	.09240	.09304
.07750	.08997	.09059	.09121	.09183	.09246	.09309	.09372	.09435	.09499	.09563
.08000	.09253	.09315	.09378	.09440	.09503	.09567	.09630	.09694	.09757	.09822
.08250	.09509	.09572	.09635	.09698	.09761	.09824	.09888	.09952	.10016	.10081
.08500	.09766	.09828	.09891	.09955	.10018	.10082	.10146	.10210	.10275	.10340
.08750	.10022	.10085	.10148	.10212	.10276	.10340	.10404	.10469	.10534	.10599
.09000	.10278	.10341	.10405	.10469	.10533	.10598	.10662	.10727	.10792	.10858
.09250	.10534	.10598	.10662	.10726	.10791	.10856	.10921	.10986	.11051	.11117
.09500	.10791	.10855	.10919	.10984	.11048	.11113	.11179	.11244	.11310	.11376
.09750	.11047	.11111	.11176	.11241	.11306	.11371	.11437	.11503	.11569	.11636
.10000	.11303	.11368	.11433	.11498	.11564	.11630	.11696	.11762	.11828	.11895
.10250	.11560	.11625	.11690	.11756	.11822	.11888	.11954	.12021	.12088	.12155
.10500	.11816	.11882	.11947	.12013	.12079	.12146	.12213	.12280	.12347	.12414
.10750	.12073	.12139	.12205	.12271	.12337	.12404	.12471	.12538	.12606	.12674
.11000	.12330	.12396	.12462	.12528	.12595	.12662	.12730	.12797	.12865	.12934
.11250	.12586	.12653	.12719	.12786	.12853	.12921	.12988	.13056	.13125	.13193
.11500	.12843	.12910	.12977	.13044	.13111	.13179	.13247	.13316	.13384	.13453
.11750	.13100	.13167	.13234	.13302	.13370	.13438	.13506	.13575	.13644	.13713
.12000	.13356	.13424	.13492	.13559	.13628	.13696	.13765	.13834	.13903	.13973
.12250	.13613	.13681	.13749	.13817	.13886	.13955	.14024	.14093	.14163	.14233
.12500	.13870	.13938	.14007	.14075	.14144	.14213	.14283	.14353	.14423	.14493
.12750	.14127	.14196	.14264	.14333	.14403	.14472	.14542	.14612	.14682	.14753
.13000	.14384	.14453	.14522	.14591	.14661	.14731	.14801	.14872	.14942	.15013
.13250	.14641	.14710	.14780	.14849	.14919	.14990	.15060	.15131	.15202	.15274
.13500	.14898	.14968	.15037	.15108	.15178	.15249	.15319	.15391	.15462	.15534
.13750	.15155	.15225	.15295	.15366	.15436	.15507	.15579	.15650	.15722	.15794
.14000	.15412	.15483	.15553	.15624	.15695	.15766	.15838	.15910	.15982	.16055
.14250	.15670	.15740	.15811	.15882	.15954	.16025	.16098	.16170	.16243	.16315
.14500	.15927	.15998	.16069	.16141	.16212	.16285	.16357	.16430	.16503	.16576
.14750	.16184	.16255	.16327	.16399	.16471	.16544	.16617	.16690	.16763	.16837
.15000	.16441	.16513	.16585	.16657	.16730	.16803	.16876	.16950	.17023	.17098
.15250	.16699	.16771	.16843	.16916	.16989	.17062	.17136	.17210	.17284	.17358
.15500	.16956	.17029	.17101	.17174	.17248	.17321	.17395	.17470	.17544	.17619
.15750	.17214	.17287	.17360	.17433	.17507	.17581	.17655	.17730	.17805	.17880
.16000	.17471	.17544	.17618	.17692	.17766	.17840	.17915	.17990	.18066	.18141
.16250	.17729	.17802	.17876	.17950	.18025	.18100	.18175	.18250	.18326	.18402
.16500	.17986	.18060	.18135	.18209	.18284	.18359	.18435	.18511	.18587	.18663
.16750	.18244	.18318	.18393	.18468	.18543	.18619	.18695	.18771	.18848	.18925
.17000	.18502	.18576	.18652	.18727	.18803	.18879	.18955	.19032	.19109	.19186
.17250	.18759	.18835	.18910	.18986	.19062	.19138	.19215	.19292	.19370	.19447
.17500	.19017	.19093	.19169	.19245	.19321	.19398	.19475	.19553	.19631	.19709
.17750	.19275	.19351	.19427	.19504	.19581	.19658	.19736	.19813	.19892	.19970
.18000	.19533	.19609	.19686	.19763	.19840	.19918	.19996	.20074	.20153	.20232
.18250	.19791	.19868	.19945	.20022	.20100	.20178	.20256	.20335	.20414	.20493
.18500	.20049	.20126	.20203	.20281	.20359	.20438	.20517	.20596	.20675	.20755
.18750	.20307	.20384	.20462	.20540	.20619	.20698	.20777	.20857	.20937	.21017
.19000	.20565	.20643	.20721	.20800	.20879	.20958	.21038	.21118	.21198	.21279
.19250	.20823	.20901	.20980	.21059	.21138	.21218	.21298	.21379	.21459	.21541
.19500	.21081	.21160	.21239	.21318	.21398	.21478	.21559	.21640	.21721	.21802
.19750	.21339	.21419	.21498	.21578	.21658	.21739	.21820	.21901	.21983	.22065
.20000	.21598	.21677	.21757	.21837	.21918	.21999	.22080	.22162	.22244	.22327
.20250	.21856	.21936	.22016	.22097	.22178	.22259	.22341	.22423	.22506	.22589
.20500	.22114	.22195	.22275	.22357	.22438	.22520	.22602	.22685	.22768	.22851
.20750	.22373	.22453	.22535	.22616	.22698	.22780	.22863	.22946	.23029	.23113

ANNUAL PERCENTAGE RATE TABLES: TERM OF MORTGAGE: 120 MONTHS

INTEREST RATE	POINTS CHARGED .07750	.08000	.08250	.08500	.08750	.09000	.09250	.09500	.09750	.10000
.07000	.08850	.08913	.08977	.09040	.09105	.09169	.09234	.09298	.09364	.09429
.07250	.09109	.09172	.09236	.09300	.09365	.09430	.09495	.09560	.09625	.09691
.07500	.09368	.09432	.09496	.09560	.09625	.09690	.09756	.09821	.09887	.09953
.07750	.09627	.09691	.09756	.09821	.09886	.09951	.10017	.10083	.10149	.10215
.08000	.09886	.09951	.10016	.10081	.10146	.10212	.10278	.10344	.10411	.10477
.08250	.10145	.10210	.10276	.10341	.10407	.10473	.10539	.10606	.10673	.10740
.08500	.10405	.10470	.10536	.10601	.10668	.10734	.10801	.10867	.10935	.11002
.08750	.10664	.10730	.10796	.10862	.10928	.10995	.11062	.11129	.11197	.11265
.09000	.10924	.10990	.11056	.11122	.11189	.11256	.11324	.11391	.11459	.11527
.09250	.11183	.11249	.11316	.11383	.11450	.11517	.11585	.11653	.11721	.11790
.09500	.11443	.11509	.11576	.11644	.11711	.11779	.11847	.11915	.11984	.12053
.09750	.11702	.11769	.11837	.11904	.11972	.12040	.12109	.12177	.12246	.12315
.10000	.11962	.12030	.12097	.12165	.12233	.12302	.12370	.12439	.12509	.12578
.10250	.12222	.12290	.12358	.12426	.12495	.12563	.12632	.12702	.12771	.12841
.10500	.12482	.12550	.12618	.12687	.12756	.12825	.12894	.12964	.13034	.13105
.10750	.12742	.12810	.12879	.12948	.13017	.13087	.13157	.13227	.13297	.13368
.11000	.13002	.13071	.13140	.13209	.13279	.13349	.13419	.13489	.13560	.13631
.11250	.13262	.13331	.13401	.13470	.13540	.13610	.13681	.13752	.13823	.13894
.11500	.13522	.13592	.13661	.13732	.13802	.13872	.13943	.14015	.14086	.14158
.11750	.13783	.13852	.13922	.13993	.14064	.14135	.14206	.14277	.14349	.14421
.12000	.14043	.14113	.14183	.14254	.14325	.14397	.14468	.14540	.14613	.14685
.12250	.14303	.14374	.14445	.14516	.14587	.14659	.14731	.14803	.14876	.14949
.12500	.14564	.14635	.14706	.14777	.14849	.14921	.14994	.15066	.15139	.15213
.12750	.14824	.14895	.14967	.15039	.15111	.15184	.15256	.15330	.15403	.15477
.13000	.15085	.15156	.15228	.15301	.15373	.15446	.15519	.15593	.15667	.15741
.13250	.15345	.15417	.15490	.15562	.15635	.15709	.15782	.15856	.15930	.16005
.13500	.15606	.15679	.15751	.15824	.15898	.15971	.16045	.16120	.16194	.16269
.13750	.15867	.15940	.16013	.16086	.16160	.16234	.16308	.16383	.16458	.16533
.14000	.16128	.16201	.16274	.16348	.16422	.16497	.16572	.16647	.16722	.16798
.14250	.16389	.16462	.16536	.16610	.16685	.16760	.16835	.16910	.16986	.17062
.14500	.16650	.16724	.16798	.16873	.16947	.17023	.17098	.17174	.17250	.17327
.14750	.16911	.16985	.17060	.17135	.17210	.17286	.17362	.17438	.17515	.17592
.15000	.17172	.17247	.17322	.17397	.17473	.17549	.17625	.17702	.17779	.17856
.15250	.17433	.17508	.17584	.17660	.17736	.17812	.17889	.17966	.18043	.18121
.15500	.17694	.17770	.17846	.17922	.17999	.18075	.18153	.18230	.18308	.18386
.15750	.17956	.18032	.18108	.18185	.18262	.18339	.18416	.18494	.18573	.18651
.16000	.18217	.18294	.18370	.18447	.18525	.18602	.18680	.18759	.18837	.18916
.16250	.18479	.18555	.18633	.18710	.18788	.18866	.18944	.19023	.19102	.19182
.16500	.18740	.18817	.18895	.18973	.19051	.19129	.19208	.19287	.19367	.19447
.16750	.19002	.19079	.19157	.19236	.19314	.19393	.19472	.19552	.19632	.19712
.17000	.19264	.19342	.19420	.19499	.19578	.19657	.19737	.19817	.19897	.19978
.17250	.19525	.19604	.19683	.19762	.19841	.19921	.20001	.20081	.20162	.20243
.17500	.19787	.19866	.19945	.20025	.20105	.20185	.20265	.20346	.20427	.20509
.17750	.20049	.20128	.20208	.20288	.20368	.20449	.20530	.20611	.20693	.20775
.18000	.20311	.20391	.20471	.20551	.20632	.20713	.20794	.20876	.20958	.21041
.18250	.20573	.20653	.20734	.20814	.20896	.20977	.21059	.21141	.21224	.21307
.18500	.20835	.20916	.20997	.21078	.21159	.21241	.21324	.21406	.21489	.21573
.18750	.21097	.21178	.21260	.21341	.21423	.21506	.21588	.21672	.21755	.21839
.19000	.21360	.21441	.21523	.21605	.21687	.21770	.21853	.21937	.22021	.22105
.19250	.21622	.21704	.21786	.21869	.21951	.22035	.22118	.22202	.22287	.22372
.19500	.21884	.21967	.22049	.22132	.22216	.22299	.22383	.22468	.22553	.22638
.19750	.22147	.22230	.22313	.22396	.22480	.22564	.22649	.22733	.22819	.22905
.20000	.22409	.22493	.22576	.22660	.22744	.22829	.22914	.22999	.23085	.23171
.20250	.22672	.22756	.22840	.22924	.23009	.23094	.23179	.23265	.23351	.23438
.20500	.22935	.23019	.23103	.23188	.23273	.23359	.23444	.23531	.23618	.23705
.20750	.23197	.23282	.23367	.23452	.23538	.23624	.23710	.23797	.23884	.23972

ANNUAL PERCENTAGE RATE TABLES: TERM OF MORTGAGE: 120 MONTHS

POINTS CHARGED

INTEREST RATE	.10250	.10500	.10750	.11000	.11250	.11500	.11750	.12000	.12250	.12500
.07000	.09495	.09561	.09627	.09693	.09760	.09827	.09895	.09962	.10030	.10098
.07250	.09757	.09823	.09890	.09957	.10024	.10091	.10159	.10227	.10295	.10364
.07500	.10019	.10086	.10153	.10220	.10288	.10355	.10423	.10492	.10560	.10629
.07750	.10282	.10349	.10416	.10484	.10551	.10620	.10688	.10757	.10826	.10895
.08000	.10544	.10612	.10679	.10747	.10815	.10884	.10953	.11022	.11091	.11161
.08250	.10807	.10875	.10943	.11011	.11079	.11148	.11217	.11287	.11356	.11426
.08500	.11070	.11138	.11206	.11275	.11344	.11413	.11482	.11552	.11622	.11692
.08750	.11333	.11401	.11470	.11539	.11608	.11677	.11747	.11817	.11888	.11958
.09000	.11596	.11664	.11733	.11803	.11872	.11942	.12012	.12083	.12154	.12225
.09250	.11859	.11928	.11997	.12067	.12137	.12207	.12277	.12348	.12419	.12491
.09500	.12122	.12191	.12261	.12331	.12401	.12472	.12543	.12614	.12686	.12757
.09750	.12385	.12455	.12525	.12595	.12666	.12737	.12808	.12880	.12952	.13024
.10000	.12648	.12718	.12789	.12860	.12931	.13002	.13074	.13146	.13218	.13291
.10250	.12912	.12982	.13053	.13124	.13196	.13267	.13339	.13412	.13484	.13557
.10500	.13175	.13246	.13317	.13389	.13461	.13533	.13605	.13678	.13751	.13824
.10750	.13439	.13510	.13582	.13653	.13726	.13798	.13871	.13944	.14018	.14091
.11000	.13702	.13774	.13846	.13918	.13991	.14064	.14137	.14210	.14284	.14358
.11250	.13966	.14038	.14111	.14183	.14256	.14329	.14403	.14477	.14551	.14626
.11500	.14230	.14302	.14375	.14448	.14522	.14595	.14669	.14743	.14818	.14893
.11750	.14494	.14567	.14640	.14713	.14787	.14861	.14935	.15010	.15085	.15161
.12000	.14758	.14831	.14905	.14978	.15053	.15127	.15202	.15277	.15352	.15428
.12250	.15022	.15096	.15170	.15244	.15318	.15393	.15468	.15544	.15620	.15696
.12500	.15286	.15360	.15435	.15509	.15584	.15659	.15735	.15811	.15887	.15964
.12750	.15551	.15625	.15700	.15775	.15850	.15926	.16002	.16078	.16155	.16232
.13000	.15815	.15890	.15965	.16040	.16116	.16192	.16269	.16345	.16422	.16500
.13250	.16080	.16155	.16230	.16306	.16382	.16459	.16536	.16613	.16690	.16768
.13500	.16344	.16420	.16496	.16572	.16648	.16725	.16803	.16880	.16958	.17036
.13750	.16609	.16685	.16761	.16838	.16915	.16992	.17070	.17148	.17226	.17305
.14000	.16874	.16950	.17027	.17104	.17181	.17259	.17337	.17415	.17494	.17573
.14250	.17139	.17215	.17293	.17370	.17448	.17526	.17604	.17683	.17762	.17842
.14500	.17404	.17481	.17558	.17636	.17715	.17793	.17872	.17951	.18031	.18111
.14750	.17669	.17746	.17824	.17903	.17981	.18060	.18140	.18219	.18299	.18380
.15000	.17934	.18012	.18090	.18169	.18248	.18328	.18407	.18487	.18568	.18649
.15250	.18199	.18278	.18357	.18436	.18515	.18595	.18675	.18756	.18837	.18918
.15500	.18465	.18544	.18623	.18702	.18782	.18863	.18943	.19024	.19106	.19187
.15750	.18730	.18809	.18889	.18969	.19049	.19130	.19211	.19293	.19374	.19457
.16000	.18996	.19075	.19155	.19236	.19317	.19398	.19479	.19561	.19644	.19726
.16250	.19261	.19342	.19422	.19503	.19584	.19666	.19748	.19830	.19913	.19996
.16500	.19527	.19608	.19689	.19770	.19852	.19934	.20016	.20099	.20182	.20266
.16750	.19793	.19874	.19955	.20037	.20119	.20202	.20285	.20368	.20451	.20535
.17000	.20059	.20140	.20222	.20304	.20387	.20470	.20553	.20637	.20721	.20805
.17250	.20325	.20407	.20489	.20572	.20655	.20738	.20822	.20906	.20991	.21076
.17500	.20591	.20673	.20756	.20839	.20923	.21007	.21091	.21175	.21260	.21346
.17750	.20857	.20940	.21023	.21107	.21191	.21275	.21360	.21445	.21530	.21616
.18000	.21124	.21207	.21291	.21375	.21459	.21544	.21629	.21714	.21800	.21887
.18250	.21390	.21474	.21558	.21642	.21727	.21812	.21898	.21984	.22070	.22157
.18500	.21657	.21741	.21825	.21910	.21996	.22081	.22167	.22254	.22341	.22428
.18750	.21923	.22008	.22093	.22178	.22264	.22350	.22437	.22524	.22611	.22699
.19000	.22190	.22275	.22360	.22446	.22533	.22619	.22706	.22794	.22882	.22970
.19250	.22457	.22542	.22628	.22715	.22801	.22888	.22976	.23064	.23152	.23241
.19500	.22724	.22810	.22896	.22983	.23070	.23158	.23246	.23334	.23423	.23512
.19750	.22991	.23077	.23164	.23251	.23339	.23427	.23515	.23604	.23694	.23783
.20000	.23258	.23345	.23432	.23520	.23608	.23696	.23785	.23875	.23965	.24055
.20250	.23525	.23612	.23700	.23788	.23877	.23966	.24056	.24145	.24236	.24326
.20500	.23792	.23880	.23968	.24057	.24146	.24236	.24326	.24416	.24507	.24598
.20750	.24060	.24148	.24237	.24326	.24415	.24506	.24596	.24687	.24778	.24870

ANNUAL PERCENTAGE RATE TABLES: TERM OF MORTGAGE: 120 MONTHS

INTEREST RATE	POINTS CHARGED .12750	.13000	.13250	.13500	.13750	.14000	.14250	.14500	.14750	.15000
.07000	.10167	.10235	.10304	.10374	.10443	.10513	.10584	.10654	.10725	.10796
.07250	.10432	.10502	.10571	.10641	.10711	.10781	.10852	.10922	.10994	.11065
.07500	.10698	.10768	.10838	.10908	.10978	.11049	.11120	.11191	.11262	.11334
.07750	.10964	.11034	.11104	.11175	.11245	.11316	.11388	.11459	.11531	.11604
.08000	.11230	.11301	.11371	.11442	.11513	.11584	.11656	.11728	.11800	.11873
.08250	.11497	.11567	.11638	.11709	.11781	.11852	.11925	.11997	.12070	.12143
.08500	.11763	.11834	.11905	.11977	.12049	.12121	.12193	.12266	.12339	.12412
.08750	.12029	.12101	.12172	.12244	.12316	.12389	.12462	.12535	.12609	.12682
.09000	.12296	.12368	.12440	.12512	.12585	.12658	.12731	.12804	.12878	.12952
.09250	.12563	.12635	.12707	.12780	.12853	.12926	.13000	.13074	.13148	.13223
.09500	.12829	.12902	.12975	.13048	.13121	.13195	.13269	.13343	.13418	.13493
.09750	.13096	.13169	.13242	.13316	.13390	.13464	.13538	.13613	.13688	.13763
.10000	.13363	.13437	.13510	.13584	.13658	.13733	.13808	.13883	.13958	.14034
.10250	.13631	.13704	.13778	.13852	.13927	.14002	.14077	.14153	.14229	.14305
.10500	.13898	.13972	.14046	.14121	.14196	.14271	.14347	.14423	.14499	.14576
.10750	.14165	.14240	.14314	.14390	.14465	.14541	.14617	.14693	.14770	.14847
.11000	.14433	.14508	.14583	.14658	.14734	.14810	.14887	.14963	.15041	.15118
.11250	.14701	.14776	.14851	.14927	.15003	.15080	.15157	.15234	.15312	.15389
.11500	.14968	.15044	.15120	.15196	.15273	.15350	.15427	.15505	.15583	.15661
.11750	.15236	.15312	.15389	.15465	.15542	.15620	.15697	.15775	.15854	.15933
.12000	.15504	.15581	.15657	.15735	.15812	.15890	.15968	.16046	.16125	.16204
.12250	.15772	.15849	.15926	.16004	.16082	.16160	.16239	.16317	.16397	.16476
.12500	.16041	.16118	.16195	.16273	.16352	.16430	.16509	.16589	.16668	.16748
.12750	.16309	.16387	.16465	.16543	.16622	.16701	.16780	.16860	.16940	.17021
.13000	.16578	.16656	.16734	.16813	.16892	.16972	.17051	.17132	.17212	.17293
.13250	.16846	.16925	.17004	.17083	.17162	.17242	.17323	.17403	.17484	.17566
.13500	.17115	.17194	.17273	.17353	.17433	.17513	.17594	.17675	.17757	.17838
.13750	.17384	.17463	.17543	.17623	.17703	.17784	.17865	.17947	.18029	.18111
.14000	.17653	.17733	.17813	.17893	.17974	.18055	.18137	.18219	.18301	.18384
.14250	.17922	.18002	.18083	.18164	.18245	.18327	.18409	.18491	.18574	.18657
.14500	.18191	.18272	.18353	.18434	.18516	.18598	.18681	.18764	.18847	.18931
.14750	.18460	.18542	.18623	.18705	.18787	.18870	.18953	.19036	.19120	.19204
.15000	.18730	.18812	.18894	.18976	.19059	.19142	.19225	.19309	.19393	.19478
.15250	.19000	.19082	.19164	.19247	.19330	.19413	.19497	.19582	.19666	.19752
.15500	.19269	.19352	.19435	.19518	.19601	.19685	.19770	.19855	.19940	.20025
.15750	.19539	.19622	.19705	.19789	.19873	.19958	.20043	.20128	.20213	.20299
.16000	.19809	.19893	.19976	.20060	.20145	.20230	.20315	.20401	.20487	.20574
.16250	.20079	.20163	.20247	.20332	.20417	.20502	.20588	.20674	.20761	.20848
.16500	.20349	.20434	.20518	.20604	.20689	.20775	.20861	.20948	.21035	.21122
.16750	.20620	.20705	.20790	.20875	.20961	.21048	.21134	.21222	.21309	.21397
.17000	.20890	.20976	.21061	.21147	.21234	.21320	.21408	.21495	.21583	.21672
.17250	.21161	.21247	.21333	.21419	.21506	.21593	.21681	.21769	.21858	.21947
.17500	.21432	.21518	.21604	.21691	.21779	.21867	.21955	.22043	.22132	.22222
.17750	.21702	.21789	.21876	.21964	.22052	.22140	.22229	.22318	.22407	.22497
.18000	.21973	.22061	.22148	.22236	.22324	.22413	.22502	.22592	.22682	.22773
.18250	.22245	.22332	.22420	.22509	.22597	.22687	.22776	.22867	.22957	.23048
.18500	.22516	.22604	.22692	.22781	.22871	.22960	.23051	.23141	.23232	.23324
.18750	.22787	.22876	.22965	.23054	.23144	.23234	.23325	.23416	.23508	.23600
.19000	.23058	.23148	.23237	.23327	.23417	.23508	.23599	.23691	.23783	.23876
.19250	.23330	.23420	.23510	.23600	.23691	.23782	.23874	.23966	.24059	.24152
.19500	.23602	.23692	.23782	.23873	.23965	.24056	.24149	.24241	.24334	.24428
.19750	.23874	.23964	.24055	.24147	.24238	.24331	.24424	.24517	.24610	.24705
.20000	.24146	.24237	.24328	.24420	.24512	.24605	.24699	.24792	.24886	.24981
.20250	.24418	.24509	.24601	.24694	.24787	.24880	.24974	.25068	.25163	.25258
.20500	.24690	.24782	.24874	.24967	.25061	.25155	.25249	.25344	.25439	.25535
.20750	.24962	.25055	.25148	.25241	.25335	.25430	.25524	.25620	.25715	.25812

ANNUAL PERCENTAGE RATE TABLES: TERM OF MORTGAGE: 180 MONTHS

INTEREST RATE	POINTS CHARGED .00250	.00500	.00750	.01000	.01250	.01500	.01750	.02000	.02250	.02500
.07000	.07040	.07081	.07121	.07162	.07203	.07244	.07285	.07326	.07368	.07409
.07250	.07291	.07331	.07372	.07413	.07454	.07496	.07537	.07579	.07621	.07662
.07500	.07541	.07582	.07623	.07664	.07706	.07747	.07789	.07831	.07873	.07916
.07750	.07791	.07832	.07874	.07916	.07957	.07999	.08041	.08084	.08126	.08169
.08000	.08041	.08083	.08125	.08167	.08209	.08251	.08294	.08336	.08379	.08422
.08250	.08292	.08334	.08376	.08418	.08460	.08503	.08546	.08589	.08632	.08675
.08500	.08542	.08584	.08627	.08669	.08712	.08755	.08798	.08841	.08884	.08928
.08750	.08792	.08835	.08878	.08921	.08964	.09007	.09050	.09094	.09137	.09181
.09000	.09043	.09086	.09129	.09172	.09215	.09259	.09302	.09346	.09390	.09434
.09250	.09293	.09336	.09380	.09423	.09467	.09511	.09555	.09599	.09643	.09688
.09500	.09543	.09587	.09631	.09674	.09718	.09763	.09807	.09851	.09896	.09941
.09750	.09794	.09838	.09882	.09926	.09970	.10015	.10059	.10104	.10149	.10194
.10000	.10044	.10088	.10132	.10177	.10222	.10267	.10312	.10357	.10402	.10448
.10250	.10294	.10339	.10383	.10428	.10473	.10519	.10564	.10609	.10655	.10701
.10500	.10545	.10589	.10635	.10680	.10725	.10771	.10816	.10862	.10908	.10955
.10750	.10795	.10840	.10886	.10931	.10977	.11023	.11069	.11115	.11161	.11208
.11000	.11045	.11091	.11137	.11182	.11228	.11275	.11321	.11368	.11414	.11461
.11250	.11296	.11342	.11388	.11434	.11480	.11527	.11574	.11621	.11668	.11715
.11500	.11546	.11592	.11639	.11685	.11732	.11779	.11826	.11873	.11921	.11969
.11750	.11796	.11843	.11890	.11937	.11984	.12031	.12078	.12126	.12174	.12222
.12000	.12047	.12094	.12141	.12188	.12235	.12283	.12331	.12379	.12427	.12476
.12250	.12297	.12344	.12392	.12439	.12487	.12535	.12584	.12632	.12681	.12729
.12500	.12547	.12595	.12643	.12691	.12739	.12787	.12836	.12885	.12934	.12983
.12750	.12798	.12846	.12894	.12942	.12991	.13040	.13089	.13138	.13187	.13237
.13000	.13048	.13097	.13145	.13194	.13243	.13292	.13341	.13391	.13441	.13490
.13250	.13299	.13347	.13396	.13445	.13495	.13544	.13594	.13644	.13694	.13744
.13500	.13549	.13598	.13647	.13697	.13746	.13796	.13846	.13897	.13947	.13998
.13750	.13799	.13849	.13898	.13948	.13998	.14049	.14099	.14150	.14201	.14252
.14000	.14050	.14100	.14150	.14200	.14250	.14301	.14352	.14403	.14454	.14506
.14250	.14300	.14350	.14401	.14451	.14502	.14553	.14605	.14656	.14708	.14760
.14500	.14550	.14601	.14652	.14703	.14754	.14806	.14857	.14909	.14961	.15014
.14750	.14801	.14852	.14903	.14954	.15006	.15058	.15110	.15162	.15215	.15267
.15000	.15051	.15103	.15154	.15206	.15258	.15310	.15363	.15415	.15468	.15521
.15250	.15302	.15353	.15405	.15458	.15510	.15563	.15616	.15669	.15722	.15775
.15500	.15552	.15604	.15657	.15709	.15762	.15815	.15868	.15922	.15976	.16030
.15750	.15802	.15855	.15908	.15961	.16014	.16067	.16121	.16175	.16229	.16284
.16000	.16053	.16106	.16159	.16212	.16266	.16320	.16374	.16428	.16483	.16538
.16250	.16303	.16357	.16410	.16464	.16518	.16572	.16627	.16682	.16737	.16792
.16500	.16554	.16607	.16661	.16716	.16770	.16825	.16880	.16935	.16990	.17046
.16750	.16804	.16858	.16913	.16967	.17022	.17077	.17133	.17188	.17244	.17300
.17000	.17054	.17109	.17164	.17219	.17274	.17330	.17386	.17442	.17498	.17554
.17250	.17305	.17360	.17415	.17471	.17526	.17582	.17639	.17695	.17752	.17809
.17500	.17555	.17611	.17666	.17722	.17778	.17835	.17892	.17948	.18006	.18063
.17750	.17806	.17862	.17918	.17974	.18031	.18087	.18145	.18202	.18259	.18317
.18000	.18056	.18112	.18169	.18226	.18283	.18340	.18398	.18455	.18513	.18572
.18250	.18307	.18363	.18420	.18477	.18535	.18593	.18651	.18709	.18767	.18826
.18500	.18557	.18614	.18672	.18729	.18787	.18845	.18904	.18962	.19021	.19080
.18750	.18807	.18865	.18923	.18981	.19039	.19098	.19157	.19216	.19275	.19335
.19000	.19058	.19116	.19174	.19233	.19291	.19350	.19410	.19469	.19529	.19589
.19250	.19308	.19367	.19425	.19484	.19544	.19603	.19663	.19723	.19783	.19844
.19500	.19559	.19618	.19677	.19736	.19796	.19856	.19916	.19977	.20037	.20098
.19750	.19809	.19868	.19928	.19988	.20048	.20109	.20169	.20230	.20291	.20353
.20000	.20060	.20119	.20179	.20240	.20300	.20361	.20422	.20484	.20545	.20607
.20250	.20310	.20370	.20431	.20492	.20553	.20614	.20676	.20737	.20800	.20862
.20500	.20560	.20621	.20682	.20743	.20805	.20867	.20929	.20991	.21054	.21117
.20750	.20811	.20872	.20934	.20995	.21057	.21119	.21182	.21245	.21308	.21371

ANNUAL PERCENTAGE RATE TABLES: TERM OF MORTGAGE: 180 MONTHS

INTEREST RATE	POINTS CHARGED .02750	.03000	.03250	.03500	.03750	.04000	.04250	.04500	.04750	.05000
.07000	.07451	.07493	.07535	.07578	.07620	.07663	.07705	.07748	.07791	.07835
.07250	.07705	.07747	.07789	.07832	.07875	.07918	.07961	.08004	.08047	.08091
.07500	.07958	.08001	.08043	.08086	.08129	.08173	.08216	.08260	.08303	.08347
.07750	.08211	.08254	.08297	.08341	.08384	.08428	.08471	.08515	.08559	.08604
.08000	.08465	.08508	.08551	.08595	.08639	.08683	.08727	.08771	.08815	.08860
.08250	.08718	.08762	.08806	.08849	.08893	.08938	.08982	.09027	.09071	.09116
.08500	.08972	.09016	.09060	.09104	.09148	.09193	.09238	.09283	.09328	.09373
.08750	.09225	.09269	.09314	.09358	.09403	.09448	.09493	.09538	.09584	.09629
.09000	.09479	.09523	.09568	.09613	.09658	.09703	.09749	.09794	.09840	.09886
.09250	.09732	.09777	.09822	.09868	.09913	.09959	.10004	.10050	.10097	.10143
.09500	.09986	.10031	.10077	.10122	.10168	.10214	.10260	.10306	.10353	.10400
.09750	.10240	.10285	.10331	.10377	.10423	.10469	.10516	.10563	.10609	.10656
.10000	.10493	.10539	.10585	.10632	.10678	.10725	.10772	.10819	.10866	.10913
.10250	.10747	.10793	.10840	.10887	.10933	.10980	.11028	.11075	.11123	.11170
.10500	.11001	.11048	.11094	.11141	.11189	.11236	.11284	.11331	.11379	.11427
.10750	.11255	.11302	.11349	.11396	.11444	.11492	.11540	.11588	.11636	.11684
.11000	.11509	.11556	.11603	.11651	.11699	.11747	.11796	.11844	.11893	.11942
.11250	.11762	.11810	.11858	.11906	.11954	.12003	.12052	.12101	.12150	.12199
.11500	.12016	.12064	.12113	.12161	.12210	.12259	.12308	.12357	.12407	.12456
.11750	.12270	.12319	.12367	.12416	.12465	.12515	.12564	.12614	.12664	.12714
.12000	.12524	.12573	.12622	.12671	.12721	.12770	.12820	.12870	.12921	.12971
.12250	.12778	.12828	.12877	.12927	.12976	.13026	.13077	.13127	.13178	.13228
.12500	.13032	.13082	.13132	.13182	.13232	.13282	.13333	.13384	.13435	.13486
.12750	.13286	.13336	.13387	.13437	.13488	.13538	.13589	.13641	.13692	.13744
.13000	.13541	.13591	.13642	.13692	.13743	.13794	.13846	.13897	.13949	.14001
.13250	.13795	.13846	.13896	.13948	.13999	.14051	.14102	.14154	.14207	.14259
.13500	.14049	.14100	.14151	.14203	.14255	.14307	.14359	.14411	.14464	.14517
.13750	.14303	.14355	.14406	.14458	.14511	.14563	.14616	.14668	.14722	.14775
.14000	.14557	.14609	.14662	.14714	.14766	.14819	.14872	.14926	.14979	.15033
.14250	.14812	.14864	.14917	.14969	.15022	.15076	.15129	.15183	.15237	.15291
.14500	.15066	.15119	.15172	.15225	.15278	.15332	.15386	.15440	.15494	.15549
.14750	.15320	.15374	.15427	.15481	.15534	.15588	.15643	.15697	.15752	.15807
.15000	.15575	.15628	.15682	.15736	.15790	.15845	.15900	.15955	.16010	.16065
.15250	.15829	.15883	.15937	.15992	.16047	.16101	.16157	.16212	.16268	.16323
.15500	.16084	.16138	.16193	.16248	.16303	.16358	.16414	.16469	.16525	.16582
.15750	.16338	.16393	.16448	.16503	.16559	.16615	.16671	.16727	.16783	.16840
.16000	.16593	.16648	.16703	.16759	.16815	.16871	.16928	.16985	.17041	.17099
.16250	.16847	.16903	.16959	.17015	.17071	.17128	.17185	.17242	.17300	.17357
.16500	.17102	.17158	.17214	.17271	.17328	.17385	.17442	.17500	.17558	.17616
.16750	.17356	.17413	.17470	.17527	.17584	.17642	.17699	.17758	.17816	.17874
.17000	.17611	.17668	.17725	.17783	.17841	.17899	.17957	.18015	.18074	.18133
.17250	.17866	.17923	.17981	.18039	.18097	.18156	.18214	.18273	.18332	.18392
.17500	.18121	.18178	.18237	.18295	.18354	.18412	.18472	.18531	.18591	.18651
.17750	.18375	.18434	.18492	.18551	.18610	.18670	.18729	.18789	.18849	.18910
.18000	.18630	.18689	.18748	.18807	.18867	.18927	.18987	.19047	.19108	.19168
.18250	.18885	.18944	.19004	.19063	.19123	.19184	.19244	.19305	.19366	.19427
.18500	.19140	.19199	.19259	.19320	.19380	.19441	.19502	.19563	.19625	.19687
.18750	.19395	.19455	.19515	.19576	.19637	.19698	.19760	.19821	.19883	.19946
.19000	.19650	.19710	.19771	.19832	.19894	.19955	.20017	.20080	.20142	.20205
.19250	.19905	.19966	.20027	.20089	.20150	.20213	.20275	.20338	.20401	.20464
.19500	.20160	.20221	.20283	.20345	.20407	.20470	.20533	.20596	.20660	.20723
.19750	.20415	.20477	.20539	.20601	.20664	.20727	.20791	.20854	.20918	.20983
.20000	.20670	.20732	.20795	.20858	.20921	.20985	.21049	.21113	.21177	.21242
.20250	.20925	.20988	.21051	.21114	.21178	.21242	.21307	.21371	.21436	.21502
.20500	.21180	.21243	.21307	.21371	.21435	.21500	.21565	.21630	.21695	.21761
.20750	.21435	.21499	.21563	.21627	.21692	.21757	.21823	.21888	.21954	.22021

ANNUAL PERCENTAGE RATE TABLES: TERM OF MORTGAGE: 180 MONTHS

INTEREST RATE	POINTS CHARGED .05250	.05500	.05750	.06000	.06250	.06500	.06750	.07000	.07250	.07500
.07000	.07878	.07922	.07966	.08009	.08054	.08098	.08142	.08187	.08232	.08277
.07250	.08135	.08179	.08223	.08267	.08311	.08356	.08401	.08446	.08491	.08536
.07500	.08391	.08436	.08480	.08525	.08569	.08614	.08660	.08705	.08750	.08796
.07750	.08648	.08693	.08737	.08782	.08827	.08873	.08918	.08964	.09010	.09056
.08000	.08905	.08950	.08995	.09040	.09086	.09131	.09177	.09223	.09269	.09316
.08250	.09161	.09207	.09252	.09298	.09344	.09390	.09436	.09482	.09529	.09576
.08500	.09418	.09464	.09510	.09556	.09602	.09648	.09695	.09742	.09789	.09836
.08750	.09675	.09721	.09767	.09814	.09860	.09907	.09954	.10001	.10048	.10096
.09000	.09932	.09979	.10025	.10072	.10119	.10166	.10213	.10261	.10308	.10356
.09250	.10189	.10236	.10283	.10330	.10377	.10425	.10472	.10520	.10568	.10617
.09500	.10446	.10494	.10541	.10588	.10636	.10684	.10732	.10780	.10828	.10877
.09750	.10704	.10751	.10799	.10847	.10895	.10943	.10991	.11040	.11089	.11138
.10000	.10961	.11009	.11057	.11105	.11153	.11202	.11251	.11300	.11349	.11398
.10250	.11218	.11266	.11315	.11363	.11412	.11461	.11510	.11560	.11609	.11659
.10500	.11476	.11524	.11573	.11622	.11671	.11720	.11770	.11820	.11870	.11920
.10750	.11733	.11782	.11831	.11881	.11930	.11980	.12030	.12080	.12130	.12181
.11000	.11991	.12040	.12090	.12139	.12189	.12239	.12290	.12340	.12391	.12442
.11250	.12248	.12298	.12348	.12398	.12448	.12499	.12550	.12601	.12652	.12703
.11500	.12506	.12556	.12606	.12657	.12708	.12759	.12810	.12861	.12913	.12965
.11750	.12764	.12814	.12865	.12916	.12967	.13018	.13070	.13122	.13174	.13226
.12000	.13022	.13073	.13124	.13175	.13226	.13278	.13330	.13382	.13435	.13487
.12250	.13280	.13331	.13382	.13434	.13486	.13538	.13590	.13643	.13696	.13749
.12500	.13538	.13589	.13641	.13693	.13746	.13798	.13851	.13904	.13957	.14011
.12750	.13796	.13848	.13900	.13952	.14005	.14058	.14111	.14165	.14219	.14272
.13000	.14054	.14106	.14159	.14212	.14265	.14318	.14372	.14426	.14480	.14534
.13250	.14312	.14365	.14418	.14471	.14525	.14579	.14633	.14687	.14742	.14796
.13500	.14570	.14623	.14677	.14731	.14785	.14839	.14893	.14948	.15003	.15058
.13750	.14828	.14882	.14936	.14990	.15045	.15099	.15154	.15210	.15265	.15321
.14000	.15087	.15141	.15195	.15250	.15305	.15360	.15415	.15471	.15527	.15583
.14250	.15345	.15400	.15455	.15510	.15565	.15621	.15676	.15732	.15789	.15845
.14500	.15604	.15659	.15714	.15769	.15825	.15881	.15937	.15994	.16051	.16108
.14750	.15862	.15918	.15973	.16029	.16086	.16142	.16199	.16256	.16313	.16370
.15000	.16121	.16177	.16233	.16289	.16346	.16403	.16460	.16517	.16575	.16633
.15250	.16380	.16436	.16493	.16549	.16606	.16664	.16721	.16779	.16837	.16896
.15500	.16638	.16695	.16752	.16809	.16867	.16925	.16983	.17041	.17100	.17159
.15750	.16897	.16954	.17012	.17070	.17128	.17186	.17244	.17303	.17362	.17422
.16000	.17156	.17214	.17272	.17330	.17388	.17447	.17506	.17565	.17625	.17685
.16250	.17415	.17473	.17532	.17590	.17649	.17708	.17768	.17828	.17888	.17948
.16500	.17674	.17733	.17792	.17851	.17910	.17970	.18030	.18090	.18150	.18211
.16750	.17933	.17992	.18052	.18111	.18171	.18231	.18292	.18352	.18413	.18474
.17000	.18192	.18252	.18312	.18372	.18432	.18493	.18554	.18615	.18676	.18738
.17250	.18452	.18512	.18572	.18632	.18693	.18754	.18816	.18877	.18939	.19001
.17500	.18711	.18771	.18832	.18893	.18954	.19016	.19078	.19140	.19202	.19265
.17750	.18970	.19031	.19092	.19154	.19216	.19278	.19340	.19403	.19466	.19529
.18000	.19230	.19291	.19353	.19415	.19477	.19540	.19602	.19666	.19729	.19793
.18250	.19489	.19551	.19613	.19676	.19738	.19801	.19865	.19928	.19992	.20057
.18500	.19749	.19811	.19874	.19937	.20000	.20063	.20127	.20191	.20256	.20321
.18750	.20008	.20071	.20134	.20198	.20262	.20326	.20390	.20455	.20519	.20585
.19000	.20268	.20331	.20395	.20459	.20523	.20588	.20653	.20718	.20783	.20849
.19250	.20528	.20592	.20656	.20720	.20785	.20850	.20915	.20981	.21047	.21113
.19500	.20787	.20852	.20916	.20981	.21047	.21112	.21178	.21244	.21311	.21378
.19750	.21047	.21112	.21177	.21243	.21309	.21375	.21441	.21508	.21575	.21642
.20000	.21307	.21373	.21438	.21504	.21570	.21637	.21704	.21771	.21839	.21907
.20250	.21567	.21633	.21699	.21766	.21832	.21900	.21967	.22035	.22103	.22171
.20500	.21827	.21894	.21960	.22027	.22095	.22162	.22230	.22298	.22367	.22436
.20750	.22087	.22154	.22221	.22289	.22357	.22425	.22493	.22562	.22631	.22701

ANNUAL PERCENTAGE RATE TABLES: TERM OF MORTGAGE: 180 MONTHS

INTEREST RATE	POINTS CHARGED .07750	.08000	.08250	.08500	.08750	.09000	.09250	.09500	.09750	.10000
.07000	.08322	.08367	.08413	.08459	.08505	.08551	.08597	.08644	.08690	.08737
.07250	.08582	.08628	.08674	.08720	.08766	.08813	.08859	.08906	.08953	.09000
.07500	.08842	.08888	.08934	.08981	.09028	.09074	.09121	.09169	.09216	.09264
.07750	.09102	.09149	.09195	.09242	.09289	.09336	.09384	.09431	.09479	.09527
.08000	.09362	.09409	.09456	.09503	.09551	.09598	.09646	.09694	.09742	.09791
.08250	.09623	.09670	.09717	.09765	.09813	.09861	.09909	.09957	.10006	.10054
.08500	.09883	.09931	.09978	.10026	.10074	.10123	.10171	.10220	.10269	.10318
.08750	.10144	.10192	.10240	.10288	.10337	.10385	.10434	.10483	.10533	.10582
.09000	.10404	.10453	.10501	.10550	.10599	.10648	.10697	.10747	.10796	.10846
.09250	.10665	.10714	.10763	.10812	.10861	.10910	.10960	.11010	.11060	.11111
.09500	.10926	.10975	.11024	.11074	.11123	.11173	.11223	.11274	.11324	.11375
.09750	.11187	.11236	.11286	.11336	.11386	.11436	.11487	.11537	.11588	.11639
.10000	.11448	.11498	.11548	.11598	.11649	.11699	.11750	.11801	.11853	.11904
.10250	.11709	.11759	.11810	.11860	.11911	.11962	.12014	.12065	.12117	.12169
.10500	.11970	.12021	.12072	.12123	.12174	.12226	.12277	.12329	.12381	.12434
.10750	.12232	.12283	.12334	.12385	.12437	.12489	.12541	.12594	.12646	.12699
.11000	.12493	.12545	.12596	.12648	.12700	.12753	.12805	.12858	.12911	.12964
.11250	.12755	.12807	.12859	.12911	.12964	.13016	.13069	.13122	.13176	.13230
.11500	.13017	.13069	.13121	.13174	.13227	.13280	.13333	.13387	.13441	.13495
.11750	.13278	.13331	.13384	.13437	.13490	.13544	.13598	.13652	.13706	.13761
.12000	.13540	.13593	.13647	.13700	.13754	.13808	.13862	.13917	.13971	.14026
.12250	.13802	.13856	.13909	.13963	.14018	.14072	.14127	.14182	.14237	.14292
.12500	.14064	.14118	.14172	.14227	.14282	.14336	.14392	.14447	.14503	.14558
.12750	.14327	.14381	.14436	.14490	.14545	.14601	.14656	.14712	.14768	.14825
.13000	.14589	.14644	.14699	.14754	.14810	.14865	.14921	.14978	.15034	.15091
.13250	.14851	.14907	.14962	.15018	.15074	.15130	.15186	.15243	.15300	.15357
.13500	.15114	.15170	.15225	.15282	.15338	.15395	.15452	.15509	.15566	.15624
.13750	.15376	.15433	.15489	.15546	.15603	.15660	.15717	.15775	.15833	.15891
.14000	.15639	.15696	.15753	.15810	.15867	.15925	.15983	.16041	.16099	.16158
.14250	.15902	.15959	.16016	.16074	.16132	.16190	.16248	.16307	.16366	.16425
.14500	.16165	.16222	.16280	.16338	.16397	.16455	.16514	.16573	.16632	.16692
.14750	.16428	.16486	.16544	.16603	.16661	.16720	.16780	.16839	.16899	.16959
.15000	.16691	.16750	.16808	.16867	.16926	.16986	.17046	.17106	.17166	.17227
.15250	.16954	.17013	.17072	.17132	.17192	.17252	.17312	.17372	.17433	.17494
.15500	.17218	.17277	.17337	.17397	.17457	.17517	.17578	.17639	.17700	.17762
.15750	.17481	.17541	.17601	.17662	.17722	.17783	.17844	.17906	.17968	.18030
.16000	.17745	.17805	.17866	.17927	.17988	.18049	.18111	.18173	.18235	.18298
.16250	.18008	.18069	.18130	.18192	.18253	.18315	.18377	.18440	.18503	.18566
.16500	.18272	.18333	.18395	.18457	.18519	.18581	.18644	.18707	.18770	.18834
.16750	.18536	.18598	.18660	.18722	.18785	.18848	.18911	.18975	.19038	.19102
.17000	.18800	.18862	.18925	.18988	.19051	.19114	.19178	.19242	.19306	.19371
.17250	.19064	.19127	.19190	.19253	.19317	.19381	.19445	.19510	.19574	.19640
.17500	.19328	.19391	.19455	.19519	.19583	.19647	.19712	.19777	.19843	.19908
.17750	.19592	.19656	.19720	.19785	.19849	.19914	.19980	.20045	.20111	.20177
.18000	.19857	.19921	.19986	.20050	.20116	.20181	.20247	.20313	.20380	.20446
.18250	.20121	.20186	.20251	.20316	.20382	.20448	.20515	.20581	.20648	.20715
.18500	.20386	.20451	.20517	.20582	.20649	.20715	.20782	.20849	.20917	.20985
.18750	.20650	.20716	.20782	.20849	.20915	.20983	.21050	.21118	.21186	.21254
.19000	.20915	.20981	.21048	.21115	.21182	.21250	.21318	.21386	.21455	.21524
.19250	.21180	.21247	.21314	.21381	.21449	.21517	.21586	.21655	.21724	.21793
.19500	.21445	.21512	.21580	.21648	.21716	.21785	.21854	.21923	.21993	.22063
.19750	.21710	.21778	.21846	.21914	.21983	.22053	.22122	.22192	.22262	.22333
.20000	.21975	.22043	.22112	.22181	.22251	.22320	.22391	.22461	.22532	.22603
.20250	.22240	.22309	.22378	.22448	.22518	.22588	.22659	.22730	.22801	.22873
.20500	.22505	.22575	.22645	.22715	.22785	.22856	.22928	.22999	.23071	.23143
.20750	.22770	.22841	.22911	.22982	.23053	.23124	.23196	.23268	.23341	.23414

ANNUAL PERCENTAGE RATE TABLES: TERM OF MORTGAGE: 180 MONTHS

INTEREST RATE	POINTS CHARGED .10250	.10500	.10750	.11000	.11250	.11500	.11750	.12000	.12250	.12500
.07000	.08784	.08832	.08879	.08927	.08975	.09023	.09071	.09120	.09168	.09217
.07250	.09048	.09096	.09143	.09191	.09240	.09288	.09337	.09386	.09435	.09484
.07500	.09312	.09360	.09408	.09456	.09505	.09554	.09603	.09652	.09702	.09751
.07750	.09575	.09624	.09672	.09721	.09770	.09819	.09869	.09919	.09969	.10019
.08000	.09839	.09888	.09937	.09986	.10036	.10085	.10135	.10185	.10236	.10286
.08250	.10103	.10153	.10202	.10252	.10301	.10351	.10402	.10452	.10503	.10554
.08500	.10368	.10417	.10467	.10517	.10567	.10618	.10668	.10719	.10770	.10822
.08750	.10632	.10682	.10732	.10782	.10833	.10884	.10935	.10986	.11038	.11090
.09000	.10896	.10947	.10997	.11048	.11099	.11150	.11202	.11254	.11306	.11358
.09250	.11161	.11212	.11263	.11314	.11366	.11417	.11469	.11521	.11574	.11626
.09500	.11426	.11477	.11528	.11580	.11632	.11684	.11736	.11789	.11842	.11895
.09750	.11691	.11742	.11794	.11846	.11899	.11951	.12004	.12057	.12110	.12163
.10000	.11956	.12008	.12060	.12113	.12165	.12218	.12271	.12325	.12378	.12432
.10250	.12221	.12274	.12326	.12379	.12432	.12486	.12539	.12593	.12647	.12701
.10500	.12486	.12539	.12592	.12646	.12699	.12753	.12807	.12861	.12916	.12971
.10750	.12752	.12805	.12859	.12913	.12967	.13021	.13075	.13130	.13185	.13240
.11000	.13018	.13071	.13125	.13179	.13234	.13289	.13344	.13399	.13454	.13510
.11250	.13283	.13336	.13392	.13447	.13501	.13557	.13612	.13668	.13723	.13780
.11500	.13549	.13604	.13659	.13714	.13769	.13825	.13881	.13937	.13993	.14050
.11750	.13815	.13870	.13926	.13981	.14037	.14093	.14149	.14206	.14263	.14320
.12000	.14082	.14137	.14193	.14249	.14305	.14362	.14418	.14475	.14533	.14590
.12250	.14348	.14404	.14460	.14517	.14573	.14630	.14687	.14745	.14803	.14861
.12500	.14615	.14671	.14728	.14784	.14842	.14899	.14957	.15015	.15073	.15131
.12750	.14881	.14938	.14995	.15053	.15110	.15168	.15226	.15285	.15343	.15402
.13000	.15148	.15205	.15263	.15321	.15379	.15437	.15496	.15555	.15614	.15673
.13250	.15415	.15473	.15531	.15589	.15648	.15707	.15766	.15825	.15885	.15945
.13500	.15682	.15740	.15799	.15858	.15917	.15976	.16036	.16095	.16156	.16216
.13750	.15949	.16008	.16067	.16126	.16186	.16246	.16306	.16366	.16427	.16488
.14000	.16217	.16276	.16335	.16395	.16455	.16515	.16576	.16637	.16698	.16759
.14250	.16484	.16544	.16604	.16664	.16725	.16785	.16846	.16908	.16969	.17031
.14500	.16752	.16812	.16872	.16933	.16994	.17055	.17117	.17179	.17241	.17304
.14750	.17020	.17080	.17141	.17202	.17264	.17326	.17388	.17450	.17513	.17576
.15000	.17288	.17349	.17410	.17472	.17534	.17596	.17659	.17722	.17785	.17848
.15250	.17556	.17617	.17679	.17741	.17804	.17867	.17930	.17993	.18057	.18121
.15500	.17824	.17886	.17948	.18011	.18074	.18138	.18201	.18265	.18329	.18394
.15750	.18092	.18155	.18218	.18281	.18345	.18408	.18473	.18537	.18602	.18667
.16000	.18361	.18424	.18487	.18551	.18615	.18680	.18744	.18809	.18875	.18940
.16250	.18629	.18693	.18757	.18821	.18886	.18951	.19016	.19082	.19147	.19214
.16500	.18898	.18962	.19027	.19092	.19157	.19222	.19288	.19354	.19420	.19487
.16750	.19167	.19232	.19297	.19362	.19428	.19494	.19560	.19627	.19694	.19761
.17000	.19436	.19501	.19567	.19633	.19699	.19765	.19832	.19899	.19967	.20035
.17250	.19705	.19771	.19837	.19903	.19970	.20037	.20105	.20172	.20240	.20309
.17500	.19974	.20041	.20107	.20174	.20242	.20309	.20377	.20445	.20514	.20583
.17750	.20244	.20311	.20378	.20445	.20513	.20581	.20650	.20719	.20788	.20857
.18000	.20513	.20581	.20649	.20717	.20785	.20854	.20923	.20992	.21062	.21132
.18250	.20783	.20851	.20919	.20988	.21057	.21126	.21196	.21266	.21336	.21407
.18500	.21053	.21121	.21190	.21259	.21329	.21399	.21469	.21539	.21610	.21682
.18750	.21323	.21392	.21461	.21531	.21601	.21671	.21742	.21813	.21885	.21957
.19000	.21593	.21663	.21732	.21803	.21873	.21944	.22016	.22087	.22159	.22232
.19250	.21863	.21933	.22004	.22075	.22146	.22217	.22289	.22362	.22434	.22507
.19500	.22133	.22204	.22275	.22347	.22418	.22491	.22563	.22636	.22709	.22783
.19750	.22404	.22475	.22547	.22619	.22691	.22764	.22837	.22910	.22984	.23058
.20000	.22675	.22746	.22819	.22891	.22964	.23037	.23111	.23185	.23259	.23334
.20250	.22945	.23018	.23090	.23164	.23237	.23311	.23385	.23460	.23535	.23610
.20500	.23216	.23289	.23362	.23436	.23510	.23585	.23660	.23735	.23810	.23886
.20750	.23487	.23561	.23635	.23709	.23784	.23859	.23934	.24010	.24086	.24163

ANNUAL PERCENTAGE RATE TABLES: TERM OF MORTGAGE: 180 MONTHS

INTEREST RATE	POINTS CHARGED .12750	.13000	.13250	.13500	.13750	.14000	.14250	.14500	.14750	.15000
.07000	.09266	.09316	.09365	.09415	.09465	.09515	.09566	.09616	.09667	.09718
.07250	.09534	.09583	.09633	.09684	.09734	.09785	.09835	.09887	.09938	.09989
.07500	.09801	.09851	.09902	.09952	.10003	.10054	.10105	.10157	.10209	.10261
.07750	.10069	.10119	.10170	.10221	.10272	.10324	.10376	.10427	.10480	.10532
.08000	.10337	.10388	.10439	.10490	.10542	.10594	.10646	.10698	.10751	.10804
.08250	.10605	.10656	.10708	.10760	.10812	.10864	.10916	.10969	.11022	.11075
.08500	.10873	.10925	.10977	.11029	.11082	.11134	.11187	.11240	.11294	.11348
.08750	.11142	.11194	.11246	.11299	.11352	.11405	.11458	.11512	.11566	.11620
.09000	.11410	.11463	.11516	.11569	.11622	.11676	.11729	.11784	.11838	.11892
.09250	.11679	.11732	.11785	.11839	.11893	.11947	.12001	.12055	.12110	.12165
.09500	.11948	.12001	.12055	.12109	.12163	.12218	.12272	.12327	.12383	.12438
.09750	.12217	.12271	.12325	.12380	.12434	.12489	.12544	.12600	.12655	.12711
.10000	.12486	.12541	.12595	.12650	.12705	.12761	.12816	.12872	.12928	.12985
.10250	.12756	.12811	.12866	.12921	.12977	.13033	.13089	.13145	.13202	.13258
.10500	.13026	.13081	.13136	.13192	.13248	.13305	.13361	.13418	.13475	.13532
.10750	.13296	.13351	.13407	.13464	.13520	.13577	.13634	.13691	.13749	.13806
.11000	.13566	.13622	.13678	.13735	.13792	.13849	.13907	.13964	.14022	.14081
.11250	.13836	.13893	.13950	.14007	.14064	.14122	.14180	.14238	.14297	.14355
.11500	.14106	.14164	.14221	.14279	.14336	.14395	.14453	.14512	.14571	.14630
.11750	.14377	.14435	.14493	.14551	.14609	.14668	.14727	.14786	.14845	.14905
.12000	.14648	.14706	.14764	.14823	.14882	.14941	.15000	.15060	.15120	.15180
.12250	.14919	.14977	.15036	.15095	.15155	.15214	.15274	.15335	.15395	.15456
.12500	.15190	.15249	.15308	.15366	.15428	.15488	.15548	.15609	.15670	.15732
.12750	.15462	.15521	.15581	.15641	.15701	.15762	.15823	.15884	.15946	.16007
.13000	.15733	.15793	.15853	.15914	.15975	.16036	.16097	.16159	.16221	.16284
.13250	.16005	.16065	.16126	.16187	.16249	.16310	.16372	.16435	.16497	.16560
.13500	.16277	.16338	.16399	.16461	.16523	.16585	.16647	.16710	.16773	.16837
.13750	.16549	.16610	.16672	.16734	.16797	.16859	.16922	.16986	.17049	.17113
.14000	.16821	.16883	.16946	.17008	.17071	.17134	.17198	.17262	.17326	.17390
.14250	.17094	.17156	.17219	.17282	.17346	.17409	.17474	.17538	.17603	.17668
.14500	.17366	.17429	.17493	.17556	.17620	.17685	.17749	.17814	.17880	.17945
.14750	.17639	.17703	.17767	.17831	.17895	.17960	.18025	.18091	.18157	.18223
.15000	.17912	.17976	.18041	.18106	.18171	.18236	.18302	.18368	.18434	.18501
.15250	.18185	.18250	.18315	.18380	.18446	.18512	.18578	.18645	.18712	.18779
.15500	.18459	.18524	.18590	.18655	.18722	.18788	.18855	.18922	.18989	.19057
.15750	.18732	.18798	.18864	.18931	.18997	.19064	.19132	.19199	.19267	.19336
.16000	.19006	.19072	.19139	.19206	.19273	.19341	.19409	.19477	.19546	.19615
.16250	.19280	.19347	.19414	.19482	.19549	.19617	.19686	.19755	.19824	.19893
.16500	.19554	.19622	.19689	.19757	.19826	.19894	.19963	.20033	.20103	.20173
.16750	.19828	.19896	.19965	.20033	.20102	.20171	.20241	.20311	.20381	.20452
.17000	.20103	.20171	.20240	.20309	.20379	.20449	.20519	.20590	.20660	.20732
.17250	.20377	.20447	.20516	.20586	.20656	.20726	.20797	.20868	.20940	.21012
.17500	.20652	.20722	.20792	.20862	.20933	.21004	.21075	.21147	.21219	.21292
.17750	.20927	.20997	.21068	.21139	.21210	.21282	.21354	.21426	.21499	.21572
.18000	.21202	.21273	.21344	.21416	.21488	.21560	.21632	.21705	.21779	.21852
.18250	.21478	.21549	.21621	.21693	.21765	.21838	.21911	.21985	.22059	.22133
.18500	.21753	.21825	.21897	.21970	.22043	.22117	.22190	.22264	.22339	.22414
.18750	.22029	.22101	.22174	.22247	.22321	.22395	.22470	.22544	.22619	.22695
.19000	.22305	.22378	.22451	.22525	.22599	.22674	.22749	.22824	.22900	.22976
.19250	.22581	.22654	.22728	.22803	.22878	.22953	.23029	.23105	.23181	.23258
.19500	.22857	.22931	.23006	.23081	.23156	.23232	.23308	.23385	.23462	.23539
.19750	.23133	.23208	.23283	.23359	.23435	.23511	.23588	.23666	.23743	.23821
.20000	.23409	.23485	.23561	.23637	.23714	.23791	.23868	.23946	.24025	.24103
.20250	.23686	.23762	.23839	.23916	.23993	.24071	.24149	.24227	.24306	.24386
.20500	.23963	.24040	.24117	.24194	.24272	.24351	.24429	.24509	.24588	.24668
.20750	.24240	.24317	.24395	.24473	.24552	.24631	.24710	.24790	.24870	.24951

ANNUAL PERCENTAGE RATE TABLES: TERM OF MORTGAGE: 240 MONTHS

INTEREST RATE	POINTS CHARGED .00250	.00500	.00750	.01000	.01250	.01500	.01750	.02000	.02250	.02500
.07000	.07032	.07065	.07097	.07130	.07163	.07196	.07229	.07262	.07296	.07329
.07250	.07283	.07315	.07348	.07381	.07415	.07448	.07481	.07515	.07549	.07582
.07500	.07533	.07566	.07599	.07633	.07666	.07700	.07734	.07768	.07802	.07836
.07750	.07783	.07817	.07850	.07884	.07918	.07952	.07986	.08020	.08055	.08089
.08000	.08034	.08067	.08101	.08135	.08170	.08204	.08238	.08273	.08306	.08343
.08250	.08284	.08318	.08352	.08387	.08421	.08456	.08491	.08526	.08561	.08596
.08500	.08534	.08569	.08603	.08638	.08673	.08708	.08743	.08779	.08814	.08850
.08750	.08785	.08820	.08854	.08890	.08925	.08960	.08996	.09031	.09067	.09103
.09000	.09035	.09070	.09106	.09141	.09177	.09212	.09248	.09284	.09320	.09357
.09250	.09285	.09321	.09357	.09392	.09428	.09464	.09501	.09537	.09574	.09610
.09500	.09536	.09572	.09608	.09644	.09680	.09717	.09753	.09790	.09827	.09864
.09750	.09786	.09822	.09859	.09895	.09932	.09969	.10006	.10043	.10080	.10118
.10000	.10036	.10073	.10110	.10147	.10184	.10221	.10258	.10296	.10334	.10372
.10250	.10287	.10324	.10361	.10398	.10436	.10473	.10511	.10549	.10587	.10625
.10500	.10537	.10575	.10612	.10650	.10688	.10726	.10764	.10802	.10841	.10879
.10750	.10788	.10825	.10863	.10901	.10940	.10978	.11017	.11055	.11094	.11133
.11000	.11038	.11076	.11114	.11153	.11192	.11230	.11269	.11308	.11348	.11387
.11250	.11288	.11327	.11366	.11404	.11443	.11483	.11522	.11561	.11601	.11641
.11500	.11539	.11578	.11617	.11656	.11695	.11735	.11775	.11815	.11855	.11895
.11750	.11789	.11828	.11868	.11906	.11947	.11987	.12028	.12068	.12108	.12149
.12000	.12040	.12079	.12119	.12159	.12199	.12240	.12280	.12321	.12362	.12403
.12250	.12290	.12330	.12370	.12411	.12452	.12492	.12533	.12574	.12616	.12657
.12500	.12540	.12581	.12622	.12663	.12704	.12745	.12786	.12828	.12870	.12911
.12750	.12791	.12832	.12873	.12914	.12956	.12997	.13039	.13081	.13123	.13166
.13000	.13041	.13083	.13124	.13166	.13208	.13250	.13292	.13334	.13377	.13420
.13250	.13292	.13333	.13375	.13418	.13460	.13502	.13545	.13588	.13631	.13674
.13500	.13542	.13584	.13627	.13669	.13712	.13755	.13798	.13841	.13885	.13929
.13750	.13792	.13835	.13878	.13921	.13964	.14008	.14051	.14095	.14139	.14183
.14000	.14043	.14086	.14129	.14173	.14216	.14260	.14304	.14348	.14393	.14437
.14250	.14293	.14337	.14381	.14424	.14468	.14513	.14557	.14602	.14647	.14692
.14500	.14544	.14588	.14632	.14676	.14721	.14765	.14810	.14855	.14901	.14946
.14750	.14794	.14839	.14883	.14928	.14973	.15018	.15063	.15109	.15155	.15201
.15000	.15045	.15089	.15135	.15180	.15225	.15271	.15317	.15363	.15409	.15455
.15250	.15295	.15340	.15386	.15432	.15477	.15524	.15570	.15616	.15663	.15710
.15500	.15546	.15591	.15637	.15683	.15730	.15776	.15823	.15870	.15917	.15965
.15750	.15796	.15842	.15889	.15935	.15982	.16029	.16076	.16124	.16171	.16219
.16000	.16046	.16093	.16140	.16187	.16234	.16282	.16330	.16377	.16426	.16474
.16250	.16297	.16344	.16391	.16439	.16487	.16535	.16583	.16631	.16680	.16729
.16500	.16547	.16595	.16643	.16691	.16739	.16787	.16836	.16885	.16934	.16983
.16750	.16798	.16846	.16894	.16943	.16991	.17040	.17089	.17139	.17188	.17238
.17000	.17048	.17097	.17146	.17195	.17244	.17293	.17343	.17393	.17443	.17493
.17250	.17299	.17348	.17397	.17447	.17496	.17546	.17596	.17647	.17697	.17748
.17500	.17549	.17599	.17648	.17698	.17749	.17799	.17850	.17900	.17952	.18003
.17750	.17800	.17850	.17900	.17950	.18001	.18052	.18103	.18154	.18206	.18258
.18000	.18050	.18101	.18151	.18202	.18253	.18305	.18356	.18408	.18460	.18513
.18250	.18301	.18352	.18403	.18454	.18506	.18558	.18610	.18662	.18715	.18768
.18500	.18551	.18603	.18654	.18706	.18758	.18811	.18863	.18916	.18969	.19023
.18750	.18802	.18854	.18906	.18958	.19011	.19064	.19117	.19170	.19224	.19278
.19000	.19052	.19105	.19157	.19210	.19263	.19317	.19371	.19424	.19479	.19533
.19250	.19303	.19356	.19409	.19462	.19516	.19570	.19624	.19678	.19733	.19788
.19500	.19553	.19607	.19660	.19714	.19769	.19823	.19878	.19933	.19988	.20043
.19750	.19804	.19858	.19912	.19966	.20021	.20076	.20131	.20187	.20242	.20298
.20000	.20054	.20109	.20163	.20218	.20274	.20329	.20385	.20441	.20497	.20554
.20250	.20305	.20360	.20415	.20470	.20526	.20582	.20639	.20695	.20752	.20809
.20500	.20555	.20611	.20667	.20723	.20779	.20835	.20892	.20949	.21007	.21064
.20750	.20806	.20862	.20918	.20975	.21031	.21089	.21146	.21203	.21261	.21319

ANNUAL PERCENTAGE RATE TABLES: TERM OF MORTGAGE: 240 MONTHS

INTEREST RATE	POINTS CHARGED .02750	.03000	.03250	.03500	.03750	.04000	.04250	.04500	.04750	.05000
.07000	.07363	.07397	.07430	.07464	.07499	.07533	.07567	.07602	.07637	.07671
.07250	.07616	.07650	.07685	.07719	.07754	.07788	.07823	.07858	.07893	.07928
.07500	.07870	.07905	.07939	.07974	.08009	.08044	.08079	.08114	.08149	.08185
.07750	.08124	.08159	.08194	.08229	.08264	.08299	.08335	.08370	.08406	.08442
.08000	.08378	.08413	.08448	.08483	.08519	.08555	.08591	.08627	.08663	.08699
.08250	.08631	.08667	.08703	.08738	.08774	.08810	.08847	.08883	.08920	.08956
.08500	.08885	.08921	.08957	.08993	.09030	.09066	.09103	.09139	.09176	.09213
.08750	.09139	.09175	.09212	.09248	.09285	.09322	.09359	.09396	.09433	.09471
.09000	.09393	.09430	.09467	.09503	.09541	.09578	.09615	.09653	.09690	.09728
.09250	.09647	.09684	.09721	.09759	.09796	.09834	.09871	.09909	.09947	.09986
.09500	.09901	.09939	.09976	.10014	.10052	.10090	.10128	.10166	.10205	.10243
.09750	.10155	.10193	.10231	.10269	.10307	.10346	.10384	.10423	.10462	.10501
.10000	.10410	.10448	.10486	.10524	.10563	.10602	.10641	.10680	.10719	.10759
.10250	.10664	.10702	.10741	.10780	.10819	.10858	.10897	.10937	.10977	.11016
.10500	.10918	.10957	.10996	.11035	.11075	.11114	.11154	.11194	.11234	.11274
.10750	.11172	.11212	.11251	.11291	.11331	.11371	.11411	.11451	.11492	.11532
.11000	.11427	.11466	.11506	.11546	.11587	.11627	.11668	.11708	.11749	.11790
.11250	.11681	.11721	.11761	.11802	.11843	.11884	.11925	.11966	.12007	.12049
.11500	.11935	.11976	.12017	.12058	.12099	.12140	.12181	.12223	.12265	.12307
.11750	.12190	.12231	.12272	.12313	.12355	.12397	.12439	.12481	.12523	.12565
.12000	.12444	.12486	.12527	.12569	.12611	.12653	.12696	.12738	.12781	.12824
.12250	.12699	.12741	.12783	.12825	.12867	.12910	.12953	.12996	.13039	.13082
.12500	.12954	.12996	.13038	.13081	.13124	.13167	.13210	.13253	.13297	.13341
.12750	.13208	.13251	.13294	.13337	.13380	.13424	.13467	.13511	.13555	.13599
.13000	.13463	.13506	.13549	.13593	.13637	.13681	.13725	.13769	.13814	.13858
.13250	.13718	.13761	.13805	.13849	.13893	.13938	.13982	.14027	.14072	.14117
.13500	.13972	.14016	.14061	.14105	.14150	.14195	.14240	.14285	.14330	.14376
.13750	.14227	.14272	.14316	.14361	.14406	.14452	.14497	.14543	.14589	.14635
.14000	.14482	.14527	.14572	.14618	.14663	.14709	.14755	.14801	.14847	.14894
.14250	.14737	.14782	.14828	.14874	.14920	.14966	.15013	.15059	.15106	.15153
.14500	.14992	.15038	.15084	.15130	.15177	.15223	.15270	.15318	.15365	.15412
.14750	.15247	.15293	.15340	.15387	.15434	.15481	.15528	.15576	.15624	.15672
.15000	.15502	.15549	.15596	.15643	.15691	.15738	.15786	.15834	.15883	.15931
.15250	.15757	.15804	.15852	.15900	.15948	.15996	.16044	.16093	.16142	.16191
.15500	.16012	.16060	.16108	.16156	.16205	.16253	.16302	.16351	.16401	.16450
.15750	.16267	.16316	.16364	.16413	.16462	.16511	.16560	.16610	.16660	.16710
.16000	.16522	.16571	.16620	.16669	.16719	.16769	.16818	.16869	.16919	.16969
.16250	.16778	.16827	.16876	.16926	.16976	.17026	.17077	.17127	.17178	.17229
.16500	.17033	.17083	.17133	.17183	.17233	.17284	.17335	.17386	.17437	.17489
.16750	.17288	.17339	.17389	.17440	.17491	.17542	.17593	.17645	.17697	.17749
.17000	.17544	.17594	.17645	.17697	.17748	.17800	.17852	.17904	.17956	.18009
.17250	.17799	.17850	.17902	.17953	.18005	.18058	.18110	.18163	.18216	.18269
.17500	.18054	.18106	.18158	.18210	.18263	.18316	.18369	.18422	.18475	.18529
.17750	.18310	.18362	.18415	.18467	.18520	.18574	.18627	.18681	.18735	.18789
.18000	.18565	.18618	.18671	.18724	.18778	.18832	.18886	.18940	.18995	.19050
.18250	.18821	.18874	.18928	.18982	.19036	.19090	.19145	.19199	.19254	.19310
.18500	.19076	.19130	.19184	.19239	.19293	.19348	.19403	.19459	.19514	.19570
.18750	.19332	.19386	.19441	.19496	.19551	.19606	.19662	.19718	.19774	.19831
.19000	.19588	.19643	.19698	.19753	.19809	.19865	.19921	.19977	.20034	.20091
.19250	.19843	.19899	.19954	.20010	.20067	.20123	.20180	.20237	.20294	.20352
.19500	.20099	.20155	.20211	.20268	.20324	.20381	.20439	.20496	.20554	.20612
.19750	.20355	.20411	.20468	.20525	.20582	.20640	.20698	.20756	.20814	.20873
.20000	.20610	.20667	.20725	.20782	.20840	.20898	.20957	.21016	.21075	.21134
.20250	.20866	.20924	.20982	.21040	.21098	.21157	.21216	.21275	.21335	.21395
.20500	.21122	.21180	.21239	.21297	.21356	.21416	.21475	.21535	.21595	.21655
.20750	.21378	.21437	.21496	.21555	.21614	.21674	.21734	.21795	.21855	.21916

ANNUAL PERCENTAGE RATE TABLES: TERM OF MORTGAGE: 240 MONTHS

POINTS CHARGED

INTEREST RATE	.05250	.05500	.05750	.06000	.06250	.06500	.06750	.07000	.07250	.07500
.07000	.07706	.07741	.07777	.07812	.07848	.07883	.07919	.07955	.07991	.08028
.07250	.07964	.07999	.08035	.08070	.08106	.08142	.08179	.08215	.08251	.08288
.07500	.08221	.08257	.08293	.08329	.08365	.08401	.08438	.08475	.08512	.08549
.07750	.08478	.08514	.08551	.08587	.08624	.08661	.08698	.08735	.08772	.08810
.08000	.08736	.08772	.08809	.08846	.08883	.08920	.08957	.08995	.09033	.09070
.08250	.08993	.09030	.09067	.09104	.09142	.09179	.09217	.09255	.09293	.09331
.08500	.09251	.09288	.09326	.09363	.09401	.09439	.09477	.09515	.09554	.09593
.08750	.09508	.09546	.09584	.09622	.09660	.09699	.09737	.09776	.09815	.09854
.09000	.09766	.09804	.09843	.09881	.09920	.09959	.09997	.10037	.10076	.10115
.09250	.10024	.10063	.10101	.10140	.10179	.10218	.10258	.10297	.10337	.10377
.09500	.10282	.10321	.10360	.10399	.10439	.10478	.10518	.10558	.10598	.10639
.09750	.10540	.10579	.10619	.10659	.10699	.10739	.10779	.10819	.10860	.10900
.10000	.10798	.10838	.10878	.10918	.10958	.10999	.11039	.11080	.11121	.11162
.10250	.11056	.11097	.11137	.11178	.11218	.11259	.11300	.11342	.11383	.11425
.10500	.11315	.11355	.11396	.11437	.11478	.11520	.11561	.11603	.11645	.11687
.10750	.11573	.11614	.11656	.11697	.11739	.11780	.11822	.11864	.11907	.11949
.11000	.11832	.11873	.11915	.11957	.11999	.12041	.12083	.12126	.12169	.12212
.11250	.12090	.12132	.12174	.12217	.12259	.12302	.12345	.12388	.12431	.12474
.11500	.12349	.12391	.12434	.12477	.12520	.12563	.12606	.12650	.12693	.12737
.11750	.12608	.12651	.12694	.12737	.12780	.12824	.12868	.12911	.12956	.13000
.12000	.12867	.12910	.12953	.12997	.13041	.13085	.13129	.13174	.13218	.13263
.12250	.13126	.13169	.13213	.13257	.13302	.13346	.13391	.13436	.13481	.13526
.12500	.13385	.13429	.13473	.13518	.13563	.13608	.13653	.13698	.13744	.13789
.12750	.13644	.13689	.13733	.13778	.13824	.13869	.13915	.13961	.14007	.14053
.13000	.13903	.13948	.13994	.14039	.14085	.14131	.14177	.14223	.14270	.14316
.13250	.14162	.14208	.14254	.14300	.14346	.14392	.14439	.14486	.14533	.14580
.13500	.14422	.14468	.14514	.14561	.14607	.14654	.14701	.14749	.14796	.14844
.13750	.14681	.14728	.14775	.14822	.14869	.14916	.14964	.15012	.15060	.15108
.14000	.14941	.14988	.15035	.15083	.15130	.15178	.15226	.15275	.15323	.15372
.14250	.15201	.15248	.15296	.15344	.15392	.15440	.15489	.15538	.15587	.15636
.14500	.15460	.15508	.15556	.15605	.15654	.15702	.15752	.15801	.15850	.15900
.14750	.15720	.15769	.15817	.15866	.15915	.15965	.16014	.16064	.16114	.16165
.15000	.15980	.16029	.16078	.16128	.16177	.16227	.16277	.16328	.16378	.16429
.15250	.16240	.16289	.16339	.16389	.16439	.16490	.16540	.16591	.16642	.16694
.15500	.16500	.16550	.16600	.16651	.16701	.16752	.16804	.16855	.16907	.16959
.15750	.16760	.16811	.16861	.16912	.16964	.17015	.17067	.17119	.17171	.17223
.16000	.17020	.17071	.17123	.17174	.17226	.17278	.17330	.17383	.17435	.17488
.16250	.17281	.17332	.17384	.17436	.17488	.17541	.17594	.17647	.17700	.17754
.16500	.17541	.17593	.17645	.17698	.17751	.17804	.17857	.17911	.17965	.18019
.16750	.17801	.17854	.17907	.17960	.18013	.18067	.18121	.18175	.18229	.18284
.17000	.18062	.18115	.18168	.18222	.18276	.18330	.18385	.18439	.18494	.18550
.17250	.18322	.18376	.18430	.18484	.18539	.18594	.18649	.18704	.18759	.18815
.17500	.18583	.18637	.18692	.18747	.18802	.18857	.18912	.18968	.19024	.19081
.17750	.18844	.18899	.18954	.19009	.19065	.19120	.19176	.19233	.19290	.19346
.18000	.19105	.19160	.19216	.19271	.19328	.19384	.19441	.19498	.19555	.19612
.18250	.19365	.19421	.19478	.19534	.19591	.19648	.19705	.19762	.19820	.19878
.18500	.19626	.19683	.19740	.19797	.19854	.19911	.19969	.20027	.20086	.20144
.18750	.19887	.19944	.20002	.20059	.20117	.20175	.20234	.20292	.20351	.20410
.19000	.20148	.20206	.20264	.20322	.20380	.20439	.20498	.20557	.20617	.20677
.19250	.20410	.20468	.20526	.20585	.20644	.20703	.20763	.20822	.20883	.20943
.19500	.20671	.20729	.20788	.20848	.20907	.20967	.21027	.21088	.21148	.21209
.19750	.20932	.20991	.21051	.21111	.21171	.21231	.21292	.21353	.21414	.21476
.20000	.21193	.21253	.21313	.21374	.21434	.21496	.21557	.21618	.21680	.21743
.20250	.21455	.21515	.21576	.21637	.21698	.21760	.21822	.21884	.21946	.22009
.20500	.21716	.21777	.21838	.21900	.21962	.22024	.22087	.22150	.22213	.22276
.20750	.21978	.22039	.22101	.22163	.22226	.22289	.22352	.22415	.22479	.22543

ANNUAL PERCENTAGE RATE TABLES: TERM OF MORTGAGE: 240 MONTHS

INTEREST RATE	POINTS CHARGED .07750	.08000	.08250	.08500	.08750	.09000	.09250	.09500	.09750	.10000
.07000	.08064	.08101	.08137	.08174	.08211	.08249	.08286	.08323	.08361	.08399
.07250	.08325	.08362	.08399	.08436	.08474	.08511	.08549	.08587	.08625	.08663
.07500	.08586	.08623	.08661	.08699	.08736	.08774	.08813	.08851	.08889	.08928
.07750	.08847	.08885	.08923	.08961	.08999	.09038	.09076	.09115	.09154	.09193
.08000	.09108	.09147	.09185	.09223	.09262	.09301	.09340	.09379	.09418	.09458
.08250	.09370	.09408	.09447	.09486	.09525	.09564	.09604	.09643	.09683	.09723
.08500	.09631	.09670	.09710	.09749	.09788	.09828	.09868	.09908	.09948	.09988
.08750	.09893	.09933	.09972	.10012	.10052	.10092	.10132	.10172	.10213	.10254
.09000	.10155	.10195	.10235	.10275	.10315	.10356	.10396	.10437	.10478	.10520
.09250	.10417	.10457	.10498	.10538	.10579	.10620	.10661	.10702	.10744	.10785
.09500	.10679	.10720	.10761	.10802	.10843	.10884	.10926	.10968	.11009	.11052
.09750	.10941	.10982	.11024	.11065	.11107	.11149	.11191	.11233	.11275	.11318
.10000	.11204	.11245	.11287	.11329	.11371	.11413	.11456	.11498	.11541	.11584
.10250	.11466	.11508	.11550	.11593	.11635	.11678	.11721	.11764	.11807	.11851
.10500	.11729	.11771	.11814	.11857	.11900	.11943	.11986	.12030	.12074	.12118
.10750	.11992	.12035	.12078	.12121	.12165	.12208	.12252	.12296	.12340	.12385
.11000	.12255	.12298	.12342	.12385	.12429	.12473	.12518	.12562	.12607	.12652
.11250	.12518	.12562	.12606	.12650	.12694	.12739	.12784	.12829	.12874	.12919
.11500	.12781	.12825	.12870	.12915	.12959	.13005	.13050	.13095	.13141	.13187
.11750	.13045	.13089	.13134	.13179	.13225	.13270	.13316	.13362	.13408	.13455
.12000	.13308	.13353	.13399	.13444	.13490	.13536	.13583	.13629	.13676	.13723
.12250	.13572	.13617	.13663	.13709	.13756	.13802	.13849	.13896	.13943	.13991
.12500	.13835	.13882	.13928	.13975	.14022	.14069	.14116	.14163	.14211	.14259
.12750	.14099	.14146	.14193	.14240	.14287	.14335	.14383	.14431	.14479	.14527
.13000	.14363	.14411	.14458	.14506	.14553	.14602	.14650	.14698	.14747	.14796
.13250	.14628	.14675	.14723	.14771	.14820	.14868	.14917	.14966	.15015	.15065
.13500	.14892	.14940	.14988	.15037	.15086	.15135	.15184	.15234	.15284	.15334
.13750	.15156	.15205	.15254	.15303	.15353	.15402	.15452	.15502	.15552	.15603
.14000	.15421	.15470	.15520	.15569	.15619	.15669	.15720	.15770	.15821	.15872
.14250	.15686	.15735	.15785	.15835	.15886	.15937	.15988	.16039	.16090	.16142
.14500	.15950	.16001	.16051	.16102	.16153	.16204	.16256	.16307	.16359	.16412
.14750	.16215	.16266	.16317	.16368	.16420	.16472	.16524	.16576	.16629	.16681
.15000	.16480	.16532	.16583	.16635	.16687	.16739	.16792	.16845	.16898	.16951
.15250	.16745	.16797	.16849	.16902	.16954	.17007	.17061	.17114	.17168	.17221
.15500	.17011	.17063	.17116	.17169	.17222	.17275	.17329	.17383	.17437	.17492
.15750	.17276	.17329	.17382	.17436	.17490	.17544	.17598	.17652	.17707	.17762
.16000	.17542	.17595	.17649	.17703	.17757	.17812	.17867	.17922	.17977	.18033
.16250	.17807	.17861	.17916	.17970	.18025	.18080	.18136	.18191	.18247	.18304
.16500	.18073	.18128	.18183	.18238	.18293	.18349	.18405	.18461	.18518	.18575
.16750	.18339	.18394	.18450	.18505	.18561	.18618	.18674	.18731	.18788	.18846
.17000	.18605	.18661	.18717	.18773	.18830	.18887	.18944	.19001	.19059	.19117
.17250	.18871	.18927	.18984	.19041	.19098	.19156	.19213	.19271	.19330	.19388
.17500	.19137	.19194	.19251	.19309	.19367	.19425	.19483	.19542	.19601	.19660
.17750	.19404	.19461	.19519	.19577	.19635	.19694	.19753	.19812	.19872	.19931
.18000	.19670	.19728	.19787	.19845	.19904	.19963	.20023	.20083	.20143	.20203
.18250	.19937	.19995	.20054	.20113	.20173	.20233	.20293	.20353	.20414	.20475
.18500	.20203	.20263	.20322	.20382	.20442	.20502	.20563	.20624	.20686	.20747
.18750	.20470	.20530	.20590	.20650	.20711	.20772	.20834	.20895	.20957	.21019
.19000	.20737	.20797	.20858	.20919	.20980	.21042	.21104	.21166	.21229	.21292
.19250	.21004	.21065	.21126	.21188	.21250	.21312	.21375	.21438	.21501	.21564
.19500	.21271	.21332	.21394	.21457	.21519	.21582	.21645	.21709	.21773	.21837
.19750	.21538	.21600	.21663	.21726	.21789	.21852	.21916	.21980	.22045	.22110
.20000	.21805	.21868	.21931	.21995	.22059	.22123	.22187	.22252	.22317	.22383
.20250	.22072	.22136	.22200	.22264	.22328	.22393	.22458	.22524	.22589	.22656
.20500	.22340	.22404	.22468	.22533	.22598	.22664	.22729	.22795	.22862	.22929
.20750	.22607	.22672	.22737	.22803	.22868	.22934	.23001	.23067	.23134	.23202

ANNUAL PERCENTAGE RATE TABLES: TERM OF MORTGAGE: 240 MONTHS

INTEREST RATE	POINTS CHARGED .10250	.10500	.10750	.11000	.11250	.11500	.11750	.12000	.12250	.12500
.07000	.08437	.08475	.08514	.08552	.08591	.08630	.08669	.08708	.08747	.08787
.07250	.08702	.08740	.08779	.08818	.08857	.08896	.08936	.08976	.09015	.09055
.07500	.08967	.09006	.09045	.09084	.09124	.09164	.09203	.09244	.09284	.09324
.07750	.09232	.09272	.09311	.09351	.09391	.09431	.09471	.09512	.09552	.09593
.08000	.09497	.09537	.09577	.09618	.09658	.09698	.09739	.09780	.09821	.09863
.08250	.09763	.09803	.09844	.09884	.09925	.09966	.10007	.10049	.10090	.10132
.08500	.10029	.10070	.10110	.10152	.10193	.10234	.10276	.10318	.10360	.10402
.08750	.10295	.10336	.10377	.10419	.10461	.10502	.10545	.10587	.10629	.10672
.09000	.10561	.10603	.10644	.10686	.10729	.10771	.10813	.10856	.10899	.10942
.09250	.10827	.10869	.10912	.10954	.10997	.11039	.11083	.11126	.11169	.11213
.09500	.11094	.11136	.11179	.11222	.11265	.11308	.11352	.11396	.11439	.11483
.09750	.11361	.11404	.11447	.11490	.11534	.11577	.11621	.11666	.11710	.11755
.10000	.11628	.11671	.11715	.11758	.11803	.11847	.11891	.11936	.11981	.12026
.10250	.11895	.11939	.11983	.12027	.12072	.12116	.12161	.12206	.12252	.12297
.10500	.12162	.12206	.12251	.12296	.12341	.12386	.12431	.12477	.12523	.12569
.10750	.12429	.12474	.12519	.12565	.12610	.12656	.12702	.12748	.12794	.12841
.11000	.12697	.12743	.12788	.12834	.12880	.12926	.12973	.13019	.13066	.13113
.11250	.12965	.13011	.13057	.13103	.13150	.13196	.13243	.13291	.13338	.13386
.11500	.13233	.13279	.13326	.13373	.13420	.13467	.13515	.13562	.13610	.13658
.11750	.13501	.13548	.13595	.13643	.13690	.13738	.13786	.13834	.13882	.13931
.12000	.13770	.13817	.13865	.13913	.13961	.14009	.14057	.14106	.14155	.14204
.12250	.14038	.14086	.14134	.14183	.14231	.14280	.14329	.14378	.14428	.14478
.12500	.14307	.14356	.14404	.14453	.14502	.14552	.14601	.14651	.14701	.14751
.12750	.14576	.14625	.14674	.14724	.14773	.14823	.14873	.14924	.14974	.15025
.13000	.14845	.14895	.14944	.14994	.15045	.15095	.15146	.15197	.15248	.15299
.13250	.15115	.15165	.15215	.15265	.15316	.15367	.15418	.15470	.15521	.15573
.13500	.15384	.15435	.15485	.15537	.15588	.15639	.15691	.15743	.15795	.15848
.13750	.15654	.15705	.15756	.15808	.15860	.15912	.15964	.16017	.16070	.16123
.14000	.15924	.15975	.16027	.16079	.16132	.16184	.16237	.16290	.16344	.16398
.14250	.16194	.16246	.16298	.16351	.16404	.16457	.16511	.16564	.16618	.16673
.14500	.16464	.16517	.16570	.16623	.16677	.16730	.16784	.16839	.16893	.16948
.14750	.16734	.16788	.16841	.16895	.16949	.17004	.17058	.17113	.17168	.17224
.15000	.17005	.17059	.17113	.17167	.17222	.17277	.17332	.17388	.17443	.17499
.15250	.17276	.17330	.17385	.17440	.17495	.17551	.17606	.17662	.17719	.17775
.15500	.17547	.17602	.17657	.17712	.17768	.17824	.17881	.17937	.17994	.18052
.15750	.17818	.17873	.17929	.17985	.18042	.18098	.18155	.18213	.18270	.18328
.16000	.18089	.18145	.18201	.18258	.18315	.18373	.18430	.18488	.18546	.18605
.16250	.18360	.18417	.18474	.18531	.18589	.18647	.18705	.18764	.18822	.18882
.16500	.18632	.18689	.18747	.18805	.18863	.18921	.18980	.19039	.19099	.19159
.16750	.18903	.18961	.19020	.19078	.19137	.19196	.19256	.19315	.19375	.19436
.17000	.19175	.19234	.19293	.19352	.19411	.19471	.19531	.19592	.19652	.19713
.17250	.19447	.19506	.19566	.19626	.19686	.19746	.19807	.19868	.19929	.19991
.17500	.19719	.19779	.19839	.19900	.19960	.20021	.20083	.20144	.20206	.20269
.17750	.19992	.20052	.20113	.20174	.20235	.20297	.20359	.20421	.20484	.20547
.18000	.20264	.20325	.20386	.20448	.20510	.20572	.20635	.20698	.20761	.20825
.18250	.20537	.20598	.20660	.20722	.20785	.20848	.20911	.20975	.21039	.21103
.18500	.20809	.20872	.20934	.20997	.21060	.21124	.21188	.21252	.21317	.21382
.18750	.21082	.21145	.21208	.21272	.21336	.21400	.21465	.21529	.21595	.21660
.19000	.21355	.21419	.21483	.21547	.21611	.21676	.21741	.21807	.21873	.21939
.19250	.21628	.21692	.21757	.21822	.21887	.21953	.22018	.22085	.22151	.22218
.19500	.21901	.21966	.22031	.22097	.22163	.22229	.22296	.22363	.22430	.22497
.19750	.22175	.22240	.22306	.22372	.22439	.22506	.22573	.22641	.22708	.22777
.20000	.22448	.22514	.22581	.22648	.22715	.22783	.22850	.22919	.22987	.23056
.20250	.22722	.22789	.22856	.22923	.22991	.23059	.23128	.23197	.23266	.23336
.20500	.22996	.23063	.23131	.23199	.23268	.23337	.23406	.23475	.23545	.23616
.20750	.23270	.23338	.23406	.23475	.23544	.23614	.23684	.23754	.23825	.23896

ANNUAL PERCENTAGE RATE TABLES: TERM OF MORTGAGE: 240 MONTHS

INTEREST RATE	POINTS CHARGED .12750	.13000	.13250	.13500	.13750	.14000	.14250	.14500	.14750	.15000
.07000	.08826	.08866	.08906	.08947	.08987	.09028	.09069	.09110	.09151	.09192
.07250	.09095	.09136	.09176	.09217	.09258	.09299	.09340	.09382	.09423	.09465
.07500	.09365	.09406	.09446	.09488	.09529	.09570	.09612	.09654	.09696	.09738
.07750	.09634	.09675	.09717	.09758	.09800	.09642	.09884	.09927	.09969	.10012
.08000	.09904	.09946	.09988	.10030	.10072	.10114	.10157	.10200	.10243	.10286
.08250	.10174	.10216	.10258	.10301	.10344	.10387	.10430	.10473	.10517	.10560
.08500	.10444	.10487	.10530	.10573	.10616	.10659	.10703	.10747	.10791	.10835
.08750	.10715	.10758	.10801	.10845	.10888	.10932	.10976	.11020	.11065	.11110
.09000	.10986	.11029	.11073	.11117	.11161	.11205	.11250	.11295	.11340	.11385
.09250	.11257	.11301	.11345	.11389	.11434	.11479	.11524	.11569	.11615	.11660
.09500	.11528	.11572	.11617	.11662	.11707	.11752	.11798	.11844	.11890	.11936
.09750	.11799	.11844	.11889	.11935	.11981	.12026	.12072	.12119	.12165	.12212
.10000	.12071	.12117	.12162	.12208	.12254	.12301	.12347	.12394	.12441	.12488
.10250	.12343	.12389	.12435	.12482	.12528	.12575	.12622	.12670	.12717	.12765
.10500	.12615	.12662	.12708	.12755	.12803	.12850	.12898	.12946	.12994	.13042
.10750	.12888	.12935	.12982	.13029	.13077	.13125	.13173	.13222	.13270	.13319
.11000	.13160	.13208	.13256	.13304	.13352	.13400	.13449	.13498	.13547	.13597
.11250	.13433	.13481	.13530	.13578	.13627	.13676	.13725	.13775	.13825	.13875
.11500	.13707	.13755	.13804	.13853	.13902	.13952	.14002	.14052	.14102	.14153
.11750	.13980	.14029	.14079	.14128	.14178	.14228	.14278	.14329	.14380	.14431
.12000	.14254	.14303	.14353	.14403	.14454	.14505	.14555	.14607	.14658	.14710
.12250	.14528	.14578	.14628	.14679	.14730	.14781	.14833	.14884	.14936	.14989
.12500	.14802	.14853	.14904	.14955	.15006	.15058	.15110	.15163	.15215	.15268
.12750	.15076	.15128	.15179	.15231	.15283	.15335	.15388	.15441	.15494	.15548
.13000	.15351	.15403	.15455	.15507	.15560	.15613	.15666	.15720	.15773	.15827
.13250	.15626	.15678	.15731	.15784	.15837	.15891	.15944	.15999	.16053	.16108
.13500	.15901	.15954	.16007	.16061	.16115	.16169	.16223	.16278	.16333	.16388
.13750	.16176	.16230	.16284	.16338	.16392	.16447	.16502	.16557	.16613	.16669
.14000	.16452	.16506	.16560	.16615	.16670	.16725	.16781	.16837	.16893	.16950
.14250	.16727	.16782	.16837	.16893	.16948	.17004	.17060	.17117	.17174	.17231
.14500	.17003	.17059	.17114	.17170	.17227	.17283	.17340	.17397	.17455	.17512
.14750	.17279	.17335	.17392	.17448	.17505	.17562	.17620	.17678	.17736	.17794
.15000	.17556	.17612	.17669	.17727	.17784	.17842	.17900	.17958	.18017	.18076
.15250	.17832	.17890	.17947	.18005	.18063	.18122	.18180	.18239	.18299	.18358
.15500	.18109	.18167	.18225	.18284	.18342	.18402	.18461	.18521	.18581	.18641
.15750	.18386	.18445	.18504	.18563	.18622	.18682	.18742	.18802	.18863	.18924
.16000	.18664	.18723	.18782	.18842	.18902	.18962	.19023	.19084	.19145	.19207
.16250	.18941	.19001	.19061	.19121	.19182	.19243	.19304	.19366	.19428	.19490
.16500	.19219	.19279	.19340	.19401	.19462	.19524	.19586	.19648	.19711	.19773
.16750	.19497	.19558	.19619	.19680	.19742	.19805	.19867	.19930	.19994	.20057
.17000	.19775	.19836	.19898	.19960	.20023	.20086	.20149	.20213	.20277	.20341
.17250	.20053	.20115	.20178	.20241	.20304	.20368	.20432	.20496	.20560	.20625
.17500	.20331	.20394	.20457	.20521	.20585	.20649	.20714	.20779	.20844	.20910
.17750	.20610	.20673	.20737	.20802	.20866	.20931	.20997	.21062	.21128	.21195
.18000	.20889	.20953	.21018	.21083	.21148	.21213	.21279	.21346	.21413	.21480
.18250	.21168	.21233	.21298	.21364	.21430	.21496	.21563	.21630	.21697	.21765
.18500	.21447	.21512	.21578	.21645	.21711	.21778	.21846	.21914	.21982	.22050
.18750	.21726	.21793	.21859	.21926	.21993	.22061	.22129	.22198	.22267	.22336
.19000	.22006	.22073	.22140	.22208	.22276	.22344	.22413	.22482	.22552	.22622
.19250	.22285	.22353	.22421	.22489	.22558	.22627	.22697	.22767	.22837	.22908
.19500	.22565	.22634	.22702	.22771	.22841	.22911	.22981	.23051	.23122	.23194
.19750	.22845	.22914	.22984	.23054	.23124	.23194	.23265	.23336	.23408	.23480
.20000	.23126	.23195	.23265	.23336	.23407	.23478	.23550	.23622	.23694	.23767
.20250	.23406	.23476	.23547	.23618	.23690	.23762	.23834	.23907	.23980	.24054
.20500	.23686	.23758	.23829	.23901	.23973	.24046	.24119	.24192	.24266	.24341
.20750	.23967	.24039	.24111	.24184	.24257	.24330	.24404	.24478	.24553	.24628

ANNUAL PERCENTAGE RATE TABLES: TERM OF MORTGAGE: 300 MONTHS

INTEREST RATE	POINTS CHARGED .00250	.00500	.00750	.01000	.01250	.01500	.01750	.02000	.02250	.02500
.07000	.07028	.07056	.07084	.07112	.07140	.07168	.07197	.07225	.07254	.07282
.07250	.07278	.07306	.07335	.07363	.07392	.07420	.07449	.07478	.07507	.07536
.07500	.07528	.07557	.07586	.07615	.07643	.07672	.07702	.07731	.07760	.07790
.07750	.07779	.07808	.07837	.07866	.07895	.07925	.07954	.07984	.08014	.08043
.08000	.08029	.08058	.08088	.08117	.08147	.08177	.08207	.08237	.08267	.08297
.08250	.08280	.08309	.08339	.08369	.08399	.08429	.08459	.08490	.08520	.08551
.08500	.08530	.08560	.08590	.08620	.08651	.08681	.08712	.08743	.08774	.08805
.08750	.08780	.08811	.08841	.08872	.08903	.08934	.08965	.08996	.09027	.09059
.09000	.09031	.09062	.09092	.09124	.09155	.09186	.09218	.09249	.09281	.09313
.09250	.09281	.09312	.09344	.09375	.09407	.09438	.09470	.09502	.09534	.09567
.09500	.09531	.09563	.09595	.09627	.09659	.09691	.09723	.09756	.09788	.09821
.09750	.09782	.09814	.09846	.09878	.09911	.09943	.09976	.10009	.10042	.10075
.10000	.10032	.10065	.10097	.10130	.10163	.10196	.10229	.10262	.10296	.10329
.10250	.10283	.10316	.10349	.10382	.10415	.10448	.10482	.10516	.10549	.10583
.10500	.10533	.10566	.10600	.10633	.10667	.10701	.10735	.10769	.10803	.10838
.10750	.10784	.10817	.10851	.10885	.10919	.10953	.10988	.11022	.11057	.11092
.11000	.11034	.11068	.11102	.11137	.11171	.11206	.11241	.11276	.11311	.11346
.11250	.11284	.11319	.11354	.11388	.11423	.11459	.11494	.11529	.11565	.11601
.11500	.11535	.11570	.11605	.11640	.11676	.11711	.11747	.11783	.11819	.11855
.11750	.11785	.11821	.11856	.11892	.11928	.11964	.12000	.12036	.12073	.12110
.12000	.12036	.12072	.12108	.12144	.12180	.12217	.12253	.12290	.12327	.12364
.12250	.12286	.12322	.12359	.12396	.12432	.12469	.12506	.12544	.12581	.12619
.12500	.12537	.12573	.12610	.12647	.12685	.12722	.12760	.12797	.12835	.12873
.12750	.12787	.12824	.12862	.12899	.12937	.12975	.13013	.13051	.13090	.13128
.13000	.13038	.13075	.13113	.13151	.13189	.13228	.13266	.13305	.13344	.13383
.13250	.13288	.13326	.13364	.13403	.13442	.13480	.13519	.13559	.13598	.13638
.13500	.13538	.13577	.13616	.13655	.13694	.13733	.13773	.13813	.13852	.13892
.13750	.13789	.13828	.13867	.13907	.13946	.13986	.14026	.14066	.14107	.14147
.14000	.14039	.14079	.14119	.14159	.14199	.14239	.14280	.14320	.14361	.14402
.14250	.14290	.14330	.14370	.14411	.14451	.14492	.14533	.14574	.14616	.14657
.14500	.14540	.14581	.14622	.14663	.14704	.14745	.14786	.14828	.14870	.14912
.14750	.14791	.14832	.14873	.14915	.14956	.14998	.15040	.15082	.15125	.15167
.15000	.15041	.15083	.15125	.15167	.15209	.15251	.15293	.15336	.15379	.15422
.15250	.15292	.15334	.15376	.15419	.15461	.15504	.15547	.15590	.15634	.15677
.15500	.15542	.15585	.15628	.15671	.15714	.15757	.15801	.15844	.15888	.15932
.15750	.15793	.15836	.15879	.15923	.15966	.16010	.16054	.16098	.16143	.16188
.16000	.16043	.16087	.16131	.16175	.16219	.16263	.16308	.16353	.16398	.16443
.16250	.16294	.16338	.16382	.16427	.16471	.16516	.16561	.16607	.16652	.16698
.16500	.16544	.16589	.16634	.16679	.16724	.16769	.16815	.16861	.16907	.16953
.16750	.16795	.16840	.16885	.16931	.16977	.17023	.17069	.17115	.17162	.17209
.17000	.17045	.17091	.17137	.17183	.17229	.17276	.17323	.17369	.17417	.17464
.17250	.17296	.17342	.17389	.17435	.17482	.17529	.17576	.17624	.17671	.17719
.17500	.17546	.17593	.17640	.17687	.17735	.17782	.17830	.17878	.17926	.17975
.17750	.17797	.17844	.17892	.17939	.17987	.18035	.18084	.18132	.18181	.18230
.18000	.18048	.18095	.18143	.18192	.18240	.18289	.18338	.18387	.18436	.18486
.18250	.18298	.18346	.18395	.18444	.18493	.18542	.18591	.18641	.18691	.18741
.18500	.18549	.18597	.18647	.18696	.18745	.18795	.18845	.18896	.18946	.18997
.18750	.18799	.18849	.18898	.18948	.18998	.19049	.19099	.19150	.19201	.19252
.19000	.19050	.19100	.19150	.19200	.19251	.19302	.19353	.19404	.19456	.19508
.19250	.19300	.19351	.19402	.19452	.19504	.19555	.19607	.19659	.19711	.19764
.19500	.19551	.19602	.19653	.19705	.19756	.19809	.19861	.19913	.19966	.20019
.19750	.19801	.19853	.19905	.19957	.20009	.20062	.20115	.20168	.20221	.20275
.20000	.20052	.20104	.20157	.20209	.20262	.20315	.20369	.20422	.20476	.20531
.20250	.20302	.20355	.20408	.20461	.20515	.20569	.20623	.20677	.20731	.20786
.20500	.20553	.20606	.20660	.20714	.20768	.20822	.20877	.20932	.20987	.21042
.20750	.20804	.20857	.20912	.20966	.21021	.21076	.21131	.21186	.21242	.21298

ANNUAL PERCENTAGE RATE TABLES: TERM OF MORTGAGE: 300 MONTHS

INTEREST RATE	POINTS CHARGED .02750	.03000	.03250	.03500	.03750	.04000	.04250	.04500	.04750	.05000
.07000	.07311	.07340	.07369	.07399	.07428	.07457	.07487	.07517	.07547	.07577
.07250	.07565	.07595	.07624	.07654	.07683	.07713	.07743	.07773	.07804	.07834
.07500	.07819	.07849	.07879	.07909	.07939	.07969	.08000	.08030	.08061	.08091
.07750	.08073	.08104	.08134	.08164	.08195	.08225	.08256	.08287	.08318	.08349
.08000	.08328	.08358	.08389	.08420	.08450	.08481	.08513	.08544	.08575	.08607
.08250	.08582	.08613	.08644	.08675	.08706	.08738	.08769	.08801	.08833	.08865
.08500	.08836	.08867	.08899	.08930	.08962	.08994	.09026	.09058	.09090	.09123
.08750	.09090	.09122	.09154	.09186	.09218	.09250	.09283	.09315	.09348	.09381
.09000	.09345	.09377	.09409	.09441	.09474	.09507	.09540	.09572	.09606	.09639
.09250	.09599	.09632	.09664	.09697	.09730	.09763	.09796	.09830	.09863	.09897
.09500	.09854	.09887	.09920	.09953	.09986	.10020	.10054	.10087	.10121	.10155
.09750	.10108	.10142	.10175	.10209	.10243	.10277	.10311	.10345	.10379	.10414
.10000	.10363	.10397	.10431	.10465	.10499	.10533	.10568	.10603	.10637	.10672
.10250	.10617	.10652	.10686	.10721	.10755	.10790	.10825	.10860	.10896	.10931
.10500	.10872	.10907	.10942	.10977	.11012	.11047	.11083	.11118	.11154	.11190
.10750	.11127	.11162	.11197	.11233	.11268	.11304	.11340	.11376	.11412	.11449
.11000	.11382	.11417	.11453	.11489	.11525	.11561	.11598	.11634	.11671	.11708
.11250	.11637	.11673	.11709	.11745	.11782	.11818	.11855	.11892	.11930	.11967
.11500	.11891	.11928	.11965	.12002	.12039	.12076	.12113	.12151	.12188	.12226
.11750	.12146	.12183	.12221	.12258	.12295	.12333	.12371	.12409	.12447	.12485
.12000	.12401	.12439	.12477	.12514	.12552	.12590	.12629	.12667	.12706	.12745
.12250	.12657	.12694	.12733	.12771	.12809	.12848	.12887	.12926	.12965	.13004
.12500	.12912	.12950	.12989	.13027	.13066	.13105	.13145	.13184	.13224	.13264
.12750	.13167	.13206	.13245	.13284	.13324	.13363	.13403	.13443	.13483	.13523
.13000	.13422	.13461	.13501	.13541	.13581	.13621	.13661	.13702	.13742	.13783
.13250	.13677	.13717	.13757	.13798	.13838	.13879	.13919	.13960	.14002	.14043
.13500	.13933	.13973	.14014	.14054	.14095	.14136	.14178	.14219	.14261	.14303
.13750	.14188	.14229	.14270	.14311	.14353	.14394	.14436	.14478	.14521	.14563
.14000	.14443	.14485	.14526	.14568	.14610	.14652	.14695	.14737	.14780	.14823
.14250	.14699	.14741	.14783	.14825	.14868	.14910	.14953	.14996	.15040	.15083
.14500	.14954	.14997	.15039	.15082	.15125	.15169	.15212	.15256	.15299	.15344
.14750	.15210	.15253	.15296	.15339	.15383	.15427	.15471	.15515	.15559	.15604
.15000	.15465	.15509	.15553	.15597	.15641	.15685	.15729	.15774	.15819	.15864
.15250	.15721	.15765	.15809	.15854	.15898	.15943	.15988	.16034	.16079	.16125
.15500	.15977	.16021	.16066	.16111	.16156	.16202	.16247	.16293	.16339	.16385
.15750	.16232	.16278	.16323	.16368	.16414	.16460	.16506	.16553	.16599	.16646
.16000	.16488	.16534	.16580	.16626	.16672	.16719	.16765	.16812	.16859	.16907
.16250	.16744	.16790	.16837	.16883	.16930	.16977	.17024	.17072	.17120	.17168
.16500	.17000	.17047	.17094	.17141	.17188	.17236	.17284	.17332	.17380	.17428
.16750	.17256	.17303	.17350	.17398	.17446	.17494	.17543	.17591	.17640	.17689
.17000	.17512	.17559	.17608	.17656	.17704	.17753	.17802	.17851	.17901	.17950
.17250	.17768	.17816	.17865	.17913	.17963	.18012	.18061	.18111	.18161	.18212
.17500	.18024	.18072	.18122	.18171	.18221	.18271	.18321	.18371	.18422	.18473
.17750	.18280	.18329	.18379	.18429	.18479	.18530	.18580	.18631	.18682	.18734
.18000	.18536	.18586	.18636	.18687	.18737	.18788	.18840	.18891	.18943	.18995
.18250	.18792	.18842	.18893	.18944	.18996	.19047	.19099	.19151	.19204	.19257
.18500	.19048	.19099	.19150	.19202	.19254	.19306	.19359	.19412	.19465	.19518
.18750	.19304	.19356	.19408	.19460	.19513	.19565	.19619	.19672	.19726	.19779
.19000	.19560	.19612	.19665	.19718	.19771	.19825	.19878	.19932	.19986	.20041
.19250	.19816	.19869	.19922	.19976	.20030	.20084	.20138	.20193	.20247	.20303
.19500	.20072	.20126	.20180	.20234	.20288	.20343	.20398	.20453	.20508	.20564
.19750	.20329	.20383	.20437	.20492	.20547	.20602	.20658	.20713	.20769	.20826
.20000	.20585	.20640	.20695	.20750	.20806	.20861	.20918	.20974	.21031	.21088
.20250	.20841	.20897	.20952	.21008	.21064	.21121	.21177	.21234	.21292	.21349
.20500	.21098	.21154	.21210	.21266	.21323	.21380	.21437	.21495	.21553	.21611
.20750	.21354	.21411	.21467	.21524	.21582	.21639	.21697	.21756	.21814	.21873

ANNUAL PERCENTAGE RATE TABLES: TERM OF MORTGAGE: 300 MONTHS

POINTS CHARGED

INTEREST RATE	.05250	.05500	.05750	.06000	.06250	.06500	.06750	.07000	.07250	.07500
.07000	.07607	.07637	.07667	.07698	.07728	.07759	.07790	.07821	.07852	.07883
.07250	.07864	.07895	.07926	.07957	.07988	.08019	.08050	.08081	.08113	.08144
.07500	.08122	.08153	.08184	.08216	.08247	.08279	.08310	.08342	.08374	.08406
.07750	.08380	.08412	.08443	.08475	.08507	.08539	.08571	.08603	.08635	.08668
.08000	.08638	.08670	.08702	.08734	.08767	.08799	.08831	.08864	.08897	.08930
.08250	.08897	.08929	.08961	.08994	.09027	.09059	.09092	.09125	.09159	.09192
.08500	.09155	.09188	.09221	.09254	.09287	.09320	.09353	.09387	.09420	.09454
.08750	.09414	.09447	.09480	.09513	.09547	.09580	.09614	.09648	.09682	.09717
.09000	.09672	.09706	.09739	.09773	.09807	.09841	.09876	.09910	.09945	.09979
.09250	.09931	.09965	.09999	.10033	.10068	.10102	.10137	.10172	.10207	.10242
.09500	.10190	.10224	.10259	.10293	.10328	.10363	.10398	.10434	.10469	.10505
.09750	.10449	.10483	.10519	.10554	.10589	.10625	.10660	.10696	.10732	.10768
.10000	.10708	.10743	.10778	.10814	.10850	.10886	.10922	.10958	.10995	.11031
.10250	.10967	.11003	.11039	.11075	.11111	.11147	.11184	.11221	.11258	.11295
.10500	.11226	.11262	.11299	.11335	.11372	.11409	.11446	.11483	.11521	.11558
.10750	.11485	.11522	.11559	.11596	.11633	.11671	.11708	.11746	.11784	.11822
.11000	.11745	.11782	.11819	.11857	.11895	.11933	.11971	.12009	.12047	.12086
.11250	.12004	.12042	.12080	.12118	.12156	.12195	.12233	.12272	.12311	.12350
.11500	.12264	.12302	.12341	.12379	.12418	.12457	.12496	.12535	.12575	.12614
.11750	.12524	.12563	.12601	.12640	.12680	.12719	.12759	.12798	.12838	.12879
.12000	.12784	.12823	.12862	.12902	.12942	.12982	.13022	.13062	.13102	.13143
.12250	.13044	.13083	.13123	.13163	.13204	.13244	.13285	.13325	.13367	.13408
.12500	.13304	.13344	.13384	.13425	.13466	.13507	.13548	.13589	.13631	.13672
.12750	.13564	.13605	.13646	.13687	.13728	.13769	.13811	.13853	.13895	.13937
.13000	.13824	.13865	.13907	.13949	.13990	.14032	.14075	.14117	.14160	.14203
.13250	.14085	.14126	.14168	.14210	.14253	.14295	.14338	.14381	.14424	.14468
.13500	.14345	.14387	.14430	.14473	.14515	.14559	.14602	.14645	.14689	.14733
.13750	.14606	.14648	.14691	.14735	.14778	.14822	.14866	.14910	.14954	.14999
.14000	.14866	.14910	.14953	.14997	.15041	.15085	.15130	.15174	.15219	.15264
.14250	.15127	.15171	.15215	.15259	.15304	.15349	.15394	.15439	.15484	.15530
.14500	.15388	.15432	.15477	.15522	.15567	.15612	.15658	.15704	.15750	.15796
.14750	.15649	.15694	.15739	.15784	.15830	.15876	.15922	.15968	.16015	.16062
.15000	.15910	.15955	.16001	.16047	.16093	.16140	.16187	.16233	.16281	.16328
.15250	.16171	.16217	.16263	.16310	.16357	.16404	.16451	.16499	.16546	.16594
.15500	.16432	.16479	.16526	.16573	.16620	.16668	.16716	.16764	.16812	.16861
.15750	.16693	.16740	.16788	.16836	.16884	.16932	.16980	.17029	.17078	.17127
.16000	.16954	.17002	.17050	.17099	.17147	.17196	.17245	.17294	.17344	.17394
.16250	.17216	.17264	.17313	.17362	.17411	.17460	.17510	.17560	.17610	.17660
.16500	.17477	.17526	.17576	.17625	.17675	.17725	.17775	.17826	.17876	.17927
.16750	.17739	.17788	.17838	.17888	.17939	.17989	.18040	.18091	.18143	.18194
.17000	.18000	.18051	.18101	.18152	.18203	.18254	.18305	.18357	.18409	.18461
.17250	.18262	.18313	.18364	.18415	.18467	.18519	.18571	.18623	.18676	.18728
.17500	.18524	.18575	.18627	.18679	.18731	.18783	.18836	.18889	.18942	.18996
.17750	.18786	.18838	.18890	.18942	.18995	.19048	.19101	.19155	.19209	.19263
.18000	.19048	.19100	.19153	.19206	.19259	.19313	.19367	.19421	.19476	.19530
.18250	.19309	.19363	.19416	.19470	.19524	.19578	.19633	.19687	.19743	.19798
.18500	.19571	.19625	.19679	.19734	.19788	.19843	.19898	.19954	.20010	.20066
.18750	.19834	.19888	.19943	.19998	.20053	.20108	.20164	.20220	.20277	.20333
.19000	.20096	.20151	.20206	.20262	.20317	.20374	.20430	.20487	.20544	.20601
.19250	.20358	.20414	.20469	.20526	.20582	.20639	.20696	.20753	.20811	.20869
.19500	.20620	.20676	.20733	.20790	.20847	.20904	.20962	.21020	.21078	.21137
.19750	.20882	.20939	.20997	.21054	.21112	.21170	.21228	.21287	.21346	.21405
.20000	.21145	.21202	.21260	.21318	.21377	.21435	.21494	.21554	.21613	.21673
.20250	.21407	.21465	.21524	.21583	.21642	.21701	.21761	.21821	.21881	.21941
.20500	.21670	.21728	.21788	.21847	.21907	.21967	.22027	.22087	.22148	.22210
.20750	.21932	.21992	.22051	.22111	.22172	.22232	.22293	.22355	.22416	.22478

ANNUAL PERCENTAGE RATE TABLES: TERM OF MORTGAGE: 300 MONTHS

INTEREST RATE	POINTS CHARGED .07750	.08000	.08250	.08500	.08750	.09000	.09250	.09500	.09750	.10000
.07000	.07914	.07946	.07978	.08009	.08041	.08073	.08106	.08138	.08170	.08203
.07250	.08176	.08208	.08240	.08272	.08305	.08337	.08370	.08403	.08436	.08469
.07500	.08438	.08471	.08503	.08536	.08569	.08601	.08635	.08668	.08701	.08735
.07750	.08701	.08733	.08766	.08799	.08833	.08866	.08899	.08933	.08967	.09001
.08000	.08963	.08996	.09029	.09063	.09097	.09130	.09164	.09199	.09233	.09267
.08250	.09225	.09259	.09293	.09327	.09361	.09395	.09430	.09464	.09499	.09534
.08500	.09488	.09522	.09557	.09591	.09626	.09660	.09695	.09730	.09765	.09801
.08750	.09751	.09786	.09820	.09855	.09890	.09926	.09961	.09996	.10032	.10068
.09000	.10014	.10049	.10084	.10120	.10155	.10191	.10227	.10263	.10299	.10335
.09250	.10277	.10313	.10349	.10384	.10420	.10457	.10493	.10529	.10566	.10603
.09500	.10541	.10577	.10613	.10649	.10686	.10722	.10759	.10796	.10833	.10871
.09750	.10804	.10841	.10877	.10914	.10951	.10988	.11026	.11063	.11101	.11139
.10000	.11068	.11105	.11142	.11179	.11217	.11255	.11292	.11330	.11369	.11407
.10250	.11332	.11369	.11407	.11445	.11483	.11521	.11559	.11598	.11636	.11675
.10500	.11596	.11634	.11672	.11710	.11749	.11788	.11826	.11865	.11905	.11944
.10750	.11860	.11899	.11937	.11976	.12015	.12054	.12094	.12133	.12173	.12213
.11000	.12125	.12164	.12203	.12242	.12282	.12321	.12361	.12401	.12442	.12482
.11250	.12389	.12429	.12468	.12508	.12548	.12589	.12629	.12670	.12710	.12751
.11500	.12654	.12694	.12734	.12775	.12815	.12856	.12897	.12938	.12979	.13021
.11750	.12919	.12959	.13000	.13041	.13082	.13123	.13165	.13207	.13249	.13291
.12000	.13184	.13225	.13266	.13308	.13349	.13391	.13433	.13475	.13518	.13561
.12250	.13449	.13491	.13532	.13574	.13617	.13659	.13702	.13745	.13788	.13831
.12500	.13714	.13757	.13799	.13841	.13884	.13927	.13970	.14014	.14057	.14101
.12750	.13980	.14023	.14066	.14109	.14152	.14195	.14239	.14283	.14327	.14372
.13000	.14246	.14289	.14332	.14376	.14420	.14464	.14508	.14553	.14597	.14642
.13250	.14511	.14555	.14599	.14643	.14688	.14732	.14777	.14822	.14868	.14913
.13500	.14777	.14822	.14866	.14911	.14956	.15001	.15047	.15092	.15138	.15184
.13750	.15043	.15088	.15133	.15179	.15224	.15270	.15316	.15363	.15409	.15456
.14000	.15309	.15355	.15401	.15447	.15493	.15539	.15586	.15633	.15680	.15727
.14250	.15576	.15622	.15668	.15715	.15762	.15809	.15856	.15903	.15951	.15999
.14500	.15842	.15889	.15936	.15983	.16030	.16078	.16126	.16174	.16222	.16271
.14750	.16109	.16156	.16204	.16251	.16299	.16348	.16396	.16445	.16494	.16543
.15000	.16376	.16423	.16472	.16520	.16568	.16617	.16666	.16716	.16765	.16815
.15250	.16642	.16691	.16740	.16789	.16838	.16887	.16937	.16987	.17037	.17087
.15500	.16909	.16958	.17008	.17057	.17107	.17157	.17208	.17258	.17309	.17360
.15750	.17177	.17226	.17276	.17326	.17377	.17427	.17478	.17529	.17581	.17633
.16000	.17444	.17494	.17545	.17595	.17646	.17698	.17749	.17801	.17853	.17905
.16250	.17711	.17762	.17813	.17865	.17916	.17968	.18020	.18073	.18125	.18178
.16500	.17979	.18030	.18082	.18134	.18186	.18239	.18292	.18345	.18398	.18452
.16750	.18246	.18298	.18351	.18403	.18456	.18509	.18563	.18617	.18671	.18725
.17000	.18514	.18567	.18620	.18673	.18726	.18780	.18834	.18889	.18943	.18998
.17250	.18782	.18835	.18889	.18943	.18997	.19051	.19106	.19161	.19216	.19272
.17500	.19049	.19103	.19158	.19212	.19267	.19322	.19378	.19433	.19489	.19546
.17750	.19317	.19372	.19427	.19482	.19538	.19593	.19650	.19706	.19763	.19820
.18000	.19585	.19641	.19696	.19752	.19808	.19865	.19922	.19979	.20036	.20094
.18250	.19854	.19910	.19966	.20022	.20079	.20136	.20194	.20251	.20309	.20368
.18500	.20122	.20178	.20235	.20293	.20350	.20408	.20466	.20524	.20583	.20642
.18750	.20390	.20448	.20505	.20563	.20621	.20679	.20738	.20797	.20857	.20916
.19000	.20659	.20717	.20775	.20833	.20892	.20951	.21011	.21070	.21130	.21191
.19250	.20927	.20986	.21045	.21104	.21163	.21223	.21283	.21344	.21404	.21465
.19500	.21196	.21255	.21315	.21374	.21435	.21495	.21556	.21617	.21678	.21740
.19750	.21465	.21524	.21585	.21645	.21706	.21767	.21829	.21890	.21952	.22015
.20000	.21733	.21794	.21855	.21916	.21977	.22039	.22101	.22164	.22227	.22290
.20250	.22002	.22063	.22125	.22187	.22249	.22312	.22374	.22438	.22501	.22565
.20500	.22271	.22333	.22395	.22458	.22521	.22584	.22647	.22711	.22775	.22840
.20750	.22540	.22603	.22666	.22729	.22792	.22856	.22920	.22985	.23050	.23115

ANNUAL PERCENTAGE RATE TABLES: TERM OF MORTGAGE: 300 MONTHS

POINTS CHARGED

INTEREST RATE	.10250	.10500	.10750	.11000	.11250	.11500	.11750	.12000	.12250	.12500
.07000	.08236	.08269	.08302	.08335	.08368	.08402	.08435	.08469	.08503	.08537
.07250	.08502	.08535	.08569	.08602	.08636	.08670	.08704	.08739	.08773	.08808
.07500	.08768	.08802	.08836	.08870	.08904	.08939	.08974	.09008	.09043	.09078
.07750	.09035	.09069	.09104	.09138	.09173	.09208	.09243	.09278	.09314	.09349
.08000	.09302	.09337	.09371	.09407	.09442	.09477	.09513	.09548	.09584	.09620
.08250	.09569	.09604	.09640	.09675	.09711	.09747	.09783	.09819	.09855	.09892
.08500	.09836	.09872	.09908	.09944	.09980	.10016	.10053	.10090	.10127	.10164
.08750	.10104	.10140	.10176	.10213	.10250	.10287	.10324	.10361	.10398	.10436
.09000	.10372	.10408	.10445	.10482	.10519	.10557	.10594	.10632	.10670	.10708
.09250	.10640	.10677	.10714	.10752	.10790	.10827	.10865	.10904	.10942	.10981
.09500	.10908	.10946	.10984	.11022	.11060	.11098	.11137	.11176	.11215	.11254
.09750	.11177	.11215	.11253	.11292	.11331	.11369	.11409	.11448	.11487	.11527
.10000	.11445	.11484	.11523	.11562	.11601	.11641	.11680	.11720	.11760	.11801
.10250	.11714	.11754	.11793	.11833	.11872	.11912	.11953	.11993	.12034	.12074
.10500	.11984	.12023	.12063	.12103	.12144	.12184	.12225	.12266	.12307	.12348
.10750	.12253	.12293	.12334	.12375	.12415	.12457	.12498	.12539	.12581	.12623
.11000	.12523	.12564	.12605	.12646	.12687	.12729	.12771	.12813	.12855	.12898
.11250	.12793	.12834	.12876	.12917	.12959	.13002	.13044	.13087	.13129	.13173
.11500	.13063	.13105	.13147	.13189	.13232	.13274	.13317	.13361	.13404	.13448
.11750	.13333	.13375	.13418	.13461	.13504	.13548	.13591	.13635	.13679	.13723
.12000	.13603	.13647	.13690	.13733	.13777	.13821	.13865	.13910	.13954	.13999
.12250	.13874	.13918	.13962	.14006	.14050	.14095	.14139	.14184	.14230	.14275
.12500	.14145	.14189	.14234	.14279	.14323	.14369	.14414	.14459	.14505	.14551
.12750	.14416	.14461	.14506	.14551	.14597	.14643	.14689	.14735	.14781	.14828
.13000	.14688	.14733	.14779	.14825	.14871	.14917	.14964	.15010	.15057	.15105
.13250	.14959	.15005	.15051	.15098	.15145	.15191	.15239	.15286	.15334	.15382
.13500	.15231	.15277	.15324	.15371	.15419	.15466	.15514	.15562	.15610	.15659
.13750	.15503	.15550	.15597	.15645	.15693	.15741	.15790	.15838	.15887	.15936
.14000	.15775	.15823	.15871	.15919	.15968	.16016	.16066	.16115	.16164	.16214
.14250	.16047	.16096	.16144	.16193	.16242	.16292	.16342	.16392	.16442	.16492
.14500	.16320	.16369	.16418	.16468	.16517	.16568	.16618	.16668	.16719	.16770
.14750	.16592	.16642	.16692	.16742	.16793	.16843	.16894	.16946	.16997	.17049
.15000	.16865	.16915	.16966	.17017	.17068	.17119	.17171	.17223	.17275	.17328
.15250	.17138	.17189	.17240	.17292	.17344	.17396	.17448	.17500	.17553	.17606
.15500	.17411	.17463	.17515	.17567	.17619	.17672	.17725	.17778	.17832	.17886
.15750	.17685	.17737	.17789	.17842	.17895	.17949	.18002	.18056	.18110	.18165
.16000	.17958	.18011	.18064	.18118	.18171	.18225	.18280	.18334	.18389	.18444
.16250	.18232	.18285	.18339	.18393	.18448	.18502	.18557	.18613	.18668	.18724
.16500	.18506	.18560	.18614	.18669	.18724	.18780	.18835	.18891	.18947	.19004
.16750	.18780	.18834	.18890	.18945	.19001	.19057	.19113	.19170	.19227	.19284
.17000	.19054	.19109	.19165	.19221	.19278	.19334	.19391	.19449	.19506	.19564
.17250	.19328	.19384	.19441	.19497	.19555	.19612	.19670	.19728	.19786	.19845
.17500	.19602	.19659	.19716	.19774	.19832	.19890	.19948	.20007	.20066	.20125
.17750	.19877	.19934	.19992	.20050	.20109	.20168	.20227	.20286	.20346	.20406
.18000	.20152	.20210	.20268	.20327	.20386	.20446	.20506	.20566	.20626	.20687
.18250	.20426	.20485	.20544	.20604	.20664	.20724	.20785	.20845	.20907	.20968
.18500	.20701	.20761	.20821	.20881	.20942	.21003	.21064	.21125	.21187	.21249
.18750	.20976	.21037	.21097	.21158	.21219	.21281	.21343	.21405	.21468	.21531
.19000	.21251	.21312	.21374	.21435	.21497	.21560	.21622	.21685	.21749	.21812
.19250	.21527	.21588	.21650	.21713	.21776	.21839	.21902	.21966	.22030	.22094
.19500	.21802	.21865	.21927	.21990	.22054	.22118	.22182	.22246	.22311	.22376
.19750	.22078	.22141	.22204	.22268	.22332	.22397	.22461	.22527	.22592	.22658
.20000	.22353	.22417	.22481	.22546	.22611	.22676	.22741	.22807	.22874	.22940
.20250	.22629	.22694	.22758	.22824	.22889	.22955	.23021	.23088	.23155	.23223
.20500	.22905	.22970	.23036	.23102	.23168	.23235	.23302	.23369	.23437	.23505
.20750	.23181	.23247	.23313	.23380	.23447	.23514	.23582	.23650	.23719	.23787

ANNUAL PERCENTAGE RATE TABLES: TERM OF MORTGAGE: 300 MONTHS

POINTS CHARGED

INTEREST RATE	.12750	.13000	.13250	.13500	.13750	.14000	.14250	.14500	.14750	.15000
.07000	.08572	.08606	.08641	.08675	.08710	.08745	.08781	.08816	.08852	.08887
.07250	.08842	.08877	.08912	.08948	.08983	.09019	.09054	.09090	.09126	.09163
.07500	.09113	.09149	.09184	.09220	.09256	.09292	.09328	.09365	.09401	.09438
.07750	.09385	.09421	.09457	.09493	.09529	.09566	.09603	.09640	.09677	.09714
.08000	.09657	.09693	.09729	.09766	.09803	.09840	.09877	.09915	.09953	.09990
.08250	.09929	.09965	.10002	.10040	.10077	.10115	.10153	.10190	.10229	.10267
.08500	.10201	.10238	.10276	.10314	.10352	.10390	.10428	.10466	.10505	.10544
.08750	.10473	.10511	.10549	.10588	.10626	.10665	.10704	.10743	.10782	.10821
.09000	.10746	.10785	.10823	.10862	.10901	.10940	.10980	.11019	.11059	.11099
.09250	.11020	.11059	.11098	.11137	.11177	.11216	.11256	.11296	.11337	.11377
.09500	.11293	.11333	.11372	.11412	.11452	.11493	.11533	.11574	.11615	.11656
.09750	.11567	.11607	.11647	.11688	.11728	.11769	.11810	.11851	.11893	.11935
.10000	.11841	.11882	.11922	.11963	.12005	.12046	.12088	.12130	.12172	.12214
.10250	.12115	.12157	.12198	.12239	.12281	.12323	.12365	.12408	.12451	.12493
.10500	.12390	.12432	.12474	.12516	.12558	.12601	.12644	.12687	.12730	.12773
.10750	.12665	.12707	.12750	.12793	.12836	.12879	.12922	.12966	.13010	.13054
.11000	.12940	.12983	.13026	.13070	.13113	.13157	.13201	.13245	.13290	.13334
.11250	.13216	.13259	.13303	.13347	.13391	.13435	.13480	.13525	.13570	.13615
.11500	.13492	.13536	.13580	.13625	.13669	.13714	.13759	.13805	.13851	.13896
.11750	.13768	.13812	.13857	.13902	.13948	.13993	.14039	.14085	.14132	.14178
.12000	.14044	.14089	.14135	.14181	.14227	.14273	.14319	.14366	.14413	.14460
.12250	.14321	.14367	.14413	.14459	.14506	.14553	.14600	.14647	.14695	.14742
.12500	.14598	.14644	.14691	.14738	.14785	.14833	.14880	.14928	.14977	.15025
.12750	.14875	.14922	.14969	.15017	.15065	.15113	.15161	.15210	.15259	.15308
.13000	.15152	.15200	.15248	.15296	.15345	.15393	.15443	.15492	.15541	.15591
.13250	.15430	.15478	.15527	.15576	.15625	.15674	.15724	.15774	.15824	.15875
.13500	.15708	.15757	.15806	.15856	.15905	.15956	.16006	.16057	.16107	.16159
.13750	.15986	.16036	.16086	.16136	.16186	.16237	.16288	.16339	.16391	.16443
.14000	.16264	.16315	.16365	.16416	.16467	.16519	.16570	.16622	.16675	.16727
.14250	.16543	.16594	.16645	.16697	.16749	.16801	.16853	.16906	.16959	.17012
.14500	.16822	.16874	.16925	.16978	.17030	.17083	.17136	.17189	.17243	.17297
.14750	.17101	.17153	.17206	.17259	.17312	.17365	.17419	.17473	.17528	.17582
.15000	.17380	.17433	.17487	.17540	.17594	.17648	.17703	.17757	.17812	.17868
.15250	.17660	.17714	.17768	.17822	.17876	.17931	.17986	.18042	.18098	.18154
.15500	.17940	.17994	.18049	.18104	.18159	.18214	.18270	.18326	.18383	.18440
.15750	.18220	.18275	.18330	.18386	.18442	.18498	.18554	.18611	.18668	.18726
.16000	.18500	.18556	.18612	.18668	.18725	.18782	.18839	.18896	.18954	.19013
.16250	.18780	.18837	.18893	.18950	.19008	.19065	.19123	.19182	.19240	.19299
.16500	.19061	.19118	.19175	.19233	.19291	.19350	.19408	.19467	.19527	.19586
.16750	.19342	.19399	.19458	.19516	.19575	.19634	.19693	.19753	.19813	.19874
.17000	.19622	.19681	.19740	.19799	.19859	.19919	.19979	.20039	.20100	.20161
.17250	.19904	.19963	.20023	.20082	.20143	.20203	.20264	.20326	.20387	.20449
.17500	.20185	.20245	.20305	.20366	.20427	.20488	.20550	.20612	.20674	.20737
.17750	.20466	.20527	.20588	.20650	.20711	.20773	.20836	.20899	.20962	.21025
.18000	.20748	.20810	.20871	.20934	.20996	.21059	.21122	.21186	.21249	.21314
.18250	.21030	.21092	.21155	.21218	.21281	.21344	.21408	.21473	.21537	.21602
.18500	.21312	.21375	.21438	.21502	.21566	.21630	.21695	.21760	.21825	.21891
.18750	.21594	.21656	.21722	.21786	.21851	.21916	.21981	.22047	.22113	.22180
.19000	.21877	.21941	.22006	.22071	.22136	.22202	.22268	.22335	.22402	.22469
.19250	.22159	.22224	.22290	.22355	.22422	.22488	.22555	.22623	.22690	.22758
.19500	.22442	.22508	.22574	.22640	.22707	.22775	.22842	.22911	.22979	.23048
.19750	.22724	.22791	.22858	.22925	.22993	.23061	.23130	.23199	.23268	.23338
.20000	.23007	.23075	.23142	.23211	.23279	.23348	.23417	.23487	.23557	.23628
.20250	.23290	.23358	.23427	.23496	.23565	.23635	.23705	.23775	.23846	.23918
.20500	.23573	.23642	.23712	.23781	.23851	.23922	.23993	.24064	.24136	.24208
.20750	.23857	.23926	.23996	.24067	.24138	.24209	.24281	.24353	.24425	.24498

ANNUAL PERCENTAGE RATE TABLES: TERM OF MORTGAGE: 348 MONTHS

POINTS CHARGED

INTEREST RATE	.00250	.00500	.00750	.01000	.01250	.01500	.01750	.02000	.02250	.02500
.07000	.07025	.07051	.07076	.07102	.07128	.07153	.07179	.07205	.07232	.07258
.07250	.07276	.07301	.07327	.07353	.07379	.07406	.07432	.07458	.07485	.07512
.07500	.07526	.07552	.07579	.07605	.07631	.07658	.07685	.07712	.07738	.07765
.07750	.07776	.07803	.07830	.07856	.07883	.07910	.07937	.07965	.07992	.08019
.08000	.08027	.08054	.08081	.08108	.08135	.08163	.08190	.08218	.08246	.08273
.08250	.08277	.08305	.08332	.08360	.08387	.08415	.08443	.08471	.08499	.08528
.08500	.08528	.08555	.08583	.08611	.08639	.08668	.08696	.08724	.08753	.08782
.08750	.08778	.08806	.08834	.08863	.08891	.08920	.08949	.08978	.09007	.09036
.09000	.09028	.09057	.09086	.09115	.09144	.09173	.09202	.09231	.09261	.09290
.09250	.09279	.09308	.09337	.09366	.09396	.09425	.09455	.09484	.09514	.09544
.09500	.09529	.09559	.09588	.09618	.09648	.09678	.09708	.09738	.09768	.09799
.09750	.09780	.09810	.09840	.09870	.09900	.09930	.09961	.09991	.10022	.10053
.10000	.10030	.10060	.10091	.10121	.10152	.10183	.10214	.10245	.10276	.10308
.10250	.10281	.10311	.10342	.10373	.10404	.10436	.10467	.10499	.10530	.10562
.10500	.10531	.10562	.10594	.10625	.10657	.10688	.10720	.10752	.10784	.10817
.10750	.10782	.10813	.10845	.10877	.10909	.10941	.10973	.11006	.11039	.11071
.11000	.11032	.11064	.11096	.11129	.11161	.11194	.11227	.11260	.11293	.11326
.11250	.11282	.11315	.11348	.11381	.11414	.11447	.11480	.11513	.11547	.11581
.11500	.11533	.11566	.11599	.11632	.11666	.11700	.11733	.11767	.11801	.11836
.11750	.11783	.11817	.11851	.11884	.11918	.11952	.11987	.12021	.12056	.12090
.12000	.12034	.12068	.12102	.12136	.12171	.12205	.12240	.12275	.12310	.12345
.12250	.12284	.12319	.12353	.12388	.12423	.12458	.12493	.12529	.12564	.12600
.12500	.12535	.12570	.12605	.12640	.12676	.12711	.12747	.12783	.12819	.12855
.12750	.12785	.12821	.12856	.12892	.12928	.12964	.13000	.13037	.13073	.13110
.13000	.13036	.13072	.13108	.13144	.13181	.13217	.13254	.13291	.13328	.13365
.13250	.13286	.13323	.13359	.13396	.13433	.13470	.13507	.13545	.13583	.13620
.13500	.13537	.13574	.13611	.13648	.13686	.13723	.13761	.13799	.13837	.13876
.13750	.13787	.13825	.13862	.13900	.13938	.13976	.14015	.14053	.14092	.14131
.14000	.14038	.14076	.14114	.14152	.14191	.14229	.14268	.14307	.14347	.14386
.14250	.14288	.14327	.14365	.14404	.14443	.14483	.14522	.14562	.14601	.14641
.14500	.14539	.14578	.14617	.14656	.14696	.14736	.14776	.14816	.14856	.14897
.14750	.14789	.14829	.14869	.14909	.14949	.14989	.15029	.15070	.15111	.15152
.15000	.15040	.15080	.15120	.15161	.15201	.15242	.15283	.15324	.15366	.15407
.15250	.15290	.15331	.15372	.15413	.15454	.15495	.15537	.15579	.15621	.15663
.15500	.15541	.15582	.15623	.15665	.15707	.15749	.15791	.15833	.15876	.15918
.15750	.15791	.15833	.15875	.15917	.15959	.16002	.16045	.16087	.16131	.16174
.16000	.16042	.16084	.16127	.16169	.16212	.16255	.16298	.16342	.16385	.16429
.16250	.16293	.16335	.16378	.16421	.16465	.16508	.16552	.16596	.16640	.16685
.16500	.16543	.16586	.16630	.16674	.16718	.16762	.16806	.16851	.16896	.16941
.16750	.16794	.16838	.16882	.16926	.16970	.17015	.17060	.17105	.17151	.17196
.17000	.17044	.17089	.17133	.17178	.17223	.17268	.17314	.17360	.17406	.17452
.17250	.17295	.17340	.17385	.17430	.17476	.17522	.17568	.17614	.17661	.17708
.17500	.17545	.17591	.17637	.17683	.17729	.17775	.17822	.17869	.17916	.17963
.17750	.17796	.17842	.17888	.17935	.17982	.18029	.18076	.18123	.18171	.18219
.18000	.18046	.18093	.18140	.18187	.18235	.18282	.18330	.18378	.18426	.18475
.18250	.18297	.18344	.18392	.18439	.18487	.18536	.18584	.18633	.18681	.18731
.18500	.18548	.18595	.18643	.18692	.18740	.18789	.18838	.18887	.18937	.18986
.18750	.18798	.18847	.18895	.18944	.18993	.19042	.19092	.19142	.19192	.19242
.19000	.19049	.19098	.19147	.19196	.19246	.19296	.19346	.19397	.19447	.19498
.19250	.19299	.19349	.19399	.19449	.19499	.19549	.19600	.19651	.19703	.19754
.19500	.19550	.19600	.19650	.19701	.19752	.19803	.19854	.19906	.19958	.20010
.19750	.19800	.19851	.19902	.19953	.20005	.20057	.20108	.20161	.20213	.20266
.20000	.20051	.20102	.20154	.20206	.20258	.20310	.20363	.20415	.20469	.20522
.20250	.20302	.20354	.20406	.20458	.20511	.20564	.20617	.20670	.20724	.20778
.20500	.20552	.20605	.20657	.20710	.20764	.20817	.20871	.20925	.20979	.21034
.20750	.20803	.20856	.20909	.20963	.21017	.21071	.21125	.21180	.21235	.21290

ANNUAL PERCENTAGE RATE TABLES: TERM OF MORTGAGE: 348 MONTHS

POINTS CHARGED

INTEREST RATE	.02750	.03000	.03250	.03500	.03750	.04000	.04250	.04500	.04750	.05000
.07000	.07284	.07311	.07337	.07364	.07391	.07418	.07445	.07472	.07499	.07526
.07250	.07538	.07565	.07592	.07619	.07646	.07674	.07701	.07729	.07756	.07784
.07500	.07793	.07820	.07847	.07875	.07902	.07930	.07958	.07986	.08014	.08042
.07750	.08047	.08075	.08102	.08130	.08158	.08187	.08215	.08243	.08272	.08300
.08000	.08301	.08330	.08358	.08386	.08415	.08443	.08472	.08501	.08530	.08559
.08250	.08556	.08584	.08613	.08642	.08671	.08700	.08729	.08758	.08787	.08817
.08500	.08810	.08839	.08868	.08898	.08927	.08956	.08986	.09016	.09046	.09076
.08750	.09065	.09094	.09124	.09154	.09183	.09213	.09243	.09273	.09304	.09334
.09000	.09320	.09350	.09380	.09410	.09440	.09470	.09501	.09531	.09562	.09593
.09250	.09575	.09605	.09635	.09666	.09696	.09727	.09758	.09789	.09820	.09852
.09500	.09829	.09860	.09891	.09922	.09953	.09984	.10016	.10047	.10079	.10111
.09750	.10084	.10115	.10147	.10178	.10210	.10241	.10273	.10305	.10338	.10370
.10000	.10339	.10371	.10403	.10434	.10467	.10499	.10531	.10564	.10596	.10629
.10250	.10594	.10626	.10658	.10691	.10723	.10756	.10789	.10822	.10855	.10888
.10500	.10849	.10882	.10914	.10947	.10980	.11014	.11047	.11080	.11114	.11148
.10750	.11104	.11137	.11171	.11204	.11237	.11271	.11305	.11339	.11373	.11407
.11000	.11359	.11393	.11427	.11461	.11495	.11529	.11563	.11598	.11632	.11667
.11250	.11615	.11649	.11683	.11717	.11752	.11786	.11821	.11856	.11891	.11927
.11500	.11870	.11904	.11939	.11974	.12009	.12044	.12080	.12115	.12151	.12187
.11750	.12125	.12160	.12196	.12231	.12266	.12302	.12338	.12374	.12410	.12447
.12000	.12381	.12416	.12452	.12488	.12524	.12560	.12596	.12633	.12670	.12707
.12250	.12636	.12672	.12708	.12745	.12781	.12818	.12855	.12892	.12929	.12967
.12500	.12892	.12928	.12965	.13002	.13039	.13076	.13114	.13151	.13189	.13227
.12750	.13147	.13184	.13222	.13259	.13297	.13334	.13372	.13411	.13449	.13487
.13000	.13403	.13440	.13478	.13516	.13554	.13593	.13631	.13670	.13709	.13748
.13250	.13658	.13697	.13735	.13773	.13812	.13851	.13890	.13929	.13969	.14008
.13500	.13914	.13953	.13992	.14031	.14070	.14109	.14149	.14189	.14229	.14269
.13750	.14170	.14209	.14248	.14288	.14328	.14368	.14408	.14448	.14489	.14530
.14000	.14426	.14465	.14505	.14546	.14586	.14626	.14667	.14708	.14749	.14791
.14250	.14681	.14722	.14762	.14803	.14844	.14885	.14926	.14968	.15010	.15051
.14500	.14937	.14978	.15019	.15061	.15102	.15144	.15186	.15228	.15270	.15312
.14750	.15193	.15235	.15276	.15318	.15360	.15402	.15445	.15488	.15530	.15573
.15000	.15449	.15491	.15533	.15576	.15618	.15661	.15704	.15747	.15791	.15835
.15250	.15705	.15748	.15791	.15833	.15877	.15920	.15964	.16007	.16052	.16096
.15500	.15961	.16004	.16048	.16091	.16135	.16179	.16223	.16268	.16312	.16357
.15750	.16217	.16261	.16305	.16349	.16393	.16438	.16483	.16528	.16573	.16618
.16000	.16473	.16518	.16562	.16607	.16652	.16697	.16742	.16788	.16834	.16880
.16250	.16730	.16774	.16819	.16865	.16910	.16956	.17002	.17048	.17095	.17141
.16500	.16986	.17031	.17077	.17123	.17169	.17215	.17262	.17309	.17356	.17403
.16750	.17242	.17288	.17334	.17381	.17427	.17474	.17522	.17569	.17617	.17664
.17000	.17498	.17545	.17592	.17639	.17686	.17734	.17781	.17829	.17878	.17926
.17250	.17754	.17802	.17849	.17897	.17945	.17993	.18041	.18090	.18139	.18188
.17500	.18011	.18059	.18107	.18155	.18203	.18252	.18301	.18350	.18400	.18450
.17750	.18267	.18316	.18364	.18413	.18462	.18512	.18561	.18611	.18661	.18711
.18000	.18524	.18573	.18622	.18671	.18721	.18771	.18821	.18872	.18922	.18973
.18250	.18780	.18830	.18879	.18929	.18980	.19030	.19081	.19132	.19184	.19235
.18500	.19036	.19087	.19137	.19188	.19239	.19290	.19341	.19393	.19445	.19497
.18750	.19293	.19344	.19395	.19446	.19498	.19549	.19602	.19654	.19706	.19759
.19000	.19549	.19601	.19652	.19704	.19757	.19809	.19862	.19915	.19968	.20021
.19250	.19806	.19858	.19910	.19963	.20015	.20069	.20122	.20176	.20229	.20284
.19500	.20062	.20115	.20168	.20221	.20275	.20328	.20382	.20436	.20491	.20546
.19750	.20319	.20372	.20426	.20479	.20534	.20588	.20642	.20697	.20753	.20808
.20000	.20575	.20629	.20683	.20738	.20793	.20848	.20903	.20958	.21014	.21070
.20250	.20832	.20887	.20941	.20996	.21052	.21107	.21163	.21219	.21276	.21333
.20500	.21089	.21144	.21199	.21255	.21311	.21367	.21424	.21480	.21538	.21595
.20750	.21345	.21401	.21457	.21513	.21570	.21627	.21684	.21741	.21799	.21857

ANNUAL PERCENTAGE RATE TABLES: TERM OF MORTGAGE: 348 MONTHS

INTEREST RATE	POINTS CHARGED .05250	.05500	.05750	.06000	.06250	.06500	.06750	.07000	.07250	.07500
.07000	.07554	.07581	.07609	.07637	.07665	.07693	.07721	.07749	.07778	.07806
.07250	.07812	.07840	.07868	.07897	.07925	.07953	.07982	.08011	.08040	.08069
.07500	.08071	.08099	.08128	.08156	.08185	.08214	.08243	.08272	.08302	.08331
.07750	.08329	.08358	.08387	.08416	.08445	.08475	.08504	.08534	.08564	.08594
.08000	.08588	.08617	.08647	.08676	.08706	.08736	.08766	.08796	.08826	.08856
.08250	.08847	.08876	.08906	.08936	.08967	.08997	.09027	.09058	.09089	.09119
.08500	.09106	.09136	.09166	.09197	.09227	.09258	.09289	.09320	.09351	.09383
.08750	.09365	.09395	.09426	.09457	.09488	.09520	.09551	.09582	.09614	.09646
.09000	.09624	.09655	.09686	.09718	.09749	.09781	.09813	.09845	.09877	.09909
.09250	.09883	.09915	.09947	.09979	.10011	.10043	.10075	.10108	.10140	.10173
.09500	.10143	.10175	.10207	.10239	.10272	.10305	.10338	.10371	.10404	.10437
.09750	.10402	.10435	.10468	.10500	.10534	.10567	.10600	.10634	.10667	.10701
.10000	.10662	.10695	.10728	.10762	.10795	.10829	.10863	.10897	.10931	.10965
.10250	.10922	.10955	.10989	.11023	.11057	.11091	.11126	.11160	.11195	.11230
.10500	.11182	.11216	.11250	.11284	.11319	.11354	.11389	.11424	.11459	.11494
.10750	.11442	.11476	.11511	.11546	.11581	.11616	.11652	.11687	.11723	.11759
.11000	.11702	.11737	.11772	.11808	.11843	.11879	.11915	.11951	.11988	.12024
.11250	.11962	.11998	.12034	.12070	.12106	.12142	.12179	.12215	.12252	.12289
.11500	.12223	.12259	.12295	.12332	.12368	.12405	.12442	.12479	.12517	.12554
.11750	.12483	.12520	.12557	.12594	.12631	.12668	.12706	.12744	.12782	.12820
.12000	.12744	.12781	.12818	.12856	.12894	.12932	.12970	.13008	.13047	.13085
.12250	.13004	.13042	.13080	.13118	.13157	.13195	.13234	.13273	.13312	.13351
.12500	.13265	.13304	.13342	.13381	.13420	.13459	.13498	.13537	.13577	.13617
.12750	.13526	.13565	.13604	.13643	.13683	.13722	.13762	.13802	.13843	.13883
.13000	.13787	.13827	.13866	.13906	.13946	.13986	.14027	.14067	.14108	.14149
.13250	.14048	.14088	.14128	.14169	.14209	.14250	.14291	.14332	.14374	.14415
.13500	.14309	.14350	.14391	.14432	.14473	.14514	.14556	.14598	.14640	.14682
.13750	.14571	.14612	.14653	.14695	.14737	.14778	.14821	.14863	.14906	.14948
.14000	.14832	.14874	.14916	.14958	.15000	.15043	.15086	.15129	.15172	.15215
.14250	.15094	.15136	.15178	.15221	.15264	.15307	.15351	.15394	.15438	.15482
.14500	.15355	.15398	.15441	.15484	.15528	.15572	.15616	.15660	.15704	.15749
.14750	.15617	.15660	.15704	.15748	.15792	.15836	.15881	.15926	.15971	.16016
.15000	.15878	.15923	.15967	.16011	.16056	.16101	.16146	.16192	.16237	.16283
.15250	.16140	.16185	.16230	.16275	.16320	.16366	.16412	.16458	.16504	.16551
.15500	.16402	.16447	.16493	.16539	.16585	.16631	.16677	.16724	.16771	.16818
.15750	.16664	.16710	.16756	.16802	.16849	.16896	.16943	.16990	.17038	.17085
.16000	.16926	.16973	.17019	.17066	.17113	.17161	.17209	.17257	.17305	.17353
.16250	.17188	.17235	.17283	.17330	.17378	.17426	.17474	.17523	.17572	.17621
.16500	.17450	.17498	.17546	.17594	.17643	.17691	.17740	.17790	.17839	.17889
.16750	.17713	.17761	.17810	.17858	.17907	.17957	.18006	.18056	.18106	.18157
.17000	.17975	.18024	.18073	.18123	.18172	.18222	.18272	.18323	.18374	.18425
.17250	.18237	.18287	.18337	.18387	.18437	.18488	.18539	.18590	.18641	.18693
.17500	.18500	.18550	.18600	.18651	.18702	.18753	.18805	.18857	.18909	.18961
.17750	.18762	.18813	.18864	.18915	.18967	.19019	.19071	.19124	.19176	.19229
.18000	.19025	.19076	.19128	.19180	.19232	.19285	.19338	.19391	.19444	.19498
.18250	.19287	.19339	.19392	.19444	.19497	.19551	.19604	.19658	.19712	.19766
.18500	.19550	.19603	.19656	.19709	.19763	.19816	.19871	.19925	.19980	.20035
.18750	.19813	.19866	.19920	.19974	.20028	.20082	.20137	.20192	.20248	.20303
.19000	.20075	.20129	.20184	.20238	.20293	.20348	.20404	.20460	.20516	.20572
.19250	.20338	.20393	.20448	.20503	.20559	.20614	.20671	.20727	.20784	.20841
.19500	.20601	.20656	.20712	.20768	.20824	.20881	.20937	.20994	.21052	.21110
.19750	.20864	.20920	.20976	.21033	.21090	.21147	.21204	.21262	.21320	.21378
.20000	.21127	.21183	.21240	.21298	.21355	.21413	.21471	.21530	.21588	.21647
.20250	.21390	.21447	.21505	.21562	.21621	.21679	.21738	.21797	.21857	.21916
.20500	.21653	.21711	.21769	.21827	.21886	.21946	.22005	.22065	.22125	.22186
.20750	.21916	.21974	.22033	.22093	.22152	.22212	.22272	.22333	.22393	.22455

ANNUAL PERCENTAGE RATE TABLES: TERM OF MORTGAGE: 348 MONTHS

POINTS CHARGED

INTEREST RATE	.07750	.08000	.08250	.08500	.08750	.09000	.09250	.09500	.09750	.10000
.07000	.07835	.07864	.07893	.07922	.07951	.07981	.08010	.08040	.08069	.08099
.07250	.08098	.08127	.08156	.08186	.08216	.08245	.08275	.08305	.08336	.08366
.07500	.08361	.08390	.08420	.08450	.08480	.08511	.08541	.08572	.08602	.08633
.07750	.08624	.08654	.08684	.08715	.08745	.08776	.08807	.08838	.08869	.08900
.08000	.08887	.08918	.08948	.08979	.09010	.09042	.09073	.09104	.09136	.09168
.08250	.09150	.09182	.09213	.09244	.09276	.09307	.09339	.09371	.09403	.09436
.08500	.09414	.09446	.09477	.09509	.09541	.09574	.09606	.09638	.09671	.09704
.08750	.09678	.09710	.09742	.09775	.09807	.09840	.09873	.09906	.09939	.09972
.09000	.09942	.09974	.10007	.10040	.10073	.10106	.10140	.10173	.10207	.10241
.09250	.10206	.10239	.10272	.10306	.10339	.10373	.10407	.10441	.10475	.10510
.09500	.10470	.10504	.10538	.10572	.10606	.10640	.10675	.10709	.10744	.10779
.09750	.10735	.10769	.10803	.10838	.10873	.10907	.10942	.10977	.11013	.11048
.10000	.11000	.11034	.11069	.11104	.11139	.11175	.11210	.11246	.11282	.11318
.10250	.11265	.11300	.11335	.11371	.11406	.11442	.11478	.11515	.11551	.11588
.10500	.11530	.11566	.11601	.11638	.11674	.11710	.11747	.11784	.11820	.11858
.10750	.11795	.11831	.11868	.11904	.11941	.11978	.12015	.12053	.12090	.12128
.11000	.12061	.12097	.12134	.12172	.12209	.12247	.12284	.12322	.12360	.12398
.11250	.12326	.12364	.12401	.12439	.12477	.12515	.12553	.12592	.12630	.12669
.11500	.12592	.12630	.12668	.12706	.12745	.12784	.12822	.12862	.12901	.12940
.11750	.12858	.12897	.12935	.12974	.13013	.13052	.13092	.13132	.13171	.13211
.12000	.13124	.13163	.13203	.13242	.13282	.13321	.13362	.13402	.13442	.13483
.12250	.13391	.13430	.13470	.13510	.13550	.13591	.13631	.13672	.13713	.13754
.12500	.13657	.13697	.13738	.13778	.13819	.13860	.13901	.13943	.13984	.14026
.12750	.13924	.13964	.14005	.14047	.14088	.14130	.14172	.14214	.14256	.14298
.13000	.14190	.14232	.14273	.14315	.14357	.14399	.14442	.14485	.14527	.14571
.13250	.14457	.14499	.14541	.14584	.14627	.14669	.14712	.14756	.14799	.14843
.13500	.14724	.14767	.14810	.14853	.14896	.14940	.14983	.15027	.15071	.15116
.13750	.14991	.15035	.15078	.15122	.15166	.15210	.15254	.15299	.15343	.15388
.14000	.15259	.15303	.15347	.15391	.15435	.15480	.15525	.15570	.15616	.15661
.14250	.15526	.15571	.15615	.15660	.15705	.15751	.15796	.15842	.15888	.15935
.14500	.15794	.15839	.15884	.15930	.15976	.16022	.16068	.16114	.16161	.16208
.14750	.16061	.16107	.16153	.16199	.16246	.16292	.16339	.16386	.16434	.16481
.15000	.16329	.16376	.16422	.16469	.16516	.16563	.16611	.16659	.16707	.16755
.15250	.16597	.16644	.16691	.16739	.16787	.16835	.16883	.16931	.16980	.17029
.15500	.16865	.16913	.16961	.17009	.17057	.17106	.17155	.17204	.17253	.17303
.15750	.17134	.17182	.17230	.17279	.17328	.17377	.17427	.17477	.17527	.17577
.16000	.17402	.17451	.17500	.17549	.17599	.17649	.17699	.17750	.17800	.17851
.16250	.17670	.17720	.17770	.17820	.17870	.17921	.17971	.18023	.18074	.18126
.16500	.17939	.17989	.18039	.18090	.18141	.18192	.18244	.18296	.18348	.18400
.16750	.18207	.18258	.18309	.18361	.18412	.18464	.18517	.18569	.18622	.18675
.17000	.18476	.18528	.18579	.18631	.18684	.18736	.18789	.18842	.18896	.18950
.17250	.18745	.18797	.18849	.18902	.18955	.19009	.19062	.19116	.19170	.19225
.17500	.19014	.19067	.19120	.19173	.19227	.19281	.19335	.19390	.19445	.19500
.17750	.19283	.19336	.19390	.19444	.19498	.19553	.19608	.19663	.19719	.19775
.18000	.19552	.19606	.19660	.19715	.19770	.19826	.19881	.19937	.19994	.20050
.18250	.19821	.19876	.19931	.19986	.20042	.20098	.20155	.20211	.20268	.20325
.18500	.20090	.20146	.20201	.20258	.20314	.20371	.20428	.20485	.20543	.20601
.18750	.20359	.20416	.20472	.20529	.20586	.20644	.20701	.20759	.20818	.20877
.19000	.20629	.20686	.20743	.20800	.20858	.20916	.20975	.21034	.21093	.21152
.19250	.20898	.20956	.21014	.21072	.21130	.21189	.21249	.21308	.21368	.21428
.19500	.21168	.21226	.21285	.21344	.21403	.21462	.21522	.21582	.21643	.21704
.19750	.21437	.21496	.21556	.21615	.21675	.21735	.21796	.21857	.21918	.21980
.20000	.21707	.21767	.21827	.21887	.21948	.22009	.22070	.22132	.22193	.22256
.20250	.21977	.22037	.22098	.22159	.22220	.22282	.22344	.22406	.22469	.22532
.20500	.22246	.22307	.22369	.22431	.22493	.22555	.22618	.22681	.22744	.22808
.20750	.22516	.22578	.22640	.22702	.22765	.22828	.22892	.22956	.23020	.23084

ANNUAL PERCENTAGE RATE TABLES: TERM OF MORTGAGE: 348 MONTHS

POINTS CHARGED

INTEREST RATE	.10250	.10500	.10750	.11000	.11250	.11500	.11750	.12000	.12250	.12500
.07000	.08129	.08159	.08190	.08220	.08251	.08281	.08312	.08343	.08374	.08406
.07250	.08396	.08427	.08458	.08489	.08520	.08551	.08582	.08614	.08645	.08677
.07500	.08664	.08695	.08726	.08758	.08789	.08821	.08853	.08885	.08917	.08949
.07750	.08932	.08963	.08995	.09027	.09059	.09091	.09124	.09156	.09189	.09222
.08000	.09200	.09232	.09264	.09297	.09329	.09362	.09395	.09428	.09461	.09494
.08250	.09468	.09501	.09534	.09566	.09600	.09633	.09666	.09700	.09733	.09767
.08500	.09737	.09770	.09803	.09837	.09870	.09904	.09938	.09972	.10006	.10041
.08750	.10006	.10039	.10073	.10107	.10141	.10175	.10210	.10245	.10279	.10314
.09000	.10275	.10309	.10343	.10378	.10412	.10447	.10482	.10517	.10553	.10588
.09250	.10544	.10579	.10614	.10649	.10684	.10719	.10755	.10791	.10827	.10863
.09500	.10814	.10849	.10884	.10920	.10956	.10992	.11028	.11064	.11101	.11137
.09750	.11084	.11120	.11156	.11192	.11228	.11264	.11301	.11338	.11375	.11412
.10000	.11354	.11390	.11427	.11463	.11500	.11537	.11575	.11612	.11650	.11688
.10250	.11624	.11661	.11698	.11736	.11773	.11811	.11849	.11887	.11925	.11963
.10500	.11895	.11932	.11970	.12008	.12046	.12084	.12123	.12161	.12200	.12239
.10750	.12166	.12204	.12242	.12281	.12319	.12358	.12397	.12436	.12476	.12515
.11000	.12437	.12476	.12514	.12553	.12593	.12632	.12672	.12712	.12752	.12792
.11250	.12708	.12748	.12787	.12827	.12866	.12906	.12947	.12987	.13028	.13069
.11500	.12980	.13020	.13060	.13100	.13140	.13181	.13222	.13263	.13304	.13346
.11750	.13252	.13292	.13333	.13374	.13415	.13456	.13497	.13539	.13581	.13623
.12000	.13524	.13565	.13606	.13647	.13689	.13731	.13773	.13816	.13858	.13901
.12250	.13796	.13838	.13880	.13922	.13964	.14006	.14049	.14092	.14135	.14179
.12500	.14068	.14111	.14153	.14196	.14239	.14282	.14325	.14369	.14413	.14457
.12750	.14341	.14384	.14427	.14470	.14514	.14558	.14602	.14646	.14691	.14735
.13000	.14614	.14657	.14701	.14745	.14790	.14834	.14879	.14924	.14969	.15014
.13250	.14887	.14931	.14976	.15020	.15065	.15110	.15156	.15201	.15247	.15293
.13500	.15160	.15205	.15250	.15295	.15341	.15387	.15433	.15479	.15526	.15572
.13750	.15434	.15479	.15525	.15571	.15617	.15664	.15710	.15757	.15804	.15852
.14000	.15707	.15753	.15800	.15846	.15893	.15940	.15988	.16035	.16083	.16131
.14250	.15981	.16028	.16075	.16122	.16170	.16218	.16266	.16314	.16363	.16411
.14500	.16255	.16303	.16350	.16398	.16446	.16495	.16544	.16593	.16642	.16691
.14750	.16529	.16577	.16626	.16674	.16723	.16773	.16822	.16872	.16922	.16972
.15000	.16804	.16852	.16902	.16951	.17000	.17050	.17100	.17151	.17201	.17252
.15250	.17078	.17128	.17177	.17227	.17278	.17328	.17379	.17430	.17481	.17533
.15500	.17353	.17403	.17453	.17504	.17555	.17606	.17658	.17710	.17762	.17814
.15750	.17628	.17678	.17730	.17781	.17833	.17885	.17937	.17989	.18042	.18095
.16000	.17903	.17954	.18006	.18058	.18110	.18163	.18216	.18269	.18323	.18376
.16250	.18178	.18230	.18282	.18335	.18388	.18442	.18495	.18549	.18603	.18658
.16500	.18453	.18506	.18559	.18612	.18666	.18720	.18775	.18829	.18884	.18940
.16750	.18728	.18782	.18836	.18890	.18944	.18999	.19054	.19110	.19165	.19221
.17000	.19004	.19058	.19113	.19168	.19223	.19278	.19334	.19390	.19447	.19503
.17250	.19279	.19334	.19390	.19445	.19501	.19558	.19614	.19671	.19728	.19786
.17500	.19555	.19611	.19667	.19723	.19780	.19837	.19894	.19952	.20010	.20068
.17750	.19831	.19887	.19944	.20001	.20059	.20116	.20174	.20233	.20291	.20350
.18000	.20107	.20164	.20222	.20279	.20338	.20396	.20455	.20514	.20573	.20633
.18250	.20383	.20441	.20499	.20558	.20617	.20676	.20735	.20795	.20855	.20916
.18500	.20659	.20718	.20777	.20836	.20896	.20956	.21016	.21076	.21137	.21198
.18750	.20936	.20995	.21055	.21115	.21175	.21235	.21296	.21358	.21419	.21481
.19000	.21212	.21272	.21332	.21393	.21454	.21516	.21577	.21639	.21702	.21765
.19250	.21488	.21549	.21610	.21672	.21734	.21796	.21858	.21921	.21984	.22048
.19500	.21765	.21827	.21888	.21951	.22013	.22076	.22139	.22203	.22267	.22331
.19750	.22042	.22104	.22167	.22229	.22293	.22356	.22420	.22485	.22549	.22615
.20000	.22318	.22381	.22445	.22508	.22573	.22637	.22702	.22767	.22832	.22898
.20250	.22595	.22659	.22723	.22788	.22852	.22917	.22983	.23049	.23115	.23182
.20500	.22872	.22937	.23002	.23067	.23132	.23198	.23264	.23331	.23398	.23465
.20750	.23149	.23214	.23280	.23346	.23412	.23479	.23546	.23613	.23681	.23749

ANNUAL PERCENTAGE RATE TABLES: TERM OF MORTGAGE: 348 MONTHS

POINTS CHARGED

INTEREST RATE	.12750	.13000	.13250	.13500	.13750	.14000	.14250	.14500	.14750	.15000
.07000	.08437	.08469	.08500	.08532	.08564	.08596	.08629	.08661	.08694	.08727
.07250	.08709	.08741	.08773	.08806	.08838	.08871	.08904	.08937	.08970	.09003
.07500	.08982	.09014	.09047	.09080	.09113	.09146	.09180	.09213	.09247	.09281
.07750	.09254	.09288	.09321	.09354	.09388	.09422	.09456	.09490	.09524	.09558
.08000	.09528	.09561	.09595	.09629	.09663	.09698	.09732	.09767	.09802	.09837
.08250	.09801	.09835	.09870	.09904	.09939	.09974	.10009	.10044	.10080	.10115
.08500	.10075	.10110	.10145	.10180	.10215	.10251	.10286	.10322	.10358	.10394
.08750	.10349	.10385	.10420	.10456	.10492	.10528	.10564	.10600	.10637	.10673
.09000	.10624	.10660	.10696	.10732	.10768	.10805	.10842	.10879	.10916	.10953
.09250	.10899	.10935	.10972	.11009	.11046	.11083	.11120	.11158	.11196	.11233
.09500	.11174	.11211	.11248	.11286	.11323	.11361	.11399	.11437	.11476	.11514
.09750	.11450	.11487	.11525	.11563	.11601	.11640	.11678	.11717	.11756	.11795
.10000	.11726	.11764	.11802	.11841	.11880	.11919	.11958	.11997	.12037	.12076
.10250	.12002	.12041	.12080	.12119	.12158	.12198	.12238	.12278	.12318	.12358
.10500	.12278	.12318	.12357	.12397	.12437	.12477	.12518	.12558	.12599	.12640
.10750	.12555	.12595	.12635	.12676	.12717	.12757	.12798	.12840	.12881	.12923
.11000	.12832	.12873	.12914	.12955	.12996	.13038	.13079	.13121	.13163	.13206
.11250	.13110	.13151	.13193	.13234	.13276	.13318	.13361	.13403	.13446	.13489
.11500	.13387	.13429	.13472	.13514	.13556	.13599	.13642	.13686	.13729	.13773
.11750	.13666	.13708	.13751	.13794	.13837	.13881	.13924	.13968	.14012	.14057
.12000	.13944	.13987	.14030	.14074	.14118	.14162	.14207	.14251	.14296	.14341
.12250	.14222	.14266	.14310	.14355	.14399	.14444	.14489	.14534	.14580	.14626
.12500	.14501	.14546	.14591	.14636	.14681	.14726	.14772	.14818	.14864	.14911
.12750	.14780	.14826	.14871	.14917	.14963	.15009	.15055	.15102	.15149	.15196
.13000	.15060	.15106	.15152	.15198	.15245	.15292	.15339	.15386	.15434	.15482
.13250	.15339	.15386	.15433	.15480	.15527	.15575	.15623	.15671	.15719	.15768
.13500	.15619	.15667	.15714	.15762	.15810	.15858	.15907	.15955	.16004	.16054
.13750	.15899	.15947	.15996	.16044	.16093	.16142	.16191	.16240	.16290	.16340
.14000	.16180	.16228	.16277	.16326	.16376	.16426	.16476	.16526	.16576	.16627
.14250	.16460	.16510	.16559	.16609	.16659	.16710	.16760	.16811	.16863	.16914
.14500	.16741	.16791	.16842	.16892	.16943	.16994	.17046	.17097	.17149	.17202
.14750	.17022	.17073	.17124	.17175	.17227	.17279	.17331	.17383	.17436	.17489
.15000	.17303	.17355	.17407	.17459	.17511	.17564	.17617	.17670	.17723	.17777
.15250	.17585	.17637	.17690	.17742	.17795	.17849	.17902	.17956	.18011	.18065
.15500	.17867	.17920	.17973	.18026	.18080	.18134	.18189	.18243	.18298	.18354
.15750	.18148	.18202	.18256	.18310	.18365	.18420	.18475	.18530	.18586	.18642
.16000	.18430	.18485	.18540	.18595	.18650	.18705	.18761	.18818	.18874	.18931
.16250	.18713	.18768	.18823	.18879	.18935	.18991	.19048	.19105	.19162	.19220
.16500	.18995	.19051	.19107	.19164	.19220	.19278	.19335	.19393	.19451	.19509
.16750	.19278	.19334	.19391	.19448	.19506	.19564	.19622	.19681	.19739	.19799
.17000	.19560	.19618	.19675	.19733	.19792	.19850	.19909	.19969	.20028	.20088
.17250	.19843	.19901	.19960	.20019	.20078	.20137	.20197	.20257	.20317	.20378
.17500	.20126	.20185	.20244	.20304	.20364	.20424	.20485	.20545	.20607	.20668
.17750	.20410	.20469	.20529	.20589	.20650	.20711	.20772	.20834	.20896	.20958
.18000	.20693	.20753	.20814	.20875	.20937	.20998	.21060	.21123	.21186	.21249
.18250	.20976	.21038	.21099	.21161	.21223	.21286	.21349	.21412	.21475	.21539
.18500	.21260	.21322	.21384	.21447	.21510	.21573	.21637	.21701	.21765	.21830
.18750	.21544	.21606	.21670	.21733	.21797	.21861	.21925	.21990	.22055	.22121
.19000	.21828	.21891	.21955	.22019	.22084	.22149	.22214	.22279	.22346	.22412
.19250	.22112	.22176	.22240	.22305	.22371	.22436	.22503	.22569	.22636	.22703
.19500	.22396	.22461	.22526	.22592	.22658	.22725	.22791	.22859	.22926	.22994
.19750	.22680	.22746	.22812	.22878	.22945	.23013	.23080	.23148	.23217	.23286
.20000	.22964	.23031	.23098	.23165	.23233	.23301	.23369	.23438	.23508	.23577
.20250	.23249	.23316	.23384	.23452	.23520	.23589	.23659	.23728	.23798	.23869
.20500	.23533	.23601	.23670	.23739	.23808	.23878	.23948	.24019	.24089	.24161
.20750	.23818	.23887	.23956	.24026	.24096	.24166	.24237	.24309	.24380	.24453

ANNUAL PERCENTAGE RATE TABLES: TERM OF MORTGAGE: 360 MONTHS

POINTS CHARGED

INTEREST RATE	.00250	.00500	.00750	.01000	.01250	.01500	.01750	.02000	.02250	.02500
.07000	.07025	.07050	.07075	.07100	.07125	.07150	.07176	.07201	.07227	.07253
.07250	.07275	.07300	.07326	.07351	.07377	.07403	.07429	.07454	.07480	.07507
.07500	.07526	.07551	.07577	.07603	.07629	.07655	.07681	.07708	.07734	.07761
.07750	.07776	.07802	.07828	.07855	.07881	.07907	.07934	.07961	.07988	.08015
.08000	.08026	.08053	.08079	.08106	.08133	.08160	.08187	.08214	.08241	.08269
.08250	.08277	.08304	.08331	.08358	.08385	.08412	.08440	.08467	.08495	.08523
.08500	.08527	.08554	.08582	.08609	.08637	.08665	.08693	.08721	.08749	.08777
.08750	.08778	.08805	.08833	.08861	.08889	.08917	.08946	.08974	.09003	.09031
.09000	.09028	.09056	.09084	.09113	.09141	.09170	.09199	.09227	.09256	.09286
.09250	.09278	.09307	.09336	.09364	.09393	.09422	.09452	.09481	.09510	.09540
.09500	.09529	.09558	.09587	.09616	.09646	.09675	.09705	.09734	.09764	.09794
.09750	.09779	.09809	.09838	.09868	.09898	.09928	.09958	.09988	.10018	.10049
.10000	.10030	.10060	.10090	.10120	.10150	.10180	.10211	.10242	.10272	.10303
.10250	.10280	.10311	.10341	.10372	.10402	.10433	.10464	.10495	.10527	.10558
.10500	.10531	.10561	.10592	.10623	.10655	.10686	.10717	.10749	.10781	.10813
.10750	.10781	.10812	.10844	.10875	.10907	.10939	.10971	.11003	.11035	.11067
.11000	.11032	.11063	.11095	.11127	.11159	.11192	.11224	.11257	.11289	.11322
.11250	.11282	.11314	.11347	.11379	.11412	.11444	.11477	.11510	.11544	.11577
.11500	.11533	.11565	.11598	.11631	.11664	.11697	.11731	.11764	.11798	.11832
.11750	.11783	.11816	.11849	.11883	.11916	.11950	.11984	.12018	.12052	.12087
.12000	.12033	.12067	.12101	.12135	.12169	.12203	.12238	.12272	.12307	.12342
.12250	.12284	.12318	.12352	.12387	.12421	.12456	.12491	.12526	.12561	.12597
.12500	.12534	.12569	.12604	.12639	.12674	.12709	.12745	.12780	.12816	.12852
.12750	.12785	.12820	.12855	.12891	.12926	.12962	.12998	.13034	.13070	.13107
.13000	.13035	.13071	.13107	.13143	.13179	.13215	.13252	.13288	.13325	.13362
.13250	.13286	.13322	.13358	.13395	.13431	.13468	.13505	.13542	.13580	.13617
.13500	.13536	.13573	.13610	.13647	.13684	.13721	.13759	.13797	.13834	.13872
.13750	.13787	.13824	.13861	.13899	.13937	.13975	.14013	.14051	.14089	.14128
.14000	.14038	.14075	.14113	.14151	.14189	.14228	.14266	.14305	.14344	.14383
.14250	.14288	.14326	.14365	.14403	.14442	.14481	.14520	.14559	.14599	.14638
.14500	.14539	.14577	.14616	.14655	.14695	.14734	.14774	.14814	.14854	.14894
.14750	.14789	.14828	.14868	.14907	.14947	.14987	.15027	.15068	.15108	.15149
.15000	.15040	.15079	.15119	.15160	.15200	.15241	.15281	.15322	.15363	.15405
.15250	.15290	.15331	.15371	.15412	.15453	.15494	.15535	.15577	.15618	.15660
.15500	.15541	.15582	.15623	.15664	.15705	.15747	.15789	.15831	.15873	.15916
.15750	.15791	.15833	.15874	.15916	.15958	.16000	.16043	.16085	.16128	.16171
.16000	.16042	.16084	.16126	.16168	.16211	.16254	.16297	.16340	.16383	.16427
.16250	.16292	.16335	.16378	.16421	.16464	.16507	.16551	.16594	.16638	.16683
.16500	.16543	.16586	.16629	.16673	.16717	.16760	.16805	.16849	.16893	.16938
.16750	.16793	.16837	.16881	.16925	.16969	.17014	.17059	.17103	.17149	.17194
.17000	.17044	.17088	.17133	.17177	.17222	.17267	.17313	.17358	.17404	.17450
.17250	.17295	.17339	.17384	.17430	.17475	.17521	.17567	.17613	.17659	.17705
.17500	.17545	.17590	.17636	.17682	.17728	.17774	.17821	.17867	.17914	.17961
.17750	.17796	.17842	.17888	.17934	.17981	.18028	.18075	.18122	.18169	.18217
.18000	.18046	.18093	.18139	.18186	.18234	.18281	.18329	.18376	.18425	.18473
.18250	.18297	.18344	.18391	.18439	.18486	.18534	.18583	.18631	.18680	.18729
.18500	.18547	.18595	.18643	.18691	.18739	.18788	.18837	.18886	.18935	.18985
.18750	.18798	.18846	.18895	.18943	.18992	.19041	.19091	.19141	.19190	.19241
.19000	.19049	.19097	.19146	.19196	.19245	.19295	.19345	.19395	.19446	.19497
.19250	.19299	.19349	.19398	.19448	.19498	.19549	.19599	.19650	.19701	.19752
.19500	.19550	.19600	.19650	.19700	.19751	.19802	.19853	.19905	.19956	.20008
.19750	.19800	.19851	.19902	.19953	.20004	.20056	.20107	.20160	.20212	.20264
.20000	.20051	.20102	.20153	.20205	.20257	.20309	.20362	.20414	.20467	.20520
.20250	.20301	.20353	.20405	.20457	.20510	.20563	.20616	.20669	.20723	.20776
.20500	.20552	.20604	.20657	.20710	.20763	.20816	.20870	.20924	.20978	.21033
.20750	.20803	.20856	.20909	.20962	.21016	.21070	.21124	.21179	.21234	.21289

ANNUAL PERCENTAGE RATE TABLES: TERM OF MORTGAGE: 360 MONTHS

POINTS CHARGED

INTEREST RATE	.02750	.03000	.03250	.03500	.03750	.04000	.04250	.04500	.04750	.05000
.07000	.07279	.07305	.07331	.07357	.07383	.07409	.07436	.07463	.07489	.07516
.07250	.07533	.07559	.07586	.07612	.07639	.07666	.07693	.07720	.07747	.07774
.07500	.07787	.07814	.07841	.07868	.07895	.07922	.07950	.07977	.08005	.08032
.07750	.08042	.08069	.08096	.08124	.08151	.08179	.08207	.08234	.08262	.08291
.08000	.08296	.08324	.08351	.08379	.08407	.08435	.08464	.08492	.08520	.08549
.08250	.08551	.08579	.08607	.08635	.08664	.08692	.08721	.08750	.08778	.08807
.08500	.08805	.08834	.08862	.08891	.08920	.08949	.08978	.09007	.09037	.09066
.08750	.09060	.09089	.09118	.09147	.09176	.09206	.09235	.09265	.09295	.09325
.09000	.09315	.09344	.09374	.09403	.09433	.09463	.09493	.09523	.09553	.09584
.09250	.09570	.09599	.09629	.09659	.09690	.09720	.09750	.09781	.09812	.09843
.09500	.09825	.09855	.09885	.09916	.09946	.09977	.10008	.10039	.10071	.10102
.09750	.10079	.10110	.10141	.10172	.10203	.10235	.10266	.10298	.10329	.10361
.10000	.10334	.10366	.10397	.10429	.10460	.10492	.10524	.10556	.10588	.10620
.10250	.10590	.10621	.10653	.10685	.10717	.10749	.10782	.10814	.10847	.10880
.10500	.10845	.10877	.10909	.10942	.10974	.11007	.11040	.11073	.11106	.11140
.10750	.11100	.11133	.11165	.11198	.11231	.11265	.11298	.11332	.11365	.11399
.11000	.11355	.11388	.11422	.11455	.11489	.11522	.11556	.11590	.11625	.11659
.11250	.11610	.11644	.11678	.11712	.11746	.11780	.11815	.11849	.11884	.11919
.11500	.11866	.11900	.11934	.11969	.12003	.12038	.12073	.12108	.12144	.12179
.11750	.12121	.12156	.12191	.12226	.12261	.12296	.12332	.12367	.12403	.12439
.12000	.12377	.12412	.12447	.12483	.12518	.12554	.12590	.12626	.12663	.12699
.12250	.12632	.12668	.12704	.12740	.12776	.12812	.12849	.12886	.12923	.12960
.12500	.12888	.12924	.12960	.12997	.13034	.13071	.13108	.13145	.13182	.13220
.12750	.13143	.13180	.13217	.13254	.13292	.13329	.13367	.13404	.13442	.13481
.13000	.13399	.13436	.13474	.13512	.13549	.13587	.13626	.13664	.13702	.13741
.13250	.13655	.13693	.13731	.13769	.13807	.13846	.13885	.13924	.13963	.14002
.13500	.13911	.13949	.13988	.14026	.14065	.14104	.14144	.14183	.14223	.14263
.13750	.14166	.14205	.14245	.14284	.14323	.14363	.14403	.14443	.14483	.14524
.14000	.14422	.14462	.14501	.14541	.14581	.14622	.14662	.14703	.14744	.14785
.14250	.14678	.14718	.14759	.14799	.14840	.14880	.14921	.14963	.15004	.15046
.14500	.14934	.14975	.15016	.15057	.15098	.15139	.15181	.15223	.15265	.15307
.14750	.15190	.15231	.15273	.15314	.15356	.15398	.15440	.15483	.15525	.15568
.15000	.15446	.15488	.15530	.15572	.15614	.15657	.15700	.15743	.15786	.15829
.15250	.15702	.15745	.15787	.15830	.15873	.15916	.15959	.16003	.16047	.16091
.15500	.15958	.16001	.16044	.16088	.16131	.16175	.16219	.16263	.16307	.16352
.15750	.16215	.16258	.16302	.16346	.16390	.16434	.16479	.16523	.16568	.16613
.16000	.16471	.16515	.16559	.16604	.16648	.16693	.16738	.16784	.16829	.16875
.16250	.16727	.16772	.16816	.16862	.16907	.16952	.16998	.17044	.17090	.17137
.16500	.16983	.17028	.17074	.17120	.17165	.17212	.17258	.17304	.17351	.17398
.16750	.17240	.17285	.17331	.17378	.17424	.17471	.17518	.17565	.17612	.17660
.17000	.17496	.17542	.17589	.17636	.17683	.17730	.17778	.17826	.17874	.17922
.17250	.17752	.17799	.17846	.17894	.17942	.17990	.18038	.18086	.18135	.18184
.17500	.18009	.18056	.18104	.18152	.18200	.18249	.18298	.18347	.18396	.18446
.17750	.18265	.18313	.18362	.18410	.18459	.18508	.18558	.18608	.18657	.18708
.18000	.18521	.18570	.18619	.18669	.18718	.18768	.18818	.18868	.18919	.18970
.18250	.18778	.18827	.18877	.18927	.18977	.19028	.19078	.19129	.19180	.19232
.18500	.19034	.19084	.19135	.19185	.19236	.19287	.19338	.19390	.19442	.19494
.18750	.19291	.19342	.19393	.19444	.19495	.19547	.19599	.19651	.19703	.19756
.19000	.19548	.19599	.19650	.19702	.19754	.19806	.19859	.19912	.19965	.20018
.19250	.19804	.19856	.19908	.19960	.20013	.20066	.20119	.20173	.20226	.20280
.19500	.20061	.20113	.20166	.20219	.20272	.20326	.20380	.20434	.20488	.20543
.19750	.20317	.20370	.20424	.20477	.20531	.20586	.20640	.20695	.20750	.20805
.20000	.20574	.20628	.20682	.20736	.20791	.20845	.20900	.20956	.21012	.21067
.20250	.20831	.20885	.20940	.20994	.21050	.21105	.21161	.21217	.21273	.21330
.20500	.21087	.21142	.21198	.21253	.21309	.21365	.21421	.21478	.21535	.21592
.20750	.21344	.21400	.21455	.21512	.21568	.21625	.21682	.21739	.21797	.21855

ANNUAL PERCENTAGE RATE TABLES: TERM OF MORTGAGE: 360 MONTHS

POINTS CHARGED

INTEREST RATE	.05250	.05500	.05750	.06000	.06250	.06500	.06750	.07000	.07250	.07500
.07000	.07543	.07570	.07597	.07625	.07652	.07680	.07707	.07735	.07763	.07791
.07250	.07802	.07829	.07857	.07884	.07912	.07940	.07968	.07997	.08025	.08053
.07500	.08060	.08088	.08116	.08144	.08173	.08201	.08230	.08258	.08287	.08316
.07750	.08319	.08347	.08376	.08404	.08433	.08462	.08491	.08520	.08549	.08579
.08000	.08578	.08606	.08635	.08664	.08694	.08723	.08752	.08782	.08812	.08842
.08250	.08837	.08866	.08895	.08925	.08955	.08984	.09014	.09044	.09075	.09105
.08500	.09096	.09125	.09155	.09185	.09215	.09246	.09276	.09307	.09337	.09368
.08750	.09355	.09385	.09415	.09446	.09477	.09507	.09538	.09569	.09600	.09632
.09000	.09614	.09645	.09676	.09707	.09738	.09769	.09801	.09832	.09864	.09896
.09250	.09874	.09905	.09936	.09968	.09999	.10031	.10063	.10095	.10127	.10159
.09500	.10133	.10165	.10197	.10229	.10261	.10293	.10326	.10358	.10391	.10424
.09750	.10393	.10425	.10458	.10490	.10523	.10555	.10588	.10621	.10655	.10688
.10000	.10653	.10686	.10718	.10751	.10785	.10818	.10851	.10885	.10918	.10952
.10250	.10913	.10946	.10979	.11013	.11047	.11080	.11114	.11148	.11183	.11217
.10500	.11173	.11207	.11241	.11275	.11309	.11343	.11377	.11412	.11447	.11482
.10750	.11433	.11467	.11502	.11536	.11571	.11606	.11641	.11676	.11711	.11747
.11000	.11694	.11728	.11763	.11798	.11833	.11869	.11904	.11940	.11976	.12012
.11250	.11954	.11989	.12025	.12060	.12096	.12132	.12168	.12204	.12241	.12277
.11500	.12215	.12250	.12286	.12322	.12359	.12395	.12432	.12469	.12506	.12543
.11750	.12475	.12512	.12548	.12585	.12622	.12659	.12696	.12733	.12771	.12809
.12000	.12736	.12773	.12810	.12847	.12885	.12922	.12960	.12998	.13036	.13074
.12250	.12997	.13034	.13072	.13110	.13148	.13186	.13224	.13263	.13301	.13340
.12500	.13258	.13296	.13334	.13372	.13411	.13450	.13489	.13528	.13567	.13606
.12750	.13519	.13558	.13596	.13635	.13674	.13714	.13753	.13793	.13833	.13873
.13000	.13780	.13819	.13859	.13898	.13938	.13978	.14018	.14058	.14098	.14139
.13250	.14041	.14081	.14121	.14161	.14201	.14242	.14282	.14323	.14364	.14406
.13500	.14303	.14343	.14384	.14424	.14465	.14506	.14547	.14589	.14630	.14672
.13750	.14564	.14605	.14646	.14687	.14729	.14770	.14812	.14854	.14897	.14939
.14000	.14826	.14867	.14909	.14951	.14993	.15035	.15077	.15120	.15163	.15206
.14250	.15087	.15129	.15172	.15214	.15257	.15300	.15343	.15386	.15429	.15473
.14500	.15349	.15392	.15435	.15478	.15521	.15564	.15608	.15652	.15696	.15740
.14750	.15611	.15654	.15698	.15741	.15785	.15829	.15873	.15918	.15963	.16008
.15000	.15873	.15917	.15961	.16005	.16049	.16094	.16139	.16184	.16230	.16275
.15250	.16135	.16179	.16224	.16269	.16314	.16359	.16405	.16450	.16496	.16543
.15500	.16397	.16442	.16487	.16533	.16578	.16624	.16670	.16717	.16763	.16810
.15750	.16659	.16705	.16750	.16797	.16843	.16889	.16936	.16983	.17031	.17078
.16000	.16921	.16967	.17014	.17061	.17108	.17155	.17202	.17250	.17298	.17346
.16250	.17183	.17230	.17277	.17325	.17372	.17420	.17468	.17517	.17565	.17614
.16500	.17446	.17493	.17541	.17589	.17637	.17686	.17734	.17783	.17833	.17882
.16750	.17708	.17756	.17805	.17853	.17902	.17951	.18001	.18050	.18100	.18150
.17000	.17970	.18019	.18068	.18117	.18167	.18217	.18267	.18317	.18368	.18418
.17250	.18233	.18282	.18332	.18382	.18432	.18482	.18533	.18584	.18635	.18687
.17500	.18495	.18545	.18596	.18646	.18697	.18748	.18800	.18851	.18903	.18955
.17750	.18758	.18809	.18860	.18911	.18962	.19014	.19066	.19118	.19171	.19224
.18000	.19021	.19072	.19124	.19175	.19228	.19280	.19333	.19386	.19439	.19492
.18250	.19283	.19335	.19388	.19440	.19493	.19546	.19599	.19653	.19707	.19761
.18500	.19546	.19599	.19652	.19705	.19758	.19812	.19866	.19920	.19975	.20030
.18750	.19809	.19862	.19916	.19970	.20024	.20078	.20133	.20188	.20243	.20298
.19000	.20072	.20126	.20180	.20234	.20289	.20344	.20400	.20455	.20511	.20567
.19250	.20335	.20389	.20444	.20499	.20555	.20610	.20666	.20723	.20779	.20836
.19500	.20598	.20653	.20708	.20764	.20820	.20877	.20933	.20990	.21048	.21105
.19750	.20861	.20917	.20973	.21029	.21086	.21143	.21200	.21258	.21316	.21374
.20000	.21124	.21180	.21237	.21294	.21352	.21409	.21467	.21526	.21584	.21643
.20250	.21387	.21444	.21501	.21559	.21617	.21676	.21734	.21793	.21853	.21912
.20500	.21650	.21708	.21766	.21824	.21883	.21942	.22002	.22061	.22121	.22182
.20750	.21913	.21972	.22030	.22090	.22149	.22209	.22269	.22329	.22390	.22451

ANNUAL PERCENTAGE RATE TABLES: TERM OF MORTGAGE: 360 MONTHS

POINTS CHARGED

INTEREST RATE	.07750	.08000	.08250	.08500	.08750	.09000	.09250	.09500	.09750	.10000
.07000	.07819	.07847	.07876	.07904	.07933	.07962	.07991	.08020	.08049	.08078
.07250	.08082	.08111	.08140	.08169	.08198	.08227	.08256	.08286	.08315	.08345
.07500	.08345	.08374	.08404	.08433	.08463	.08492	.08522	.08552	.08582	.08613
.07750	.08608	.08638	.08668	.08698	.08728	.08758	.08788	.08819	.08849	.08880
.08000	.08872	.08902	.08932	.08963	.08993	.09024	.09055	.09086	.09117	.09148
.08250	.09135	.09166	.09197	.09228	.09259	.09290	.09321	.09353	.09384	.09416
.08500	.09399	.09430	.09462	.09493	.09525	.09556	.09588	.09620	.09652	.09685
.08750	.09663	.09695	.09727	.09759	.09791	.09823	.09855	.09888	.09920	.09953
.09000	.09928	.09960	.09992	.10024	.10057	.10090	.10122	.10156	.10189	.10222
.09250	.10192	.10225	.10257	.10290	.10323	.10357	.10390	.10424	.10457	.10491
.09500	.10457	.10490	.10523	.10557	.10590	.10624	.10658	.10692	.10726	.10761
.09750	.10721	.10755	.10789	.10823	.10857	.10891	.10926	.10961	.10995	.11030
.10000	.10986	.11021	.11055	.11090	.11124	.11159	.11194	.11229	.11265	.11300
.10250	.11252	.11286	.11321	.11356	.11392	.11427	.11463	.11498	.11534	.11570
.10500	.11517	.11552	.11588	.11623	.11659	.11695	.11731	.11768	.11804	.11841
.10750	.11783	.11818	.11854	.11891	.11927	.11963	.12000	.12037	.12074	.12111
.11000	.12048	.12085	.12121	.12158	.12195	.12232	.12269	.12307	.12344	.12382
.11250	.12314	.12351	.12388	.12426	.12463	.12501	.12539	.12577	.12615	.12653
.11500	.12580	.12618	.12655	.12693	.12731	.12770	.12808	.12847	.12886	.12925
.11750	.12846	.12885	.12923	.12961	.13000	.13039	.13078	.13117	.13157	.13196
.12000	.13113	.13152	.13190	.13230	.13269	.13308	.13348	.13388	.13428	.13468
.12250	.13379	.13419	.13458	.13498	.13538	.13578	.13618	.13659	.13699	.13740
.12500	.13646	.13686	.13726	.13766	.13807	.13847	.13888	.13929	.13971	.14012
.12750	.13913	.13953	.13994	.14035	.14076	.14117	.14159	.14201	.14243	.14285
.13000	.14180	.14221	.14262	.14304	.14346	.14387	.14430	.14472	.14514	.14557
.13250	.14447	.14489	.14531	.14573	.14615	.14658	.14700	.14743	.14787	.14830
.13500	.14714	.14757	.14799	.14842	.14885	.14928	.14971	.15015	.15059	.15103
.13750	.14982	.15025	.15068	.15111	.15155	.15199	.15243	.15287	.15331	.15376
.14000	.15249	.15293	.15337	.15381	.15425	.15469	.15514	.15559	.15604	.15649
.14250	.15517	.15561	.15606	.15650	.15695	.15740	.15786	.15831	.15877	.15923
.14500	.15785	.15830	.15875	.15920	.15966	.16011	.16057	.16103	.16150	.16197
.14750	.16053	.16098	.16144	.16190	.16236	.16282	.16329	.16376	.16423	.16470
.15000	.16321	.16367	.16413	.16460	.16507	.16554	.16601	.16649	.16696	.16744
.15250	.16589	.16636	.16683	.16730	.16778	.16825	.16873	.16921	.16970	.17018
.15500	.16857	.16905	.16952	.17000	.17048	.17097	.17145	.17194	.17243	.17293
.15750	.17126	.17174	.17222	.17271	.17319	.17369	.17418	.17467	.17517	.17567
.16000	.17394	.17443	.17492	.17541	.17591	.17640	.17690	.17741	.17791	.17842
.16250	.17663	.17712	.17762	.17812	.17862	.17912	.17963	.18014	.18065	.18116
.16500	.17932	.17982	.18032	.18083	.18133	.18184	.18236	.18287	.18339	.18391
.16750	.18201	.18251	.18302	.18353	.18405	.18457	.18509	.18561	.18613	.18666
.17000	.18469	.18521	.18572	.18624	.18676	.18729	.18782	.18835	.18888	.18941
.17250	.18738	.18790	.18843	.18895	.18948	.19001	.19055	.19108	.19162	.19217
.17500	.19008	.19060	.19113	.19166	.19220	.19274	.19328	.19382	.19437	.19492
.17750	.19277	.19330	.19384	.19438	.19492	.19546	.19601	.19656	.19712	.19767
.18000	.19546	.19600	.19654	.19709	.19764	.19819	.19875	.19930	.19986	.20043
.18250	.19815	.19870	.19925	.19980	.20036	.20092	.20148	.20205	.20261	.20318
.18500	.20085	.20140	.20196	.20252	.20308	.20365	.20422	.20479	.20536	.20594
.18750	.20354	.20410	.20467	.20523	.20580	.20638	.20695	.20753	.20811	.20870
.19000	.20624	.20681	.20738	.20795	.20853	.20911	.20969	.21028	.21087	.21146
.19250	.20893	.20951	.21009	.21067	.21125	.21184	.21243	.21302	.21362	.21422
.19500	.21163	.21221	.21280	.21338	.21398	.21457	.21517	.21577	.21637	.21698
.19750	.21433	.21492	.21551	.21610	.21670	.21730	.21791	.21852	.21913	.21974
.20000	.21703	.21762	.21822	.21882	.21943	.22004	.22065	.22126	.22188	.22250
.20250	.21972	.22033	.22093	.22154	.22215	.22277	.22339	.22401	.22464	.22527
.20500	.22242	.22303	.22365	.22426	.22488	.22550	.22613	.22676	.22739	.22803
.20750	.22512	.22574	.22636	.22698	.22761	.22824	.22887	.22951	.23015	.23080

ANNUAL PERCENTAGE RATE TABLES: TERM OF MORTGAGE: 360 MONTHS

INTEREST RATE	POINTS CHARGED .10250	.10500	.10750	.11000	.11250	.11500	.11750	.12000	.12250	.12500
.07000	.08108	.08137	.08167	.08197	.08227	.08257	.08287	.08318	.08348	.08379
.07250	.08375	.08405	.08435	.08466	.08496	.08527	.08558	.08589	.08620	.08651
.07500	.08643	.08674	.08704	.08735	.08766	.08797	.08828	.08860	.08891	.08923
.07750	.08911	.08942	.08973	.09005	.09036	.09068	.09100	.09132	.09164	.09196
.08000	.09179	.09211	.09243	.09275	.09307	.09339	.09371	.09404	.09436	.09469
.08250	.09448	.09480	.09512	.09545	.09577	.09610	.09643	.09676	.09709	.09742
.08500	.09717	.09750	.09782	.09815	.09848	.09882	.09915	.09948	.09982	.10016
.08750	.09986	.10019	.10053	.10086	.10120	.10153	.10187	.10221	.10256	.10290
.09000	.10256	.10289	.10323	.10357	.10391	.10426	.10460	.10495	.10530	.10565
.09250	.10525	.10559	.10594	.10628	.10663	.10698	.10733	.10768	.10804	.10839
.09500	.10795	.10830	.10865	.10900	.10935	.10971	.11006	.11042	.11078	.11114
.09750	.11065	.11101	.11136	.11172	.11208	.11244	.11280	.11316	.11353	.11390
.10000	.11336	.11372	.11408	.11444	.11481	.11517	.11554	.11591	.11628	.11666
.10250	.11607	.11643	.11680	.11717	.11754	.11791	.11828	.11866	.11904	.11942
.10500	.11878	.11915	.11952	.11989	.12027	.12065	.12103	.12141	.12179	.12218
.10750	.12149	.12187	.12224	.12262	.12301	.12339	.12378	.12416	.12455	.12495
.11000	.12420	.12459	.12497	.12536	.12574	.12613	.12653	.12692	.12732	.12772
.11250	.12692	.12731	.12770	.12809	.12849	.12888	.12928	.12968	.13008	.13049
.11500	.12964	.13003	.13043	.13083	.13123	.13163	.13204	.13244	.13285	.13326
.11750	.13236	.13276	.13317	.13357	.13398	.13439	.13480	.13521	.13562	.13604
.12000	.13509	.13549	.13590	.13631	.13673	.13714	.13756	.13798	.13840	.13882
.12250	.13781	.13822	.13864	.13906	.13948	.13990	.14032	.14075	.14118	.14161
.12500	.14054	.14096	.14138	.14180	.14223	.14266	.14309	.14352	.14396	.14439
.12750	.14327	.14370	.14412	.14455	.14499	.14542	.14586	.14630	.14674	.14718
.13000	.14600	.14643	.14687	.14731	.14774	.14819	.14863	.14907	.14952	.14997
.13250	.14874	.14917	.14962	.15006	.15050	.15095	.15140	.15185	.15231	.15277
.13500	.15147	.15192	.15236	.15281	.15327	.15372	.15418	.15464	.15510	.15556
.13750	.15421	.15466	.15512	.15557	.15603	.15649	.15696	.15742	.15789	.15836
.14000	.15695	.15741	.15787	.15833	.15880	.15927	.15974	.16021	.16068	.16116
.14250	.15969	.16016	.16062	.16109	.16157	.16204	.16252	.16300	.16348	.16397
.14500	.16243	.16291	.16338	.16386	.16434	.16482	.16530	.16579	.16628	.16677
.14750	.16518	.16566	.16614	.16662	.16711	.16760	.16809	.16858	.16908	.16958
.15000	.16793	.16841	.16890	.16939	.16988	.17038	.17088	.17138	.17188	.17239
.15250	.17067	.17117	.17166	.17216	.17266	.17316	.17367	.17418	.17469	.17520
.15500	.17342	.17392	.17442	.17493	.17544	.17595	.17646	.17697	.17749	.17801
.15750	.17618	.17668	.17719	.17770	.17822	.17873	.17925	.17977	.18030	.18083
.16000	.17893	.17944	.17996	.18048	.18100	.18152	.18205	.18258	.18311	.18365
.16250	.18168	.18220	.18272	.18325	.18378	.18431	.18484	.18538	.18592	.18646
.16500	.18444	.18496	.18549	.18603	.18656	.18710	.18764	.18819	.18873	.18928
.16750	.18719	.18773	.18826	.18880	.18935	.18989	.19044	.19099	.19155	.19211
.17000	.18995	.19049	.19104	.19158	.19213	.19269	.19324	.19380	.19436	.19493
.17250	.19271	.19326	.19381	.19436	.19492	.19548	.19605	.19661	.19718	.19775
.17500	.19547	.19603	.19659	.19715	.19771	.19828	.19885	.19942	.20000	.20058
.17750	.19823	.19880	.19936	.19993	.20050	.20108	.20166	.20224	.20282	.20341
.18000	.20099	.20156	.20214	.20271	.20329	.20388	.20446	.20505	.20564	.20624
.18250	.20376	.20434	.20492	.20550	.20609	.20668	.20727	.20787	.20847	.20907
.18500	.20652	.20711	.20770	.20829	.20888	.20948	.21008	.21068	.21129	.21190
.18750	.20929	.20988	.21048	.21107	.21168	.21228	.21289	.21350	.21411	.21473
.19000	.21205	.21265	.21326	.21386	.21447	.21508	.21570	.21632	.21694	.21757
.19250	.21482	.21543	.21604	.21665	.21727	.21789	.21851	.21914	.21977	.22040
.19500	.21759	.21820	.21882	.21944	.22007	.22069	.22132	.22196	.22260	.22324
.19750	.22036	.22098	.22161	.22223	.22286	.22350	.22414	.22478	.22543	.22608
.20000	.22313	.22376	.22439	.22503	.22566	.22631	.22695	.22760	.22826	.22891
.20250	.22590	.22654	.22718	.22782	.22846	.22912	.22977	.23043	.23109	.23175
.20500	.22867	.22931	.22996	.23061	.23127	.23192	.23259	.23325	.23392	.23459
.20750	.23144	.23209	.23275	.23341	.23407	.23473	.23540	.23608	.23675	.23743

ANNUAL PERCENTAGE RATE TABLES: TERM OF MORTGAGE: 360 MONTHS

INTEREST RATE	POINTS CHARGED .12750	.13000	.13250	.13500	.13750	.14000	.14250	.14500	.14750	.15000
.07000	.08410	.08441	.08472	.08503	.08535	.08566	.08598	.08630	.08662	.08694
.07250	.08682	.08714	.08745	.08777	.08809	.08841	.08874	.08906	.08939	.08971
.07500	.08955	.08987	.09019	.09052	.09084	.09117	.09150	.09183	.09216	.09249
.07750	.09228	.09261	.09294	.09326	.09360	.09393	.09426	.09460	.09493	.09527
.08000	.09502	.09535	.09568	.09602	.09635	.09669	.09703	.09737	.09771	.09806
.08250	.09776	.09809	.09843	.09877	.09911	.09946	.09980	.10015	.10050	.10085
.08500	.10050	.10084	.10119	.10153	.10188	.10223	.10258	.10293	.10329	.10364
.08750	.10325	.10360	.10394	.10430	.10465	.10500	.10536	.10572	.10608	.10644
.09000	.10600	.10635	.10671	.10706	.10742	.10778	.10815	.10851	.10888	.10924
.09250	.10875	.10911	.10947	.10983	.11020	.11057	.11093	.11130	.11168	.11205
.09500	.11151	.11187	.11224	.11261	.11298	.11335	.11373	.11410	.11448	.11486
.09750	.11427	.11464	.11501	.11539	.11576	.11614	.11652	.11691	.11729	.11768
.10000	.11703	.11741	.11779	.11817	.11855	.11894	.11932	.11971	.12010	.12050
.10250	.11980	.12018	.12057	.12095	.12134	.12173	.12213	.12252	.12292	.12332
.10500	.12257	.12296	.12335	.12374	.12414	.12453	.12493	.12534	.12574	.12615
.10750	.12534	.12574	.12613	.12653	.12694	.12734	.12775	.12815	.12856	.12898
.11000	.12812	.12852	.12892	.12933	.12974	.13015	.13056	.13098	.13139	.13181
.11250	.13089	.13130	.13171	.13213	.13254	.13296	.13338	.13380	.13422	.13465
.11500	.13368	.13409	.13451	.13493	.13535	.13577	.13620	.13663	.13706	.13749
.11750	.13646	.13688	.13731	.13773	.13816	.13859	.13902	.13946	.13990	.14034
.12000	.13925	.13968	.14011	.14054	.14098	.14141	.14185	.14229	.14274	.14319
.12250	.14204	.14247	.14291	.14335	.14379	.14424	.14468	.14513	.14558	.14604
.12500	.14483	.14527	.14572	.14616	.14661	.14706	.14752	.14797	.14843	.14889
.12750	.14763	.14808	.14853	.14898	.14944	.14989	.15035	.15082	.15128	.15175
.13000	.15043	.15088	.15134	.15180	.15226	.15273	.15319	.15367	.15414	.15461
.13250	.15323	.15369	.15415	.15462	.15509	.15556	.15604	.15652	.15700	.15748
.13500	.15603	.15650	.15697	.15745	.15792	.15840	.15888	.15937	.15986	.16035
.13750	.15884	.15931	.15979	.16027	.16076	.16124	.16173	.16222	.16272	.16322
.14000	.16164	.16213	.16261	.16310	.16359	.16409	.16458	.16508	.16558	.16609
.14250	.16445	.16494	.16544	.16593	.16643	.16693	.16744	.16794	.16845	.16897
.14500	.16727	.16776	.16826	.16877	.16927	.16978	.17029	.17081	.17132	.17184
.14750	.17008	.17059	.17109	.17160	.17212	.17263	.17315	.17367	.17420	.17473
.15000	.17290	.17341	.17392	.17444	.17496	.17549	.17601	.17654	.17707	.17761
.15250	.17572	.17624	.17676	.17728	.17781	.17834	.17888	.17941	.17995	.18050
.15500	.17854	.17906	.17959	.18013	.18066	.18120	.18174	.18229	.18283	.18338
.15750	.18136	.18189	.18243	.18297	.18351	.18406	.18461	.18516	.18572	.18627
.16000	.18418	.18473	.18527	.18582	.18637	.18692	.18748	.18804	.18860	.18917
.16250	.18701	.18756	.18811	.18867	.18922	.18979	.19035	.19092	.19149	.19206
.16500	.18984	.19039	.19095	.19152	.19208	.19265	.19322	.19380	.19438	.19496
.16750	.19267	.19323	.19380	.19437	.19494	.19552	.19610	.19668	.19727	.19786
.17000	.19550	.19607	.19664	.19722	.19780	.19839	.19898	.19957	.20016	.20076
.17250	.19833	.19891	.19949	.20008	.20067	.20126	.20185	.20245	.20306	.20366
.17500	.20116	.20175	.20234	.20293	.20353	.20413	.20474	.20534	.20595	.20657
.17750	.20400	.20459	.20519	.20579	.20640	.20701	.20762	.20823	.20885	.20947
.18000	.20684	.20744	.20804	.20865	.20927	.20988	.21050	.21112	.21175	.21238
.18250	.20968	.21028	.21090	.21151	.21214	.21276	.21339	.21402	.21465	.21529
.18500	.21251	.21313	.21375	.21438	.21501	.21564	.21627	.21691	.21755	.21820
.18750	.21536	.21598	.21661	.21724	.21788	.21852	.21916	.21981	.22046	.22111
.19000	.21820	.21883	.21947	.22011	.22075	.22140	.22205	.22271	.22336	.22403
.19250	.22104	.22168	.22233	.22297	.22363	.22428	.22494	.22560	.22627	.22694
.19500	.22388	.22453	.22518	.22584	.22650	.22716	.22783	.22850	.22918	.22986
.19750	.22673	.22739	.22805	.22871	.22938	.23005	.23073	.23140	.23209	.23278
.20000	.22957	.23024	.23091	.23158	.23226	.23294	.23362	.23431	.23500	.23569
.20250	.23242	.23309	.23377	.23445	.23513	.23582	.23651	.23721	.23791	.23861
.20500	.23527	.23595	.23663	.23732	.23801	.23871	.23941	.24011	.24082	.24153
.20750	.23812	.23881	.23950	.24019	.24089	.24160	.24231	.24302	.24374	.24446

ANNUAL PERCENTAGE RATE TABLES: TERM OF MORTGAGE: 420 MONTHS

INTEREST RATE	POINTS CHARGED .00250	.00500	.00750	.01000	.01250	.01500	.01750	.02000	.02250	.02500
.07000	.07023	.07046	.07069	.07092	.07115	.07138	.07162	.07185	.07209	.07233
.07250	.07273	.07297	.07320	.07344	.07367	.07391	.07415	.07439	.07463	.07487
.07500	.07524	.07547	.07571	.07595	.07619	.07643	.07668	.07692	.07716	.07741
.07750	.07774	.07798	.07823	.07847	.07871	.07896	.07921	.07945	.07970	.07995
.08000	.08024	.08049	.08074	.08099	.08124	.08149	.08174	.08199	.08224	.08250
.08250	.08275	.08300	.08325	.08350	.08376	.08401	.08427	.08452	.08478	.08504
.08500	.08525	.08551	.08576	.08602	.08628	.08654	.08680	.08706	.08732	.08759
.08750	.08776	.08802	.08828	.08854	.08880	.08907	.08933	.08960	.08986	.09013
.09000	.09026	.09053	.09079	.09106	.09133	.09159	.09186	.09213	.09241	.09268
.09250	.09277	.09304	.09331	.09358	.09385	.09412	.09440	.09467	.09495	.09523
.09500	.09527	.09555	.09582	.09610	.09637	.09665	.09693	.09721	.09749	.09777
.09750	.09778	.09805	.09833	.09861	.09890	.09918	.09946	.09975	.10003	.10032
.10000	.10028	.10056	.10085	.10113	.10142	.10171	.10200	.10229	.10258	.10287
.10250	.10279	.10307	.10336	.10365	.10394	.10424	.10453	.10483	.10512	.10542
.10500	.10529	.10558	.10588	.10617	.10647	.10677	.10707	.10737	.10767	.10797
.10750	.10780	.10809	.10839	.10869	.10899	.10930	.10960	.10991	.11021	.11052
.11000	.11030	.11060	.11091	.11121	.11152	.11183	.11214	.11245	.11276	.11307
.11250	.11281	.11311	.11342	.11373	.11404	.11436	.11467	.11499	.11531	.11562
.11500	.11531	.11562	.11594	.11625	.11657	.11689	.11721	.11753	.11785	.11818
.11750	.11782	.11813	.11845	.11877	.11910	.11942	.11974	.12007	.12040	.12073
.12000	.12032	.12064	.12097	.12129	.12162	.12195	.12228	.12261	.12295	.12328
.12250	.12283	.12315	.12348	.12382	.12415	.12448	.12482	.12516	.12550	.12584
.12500	.12533	.12567	.12600	.12634	.12668	.12702	.12736	.12770	.12804	.12839
.12750	.12784	.12818	.12852	.12886	.12920	.12955	.12989	.13024	.13059	.13094
.13000	.13034	.13069	.13103	.13138	.13173	.13208	.13243	.13279	.13314	.13350
.13250	.13285	.13320	.13355	.13390	.13426	.13461	.13497	.13533	.13569	.13606
.13500	.13535	.13571	.13607	.13642	.13678	.13715	.13751	.13788	.13824	.13861
.13750	.13786	.13822	.13858	.13895	.13931	.13968	.14005	.14042	.14079	.14117
.14000	.14036	.14073	.14110	.14147	.14184	.14221	.14259	.14296	.14334	.14372
.14250	.14287	.14324	.14362	.14399	.14437	.14475	.14513	.14551	.14589	.14628
.14500	.14538	.14575	.14613	.14651	.14690	.14728	.14767	.14806	.14845	.14884
.14750	.14788	.14826	.14865	.14904	.14942	.14981	.15021	.15060	.15100	.15140
.15000	.15039	.15078	.15117	.15156	.15195	.15235	.15275	.15315	.15355	.15395
.15250	.15289	.15329	.15368	.15408	.15448	.15488	.15529	.15569	.15610	.15651
.15500	.15540	.15580	.15620	.15660	.15701	.15742	.15783	.15824	.15865	.15907
.15750	.15790	.15831	.15872	.15913	.15954	.15995	.16037	.16079	.16121	.16163
.16000	.16041	.16082	.16123	.16165	.16207	.16249	.16291	.16333	.16376	.16419
.16250	.16292	.16333	.16375	.16417	.16460	.16502	.16545	.16588	.16631	.16675
.16500	.16542	.16584	.16627	.16670	.16713	.16756	.16799	.16843	.16887	.16931
.16750	.16793	.16836	.16879	.16922	.16966	.17009	.17053	.17098	.17142	.17187
.17000	.17043	.17087	.17131	.17174	.17219	.17263	.17308	.17352	.17397	.17443
.17250	.17294	.17338	.17382	.17427	.17472	.17517	.17562	.17607	.17653	.17699
.17500	.17544	.17589	.17634	.17679	.17725	.17770	.17816	.17862	.17908	.17955
.17750	.17795	.17840	.17886	.17932	.17978	.18024	.18070	.18117	.18164	.18211
.18000	.18046	.18092	.18138	.18184	.18231	.18277	.18324	.18372	.18419	.18467
.18250	.18296	.18343	.18389	.18436	.18484	.18531	.18579	.18626	.18675	.18723
.18500	.18547	.18594	.18641	.18689	.18737	.18785	.18833	.18881	.18930	.18979
.18750	.18797	.18845	.18893	.18941	.18990	.19038	.19087	.19136	.19186	.19235
.19000	.19048	.19096	.19145	.19194	.19243	.19292	.19341	.19391	.19441	.19491
.19250	.19299	.19348	.19397	.19446	.19496	.19546	.19596	.19646	.19697	.19747
.19500	.19549	.19599	.19648	.19698	.19749	.19799	.19850	.19901	.19952	.20004
.19750	.19800	.19850	.19900	.19951	.20002	.20053	.20104	.20156	.20208	.20260
.20000	.20050	.20101	.20152	.20203	.20255	.20307	.20359	.20411	.20463	.20516
.20250	.20301	.20352	.20404	.20456	.20508	.20560	.20613	.20666	.20719	.20772
.20500	.20552	.20604	.20656	.20708	.20761	.20814	.20867	.20921	.20974	.21028
.20750	.20802	.20855	.20908	.20961	.21014	.21068	.21121	.21176	.21230	.21285

ANNUAL PERCENTAGE RATE TABLES: TERM OF MORTGAGE: 420 MONTHS

INTEREST RATE	POINTS CHARGED .02750	.03000	.03250	.03500	.03750	.04000	.04250	.04500	.04750	.05000
.07000	.07256	.07280	.07304	.07328	.07353	.07377	.07401	.07426	.07451	.07475
.07250	.07511	.07535	.07560	.07584	.07609	.07634	.07659	.07684	.07709	.07734
.07500	.07766	.07790	.07815	.07840	.07865	.07891	.07916	.07941	.07967	.07993
.07750	.08020	.08046	.08071	.08096	.08122	.08148	.08174	.08199	.08225	.08252
.08000	.08275	.08301	.08327	.08353	.08379	.08405	.08431	.08458	.08484	.08511
.08250	.08530	.08556	.08583	.08609	.08636	.08662	.08689	.08716	.08743	.08770
.08500	.08785	.08812	.08839	.08865	.08892	.08919	.08947	.08974	.09002	.09029
.08750	.09040	.09067	.09095	.09122	.09149	.09177	.09205	.09232	.09260	.09289
.09000	.09295	.09323	.09351	.09378	.09406	.09435	.09463	.09491	.09520	.09548
.09250	.09551	.09579	.09607	.09635	.09664	.09692	.09721	.09750	.09779	.09808
.09500	.09806	.09834	.09863	.09892	.09921	.09950	.09979	.10009	.10038	.10068
.09750	.10061	.10090	.10119	.10149	.10178	.10208	.10238	.10267	.10297	.10328
.10000	.10317	.10346	.10376	.10406	.10436	.10466	.10496	.10526	.10557	.10588
.10250	.10572	.10602	.10632	.10663	.10693	.10724	.10755	.10786	.10817	.10848
.10500	.10828	.10858	.10889	.10920	.10951	.10982	.11013	.11045	.11076	.11108
.10750	.11083	.11114	.11146	.11177	.11209	.11240	.11272	.11304	.11336	.11369
.11000	.11339	.11370	.11402	.11434	.11466	.11499	.11531	.11564	.11596	.11629
.11250	.11595	.11627	.11659	.11692	.11724	.11757	.11790	.11823	.11856	.11890
.11500	.11850	.11883	.11916	.11949	.11982	.12016	.12049	.12083	.12117	.12151
.11750	.12106	.12139	.12173	.12206	.12240	.12274	.12308	.12342	.12377	.12411
.12000	.12362	.12396	.12430	.12464	.12498	.12533	.12567	.12602	.12637	.12672
.12250	.12618	.12652	.12687	.12722	.12756	.12791	.12827	.12862	.12898	.12933
.12500	.12874	.12909	.12944	.12979	.13015	.13050	.13086	.13122	.13158	.13195
.12750	.13130	.13165	.13201	.13237	.13273	.13309	.13346	.13382	.13419	.13456
.13000	.13386	.13422	.13458	.13495	.13531	.13568	.13605	.13642	.13680	.13717
.13250	.13642	.13679	.13716	.13753	.13790	.13827	.13865	.13902	.13940	.13979
.13500	.13898	.13935	.13973	.14010	.14048	.14086	.14124	.14163	.14201	.14240
.13750	.14154	.14192	.14230	.14268	.14307	.14345	.14384	.14423	.14462	.14502
.14000	.14411	.14449	.14488	.14526	.14565	.14605	.14644	.14684	.14723	.14763
.14250	.14667	.14706	.14745	.14784	.14824	.14864	.14904	.14944	.14984	.15025
.14500	.14923	.14963	.15003	.15043	.15083	.15123	.15164	.15205	.15246	.15287
.14750	.15180	.15220	.15260	.15301	.15342	.15383	.15424	.15465	.15507	.15549
.15000	.15436	.15477	.15518	.15559	.15600	.15642	.15684	.15726	.15768	.15810
.15250	.15692	.15734	.15775	.15817	.15859	.15901	.15944	.15987	.16029	.16072
.15500	.15949	.15991	.16033	.16075	.16118	.16161	.16204	.16247	.16291	.16335
.15750	.16205	.16248	.16291	.16334	.16377	.16420	.16464	.16508	.16552	.16597
.16000	.16462	.16505	.16548	.16592	.16636	.16680	.16724	.16769	.16814	.16859
.16250	.16718	.16762	.16806	.16851	.16895	.16940	.16985	.17030	.17075	.17121
.16500	.16975	.17019	.17064	.17109	.17154	.17199	.17245	.17291	.17337	.17383
.16750	.17231	.17277	.17322	.17367	.17413	.17459	.17505	.17552	.17599	.17646
.17000	.17488	.17534	.17580	.17626	.17672	.17719	.17766	.17813	.17860	.17908
.17250	.17745	.17791	.17838	.17884	.17931	.17979	.18026	.18074	.18122	.18170
.17500	.18001	.18048	.18096	.18143	.18191	.18239	.18287	.18335	.18384	.18433
.17750	.18258	.18306	.18353	.18402	.18450	.18498	.18547	.18596	.18646	.18695
.18000	.18515	.18563	.18611	.18660	.18709	.18758	.18808	.18857	.18907	.18958
.18250	.18772	.18820	.18869	.18919	.18968	.19018	.19068	.19119	.19169	.19220
.18500	.19028	.19078	.19127	.19177	.19228	.19278	.19329	.19380	.19431	.19483
.18750	.19285	.19335	.19386	.19436	.19487	.19538	.19590	.19641	.19693	.19745
.19000	.19542	.19593	.19644	.19695	.19746	.19798	.19850	.19903	.19955	.20008
.19250	.19799	.19850	.19902	.19954	.20006	.20058	.20111	.20164	.20217	.20271
.19500	.20055	.20107	.20160	.20212	.20265	.20318	.20372	.20425	.20479	.20533
.19750	.20312	.20365	.20418	.20471	.20525	.20578	.20632	.20687	.20741	.20796
.20000	.20569	.20622	.20676	.20730	.20784	.20838	.20893	.20948	.21003	.21059
.20250	.20826	.20880	.20934	.20989	.21043	.21098	.21154	.21209	.21265	.21322
.20500	.21083	.21137	.21192	.21247	.21303	.21359	.21415	.21471	.21528	.21584
.20750	.21340	.21395	.21450	.21506	.21562	.21619	.21675	.21732	.21790	.21847